Handbook of Research on Big Data and the IoT

Gurjit Kaur
Delhi Technological University, India

Pradeep Tomar
Gautam Buddha University, India

A volume in the Advances in Data Mining and Database Management (ADMDM) Book Series

Published in the United States of America by
IGI Global
Engineering Science Reference (an imprint of IGI Global)
701 E. Chocolate Avenue
Hershey PA, USA 17033
Tel: 717-533-8845
Fax: 717-533-8661
E-mail: cust@igi-global.com
Web site: http://www.igi-global.com

Library of Congress Cataloging-in-Publication Data

Names: Kaur, Gurjit, 1980- editor. | Tomar, Pradeep, 1976- editor.
Title: Handbook of research on big data and the IoT / Gurjit Kaur and Pradeep Tomar, editors.
Description: Hershey, PA : Engineering Science Reference, [2019] | Includes bibliographical references.
Identifiers: LCCN 2018031760| ISBN 9781522574323 (h/c) | ISBN 9781522574330 (eISBN)
Subjects: LCSH: Big data--Research--Handbooks, manuals, etc. | Internet of things--Research--Handbooks, manuals, etc.
Classification: LCC QA76.9.B45 H365 2019 | DDC 005.7--dc23 LC record available at https://lccn.loc.gov/2018031760

This book is published in the IGI Global book series Advances in Data Mining and Database Management (ADMDM) (ISSN: 2327-1981; eISSN: 2327-199X)

British Cataloguing in Publication Data
A Cataloguing in Publication record for this book is available from the British Library.

For electronic access to this publication, please contact: eresources@igi-global.com.

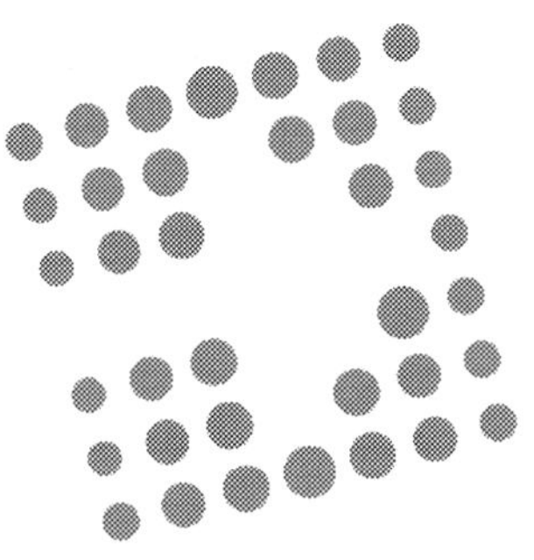

Advances in Data Mining and Database Management (ADMDM) Book Series

David Taniar
Monash University, Australia

ISSN:2327-1981
EISSN:2327-199X

Mission

With the large amounts of information available to organizations in today's digital world, there is a need for continual research surrounding emerging methods and tools for collecting, analyzing, and storing data.

The **Advances in Data Mining & Database Management (ADMDM)** series aims to bring together research in information retrieval, data analysis, data warehousing, and related areas in order to become an ideal resource for those working and studying in these fields. IT professionals, software engineers, academicians and upper-level students will find titles within the ADMDM book series particularly useful for staying up-to-date on emerging research, theories, and applications in the fields of data mining and database management.

Coverage

- Sequence analysis
- Profiling Practices
- Educational Data Mining
- Data quality
- Web Mining
- Data Warehousing
- Information Extraction
- Neural Networks
- Decision Support Systems
- Heterogeneous and Distributed Databases

IGI Global is currently accepting manuscripts for publication within this series. To submit a proposal for a volume in this series, please contact our Acquisition Editors at Acquisitions@igi-global.com or visit: http://www.igi-global.com/publish/.

The Advances in Data Mining and Database Management (ADMDM) Book Series (ISSN 2327-1981) is published by IGI Global, 701 E. Chocolate Avenue, Hershey, PA 17033-1240, USA, www.igi-global.com. This series is composed of titles available for purchase individually; each title is edited to be contextually exclusive from any other title within the series. For pricing and ordering information please visit http://www.igi-global.com/book-series/advances-data-mining-database-management/37146. Postmaster: Send all address changes to above address.

Titles in this Series

For a list of additional titles in this series, please visit: www.igi-global.com/book-series

Optimizing Big Data Management and Industrial Systems With Intelligent Techniques
Sultan Ceren Öner (Istanbul Technical University, Turkey) and Oya H. Yüregir (Çukurova University, Turkey)
Engineering Science Reference • copyright 2019 • 238pp • H/C (ISBN: 9781522551379) • US $205.00 (our price)

Big Data Processing With Hadoop
T. Revathi (Mepco Schlenk Engineering College, India) K. Muneeswaran (Mepco Schlenk Engineering College, India) and M. Blessa Binolin Pepsi (Mepco Schlenk Engineering College, India)
Engineering Science Reference • copyright 2019 • 244pp • H/C (ISBN: 9781522537908) • US $195.00 (our price)

Extracting Knowledge From Opinion Mining
Rashmi Agrawal (Manav Rachna International Institute of Research and Studies, India) and Neha Gupta (Manav Rachna International Institute of Research and Studies, India)
Engineering Science Reference • copyright 2019 • 346pp • H/C (ISBN: 9781522561170) • US $225.00 (our price)

Intelligent Innovations in Multimedia Data Engineering and Management
Siddhartha Bhattacharyya (RCC Institute of Information Technology, India)
Engineering Science Reference • copyright 2019 • 316pp • H/C (ISBN: 9781522571070) • US $225.00 (our price)

Data Clustering and Image Segmentation Through Genetic Algorithms Emerging Research and Opportunities
S. Dash (North Orissa University, India) and B.K. Tripathy (VIT University, India)
Engineering Science Reference • copyright 2019 • 160pp • H/C (ISBN: 9781522563198) • US $165.00 (our price)

Optimization Techniques for Problem Solving in Uncertainty
Surafel Luleseged Tilahun (University of Zululand, South Africa) and Jean Medard T. Ngnotchouye (University of KwaZulu-Natal, South Africa)
Engineering Science Reference • copyright 2018 • 313pp • H/C (ISBN: 9781522550914) • US $195.00 (our price)

Predictive Analysis on Large Data for Actionable Knowledge Emerging Research and Opportunities
Muhammad Usman (Shaheed Zulfikar Ali Bhutto Institute of Science and Technology, Pakistan) and M. Usman (Pakistan Scientific and Technological Information Center (PASTIC), Pakistan)
Information Science Reference • copyright 2018 • 177pp • H/C (ISBN: 9781522550297) • US $135.00 (our price)

Handbook of Research on Big Data Storage and Visualization Techniques
Richard S. Segall (Arkansas State University, USA) and Jeffrey S. Cook (Independent Researcher, USA)
Engineering Science Reference • copyright 2018 • 917pp • H/C (ISBN: 9781522531425) • US $565.00 (our price)

701 East Chocolate Avenue, Hershey, PA 17033, USA
Tel: 717-533-8845 x100 • Fax: 717-533-8661
E-Mail: cust@igi-global.com • www.igi-global.com

List of Contributors

Table of Contents

Detailed Table of Contents

Big data and the Internet of Things (IoT) are the recent innovations in this era of smart world. Both of these technologies are proving very beneficial for today's fast-moving lifestyle. Both technologies are connected to each other and used together in many real-world applications. Big data and IoT have their uses and applications in almost every area from homes to industries, from agriculture to manufacturing, from transportation to warehousing, from food industries to entertainment industry, even from our shoe to robotics. This chapter discusses various applications of big data and IoT in detail and also discusses how both the technologies are affecting our daily life and how it can make things better.

In recent years, enormous amounts of digital data have been generated. In parallel, data collection, storage, and analysis technologies have developed. Recently, there has been an increasing trend of people moving towards urban areas. By 2030 more than 60% of the world's population will live in an urban environment. Urban areas are big data resource because they include millions of citizens, technological devices, and vehicles which generate data continuously. Besides, rapid urbanization brings many challenges, such as environmental pollution, traffic congestion, health problems, energy management, etc. Some policies for countries are required to cope with urbanization problems. One of these policies is to build smart cities. Smart cities integrate information and communication technology and various physical devices connected to the network (the internet of things or IoT) to both improve the quality of government services and citizen welfare. This chapter presents a literature review of big data, smart cities, IoT, green-IoT concepts, using technology and methods, and applications worldwide.

the aim of this chapter is to provide a holistic study of big data and IoT opportunities, challenges, and applications within the SMEs context. The authors hope that the outcome of this study would provide foundational information on how the SMEs can partake with the new wave technological advancement and in turn, spurring more SMEs for adoption.

In recent years, everyday objects and locating of people become an active area in IoT-based visual surveillance system. Internet of things (IoT) is basically transferring data with numerous other things. In visual surveillance systems, conventional methods are very easily susceptible to the environmental changes (i.e., illumination changing, slow motion in the background due to waving tree leaves, rippling of water, and variation in lightening condition). This chapter describes the current challenging issues present in literature along with major application areas, resources and dataset, tools and advantages of IoT-based visual surveillance systems.

Information technology, computer science, etc. have been developed more and more in many countries in the world. Their subfields have already had many very crucial contributions to everyone life: production, politics, advertisement, etc. Especially, big data semantics, scientific and knowledge discovery, and intelligence are the subareas that are gaining more interest. Therefore, the authors display semantics for massive data sets fully in this chapter. This is very significant for commercial applications, studies, researchers, etc. in the world.

The internet of things (IoT) generates large amounts of data that are sent to the cloud to be stored, processed, and analyzed to extract useful information. However, the cloud-based big data analytics approach is not completely appropriate for the analysis of IoT data sources, and presents some issues and limitations, such as inherent delay, late response, and high bandwidth occupancy. Fog computing emerges as a possible solution to address these cloud limitations by extending cloud computing capabilities at the network edge (i.e., gateways, switches), close to the IoT devices. This chapter presents a comprehensive overview of IoT big data analytics architectures, approaches, and solutions. Particularly, the fog-cloud reference architecture is proposed as the best approach for performing big data analytics in IoT ecosystems. Moreover, the benefits of the fog-cloud approach are analyzed in two IoT application case studies. Finally, fog-cloud open research challenges are described, providing some guidelines to researchers and application developers to address fog-cloud limitations.

Interoperability refers to the ability of IoT systems and components to communicate and share information among them. This crucial feature is key to unlock all of the IoT paradigm´s potential, including immense technological, economic, and social benefits. Interoperability is currently a major challenge in IoT, mainly due to the lack of a reference standard and the vast heterogeneity of IoT systems. IoT interoperability has also a significant importance in big data analytics because it substantively eases data processing. This chapter analyzes the critical importance of IoT interoperability, its different types, challenges to face, diverse use cases, and prospective interoperability solutions. Given that it is a complex concept that involves multiple aspects and elements of IoT, for a deeper insight, interoperability is studied across different levels of IoT systems. Furthermore, interoperability is also re-examined from a global approach among platforms and systems.

In this chapter, the authors collected data from issues related to threats in the applications of IoT-based technologies that describe the security and privacy issues from 30 peer reviewed publications from 2014 to 2017. Further, they analyzed each threat type and its percentages in each application of the internet of things. The results indicated that the applications of smart transportation (20%) face the highest amount of security and privacy issues followed by smart home (19%) and smart cities (18%) compared to the rest of the applications. Further, they determined that the biggest threats were denial of service attack (9%) followed by eavesdropping (5%), man in the middle (4%), and replay (4%). Denial of service attacks and man in the middle attack are active attacks that can severely damage human life whereas eavesdropping is a passive attack that steals information. This study has found that privacy issues have the biggest impacts on people. Therefore, researchers need to find possible solutions to these threats to improve the quality of IoT applications.

There are higher rates of mobile devices in current networks that are associated with each other intelligently using internet of things (IoT) domain to make diverse communication in various applications. Therefore, security issues are a major concern to accomplish a protected communication. There are many functions and cryptographic algorithms developed during research which can be utilized as a part of the communication trade among the devices to make secure internet of things networks in an approach to ensure right transmission. Big data is the most demanding concept used in business analytics and massive data processing. It is heard all over the place, particularly in the social insurance industry. Traditionally, the tremendous measure of data produced by the medicinal services industry was put away as printed version. This data has the ability to help an extensive variety of medicinal services and restorative capacities. The digitization of such data is called big data. The chapter features critical security issues in IoT-associated devices both in wireless network and big data analytics along with all other widely used area where IoT environment has been implemented. It also describes security issues in IoT systems particularly when IoT computing devices are used in critical real-time applications such as utilizing IoT frameworks involving information transmission with mobile phones, existing secured systems for enormous information, and individual information security including verification and secured correspondence in IoT.

The problem of hazard detection and the robotic exploration of the hazardous environment is the need of the of the hour due to the continuous increase of the hazardous gases owing to the industry proliferation and modernization of the infrastructure. It includes radiological materials and toxic gases with long term harmful effects. The definition of a hazardous environment and extracting the parameters for the same is itself a complicated task. The chapter proposes the alarming solution to warn about the level of hazardous effects for a particular environment area. The need of the hour is to build complete systems that can autosense the hazardous environment even in low visibility environment and raise an alarm. The combination of IoT and machine learning can be best used for getting the real-time data and using the real-time data for analyzing the accurate current hazardous level as well as prediction of future hazards by reading the parameters for detection and also selecting the useful parameters from them.

The internet of things (IoT) transforms the world in many ways. It combines many types of hardware and software with a variety of communication technologies to enable the development of innovative applications. A typical IoT system consists of IoT device, IoT gateway, IoT platform, and IoT application. Developing these elements and delivering an IoT system for fulfilling business requirements encompasses many activities to be executed and is not straightforward. To expedite these activities, some major vendors provide software development kits (SDK), integrated development environments (IDE), and utility tools for developing software to be executed on IoT devices/gateways. Moreover, these vendors utilize their cloud platforms to provide fundamental services, such as data storage, analytics, stream processing, for developing IoT systems. These vendors also developed IoT specific cloud-based services, such as connectivity and device management, to support IoT system development. This chapter presents an overview of tools and platforms provided by five major vendors.

Artificial intelligence (ARTINT) and information have been famous fields for many years. A reason has been that many different areas have been promoted quickly based on the ARTINT and information, and they have created many significant values for many years. These crucial values have certainly been used more and more for many economies of the countries in the world, other sciences, companies, organizations, etc. Many massive corporations, big organizations, etc. have been established rapidly because these economies have been developed in the strongest way. Unsurprisingly, lots of information and large-scale data sets have been created clearly from these corporations, organizations, etc. This has been the major challenges for many commercial applications, studies, etc. to process and store them successfully. To handle this problem, many algorithms have been proposed for processing these big data sets.

With the new developments in information technologies, personal and business data have become easily accessible through different channels. The huge amounts of personal data across global networks and databases have provided crucial benefits in a scientific manner and many business opportunities, also in the meeting, incentive, convention, and exhibition (MICE) industry. In this chapter, the authors focus on the analysis of MICE industry with regards to the new regulation (GDPR) of personal data protection of all EU citizens and how the industry professionals can adapt their way of business in light of this new regulation. The authors conducted an online interview with five different meetings industry professionals to have more insight about the data produced with its content and new regulations applied to the industry. The importance of personal data privacy and protection is discussed, and the most suitable anonymization techniques for personal data privacy are proposed.

The equilibration that underscores the internet of things (IoT) and big data analytics (BDA) cannot be underestimated at the behest of real-life social challenges and significant policy data generated to redress the concerns of epistemic communities, such as political policy actors, stakeholders, and the citizenry. The cognitive balancing of new information gathered by BDA and assimilated across the IoT is at the

Preface

The significant increase in connected devices in Internet of Things will lead to an exponential increase in the data that an organization is required to manage. This is the point when IoT intersects wonderfully with big data and it becomes evident that the two trends fit one another very effectively. Big Data, on the other hand use analytics tools designed to handle large and fast-changing volumes of information. Big Data capacity is a prerequisite to tapping into the Internet of Things. Without the proper data-gathering in place, it'll be impossible for businesses to sort through all the information flowing in from embedded sensors. What that means is that, without Big Data, the Internet of Things can offer an enterprise little more than noise. So, the Big Data and IoT has drawn great attention from both academia and industry, since it offers challenging notion of creating a world where all the things, known as smart objects around us are connected, typically in a wireless manner, to the Internet and communicate with each other with minimum human intervention. Another component set to help Big Data and IoT succeed is cloud computing, which acts as a sort of front end. IoT and Big Data is also fuelled by the advancement of digital technologies. The use of Artificial Intelligence technologies like deep learning will be a key differentiator to derive insights rapidly from massive streams of data. With IoT, Big Data analytics would also move at the edge for real-time decision making. Machine learning and predictive analytics open up new opportunities for enterprises, Internet of Things has moved from being hype to becoming a reality. All these new solutions require new skill sets and qualities, which also force cultural change within organizations. To sum it up, the combination of Big Data and IoT will enable new monitoring services and powerful processing of sensory data streams. These applications alongside implementation details and challenges should also be explored for successful mainstream adoption.

Recently, IoT and Big Data have been widely studied and applied in many fields, as they can provide a new method for intelligent perception and connection from M2M (including man-to-man, man-to-machine, and machine-to-machine), and on-demand use and efficient sharing of resources, respectively. A novel paradigm where Big Data and IoT are merged together is foreseen as disruptive and an enabler of a large number of application scenarios. In this book, we will focus our attention on the concept of Big Data and IoT. We had tried to cover various aspects of Big Data and IoT system, the need for integrating them, the challenges deriving from such integration, and how these issues have been tackled. Apart from them we also tried to describe various applications to manage the database of IoT based smart cities, smart homes, and smart e-health services etc. We explored various big data and IoT integration technologies. Apart from that major emphasis is given to energy efficiency of the IoT system with Big Data. Overview about Big Data and IoT with standards, protocols, architecture and system design, integration with existing standards and protocols of Big Data and IoT, data management and technology involved in Big Data and IoT, Applications of Big Data and IoT with challenges and Solutions are discussed in a detailed manner.

The main objective of this book is to explore potential applications of Big data and IOT by both researchers and practitioners. The overall objectives are:

- To study, analyze and present the IoT and Big Data related technologies and standards.
- To present and describe the recent research and development in the Big Data Analytics and IoT.
- To present recent emerging trends and technological advances of the big data based IoT.
- To present recent and innovative applications of the Big Data and IoT.
- To present implementation, challenges and implication issues on society.

This book contains 24 chapters authored by several leading experts in the field of IoT and Big Data. The book is presented in a coordinated and integrated manner starting with the fundamentals, and followed by the technologies that implement them. The primary target audiences for this discourse are educators and learning practitioners in higher education, industry, as well as governmental agencies and industrialist and professional those are interested in exploring and implementing the Big Data, IoT and related technologies. This book will serve as a reference book of scholarly value for advanced level students, researchers, and professionals. Graduate students, researchers, academicians, industrialists and professionals that are interested in exploring and implementing the IoT and related technologies of Big Data and IoT Research Groups.

The content of the book is organized as follows:

INTRODUCTION: ROLE OF RECENT TECHNOLOGIES OF BIG DATA AND IOT IN HUMAN LIFE

The authors describe top technologies used to store and analyses Big Data and also it categories them into two (storage and Querying/Analysis). Apache Hadoop, Microsoft HD Insight, NoSQL, Hive, Spoop, Ploybase, Big Data in excel and presto are some of big data technologies. The authors also describe technologies involved in IoT like LAWAN, Cellular, BLE (Bluetooth Low Energy, Zigbee, NFC, RFID, WiFi, Ethernet all are represent in network access and physical layers of IOT network technology.

CHAPTER 1: BIG DATA AND IoT APPLICATIONS IN REAL-LIFE ENVIRONMENTS

Big data and IoT have their use and applications in almost every area from homes to industries, from agriculture to manufacturing, from transportation to warehousing, from food industries to entertainment industry, even from our shoe to robotics. In this chapter, authors explored various applications of big data and IoT in detail and also discusses how both the technologies are affecting our daily life and how it can make things better.

CHAPTER 2: APPLICATIONS OF BIG DATA AND GREEN IoT-ENABLING TECHNOLOGIES FOR SMART CITIES

Besides, rapid urbanization brings many challenges such as environment pollution, traffic congestion, health problems, energy management etc. Some policies for countries are required to cope with urbanization problems. One of these policies is to build smart cities. Smart cities integrate information and communication technology and various physical devices connected to the network (the Internet of things or IoT) improve both the quality of government services and citizen welfare. This chapter presents literature review on big data, smart city, IoT, green-IoT concepts; used technology and methods, and applications worldwide.

CHAPTER 3: BIG DATA UTILIZATION – BENEFITS AND CHALLENGES FOR SMART CITY IMPLEMENTATION

This chapter discusses the Big Data utilization for making smart cities and also throws light on various applications where efficient analysis of services can be carried out using Big Data technique. The main objective of this chapter is to provide knowledge of big data implementation for the smart city and its services. This chapter also investigate various prospects, benefits and challenges of absorbing big data utilization for smart cities. It discusses some case studies related to big data applications for smart city services and also propose some open issues related to big data implementation for the smart city.

CHAPTER 4: BIG DATA AND THE INTERNET OF THINGS – CURRENT INDUSTRY PRACTICES AND THEIR IMPLICATIONS FOR CONSUMER PRIVACY AND PRIVACY LITERACY

To protect consumer's privacy a wide range of approaches to informational privacy protections exist. However, individuals are increasingly required to actively respond to control and manage their informational privacy rather than rely on any protection mechanisms. This chapter highlights privacy issues across consumer's use of IoT and identifies existing responses to enhance privacy awareness as a way of enabling IoT users to protect their privacy.

CHAPTER 5: BIG DATA AND IoT OPPORTUNITIES FOR SMALL AND MEDIUM-SIZED ENTERPRISES (SMEs)

The advancement of technology and emergence of Internet-of-Things (IoT) has exponentially caused a data explosion in the 21st Century era. As such, the arrival of IoT is set to revolutionize the development of the Small and Medium-Sized Enterprise (SME) organizations – by shaping it into a more universal and integrated ecosystem. Despite evidential studies of the potential of advanced technologies for businesses, the SMEs are apprehensive towards new technologies adoption such as big data analytics and

IoT. So this chapter provides a holistic study of big data and IoT opportunities, challenges and, applications within the SMEs context and discuss how the SMEs can partake with the new wave technological advancement and in turn, spurring more SMEs for adoption.

CHAPTER 6: INTERNET OF THINGS WITH OBJECT DETECTION

In visual surveillance system, conventional methods are very easily susceptible to the environmental changes i.e. illumination changing, slow leafy motion in the background, rippling of water, and variation in lightening condition. This chapter describes the current challenging issues present in literature along with major application areas, resources and dataset, tools and advantages of IoT based visual surveillance system.

CHAPTER 7: SEMANTICS FOR BIG DATA SETS

Information technology, computer science have been developed more and more in many countries in the world. Their sub-fields have already had many very crucial contributions to everyone life: production, politics, advertisement, and etc. Especially, big data semantics, scientific and knowledge discovery, and intelligence are the sub-areas which are great interested more and more. Therefore, the authors display semantics for massive data sets fully in this chapter. This is very significant for commercial applications, studies, researchers, and etc. in the world.

CHAPTER 8: IoT BIG DATA ARCHITECTURES, APPROACHES, AND CHALLENGES

As Fog computing emerges as a possible solution to address these cloud limitations by extending cloud computing capabilities at the network edge (i.e. gateways, switches), close to the IoT devices. This chapter discuss a comprehensive overview of IoT big data analytics architectures, approaches, and solutions. Author proposed a fog-cloud reference architecture for performing big data analytics in IoT ecosystems. Moreover, the benefits of the fog-cloud approach are analyzed in two IoT application case studies. Finally, fog-cloud open research challenges are described, providing some guidelines to researchers and application developers to address fog-cloud limitations.

CHAPTER 9: INTEROPERABILITY IN IoT

Interoperability is currently a major challenge in IoT, mainly due to the lack of a reference standard and the vast heterogeneity of IoT systems. IoT interoperability has also a significant importance in Big Data analytics because it substantively eases data processing. In this chapter, authors has analyzed the critical importance of IoT interoperability, its different types, challenges to face, diverse use cases and prospective interoperability solutions. Furthermore, interoperability is also re-examined from a global approach among platforms and systems.

CHAPTER 10: CRITICAL ISSUES IN THE INVASION OF THE INTERNET OF THINGS (IoT): SECURITY, PRIVACY, AND OTHER VULNERABILITIES

This chapter describes the issues related to threats in the applications of IoT based technologies specially the security and privacy. Authors analysed each type of threat and its percentages in each application of the Internet of things where their results indicated that the applications of smart transportation (20%) face the highest amount of security and privacy issues followed by smart home (19%) and smart cities (18%) compared to the rest of the applications. Further, they determined that the biggest threats were Denial of service attack (9%) followed by Eavesdropping (5%), Man in the Middle (4%) and Replay (4%). Their study reveals that the Denial of service attacks and Man in the middle attack are Active attacks that can severely damage human life whereas Eavesdropping is a passive attack that steals information.

CHAPTER 11: SECURITY IN IoT AND BIG DATA WITH TECHNICAL CHALLENGES

In current technology based development there is an incredible collection of mobile devices associated with each other intelligently in Internet of Things (IoT) domain to make diverse communication in various applications. Therefore, security issues play major concern to accomplish a protected communication. There are many functions and cryptographic algorithms developed during research which can be utilized as a part of the communication trade among the devices to make secure Internet of Things networks in an approach to ensure right transmission. In this chapter, authors discussed about the security in IOT and Big data with technical challenges.

CHAPTER 12: DISASTER MANAGEMENT USING INTERNET OF THINGS

The problem of hazard detection and the robotic exploration of the hazardous environment is need the of the hour due to the continuous increase of the hazardous gases owing to the industry proliferation and modernization of the infrastructure . It includes radiological materials and toxic gases with long term harmful effects. The definition of a hazardous environment and extracting out the parameters for the same is itself a complicated task. The chapter aims to set up the alarming solution to warn about the level of hazardous effects for a particular environment area.

CHAPTER 13: TOOLS AND PLATFORMS FOR DEVELOPING IoT SYSTEMS

As an IoT system consists of IoT device, IoT gateway, IoT platform, and IoT application. Developing these elements and delivering an IoT system for fulfilling business requirements encompasses many activities to be executed and is not straightforward. To expedite these activities, some major vendors provide Software Development Kits (SDK), Integrated Development Environments (IDE) and utility tools for developing software to be executed on IoT devices/gateways and utilize vendors utilize their cloud platforms to provide fundamental services, such as data storage, analytics, stream processing, for developing IoT systems. These vendors also developed IoT specific cloud-based services, such as connectivity and device management, to support IoT system development. This chapter presents an overview of tools and platforms provided by five major vendors.

CHAPTER 14: AN INTERNET OF THINGS AMBIENT LIGHT MONITORING SYSTEM

In this chapter, authors designed a system to measure the light measurement autonomously and continuously without human involvement. Through their system the end-users are able to access the real-time information of the collected data via internet through a cloud based IoT platform with analytics capabilities. This system also provide significant benefits to the campus community in terms of creating a more conducive environment, increased productivity and improved health condition. Furthermore, its implementation can be easily extended to other human spaces to create even greater benefits to society at large.

CHAPTER 15: CHALLENGES AND SOLUTIONS OF BIG DATA AND IoT

To manage big data in a continuous network that keeps expanding leads to few issues related to data collection, data processing, analytics and security. To address these issues, authors has examined certain solution using bigdata approach in IoT. Even-though number of research are being done on big data analytics and IoT, combining these two areas provides several opportunities developing new systems and identify advanced techniques to solve challenges on bigdata and IoT.

CHAPTER 16: ROLE OF BIG DATA IN INTERNET OF THINGS NETWORKS

As a large number of devices connected for various applications, the networks generates an enormous amount of data. This leads to problems in data storage, efficient data processing and intelligent data analytics. In this chapter, authors discuss the role of Big Data and related challenges in IoT networks and various data analytics platforms used for the IoT domain. In addition to this, they discuss the architectural model of Big Data in IoT along with various future research challenges. At the end authors also discuss Smart Health and Smart Transportation as a case study, to supplement their presented architectural model.

CHAPTER 17: ROLE OF COMMUNICATION TECHNOLOGIES FOR SMART APPLICATIONS IN IoT

New technologies like ICTs are recognized as key player in building smart applications for IoT. The use of sensors and actuators can efficiently control the whole communication system and will provide application based solution for smart applications. In this chapter authors discussed the various communication technologies which can be used for smart applications in IoT.

CHAPTER 18: MACHINE LEARNING, DATA MINING FOR IoT-BASED SYSTEMS

This chapter describes the challenges with the Internet of things (IoT) and Machine learning (ML), the how a bit of the trouble of Machine Learning executions are recorded here and should be recalled while arranging the game plan, the decision of right figuring. Existing examination in ML and IoT was center around discovering how Garbage in will convey Garbage out, which is extraordinarily suitable for the extent of the enlightening list for machine learning. The quality, aggregate, availability, and decision of data are essential to the accomplishment of a machine learning game plan. This chapter discuss the outline of how the framework can utilize advancements alongside machine learning and difficulties get a kick out of the chance to understand the security challenges IoT can be bolstered.

CHAPTER 19: CREATING A RESEARCH LABORATORY ON BIG DATA AND INTERNET OF THINGS FOR THE STUDY AND DEVELOPMENT OF DIGITAL TRANSFORMATION

This chapter discusses the problems associated with the design of the business model in the new context of Big Data and the Internet of things to create a research laboratory for studying and improving digital transformations. In the chapter, the business model of the ecosystem is considered as a model consisting of signs fixed in ecosystems and focuses on creating the cost of the laboratory, and fixing the value of the ecosystem in which the created laboratory operates.

CHAPTER 20: BIG DATA ANALYTICS AND INTERNET OF THINGS IN INDUSTRIAL INTERNET IN FORMER SOVIET UNION COUNTRIES

In this chapter the authors explore the integration of three concepts: "Big Data", "Internet of Things" and "Internet Signs" in the countries of the former Soviet Union. Some potential applications of the integration of these three concepts are also discussed. These applications included continuous monitoring of accounting data, continuous verification and validation and use of "Big Data", location information and other data, for example, to control fraudsters in the countries of the former Soviet Union.

CHAPTER 21: GREEN INTERNET OF THINGS (G-IoT) – ICT TECHNOLOGIES, PRINCIPLES, APPLICATIONS, PROJECTS, AND CHALLENGES

This chapter explores an in-depth analysis of principles of G-IoT, making significant progress towards improvising the quality of life and sustainable environment. In addition to this, the chapter outlines various Green ICT technologies explores potential towards diverse real-time areas and also highlights various challenges acting as a barrier towards G-IoT implementation in the real world.

CHAPTER 22: ARTIFICIAL NEURAL NETWORK MODELS FOR LARGE-SCALE DATA

Artificial Intelligence (ARTINT) and Information have been famous fields for many years. A reason has been that many different areas have been promoted quickly based on the ARTINT and information. This chapter explores Artificial Neural Network Models for large scale data.

CHAPTER 23: PERSONAL DATA PRIVACY AND PROTECTION IN THE MEETING, INCENTIVE, CONVENTION, AND EXHIBITION (MICE) INDUSTRY

In this chapter, the authors focus on the analysis of MICE industry with regards to the new regulation (GDPR) of personal data protection of all EU citizens and how the industry professionals can adapt their way of business in light of this new regulation. Authors conducted an online interview with five different meetings industry professionals to have more insight about the data produced with its content and new regulations applied to the industry. The importance of personal data privacy and protection is discussed and the most suitable anonymization techniques for personal data privacy are proposed.

CHAPTER 24: PUBLIC ADMINISTRATION CURRICULUM-BASED BIG DATA POLICY-ANALYTIC EPISTEMOLOGY

The cognitive balancing of new information gathered by BDA and assimilated across the IoT is at the crossroads of ascertaining how the growing increases of such BDA can be managed to transition from the big data state of disequilibration to reach a more stable equilibrium of policy data usefulness. In the quest for explicating the equilibration of policy data usefulness, an account of the curriculum-based MPA Policy Analysis and Analytics concentration program at Norwich University is described as a case example of big data policy-analytic epistemology. The case study in this chapter offers a symbolic ideology of an IoT action-learning solution model as a recommendation for fostering the stable equilibration of policy data usefulness.

Gurjit Kaur
Delhi Technological University, India

Pradeep Tomar
Gautam Buddha University, India

Introduction

ROLE AND RELATIONSHIP OF RECENT TECHNOLOGIES OF BIG DATA AND IOT IN HUMAN LIFE

1. Introduction

The term big data refers to collection of complex and very large data sets that are often very difficult to perform using traditional tools and applications. With increasing data, size exceeds in terabytes of memory because of the variety of data it encompasses, big data comes with a number of challenges mainly related to its complexity and volume. A survey conducted recently shows that around 80% of the data that is created in the world belongs to the unstructured category. One challenge is to how these data which belongs to the unstructured category can become structured, in order to make an attempt to capture and understand the most important data. Another challenge is how we can store it. In this Introduction we describe how recent top technologies used to analyze and store Big Data.

Internet of Things (IoT) presents new change in individual enterprises productivity and quality of life. Through a local network of intelligent smart devices i.e. IoT has the potential to enhance and enable extensions to fundamental services in logistics, transportation, utilities, education, security, healthcare and other areas, while providing a new environment for the development of new upcoming application. To move the industry towards maturity and beyond the early stages of development of market a sincere effort is required, driven by common understanding of the nature of the different applications. IoT or Internet of Things has seen an exponential growth in the number of gadgets and devices connected to it and the massive increase in the consumption of data, this shows how the growth of big data overlaps with IoT. (A. Kaklauskas, 2016) Management becomes difficult because of the non-trivial concerns regarding data processing, data collection efficiency, security and analytics because of the continuously expanding of big data network. Researchers have examined the success of deployment of IoT and its challenges associated. Despite the large number of researches on IoT, analytics and big data, these areas converge to create several opportunities for IoT systems for analytics of big data. Recent advancement in big data analytics is explored in this Introduction for an IoT environment and IoT systems and also the key requirements for enabling analytics and managing big data. From the convergence of analytics, IoT and big data this Introduction tried to identify the opportunity and discuss IoT applications and big data analytics role in these IoT applications. The increase in the volume of data is the first thing that pops up in mind when talking about Big Data and IoT which actually hit the companies data storage system. Additional data load needs to be handled by setting up new data centers.

A cloud-based solution, Platform-as-a-Service model, is now been implemented by organizations because of the enormous impact of IoT on data storage infrastructure as opposed to their own storage infrastructure's maintenance. (Adibi, 2013) PaaS provides scalability, flexibility, a smart architecture and compliance to store all valuable and necessary IoT data. Unlike, systems like in-house data systems where if the data load increases, the system needs to be constantly updated. Private, public and hybrid models are options included in cloud storage. If a company has sensitive data that require heightened security, using a private cloud would be the best course of action if the data is subject to any regulatory compliance requirements for other companies, for the storage of IoT data, a hybrid or public cloud can be used. To handle the large amounts of IoT data, most organizations make their adaptable technologies. IoT-linked devices send and receive data. The devices are connected to each other via Wi-Fi, Bluetooth or any other suited technology. The MQTT or Message Queue Telemetry Transport is one of the most widely used protocol Hadoop and Hive are used to store data by a lot of companies. For IoT data, NoSQL databases like Apache CouchDB are more suitable as they offer high throughput and low latency. (Adibi, 2013) The kinds of data generated by the devices and the devices that makes up the IoT vary by nature. Different data security risks are carried by the data types which include communication protocols, processed data, raw data etc. Security professionals are still very new to IoT, who are not effective and lacks experience in dealing with IoT-based security threats, as a result, risks is increased. Attacks which can be of any kind can threaten the data. The devices are also at the risk of damage which are connected to the network. Organizations necessity to make crucial changes to their security landscape in this type of world. IoT devices located outside the network must be able to communicate with corporate applications as they come in various shapes and sizes. Therefore, for authentication purpose a non-repudiation identifier must be in every device. Enterprises for an audit purpose should be able store them. A multi-layered system for proper segmentation and security of the network can also be used to avoid corrupting the other parts of the network and can help to prevent attacks. A properly configured IoT system can be used to check that which of the IoT devices are allowed to connect by following an access control policy of a finely-tuned network. To ensure dynamic network segmentation, SDN technologies or Software-defined networking are combined with appropriate access policies and network identity. SDN segmentation-based network must and can also be used for point-to-multipoint and point-to-point encryption.

The use of intelligently connected systems and devices to leverage data gathered by embedded actuators and sensors in physical objects and machines refer to as IoT or the Internet of Things. Over the coming years IoT is expected to spread rapidly and a new dimension of services will be unleash by this convergence that improve productivity of enterprises and the quality of life of consumers, unlocking an opportunity 'Connected Life' as referred by the GSMA. The IoT has the potential to deliver solutions for consumers that improve many other aspects of daily life like security, energy efficiency, education and health dramatically. IoT can underpin solutions for enterprises that improve productivity and decision-making in agriculture, retail, manufacturing and other sectors. M2M or Machine to Machine solutions (Adibi, 2013) – IoT's subset – with minimal direct human intervention, already use wireless networks to connect to the Internet and devices to each other, the needs of a wide range of industries that meet deliver services. IoT's impact is considerable, to move beyond this early stage an effort is required, a common understanding of the opportunity and its distinct nature is required, in order to optimize the market's development. To date, there are several key distinctive features have been identified by the mobile operators (Adibi, 2013). The next wave of life-enhancing services can be enabled by The Internet of Things across several fundamental sectors of the economy. Also the meeting the needs of customers may require consistent global services and global distribution models. IoT can support mass global deployments the Internet of Things presents an opportunity for new commercial models. The majority of revenue will arise from the provision of value-added services and mobile operators are building new capabilities to enable these new service areas. Also new and varying demands on mobile networks will be placed by Device and application behaviour.

An enormous impact of the Internet of Things will ultimately have an on society, enterprises and consumers as a whole, development is still at an early stage. New services pilot by mobile operators and their partners across ranging from health to automotive, multiple sectors, as several distinct features of the IoT have been identified. As the IoT evolves, the proliferation of smart connected devices providing pervasive seamless connectivity supported by mobile networks, opportunities will be unlocked to boost productivity for enterprises and to provide life-enhancing services for consumers. Quality of life of consumers in multiple ways could enhance connectivity provided by the IoT, but not limited to, such as, security and energy efficiency in the city and at the home. In the home, the integration cloud-based services and connected smart devices will help address the pressing issue of security and energy efficiency. Connected smart devices will improve home security via remote monitoring and also enable a reduction in outages and utility bills. The IoT will improve quality of health and education and also help widen access. As demand doubles for healthcare, this challenge will be addressed by connected smart devices by improving enable and access monitoring of age-related conditions and chronic diseases in the home, supporting a range of e-health services. The ability of IoT, for enterprises, to combine innovations in 3D printing, data analytics and sensors, will improve productivity by enabling a step change in the efficiency of production, quality of decision making, productivity of food production and personalization of retail.

2. Big Data in Human Life

Big Data is growing at an exponential rate and it is expected that most of the customers will be attracted to it in the upcoming year due to its tremendous prospect of progressing a business. There has been an enormous increase in the variety, volume, and velocity of the data, which is a proof that future applications require this. Experts have predicted Big Data's various technologies. The top predictions are:

1. The tasks that are related to the human intelligence demand main attention and to give proper attention to it, cognitive technologies are emerging in a great way. This will automate the human-induced activities like writing and face recognition. Along with it, the intellectual aspects of the human-like reasoning, conceptualizing, and learning, will also be taken care of this technology. With the advent of this technology, the activities that needed human intervention can be easily accomplished with the help of automation.
2. The performance of the business will improve by optimizing, discovering, evaluating, and deploying the predictive models. This will allow the Big Data to be analyzed, which will deplete the risks and accentuate the potential.
3. One of the most important aspect of IoT is the Big Data (Supriya, 2017) and the world is about to see an enormous change in the coming year. People are relying more on the Smartphones and tablets for their daily activities as well as for important transactions. Hence, the companies are spending more time and capital on the IoT to get the required information seamlessly. The sensor-based analytics have mutually benefited the clients as well as the entrepreneurs. Hence, it is evident that the integrated impact of the IoT on Big Data will be something to look forward to. The most alluring advantage of IoT is that business from any domain can enjoy the benefits.

4. The searching tools and technologies, which will help derive the information from the pool of data, will help save the time and hassle immensely. Along with it, the mammoth archive of the structured and unstructured data that is stored in the various sources of files like APIs, Databases, file systems, etc. will also be easy to access, irrespective of the platforms and applications.
5. Machine Learning is growing in a huge way in order to cope up with the increasing demands. It is predicted that it will be able to analyze enormous volume and process complicated data at a faster pace with accuracy. This will be achieved with the help of improvised hardware, algorithm and enormous data. As a result, the process will also be managed in a better way, which will attract better results. Machine Learning is predicted to accentuate the performance of the business with the help of fraud detection, data analysis, real-time advertisements, etc.
6. In future the businesses will approach a safer and secure way of accomplishing the activities. Artificial Intelligence (AI) will be taking the security breaches seriously, making it difficult for the spammers to break the security code. It is expected that the machines will be able to envision the human psychology in a better way. The machines will also be able to understand the unlabeled data accurately without any intervention from a human. With the help of these technologies, AI will be able to establish itself as a powerful tool that will proficiently safeguard the data. Before the onset of digitization, data was maintained manually. Hence, there is a huge part of the data that is yet to be digitized. This data is called the dark data that requires attention on an urgent basis. With the improvisation of Big Data, the dark data will be taken into account and recovered. The recovery will make the trends and product cycles prominent, which will help understand the predictions in a better way. This is a unique technology that helps produce information from various sources of data that includes Big Data source like Hadoop. It also utilizes the distributed data storage in real-time. It relates to the products that are in relation to the data cleansing, along with the high-velocity sets of data and enrichment of the giant. It also uses parallel operation on databases. Composition of data through various solutions like Apache, Apache Spark, Hive, Apache Pig, Hadoop, MapReduce, Couchbase, Amazon Elastic Map Reduce (EMR), and MongoDB is accomplished. This will be utilized to offer streamlined database for enhanced efficiency.

Reasonable developments in the applications of the Big Data world burst the bubble around Big Data. Well, now most are familiar with terms like Hadoop, NO-SQL, Spark, Cloud, Hive, etc. A number of other Big Data solutions and at least 20 NO-SQL databases emerge every month. But which technology has the prospects to go forward and which technology will fetch big benefits. Enterprises have widely adopted Hadoop in the past years for their data warehouse needs. In the coming year the trend seems to grow and continue as well. Its applications and advantages will be seen by companies that have not explored Hadoop so far. Hadoop would be more enterprise ready as it comes up with features in terms of the technological developments, Hadoop's implementation will expand across many more companies and sectors can use the solutions without much of security concerns once Hadoop security projects like Rhino, Sentry etc. gain stability. All the companies now know how to process and store Big Data. For better business decisions the real difference is going to be its analytics solutions and how fast can they deliver it. Big Data solution's processing capabilities will certainly increase. With this aspect in mind Projects like Storm, Kafka, Spark etc. were developed. Data generation is on its increase with IoT or Internet of Things taking front seat. Huge volumes of Data require perfect scalable solution for applications involving IOT. Cloud services is better than others. The advantages of using Hadoop on cloud by many technologies and organizations has already been realized pertaining to the coupling of Big Data technologies like cloud, Hadoop, IOT and Spark is expected to rise in the coming years.

3. Role of Big Data and the Internet of Things in Human Life

IoT will generate a vast amount of data in near future, data which is well-analyzed in today's world is extremely valuable. The company will be forces to upgrade as soon as possible their current tools, technology and processes because of the impact of the Big Data universe which, in turn, take advantage of insights which will be delivered to accommodate massive data volumes by Big Data. The increase in the volume of data is the first thing that pops up in mind when talking about Big Data and IoT which will hit the companies' data storage framework. Additional data load needs to be handled by setting up new data centers.

Data storage infrastructure will have an enormous impact of IoT if taken into consideration. As opposed to the maintenance of their own storage infrastructure, cloud-based solution, the Platform-as-a-Service model, is what the organizations have begun to move towards. PaaS provides scalability, flexibility, a sophisticated architecture and compliance to store all valuable and necessary IoT data. Unlike, systems like in-house data systems where if the data load increases, the system needs to be constantly updated. Private, public and hybrid models are options included in cloud storage. If a company has sensitive data that require heightened security, using a private cloud would be the best course of action if the data is subject to any regulatory compliance requirements for other companies, for the storage of IoT data, a hybrid or public cloud can be used. To handle the large amounts of IoT data, most organizations will have to adapt their technologies.

4. The Relationship Between Big Data and IoT

"IoT is the senses, Big Data is the fuel, and AI is the brain to realize the future of a smart connected world." IoT is about data, devices and their connectivity. Creating delivering intelligent insights, providing new business outcomes and smarter products is the real value of Internet of Things. Massive in flow of Big Data will trigger internet of things as millions of devices get connected. Various types of data (unstructured, structured, real-time, images, dark data, contextual), the key challenge is uncovering and visualizing insights from and in context of your applications. The key enabler for connected world and smarter devices is by deriving intelligence using AI technologies from Big Data.

The end goal is to harness the data coming from other contextual information and sensors to correlations and discover patterns to positively impact businesses in real-time. Augmentation of existing Big Data technologies need to be to effectively extract value, manage and store continuous streams of data from sensor. It is estimated, for instance that, every hour 25 gigabytes of data will be send by connected cars to the cloud. To make sense of this data is the biggest challenge, identifying data and quickly acted upon consumed data to derive actionable events. Technologies like deep learning uses AI, insights are derived rapidly from massive streams of data which will be a key differentiator. Real-time decision making with Big Data analytics, for instance detecting suspicious activities at ATMs, predicting driver behavior for a connected car or in agriculture plants detecting crop patterns using drones at remote places.

In technology, currently the hottest buzzword is AI. And with reasons which cannot be denied-science fiction slowly transforms into reality in the last few years and a number of techniques that previously were fiction. AI is looked by experts as a factor of production which change the way work is done across industries and has the potential to introduce new sources of growth. According to How AI Boosts Industry Profits and Innovations report, increase in economic growth by an average of 1.7 percent as predicted by AI across 16 industries by 2035. By 2035, the report says that, 40 percent or more, could increase in labor productivity by AI technologies, there by 12 developed nations economic growth will be doubled, which will continue to draw experienced and talented professionals to work in this domain.

AI is a method of making software, a computer-controlled robot, a computer that is like human mind which think intelligently. By analyzing the cognitive process and by studying the patterns of the human brain, AI is accomplished. The intelligent software and systems are developed based on the outcome of these studies. The goals of AI are extended by researchers to the following: Logical Reasoning, Knowledge Representation (Suzanne Skublics, 1991), Planning & Navigation, Natural Language Processing, Perception, and Emergent Intelligence:

5. Conclusion

Starting from cognitive technology to retrieving the dark data, Big Data will take care of the backlogs and will make sure the security breaches are managed in a strategic manner. Let's hope that the latest technologies and the enhanced version of Big Data will make the technology highly advanced as well as secured. In the development of the internet, the emerging third wave, the Internet of Things (IoT) which can be accessed via the Internet is a network of physical objects. These objects contain embedded technology which includes items used in everyday life from cars to dishwashers that can regulate and interact with the internal states and with an external environment.

Pradeep Tomar
Gautam Buddha University, India

Gurjit Kaur
Delhi Technological University, India

REFERENCES

Adibi, Mobasher, & Tofigh. (2016). LTE networking: Extending the reach for sensors in mHealth applications. *Transactions on Emerging Telecommunications Technologies*.

Kaklauskas & Gudauskas. (1991). *Intelligent decision-support systems and the Internet of Things for the smart built environment*. Elsevier BV.

Skublics, S., & White, P. (2013). *Teaching Smalltalk as a first programming language*. ACM SIGCSE Bulletin.

Supriya, M., & Deepa, A. J. (2017). A Survey on Prediction Using Big Data Analytics. *International Journal of Big Data and Analytics in Healthcare*, *2*(1), 1–15. doi:10.4018/IJBDAH.2017010101

Chapter 1
Big Data and IoT Applications in Real Life Environment

Anjali Chaudhary
Noida International University, India

Pradeep Tomar
Gautam Buddha University, India

ABSTRACT

Big data and the Internet of Things (IoT) are the recent innovations in this era of smart world. Both of these technologies are proving very beneficial for today's fast-moving lifestyle. Both technologies are connected to each other and used together in many real-world applications. Big data and IoT have their uses and applications in almost every area from homes to industries, from agriculture to manufacturing, from transportation to warehousing, from food industries to entertainment industry, even from our shoe to robotics. This chapter discusses various applications of big data and IoT in detail and also discusses how both the technologies are affecting our daily life and how it can make things better.

INTRODUCTION

Nowadays human life is very much affected by scientific advancement; internet of things has a great role in making human life more comfortable and has potentials to provide a smart environment around by establishing communication between man, machines & objects or machine to machine transmission/ communication. IoT symbolizes a system which comprises things in the material world where sensors dedicated to these IoT things that are connected to the internet in a network structure whether wired or wireless. IoT sensors can be connected by using various technologies like GPRS, RFID, Wi-Fi, GSM, Bluetooth, ZigBee, 3G, and LTE. IoT-empowered devices will share the info about the situation of the surroundings with persons, systems & other machines. IoT makes the world smarter in each aspect; IoT will lead to smart cities, smart homes, smart healthcare, smart transportation smart buildings, smart energy management and smart waste management. Millions of dollars have been spending on research of IoT, worldwide.

DOI: 10.4018/978-1-5225-7432-3.ch001

In this era of digitization, the use of big data is not only to store massive amount of heterogeneous data but also it includes the analysis of the data which is commonly known as big data analytics. Big data can be beneficial for an organization in such a way that big data analytics uses different analytical and mining tool to extract useful information from the huge data which can be very useful for the progress of the organization (Mohsen et al, 2017; Kwon et al, 2014). In many domains big data has brought a tremendous change. The major goal of big data applications is to analyze the large data with the various tools and to help companies or organizations to predict what can happen in future and then take decisions according to the situations. Along with the private sectors public sectors are also benefited with big data. Big data applications store data by servers, internet click streams, social media mobile phone records, sensors, etc. Nowadays various domains are hiring big data analytics to analyze the big data to know the hidden pattern, risks, relations between data, customer choice or priority and much other business information.

IoT and big data are connected with each other. Even both the technologies have almost same applications. While we are using IoT devices and network everywhere in future world, the data that is produced by these sensors is heterogeneous big-data files required to be stored to process in future to predict potential solutions to modern world problems.

Government has also embraced the arena of "Big Data" and "Internet of Things" as a National Digital Mission to attain their aim to be a prominent country in the field of hyper connected domain with a promotional scheme of strengthening the affordability in software sensor devices; also providing training to produce specialists that will internalize security for IoT services and big data analytics so that data can be analyzed.

Some major applications of IoT and big data are explained in detail in this chapter that will help to learn the use of IoT and big data in real world.

BIG DATA APPLICATIONS

Figure 1 represents various domains of big data.

Let us discuss various domains of big data applications:

Banking and Finance

Banking is the most prominent area which is benefited by data science or big data. Nowadays almost every person has bank account, and while someone opens his or her account bank demands a lot of information and thus this process produce a large amount of digital data that is big data. The aim of banks is not only to store this data but also to analyze the data. This big unstructured and heterogeneous data can be analyzed using several techniques and very useful information can be extracted as per the need of the bank. Big data is also useful in financial market as it can be used to track illegal trading activities. But keeping the records of customers safe is the most concern as distributing data among various departments and applying analytics techniques makes data more prone to leak or breach (Sravanthi & Reddy, 2015).

Some common actions which can be taken by banks using big data can be concluded as follows:

Figure 1. Big Data applications

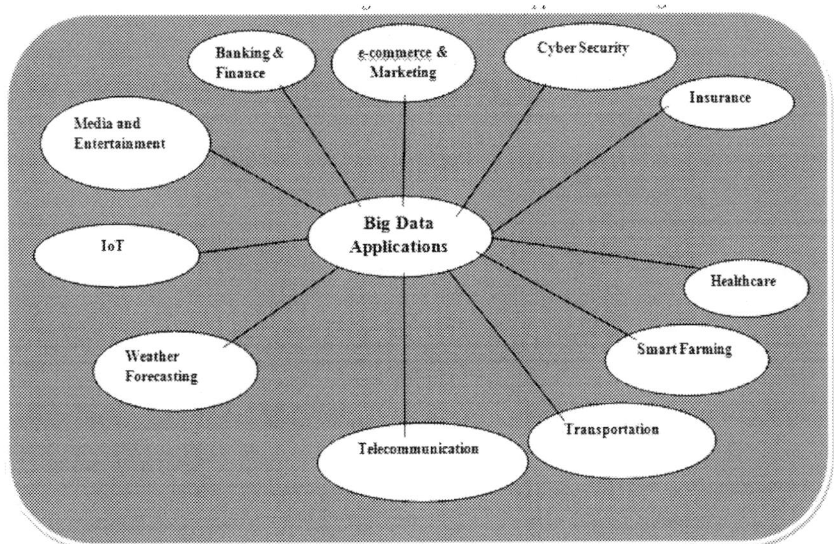

- **Fraud Detection:** Using big data analytics and machine learning banks and financial firms can differentiate between a normal and abnormal transaction based on the historical statistics of a customer. For example, if some unusual high transaction occurs from a customer's account and if bank's fraud detection system analyzes it, immediately transaction can be abort until customer verifies it.
- **Regular Monitoring:** Financial firms perform regular monitoring of the financial activities for example shares and stocks and they are also supposed to maintain report of the data. Moreover, with the help of data a pattern for example closing, lows or high stocks or shares within a period of time can be identified. This analysis can be useful in prediction and can reduce various financial risks.
- **Customer Division & Personalized Marketing:** Customer segmentation is to divide customers into different sets depending on their age, income, region, online transactions, and frequency of transactions. This type of segmentation is to understand the customers which can definitely improve promotions and marketing campaigns since we can know which type of promotions and marketing campaigns is needed for which segment of customer.
- **Risk Management:** Financial firms are always critical to various types of risks for example credit risk, market risk, operational risk, liquidity risk, reputational risk etc. Risks can be monitored and controlled using the analysis of data.
- **Customer Support:** For any type of organization the key of success is excellent customer support. Data science makes this process better automated, more accurate, personal, direct, and productive, and less costly concerning employee time.
- **Life Time Value Prediction:** Big data helps to predict or determine the future marketing strategies based on user data, it also helps to maintain good customer relations during each customer's lifetime which gives opportunity of growth and profit.

Electronic: Commerce and Marketing

Buying or selling things electronically is a very common trend nowadays due to the easy availability of internet and electronic devices for example smart phones and laptops. The large volume data that is produced during e-commerce acting a very important role in determining, assessing the interest of the customers. This data is analyzed using analytical tools and provide very meaningful information about what customer wants and thus improves business strategy.

Social media analytics that is analysis of data produced by social sites playing an acute role in the growth of e-commerce. Social media is such type of platform where users interact and exchange views with each other and affects each other thus can influence a brand. E- Commerce vendors uses social media analytics to gain knowledge about what people talking about, what are their likes and opinions. Using this data vendors advertise their product accordingly and enhance the business.

Real life examples of E-commerce business are Amazon, Myntra, Jabong, etc. These shopping websites analyzes cookies (a text piece, stored by web server in user's hard disk) to identify either the customer has visited website before or he/she is an existing customer, number of customers who visited the website, the frequency of a customer to visit the website, to identify the preferences of the customer. Moreover, cookies are helpful to track what customer has in her/his bag. So, by using such type of information it can be easily identified what a customer is browsing, what are his/her preferences, etc., and thus a better service and advertising policy can be made Edosio, 2014).

Many industries are now adopting big data analytics to optimize their profit and to achieve their goals. Data analysis helps industrialists to take decisions. It saves time and money. Data analytics helps marketers to investigate valuable customers. Digital customers keep producing lots of data with each click by using mobile phones, laptops and internet. This information can cultivate very useful information to improve the manufacturing process, can be helpful to predict failures, and also can be helpful to analyze right time to launch a product.

Big data analytics can also work as predictive insight which can be useful to predict demand of a particular product. This will directly impact to transportation and logistics industries (Elgendy & Elragal, 2014).

Cyber Security

Easy availability and accessibility of internet has made our life easier but on the other hand it brought a lot of cyberattacks. There are many cyber security solutions available but due to the production of large amount of data over internet that is increasing day by day than before solely traditional cyber security solutions are not feasible. To solve this problem cyber security analytics comes into the picture that is analyzing the data present on network.

Combination of traditional cyber security solutions and big data tools has given birth to the term 'Big Data Cybersecurity Analytics' that is the analysis of massive amount of data collected from various sources for example social sites, clouds, servers, databases, networks, firewalls, applications etc.

Big data cyber security analytics system of a particular company or organization monitors the activities of the concerned people of the company and other details like IP addresses to which or from they communicate. This analysis gives a pattern usage network. For instance, if an IP address is found that is trying to connect with the company server that IP ca n be considered suspicious and appropriate action can be taken (Mahmood & Afzal, 2013).

Insurance

Data is a centric part of insurance company. Data has always been advantageous for the insurers as insurers analyze the data to give more profit and policies to the customer, identify and remove the risks, and make financial model which can ensure growth. But in this era of digitization the nature of data has been changed. Data is now large in volume then before, it is heterogeneous and increases rapidly. In older days the only method for the insurance agents was to meet their customers personally but nowadays, agents use real time methods to collect information about the customer, for example real-time climate feeds, geospatial data, public records, social media, cookies and click streams along with the traditional structured data. With the help of analytical tools this data can be analyzed and more precise information can be gathered from this massive data, which can be helpful to mitigate risk, to generate more detailed reports, more satisfied users and business enhancement.

Some common actions which can be taken by insurance companies using big data can be concluded as follows:

- **Risk or threat Assessment:** The primary concern of insurers is to determine the policy premium. When a customer comes to the insurance company, before giving insurance insurers want to know what the adverse things possible with the customer for which customer wants to make a claim. Big data makes this task of policy setting easier as it provides a lot of data of the customer. For example, if a customer wants an insurance for a car then insurance company can analyze that in which areas car travels most, how much that area is vulnerable to the road accidents and damage etc. So, keeping all these points in mind insurance company can decide the policy premium without any losses.
- **Fraud Detection:** fraudulency is a very common practice in insurance. It is undesirable for the insurers. Big data can help in this case in a very broad way. For example, if a customer demands an insurance, company can check the post claims of the person and can predict the probability of fraud and can take appropriate action.
- **Gaining satisfied customers:** With the use of big data in insurance, information about a customer can be collected from different sources. This data can be helpful to predict which policy would be most beneficial for the customer, and policy agents would be able to give more satisfied answers to the customers because they know the history (policies held by the customer, earning, etc.) and requirement of the customer in advance. Thus in this way big data can help insurance agencies to meet their objectives because more satisfied users leads to more profit for an organization.
- **Marketing:** After analyzing the customer data insurance agents can understand what exactly customer need and can suggest appropriate services or product. Moreover, agents can give special offers to the customer according to the circumstances (home. Health, vehicle insurance).
- **Smarter Work and Finance:** With the advance use of big data, machine learning, and data mining insurers can save his/her time and can prioritize policies according to the customer.

Healthcare

Big data is a technical sensation nowadays. Even healthcare sector is not untouched with big data. Nowadays hospitals maintain the patients record electronically, and by using analytics tools desired information can be extracted. Hospitals can collect massive amount of unstructured and different data from different sources like patient health record, test result, electronic medical equipment, social media, health insurance data, drug research, genome research, clinical outcome, transaction. Data analytics can manage this data using analytics tool and can extract meaningful information (Ojha & Mathur, 2016).

One of the favorable areas where big data can be useful is healthcare. Many countries are also using big data in this area to make the things easier. Since healthcare professionals also produces lots of data on daily basis this data can be helpful in various ways. Even some of the countries have also been adopted big data in health sector.

Few hospitals in Paris are analyzing data gathered from different sources and predict number of customers on daily and hourly interval. This solves the problem of staff size. By predicting number of customers in advance staff size can be increased or decreased which is beneficial for both patients as it optimizes the service and for the management as it can reduce the cost.

Moreover, data scientists are working on "time series analysis technique" in which old record of patient admission is analyzed and patient rate can be predicted in different weathers. Using machine algorithm an algorithm can be made which can forecast future admission patterns.

The next application which is using big data is Electronic Health Record (EHR). US has installed EHR in about 90 percent hospitals, however many countries are struggling for this. EHR is a digitized collection of patients. It contains all the information about a customer for example medical history, allergies detail, medication, age, weight, lab test details etc. details of EHR can be shared among healthcare. One modifiable file is also attached along with the record, this file can be modified by the doctor. Thus, EHR reduces the paper work and gives correct and unambiguous detail of a patient.

America and Canada used big data analytics to tackle the problem of misused opioids. With the help of big data, information about chronic disease and population can be gathered. It can also be predicted which region don't have sufficient health facility. Big data can also help to bio researchers to study about chronic diseases for example cancer, tumors etc. Researchers can study tumor samples stored in bio banks linked with patient treatment records. This research can give unexpected results.

Smart Farming

Big data is playing a very important role in smart farming. Smart farming is a phenomenon which uses IoT, Cloud Computing and AI in farming. These all technologies are surrounded by big data as smart farming uses smart devices, which are basically an extension of traditional devices with sensors and intelligence. Machine sensors can collect various type of data like temperature, water levels of a particular area, historical weather, soil and water consumption, growth, gene sequencing of a particular plant and this information can be used to know desired conditions for a particular plant (Wolfert, Ge, Verdouw et al., 2015). Moreover, this information can help to predict feasible amount of fertilizers and seeds for a crop.

Not only traditional area of farming even livestock economy is also affected by digitization. Livestock plays a very important role in the economy. It is a great source of milk, meat, eggs which gives employment to many people. Sensors and robots are being used in a very smart way (Schönfeld, Heil & Bittner (2017).

A smart farm uses GPS to collect information about a particular region or the position of the animals in the farm. This data is fed in to the computers and based on the data and programs computer analyze what should be the feasible composition of seeds and fertilizers for a specific area. Even researchers are doing research on robots that can maintain the farms and can take decisions (Schönfeld, Heil & Bittner, 2017) Drones are also being used for the surveillance of the farm. Drones are used to take images to gather data about the field. This data (Collected by the drones) and sensors help to gain information for example to create digital map of a specific area (Schönfeld, Heil & Bittner, 2017).

Big data is helpful in farm animals too. Microchips and sensors can be put in the collars of the animals which can measure the temperature and other important data. Analysis of data can be helpful in regular monitoring of the animals. Farmers and doctors can be notified for the same (Schönfeld, Heil & Bittner, 2017; Poppe, Wolfert & Verdouw, 2015).

Transportation

In transportation big data brought lots of possibilities by which we can make our transportation system as smart transportation system which will be efficient to solve many problems we face in our daily routine. A smart transportation system is a system which contains information about accidents, road congestion and route suggestions.

A smart transportation system collects a large amount of data from social signals, drivers' GPS coordinates, mobile phones' billing records to messages post on social media, record spatial, temporal and emotional information and establish the data foundation for social transportation research (Zheng, Chen, Wang et al., 2015; Wang, 2014). For example, if we talk about social signals, people are very active on social sites e.g.: Facebook, Twitter, etc. it is a virtual community where people keep sharing their location, information about accidents, traffic congestion, this data works as an input data to the smart transportation system. Many applications using this data for example the Waze app, which is a GPS navigation app, works on smartphones and tablets. Another example of SMT is Google map which takes data from the sensors and uses GPS coordinators to guide the user for the destination, also suggest path which leads to minimum traffic and helps passenger to reach the destination in minimum time. Moreover, while we travel in public transport for example metro millions of passengers daily generate massive amount of data by using cards. These social signals record temporal information of passengers is being used by the researchers to optimize transportation system (Zheng, Chen, Wang et al., 2015). With the help of big data government can understand the need of the people and can map the route accordingly. Government can use this data to identify which type of transportation can make people life simpler, number of buses or trains for a route and the size of the vehicle. By analyzing the data collected by the sensors (implemented in the vehicles) it can be predicted in advance which part of the vehicle need maintenance before the failure of the part. It is also beneficial for the safety of the passengers. Many private transportation industries for example uber, Ola are also based on big data. These industries maintain the database of all the drivers of all the covered cities, and when a passenger asks for a ride they provide a driver after analyzing the database. With the help of data collected by sensors and GPS fare is calculated.

Telecommunication

In the telecommunication sector, big data is helping operators in a very broad way. Using big data analytics operators can understand the demand of the customers and can get more satisfied users and with a big profit. Because of internet and mobile devices telecommunication sector need to store various type of information in bulk which keeps changing rapidly. Telecommunication sector collets a big amount of data such as call detail, user online data usage, user location data, network performance data, server log data, billing data etc.

The analysis of data can help operators in different ways, for example operators can examine a new plan that how much it is being liked by the customers and hence they can get more satisfied users, fault detection can be done before failure, they can predict how much bandwidth is needed in advance, they can identify the problems of customers and can resolve them and even they can give more secured network to their customers (Su & Peng, 2016) Figure 2 represents how big data can be useful in telecommunication sector.

Media and Entertainment

For media and entertainment companies, big data has been proven as an asset to attract more and more customers and producing more revenue. Companies are analyzing the data collected from various sources to identify what customer need what for example music, video, sows etc. moreover it can also be predicted what is the favorable time for a show. Media is adopting big data in a very broad way because big data has given an opportunity to media market for digital revolution as big data analysis gave the opportunity to use data not even within the organization but also from outside the organization (Lippell, 2016). Now media owners know what their customers want more precisely than before.

Media companies which are using big data are more capable in marketing or publishing their content more intelligently (Lippell, 2016). Many companies, for example, Netflix, Amazon, etc., use big data to understand their customers more precisely.

IoT

IoT, the Internet of Things, is a network of smart devices which can interact with each other without human interaction. Smart city and smart home are prominent applications of IoT. A city becomes smart when it has smart workplaces, smart farming, smart banking, smart transportation, smart cultivation and smart energy, etc., (Al Nuaimi, Al Neyadi, Mohamed et al, 2015; Gubbi, Buyya, Marusic et al., 2013) and a home becomes smart when it has smart devices like sensors which are able to communicate. Big data and IoT can be thought as two sides of a coin. Big data and IoT both are affecting all the fields of technologies and providing large scope and opportunity of growth. Due to the increased use of IoT the use of big data has also grown, as sensors collect and deal with the data by taking input data from other sensors and at the same time by providing input to other sensors in the IoT environment. By analyzing this huge amount of data organizations and individuals may get more profit by taking right decisions on right time.

Figure 2. Big Data in telecommunication

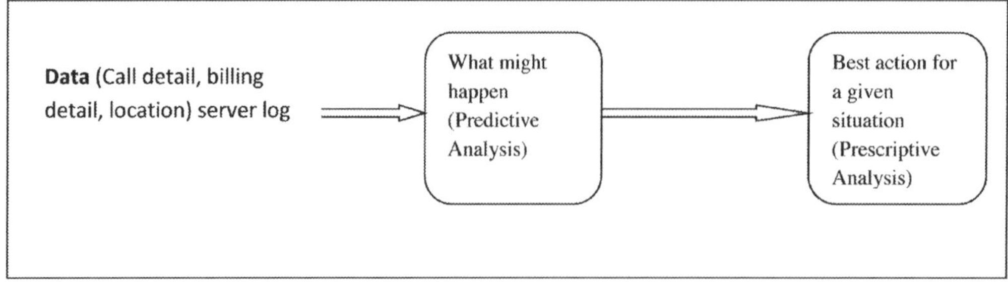

In figure 3 (Marjani, Nasaruddin, Gani et al., 2017) the relationship between big data and IoT is shown. This figure can be partitioned into three parts; first part depicts the communication between smart sensor devices such as CCTV cameras, smart traffic lights, and smart home devices etc. This data can be stored on cloud which is big and heterogeneous and increases rapidly. In second part this huge data known as big data is stored in big data files in shared distributed fault- tolerant databases. In last part comprises analytics tool which can analyze the data generated due to IoT (Marjani, Nasaruddin, Gani et al., 2017).

Weather Forecasting

Predicting weather has always been a tough task. Scientist is trying hard to predict it. Since, to predict whether it is important to analyze data becomes very advantageous for weather forecasting. So it will be useful for saving lives, improving the quality of life, reducing risks, enhancing profitability and humanity. Some examples of these domains include Forecasting Solar Power for Utility Operations, large-scale crop production forecasts for global food security (Jain & Jain, 2017). Example: IBM's Deep Thunder was developed by IBM which forecast the weather for a specific location and identifies how weather will influence the people and communications there. It is focused on much more short-term forecasts. Deep Thunder was used during the 1996 Atlanta Olympic Games to precisely forecast that there would be no rain during the closing ceremony. It was also used for the 2016 Summer Olympics in Rio de Janeiro. To predict the weather deep thunder takes data from public satellites, historic statistic data and many other private sources as well as local sensors and data a location may have.

APPLICATIONS OF IOT

IoT in Homes

Smart Homes is a technology that was started decades back by introducing the idea of interacting devices and networking equipment in the houses. The best description of smart homes is: the combination of technology and amenities in home network for an enhanced quality of existence. Most of the equipment that are commonly used in computer can also be assimilated in Smart Homes. In this topic, we will study the tools & Technologies that can be applied in Smart Home structures.

Smart Home Systems

Smart home is the phenomena generally used to describe a home that uses a home automation controller system. Generally, most prevalent home controller systems are connected to a computer system all

Figure 3. Relationship between Big Data and IoT

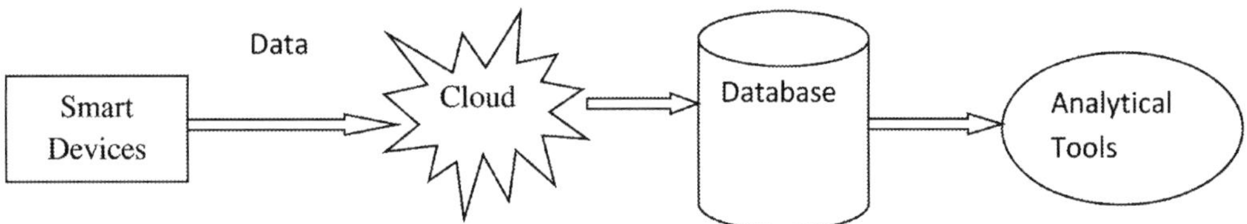

through program design only, and left to accomplish the home controller system responsibilities unconnected. Assimilating the home controller system devices permits them to interconnect with each other via the controller system, thus empowering one single particular button and speech controller of the different controller systems all together, in already programmed set-ups or operational modes. This field is escalating promptly as electronic tools unite.

Smart Home Technology

PCS technology (Powerline Carrier Systems) is used to send signals in a home controller system's electrical system to programmed outlets (Robles & Kim, 2010). These signals commands those connected devices how to operate corresponding to that location. PCS transmitter send the signal via home connections and the receiver device plugged in home will receive that signal and then perform the required operation on the appliances plugged with it. PCS has a common protocol X10 to control remotely plugged device by using short radio frequency. European countries use *InstaBus* to install home controller devices. This control protocol consists of a 2-wire bus line installed with normal wiring system which connects all appliances in the home to a decentralized transmission system and operates as an old telephone line system which in turns controls all the appliances. Except these other technologies are also present like Z-wave, ZigBee, insteon, etc. In smart home automation technology commonly connected appliances and some famous services of IoT are controlling curtains, garage shutters, kitchen appliances, garden sprinkles, managing lighting, security, eCAMs, etc.

Installation of Home Automation System

- Manufacturers and industries have produced various smart home appliances with systems like X10, Z-wave, Zig Bee etc. some illustrations of smart home appliances are presented here for better understanding of the topic.
- E-CAM that can capture pictures of exterior of home even at night.
- Motion sensors that can sense movement around home and that can differentiate between pets and burglars.
- Video doorbell in which your visitors can be checked before opening the door.
- Door locks with code or door handles with fingerprint sensors.
- Smart equipment to make physically handicapped people's life easy.

The requirements for smart home controller technologies: smart home networks must have provision for varied technologies to be able to run several services simultaneously. The server installed for home network is the soul of the Network that supports most of the applications. Third party services run on a distinct virtual machine (VM) that is connected to the server with the help of a typical interface. Some other server attributes that have to be considered are security& safety, maintenance and its ability to upgrade (Das, 2013).

Some noticeable features of home servers are the following:

- IP set-top box and servers have a virtualized design.
- Operating system used is Linux.
- Virtual Machines are focused on the top most layer of Linux.

- Virtual Machines construction is done in Security Layer according to the service application it runs.
- Virtual machines are isolated by the Security Layer that is built on Fuzzy Logic.

IoT in Transportation

Transportation is essential for the relocation of goods, animals and, humans; for transportation various kind of vehicles and modes are used by humans. A manageable and ecological transportation system permits fundamental and development requirements of public and societies to be met. Therefore, the interest of public in internet of things (IoT) potential is growing to see potential changes in transportation. The approach of internet of things in the form of connected appliances, devices and new technologies emerging rapidly signifies the emerging hyper-connected world. With the help of IoT we can modifies the advantages of steady internet to constantly connected controlled remote devices and goods in real world. IoT makes everything in this world accessible and connected with wireless sensors to make transportation more convenient for everybody even for physically challenged peoples. Government division of transportation plays a pivot role to implement up-to-date and well equipped, IoT enabled mode of transportation and to make it available to public instead of regular public transport. In this topic we will see what benefits can be there by adopting new technologies in transportation; the problem here is: "What would be the part of IoT in attaining feasibility in transportation supervision and control." The aim of IoT in transportation would be:

- To recognize the areas where we can apply IoT in the field of transportation.
- To identify the probable contribution of IoT to be applied in transport management.

The domains recognized for IoT enabled transportation were highway network regulation, road safety, aeronautics management, traffic supervision, naval facilities, and train services. These domains are further divided into sub domains to ease the administration of transport department (NomusaDlodlo, 2015). Here we have included some diagrams to make things clear.

In route network management, some sub domains have to be considered as shown in figure 4 like roadway management, quick reaction to emergency, observing and managing of road conditions etc. highways and route network is the most important resources in the development of any country. Roadways

Figure 4. Sub-domains of route network management

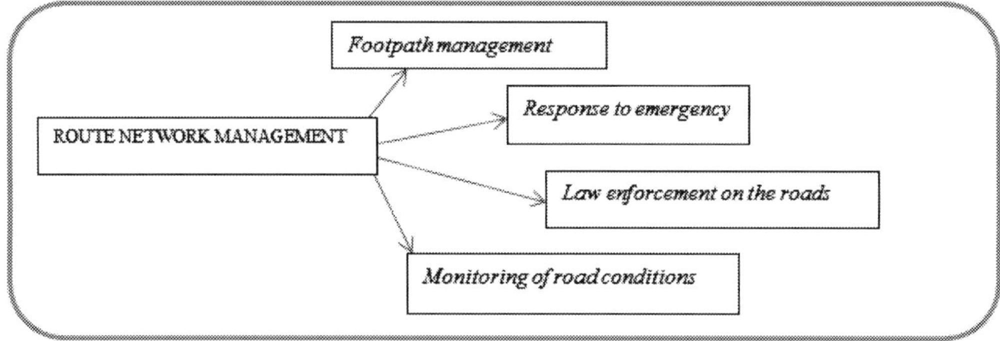

management or footpath management is the policy of maintaining and repairing the paved facilities and enforcing laws for the safety of public. IoT enabled small electric vehicles with the help of GPS system can help in route network management; it will collect data about the road conditions and will send the data directly to the maintenance department.

In road security management, important sub domains to be considered as shown in figure 5 are security awareness, load bearing capacity of roads and bridges, importance of traffic rules and regulations, control on speed of vehicles and pollution. Road security generally refers to various measures that ensure safety of public travelling on roads and highways including pedestrians, animals, cyclists, bikers, private vehicles, commercial vehicles and public transport. Visibility on roads is sometimes not clear, may be because of bad lighting, dark, bad weather; in that case IoT can help in detecting other vehicles and pedestrians on roads with the help of sensors. IoT enabled devices can also help in controlling “drink and drive cases” with help of the equipment that can detect alcohol in blood. IoT devices can also detect the speed of the moving vehicles that help police in managing over speed traffic in roads; that will also reduce road accident cases. IoT enabled devices also help in calculating the load bearing capacity of any road, bridge, train rails and infrastructure of subways, over crossing buildings. These sensors can generate early warning about changing potential conditions or about the need of repair, renovation and inspection. IoT enabled vehicles can generate alarm for the need of engine, fuel and other maintenance issues. Emergency sensors will automatically send emergency call and data directly to the help centre instead of manually calling for help; this will reduce the risk of sudden engine failure on highway.

IoT is helpful in traffic management also. Sub-domains of road traffic management are shown in figure 6. IoT is helpful in accident investigation, road networking policing, communications and route management etc.

Similarly, in the aircraft management and marine vehicles management as shown in figure 7 and figure 8 IoT devices can help in security, tracing and managing the movement of aircraft and ships. Database management and wireless communication is used to trace and rescue of any lost ship with the help of GPS & GIS enabled vehicles in ocean. To make the safety inspection effective and efficient metal detectors and sensors are used for Safety at port and airports as well as parking of airplanes and ships can be easily managed with the help of IoT devices. Passengers can check their schedule on their

Figure 5. Sub-domains of road security management

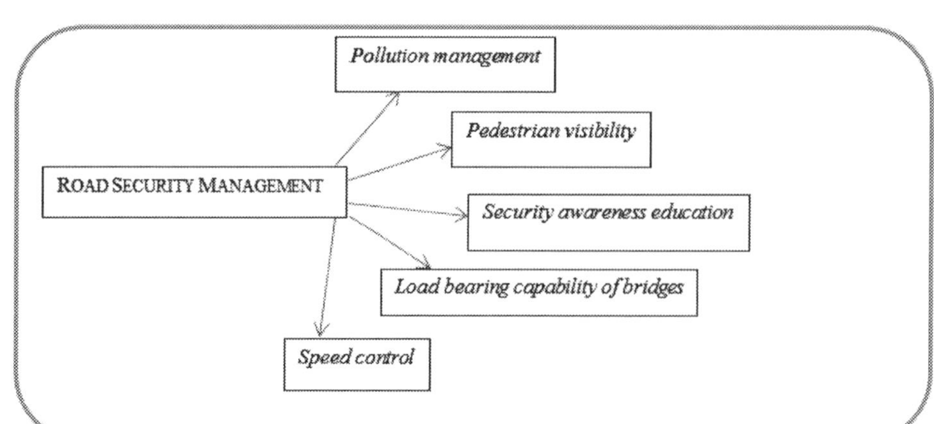

Figure 6. Sub-domains of road traffic management

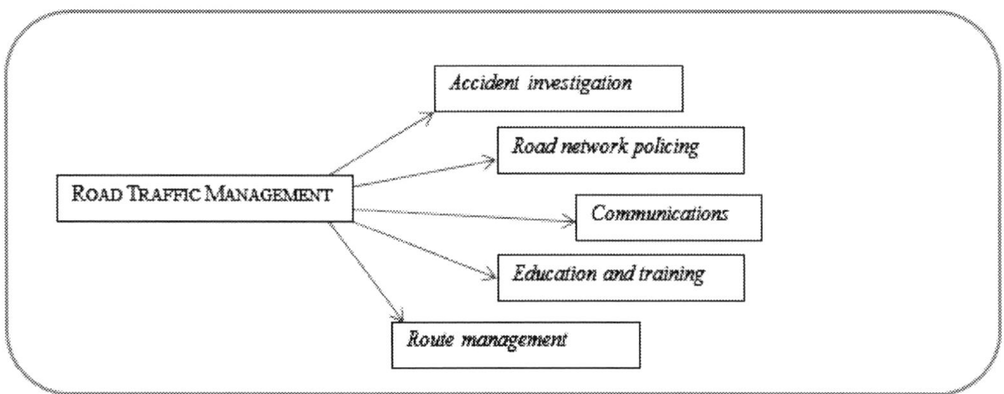

Figure 7. Sub-domains of aviation management

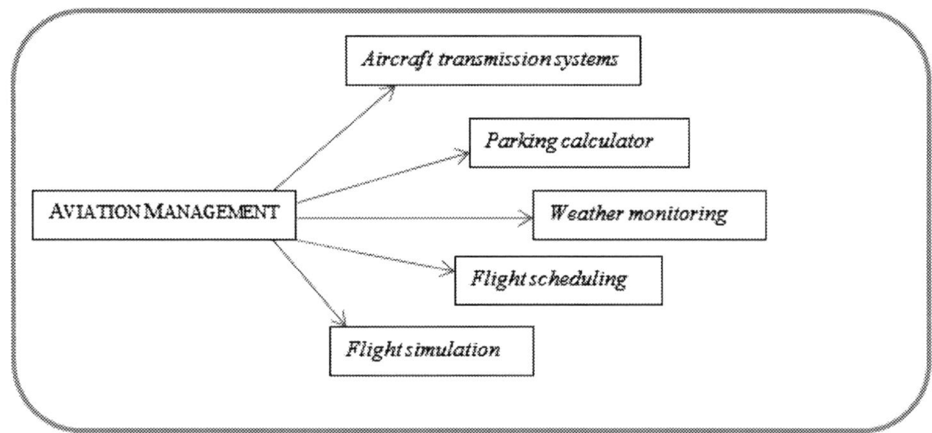

Figure 8. Sub-domains of maritime services management

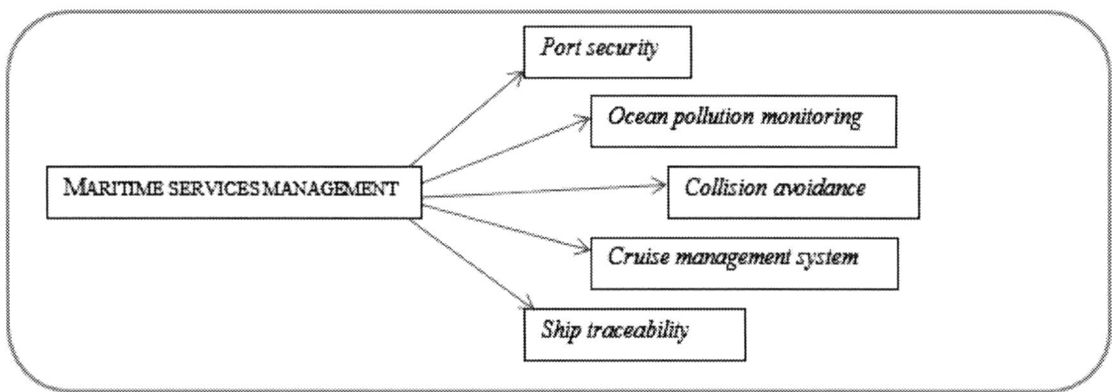

smart phones and laptops; Google also provide 3D simulation of flight; *Google Earth Flight Simulators*, passengers can feel the experience of flight while sitting in their living rooms. IoT enabled devices also help in monitoring the weather to avoid any unfortunate incident, collisions or mishaps during air travel and in the ocean. Pollution in oceans can be traced and managed with the sensors that can detect their surrounding objects, oil spills, seepages; garbage dumping etc. that data will be stored and used in pollution control as well as in Collison control.

IoT in Agriculture: Smart Agriculture

Farming till now is done by mundane, manual ways in India. Most of the farmers do not have proper knowledge about the modern methods. A huge percentage of agricultural activities depend on the predictions, due to this Farmers generally bear enormous losses and their loss forces them to commit suicide. Since it is known that benefits of appropriate soil moisture, irrigation etc.; these parameters can't be overlooked while growing harvests.

Therefore, in this topic we will study about the new ideas of monitoring the crops and uses of IoT in agribusiness; it will provide reliability &distant monitoring. Digitalizing agricultural activities enable farmers to check the requirements of their harvest and precisely predict growth of their crops. This notion of IoT in agriculture will certainly speed up the agribusiness to attain new heights; its success basically depends on the responsiveness and attentiveness among farmers.

Internet of things is the term that refers to a world where every object is connected with every other objects of our daily use; every machine transmit data continuously just like man to man communication. Similarly, agriculture appliances and tools can also be connected via IoT, various sensors like temperature sensor, crop quality checking tools; humidity sensors etc. can be installed in fields to collect the data to be processed and to send recommendation to the farmers so that their harvest growth can be improved. Every sensor sends data after a particular time interval to the IoT based server where this data is examined by agriculture experts and scientists; for e.g. soil sensor collects data about the soil conditions on a regular basis in every season, with the help of this data experts calculates the effect on nutrients in soil, humidity variance in soil, pesticides effects etc. which help scientists to make decisions. Similarly, other sensors and appliances sends their data, various information was then combined into one database set, this database is processed using machine learning techniques by the IoT based agriculture expert systems. Different IoT expert systems have been generated for rabbi crops, kharif crops and other various crops based on their required conditions for growth; like wheat crop require different condition than sugarcane, rice paddy require different condition than Aloe-Vera plant. All IoT based agriculture expert systems generally works on some common modules as discussed here moreover communication among these modules is shown in figure 9 (Shahzadi, Ferzund, Tausif et al., 2016):

- User interface
- Knowledge base
- Storage memory
- Trained algorithms
- Database set

Figure 9. Various parameters of smart agriculture

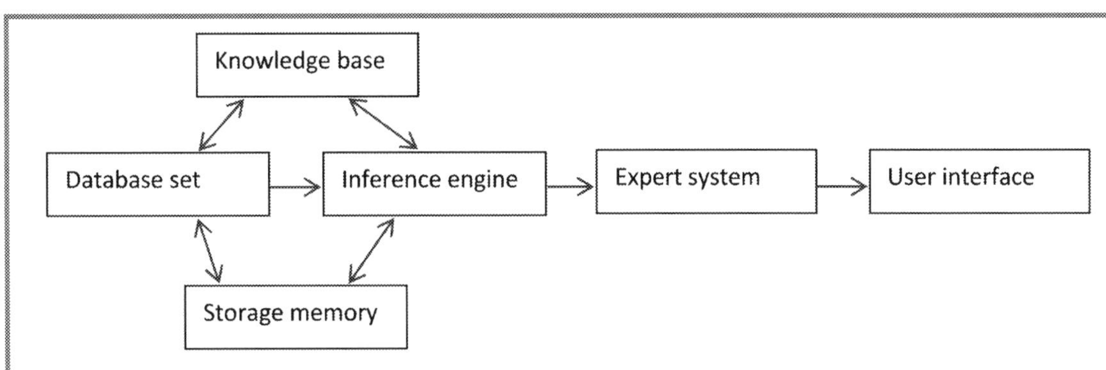

Recommendations are sending to the farmers on their mobile phones for the accessibility of uneducated farmers; some android applications are also developed for the use of farmers in various local languages. The server sends the predicted results to the farmers in their convenient languages.

IoT in Healthcare

Real-time monitoring of health for elderly people provides improved life care in countryside areas. This technology was used to cut down the cost of treatment for population; this will improve the life quality of aged population living hood. Implanted sensors collect the data for detecting the ups and downs in individual's health. Recognizing the problematic changes in beginning phase will makes the cure easy comparatively. This technology is more useful for citizens above 60 years; this technology ensures consistent and healthy aging. This method is for monitoring pulse and body temperature of the patient regularly for self-regulating living.

IoT enabled devices are used to generate, assemble, compile and then for uploading the code for input from the installed sensors, sending data to server & storing and for connecting the hardware devices to internet. Whenever the nursing staff clicks the button on webpage then a query is triggered, and a request for data will be directed to the Server via internet, System there get that request and establish a connection to webpage of user, and instantly start collecting data from the assimilated sensors, the data collected is sent to server over the internet. This information will be shown on webpage after every 5 sec the data is updated and shown in a bar graph to make it easy to read. These embedded sensors help in monitoring the patient from home for gathering data about changes in his health condition (Kumar & Prabu, 2016). This calculation helps in capturing real-time health pattern. These results are shown to the experts who are helpful for medical examiners and the IoT system delivers spontaneous health alerts to recognize various health issues in the beginning phase for the potential treatment. This technology is very useful in monitoring patients with IoT enabled devices especially in those rural areas where the doctor cannot be available physically. Doctor can easily analyze patient continuously using web browser, moreover the biggest advantage of IoT devices is that it makes the treatment cost effective and also diminish casualties.

IoT devices has made senior citizens life better while it has also improved the living conditions of physically & mentally challenged people. Nowadays, we see so advanced devices like smart watches which keep track of individuals heart rate, calories burned, distance covered walking, body temperature etc. some small IoT devices used by patients at their homes to keep a check on their blood pressure, blood sugar, cholesterol. Earlier patients have to visit hospitals and labs for every small test but now most of the thing are available at the comfort of their home. Except these small devices there are some major appliances or tools; you can say, that help physically challenged person. Artificial body parts which are developed with the help of these IoT appliances, successfully gave a new life to many people. New modern IoT enabled wheel chairs which the patient himself or herself operate, made the movement of bed-ridden individual life beautiful and easy. Not just humans, animals are also getting advantage of IoT technology, veterinary scientist and experts has worked a lot to provide better treatment to their patients; as a result now artificial legs for animals taking the market to sky high. IoT Embedded sensors can also be very beneficial in keeping track of wild animal in wild life reserves and bird sanctuaries; tracking the movement of birds, animals and the tourist will be very useful in avoiding any life threating danger for both animals as well as humans.

Not only healthcare sector but the insurance sector is also not untouched by IoT, and are also getting benefits of the internet of things; although the use of IoT in insurance sector is not as much as in healthcare sector. The database that is generate by smart homes, smart vehicles, smart home and garden appliances, smart watches, smart medical equipment will be used by the insurance companies to check the health risk, vehicles breakdown risk, appliances failure risk etc. before ensuring the demanded insured amount. In the USA an insurance company uses a special IoT technique known as uses-based-insurance (UBI) to monitor how the customer drives its vehicle. With the help of machine learning and data analytics, the insurer can efficiently judge a driver's performance on each of his journey. This technique ensures a more accurate price to all individuals and this also boots safe driving with bargain premiums. Till now the organization has done 1.7 trillion observations of drivers based on this technique rather than traditional factors.

The participation of Internet of Things in insurance industry will propagate now as insurers are becoming more technically adequate, with this technology insurers will be having a huge amount of data to cope with. Insurers are looking forward to leveraging this money to expand their business by rewarding their customers believed to be better and safe than others. The future is possibly be affected by increasing machine-to-machine transmission network, artificial intelligence, data analysis and cloud computing, with various algorithms shaping our activities and actions.

IoT in Industries

Industrial IoT is a term which refers to the coming era of industrial uprising, also known as "industry 4.0." Industrial IoT has more sounding potential of proficiencies over automation, connectivity and analytics. Concentration of industrial IoT is on those sectors where the use of IoT can increase the production and take the business forward in a more efficient way. Some industries which are using IoT are related to agriculture, logistic, production, construction, manufacturing, engineering, supply and mining, airbus, warehousing, robotics etc. *Digitally connected factories:* IoT enabled machine transmits operative data to the company associates and field engineers about original equipment and producers. This technique enables process managers and industrial unit heads to distantly monitor the manufacturing and enable them to yield benefits of development automation, mechanization and optimization. Along with it, a digitally linked division establishes better commands and categorizes key result zones.

Managing flow of manufacture: IoT in production enables managers to monitor the production process initially from refining method to packaging ultimate goods. This whole monitoring process in real world offers prospect to end or reduce alterations in procedures for improved supervision of operational expenses. Additionally, this kind of close supervision enables managers to overcome lags in manufacture, eliminating excessive workload in progress. *Security and safety in factories*: IoT with data analysis improves the safety of the workers in organization. By supervising Key Indicators of health and safety, like the frequency of getting injured, near-misses, illness, type of illness, absences, vehicle accidents, property loss or any other loss during working hours; because operational supervision ensures enhanced safety methods. IoT indicators and sensors ensure proper well-being, protection, and surroundings issues. Industrial IoT is also useful in getting information about real time supply and tracking goods. This technique enables manufacturers and other parties associated with the organization to keep track of interdependencies, production cycle time, delivery time, goods flow and other data. This data is very helpful for managers, manufacturers, cuts prediction issues, & reduces capital requirements.

Quality controller: IoT sensors gather goods data and third-party information of various phases in a production cycle. This information checked in alignment of raw material, employee's working environment, temperature and trashes, transportation etc. on the finalized goods. Besides, IoT devices make information available about the client sentiments after using company goods. Later, all this information is analyzed for detection and correction of quality concerns. *Capacity management:* IoT devices and sensors in engineering equipment permits maintenance alerts based on situations. Now-a-days many vital IoT machines specifically developed to operate in specific temperature and trembling ranges. IoT Sensors efficiently observe these IoT enabled machines and send warning when the installed tools & equipment differs from pre-set parameters. IoT also helpful in reducing cost, saving energy, eliminating downtime of machines and for increasing working efficiency. As more and more consumers are shifting to online shopping now days, E-commerce is also getting benefited by IoT. 60-70% of the sellers have opted for IoT to improve their customer shopping experience. Latest IoT devices have captured the market for e.g. smart mirrors in stores for trial of dresses virtually; that means anybody can try different clothes virtually without actually wearing those clothes. Amazon has opted for a new IoT technique which allows users to reorder their desired items with just a click; IoT has entirely changed the shopping experience.

IoT in City Administration

With emerging technology of IoT homes, vehicles, medical facilities, retail, industries have already opted for latest IoT technologies and it's time to change cities into smart cities. A smart city is the municipal area that has various technologies, devices and sensors for collecting electronic data to stream info that can be used to manage resources efficiently. This data collection is done from various devices, citizens and resources. This info is processed and examined to monitor public transport, water supply network, power plants & industries, waste management, law implementation, universities, schools, public library, medical facilities etc. The concept of smart cities incorporates info and transmission technology, various other physical devices are also linked to the IoT network to enhance the productivity of city services which connect the citizens. This expertise permits city bureaucrats to interrelate directly with the community for monitoring how the development of the city is progressing. IoT technique is used to improve the worth, performance and inter-mutuality of the services in urban area, to lessen the costs and the consumption of various resources and for increasing the interaction between the government and the citizens. So, smart cities must be more equipped to handle the challenges.

Currently, so many initiatory moves have been intended at investigating the beginning procedure, positioning approaches or consequences of Smart City ventures with the help of IoT network; established in numerous areas. Since its beginning, Smart City concept has progressed from the implementation of some specific missions to the execution of worldwide stratagems to tackle varied city disputes and defiance. Any Smart City should respond to the actual challenges of the cities in 21st century; like availability of parking space, monitoring traffic, controlling pollution, reducing crime rate, better administration within city and improved public transportation, medical and other basic facilities etc. it offers a wide-ranging outline of the accessible opportunities. Initiatives in this direction will be offered for establishing relations among the 'known city challenges' & 'actual solutions' provided by IoT network to support smart city venture. A Project Escort has established for the execution of Smart City ventures that professionally handle various complex urban problems without bargaining their progress as well as improving life quality of citizens. The objectives of smart city ventures are (Monzon, 2015):

- To outline the concept of smart city with the help of IoT devices and to find out how this project can help in achieving urban development main concerns.
- To establish a procedure to evaluate and prioritize better economy and flexible governance in these Smart City ventures.
- To set guidelines for implementing and managing environmental conditions and affordable housing in Smart Cities.
- To improve unemployment and exchangeability strategies for Smart Cities.

Problems in today's metropolitan cities specifically in Asian cities are categories in six major sections namely administration of the city, economy, transportation, environmental conditions, population and living conditions which are further explained with sub sections for better understanding; that are shown here in a table. In spite of the IoT technologies discussed above in this chapter like smart homes, smart transportation, smart industries etc. IoT can help in reducing the challenges which are discussed in the given table to achieve the goal of smart cities. This table gives a wide overview of the area where the IoT devices can be beneficial to turn a city into smart city.

Poverty, unemployment and uncertainty in safety are the major issues to tackle. Living standards in these cities are not so attractive, that has also affected the capability of attracting fresh innovative businesses. Instability of government sometimes invites fierceness and bribery. By refining these social conditions founds the grounds for constructing a better future.

IoT and Animal Husbandry

Animal husbandry and dairy farming are the branches of science that are related to animals that are upraised to fulfill human necessities like milk and milk products, fiber, eggs, wool, meat etc. It comprises everyday care of animals and selective breeding. Modern husbandry production depends on the availability of land type, for example cattle that are kept for beef; they require high concentration feedlots, where as thousands of hens and chickens might be raised up in very confined battery houses. Sometimes in such cases animal health gets ignored although various laws has been made for animal rights but technology can also help in managing health of animals. IoT sensors use for managing animal's health, are gaining popularity very fast in international market. Some sensors are produced for animal fitness at various stages; these sensors generate precise health status and sickness prediction which are relevant to humans. Correct animal breeding practice include a widespread extent of superior technology applied, like sound analyzers, location detector, micro fluidics, sweat sensors, salivary sensing strategy etc.

There generated a need to assimilate these available sensing technologies to create a proficient gadget for on-line monitoring in order to monitor animal health in real time. In this topic we will discuss the possibility of various wearable gadgets for animals and Nano molecular sensors with superior diagnose technique for many infections in cattle. IoT not only propose the apparatus for data collection in streamlined manner, but also provides interpretable, relevant and meaningful data. Nowadays, farming does not depend on conventional knowledge; sensor-driven information in farming permits great tracking of crucial factors for great profit. As population is increasing day by day demand for is also increasing, it is predicted that this increasing demand for dairy products and livestock can be fulfilled efficiently with IoT; it enables us to breed more livestock per farm with modern technique for feeding, milking and other tasks. Small IoT chip attached to an animal's legs or ear gives exact data about their health, age, growth rates, meat quality, etc., which can be used to predict the best time to slaughter the livestock to get maximum profit and to reduce cost of drugs and veterinary care.

The structure of unstable natural compounds in inhaling can be very helpful in understanding the glucose level in blood; these organic Compounds are computed for the same cause. Normally, blood-glucose level is associated with ketone, ethanol, and exogenous mixes in animal's body. Besides, hazardous configuration of exhaled air used for analysis of the breath—a forward technique for critical diagnosis in which puncturing animal's body is not required. These ailments involve many circulatory and chronic breathing diseases. The composition of respiration shows the configuration of blood-stream; a whole frame of animal's digestion. Cattle tuberculosis is a sickness in livestock with universal health impact. The capability to find out unstable organic compounds formed by means of microorganisms has developed the curiosity in veterinary scientist for diagnosing this illness. Many software Applications has been established to strengthen the link between veterinaries and pet owners. Engineers nowadays are busy in developing computer-generated peer group to mollify the desires of puppy owners, dairy owners, cattle managers and farmers.

Pharmacological firms use software applications for their medication manufacture items portfolio for providing transparency in health status of each and every animal at any point of time in its lifecycle. Governing bodies and strategy planers have also understood the benefits of IoT, nowadays some of the European countries involve this data collected by IoT sensors on antibiotic use. The IoT for animal health will generate an innovative level of translucency and turn into a requirement for international research initiatives. With these latest IoT technologies, there is a communal accountability also to use this data in optimistic manner to make the most of the production sequence, whereas defending the constitutional rights of animals. The usage of this sensor generated data in seclusion does not achieve its possible benefits: better translucency in food chain, enhanced traceability, further advances to animal welfare. This big-data is also vital when describing legislative policies, classifying trends and cultural swings in population.

CONCLUSION

This chapter first gives general idea about big data and IoT, and further discusses the various applications of big data and IoT in various fields of today's life. Big Data and IoT are the technology booming rapidly now a day. The biggest resource of big data is IoT applications. Both are connected in some or the other way. Big data and IoT applications have huge scope in every major field of human life as well as everyday life chores. Many applications of both the technologies are discussed in this chapter but there are many more applications like controlling traffic on highways, training robots, developing artificial intelligence applications, inventing voice commanding devices etc. Every new smart technology invented to make human life easy is either related to big data or IoT. These two technologies are also proving beneficial for animals and environment as well for e.g. stopping deforestation, to stop poaching, in poultry farming, reducing human intervention in animal reserves, to stop hunting, saving under extinction animals etc. The future of Big data and IoT is very Enthralling than this where billions of devices will be talking to each other, these technologies will bring macro shift in the way we live and work.

REFERENCES

Al Nuaimi, E., Al Neyadi, H., Mohamed, N., & Al-Jaroodi, J. (2015). Applications of big data to smart cities. *Journal of Internet Services and Applications*, *6*(1), 25. doi:10.118613174-015-0041-5

Das, S. (2013). Technology for Smart Home. In *Proceedings of International Conference on VLSI, Communication, Advanced Devices, Signals & Systems and Networking (VCASAN-2013)* (pp. 7-12). Springer, India. Retrieved from http://www.springer.com/978-81-322-1523-3

Dlodlo, N. (2015). The internet of things in transportation in south Africa. In *2015 International Conference on Emerging Trends in Networks and Computer Communications*. IEEE.

Edosio, U. Z. (2014). Big data Analytics and its Application in E-commerce. *E-Commerce Technologies, 1*. Retrieved from https://www.researchgate.net/publication/264129339_Big_Data_Analytics_and_its_Application_in_E-Commerce

Elgendy, N., & Elragal, A. (2014, July). Big data analytics: a literature review paper. In *Industrial Conference on Data Mining* (pp. 214-227). Springer, Cham.

Gubbi, J., Buyya, R., Marusic, S., & Palaniswami, M. (2013). Internet of Things (IoT): A vision architectural elements and future directions. *Future Generation Computer Systems*, *29*(7), 1645–1660. doi:10.1016/j.future.2013.01.010

Jain, H., & Jain, R. (2017, March). Big data in weather forecasting: Applications and challenges. In *2017 International Conference on Big Data Analytics and Computational Intelligence (ICBDAC)* (pp. 138-142). IEEE.

Kumar, R., & Prabu, S. (2016). Smart healthcare monitoring system for rural area using IoT. *International Journal of Pharmacy & Technology*, *8*(4), 21821–21826.

Kwon, O., Lee, N., & Shin, B. (2014). Data quality management, data usage experience and acquisition intention of big data analytics. *International Journal of Information Management*, *34*(3), 387–394.

Lippell, H. (2016). Big Data in the Media and Entertainment Sectors. In *New Horizons for a Data-Driven Economy* (pp. 245–259). Cham: Springer.

Mahmood, T., & Afzal, U. (2013, December). Security analytics: Big data analytics for cybersecurity: A review of trends, techniques and tools. In *2013 2nd national conference on Information assurance (NCIA)* (pp. 129-134). IEEE.

Marjani, M., Nasaruddin, F., Gani, A., Karim, A., Hashem, I. A. T., Siddiqa, A., & Yaqoob, I. (2017). Big IoT data analytics: Architecture, opportunities, and open research challenges. *IEEE Access: Practical Innovations, Open Solutions*, *5*, 5247–5261.

Monzon, A. (2015, May). Smart cities concept and challenges: Bases for the assessment of smart city projects. In *2015 International Conference on Smart Cities and Green ICT Systems (SMARTGREENS)* (pp. 1-11). IEEE.

Ojha, M., & Mathur, K. (2016, March). Proposed application of big data analytics in healthcare at Maharaja Yeshwantrao Hospital. In *2016 3rd MEC International Conference on Big Data and Smart City (ICBDSC)* (pp. 1-7). IEEE.

Poppe, K., Wolfert, S., & Verdouw, C. N. (2015). A European Perspective on the Economics of Big Data. *OECD*. Retrieved from https://www.oecd.org/tad/events/Autumn15_Journal_Poppe.et.al.pdf

Robles, R. J., & Kim, T. H. (2010). Applications, systems and methods in smart home technology. *Int. Journal of Advanced Science And Technology, 15*.

Schönfeld, M., Heil, R., & Bittner, L. (2017). Big Data in a Farm- Smart Farming. In *Big Data in Context* (pp. 109–120). Springer.

Shahzadi, R., Ferzund, J., Tausif, M., & Suryani, M. A. (2016). Internet of Things based Expert System for Smart Agriculture. *International Journal of Advanced Computer Science and Applications*, *7*(9), 341–350.

Sravanthi, K., & Reddy, T. S. (2015). Applications of Big data in Various Fields. *International Journal of Computer Science and Information Technologies*, *6*(5), 4629–4632.

Su, F., & Peng, Y. (2016). The research of big data architecture on telecom industry. In *2016 16th International Symposium on Communications and Information Technologies (ISCIT)*. IEEE. doi:10.1109/ISCIT.2016.7751636

Wang, F. (2014). Scanning the Issue and Beyond; Parallel driving with software vehicular robots for safety and smartness. *IEEE Transactions on Intelligent Transportation Systems*, *15*(4), 1381–1387. doi:10.1109/TITS.2014.2342451

Wanichayapong, N., Pruthipunyaskul, W., Pattara-Atikom, W., & Chaovalit, P. (2011, August). Social-based traffic information extraction and classification. In *2011 11th International Conference on ITS Telecommunications (ITST)* (pp. 107-112). IEEE.

Wolfert, S., Ge, L., Verdouw, C., & Bogaardt, M. J. (2017). Big data in smart farming–a review. *Agricultural Systems*, *153*, 69-80. Retrieved from https://www.sciencedirect.com/science/article/pii/S0308521X16303754

Zheng, X., Chen, W., Wang, P., Shen, D., Chen, S., Wang, X., ... Yang, L. (2016). Big data for social transportation. *IEEE Transactions on Intelligent Transportation Systems*, *17*(3), 620–630.

Chapter 2
Applications of Big Data and Green IoT-Enabling Technologies for Smart Cities

Onur Dogan
Istanbul Technical University, Turkey

Omer Faruk Gurcan
Istanbul Technical University, Turkey

ABSTRACT

In recent years, enormous amounts of digital data have been generated. In parallel, data collection, storage, and analysis technologies have developed. Recently, there has been an increasing trend of people moving towards urban areas. By 2030 more than 60% of the world's population will live in an urban environment. Urban areas are big data resource because they include millions of citizens, technological devices, and vehicles which generate data continuously. Besides, rapid urbanization brings many challenges, such as environmental pollution, traffic congestion, health problems, energy management, etc. Some policies for countries are required to cope with urbanization problems. One of these policies is to build smart cities. Smart cities integrate information and communication technology and various physical devices connected to the network (the internet of things or IoT) to both improve the quality of government services and citizen welfare. This chapter presents a literature review of big data, smart cities, IoT, green-IoT concepts, using technology and methods, and applications worldwide.

INTRODUCTION

Data increases at exponential growth rate year after year. Advances in several technologies such as communications, sensors and mobile devices have enabled data collection (Yakoob et al., 2016). In the 2012 World Economic Forum, it is reported that big data has become an economic resource, which has a significance to gold and currency (Alharthi et al., 2017). Jeanne Ross from MIT (cited in Akoka et al., 2017) suggests the SMACIT factors (Social media, Mobile systems, Analytics, Cloud and Internet of Things) that have critical parts of digital transformation. This classification has the goal of focusing on

DOI: 10.4018/978-1-5225-7432-3.ch002

the link of SMACIT and Big Data (Akoka et al., 2017). With advances in IoT technology, interconnection of different networked embedded tools, such as sensors, cameras and home appliances associated with Internet (Jaradat et al., 2015; Zanella et al., 2014). Internet of Things (IoT) provides new services and facilitates human life considerably in different areas of life such as healthcare, transportation and emergency (Zanella et al., 2014; Rathore et al., 2016).

More than 53.86% of the population in the world was living in cities as of 2015. On the other hand, Turkey has an urban population of 73.40%. Cities go on to grow and a prediction declares that 70% of the people will live in urban areas by 2050 (URL 11). The growth increases management and complexity problems for authorities in many areas such as waste management, supply of energy, traffic management, healthcare environment, education and safety. With the increasing population, tremendous devices contact with each other. Significant increase in device variety, volume of data and sensor technologies have offered opportunities to build smart cities for countries (Rathore et al., 2016; Holler et al., 2014; Joshi et al., 2016; Souza et al., 2016). According to Doran et al. (2013) sensors are useful to determine what is happening, on the other hand, they are not successful to occur information about why and how. Cities have been equipped with many strategies to become smart and easy-to-manage.

The Smart City was a concept firstly introduced in the "Strategic Energy Technology Plan" (URL 12). In the plan smart city is defined as "…a city that makes a conscious effort to innovatively employ information and communication technologies (ICT) to support a more inclusive, diverse and sustainable urban environment…" (Rosati & Conti, 2016). According to Pike Research on Smart Cities, the smart city market is estimated at hundreds of billion dollars by 2020 (URL 13). The basic goal of the smart cities is solving common public problems for people (Consoli et al., 2017). Urban big data is a significant resource for smart city development projects. It is a huge amount of data collected from the subjects and objects including people, companies and other urban facilities (Pan et al., 2016). Smart city applications can be made on transportation systems, education, healthcare, energy management etc. with private companies and urban administration cooperation. Smart city applications offer both improved delivery of services to citizens and reduced environmental impact (Holler et al., 2014).

SMART CITY

Urban area has higher population than the rural area in the worldwide since 2008 and it is predicted that increase in population will not only go on but also be strengthened (United Nations, 2012). The fact means that there will be many difficulties for economies in cities with respect to efficiently use of resources and sustainability in the near future (Angelidou, 2015). High ratio of urbanization brings some problems related to health, traffic management, education, energy management, pollution and waste management. Table 1 presents implementation areas related to mentioned problems. These problems require to develop new strategies about the environment design. The digital developments have made easy cities and policy makers to recognize the relationship between technology benefits and urbanization. As a response, various conceptualizations have been introduced such as digital cities, wired cities, cyber cities, real-time city, techno cities, WIKI cities and networked cities. Although there are variety of city descriptions, the smart city concept has become most recognized among practitioners and urban researchers (Steenbruggen et al., 2015).

Smart city is a term introduced in 1994. EU has supported smart city projects since 2010. It has become a popular topic in academia and industry. Some big companies such as Microsoft, IBM and

Table 1. Studies related to urbanization problems

Implementation	The study presents ...	Study
Health	an IoT hybrid monitoring system for health industry by combining RFID and WSN technologies.	Adame et al., 2018
	a novel term as smart health. Smart health uses mobile phones including context-aware complement in smart cities.	Solanas et al. 2014
	remote monitoring system based on daily living activity by supporting elderly people.	Maki et al, 2011
Traffic Management	a pilot system for public safety integrated in a campus microgrid. In addition, the system uncovers cyber security problems.	Jin et al, 2016
	An evaluation of passenger and commercial vehicles performance.	Melo et al. 2017
	a monitoring system based on mobility and some implementations related to traffic flows, security improvement and inside building energy.	Fernández-Ares et al., 2017
	an evaluation dynamic traffic network of a hotel service centers.	Yang et al., (in press)
Education	a study on integration of whole population and social inclusion in schools.	Aguaded-Ramírez, 2017
	a smart classroom environment for engineering education to develop co-learning.	Alelaiwi et al., 2015
	a smart class environment. It has a goal to generalize the Ambient Intelligence (AmI) vision in schools.	Santana-Mancilla et al. 2013
Energy Management	planning and operation models in the smart city based on energy.	Calvillo et al. 2016
	a load profile in buildings by analyzing the consumption of energy in a cooling/heating mechanical room	Capozzoli et al. 2017
	new method for operational management and mobile power infrastructure planning in smart cities.	Meenaa et al. 2017
	smart mobility solutions to manage energy savings with four main steps.	Chen et al. 2017
Pollution Monitoring	a study related to coastal and water areas, that is, pollution load in the coastal and modelling of dynamics in water.	Rahmat et al. 2016
Waste Management	different collection and transportation methods for solid waste.	Lella et al. 2017

Oracle have adopted smart city term to their visions since 2005 (Sta, 2016). Smart cities provide a smart economy, smart environment, smart living and smart governance by integration of technology, government and people. (Ahvenniemi et al., 2017). Townsend (2013) defines smart cities as "…places where information technology is combined with infrastructure, architecture, everyday objects, and even our bodies to address social, economic, and environmental problems…"

Smart city implementations aim to get the right information at the right place and on the right device to make a city-based decision with ease and to aid citizens more quickly (Rathore et al., 2016). The smart cities include millions of data sources. Sta (2016) expected that 50 billion devices would connect by IoT devices in 2020. A smart city monitors streets, people and objects continuously and gathers, analyses and uses data from different sources such as websites, smart phones and weblogs (Van de Pas et al., 2015). Smart cities have successful implementations in several areas such as smart mobility, smart living, smart environment, smart governance and smart economy (Del Chiappa & Baggio, 2015). Figure 1 presents a smart city concept with respect to big data sources and implementation areas.

Smart Cities supported by Big Data and IoT help provide sustainable environment. They provide optimizing infrastructures, network security, convenience of the public services, better life environment,

Figure 1. Smart city concept

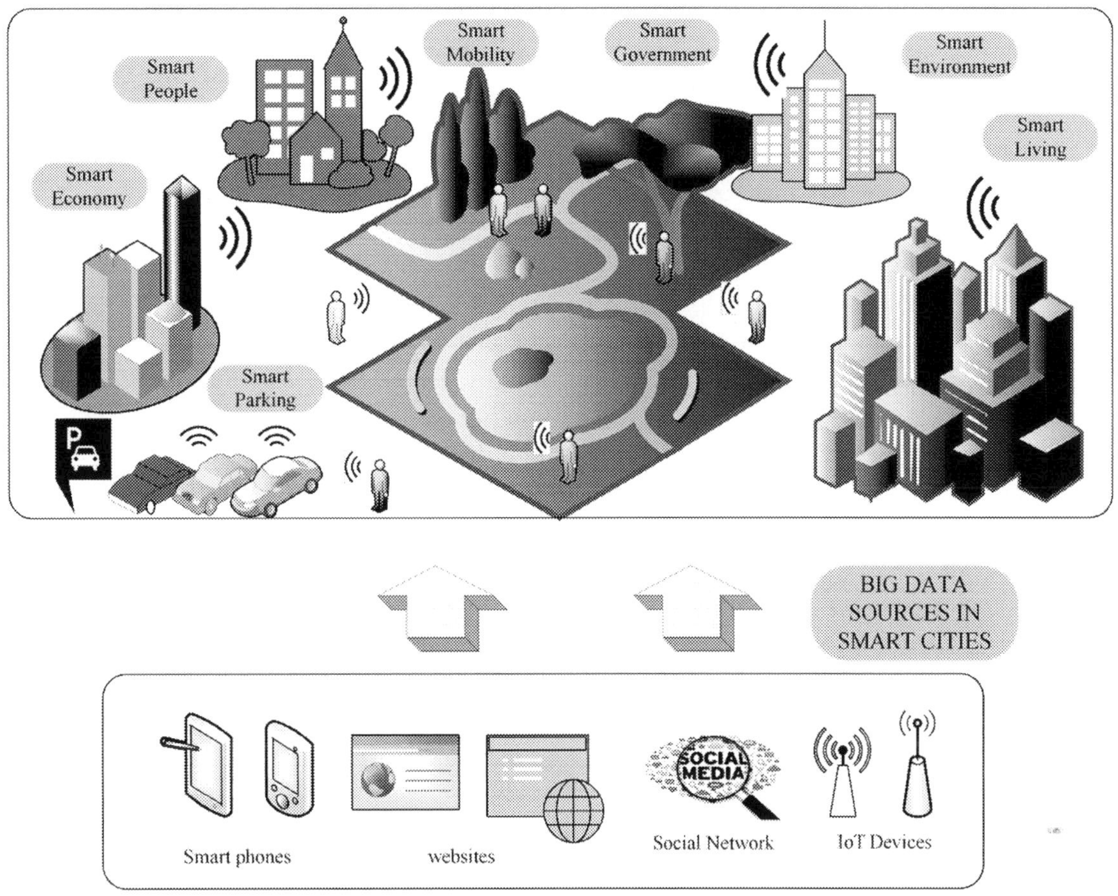

efficiency in city management and services, industry that is more modern and a dynamic and innovative economy (Susanti et al., 2016). Smart cities have also some economic outcomes such as workforce development and business or job creation (Joshi et al., 2016). At the same time, smart city initiatives with urban big data can increase people awareness and motivate the citizens to participate actively in public administration (Zanella et al., 2014).

BIG DATA

The volume of data has dramatically increased over the last decades with the use of several digital devices because of continuously huge amount of data generation. The generated data are generally heterogeneous, structured or unstructured data. Traditional database systems are inefficient with respect to storage, processing and analysis for big data. As an example of big data generation, Walmart tackles over 1 million transactions data and this value contains over 2.5 petabyte of data each hour (Yakoob et al., 2016).

Big data is a well-known concept arising from the requirement of big companies such as Google and Facebook that aim to analyze huge amount of data. Huge amounts of generated data are often called as big data. Various dimensions have been used to define big data. In 2001, Laney (2001) proposed the three dimensions of big data: volume, variety and velocity. Then the 3Vs have been accepted as a widespread big data concept (Chen et al., 2012; Kwon et al., 2014; Furht & Villanustre, 2016; Lee, 2017).

Volume is related to the collected and/or generated data. Sensors, social media, organizations and individuals generate large amount of unstructured data such as text, audio, images, and video (Anshari & Alas, 2015). John Gantz and David Reinsel (2011) put forward that the generated data volume in the world was 1.8 zettabytes (ZB), that 1 ZB equals to 1 trillion gigabytes, and it will be 35 ZB in 2020.

Velocity indicates the speed of created and processed data. The data velocity accelerates day by day. At the beginning, while companies analyzed their data with batch processing systems, today real time data processing has become well-advised because of high speed of data generating and processing. For instance, over one billion users open Youtube in each month and 100 hours of new videos of every few minutes. As another example to Big Data speed, users upload over 100 terabytes of data to Facebook in each day. Gartner (2015), a research and advisory company, forecasted that by 2020, the number of contacted devices will be 20.8 billion.

Variety indicates types of data. Big data are produced in various formats such as image, audio, text or clickstream using today's technologies (Yakoob et al., 2016). The generated data sets include several types of data such as complete or incomplete, structured, semi-structured or unstructured data and private or public (Oussous et al., 2017). According to the data type, analysis difficulty changes. For example, while structured data meet certain structural needs of applications, on the other hand, some extra transactions are applied to unstructured data.

In addition to the basic 3Vs, a number of new dimensions have introduced day by day, which help to understand big data. IBM put the fourth dimension as veracity, which presents the uncertainty because to data ambiguities, incompleteness and inconsistency. SAS introduced two additional concepts as variability and complexity. Variability means to the variation in data flow rates that may change due to unpredictable peaks and troughs. Complexity represents the number of data sources. Since big data are obtained from various sources, data formats and types make harder to analyze. Oracle added value as another dimension of big data. Value indicates worth of hidden insights in big data. Understanding the importance of using big is possible to uncover hidden information in collected data. Lee (2017) proposed decay that indicates the decreasing value of data in time. Because analyzing is a time-critical step of big data in different areas such as patient surveillance and environmental safety, decay of data is a significant element with respect to big data. Figure 2 shows the mentioned big data dimensions.

Multimedia data are created in different type such as video, audio, images, text and clickstream from several data sources such as organizations and individuals. For example, each individual generates data by connecting to the Internet at any moment. Facebook, Twitter, LinkedIn, YouTube and so on as social media platforms collect the generated huge amount of data (Bello-Orgaz et al., 2016). At the same time millions of people lives in urban areas which are big data resources. City data is obtained from individual citizens and visitors, private and public stakeholders and various governmental departments (van Zoonen, 2016). Notice that hidden patterns, correlations or other insight from city data can offer city planners to make successful urban policies and it can increase life quality of citizens.

Collected data from various sources as big data is used in many studies that provide collecting, observing, managing and analyzing for data-based decision making and various application goals (Işik et al., 2013; Jia et al., 2015; Jiang and Gallupe, 2015; Kung et al., 2015). In addition to the literature, organizations capitalize on big data by taking care of data flows (Akoka, 2017). Big data has an important effect for companies in generating new businesses, creating new services and products and developing business

Figure 2. Big data dimensions

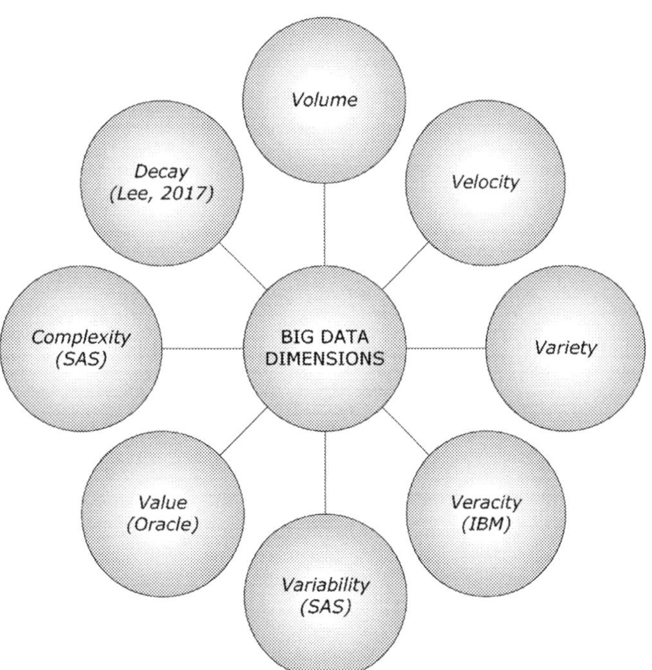

processes (Lee, 2017). Daimler produces about 10,000 cylinder heads used in car engine manufacturing. During the production process, Daimler gathers over 500 different data belonging to the product. The company analyzes the data, predicts errors and verifies variances before the production defects occur. Daimler cylinder manufacturing increased by approximately 25% after two years (Alharthi et al., 2017). Companies using data analytics in the processes have more effective and quick responses time to supply chain management. Southwest Airlines uses social media analytics to better meeting of customer requirements and representing better service. Tesco analyzes refrigerator data to decrease energy cost and achieved the saving near to $25 million in a year. Sears analyzes big data related to local weather conditions, prices at other retailers and product availability in the stores to determine prices dynamically. Innovative firms have applied social media to evaluate the credit risk and financing requirements of potential customers. They enable new types of financial items (Lee, 2017). Big data may enhance the potential value of the medical sector in US estimated at 300 billion $. When retailers exactly benefit from Big Data, they can raise the profit over 60% (Akoka, 2017).

Today, most of the people may be used as agents to gather data for real-time spatial observations (Steenbruggen et al., 2015). The applications are the basic data sources of generating big data (Yakoob et al., 2016). Social media can give information about the situation of traffic, environmental conditions, public transport and safety (Souza et al., 2016). Smart-phones, sensors, personal computers, cameras, intelligent/smart cars, Personal Digital Assistants (PDAs), social networking sites are possible data sources which generates big data (Hashem et al., 2016). Especially developed mobile operating systems have caused the smartphone as a necessary device in human life. One of the most critical characteristic of smartphones is the internet connectivity which provides to access internet at any moment (Anshari & Alas, 2017).

The Role of Data Analytics in IoT Applications

Big data analytics allow to store and process data in an IoT, rather than offering better decisions for business. IoT applications are one of the critical tools of big data. This subsection clarifies the role of big data and analytics in various IoT applications which include e-health, public utilities, transportation and logistics and smart inventory systems (Hashem et al., 2016; Al Nuaimi et al., 2015). Figure 3 presents a common framework for big data flow, which begins from IoT sources and results in useful information using various big data analytics.

Smart grid case: Smart grids generate rapidly data from different data sources such as (Hashem et al., 2016). Monitoring smart grids operations and managing electronic power consumption and in real time are critical. This is achieved by connecting multiple IoT elements such as sensors, smart meters and control centers (Ahmed et al., 2017). Proper big data analytics helps to make correct decisions by detecting abnormal behaviors of the connected devices and identifying risk level of transformers. A real time analysis can simulate a model for incident scenarios. Energy consumption analytics can guide for management of power demand load (Stimmel, 2014).

- **Transportation:** Many transportation companies use RFID (Radio Frequency Identification) and GPS (Global Positioning System) systems to track and monitor vehicles (Rajaraman, 2016). These tracking systems can provide interesting information about passengers, routes and accidents after analysis of collected data. For example, mining big data can recommend different routes or frequency of trips for buses according to traffic jam or accident in the city. Passengers can obtain useful information about alternative ways to go to the desired destination. Big data analytics uses trips history of passengers to predict alternatives. Using real time systems provides valuable information for both passengers and bus routes. Passengers can get information on expected arrival time of buses and city planners have opportunity to change daily bus routes if needed. Collected data can be used to predict accident circumstances. It can define parameters causing an accident from previous accident. Therefore, number of road accidents can be minimized.

Figure 3. Big data flow

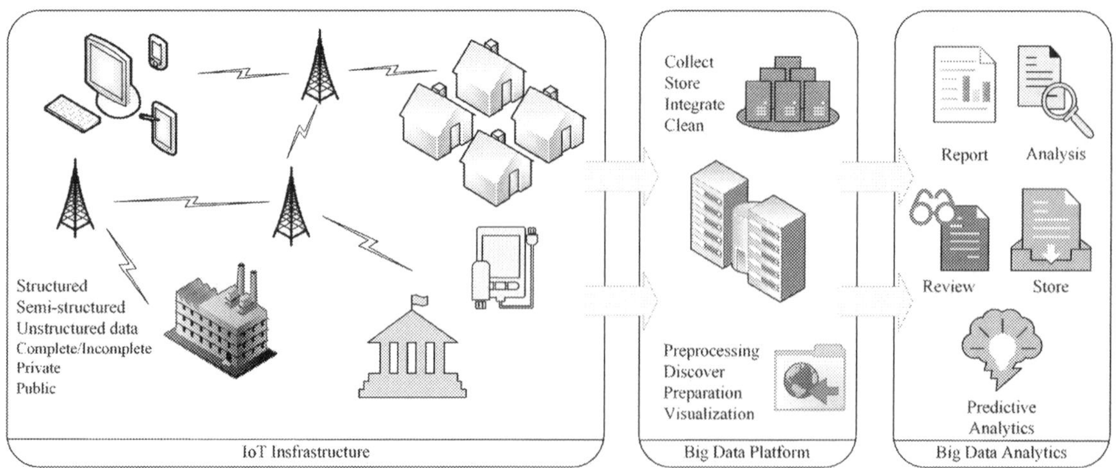

- **E-Health:** The basic idea on a big data application for healthcare is to personalize. To individualize health services, different health platforms are connected (Nambiar et al.,2013). As a result, large amount of data has been created in the healthcare sector over the last few years (Ahmed et al., 2017). Unless e-health analytics analyzes collected big data, personalization of healthcare is impossible. E-health analytics helps to analyze patients' data, created from several sources such as hospitals operations and clinical results data to learn their disease history. It is also used to optimize healthcare operations. In addition, insurance companies can benefit from big data e-health analytics to prepare policies.
- **Public Utilities:** Water supply and natural gas companies as an example of utilities use sensors in pipelines to observe and check flow of water/gas. A real-time tracking system to catch leakages and then control valves remotely to enable equitable supply of water/gas to different areas in the city (Oussous et al., in press). Big data public utilities analytics helps to decrease the number of operators accordingly reduce labor cost. In addition, it reduces time to identify and fix pipelines.
- **Smart Inventories:** It is used to monitor the flow of products in a company, create purchase orders, invoices and receipts etc. and control accounting related to inventory. The big data inventory analytics extract information on market trends, product recommendations and fraud detection from big data of inventory systems (Ahmed et al., 2017).

IoT and Green IoT

The term IoT first emerged in 1999. The data collection with various RFID tags and sensor technologies with the developments on Artificial Intelligence, Machine to Machine architectures, Wireless Sensor Networks and semantic technologies increased the applications of IoT (Hui et al., 2017).

IoT connectivity involves people, machines, tools and places such as mobile phones, watches, computers, cars, appliances using sensors, actuators, RFID, laser scanners, GPS etc. with unique addresses and enable these objects to interact with each other. Daily life devices such as fridge, air conditioning, switch, washing-machine can be easily communicated and managed with various Internet-based protocols. Many of these devices without IP support are resource constrained devices (Zhu et al., 2015; Kaur & Maheshwari, 2016; Bibri, 2018).

According to Zhu et al. (2015), IoT has six elements. These are identification, sensing, communication technologies, computation, services and semantic. Identification helps in naming and matching services with their demand. Electronic product codes are examples of identification methods used for the IoT. Sensing enables collecting data mostly from sensors and sending it to a database, data center, data warehouse etc. Communication technologies connect heterogeneous objects. Some protocols for the IoT are used such as Bluetooth, Wi-Fi, ultra-wide bandwidth etc. Computation is fulfilled by the hardware processing units and software applications. Cloud computing is essential in computation part of IoT. The services in IoT include identity-related services, information aggregation services, collaborative-aware services and ubiquitous services. Semantic aims to extract knowledge intelligently. The most frequently used semantic technologies are web ontology language (OWL), efficient XML interchange (EXI), etc. IoT has interconnection with Big Data and Cloud Computing to offer intelligent applications. The data is collected from various resources in a Smart City can be integrated with Cloud Computing (Albreem et al., 2017).

Green IoT aims a sustainable smart world, by decreasing the energy consumption of IoT (Zhu et al., 2015). The connected devices' number will be about 50 billion by 2020. Energy prices and carbon emissions increase correspondingly. Taking care of environmental issues through reducing the carbon dioxide emissions and greenhouse effects of devices, sensors, services etc. is crucial to acquire a green IoT reliability and smart city applications. Green RFID tags (such as reducing size of tags, producing printable and energy efficient tags), green sensing network (such as using renewable energy for charging, using energy saving optimization techniques, using context and data awareness algorithms to decrease data size) and green cloud computing networks (these networks have hardware that consumes less energy without losing performance and software that consumes less energy with minimum resource use) are some green IoT systems (Albreem et al., 2017).

BIG DATA AND IoT APPLICATIONS FOR SMART CITIES

Modern cities are getting smarter because technology grows rapidly. Problems can be prevented or their effects can be mitigated by analyzing huge data from variety of resources. This is where Big Data arises (Joshi et al., 2016). The need for smart cities has been emerging because of the increasing urbanization accompanies many problems. The processing power and storage capacity of computer technology increased with mobile broadband. Generated data from technological devices provides some of the solutions to urbanization problems by reducing environmental impact, creating new jobs, innovations, economic growth also helping traffic congestion, energy consumption, and behavioral change (Holler et al., 2014). According to van Zoonen (2016) data can be categorized as personal and impersonal that can be used service to citizens or surveillance of citizens in smart city applications.

Mobile phone data is one of the resources for smart city applications. Most of the people spend their time at a few places. To know these location points and routes can be used in effective network management and city management. Mobile phone data helps to find temporal and spatial level patterns. Then after analyzed properly, this data offers many benefits to city officers such as knowing where workers live and work can help manage public transportation traffic flows and plan services. As another example, knowing where and what times people come together for social activities, cultural or business institutions can target and price better their outdoor advertising as well as increase opening times and schedule of events. In city government point of view, mobile phone data can be used in crowd modeling. The smart city applications can appear in critical issues such as preventing dangerous situations, crime or planning an emergency evacuation (Steenbruggen, 2015).

The expansion of the IoT parallel to big data analytics is increasingly stimulating smart city applications. The amount of digital urban data which is enabled by the IoT increase exponentially (Bibri, 2018). These big data have many application areas for cities.

With the use of IoT, all citizen's cyber, physical, social and mental condition will be interconnected and intelligent. Citizens can obtain knowledge about their surroundings. For example, an audio sensor of a citizen's mobile phone will be able to detect any abnormality in citizen's voice to determine whether the person is ill or not (Zhu et al., 2015).

Big data is collected from different sources, such as energy utilization habits or energy consumption of citizen data which are measured by smart meters. When big data is analyzed, future need of power supply can be predicted, specific pricing plans can be made. Smart grids aim to manage the power supply of cities effectively. Information flow is very important subject in smart grid. Information flow and energy flow are integrated and large amounts of and various types of data are collected in smart grids. Such as device status, customer interaction data. Big data analysis enables accurate electricity demand prediction so firms can optimize power generation, firms can develop dynamic pricing using customers' electricity consumption patterns. Smart healthcare applications are related such as remote monitoring systems, management of electronic records or hospital asset management. When big healthcare data analyzed properly, epidemics, cures, and diseases can be predicted. Personalized medicine can be improved. Large amounts of traffic data can be used in traffic congestion problem by offering alternative routes, transport data can be used to optimize shipping movements or some solutions for parking, public transport can be developed. Smart education includes eLearning, massive open online courses (MOOCs). Smart buildings have smart meters, various sensors, heating, light or water and waste management systems (Hashem et al., 2016; Holler et al., 2016; Jaradat et al., 2015; Zhou et al., 2016).

When smart energy management is succeeded, energy big data has potential benefits in terms of operational efficiency and cost control, system stability and reliability, energy efficiency and environmental issues, customer engagement and service satisfaction improvement, renewable energy management (Zhou et al., 2016). City administrators or firms can increase comfort level of citizens besides decreasing heating/cooling costs by monitoring temperature and the salubrity of the environment in public buildings such as administration offices with different types of sensors (Zanella et al., 2014). Smart parking helps citizens using sensor and monitor technologies and tracks cars and empty places in parking areas. Drivers can use some applications and they can obtain free parking areas in nearest area or more suitable places to them (Rathore et al., 2016).

Smart governance is related to citizen participation and private/public partnerships. Smart governance enables service integration, collaboration, communication and data exchange (Joshi et al., 2016). Smart technologies can be used in waste management of cities to reduce cost and enhance efficiency. Predictive policing can be made collecting individual and aggregate data. Such as crime patterns can be analyzed and then police departments' performance is increased (van Zoonen, 2016).

Security is one of the most critical smart city subject for the citizens. Smart public safety initiatives by feeding real-time information such as continuous video monitoring to fire and police departments enables safety personnel to arrive quickly to emergency situation area. Another example is face recognition systems that can be helpful in criminal cases (Rathore et al., 2016; Washburn et al. 2009). The effects of light earthquakes on buildings can be observed with sensor data such as vibration and deformation sensors, and then building stress can be monitored (Zanella et al., 2014). The smart tourism destination concept is also a smart city application (Del Chiappa & Baggio, 2015).

Urban Big Data Lab project is developed by some universities and local government of Rotterdam. It aims to understand and use big and open data for smart applications and city planning (van Zoonen, 2016). Some sensors are placed on bins where how full the bins are measured. When a bin collects a certain level of waste, a dustcart will be warned to collect the waste. This application can save about 50% of waste logistics costs (van Zoonen, 2016). Dubai Roads and Transport Authority has smart city projects. Smart Parking collects sensors data from parking spots, and finds free parking spaces for citizens (Kaur & Maheshwari, 2016). In Padova Smart City project, environmental data such as air temperature and humidity, CO level, noise, vibrations are collected with different kind of sensors which are settled on street lights (Avijit & Chinnaiyan, 2018).

There are many smart cities in the world applying mentioned big data and IoT applications. Seoul is one of the leading cities using smart technology in mobility and transportation. Especially in healthcare facilities for disabled and elderly using mobile devices to assure they received timely medical attention. Rio de Janeiro, hosting the 2014 World Cup and the 2016 Olympics, had a partnership with IBM to be a smart city with offering advanced emergency and traffic services to visitors and citizens (Angelidou,

2015). Istanbul has worked on IoT since 2009 for smart transportation. Collecting sensor information from 6000 buses and 1050 bus stops, passengers are informed with an application where the bus is, how many minutes later it will arrive etc. There is also a black box project. In this project scope, more than 80 varied data (Indoor temperature, fuel saving, breaking number, engine temperature, breakdown information, idle running time etc.) are collected with communication technology infrastructure in buses. It offers to increase passenger satisfaction level. New York City decreased crime rate by 27% with gathering data in a central location and delivering real time information to officers instantly. Police department has real-time dashboards which shows a single view of emergency needs and its resources. The department can access event notifications using a web portal, email and handheld devices (Washburn et al., 2009). The Virtual Power Operating Center (Vi-POC) project is developed to support renewable energy providers in Italy. Data is collected from heterogeneous energy production plants (such as geothermal, wind etc.) using sensors in a wide territory. Weather information is also collected from related institutions. Combining these data sources, real-time energy production of power plants is predicted (Bergamaschi et al., 2016). National New Urbanization Planning of China has smart city initiatives such as informationized planning and management, modernized industrial development and elaborate social governance, broadband access of network, smart infrastructures, convenient provision of public service (Wu et al., 2018). Stockholm uses laser scanning, radio frequency identification and automatic photographing sensors in urban roads. These sensors monitor traffic in downtown area. Based on collected data, special taxes can be collected from drivers to help traffic jam and decrease greenhouse gas emission (Wu et al., 2018).

According to the study of Vidiasova et al. (2017), smart transportation is very popular for Hague (URL 1), Chicago (Buntz, 2016), New York (Ratnikova, 2015), Toronto (Marshalls, 2016), Bangkok (Oko, 2016), Dubai (URL 2), Hong Kong (URL 3) and Moscow (URL 4). Smart living applications, which refer quality of life for citizens, has an important interest in Berlin (URL 5), Canberra (URL 6) and Melbourne (URL 7). Smart environmental projects have been implemented in Buenos Aires (Donato, 2016), Delft (URL 8), Bodo (URL 9), Helsinki (URL 10) and Malmo (Graham, 2016). While Buenos Aires and Delft have are interested for a smart response to the flooding, on the other hand, Scandinavian cities such as Bodo, Helsinki and Malmo have detected project related to sustainable environment and ecology.

TECHNIQUES AND METHODS

Data Analytics

There are three types of analytics. These are descriptive, predictive and prescriptive. Descriptive analytics summarize the data and show what happened before such as Twitter posts. Predictive one analyzes statistical data to predict the future and, the prescriptive analysis helps to make suggestion to take action or can also be used to identify necessary solutions (Anshari & Alas, 2015).

The entire data processing can be summarized as follows: Firstly, data is acquired and stored, and according to requirements of user pattern extraction and filtering is done from data stores. Then cleaning and preprocessing such as data filling, data merging, data optimization, data consistency check, data normalization is done. So, data is prepared to be processed by establishing the dataset. Next step is processing and analyzing prepared data set. This kind of processing includes such as linear or nonlinear analysis, sequential analysis, factor analysis, regression, bivariate statistics. Data is categorized and the inter data and inter category relationships are analyzed with algorithms such as support vector machine, random forest, logistic regression, naive bayes. Next among the categorized data, inherent relationships are observed and further patterns or rules are uncovered using algorithms such as neural network, genetic algorithm, cross media algorithm. Lastly relationships among the variables are explained interactively and visually to present deeper understanding of obtained results (Pan et al., 2016).

Big Data Analytics

Although the information and communication technologies' important role in collecting, transmitting, and storing the big data, smart city development and maintaining depends on mining the useful information existed in data storages (Wu et al., 2018). Most of the big data is unstructured data which is about 95%, so new analytic tools, methods or techniques specific to such data sets are needed (Miah et al., 2017).

Big data analytics have similarities with business intelligence (BI). Both concepts use data management technologies and computer-based analytical tools to discover actionable knowledge and to facilitate decision making. BI is often used on organizational data architecture which relies on finite set of highly structured and offline mode data sources. On the other hand, big data aims to develop data management technologies and analytical tools that can overcome an infinite number of data sets, highly complex and dispersed data in real-time formats (Alharthi et al., 2017). Big data analytics capabilities consist of descriptive, exploratory, inferential, predictive, causal and mechanistic techniques (Janssen et al., 2017).

Some techniques analyze considerable amounts of data in a certain time. Data mining, social network analysis, web mining, machine learning, deep learning, visualization approaches, computer vision and optimization methods are helpful big data analytic techniques. Data mining includes classification, regression, cluster analysis and association rule of learning; and uses statistical methods and machine learning algorithms extracting meaningful information from data. Web mining is used to obtain a pattern from large web repositories. It includes web content and web structure mining. Visualization approaches generate tables, figures or diagrams to understand the data. Visualization enables to identify patterns and relationships. Quantifiable problems can be solved with optimization methods. Some strategies to solve the problem quickly and find a solution near to optimum are quantum annealing, simulated annealing, swarm optimization, and genetic algorithms. Computer vision helps to gain high level of understandings from digital data. Lastly, social network analysis is applied to view social relationships in social network theory (Yakoob et al., 2016).

Machine learning and text mining are the main techniques for location and mobility mining. The core techniques used in literature are: k-Means, Self-organizing map, Density-based clustering, Spectral clustering and Mean-shift (Sacco et al., 2013).

Constraint programming, fuzzy possibilistic model, dynamic programming, Particle swarm optimization based method, Biogeography-based optimization algorithm, Time series models, autoregressive models, artificial neural network, Bayesian networks, support vector machine, quantile regression, artificial neural network, Sequential Monte Carlo simulation, Ant colony optimization, K-means clustering, Hierarchical clustering, Self-organized Mapping, fault tree analysis, autoregressive models are big data driven smart grid management methods (Zhou et al., 2016).

City data as a big data has various kinds of imperfection. These are imprecision, uncertainty, ambiguity. Several theories are applied to model these imperfections such as fuzzy set logic to model ambiguity and imprecise data, probability theory to model incomplete data, and possibility theory to model imprecise data. The bipolar logic and the set approximate (Rough Sets) and the Dempster, Shafer, theory are also used (Sta, 2017).

Architecture of Smart City and Big data is presented in Table 2. It is a 4-tier model and includes data resources, human resources, technologies, and tools. Developed smart city applications should be environment friend. Examples for each tier is given in Table 2.

CONCLUSION

Big Data is a new resource to maintain the high growth of the information industry. Today, firms' competitiveness is highly dependent on their skills to leverage the technologies related to Big Data (Akoka, Comyn-Wattiau, & Laoufi, 2017).

People produces digital signs increasingly interacting with devices, social media and other technological systems. This data gives many opportunities to support policies and planners in satisfying citizens' needs (Bergamaschi et al., 2016). Uncovering hidden patterns, correlations, and some other insights from big data offer organizations to improve their businesses and satisfy their customers (Hashem et al., 2016).

Rapid urbanization and growth of urban populations require some policies for countries. One of these policies is to build smart environments. Smart City applications are oriented on the strategic use of new technology and innovativeness to increase the efficiencies and the competitiveness of cities (Sta, 2016). Smart homes, smart transportation, smart grids and smart health cares have been introduced recently. Big data has the potential for especially for metropolis to get valuable insights from huge amount of data which is collected with variety of sources (Hashem et al., 2016). Big data can be shared, integrated, analyzed and mined to enable users a better understanding of urban operations. More informed decisions about urban administration can be taken with more scientific approaches (Pan, Tian, Liu, Gu, & Hua, 2016).

Table 2. Architecture of smart city and big data

Data Resource	Human Resource	Technology	Tools
Machine data captured by sensors, meters etc.	Citizens	Mobile Phone	Data mining
Data from mobile phones	Data scientists	Network (4G LTE, LTE-A, and 5G)	Hadoop and its companion tools
Internet data	Predictive modellers	Smart meters	Predictive analytics
Web server logs	Statisticians	Sensors, screens	Machine learning
Social media	Other analytics professionals	Vehicle technology	Deep learning
GPS	Government officials	RFID	Cloud computing
Various records such as hospital data	Industry managers	PCs	Text mining
Other mobile phone data	Municipal authority	Wi-Fi, Ultra-wideband, ZigBee, and Bluetooth	Statistical analysis
Weather data		Camera	Data visualization tools
Vehicles		Wearable devices	Web mining
Applications			

Smart cities have challenges about some regulatory issues, legal compliances and environmental issues. Both political and legal components are important to develop a smart city (Joshi, Saxena, Godbole, & Shreya, 2016). Becoming a smart city has technical, organizational or educational challenges (Holler et al., 2014). Another challenge in building smart cities is the extraction of relevant information from the information communication technology infrastructure of cities (Souza, Figueredo, Cacho, Araújo, & Prolo, 2016). A well-planned infrastructure should be set up and developed. The use of a variety of sensors have some challenges that are related to restricted physical capabilities (as energy, processing, and memory) (Souza, Figueredo, Cacho, Araújo, & Prolo, 2016).

While some argue that proper usage of big data makes cities cleaner, richer and more efficient, contrary to this, some argue that cities will turn into robotic places which are data driven. So creativity of these cities disappears (van Zoonen, 2016). Data is collected from various sources and has various kinds of imperfection: imprecision, uncertainty, ambiguity (Sta, 2016). Lack of data science skills in organizations, organizational cultures that are not leading to data driven operations or data driven decision making are another barrier (Alharthi et al., 2017).

REFERENCES

Adame, T., Bel, A., Carreras, A., Melià-Seguí, J., Oliver, M., & Pous, R. (2018). CUIDATS: An RFID–WSN hybrid monitoring system for smart health care environments. *Future Generation Computer Systems*, *78*(2), 602–615. doi:10.1016/j.future.2016.12.023

Aguaded-Ramírez, E. (2017). Smart city and Intercultural Education. *Procedia: Social and Behavioral Sciences*, *237*, 326–333. doi:10.1016/j.sbspro.2017.02.010

Ahmed, E., Yaqoob, I., Hashem, I. A. T., Khan, I., Ahmed, A. I. A., Imran, M., & Vasilakos, A. V. (2017). The role of big data analytics in Internet of Things. *Computer Networks*, *129*, 459–471. doi:10.1016/j.comnet.2017.06.013

Ahvenniemi, H., Huovila, A., Pinto-Seppä, I., & Airaksinen, M. (2017). What are the differences between sustainable and smart cities? *Cities (London, England)*, *60*, 234–245. doi:10.1016/j.cities.2016.09.009

Akoka, J., Comyn-Wattiau, I., & Laoufi, N. (2017). Research on Big Data–A systematic mapping study. *Computer Standards & Interfaces*, *54*, 105–115. doi:10.1016/j.csi.2017.01.004

Al Nuaimi, E., Al Neyadi, H., Mohamed, N., & Al-Jaroodi, J. (2015). Applications of big data to smart cities. *Journal of Internet Services and Applications*, *6*(1), 25–40. doi:10.118613174-015-0041-5

Albreem, M. A., El-Saleh, A. A., Isa, M., Salah, W., Jusoh, M., Azizan, M. M., & Ali, A. (2017). Green internet of things (IoT): An overview. In: Smart Instrumentation, Measurement and Application (ICSIMA), 2017 IEEE 4th International Conference on. IEEE, 2017. p. 1-6.

Alelaiwi, A., Alghamdi, A. Shorfuzzaman, M., Rawashdeh, M., Hossain, M.S. & Muhammad, G. (2015). Enhanced engineering education using smart class environment. *Computers in Human Behavior, 51(Part B)*, 852-856.

Alharthi, A., Krotov, V., & Bowman, M. (2017). Addressing barriers to big data. *Business Horizons*, *60*(3), 285–292. doi:10.1016/j.bushor.2017.01.002

Angelidou, M. (2015). Smart cities: A conjuncture of four forces. *Cities (London, England)*, *47*, 95–106. doi:10.1016/j.cities.2015.05.004

Anshari, M., & Alas, Y. (2015). Smartphones habits, necessities, and big data challenges. *The Journal of High Technology Management Research*, *26*(2), 177–185. doi:10.1016/j.hitech.2015.09.005

Avijit, K., & Chinnaiyan, R. (2018). IOT for Smart Cities. International Journal of Scientific Research in Computer Science. *Engineering and Information Technology*, *3*(4), 1126–1139.

Bello-Orgaz, G., Jung, J. J., & Camacho, D. (2016). Social big data: Recent achievements and new challenges. *Information Fusion*, *28*, 45–59. doi:10.1016/j.inffus.2015.08.005

Bergamaschi, S., Carlini, E., Ceci, M., Furletti, B., Giannotti, F., Malerba, D., ... Perego, R. (2016). Big Data Research in Italy: A Perspective. *Engineering*, *2*(2), 163–170. doi:10.1016/J.ENG.2016.02.011

Bibri, S. E. (2018). The IoT for Smart Sustainable Cities of the Future: An Analytical Framework for Sensor-Based Big Data Applications for Environmental Sustainability. *Sustainable Cities and Society*, *38*, 230–253. doi:10.1016/j.scs.2017.12.034

Buntz, B. (2016). *Why Chicago is a Smart City King*. Retrieved 08 January, 2018 from http://www.ioti.com/smart-cities/why-chicago-smart-city-king

Calvillo, C. F., Sánchez-Miralles, A., & Villar, J. (2016). Energy management and planning in smart cities. *Renewable & Sustainable Energy Reviews*, *55*, 273–287. doi:10.1016/j.rser.2015.10.133

Capozzoli, A., Piscitelli, M. S., & Brandi, S. (2017). Mining typical load profiles in buildings to support energy management in the smart city context. *Energy Procedia*, *134*, 865–874. doi:10.1016/j.egypro.2017.09.545

Chen, H., Chiang, R. H. L., & Storey, V. C. (2012). Business intelligence and analytics: From big data to big impact. *Management Information Systems Quarterly*, *36*(4), 1165–1188. doi:10.2307/41703503

Chen, Y., Ardila-Gomez, A., & Frame, G. (2017). Achieving energy savings by intelligent transportation systems investments in the context of smart cities. *Transportation Research Part D, Transport and Environment*, *54*, 381–396. doi:10.1016/j.trd.2017.06.008

Cities Digest. (2017). *Smart City Moscow*. CitiesDigest. Retrieved from https://www.citiesdigest.com/2017/07/03/smart-city-moscow

CMD. (2014). *Digital Canberra: Action Plan 2014-2018*. Retrieved from http://www.cmd.act.gov.au/__data/assets/pdf_file/0006/565566/digcbractionplan_print.pdf

Consoli, S., Presutti, V., Recupero, D. R., Nuzzolese, A. G., Peroni, S., & Gangemi, A. (2017). Producing linked data for smart cities: The case of Catania. *Big Data Research*, *7*, 1–15. doi:10.1016/j.bdr.2016.10.001

Cumgeek. (2017). *Hong Kong becomes a Smart City*. (in Russian) Retrieved from https://cumgeek.com/articles/gonkong-skoro-stanet-umnym-gorodom

Del Chiappa, G., & Baggio, R. (2015). Knowledge transfer in smart tourism destinations: Analyzing the effects of a network structure. *Journal of Destination Marketing & Management*, *4*(3), 145–150. doi:10.1016/j.jdmm.2015.02.001

Delft, The Netherlands. (2015). *Delft Smart City*. Retrieved from https://www.delft.nl/Bedrijven/Stad_van_innovatie/Delft_Smart_City

Donato, C. (2016). Buenos Aires Preserves Old Charm by Becoming a Smart City. *SAP News Center*. Retrieved from http://news.sap.com/buenos-aires-preserves-old-charm-by-becoming-a-smart-city/

Doran, D., Gokhale, S., & Dagnino, A. (2013). Human sensing for smart cities. In *Proceedings of the 2013 IEEE/ACM International Conference on Advances in Social Networks Analysis and Mining* (pp. 1323-1330). ACM.

Economist. (2016). *The world`s most livable cities*. Retrieved from https://www.economist.com/blogs/graphicdetail/2016/08/daily-chart-14

EU Smartcities. (2017). *The Hague- Smart communities market place*. Retrieved from https://eu-smartcities.eu/place/hague

European Commission. (n.d.). Strategic Energy Technology Plan. Retrieved from https://ec.europa.eu/energy/en/topics/technology-and-innovation/strategic-energy-technology-plan

Fernández-Ares, A., Mora, A. M., Arenas, M. G., García-Sanchez, P., Romero, G., Rivas, V., ... Merelo, J. J. (2017). Studying real traffic and mobility scenarios for a Smart City using a new monitoring and tracking system. *Future Generation Computer Systems*, *76*, 163–179. doi:10.1016/j.future.2016.11.021

Furht, B., & Villanustre, F. (2016). Introduction to big data. In B. Furht & F. Villanustre (Eds.), *Big Data Technology and Application* (pp. 3–11). Cham: Springer International Publishing. doi:10.1007/978-3-319-44550-2_1

Gantz, J. & Reinsel, D. (2011). Extracting value from chaos. *IDC iView Report*.

Gartner. (2015). Gartner says 6.4 billion connected things will be in use in 2016, up 30 percent from. Retrieved from https://www.gartner.com/newsroom/id/3165317

Graham, T. (2016). Smart city Malmo. *EIB*. Retrieved from http://www.eib.org/attachments/documents/smart_city_initiatives_and_projects_in_malmo_sweden_en.pdf

Hashem, I. A. T., Chang, V., Anuar, N. B., Adewole, K., Yaqoob, I., Gani, A., ... Chiroma, H. (2016). The role of big data in smart city. *International Journal of Information Management*, *36*(5), 748–758. doi:10.1016/j.ijinfomgt.2016.05.002

Helsinki Smart Region. (2016). Retrieved from https://www.helsinkismart.fi

Holler, J., Tsiatsis, V., Mulligan, C., Avesand, S., Karnouskos, S., & Boyle, D. (2014). *From Machine-to-machine to the Internet of Things: Introduction to a New Age of Intelligence*. Cambridge: Academic Press.

Hui, T. K., Sherratt, R. S., & Sánchez, D. D. (2017). Major requirements for building Smart Homes in Smart Cities based on Internet of Things technologies. *Future Generation Computer Systems*, *76*, 358–369. doi:10.1016/j.future.2016.10.026

Işık, Ö., Jones, M. C., & Sidorova, A. (2013). Business intelligence success: The roles of BI capabilities and decision. *Information & Management*, *50*(1), 13–23. doi:10.1016/j.im.2012.12.001

Janssen, M., van der Voort, H., & Wahyudi, A. (2017). Factors influencing big data decision-making quality. *Journal of Business Research*, *70*, 338–345. doi:10.1016/j.jbusres.2016.08.007

Jaradat, M., Jarrah, M., Bousselham, A., Jararweh, Y., & Al-Ayyoub, M. (2015). The internet of energy: Smart sensor networks and big data management for smart grid. *Procedia Computer Science*, *56*(6), 592–597. doi:10.1016/j.procs.2015.07.250

Jia, L., Hall, D., & Song, J. (2015). The conceptualization of data-driven decision making capability. In *Proceedings of the Twenty-First Americas Conference on Information Systems*, Puerto Rico, August 13–15.

Jiang, J., & Gallupe, R. B. (2015). Environmental scanning and business insight capability: the role of business analytics and knowledge integration. In *Proceedings of the Twenty-First Americas Conference on Information Systems*, Puerto Rico, August 13–15.

Jin, D., Hannon, C., Li, Z., Cortes, P., Ramaraju, S., Burgess, P., ... Shahidehpour, M. (2016). Smart street lighting system: A platform for innovative smart city applications and a new frontier for cyber-security. *The Electricity Journal*, *29*(10), 28–35. doi:10.1016/j.tej.2016.11.011

Joshi, S., Saxena, S., Godbole, T., & Shreya. (2015). Developing Smart Cities: An Integrated Framework. *Procedia Computer Science*, *93*, 902–909. doi:10.1016/j.procs.2016.07.258

Kaur, M. J., & Maheshwari, P. (2016, March). Building smart cities applications using IoT and cloud-based architectures. In *2016 International Conference on Industrial Informatics and Computer Systems (CIICS)* (pp. 1-5). IEEE. 10.1109/ICCSII.2016.7462433

Kim, T. H., Ramos, C., & Mohammed, S. (2017). Smart city and IoT.

Kung, L., Kung, H., Jones-Framer, A., & Wang, Y. (2015). Managing big data for firm performance: a configurational approach. In *Proceedings of the Twenty-First Americas Conference on Information Systems*, Puerto Rico, August 13–15.

Kwon, O., Lee, N., & Shin, B. (2014). Data quality management, data usage experience, and acquisition intention of big data analytics. *International Journal of Information Management*, *34*(3), 387–394. doi:10.1016/j.ijinfomgt.2014.02.002

Laney, D. (2001). 3D data management: Controlling data volume, velocity, and variety. *Gartner*. Retrieved from http://blogs.gartner.com/doug-laney/files/2012/01/ad949-3D-Data-Management-Controlling-Data-Volume-Velocity-and-Variety.pdf

Lee, I. (2017). Big data: Dimensions, evolution, impacts, and challenges. *Business Horizons*, *60*(3), 293–303. doi:10.1016/j.bushor.2017.01.004

Lella, J., Mandla, V. R., & Zhu, X. (2017). Solid waste collection/transport optimization and vegetation land cover estimation using Geographic Information System (GIS): A case study of a proposed smart-city. *Sustainable Cities and Society*, *35*, 336–349. doi:10.1016/j.scs.2017.08.023

Maki, H., Ogawa, H., Matsuoka, S., Yonezawa, Y., & Caldwell, W. M. (2011). A daily living activity remote monitoring system for solitary elderly people. In *Proceedings of 2011 annual international conference of the IEEE engineering in medicine and biology society* (pp. 5608–5611). 10.1109/IEMBS.2011.6091357

Marshalls, A. (2016). How Toronto is becoming a smarter city. *Torontoist*. Retrieved from http://torontoist.com/2016/06/how-toronto-is-becoming-a-smarter-city

Meena, N. K., Parashar, S., Swarnkar, A., Gupta, N., Niazi, K. R., & Bansal, R. C. (2017). Mobile Power Infrastructure Planning and Operational Management for Smart City Applications. *Energy Procedia*, *142*, 2202–2207. doi:10.1016/j.egypro.2017.12.589

Melo, S., Macedo, J., & Baptista, P. (2017). Guiding cities to pursue a smart mobility paradigm: An example from vehicle routing guidance and its traffic and operational effects. *Research in Transportation Economics*, *65*, 24–33. doi:10.1016/j.retrec.2017.09.007

Miah, S. J., Vu, H. Q., Gammack, J., & McGrath, M. (2017). A big data analytics method for tourist behaviour analysis. *Information & Management*, *54*(6), 771–785. doi:10.1016/j.im.2016.11.011

Nambiar, R., Bhardwaj, R., Sethi, A., & Vargheese, R. (2013). A look at challenges and opportunities of Big Data analytics in healthcare. In *IEEE International Conference on Big Data*, Santa Clara, October 6-9. 10.1109/BigData.2013.6691753

Oko, Y. (2016). Bangkok strives to be 'smart city' to ease traffic. *Asian Review*. Retrieved from http://asia.nikkei.com/Business/Trends/Bangkok-strives-to-be-smart-city-to-ease-traffic

Oussous, A., Benjelloun, F.Z., Lahcen, A.A. & Belfkih, S. (in press). Big Data technologies: A survey. *Journal of King Saud University – Computer and Information Sciences*.

Pan, Y., Tian, Y., Liu, X., Gu, D., & Hua, G. (2016). Urban big data and the development of city intelligence. *Engineering*, *2*(2), 171–178. doi:10.1016/J.ENG.2016.02.003

Rahmat, A., Syadiah, N., & Subur, B. (2016). Smart Coastal City: Sea Pollution Awareness for People in Surabaya Waterfront City. *Procedia: Social and Behavioral Sciences*, *227*, 770–777. doi:10.1016/j.sbspro.2016.06.144

Rajaraman, V. (2016). Big Data Analytics. *Resonance*, *21*(8), 695–716. doi:10.100712045-016-0376-7

Rathore, M. M., Ahmad, A., Paul, A., & Rho, S. (2016). Urban planning and building smart cities based on the Internet of Things using Big Data analytics. *Computer Networks*, *101*(3), 63–80. doi:10.1016/j.comnet.2015.12.023

Ratnikova, L. (2015). 11 Ecological initiatives in megapolicies. *Recyclemag*. Retrieved from http://recyclemag.ru/article/11-ekologicheskih-initsiativ-mirovyh-megapolisov

Rosati, U., & Conti, S. (2016). What is a smart city project? An urban model or a corporate business plan? *Procedia: Social and Behavioral Sciences*, *223*, 968–973. doi:10.1016/j.sbspro.2016.05.332

Sacco, D., Motta, G., You, L., Bertolazzo, N., Chen, C., Pavia, U., & Pv, P. (2013). *Smart cities, urban sensing and big data: mining geo-location in social networks*. Salerno, Italy: AICA.

Santana-Mancilla, P. C., Echeverría, M. A. M., Santos, J. C. R., Castellanos, J. A. N. C., & Díaz, A. P. S. (2013). Towards Smart Education: Ambient Intelligence in the Mexican Classrooms. *Procedia: Social and Behavioral Sciences*, *106*, 3141–3148. doi:10.1016/j.sbspro.2013.12.363

Smart Cities Council. (n.d.). Pike research. Retrieved from http://smartcitiescouncil.com/tags/pike-research

Smart Dubai. (2016). *Smart Dubai*. Retrieved from http://www.smartdubai.ae

Solanas, A., Patsakis, C., Conti, M., Vlachos, I. S., Ramos, V., Falcone, F., ... Martinez-Balleste, A. (2014). Smart health: A context-aware health paradigm within smart cities. *IEEE Communications Magazine*, *52*(8), 74–81. doi:10.1109/MCOM.2014.6871673

Souza, A., Figueredo, M., Cacho, N., Araújo, D., & Prolo, C. A. (2016). Using Big Data and Real-Time Analytics to Support Smart City Initiatives. *IFAC-PapersOnLine*, *49*(30), 257–262. doi:10.1016/j.ifacol.2016.11.121

Sta, H. B. (2016). Quality and the efficiency of data in "Smart-Cities". *Future Generation Computer Systems*, *74*, 409–416. doi:10.1016/j.future.2016.12.021

Stadtentwicklung. (2015). *Smart City Strategy Berlin. State Department for Urban Development and the Environment*. Retrieved from http://www.stadtentwicklung.berlin.de/planen/foren_initiativen/smart-city/download/Strategie_Smart_City_Berlin_en.pdf

Steenbruggen, J., Tranos, E., & Nijkamp, P. (2015). Data from mobile phone operators: A tool for smarter cities? *Telecommunications Policy*, *39*(3), 335–346. doi:10.1016/j.telpol.2014.04.001

Stimmel, C. L. (2014). *Big Data Analytics Strategies for the Smart Grid*. CRC Press. doi:10.1201/b17228

Susanti, R., Soetomo, S., Buchori, I., & Brotosunaryo, P. M. (2016). Smart Growth, Smart City and Density: In Search of The Appropriate Indicator for Residential Density in Indonesia. *Procedia: Social and Behavioral Sciences*, *227*, 194–201. doi:10.1016/j.sbspro.2016.06.062

Townsend, A. M. (2013). *Smart cities: Big data, civic hackers, and the quest for a new utopia*. New York: WW Norton & Company.

United Nations. (2012). *World urbanization prospects; the 2011 revision*. New York: Department of Economic and Social Affairs.

van de Pas, J., van Bussel, G. J., Veenstra, M., & Jorna, F. (2015). Digital data and the city: An exploration of the building blocks of a smart city architecture. In D. Baker & W. Evans (Eds.), *Digital Information Strategies: From Applications and Content to Libraries* (pp. 185–198). Chandos Publishing.

van Zoonen, L. (2016). Privacy concerns in smart cities. *Government Information Quarterly*, *33*(3), 471–480. doi:10.1016/j.giq.2016.06.004

Vegvesen. (2015). *Smart Bodo*. Retrieved from https://www.vegvesen.no/_attachment/1103917/binary/1076326?fast_title=Visjonen+om+verdens+smarteste+by+%E2%80%93+SMART+Bod%C3%B8+-+Asgeir+Jordbru.pdf

Vidiasova, L., Kachurina, P., & Cronemberger, P. (2017). Smart Cities Prospects from the Results of the World Practice Expert Benchmarking. *Procedia Computer Science*, *119*, 269–277. doi:10.1016/j.procs.2017.11.185

Washburn, D., Sindhu, U., Balaouras, S., Dines, R. A., Hayes, N., & Nelson, L. E. (2009). *Helping CIOs understand "smart city" initiatives*. Cambridge: Forrester.

World Bank. (n.d.). Retrieved from data.worldbank.org/indicator/SP.URB.TOTL.IN.ZS?end=2015&start=1960&view=chart

Wu, Y., Zhang, W., Shen, J., Mo, Z., & Peng, Y. (2018). Smart City with Chinese Characteristics against the Background of Big Data: Idea, Action and Risk. *Journal of Cleaner Production*, *173*, 60–66. doi:10.1016/j.jclepro.2017.01.047

Yang, J., Han, Y., Wang, Y., Jiang, B., Lv, Z., & Song, H. (in press). Optimization of real-time traffic network assignment based on IoT data using DBN and clustering model in smart city. *Future Generation Computer Systems*.

Yaqoob, I., Hashem, I. A. T., Gani, A., Mokhtar, S., Ahmed, E., Anuar, N. B., & Vasilakos, A. V. (2016). Big data: From beginning to future. *International Journal of Information Management*, *36*(6), 1231–1247. doi:10.1016/j.ijinfomgt.2016.07.009

Zanella, A., Bui, N., Castellani, A., Vangelista, L., & Zorzi, M. (2014). Internet of things for smart cities. *IEEE Internet of Things Journal*, *1*(1), 22–32. doi:10.1109/JIOT.2014.2306328

Zhou, K., Fu, C., & Yang, S. (2016). Big data driven smart energy management: From big data to big insights. *Renewable & Sustainable Energy Reviews*, *56*, 215–225. doi:10.1016/j.rser.2015.11.050

Zhu, C., Leung, V. C., Shu, L., & Ngai, E. C. H. (2015). Green internet of things for smart world. *IEEE Access: Practical Innovations, Open Solutions*, *3*, 2151–2162. doi:10.1109/ACCESS.2015.2497312

Chapter 3
Big Data Utilization, Benefits, and Challenges for Smart City Implementation

Sonali Vyas
Amity University Jaipur, India

Deepshikha Bhargava
University of Petroleum and Energy Studies, India

ABSTRACT

With the rapid advancement of technology, everything is transforming into smarter versions. The term smart city means a technologically strengthened and advanced version of the city. Smart cities utilize digital information and techniques for improving services like performance, quality, etc. Big data technology and methods are utilized for handling the vast volume, high velocity and wide variety of data related to cities. This chapter discusses the big data utilization for making smart cities and also throws light on various applications where efficient analysis of services can be carried out using Big Data techniques. The main objective of this chapter will be to provide knowledge of big data implementation for the smart city and its services. This chapter will also investigate various prospects, benefits, and challenges of absorbing big data utilization for smart cities. It will also discuss some case studies related to big data applications for smart city services. It will also propose some open issues related to big data implementation for the smart city.

INTRODUCTION

In the recent scenario each city is transforming into smart city by implementing various techniques and infrastructures. These technologies help in improving not only the look of city but will enhance the performance of various activities related to health, communication, education, transportation, business, utilization of resources and help citizens to sustain comfortable living. The idea behind smart city is to upgrade the standards of services provided to citizens and also regulate costs and time. The term Smart City means technologically strengthened and advanced version of city, which analyses its environment

DOI: 10.4018/978-1-5225-7432-3.ch003

using data analysis so that it can easily adapt changes and resolves problems and to advance living quality of residents. As digitization era is upgrading day by day data storage and retrieval becomes crucial tasks and in order to make city smarter and enhance its services Big Data Analytics plays a vital role (Al Nuaimi et. al, 2015). It helps in managing huge amount of data and its retrieval to various useful application areas.

SMART CITY

Smart cities utilize digital information and techniques for improving services like performance, quality etc. Smart city helps in reducing cost and consumption of resources and active engagement of residents. The main goal behind development of smart city applications is improvement of management techniques of urban flows and also allows real time data response and various challenges associated with it. Smart city helps in enhancing the process of decision-making combining Information Technology. Smart city characteristics are as follows:

- **Instrumented City:** City's data of data sources are sensed and measured
- **Interconnected City**: Consists of physical phase and logical phase. Physical phase refers to the networks which integrates systems and also attach devices. Logical phase deals with the combination of data from various sources and also mentions relationships between data.
- **Intelligent City:** Utilizes various advance logical techniques to set perceptions for events of city and tools for visualization to envisage behavior of city.

Figure 1. Smart city concepts

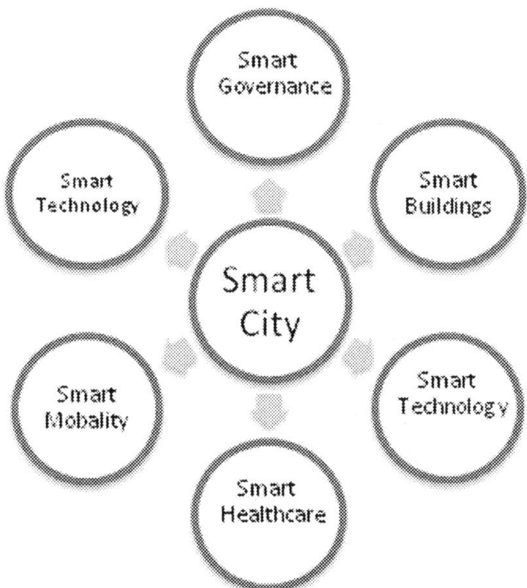

BIG DATA

Big Data is a technology for describing vast volumes of data both structured as well as unstructured. Since the volume of data is huge that's why it turns to be tricky to process data using conventional data management techniques. The big data term involves properties like sorting data, streaming live data, despite of format of data i.e. text, audio, video, etc. Big data characteristics are as follows:

- **Volume:** data size or amount of data.
- **Variety:** data from various sources in structured as well as unstructured format.
- **Velocity:** the rate of flow of data from various sources where flow is huge and continuous.
- **Veracity:** data uncertainty which deals with quality, accuracy, reliability of data.

Big data characteristics reveals large potential regarding advancement and possibilities are continuous which are bound to the tools and technologies available. In order to attain goals and services in smart city big data entails analysis of tools and techniques which are categorized efficiently and effectively.

Relationship Between Big Data and Smart City

Applications of Smart city produces enormous data where big data systems utilizes this data for producing information in order to improve smart city functions. Big data systems help in storing, processing and mining information of smart city applications efficiently. Big data also aids in decision making process for any advancement in resources, services and areas related to smart city.

Big Data Utilization in Smart Cities

Big data systems have ability to hand out various zones of smart city. It facilitates better customer knowledge and services for improving performance. Utilization of big data in smart city implementation can be done in following areas:

Figure 2. Big Data V's

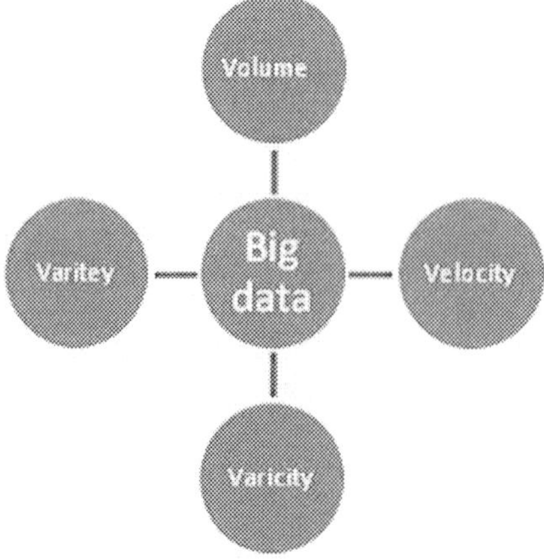

Smart Health Care

Advancement in health care is done by improving care services, diagnosis and tools, patient care, record management etc. Big data helps in increasing the amount of real time data of patient's health with the help of smart devices that records data regarding attributes like blood pressure, sleeping patterns etc.

Smart Transportation System

Big data is used to identify patterns of traffic by analyzing real time data. It also helps in minimizing congestion on roads by estimating traffic conditions and controlling it. Big data is used to provide feedback for particular objects for taking actions to minimize traffic issues. Big data also helps in optimizing routes, schedules, and put up for changing demands and making it more environment friendly.

Smart Learning

These applications of smart city will attract people for active learning which permits them to adjust changes in society. By depending on big data gathered in field and accurately processed for generating information needed, this will have positive impact on knowledge standards. Utilizing ICT and Big data will also aid in building knowledge- based society, for enhancing competitiveness Big data in education can be used for observing shortcomings related to education and helps in enhancing study curriculums.

Smart Public Safety Systems

Big data is helpful in making public safety systems which are more practical regarding events. It means smart public safety systems offer sensing automation, detection and alerting for incidents utilizing analysis and visualization tools.

Crowd Control

Big data is already proved very much beneficial in this area. At any point of time large group of people gather together at one place, requirement for services is needed in that area. It may include requirements of crowd like food, drink etc. and guarantee their safety. As word's population is augmenting, such events happen more frequent and it becomes necessary to forecast and recognize them. Huge groups of people represent enormous amount of data generation. In such case big data is put in action for understanding the reason behind crowd formation and to forecast their actions.

The utilization boundary of big data in smart city implementation is not restricted to this only, also helps in waste management, water management, etc., by executing innovations for managing services effectively.

Benefits of Big Data in Smart Cities

Presently, many cities are competing for becoming smart cities for gaining benefits economically and socially. Therefore, for making successful big data analytics is utilized in smart cities applications. The benefits of utilizing big data in smart city implementation include:

Efficient Utilization of Resources

For better and efficient utilization of resources in controlled way it is necessary to integrate different solutions together. Technological systems like ERP and GIS will be beneficial and with the help of monitoring systems it becomes easy to find out waste points and efficiently distribute resources by regulating costs, consumption and reduction of energy. One of the main features of smart city applications is that it is designed for interconnectivity and collection of data which helps in collaborating applications and services.

Enhanced Quality of Life

Smart city promises better quality of life by better services, efficient living models, less time and resource consumption. It includes better living plans, work locations, efficient transport facility, fast services and better information systems for better decision making.

Higher Transparency Levels

In order to manage and control different smart city applications in better way the interoperability and transparency is needed at higher levels. The main norm is data and resource sharing. This also enhances transparency of information for everyone and encourages association and communication between different entities and creates more services and applications for further enhancing smart city.

In order to gain these benefits, investment in technology, efficient development efforts and effective utilization of big data. There is also requirement of setting rules for ensuring accuracy, quality, security, privacy and control of data and also focuses on documentation of data for providing guidance regarding content and dataset utilization.

In many sectors of smart city big data applications provides better services and customer experiences which helps in achieving better performance and increased profits in businesses. It also provides improved healthcare by enhancing care services, diagnosis tools, healthcare record management and care of patient. Big data greatly improves transport system in smart city by optimizing routes and schedules and also accommodates varying demands.

Challenges Related to Big Data in Smart City Implementation

The environment of smart cities is dynamic and emerging one. But there are some challenges associated with implementation of smart city using big data. Most challenges are associated with the designing, developing and deploying of big data for smart cities. It is crucial to overcome these challenges for effective implementation of smart cities. These are related to accessible big data tools, real-time analytics, precision, illustration, cost, and accessibility (Fan and Bifet, 2013). These challenges can influence smart city service performance depending on big data. Some of the basic challenges are:

Data Size and Sources

In smart city, data is generated from various sources and in different formats like structured, unstructured and semi-structured and traditional software is not useful in processing and managing such data.

This data needs to be maintained and transformed in structured form using advance database system (Michalik, Stofa, and Zolotova, 2014). While designing smart city it is necessary for considering data formats and sources and simplified into solution. It is also complicated to foresee the expansion of data because of evolving environment. In addition to this, future challenges may include analytics, mining distributed data, real-time data, visualizing, compressing and evaluating big data (Fan and Bifet, 2013).

Data Sharing and Information

Data and information sharing amongst various cities and departments is a big challenge. Each department and city have their own data warehouses. Some data may be having some kind of security constraints which restricts its sharing among other cities or departments. The idea of smart city involves the guarantee of combining data from various organizations, environments and various intelligent devices. It is a challenge in integrating data from multiple sources. There are also many legal important security and privacy requirements like DPA (Data Protection Act) to ensure privacy and security of information. Smart city implementation needs to derive methods for securing and reducing obstacles for achieving flawless sharing information among various entities (Hirawat and Bharagava, 2015). So, it becomes difficult for creating a integrated data semantics and extraction of new knowledge on basis of real-time data. Therefore, it becomes challenging for creating knowledge base of smart city.

Quality of Data

Data in smart city is from multiple assorted systems and in varied formats, so maintenance of data quality can be a challenge. In transactional systems data is required to be in single format and in case of big data warehouse data is gathered from various sources requires a precise format without considering data quality. If data is retrieved from third party, it requires ensuring proper mechanism to maintain quality of data.

Security of Data

Violations of big data are big with potential to more severe damages and legal consequences. It is a big challenge in smart city implementation to secure movement of data across multiple sources. Security means giving right information to right person in right time and at right place. It is very important in smart city implementation that how data is masked and secured so that it does not reach to unauthorized persons.

Technology Advancement

The smart city implementation should be done in such a way that with enhancement in technology, advancement of existing solution can be obtained with minimum efforts.

Skill Gaps

Lacking data skills can be the obstacle for effective utilization of big data for smart city management. Management and analysis of huge data sets and development of insights for effective making of policies needs skills which are less supplied mostly in public sector.

Lack of Standards

In smart city development, standards play an essential role in holding onto common platform. Presently, lack of standards is there regarding integration of data, policies, procedures and formats which requires to be handled.

Big Data Applications in Smart City

The implementation of smart city using big data has many applications which can be categorized in two types: Offline big data applications and Real-time big data applications. Real-time big data application relies on instant input and immediate analysis for making decision in short and specific time. But if decisions are not made within specified time then it is useless. Therefore it is necessary to make data available in time and analysis should be done fast and reliable way. Applications of big data for smart city in field like energy, education, healthcare and traffic come under offline category. Whereas, applications needing interactive actions, improvements and control for smart applications are real-time types.

Big data application driving smart cities:

Smart Education

ICT gives a solution for enhancing process of education efficiently and effectively with the help of smart devices and services which are intelligent for utilizing information, enhancing control and supporting life-long education of people. By making use of big data, desired information is processed accurately and influence levels of knowledge and teaching/learning tools for delivering knowledge. Utilizing ICT and Big Data helps in developing knowledge based society, enhancing learning standards, making opportunities available anytime, anywhere and in desirable way. Big data helps in creating useful resource for analyzing and fetching useful information for more enhanced and better education.

Figure 3. Smart city and big data relationship
(E. Al Nuaimi, el. at. 2015)

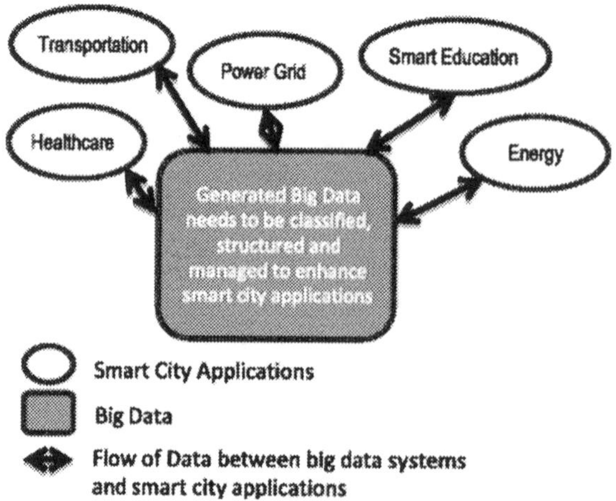

Smart Traffic Management

For a smart city it is important to have a good traffic management and flow in city, this improves transportation system and traffic pattern. As traffic problems are increasing day by day with increase in population, need for smart traffic management also increases. This is implemented by use of smart traffic lights and signals which helps in dealing with high volume of traffic and congestions. Smart traffic lights and signals are interlocked athwart the traffic grids for presenting extra information related to traffic patterns. Each sensor helps in detecting various parameters related to the traffic flow like speed of car, waiting time, traffic jam, etc. The system builds decisions on the basis of these parameter values and provides right instructions to the lights and signals. Thus, for making more efficient decisions more data should be made available to the system. So as to provide efficient services in smart traffic management it will be good to gather data from every traffic light across the city and develop smart decision systems with the help of this data. It requires big data management and analytics for managing and analyzing real time data.

Smart Grid

Smart grid is essential element of a smart city. It is understood as a advanced electrical grid system which makes use of information and technology in order to gather and act on available data (Yin et al, 2013). It helps in improving efficiency, consistency and sustainability of distribution and generation of electricity. It uses computer oriented remote controls with two way communication system between producers and consumers for maximizing efficiency of grid and reliability using feedback and self-monitoring system. This engages smart sensors and meters for production, consumption, and distribution systems. It also helps in gathering real time data about power consumption and faults at customer points. It put into practice flexible pricing models for power usage for stabilizing high charges at peak times and minimizes charges at normal times. It provides consumers real time information about use of energy and permits them to maintain their usage depending on their requirements and prices. Even though smart grids have huge benefits, it needs huge amount of data from power producers, transmitters, distributors and consumers. (Mohamed and Al-Jaroodi, 2014). Also it needs processing of data collected, which is done using big data analytics, in real time scenario for sending back control information in order to improve performance of electric power systems. (Vyas, Saxena, and Bhargava, 2015).

Smart Healthcare

Big data allows medical practitioners for gathering, analyzing and utilizing information of a patient for use by various insurance agencies, government organizations and future diagnosis. By using big data in healthcare it becomes efficient to process complex data generated by various healthcare devices and monitoring and analyzing health related issues on daily or demand basis. It helps in capturing real time data for patient's health by smart devices for monitoring issues like blood pressure, sleeping patterns etc. and giving response to health issues in time and also maintains history of patient's health.

Smart Governance

Smart Governance is an important component of a smart city. For developing smart governance big data implementation is needed. It helps in supporting assimilation and association of various government companies and streamlining their activities. This will help in carrying out more efficient processes and controlling sharing of data. It also provides good and efficient management of regulations and government policies. It also helps in improving decision making for businesses. Big data analytics helps in analyzing economic growth of a firm and comparing to its competitors and making more effective decisions in support to production strategies. It helps government agencies to spotlight concerns of citizens in area of health, housing, education and various issues.

Big data provides various analysis and management techniques to handle real-time data in more efficient and effective way in support to the development of smart city.

Requirements of Big Data for Smart City Implementation

Big Data Management

As large volume of data is originated in smart city in multiple formats and from multiple sources like traffic, energy, education and healthcare therefore management of data becomes important.

Big Data Processing Platform

It presents high performance, computation capability, optimized hardware use, stream processing support etc. For this, various platforms are there like Hadoop, MapReduce, HPCC stratosphere etc.

Smart Network Infrastructure

Smart networks are needed in smart city for establishing connections between components involving resident equipment such as cars, smart house devices and smart phones.

Advanced Algorithms

Some advance algorithms are needed for optimizing huge volume of data, varied data types, decision making time constraints and components distributed at multiple locations.

Open Standard Technology

It includes huge heterogeneous data and system. It helps in obtaining flexibility regarding advancement, maintenance and appending more applications for implementing smart city.

Security and Privacy

It becomes essential to ensure levels of security and privacy of all applications as huge data is gathered and processed in smart city.

Open Issues Related to Big Data for Smart Cities Implementation

- **Security and privacy issues:** These are essential requirements of smart cities and should be taken into consideration. Since systems are amalgamated, data is distributed among various bodies in smart city. Thus, security of infrastructures and platforms must be ensured and privacy should be conserved so that information is also conserved.
- **Political Issues:** The deliberation of politics and its impact on city decides how actions are to me performed for smart city implementations. The right of access regarding information by various people in various political positions should be considered and taken care.
- **Qualified People:** Highly qualified people are needed for designing, developing, deploying and operating smart city structure and applications. For this purpose special education and training is offered to make this type of personnel.
- **Monitoring and Control:** Some monitoring and control policies need to be set for smart city applications. Various tools and techniques are needed for monitoring and control of implementation in smart cities for ensuring efficiency, effectiveness and quality of applications.

CASE STUDIES: SMART HEALTHCARE USING BIG DATA

Medical practices are transforming from informal and one-sided decision process to objective and up-to-date proof-based healthcare. This evidence is data collected by Electronic Health Record (EHR) Systems, Capturing devices, sensors, etc. These resources fabricate huge amounts of complex datasets, which are not easy to handle and process by using traditional data processing and management tools.

Big Data Applications in Healthcare

- Presently, in Intensive Care Units (ICUs) generates real time data which is difficult to gather, process and utilized for analysis purposes. The use of user interactive platform for processing and evaluating huge data volumes can influence knowledge mining and quality enhancement of health care. The requirement of quick computation and analysis of ICUs data hampers use of traditional databases and requires use of big data management systems.
- Electronic Health Records (EHRs) is a most prevalent big data application in health care. In HER each patient has a record which contains demographics, test reports, medical history, etc. Every record is shared via information systems and made available to private and public sectors. These records have one flexible file so that doctors can update it when needed without replicating data. EHRs generate alerts and reminders whenever patient gets new test or keeps track of patient's activities.
- Real Time Alerts is another example of big data implementation in healthcare. Clinical Decision Support (CDS) helps in analyzing data in real time and benefit doctors in taking prescriptive decisions on the basis of analysis done. Personal analytics devices or smart wearable devices collects patient's health information and save this data in cloud. This data can be accessed for health analysis and permits doctors to make comparison in socioeconomic area for giving prescriptions as and when needed.

- Improving patient's rendezvous and awareness by introducing smart devices which helps in tracking each step and activity of patient. It also keep them updated regarding their blood pressure level and heart rates so that during emergency situation they can take corrective measures.
- Predictive analysis has become one of the major trends in healthcare and business intelligence. The main aim of healthcare intelligence is to provide doctors with ability to take decisions based on data in few seconds and thus improving patient's health. This proves beneficial for patients with multiple sufferings or difficult medical record. Various tools can also predict risk of diabetes, etc., so that doctors can advise them with precautions to minimize its levels.

All these above cases prove that big data in healthcare proves to be helpful for analysis and keeping updated records of patient's medical process. It also permits predictive analysis of patients and suggests preventing actions.

CONCLUSION

Big data utilization in smart city implementation helps in developing cities more efficient and helps in achieving sustainability and flexibility. It also helps in improving quality of life and efficient utilization of resources. This chapter explores various areas of big data applications in smart city implementations. In spite of various definitions of each concept poses unique characteristics. Depending on these characteristics it becomes easy to recognize benefits of big data utilization for designing and supporting smart city implementation. After this various opportunities and challenges of utilizing big data in smart city applications. It also identifies various issues which may affect big data applications and on this basis list of requirements for big data uses in smart city applications are also discussed. These requirements also help in addressing challenges and also proposed various techniques to overcome them and producing efficient results. It also discusses open issues which needs further investigation and concentrate on reaching to more inclusive view of smart cities and developing a holistic thought model. Finally, it discusses case of big data utilization in healthcare for maintain real time data of patients and also helps in predictive analysis of medical reports. Therefore, big data is very important in implementing Smart City concept.

REFERENCES

Ahmed, E., Yaqoob, I., Hashem, I. A. T., Khan, I., Ahmed, A. I. A., Imran, M., & Vasilakos, A. V. (2017). The role of big data analytics in Internet of Things. *Computer Networks*, *129*, 459–471. doi:10.1016/j.comnet.2017.06.013

Al Nuaimi, E., Al Neyadi, H., Mohamed, N., & Al-Jaroodi, J. (2015). Applications of big data to smart cities. *Journal of Internet Services and Applications*, *6*(1), 25. doi:10.118613174-015-0041-5

Alshawish, R. A., Alfagih, S. A., & Musbah, M. S. (2016, September). Big data applications in smart cities. In International Conference on Engineering & MIS (ICEMIS) (pp. 1-7). IEEE.

Barkham, R., Bokhari, S., & Saiz, A. (2018). *Urban Big Data: City Management and Real Estate Markets*. New York, NY: GovLab Digest.

Batty, M. (2013). Big data, smart cities and city planning. *Dialogues in Human Geography*, *3*(3), 274–279. doi:10.1177/2043820613513390 PMID:29472982

Batty, M., Axhausen, K. W., Giannotti, F., Pozdnoukhov, A., Bazzani, A., Wachowicz, M., ... Portugali, Y. (2012). Smart cities of the future. *The European Physical Journal. Special Topics*, *214*(1), 481–518. doi:10.1140/epjst/e2012-01703-3

Bettencourt, L. M. (2014). The uses of big data in cities. *Big Data*, *2*(1), 12–22. doi:10.1089/big.2013.0042 PMID:27447307

Bhargava, D., & Sinha, M. (2012). Design and implementation of agent based inter process synchronization manager. *International Journal of Computers and Applications*, *46*(21), 17–22.

Bi, Z., & Cochran, D. (2014). Big data analytics with applications. *Journal of Management Analytics*, *1*(4), 249–265. doi:10.1080/23270012.2014.992985

Chen, M., Mao, S., & Liu, Y. (2014). Big data: A survey. *Mobile Networks and Applications*, *19*(2), 171–209. doi:10.100711036-013-0489-0

Chourabi, H., Nam, T., Walker, S., Gil-Garcia, J. R., Mellouli, S., Nahon, K., . . . Scholl, H. J. (2012, January). Understanding smart cities: An integrative framework. In 2012 45th Hawaii International Conference on System Science (HICSS) (pp. 2289-2297). IEEE.

Dhaka, V. S., & Vyas, S. (2014). Analysis of Server Performance with Different Techniques of Virtual Databases. *Journal of Emerging Trends in Computing and Information Sciences*, *5*(10).

Elhoseny, H., Elhoseny, M., Riad, A. M., & Hassanien, A. E. (2018, February). A framework for big data analysis in smart cities. In *International Conference on Advanced Machine Learning Technologies and Applications* (pp. 405-414). Springer, Cham. 10.1007/978-3-319-74690-6_40

Fan, W., & Bifet, A. (2013). Mining big data: current status, and forecast to the future. ACM *sIGKDD Explorations Newsletter*, *14*(2), 1-5.

Groves, P., Kayyali, B., Knott, D., & Van Kuiken, S. (2013). The 'big data' revolution in healthcare. *The McKinsey Quarterly*, *2*(3).

Hashem, I. A. T., Chang, V., Anuar, N. B., Adewole, K., Yaqoob, I., Gani, A., ... Chiroma, H. (2016). The role of big data in smart city. *International Journal of Information Management*, *36*(5), 748–758. doi:10.1016/j.ijinfomgt.2016.05.002

Hirawat, A., & Bhargava, D. (2015). Enhanced accident detection system using safety application for emergency in mobile environment: Safeme. In *Proceedings of Fourth International Conference on Soft Computing for Problem Solving* (pp. 177-183). Springer New Delhi. 10.1007/978-81-322-2220-0_14

Khan, Z., Anjum, A., & Kiani, S. L. (2013, December). Cloud based big data analytics for smart future cities. In *Proceedings of the 2013 IEEE/ACM 6th international conference on utility and cloud computing* (pp. 381-386). IEEE Computer Society. 10.1109/UCC.2013.77

Kitchin, R. (2014). The real-time city? Big data and smart urbanism. *GeoJournal*, *79*(1), 1–14. doi:10.100710708-013-9516-8

Michalik, P., Stofa, J., & Zolotova, I. (2014, January). Concept definition for Big Data architecture in the education system. In *2014 IEEE 12th International Symposium on Applied Machine Intelligence and Informatics (SAMI)* (pp. 331-334). IEEE. 10.1109/SAMI.2014.6822433

Mohamed, N., & Al-Jaroodi, J. (2014, July). Real-time big data analytics: Applications and challenges. In *2014 International Conference on High Performance Computing & Simulation (HPCS)* (pp. 305-310). IEEE.

Moreno, M. V., Terroso-Sáenz, F., González-Vidal, A., Valdés-Vela, M., Skarmeta, A. F., Zamora, M. A., & Chang, V. (2017). Applicability of big data techniques to smart cities deployments. *IEEE Transactions on Industrial Informatics*, *13*(2), 800–809. doi:10.1109/TII.2016.2605581

Neirotti, P., De Marco, A., Cagliano, A. C., Mangano, G., & Scorrano, F. (2014). Current trends in Smart City initiatives: Some stylised facts. *Cities (London, England)*, *38*, 25–36. doi:10.1016/j.cities.2013.12.010

Pantelis, K., & Aija, L. (2013, October). Understanding the value of (big) data. In *2013 IEEE International Conference on Big Data* (pp. 38-42). IEEE.

Pramanik, M. I., Lau, R. Y., Demirkan, H., & Azad, M. A. K. (2017). Smart health: Big data enabled health paradigm within smart cities. *Expert Systems with Applications*, *87*, 370–383. doi:10.1016/j.eswa.2017.06.027

Raja, L., & Vyas, S. (2018). The Study of Technological Development in the Field of Smart Farming. *Smart Farming Technologies for Sustainable Agricultural Development, 1*.

Su, K., Li, J., & Fu, H. (2011, September). Smart city and the applications. In *2011 International Conference on Electronics, Communications and Control (ICECC)* (pp. 1028-1031). IEEE. 10.1109/ICECC.2011.6066743

Van Zoonen, L. (2016). Privacy concerns in smart cities. *Government Information Quarterly*, *33*(3), 472–480. doi:10.1016/j.giq.2016.06.004

Vyas, V., Saxena, S., & Bhargava, D. (2015). Mind Reading by Face Recognition Using Security Enhancement Model. In *Proceedings of Fourth International Conference on Soft Computing for Problem Solving* (pp. 173-180). Springer New Delhi. 10.1007/978-81-322-2217-0_15

Yin, J., Sharma, P., Gorton, I., & Akyoli, B. (2013, March). Large-scale data challenges in future power grids. In *2013 IEEE Seventh International Symposium on Service-Oriented System Engineering* (pp. 324-328). IEEE.

Chapter 4
Big Data and the Internet of Things:
Current Industry Practices and Their Implications for Consumer Privacy and Privacy Literacy

Zablon Pingo
https://orcid.org/0000-0002-0433-605X
University of Technology Sydney, Australia

Bhuva Narayan
University of Technology Sydney, Australia

ABSTRACT

The privacy construct is an important aspect of internet of things (IoT) technologies as it is projected that over 20 billion IoT devices will be in use by 2022. Among other things, IoT produces big data and many industries are leveraging this data for predictive analytics to aid decision making in health, education, business, and other areas. Despite benefits in some areas, privacy issues have persisted in relation to the use of the data produced by many consumer products. The practices surrounding IoT and Big Data by service providers and third parties are associated with a negative impact to individuals. To protect consumers' privacy, a wide range of approaches to informational privacy protections exist. However, individuals are increasingly required to actively respond to control and manage their informational privacy rather than rely on any protection mechanisms. This chapter highlights privacy issues across consumers' use of IoT and identifies existing responses to enhance privacy awareness as a way of enabling IoT users to protect their privacy.

DOI: 10.4018/978-1-5225-7432-3.ch004

INTRODUCTION

Current information technology innovations such as the Internet of Things (IoT) is generating a huge amount of data popularly referred to as Big Data, which have significantly disrupted decision making in various sectors including health, manufacturing, education, agriculture, energy, retail, insurance, automotive and crime detection (Dutton, 2013; Federal Trade Commission, 2015; Richardson et al., 2017a). The IoT have increasingly become prevalent amongst consumers, promising to benefit our lives in many positive ways (Richardson et al., 2017). While the conversation around Big Data and IoT centers on the benefits, privacy and security vulnerabilities have also risen to the surface. When organizations such as service providers and data brokers collect personal information from multiple sources such including IoT devices and integrate them to create Big Data, as is often the practice under some business models (Rappa, 2003), it poses an imminent privacy and security risk to consumers. To address these privacy and security issues, several researchers have proposed technical and legal approaches, but there are limited accounts of how users of IoT respond to these privacy concerns, and about their privacy literacy. Privacy awareness is defined as individuals "cognitive ability to identify" and respond to privacy concerns in specific environments or information technology artifacts (Omoronyia, 2016). Awareness as part of literacy, thus privacy literacy is conceptualized as one's level of understanding and awareness of how information is tracked and used in online environments and how that information can retain or lose its private nature (Givens, 2015).

This chapter provides an account of how users/consumers, service providers, and regulators/policy makers need to be aware of in light of these data practices and privacy concerns. This is important as the Internet industry has a growing interest in generating value out of the Big Data both for social good and for commercial purposes. To safeguard users' privacy and personal data, various legal and structural frameworks have been proposed or put in place across many countries. However, the increased innovations of IoT and the leveraging of Big Data has opened up new challenges. These challenges also raise the question of the need to balance between regulation to protect the information privacy of users and maintaining flexibility for economic value. Thus, the data practices attract both opportunities and potential risks, particularly in how the information is collected, processed and used by the data controllers. Scholars note the challenges arise from linking users' personal information, lack of transparency, possible misuse of the data among others practices that pose risks or harm to data subjects (Crawford & Schultz, 2014; Dutton, 2013; Federal Trade Commission, 2015; Haynes & Robinson, 2015).

Increased innovation and popularity of lifelogging technologies categorized as a subset of the Internet of Things has attracted a lot of attention in research and business (Federal Trade Commission, 2015). The IoT devices have the ability to collect, process and communicate to other devices and humans. The IoT makes users both subjects and recipients of the data (Tuninetti Ferrari, 2017). Privacy is an important area for users' of IoT, for they need to be protected and have necessary awareness on how personal data collected is used by other parties, given the complexity of data sharing, business models and privacy in the technologies (boyd & Hargittai, 2010; Park, 2013; Rappa, 2003; Solove & Schwartz, 2014; Torre, Sanchez, Koceva, & Adorni, 2017). As the IoT become common and pervasive, there is a need for people to enhance their ability to evaluate the privacy/security associated with particular data practices (Zhou & Piramuthu, 2014).

Since privacy is a socially and economically negotiated concept that can be contextual, it is important for service providers to ensure an enabling environment for such negotiation to happen. Various stakeholders such as technology designers, device manufacturers, service providers, educators, privacy advocates, privacy and personal information regulators and consumers, all have a role in enhancing information privacy. Some governments have also responded to this issue through legislations to protect people from any potential harmful acts. While the organizations, manufacturers and service providers have the obligation to comply with the regulations to address these privacy issues, users still need enough information and knowledge to make decisions on how to manage personal information and privacy.

BACKGROUND

Privacy awareness is important for users to understand how IoT can potentially open-up access to personal information, consequently exposing users to risks and security vulnerabilities imposed by data practices about personal information collection, storage, processing, and subsequent use and dissemination practices (Solove, 2006). As some of the practices surrounding Big Data collection through IoT are technical in nature, it makes it difficult for individuals to determine the potential of real privacy risks. Additionally, with the increase of data-dependent economies, most technology users are unaware of what type of information/data generated on a particular platform or devices and the risks associated with it.

Current approaches to privacy protections have "the assumption [that] users of digital technologies are omni-competent" in evaluating the present benefits and potential risks (Park, 2013). Privacy scholars also observe that with the increased use of information technologies most of them have an impact on users' privacy (Petronio, 2002), although the informational privacy of individuals is assumed as protected by mechanisms such as legal regulations, self-regulations, and privacy-enhancing technologies (Debatin, 2011). However, the lack of sufficient privacy protection through these channels is now increasingly evident (Crow, Wiles, Heath, & Charles, 2006). For instance, the global nature of digital technologies means that the legal frameworks we have in some countries or jurisdictions do not protect users effectively (Svantesson & Clarke, 2010). The legal systems also do not keep up with the innovations in digital technologies (Caron, Bosua, Maynard, & Ahmad, 2016; Haddadi et al., 2015; Schwartz & Solove, 2011). On the other hand, system design approaches embrace privacy-enhancing technologies by incorporating privacy by design mechanisms (Cavoukian & Jonas, 2012), but given the affordances from the convergence of technologies, information can be derived from combined sets of integrated data (or hashing) and this subverts the intended goals of enhancing informational privacy.

Researchers have demonstrated further that personal information can permeate beyond the system's design or personal data anonymizations (Sweeney, Abu, & Winn, 2013). For example, on social networking sites, personality traits and personal preferences can be derived simply from behavioral data such as "likes" or "shares" on Facebook (Clarke, 2014a; Lambiotte & Kosinski, 2014) which is unknown to many users of the platforms. Other researchers have also exposed security and privacy vulnerabilities in IoT devices like fitness trackers by demonstrating how some of the devices can easily be turned into surveillance tools (Barcena, Wueest, & Lau, 2014; Fereidooni, Frassetto, Miettinen, Sadeghi, & Conti, 2017) through the ability of some to share data with third parties (Torre et al., 2017). Hence, the onus of protecting personal data in online and Internet-connected devices has both a legal and technical aspect, but both fall in the hands of the individuals to manage, which raises the question: Do IoT users have the privacy literacy to manage this responsibility? What steps should stakeholders take to enhance privacy awareness and facilitate decision making about informational privacy management? This chapter also introduces various theories applicable to understand privacy awareness among IoT users. These frameworks are important to enable all stakeholders to respond to informational privacy concerns in IoT.

Internet of Things and Data Practices

Internet of Things are defined as "Internet-enabled applications based on physical objects and the environment seamlessly integrating into the information network" (Dutton, 2013). The IoT include consumer products with multiple capabilities and functionalities to facilitate constant information flow (send and receive data) to/from the users, service providers, servers and other third parties (Federal Trade Commission, 2015; Helberger, 2016). In business environments, IoT facilitates transaction and movement of products and services in a global supply chain network with the example of Radio-Frequently Identification (RFID) (Weber, 2010).

The IoT devices also connect people and things anytime and anywhere (Schneier, 2015) using sensors, microphones, webcams, tracking devices, GPS navigation devices, and smart phones (Dutton, 2013). With a sharp increase in IoT adoption, it is estimated individuals will be in possession of an average of 3.4 networked devices within a decade with an increased projection of 20.4 billion of consumer and cross-industry devices by 2020 (Gartner, 2017). The IoT products are in use in our homes and for personal use in our daily lives and in business applications (Dutton, 2013). The users of these products can get continual monitoring of bodily activities, environmental conditions, energy consumption in houses, car and driver data and so on. The IoT devices are connected to smartphones, apps, and activity trackers to collect and exchange information for various purposes like monitoring energy consumption, health and fitness, and locational tracking, among others. This means that the consumers are voluntarily or inadvertently sending information continually to the manufacturers and service providers.

IoT are projected to facilitate significant growth in social, economic and service delivery (Dutton, 2013). For instance, IoT offer a range of benefits to consumers in providing remote monitoring of patients by medical professionals (Federal Trade Commission, 2015) in addition devices like fitness trackers (e.g. Fitbit, Jawbone, Nike fuel band, etc.) that can record and provide basic health information for personal fitness and health monitoring purposes (Christovich, 2016; Lupton, 2016; Rose, 2014). Some of the consumer IoT devices have the ability to collect, process and communicate to other devices and humans, rendering users both subjects and recipients of the data (Tuninetti Ferrari, 2017). IoT are distinguished by five distinct characteristics (Ziegeldorf, Morchon, & Wehrle, 2014):

1. Interaction between the smart devices,
2. Data collection,
3. Processing which refers analysis of information to provide the desired services
4. Dissemination of processed data towards the data subjects or service providers, and,
5. Presentation, which essentially means providing information in a usable format (graphs, advert, profiling, etc.).

The data collected from the above is often implicitly or actively shared with other parties depending on what one wants in return for the data. For example, health devices and applications collect data for personal health management purposes and for self-monitoring purposes with possible sharing of the data to trainers or third-party applications for additional services (Lo, Ip, & Yang, 2016; Lupton, 2014). Therefore, despite all the benefits, consumers may be exposed to risks including unauthorized access and misuse of personal data, personal safety risks, and attacks on systems and identification of an individual condition (Caron et al., 2016; Weber, 2015). Researchers and privacy experts argue that when a consumer buys a product they not only pay with money but also pay with data about themselves

(Helberger, 2016, p. 7). In addition, the collected data plays multiple roles: to enhance functionality and enable product improvement, and other purposes such as marketing, profiling, selling of the data and re-adjusting terms of service in favor of service providers (Helberger, 2016). Other implications include privacy-related risks involving collecting "actionable data" related to individuals (Lupton & Williamson, 2017) and monitoring an individual's habits, locations, and physical conditions (Lupton, 2016; Neff & Nafus, 2016)

Big Data

Big Data is defined using descriptors of volume, variety, veracity, value, and velocity of data, essentially referring to data size and type. Gartner defines big data as "high-volume, high-velocity and high-variety information assets that demand cost-effective, innovative forms of information processing for enhanced insight and decision-making" (Garner, 2013; Beyer & Laney, 2012). However, other researchers have noted a disparity in the conceptualization of big data, arguing whatever is referred to as "big data" today might potentially be the small data of the future (Casanovas, De Koker, Mendelson, & Watts, 2017). Data science researchers note that this disparity exists in the definition due to industry-specific and dependent perspectives (Dutcher, 2014). Nevertheless, increased innovations and production of social data from apps and IoT devices in everyday life prompted Lemov (2016) to argue that this conceptualization should account for the humanness of the data produced as a result of human activities and bodies captured by digital objects, for smartphones, social media applications and IoT devices among other information technologies produce a variety of data as a result of human activities (Lemov, 2016).

Schneier (2010); Tuninetti Ferrari (2017) provide a taxonomy (Figure 1) to distinguish various types of data as detailed below:

1. **Corporate performance data** is a category of data that includes business performance *e.g.* stocks, sales, prices, customers, suppliers, accounting and so on.

Figure 1. Sources of big data
Source: (Tuninetti Ferrari, 2017)

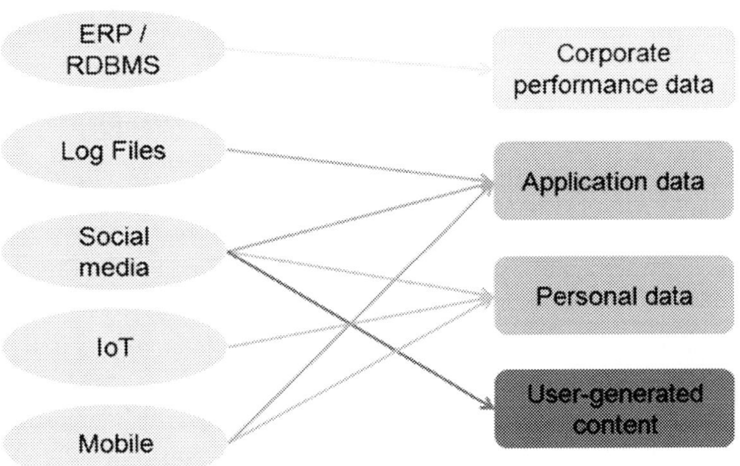

2. **Application data** refers to "any possible records of a particular activity that was performed by human and/or machine and can be tracked in a log file by an application of IoT sensors, e.g. logins and access records (for the activities performed on websites or software platforms)".
3. **Personal data** refers to any information, which may lead to identify a person directly or indirectly. This includes identifiers such as names, identification numbers, physical or location address and online identifiers. In the social media personal data is categorized into various types of information into incidental, private, personalized, privatized, derived, behavioral (Schneier, 2010).
4. **User generated content** includes any form of incidental data, behavioral data, disclosed data generated or uploaded in or to social media e.g. posts, blogs, videos, wikis, comments, likes, or dislikes on social media applications and is readily available to service providers (Schneier, 2010). The application and user generated data are attributed to human elements in the production of big data (Lemov, 2016) which service providers together with data brokers and marketers (or third parties) collect, mine, combine, analyzed, disclose and act upon for the purposes of targeted advertising among other uses raising potential privacy risks and concerns (Christl, Kopp, & Riechert, 2017; Lemov, 2016; Navetta, 2013). The richness of big data is a result of constant production and multiplicity of sources i.e. through use of devices, social networks, websites, search engines, smartphones and Internet-connected appliances (Agnellutti, 2014).

Dataveillance Practices in Big Data and Internet of Things Era

Dataveillance refers to the collection and monitoring of people through data (Clarke, 1988, 1999). These practices have been further facilitated by the use of IoT devices in practice. Michael & Michael (2007) refer to as uberveillance. The IoT devices have also enhanced surveillance of people at a very granular level- monitoring bodily functions heart rate, sleep patterns, menstrual cycles, and other factors, thus watching from "under the skin" (Michael, 2017; Michael & Michael, 2007). In short, IoT devices are proving to be effective in collecting a variety of data about users (Ferrari, 2017).

Due to these data practices, researchers and privacy advocates are increasingly concerned about the manner in which the data is collected by IoT and used or repurposed without the subject's knowledge (Clarke, 1999; Etzioni, 2015; Lupton, 2015; Michael, 2015). The prevalence of dataveillance practices and increasing uptake of IoT have accelerated commercial entities exploitation of socially produced data with users unknowingly paying for the applications, accounts or services with such large datasets (Clarke, 2014b).

Data Practices: Privacy Risks and Harms in the Data Driven Economies

Big Data and IoT still present opportunities amidst various privacy and security challenges (Crawford & Schultz, 2014; Federal Trade Commission, 2015; K. Michael & Miller, 2013). The ever-increasing challenge is of informational privacy related to data collection, sharing and processing using predictive data analytics tools that allow cross-matching information about consumers (Christiansen, 2011; Crawford & Schultz, 2014). Cyber security experts note that the practices surrounding big data processing pose great challenges to the normative perspectives to privacy (Schneier, 2015). Although consumers might consider privacy risks as distant events unlikely to happen in real-life it is increasingly evident that users of these technologies have witnessed a impact related to social and economic inequality, coercion, manipulation and hidden influence, financial loss or identity theft, discrimination, seclusion among others (Acquisti, Brandimarte, & Loewenstein, 2015; Haynes & Robinson, 2015; Rosenblat, Kneese, & Boyd, 2014; Yao, 2011).

Privacy risks have direct negative impact on individuals if used to determine health conditions and assess credit worthiness and employability without the data subject knowledge, or having an option to correct the information held about them (Federal Trade Commission, 2015; (Haynes & Robinson, 2015; Rosenblat, Kneese & boyd, 2014). Researchers note that although most people are aware of corporations collecting information about them through various technologies, they are unaware of the extent and the scope of the invasion of privacy that are now widespread (Frank, 2014). For instance, data brokerage companies and government agencies now keep massive data about individuals: divorces, political leanings, adult entertainment use, and gambling, but it is largely unknown how the information is used and to what consequence (Christl et al., 2017; Etzioni, 2015; Frank, 2014). With the increased innovation in IoT and use of Big Data, privacy risks are bound to increase if privacy concerns are not addressed. Table 1 summarizes the evidence from the literature.

PRIVACY LITERACY AND AWARENESS FRAMEWORKS

Researchers study privacy from multiple disciplines and theoretical perspectives: sociological, psychological, legal, environmental and economic (Newell, 1995). Empirical research evaluating users of IoT devices and social media literacy (Pingo & Narayan, 2016, Bartsch, 2016) and regulatory awareness (Richardson et al., 2017) have emerged in recent years. Scholars have noted the discussion of privacy

Table 1. Summary of privacy risks and harms raised in big data and IoT era

Privacy risks or Outcome of the data practices	Consequences facilitated by use of personal data
Lack of trust	Lack of openness of how the data is compiled and used have emerged with data subjects having no understanding or control over; for example, in relation the use of data by data brokerage and analysis companies (Christl & Spiekerman, 2016) Lack of transparency may lead to users avoiding using specific products or services (Information and Privacy Commissioner, 2017)
Financial risks and loss (e.g. job or insurance costs, determining tax, determine loan application)	The possibility of inflated health insurance premium rates due risks based on data collected from IoT like, fitness trackers and pacemakers due to perceived health, exposure to hazards, risky behavior (Haynes & Robinson, 2015; K. Michael, 2017) Pricing and assessing individual's financial bankability or financial liability based on the SNS friend and family lists (Meyer, 2015) and personal information collected on SNSs, fitness trackers, driving habits based on the car tracking systems. (Moncrief, 2015)
Limited access to services and products	Use of Big Data models limit individuals' access to advertisements on financial services due to their low credit scores (Fertik, 2013). Secondary use of Big Data beyond users understanding (aggregated or personally identifiable information) with potential use by advertisers for price discrimination purposes to consumers (Fertik, 2013; Fornaciari, 2014)
Breach of confidentiality	Deliberate or accidental release or leakage of sensitive information (Haynes & Robinson, 2015)
Regulatory non-compliance	Failure of service providers and third parties to comply with the regulatory frameworks leads to misuse of personal information beyond user's expectation or knowledge leading to adverse effects to individuals (Haynes & Robinson, 2015)
Power imbalance	The information asymmetry between data controllers and data subjects leading to inaccurate decision-making without the knowledge of the subjects (Tuninetti Ferrari, 2017)

shifting from structuralistic to individualistic due to disruptions brought by economic and technological contexts, requiring individuals to negotiate and manage their own privacy (Fornaciari, 2014). It is important for individuals to have knowledge to evaluate the risks of using such technologies and possible exposure of personal information. This means consumers' need to have awareness and understanding of such responsibilities in managing their privacy and personal information. Researchers have also noted that although technical and legal means exist to protect users' privacy, user awareness of such vulnerabilities is important (Solove, 2012; Torre et al., 2017). Privacy studies apply various theoretical frameworks including privacy as a right (Warren & Brandeis, 1890), privacy as contextual integrity (Nissenbaum, 2004), communication privacy management (Petronio, 2002) and Westin's (1967) perspective of privacy as a claim to control and determine to what extent, to whom and how their information is shared to others. In addition other scholars have explored privacy and security protection online using the theory of planned behavior (Yao, 2011) and protection motivation (De Santo & Gaspoz, 2015). The following section highlights some of the frameworks used to analyze consumers' informational privacy awareness in IoT and other digital technologies.

PRIVACY LITERACY FRAMEWORK

Rotman (2009) identified critical skills/aspects that users of information technologies need to posses to enable them to manage online information privacy. The privacy literacy framework explains the need for people to understand what happens to personal information when collected in databases and how to actively protect this information. The users of digital technologies should apply their knowledge to understand how personal information is collected, stored, processed, used or disseminated (Solove, 2006) and make decisions against their privacy expectations. The theory provides five key elements to analyze privacy awareness: understanding, recognizing, realizing, evaluating and deciding (Rotman, 2009). The understanding of how personal information is used by organizations, recognizing potential places of personal exposure, realizing the consequences of exposing personal information, evaluating the risks and benefits the sharing personal data across digital technologies, and finally, making decision over the appropriateness of the personal data to be shared online (Rotman, 2009). The framework provides cognitive tools to evaluate privacy risks and concerns in social technologies but also possible to use in IoT technologies since they part of our everyday life.

Informational Privacy Awareness (IPA) and Informational Privacy Situational Awareness (IPSA)

With the increased use of various information technologies in our everyday life, users are faced with the challenge of managing privacy against the organizations seeking to access personal information, and from exposure to unexpected parties. Consumers' privacy awareness, literacy, and knowledge have become extremely important to enable consumers in decision making on how to control personal information exposure of while using a range of information technologies (Xu, Dinev, Smith, & Hart, 2011).

Privacy scholars have proposed informational privacy situational awareness (IPSA) (Sim, Liginlal, & Khansa, 2012) and informational privacy awareness (IPA) (Correia & Compeau, 2017) as frameworks to explain information disclosure practices in technologies. Thus, to understand privacy awareness, attitudes or concerns in IoT, the theory of information privacy awareness (Correia & Compeau, 2017) provides elaborate mechanisms to evaluate common practices and information disclosure across information technologies platforms.

IPSA (Sim et al., 2012) and IPA (Correia & Compeau, 2017) both build on the situational awareness theory (Endsley, 1995b). The situational awareness (SA) is conceptualized as a "perception of elements in an environment within a volume of time and space, the comprehension of their meaning and the projection of their status in the near future" (Endsley, 1988). The Situational awareness model has largely been applied to evaluate decision-making in particular operational tasks of dynamic and complex systems (Endsley, 1995a). Building on SA theory, the IPSA and IPA construct have developed the tools to measure various aspects of information privacy awareness. Endsley (1995a) observes the lack of situation awareness in human decision-making leads to errors while situational analysis about a situation leads to optimum performance.

The IPA and IPSA constructs presume that individuals with knowledge and awareness about a situation are likely to take a more adaptive response to privacy risks and the lack of it may lead to erratic decisions to disclose or expose personal information (Correia & Compeau, 2017; Sim et al., 2012). In this section the focus is to highlight various aspects of IPA relevant to privacy awareness in IoT and related information technologies. The situational analysis in informational privacy may be perceived as individuals being well-informed and having a good knowledge on how technologies and service providers collect and use personal data (Correia & Compeau, 2017). In addition, individuals must have the ability to anticipate consequences of their actions in particular situations while using information technologies. Privacy research increasingly examines individual's privacy behavior and what influences decision-making in personal information disclosures (Sim et al., 2012). Some of the privacy research findings indicate that individuals are still vulnerable towards disclosing personal information to untrustworthy third parties even after situational analysis of potential or real privacy loss (Xia, Wang, Huang, & Shah, 2017).

Information privacy awareness (IPA) focuses on building requisite knowledge about the factors related to information privacy (type 1), the understanding of the existence of elements that might possibly compromise privacy in an environment (type 2) and the anticipation of their future risks to privacy (type 3) (Correia & Compeau, 2017). The core elements in this framework are technology, regulations and the information practices (collection, processing, transfer and use) of individuals and organizations. The environment encompasses the technological infrastructure that facilitates information flow from individuals to all other destinations (servers, other users, third parties, etc.). The informational privacy awareness covers three major areas that individuals need to be build knowledge on: technology, regulations, and common data practices (Correia & Compeau, 2017). The IPA construct introduces three-dimensions of an informational privacy awareness evaluation matrix consisting of: technology informational privacy awareness (TIPA), regulatory informational privacy awareness (RIPA) and common practices in informational privacy (CPIPA).

The technology informational privacy awareness (TIPA) covers knowledge of technical elements related to informational privacy type 1, 2 and 3. The technical elements include the information infrastructure of both physical objects and software used by individuals and companies to collect, use and disseminate data. The environment is the technological platforms used to send, collect, process, organize and store the information. And finally, the knowledge about implications continued technological innovations and information privacy. The regulatory information privacy awareness (RIPA) covers knowledge of data governance and regulatory elements related to information privacy (type 1), the understanding of the regulatory elements that exist in the environment (type 2) and the anticipation of their implications in the future. The elements in these contexts are regulatory laws and principles that mediate between the individuals and the data collecting and processing entities. And finally type 3 awareness relates to users' anticipation of change in laws that impact on personal information collection processing, use and dissemination.

The common practices in information privacy awareness (CPIPA) cover knowledge of the practices or elements related to information privacy (type 1), knowledge about the privacy components that exist in the IoT/digital technologies environment (type 2), and an understanding of their future potential implications to privacy (type 3). The common practices refer to the data practices that organizations use to collect, process and use personal information for economic purposes. The environment refers to how the information flows from individuals to entities through the information infrastructure. The construct of type 1 includes understanding of the information technology tools and the data practices used by organizations or service providers, and type 2 is the knowledge and awareness of the existence of the practices within the technologies, while type 3 is the knowledge of the risks associated with the ever-changing data practices, which pose privacy risks to individuals.

APPROACHES TO ADDRESS PRIVACY CONCERNS IN DIGITAL TECHNOLOGIES

Among the strategies to address privacy protections, legal protections exist in many jurisdictions under privacy acts, data protection acts, consumer rights protection laws, privacy principles, and fair information principles (Debatin, 2011; Richardson et al., 2017; Solove & Schwartz, 2014). Although individuals are assured of their privacy through regulatory means, especially when personal information is collected directly or indirectly, used, transferred or disclosed through consent and notice (Mantelero, 2014). However, the ever-growing ease of access and transmission of information in online or digital environments and the increased predictive data analytics challenge the existing privacy protections (Crawford & Schultz, 2014; Mantelero, 2014). Earlier research on privacy considered informational privacy as a design problem

Figure 2. Informational privacy awareness
(Correia & Compeau, 2017)

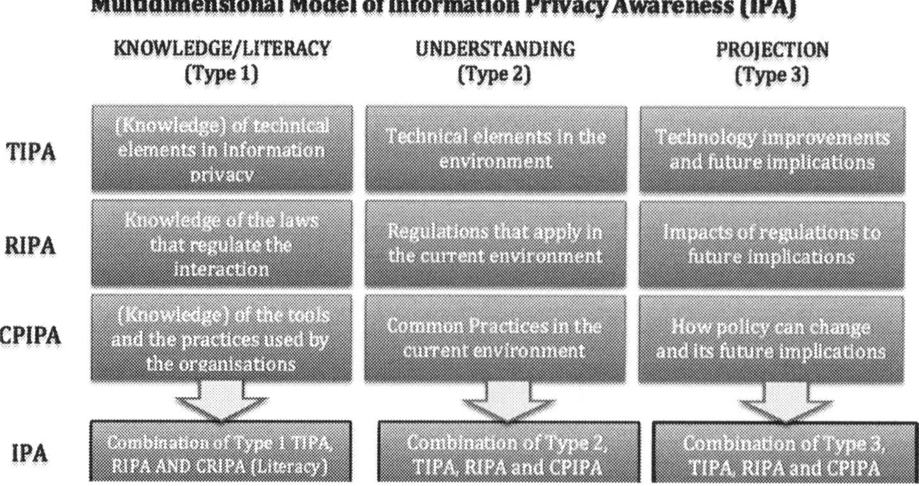

from an information systems perspective (Lehikoinen, 2008), which Cavoukian and Jonas (2012, p. 863) assert can be addressed by incorporating "privacy by design" approaches and use of Fair Information Practice Principles (FIPP). On the contrary, King and Forder (2016) observe that the current practices of recording mediated communication, combining and deriving meaning from the data (collected from myriad gadgets/ IoT) to gain insights into users' behaviors for wider profiling practices, makes it harder to have one definitive way to deal with informational privacy. This chapter contributes to the need for organizations or IoT data holders to have elaborate means to enhance privacy, including privacy literacy, as a complimentary mechanism to privacy-enhancing technologies and legal frameworks, which should be manifested through stakeholders' awareness and creation of strategies and educational programs to all consumers and non-consumers of the IoT. In addition to these, increasing transparency, ethical self-regulation and co-regulation (through use of transparent and open consent, choices, notices and systems designs) are needed to protect and bolster privacy in new technologies and use of personal data.

Ethical Self-Regulation

According to Brown and Marsden (2013), self-regulation refers to "a rule of the formation of norms: it exercises functions that shapes or controls the behavior of actors in that environment…." Self-regulation in this context refers to IoT service providers' practices in managing consumers' personal information using internal regulations in data-based economies. For instance, global social networking service providers like Facebook and LinkedIn among others, claim to self-regulate in managing personal information (Haynes, 2015). However, the self-regulation mechanisms have been faulted due their lack of transparency and the unfairness in the way they present privacy policies and data sharing practices to their consumers (Christl & Spiekerman, 2016; Hans, 2012).

Privacy scholars are in constant contemplation of whether IoT innovations and surrounding synergies should be regulated or self-regulate (R. Weber, 2010). Often regulatory mechanisms are categorized into hard (legally binding) or soft laws, with the latter serving the legal purposes of the adopting parties (Karine, 2017). Further legal scholars suggest that soft regulation should be used as a means of the regulation of IoT and their derivative data practices. Soft regulation is presented as an ideal to allow consensus-based norms to Internet industry activities (Karine, 2017).

Due to the global nature of technology services, self-regulation often manifests through different mechanisms in different countries guided by government agencies mandated to monitor use of technologies and the data practices surrounding them (Haynes, 2015), but since this very global nature of technology services also make the information accessible globally, and there is often a disconnect between regulations and reality. As IoT based service providers negotiate and envisage to protect against legal liabilities, protecting users' privacy and personal data through self-regulation mechanisms should also be given equal priority (Gasser & Schultz, 2015). In addition to internal self-regulation, proper guidance and supervision from various stakeholders like information and privacy commissioners, legislations, and privacy commissioners is important. For example, in the Australian context, the Australian Privacy Principles and Privacy and Personal Information Act 1998 is informed by Privacy by Design (Cavoukian, 2009) and key regulatory frameworks guide service providers in protecting citizens' privacy and the processing of users' personal data.

Privacy scholars examine privacy principles and regulations, and should ideally be embedded in privacy policies and systems design with manifestation in: consents, choices (opt-in and opt-out options), anonymity, transparency, notices and accountability and openness (Cavoukian & Jonas, 2012; Custers,

2016; Langheinrich, 2002; Minelli, Chambers, & Dhiraj, 2013). The goals of these principles are to guide organizations, or rather service providers, to protect both consumers and organizational interests (Pierson, 2012). Currently, tension exists in their efficacy due to the complexities and lack of transparency and proper implementation evidenced by how organizations handle the collected data (Solove, 2012). For example, in Australia, the Privacy Act of 1988 and the Australian Privacy Principles provide privacy guidelines in personal data protection (Office of the Australian Information Commissioner, 2014); however, privacy researchers have expressed concerns about the transparency and efficacy in their implementation as consumers still lack real choices (King & Forder, 2016; Svantesson & Clarke, 2010). Organizations that provide online services also have an obligation to provide:

- Transparent, open and easy to understand notices to explain the use of the collected personal information
- Provide easy opt-in or out options with respect to collection and use of data
- Provide easily accessible means for consumers to lodge complaints directly with entities (Briedis, Webb, & Fraser, 2016).

Nevertheless, privacy scholars have noted a lack of openness in current data processing practices (Christl et al., 2017). Table 2 lists the key components proposed to ensure realization of efficient self-regulation as observed by regulators, scholars, and privacy experts.

Transparency in Data Practices

Transparency is understood as "the principle of enabling the public to gain information about the operations and structures of a given entity" (Etzioni, 2010). Most of the online service providers are for-profit companies, with their income dependent on online commercial services (Christl & Spiekerman, 2016); in their perspective, consumers are benefiting through the use of their free online services and in return pay with personal data including user generated content which service providers claim ownership over (Christl & Spiekerman, 2016; Pierson, 2012). Scholars note that this kind of trade-off between the service

Table 2. Fair information practice principles

Principles	Description
Notice	As part of self-regulation obligations, organizations should inform individuals on how the collected data is used
Choice	Individuals should be given choices to opt-in or opt-out of data practices involving collection, processing and transferring of data in an explicit manner
Consent	The data subjects should be able to give explicit consent to the collection and use of any personal data collected and generated
Security	Organizations should protect personal data from any loss, misuse, unauthorized access, disclosure, alteration, and destructions (Kitchin, 2014).
Integrity	The data processors should make sure the data is reliable, accurate, complete and current for any consequent decision making based on such data
Access	Provide means for individuals to access, check, and verify data about themselves
Accountability	Data controllers need to ensure they follow the information principles and regulatory mechanisms

Source: (OECD, 1980)

providers and consumers is not problematic but needs each party to clearly understand the terms and conditions presented in privacy policies in an open manner (McDonald & Cranor, 2009).

Transparency is integral in data processing for organizations or technology service providers to enhance and build consumer trust (Liu, Marchewka, Lu, & Yu, 2005). In recent times, increased cases of data breaches have prompted governments to enforce new regulation to ensure transparency in how the companies handle consumer personal data with requirement to notify data subjects of any data breaches, present consents and set of data subjects right (European Commission, 2016). In response, some privacy advocacy organizations have emerged such as Terms of Services Didn't Read (ToS; DR) (Terms of Services Didn't Read, 2017), with the aim of analyzing terms of services of global technology companies to inform and enable consumers to understand how the organizations collect, processes, and handle personal data. These actions have also prompted increased awareness and reflection on how corporations lack transparency in handling personal information and wield power over the data subjects and regulators (Travis & Arthur, 2014). This mechanism attempts to push corporations to be transparent on how they handle personal data. Therefore, regulators are presented with the challenge of determining the standards of transparency to technology service providers and monitoring mechanisms to ensure adherence and respect for transparency (Karine, 2017).

Accountability in Data Practices

The service providers and data brokers have demonstrated lack of accountability in several incidents of data breaches (Christl et al., 2017). In the most recent case in 2018 involving Facebook Corporation and Cambridge Analytica, more than 87 million users' personal data was compromised without the subjects being informed. Accountability has always been conceived as a preserve of public organizations' governance; however, drawing on Mulgan's (2000) work, accountability covers both public and private organizations that provide services to the public. According to Mulgan (2000) accountability refers to "...certain obligations that arise within a relationship of responsibility, where one person or body is responsible to another for the performance of particular services..." Mulgan (2000) observes that individual consumers are powerless when in conflict with large private organizations. Thus, private organizations should be made publicly accountable to consumers of such services (Mulgan, 2000). Therefore, as organizations engage in various data collection, processing and use practices using a variety of information technologies, they need to be accountable for any possible harm to consumers when using the data generated from IoT.

Building on Mulgan's work, scholars declare that Internet industry actors are obligated to take care of their infrastructure and customers, which means they should be responsible and accountable for any potential threats, risks or vulnerabilities to the users. Thus, accountability entails the "identification of who is accountable, to whom and for what" (Morgan & Yeung, 2007).

In relation to IoT service providers, accountability is presented as one of the core means to hold data controllers responsible for any consequences that may result from data practices (privacy breaches and security exposures). For instance, the new European Union new data protection regulation- General Data Protection Regulation (GDPR, 2016) intends to provide comprehensive guidelines to regulate data practices (includes IoT and other technologies) requiring technology service providers to be more transparent and accountable in their data practices (data collection and use) and also make cases of data breaches openly known to data subjects.

STAKEHOLDERS' RESPONSIBILITIES IN ENHANCING PRIVACY AWARENESS AND PROTECTION

The normative approaches to privacy protection heavily rely on social norms and legal traditions (Solove & Schwartz, 2014), but this increases the threats to personal and information privacy faced in digital environments if users of the technologies are not aware of the existing privacy vulnerabilities (Acquisti et al., 2015). Legal and technology researchers increasingly support awareness as a complimentary mechanism to existing approaches (Solove, 2012). Thus, the IoT devices and Internet users cannot rely solely on legal regulations to protect information privacy (Weber, 2010), nor can they expect users to

Table 3. Responsibilities to enhance privacy awareness/literacy

Stakeholders	Spectrum Of Responsibilities To Data And Privacy Protection Enhancement
Individuals (consumers/ Non-consumers)	• Consumers need to educate themselves on privacy and security threats and risks when using online platforms • Increase privacy awareness about the implications of the data exposure to both implicit and explicit data practices on digital technologies • Actively enact privacy settings on social technologies and other online platforms • Acquire relevant knowledge to protect information /online privacy • To be cautious about social sharing features on application and devices • Understand the value and need for personal and informational privacy in cyberspace (Culver & Grizzle, 2017). • Build awareness of possible use or commodification of the personal information collected from online applications and devices • Ability to assess and make judgments when sharing personal information offline and online • Ethical use of others' personal information and respect for the privacy of others (Culver & Grizzle, 2017) • Actively controlling and determining how personal information is shared or used
Service providers/ Manufacturers	• Enhance Privacy-preserving technologies • Allow transfer of information or deletion of information or account in the applications • Improve consumer controls and awareness with open practices that requires consumer consents (Briedis et al., 2016) • Minimize risk and harm in data collection, storage and use processes • Incorporate privacy by design in the applications from the start (Cavoukian, 2009) • Provide list of features and the authorization needed to activate the feature (privacy by default features) in applications • Minimize the collection of data by collecting only necessary data to provide services to users or enhance the technologies • Provide user-friendly privacy policies to users of the devices and applications • Ensure that the organization trains staff to handle sensitive data ethically • Comply with relevant data protection and privacy regulations • Ensure that devices are used in the manner they are intended not for other purposes. • Use secure data transferring protocols (Barcena et al., 2014)
Third-parties/ advertisers	• Explicitly state the processing and use of the collected personal information • Ensure transparency in the data practices by explicitly informing data subjects on the data collection, storage, processing, sharing and use of the personal data • Provide consumer friendly privacy policies • Openness in personal data management processes • Friendly opt-in/opt-out options • Communicate privacy of information clearly to the consumers • Comply with data protections and privacy laws • Improved privacy communication to consumers
Governments and regulatory bodies (Privacy commissioners)	• Promote privacy awareness to general public • Collaboration with service providers to ensure transparency • Provide clear guidelines on privacy preservation by technology developers and third parties services providers • Evaluate legitimate limitations of privacy online (Culver & Grizzle, 2017) • Enforce standards and certification process in technology • Promote Privacy Impact Assessment in organizations

use social and cultural norms to navigate the existing information practices and complexities in the digital era. Acquisti, et.al (2015) note that although some technologies seem to provide 'controls', they simply create an illusion of control and encourage greater sharing of personal data. This is because it is harder for people to understand the digital architecture and the network of the Internet than it is for them understand the architecture of the real spaces (boyd, 2010). The ubiquity of digital technologies has made it impossible for people to be off the grid, and as technologies keep evolving at a faster rate, users are unable to keep up with how it changes the rules on them (Bartsch & Dienlin, 2016). It is important for all stakeholders to take an active role in ensuring information technology consumers are protected besides the commercial interests. Table 3 highlights some of the light-touch approaches to enhance consumer privacy awareness.

CONCLUSION

This chapter identified privacy risks and stakeholders' roles in providing an environment for users to understand and have control of how information is collected, processed, shared and used in digital economies. The authors take the view that all the stakeholders: scholars, media, privacy advocates, manufacturers and technology designers, controllers and regulators, have responsibility to educate the public on possible privacy and security risks in the new IoT innovations. The service providers should ensure consumers are aware of how the technologies open possibilities for data breaches and the consequences of their misuse that sometimes consumers are unaware of. The data subjects equally have responsibility to acquire knowledge about the technologies, regulations and understanding of the technology environment to manage informational privacy while using them.

Privacy awareness is important for users to take control of in managing the exposure of personal information in information technologies. As the Internet industry generates value and benefits from the Big Data generated from IoT and other digital technologies, privacy of the users should be safeguarded by incorporating transparency and accountability in data practices; for example, the provision of simplified, plain language, and user-friendly privacy policies and terms-of-service and choices to opt-in rather using bottleneck opt-out options into data practices will greatly help in this area. Finally, for the users to negotiate and manage information privacy, it is imperative for each stakeholder to participate in ensuring that contextual integrity (Nissenbaum, 2004) is maintained in handling big data, and that data subjects have a reasonable understanding of these data practices.

REFERENCES

Acetech. (2013). Internet Privacy. Options for adequate realization. In J. Buchmann (Ed.), *Interdisciplinary perspectives on internet applications and privacy options*. Heidelberg: Springer Verlag.

Acquisti, A., Brandimarte, L., & Loewenstein, G. (2015). Privacy and human behavior in the age of information. *Science*, *347*(6221), 509–514. doi:10.1126cience.aaa1465 PMID:25635091

Agnellutti, C. (2014). *Big Data: An Exploration of Opportunities, Values, and Privacy Issues*. New York: Nova Science Publishers, Inc.

Barcena, M. B., Wueest, C., & Lau, H. (2014). *How safe is your quantified self*. Mountain View, CA: Symantech.

Bartsch, M., & Dienlin, T. (2016). Control your Facebook: An analysis of online privacy literacy. *Computers in Human Behavior, 56*, 147–154. doi:10.1016/j.chb.2015.11.022

Beyer, M. A., & Laney, D. (2012). *The importance of 'big data': a definition*. Gartner.

Boyd, D. (2010). Austin, Texas: Making Sense of Privacy and Publicity. In SXSW; Retrieved from http://www.danah.org/papers/talks/2010/SXSW2010.html

boyd, D., & Hargittai, E. (2010). Facebook privacy settings: Who cares. *First Monday, 15*(8), 1-23.

Briedis, M., Webb, J., & Fraser, M. (2016). *Improving the Communication of Privacy Information for Consumers*. Retrieved from Sydney https://goo.gl/zWZS3T

Brown, & Marsden, C. T. (2013). *Regulating code: Good governance and better regulation in the information age*. Cambridge: MIT Press.

Caron, X., Bosua, R., Maynard, S. B., & Ahmad, A. (2016). The Internet of Things (IoT) and its impact on individual privacy: An Australian perspective. *Computer Law & Security Review, 32*(1), 4–15. doi:10.1016/j.clsr.2015.12.001

Casanovas, P., De Koker, L., Mendelson, D., & Watts, D. (2017). Regulation of Big Data: Perspectives on strategy, policy, law and privacy. *Health and Technology*, 1–15. doi:10.100712553-017-0190-6

Cavoukian, A. (2009). *Privacy by design: The 7 foundational principles. implementation and mapping of fair information practices*. Canada: Information and Privacy Commissioner of Ontario.

Cavoukian, A., & Jonas, J. (2012). *Privacy by Design in the Age of Big Data*. Ontario, Canada: Information & Privacy Commissioner.

Chaudhry, A., Crowcroft, J., Howard, H., Madhavapeddy, A., Mortier, R., Haddadi, H., & McAuley, D. (2015, August). Personal data: thinking inside the box. In *Proceedings of the fifth decennial Aarhus conference on critical alternatives* (pp. 29-32). Aarhus University Press.

Christiansen, L. (2011). Personal privacy and Internet marketing: An impossible conflict or a marriage made in heaven? *Business Horizons, 54*(6), 509–514. doi:10.1016/j.bushor.2011.06.002

Christl, W., Kopp, K., & Riechert, P. U. (2017). How companies use personal information against people: Automated Disadvantage, Personalized Persuasion, and the Societal Ramifications of the Commercial Use of Personal Information. *Cracked Labs*. Retrieved from https://crackedlabs.org/en/data-against-people

Christl, W., & Spiekerman, S. (2016). *Networks of control: A report on corporate surveillance, digital tracking, big data & privacy*. Vienna, Austria: Facultas.

Christovich, M. M. (2016). Why should we care what Fitbit shares-a proposed statutory solution to protect sensitive personal fitness information. *Hastings Communication & Entertainment Law Journal, 38*, 91–116.

Clarke, R. (1988). Information technology and dataveillance. *Communications of the ACM*, *31*(5), 498–512. doi:10.1145/42411.42413

Clarke, R. (1999). Introduction to dataveillance and information privacy, and definitions of terms. Retrieved from http://www.rogerclarke.com/DV/CACM88.html

Clarke, R. (2014b). The Prospects for Consumer-Oriented Social Media. *Organizacija*, *47*(4), 219–230. doi:10.2478/orga-2014-0024

Correia, J., & Compeau, D. (2017). Information Privacy Awareness (IPA): A Review of the Use, Definition and Measurement of IPA. *Paper presented at the Proceedings of the 50th Hawaii International Conference on System Sciences*, Hawaii. Retrieved from http://hdl.handle.net/10125/41646

Crawford, K., & Schultz, J. (2014). Big data and due process: Toward a framework to redress predictive privacy harms. *Boston College Law Review. Boston College. Law School*, *55*(1), 39–92.

Crow, G., Wiles, R., Heath, S., & Charles, V. (2006). Research ethics and data quality: The implications of informed consent. *International Journal of Social Research Methodology*, *9*(2), 83–95. doi:10.1080/13645570600595231

Culver, S. H., & Grizzle, A. (2017). *Survey on privacy in media and information literacy with youth perspectives*. Paris: UNESCO.

Custers, B. (2016). Click here to consent forever: Expiry dates for informed consent. *Big Data & Society*, *3*(1).

Data privacy Lab, IQSS, Harvard University. (n.d.). White Paper. Retrieved 21 December 2018 from https://dataprivacylab.org/projects/pgp/1021-1.pdf

De Santo, A., & Gaspoz, C. (2015). *Influence of risks and privacy literacy on coping responses to privacy threats*. Paper presented at the In Proceedings of the 20th Association Information Management Conference. Retrieved from http://bit.ly/2dGrUfk

Debatin, B. (2011). Ethics, privacy, and self-restraint in social networking. In R. L. Trepte (Ed.), Privacy online (pp. 47-60). Berlin: Springer. doi:10.1007/978-3-642-21521-6_5

Dutcher, J. (2014). What is Big data? Retrieved from https://datascience.berkeley.edu/what-is-big-data/

Dutton, W. H. (2013). The Internet of things. doi:https://ssrn.com/abstract=2324902 or doi:10.2139srn.2324902

Endsley, M. R. (1988). Situation awareness global assessment technique (SAGAT). *Paper presented at the IEEE Aerospace and Electronics Conference, 1988. NAECON 1988.*

Endsley, M. R. (1995a). Measurement of Situation Awareness in Dynamic Systems. *Human Factors*, *37*(1), 65–84. doi:10.1518/001872095779049499

Endsley, M. R. (1995b). Toward a Theory of Situation Awareness in Dynamic Systems. *Human Factors*, *37*(1), 32–64. doi:10.1518/001872095779049543

Etzioni, A. (2010). Is Transparency the Best Disinfectant? *Journal of Political Philosophy*, *18*(4), 389–404. doi:10.1111/j.1467-9760.2010.00366.x

Etzioni, A. (2015). *A Cyber Age Privacy Doctrine: policy and practice*. New York: Palgrave Macmillan. doi:10.1057/9781137513960

European Commission. (2016). *General Data Protection Regulation*. Retrieved from https://goo.gl/JxYRUK

Federal Trade Commission. (2015). *Internet of things: privacy and security in a connected world*. Retrieved from https://goo.gl/qAhiAH

Fereidooni, H., Frassetto, T., Miettinen, M., Sadeghi, A.-R., & Conti, M. (2017). Fitness Trackers: Fit for Health but Unfit for Security and Privacy. *Paper presented at the Connected Health Applications, Systems and Engineering Technologies (CHASE) Conference*. IEEE.

Fertik, M. (Feb.1 2013). The Rich See a Different Internet Than the Poor. *Scientific American*. Retrieved from https://goo.gl/gVLnxK

Fornaciari, F. (2014). Pricey privacy: Framing the economy of information in the digital age. *First Monday*, *19*(12). doi:10.5210/fm.v19i12.5008

Frank, P. (2014). The Dark Market for Personal Data. *The New York Times*. Retrieved from https://goo.gl/v5k5Kf

Gartner. (2013). IT Glossary. Retrieved from https://www.gartner.com/it-glossary/big-data/

Gartner. (2017). Gartner Says 8.4 Billion Connected "Things" Will Be in Use in 2017, Up 31 Percent From 2016. Retrieved from https://www.gartner.com/newsroom/id/3598917

Gasser, U., & Schultz, J. (2015). Governance of online intermediaries: Observation from series of national case studies. *The Berkman Centre for Internet & Society Research publication series No. 2015-5*. doi:10.2139srn.2566364

Hans, G. (2012). Privacy Policies, Terms of Service, and FTC Enforcement: Broadening Unfairness Regulation for a New Era. *Michigan Telecommunications and Technology Law Review*, *19*, 163.

Haynes, D. (2015). *Risk and regulation of access to personal data on online social networking services in the UK*. Unpublished doctoral dissertation, City University London, London. Retrieved from http://openaccess.city.ac.uk/11972/

Haynes, D., & Robinson, L. (2015). Defining user risk in social networking services. *Aslib Journal of Information Management*, *67*(1), 94–115. doi:10.1108/AJIM-07-2014-0087

Helberger, N. (2016). Profiling and Targeting Consumers in the Internet of Things – A New Challenge for Consumer Law. *SSRN Electronic Journal*. doi:10.2139srn.2728717

Karine, K. (2017). How industry can help us fight against botnets: Notes on regulating private-sector intervention. *International Review of Law Computers & Technology*, *31*(1), 105–130. doi:10.1080/13600869.2017.1275274

King, N. J., & Forder, J. (2016). Data analytics and consumer profiling: Finding appropriate privacy principles for discovered data. *Computer Law & Security Review*, *32*(5), 696–714. doi:10.1016/j.clsr.2016.05.002

Kitchin, R. (2014). *The data revolution: Big data, open data, data infrastructures and their consequences*. Los Angeles: Sage.

Lambiotte, R., & Kosinski, M. (2014). Tracking the digital footprints of personality. *Proceedings of the IEEE*, *102*(12), 1934–1939. doi:10.1109/JPROC.2014.2359054

Langheinrich, M. (2002). A privacy awareness system for ubiquitous computing environments. In H. L. E. G. Borriello (Ed.), *International conference on Ubiquitous Computing*. Springer. 10.1007/3-540-45809-3_19

Lehikoinen, J. T. (2008). Theory and Application of the Privacy Regulation Model. In J. Lumsden (Ed.), *Handbook of Research on User Interface Design and Evaluation for Mobile Technology* (pp. 863–876). Hershey, PA: IGI Global; doi:10.4018/978-1-59904-871-0.ch051

Lemov, R. (2016). Big data is people: why big data is actually small personal and very human. *Aeon*. Retrieved from https://goo.gl/gRsu8L

Liu, C., Marchewka, J. T., Lu, J., & Yu, C. S. (2005). Beyond concern—A privacy-trust-behavioral intention model of electronic commerce. *Information & Management*, *42*(2), 289–304. doi:10.1016/j.im.2004.01.003

Lo, B. P., Ip, H., & Yang, G.-Z. (2016). Transforming health care: Body sensor networks, wearables, and the Internet of Things. *IEEE Pulse*, *7*(1), 4–8. doi:10.1109/MPUL.2015.2498474 PMID:26799719

Lupton, D. (2014). You are your data: Self-tracking practices and concepts of data. In S. Selke (Ed.) Lifelogging (pp. 61-79). doi:10.1007/978-3-658-13137-1_4

Lupton, D. (2015). *Digital sociology*. London: Routledge.

Lupton, D. (2016). *The quantified self*. Malden, MA: Polity Press.

Lupton, D., & Williamson, B. (2017). The datafied child: The dataveillance of children and implications for their rights. *New Media & Society*, *19*(5), 780–794. doi:10.1177/1461444816686328

Mantelero, A. (2014). The future of consumer data protection in the EU Re-thinking the "notice and consent" paradigm in the new era of predictive analytics. *Computer Law & Security Review*, *30*(6), 643–660. doi:10.1016/j.clsr.2014.09.004

McDonald, A. M., & Cranor, L. F. (2009). The cost of reading privacy policies. *A Journal of Law and Policy for the Information Society*, *4*(3), 543-568.

Meyer, R. (2015, September 25). Could a Bank Deny Your Loan Based on Your Facebook Friends? *The Atlantic*. Retrieved from https://goo.gl/HauP6P

Michael, K. (2015). Wearables and Lifelogging: The socioethical implications. *IEEE Consumer Electronics Magazine*, *4*(2), 79–81. doi:10.1109/MCE.2015.2392998

Michael, K. (2017). Implantable Medical Device Tells All: Uberveillance Gets to the Heart of the Matter. *IEEE Consumer Electronics Magazine*, *6*(4), 107–115. doi:10.1109/MCE.2017.2714279

Michael, K., & Miller, K. W. (2013). Big data: New opportunities and new challenges. *Computer*, *46*(6), 22–24. doi:10.1109/MC.2013.196

Michael, M. G., & Michael, K. A. (2007). A Note on Uberveillance, From Dataveillance to Überveillance and the Realpolitik of the Transparent Society. In *The Second Workshop on Social Implications of National Security*, Wollongong, Australia, October 29. Retrieved from https://ro.uow.edu.au/infopapers/560/

Moncrief, M. (2015, August 15). Your Facebook friends could make or break that loan application. *The Sydney Morning Herald*. Retrieved from https://goo.gl/szE4Aj

Morgan, B., & Yeung, K. (2007). *An introduction to Law and Regulation*. Cambridge: Cambridge University Press. doi:10.1017/CBO9780511801112

Mulgan, R. (2000). Comparing accountability in the public and private sectors. *Australian Journal of Public Administration*, *59*(1), 87–97. doi:10.1111/1467-8500.00142

Navetta, D. (2013). Legal Implications of Big Data, a Primer. *Computer & Internet Lawyer*, *11*(3), 14–19.

Neff, G., & Nafus, D. (2016). *The Self-Tracking*. Cambridge, MA: MIT Press. doi:10.7551/mitpress/10421.001.0001

Newell, P. B. (1995). Perspectives on privacy. *Journal of Environmental Psychology*, *15*(2), 87–104. doi:10.1016/0272-4944(95)90018-7

Nissenbaum, H. (2004). Privacy as contextual integrity. *Washington Law Review (Seattle, Wash.)*, *79*, 119.

OECD. (1980). *OECD Guidelines on the Protection of Privacy and Transborder Flows of Personal Data*. Retrieved 21 December 2018 from http://www.oecd.org/internet/ieconomy/oecdguidelinesontheprotectionofprivacyandtransborderflowsofpersonaldata.htm

Office of the Australian Information Commissioner. (2014). *Privacy fact sheet 17: Australia Privacy Principles* Retrieved from https://goo.gl/ZSswXH

Office of the Australian Information Commissioner. (2017). *Australian Community Attitudes to Privacy Survey 2017*. Retrieved from https://goo.gl/7zembF

Office of the Privacy Commissioner. (2015, December 21). *Report of the privacy commissioner under section 61B of the privacy and personal information protection act 1988*.

Omoronyia, I. (2016). The case for privacy awareness requirements. *International Journal of Secure Software Engineering*, *7*(2), 19–36. doi:10.4018/IJSSE.2016040102

Park, Y. J. (2013). Digital literacy and privacy behavior online. *Communication Research*, *40*(2), 215–236. doi:10.1177/0093650211418338

Petronio, S. (2002). *Boundaries of privacy: Dialectic of disclosure*. Albany, NY: State University of New York Press.

Pierson, J. (2012). Online privacy in social media: A conceptual exploration of empowerment and vulnerability. *Communications & Stratégies*, *88*(4), 99–120.

Pingo, Z., & Narayan, B. (2016). When Personal Data Becomes Open Data: An Exploration of Lifelogging, User Privacy, and Implications for Privacy Literacy. In R. A. Morishima & C. Liew (Ed.), Digital Libraries: Knowledge, Information, and Data in an Open Access Society (pp. 3-9). Cham: Springer.

Rappa, M. (2003). Business models on the web. In *Managing the Digital Enterprise*. Retrieved from http://digitalenterprise.org/privacy/privacy.html

Richardson, M., Bosua, R., Clark, K., Webb, J., Ahmad, A., & Maynard, S. (2017a). Towards responsive regulation of the Internet of Things: Australian perspectives. *Internet Policy Review, 6*(1).

Rose, B. (2014). The Best Fitness Tracker for Every Need. *Gizmodo*. Retrieved 21 December 2018 from https://www.gizmodo.com.au/2014/12/the-best-fitness-tracker-for-every-exercise/

Rosenblat, A., Kneese, T., & boyd, d. (2014). *Networked Employment Discrimination*. Data & Society Research Institute. Retrieved 21 December 2018 from doi:10.2139srn.2543507

Rotman, D. (2009). *Are You Looking At Me? Social Media and Privacy Literacy*. Paper presented at the 4th iSchool Conference 2009, Chapel Hill, NC. Retrieved 21 December 2018 from http://hdl.handle.net/2142/15339

Schneier, B. (2010). A taxonomy of social networking data. *Security & Privacy, IEEE*, *8*(4), 88–88. doi:10.1109/MSP.2010.118

Schneier, B. (2015). *Data and Goliath: The hidden battles to collect your data and control your world*. New York: WW Norton & Company.

Schwartz, P. M., & Solove, D. J. (2011). PII problem: Privacy and a new concept of personally identifiable information, the. *New York University Law Review*, *86*, 1814.

Sim, I., Liginlal, D., & Khansa, L. (2012). Information Privacy Situation Awareness: Construct and Validation. *Journal of Computer Information Systems*, *53*(1), 57–64. doi:10.1080/08874417.2012.11645597

Solove, D. J. (2006). A taxonomy of privacy. *University of Pennsylvania Law Review*, *154*(3), 477–564. doi:10.2307/40041279

Solove, D. J. (2012b). Privacy self-management and the consent dilemma. *Harvard Law Review*, *126*, 1880–1903.

Solove, D. J., & Schwartz, P. M. (2014). *Consumer Privacy and Data Protection* (5th ed.). New York: Wolters Kluwer.

Svantesson, D., & Clarke, R. (2010). A best practice model for e-consumer protection. *Computer Law & Security Review*, *26*(1), 31–37. doi:10.1016/j.clsr.2009.11.006

Sweeney, L., Abu, A., & Winn, J. (2013). *Identifying participants in the personal genome project by name*. Academic Press.

Terms of Service Didn't Read. (2017). *I have read and agree to the Terms is the biggest lie on the web. We aim to fix that.* Retrieved 21 December 2018 from https://tosdr.org/index.html

Torre, I., Sanchez, O. R., Koceva, F., & Adorni, G. (2017). Supporting users to take informed decisions on privacy settings of personal devices. *Personal and Ubiquitous Computing*, 1–20.

Travis, A., & Arthur, C. (2014, May 13). EU court backs 'right to be forgotten': Google must amend results on request. *The Guardian*. Retrieved from https://www.theguardian.com/technology/2014/may/13/right-to-be-forgotten-eu-court-google-search-results

Tuninetti Ferrari, A. (2017). *Big Data: balancing the web user's and the service provider's rights in the Big Data era* (Unpublished doctoral thesis). Università degli Studi di Parma. Dipartimento di Giurisprudenza. Retrieved 21 December 2018 from http://dspace-unipr.cineca.it/handle/1889/3333

Warren, S., & Brandeis, L. (1890). The right to privacy. *Harvard Law Review, 4*(5), 193-220. Retrieved 21 December 2018 from https://www.cs.cornell.edu/~shmat/courses/cs5436/warren-brandeis.pdf

Weber, R. (2010). Internet of Things – New security and privacy challenges. *Computer Law & Security Review, 26*(1), 23–30. doi:10.1016/j.clsr.2009.11.008

Weber, R. (2015). Internet of things: Privacy issues revisited. *Computer Law & Security Review, 31*(5), 618–627. doi:10.1016/j.clsr.2015.07.002

Weber, R. H. (2010). Internet of Things–New security and privacy challenges. *Computer Law & Security Review, 26*(1), 23–30. doi:10.1016/j.clsr.2009.11.008

Westin, A. F. (1967). *Privacy and freedom*. New York: Athenaeum.

Xia, H., Wang, Y., Huang, Y., & Shah, A. (2017). "Our Privacy Needs to be Protected at All Costs": Crowd Workers' Privacy Experiences on Amazon Mechanical Turk. *ACM Human Computer Interaction, 1*(2), 22. doi:10.1145/3134748

Xu, H., Dinev, T., Smith, J., & Hart, P. (2011). Information privacy concerns: Linking individual perceptions with institutional privacy assurances. *Journal of the Association for Information Systems, 12*(12), 798–824. doi:10.17705/1jais.00281

Yao, M. Z. (2011). Self-protection of online privacy: A behavioral approach. In R. L. Trepte S. (Ed.), Privacy Online (pp. 111-125). Berlin: Springer. doi:10.1007/978-3-642-21521-6_9

Zhou, W., & Piramuthu, S. (2014). *Security/privacy of wearable fitness tracking IoT devices*. Paper presented at the 9th Iberian Conference on Information Systems and Technologies (CISTI), Barcelona, Spain. 10.1109/CISTI.2014.6877073

Ziegeldorf, J. H., Morchon, O. G., & Wehrle, K. (2014). Privacy in the Internet of Things: Threats and challenges. *Security and Communication Networks, 7*(12), 2728–2742. doi:10.1002ec.795

Chapter 5
Big Data and IoT Opportunities for Small and Medium-Sized Enterprises (SMEs)

Siti Aishah Mohd Selamat
https://orcid.org/0000-0003-2844-9806
Bournemouth University, UK

Simant Prakoonwit
Bournemouth University, UK

Reza Sahandi
Bournemouth University, UK

Wajid Khan
Bournemouth University, UK

ABSTRACT

The advancement of technology and emergence of internet of things (IoT) has exponentially caused a data explosion in the 21st century era. As such, the arrival of IoT is set to revolutionize the development of the small and medium-sized enterprise (SME) organizations by shaping it into a more universal and integrated ecosystem. Despite evidential studies of the potential of advanced technologies for businesses, the SMEs are apprehensive towards new technologies adoption such as big data analytics and IoT. Therefore, the aim of this chapter is to provide a holistic study of big data and IoT opportunities, challenges, and applications within the SMEs context. The authors hope that the outcome of this study would provide foundational information on how the SMEs can partake with the new wave technological advancement and in turn, spurring more SMEs for adoption.

DOI: 10.4018/978-1-5225-7432-3.ch005

INTRODUCTION

The advancement of technology and emergence of Internet-of-Things (Woodward et al.) has exponentially caused a data explosion in the 21st Century era. It is predicted that the magnitude of data is set to scale up to fifty billion Terabytes by 2020 (Arora & Rahman, 2016). The arrival of IoT is set to revolutionize the development of a Small and Medium-Sized Enterprise (SME) organisation – by shaping it into a more universal and integrated ecosystem. The inpouring of data can pose as a potential treasure for the SMEs organisation if the data collected are inherently translated to become useful knowledge (Chudik, Kapetanios, & Pesaran, 2016). Despite being in a progressive business condition, loaded with interconnectedness; a business long-term positioning remains 'uncertain'. It is, therefore, crucial to study the opportunities of big data and IoT for the SMEs. In addition, analysing also its implications and effect, should the SMEs organization fails to jump on-board on the new technological advancement wave. An extensive report from the European (EU) Commission indicates that SMEs are the core financial driver of growth in the EU region. In 2015, the EU Commission unveils that the SMEs contributed up to approximate of 4 trillionn euros to the EU economy (Eurostat 2018). Further to this, it has been highlighted that the SMEs are contributing twice as much in comparison to the larger organizations available in the EU continents. SMEs organizations can aspect to accelerate their growth by up to two to three times faster when they embrace new digital technologies like big data and IoT (Commission, 2013). The untapped potential here for the SME is really immense. For instance, a recent study by the EU Commission denotes that most digitally mature SMEs in France observed a growth rate of up to six times in comparison to the digitally less mature SMEs. By incorporating new technologies into the business, the French SMEs doubled their revenue growth rates (Commission, 2017). Another study conducted in the Swedish context reveals a similar result. Despite the momentous opportunities and advantages, SME businesses are slow to change and labeled as laggards in new technologies adoption in comparison to its larger enterprise counterpart. It is reported that close to 9.2 million (41%) of EU SMEs have yet to adopt any of a set of the four advanced technologies like social media, mobile, big data and cloud computing. Focusing in specific to the big data solution adoption rate; an alarming figure of 20.7 million EUs SMEs has yet to adopt big data technologies in 2015 (Commission, 2013). These startling findings insinuate that these SMEs will not be ready to welcome the IoT technologies either. Reason being, big data capability is mandatory for connecting into the IoT ecosystem. It would be unattainable for the EU SMEs to manage the incoming data flow from the embedded sensors from the IoT without having the big data solutions in place first. It is undeniable that the EU SMEs needs to revolutionize itself in order to remain competitive and relevant in the business sphere. As recount earlier, the business environment is unpredictable; the EU SMEs unpreparedness could eventually be overtaken by the larger enterprises.

The key objective of the chapter is to outline a holistic research of big data and IoT opportunities, challenges and, applications within the SMEs context. It is with the hope that the outcome of this study would provide foundational information on how the SMEs can partake with the new wave technological advancement – in turn spurring more SMEs for adoption. This chapter would provide a unique contribution to the research handbook by providing the readers with a comprehensive breakdown of big data and IoT study in the SMEs context. The target audience of this chapter is aimed at researchers, business leaders and policymakers' with a special interest in the research and study of SME developments. The contribution of this chapter anticipates in elevating the awareness on the study of big data and IoT, providing aid to the SMEs' understanding and business capitalization. To ensure the relevance and applicability of this chapter, the literature collections are limited to publication within the last 10 years' time period.

The literature selection includes papers relating to the SMEs hindrance factors in big data technology application, the potential benefits and advantages of big data and IoT application in the various SMEs industry and the probable challenges and drawback. The literature collected is screened to validate the relevance and applicability of the literature content. Upon the literature screening, only fitting articles are used for this research. The works of literature were cited from credible research databases like Science Direct, Association for Computing Machinery Digital Library, EJS E-Journals, Google Scholar, Springer, Science Direct, Semantic Scholar and last but not least, International Publisher of Information Science and Technology Research. In the next section, this study will provide an overview background of the SME's deterrent factors against big data analytics (BDAs). The third section will identify the additional organisational barriers faced by the SMEs in BDA applications. The fourth and fifth section will present an overview of BDA and IoT subject. This is followed by, a run through of the technology applications within the SMEs context. The sixth and seventh sections will cover the potential benefits and challenges of BDA and IoT applications for SMEs. The eighth section of this chapter will include with a general guideline for SMEs to consider when adopting the BDA and IoT applications. Lastly, this chapter will conclude the overall contribution of this chapter.

SME'S DETERRENT FACTORS AGAINST BIG DATA ANALYTICS (BDA)

Based on several key research, it is evident that the SME group are skeptic towards new technological adoption – especially so, in the area of BDA application (Mohd Selamat, Prakoonwit, Sahandi, Khan, & Ramachandran, 2018). According to Coleman (2016), there are several key resistant factors towards BDA application. And these key factors can be classified into three components – knowledge, resources and data management. The illustration of each component (knowledge, resources and data management) will be discussed in the next sub-sections. The discussion will include research examples to support and justify the three individual components.

Resources

One of the major obstacles of the SMEs in adopting the BDA technology relates to resources. The reason includes (1) the shortfall in financial source to invest in the used of brand-new technologies (2) the limitation in the value for money analytics consulting solution available for SMEs (3) the lack and shortage of internal data analytics professional within the SMEs domain and lastly (4) the analytics software package available in the market is highly complex. First and foremost, the shortfalls of capable, adequate and licensed BDA specialist in the market generate the paucity of in-house experts in the BDA domain. Within the United States of America (USA) it is predicted and envisage that by year-end 2018, there will be an estimated of two hundred thousand deficit of proficient analytics talent and a further close to an additional one and half million analytics senior executive equipped with the suitable proficiency to make strategic business decision(s) with big data (Manyika et al., 2011). In a study conducted with the UK recruiters, it is revealed that an estimate of 60% of the recruiting agent is experiencing talent scarcity in the BDA domain (UK, 2013)This would evidently have a great implication in the BDA evolvement within the EU context. The available analytics software in the market is expected to curb the impending deficit of BDA talent supply. Although there is plenty of analytics solution readily available for the SMEs purchase – to narrow down a feasible solution that is installed with robust and user-friendly analytic functions is sparse. The requirement of a simple and straightforward user interface would facilitate a shorter learning experience and in turn, enabling a quicker technology implementation time frames (Probst et al., 2014). Additionally, the end users will little or nil proficiency in the technology may face difficulties in choosing the right analytics solution given that the evaluation platforms provided by the vendor are vendor biased. A lower price-performance ratio solution in the market would ease the impending financial resource limitation of the SMEs (S. Coleman et al., 2016).

Knowledge

The second key obstacles faced by the SMEs in BDA technology application are associated with knowledge elements such as (1) the lack of comprehension in the BDA domain (2) minimal interest in new upcoming management trends in the business sphere and lastly, (3) the inadequacy and availability of successful SMEs case studies to make reference of. The lack of comprehension in the BDA domain by the SMEs' staff can be seen in the UK (UK, 2013) and Germany (S. Y. Coleman, 2016) based on a survey conducted by two separate researches. Notably, the SMEs at large are unaware of the potential residing within the business datasets, in consequence, creating doubt on the BDA capabilities to derive the expected advantages from it. Although there are general guidelines for the SMEs to refer to, there are little or nil exemplary research case studies of successful BDA implementation in the SMEs context (Mohd Selamat et al., 2018). The current BDA case studies collected in the EU context does not generally correspond with the SMEs' needs as the use cases are in relation to the larger enterprises. Given that the function and operation of the SMEs differ greatly to the larger organization, the availability of more case studies in the SME context is needed to boost the SMEs zeal in BDA adoption.

Data Management

The last obstacles component encountered by the SMEs relates to data management. The SMEs stakeholders have concerns regarding data security, protection and privacy. In a global survey conducted, out of the 82 SMEs organizations surveyed, more than half percent of the organizations had identified data protection and security has a key concern and barrier to BDA application (S. Y. Coleman, 2016). Unlike the larger organizations, the SME group in totality lacks the aptitude and capability to build up its information technology safety measure (Lacey & James, 2010). The current usage in regards to the outdated database management system by the SMEs may make them more vulnerable against intrusions and cyber-attacks. In addition, SMEs in the EU continent will need to abide by the EU data regulation (Rights, 2016) on data privacy and protection when managing its customer's data. In view of the lengthy EU data protection law and that the SMEs has financial constraint, the SMEs would not be able to supplement the financial expense in engaging a legal expert to administer the legality aspect of EU data legislation requirements.

Additional Organisational Barriers

Apart from the barrier in association to resource, knowledge and data management, it is worthy to note that there are other incorporeal drawbacks that are preventing the SMEs from applying the BDA initiative in its business. These barriers are in relation to the SMEs' internal management matters such as organisational culture, structure and decision-making. Although these matters are elusive in nature, its impact and implication are paramount to the SMEs. In the area of organisational culture – customary, the SMEs leaders have minimal or zero engrossment in contemporary and emerging executive trends that could be useful to the organisation (Goebel, Norman, & Karanasios, 2015). As such, the inherent traditionalism value of the SMEs' leaders perceives the application of BDA as rising business hype only. The second organisational barrier relates to the SMEs' management structure, whereby a felicitous management formation is needed in order to have a fluent BDA executive. Traditionally, unlike the larger organisations, a majority of the SMEs organisational hierarchy are flat with minimal or zero middle authority amongst the general staffs and executive employees (Capgemini, 2012). How SMEs are being organised will impact the way in which decisions are being made. Generally, in the SMEs environment, the business owners are usually the decision makers. How the business owners make their decisions are occasionally mirrored by the individual's life and identity (Goebel et al., 2015). The presence of a hierarchical structure in the larger organization makes the decision making the process more rational in comparison to the SMEs, which are mainly driven by the company owner's instinct or experiences (Culkin & Smith, 2000). In summation, should business owners are not personally inclined towards learning and keeping him or herself updated with the new management trends of BDA – it will pose a great challenge to overcome.

BDA AND INTERNET OF THINGS

BDA is at present gaining momentous attraction globally. As defined by Gartner, big data refers to the high volume, velocity, variety of information assets that require processing in order to churn out new and unique insights to facilitate strategic decision making and process optimization (Beyer, 2011). Adding additional Vs of veracity; variability and value proposition to the initial 3Vs (Lugmayr et al., 2016) – the consolidation of first five Vs (volume, velocity, variety, veracity, and variability) would provide the final V of value proposition, which is important for all organizations. The emergence of big data has created a great demand for companies to engage data scientists that are equipped with the relevant skills to analyse and churn out unique business insights from various data source pool (Bagnoli, 2015). For the organization to deliver a successful analytics undertaking – they are seven key factors to take note of. The seven factors consist of (1) a well-defined business needs (2) a solid and committed benefactor (3) a clear calibration of the business and technology strategy (4) a data-driven decision making business culture (5) a well-founded data structure (6) the relevant appropriate analytical contrivance and lastly, (7) a group of well-skilled employees in the analytical domain (Turban, King, Sharda, & Delen, 2013). In summary, to build a data-driven organization, both the technical and organisational needs are required to be in place in order to implement the BDA undertakings successfully. Big data then comes in various sources, which are considerably big in volume and are generally in actual-time environment. The trend is shaping broadly from the presence of mobile phones and social media gadgets. The IoT platform on the other hand are driven with the presence of radio frequency identification (RFID) and the various sensor or tracking medium (Strohbach, Ziekow, Gazis, & Akiva, 2015). IoT is commonly defined as the global network and chain of interconnected gadgets, which are uniquely identified, based on the common communication protocols (Y. Sun, Song, Jara, & Bie, 2016). It is predicted that the volume of connected on IoT is estimated to reach 75 billion by the year 2020 (Shanthamallu, Spanias, Tepedelenlioglu, & Stanley, 2017). The presence of IoT will become pervasive in the coming years, generating a massive volume of data. As such, these data are needed for analysis in order to create value for a particular organization or society. The function of IoT would facilitate the tracing and tracking of all tagged mobile devices as it maneuvers around or is in a stationary position to audit its changeable environment. This could include object going through the supply line of chain, devices, and machinery in the hospital or factory setting or lastly, even a self-driving automobile. Stationary objects with embedded control and sensor capabilities that are connected to the IoT are able to (1) oversee its overall circumferential surrounding (2) carry out conditional reporting (3) change its state and the state of any connected devices and lastly (4) make amendments to its encompassing environment (Lee & Lee, 2015). The predicted 75 billion connected objects as envisioned by Morgan Stanley – would indefinitely provide momentous strategic and operational benefits for an organization that is capable to take advantage of the IoT technology functionality. In order to effectively manage the IoT automation demands, BDA is required to collect, converge and analyse the data streaming from the various sources such as sensors, RFID tags, social media feeds, video, images and mobile devices (Riggins & Wamba, 2015). It is evident that the role of BDA and IoT can spur tremendous opportunities for organization of the various industries.

OPPORTUNITIES OF BDA AND IoT

Through this chapter, two opportunities of IoT platform have been identified (as refered in Table 1) – cyber-physical cloud computing (CPCC) and mobile crowdsensing (MCS). The illustrations of both platforms are shown in Table 1.

The accumulations of a large volume of data collected through the IoT platform present the utilization of BDA application to process analysed and interpret the collected data for strategic decision-making and control.

Table 1. IoT platform opportunities

Mobile Crowdsensing (MCS) (Ganti, Ye, & Lei, 2011)	Mobile crowdsensing (MCS) makes up one class of the IoT application that depends heavily on the data collected from an extensive volume of mobile sensing gadgets such as mobile phones. The MCS application can be classified into three different groups – (1) social (2) infrastructure and (3) environmental. Within the social MCS applications, individuals are sharing sensed information amongst themselves. For an instance, an individual can be sharing about their personal exercise data and compare their personal exercise data amongst the entire community. This would assist the individual to improve their exercise routines. Within the environmental MCS applications, data of the concerning the natural environment are measured. For instance, measuring the noise or air pollution levels in a particular city. Within the infrastructure MCS applications, data of the public infrastructure are being measured. For instance, the traffic congestion, condition, power outage, parking vacancy and transit tracking are being measured. The benefits of MCS include: • Having significantly large storage, communication and computation are fitted with multimodality sensing functionalities • Preventing high deployment cost and time of setting up big-scale wireless sensor networks. In the 21st century, it is normality for the majority of the individuals to be carrying their mobile devices.
Cyber-Physical Cloud Computing (CPCC) (Colombo et al., 2014)	Cyber-Physical Could Computing (CPCC) refers to a networking framework for cyber-physical systems (CPS). CPS refers to smart networked systems with integrated sensors, actuators and, processors that are constructed to interact and sense with the human users and also, support real-time safety-critical applications. The benefit of CPCC includes the effective usage of resources, smart adaption to the environment in every scale, reliable and resilient. The CPCC paradigm plays an integral role in the smart city infrastructure like smart transportation, smart disaster management, smart healthcare and many more.

CHALLENGES OF BDA AND IoT

In regards to the challenges, two probable challenges of IoT has been identified (as refered in Table 2)– resource limitations and cyber security and privacy. The illustrations of both challenges are shown in Table 2.

Most often, the data collected through the IoT platform are diverse and heterogeneous in state. For an instance, data in relation to smart buildings does not consist only the energy-consumption data, weather data, but in addition, the data on the thermostat settings, the state of the windows and doors, airows, room occupancy, building materials and structure and many more. Therefore, translating social variable, biological and physical into a concise and indicative electrical signal is a demanding task. For an instance, occupancy in a building can be obtained from appliance acoustics, usage, infrared signatures, motion detection, vibration, imaging, disruption and many other – but in all, these only serve as noisy indicators of room occupancy (Lee & Lee, 2015)

BDA AND IoT APPLICATION FOR SMEs

The BDA and IoT application is not only limited to the large organization but rather, it also provides tremendous opportunities for SMEs too. The SMEs can be equivalently competitive and yet remaining small by channeling its focus over technology and applications over its headcount. The opportunity to tap on both the BDA and IoT capabilities is limitless. As illustrated below are several use cases on how BDA and IoT can be applied in the SMEs' industrial practice of various areas – as refered in Table 3.

Based on the examples provided, it is evident that the application of BDA and IoT are implementable in various sector and industries. For an example, from streamlining the supply chain cycle, enhancing the business product and services, managing operational efficiencies and many more. It is important to highlight that for the application of BDA and IoT to be carried out; the need for connectivity is an important element. The data collected from the devices and remote sensors need to be converging with at least one of the SME's management system for the information to be processed and reported in the system's dashboard. The SMEs companies can explore the integration platform with in-memory computing functionalities to furnish real-time processing of the large volume of data churned out by the IoT systems. In summation, as recount earlier, the BDA and IoT application would provide vast opportunities for the SMEs' business growth.

Table 2. IoT probable challenges

Resource Limitations (Van Kranenburg & Bassi, 2012)	The mobile devices collecting the sensor data are high-powered in its capabilities and availability as such, predicting the bandwidth and energy requirement in an IoT application is challenging. Additionally, scheduling and identifying communication and sensing tasks amongst the large volume of devices with the wide variation of sensing functionalities can be a very daunting task.
Cyber Security and Privacy (Zhou, Cao, Dong, & Vasilakos, 2017)	The second key challenge in an IoT application is the preservation of the individual's personal privacy and security – from which sensitive data in relation to the individual are being collected through sensors. For an instance, GPS sensor data, which are used to gauge the traffic condition level, can also be used to read personal information of the individual's daily route to work, home or social meet-up locations. As such, the security and privacy regulation can implicate the access management of data records within and across the IoT services.

Table 3. SMEs industrial applications

Area	Application
Product Design and Marketing (Porter & Heppelmann, 2014)	The sensor functionality can aid in reporting how, when and where a particular product is being used – providing valueable inputs to designing and marketing process. The channel for collecting real-time data can provide the business a more effective and accurate information in comparison to the traditional customer survey or market research.
Product Sales (Perera, Liu, Jayawardena, & Chen, 2014)	Through monitoring the inventory and usage of a particular product or connected elements – the SMEs can preempt when the customers will need a supplement order or parts. The SMEs sales department will then need to ensure that the required products are available in the inventory stock. By having the relevant information readily at hand, the sales department can be proactive in its delivery in order to avoid any potential loss of revenue to the competitors.
Product Maintenance (Tao, Cheng, Da Xu, Zhang, & Li, 2014)	In relation to product maintenance, real-time data on operational wear and tear can enable in reducing operating and maintenance cost by identifying in advance possible equipment failure. This is would, in turn, avoid at downtime period in the organization operational activities. For an instance, in a printing business, if one of the machines were to break down during a print run, the business could a substantial amount of monetary loss. And this including incurring additional cost to request for emergency servicing request in an emergency situation. In overall, this would implicate the service delivery timeline for the customer – if the delivery is delayed, the business will need to compensate the customer accordingly. Potential equipment failure can be deduced by sensing the heat indication or vibration of the machinery. By doing so, the technician can be primitively dispatched to avoid a plausible equipment failure.
Logistics (C. Sun, 2012)	For logistic SMEs, the application of sensor in shipping containers can allow the company to receive real-time data on the package location and condition. By connecting the real-time information to the SMEs warehouse management system (WMS), it would enhance the business efficiencies, service delivery and boost customer service.
Product Engineering (Perera et al., 2014)	In product engineering, the selection of product design and material can be improved by monitoring the machine's condition, configuration and, overall usage.
Manufacturing Processes (Bandyopadhyay & Sen, 2011)	In relation to the manufacturing processes; a potential issue that impacts the production's output level can be distinguished earlier so as to schedule the necessary corrective measure. Monitoring the configuration, condition, and usage of the production machinery can carry this out.
Transportation (Chunli, 2012)	Within the transportation context, SMEs can provide IoT services to supplement the smart city initiative. For an instance, smart parking can be offered to provide driving commuters real-time update on the parking availability and also enabling the user to make the parking payment with their mobile phone. In the context of public transport, real-time update on the transport arrival and seat availability can be shown on the bus stops dashboard or mobile application.
Fleet Maintenance (Chen, Xu, Liu, Hu, & Wang, 2014)	Under the fleet maintenance, the sensory function can be applied to monitor the fleet's speed, mileage, and engine health. By collecting data on the vehicle's condition and usage, an advance servicing can be scheduled to prevent any fleet downtime. In addition, by learning the driving behavior of the fleet driver, customized driving tips for the drivers' improvement can be provided. Through an effective driving and maintenance, it can reduce the CO^2 emissions and prolong the vehicle life expectancy.
Agriculture (Minbo, Zhu, & Guangyu, 2013)	SMEs in the agriculture line of business can employ the use of the sensory application to track the soil and air temperature, humidity, speed, leaf wetness, rainfall, and fruit color. The farmers can, in turn, use the collected data, to amendment accordingly the watering amount, time and the picking schedules.
Medical (Wang, Wang, Zhang, & Song, 2013)	Within the medical context, the use of IoT can enable the medical doctors and hospitals to collect real-time information on the patient's data using wearable gadgets or home health's monitors. Medical doctors can utilize the real-time data collected to monitor and improve the patient care. In addition, provide better diagnosis and treatment.

TECHNOLOGY READINESS FOR BDA-IoT

Technology readiness refers to the organisational's employees proneness to adapt and accept the usage of new technology in order to achieve work or home life goals (Parasuraman & Grewal, 2000). In theory, there are four core elements that constitute technology readiness –insecurity, innovativeness, optimism and discomfort. Optimism is defined as the positive effect of new technology on the user lives which he or she has control over it. Innovativeness refers to individuals that are positive towards new technology adoption. Discomfort is the opposite of the classification of optimism whereby the individual would discern new technology adoption as overwhelming. Lastly, insecurity refers to the negative reaction and perception towards new technology, assuming that the new technology will not function effectively as intended (Godoe & Johansen, 2012). It is suggesting that the innovativeness and optimism elements act as key motivators in embracing new technology application, whereby, the elements of insecurity and discomfort are deterrence factors (Parasuraman & Colby, 2015).

There are two related measurements available in measuring the scale of technology readiness – technology readiness index (Probst et al.) and technology readiness level (TRL). First and foremost, it is important to distinguish that TRI and TRL serve two different purposes and usage. TRI is being measured using a marketing-based measurement scale, which uses the survey to retrieve the individual feedback towards new technology adoption within the service domain – for instance, using the Internet platform (Parasuraman & Grewal, 2000). Unlike the TRI, TRL measurement is technical-based centric which is used to evaluate the maturity level of a specific technology and making a comparison against other various types of technology – for instance, NASA is applying it for its technology planning task (Clausing & Holmes, 2010). It is fundamental for SMEs to assess its technology readiness before galvanizing into the BDA-IOT implementation.

CONCLUSION

Based on the study of this chapter, it is evident that IoT is set to revolutionize the business environment. And due to IoT, the collection of data is envisioned to grow rapidly as it is already. It is further evidential that data is the new oil and asset for companies in this 21st century. When the data are processed and translated, it can provide companies with unique and new insights into enhanced strategic decision making and forecasting. Despite the momentous opportunities and advantages of advanced technologies, the SME businesses groups are slow in its adoption. From this study, it was uncovered that the key resistant factors towards BDA application are within the aspect of knowledge, resources and data governance. An additional organisational barrier like organisational decision-making, structure and culture further raises the resistant factors of the SMEs in the application BDA in its business. It is key that the SME businesses are acquainted with the BDA application, as the presence of IoT will further generate a massive volume of data. And these data will need to be analysed in order to create value for the SMEs. Through this chapter, two opportunities of IoT platform that the SMEs can explore are the cyber-physical cloud computing (CPCC) and mobile crowdsensing (MCS) platforms. The probable challenges of IoT and BDA, on the other hand, includes resource limitations, cybersecurity and privacy and the heterogeneous state of the data collected. The overall encapsulation of this chapter identifies that BDA and IoT application are not only limited to the large organization but rather, it also provides tremendous opportunities for SMEs – and this is evident with the several industrial application provided. The SMEs can be equivalently competitive and yet remaining small by channeling its focus over technology and applications over its headcount. The opportunity to tap on both the BDA and IoT capabilities is limitless. In order to measure the scale of technology readiness before the application of BDA and IoT, SMEs can adopt either one or both the technology readiness measurement method. There is technology readiness index (Probst et al.) and technology readiness level (TRL). It is fundamental for SMEs to assess its technology readiness before galvanizing into the BDA-IoT implementation to ensure that the organization is equipped to implement the BDA-IoT application. In conclusion, as much as there are immense opportunities of entry for the SMEs to tap on the BDA-IoT – the SMEs will need to step out of its comfort zone and be willing to explore the potential of new advanced technologies. This is key in order to remain relevant and competitive in the ever-changing business environment.

REFERENCES

Arora, B., & Rahman, Z. (2016). Using Big Data Analytics for Competitive Advantage. *International Journal of Innovative Research and Development*, *5*(2).

Bagnoli, V. (2015). Competition for the Effectiveness of Big Data Benefits. *IIC-International Review of Intellectual Property and Competition Law*, *46*(6), 629–631. doi:10.100740319-015-0382-4

Bandyopadhyay, D., & Sen, J. (2011). Internet of things: Applications and challenges in technology and standardization. *Wireless Personal Communications*, *58*(1), 49–69. doi:10.100711277-011-0288-5

Beyer, M. (2011). *Gartner Says Solving 'Big Data' Challenge Involves More Than Just Managing Volumes of Data.* Gartner.

Capgemini. (2012). Measuring Organizational Maturity in Predictive Analytics: the First Step to Enabling the Vision. *Resource*.

Chen, S., Xu, H., Liu, D., Hu, B., & Wang, H. (2014). A Vision of IoT: Applications, Challenges, and Opportunities With China Perspective. *IEEE Internet of Things Journal*, *1*(4), 349–359. doi:10.1109/JIOT.2014.2337336

Chudik, A., Kapetanios, G., & Pesaran, M. H. (2016). *Big Data Analytics: A New Perspective*. Federal Reserve Bank of Dallas Globalization and Monetary Policy Institute.

Chunli, L. (2012). *Intelligent transportation based on the Internet of Things*. Paper presented at the 2012 2nd International Conference on Consumer Electronics, Communications and Networks (CECNet).

Clausing, D., & Holmes, M. (2010). Technology readiness. *Research Technology Management*, *53*(4), 52–59. doi:10.1080/08956308.2010.11657640

Coleman, S., Göb, R., Manco, G., Pievatolo, A., Tort-Martorell, X., & Reis, M. S. (2016). How Can SMEs Benefit from Big Data? Challenges and a Path Forward. *Quality and Reliability Engineering International*, *32*(6), 2151–2164. doi:10.1002/qre.2008

Coleman, S. Y. (2016). Data-Mining Opportunities for Small and Medium Enterprises with Official Statistics in the UK. *Journal of Official Statistics*, *32*(4), 849–865. doi:10.1515/jos-2016-0044

Colombo, A. W., Bangemann, T., Karnouskos, S., Delsing, J., Stluka, P., Harrison, R., & Lastra, J. L. (2014). *Industrial cloud-based cyber-physical systems*. The IMC-AESOP Approach. doi:10.1007/978-3-319-05624-1

Commission, E. (2013). Business Opportunities. *Big Data*.

Commission, E. (2017). *Annual Report on European SMEs 2015/2016 – SME recovery continues*. Academic Press.

Culkin, N., & Smith, D. (2000). An emotional business: A guide to understanding the motivations of small business decision takers. *Qualitative Market Research*, *3*(3), 145–157. doi:10.1108/13522750010333898

Ganti, R. K., Ye, F., & Lei, H. (2011). Mobile crowdsensing: Current state and future challenges. *IEEE Communications Magazine*, *49*(11), 32–39. doi:10.1109/MCOM.2011.6069707

Godoe, P., & Johansen, T. (2012). Understanding adoption of new technologies: Technology readiness and technology acceptance as an integrated concept. *Journal of European Psychology Students*, *3*(1).

Goebel, R., Norman, A., & Karanasios, S. (2015). *Exploring the Value of Business Analytics Solutions for SMEs*. Association for Information Systems AIS Electronic Library (AISeL).

Lacey, D., & James, B. E. (2010). Review of availability of advice on security for small/medium sized organisations. *Retrieved*, *2*(28), 2013.

Lee, I., & Lee, K. (2015). The Internet of Things (IoT): Applications, investments, and challenges for enterprises. *Business Horizons*, *58*(4), 431–440. doi:10.1016/j.bushor.2015.03.008

Lugmayr, A., Stockleben, B., Scheib, C., Mailaparampil, M., Mesia, N., & Ranta, H. (2016). *A Comprehensive Survey on Big-Data Research and its Implications-What is Really'New'in Big Data?-IT's Cognitive Big Data!* Paper presented at the PACIS.

Minbo, L., Zhu, Z., & Guangyu, C. (2013). Information Service System Of Agriculture IoT. *Automatika (Zagreb)*, *54*(4), 415–426. doi:10.7305/automatika.54-4.413

Mohd Selamat, S. A., Prakoonwit, S., Sahandi, R., Khan, W., & Ramachandran, M. (2018). Big data analytics—A review of data-mining models for small and medium enterprises in the transportation sector. *Wiley Interdisciplinary Reviews. Data Mining and Knowledge Discovery*, *8*(3), e1238. doi:10.1002/widm.1238

Parasuraman, A., & Colby, C. L. (2015). An updated and streamlined technology readiness index: TRI 2.0. *Journal of Service Research*, *18*(1), 59–74. doi:10.1177/1094670514539730

Parasuraman, A., & Grewal, D. (2000). The impact of technology on the quality-value-loyalty chain: A research agenda. *Journal of the Academy of Marketing Science*, *28*(1), 168–174. doi:10.1177/0092070300281015

Perera, C., Liu, C. H., Jayawardena, S., & Chen, M. (2014). A survey on internet of things from industrial market perspective. *IEEE Access : Practical Innovations, Open Solutions*, *2*, 1660–1679. doi:10.1109/ACCESS.2015.2389854

Porter, M. E., & Heppelmann, J. E. (2014). How smart, connected products are transforming competition. *Harvard Business Review*, *92*(11), 64–88.

Probst, L., Frideres, L., Demetri, D., Vomhof, B., Lonkeu, O.-K., & Luxembourg, P. (2014). Business Innovation Observatory - Customer Experience. *European Union*.

Riggins, F. J., & Wamba, S. F. (2015). *Research directions on the adoption, usage, and impact of the internet of things through the use of big data analytics.* Paper presented at the System Sciences (HICSS), 2015 48th Hawaii International Conference on. 10.1109/HICSS.2015.186

Rights, E. U. A. F. (2016). *Handbook on European data protection law.* Retrieved from http://fra.europa.eu/en/publication/2014/handbook-european-data-protection-law

Shanthamallu, U. S., Spanias, A., Tepedelenlioglu, C., & Stanley, M. (2017). *A brief survey of machine learning methods and their sensor and IoT applications.* Paper presented at the Information, Intelligence, Systems & Applications (IISA), 2017 8th International Conference on. 10.1109/IISA.2017.8316459

Strohbach, M., Ziekow, H., Gazis, V., & Akiva, N. (2015). *Towards a big data analytics framework for IoT and smart city applications. In Modeling and processing for next-generation big-data technologies* (pp. 257–282). Springer.

Sun, C. (2012). Application of RFID technology for logistics on internet of things. *AASRI Procedia*, *1*, 106–111. doi:10.1016/j.aasri.2012.06.019

Sun, Y., Song, H., Jara, A. J., & Bie, R. (2016). Internet of things and big data analytics for smart and connected communities. *IEEE Access : Practical Innovations, Open Solutions*, *4*, 766–773. doi:10.1109/ACCESS.2016.2529723

Tao, F., Cheng, Y., Da Xu, L., Zhang, L., & Li, B. H. (2014). CCIoT-CMfg: Cloud computing and internet of things-based cloud manufacturing service system. *IEEE Transactions on Industrial Informatics*, *10*(2), 1435–1442. doi:10.1109/TII.2014.2306383

Turban, E., King, D., Sharda, R., & Delen, D. (2013). *Business intelligence: a managerial perspective on analytics.* Prentice Hall.

Van Kranenburg, R., & Bassi, A. (2012). IoT challenges. *Communications in Mobile Computing*, *1*(1), 9. doi:10.1186/2192-1121-1-9

Wang, X., Wang, J. T., Zhang, X., & Song, J. (2013). *A multiple communication standards compatible IoT system for medical usage.* Paper presented at the 2013 IEEE Faible Tension Faible Consommation. 10.1109/FTFC.2013.6577775

Woodward, W. A., Gray, H. L., & Elliott, A. C. (2017). *Applied Time Series Analysis with R.* CRC press.

Zhou, J., Cao, Z., Dong, X., & Vasilakos, A. V. (2017). Security and privacy for cloud-based IoT: Challenges. *IEEE Communications Magazine*, *55*(1), 26–33. doi:10.1109/MCOM.2017.1600363CM

Chapter 6
Internet of Things With Object Detection:
Challenges, Applications, and Solutions

Lavanya Sharma
Uttarakhand Technical University, India

Nirvikar Lohan
College of Engineering Roorkee, India

ABSTRACT

In recent years, everyday objects and locating of people become an active area in IoT-based visual surveillance system. Internet of things (IoT) is basically transferring data with numerous other things. In visual surveillance systems, conventional methods are very easily susceptible to the environmental changes (i.e., illumination changing, slow motion in the background due to waving tree leaves, rippling of water, and variation in lightening condition). This chapter describes the current challenging issues present in literature along with major application areas, resources and dataset, tools and advantages of IoT-based visual surveillance systems.

1. INTRODUCTION

Over the last few decades, the object detection is the initial step, and plays an important role in various applications of computer vision. It is the first step applied to extricate the most informative pixel from the sequence of video captured from CCTV cameras or IP cameras. Till now in literatures various algorithms are presents in literature for the detection of object from video sequence. This chapter provides a detailed overview of Internet of things with Object Detection: Challenges, Applications and Solutions (OGC Senor, 2016; Ren et.al., 2018). Internet of Things is an emerging field wherein a lot of classical approaches can be inculcated. Detection of motion based object is considered as a complicated task because the object may vary in shape, size or color.

DOI: 10.4018/978-1-5225-7432-3.ch006

Since, 1990's this approach has been broadly studied and applied by several authors for motion detection, object detection, locating people, indoor- outdoor sequence, logo detection, unusual activity detection, industrial automation, traffic monitoring, medical analysis and other commercial appliances. In computer vision, the effectiveness usage of internet of things, GPS trajectory, and location prediction can be carried out by maintaining a connection between an IP cameras with visual output devices over internet protocol (Felzenszwalb et.al., 2010; Brown, E., 2016; Aribas & Daglarli, 2017; Hu & Giang, 2017).

Mining motion based object data such as trajectory prediction (GPS), and location prediction in rapidly increasingly day by day. Trajectory classification can be best suited to utilize the video sequences of the locations that are visited by the moving or motion based object. Location prediction also plays another important key role in predicting the historical location of motion based object, basically it aims to forecast that the object may visit (Overview of Internet of Things, 2018). The upcoming or next location of moving object can be predicted by comparing the current object location. In this chapter a detailed overview with combination of object detection technique with Internet of Things (IoT) concept is presented in this chapter. The first step in any computer vision and digital image processing is to detect the most informative object from the video sequence to perform any task related to it. The Five waves of IoT is shown in Figure 1.

Now days, computer vision is an emerging research area in various applications, it becomes necessary to have an robust system that efficiently detect, track and recognize the object from video sequence. The need of object detection is increasing day by and can be easily visualized in various applications such as industrial automation, military, and other commercial appliances. The Internet also plays a vital role in numerous areas of computation such as banking, social Networking, online bookings and so on.

Figure 1.

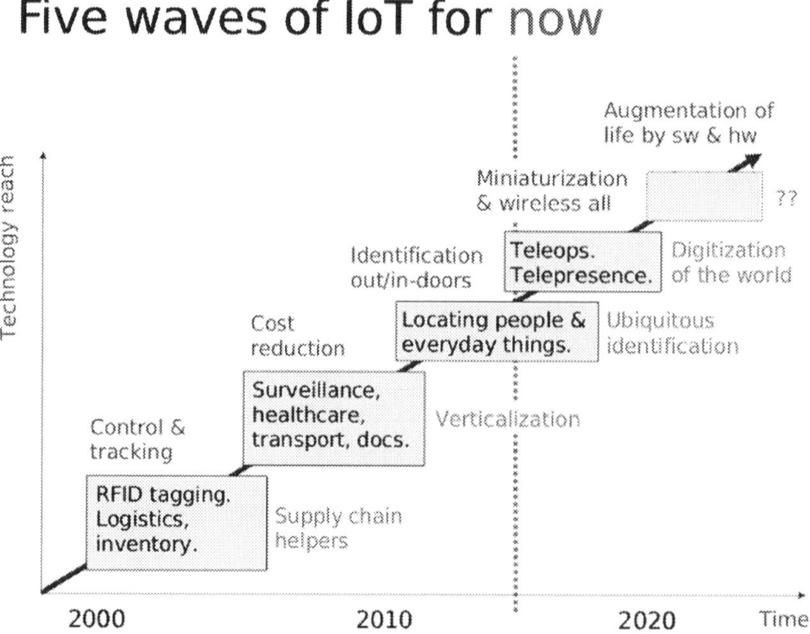

This terminology is considered a revolution in network and communication technology and becomes more popular day by day because it can be seen as "Everything-as-a-service" (Felzenszwalb et.al., 2010; Chen et.al., 2014).

This terminology is a combination of physical address with internet protocol. This concept also involve human and can be applicable on a large number of applications such as smart home, industrial surveillance, medical surveillance and so on. Due to dynamics that keeps on changing, sometimes it becomes more difficult to detect and track the motion based object from the video sequence. The databases for the computer vision also have limitation due to memory requirement, time constraints and hence many of the objects such as person or human detection may be unknown to the system (Li & Wang, 2012). It is very difficult to get critical information about such things because no resource is available which can tell us about it. So, this chapter deals with the above listed scenarios including applications, challenges, solution of internet of things with object detection.

In this chapter, Section 1 has covered the detailed description, major application domains and current challenging issues of surveillance system. In section 2, explores the work done by various authors in this specific domain. Section 3 deals with major challenging issues. Section 4 explores major applications in this relevant area. In section 5, various resources such as datasets and programming tools are discussed. Section 6 focuses on advantages of IoT in visual surveillance system. Finally, in section 7, conclusion and future direction are discussed.

2. LITERATURE REVIEW

In the current research there are various challenging issues in IoT technology based surveillance systems. (Ren et.al., 2018) proposed an architecture in their research work. In this work, a case study with their preliminary solution in terms of performance evaluation on various parameters. Author also explored the associated major challenging issues in the implementation of architecture. At last, future work directions are discussed for additional studies. (Aribas & Daglarli, 2017). discussed the detection of object in IoT environment. Author also discussed the Gaps in methodology, unidentified concepts and lacks of mathematical concept which mak very difficult to design the computing algorithms. Algorithm or proposed model in in this area can be developed with machine learning and/or numerical methodologies which are available in literature. Finally authors concludes that yolo algorithm performs better for detection of most informative object in IoT. A protocol for secure tracking and detections of most salient object was developed. It also ensured the visibility and traceability of the particular tracked object to support the Internet of Things (IoT). The proposed work is based on RFID system which identifies the IoT objects globally (OGC Senor, 2016) (Brown, 2016) modeled a protocol using SPDL(security protocol description language) and simulated using the Synther verification tool. In this work, the protocol used lightweight cryptographic primitive to ensure the secure object detection and tracking. (Hu & Giang, 2017) presents a novel unified approach of automated object detection in case of urban surveillance. In this work, the proposed method first determine and the pick out the highest energy frequency regions of the still or images using digital camera imaging sensors. The proposed work detects the object vehicles rapidly and accurately as compared to the others but also results in reducing big data level which needed to be stored in urban surveillance systems. (Quack1 & Gool, 2008) presents a system that allows to request information on the basis of physical objects by capturing their images. In this manner, with the help of a mobile phone users can easily interact with the particular objects in an efficient and simplify way. In this work, author also presents two major applications for system, namely slide tagging application for presentation screens in smart rooms and another a city guide on a mobile device Experimental evaluation also depicts that the performance of proposed method in both application areas results in better object recognition under challenging scenarios.

3. MAJOR CHALLENGING ISSUES

This section explore various current challenging issues which are generated due to the background environment complexity.

- **Dynamic or cluttered Background:** In some cases the background highly dynamic or cluttered it is not easy to distinguish a pixel as whether belongs to a foreground (FG) or background (BG) which results in false detection of moving pixel such as waving motion, rippling of water (Haque & Paul, 2008; The Open Innotation Tool, Dataset, 2016).
- **Noise image:** Digital images are susceptible to noise. Noise present in an image are result of a poor quality image source such as images captured from a web cameras or sometimes images are compressed (Jung, C.R., 2009; Tuan & Westerlund, 2015). For e.g. salt & pepper noise, gaussian noise.
- **Camera jitter:** Shaking of camera is another chronic issue in real world scenario that may results in blur motion. In some cases, camera is displaced due to high motion of wind and often causes a nominal motion which lead tp false detection of pixels (Jung, C.R., 2009; Yadav & Singh, 2015).
- **Illumination changes:** When an object is moving from brighten to darkness or from darkness to lightness the intensity value of a pixel changes that result in illumination variations. There can be gradual illumination changes such as light switch on or off .that can lead to intensity changes .which further results in false alarms (The Open Innotation Tool, Dataset, 2016; Aribas & Daglarli, 2017; Hu & Giang, 2017).
- **Bootstrapping:** During the training stage, sometimes background is not present. Then, in that case it becomes very difficult to compute an illustrative background (Toyama & Meyers, 1999; Jung, C.R., 2009; Yadav & Singh, 2015; Yadav & Singh, 2015).
- **Moved background Object:** In some cases, background's object is moved and cannot be consider as a part of foreground. So, both initial and existing object position are detected without an efficient background maintenance method (Sharma et.al., 2015; Internet of Things, 2017).
- **Camouflage:** Sometimes the color of a background is quite similar to the foreground that pixel's corresponds to the background are falsely computed as foreground (Toyama & Meyers, 1999; Jung, C.R., 2009).
- **Inserted background object:** In case a new background object is inserted then this object cannot be considered as foreground because this object is detected without any effective maintenance mechanism (Felzenszwalb et.al., 2010; Scene Background Initialization (SBI) dataset, 2015; Sharma et.al., 2015; Tuan et.al., 2015; Aribas & Daglarli, 2017).
- **Leaves, rippling of water, water surface etc:** In realistic environment background is not static it keeps on changing, due to rippling of water or slow leafy movement in the background makes it more complex and dynamic due to present of these environmental factors background pixels can

be falsely are considered as foreground and often lead to misinterpretation of pixels (Handte et.al., 2016; Right Sensors for Object Tracking, 2016; The Open Innotation Tool, Dataset, 2016).

- **Sleeping foreground object:** Motionless or Sleeping foreground objects are known as background. Due to its unmoving phenomenon it becomes very difficult to differentiate between a non moving objects from background, and considered as a background pixel (Stauffer & Grimson, 1999; CAVIAR Test Case Scenarios, 2003; Change Detection Dataset, 2015; Felzenszwalb et.al., 2010; Aribas & Daglarli, 2017; Overview of Internet of Things, 2018).
- **Shadowing:** Shadow detection is a challenging research domain itself and can be detected as foreground comes from moving object (Sharma et.al., 2015; Yadav & Singh, 2015).

Sometimes other challenges also arise during capturing or transmission of data from one end to another end that results in loss of information as shown in Figure 2. (Sharma & Yadav, 2016). Some of the critical challenges are listed below:

- Challenging Issues of visual Surveillance System.
- Failure of hardware device or insufficient amount of space issue on a server or cloud
- Technical problem arises due to internet problems such as incorrect IP address allocation, or during transmission the data transmitted was not correct and many more.
- Connection failure from client side to the cloud server or any IoT device to the Cloud server.

4. MAJOR APPLICATIONS

Moving Object Detection from video streaming is the first and basic step of any machine or computer vision application. It is also a very challenging research domain due to the environmental factors present in the background which make the extraction process difficult and also makes the background more complex. Some of the major real time applications that use this research area are shown in Figure 3.

Figure 2.

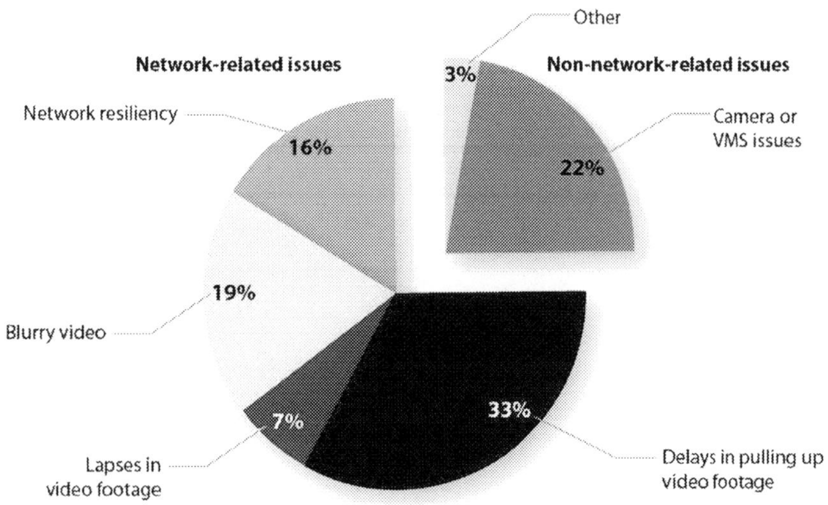

Figure 3.

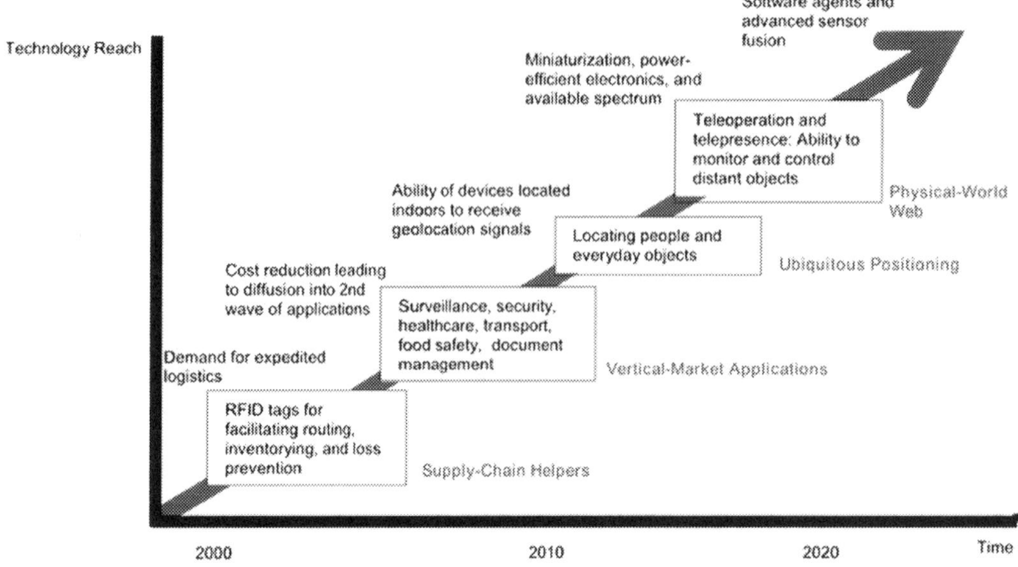

- **IoT in Intelligent Visual Surveillances of human actions:** The main motive of IoT based Intelligent visual surveillance of human actions is to detect and track the motion based object from video streaming with the help of CCTV or IP camera etc as shown in Figure 4. This is applicable in various realistic environments such as Traffic monitoring, Surveillance of illegal activities,

Figure 4.

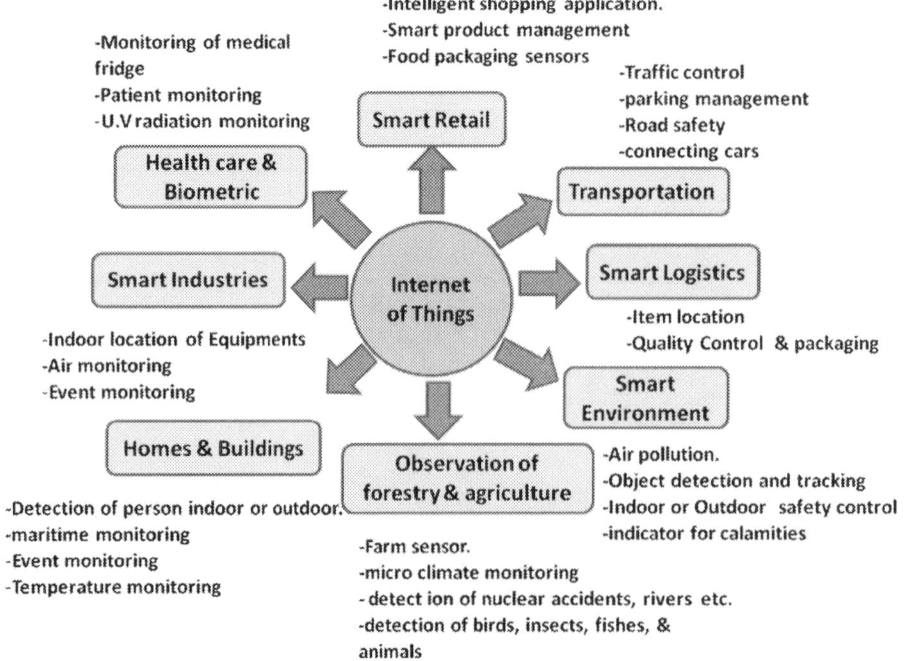

maritime traffic monitoring, public places or events, Maritime traffic Surveillance, temperature monitoring, aerial monitoring, medical surveillance, leak detection, monitoring of solar panel, Border surveillance including Navy, Army and many more (Haque & Paul, 2008; Tuan et.al., 2015). This system seems to be more specific in case of shopping complexes, General stores, indoor or outdoor surveillance.

- **IoT in Intelligent Visual observation of Forestry:** The IoT based Visual surveillance system can efficiently detect the activities of birds, insects, fishes, and other animals in restricted or protected zone such as national parks and zoo's (Haque & Paul, 2008; Sharma et.al., 2015; Yadav & Singh, 2015; Tuan et.al., 2015).
- **IoT in Intelligent Visual observation of Forestry:** The IOT based surveillance systems can detect the nuclear accidents, surveillance of Dike, River or coastal areas observed activities including objects, people and woods (Sharma et.al., 2015).
- **IoT in Biometric:** This system deals with Face detection, finger prints detection, hand geometry, iris pattern detection (Lavanya Sharma, 2018).
- **IoT in Healthcare Surveillance***:* In today's scenarios most of the health care groups can results in reduction of cost of patient's activities using IoT devices. In emergency cases this system provides better facilities to treat the patient on life saving mode. There are numerous services that can be combine video streaming and IoT sensors with cloud (Tuan et.al., 2015).
- **IoT In human Computer Interaction:** In recent years IoT and Big data based real time applications needs interaction of human with the computers via video captured by non moving cameras which sounds to be very fruitful in case of gaming and ludo programming (Gharavi & Ghafurian, 2011; Sharma et.al., 2014).
- **Wearable IoT Devices to connect via network:** In todays world wearable devices such as shoes, watches or glasses can be used to the biometric information. These devices can effectively collect the information as Wearable IoT a devices that connect the networks and then communicate with control hub via. Internet as shown in Figure 5. (Gharavi & Ghafurian, 2011; Scene Background Initialization (SBI) dataset, 2015; Sharma & Yadav, 2016).

Figure 5.

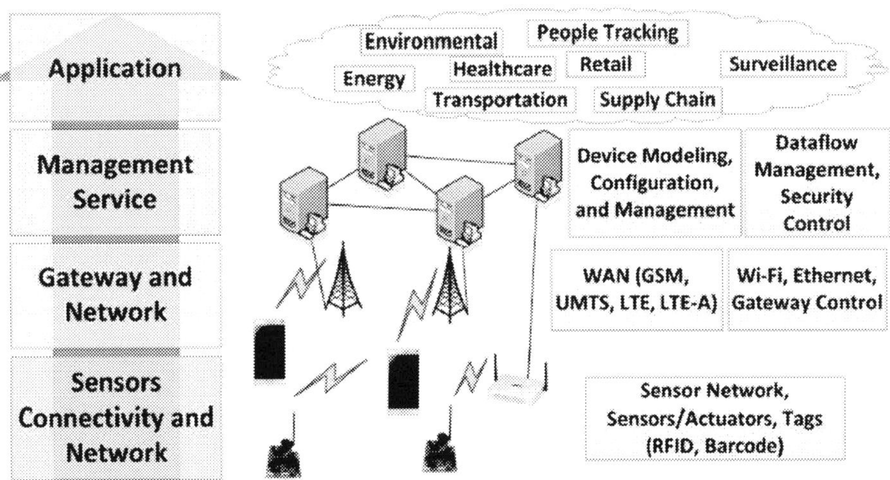

5. RESOURCES AND DATASETS

This chapter explores various existing resources and datasets using non moving or still camera which are not used in IoT environment. But in realistic scenarios it a basic need to detect and locate the people using IoT or cloud computing. These real time applications can be implemented using MATlab, open CV or python. In order to detect and track the motion based object one ground truth image or template is required (Haque & Paul, 2008; Hong et.al., 2010; Gharavi & Ghafurian, 2011; Sanaz et.al., 2014; Sharma et.al., 2015; Yadav & Singh, 2015; Tuan et.al., 2015). Some of the major datasets and resources are listed below in Table 1. In Figure 6, Left to Right: (a) original frame sequence, (b) generated background ground truth (GT), (c) foreground mask. All the shown images or frames are taken from change detection dataset (Change Detection Dataset, 2015).

6. ADVANTAGES OF IOT BASED SURVEILLANCE SYSTEM

The surveillance systems using IoT are designed for the security aspects in today's scenarios. These systems mainly support the continuous locating of people (crime or threat) or moving objects, transmission and

Figure 6.

Table 1. Major datasets and resources

Datasets/ Resources	Current Challenging Issues
Microsoft's Wall-flower Dataset (Toyama et.al., 1999)	Dynamic background, illumination variation, camouflage, Foreground aperture, light switch on or off, bootstrapping. (http://classif.ai/dataset/wallflower-dataset/)
Labelme dataset (The Open Annotation Tool, Dataset, 2016).	Moving persons, complex background (http://labelme.csail.mit.edu/Release3.0/browserTools/php/dataset.php)
Change Detection Dataset (Change Detection Dataset, 2015).	Camera Jitter, dynamic background, intermittent object motion, shadow. (http://changedetection.net/)
SBMI 2015 dataset (Scene Background Initialization (SBI) dataset, (2015)	Dynamic background or illumination variation (http://sbmi2015.na.icar.cnr.it/)
CSIR-CSIO Dataset (Yadav et.al., 2014)	Background motion, illumination variation. (http://www.vcipl.okstate.edu/otcbvs/bench/)
CBCL Car Dataset (Poggio & Tomaso, 2016).	Moving person with moving background in thermal (http://cbcl.mit.edu/software-datasets/CarData.html)
DIAMLER Dataset (Flohr, & Gavrila, 2016)	Dynamic background, locating people (http://www.gavrila.net/Datasets/Daimler_Pedestrian_Benchmark_D/daimler_pedestrian_benchmark_d.html)
CAVIAR dataset(CAVIAR Test Case Scenarios, 2003).	Indoor or outdoor sequence focuses on moving people (http://homepages.inf.ed.ac.uk/rbf/CAVIARDATA1/)
FGNET Dataset (Wallhoff, & München, 2000).	Background motion, illumination variation (http://www-prima.inrialpes.fr/FGnet/html/benchmarks.html)

recording for future purpose that helps the law enforcement systems for securities reasons (Sanaz et.al., 2014; Sharma et.al., 2014; Yadav & Singh, 2015; Tuan et.al., 2015; Sharma & Yadav, 2016; Sharma & Lohan, 2017). Some of the major advantages of the IoT based surveillance are listed below in Table 2.

7. CONCLUSION AND FUTURE WORK

This chapter explores the basic architecture of IoT environment, current challenging issues and their applications including leak monitoring, temperature monitoring, traffic monitoring indoor and outdoor

Table 2. IoT based surveillance

Advantages	Description
Act as a crime deterrent	It Allows authoritative individual to continuous monitor the motion based persons, and detect the critical, or restricted domains
Remote video monitoring	Monitor the person for medical facilities in remote areas using IoT. The emergency facility can be easily achieved using IP based visual surveillance in IoT environment.
Evidence gathering	With IoT based video surveillance system, the legal authorities can comes to conclusion about the sequence of actions occurred at the time of crime.
Improve productivity	Such system results in improvement of the productivity of manufacturing goods, automobiles, even in small scale industries to keep an eye on the activities of employees
Prevent dishonest Claims	To challenge the allegation of false information in case of misbehave, crime or threat.
Data is storage digitally	IoT devices including wearable devices such as glasses, watches be used to store the data.

activity monitoring, defence, marine surveillance, emergency department and many more. Then, we also discussed about various datasets and resources available in literature. Advantages of IoT based Surveillance is also explore in this chapter. In future work, we work on detection of everyday object using some hardware resources such as IP camera's or Raspberry-Pi to get the valuable information from the streamed video. Then, after capturing we will use cloud as storage, and retrieval of data from cloud for further processing.

REFERENCES

Aribas, E., & Daglarli, E. (2017). Realtime object detection in IoT (Internet of Things) devices. *25th Signal Processing and Communications Applications Conference (SIU)*, 1-6. 10.1109/SIU.2017.7960690

Brown, E. (2016). *Who Needs the Internet of Things*. Retrieved May 2018, from https://www.linux.com/news/who-needs-internet-things

CAVIAR Test Case Scenarios. (2003). Retrieved, May 2018 from http://homepages.inf.ed.ac.uk/rbf/CAVIARDATA1/

Change Detection Dataset. (2015). Retrieved, March 2018, from http://changedetection.net/

Chen, S., Xu, H., Liu, D., Hu, B., & Wang, H. (2014). A vision of IoT: Applications challenges and opportunities with China perspective. *IEEE Internet Things Journal*, *1*(4), 349–359. doi:10.1109/JIOT.2014.2337336

Detection and Ranging for the Internet of Things. (2018). Retrieved April 2018, from http://www.kritikalsolutions.com/internet-of-things

Enabling Detection and Ranging for the Internet of Things and Beyond. (2018). Retrieved May 2018, from https://leddartech.com/enabling-detection-and-ranging-for-the-internet-of-things-and-beyond/

Felzenszwalb, F., Girshick, R. B., McAllester, D., & Ramanan, D. (2010). Object detection with discriminatively trained part based models. *IEEE Transactions on Pattern Analysis and Machine Intelligence*, *32*(9), 1627–1645. doi:10.1109/TPAMI.2009.167 PMID:20634557

Flohr, F., & Gavrila, M. (2016). *Daimler Pedestrian Segmentation Benchmark Dataset*. Retrieved, May 2018 from, http://www.gavrila.net/Datasets/Daimler_Pedestrian_Benchmark_D/daimler_pedestrian_benchmark_d.html

Gharavi, H., & Ghafurian, R. (2011). Smart grid: The electric energy system of the future. *Proceedings of the IEEE*, *99*(6), 917–921. doi:10.1109/JPROC.2011.2124210

Handte, M., Foell, S., Wagner, S., Kortuem, G., & Marrón, P. (2016). An Internet-of-Things enabled connected navigation system for urban bus rider. *IEEE Internet Things Journal*, *3*(5), 735–744. doi:10.1109/JIOT.2016.2554146

Haque, M., Murshed, M., & Paul, M. (2008). On stable dynamic background generation technique using gaussian mixture models for robust object detection. *5th International Conference on Advanced Video and Signal Based Surveillance*, 41–48. 10.1109/AVSS.2008.12

Hong, S., Kim, D., Park, S., Jung, W., & Kim, E. (2010). SNAIL: An IP-based wireless sensor network approach to the internet of things. *IEEE Wireless Communications*, *17*(6), 34–42. doi:10.1109/MWC.2010.5675776

Hu, L., & Giang, N. (2017). IoT-Driven Automated Object Detection Algorithm for Urban Surveillance Systems in Smart Cities. *IEEE Internet of Things Journal*, *5*(2), 747–754. doi:10.1109/JIOT.2017.2705560

Initialization, S. B. (SBI) dataset. (2015). Retrieved, April 2018, from, http://sbmi2015.na.icar.cnr.it/

Internet of Things. (2017). Retrieved, May 2018 from, https://arxiv.org/ftp/arxiv/papers/1708/1708.04560.pdf

Jung, C. R. (2009). Efficient background subtraction and shadow removal for monochromatic video sequences. *IEEE Transactions on Multimedia*, *11*(3), 571–577. doi:10.1109/TMM.2009.2012924

Li, B., Tian, B., Yao, Q., & Wang, K. (2012). A vehicle license plate recognition system based on analysis of maximally stable extremal regions. In *Proceedings of 9th IEEE Int. Conference Network Sensors Control (pp.* 399-404). 10.1109/ICNSC.2012.6204952

OGC Senor. (2016). *OGC Sensor Things API standard specification*. Retrieved April 2018, from http://www.opengeospatial.org/standards/sensorthings

Overview of Internet of Things. (2018). Retrieved, June 2018 from https://cloud.google.com/solutions/iot-overview

Poggio, A., & Tomaso, D. (2016). *The Center for Biological & Computational Learning (CBCL)*. Retrieved, May 2018, from http://cbcl.mit.edu/software-datasets/CarData.html

Quack, T., & Gool, L. (2008). Object Recognition for the Internet of Things. *Lecture Notes in Computer Science, 4952*, 230–246.

Ren, J., Guo, Y., Liu, Q., & Zhang, Y. (2018). Distributed and Efficient Object Detection in Edge Computing: Challenges and Solutions. *IEEE Network*, *1*, 1–7.

Right Sensors for Object Tracking. (2016). Retrieved April 2018, from https://www.hcltech.com/blogs/right-sensors-object-tracking-iot-part-1

Sanaz, R., Moosavi, R., Mohammad, R., & Yang, P. Tenhunen, h. (2014). Pervasive Health Monitoring Based on Internet of Things: Two Case Studies. *Wireless Mobile Communication and Healthcare (Mobihealth) 2014 EAI 4th International Conference*, 275-278.

Sharma, L. (2018). *Object Detection with Background Subtraction. LAP LAMBERT Academic Publishing*.

Sharma, L., & Lohan, N. (2017) Performance enhancement through Handling of false classification in video surveillance. *Journal of Pure and applied Science & Technology, 7*(2), 9-17.

Sharma, L., & Yadav, D. (2016). Fisher's Linear Discriminant Ratio based Threshold for Moving Human Detection in Thermal Video. *Infrared Physics and Technology, 78*, 118-128.

Sharma, L., Yadav, D., & Bharti, S. (2015). An improved method for visual surveillance using background subtraction technique. *2nd Int. Conf. on Signal Processing and Integrated Networks (SPIN)*, 421-426. 10.1109/SPIN.2015.7095253

Stauffer, C., & Grimson, W. E. L. (1999). Adaptive background mixture models for real-time tracking. *IEEE Computer Society Conference on Computer Vision and Pattern Recognition*, 2, 246–252 10.1109/CVPR.1999.784637

The Open Innotation Tool Dataset. (2016). *Dataset from MIT lab*. Retrieved, March 2018, from http://labelme.csail.mit.edu/Release3.0/browserTools/php/dataset.php

Toyama, K., Krumm, J., Brumitt, B., & Meyers, B. (1999). Wallflower: principles and practice of background maintenance. *7th International Conference on Computer Vision,* 255–261. 10.1109/ICCV.1999.791228

Tuan, N., Mohammad, G., Rahmani, T., & Westerlund, L. (2015). Fault Tolerant and Scalable IoT-based Architecture for Health Monitoring. *Sensors Applications Symposium (SAS)*, 1-6.

Wallhoff, F., & München, T. (2000). *FGNet Facial Emotions and Expressions Database*. Retrieved, May 2018, from http://www-prima.inrialpes.fr/FGnet/html/benchmarks.html

Yadav, D., Sharma, L., & Bharti, S. (2014). *Moving Object Detection in Real-Time Visual Surveillance using Background Subtraction Technique. In 14th International conference on Hybrid Intelligent Systems (HIS2014)* (pp. 79–84). IEEE.

Yadav, D., & Singh, K. (2015). Moving Object Detection for Visual Surveillance Using Quasi-Euclidian Distance, IC3T-2015. *LNCS, Advances in Intelligent Systems and Computing Series, Springer*, *381*, 225–233. doi:10.1007/978-81-322-2526-3_25

Yadav, D., & Singh, K. (2015). A Combined Approach of Kullback-Leibler Divergence Method and Background Subtraction for Moving Object Detection in Thermal Video. *Infrared Physics and Technology, Elsevier*, *76*, 21–31. doi:10.1016/j.infrared.2015.12.027

Chapter 7
Semantics for Big Data Sets

Vo Ngoc Phu
Duy Tan University, Vietnam

Vo Thi Ngoc Tran
Ho Chi Minh City University of Technology, Vietnam

ABSTRACT

Information technology, computer science, etc. have been developed more and more in many countries in the world. Their subfields have already had many very crucial contributions to everyone life: production, politics, advertisement, etc. Especially, big data semantics, scientific and knowledge discovery, and intelligence are the subareas that are gaining more interest. Therefore, the authors display semantics for massive data sets fully in this chapter. This is very significant for commercial applications, studies, researchers, etc. in the world.

INTRODUCTION

The massive corporations, large-scale organizations, and etc. have already been built more and more from the strong development of the economies of the countries in the word for the recent years. They have already generated a lot of information, knowledge, and etc. We have already called these information, knowledge, and etc. as many big data sets (BIGDSs).

According to our knowledge, the BIGDS has been a data set which has been millions of data samples (or billions of data records) or a massive size (or a big volume) about over billions of bytes, etc.

These large-scale data sets (LARSDSs) have been wondered whether they have been very crucial for the corporations, organizations, and etc. Therefore, the corporations, organizations, and etc. have needed whether the massive data sets (MASDSs) have been handled fully, successfully, and etc. In addition, they have needed whether the BIGDSs have been extracted many significant values automatically, etc.

The LARSDSs has comprised many different areas such as natural language processing (NLP), machine learning (ML), data mining (DM), artificial intelligence (AI), expert systems (ES), and etc. There have been many commercial applications and many surveys of these fields which have been studied, developed, and etc. for the MASDSs. Furthermore, these areas have been very significant for the corporations, organizations, and etc. in the world. However, there have not been enough the commercial applications and the studies for the BIGDSs yet in the world for the recent years.

DOI: 10.4018/978-1-5225-7432-3.ch007

Based on the above proofs and our opinion, we have presented the semantic analysis (SEMANA) for the LARSDSs in this book chapter.

According to our opinion, the classification has been a process of identifying the semantic values and the sentiment polarities of many words, many phrases, many sentences, many documents, and etc.

The sentiment polarity has been positive, negative, or neutral. When a word has been displayed positive attitudes such as like, love, etc., this word has been the positive polarity. When a word has been shown negative attitudes such as dislike, hate, etc., this word has been the negative polarity. When a word has been presented neutral attitudes such as drink, eat, etc., this word has been the neutral polarity.

Based on the opinion polarity of a word, when a phrase has been shown positive attitudes, this phrase has been the positive polarity. When a phrase has been presented negative attitudes, this phrase has been the negative polarity. When a phrase has been displayed neutral attitudes, this phrase has been the neutral polarity.

According to the sentiment polarity of a word and the opinion polarity of a phrase, when a sentence has been shown positive attitudes, this sentence has been the positive polarity. When a sentence has been displayed negative attitudes, this sentence has been the negative polarity. When a sentence has been presented neutral attitudes, this sentence has been the neutral polarity.

Based on the semantic polarity of a word/phrase/sentence, when a document has been presented positive attitudes, this document has been the positive polarity. When a document has been shown negative attitudes, this document has been the negative polarity. When a document has been displayed neutral attitudes, this document has been the neutral polarity.

The semantic value (or the sentiment score, or the valence) has been a value of a word/phrase/sentence/document. The valence of a word has been greater than 0 when the sentiment polarity of this word has been the positive. The sentiment score of a word has been less than 0 when the opinion polarity of this word has been the negative. The opinion value of a word has been as equal as 0 when the semantic polarity of this word has been the neutral.

According to the valence of a word, the sentiment score of a phrase has been greater than 0 when the opinion polarity of this phrase has been the positive. The opinion value of a phrase has been less than 0 when the semantic polarity of this phrase has been the negative. The valence of a phrase has been as equal as 0 when the valence of this phrase has been the neutral.

Based on the opinion value of a word, and a phrase, the valence of a sentence has been greater than 0 when this sentence has been the positive polarity. The opinion score of a sentence has been less than 0 when this sentence has been the negative polarity. The sentiment value of a sentence has been as equal as 0 when this sentence has been the neutral polarity.

According to the valence of a word/phrase/sentence, the opinion score of a document has been greater than 0 when this document has been the positive polarity. The valence of a document has been less than 0 when this document has been the negative polarity. The sentiment value of a document has been as equal as 0 when this document has been the neutral polarity.

We have presented the latest surveys of the SEMANA for the BIGDSs into the 3 categories: supervised approach (SUPLEARN), semi-supervised approach (SESUPLEARN), and un-supervised learning (UNSUPLEARN).

The SUPLEARN has been an algorithm, a method, a model, etc., and it has been a least a training stage and a learning stage. It has been a least a testing data set (TSTDS) and a training data set (TRNDS). This training stage has used the TRNDS, and this learning stage has used the TSTDS. This training stage has been a stage which has been used for the learning stage. This learning stage has been used to identify the results of this algorithm, this method, this model, and etc.

The SESUPLEARN has also been an algorithm, a method, a model, etc., and it has been only a training stage and a least a learning stage. It has been a least a TSTDS and only a TRNDS. This TRNDS has been less than the 50% of the task of the TRNDS of the SUPLEARN. This training stage has also used the TRNDS, and this learning stage has also used the TSTDS. This training stage has been less than the 50% of the task of the training stage of the SUPLEARN. This training stage has also been a stage which has also been used for the learning stage. However, this learning stage has not been dependent on the training stage fully. This learning stage has also been used to determine the results of this algorithm, this method, this model, and etc.

The UNSUPLEARN has also been an algorithm, a method, a model, etc., and it has been at least a learning stage. Furthermore, it has not been any training stages. It has been a least a TSTDS, and it has not been any TRNDSs. This UNSUPLEARN has used this learning stage itself to identify the results of this algorithm, this method, this model, and etc.

The main contributions of this book chapter to the problem from many surveys related to lots of new computational models for the LARSDSs have been as follows:

1. We have believed that the readers of this chapter have lots of significant information and knowledge about the BIGDSs.
2. We have also believed that the readers certainly understand most of all the latest algorithms, the latest methods, the latest models of the BIGDSs
3. We have displayed most of all the latest algorithms, the latest methods, the latest models of the MASDSs of the SEMANA in both many sequential environments (SEQENVIRs) and many parallel network environments (PANETENVIRs) on more details.
4. Based on the information of (1), (2), and (3), the readers including scientists, researchers, CEO, managers, and etc. can build, develop, and deploy many commercial applications, surveys, and etc. so much.
5. We have carefully shown the different technologies of the algorithms, methods, and models on more details.
6. In this book chapter, we have already considered that the algorithms, methods, models, and etc. having been applied to the MASDSs must be over the 500,000 data samples or the 1,000,000 data records in the SEQENVIR and the PANETENVIR.
7. …etc.

We have displayed the contribution original of this book chapter as follows:

1. We have believed that the readers can understand the simple concepts of the SEMANA, the semantic polarity, the sentiment score, the SUPLEARN, the SESUPLEARN, the UNSUPLEARN, the BIGDSs, and etc. through this book chapter.
2. We have also believed that the readers can understand the algorithms, methods, models, and etc. of the SEMANA for the LARSDSs fully in the SEQENVIR and the PANETENVIR.
3. We have proposed a novel model of the SEMANA for the MASDSs in the SEQENVIR and the PANETENVIR successfully for this book chapter.

4. We have believed that many commercial applications, surveys, and etc. can be studied, developed, and deployed for the SEMANA of the BIGDSs successfully.
5. …etc.

We have presented the contribution non-trivial as follows: We have proposed a novel model of the SEMANA for a BIGDS to give an example in this book chapter fully. We have performed this proposed model in both a SEQENVIR and a PANETENVIR. This PANETENVIR has been a Cloudera distributed network system (CLOUDDISNS). Furthermore, we have used Hadoop Map (M), and Hadoop Reduce (R) for this approach. We have also used a K-Means algorithm (KMEANAL) and many multi-dimensional vectors (MULTDVECTs) for this example. We have already tested this survey on the 2,000,000 reviews of a TSTDS according to the 2,000,000 documents of a TRNDS in English, and we have already achieved 85.23% accuracy of this novel model. Based on the results of this survey, we have believed that the sentiments (positive/negative/neutral) of millions of the documents in English can be identified successfully in the PANETENVIR.

In this book chapter, we have shown a variety of models of the SEMANA for handling the LARSDS in the SEQENVIR and the PANETENVIR. These models have been divided into the 3 categories such as the SUPLEARN, the SESUPLEARN, and the UNSUPLEARN. We have presented each model of each category in the 3 categories on more details.

BACKGROUND

We have briefly summarized the surveys related to the proposed model of this example in this book chapter such as the KMEANAL, vector space model (VSM), Hadoop, the CLOUDDISNS, and etc.

There have been the studies of the VSM presented in the survey [(Vaibhav Kant Singh, & Vinay Kumar Singh, 2015), (Víctor Carrera-Trejo, &et al, 2015), and (Pascal Soucy, & Guy W. Mineau, 2015)]. The VSM, an information retrieval technique and its variation, has been examined in the research (Vaibhav Kant Singh, & Vinay Kumar Singh, 2015). The VSM has been an algebraic model used for information retrieval, which has represented many natural language documents by using vectors in a multi-dimensional space, etc. The authors have also displayed the VSM in the survey (Víctor Carrera-Trejo, &et al, 2015), etc.

The algorithms, applications, surveys have been launched in a PANETENVIR according to the works [(Hadoop, 2017), (Apache, 2017), and (Cloudera, 2017)]. In addition, the Hadoop has been an Apache-based framework which has been used to process massive data sets on the clusters consisting of the multiple computers by using the M and R programming model in (Hadoop, 2017) and (Apache, 2017). There have been the two main tasks of the Hadoop: the M and the R, etc. Furthermore, Cloudera has been the global provider of the platforms (fastest, easiest, and most secure data management and analytics) built on Apache Hadoop in (Cloudera, 2017). Cloudera has been a PANETENVIR for many algorithms, methods, models, and etc. to be implemented in a parallel way, etc.

The authors have displayed the KMEANAL in the studies [(K. Krishna, & M. Narasimha Murty, 1999), (Zhexue Huang, 1998), (Kiri Wagstaff, & et al, 2001), (Anil K. Jain, 2010), (Liping Jing, & et al, 2007), (J.M Peña, & et al, 1999), (B.-H. Juang, & L.R. Rabiner, 1990), (Mu-Chun Su, & Chien-Hsing Chou, 2001), (Alsabti, Khaled; & et al, 1997), (Vance Faber, 1994), (Greg Hamerly, & Charles Elkan, 2002), (Aristidis Likas, & et al, 2003), (J.Z. Huang, & et al, 2005), (Sanghamitra Bandyopadhyay, & Ujjwal Maulik, 2002), and (T. Kanungo, D.M. Mount, & et al, 2002)]. A globally optimal partition of a sample has been found by a novel hybrid genetic algorithm using the KMEANAL into a specified number of the clusters in the study (K. Krishna, & M. Narasimha Murty, 1999), etc. The authors have extended the KMEANAL by using mixed numeric and categorical values for categorical domains and domains in the work (Zhexue Huang, 1998), etc.

All the documents of the TSTDS and the TRNDS have automatically been extracted from Facebook, websites, social networks, and etc. in the movie area in English. These documents must be standardized. These documents must be pre-processed carefully (online text cleaning/white space removal/expanding abbreviation/stemming, and stop words removal). Furthermore, we have labeled positive and negative for these documents fully.

The TRNDS of the novel model of this example has been the 2,000,000 documents (the 1,000,000 English positive, and the 1,000,000 English negative).

In addition, the TSTDS of the proposed approach of this example has also been the 2,000,000 documents including the 1,000,000 English positive and the 1,000,000 English negative.

The accuracy of this novel model has been dependent on the accuracy of the TSTDS and the TRNDS.

The accuracy of the TSTDS and the TRNDS has been dependent on the factors as follows:

1. The TSTDS and the TRNDS: TSTDS must be close to the TRNDS.
2. The sizes of the TSTDS and the TRNDS: the number of the documents of the TSTDS and the TRNDS.
3. The documents of the TSTDS and the TRNDS must be standardized and pre-processed carefully.

MAIN FOCUS OF THE CHAPTER

Issues, Controversies, Problems

We have presented all the possible novel models of the SEMANA for the MASDSs into the 3 categories: the SUPLEARN, the SESUPLEARN, and the UNSUPLEARN in this section. In addition, we have given an approach model of the SEMANA for the BIGDSs as an example of this book chapter.

These models of this part in this book chapter have been divided into the two environments: the SEQENVIRs and the PANETENVIRs.

We have already considered that the algorithms, methods, models, and etc. having been applied to the MASDSs must be over the 500,000 data samples or the 1,000,000 data records in the SEQENVIR and the PANETENVIR in this book chapter.

When these approaches of the SEMANA having been implemented in the SEQENVIR must be over the 500,000 data samples or the 1,000,000 data records, we have seen that the approaches have handled the LARSDSs certainly.

When these approaches of the SEMANA have been performed in the PANETENVIR, the approaches have processed the BIGDSs certainly, and the approaches must not be over the 500,000 data samples or the 1,000,000 data records because the PANETENVIR has been an environment for the MASDSs certainly, fully, and successfully.

We have already looked for the unsupervised approaches of the SEMANA for the MASDSs in the SEQENVIRs on the internet through many search engines (Google search engine (GOOGSE), Yahoo search engine (YSE), and etc.). However, we have not found any the unsupervised approaches of the SEMANA for the BIGDSs in the SEQENVIRs.

In addition, according to our opinion, information, and knowledge, we have not been many unsupervised approaches of the SEMANA for the MASDSs in the SEQENVIRs in the world.

We have already found the unsupervised approaches of the SEMANA in the world such as (Vo Ngoc Phu, &et al, 2017a), (Vo Ngoc Phu, &et al, 2017b), (Vo Ngoc Phu, &et al, 2017c), (Vo Ngoc Phu, &et al, 2017d), (Vo Ngoc Phu, &et al, 2017e), and etc.

According to the results of looking for the supervised approaches of the SEMANA for the LARSDSs and according to our opinion, information, and knowledge, there have been the supervised algorithms, the supervised methods, the supervised models, and etc. of the SEMANA for the MASDSs in both the SEQENVIRs and the PANETENVIRs.

Based on the results of looking for the semi-supervised approaches of the SEMANA for the BIGDSs and based on our opinion, information, and knowledge, there have been the semi-supervised algorithms, the semi-supervised methods, the semi-supervised models, and etc. of the SEMANA for the LARSDSs in both the SEQENVIRs and the PANETENVIRs.

According to the above proofs, we have firstly displayed the unsupervised approaches (comprising the algorithms, the methods, the models, and etc.) in the SEQENVIR and the PANETENVIR. Then, we have secondly presented the supervised approaches (including the algorithms, the methods, the models, and etc.) in the SEQENVIR and the PANETENVIR. Next, we have thirdly displayed the semi-supervised approaches (comprising the algorithms, the methods, the models, and etc.) in the SEQENVIR and the PANETENVIR. Finally, we have given an example of the SEQENVIR for the MASDS in the SEQENVIR and the PANETENVIR by showing a novel model in the next section on more details.

Based on the execution environments of the SEMANA models, we have presented the SEMANA models for the MASDSs in the SEQENVIR and PANETENVIR in the 3 categories (the UNSUPLEARN, the SUPLEARN, and the SESUPLEARN).

In the time of the finished book chapter, we have found only the 3 unsupervised surveys of the SEMANA for the LARSDS in the SEQENVIR as follows: (Vo Ngoc Phu, & Vo Thi Ngoc Tran, 2017a), (Vo Ngoc Phu, & Vo Thi Ngoc Tran, 2018a), (Vo Ngoc Phu, & Vo Thi Ngoc Tran, 2018b), and etc.

The authors of the work in (Vo Ngoc Phu, & Vo Thi Ngoc Tran, 2017a) have already used an unsupervised model of the SEMANA for the MASDS in the SEQENVIR. This model has been used to classify the semantics (positive, negative, or neutral) for the 5,000,000 documents of the TSTDS in English, and in addition, the authors have not used any TRNDSs for this survey. A Johnson measure (JOHNSM) has been used through the Google search engine (GOOGSE) with the AND operator and OR operator (ANDOROPs) in this study. This novel work has been achieved 87.56% accuracy of the TSTDS, etc.

In the survey (Vo Ngoc Phu, & Vo Thi Ngoc Tran, 2018a), the authors have also used the opinion scores of the lexicons of a Kuhns-II Coefficient (KUHS_II_CO) for the unsupervised model of the SEMANA for the LARSDS in English in SEQENVIR. The authors have not also used any TRNDSs for this survey which have been used for the SEMANA of the 8,500,000 documents of the TSTDS, etc.

A unsupervised model have been proposed for the SEMANA of the BIGDS in the SEQENVIR by using the multi-dimensional vectors (MULTDMVECTs) and the Yule-II coefficient (YIICOEFF) for a Self-Organizing Map algorithm (SELFOM) in the study (Vo Ngoc Phu, & Vo Thi Ngoc Tran, 2018b), etc.

In the near future, we can find the unsupervised studies of the SEMANA for the BIGDS more and more in the SEQENVIR

In the time of the finished book chapter, we have found lots of the unsupervised surveys of the SEMANA for the LARSDS in the PANETENVIR as follows:

The authors of the work in (Vo Ngoc Phu, & Vo Thi Ngoc Tran, 2017a) have already used an unsupervised model of the SEMANA for the MASDS in the PANETENVIR. This model has been used to classify the semantics (positive, negative, or neutral) for the 5,000,000 documents of the TSTDS in English, and in addition, the authors have not used any TRNDSs for this survey. A Johnson measure (JOHNSM) has been used through the Google search engine (GOOGSE) with the AND operator and OR operator (ANDOROPs) in this study. This novel work has been achieved 87.56% accuracy of the TSTDS, etc.

In the survey (Vo Ngoc Phu, & Vo Thi Ngoc Tran, 2018a), the authors have also used the opinion scores of the lexicons of a Kuhns-II Coefficient (KUHS_II_CO) for the unsupervised model of the SEMANA for the LARSDS in English in PANETENVIR. The authors have not also used any TRNDSs for this survey which have been used for the SEMANA of the 8,500,000 documents of the TSTDS, etc.

A unsupervised model have been proposed for the SEMANA of the BIGDS in the PANETENVIR by using the multi-dimensional vectors (MULTDMVECTs) and the Yule-II coefficient (YIICOEFF) for a Self-Organizing Map algorithm (SELFOM) in the study (Vo Ngoc Phu, & Vo Thi Ngoc Tran, 2018b), etc.

Next, we have displayed a lot of the supervised learning surveys of the SEMANA of the MASDS in the SEQENVIR and the PANETENVIR as follows: (Nguyen Duy Dat, & et al, 2017), (Vo Ngoc Phu, & et al, 2017f), (Vo Ngoc Phu, &et al, 2017g), (Vo Ngoc Phu, &Vo Thi Ngoc Tran, 2017b), (Vo Ngoc Phu, &Vo Thi Ngoc Tran, 2018c), (Vo Ngoc Phu, &Vo Thi Ngoc Tran, 2018d), (Vo Ngoc Phu, &et al, 2018), (Vo Ngoc Phu, &Vo Thi Ngoc Tran, 2018e), (Vo Ngoc Phu, &Vo Thi Ngoc Tran, 2018f), (Vo Ngoc Phu, &Vo Thi Ngoc Tran, 2018g), (Vo Ngoc Phu, &Vo Thi Ngoc Tran, 2018h), and etc.

The authors have developed a supervised model of the SEMANA of the LARSDS in the SEQENVIR and the PANETENVIR by using the STING algorithm to classify the opinions for the 25,000 documents of the TSTDS according to the 90,000 sentences of the TRNDS in English, and they have already achieved 61.2% accuracy of the proposed approach in the survey (Nguyen Duy Dat, & et al, 2017), etc.

According to the work (Vo Ngoc Phu, & et al, 2017f), the authors have developed a supervised survey using the Fuzzy C-Means algorithm for the SEMANA of the BIGDS in the SEQENVIR and the PANETENVIR. This novel approach has been used to identify the semantics of the 25,000 reviews of the TSTDS based on the 60,000 sentences of the TRNDS in English. Furthermore, the accuracy of this survey has been achieved 60.2% of the TSTDS, etc.

The authors have already used a SVM algorithm for the SEMANA of the BIGDS in the SEQENVIR and the PANETENVIR in the study (Vo Ngoc Phu, & et al, 2017g) on the 25,000 documents of the TSTDS based on the 90,000 sentences of the TRNDS in English, etc.

A novel approach has been developed for the SEMANA of the MASDS in the SEQENVIR and the PANETENVIR by using the Statistical Information Grid algorithm and the MULTDVECTs to classify the 1,000,000 reviews of the TSTDS into the positive/the negative according to the 2,000,000 documents of the TRNDS in English in the study (Vo Ngoc Phu, &Vo Thi Ngoc Tran, 2017b). Therefore, we have already achieved 83.92% accuracy of this model on the TSTDS, etc.

In the study (Vo Ngoc Phu, & Vo Thi Ngoc Tran, 2018c), the authors have developed a supervised survey of a Genetic Algorithm (GA) and a Gower-2 Coefficient (HA) with a Fitness proportionate Selection (FPS) to identify the opinions for the 8,000,000 documents of the TSTDS into the positive/the negative based on the 7,000,000 sentences of the TRNDS for the SEMANA of the LARSDS in the SEQENVIR and the PANETENVIR, etc. We have already achieved 88.12% accuracy of the SEMANA, etc.

The authors of the work (Vo Ngoc Phu, & Vo Thi Ngoc Tran, 2018d) have already built a proposed approach using the Dennis Coefficient (DennisCOEFF) and the Latent Semantic Analysis (LatentSA) for the SEMANA of the BIGDS in the SEQENVIR and the PANETENVIR to classify the 11,000,000 documents of the TSTDS into either the positive or the negative according to the 5,000,000 documents of the TRNDS in English, etc. and so, the accuracy of this supervised model has been achieved 88.76% on the TSTDS, etc.

The authors have already proposed the supervised model of the Clustering Using Representatives algorithm for the SEMANA of the MASDS in the SEQENVIR and the PANETENVIR in Vietnamese in the survey (Vo Ngoc Phu, & et al, 2018), and we have already achieved 62.92% accuracy of the TSTDS based on the sentences of the TRNDS, etc.

The authors of the study (Vo Ngoc Phu, &Vo Thi Ngoc Tran, 2018e) have already presented a supervised model using a Genetic Algorithm (GEAL) and a Fager & MacGowan Coefficient (FAMACC) with a Rank Selection (RASE) for the SEMANA of the BIGDS in the SEQENVIR and the PANETENVIR to classify the 7,500,000 documents of the TSTDS into the positive/the negative based on the 7,000,000 sentences of the TRNDS, etc. This model has achieved 88.21% accuracy of the TSTDS, etc.

Then, we have displayed the semi-supervised learning surveys of the SEMANA for the LARSDS in the SEQENVIR and the PANETENVIR as follows: (Vo Ngoc Phu, & Vo Thi Ngoc Tran, 2018i), (Vo Ngoc Phu, & Vo Thi Ngoc Tran, 2018j), (Vo Ngoc Phu, & Vo Thi Ngoc Tran, 2018k), (Vo Ngoc Phu, & Vo Thi Ngoc Tran, 2018l), (Vo Ngoc Phu, & Vo Thi Ngoc Tran, 2018m), and etc.

The authors have developed a semi-supervised novel model by using the Co-Training algorithm (COTRAL), the Fuzzy C-Means algorithm (FUZZCM), and the MULTDVECTs of an Otsuka coefficient (OTCOEFF) for the SEMANA of the MASDS in the SEQENVIR and the PANETENVIR, and they have already achieved 89.25% accuracy of the TSTDS in the work (Vo Ngoc Phu, & Vo Thi Ngoc Tran, 2018i), etc.

In the survey (Vo Ngoc Phu, & Vo Thi Ngoc Tran, 2018j), a semi-supervised model has already been displayed by using a Self-Training algorithm, a K-NN algorithm, and the MULTDVECTs of a S6 coefficient for the SEMANA of the BIGDS in the SEQENVIR and the PANETENVIR. Furthermore, we have already achieved 89.13% accuracy of the TSTDS, etc.

The survey (Vo Ngoc Phu, & Vo Thi Ngoc Tran, 2018k) has already shown a semi-supervised approach by using the OCHIAI coefficient (OCHCOEFF) for the SEMANA of the MASDS in the SEQENVIR and the PANETENVIR to get 87.5% accuracy of the testing data set, etc.

The authors have already proposed a semi-supervised approach using the YULEQ coefficient and the one-dimensional vectors for the SEMANA of the MASDS in the SEQENVIR and the PANETENVIR to achieved 87.85% accuracy of the TSTDS in English in the study (Vo Ngoc Phu, &Vo Thi Ngoc Tran, 2018l), etc.

The authors of the survey (Vo Ngoc Phu, &Vo Thi Ngoc Tran, 2018m) have already used the binary bits and the opinion lexicons of the Yules Sigma measure (YUSIGMEAS) for the semi-supervised approach of the SEMANA for the LARSDS in the SEQENVIR and the PANETENVIR to have the 89.01% accuracy of the TSTDS, etc.

In the below sub-section "Solutions and Recommendations", we have already displayed the supervised approach as an example of this book chapter by using the KMEANAL and the MULTDVECTs for the SEMANA of the MASDS in the SEQENVIR and the CLOUDDISNS (with the M and the R) to classify the semantics of the 2,000,000 documents of the TSTDS into the positive/the negative polarity according to the 2,000,000 documents of the TRNDS in English. Then, the 85.23% accuracy has been the accuracy of this proposed model, etc.

SOLUTIONS AND RECOMMENDATIONS

In this part of this book chapter, we have already proposed the basic principles as follows:

1. Each sentence has been m words/phrases in English.
2. The maximum number of one sentence has been m_max in English. It has meant that m has been less than m_max or m has been as equal as m_max.
3. Each document has been n sentences in English.
4. The maximum number of one document has been n_max in English. It has meant that n has been less than n_max or n has been as equal as n_max.
5. Each sentence has been transferred into one one-dimensional vector in English. Therefore, the length of the vector has been m. When m has been less than m_max, each element of the vector from m to_max-1 has been 0 (zero).
6. Each document has been transformed into one MULTDVECT in English. Thus, the MULTDVECT has been n rows and m columns. When n has been less than n_max, each element of the MULTDVECT from n to n_max-1 has been 0 (zero vector).
7. We have already transformed all the documents of the TRNDS into the MULTDVECTs in English. In addition, the positive documents of the TRNDS has been transferred into the positive MULTDVECTs, called the positive MULTDVECT group (POSMULTDVECTGR). The negative documents of the TRNDS has been transferred into the negative MULTDVECTs, called the negative MULTDVECT group (NEGMULTDVECTGR).
8. We have already transferred all the documents of the TSTDS into the MULTDVECTs in English.
9. When one MULTDVECT has been classified into the POSMULTDVECTGR, this MULTDVECT has been the positive polarity (corresponding to one document in the TSTDS in English)
10. When one MULTDVECT has been classified into the NEGMULTDVECTGR, this MULTDVECT has been the negative polarity (corresponding to one document in the TSTDS in English)
11. When one MULTDVECT has been classified into neither the NEGMULTDVECTGR nor the POSMULTDVECTGR, this MULTDVECT has been the neutral polarity (corresponding to one document in the TSTDS in English)

There have been the crucial contributions of this proposed approach to the commercial applications and the surveys as follows:

1. The algorithms of the DM and the ML have been applicable to the SEMANA of the natural language processing.
2. This survey has also proved that the scientific research in the different fields can be related in many ways.
3. We have believed that millions of documents in English have been handled for the SEMANA successfully.

4. We have also believed that we can apply the results of this model into the surveys and the commercial applications certainly
5. The SEMANA has been launched in the CLOUDDISNS
6. We have proposed the significant principles in this survey.
7. The SEMANA of the document has been implemented on the documents in English.
8. We have also believed that this proposed model can be applied other languages easily and successfully.
9. The CLOUDDISNS, the M and the R have been used for this supervised model successfully.
10. We have believed that we can apply this proposed model to other parallel systems.
11. This novel survey have already used the M and the R.
12. We have believed that we can apply this proposed study to many different distributed network systems such as a Cloudera system, etc.
13. We have believed that we can apply this proposed work to many different parallel functions such as the M and the R.
14. We have developed the algorithms related to the K-Means algorithm for this survey.

This section has been two parts: the SEMANA for the documents of the TSTDS in the SEQENVIR has been presented in the first part. In the second part, the SEMANA for the documents of the TSTDS in the PANETENVIR has been displayed.

We have been the two groups of the TRNDS as follows: The first group has been the positive documents and the second group has been the negative documents. The first group has been called the positive cluster. The second group has been called the negative cluster.

Moreover, all documents in both the two groups have gone through the segmentation of words, and stop-words removal. Then, they have been transferred into the MULTDMVECTs (vector representation).

The documents of the positive cluster have been transformed into the positive MULTDMVECTs, called POSMULTDVECTGR.

The negative documents of the negative cluster have been transferred into the negative MULTDMVECTs, called NEGMULTDVECTGR.

Thus, the TRNDS has been POSMULTDVECTGR and NEGMULTDVECTGR.

The authors have already presented the vector space modeling (VSM) in the surveys [1-3] on more details.

Each sentence in English has been transferred into the one one-dimensional vector (ONDIMVECT) similar to the VSM [1-3].

Performing the KMEANAL in the SEQENVIR

In Figure 1, the documents of the TSTDS have been transferred to the MULTDVECTs in the SEQENVIR as follows: Each sentence of one document of the TSTDS has been transformed to the ONDIMVECT similar to the VSM [1-3]. Based on this result, each document of the documents of the TSTDS has been transferred to the MULTDVECT.

Then, the positive documents of the TRNDS have been transformed to the positive MULTDVECTs, called POSMULTDVECTGR as follows: Each sentence of one document of the positive documents of the TRNDS has been transferred to the ONDIMVECT similar to the VSM [(Vaibhav Kant Singh, & Vinay Kumar Singh, 2015), (Víctor Carrera-Trejo, &et al, 2015), and (Pascal Soucy, & Guy W. Mineau, 2015)]. According to this result, each document of the positive documents of the TRNDS has been

Figure 1.

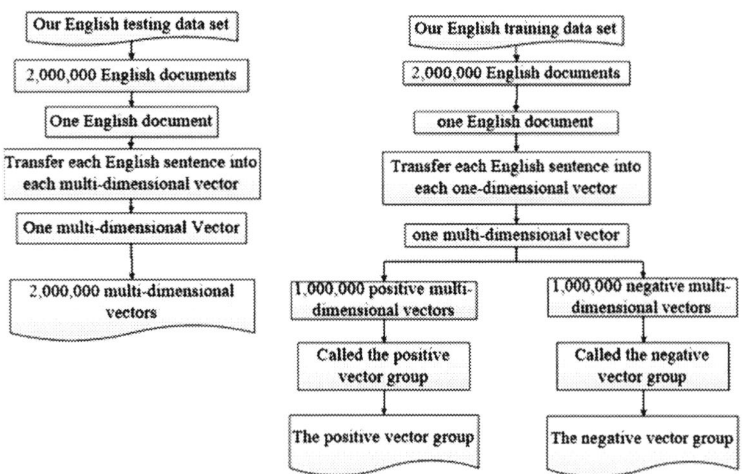

transformed to the MULTDVECT. Based on this results, all the positive documents of the TRNDS have been transferred to the positive MULTDVECTs.

Next, the negative documents of the TRNDS have been transformed to the negative MULTDVECTs, called NEGVMULTDVECTGR as follows: Each sentence of one document of the negative documents of the TRNDS has been transferred to the ONDIMVECT similar to the VSM [(Vaibhav Kant Singh, & Vinay Kumar Singh, 2015), (Víctor Carrera-Trejo, &et al, 2015), and (Pascal Soucy, & Guy W. Mineau, 2015)]. According to this result, each document of the negative documents of the TRNDS has been transformed to the MULTDVECT. Based on this results, all the negative documents of the TRNDS have been transferred to the negative MULTDVECTs.

We have already performed this part in Figure 2: The KMEANAL has been implemented to cluster one MULTDVECT (called A) of the MULTDVECT into the POSMULTDVECTGR or the NEGMULTDVECTGR. When A has been clustered into the POSMULTDVECTGR, the document corresponding to A has been the positive polarity. When A has been clustered into the NEGMULTDVECTGR, the document corresponding to A has been the negative polarity. When A has been clustered into neither the NEGMULTDVECTGR nor the POSMULTDVECTGR, the document corresponding to A has been the neutral polarity.

We have developed the algorithms to perform the KMEANAL in the SEQENVIR.

We have proposed the algorithm 1 to transfer one document into one MULTDVECT. Each document has been separated into the sentences. Each sentence in the sentences has been transferred to one ONDIMVECT based on the VSM [(Vaibhav Kant Singh, & Vinay Kumar Singh, 2015), (Víctor Carrera-Trejo, &et al, 2015), and (Pascal Soucy, & Guy W. Mineau, 2015)] in the SEQENVIR. We have inserted all the ONDIMVECTs of the sentences into one MULTDVECT of one document

Input: One document in English

Output: One MULTDVECT

1. Split the English document into the separate sentences based on "." Or "!" or "?";
2. Each sentence in the n sentences of this document, do repeat:

Figure 2.

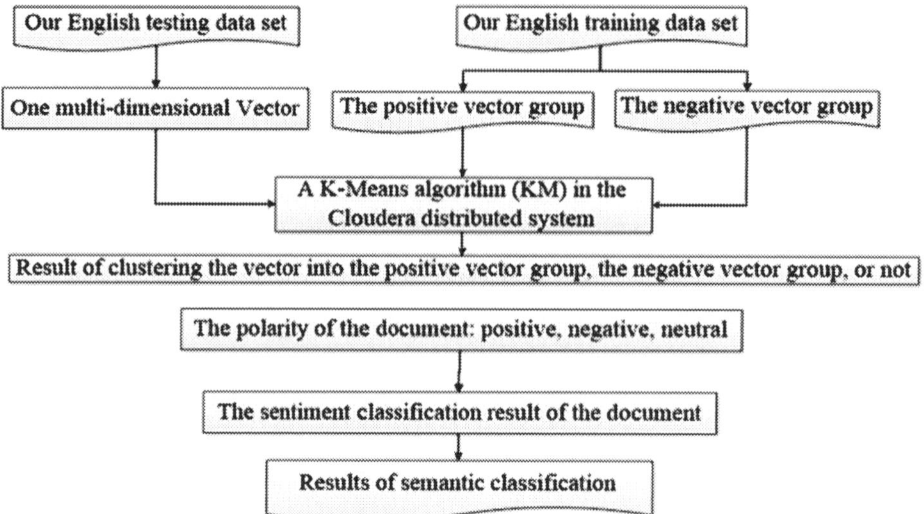

3. Transfer this sentence into one ONDIMVECT based on the VSM [(Vaibhav Kant Singh, & Vinay Kumar Singh, 2015), (Víctor Carrera-Trejo, &et al, 2015), and (Pascal Soucy, & Guy W. Mineau, 2015)];
4. Add the transferred vector into one MULTDVECT;
5. End Repeat – End (2);
6. Return one MULTDVECT;

We have built the algorithm 2 to create the positive vector group – POSMULTDVECTGR: Each document of the positive documents of the TRNDS in English has been separated into the sentences. Each sentence of the document has been transferred to one ONDIMVECT based on the VSM [(Vaibhav Kant Singh, & Vinay Kumar Singh, 2015), (Víctor Carrera-Trejo, &et al, 2015), and (Pascal Soucy, & Guy W. Mineau, 2015)] in the SEQENVIR. We have inserted all the ONDIMVECTs of the sentences of the document into one MULTDVECT of the document. Then, the positive documents of the TRNDS have been transferred to the positive MULTDVECTs.

Input: The positive documents of the TRNDS in English
Output: The positive vector group POSMULTDVECTGR

1. Each document in the positive document of the TRNDS, do repeat:
2. OneMultiDimensionalVector:= Call Algorithm 1 with the positive document in the TRNDS;
3. Add OneMultiDimensionalVector into POSMULTDVECTGR;
4. End Repeat – End (1)
5. Return POSMULTDVECTGR;

We have developed the algorithm 3 to create the negative vector group - NEGMULTDVECTGR. Each document of the negative documents of the TRNDS has been separated into the sentences. Each sentence of the document has been transferred to one ONDIMVECT based on the VSM [(Vaibhav Kant

Singh, & Vinay Kumar Singh, 2015), (Víctor Carrera-Trejo, &et al, 2015), and (Pascal Soucy, & Guy W. Mineau, 2015)] in the SEQENVIR. We have inserted all the ONDIMVECTs of the sentences of the document into one MULTDVECT of the document. Then, the negative documents of the TRNDS have been transferred to the negative MULTDVECTs.

Input: The negative documents of the TRNDS in English

Output: The negative vector group NEGMULTDVECTGR

1. Each document in the negative document of the TRNDS, do repeat:
2. OneMultiDimensionalVector:= Call Algorithm 1 with the negative document of the TRNDS in English;
3. Add OneMultiDimensionalVector into NEGMULTDVECTGR;
4. End Repeat – End (1)
5. Return NEGMULTDVECTGR;

We have proposed the algorithm 4 to cluster a MULTDVECT (of a document of the TSTDS in English) into either the NEGMULTDVECTGR or the POSMULTDVECTGR

Input: One MULTDVECT A (corresponding to one document of the TSTDS in English), the NEGMULTDVECTGR and the POSMULTDVECTGR;

Output: Positive, negative, neutral;

1. Implement the KMEANAL based on the KMEANAL in [(K. Krishna, & M. Narasimha Murty, 1999), (Zhexue Huang, 1998), (Kiri Wagstaff, & et al, 2001), (Anil K. Jain, 2010), (Liping Jing, & et al, 2007), (J.M Peña, & et al, 1999), (B.-H. Juang, & L.R. Rabiner, 1990), (Mu-Chun Su, & Chien-Hsing Chou, 2001), (Alsabti, Khaled; & et al, 1997), (Vance Faber, 1994), (Greg Hamerly, & Charles Elkan, 2002), (Aristidis Likas, & et al, 2003), (J.Z. Huang, & et al, 2005), (Sanghamitra Bandyopadhyay, & Ujjwal Maulik, 2002), and (T. Kanungo, D.M. Mount, & et al, 2002)] with the input has been one MULTDVECT (corresponding to one document of the TSTDS in English), the NEGMULTDVECTGR and the POSMULTDVECTGR;
2. According to the results of (1), If the vector has been clustered into the POSMULTDVECTGR Then Return positive;
3. Else If the vector has been clustered into the NEGMULTDVECTGR Then Return negative;
4. End If – End (2);
5. Return neutral;

The KMEANAL has used the Euclidean measure to calculate the distance of the vector A and the vector B.

Implementing the KMEANAL in the PANETENVIR

In Figure 3, all the documents of the TSTDS and the TRNDS have been transformed into all the MULTDVECTs in the CLOUDDISNS.

We have already transferred the documents of the TRNDS in English into the MULTDVECTs by using the M and the R in the CLOUDDISNS to shorten the execution time of this task.

Figure 3.

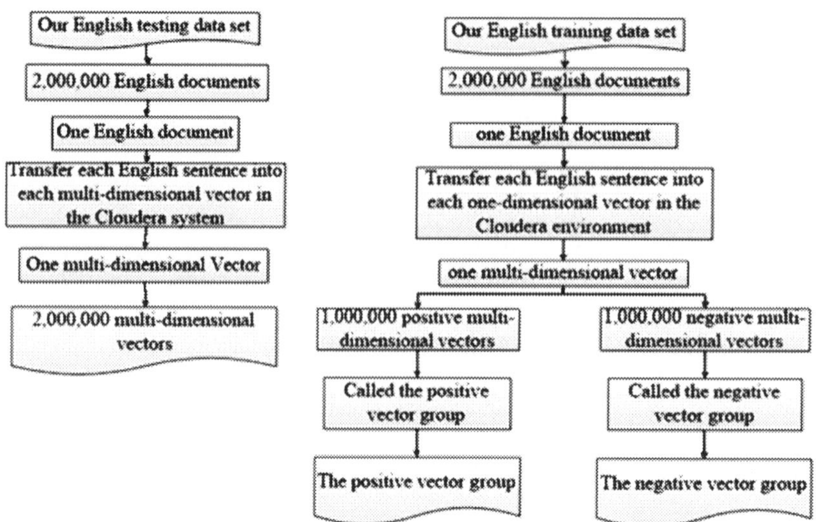

The positive documents of the TRNDS have been transformed into the positive MULTDVECTs in the CLOUDDISNS, called POSMULTDVECTGR.

The negative documents of the TRNDS have been transferred into the negative MULTDVECTs in the CLOUDDISNS, called POSMULTDVECTGR.

In addition, the documents of the TSTDS have been transformed into the MULTDVECTs by using the M and the R in the CLOUDDISNS

We have already performed this section in Figure 4: In the CLOUDDISNS, by using the KMEANAL, one MULTDVECT (called A) of one document of the TSTDS in English has been clustered into either the POSMULTDVECTGR or the NEGMULTDVECTGR. When A has been classified into the POS-

Figure 4.

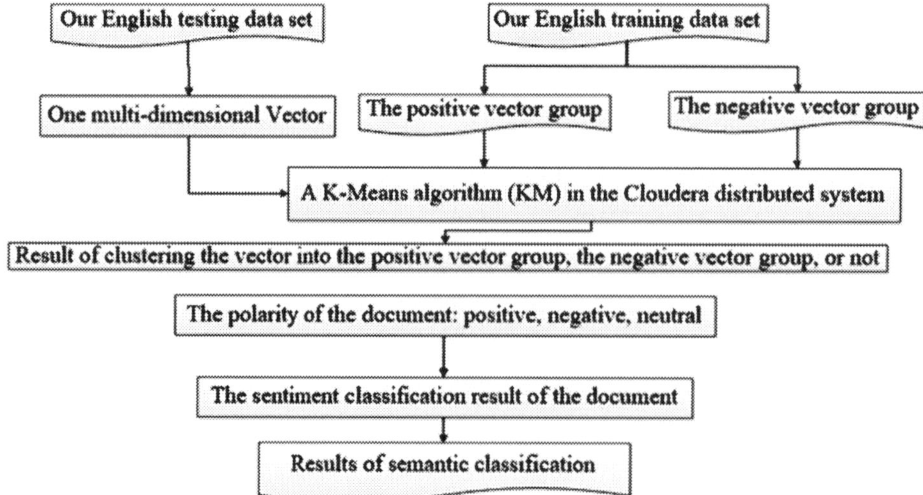

MULTDVECTGR, the document (corresponding to A) has been the positive polarity. When A has been classified into the NEGMULTDVECTGR, the document (corresponding to A) has been the negative polarity. When A has been clustered into neither the NEGMULTDVECTGR nor the POSMULTD-VECTGR, the document (corresponding to A) has been the neutral polarity.

We have already presented the transferring each document t in English into one MULTDVECT in Figure 5 as follows: the M and the R. The input of the M has been one document, and the output of the M has been the components of one ONDIMVECT of a sentence. One document of the input of the M has been separated into the sentences. Each sentence in the sentences in English has been transformed into one ONDIMVECT based on the VSM[(Vaibhav Kant Singh, & Vinay Kumar Singh, 2015), (Víctor Carrera-Trejo, &et al, 2015), and (Pascal Soucy, & Guy W. Mineau, 2015)]. This has been repeated for all the sentences of the document until all the sentences have been transferred into all the ONDIMVECTs of the document. After finishing to transfer each sentence of the document into one ONDIMVECT, the M of the CLOUDDISNS has automatically transferred the ONDIMVECT into the R phase. The input of the R has been the output of the M, and this input has comprised the components (the ONDIMVECTs) of a MULTDVECT. The output of the R has been a MULTDVECT corresponding the document. In the R of the CLOUDDISNS, these ONDIMVECTs have been built into one MULTDVECT.

The documents of the TSTDS in English have been transferred into the MULTDVECTs based on Figure 5.

The KMEANAL in the CLOUDDISNS has been the first main phase and the second main phase: The first phase has been the M in the CLOUDDISNS, and the second phase has been the R in the CLOUDDISNS.

In the M of the CLOUDDISNS, the input has been the MULTDVECT of a document in English (which has been classified), the POSMULTDVECTGR and the NEGMULTDVECTGR. In addition, the output of this phase has been the results of clustering of the MULTDVECT of the document into either the POSMULTDVECTGR or the NEGMULTDVECTGR.

Figure 5.

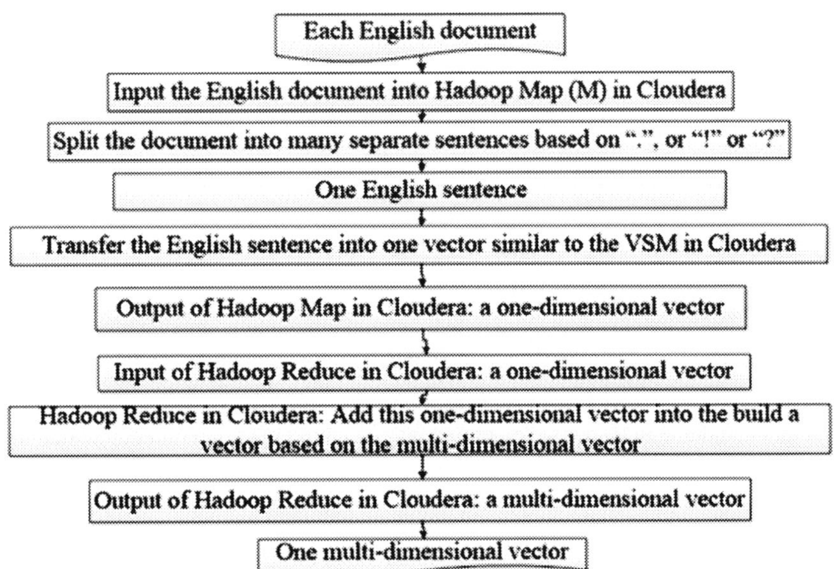

In the R of the CLOUDDISNS, the input has been the output of the M of the CLOUDDISNS, and this input has been the results of clustering of the MULTDVECT of the document into either the POSMULTDVECTGR or the NEGMULTDVECTGR. Furthermore, the output has been the result of the SEMANA of the document into either the POSMULTDVECTGR or the NEGMULTDVECTGR.

In the R, when the MULTDVECT has been clustered into the POSMULTDVECTGR, the document has been classified into the positive emotion. When the MULTDVECT has been clustered into the NEGMULTDVECTGR, the document has been classified into the negative emotion. When the MULTDVECT has been clustered into neither the NEGMULTDVECTGR nor the POSMULTDVECTGR, the document has been classified into the neutral emotion.

The M Phase

We have already performed this phase in Figure 6 as follows: The KMEANAL in the CLOUDDISNS has been based on the KMEANAL of the surveys [(K. Krishna, & M. Narasimha Murty, 1999), (Zhexue Huang, 1998), (Kiri Wagstaff, & et al, 2001), (Anil K. Jain, 2010), (Liping Jing, & et al, 2007), (J.M Peña, & et al, 1999), (B.-H. Juang, & L.R. Rabiner, 1990), (Mu-Chun Su, & Chien-Hsing Chou, 2001), (Alsabti, Khaled; & et al, 1997), (Vance Faber, 1994), (Greg Hamerly, & Charles Elkan, 2002), and (Aristidis Likas, & et al, 2003)]. The input has been one MULTDVECT in the TSTDS, the NEGMULTDVECTGR and the POSMULTDVECTGR of the TRNDS. The output has been the clustering results of the MULTDVECT into either the POSMULTDVECTGR or the NEGMULTDVECTGR

1. Select k centers (centroid) of k clusters randomly. Each cluster has been represented by using the center of this cluster: in this survey, we choose K = 2;
2. Identify the distance of the objects to k centers (using Euclidean measure).
3. Group objects to the closest group
4. Calculate the new center of the clusters.
5. Repeat (step 2) until no change groups of objects.

The KMEANAL has used the Euclidean measure to calculate the distance of the vector A and the vector B

Figure 6.

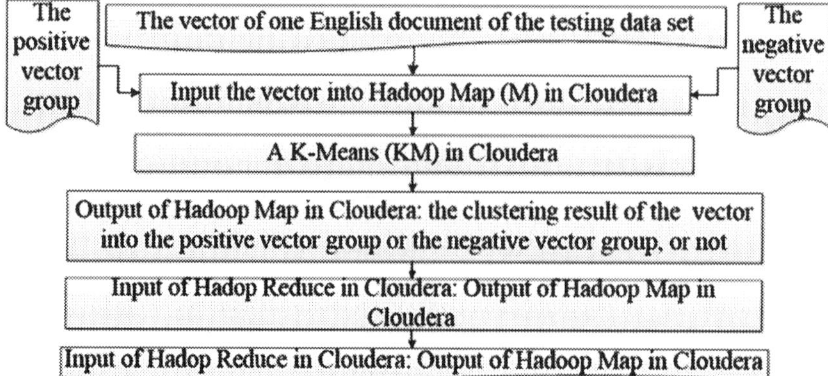

After finishing to cluster the MULTDVECT into either the POSMULTDVECTGR or the NEGMULTDVECTGR, the M has transferred this results into the R in the Cloudera

The R Phase

We have already implemented in Figure 7: After receiving the clustering result of the M, the R has labeled the semantic polarity (positive, negative, or neutral) for the MULTDVECT which has been classified. Then, the output of the R has returned the semantic polarity of one document (corresponding to the MULTDVECT) in the TSTDS in English. When the MULTDVECT has been clustered into the POSMULTDVECTGR, the document has been the positive polarity. When the MULTDVECT has been clustered into the NEGMULTDVECTGR, the document has been the negative polarity. When the MULTDVECT has been clustered into neither the NEGMULTDVECTGR nor the POSMULTDVECTGR, the document has been the neutral polarity.

An Accuracy (A) measure has already been used to identify the accuracy of the results of the SEMANA.

The Java language (JAVAPL) has been used for programming to save the data sets, and performing our proposed survey to classify the documents of the TSTDS.

The SEQENVIR in this research has included 1 node (1 server). The JAVAPL has been used in programming the KMEANAL.

The SEQENVIR has been the configuration as follows: Intel® Server Board S1200V3RPS, Intel® Pentium® Processor G3220 (3M Cache, 3.00 GHz), 2GB PC3-10600 ECC 1333 MHz LP Unbuffered DIMMs. The server has been the operating system as follows: Cloudera system.

We have performed the KMEANAL in the CLOUDDISNS. This Cloudera system has included 9 nodes (9 servers). The JAVAPL has been in programming the application of the KMEANAL in the CLOUDDISNS.

Each server has been the configuration in the CLOUDDISNS as follows: Intel® Server Board S1200V3RPS, Intel® Pentium® Processor G3220 (3M Cache, 3.00 GHz), 2GB PC3-10600 ECC 1333

Figure 7.

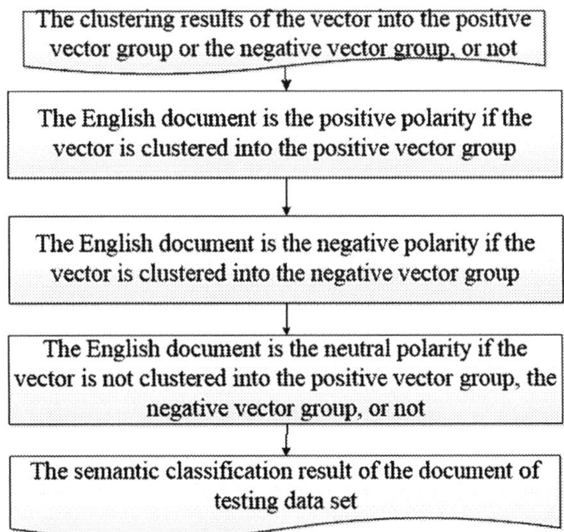

MHz LP Unbuffered DIMMs. Each server in the 9 servers has been the operating system as follows: Cloudera system. All the 9 nodes have been the same configuration.

We have presented the results of the SEMANA of the documents of the TSTDS in English in Table 1.

We have already displayed the accuracy of the SEMANA of the documents of the TSTDS in Table 2

In Table 3, we have already displayed the average execution time of the SEMANA of our new model for the documents of the TSTDS in English.

Although we have tested this novel survey on our TSTDS in English, we can apply it to other languages. In this book chapter, our study has been tested on the 2,000,000 English documents of the TSTDS. However, we can apply our model to many large-scale data sets with millions of the documents in English in the shortest time.

In this work, a new model has been developed to classify the sentiments of English documents using the KMEANAL with the M and the R in the CLOUDDISNS. With our proposed novel survey, we have already achieved 85.23% accuracy of the TSTDS.

We have been the information of the average execution times in Table 3 as follows:

1. The average execution time of the SEMANA of this novel model in the SEQENVIR has been 11,011,096 /2,000,000 documents in English, and it has been greater than the execution time of the SEMANA of this proposed model in the CLOUDDISNS – 3 nodes which has been 3,578,369 seconds /1,000,000 English documents.

Table 1. The results of the SEMANA of the documents of the TSTDS in English

	Testing Dataset	Correct Classification	Incorrect Classification
Negative	1,000,000	844,299	155,701
Positive	1,000,000	860,301	139,699
Summary	2,000,000	1,704,600	295,400

Table 2. The accuracy of the SEMANA of the documents of the TSTDS

Proposed Model	Class	Accuracy
Our new model	Negative	85.23%
	Positive	

Table 3. The average execution time of the SEMANA of our new model for the documents of the TSTDS in English

	The average execution time of the classification /2,000,000 English documents.
The novel model in the SEQENVIR	11,011,096 seconds
The novel model in the CLOUDDISNS – 3 nodes	3,578,369 seconds
The novel model in the CLOUDDISNS – 6 nodes	1,843,982 seconds
The novel model in the CLOUDDISNS – 9 nodes	1,243,455 seconds

2. The average execution time of the SEMANA of this novel approach in the CLOUDDISNS – 9 nodes has been the shortest time and it has been 1,243,455 seconds /1,000,000 English documents
3. The average execution time of the SEMANA of this proposed approach in the CLOUDDISNS – 6 nodes has been 1,843,982 seconds /1,000,000 English documents

The accuracy of the proposed model has been dependent on the factors as follows:

1. The algorithms related to the KMEANAL
2. The TSTDS and the TRNDS
3. The documents of the TSTDS and the TRNDS must be standardized carefully.
4. Transferring one document into one MULTDVECT
5. etc.

The execution time of the proposed model has been dependent on the factors as follows:

1. The parallel network environment such as the Cloudera system.
2. The distributed functions such as Hadoop Map (M) and Hadoop Reduce (R).
3. The algorithms related to the KMEANAL
4. The performance of the distributed network system.
5. The number of nodes of the parallel network environment.
6. The performance of each node (each server) of the distributed environment.
7. The sizes of the TSTDS and the TRNDS
8. Transferring one document into one MULTDVECT
9. etc.

We have been the advantages and disadvantages of this novel model as follows:

1. There have been the advantages as follows: It has used the KMEANAL to classify the semantics of the documents of the TSTDS according to the documents of the TRNDS. This survey can be implemented in many parallel network systems. We can apply it to other languages.
2. There have been the disadvantages as follows: It has been a low rate of the accuracy. We have already spent too much cost, and spent too much time to perform this novel model successfully.

FUTURE RESEARCH DIRECTIONS

From those results of this novel model and according to the above proofs, we are going to study this model for applying to billions of English documents in both the SE and the PNE. In addition, we are also going to research this approach for being performed in the PNE with over 50 nodes. Furthermore, the accuracy of this new computational model can be studied to improve certainly.

From the results of this chapter, many algorithms, methods, models, and etc. are going to be developed more and more for handling the massive data sets fully in the near future.

CONCLUSION

In this chapter, we have shown the possible novel computational models for the big data sets of the semantic analysis successfully on more details.

We have also presented a novel model using the KMEANAL for the big data opinion analysis in both the SS and PNE.

These models can be performed in the sequential system or the parallel environment fully.

These models have been divided into the 3 categories: supervised learning; semi-supervised learning; and un-supervised learning.

There can be many models for the large-scale data sets, which have not been presented in this chapter yet.

In the near future, many novel computational models are going to be developed more and more for the massive data sets. This is very significant for many organizations, economies, governments, countries, commercial applications, researches, and etc. in the world.

ABBREVIATIONS

Natural language processing: NLP
semantic analysis: SEMANA
big data sets: BIGDSs
large-scale data sets: LARSDSs
massive data sets: MASDSs
natural language processing: NLP
machine learning: ML
data mining: DM
artificial intelligence: AI
expert systems: ES
Yahoo search engine: YSE
supervised learning: SUPLEARN
semi-supervised learning: SESUPLEARN
un-supervised learning: UNSUPLEARN
testing data set: TSTDS
training data set: TRNDS
sequential environments: SEQENVIRs
parallel network environments: PANETENVIRs
Cloudera distributed network system: CLOUDDISNS
Hadoop Map: M
Hadoop Reduce: R
K-Means algorithm: KMEANAL
multi-dimensional vectors: MULTDVECTs
vector space model: VSM
Johnson measure: JOHNSM

Google search engine: GOOGSE
AND operator and OR operator: ANDOROPs
Kuhns-II Coefficient: KUHS_II_CO
Yule-II coefficient: YIICOEFF
Self-Organizing Map algorithm: SELFOM
Gower-2 Coefficient: HA
Genetic Algorithm: GA
Fitness proportionate Selection: FPS
Latent Semantic Analysis: LatentSA
Dennis Coefficient: DennisCOEFF
Fager & MacGowan Coefficient: FAMACC
Genetic Algorithm: GEAL
Rank Selection: RASE
Co-Training algorithm: COTRAL
Fuzzy C-Means algorithm: FUZZCM
Otsuka coefficient: OTCOEFF
Yules Sigma measure: YUSIGMEAS
positive MULTDVECT group: POSMULTDVECTGR
negative MULTDVECT group: NEGMULTDVECTGR
one-dimensional vector: ONDIMVECT
Java programming language: JAVAPL

ACKNOWLEDGMENT

This book chapter is funded by Institute of Research and Development, Duy Tan University-DTU, Da Nang, Vietnam

REFERENCES

Alsabti, K., Ranka, S., & Singh, V. (1997). An efficient k-means clustering algorithm. *Electrical Engineering and Computer Science*, *43*. Retrieved from http://surface.syr.edu/eecs/43

Apache. (2017). Retrieved from http://apache.org

Bandyopadhyay, S., & Maulik, U. (2002). An evolutionary technique based on K-Means algorithm for optimal clustering in RN. *Information Sciences*, *146*(1–4), 221–237. doi:10.1016/S0020-0255(02)00208-6

Carrera-Trejo, V., Sidorov, G., Miranda-Jiménez, S., Ibarra, M. M., & Martínez, R. C. (2015). Latent Dirichlet Allocation complement in the vector space model for Multi-Label Text Classification. *International Journal of Combinatorial Optimization Problems and Informatics*, *6*(1), 7–19.

Cloudera. (2017). Retrieved from http://www.cloudera.com

Dat, N. D., Phu, V. N., Vo, T. N. C., Vo, T. N. T., & Nguyen, T. A. (2017). STING Algorithm used English Sentiment Classification in A Parallel Environment. International Journal of Pattern Recognition and Artificial Intelligence, 31(7). doi:10.1142/S0218001417500215

Faber. (1994). Clustering and the Continuous k-Means Algorithm. *Los Alamos Science, 22*.

Hadoop. (2017). Retrieved from http://hadoop.apache.org

Hamerly, G., & Elkan, C. (2002). Alternatives to the k-means algorithm that find better clusterings. *CIKM '02 Proceedings of the eleventh international conference on Information and knowledge management*, 600-607.

Huang, Ng, Rong, & Li. (2005). Automated variable weighting in k-means type clustering. *IEEE Transactions on Pattern Analysis and Machine Intelligence, 27*(5). Doi:10.1109/TPAMI.2005.95

Huang, Z. (1998). Extensions to the k-Means Algorithm for Clustering Large Data Sets with Categorical Values. *Data Mining and Knowledge Discovery*, *2*(3), 283–304. doi:10.1023/A:1009769707641

Jain, A. K. (2010). Data clustering: 50 years beyond K-means. *Pattern Recognition Letters*, *31*(8), 651–666. doi:10.1016/j.patrec.2009.09.011

Jing, Ng, & Huang. (2007). An Entropy Weighting k-Means Algorithm for Subspace Clustering of High-Dimensional Sparse Data. *IEEE Transactions on Knowledge and Data Engineering*, *19*(8). Doi:10.1109/TKDE.2007.1048

Juang & Rabiner. (1990). The segmental K-means algorithm for estimating parameters of hidden Markov models. *IEEE Transactions on Acoustics, Speech, and Signal Processing*, *38*(9). Doi:10.1109/29.60082

Kanungo, Mount, Netanyahu, Piatko, Silverman, & Wu. (2002). An efficient k-means clustering algorithm: analysis and implementation. *IEEE Transactions on Pattern Analysis and Machine Intelligence*, *24*(7). Doi:10.1109/TPAMI.2002.1017616

Krishna, & Narasimha Murty. (1999). Genetic K-means algorithm. *IEEE Transactions on Systems, Man, and Cybernetics, Part B (Cybernetics)*, *29*(3). Doi:10.1109/3477.764879

Likas, A., Vlassis, N., & Verbeek, J. J. (2003). The global k-means clustering algorithm. *Pattern Recognition*, *36*(2), 451–461. doi:10.1016/S0031-3203(02)00060-2

Peña, J. M., Lozano, J. A., & Larrañaga, P. (1999). An empirical comparison of four initialization methods for the K-Means algorithm. *Pattern Recognition Letters*, *20*(10), 1027–1040. doi:10.1016/S0167-8655(99)00069-0

Phu, V. N., Dat, N. D., Vo, T. N. T., Vo, T. N. C., & Nguyen, T. A. (2017f). Fuzzy C-means for english sentiment classification in a distributed system. *International Journal of Applied Intelligence*, *46*(3), 717–738. doi:10.100710489-016-0858-z

Phu, V. N., Vo, T. N. C., Dat, N. D., Vo, T. N. T., & Nguyen, T. A. (2017b). A Valences-Totaling Model for English Sentiment Classification. International Journal of Knowledge and Information Systems. doi:10.100710115-017-1054-0

Phu, V. N., Vo, T. N. C., & Vo, T. N. T. (2017c). Shifting Semantic Values of English Phrases for Classification. International Journal of Speech Technology. doi:10.1007/S13772-017-9420-6

Phu, V. N., Vo, T. N. C., & Vo, T. N. T. (2017g). *SVM for English Semantic Classification in Parallel Environment. International Journal of Speech Technology*. doi:10.100710772-017-9421-5

Phu, V. N., Vo, T. N. C., Vo, T. N. T., & Dat, N. D. (2017a). A Vietnamese adjective emotion dictionary based on exploitation of Vietnamese language characteristics. International Journal of Artificial Intelligence Review. doi:10.1007/S13462-017-9538-6

Phu, V. N., Vo, T. N. C., Vo, T. N. T., Dat, N. D., & Khanh, L. D. D. (2017d). A Valence-Totaling Model for Vietnamese Sentiment Classification. International Journal of Evolving Systems. doi:10.100712530-017-9187-7

Phu, V. N., Vo, T. N. C., Vo, T. N. T., Dat, N. D., & Khanh, L. D. D. (2017e). Semantic Lexicons of English Nouns for Classification. International Journal of Evolving Systems. doi:10.100712530-017-9188-6

Phu, V. N., & Vo, T. N. T. (2017a). English Sentiment Classification using Only the Sentiment Lexicons with a JOHNSON Coefficient in a Parallel Network Environment. American Journal of Engineering and Applied Sciences. doi:10.3844/ajeassp.2017

Phu, V. N., & Vo, T. N. T. (2017b). A STING Algorithm and Multi-dimensional Vectors Used for English Sentiment Classification in a Distributed System. American Journal of Engineering and Applied Sciences. doi:10.3844/ajeassp.2017

Phu, V. N., & Vo, T. N. T. (2018a). Sentiment Classification using The Sentiment Scores Of Lexicons Based on A Kuhns-II Coefficient in English. International Journal of Tomography & Simulation, 31(3).

Phu, V. N., & Vo, T. N. T. (2018b). The Multi-dimensional Vectors and An Yule-II Measure Used for A Self-Organizing Map Algorithm of English Sentiment Classification in A Distributed Environment. *Journal of Theoretical and Applied Information Technology*, *96*(10).

Phu, V. N., & Vo, T. N. T. (2018c). English Sentiment Classification using A Gower-2 Coefficient and A Genetic Algorithm with A Fitness-proportionate Selection in a Parallel Network Environment. *Journal of Theoretical and Applied Information Technology*, *96*(4), 1-50.

Phu, V. N., & Vo, T. N. T. (2018d). Latent Semantic Analysis using A Dennis Coefficient for English Sentiment Classification in A Parallel System. *International Journal of Computers, Communications and Control*, *13*(3), 390-410.

Phu, V. N., & Vo, T. N. T. (2018e). English sentiment classification using a Fager & MacGowan coefficient and a genetic algorithm with a rank selection in a parallel network environment. *International Journal of Computer Modelling and New Technologies*, *22*(1), 57-112.

Phu, V. N., & Vo, T. N. T. (2018f). English Sentiment Classification using A BIRCH Algorithm and The Sentiment Lexicons-Based One-dimentional Vectors in a Parallel Network Environment. *International Journal of Computer Modelling and New Technologies*, *22*(1).

Phu, V. N., & Vo, T. N. T. (2018g). A Fuzzy C-Means Algorithm and Sentiment-Lexicons-based Multi-dimensional Vectors Of A SOKAL & SNEATH-IV Coefficient Used For English Sentiment Classification. *International Journal of Theoretical and Applied Information Technology*, *96*(10).

Phu, V. N., & Vo, T. N. T. (2018h). The Bag-Of-Words Vectors And A Sokal & Sneath-Iv Coefficient Used For A K-Means Algorithm Of English Sentiment Classification In A Parallel System. *Journal of Theoretical and Applied Information Technology*, *96*(15), 1-30.

Phu, V. N., & Vo, T. N. T. (2018i). A Co-Training Model Using A Fuzzy C-Means Algorithm, A K-Means Algorithm And The Sentiment Lexicons - Based Multi-Dimensional Vectors Of An Otsuka Coefficient For English Sentiment Classification. *Journal of Theoretical and Applied Information Technology*, *96*(15), 1-29.

Phu, V. N., & Vo, T. N. T. (2018j). A Self-Training - Based Model using A K-NN Algorithm and The Sentiment Lexicons - Based Multi-dimensional Vectors of A S6 coefficient for Sentiment Classification. *International Journal of Theoretical and Applied Information Technology*, *96*(10).

Phu, V. N., & Vo, T. N. T. (2018k). English Sentiment Classification using An Ochiai similarity measure and The One-dimensional Vectors in a Parallel Network Environment. International Journal of Tomography & Simulation, 31(3).

Phu, V. N., & Vo, T. N. T. (2018l). English Sentiment Classification using An YULEQ similarity measure and The One-dimensional Vectors in a Parallel Network Environment. *Journal of Theoretical and Applied Information Technology*, *6*(11).

Phu, V. N., & Vo, T. N. T. (2018m). The Binary Bits And The Sentiment Lexicons Based On An Yules Sigma Coefficient Used For Sentiment Classification In English. *Journal of Theoretical and Applied Information Technology*, 96(15), 1-36.

Phu, V. N., Vo, T. N. T., & Max, J. (2018). A CURE Algorithm for Vietnamese Sentiment Classification in a Parallel Environment. *International Journal of Computer Science*. Retrieved from http://thescipub.com/abstract/10.3844/ofsp.11906

Singh & Singh. (2015). Vector Space Model: An Information Retrieval System. *Int. J. Adv. Engg. Res. Studies, 4*(2), 141-143.

Soucy, P., & Mineau, G. W. (2015). Beyond TFIDF Weighting for Text Categorization in the Vector Space Model. *Proceedings of the 19th International Joint Conference on Artificial Intelligence*, 1130-1135.

Su & Chou. (2001). A modified version of the K-means algorithm with a distance based on cluster symmetry. *IEEE Transactions on Pattern Analysis and Machine Intelligence*, *23*(6). Doi:10.1109/34.927466

Wagstaff, K., Cardie, C., Rogers, S., & Schroedl, S. (2001). Constrained K-means Clustering with Background Knowledge. *Proceedings of the Eighteenth International Conference on Machine Learning*, 577-584.

Chapter 8
IoT Big Data Architectures, Approaches, and Challenges: A Fog-Cloud Approach

David Sarabia-Jácome
Universitat Politècnica de València (UPV), Spain

Regel Gonzalez-Usach
Universitat Politècnica de València (UPV), Spain

Carlos E. Palau
Universitat Politècnica de València (UPV), Spain

ABSTRACT

The internet of things (IoT) generates large amounts of data that are sent to the cloud to be stored, processed, and analyzed to extract useful information. However, the cloud-based big data analytics approach is not completely appropriate for the analysis of IoT data sources, and presents some issues and limitations, such as inherent delay, late response, and high bandwidth occupancy. Fog computing emerges as a possible solution to address these cloud limitations by extending cloud computing capabilities at the network edge (i.e., gateways, switches), close to the IoT devices. This chapter presents a comprehensive overview of IoT big data analytics architectures, approaches, and solutions. Particularly, the fog-cloud reference architecture is proposed as the best approach for performing big data analytics in IoT ecosystems. Moreover, the benefits of the fog-cloud approach are analyzed in two IoT application case studies. Finally, fog-cloud open research challenges are described, providing some guidelines to researchers and application developers to address fog-cloud limitations.

INTRODUCTION

The accelerated growth of the Internet of Things (IoT) ecosystems will generate considerably even larger amounts of information in the short-term future. The analysis of IoT data sources brings enormous benefits in the wide range of application areas that IoT covers (e.g. transport and logistics, health, intelligent environments, industries, and smart cities, among many others). IoT is providing many benefits in

DOI: 10.4018/978-1-5225-7432-3.ch008

our well-being, industry and in our economy. But in order to obtain these benefits, IoT data need to be stored, processed, and analyzed. Due to the specific characteristics of data generated from IoT systems, these steps represent a difficult challenge in terms data analysis processing to find patterns, trends, or valuable information. Data sent by sound sensors, video cameras, motion sensors, temperature gauges, and other types of sensing devices describe the wide variety of IoT data sources with different formats and structures.

This heterogeneity represents an important challenge for its analysis, as far as it makes difficult data integration and the extraction of useful information. In addition, the rapid generation of these data flows in real-time exceeds the maximum storage and processing capacity of different kind of applications. For example, audio and video applications produce a very high volume of data per user. If additionally, those applications are deployed on a large scale, the very large volume of data generated cannot be supported by conventional systems. Additionally, other aspects of the data from IoT systems make necessary special management and processing functionality not supported by traditional systems. For these reasons, specific technologies suitable for big data analysis are required for handling IoT data (Chen, Mao, Zhang, & Leung, 2014).

Cloud computing is a technology capable of appropriately handling IoT data storage and processing, as far as it is adequate for big data management. This powerful technology offers resources for complex and large-scale computing hosted on the Internet. Those online resources are provided on-demand and have a secure and easy access. Moreover, cloud computing has technical advantages such as energy efficiency, optimization of resource utilization, elasticity, and flexibility. All these benefits are possible thanks to infrastructure virtualization and distributed computing that enable flexibility, scalability, high availability, and security.

Cloud computing is a fully mature technology that accomplishes the requirements to provide big data storage and analysis. However, it presents some issues handing IoT big data. As far as resources are hosted on the Internet, there is an additional delay caused by the propagation time of data across the network. Many IoT systems are very time-sensitive and require responses in real-time, so this latency can be excessive. Also, IoT big data may overload the network capacity, causing indirectly a poor cloud analysis service and higher delay. For this reason, Cisco, in 2012, introduced the fog computing concept to solve the limitations of an interconnection between IoT and cloud computing. Fog computing is a paradigm that provides distributed computing, storage, and network services using virtualization and non-virtualization technologies in between devices and cloud computing (Bonomi, Milito, Zhu, & Addepalli, 2012). To do this, fog computing places part of this capabilities closer to where the data is generated. In this way, this technology solves the disadvantages of using a centralized infrastructure generally distant from the IoT system. Fog computing allows the creation of geographically distributed services, since it is highly distributed paradigm (Aazam & Huh, 2014). Furthermore, fog computing is capable of performing an efficient IoT data management streaming. Also, it permits the reduction of latency and bandwidth occupation, along with efficient data storage.

This chapter provides an overview of big data architectures, approaches, and solutions for IoT applications.

- First, the chapter offers an overview of IoT as a big data source, describing IoT data characteristics and the specific requirements of its analysis; and the most important big data architectures, Lambda and Kappa, are briefly explained. Also, their role in IoT uses cases is discussed.

- Second, cloud computing is analyzed as a supporting technology for covering IoT data requirements. This analysis describes an IoT cloud computing reference architecture and the advantages and disadvantages of this approach.
- Next, fog computing is discussed as a solution to overcome cloud computing limitations for the IoT big data analysis. Also, a fog-cloud approach architecture is proposed as a reference to facilitate new research case studies, services, and applications development. This architecture is examined in two IoT use cases (smart city and smart health), providing solutions to technical obstacles and discussing possible difficulties in the achievement of IoT applications development.
- Finally, challenges and advances in fog computing are detailed to encourage future research along certain lines.

BACKGROUND

IoT as big data source generates many challenges and opportunities for researchers and application developers. Big data from multiple sources provides new opportunities to improve predictive models for developing innovative services. However, a proper management of IoT data is a challenging task due to IoT data requires particular requirements for its processing and exploitation through big data analytics. These requirements are related to IoT data volume, velocity, and variety. First, sensors and other smart devices generate large amounts of data. In concord with the Cisco report, IoT devices would generate 847 ZB per year by 2021—up from 218 ZB per year in 2016 (Cisco, 2018). New strategies for the storage and management of this large data volume are needed. Relational database systems are not capable of supporting the large volume of IoT data, and do not present robustness and scalability. Thus, non-relational database systems are the best option to cover these limitations, providing a distributed environment.

Second, sensors typically take measurements with a very high frequency – so high volume of data is generated in a very short time. An appropriate management of IoT data, one considering this velocity feature, enables real-time services for improving decision making. Currently, IoT systems incorporate Complex Event Processors (CEP) that analyze events and find patterns in real-time to allow a fast reaction. Unfortunately, though, CEPs are not scalable and are not efficient in large-scale systems; so distributed real-time systems are one of the best options for deploying large-scale applications and services. Thus, due to the IoT data velocity requirement, it is also necessary to use distributed real-time processing systems that provide scalability, flexibility and low latency.

Finally, regarding the aforementioned variety feature, IoT data are represented in very different formats that do not follow a specific structure. There are many formats used by the IoT platforms to represent the data models. For example, some IoT platforms use JSON (JavaScript Object Notation) files to store the data collected by the sensors; while others platforms use formats such as CSV (Comma-separated values), XML (eXtensible Markup Language), or RDF (Resource Description Framework). Also, IoT data can be semi-structured or unstructured (in some cases). Semi-structured IoT data does not follow an implicit structure; but it does present an internal organization that facilitates processing and analysis (Chen et al., 2014). Since this variety of formats in IoT data sources, the integration of this data becomes a very challenger task. This data integration is a very convenient step in big data analytics. Over-all, the data analysis from several sources provides better and more precise data mining models to extract value—more so than does the use of a single one. Furthermore, from a semantic perspective, IoT data format variety also requires mechanisms that allow for the creation of a unified data model designed to integrate data from different sources without changing the meaning of this data and metadata.

In short, IoT data volume, velocity, and variety must be considered for the design of a scalable, flexible, available, and secure data analysis architecture.

Big Data Traditional Architectures

There are two main reference architectures in the context of big data: Lambda and Kappa. The majority of system architectures for big data applications are based on one of them. Both architectures were designed to provide fault tolerance, distributed processing, and scalability. The Lambda architecture was designed by Nathan Marz to enhance Twitter systems. In a similar way, the Kappa architecture was designed by Jay Kreps to support the data generated on LinkedIn.

Lambda Architecture

The Lambda architecture is divided into a batch layer, a speed layer, and a serving layer. The batch layer performs immutable data storage tasks and processes those data (e.g. data stored in a NoSQL No Structured Query Language database is processed using batch processing platforms such as Hadoop). Results are provided as data views. The serving layer stores batch processed data results and allows to query them. For accomplishing these functions, the serving layer must be implemented on a distributed database system. The speed layer tries to compensate the latency caused by batch processing. To do so, the speed layer executes a fast processing of incoming data and updates incrementally the batch processing layer results. In this case, the real-time processing does not reprocess all the data, but only the data recently received. The Lambda architecture considers the volume characteristics through the use of batch layer and velocity by using the speed layer, while the variety is analyzed through the use of ETL (Extraction Transformation and Load) tools that are widely used in data warehouse applications (Marz & Warren, 2015).

Kappa Architecture

The Kappa architecture, unlike Lambda, has no batch processing layer. To overcome this limitation, data go through the streaming processing rapidly (Uesugi, 2014). In this way, it is necessary the use of brokers such as Kafka to send this data, as they act as data buffers, storing for a short time the data before to be injected into a streaming processing platform. The processed data is stored in a database in the service layer. Applications will connect to this database to access data through specific queries. Data is reprocessed periodically to update data results. The data stored in the Kafka buffer will be used to reprocess the data, and the results will be stored in a new table for use by applications and services ingestion. The process is repeated often, avoiding the creation of a batch processing layer. The main disadvantage is the huge growth of databases' tables due to the reprocessing task (Kreps, 2014).

Overview of Both Architectures

Both architectures have emerged to solve the processing of big amounts of data generated by social networks; and they fit big data application requirements in any domain (e.g. retail; web searching) very well. The ability of the Lambda architecture to process data in real time and in batches is an advantage for data exploitation in general. On the other hand, the Kappa architecture is more appropriate for real-time applications. Both architectures address massive data processing in different ways—providing the scalability, high availability, reliability, and security required in big data processing. Between them, the Lambda architecture is considered the best option as a reference in the IoT big data architecture design, due to its flexibility and a better support for data processing. The batch layer can be used to train machine learning models using raw data, while the additional real-time processing layer supports the high frequency with which the data is generated in IoT. Lambda is a reference architecture in IoT-big data design; but this architecture does not fully adapt to all IoT requirements.

CLOUD COMPUTING APPROACH

Cloud computing in combination with big data can provide a suitable data management for many reasons. First, traditional infrastructures for data storage, processing, and analysis are not suitable for big data management, as their resources are insufficient for handling massive amount of data. By contrast, cloud computing provides almost unlimited capabilities and resources for big data storage and management. The cloud computing service models (IaaS Infrastructure as a Service, PaaS Platform as a Service, and SaaS Software as a Service) are capable of enabling integration with big data platforms. Companies such as Google, Microsoft, Amazon, and Cloudera provide Big Data platforms as a Service (BDaaS) in their cloud computing infrastructures (Hashem et al., 2015). Thus, programming models of theirs, such as Google MapReduce, can take advantage of cloud computing. For example, in-memory computing has optimized data processing to properly handle big data velocity. Thus, cloud computing and big data platforms have intrinsic characteristics that benefit data storage, processing, and analysis to obtain valuable insights.

The existence of big data sources from IoT is relatively recent. For this reason, many of the existent cloud computing service models must be adapted to support IoT big data. Integration of IoT with cloud computing can solve IoT limitations to store, process and analyze data. This integration has created the Cloud of Things (CoT) paradigm (Aazam, Khan, Alsaffar, & Huh, 2014). Also, new cloud computing services must be generated to manage IoT. One example of them is Sensing as a Service (SenaaS), this service model takes advantage of cloud computing capabilities to store IoT data and publish it for the owner of the IoT data to achieve economic benefits (Zaslavsky, Perera, & Georgakopoulos, 2012). For example, a temperature sensor in a house can collect and store data in the cloud; and these data can be sold to an air conditioner manufacturer for improving their product's performance. The cloud computing potential is evident to solve the IoT storage and processing limitations.

The following subsections detail a general cloud-based architecture and the CoT solutions overview. Finally, the architectural approach issues are described.

Cloud-Based Reference Architecture

The extraction of information from IoT is a challenger task due to some particular features of IoT data (velocity, variety, and volume). Cloud-based architectures must be designed taking into account these IoT data characteristics. These IoT requirements will vary depending on the application and the specific IoT sources. Thus, the requirements will be unique to each application. For example, low latency in health applications is essential to detect risk situations in people's health and to react in time to save lives. In addition to increase the complexity of the IoT big data analysis, in IoT systems, sensors employed differ between applications. One IoT feature is the enormous heterogeneity of wireless technologies, communication protocols, sensors, and platforms. Moreover, another aspect to consider is the appropriate type of processing that collected data requires. The batch processing and the stream processing are suitable for management the data volume and velocity, respectively. In brief, the IoT architecture design must consider aspects such as connectivity, processing, storage, and service (depending on the application). Cloud-based IoT big data architectures are constituted by three levels, the perception level, network level, and the applications and services level, as is shown in Figure 1.

Perception Level

This level is responsible for taking sensor measurements, for converting the measurements into data and for sending the data collected to the network level. At the perception level, the sensors and embedded systems that compose it send data using protocols (e.g. CoAP (Constrained Application Protocol); MQTT (Message Queue Telemetry Transport)) and low-power wireless technologies (e.g. ZigBee; Bluetooth) or via other technologies such as Wi-Fi (Wireless Fidelity). An IoT gateway ensures connectivity of the smart devices to the Internet. Also, the IoT gateway performs a formatting task to place data in a pre-established model to be sent to the cloud layer.

Network Level

This level is responsible for the interconnection of sensors with the Internet (typically through a smart gateway), and the transmission of the sensor data information through the network, to the cloud service (at the application and the service level). This level uses wired (fiber; copper) or wireless Internet access

Figure 1. Cloud computing reference architecture

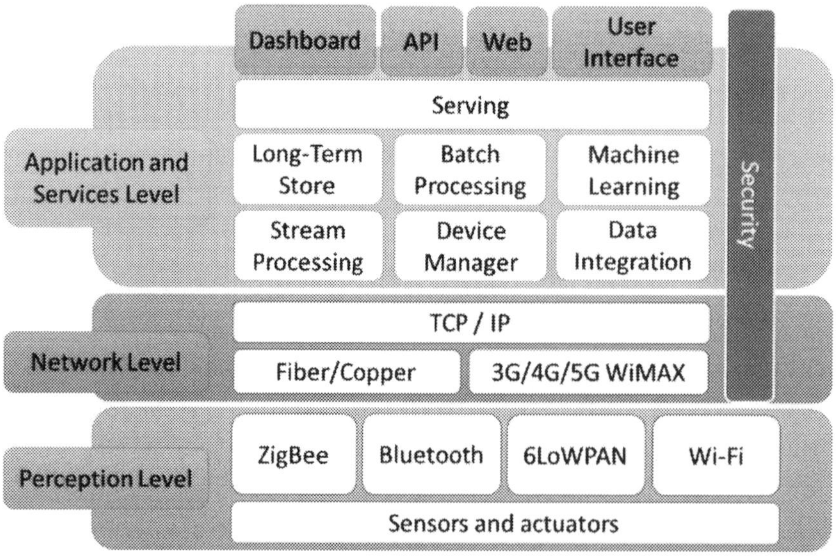

technologies (3G, 4G, 5G; WiMAX; etc.) to send data to the next level. Data is encapsulated and routed using TCP/IP protocols and routing protocols. An appropriate quality of service of the network (QoS) ensures that data is received in the application and services level, in which it will be stored.

Application and Services Level

Finally, the application and services level allows for the storing, processing, and analyzing of data to generate services to end users. This level is implemented in a cloud computing infrastructure and employs a Lambda-based big data analytics architecture. This architecture is divided into batch, speed, and serving layer. Each layer implements the modules as follows:

- **Long-Term-Store Module:** This module is responsible of data storage. It supports high-frequency data writing and provides scalability, high service availability, and privacy. For these reasons, non-relational NoSQL database systems are employed, which provide other benefits such as data immutability and data integrity. Database systems such as Apache Cassandra have good performance with regard to storing data from large-scale sensor deployments. In comparison, MongoDB has a comparatively worse performance in managing very large volumes of sensor data (Kang, Park, Rhee, & Lee, 2016). On the other hand, though, MongoDB performs better than Cassandra when they are implemented in virtualized servers (Aydin, Hallac, & Karakus, 2015). In addition to these systems, HDFS (Hadoop Distributed File System) can be an alternative to MongoDB and Cassandra for data storage (Jiang et al., 2014).
- **Batch Processing Module:** This module extracts information from the data stored in the long-term-store module. The batch processing exploits historical IoT data to obtain descriptive statistics that give more details about data. Batch processing jobs are typically designed to read data from the database, and execute some kind of statistical processing to provide descriptive data information. The most widely used batch processing programming model is MapReduce, which is enhanced by in-memory computing to reduce processing time. One example of in-memory computing is Apache Spark which improves the Hadoop MapReduce processing time by using the Resilient Distributed Dataset (RDD) technology. In addition, there is a wide variety of high-level libraries that facilitate the statistical processing using programming languages such as Java, Python, C, or Scala. For example, some platforms implement query libraries such as Pig Latin, HiveQL, Apache SparkQL, or Cassandra Query Language (CQL) to query data or easily obtain data descriptive statistics.
- **Machine Learning Module:** The machine learning module will exploit the data using data mining techniques implemented in machine or deep learning frameworks or libraries to improve decision making. The inclusion of a machine learning module in the batch layer is necessary to fully benefit from IoT data. The machine learning analysis of this data allows finding trends, patterns, correlations, and new information to detect anomalies or predict future events, to improve decision making. For example, the detection of machinery anomalies reduces the response time to solve issues and prevents machinery from going out service. Data mining techniques such as clustering, classification, and regression models are suitable for IoT data. Deep learning techniques allow to extract more hidden information than classic data mining techniques. There is an extensive variety of machine learning libraries that are included either in processing frameworks or in non-processing frameworks specifically designed to implement either machine learning or deep learning

models quickly and easily. For example, libraries such as Apache Spark MLlib, Apache FlinkML, and Apache Mahout, are included in its respective processing frameworks, while frameworks such as TensorFlow, Caffe, Torch, and Keras, among others, and are machine-learning-dedicated frameworks.

- **Stream Processing Module:** IoT data is mainly processed in real time. The speed layer implementation can exploit IoT data velocity in the cloud to improve decision making. For this aim, architecture must provide a stream processor capable of executing data aggregation based on analysis windows. The windows provide a descriptive data analysis in real-time that constantly updates the batch processing results. Also, it is necessary the design of stream pipelines using real-time platforms and libraries such as Apache Spark Stream, Apache Flink Stream, Apache Kafka Streaming, Apache Storm, and others. By doing this, applications can execute their data analytics processes with a minimum possible delay. Then, machine learning models are able to perform predictions in real time, using a continuous IoT data flow.
- **Serving module:** Facilitates the use of big data analysis results, by exposing Application Programming Interfaces (APIs) to enable access to the data. In general, the serving module is implemented using a temporary repository to store the results, such as a database system or a message system. The serving layer allows the implementation of new services that benefit from the information obtained from the IoT data analysis.

There are others submodules that ensure IoT device management, data integration and security. The security access submodule will ensure access control to information providing data security and privacy. In this way, only pre-authorized people can access to the data. Moreover, the IoT device manager submodule ensures data integrity and veracity. This submodule controls that data ingested into the cloud comes only from authorized smart devices. Finally, a data integration submodule enables an API for integrating the system with others. By doing so, other sources from different big data areas (e.g. social media; manufacturing; business) can provide more information to enrich the IoT data analytics. In short, these are the basic modules to implement an IoT big data architecture. Other modules can be found on different IoT architectures—focused on other tasks such as integration between sources, index searching, or data visualization.

'Cloud of Things' Solutions

The Cloud of Things (CoT) paradigm enables the cloud computing and IoT integration. This integration is necessary as far as IoT has insufficient scalability, interoperability, reliability, flexibility, and security. For this integration, some important aspects must be addressed – aspects such as communications, storage, and computation. CoT enables mechanisms to share data between IoT devices and the cloud. In this way, the cloud offers a solution to connect and manage the IoT devices by using customized portals. Also, CoT provides an efficient and cost-effective solution to address the high IoT data storage demand. The on-demand cloud service provides a flexible, low-cost, efficient, and secure storage system. In addition, the virtualization provides almost unlimited processing capabilities to implement data analytics platforms.

Several technological proposals have been developed to promote the IoT and cloud computing integration. The proposals are focused on the enablement of mechanisms and resources to facilitate the IoT devices' connection to the cloud. In this way, leading companies in the field of cloud computing have expanded its services portfolio for supporting this integration. In addition, several open-source projects have been developed on purpose of taking advantage of CoT by providing platforms. Similarly, several research projects related to IoT have been promoted with the aim of solving several IoT challenges—including interoperability, integration with cloud computing, and federation, among other challenges. Like so, there are some solutions for IoT and cloud computing integration promoted by technology companies, open-source initiatives, and research projects.

The aforementioned technology companies provide mechanisms to support IoT integration. Companies like Amazon, Microsoft, Google, and IBM offer platforms and services to connect the IoT physical world with the digital world. Amazon offers Amazon Web Service (AWS) IoT Core platform to provide a secure connection, routing, processing, control and interactivity with the IoT devices. This platform receives IoT devices data and routes the data to other Amazon platforms such as AWS S3, Quicksight, or Machine Learning. Additionally, Amazon provides a device management module for handling all connected devices (Amazon, 2018). This module enables device monitoring and device configuration.

Similarly, Google proposes the Google IoT Core to connect, manage, and route IoT devices data to the cloud. Google IoT Core implements two basic functions: intelligent device management, and message conversion. The intelligent devices management enables control configuration options and security options. Message conversion translates messages from the MQTT protocol to HTTP (Hypertext Transfer Protocol), and it also publishes the messages on the Google Cloud Pub / Sub platform. Messages that reach the Cloud Pub / Sub platform can be consumed by different Google platforms such as Cloud BigTable, BigQuery, Cloud ML, Data Studio, and among others (Google, 2017).

In the same way, Microsoft Azure IoT hub is an open, flexible service platform that allows the connection, management of IoT devices in a secure manner, and facilitates integration with other services to process, store, and analyze IoT data (Microsoft, 2016). In summary, technology companies have developed platforms to integrate IoT devices into the cloud through APIs and to exploit the data collected using their extensive portfolios' services.

Similarly, the development of open-source IoT platforms have enabled the CoT implementation. The most relevant open-source platforms are Fiware, OpenIoT, and Kaa. Fiware is one of the most used open-source IoT platforms for Smart Cities in Europe. Fiware has different modules, called Generic Enablers, to store, process and visualize data in the cloud. Fiware's main component is Orion Context Broker, which enables the management of data from IoT devices and provides flexibility to connect any external big data analytics platform or Generic Enablers for data analysis. Those modules can be WireCloud, Knowage, Kurento, or Cosmo, among others (FI-WARE Consortium, 2012). Likewise, OpenIoT is a middleware that facilitates the deployment and release of cloud-based services using the SenaaS concept. Unlike Fiware, OpenIoT not only connects physical sensors, but also virtual sensors. In addition, OpenIoT focuses on mobility aspects for efficient data collection and transmission energy used (Botta, de Donato, Persico, & Pescape, 2014). Equally, Kaa IoT platform is a middleware that allows to build end-to-end IoT solutions by means of toolkits. These toolkits enable the development of applications and services. In addition, the middleware provides an environment to manage data schemas and allows big data analysis platforms to be easily integrated via API REST interfaces (KAA, 2018). Other platforms such as WSO2, Xively, Thingsboard, Thinner, Eclipse IoT Kura, and Mainflux (among others) implement middleware and platforms to facilitate integration through Software Development Kit (SDK) and APIs.

The European Commission has invested in several projects for the development of IoT platforms by the end of 2020 (European Commission, 2017). In this way, projects such as symbIoTe, bIoTope, BIG IoT, AGILE, VINICITY, TagItSmart, and Inter-IoT are being developed to facilitate IoT platforms' interoperability, cloud connection, and device intelligent management of devices. IoT heterogeneity makes it difficult to integrate and enrich data from different IoT sources, so the IoT data is not exploited properly. IoT interoperability makes it possible to have a single format and a standard data model without losing the data semantics. Therefore, these projects are important for the deployment of innovative services for exploiting the IoT data.

Cloud-Based Architecture Issues

A cloud-based architecture requires that the whole computing process is centralized in a datacenter, and that data has to be transmitted to the cloud. As a result, a cloud-based approach presents setbacks derived from the use of a centralized computing model. The issues of cloud computing managing IoT big data are summarized as follows:

- **Latency:** This is one of the most important issues that arises in a big data analytics cloud-based architecture. Although cloud computing has a good stream processing performance, the latency period can be excessive as encompasses the time necessary to generate sensing data, transmit it to the cloud, process the stream, and perform an action in response (end-to-end latency). In some cases such as in health application a high end-to-end latency can be fatal in where a prompt warning service in abnormal or risky situations is required.
- **Bandwidth Occupancy:** Big data may cause network layer saturation due to a massive bandwidth occupation, as it has to be transmitted to the cloud data centers. This exaggerated occupation is comparatively more likely caused by video or audio streaming for monitoring activities. Video network access requires a high bandwidth capacity. Also, it must be noted that IoT wireless access networks (that connect IoT devices to the Internet) are well-known for their low bandwidth and high cost.
- **Geographically Centralized:** The computing resources are usually located at one or a few locations. As a result, if the sensors or users are geographically distant from these data center points, the latency increases and QoS decreases.
- **Low QoS:** Since the computational power is geographically distant from the user, a bad QoS may be perceived by the users, who may experiment a bad user experience. It must be considered that the transmission of unnecessary or redundant sensor data has an impact on data storage costs and network overload. Thus, to ensure optimum QoS with the available infrastructure and to minimize costs, it is important to design IoT systems to function in a way which avoids the transmission of data that is either unnecessary or too redundant (e.g. measurements being taken too frequently).

FOG COMPUTING APPROACH

As has been seen in the previous section, the interconnection of IoT systems with the cloud has some limitations (e.g. centralization; possibly high latency; high bandwidth occupancy; and low QoS). The fog computing approach emerges as an efficient technological proposal to address the specific technical requirements of IoT big data (velocity, variety, and volume). The combination of fog computing with cloud computing is called the *fog-cloud approach*—one which is capable of overcoming (up to a big extent) the limitations of cloud computing regarding IoT big data.

Fog computing infrastructure is composed by several fog nodes that are located within an IoT system, thus close to the sensing devices. This differs from the cloud computing approach, in which the computing nodes are placed far from such devices. These fog nodes are edge device networks: components such as gateways, routers, switches, smartphones, and fog servers. But those fog nodes have additional storage and processing functionality rather than simple network function.

Thus, fog nodes provide networking, processing, and storage capabilities to IoT devices. The fog nodes can support IoT devices protocols (e.g. CoAP; MQTT) and low-power wireless technologies (e.g. ZigBee; Bluetooth). Then, IoT devices are interconnected to each other and to the cloud through the fog nodes. Unlike simple network elements, fog nodes can process the data. This processing is known as *edge analytics*. Data received from IoT devices are processed in real-time. This data processing has two important consequences. First, it allows to perform responsively actions without the long delay inherent to a cloud approach. For example, the fog node – according to its programming – can decide to send specific orders to actuators by using the information extracted from the IoT data analysis. In this case, this order is sent without the delay derived from the transmission of the data to the cloud, in addition to the transmission of the order to the IoT system from the cloud—thus reducing the response time. Moreover, the action can be messages sent to users to notify a risky situation. In general, this type of processing can be done by using a rule-based processor (e.g. using a CEP) in the fog node to detect anomalies on time. Also, fog nodes provide temporal storage to save data processing results. In this case, IoT services or applications retrieve data information by means of querying the edge database as required.

Fog computing solves some limitations of cloud computing in IoT. First, fog computing reduces the end-to-end latency in IoT services, as compared to a cloud approach; and allows for better decision making. Edge analytics processing reduces the time it takes to send data from the IoT devices to the cloud reducing the time it takes to send an action to actuators. This particular benefit of fog computing can improve the development of innovative applications in any field of IoT, such as smart health, smart home, smart cities, smart manufacturing, and other fields. In addition, fog computing enables efficient data storage in the cloud. The pre-processing tasks (e.g. filtering and cleaning data) reduce redundant and unnecessary data. Pre-processing is a set of data preparation steps taken before performing accuracy analytics. In this way, data pre-processing on the edge provides an efficient data storage and improves data quality. Another beneficial consequence is a lower bandwidth consumption, as compared with a direct connection to the cloud. Edge analytics processing limits the data streams bandwidth by reducing the frequency at which data is sent to the cloud. In addition, edge analytics processing identifies changes in the data flow and sends the data to the cloud only when such changes occur. For example, in a video surveillance scenario, a photo and metadata context information would be sent to the cloud only when an irregularity is detected. Additionally, a data temporary storage on the edge reduces the volume of data; thereby avoiding network congestion. Finally, QoS and user experience are increased due to there being a low delay in the provision of services. Fog computing wide-spread geographical distribution computation allows for providing location awareness and mobility support due to the fog's high area of coverage.

To sum up, fog computing provides relevant benefits to the handling of IoT big data. The well-known cloud computing approach and fog computing integration empowers the IoT ecosystem. This integration provides a new perspective on the efficient management of IoT big data features. Its advantages are not only limited to reducing latency, reducing bandwidth consumption, and reducing data storage size, but also improving QoS, mobility support, location awareness, and interoperability (Bonomi, Milito, Natarajan, & Zhu, 2014). However, fog nodes are resource constrained and battery constrained, which makes it difficult for users to benefit from the advantages of using fog nodes. These limitations require attention for exploiting the advantages of using a fog-cloud approach.

Fog-Cloud Reference Architecture

The fog-cloud architecture is a multilevel system that covers the processing, storage, and network processes from the cloud to the edge. Fog-cloud architecture should facilitate IoT ecosystems' interoperability, security, scalability, programmability, reliability, availability, and agility (OpenFog Consortium Architecture Working Group, 2017). Consequently, the fog-cloud approach potentiates IoT ecosystems and the development of innovative and profitable services within them. Currently, initiatives such as the OpenFog Consortium aim to provide an open architecture of fog computing that guarantees the implemented availability of these aforementioned aspects. The OpenFog Consortium integrates research organizations and technology vendors to promote terminals and services based on standards. In addition to this initiative, several architectures have been proposed by different research groups. Typically, fog-cloud architecture proposals are composed of three levels: the smart devices level, the fog computing level, and the cloud computing level, shown in Figure 2.

The Smart Devices Level

This level has been seen within the reference architecture of cloud computing. It is composed of smart objects such as embedded devices, sensors, and actuators. Sensors take measurements; transform those measurements into data; and then send them to the fog level using low-power wireless communication, through an IoT gateway. On the other hand, actuators react to orders from the fog or from the cloud computing level. Also, IoT devices sends data to the higher level using communication protocols and low-power wireless technologies.

Figure 2. Fog-Cloud approach reference architecture

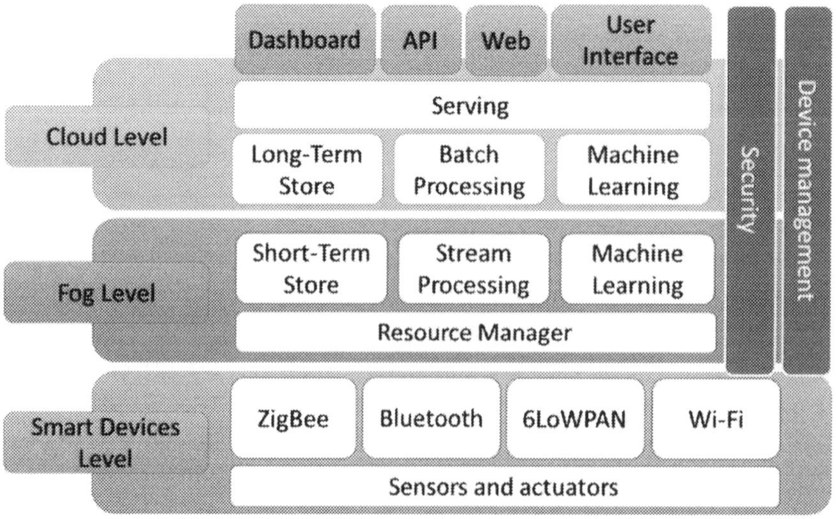

The Fog Computing Level

This level is located in the majority of the cases on the edge of the network (i.e. gateways), which is the infrastructure that provides access to the network to IoT devices. This level is composed of fog nodes which are close to smart devices. Fog nodes provides stream processing and storage capabilities for the data collected in the smart devices level. For this, fog nodes must be able to support the smart devices technologies and protocols and manage the processing and storage resources. Performing those tasks are challenging due to the very limited capabilities of the fog nodes devices.

The gateway of this level requires more functions than do gateways from the cloud computing architecture. This smart IoT gateway implements more functions than the traditional packet routing, such as data pre-processing tasks, data storage, IoT interoperability, and security smart devices connection. It must be capable of performing edge analytics processing—in addition to providing technical, syntactic and semantic interoperability. Technical interoperability ensures the wireless connection of smart devices. Syntactic interoperability ensures the conversion of data structures and of data formats if necessary. Semantic interoperability ensures the ability to interpret information correctly (Janssen, Estevez, & Janowski, 2014). The gateway has a temporary database for storing the pre-processed data. This database is temporary because of the limited resources available in fog nodes. Also, this gateway implements mechanisms to monitor and manage resources through an orchestrator, which is able to request resources from other fog or cloud nodes to process or store data (Patel, Intizar Ali, & Sheth, 2017).

Fog level scalability, security, and smart devices management is a fundamental requirement in the architecture design process. Fog nodes adopt lightweight virtualization technologies as far as they enable a very efficient usage of the fog limited resources. Generally, fog nodes are implemented using container-based technology. This technology virtualizes applications isolated at the operating system level, avoiding hardware and driver virtualization (Morabito, Petrolo, Loscrì, & Mitton, 2018). Also, platforms such as Apache Edgent or ParaDrop (Sphinx, 2018) have been developed to enable edge analytics processing implementation. Apache Edgent is a platform for real-time data processing in devices located on the edge; and it is mostly used to integrate with the IBM Watson IoT platform in the cloud.

The Cloud Computing Level

The cloud computing level retains some modules of the cloud-based architecture. Thus, this level concentrates data storage and management, machine learning processing, and historical data analysis results. In this case, the speed layer is not consider in this level, because it is performed in the fog level.

The Use of the Fog-Cloud Architecture With IoT Applications: Case Studies

IoT has an extensive variety of applications in various areas (e.g. e-health, transport and logistics, manufacturing and smart cities); and each area has its own requirements and particular features. In this section, the application of a fog-cloud approach in IoT is studied an analyzed on two very significant IoT case studies—the areas of Smart City and e-Health. In both cases, the fog computing approach is presented as being a solution to the particular challenges of both IoT scenarios. The specific requirements and features of each case study are described, as well as the challenges that are faced in the implementation of services and applications.

Smart Health

Smart Health's aim is to improve the quality of healthcare by leveraging new technologies such as IoT. The use of this technology enhances the tools of diagnosis and treatment for patients in order to improve the quality of life of people. Smart health includes eHealth and mHealth services, smart home services and smart metering devices. This area, in particular, very much benefits from the use of IoT and a fog-cloud approach. Two applications of Smart Health are studied in this section, with regard to the application and effectiveness of fog and cloud computing. These applications are a home-based monitoring of patients and the creation of an Ambient Intelligent Environment with Ambient Assisted Living (AAL) purposes (that do not include home-based health monitoring).

- **Home-based monitoring of patients:** This application is implemented to control chronic diseases, diabetes, and cardiology diseases, among other conditions. To do so, multiple vital sign monitoring services are deployed to sense patients over a long period. These services allow for finding patterns to forecast dangerous clinical events in advance (Rahim, Forkan, Khalil, & Atiquzzaman, 2017). In this context, electrocardiogram monitoring is one of the most studied health services for its potential to provide relevant information about people's health. Among other benefits, this system allows for the improvement of people's well-being, as far as facilitates patients' movement without deteriorating health service. Delay time is a critical factor in a health monitoring system. Also, home-based health systems security is very important because health information is sensitive. Security policies and access control mechanisms must be implemented to control the security of the data. Also, data anonymity can be implemented during the whole data analysis process to preserve patients' privacy. The fog-cloud approach meets the requirements of this application. All these requirements must be fulfilled, providing reliability in each of the fog-cloud layers and modules.

Figure 3. Smart health fog-cloud approach

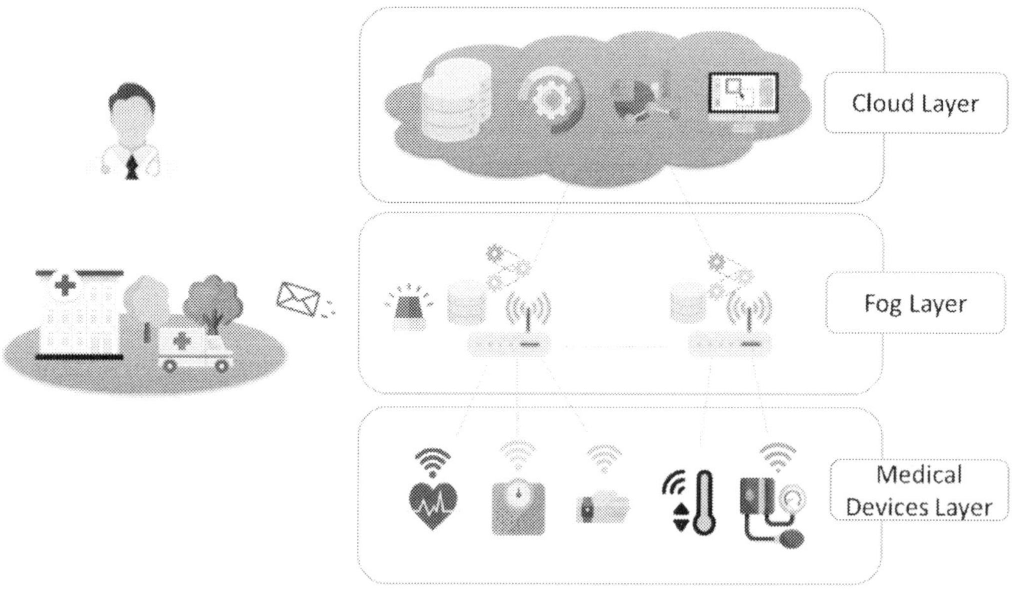

- **Ambient Assisted Living (AAL):** This application is part of the domain of Ambient Intelligent (AmI) that is focused on the creation of Ambient Intelligent Environments to promote independent living and the preservation of patients and elderly's quality life and autonomy. Such environments are sensitive to people's interaction—and respond intelligently to it. To do so, AAL system collects patients' health status, location, activities, and surrounding ambient conditions—doing so using body sensors, ambient sensors, and actuators. Traditionally, Cloud-based AAL systems have been proposed to perform the data analysis; however, this is not very efficient due to the vast data volume that these systems can generate (100 kilobytes data every second on average) (Forkan, Khalil, Ibaida, & Member, 2015). The fog-cloud approach can substantially improve the AAL systems' efficiency and response times. In addition, fog-node-distributed data analysis is potentially able to provide more intelligence to the edge—thereby improving decision making. In this way, detect aging's falls can be performed on the fog nodes; thereby reducing the response time and energy consumption (Cao, Chen, Hou, & Brown, 2015).

The fog-cloud approach meets Smart Health requirements. Figure 3 shows a Smart Health system that applies a fog-cloud approach. The fog layer is capable of reducing the latency by performing a real-time processing on the edge. By doing so, alerts and messages can be sent to medical professionals, so they can respond in time to the emergency. Additionally, the cloud facilitates integration with other systems that may be hosted in the same cloud infrastructure. The cloud layer support the data analytics for exploiting the benefits of big data through data exploratory and data mining techniques. The data exploratory provides a descriptive analysis to find disease patterns relative to outbreak of chronic diseases. Also, the descriptive analysis facilitates the designing of the treatment for each patient. The data mining techniques provides a predictive analysis to forecast the outbreak of a chronic diseases or to diagnose diseases. This performance is possible by developing machine learning models based on artificial neural networks algorithms and integrating data from alternative sources improving those machine learning algorithms and making them more efficient. In short, the fog-cloud approach provides a scalable and secure means of performing big data analytics.

Smart City

Smart City refers to the employment and leveraging of technology (especially in IoT) to transform the performance of a city and improve citizens' services, public information, and people's well-being. IoT data analysis in a city maximizes the resources of city management; turning the city into a sustainable and governable city. Data descriptive analysis provides an overview of the use of city resources. In addition, the analysis of IoT data enables an optimization of the city resources—thus increasing efficiency and availability. The prediction of city resource consumption provides, in advance, information that improves decision making. Finally, big data analytics allows the incidents or crises of a city to be better managed—thereby making that city more resilient. The fast detection of failures in public services, and the prediction of future events, each –very significantly – improves incident management and prevents harmful impacts on services and infrastructures. IoT applications in a Smart City are oriented towards facilitating an adequate management of city resources so as to provide for the sustainability of the city and the well-being of the people who inhabit it. This IoT big data analysis can be efficiently performed through fog-cloud approach.

Figure 4. High-level view of a smart city application fields

Thus, the fog-cloud approach accomplishes the requirements of Smart City applications. Fog-level processing reduces redundant information that certain applications can generate—thereby optimizing cloud storage. In addition, the real-time processing of fog nodes optimizes the bandwidth used in data communications. In the cloud, processing power will be exploited to generate models that continually identify patterns and trends in the data. In addition, the cloud provides comparatively better resources than the fog level for enabling the data to become publicly available and accessible by citizens. The fog-cloud approach can be used in all smart city applications—such as in traffic, environment, water, garbage, or parking management applications, as is shown in Figure 4. This chapter analyzes the benefits of using the fog-cloud architecture in the following smart city applications:

- **Environmental monitoring:** This application focuses on monitoring weather conditions and pollutant levels. Environmental data is collected from static and mobile stations. Each station generally censes temperature, humidity, wind velocity, wind direction, rain levels, Carbone Oxide (CO2), Sulfuric Oxide (SO2), Nitrogen Oxide (NOx), Ozone (O3), and Particulate Matter (PM10), among other data. In this case, the response time is not critical because data is not dramatically changed in a short period of time. For example, the city temperature usually does not change in at least 2 hours. However, the data redundancy is high—thereby causing unnecessary data storage occupancy and a related cost increment. The fog-cloud approach reduces the data redundancy by using an aggregate processing window in the fog node. Also, fog nodes geographically placed in the city can receive data from mobile stations. For example, mobile stations can be implemented in buses using sensor kits; and they send data to fog nodes placed in each bus station (Perera, Talagala, Liu, & Estrella, 2016). Finally, the cloud layer can perform machine learning models to predict hazard pollutant levels.
- **Traffic management:** This application focuses on monitoring road congestion, tracking accident locations, and controlling traffic lights in the city. The traffic is sensed using inductive circle recognition, infrared sensors, and video analysis, and among other means (Rizwan, Suresh, &

Babu, 2016). The fog-cloud approach reduces the bandwidth usage due to video surveillance. Fog nodes can process video using deep learning models to identify the traffic—and can send only a notification to the cloud. Moreover, fog nodes can detect ambulance lights in the video and send a notification to the control traffic lights to change their pattern to control the emergency. Also, fog nodes can be located geographically to better cover the monitoring area and produce aggregate results. In this way, edge analytics processing can produce results to send alerts and alarms to users in real-time to optimize their translation. Also, the historical data store in the cloud can be exploited using machine learning models to obtain trends and patterns for generating new traffic management strategies. By using this, the control traffic lights can be optimized in function of the traffic patterns in each road segment occupancy (Huang, Lu, & Choo, 2017).

Smart Cities' applications should be able to interact or interoperate among them – such as, for example, sharing information. Big data potential and IoT benefits will be more tangible when the data coming from different sources are correlated. For example, by using traffic congestion, the environmental monitoring can be improved to predict pollutant levels in the city (Jara, Genoud, & Bocchi, 2014). Also, Smart Cities' applications are capable of providing contextual information to enrich data analysis in other IoT applications. For example, the Smart Cities and Smart Health integration will provide contextual information to better manage and control the treatment of diseases (Sarabia-Jacome, Belsa, Palau, & Esteve, 2018). This integration can be performed in the cloud layer using a context broker manager.

FUTURE RESEARCH DIRECTIONS

Currently, the fog-cloud approach has some challenges and limitations that can be solved in the future through further research into the development and use of this technology. Fog nodes have usually low computing capabilities and low battery capacity. These limitations make it difficult to perform multi-tenancy edge analytics processing that requires more resources. Also, runtime platforms are not well-defined, as none sufficient programming models have been proposed yet to facilitate the deployment of applications in fog nodes. Conclusively, fog computing is a technology that still needs some improvements. In this section, the most relevant challenges of the fog-cloud approach are discussed. Also, some ideas are provided for researchers and applications developers as a starting point for addressing these challenges.

Interoperability

Many IoT benefits are obtained when IoT elements and systems are able to interoperate amongst themselves. In a big data context, information of different IoT sources can facilitate the enrichment of data, so that an enriched analysis can be performed to develop innovative services. However, the current lack of interoperability in IoT systems is a barrier to the use of different data sources. Nowadays, IoT platforms typically store data in an isolated way; following different standards (different data models and formats). Thus, other platforms of IoT systems are typically unable to understand this information. This data management scheme makes the integration of various sources and data exploitation difficult. Interoperability between domains allows generating a single data model and standard formats. Moreover, policies and agreements need to be implemented to enable platforms to share data to each other. In this way, the Inter-IoT project promoted by the European Commission proposes a framework to facilitate interoperability and information sharing between different IoT domains and platforms (Gravina, Manso, & Liotta, 2018). Also, a federated architecture considering fog computing is necessary so that the platforms' integration allows for a secure cooperation between nodes. In this way, fog nodes from different platforms will be able share the data following a policy-based scheme. The policies will be designed to support the operational, network, and security requirements necessary to maintain communication between them. Fog computing will provide a multi-domain integration at different levels for the interconnection and interoperability of heterogeneous devices and nodes.

Stream Processing in the Fog

As has been previously introduced, cloud processing platforms are not suitable for executing real-time IoT data analysis in fog nodes due to resource limitations. Therefore, new real-time processing platforms should be designed in consideration of fog node features, so as to have both the advantages of minimum latency and complex big data analysis. These platforms should be lightweight and should optimally exploit the highly distributed fog computing resources. For this, new programming models should be proposed to optimize operators' locations – both in consideration of a minimum resource usage expectation (Cardellini, Grassi, Lo Presti, & Nardelli, 2017), and to schedule workflows (Yin & Kosar, 2011). Also, these new stream processing engines should explore new mechanisms to exploit the elasticity of resources in highly distributed environments.

Resource Management

New algorithms must be developed to monitor Fog and Cloud resources and to optimize resource usage by external applications. Since fog nodes are distributed over various location, the fog nodes resources require discovery, orchestration, and monitoring. These actions provide information to better controlling the limited resources so as to improve the deployment of applications in fog computing. Also, this control should help to optimize resources by using algorithms to exploit those resources. For example, new algorithms that optimize processing costs need to be develop based on the management of Fog-to-Cloud resources (Ghosh, Komma, & Simmhan, 2018; Skarlat, Nardelli, Schulte, Borkowski, & Leitner, 2017). Also, algorithms based on resource sharing are required to be proposed. These algorithms must be capable of enabling computing resource among the fog nodes to facilities the execution of applications.

Mobility

Fog node mobility (e.g. a mobile gateway), though difficult, is possible; it is important to consider that, during the sensors movements, the sensors do not lose the services deployed from the cloud. Currently, new strategies need to be designed to support mobility. Covering a sensor node area implies defining a fog node as being capable of providing services which would be taking into account sensors' geolocation and mobility (Zohora, Khan, Bhuiyan, & Das, 2017). A possible strategy would be the adaptation of virtual machine migrations, usually carried out in cloud computing, to the fog computing scenario. This virtual machine migration between nodes has a high time cost due to the time required to find available resources within a fog node in which the smart device can move. Another strategy is to measure the transmitted energy usage by the IoT device to know how far is it to the fog node coverage service area

(Mach & Becvar, 2017). In this way, the resources can be previously reserved in the near fog nodes to allow stream operators the capability of migration. An environment fog computing mobility will potentiate the development of new services.

Privacy and Security

Both data privacy and security must be addressed within data transmission process and the temporary data storage. As the fog nodes are physically located in the IoT deployment, they can suffer physical manipulation and thus are more vulnerable to malicious attacks such as data hijacking and eavesdropping (Hu et al., 2017). To guarantee security to the extent possible, fog nodes must implement authentication, encryption, and access control mechanisms. Authentication techniques centralized in the cloud are not suitable for fog nodes, which are remotely located, as far as fog nodes would depend on the connection to the central server for proper operation. In other words, if the connection to the central server fails, authentication would not work properly. Moreover, encryption schemes are necessary to prevent malicious nodes from being introduced into the architecture and to avoid man-in-the-middle attacks. Similarly, access control policies are necessary to support a secure integration between heterogeneous resources. Despite some efforts have been done on the improvement of fog node security, many security problems are still unresolved. This issue is expected to receive significant research attention in the coming years due to its enormous importance.

CONCLUSION

The chapter provides a comprehensive overview of IoT big data analytics architectures, approaches, and solutions for developing IoT applications. Several architectures, models, and solutions have been designed to carry the IoT requirements to efficiently perform big data analytics. These architectures were mostly designed using the ideas presented in the well-known big data architectures Lambda and Kappa. Big data analytics architectures focus their efforts on dividing data processing into two types: batch and stream processing. The IoT characteristics indicate that stream processing is of comparatively greater concern in the development of real-time applications and services. However, batch processing is valuable in the pre-processing task relative to the development of machine learning models to identify patterns from large datasets. The adequate combination of these types of processing will enable the development of comparatively more innovative applications and services. In this way, two approaches were identified in the literature: a cloud-based and a fog-cloud approach. The cloud-based approach is the most popular approach for solving IoT limitations. IoT data requires to be stored, processed, and analyzed—and cloud computing provides an almost unlimited capacity to do so. However, some issues were identified in the cloud-based approach such as latency, bandwidth saturation, low QoS, and a centralized model. Fog computing is used to overcome these cloud-based issues, but this still needs some cloud capabilities support. As a result, fog-cloud reference architecture was proposed to facilitate developers' and researchers' development of new services.

This analysis was performed on two relevant case studies. Two well-known IoT application areas (smart health, and smart city) were analyzed, detailing the improvements of a fog-cloud architecture and the recent advances in each area. Finally, it was noted that the challenges of an open fog-cloud architecture make it difficult to exploit all the advantages described. Fog nodes usually have comparatively less computing and battery power capabilities than cloud servers, making it difficult for the nodes to handle a large amount of data.

Future research and development in this area should be focused on improving interoperability, stream processing, mobility, resource management, privacy, and security to improve the fog-cloud approach. Despite the limitations of the fog-cloud approach, big data is very significantly benefited by improving stream data handling—thereby allowing for efficient data management and optimization of information usage.

REFERENCES

Aazam, M., & Huh, E. N. (2014). Fog computing and smart gateway based communication for cloud of things. *Proceedings - 2014 International Conference on Future Internet of Things and Cloud,* 464–470.

Aazam, M., Khan, I., Alsaffar, A. A., & Huh, E. (2014). *Cloud of Things : Integrating Internet of Things and cloud computing and the issues involved*. Academic Press.

Amazon. (2018). *AWS IoT Services Overview - Amazon Web Services*. Retrieved May 15, 2018, from https://aws.amazon.com/iot/?nc1=h_ls

Aydin, G., Hallac, I. R., & Karakus, B. (2015). Architecture and Implementation of a Scalable Sensor Data Storage and Analysis System Using Cloud Computing and Big Data Technologies. *Journal of Sensors*, *2015*, 1–11. doi:10.1155/2015/834217

Bonomi, F., Milito, R., Natarajan, P., & Zhu, J. (2014). Big Data and Internet of Things: A Roadmap for Smart Environments. In Studies in Computational Intelligence (Vol. 546). Cham: Springer International Publishing.

Bonomi, F., Milito, R., Zhu, J., & Addepalli, S. (2012). Fog Computing and Its Role in the Internet of Things. In *Proceedings of the First Edition of the MCC Workshop on Mobile Cloud Computing* (pp. 13–16). New York: ACM. 10.1145/2342509.2342513

Botta, A., de Donato, W., Persico, V., & Pescape, A. (2014). On the Integration of Cloud Computing and Internet of Things. In *2014 International Conference on Future Internet of Things and Cloud* (Vol. 56, pp. 23–30). IEEE. 10.1109/FiCloud.2014.14

Cao, Y., Chen, S., Hou, P., & Brown, D. (2015). FAST: A fog computing assisted distributed analytics system to monitor fall for stroke mitigation. In *2015 IEEE International Conference on Networking, Architecture and Storage (NAS)* (pp. 2–11). IEEE. 10.1109/NAS.2015.7255196

Cardellini, V., Grassi, V., Lo Presti, F., & Nardelli, M. (2017). Optimal Operator Replication and Placement for Distributed Stream Processing Systems. *Performance Evaluation Review*, *44*(4), 11–22. doi:10.1145/3092819.3092823

Chen, M., Mao, S., Zhang, Y., & Leung, V. C. M. (2014). *Big Data*. Cham, Germany: Springer International Publishing. doi:10.1007/978-3-319-06245-7

Cisco. (2018). *Cisco Global Cloud Index: Forecast and Methodology, 2016–2021.* White Paper.

European Commission. (2017). *The Internet of Things | Digital Single Market*. Retrieved May 12, 2018, from https://ec.europa.eu/digital-single-market/en/research-innovation-iot

FI-WARE Consortium. (2012). *FI-WARE Architecture, 2004*. doi:10.1002/ejoc.201200111

Forkan, A. R. M., Khalil, I., Ibaida, A., & Member, Z. T. (2015). BDCaM: Big Data for Context-Aware monitoring-a personalized knowledge discovery framework for assisted healthcare. *IEEE Transactions on Cloud Computing*.

Ghosh, R., Komma, S. P. R., & Simmhan, Y. (2018). *Adaptive Energy-aware Scheduling of Dynamic Event Analytics across Edge and Cloud Resources*. Academic Press.

Google. (2017). *Google Cloud IoT*. Retrieved May 15, 2018, from https://cloud.google.com/iot-core/

Gravina, R., Manso, M., & Liotta, A. (2018). *Integration, Interconnection, and Interoperability of IoT Systems* (R. Gravina, C. E. Palau, M. Manso, A. Liotta, & G. Fortino, Eds.). Cham: Springer International Publishing. doi:10.1007/978-3-319-61300-0

Hashem, I. A. T., Yaqoob, I., Anuar, N. B., Mokhtar, S., Gani, A., & Ullah Khan, S. (2015). The rise of "big data" on cloud computing: Review and open research issues. *Information Systems*, *47*, 98–115. doi:10.1016/j.is.2014.07.006

Hu, P., Member, S., Ning, H., Member, S., Qiu, T., & Member, S. (2017). Security and Privacy Preservation Scheme of Face Identification and Resolution Framework Using Fog Computing in .... *Security and Privacy Preservation Scheme of Face Identification and Resolution Framework Using Fog Computing in Internet of Things*, *4*, 1143–1155.

Huang, C., Lu, R., & Choo, K. K. R. (2017). Vehicular Fog Computing: Architecture, Use Case, and Security and Forensic Challenges. *IEEE Communications Magazine*, *55*(11), 105–111. doi:10.1109/MCOM.2017.1700322

Janssen, M., Estevez, E., & Janowski, T. (2014). Interoperability in big, open, and linked data-organizational maturity, capabilities, and data portfolios. *Computer*, *47*(10), 44–49. doi:10.1109/MC.2014.290

Jara, A. J., Genoud, D., & Bocchi, Y. (2014). Big data in smart cities: From poisson to human dynamics. *Proceedings - 2014 IEEE 28th International Conference on Advanced Information Networking and Applications Workshops,* 785–790.

Jiang, L., Da Xu, L., Cai, H., Jiang, Z., Bu, F., & Xu, B. (2014). An IoT-Oriented Data Storage Framework in Cloud Computing Platform. *Industrial Informatics. IEEE Transactions On*, *10*(2), 1443–1451.

KAA. (2018). *Kaa IoT Development Platform overview*. Retrieved May 18, 2018, from https://www.kaaproject.org/

Kang, Y., Park, I., Rhee, J., & Lee, Y. (2016). MongoDB-based Repository Design for IoT- generated RFID / Sensor Big Data. *IEEE Sensors Journal*, *16*(2), 485–497. doi:10.1109/JSEN.2015.2483499

Kreps, J. (2014). *Questioning the Lambda Architecture - O'Reilly Media*. Retrieved May 8, 2018, from https://www.oreilly.com/ideas/questioning-the-lambda-architecture

Mach, P., & Becvar, Z. (2017). Mobile Edge Computing: A Survey on Architecture and Computation Offloading. *IEEE Communications Surveys and Tutorials*, *19*(3), 1628–1656. doi:10.1109/COMST.2017.2682318

Marz, N., & Warren, J. (2015). *Big data: principles and best practices of scalable realtime data systems*. Shelter Island, NY: Manning, cop. Retrieved from http://nathanmarz.com/about/

Microsoft. (2016). *Azure IoT Hub | Microsoft Azure*. Retrieved May 15, 2018, from https://azure.microsoft.com/en-us/services/iot-hub/

Morabito, R., Petrolo, R., Loscrì, V., & Mitton, N. (2018). LEGIoT: A Lightweight Edge Gateway for the Internet of Things. *Future Generation Computer Systems*, *81*, 1–15. doi:10.1016/j.future.2017.10.011

OpenFog Consortium Architecture Working Group. (2017, February). OpenFog Reference Architecture for Fog Computing. *OpenFogConsortium*, 1–162.

Patel, P., Intizar Ali, M., & Sheth, A. (2017). On Using the Intelligent Edge for IoT Analytics. *IEEE Intelligent Systems*, *32*(5), 64–69. doi:10.1109/MIS.2017.3711653

Perera, C., Talagala, D., Liu, C. H., & Estrella, J. C. (2016). *Energy Efficient Location and Activity-aware On-Demand Mobile Distributed Sensing Platform for Sensing as a Service in IoT Clouds*. Academic Press.

Rahim, A., Forkan, M., Khalil, I., & Atiquzzaman, M. (2017). ViSiBiD: A learning model for early discovery and real-time prediction of severe clinical events using vital signs as big data. *Computer Networks*, *113*, 244–257. doi:10.1016/j.comnet.2016.12.019

Rizwan, P., Suresh, K., & Babu, M. R. (2016). Real-time smart traffic management system for smart cities by using Internet of Things and big data. In *2016 International Conference on Emerging Technological Trends (ICETT)* (pp. 1–7). Academic Press. doi:10.1109/ICETT.2016.7873660

Sarabia-Jacome, D., Belsa, A., Palau, C. E., & Esteve, M. (2018). Exploiting IoT Data and Smart City Services for Chronic Obstructive Pulmonary Diseases Risk Factors Monitoring. In *2018 IEEE International Conference on Cloud Engineering (IC2E)* (pp. 351–356). IEEE. doi:10.1109/IC2E.2018.00060

Skarlat, O., Nardelli, M., Schulte, S., Borkowski, M., & Leitner, P. (2017). Optimized IoT service placement in the fog. *Service Oriented Computing and Applications*, *11*(4), 427–443. doi:10.100711761-017-0219-8

Sphinx. (2018). *ParaDrop - Enabling Edge Computing at the Extreme Edge — paradrop 0.11.2 documentation*. Retrieved May 23, 2018, from http://paradrop.readthedocs.io/en/latest/index.html

Uesugi, Sh. (2014). *Kappa Architecture - Where Every Thing Is A Stream*. Retrieved May 4, 2018, from http://milinda.pathirage.org/kappa-architecture.com/

Yin, D., & Kosar, T. (2011). A data-aware workflow scheduling algorithm for heterogeneous distributed systems. *International Conference on High Performance Computing & Simulation*, 114–120. 10.1109/HPCSim.2011.5999814

Zaslavsky, A., Perera, C., & Georgakopoulos, D. (2012). Sensing as a Service and Big Data. *Proceedings of the International Conference on Advances in Cloud Computing (ACC-2012)*, 21–29.

Zohora, F. T., Khan, M. R. R., Bhuiyan, M. F. R., & Das, A. K. (2017). Enhancing the capabilities of IoT based fog and cloud infrastructures for time sensitive events. *ICECOS 2017 - Proceeding of 2017 International Conference on Electrical Engineering and Computer Science: Sustaining the Cultural Heritage Toward the Smart Environment for Better Future*, 224–230.

ADDITIONAL READING

Chen, J., Chen, H., Wu, Z., Hu, D., & Pan, J. Z. (2017). Forecasting smog-related health hazard based on social media and physical sensor. *Information Systems*, *64*, 281–291. doi:10.1016/j.is.2016.03.011

Chen, M., Hao, Y., Hwang, K., Wang, L., & Wang, L. (2017). Disease Prediction by Machine Learning Over Big Data From Healthcare Communities. *IEEE Access: Practical Innovations, Open Solutions*, *5*, 8869–8879. doi:10.1109/ACCESS.2017.2694446

Chen, M., Yang, J., Zhou, J., Hao, Y., Zhang, J., & Youn, C. (2018). 5G-Smart Diabetes : Toward Personalized Diabetes Diagnosis with Healthcare Big Data Clouds. *IEEE Communications Magazine*, (April): 2–9.

Marjani, M., Nasaruddin, F., Gani, A., Karim, A., Hashem, I. A. T., Siddiqa, A., & Yaqoob, I. (2017). Big IoT Data Analytics: Architecture, Opportunities, and Open Research Challenges. *IEEE Access: Practical Innovations, Open Solutions*, *5*, 5247–5261. doi:10.1109/ACCESS.2017.2689040

Rahmani, A. M., Gia, T. N., Negash, B., Anzanpour, A., Azimi, I., Jiang, M., & Liljeberg, P. (2018). Exploiting smart e-Health gateways at the edge of healthcare Internet-of-Things: A fog computing approach. *Future Generation Computer Systems*, *78*, 641–658. doi:10.1016/j.future.2017.02.014

Yacchirema, D., Sarabia-Jácome, D., Palau, C. E., & Esteve, M. (2018). System for monitoring and supporting the treatment of sleep apnea using IoT and big data. *Pervasive and Mobile Computing*, *50*, 25–40. doi:10.1016/j.pmcj.2018.07.007

KEY TERMS AND DEFINITIONS

API (Application Programming Interface): External interface of a software that presents a group of well-defined methods, to be used by another software.

BDaaS (Big Data Platforms as a Service): A cloud computing model service which provides big data platforms for storing, processing and analyzing data to online users.

CEP (Complex Event Processor): A framework to enable the analysis of a stream of events to find patterns.

Cloud Computing: Paradigm that offers resources hosted on the Internet for complex and large-scale computing. Those online resources are provided on-demand and have a secure and easy access.

CoAP (Constrained Application Protocol): a lightweight web transfer protocol appropriated for constrained devices (e.g., sensors) to send telemetry information.

End-to-End Latency: In the context of cloud services, it refers to the time that takes to receive the response of a service across the network once it is triggered. In the context of IoT and cloud services, it includes the network delay of transmitting the data to the cloud, the processing time of the cloud service and finally the network transport delay of transmitting the information to the IoT system.

ETL (Extraction Transformation and Load): Process to extract, to transform, and to load data from a database to another database.

Fog Computing: Highly virtualized paradigm that provides computing and storage services between end devices (typically IoT smart objects) and cloud data centers, at the edge of the network. In this way, part of the processing performed by the cloud services is done within the system that generates big data, sparing the network end-to-end communication delay.

Fog Node: Component of the fog computing infrastructure. Edge device networks (e.g. gateways) which, in addition to simple network function, have storage and processing capabilities. Due to this fact, a fog node can perform data preprocessing and part of the cloud computing processing close to the devices within the IoT system, thus enabling a faster response to events than the cloud paradigm.

IaaS (Infrastructure as a Service): A cloud computing model service that provides online infrastructure resources through virtual machines.

MQTT (Message Queue Telemetry Transport): A lightweight communication protocol that is typically used by sensors to send telemetry information.

NoSQL (No Structured Query Language): A group of database systems which are not based on structured query language.

PaaS (Platform as a Service): A cloud computing model service which provides online platform layer resources by supporting operating systems and software for the development of frameworks.

SaaS (Software as a Service): A cloud computing model service which provides applications to end users.

Chapter 9
Interoperability in IoT

Regel Gonzalez-Usach
Universitat Politecnica de Valencia, Spain

Diana Yacchirema
Escuela Politécnica Nacional, Ecuador

Matilde Julian
Universitat Politecnica de Valencia, Spain

Carlos E. Palau
Universitat Politècnica de València, Spain

ABSTRACT

Interoperability refers to the ability of IoT systems and components to communicate and share information among them. This crucial feature is key to unlock all of the IoT paradigm´s potential, including immense technological, economic, and social benefits. Interoperability is currently a major challenge in IoT, mainly due to the lack of a reference standard and the vast heterogeneity of IoT systems. IoT interoperability has also a significant importance in big data analytics because it substantively eases data processing. This chapter analyzes the critical importance of IoT interoperability, its different types, challenges to face, diverse use cases, and prospective interoperability solutions. Given that it is a complex concept that involves multiple aspects and elements of IoT, for a deeper insight, interoperability is studied across different levels of IoT systems. Furthermore, interoperability is also re-examined from a global approach among platforms and systems.

INTRODUCTION

Interoperability is defined as the ability of different technology systems, system components or software applications to establish communication between them, exchange data, and interpret properly the received information for its use (ETSI, 2013). This property applies to interactions within a system (i.e. the internal communication of its different components), but also to the interaction between two or more systems.

In IoT interoperability plays an essential role; there is probably no other technology area in which interoperability becomes as critical and relevant as in the case of IoT (World Economic Forum, 2015).

DOI: 10.4018/978-1-5225-7432-3.ch009

Interoperability is the key that allows any set of devices to exchange information and work together in concert, acting as an actual IoT system. For example, without interoperability lights would not respond to remote switches, sensors could not be read by smartphones, and devices in general would be unable to connect to accessible networks. Moreover, according to a study by the McKinsey Global Institute in 2015 (Mckinsey Global Institute, 2015), without interoperability, at least 40% of the potential benefits of IoT cannot be achieved. This is evident considering that a transparent integration and interconnection of different IoT systems and system components would critically simplify their implementation, maximize performance and facilitate their operation with other systems. This interconnection of systems propitiates to share relevant data and to establish significant synergies, improving the quality of the information, the quality of service and the experience provided to the user. Moreover, interoperability enriches Big Data analytics using 3v model (Tanque, M., & Foxwell, 2014) through the integration of a variety of data formats, models and definitions, in a common data model to increase its effectiveness. Indeed, one of the main challenges in Big Data is to handle this data diversity properly (Chen et al., 2014).

To highlight the aforementioned advantages, let us consider an application of a bus company that calculates its optimal route. This application could benefit from interoperability with other transportation services. For instance, it could consider links with trains using the real time information that they provide. The application could also benefit from the interoperation with the traffic monitoring service of the city, capable of indicating the less congested routes. Thus, the service provided by the bus application would be more precise, complete and useful for the user.

Let us also consider some examples of IoT systems in the e-Health domain. In this area, interoperability among sensors and medical devices permit the remote monitoring of different bodily vital signals such as heart rate, blood pressure or breath rate using wearable sensors. Through this monitoring, it is possible for an IoT health system to detect any abnormality of vital signals remotely, at any moment, and automatically alert health services and caregivers. In both examples, it is necessary the interconnection and integration of systems in order to collect, analyse and use big amounts of data from heterogeneous sources.

To achieve a high degree of interoperability in an IoT system is therefore desirable, but regrettably it is still one of the most difficult and important challenges to solve in IoT. As a matter of fact, currently the different IoT systems are typically unable to communicate with each other or to interoperate in general (Diallo, Herencia-zapana, Padilla, & Tolk, 2011). The main cause of this lack of interoperability is the highly heterogeneous nature of IoT systems. The Internet of things covers a wide range of devices, protocols, technologies, networks, middleware, applications, systems and data that present a vast diversity. The heterogeneity of the underlying technologies can prevent the interoperation of smart objects and systems, as they follow different rules and standards. This diversity also affects the process of extracting value from the IoT Big Data due to its inherent heterogeneity, variety of data formats, and rapid growth (Chen et al., 2014). In this sense, the existence of a global reference standard for IoT would notably facilitate interoperability by giving rules and certain homogeneity to this heterogeneous universe. Though, currently there is no *de facto* reference standard, posing a significant problem when designing new IoT systems (Ganzha, Paprzycki, Pawlowski, Szmeja, & Wasielewska, 2016).

This chapter covers all these topics, starting with the explanation of the concept of interoperability in IoT, the different types of interoperability that exist, the problems that arise regarding their enablement and also the considerable benefits that interoperability brings. As far as standards can simplify and ease interoperability, an overview of the existing standards is provided, although so far none of them has been established as a de facto one. Also, in order to facilitate a deeper understanding of the concept, interoperability is studied in this chapter across the different layers of IoT systems: at the Device, Network and Middleware levels. Interoperability is analysed within each layer alongside with its associated problems and obstacles and potential solutions. Next, interoperability is analysed from a global perspective, implying interoperability between different IoT platforms. Finally, in order to show in practice the role of IoT interoperability in IoT systems some use cases are provided.

BACKGROUND

Definition of Interoperability

Although many interoperability definitions exist, they all agree on the same basic principles and highlight the necessary and sufficient conditions to achieve interoperability: "*Information exchange and usability of information*" (Diallo et al., 2011). Therefore, interoperability in the IoT ecosystem can be understood as the ability to exchange data and use the information across systems, applications, or system components.

Types of Interoperability

There are different types of interoperability to be considered:

- **Technical Interoperability** refers to the ability of systems, system components or applications to establish communication and share messages, without necessarily understanding their content. Hence, it does not imply awareness of data format and meaning (Molina, 2014). It typically requires the existence of network connectivity. Technical interoperability is strongly related with the elements that enable a machine-to-machine (M2M) communication (e.g. required protocols, hardware and software) (Hans van der Veer, 2008).
- **Syntactic Interoperability** refers to the ability of systems of correctly interpreting the message structure of exchanged information and, thus, being capable to read its content, although they may not be aware of the meaning of this information (Gubbi, Buyya, Marusic, & Palaniswami, 2013). An example of syntactic interoperability is a smart city system that receives information from a data center and is capable to properly recognise its specific data format (e.g. CSV) and thus correctly extract the data from the message (e.g. a set of values). Nevertheless, it may not be aware of what this data represents (for example the values could be temperatures), thus being unable to use the data within the correct context. Therefore, syntactic interoperability relies on data formats, as the messages exchanged among systems require a common data representation for the correct interpretation of the data structure and content (Yacchirema, Palau, & Esteve, 2016). The use of standardized data formats avoids ambiguity in the interpretation of data. Examples of data formats are standards such as, XML, JSON or CSV, which provide a high-level syntax.
- **Semantic Interoperability:** at this level, the systems are capable of interpreting the content and the meaning of the information exchanged. Ontologies, semantic technologies and knowledge management systems are means to facilitate semantic interoperability. In this regard, the Sensor Web Enablement (SWE) initiative of the Open Geospatial Consortium (OGC) defines data encod-

ings and Web services to enable interoperability by SensorML and O&M ontologies (Ganzha et al., 2016). As an example, semantic interoperability allows a smart city system that has correctly extracted the data received from another system, to understand the meaning and context of the information contained in this data. Then, this system can be aware that the set of values extracted actually represent temperatures of a city area. Thus, the system becomes capable of using this information in the proper context.

Importance of Interoperability in IoT

The connection of things or smart objects to the Internet generates unexpected insights and significant business value that will be positive for the citizenry and the industrial sector (Aloi et al., 2017). However, as it has been mentioned before, according to (Mckinsey Global Institute, 2015) without proper interoperability in IoT systems, it will not be possible to achieve on average 40% of the potential economic benefits of IoT.

Insufficient interoperability is the main obstacle for the development of IoT and its adoption by the market (Telecommunication Standarization Sector of ITU, 2014). It is also the cause of major technological and business issues and setbacks (Aloi et al., 2017). A typical issue is that some smart objects may not be compatible with certain IoT platforms. In addition, it causes an increased difficulty in the development of IoT applications that exploit several platforms in diverse domains. This situation produces sluggishness in the large-scale introduction of IoT technology. Some of its main drawbacks are frustration and discouragement when trying to adopt IoT technologies, increased costs, bad user experience and the non-reusability of technical solutions.

Another important issue is the existence of isolated systems due to the general lack of interoperability among platforms. The IoT market is a highly fragmented ecosystem in which several vertical systems coexist. Due to the absence of interoperability among them, these systems stand as isolated vertical silos of information that are unable to inter-operate, collaborate or share specific information (Soursos et al., 2016). These vertical systems cannot benefit from synergies and opportunities that arise in a fast-paced business landscape as a fruit of system interoperability. This has significant market drawbacks, and affects to the quality of services offered to the user.

From the point of view of Big Data, the lack of interoperability hinders substantially the integration of several IoT data sources to extract useful insight. The integration of different data sources enhances data with context information by accessing, combining, and mashing up several datasets. This data enrichment process improves the data quality and thus, data becomes more valuable (Janssen, Estevez, & Janowski, 2014). Enriched data allow for finding correlations, patterns, trends, and establishing relations of causality. However, reaching the interoperability at all levels in IoT is a very complex challenge because IoT platforms and systems use different standards, data formats, metadata, ontologies and data models. Lack of interoperability has many relevant drawbacks for the development of applications and has an enormous impact in the quality of big data analytics.

The envisioned future of IoT forecasts that all devices with communication and sensing capabilities will be able to interconnect and interact in a transparent way (Atzori, Iera, & Morabito, 2010) (Gubbi et al., 2013). According to this vision, interoperability plays a major role, as this seamless integration requires a very high degree of interoperation at all levels.

IOT STANDARDS

An effective approach to tackle interoperability is the use of standards, reference architecture models and the application of best practices in IoT deployments. In this sense, the use of a global standard in IoT can potentially solve the interoperability problem and enable compatibility among IoT systems.

Next, the most relevant standards for IoT are mentioned:

- **OneM2M:** Is the global standards initiative for IoT and Machine-to-Machine (M2M) communications. OneM2M is working on a service layer that includes technical requirements, Application Programming Interface (API) specifications, data semantics, and security solutions to enable IoT interoperability (Alaya, Banouar, Monteil, Chassot, & Drira, 2014).
- **AllJoyn:** Is an open source framework driven by the AllSeen Alliance that allows devices to communicate with other machines regardless of the communication technology or manufacturer thanks to the use of a common protocol (Allseen Alliance, 2017).
- **IoTivity:** Is an initiative from the Open Connectivity Foundation. It provides an open source framework that enables seamless interconnection and management of wired and wireless devices, independently from the device manufacturer or the operating system used (Linux Foundation, 2017).
- **ARM:** Is an IoT Reference Architectural Model proposed by the European research project IoT-A. This standardization initiative consists of a set of building blocks that represent basic concepts and components that enable the creation of interoperable IoT systems (Krco, Pokric, & Carrez, 2014).

Furthermore, other working groups have also provided their own standardization initiatives, as is the case of the organizations ITU, ETSI and IPSO Alliance. However, despite all these efforts, nowadays no global reference standard has been adopted for IoT. Moreover, none of the current standards is expected to become a referent in the medium-term future.

In this multi-standard context, the high fragmentation and development of vertical IoT systems is increasing, as systems operating on different standards are unable to communicate with each other. This produces a Babel's Tower-like situation that prevents interoperability among them.

INTEROPERABILITY LAYERED-APPROACH

IoT interoperability is a complex concept that encompasses many different aspects and elements from each layer of an IoT system. Instead of only providing a conventional holistic approach regarding interoperability, this section offers an analysis of interoperability across specific layers or levels of IoT systems: Device, Network and Middleware. This perspective offers a better comprehension of the IoT interoperability concept and its associated challenges.

The Device layer represents the set of sensors, actuators and smart objects that compose the lowest level of an IoT system. The Network layer is the level of networking and communication that encompasses networks and communication protocols. Finally, the Middleware layer represents the software infrastructure of an IT system that enables communication among its different components. Together, all these layers constitute the core of a standard IoT system.

Device Layer

The Device Layer in the context of IoT, refers to the collection of sensing devices or actuators connected to an IoT system. These are commonly known as the 'Things' in the Internet of Things. This layer is composed by smart objects (sensors, actuators and virtual devices) connected to a network that quite often have limited CPU, energy resources and memory. Devices that present these limitations are called "constrained devices". A classification of constrained devices can be found in (Bormann, 2014).

Main Issues

Interoperability at the device level refers to the ability of heterogeneous IoT smart objects to interact with other devices of an IoT system. It also means that they could be integrated into an IoT platform.

Interoperability at this layer is mainly hindered by the heterogeneity of devices regarding the protocols they use, their communication technologies, hardware specifications, providers, etc. Besides, the IoT device software is never platform-independent, since companies produce proprietary and closed solutions motivated by economic reasons. These facts make interoperability much harder to achieve.

Communication Models at the Device Layer

In order to analyze interoperability at the device layer, it is necessary to understand first the communication models of smart objects. Smart devices introduce a new communication paradigm and interoperability issues that cannot be solved by the existing patterns for traditional Internet architectures. For this reason, new communication models for smart objects have been recently defined (H. Tschofenig, J. Arkko, D. Thaler, 2015): device-to-device (D2D), device-to-gateway (D2G) and device-to-cloud (D2C).

Device-to-Device Communication Pattern (D2D)

D2D refers to direct communication between two devices. This includes M2M (e.g. direct communication between smartphones). In order to make D2D communication possible, specific communication aspects of both devices need to be defined and addressed. Such aspects comprise a common protocol stack and protocol design (e.g. supported physical layer, network technology, IP addressing, architecture, data rate constraints and transport protocol among other).

This type of communication requires a very specific solution design for each different case. Usually it is only possible between devices from the same vendor that support a common network technology.

Device-to-Cloud Communication Pattern (D2C)

In this case, the device sends directly information to a cloud platform, application or service. The cloud service provider is in charge of guaranteeing the interoperability with a wide range of devices.

Device-to-Gateway Communication (D2G)

This model refers to the communication between a smart device and a gateway, a node linking two networks that employ different protocols. Whereas the function of a bridge is to conjoin two similar types of networks, a gateway connects two dissimilar networks. The main functionality of the gateway is to convert protocols from an entering communication flow. This flow is then transmitted using a different set of protocols outside the gateway. This conversion is done at all levels (device, network, physical and application), allowing interoperability between two communication endpoints. For example, at a network level a gateway can convert between the IPv4 and IPv6 protocols; at the physical level, between 802.15.4 and 802.11, and at the application level between MQTT and CoAP.

The D2G communication model is generally employed to allow long-distance communication for constrained devices. This communication pattern is implemented in IoT systems to enable remote interactions with smart devices in real time. In that case, the gateway is permanently connected to the Internet.

Another case study of D2G is the use of a mobile gateway (e.g. a smartphone), where connectivity between the device and the Internet may be intermittent.

Interoperability Solutions in the Device Layer

Interoperability solutions for devices are typically gateway-oriented. These approaches allow the establishment of D2D and D2C communication when a direct connection is not possible due to technical limitations. In D2D, a gateway allows communication between smart devices that are not capable to communicate among them, which is the most frequent case. Both devices must be connected to the gateway. For D2C communications, a gateway is necessary when dealing with constrained devices. These devices lack resources to manage protocols for the interconnection with the cloud. In this case, the gateway acts also as an intermediary element.

Gateway-Oriented Interoperability Solutions

A gateway is a key element for providing interoperability in many IoT systems. It allows for interoperability among heterogeneous devices and between heterogeneous networks at many levels (i.e. device, application and physical) (Yacchirema, Palau, & Esteve, 2016).

Gateways for IoT, also called smart gateways, offer additional functionality to traditional gateways. A smart gateway adds a data processing stage before sending the information to its destination. Also, it usually provides connectivity for typical low-power IoT technologies (e.g. ZigBee or Bluetooth), in addition to the regular gateway connectivity (i.e. WiFi or Ethernet). This feature maximizes device interoperation, as most smart devices only use low-power technologies.

Gateways provide technical interoperability, allowing basic communication between the two endpoints (i.e. the smart device and the external destination endpoint). The data processing stage of the smart gateway facilitates syntactic and semantic interoperability. On one hand, the gateway can process the information received from a sensor, and convert it into the appropriate syntactic data format for the receiver. On the other hand, semantic metadata can be added to the sensor data using a data aggregation functionality to support semantic interoperability. This additional semantic metadata consists of information about the meaning and context of the data, and can be interpreted using the proper ontology.

An example of smart gateways are the software-defined IoT gateways. These can be implemented in any hardware featuring the necessary minimal requirements in terms of processing power (e.g., they can be installed in a low-power processor, such as a Raspberry). Some relevant examples of these gateways are:

- **Eclipse Kura:** Is an open-source Eclipse project that provides a platform for building IoT gateways. Kura offers a service API and is capable of handling events. It enables the remote management of IoT gateways. As it is Java-based, Kura is platform independent (it runs on any platform). As a disadvantage, it cannot be installed in devices with limited memory and processing power because Java requires considerable resources.
- **OneM2M middle node:** The middle node of an OneM2M platform acts as a smart IoT gateway. OneM2M middle node has a common service layer that enables interoperability and data exchange. This is done through the functions of device discovery, connectivity management and establishment of secure connections. This architecture can be easily extended by developing specific modules for new devices and protocols.
- **Mihini:** Is another Eclipse open source project that allows device interoperability and the development of M2M applications. This framework permits to build lightweight and portable smart IoT gateways, which require few processing power.
- **AGILE IoT:** Is a modular hardware and software gateway specifically conceived for the Internet of Things. It features support for protocol interoperability, device management, device data and IoT apps.
- **Intel IoT Gateway:** Intel offers a proprietary IoT gateway and a platform that allows its remote management. In addition to the software-defined gateway, Intel also provides the physical device. Intel IoT Gateway can connect both legacy industrial devices and modern smart objects to an IoT system.
- **BodyCloud:** A smart mobile gateway that can be installed on a smartphone. It was designed for medical purposes, to allow for the monitoring of a set of medical sensors on the body of a patient that carries the smartphone.

Network Layer

The network level of an IoT deployment refers to the set of protocols, systems, and devices that work on the Network layer of the OSI protocol stack (Whitmore, Agarwal, & Da Xu, 2015). This layer contains hardware elements such as switches, firewalls, routers and bridges.

In some aspects, networks in IoT environments are significantly different from traditional networks. Networks composed by an IoT gateway and smart objects have typically constrained capabilities such as unreliable channels, a narrow and erratic bandwidth, and a highly changing topology (Z. Shelby, K. Hartke, 2014). Other distinctive feature is that these networks typically support technologies and protocols for constrained devices. Most of them are wireless protocols for low rate transmission and energy saving. Examples of those technologies are ZigBee, RFID or LoRa.

This section explains how to achieve interoperability between networks or parts of a network that belong to an IoT system. At the network level, only technical interoperability is considered, given that semantic and syntactic aspects are transparent to this layer. Specific challenges in the network level include the seamless mobility of smart objects through different access networks (roaming) and secure connectivity. Other issues must be also considered, such as the difficulties inherent to the operation in highly constrained environments and the use of a wide range of heterogeneous protocols (e.g. 6LowPAN, RPL, LoRa, SIGFox, etc).

Interoperability Solutions at the Network Layer

The interoperability solutions introduced in this section are based on software-defined paradigms. They rely mainly on two approaches:

- **Software Defined Radio:** This approach can provide interoperability on the access to network, allowing seamless roaming among areas covered by SDRs, as well as a dynamic network topology.
- **Software Defined Networks:** This approach allows for a transparent and seamless interconnection of dissimilar non-adjacent IoT networks. Those networks do not need to be contiguous to act internally as a single one; they can be placed on different geographical locations.

Software Defined Radio

An obvious interoperability solution for network access is a gateway, which also allows performing protocol conversion and enables device interoperability. Another remarkable interoperability solution for network access is a Software Defined Radio (SDR), which is capable to solve very arduous interconnection problems that are inherent to IoT environments.

At present time, there is very limited spectrum available for IoT wireless networks. Thus, an effective use of the available spectrum is key to enable the connectivity of numerous wireless heterogeneous smart objects. As an additional problem, IoT environments suffer a high level of wireless interferences. To overcome this effect, communication with smart objects should be highly reliable.

A SDR represents an interoperability solution to overcome these problems and facilitate network access to multiple wireless sensors. These sensors can be working on very different radio frequencies using very different protocols/standards, or even be non-standard. A Software Defined Radio is a radio that has digital components and provides software control over radio system functionalities, such as the modulation type, the frequency and the transmit power, being digital SDR flexible and adaptable. SDR allows to combine different radio standards in a single terminal. The different standards, (e.g. GSM, UMTS or Wi-Fi) run as software modules. It is possible even to upload new or revised radio standards over-the-air. SDR software tuneable antenna system allows for efficient RF radiation over a wide range of frequencies.

As a result, SDR technology can bridge different wireless devices across different frequencies and protocols. With this approach, even non-standard devices that use a radio access network are able to interoperate with the rest of the IoT system. SDR can enhance interoperability and set up the infrastructure for future devices so that they are not restricted by bandwidth or frequency. In addition to the provision of standard two-way communication, SDR can act as repeaters in order to allow the communication among different wireless devices, engage with many different devices simultaneously, offer secure wireless nodes and provide very low latency point-to-point wireless links. This feature allows roaming of smart objects across repeaters and the creation of IoT networks with a very flexible and dynamic topology.

Software Defined Network Solution for Network Interoperability

Software Defined Network (SDN) solutions allow to interconnect different networks, enabling interoperability among them. Those networks can be on different locations, from different vendors, or with a different configuration or topology.

SDN is a set of network technologies that make the network functionality abstracted, virtualized and controlled via software. As a consequence, it can be automatized, and also accessed and controlled by a network administrator. SDN is based on these main technologies: network virtualization, functional separation and automation through programmability (Kreutz et al., 2015).

In a SDN, the network functionality is decoupled in two planes: the data plane that comprises the forwarding functions, and the control plane that represents the network control. The data plane is related with data transmission and transport, and due to this separation the network routing elements (e.g. switches, routers) become mere forwarders of data packets. On the other hand, regarding the control plane, the whole logic of routing, algorithms and other services previously provided by firewalls, middleboxes, IPS, etc. are transferred to a single point of control and decision-making called the controller. The system intelligence, the algorithms for routing and the network management become centralized. The underlying network infrastructure is abstracted, as this separation of planes allows the virtualization of the different components of the network, using the Network Function Virtualization (NFV) approach (Kreutz et al., 2015).

The NFV aims to virtualize all the functions and components within a network. Physical elements such as firewalls, routers, switches, load balancers, etc. can be virtualized and located in centralized or distributed equipment, and the underlying network can be controlled virtually (Omnes, Bouillon, Fromentoux, & Le Grand, 2015). The required hardware to use NFV is one or more servers capable of managing several virtual machines and the virtualized network elements. The physical forwarder elements of the data plane are controlled remotely by the network controller.

The centralized network control also facilitates interoperability among different SDN networks. In this case, two or more different networks can be joined and work altogether as one at a transport and networking level. Thus, their physical separation becomes transparent for the user as well as for all the connected IoT elements, which perceive the joint system as a whole. In other words, the SDN paradigm allows to create a single VLAN (Virtual Local Area Network) from a set of disjoint networks.

In addition, the SDN offers further benefits in terms of performance and interoperability. First, it facilitates specific interoperation inside a network as it provides useful features for IoT. For example, SDN provides network management based on access control and also mechanisms for WiFi (or other technologies) handoffs, and both of them enable roaming of smart objects across the network[1] (McKeown et al., 2008). Moreover, currently there is an exponential growth of data traffic in networks and SDN scalability and flexibility can overcome problems generated by this situation, unlike traditional networks.

Middleware Layer

The middleware is a software layer between applications and the communication network. It allows an application to abstract from the intricacies of how to send data to a service of another application. A middleware offers functionalities for this aim, such as to find and establish a connection to a service, negotiate the optimal wire and transport protocols, access applications data structures and encode the necessary data in a format appropriate for the selected protocol. Also, for sending the data and for receiving results back when there are any. Moreover, it can also provide additional services, such as monitoring, security and anonymization (Perera, Zaslavsky, Christen, & Georgakopoulos, 2014).

A middleware is a software that connects different and frequently complex IoT elements that were not initially conceived to be connected. This is the case of smart objects and the applications that want to interact with them. On one side, the middleware provides a connectivity layer for sensors, actuators, and networks of sensors; on the other side, it also provides a connectivity interface for applications that are willing to receive monitoring data from sensors, or perform any other interaction. The IoT middleware provides services that ensure effective communications between those elements, thus enabling interoperability among them (Perera et al., 2014).

Interoperability Challenges at Middleware Level

IoT interoperability represents a significant challenge for middleware approaches, given that applications and a vast range of heterogeneous smart devices are expected to collaborate by exchanging information. This entails high complexity in the middleware design and development, as it must be capable of supporting interoperability covering a wide range of current devices (Bandyopadhyay & Sen, 2011). Furthermore, it has also to tackle with the inclusion of potential new kinds of devices (Moumena, Mohamed, & Mohamed, 2012).

The different types of interoperability should be considered in middleware design:

- **Technical Interoperability:** To allow it, the middleware should be able to exchange information across different networks, and may use different communication technologies.
- **Syntactic Interoperation:** To achieve it, the middleware should allow for the heterogeneous formatting and encoding structures of any exchanged information.
- **Semantic Interoperability:** This should be permitted in the exchanges between devices and applications and services in IoT, in order to enable a common interpretation of the meaning of the exchanged information. Some middleware solutions have semantic support and use a specific ontology (e.g. Open-IoT and SOFIA2), while other do not (e.g. FIWARE).

There are also other challenges that should be addressed to improve interoperability at the middleware level. Firstly, an IoT middleware must be easily scalable in order to accommodate the potential growth of the IoT network and the related applications and services. Also, IoT middleware must have event management and automatic device identification to handle requests from the smart objects. Another challenge to be consider by IoT middleware would be to perform an abstraction of devices, data streams and interfaces to facilitate interoperability.

Finally, an IoT middleware should be continuously supported by developers to guarantee an up-to-date interoperability (Moumena et al., 2012).

Interoperability Solutions at Middleware Level

The development of IoT middleware is an active area of scientific and industrial research, and a considerable number of interesting solutions have been developed so far (Bandyopadhyay & Sen, 2011). Several architectures have been proposed for interoperability in IoT, such as ARM, FIWARE, OneM2M, SOFIA or UniversAAL. Some of them have been implemented, thus constituting functional IoT platforms (e.g. FIWARE or OneM2M). An IoT platform is defined as the infrastructure and middleware that allow end users to successfully interact with sensors and actuators (Mineraud, Mazhelis, Su, & Tarkoma, 2016). Therefore, a platform is a middleware solution that allows applications to seamlessly interact with the device layer, thus enabling interoperability. That means to enable the retrieval of data from sensors as well as issuing orders to actuators.

Some of the existing IoT platforms, such as FIWARE and OneM2M, are open-source, whereas others, like SOFIA2 and SORACOM, are proprietary. A specific group of these proprietary platforms are cloud-centric, which means that they are hosted in the cloud. They offer a set of services that include cloud storage as a Platform-as-a-Service (PaaS) on the Cloud, instead of a deployable self-hosted solution. Examples of cloud-centric platforms are the cloud platform solution for IoT offered by AWS, called AWS IoT, and Microsoft Azure. Next, some of the most relevant IoT platforms that represent middleware solutions for interoperability are described: FIWARE, OneM2M, UniversAAL and SOFIA2.

FIWARE is an open platform which provides diverse middleware services for distributed applications and a support framework for the Internet of Things. FIWARE provides a set of public APIs for the development of applications in multiple sectors (Fiware, 2017).

The foundation of FIWARE architecture are the General Enablers (GE), which provide general-purpose functions. FIWARE provides public specifications of the GE APIs and reference open-source implementations of each GE. Additionally, FIWARE offers domain-specific enablers that provide useful functionalities for specific sectors.

The main GE is the Context Broker, which receives data from the context producers and makes it available for the context consumers. Both context producers and context consumers communicate with the Context Broker through NGSI (Next Generation Service Interface). The main purpose of the Context Broker is to make the context consumers independent from the context producers. The context consumers can obtain the data from the Context Broker on demand or subscribe to the information on which they have taken an interest. The reference implementation of the Context Broker is called Orion.

Other GEs provide additional functionalities to the platform. For instance, the CEP (Complex Event Processing) provides real-time data analysis and sends notifications when certain situations are identified, while the Big Data Analysis GE deploys the means for the analysis of both aggregated and stream data on a Cloud Computing environment.

OneM2M provides a standard for Machine-to-Machine (M2M) interoperability, which refers to the communication between devices. Under the OneM2M functional architecture, several types of nodes are defined that can connect and communicate among them at a global scale. Every node may be composed of three kinds of logical entities:

- **Application Entity (AE):** Represents an M2M logical application
- **Common Service Entity (CSE):** Contains a set of common functions of the oneM2M architecture
- **Network Service Entity (NSE)**: Provides access to the underlying network infrastructure

The functional architecture consists of two domains: the Field Domain and the Infrastructure Domain, which are composed of different nodes. The Field Domain is made up of Application-Dedicated Nodes (ADNs), Application Service Nodes (ASNs) and Middle Nodes (MNs), which can be embodied as physical sensors or actuators, M2M devices, and M2M gateways, respectively. The Infrastructure Domain includes an Infrastructure Node (IN), which physically corresponds to the M2M server. Regarding the nodes, each of them consists of at least either a CSE or an AE. Depending on the type of node where the CSE is incorporated, this entity can be classified as:

- IN-CSE, if it is incorporated into an Infrastructure Node.
- MN-CSE, which are the CSEs incorporated into Middle Nodes.
- ASN-CSE, if the CSE is incorporated into an Application Service Node.

Several reference points defined within the Functional Architecture are used for the communications among OneM2M entities, such as

- Mca, for communication between AEs and CSEs.
- Mcn, for communication between CSEs and NSEs.
- Mcc, for communication between same domain CSEs.
- Mcc', for communication between different domain CSEs.

SOFIA2 is a proprietary platform developed by Indra Company and is based on the SOFIA architecture. SOFIA (Smart Objects For Intelligent Applications) was a research project that created a semantic interoperability platform. SOFIA2 permits the interoperability of several systems and devices in order to make real information available for IoT intelligent applications (Sofia2, 2017). The core of the platform is the Semantic Information Broker, which receives, processes and stores all the information. To provide semantic interoperability, any concept defined in the platform is represented through the use of ontologies.

UniversAAL is a semantic and distributed open-source platform designed for the development of integrated Ambient Assisted Living, e-Health and AHA applications. In UniversAAL, every component, including the services and the real world, is semantically annotated and represented in terms of ontologies. Every interaction is also modelled in a semantic way, making use of the RDF/Turtle format (Hanke et al., 2011).

GLOBAL INTEROPERABILITY

Regarding the concept of global interoperability, it must be noted that IoT platforms such as FIWARE, OneM2M or SOFIA2 provide full intra-platform interoperability across their different levels but they do not support interoperability with external IoT systems and platforms. Each platform uses its own architecture and it represents a vertical silo of isolated information, as it is not directly accessible by other IoT systems (Jacoby, Antonić, Kreiner, Łapacz, & Pielorz, 2016). For example, from a semantic perspective, platforms use different ontologies and semantic structures, so that the meaning of the information from one platform cannot be interpreted by another platform. Although semantic translations among platforms are possible, these tasks are usually complex, non-generalizable *ad hoc* solutions. Therefore, for the achievement of a more global, inter-platform interoperability, horizontal solutions for integrating those vertical silos must be provided (Jacoby et al., 2016).

An obvious solution for this problem would be the general acceptance of a common reference standard for IoT. This would facilitate interoperability at all levels, including the inter-platform case. Though, as it was mentioned before, the current multi-standard situation in IoT makes this approach very unlikely. No common de facto global standard has been foreseen for the middle-term future (Tan, L., & Wang, 2010). To overcome this situation, many partial and specific solutions have been developed. These solutions for interoperation among different IoT systems or platforms apply only to the device or data level and in an incomplete, non-transparent and non-seamless way (World Economic Forum, 2015). Although interoperability among platforms is a major concern in many application domains (e.g. e-Health), only few IoT architectures have addressed interoperability and integration issues among platforms. An example of these rare initiatives are the IoT platforms i-Core and Butler that were designed to be interoperable among them, but lacked interoperability with other platforms. Also, some other projects have recently addressed solutions for interoperability among platforms. One important example is the initiative INTER-IoT (InterIoT, 2016) that proposes a novel solution for enabling interoperability among different IoT platforms across all their levels or layers, including semantic interoperability. It also facilitates the discovery, orchestration and composition of applications and services provided by different platforms. This open-source solution aims to guarantee a seamless integration of heterogeneous IoT technologies, and a horizontal integration of vertical systems.

The INTER-IoT Solution for Global Interoperability Among IoT Platforms

Integration between heterogeneous elements is usually done at the device or network level, and it is typically limited to data collection (InterIoT, 2016). In contrast, INTER-IoT offers a more complete and global solution, based on a set of methods and interoperability solutions across all different layers.

Next, the main solutions and benefits of INTER-IoT at different levels are summarized:

- **Device Level:** INTER-IoT enables the seamless inclusion of new IoT devices and their interoperation with existing heterogeneous ones. This solution provides a Device-to-Device gateway that allows any type of data transfer, thus making the device layer more flexible by decoupling the gateway into two independent parts: a physical part that only manages network access and communication protocols, and a virtual part that handles all other gateway operations and services. If the connection is lost, the virtual part remains functional and answers the API requests. The gateway modularity allows the addition of optional service blocks in order to adapt to specific cases. It supports many network technologies such as ZigBee, LoRa, WiFi or PLC, and transport protocols (e.g. CoAP, Multipath TCP).
- **Network Level:** INTER-IoT provides transparent support for smart objects mobility (roaming) and information routing. This solution is based on SDN and NFV. It creates virtual networks that can be controlled through an API. Additionally, INTER-IoT enables offloading, roaming and secure seamless mobility, important aspects in IoT that are related to interoperability at the network level.
- **Middleware Level:** The solution provides a seamless resource discovery and management system for smart objects and their basic services. This allows the global exploitation of smart objects in large-scale IoT systems. Different modules at this level provide services to manage the virtual representation of smart objects, thus creating an abstraction layer to access all their features and information.
- **Application and Services Level:** The main benefits are the use, discovery and combination of heterogeneous services from different IoT platforms by means of the INTER-IoT service discovery, service catalog and service composition.

In addition to the technical interoperability achieved with these solutions, INTER-IoT also aims to guarantee syntactic and semantic interoperability. Regarding syntactic interoperability INTER-IoT performs a data format conversion among platforms, to put the information into the required syntax for the receiver platform. Regarding semantic interoperability, INTER-IoT allows a common interpretation of data and information from different platforms and heterogeneous data sources (Ganzha et al., 2016), with a novel approach that provides universal semantic translation among platforms.

The INTER-IoT framework can be employed as a middle element between two IoT platforms that are unable to directly interoperate among them due to the use of different standards, systems, data formats, and semantics.

USE CASES

In this section, two representative use cases of IoT strongly reliant on interoperability are analyzed: Smart Cities and e-Health.

Smart City

The use case of a smart city is a clear example of interoperability at many different levels because it includes wide sensor networks, gateways and middleware platforms that will handle and analyse the data collected from a common domain or several of them. IoT platforms enable the addition of value to the data gathered in the city to determine what applications can be used to offer useful services to the citizens. The whole set of applications and services can comprise a single domain or several of them (Cenedese, Zanella, Vangelista, & Zorzi, 2014). The potential benefits of interoperability on a large scale and across a whole city are manifold and important: relevant improvements in innovation, economic growth and well-being can be expected.

An challenging interoperability- and Big Data-related goal in smart cities is the adoption of a common standard and information model. This makes possible the fashioning of solutions, both interoperable and portable, that may be reproduced and adjusted to the perceived needs and requirements of every concerned city. Also, a common standard and information model makes possible the development of innovative services and applications that would allow the city to become more liveable, sustainable, affordable, and efficient. In particular, an enriched context information is developed by a common data model to establish easily correlational patterns for improving the city's urban planning (Ahmed et al., 2017). As a result, cities may accomplish the envisioned transformation with minimum impact, thereby merging the intervening forces to arrange an ecosystem in which systems can link up and collaborate.

Next, it is presented the analysis of Valencia Smart City, a real Smart City IoT platform implementation.

Valencia Smart City

The city of Valencia (Spain) is the first case in Europe of a practically total integration of public services in a Smart City (above 95%). Regarding the technology and tools used, Valencia Smart City presents the adoption of FIWARE open data APIs and platforms to release open data. Web and mobile applications can make use of this data to offer a variety of services, such as route calculation and real-time estimated timing of the different public transport options (subway, bus and tramlines), bike rental information (availability, nearby stations), information about parking lots, etc. Furthermore, the Valencia Smart City Platform (VLCi Platform) provides an integral view of the city and its management, and enables the improvement of the decision-making processes.

Across the city, a sensor network collects a wide variety of data from the environment, such as traffic information, public transport information, air pollution, noise, etc. Those sensors connect to several gateways, which perform data pre-processing tasks and send the data to the FIWARE Context Broker.

The Context Broker mediates between data producers and consumers in order to allow access to the information regardless of its source. The information is processed in real time by a CEP (Complex Event Processing) component of the IoT platform, which identifies patterns and triggers events based on the application of predefined rules. The CEP enables instant response to changing conditions. The gathered data is classified into different collections and stored in public repositories on CKAN, which is the most widely used software to build Open Data portals. Moreover, dynamic data is accessible in real time through the Real Time Open Data API.

Finally, a variety of applications and services make use of the available data. Applications and services can obtain data from the system upon request by making use of the defined APIs. This way, applications can retrieve data from Context Broker or CKAN and exploit the data by using Big Data platforms. As a result, general tendencies can be identified or predicted by making use of Big Data analytics on aggregated datasets. For example, a machine learning model can be implemented to identify the car traffic increment in some sites of the city due to a rainy day and make predictions about traffic behaviour in future rainy days, so the city council can use this information to make effective plans to reduce car traffic. In addition, the applications can also subscribe to events generated by the CEP or the Context Broker in order to receive information of interest whenever it is available. For instance, the information about free parking spots can be provided by a mobile application that make use of the subscription services from the Context Broker. The systems described above are possible thanks to interoperability at different levels.

Sensors and gateways interact at the device level and technical interoperability is needed in order to have network connectivity. The gateway also provides interoperability at the network level (routing) and syntactic interoperability through common data representations (JSON) and communication protocols (NGSI). At an upper level, the Context Broker receives and manages all the requests addressed to the IoT platform and provides interoperability at the middleware level. Finally, semantic interoperability is needed in order to ensure that the meaning of the data sent the IoT platform is understood by any application, system or service that consumes this information. Seeking to attain semantic interoperability in FIWARE, the authors of (Kovacs et al., 2016) propose the incorporation of knowledge-based semantic processing agents (KSPAs) to the platform. These agents can be incorporated to the FIWARE Data Model as hidden processing agents or can offer their semantic services to the applications, systems and services. Figure 1 shows the high-level architecture employed to enable the different interoperability levels in the proposed use case.

E-Health Platform

IoT interoperability can offer critical benefits in the area of health. Some of these benefits are the improvement in the comfort level of patients, the provision of remote patient monitoring (Yacchirema, Sarabia-Jácome, Palau, & Esteve, 2018) which makes it possible to provide healthcare even in remote locations, and an associated cost reduction due to a decrease in the number of hospital visits. Moreover, the use of wearable sensors and mobile devices allows for real-time monitoring and Big Data analytics can help to personalize healthcare and treatments (Farahani et al., 2017).

The development of an e-Health platform relies on interoperability at different levels. The sensors need to connect to a network in order to share their information. A gateway, which can be a physical device or an application running on a mobile device, provides access to the Internet in order to make the data available. A middleware platform provides integration and permits access to information in a transparent way, thus shielding the particulars of the devices from the applications making use of the data. In order

Figure 1. Smart City case study schema

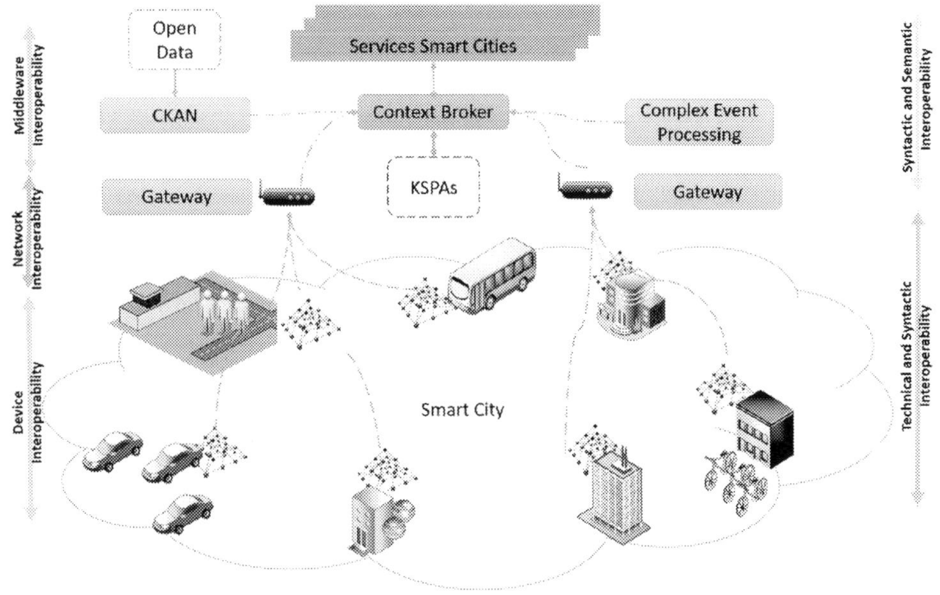

to make sure that the data shared across the system is interpreted correctly and proper actions are taken, semantic interoperability is required (Ganzha, Paprzycki, Pawłowski, Szmeja, & Wasielewska, 2018).

Next, it is presented an example of the possible use of IoT interoperability solutions in the e-Health domain. In this example, a fictional continuous care system based on OneM2M will be explained. Continuous care allows elderly people and patients with chronic disease to reduce their visits to the doctor. Figure 2 illustrates how this e-Health platform would be implemented.

Sensors and medical devices monitor physiological variables, such as heart rate and oxygen saturation. These devices communicate with the gateway using wireless protocols, such as Zigbee or Bluetooth. In the gateway, the Common Service Entity of the Middle Node (MN-CSE) sends the data to the Common Service Entity of the Infrastructure Node (IN-CSE), which in this case is hosted in the Cloud by the OneM2M provider. The Application Entities of the Infrastructure Node (IN-AE) interact with the IN-

Figure 2. e-Health case study schema

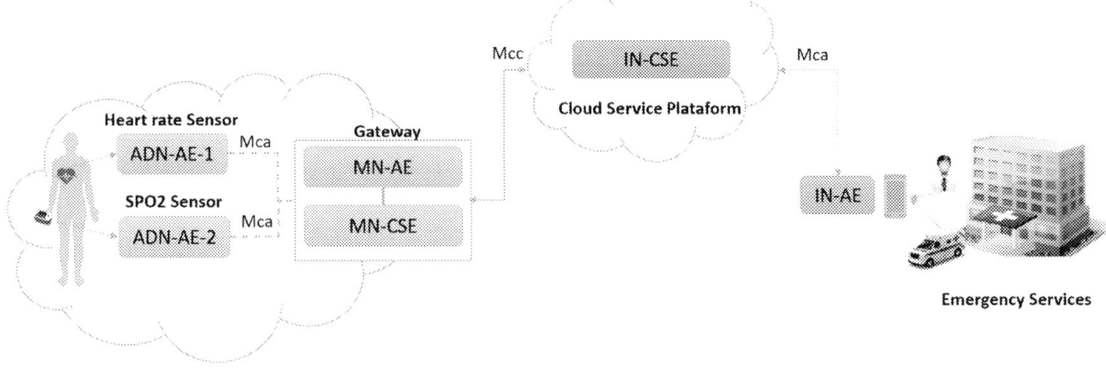

CSE and retrieve the information in order to provide health and environment monitoring services. This interaction is based on a publish/subscribe scheme. Hence, the platform sends the updated parameters to the doctor, who interprets the results. The system also performs some data processing in order to identify abnormal situations and send a warning to the emergency services when a potentially dangerous situation arises.

Regarding the different types of interoperability needed for this platform, the use of common standard wireless protocols provides device level interoperability, while the gateway provides network level interoperability. The middleware level interoperability is obtained by making use of an IoT platform. Technical interoperability is accomplished thanks to the use of communication protocols while the use of common data representations provides syntactic interoperability. Finally, the definition of data semantics though the use of ontologies allows for semantic interoperability. Ontologies, which are represented as OWL files, describe the system as well as the meaning and purpose of the data. Currently, OneM2M provides one ontology, termed the oneM2M Base Ontology, which is the minimal ontology required for interoperability. This ontology can be extended using domain-specific ontologies. Hence, semantic interoperability would be achieved by the incorporation into the platform of ontologies describing concepts from the health domain.

Stored data in the IN-CSE can be accessed by Big Data analytics platforms to effectively get valuable insights. By doing so, innovative services can be developed to provide remote patient monitoring, improve the patients' quality of life, and reduce healthcare associated cost (Ahmed et al., 2017). Rule-based processing, and event processing can be applied to monitoring a remote patient's vital signs using a CEP that identifies out of thresholds values (Farahani et al., 2017). Also, data mining and machine learning models can be applied using platforms such as Weka, Scikit-learn, or TensorFlow to predict diseases and reduce healthcare costs. For example, the prediction of obstructive sleep apnoea can be implemented by using ECG sensor to detect the disease, thus reducing the high price of a polysomnography test (Glasser et al., 2014). Furthermore, automotive reasoning algorithms can be implemented to re-configure rules in the CEP to adapt to the particular patients' habits in order to improve their quality of life (Farahani et al., 2017). For instance, a personal treatment plan can be designed based on information about sleep, physics or eating habits (Forkan, Khalil, & Tari, 2014). Regarding the possibilities that Big Data analysis offers, data scientists can find ways of improving the business model by exploiting the integrated data obtained from IoT sensors and platforms.

FUTURE RESEARCH DIRECTIONS

As a major concern in IoT, which also encompasses multiple levels and aspects, IoT interoperability is a topic that has currently open several lines of future research.

Ambient Intelligence environments (AmI) (Aarts & Wichert, 2009) represent a very important research area of IoT today. These intelligent environments aim to facilitate people's life. In special, e-Health (Scarpato, Pieroni, Di Nunzio, & Fallucchi, 2017) and Active and Healthy Ageing (AHA) domains (Bousquet, Kuh, Bewick, Standberg, & Farrell et al., 2015), in the area of Ambient Assisted Living (AAL) are very benefited from the existence of this intelligent environments that support assisted life through the leverage of IoT technology. Regarding future research directions, it must be noted that Ambient Intelligent environments evolve towards the use of transparent human interfaces completely integrated in the intelligent environment. As well, the vision of future of the IoT is an environment in which smart devices connect and interact transparently with each other, without the need of human interaction (Mishra et al., 2016). Both future predictions only can be achieved through seamless interoperability among the different components, technologies and protocols employed in those environments. Therefore, the achievement of transparent interoperability at multiple levels represents an important research aim. Also, other IoT fields, such as Smart Cities and e-Health, are specially benefited from inter-system and inter-platform interoperability. There is currently an important research effort on this direction.

From a big data point of view, the use of data from different IoT sources enriches the big data analysis, enhancing the value of the information extracted from this set, and augmenting very significantly the benefits of the big data analysis. Though, the use of multiple sources implies an effort on processing different type of data formats and semantics, and on understanding the meaning of that information (Ullah et al., 2017). The use of very different standards, formats and semantics on different IoT systems makes the integration of different sources difficult, and thus, their exploitation. Interoperability between domains allows generating a single data model and standard formats. Moreover, policies and agreements need to be implemented to enable platforms to share data to each other, although some initiatives, such as Inter-IoT facilitate interoperability and information sharing between different IoT domains and platforms (Ganzha et al., 2018).

In the field of semantic interoperability among IoT systems and platforms, solutions that enable scalability and automatic adaptation are being currently an aim of several research efforts (Ganzha, Paprzycki, Pawłowski, Szmeja, & Wasielewska, 2017). Current solutions are generally not scalable, thus is exponentially complex the addition of new systems for enabling semantic interoperability among them. However, this feature will enable systematic semantic interoperability in a broad scope.

Regarding the current evolution and growth of IoT, new protocols specifically designed for IoT are emerging. Gateways and middlewares have to be updated for working with new technologies, protocols and different syntactic formats. A modular design in the case of smart gateways allows an easier adaptation to these new protocols and technologies. In particular, research efforts for providing middleware for IoT are increasing in an accelerated rate during the last years. The development of a middleware is a research challenge that requires constant updates due to the rapid evolution of IoT. Thus, there are currently important research efforts on those directions (Razzaque, Milojevic-Jevric, Palade, & Clarke, 2016) (Yacchirema, Palau, & Esteve, 2016).

In addition, there is further research on the field of network virtualization. Interoperability, roaming, flexibility and adaptation to changing environments, such as the current exponential growth of traffic, can be solved through the use of SDN and network virtualization (Tayyaba, Shah, Khan, & Ahmed, 2017). In that sense, traditional networks are not prepared for this congestion situation and thus face collapse; nevertheless, this data traffic growth is expected to keep this unstoppable growth in the future. On the other hand, roaming of smart objects is tightly related with network interoperability and represents an important concern in IoT systems and in the field of fog computing. Due to these reasons, it is currently receiving a considerable research attention.

CONCLUSION

The concept of interoperability in IoT is defined and thoroughly explained in this chapter. Additionally, its crucial role and importance in IoT and Big Data has been discussed, alongside with the general lack of interoperability at this moment, the problems that preclude its actual achievement, and the currently existent IoT standards. Interoperability has been analysed across several layers of IoT systems by studying the challenges posed by its achievement, possible technical solutions and use cases. Finally, the concept of global interoperability has been presented and an overview of the current situation of interoperability has been discussed in main outline.

IoT is going to be the next revolution of the information era and the next step in the path of modern society towards full digitalization. Interoperability is the key to unlock an immense untapped potential of IoT. To make it possible, a global reference standard for IoT is expected and very necessary. Its existence, in conjunction with a widespread acceptance and implementation, will solve the interoperability problem and allow the world to benefit from the full potential of IoT. More than a dozen possible global standards for IoT exist already. Among others, AllJoyn is pointed out as one of the best positioned candidates for becoming the future reference standard for IoT, due to a strong support from some very relevant technological firms. IoTivity is also a promising option as it is the candidate with the strongest support from the open source community. However, at present, all these possibilities seem to be uncertain and unclear, and their chances of success are considerably slim. No global reference standard is expected for the middle-term future.

The lack of a global reference standard and the vast heterogeneity in IoT environments are the main factors preventing interoperability in IoT. In this multi-standard scenario, new initiatives for enabling global interoperability seem destined to play a major role. It is important to mention the existence of initiatives such as INTER-IoT, which will allow for interoperability among different IoT platforms and across all their levels or layers, despite the use of different standards on them. Interoperability frameworks may play an essential role in the achievement of global interoperability and the disappearance of vertical silos. Thus, new initiatives and solutions capable of solving the interoperability problem may be key to unleash the enormous latent potential of the Internet of Things, which is still waiting to be awaken.

ACKNOWLEDGMENT

This research has received funding from the "Horizon 2020" research and innovation program as part of the Interoperability of Heterogeneous IoT Platforms project (INTER-IoT) under grant agreement 687283, ACTIVAGE project under grant agreement 732679, the Ecuadorian Government through of Secretary of Higher Education, Science, Technology, and Innovation (SENESCYT) and Escuela Politécnica Nacional.

REFERENCES

Ahmed, E., Yaqoob, I., Hashem, I. A. T., Khan, I., Ahmed, A. I. A., Imran, M., & Vasilakos, A. V. (2017). The role of big data analytics in Internet of Things. *Computer Networks*, *129*, 459–471. doi:10.1016/j.comnet.2017.06.013

Allseen Alliance. (2017). *AllJoyn Framework*. Retrieved May 1, 2017, from https://allseenalliance.org/framework

Aloi, G., Caliciuri, G., Fortino, G., Gravina, R., Pace, P., Russo, W., & Savaglio, C. (2017). Enabling IoT interoperability through opportunistic smartphone-based mobile gateways. *Journal of Network and Computer Applications*, *81*, 74–84. doi:10.1016/j.jnca.2016.10.013

Atzori, L., Iera, A., & Morabito, G. (2010). The Internet of Things: A survey. *Computer Networks*, *54*(15), 2787–2805. doi:10.1016/j.comnet.2010.05.010

Bandyopadhyay, D., & Sen, J. (2011). Internet of things: Applications and challenges in technology and standardization. *Wireless Personal Communications*, *58*(1), 49–69. doi:10.100711277-011-0288-5

Ben Alaya, M., Banouar, Y., Monteil, T., Chassot, C., & Drira, K. (2014). OM2M: Extensible ETSI-compliant M2M service platform with self-configuration capability. *Procedia Computer Science*, *32*, 1079–1086. doi:10.1016/j.procs.2014.05.536

Bormann, C. M. E. A. K. (2014). *Terminology for Constrained-Node Networks RFC 7228*. Retrieved August 12, 2016, from https://tools.ietf.org/html/rfc7228#section-2.3.2

Bousquet, J., Kuh, D., Bewick, M., Standberg, T., & Farrell, J. (2015). Operational definition of Active and Healthy Ageing (AHA): A conceptual framework. *The Journal of Nutrition, Health & Aging, 19*(9), 955–960. doi:10.100712603-015-0589-6

Cenedese, A., Zanella, A., Vangelista, L., & Zorzi, M. (2014). Padova smart City: An urban Internet of Things experimentation. *Proceeding of IEEE International Symposium on a World of Wireless, Mobile and Multimedia Networks 2014, WoWMoM 2014*. 10.1109/WoWMoM.2014.6918931

Chen, M., Shiwen, M., Zhang, Y., Leung, V. C. M., Mao, S., Zhang, Y., & Leung, V. C. M. M. (2014). *Big Data-Related Technologies*. Challenges and Future Prospects; doi:10.1007/978-3-319-06245-7

Diallo, S. Y., Herencia-zapana, H., Padilla, J. J., & Tolk, A. (2011). *Understanding Interoperability*. Academic Press.

ETSI. (2013). *Interoperability Best Practices*. Retrieved from https://portal.etsi.org/CTI/Downloads/ETSIApproach/IOT_Best_Practices.pdf

Farahani, B., Firouzi, F., Chang, V., Badaroglu, M., Constant, N., & Mankodiya, K. (2017). Towards fog-driven IoT eHealth: Promises and challenges of IoT in medicine and healthcare. *Future Generation Computer Systems*. doi:10.1016/j.future.2017.04.036

Fiware. (2017). Retrieved May 1, 2017, from https://www.fiware.org/tag/iot/

Forkan, A., Khalil, I., & Tari, Z. (2014). CoCaMAAL: A cloud-oriented context-aware middleware in ambient assisted living. *Future Generation Computer Systems*, *35*, 114–127. doi:10.1016/j.future.2013.07.009

Ganzha, M., Paprzycki, M., Pawlowski, W., Szmeja, P., & Wasielewska, K. (2016). Semantic Technologies for the IoT-An Inter-IoT Perspective. In *Internet-of-Things Design and Implementation (IoTDI), 2016 IEEE First International Conference on* (pp. 271–276). Academic Press. 10.1109/IoTDI.2015.22

Ganzha, M., Paprzycki, M., Pawłowski, W., Szmeja, P., & Wasielewska, K. (2017). Semantic interoperability in the Internet of Things: An overview from the INTER-IoT perspective. *Journal of Network and Computer Applications*, *81*, 111–124. doi:10.1016/j.jnca.2016.08.007

Ganzha, M., Paprzycki, M., Pawłowski, W., Szmeja, P., & Wasielewska, K. (2018). Towards Semantic Interoperability Between Internet of Things Platforms BT - Integration, Interconnection, and Interoperability of IoT Systems. In R. Gravina, C. E. Palau, M. Manso, A. Liotta, & G. Fortino (Eds.), (pp. 103–127). Cham: Springer International Publishing; doi:10.1007/978-3-319-61300-0_6

Glasser, M., Bailey, N., McMillan, A., Goff, E., Morrell, M. J., Nam, Y., ... Da Xu, L. (2014). Multi-modal Low-Invasive System for Sleep Quality Monitoring and Improvement BT - Beyond the Internet of Things: Everything Interconnected. *Sleep*, *49*(6), 261–274. doi:10.1164/rccm.169.1160

Gubbi, J., Buyya, R., Marusic, S., & Palaniswami, M. (2013). Internet of Things (IoT): A vision, architectural elements, and future directions. *Future Generation Computer Systems*, *29*(7), 1645–1660. doi:10.1016/j.future.2013.01.010

Hanke, S., Mayer, C., Hoeftberger, O., Boos, H., Wichert, R., & Tazari, M.-R. … Furfari, F. (2011). universAAL -- An Open and Consolidated AAL Platform. In R. Wichert & B. Eberhardt (Eds.), Ambient Assisted Living: 4. AAL-Kongress 2011 (pp. 127–140). Berlin: Springer Berlin Heidelberg. doi:10.1007/978-3-642-18167-2_10

Hans van der Veer, A. W. (2008). *Achieving Technical Interoperability - the ETSI Approach*. Academic Press.

InterIoT. (2016). Retrieved June 1, 2017, from http://www.inter-iot-project.eu/

Jacoby, M., Antonić, A., Kreiner, K., Łapacz, R., & Pielorz, J. (2016). Semantic Interoperability as Key to IoT Platform Federation. In *International Workshop on Interoperability and Open-Source Solutions* (pp. 3–19). Academic Press.

Janssen, M., Estevez, E., & Janowski, T. (2014). Interoperability in Big, Open, and Linked Data--Organizational Maturity, Capabilities, and Data Portfolios. *Computer*, *47*(10), 44–49. doi:10.1109/MC.2014.290

Kovacs, E., Bauer, M., Kim, J., Yun, J., Le Gall, F., & Zhao, M. (2016). Standards-Based Worldwide Semantic Interoperability for IoT. *IEEE Communications Magazine*, *54*(12), 40–46. doi:10.1109/MCOM.2016.1600460CM

Krco, S., Pokric, B., & Carrez, F. (2014). Designing IoT architecture (s): A European perspective. In *Internet of Things (WF-IoT), 2014 IEEE World Forum on* (pp. 79–84). IEEE.

Kreutz, D., Ramos, F. M. V., Verissimo, P. E., Rothenberg, C. E., Azodolmolky, S., & Uhlig, S. (2015). Software-defined networking: A comprehensive survey. *Proceedings of the IEEE*, *103*(1), 14–76. doi:10.1109/JPROC.2014.2371999

Linux Foundation. (2017). *IoTivity*. Retrieved May 1, 2017, from https://www.iotivity.org/

McKeown, N., Anderson, T., Balakrishnan, H., Parulkar, G., Peterson, L., Rexford, J., ... Turner, J. (2008). OpenFlow: Enabling innovation in campus networks. *Computer Communication Review*, *38*(2), 69–74. doi:10.1145/1355734.1355746

McKinsey Global Institute. (2015). *The Internet of Things : Mapping the Value Beyond the Hype*. Author.

Mineraud, J., Mazhelis, O., Su, X., & Tarkoma, S. (2016). A gap analysis of Internet-of-Things platforms. *Computer Communications*, *89*, 5–16. doi:10.1016/j.comcom.2016.03.015

Mishra, D., Gunasekaran, A., Childe, S. J., Papadopoulos, T., Dubey, R., & Wamba, S. (2016). Vision, applications and future challenges of Internet of Things: A bibliometric study of the recent literature. *Industrial Management & Data Systems*, *116*(7), 1331–1355. doi:10.1108/IMDS-11-2015-0478

Molina, B. (2014). Empowering smart cities through interoperable Sensor Network Enablers. Academic Press. doi:10.1109/SMC.2014.6973876

Moumena, A., Mohamed, C., & Mohamed, N. (2012). Challenges in Middleware Solutions for the Internet of Things. *Proc. of The 2012 International Conference on Collaboration Technologies and Systems (CTS 2012).*

Omnes, N., Bouillon, M., Fromentoux, G., & Le Grand, O. (2015). A programmable and virtualized network & IT infrastructure for the internet of things: How can NFV & SDN help for facing the upcoming challenges. In *Intelligence in Next Generation Networks (ICIN), 2015 18th International Conference on* (pp. 64–69). Academic Press.

Perera, C., Zaslavsky, A., Christen, P., & Georgakopoulos, D. (2014). Context aware computing for the internet of things: A survey. *IEEE Communications Surveys and Tutorials*, *16*(1), 414–454. doi:10.1109/SURV.2013.042313.00197

Razzaque, M. A., Milojevic-Jevric, M., Palade, A., & Clarke, S. (2016). Middleware for Internet of Things: A Survey. *IEEE Internet of Things Journal*, *3*(1), 70–95. doi:10.1109/JIOT.2015.2498900

Scarpato, N., Pieroni, A., Di Nunzio, L., & Fallucchi, F. (2017). E-health-IoT universe: A review. *Management*, *21*(44), 46.

Shelby, Z., & Hartke, K. C. B. (2014). *The Constrained Application Protocol (CoAP) - RFC 7252.* Retrieved July 15, 2016, from http://coap.technology/

Sofia2. (2017). Retrieved June 1, 2017, from http://sofia2.com/

Soursos, S., Zarko, I. P., Zwickl, P., Gojmerac, I., Bianchi, G., & Carrozzo, G. (2016). Towards the cross-domain interoperability of IoT platforms. In *2016 European Conference on Networks and Communications (EuCNC)* (pp. 398–402). Academic Press. 10.1109/EuCNC.2016.7561070

Tan, L., & Wang, N. (2010). Future Internet: The Internet of Things. In *Advanced Computer Theory and Engineering (ICACTE), 3rd International Conference* (pp. 376–380). Academic Press.

Tanque, M., & Foxwell, H. J. (2014). *Big Data and Cloud Computing: A Review of Supply Chain Capabilities and Challenges*. Retrieved from http://linkinghub.elsevier.com/retrieve/pii/B9780124071926000091

Tayyaba, S. K., Shah, M. A., Khan, O. A., & Ahmed, A. W. (2017). Software Defined Network (SDN) Based Internet of Things (IoT): A Road Ahead. In *Proceedings of the International Conference on Future Networks and Distributed Systems* (p. 10). ACM. 10.1145/3102304.3102319

Telecommunication Standarization Sector of ITU. (2014). *Common requirements and capabilities of a gateway for Internet of things applications*. Retrieved from https://www.itu.int/rec/T-REC-Y.2067/en

Tschofenig, H., Arkko, J., & Thaler, D. D. M. (2015). *Architectural Considerations in Smart Object Networking - RFC 7452*. Retrieved from https://tools.ietf.org/pdf/rfc7452.pdf

Ullah, F., Habib, M. A., Farhan, M., Khalid, S., Durrani, M. Y., & Jabbar, S. (2017). Semantic interoperability for big-data in heterogeneous IoT infrastructure for healthcare. *Sustainable Cities and Society*, *34*, 90–96. doi:10.1016/j.scs.2017.06.010

Whitmore, A., Agarwal, A., & Da Xu, L. (2015). The Internet of Things—A survey of topics and trends. *Information Systems Frontiers*, *17*(2), 261–274. doi:10.100710796-014-9489-2

World Economic Forum. (2015). *Industrial Internet of Things: Unleashing the Potential of Connected Products and Services*. Retrieved from http://www3.weforum.org/docs/WEFUSA_IndustrialInternet_Report2015.pdf

Yacchirema, D., Palau, C., & Esteve, M. (2016). Smart IoT Gateway For Heterogeneous Devices Interoperability. *IEEE Latin America Transactions*, *14*(8), 3900–3906. doi:10.1109/TLA.2016.7786378

Yacchirema, D., Sarabia-Jácome, D., Palau, C. E., & Esteve, M. (2018). A Smart System for sleep monitoring by integrating IoT with big data analytics. *IEEE Access: Practical Innovations, Open Solutions*, *1*. doi:10.1109/ACCESS.2018.2849822

ADDITIONAL READING

Ahlgren, B., Hidell, M., & Ngai, E. C. (2016). Internet of Things for Smart Cities: Interoperability and Open Data. *IEEE Internet Computing*, *20*(6), 52–56. doi:10.1109/MIC.2016.124

Aloi, G., Caliciuri, G., Fortino, G., Gravina, R., Pace, P., Russo, W., & Savaglio, C. (2017). Enabling IoT interoperability through opportunistic smartphone-based mobile gateways. *Journal of Network and Computer Applications*, *81*, 74–84. doi:10.1016/j.jnca.2016.10.013

Bröring, A., Schmid, S., Schindhelm, C. K., Khelil, A., Käbisch, S., Kramer, D., ... Teniente, E. (2017). Enabling IoT Ecosystems through Platform Interoperability. *IEEE Software*, *34*(1), 54–61. doi:10.1109/MS.2017.2

Chang, W. L., Roy, A., Grady, N., Reinsch, R., Underwood, M., Fox, G., … von Laszewski, G. (2018). *NIST big data interoperability framework*.

Ganzha, M., Paprzycki, M., Pawłowski, W., Szmeja, P., & Wasielewska, K. (2017). Semantic interoperability in the Internet of Things: An overview from the INTER-IoT perspective. *Journal of Network and Computer Applications*, *81*, 111–124. doi:10.1016/j.jnca.2016.08.007

Hans van der Veer, A. W. (2008). *Achieving Technical Interoperability - the ETSI Approach*.

Interconnection Issues in CPS. (2015). *Challenges, Opportunities, and Dimensions of Cyber-Physical Systems* (pp. 61–75). Hershey, PA, USA: IGI Global; doi:10.4018/978-1-4666-7312-0.ch004

ITU-T. Smart Sustainable Cities. (n.d.). Retrieved August 12, 2016, from http://www.itu.int/en/ITU-T/ssc/Pages/default.aspx

Swetina, J., Lu, G., Jacobs, P., Ennesser, F., & Song, J. (2014). Toward a standardized common M2M service layer platform: Introduction to oneM2M. *IEEE Wireless Communications*, *21*(3), 20–26. doi:10.1109/MWC.2014.6845045

KEY TERMS AND DEFINITIONS

Constrained Device: Is a device with sensing capabilities, which presents limited CPU, energy resources, and memory.

E-Health: It is also called health information technology refers to the use of information and communications technologies like to the internet to store and manage the medical records, instead of paper files in healthcare industry.

Interoperability: Is the ability to exchange data and use the information across systems, applications, or system components.

IoT Platform: Is the infrastructure and middleware that allow end users and applications to successfully interact with sensors and actuators.

M2M or Machine-to-Machine Communication: Direct exchange of information or communication between two remote machines (e.g., dispositions, tablets, PCs, etc.) without the manual assistance of humans.

Ontology: Is a vocabulary that contains the formal naming of concepts, and the definition of their types, properties, and interrelations. It enables a common interpretation of semantic metadata, which allows systems to understand the actual meaning and context of exchanged data.

Semantic Interoperability: Ability of systems of understanding the meaning and context of the information exchanged among them. Ontologies, semantic technologies and knowledge management systems are means to facilitate semantic interoperability.

Smart City: City that employs digital technology to enhance the quality and performance of urban services (such as transportation, energy, environment, etc.) through the leverage of modern technologies such as IoT.

Smart Gateway: Is a gateway specifically designed for the connection of IoT devices. These gateways offer additional functionality in comparison to traditional gateways such as data aggregation and data pre-processing. Also, they usually provide low-power connectivity through typical IoT technologies such as ZigBee or Bluetooth.

Smart Object or Smart Device: Refers to any sensor, actuator and/or virtual device connected within an IoT system.

Syntactic Interoperability: Is the ability of systems of correctly interpreting the message structure of exchanged information, and thus, of being capable to read its content, although they may not being aware of the meaning of this information.

Technical Interoperability: Refers to the ability of systems, system components or applications to establish communication and share messages, without necessarily understanding their content.

Vertical Silo: System that is unable to communicate or interoperate with others.

ENDNOTE

1 Roaming is defined as a network service that allows mobile wireless smart objects to travel among different access points of a network maintaining uninterruptedly its connection.

Chapter 10
Critical Issues in the Invasion of the Internet of Things (IoT): Security, Privacy, and Other Vulnerabilities

Shravani Devarakonda
Charles Sturt University, Australia

Malka Halgamuge
The University of Melbourne, Australia

Azeem Mohammad
Charles Sturt University, Australia

ABSTRACT

In this chapter, the authors collected data from issues related to threats in the applications of IoT-based technologies that describe the security and privacy issues from 30 peer reviewed publications from 2014 to 2017. Further, they analyzed each threat type and its percentages in each application of the internet of things. The results indicated that the applications of smart transportation (20%) face the highest amount of security and privacy issues followed by smart home (19%) and smart cities (18%) compared to the rest of the applications. Further, they determined that the biggest threats were denial of service attack (9%) followed by eavesdropping (5%), man in the middle (4%), and replay (4%). Denial of service attacks and man in the middle attack are active attacks that can severely damage human life whereas eavesdropping is a passive attack that steals information. This study has found that privacy issues have the biggest impacts on people. Therefore, researchers need to find possible solutions to these threats to improve the quality of IoT applications.

INTRODUCTION

In the most recent decade, there has been economic growth and social transformation that has prompted the urbanization rush in the world (Zhang et al., 2017). There is a continued growth in technologies due to the Internet of Things (IoT) is in every part of the people's lives in the 21st century (Pishva, 2017). By 2030, it is estimated that urban areas population will reach 5 billion (Zhang et al., 2017) and a few

DOI: 10.4018/978-1-5225-7432-3.ch010

Figure 1. Graphical abstract of this study

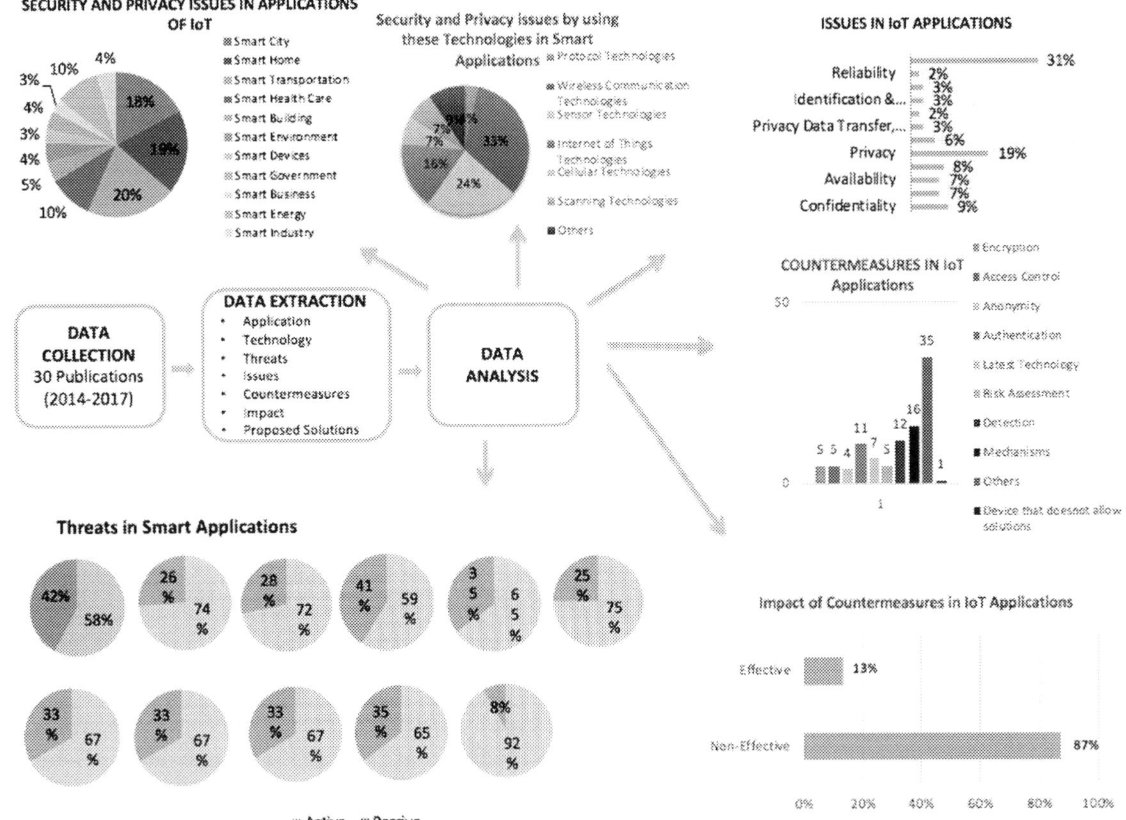

*For a more accurate representation see the electronic version.

experts are estimating that more than 50 billion things would be connected to the networking world. Most of these associates to unsecured actuators and sensors (Ronen et al., 2017) for a lower marketplace and customers demand services (Geneiatakis et al., 2017). The mission of smart cities in urban areas is quick growth that increases the opportunities (Srivastava, 2017). Some of the applications which come under the smart city concept which are shown in the Table 1.

In today's world nearly, all appliances are connected to internet technologies. Making use of electronics with a few specialized programs that have Internet access and creates intelligent networks (Pishva, 2017). The Smart Cities architecture consists of 3 worlds: Information, Communication, and Physical. Furthermore, the sensing components that make up the Physical world of IoT include wearable devices, smart sensing devices, environmental sensors, and operating and control components. Similarly, the heterogeneous network that makes up the Communication world include sensor networks, cellular networks, local servers, device-to-device communications and wireless fidelity access points. Lastly, the processing units that make up the Information world are cloud servers, control centers, decision-making methods, and data access and authorized entities. These interconnected worlds become a smart city which is made into four layers: Application, Service, Network and Sensing in the Smart Cities architecture (Zhang et al., 2017) (Alkhamisi et al., 2016).

Table 1. Diverse types of applications with sub-applications in the Internet of Things

Smart Living	✓ Smart Surveillance ✓ Smart Recycle ✓ Social Network ✓ Smart Community ✓ Smart Home
Smart Energy	✓ Smart Energy ✓ Smart Grid
Smart Services	✓ Intelligent Governance ✓ Intelligent Health Care ✓ Intelligent Transportation ✓ Smart Parking
Smart Environment	✓ Smart Weather ✓ Environment Monitoring
Smart Industry	✓ Intelligent Industry ✓ Intelligent Control

IoT is mostly focused on business models which results in better quality in the lives of people with the latest and most efficient services. Nonetheless, latest services can also result in higher risks of threats such as data retrieval and data loss (Geneiatakis et al., 2017).

The significant problems in the architecture of smart cities in relation to cybersecurity are sophisticated attacks, security products of software with vulnerabilities, as well as complexity and legislation (Khatoun et al., 2017). In the IoT, the sensing components provide data collection and transmission over wireless networks. The data during the transmission is analyzed for utilizing control to the actuators. Accordingly, the significant factor which must be guaranteed in an IoT infrastructure is security and ensuring trustworthiness for the data (Li et al., 2017).

MATERIAL AND METHODOLOGY

Issues have increasingly arisen in the security of the IoT. The increase in the sophistication of technologies has provided new services to customers. The risks involved in IoT are evolving, hence, the research issues every organization are addressing is the need to identify issues related to privacy and security with solutions for IoT. The information for this chapter was retrieved from a selection of published articles which were published from 2014 to 2017and the following aspects evaluated: threats, issues, countermeasures and proposed solutions.

Raw Data Collection

The data from the different smart city applications (in relation to IoT) was collected from thirty peer-reviewed articles and analyzed. The attributes which were compared with the smart city applications were applications, technology, threats, issues, countermeasures and proposed solutions.

Inclusion of Data

The accessing of data is done by comparing the applications with respect to the privacy and security issues by including the attributes of the application, technology, threats, issues, countermeasures, and proposed solutions.

Raw Data Analysis

The raw data analysis has done with respect to the smart city applications according to smart city applications with sub-applications which are shown in Table 2. The attributes in the peer-reviewed articles have similar types of threats, issues, countermeasures and proposed a solution.

RESULTS

See Table 3.

Analysis of Applications

The applications of smart cities are clustered according to the main classification such as smart transportation, home, healthcare, building, environment, devices, government, business, grid, industry, and city, which is shown in Table 2. The results are in Figure 2.

Figure 2. The average percentage of the security issues in the applications of Smart City

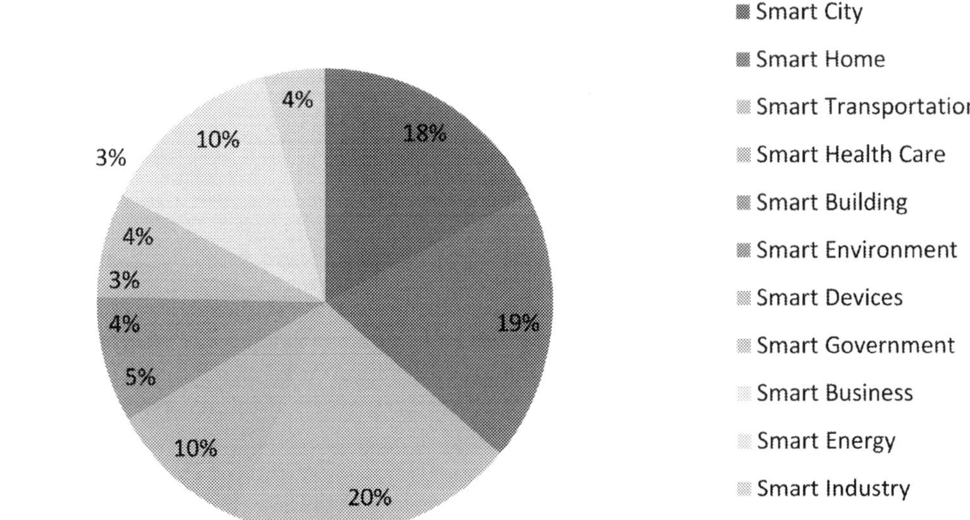

**For a more accurate representation see the electronic version.*

Table 2. Diverse types of threats, issues, and solutions in the applications for Internet of Things

NO	STUDY	APPLICATION	TECHNOLOGY	THREATS	ISSUES	COUNTERMEASURES	IMPACT	PROPOSED SOLUTION
1	Zhang et al. (2017) [1]	Smart transportation, healthcare, environment, entertainment, energy	Sensing components	*Malicious attacks *Vulnerability to privacy leakage and information *Getting information from unauthorized access, disruption, disclosure, inspection, modification, and annihilation	*Privacy leakage *Data storage and processing *Trustworthy and dependable control	*Encryption *Access control *Anonymity	*Still disclosed to the entities which are untrusted	*State-of-the-art scheme to achieve security and privacy
2	Pishva (2017) [2]	Smart home appliances	Computer and information technology, surveillance technology, OSGI technology, FAN technology	* Information leakage *Privacy infringement *Data corruption	*Implementing security on the devices	*Anonymous communication which is TOR-based in the network of IoT	*Not effective to the main users who are unaware of technology of such devices	*Essential component for security(PKI) *Easy-to-use mechanisms for authentication *An architecture to manage the issues of security through universal gateways of home
3	Ronen et al. (2017) [3]	Smart lamp	ZigBee	*City-wide disruption *Denial of service *Brute force attack*ZigBee worm which is autonomously self-spreading *ZigBee worm which is autonomously self-spreading *Bluetooth enabled cellular phone worms*Two novel attacks: a correlation power analysis attack & a takeover attack *Bricking attack *Wireless network jamming *Data infiltration and exfiltration *Epileptic seizures	*Hackers are misusing the cryptographic techniques which are Industry standard and creating new kind of attacks: difficult to stop and investigate *An explosive chain reaction starts if one lamp is infected *Unknown weakness in the ZigBee protocol implementation *The design of ZLL standard was insecure *The master key including OTA update keys also gets leaked	*The implementation of the touch link which is the part of light link protocol of ZigBee by discovering and exploiting a major bug *developed a latest version of an attack which is side channel to encrypt and authenticate the latest firmware	*overcame the problem *found difficult to manage the key by finding without looking the actual updates	*Using unique keys per bulb, hash-based signatures & asymmetric cryptography *Making sure the whole ecosystem damage by the leak of specific product key *ZigBee certification process with negative testing in the case of security and cryptographic protocols
4	Geneiatakis et al. (2017) [4]	Smart home	ZigBee, Z-wave	*Eavesdropping (active and passive type) *Denial of service (active type) *Impersonation (active type) *Software exploitation (active and passive type)	*Confidentiality *Availability *Integrity *Unauthorized access *privacy	*Manufacturers supposed to give security in the architecture underlying in smart home	*This assumption does not effect	*Proper deployment of authentication and Integrity mechanisms*Protection in the network layer *Trustworthy channels usage for the services and applications by the users *To makes users configure the device properly with strong passwords
5	Srivastava (2017) [5]	Smart city	ICT (Information and communication technology)	*Gun violence *Potential harmful threats to the earlier security systems *Suspicious anomalies *Tackled threats	*Some systems rely on rules which are set to detect anomalies but it needs programmer upgradation for constant code *Illegal or misuse of firearms *Needs of human intervention	*relying and adopting latest techniques to make secure cities	*a central stage of latest threat is taking of diminishing control and privacy of life	*Advanced Artificial intelligence (AI) systems

continued on following page

Table 2. Continued

NO	STUDY	APPLICATION	TECHNOLOGY	THREATS	ISSUES	COUNTERMEASURES	IMPACT	PROPOSED SOLUTION
6	Khatoun et al. (2017) [7]	Smart mobility, smart government, smart living, smart people, smart environment, smart economy,	Information and communication technology, Fuel cell technology, solar technology, vehicular communication technology	*MITM (man in the middle) *Denial of service *Cracking *Remote Hacking *Malicious emails	*Data confidentiality *Human life safety *Users' privacy *Privacy concern in data storage, transfer, and processing	*Stronger authentication, Forensics, modeling for threat and modeling, solutions for backup and recovery *Encryption, PKI, digital certificates, solutions for misbehavior detection, identities for pseudorandom *Leakage prevention, training for awareness, risk assessment, analysis for Insider threat *Secured Wi-fi networks, Risk assessment *Cybercrime Intelligence, Risk assessment, Intrusion detection and prevention, analysis for Insider threat *Cybercrime Intelligence, Encryption, Firewall, solutions for anti-malicious software, techniques for fraud detection and prevention, Insurance, Risk assessment	*Effective	*Further investigation of privacy preservation models
7	Li et al. (2017) [8]	Smart transportation, smart building, smart water, smart home, smart urban services, smart waste collection, smart energy, smart citizens	Wireless network technology: consumer electronics and wireless communication	• Signal propagation error • Eavesdropping or tampering • Inconsistent data • Faulty and compromised nodes • Ever-changing topology of network	• Security • Trust	• Detect malicious nodes and evaluating trustworthiness for Internet of Things	• Might do great harm to the systems of Internet of Things	• RealAlert scheme • Trust management • Malicious node detection • Policy management • Data collection
8	Kim (2017) [9]	Smart home	Information and communication technology	*Denial of service *Eavesdropping *Sensor node attack *Sensing data privacy	*Confidentiality *Authentication and access control *Availability and survivability *Integrity and Non-repudiation *Freshness *Privacy and authority control	*Heterogeneous connection	*cannot provide with security engine and conventional cryptography	*Intrusion protection and detection in the sensor networks
9	Yang et al. (2017) [10]	Smart grid	*Advanced power engineering technology *Wireless Communication Technology * Advanced Metering Infrastructure	*Data integrity attacks	*Low detection accuracy	*Min-Max model scheme	*are vulnerable if there are fluctuations in the set of data	*The detection scheme which is based on A Gaussian-mixture model

continued on following page

Table 2. Continued

NO	STUDY	APPLICATION	TECHNOLOGY	THREATS	ISSUES	COUNTERMEASURES	IMPACT	PROPOSED SOLUTION
10	Nia et al. (2017) [11]	*Smart vehicles *Health monitoring *smart buildings *Energy and construction management *Environmental monitoring *Food supply chain *Production and assembly line management	*Edge computing *RFID	*Attacks on edge nodes *Attacks on communication *Attacks on edge computing level	*Confidentiality *Integrity *Non-repudiation *Privacy *Accountability *Availability *Auditability *Trustworthiness	For Computing Nodes *Circuit modification *Side-Channel Analysis *Securing firmware update *Policy-based mechanisms and Intrusion detection systems For RFID tags *Kill/sleep command *Blocking *personal firewall *Anonymous tag *Isolation *Distance estimation *Cryptographic schemes *Circuit modification For communication *Role-based authorization *Intrusion detection system *Information flooding *Reliable routing *cryptographic schemes *De-patterning and decentralization For edge computing level *Pre-testing *Outlier detection *Intrusion detection system	*Unfortunately, in the domain of Internet of Things, the threats of security are not well-recognized	*Threats must be addressed aggressively and proactively by manufacturers and research communities of industries
11	Lin et al. (2017) [12]	Fog computing: smart transportation, smart grid, smart cities,	*RFID *6LoWPAN *Wireless Sensor Networks *Barcode *Message Queue Telemetry *IEEE 802.15.4 Transport *ZigBee *Constrained application protocol *Z-wave *Data Distribution service *Protocol of Extensible messaging and presence *Interface *Protocol of Advanced Message Queuing *Service management	*Forging the data which is collected and destroying the devices in the perception layer: Node capture attacks, False Data Injection Attacks, cryptanalysis and side channel Attacks, Malicious Code Injection Attacks, Replay Attacks, Eavesdropping and Interference, sleep Deprivation Attacks *Impacting the network resource availability in the Network Layer: wormhole, Spoofing, Denial-of-service, Man-in-the-Middle, Sybil, Routing Information Attacks, Unauthorized attacks, sinkhole attacks *software attacks in the application layer: Phishing attack Malicious virus and scripts *Attacks on privacy: Data mining and analytics, Data Aggregation, Data collection	*Confidentiality *Integrity *Availability *Identification and Authentication *Privacy *Trust	*Fog computing	*quality of service is great and response is fast	*Encryption-based privacy preservation *Perturbation-based privacy preservation *Anonymity-based privacy preservation
12	Joy et al. (2017) [13]	*Internet of vehicles *Autonomous connected car	*Sensors *cameras	*Security attacks *DDoS attacks *Waze attacks	*Security *Privacy	*Autonomous switchover experiment	*complex experiment and raises privacy concerns which are serious	*Haystack Privacy

continued on following page

Table 2. Continued

NO	STUDY	APPLICATION	TECHNOLOGY	THREATS	ISSUES	COUNTERMEASURES	IMPACT	PROPOSED SOLUTION
13	Giuliano et al. (2017) [14]	Smart City	*Wi-Fi *Bluetooth *ZigBee *6LoWPAN *Cellular Radio Technology	*Release of message content *Traffic Analysis *Masquerade *Replay *Intentional DoS *Modification of messages *Man-In-The-Middle attack	*Security *Privacy	*Assuming the availability of security layer below the level of application *Considering the identity devices of IP and non-IP	*Hard to find applicability for bidirectional devices	*Algorithms to access the security for Unidirectional Data Transmissions, Bidirectional Data Transmissions *Key generation to connect securely based on time
14	Oh et al. (2017) [15]	*Smart car *Smart building *Smart home *smart city	Sensor technology	*Fragmentation *security attacks *Unauthorized access *Brute-force attack *Dictionary attack *Buffer overflow *Spoofing *Man-in-the-middle *Sniffing	*Trust *middleware *Access control *Storage	*Security in bootstrapping and multicasting	*There is no guarantee that with only security in network can prevent the attack on security	The proposed solution which analyses the important characteristics: *Heterogeneity *Resource constraint *Dynamic environment
15	Beligianni et al. (2016) [16]	Smart grid	Information and communication technology, IoT gateways which use sensors and actuators		*Enhancing privacy *Protecting the system *Reducing the cost	*Cloud computing which is centralized architecture	*Can provide support to the applications of Internet of Things which is not efficient	*Preserving the privacy in the energy consumption to the users by the proposed software architecture
16	Ding et al. (2016) [17]	Smart health	*Data mining *Internet of things *wireless sensor networks *Ubiquitous computing	*Leakage of their location and condition of health *Eavesdropping *Skimming	*Identity Privacy *Footprint and owner privacy *Location Privacy *Query Privacy	*Uses the ICT and infrastructure of the city to provide the preventive methods	*might be some potential problems of privacy in the architecture	*Five-dimensional (5D) model
17	Srinivasan et al. (2016) [18]	Emergency response system	*GPS *Wi-Fi *Wireless sensor networks *Cellular *Bluetooth Beacons *RFID *Indoor lighting *small radar	*Attack vector	*Identity privacy protection *Misusing the Information *Data usage and control *Security *Access control *Privacy *Trust management *Data purging	*LBS architecture	*the privacy breaches are subjected by the user	*Privacy-aware architecture
18	Majeed et al. (2016) [19]	Global network of Smart devices	Internet technology	*Attack vector *Malicious Insiders *Un-intentional Insiders	*Data exploitation	*Detecting the Insider threat approach	*not sufficiently strong to address them	*The VERIS model
19	Vattapparamban et al. (2016) [20]	Smart city	Aerial Technology	*De-authentication Attack *GPS spoofing Attack	*Privacy concern	*UAVs	*Difficult to identify the drones which are unauthorized	-
20	Guo et al. (2016) [21]	*Smart home *consumer *Healthcare *Retail	Biometry technology	*Reverse Engineering *Tampering *Unauthorized access	*Reliability *Template protection and Revocability *Privacy *Signal processing is low cost and extracting the features	*combining novel biometrics	*the promising and motivating results which works in the future	*Key generation algorithm

continued on following page

Table 2. Continued

NO	STUDY	APPLICATION	TECHNOLOGY	THREATS	ISSUES	COUNTERMEASURES	IMPACT	PROPOSED SOLUTION
21	Hodo et al. (2016) [22]	Industry sector *Medical field *Logistics tracking *Smart City *Automobile	*Sensor *Cloud	*External Intruder attacks *Internal Intruder attacks *Denial of service *Malware *Data Breaches *Weakening perimeters	*Accuracy	*Intrusion detection which is based on neural network approach	*classifying normal and patterns of threat	* ANN model
22	Yadav et al. (2016) [23]	Smart grid	Smart grid technology	*Non-malicious attacks *Retrieving crucial information *Disrupting the resources *Using malware *Unauthorized access *Replay *Dos attacks *Traffic analysis	*Data confidentiality *Availability of service *Integrity of information shared	*Security mechanisms	*not much efficient	*Perilous architecture
23	Peter et al. (2016) [24]	Smart home	Communication and cryptography technology	*Physical damage *Denial-of-service *Man-in-the-middle *Replay *Node capture	*Forward security *Data confidentiality and Integrity *Privacy preservation *Mutual Authentication	*Multi-level authentication scheme	*no communication and computation efficiency	*Proposed authentication scheme
24	Pacheco et al. (2016) [25]	Smart car	*Internet *wireless sensor networks *Satellite *Internal car network infrastructures *mobile cellular networks	*Replay *Delay *Denial of service *Flooding *Sensor Impersonation *Pulse Denial of service *Noise Injection	*Trustworthy *security	*security in Ad-hoc	*experiencing challenge in securing and protecting its information services which are advanced	*IoT Security development framework which detects the known attacks and unknown attacks
25	Ahamed et al. (2016) [26]	*Smart home *Wearable devices *Smart city *Smart health *Smart Transportation and Traffic management	*Sensor technology	*Brute-force attack *Denial of service *Remote-code execution *SQL injection *Data loss *Data corruption *Man-in-the-middle attack *Compromise of Personal Information *Disclosure of Confidential Information	*Confidentiality *Integrity *Availability	*did not propose and analyze to deal with the vulnerabilities of security	*Various vulnerabilities and mapping	-
26	Dhungana et al. (2015) [27]	Smart city	*RFID, *Environmental sensors *cloud computing *smartphones *actuators *wearable sensors *sensor networks *smart household appliances	*Reconstruction Attack	*Secure Data handling *Privacy guarantee *Flexible privacy policies *Anonymity *Data provenance	* Unlocking the big data potential by capture and combine approach of data which is related to behavior and demographic from many channels	*remained a great challenge	*Aspern Research project for smart city which emphasizes the challenges of security and privacy

continued on following page

Table 2. Continued

NO	STUDY	APPLICATION	TECHNOLOGY	THREATS	ISSUES	COUNTERMEASURES	IMPACT	PROPOSED SOLUTION
27	Sun et al. (2015) [28]	Internet of vehicles	Wireless and mobile communication technology	Authentication *Sybil attack *Masquerading *GPS deception *wormhole Availability *Denial of service *Channel interference Secrecy *Eavesdropping *Interception Routing *Eavesdropping *Route modification *Denial of service *masquerading Data Authenticity *Replay *Camouflage *Tampering and Fabricating with messages *Illusion	*Leakage of confidential data *Fake evidence *Unpredictable property damage *Losing the normal response *Collapsing the system *Leakage of users' privacy *Loopholes and vulnerability *Easily captured, fabricated and forwarded	*Threat model *Key management *Secure Routing protocols *Intrusion detection system *Routing privacy protection Mechanism *Honeypot	*needs specific requirements in Internet of Vehicles for the countermeasures	
28	Tragos et al. (2014) [29]	Smart city	Information and Communication Technology	*Node Failure *Interference *Denial of Service *Eavesdropping *Data falsification	*Confidentiality *Integrity *Availability	*New advances in Internet of Things	*Security, Reliability and Privacy are not considered	*Fp7 project RERUM
29	Lee et al. (2014) [30]	Smart home	*Bluetooth *ZigBee *Wi-Fi *Gateway	Physical layer *Jamming *Tampering Data link layer *Ack attack *Killer bee *Back-off Manipulation *GTS attack Network layer *Black hole attack Transport layer *Flooding *De-synchronization Application layer *XMPPloit	*Physical access *Energy constraints *Resource constraints protocols *Unreliable communications *Heterogeneous communication	*The devices which has the nature of resource-constrained does not allow to implement the solutions of security which are standard	*has security vulnerabilities	*New algorithms for security is to do research and developed
30	Alohali et al. (2014) [31]	Smart grid	Sensor-based technology	*Replication attacks *Sybil attacks *Man-in-the-middle (MIIM) attacks	*Secure communication *Scalability *Availability *Confidentiality *Network lifetime *Security *Privacy	*Scheme of key management	*has always the security and privacy issue	*Home Area Network security scheme which is based on Cloud of things

Table 3. The applications of smart cities include their values which indicate the security issues

Smart City	• Smart city (13.04%) • Urban services (1.44%) • Waste collection (1.44%) • Water (1.44)
Smart Home	• Home (13.04%) • Living (1.44%) • People (1.44%) • Entertainment (1.44%) • Lamp (1.44%)
Smart Transportation	• Smart transportation (7.24%) • Mobility (1.44%) • Vehicles connected with internet (2.89%) • Car (4.34%) • Automobiles (1.44%) • Logistics Tracking (1.44%)
Smart Healthcare	• Smart health (8.69%) • Emergency response system (1.44%)
Smart Building	• Smart building (4.34%)
Smart Environment	• Smart environment (4.34%)
Smart Devices	• Smart devices (2.89%)
Smart Government	• Government (1.44%) • Economy (1.44%) • Citizen (1.44%)
Smart Business	• Consumer (1.44%) • Retail (1.44%)
Smart Energy	• Smart grid (7.24%) • Smart energy (2.89%)
Smart Industry	• Smart Industry (1.44%) • Production and assembly line (1.44%) • Energy and construction (1.44%)

Our results show the application which has the most security and privacy issues are transportation (20%) followed by home (19%), city (18%), healthcare (10%), energy (10%), buildings (5%), environment (4%), government (4%), industry (4%), devices (3%), and business (3%).

Analysis of Technologies in Smart Applications

The technologies in the applications of smart cities are clustered into the following main classifications: Protocol Technologies, Wireless Communication Technologies, Sensor Technologies, IoT Technologies, Cellular Technology, Scanning Technologies and Others which are shown in Table 4. The results are shown in Figure 3.

In this chapter, the issues of using technologies in smart city applications are 33% for Wireless Communication Technologies. Secondly, 24% and 16% of Sensor Technologies and Internet of Things Technologies. Thirdly, 7% for Cellular Technologies, 7% for Scanning Technologies, 4% for Protocol Technologies and 9% for Other Technologies.

Table 4. The technologies of smart cities including their values which indicates the security issues with percentages

Protocol Technologies (3.53%)	• Constrained Application Protocol (1.176%) • Protocol of Extensible Messaging and Presence (1.176%) • Protocol of Advanced Message Queuing (1.176%)
Wireless communication technologies (32.93%)	• Wireless Communication Technology (2.352%) • Wi-Fi Technology (3.529%) • Wireless Network Technology (1.176%) • Bluetooth Technology (3.529%) • ZigBee (5.882%) • Information and Communication Technology (5.882%) • Computer and Information Technology (1.176%) • Vehicular Communication Technology (2.352%) • Communication and Cryptography Technology (1.176%) • Satellite Technology (1.176%) • Z-Wave (2.352%) • IEEE 802.15.4 Technology (1.176%) • GPS (1.176%)
Sensor Technologies (23.53%)	• Sensor Technology (15.294%) • Gateway (2.352%) • Actuators (1.176%) • Surveillance Technology (2.352%) • FAN Technology (1.176%) • Indoor Lighting (1.176%)
Internet of Things Technologies (16.46%)	• Internet of Things (1.176%) • 6LoWPAN Technology (2.352%) • Internet Technology (2.352%) • Cloud Technology (2.352%) • Smart Grid Technology (1.176%) • Interface Technology (1.176%) • Smart Household Appliances (1.176%) • Edge Computing Technology (1.176%) • Data Distribution Service (1.176%) • Service Management (1.176%) • Ubiquitous Computing (1.176%)
Cellular Technologies (7.06%)	• Cellular Radio Technology (4.705%) • Smart Phone (1.176%) • Small Radar (1.176%)
Scanning Technologies (7.06%)	• Biometry Technology (1.176%) • Barcode Technology (1.176%) • RFID Technology (4.705%)
Others (9.44%)	• OSGI Technology (1.176%) • Fuel Cell Technology (1.176%) • Solar Technology (1.176%) • Advanced Power Engineering Technology (1.176%) • Advanced Metering Infrastructure Technology (1.176%) • Message Queue Telemetry Transport (1.176%) • Data Mining Technology (1.176%) • Aerial Technology (1.176%)

Figure 3. The average percentage of the security issues in the applications of smart city by using these technologies

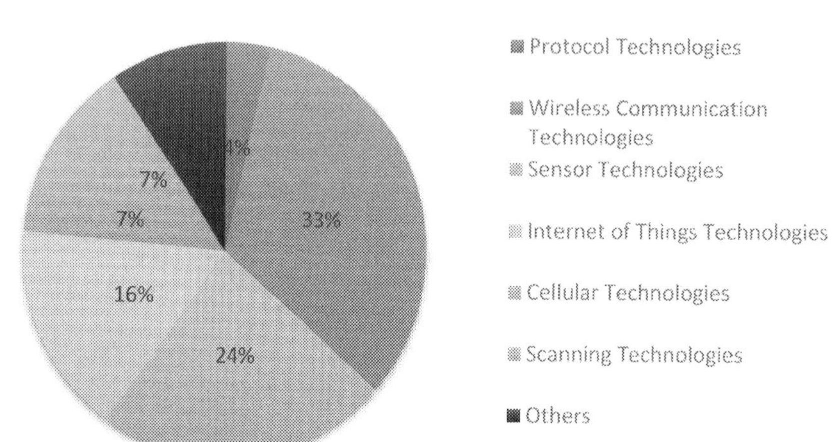

**For a more accurate representation see the electronic version.*

Analysis of Privacy and Security Threats in the Smart Applications

The threats are clustered into two main categories such as active attack and passive attack.

In Figure 4, the analysis made from this study for security and privacy threats in the applications is shown. The active and passive attacks in Smart City applications (Smart City, Smart Home, Smart Transportation, Smart HealthCare, Smart Building, Smart Environment, Smart Devices, Smart Government, Smart Business, Smart Energy and Smart Industry) are observed in Figure 4.

Analysis of Issues in Smart City Applications

The issues are clustered with many categories such as confidentiality, Integrity, Availability, Security, Privacy, Trust, Privacy Data Transfer, Storage & Processing, Non-Repudiation, Identification & Authentication, Access control, Reliability, and others.

In Figure 5. Which indicates the various types of issues from our analysis in which the highest issue percentage 19% for Privacy, 9% for Confidentiality, 8% for Security, 7% for Availability and Integrity, 6% for Trust, 3% for privacy data transfer, storage & processing, Identification & Authentication and Access control, 2% for Non-repudiation and Reliability and 31% for others.

Analysis of Countermeasures in Smart Applications

The Countermeasures in the applications of smart cities are clustered to the main classification such as Encryption, Access Control, Anonymity, Authentication, Latest Technology, Risk Assessment, Detec-

Figure 4. The analysis percentage of security and privacy threats in smart applications

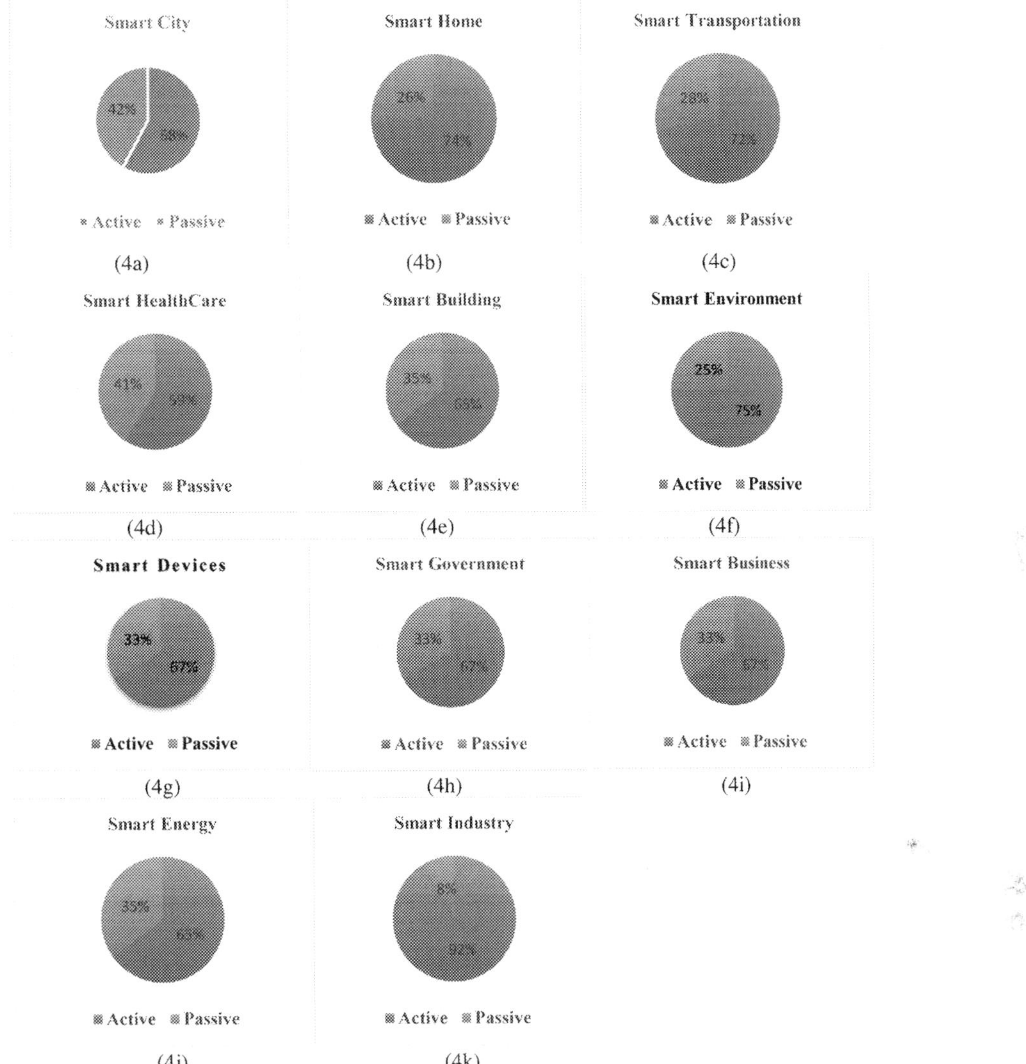

**For a more accurate representation see the electronic version.*

tion, Mechanisms, Others, and Device that does not allow solutions which are shown in Table 6. The results are shown in Figure 6.

In this chapter, the issues of using Countermeasures in smart city applications are 16% for Mechanisms. Secondly, 12% and 11% of Detection and Authentication. Thirdly, 7% for Latest Technology, 5% for Risk Assessment, 5% for Access Control and 5% for Encryption, 4% for Anonymity, 1% for Device that does not allow solutions. Finally, 35% for other Countermeasures.

Analysis of Technologies in Smart Applications

The Impact from the countermeasures in the applications of smart cities is clustered to two classifications Non-Effective and Effective which are shown in Table 7. The results are shown in Figure 7.

Table 5. The various types of issues in the applications of smart city with percentages

Issues	Percentages (%)
Confidentiality	9%
Integrity	7%
Availability	7%
Security	8%
Privacy	19%
Trust	6%
Privacy in Data Transfer, Storage & Processing	3%
Non-Repudiation	2%
Identification & Authentication	3%
Access control	3%
Reliability	2%
Others (Unauthorized Access, Human Life Safety, Dependable Control, Misuse of Cryptographic Techniques, An Explosive Chain Reaction, Unknown Weakness, Needs Programmer Up gradation, Misuse of Firearms, Human Intervention, Anonymity, Data Provenance, Accuracy, Accountability, Auditability, System Protection, Cost Reduction, Information Misuse, Data Purging, Data Usage and Control, Data Exploitation, Template Protection and Revocability, Low-Cost Signal Process, Survivability, Authority Control, Freshness, Heterogeneous Communication, Resource Constraints Protocol, Energy Constraints, Physical Access, Middleware, Fake Evidence, Property Damage, Losing the Normal Response, Collapsing the System, Loopholes & Vulnerability, Easy Capture, Fabrication, and Forward, Network Lifetime, Scalability)	31%

Figure 5. The analysis of security and privacy issues in smart applications

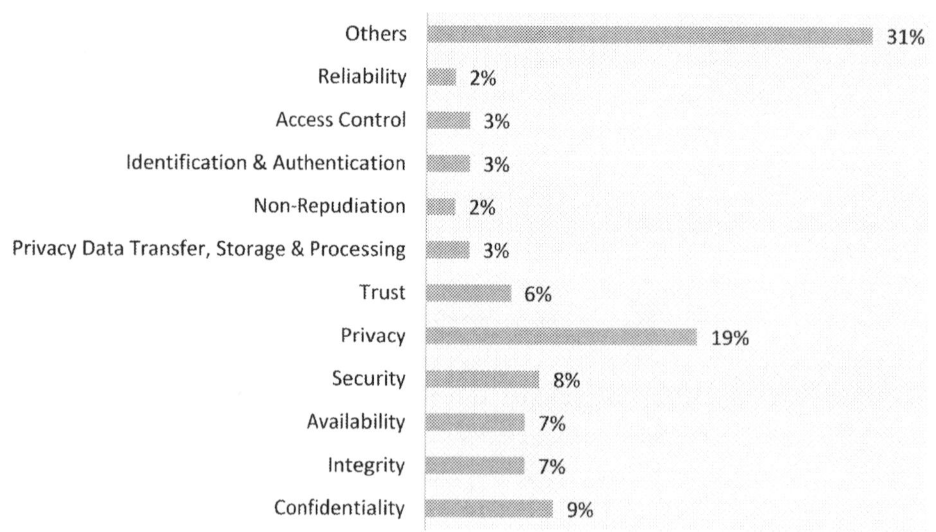

Table 6. The countermeasures of smart cities including their values which indicates the security issues with percentages

Encryption (5%)	
Access control (5%)	• Role-based authorization • Considering the identity devices of IP and non-IP • Identities for pseudorandom
Anonymity (4%)	• TOR-based anonymous communication • Anonymous tag
Authentication (11%)	• Multi-level authentication scheme • PKI • Digital Certificates • Cryptographic schemes • Firewall
Latest Technology (7%)	• New advances in Internet of Things • Fog computing • Cloud computing • Forensics • ZigBee Protocol • Latest Techniques
Risk Assessment (5%)	
Detection (12%)	• Outlier detection • Intrusion detection system • Detecting the Insider threat approach
Mechanisms (16%)	• Architecture Security • Securing firmware update • Security in bootstrapping and multicasting • security in Ad-hoc • Secure Routing protocols • Security mechanisms • Policy-based mechanisms • Routing privacy protection Mechanism • Reliable routing • Secured Wi-Fi networks • Circuit modification • Leakage Prevention
Others (35%)	• Kill/sleep command • Blocking • Isolation • Distance estimation • Information flooding • De-patterning and decentralization • Pre-testing • Autonomous switchover experiment • ICT and infrastructure • LBS architecture • UAVs • combining novel biometrics • Capture and Combine Approach • Key management • Honeypot • Insurance • Cybercrime Intelligence • Heterogeneous connection • solutions for backup and recovery • solutions for misbehaviour detection • solutions for anti-malicious software • Modelling • Threat model • Min-Max model scheme • Awareness Training • Side-Channel Analysis • Analyzing threats
Device that does not allow solutions (1%)	

Figure 6. The average percentage of the security issues in the applications of smart city by using these countermeasures

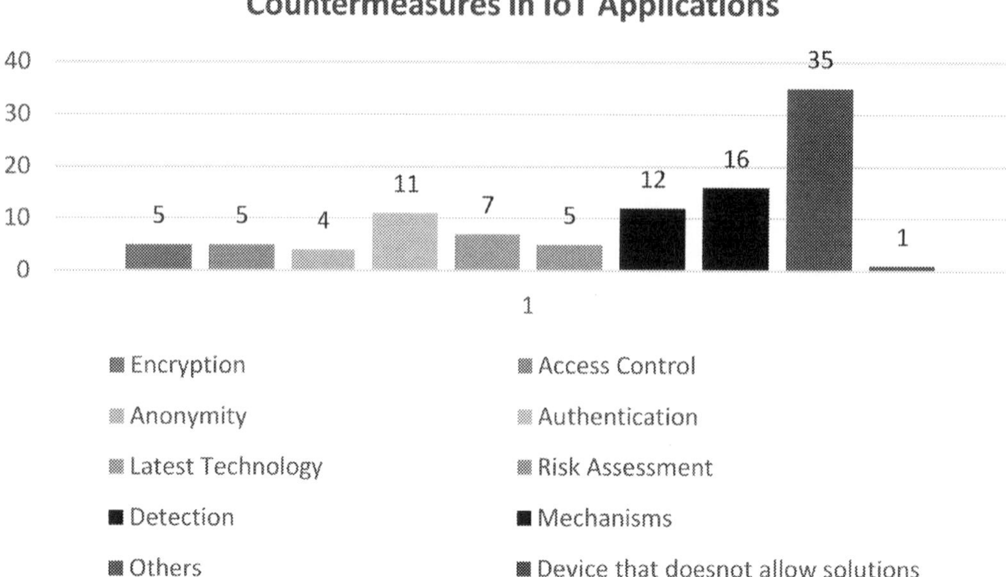

**For a more accurate representation see the electronic version.*

Table 7. The impact of countermeasures on smart cities including their values which indicates the security issues with percentages

Non-Effective	87%
Effective	13%

Figure 7. The average percentage of the security issues in the applications of Smart City after using the countermeasures

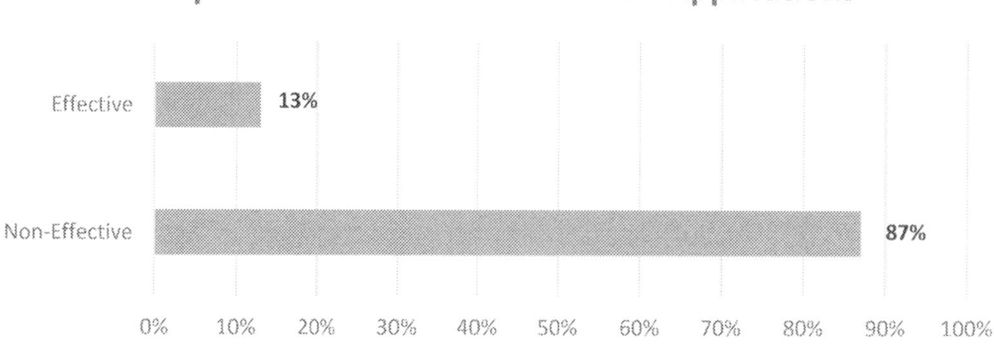

In this chapter, after using countermeasures, the security issues in smart city applications are 13% is Effective and 87% is Non-Effective.

DISCUSSION

Tremendous business possibilities that exist inside the IoT space fundamentally expanded the number of smart devices and intelligent, autonomous services allowed in IoT systems. Additionally, the dependence on IoT devices on cloud support for data transfer, storage and analysis directed the improvement of cloud-empowered IoT systems (Mai, 2017).

The quick development of IoT devices and services prompted the organization of numerous weak and insecure nodes (Giaretta, 2016). Besides, conventional user-driven security structures are of limited use in object-driven IoT networks (Alaba, 2017). Accordingly, we require particular tools, systems and procedures for defending IoT networks and gathering, protecting and investigating residual proof of IoT conditions.

The challenging task for smart cities is providing security and privacy because the smart cities need to collect and store a large amount of data in databases and perform the real-time and batch analytics. Additionally, there are many outside and inside (known and unknown) attacks which provide concern to security and privacy of smart cities. The main objective of smart cities is to enhance the quality of services as well as to provide for and improve human quality of life is the main objective of smart cities. This chapter aimed to identify the applications of IoT, threats (security and privacy) and their outcomes. The main purpose of this chapter is to provide direction for designing the system of IoT securely and to improve the understanding of the concerns and requirements of the security of the IoT.

Security issues (Munugala et al., (2017), Singh et al., (2018)], for example, privacy, access control, secure data transmission and secure data storage are getting to be critical hurdles in the IoT space (Zarpelão, 2017). Besides, each device that we make, each new sensor that we use, and each byte that is synchronized within the IoT ecosystem may sooner or later go under further investigation (Conti, 2018).

We analyzed the threats and associated issues in the applications of smart cities to identify key security and privacy issues. The major finding in our study is that the highest of percentage of security and privacy issues in the applications of smart cities were active attacks that exploited the vulnerabilities in the system. These threats are impacting the privacy and security of the data of the users.

The key challenges in the IoT are security, privacy, trust, and the CIA triangle (Confidentiality, Integrity & Availability). If we maintain some algorithms and encryption mechanisms for information in the system, then it is secured. However, the problem of security still exists in the system because new threats are always impacting on the IoT. This is particularly significant as information on the internet is especially vulnerable to threats. A few studies, including that written by and Li et al., (2017), and Tragos (2014), support the idea that these key challenges can be overcome in the IoT by using various mechanisms. In contrast to this, study by Pishva (2017), Srivastava et al., (2016) and Sun et al., (2015) suggest that new threats will increase even more. Moreover, investigating diverse strategies for big data databases [Vargas et al., (2016), Kalid et al., (2017)], prediction and pattern analysis [Gupta et al., (2016), Wanigasooriya et al., (2017)], and fog computing architecture [Ekanayake et al., (2018)] could be a fascinating way to make the Internet of Things (IoT) into the future dominating technology.

Cui et al. discussed [Cui et al., (2018)] present privacy and security protection technologies for smart city applications. Recently, various novel countermeasures have been proposed in many fields. Yet, the threats and requirements of security are being updated. With the rapid growth of smart cities, more efficient protection methods should be developed. Cui et al., (2018) suggested novel effective technologies, more attention to the smart systems in fog-based structure, development of user-friendly protection assistant, two-fold data minimization task, lightweight countermeasures development, important additional theoretical studies are required to cope up with the latest challenges. And, the categories of protection methods related to security and privacy in smart cities applications suggested by Cui et al., (2018) were Blockchain, Cryptography, Ontology, Biometrics, Machine learning data mining, and Game theory.

Our observations noted that the most common attacks in specific applications have been analyzed, nonetheless, the well-known attacks, as well as unknown attacks, also create problems for the security and privacy of the users which is not considered by the other studies. Unknown attacks are also a sign of the privacy issues of users. We paid attention to the security and privacy threats and related issues with proposed solutions in the applications of the IoT. Users should be aware of the issues and should have the knowledge not to disclose certain credentials or keys in these smart city applications. The unknown attacks should also be considered to prevent small loopholes. From these threats in the IoT applications, the devices in the IoT can become secured by algorithms and mechanisms. Even after securing the devices, the threats cannot be eradicated totally nonetheless it can be controlled to an extent. The security must be keeping on updating as new threats keep on approaching.

CONCLUSION

This chapter discussed the threats and its effects on the applications of the IoT. Based on the articles, we found that hackers are targeting the privacy of the users, and the attacks are higher in smart transportation applications (72% active attacks, 28% passive attacks) followed by smart home (74% active attacks, 26% passive attacks) and smart cities (58% active attacks, 42% passive attacks) applications. If the vulnerabilities in the devices are related to the IoT applications, they can be eradicated with proper algorithms and encryption techniques then the security and privacy issues might be minimized. Each study was investigating to emphasize the impact on the users from the security and privacy concerns and suggesting various solutions according to their study on smart cities. Based on these solutions, somehow, they can eradicate the security and privacy challenges. Users should know the proper usage of devices, hence, they can minimize the issues of authorization. Each device used by the applications of the IoT has some loopholes and has been targeted by new types of attacks, securing them can prevent the present threats. The well-known and unknown attacks should be considered so that minor loopholes in the systems can be eradicated.

AUTHOR CONTRIBUTION

S.D. and M.N.H. conceived the study idea and developed the analysis plan. S.D. analyzed the data and wrote the initial paper. M.N.H. helped preparing the figures and tables, and in finalizing the manuscript. All authors read the manuscript.

REFERENCES

Ahamed, J., & Rajan, A. V. (2016). Internet of Things (IoT): Application systems and security vulnerabilities. *2016 5th International Conference on Electronic Devices, Systems and Applications (ICEDSA)*, 1-5. 10.1109/ICEDSA.2016.7818534

Alaba, F. A., Othman, M., Hashem, I. A. T., & Alotaibi, F. (2017). Internet of Things security: A survey. *Journal of Network and Computer Applications*, *88*, 10–28. doi:10.1016/j.jnca.2017.04.002

Alkhamisi, A., Nazmudeen, M. S. H., & Buhari, S. M. (2016). A cross-layer framework for sensor data aggregation for IoT applications in smart cities. *2016 IEEE International Smart Cities Conference (ISC2)*, 1-6. 10.1109/ISC2.2016.7580853

Alohali, B., Merabti, M., & Kifayat, K. (2014). A Cloud of Things (CoT) Based Security for Home Area Network (HAN) in the Smart Grid. *2014 Eighth International Conference on Next Generation Mobile Apps, Services and Technologies*, 326-330. 10.1109/NGMAST.2014.50

Beligianni, F., Alamaniotis, M., Fevgas, A., Tsompanopoulou, P., Bozanis, P., & Tsoukalas, L. H. (2016). An internet of things architecture for preserving privacy of energy consumption. *Mediterranean Conference on Power Generation, Transmission, Distribution and Energy Conversion (MedPower 2016)*, 1-7. 10.1049/cp.2016.1096

Conti, M., Dehghantanha, A., Franke, K., & Watson, S. (2018). Internet of Things security and forensics: Challenges and opportunities. *Future Generation Computer Systems*, *78*, 544–546. doi:10.1016/j.future.2017.07.060

Cui, L., Xie, G., Qu, Y., Gao, L., & Yang, Y. (2018). Security and Privacy in Smart Cities: Challenges and Opportunities. *IEEE Access: Practical Innovations, Open Solutions*, *6*, 46134–46145. doi:10.1109/ACCESS.2018.2853985

Dhungana, D., Engelbrecht, G., Parreira, J. X., Schuster, A., & Valerio, D. (2015). Aspern smart ICT: Data analytics and privacy challenges in a smart city. *2015 IEEE 2nd World Forum on Internet of Things (WF-IoT)*, 447-452. 10.1109/WF-IoT.2015.7389096

Ding, D., Conti, M., & Solanas, A. (2016). A smart health application and its related privacy issues. *2016 Smart City Security and Privacy Workshop (SCSP-W)*, 1-5. 10.1109/SCSPW.2016.7509558

Ekanayake, B. N. B., Halgamuge, M. N., & Syed, A. (January 2018). Review: Security and Privacy Issues of Fog Computing for the Internet of Things (IoT). In *Lecture Notes on Data Engineering and Communications Technologies Cognitive Computing for Big Data Systems Over IoT, Frameworks, Tools and Applications* (Vol. 14). Springer. doi:10.1007/978-3-319-70688-7_7

Geneiatakis, D., Kounelis, I., Neisse, R., Nai-Fovino, I., Steri, G., & Baldini, G. (2017). Security and privacy issues for an IoT based smart home. *2017 40th International Convention on Information and Communication Technology, Electronics and Microelectronics (MIPRO)*, 1292-1297. 10.23919/MIPRO.2017.7973622

Giaretta, A., Balasubramaniam, S., & Conti, M. (2016). Security vulnerabilities and countermeasures for target localization in bio-nanothings communication networks. *IEEE Transactions on Information Forensics and Security*, *11*(4), 665–676. doi:10.1109/TIFS.2015.2505632

Giuliano, Mazzenga, Neri, & Vegni. (2017). Security Access Protocols in IoT Capillary Networks. *IEEE Internet of Things Journal, 4*(3), 645-657.

Guo, Z., Karimian, N., Tehranipoor, M. M., & Forte, D. (2016). Hardware security meets biometrics for the age of IoT. *2016 IEEE International Symposium on Circuits and Systems (ISCAS)*, 1318-1321. 10.1109/ISCAS.2016.7527491

Gupta, A., Mohammad, A., Syed, A., & Halgamuge, M. N. (2016). A Comparative Study of Classification Algorithms using Data Mining: Crime and Accidents in Denver City the USA. *International Journal of Advanced Computer Science and Applications*, *7*(7), 374–381. doi:10.14569/IJACSA.2016.070753

Hodo, E. (2016). Threat analysis of IoT networks using artificial neural network intrusion detection system. *2016 International Symposium on Networks, Computers and Communications (ISNCC)*, 1-6. 10.1109/ISNCC.2016.7746067

Joy, J., & Gerla, M. (2017). Internet of Vehicles and Autonomous Connected Car - Privacy and Security Issues. *2017 26th International Conference on Computer Communication and Networks (ICCCN)*, 1-9. 10.1109/ICCCN.2017.8038391

Kalid, S., Syed, A., Mohammad, A., & Halgamuge, M. N. (2017). Big-Data NoSQL Databases: Comparison and Analysis of "Big-Table", "DynamoDB", and "Cassandra". *IEEE 2nd International Conference on Big Data Analysis (ICBDA'17)*, 89-93.

Khatoun, R., & Zeadally, S. (2017). Cybersecurity and Privacy Solutions in Smart Cities. *IEEE Communications Magazine*, *55*(3), 51–59. doi:10.1109/MCOM.2017.1600297CM

Kim, J. T. (2017). Analyses of secure authentication scheme for the smart home system based on the internet on things. *2017 International Conference on Applied System Innovation (ICASI)*, 335-336. 10.1109/ICASI.2017.7988420

Lee, C., & Zappaterra, L. (2014). Kwanghee Choi and Hyeong-Ah Choi, "Securing smart home: Technologies, security challenges, and security requirements. *2014 IEEE Conference on Communications and Network Security*, 67-72.

Li, Song, & Zeng. (n.d.). Policy-based Secure and Trustworthy Sensing for an Internet of Things in Smart Cities. *IEEE Internet of Things Journal.*

Lin, Yu, Zhang, Yang, Zhang, & Zhao. (n.d.). A Survey on Internet of Things: Architecture, Enabling Technologies, Security and Privacy, and Applications. *IEEE Internet of Things Journal.*

Mai, V., & Khalil, I. (2017). Design and implementation of a secure cloud-based billing model for smart meters as an Internet of Things using homomorphic cryptography. *Future Generation Computer Systems*, *72*, 327–338. doi:10.1016/j.future.2016.06.003

Majeed, A., Haq, A. U., Jamal, A., Bhana, R., Banigo, F., & Baadel, S. (2016). Internet of everything (IoE) exploiting organisational inside threats: Global network of smart devices (GNSD). *IEEE International Symposium on Systems Engineering (ISSE)*, 1-7. 10.1109/SysEng.2016.7753152

Mohsen Nia & Jha. (n.d.). A Comprehensive Study of Security of Internet-of-Things. *IEEE Transactions on Emerging Topics in Computing*.

Munugala, Brar, Syed, Mohammad, & Halgamuge. (2017). The Much Needed Security and Data Reforms of Cloud Computing in Medical Data Storage. In *Applying Big Data Analytics in Bioinformatics and Medicine*. IGI Global.

Oh, S. R., & Kim, Y. G. (2017). Security Requirements Analysis for the IoT. *2017 International Conference on Platform Technology and Service (PlatCon)*, 1-6.

Pacheco, J., Satam, S., Hariri, S., Grijalva, C., & Berkenbrock, H. (2016). IoT Security Development Framework for building trustworthy Smart car services. *2016 IEEE Conference on Intelligence and Security Informatics (ISI)*, 237-242. 10.1109/ISI.2016.7745481

Peter, S., & Gopal, R. K. (2016). Multi-level authentication system for smart home-security analysis and implementation. *2016 International Conference on Inventive Computation Technologies (ICICT)*, 1-7. 10.1109/INVENTIVE.2016.7824790

Pishva, D. (2017). Internet of Things: Security and privacy issues and possible solution. *2017 19th International Conference on Advanced Communication Technology (ICACT)*, 797-808. 10.23919/ICACT.2017.7890229

Ronen, E., Shamir, A., Weingarten, A. O., & O'Flynn, C. (2017). IoT Goes Nuclear: Creating a ZigBee Chain Reaction. *2017 IEEE Symposium on Security and Privacy (SP)*, 195-212. 10.1109/SP.2017.14

Singh, M., Halgamuge, M. N., Ekici, G., & Jayasekara, C. S. (January 2018). A Review on Security and Privacy Challenges of Big Data. In *Lecture Notes on Data Engineering and Communications Technologies Cognitive Computing for Big Data Systems Over IoT, Frameworks, Tools and Applications* (Vol. 14). Springer. doi:10.1007/978-3-319-70688-7_8

Srinivasan, R., Mohan, A., & Srinivasan, P. (2016). Privacy conscious architecture for improving emergency response in smart cities. *2016 Smart City Security and Privacy Workshop (SCSP-W)*, 1-5. 10.1109/SCSPW.2016.7509559

Srivastava, S., Bisht, A., & Narayan, N. (2017). Safety and security in smart cities using artificial intelligence — A review. *2017 7th International Conference on Cloud Computing, Data Science & Engineering - Confluence*, 130-133. 10.1109/CONFLUENCE.2017.7943136

Sun, Y., Wu, L., Wu, S., Li, S., Zhang, T., Zhang, L., ... Xiong, Y. (2015). Security and Privacy in the Internet of Vehicles. *2015 International Conference on Identification, Information, and Knowledge in the Internet of Things (IIKI)*, 116-121. 10.1109/IIKI.2015.33

Tragos, E. Z. (2014). Enabling reliable and secure IoT-based smart city applications. *2014 IEEE International Conference on Pervasive Computing and Communication Workshops (PERCOM WORKSHOPS)*, 111-116. 10.1109/PerComW.2014.6815175

Vargas, V., Syed, A., Mohammad, A., & Halgamuge, M. N. (2016). Pentaho and Jaspersoft: A Comparative Study of Business Intelligence Open Source Tools Processing Big Data to Evaluate Performances. *International Journal of Advanced Computer Science and Applications*, *7*(10), 20–29.

Vattapparamban, E., Güvenç, İ., Yurekli, A. İ., Akkaya, K., & Uluağaç, S. (2016). Drones for smart cities: Issues in cybersecurity, privacy, and public safety. *2016 International Wireless Communications and Mobile Computing Conference (IWCMC)*, 216-221. 10.1109/IWCMC.2016.7577060

Wanigasooriya, Halgamuge, & Mohamad. (2017). The Analyzes of Anticancer Drug Sensitivity of Lung Cancer Cell Lines by Using Machine Learning Clustering Techniques. *International Journal of Advanced Computer Science and Applications, 8*(9).

Yadav, S. A., Kumar, S. R., Sharma, S., & Singh, A. (2016). A review of possibilities and solutions of cyber attacks in smart grids. *2016 International Conference on Innovation and Challenges in Cyber Security (ICICCS-INBUSH)*, 60-63. 10.1109/ICICCS.2016.7542359

Yang, Zhao, Zhang, Lin, & Yu. (2017). Toward a Gaussian-Mixture Model-Based Detection Scheme Against Data Integrity Attacks in the Smart Grid. *IEEE Internet of Things Journal, 4*(1), 147-161.

Zarpelão, B. B., Miani, R. S., Kawakani, C. T., & de Alvarenga, S. C. (2017). A survey of intrusion detection in Internet of Things. *Journal of Network and Computer Applications*, *84*, 25–37. doi:10.1016/j.jnca.2017.02.009

Zhang, K., Ni, J., Yang, K., Liang, X., Ren, J., & Shen, X. S. (2017). Security and Privacy in Smart City Applications: Challenges and Solutions. *IEEE Communications Magazine*, *55*(1), 122–129. doi:10.1109/MCOM.2017.1600267CM

Chapter 11
Security in IoT and Big Data With Technical Challenges

Mamata Rath
C. V. Raman College of Engineering, India

ABSTRACT

There are higher rates of mobile devices in current networks that are associated with each other intelligently using internet of things (IoT) domain to make diverse communication in various applications. Therefore, security issues are a major concern to accomplish a protected communication. There are many functions and cryptographic algorithms developed during research which can be utilized as a part of the communication trade among the devices to make secure internet of things networks in an approach to ensure right transmission. Big data is the most demanding concept used in business analytics and massive data processing. It is heard all over the place, particularly in the social insurance industry. Traditionally, the tremendous measure of data produced by the medicinal services industry was put away as printed version. This data has the ability to help an extensive variety of medicinal services and restorative capacities. The digitization of such data is called big data. The chapter features critical security issues in IoT-associated devices both in wireless network and big data analytics along with all other widely used area where IoT environment has been implemented. It also describes security issues in IoT systems particularly when IoT computing devices are used in critical real-time applications such as utilizing IoT frameworks involving information transmission with mobile phones, existing secured systems for enormous information, and individual information security including verification and secured correspondence in IoT.

INTRODUCTION

The design of Internet of Things (IoT) began with things with personality specialized computing devicess. The computing devicess could be followed, controlled or checked utilizing remote PCs associated through Internet. IoT broadens the utilization of Internet giving the correspondence, and in this way between system of the computing devicess and physical articles, or 'Things'. The two unmistakable words in IoT are "internet" and "things". Internet implies an immense worldwide system of associated servers, PCs,

DOI: 10.4018/978-1-5225-7432-3.ch011

tablets and mobiles utilizing the universally utilized conventions and interfacing frameworks. Internet empowers sending, getting, or imparting of data. Thing in English has number of employments and implications. Word reference significance of 'Thing' is a term used to reference to a physical question, an activity or thought, circumstance or movement, on the off chance that when we don't wish to be exact. IoT, when all is said in done comprises of between system of the computing devicess and physical items, number of articles can accumulate the information at remote areas and convey to units overseeing, gaining, sorting out and examining the information in the procedures and administrations. It gives a dream where things (wearable, watch, wake up timer, home computing devicess, encompassing items with) end up noticeably keen and carry on alive through detecting, registering and imparting by implanted little computing devicess which interface with remote articles or people through availability. The versatile and hearty nature of Cloud registering is enabling engineers to make and host their applications on it.

Figure 1 shows Various applications of IoT in different fields. The detail mechanism are discussed in the following sections.

CHALLENGES AND SECURITY IN IOT BASED APPLIANCES AND BIG DATA

New prospects for health care checking is induced by the expansion of Internet of Things (IoT) and Big data, and in addition the universal idea of little wearable bio sensors. Numerous defy presently can't seem to be routed to make a tried and true and adaptable framework for health care checking Big data investigation on IoT based Health care framework is proposed (p. Sunderavadivel et.al, 2018) and it utilizes IoT based health care observing framework that contains "Web of health sensor things". These things create gigantic volumes of data that couldn't be dealt with by the doctor. The Physicians imperative concern is that they have to settle on basic choices about their patient's health from these gigantic volumes of health data. He/she needs to isolate the data around one specific patient from the surge of health care data landing from the monstrous number of patients. Intel Galileo Gen 2 is going about as

Figure 1. Various applications of IoT

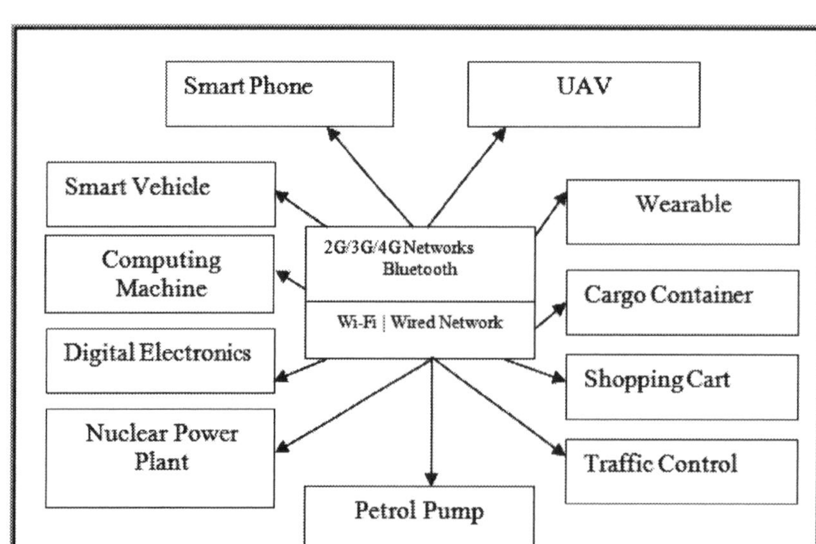

IoT operator and is utilized to convey the health data of patients into the Cloud. The could deal with the expanding volume of health data, ingeniously share the data crosswise over healthcare frameworks and give feasibility to Big data examination. Ongoing alarming of patient health data is a critical exercise in Big data which is essential in the proposed work. The Big health sensor data are investigated utilizing the Hadoop system. Since the reaction time of the proposed framework is less, it is reasonable for ongoing cautioning pharmaceutical.

The intensity of machine learning has been enormously perceived in changing different ventures and health care applications . The reason that Amazon, Netflix, and Google have changed their enterprises and have inserted learning all through each part of what they do. AEGLE enterprise focuses to construct an imaginative ICT arrangement tending to the entire data esteem chain for health in view of: distributed computing empowering dynamic asset portion, HPC frameworks for computational speeding up and propelled perception techniques.Aanalysis of the tended to Big Data health situations and the key empowering advances, and data security and administrative issues has been completed which are to be incorporated into AEGLE's bioanalytical community (T.Shah et.al, 2016) empowering propelled healthcare expository administrations, while additionally advancing related research exercises.

Basic Health Care IT Computing Systems such as life sustained devices, Health checking systems, data processing systems that give purpose of caring solution and direction to care groups are a key segment of a lifesaving exertion in Healthcare. The high trends of mobility, social, cloud joined with far reaching increment and modernity of malware, has made new difficulties and the point in time location strategies at the clinics are never again compelling and represent a major danger to the basic care systems (V. Vippalapalli 2016) . To keep up the accessibility and honesty of these basic care systems, new versatile, learning security safeguard systems are required that not just gains from the activity entering the healing facility, yet in addition proactively gains from the movement around the world. Cisco's Cloud web security (CWS) gives industry-driving security and control for the dispersed endeavor by ensuring clients all over, whenever through Cisco overall danger knowledge, propelled risk barrier abilities, and wandering client assurance. It use the huge information to perform conduct investigation, irregularity location, avoidance obstruction, quick Detection administrations utilizing stream based, signature based,

Figure 2. Application of big data applications

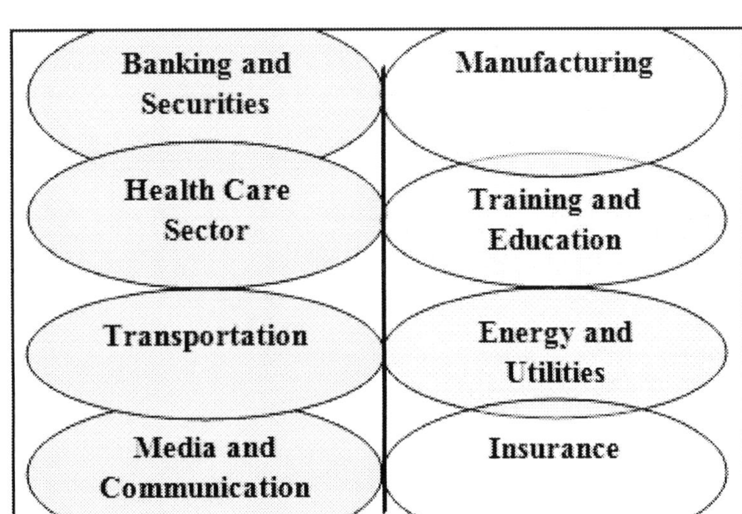

conduct based and full bundle catch models to distinguish dangers. A specialized audit takes a gander at how huge Data Analytics is utilized as a part of blend with other security capacities to proactively distinguish dangers and anticipate far reaching harm to social insurance basic resources.

Association of IoT and Big Data Analytics

Interfacing the physical world to the Internet of Things (IoT) – It takes into account the advancement of a wide assortment of utilizations. Things can be sought, overseen, examined, and even incorporated into collective amusements. Enterprises, health care, and urban areas are misusing IoT information driven systems to make these associations more productive, in this way, enhancing the lives of residents (M.K. Pusala et.al, 2016) . For making IoT a reality, information created by sensors, advanced mobile phones, watches, and different wearables should be coordinated; additionally, the importance of IoT information ought to be expressly spoken to. Nonetheless, the Big Data nature of IoT information forces challenges that should be tended to keeping in care the end goal to give versatile and productive IoT information driven foundations. These issues have been taken care of and focussed on the problems of portraying the significance of IoT spilling information utilizing philosophy and incorporating this information in a learning chart. DESERT, a SPARQL inquiry motor has been planned [80] to influence ready to on-Demand factorizE and Semantically To advance stReam information (DESERT) in a learning diagram.

Coming about learning charts show the semantics or significance of combined information as far as elements that fulfill the SPARQL inquiries and connections among those substances; in this manner, just information required for question noting is incorporated into the learning diagram. It assesses the consequences of DESERT on SRBench, a benchmark of Streaming RDF information. The trial comes about recommend that DESERT takes into consideration accelerating question execution while the extent of the learning charts remains generally low (L.Cui et,al, 2016) .One of the biggest obstacles obstructing to utilize big data in social insurance is the manner by which restorative data is spread crosswise over

Figure 3. IoT supporting concepts

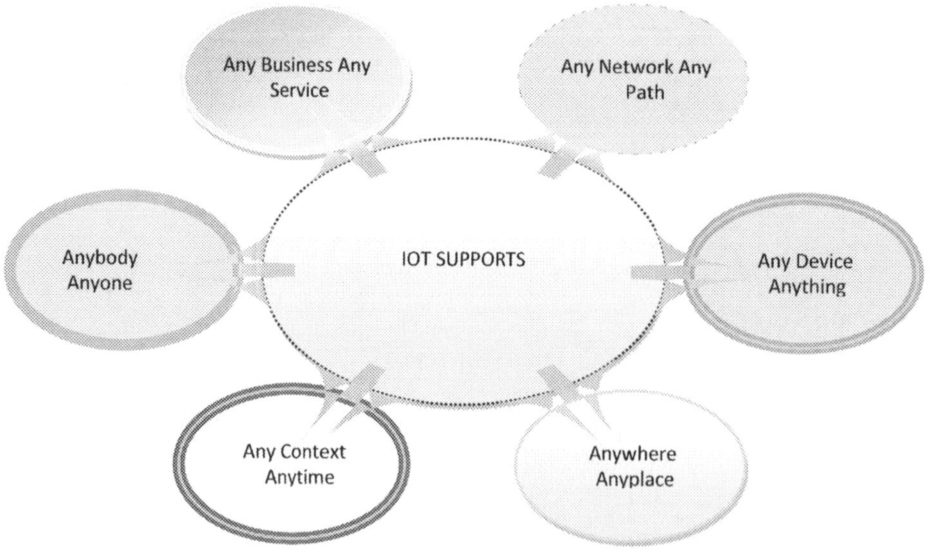

numerous sources represented by various states, clinics, and authoritative offices. Combination of these data sources would require building up another foundation where all data suppliers team up with each other. Similarly critical is actualizing new data examination instruments and procedures. Social insurance needs to get up to speed with different ventures that have effectively moved from standard relapse based techniques to more future-arranged like prescient investigation, machine learning, and chart examination.

Data Security and Real Time Applications

Data security and patient secrecy is an additional hazard. One of the benefits of paper and siloed electronic records is that they are not hackable. At the point when human services associations consider versatile application advancement to help IoT equipments, they should likewise guarantee that weakness is held within proper limits. Regardless of these dangers, wearables, sensors and portable applications are propelling the wildernesses of medicinal learning at a consistently expanding rate – particularly in battling and anticipating perilous sicknesses and immune system diseases (D. Finlay(2016 et.al, 2016) . The odds of creating tumor in one's lifetime are evaluated to be as high as one out of two (for US guys). In any case, the industry is making fast walks in battling and keeping these malignancies. Different cases of big data in human services share one pivotal usefulness – constant alarming. In doctor's facilities, Clinical Decision Support (CDS) programming breaks down restorative data on the spot, furnishing wellbeing experts with guidance as they settle on prescriptive choices ought to end up a reality.

Kaiser Permanente (a case study) is driving the path in the U.S., and could give a model to the EU to take after. They've completely executed a framework called HealthConnect that offers data over the majority of their offices and makes it less demanding to utilize EHRs. A McKinsey cover big data in human services expresses that "The incorporated framework has enhanced results in cardiovascular infection and accomplished an expected $1 billion in investment funds from lessened office visits and lab tests." In any case, there are some sublime occurrences where medicinal services doesn't fall behind, for example, EHRs (particularly in the US.) So, regardless of whether these administrations are not some tea, you are a potential patient, thus you should think about new social insurance investigation applications. In addition, it's great to investigate now and again and perceive how different ventures adapt to big data. They can motivate you to adjust and receive some smart thoughts. A gander at one great issue can be taken that any move director faces: what number of people do I put on staff at any given day on gate (D. Finlay et.al, 2016). On the off chance that you put on an excessive number of specialists, you risk having pointless work costs include. Excessively couple of specialists, you can have poor client benefit results – which can be lethal for patients in businesses like social insurance. Big data is taking care of this issue, in any event at a couple of healing centers in Paris. A Forbes article subtle elements how four doctor's facilities which are a piece of the Assistance Publique-Hôpitaux de Paris have been utilizing data from an assortment of sources to think of day by day and hourly forecasts of what number of patients are required to be at every doctor's facility.

Big data is the most demanding concept used in business analytics and massive data processing. It is heard all over the place, particularly in the social insurance industry. Traditionally, the tremendous measure of data produced by the medicinal services industry was put away as printed version. This data has the ability to help an extensive variety of medicinal services and restorative capacities. The digitization of such data is called Big Data. The total of data that is identified with understanding social insurance and prosperity makes up big data. A 2011 McKinsey report [86] assessed that the medicinal services industry could conceivably acknowledge $300 billion in yearly incentive by utilizing big data. The wide assorted variety of big data and the pace at which it is overseen makes it overpowering.

Health Care Data Solution

With the assistance of big data, the immense measure of data can be put away deliberately. Presently specialists and other human services professionals can settle on educated choices as they approach an extensive variety of data. Obviously, the data produced will develop significantly, and more up to date frameworks will have the capacity to process it rapidly and cost adequately. Tumor is quickly devastating people over the world. Big data can battle disease all the more successfully. Social insurance suppliers will have upgraded capacity to recognize and analyze illnesses in their beginning periods, doling out more efficacious treatments in view of a patient's hereditary cosmetics, and manage sedate measurements to limit symptoms and enhance adequacy. It will likewise give awesome help to parallelization and help in mapping the 3 billion DNA base sets. The utilization of big data makes it less demanding for healing facility staff to work all the more effectively. Sensors are utilized other than understanding beds to ceaselessly screen pulse, pulse and respiratory rate. Any adjustment in design is immediately alarmed to specialists and social insurance chairmen.

Medicinal services organization turns out to be much smoother with the assistance of big data. It diminishes the cost of care estimation, give the best clinical help, and deal with the number of inhabitants in danger patients. It likewise enables restorative specialists to break down data from differing sources. It enables human services suppliers to close the deviations among patients and the impacts medications have on their wellbeing. Big Data can be utilized for human services Intelligence application. This will encourage doctor's facilities, payers and medicinal services offices increase their upper hands by creating brilliant business arrangements. Big data keeps an extensive variety of mistakes in favor of wellbeing overseers as wrong measurements, wrong medications, and other human blunders. It will likewise be especially helpful to insurance agencies. They can keep an extensive variety of false claims of protection. Data science acts as an essential part in numerous ventures. In confronting enormous measures of heterogeneous data, adaptable machine learning and data mining calculations and frameworks have turned out to be critical for data researchers. The development of volume, multifaceted nature and speed in data drives the requirement for versatile data logical calculations and frameworks. In human services, large measures of heterogeneous therapeutic data have turned out to be accessible in different social insurance associations (payers, suppliers, pharmaceuticals). This data could be an empowering resource for inferring experiences for enhancing care conveyance and diminishing waste. The immensity and many-sided quality of these datasets introduce extraordinary difficulties in investigations and resulting applications to a down to earth clinical condition.

It is essential to know qualities of medicinal data and related data mining challenges in managing such data. Various calculations and frameworks for big data investigation likewise should be known to get favorable position of the apparatuses. Procedures utilized as a part of big data applications with regards to solid social insurance logical applications, for example, prescient displaying, computational phenol writing and patient similitude should be comprehended alongside the ideas, for example, Understanding the wellbeing data and big data systematic innovation, Standard wellbeing data, Scalable machine learning calculations, for example, web based learning and quick comparability seek, Big data explanatory frameworks, for example, Hadoop family (Hive, Pig, HBase), Spark and Graph DB, Deep learning models and bundles, for example, tensorflow.

Big Data is a major demanding expression in current technology. The theme has been making waves in different enterprises for quite a while, however its applications in human services are still in their developmental stages. The utilization of big data demonstrates energizing guarantee for enhancing well-being results and controlling expenses, as prove by some developing use cases, yet the training is by all accounts characterized to some degree contrastingly by every master we inquire (J. Archenaa, 2015).

The idea alludes to immense amounts of data—made by the mass appropriation of the Internet and digitization of a wide range of information, including wellbeing records—too large or complex for traditional innovation to comprehend. New big data innovations, be that as it may, hold guarantee for merging and dissecting these computerized treasure troves so as to find patterns and make forecasts. It is needed to comprehend what big data will mean for social insurance, so big data investigation and human services informatics master Dr. Russell Richmond to talk about what's in store. Dr. Richmond is a main social insurance innovation expert whose experience incorporates constructing large data examination organizations and exhorting wellbeing framework officials as a specialist at administration counselling firm McKinsey and Company.

As per Dr. Richmond, a standout amongst the most energizing ramifications for big data in social insurance is that suppliers will have the capacity to convey substantially more exact and customized mind. With a more entire, point by point picture of patients and populaces, they'll have the capacity to decide how a specific patient will react to a particular treatment, or even distinguish patients in danger before a medical problem emerges. "More information yields more granular finding, which makes the open door for more exact treatment," Dr. Richmond disclosed to me. Dr. Richmond made me ponder about organizations that are as of now making utilization of big data to impact wellbeing results. He as of late joined the top managerial staff for one such organization, Explorys. So I chose to investigate Explorys and different associations using big data today.

Success of Big Data With Improved Health Operations

Any organization of any size in any industry can profit by big data examination, however maybe it is the social insurance industry that has the most to pick up. Doctor's facilities produce a great deal of data for persistent care, tranquilize organization, tasks, protection charging, administrative consistence and a large group of different necessities, and every one of that data can be utilized to enhance the nature of care and activities. Big data investigation appears to be made for human services, and there are many utilize cases that convey a high ROI for any restorative practice.

Some important cases of Big Data Utilization in smart applications has been presented in this section.Developing countries where health care related information are not completely used to help and enhance healthcare results is because of alienated Healthcare Information Systems (HISs). Namibian healthcare scene, scratch capacities, data frameworks and the difficulties they confront. Namibia has a double healthcare framework with an open healthcare part that works in parallel with secretly subsidized healthcare arrangement. The data and data being gathered or firmly pertinent to the Namibia HIS are assembled into three principle classifications gathered, stockpiling and oversaw as of now in different HIS that are divided and crumbled. Thus, there is requirement for a coordinated HIS. We investigate two conceivable methodologies, and related reference engineering with their difficulties. Another way to deal with enhance the Lambda design restrictions has been proposed (Fatima et.al, 2017) utilizing abilities and ideas of administration situated engineering and virtualization.

While examining data where the connections between factors are not completely comprehended, it is commonplace to participate in visual investigation. In any case, this is moderate and physically concentrated, and fascinating patterns could conceivably be missed. (Richard K et.al, 2017) centers around examples and areas inside the data that are fascinating, for example, noteworthy bunches and exceptions. It introduce a novel iterative k-implies grouping calculation to proficiently distinguish bunches in substantial datasets. This encourages quick visual investigation of new datasets. The system has been shown by playing out a nitty gritty examination of open health care data discharged by the US Government and New York State. Iterative k-implies calculation has been utilized to recognize groups of patterns in labor compel cooperation to introduce a remarkable point of view by zone of restorative claim to fame over a 50-year time frame. Claims to fame, for example, nurture experts have seen a huge increment in the quantity of specialists with respect to inner pha

Another novel approach has been anticipated that assesses the right model for post commitment and opportunity on Facebook. Also, it gives knowledge into significant markers that prompt higher commitment with health care posts on Facebook. Both directed and unsupervised learning procedures are utilized to accomplish this objective. This exploration expects to add to technique of health-care associations to connect with consistent clients and assemble preventive systems over the long haul through useful health-care content posted on Facebook. In the present Indian situation, healthcare data is freely kept up by doctor's facilities, foundations and not promptly open in a brought together, educated way. This extraordinarily restrains the health suppliers' endeavors to enhance quality and proficiency. The issue of data from numerous sources into one place in realtime situation has been fathomed (H. Qiu et.al, 2015) which can be genuinely life sparing. Additionally, low proportion of specialist to understanding and the low per capita wage in India climbs the medicinal costs consequently expanding the patient's detachment to get appropriate health care in their scope particularly for individuals in the provincial regions. A methods by which the extension between the patients and specialists can be gapped and how patients can be dealt with at a lower cost is the prime concern. It likewise centers around the improvement of a versatile/web application, through which patients sends their symptomatic question to the specialists through a server. The versatile application will be furnished with medical aid guidelines, as per the nature and seriousness of the side effects, either the patients are coordinated to separate divisions or given crisis help for promote treatment. Inside the time gigantic measure of data is gathered from clients and specialists, this big data will be utilized to prepare machines to computerize the assignments to some degree. The data picked up from breaking down enormous measures of accumulated health data can give helpful knowledge to enhance quality and proficiency for suppliers and back up plans alike. This influences the patients to connect for healthcare arrangements effectively and economically and makes healthcare a simple reach for the unprivileged too. In this manner, this brought together model can fill in as a data accumulation, conveyance and in addition a scientific device in the healthcare space. In the event of health problems in human life, medications are prescribed to cure medicinal problems by health care proficient; accumulation of this record makes Medical Big Data (MBD) . It incorporates therapeutic history and solution reports, test reports, X-Ray, CT Scan, and some different kinds of restorative finding. E-Health and Telemedicine systems are being produced to diminish information accessibility (Rath et.al, 2018) to understanding, and is refreshed at the specialist end and kept up in the cloud based foundations. Enormous Medical information is compacted to keep up more record. This has broadened the spaces that are related with MBD. Most recent advancements give better helps to make MBD a piece of information accumulation, handling and dependable shape for future recommendation.

Secured Approach of Big Data and IoT in Smart Traffic

Designing smart traffic control systems for smart cities is a challenging task for network developers. (Pattanayak et.al, 2014) Use of control operators for coordinating parts in a network of collaborating dynamic frameworks is an emblematic approach. In this technique, every nearby control operator must guarantee that every single neighborhood detail are met, however in the meantime should guarantee that the distinctive segments help each other in accomplishing great worldwide conduct and great neighborhood conduct. This is shown by utilizing urban traffic control and smart electric power frameworks as illustrations. Brought together or various leveled control approaches are not powerful against disappointments in correspondence networks (Rath et.al, 2014), and require doubtful presumptions on the information of every specialist about the general model. A totally decentralized approach, where every nearby control specialist egotistically attempts to accomplish its neighborhood particulars just, runs a high danger of worldwide associations that may destabilize the framework, making it difficult to accomplish the determinations. There are two ideal models for distributed input control (Enji et.al, 2012) that require next to no data trade and almost no worldwide model learning. The pioneer/supporter control worldview is delineated for urban traffic control: vigorously stacked pioneer operators send messages to their adherent neighbors asking for that these devotees give green just to companies of vehicles going towards the pioneer crossing point at those occasions when this will be ideal for the execution of the pioneer. Another coordination worldview is known as the organizing model prescient control (CMPC). A power transmission network (Rath et.al, 2016) might be viewed as that has been divided in collaborating areas, where CMPC is utilized keeping in mind the end goal to keep the spread of the unsettling influences following occurrences like line or machine disappointment. CMPC attempts to determine this by having every nearby control operator apply a model prescient controller, utilizing as on-line accessible data the nearby voltage and current estimations, as well as data on the arranged grouping of future control activities of neighboring specialists, (Aamir Hussain, 2015) conveyed to it now and again. This review talks about a portion of the minimum need for demonstrating, correspondence and control specialist set-up keeping in mind the end goal to vigorously accomplish determinations utilizing distributed control.

The information model is expected to portray information procedures and information streams, parameters, and properties of the control framework for traveler traffic enlistment in broad daylight transport of "smart" city that guarantees viable working of the created framework. The viable implementation of the information show includes utilizing the rundown information structures and XML.Traffic overburden is a squeezing problem for some urban areas these days and they are attempting to discover smart arrangements. In this manner urban communities are presenting traffic control frameworks (Rath et.al, 2019) that encourage a more unique travel through the city for travel traffic while advancing the control of individual intersections outfitted with light flagging. Assessment of traffic control parameters is normally in light of preparing of information from traffic overviews.

Urban city and congestion created with general smart society transport framework's creates disappointment, in taking care of the people's rising demand for a powerful transport methodology remain as significant reasons tempting the Sfax city (Bahar et.al, 2018) occupants to request for the private methods for transport instead of picking people in general transport benefit (80% versus 20%). It is really this reality which lies as the real hotspot for the astounding obstructed traffic and street clog, and additionally the constantly irritating pollution issues describing the city's condition. It is in this setting the proposed study can be set with a top to bottom research planned to examine the genuine condition of traffic on the light of hindrance focuses' assurance contemplate (red spots) as enduring on the city's street network (Rath et.al, 2015). As a major aspect of the attempted exploratory investigation, a unique crusade has been actualized on leading body of the SORETRAS, the general population transport transporting organization's vehicles to gauge and assess the general overwhelming business speed. The measure has been directed through utilization of the ways' genuine term timing strategy, notwithstanding recognizable proof of the red spots and comparing stop span ID approach. The conceived structure includes concocting an extraordinary Smart control and urban administration by methods for a clever transportation framework. The last would serve to help in viably advancing the utilization of transport foundations through limiting street clog. It depends on the accompanying advances: obtaining the constant information of traffic status at each point as recognized from the reconnaissance cameras, gathering information, from that point, in an accumulation focus and as an extreme advance, investigating and settling on the correct choice with respect to the traffic circumstance. Such an arbitration, redirecting traffic, alongside establishment of police robots, watch dispatching and programmed direction. Notwithstanding many years of reformative enactment with respect to the security of drivers and enormous activities by developers to enhance vehicle security features, engine vehicle defect identified with speed killed around 3000 young people (matured 16-19) every year. A detailed report [44] proposes an implanted smart control framework to constrain the vehicle speed to the most extreme admissible street speed. This can be accomplished by setting up a live correspondence between the voyage control framework and the locally available GPS module. Utilizing the Engine Control Unit (ECU) to control the electronic throttle and air valve, the most extreme rotational velocity of the motor can be restricted with the goal that the vehicle's speed does not outperform a street speed confine. By executing this installed framework to control the speed of the engine vehicle, this framework can possibly diminish the quantity of speeding-related mischances. The investigation assesses the practicability of the proposed inserted framework and talks about option controlling techniques. For this reason, a graphical UI (GUI) module is likewise created to make the framework more easy to use. The information used to test the framework was gathered through a GPS benefit from the boulevards around the grounds of the University of Central Oklahoma.

Correspondence based prepare control (CBTC) frameworks utilize remote neighborhood for information transmission amongst trains and wayside gear. Since unavoidable bundle deferral and drop are presented in prepare wayside interchanges, information vulnerabilities in trains' states will prompt impromptu footing/braking requests, and also squander in electrical vitality (M.Hossain et.al, 2017) . Also, with the presentation of regenerative braking innovation, control networks in CBTC frameworks are developing to smart lattices, and cost-mindful power administration ought to be utilized to decrease the aggregate monetary cost of devoured electrical vitality. In this paper, an intellectual control technique for CBTC frameworks with smart networks is displayed to upgrade both prepare activity execution and cost effectiveness (Rathg et.al, 2017). A psychological control framework show has been detailed for CBTC frameworks. The information hole in subjective control is computed to break down how the prepare wayside interchanges influence the activity of trains. The Q-learning calculation is utilized in the proposed intellectual control strategy, and a joint target work made out of the information hole and the aggregate money related cost is applied to create ideal approach. The medium-get to control layer retry-restrain adaption and footing procedure choice are embraced as psychological activities. Broad reenactment results demonstrate that the cost productivity and prepare activity execution of CBTC frameworks are significantly enhanced utilizing our proposed subjective control strategy.

CONCLUSION

The development rate of information generation has expanded radically over the previous years with the multiplication of brilliant and sensor gadgets. The collaboration amongst IoT and big data analytics is presently at a phase where preparing, changing, and breaking down a lot of information at a high recurrence are essential. We directed this review with regards to security of enormous IoT information and investigation. In the first place, we investigated late inspection activities. The relationship between enormous information examination and IoT was additionally talked about. Next we have presented issues related to security in IoT using Big Data analytics with informative exploration. Many open house research challenges were highlighted and discussed from application point of view. At last impact of big data in social platforms and their important contribution in health care appliances was depicted in order to give a multi dimensional review to the subject.

REFERENCES

Archenaa, J., & Mary Anita, E. A. (2015). A Survey of Big Data Analytics in Healthcare and Government. *Procedia Computer Science, 50*, 408-413. doi:10.1016/j.procs.2015.04.021

Cui, L., Yu, F. R., & Yan, Q. (2016). When big data meets software-defined networking: SDN for big data and big data for SDN. IEEE Netw., 30, 58–65.

Farahani, B., Firouzi, F., Chang, V., Badaroglu, M., Constant, N., & Mankodiya, K. (2018). Towards fog-driven IoT eHealth: Promises and challenges of IoT in medicine and healthcare. *Future Generation Computer Systems, 78*(2), 659-676.

Finlay, D. (2016). Article Seven - Connected Health Approaches to Wound Monitoring. In J. Davis, A. McLister, J. Cundell, & D. Finlay (Eds.), *Smart Bandage Technologies* (pp. 229–244). Academic Press. doi:10.1016/B978-0-12-803762-1.00007-2

Hossain, Islam, Ali, Kwak, & Hasan. (2017). An Internet of Things-based health prescription assistant and its security system design. *Future Generation Computer Systems.*

Hussain, A., & Rao, W. (2015). Health and emergency-care platform for the elderly and disabled people in the Smart City. *Journal of Systems and Software, 110*, 253-263.

Jeste, Blazer, Buckwalter, Cassidy, Fishman, Gwyther, … Feather. (2016). Age-Friendly Communities Initiative: Public Health Approach to Promoting Successful Aging. *The American Journal of Geriatric Psychiatry, 24*(12), 1158-1170.

Lomotey, Pry, & Sriramoju. (2017). Wearable IoT data stream traceability in a distributed health information system. *Pervasive and Mobile Computing, 40*, 692-707.

Mamata, R. B. P. (2018). Communication Improvement and Traffic Control Based on V2I in Smart City Framework. *International Journal of Vehicular Telematics and Infotainment Systems, 2*(1).

Pattanayak, B., & Rath, M. (2014). A Mobile Agent Based Intrusion Detection System Architecture For Mobile Ad Hoc Networks. *Journal of Computational Science, 10*(6), 970–975. doi:10.3844/jcssp.2014.970.975

Pusala, M. K., Salehi, M. A., Katukuri, J. R., Xie, Y., & Raghavan, V. (2016). *Massive Data Analysis: Tasks, Tools, Applications, and Challenges, Big Data Analytics*. Springer.

Qiu, H. J. F., Ho, I. W. H., Tse, C. K., & Xie, Y. (2015). A Methodology for Studying 802.11p VANET Broadcasting Performance With Practical Vehicle Distribution. *IEEE Transactions on Vehicular Technology, 64*(10), 4756–4769. doi:10.1109/TVT.2014.2367037

Rath, M. (2017). Resource provision and QoS support with added security for client side applications in cloud computing. *International Journal of Information Technology, 9*(3), 1–8.

Rath, M., & Oreku, G. S. (2018). Security Issues in Mobile Devices and Mobile Adhoc Networks. In Mobile Technologies and Socio-Economic Development in Emerging Nations. IGI Global. doi:10.4018/978-1-5225-4029-8.ch009

Rath, M. (2018a). An Exhaustive Study and Analysis of Assorted Application and Challenges in Fog Computing and Emerging Ubiquitous Computing Technology. *International Journal of Applied Evolutionary Computation, 9*(2), 17-32. Retrieved from www.igi-global.com/ijaec

Rath, M. (2018b). A Methodical Analysis of Application of Emerging Ubiquitous Computing Technology With Fog Computing and IoT in Diversified Fields and Challenges of Cloud Computing. *International Journal of Information Communication Technologies and Human Development, 10*(2). Doi:10.4018/978-1-5225-4100-4.ch002

Rath, M. (2018e). Smart Traffic Management System for Traffic Control using Automated Mechanical and Electronic Devices. *I Mater. Sci. Eng., 377*. /10.1088/1757-899X/377/1/012201

Rath, M., & Panda, M. R. (2017). MAQ system development in mobile ad-hoc networks using mobile agents. *IEEE 2nd International Conference on Contemporary Computing and Informatics (IC3I)*, 794-798.

Rath, M., & Panigrahi, C. (2016). Prioritization of Security Measures at the Junction of MANET and IoT. In *Second International Conference on Information and Communication Technology for Competitive Strategies*. ACM Publication. 10.1145/2905055.2905187

Rath, M., & Pati, B. (2017). *Load balanced routing scheme for MANETs with power and delay optimization. International Journal of Communication Network and Distributed Systems*, 19.

Rath, M., Pati, B., & Pattanayak, B. (2015). Energy Competent Routing Protocol Design in MANET with Real time Application Provision. *International Journal of Business Data Communications and Networking, IGI Global, 11*(1), 50–60. doi:10.4018/IJBDCN.2015010105

Rath, M., Pati, B., & Pattanayak, B. (2015). Delay and power based network assessment of network layer protocols in MANET. *2015 Intern-ational Conference on Control, Instrumentation, Communication and Computational Technologies (IEEE ICCICCT)*, 682-686. 10.1109/ICCICCT.2015.7475365

Rath, M., Pati, B., & Pattanayak, B. (2016). Energy Efficient MANET Protocol Using Cross Layer Design for Military Applications. *Defence Science Journal, 66*(2), 146. doi:10.14429/dsj.66.9705

Rath, M., Pati, B., & Pattanayak, B. (2016). Comparative analysis of AODV routing protocols based on network performance parameters in Mobile Adhoc Networks. In Foundations and Frontiers in Computer, Communication and Electrical Engineering (pp. 461-466). CRC Press, Taylor & Francis.

Rath, M., Pati, B., & Pattanayak, B. (2016). Resource Reservation and Improved QoS for Real Time Applications in MANET. *Indian Journal of Science and Technology*, *9*(36). doi:10.17485/ijst/2016/v9i36/100910

Rath, M., Pati, B., & Pattanayak, B. (2016). QoS Satisfaction in MANET Based Real Time Applications. *International Journal of Control Theory and Applications, 9*(7), 3069-3083.

Rath, M., Pati, B., & Pattanayak, B. K. (2016). Inter-Layer Communication Based QoS Platform for Real Time Multimedia Applications in MANET. Wireless Communications, Signal Processing and Networking (IEEE WiSPNET), 613-617. doi:10.1109/WiSPNET.2016.7566203

Rath, M., Pati, B., & Pattanayak, B. K. (2017). Cross layer based QoS platform for multimedia transmission in MANET. *11th International Conference on Intelligent Systems and Control (ISCO)*, 402-407. 10.1109/ISCO.2017.7856026

Rath, M., Pati, B., & Pattanayak, B. K. (2018). Relevance of Soft Computing Techniques in the Significant Management of Wireless Sensor Networks. In Soft Computing in Wireless Sensor Networks (pp. 86-106). Chapman and Hall/CRC, Taylor & Francis Group. doi:10.1201/9780429438639-4

Rath, M., Pati, B., & Pattanayak, B. K. (2019). Mobile Agent-Based Improved Traffic Control System in VANET. In A. Krishna, K. Srikantaiah, & C. Naveena (Eds.), *Integrated Intelligent Computing, Communication and Security. Studies in Computational Intelligence* (Vol. 771). Singapore: Springer. doi:10.1007/978-981-10-8797-4_28

Rath, M., & Pattanayak, B. (2016). A Contemporary Survey and Analysis of Delay and Power Based Routing Protocols in MANET. *Journal of Engineering and Applied Sciences (Asian Research Publishing Network), 11*(1), 536–540.

Rath, M., & Pattanayak, B. (2017). MAQ:A Mobile Agent Based QoS Platform for MANETs. *International Journal of Business Data Communications and Networking, IGI Global, 13*(1), 1–8. doi:10.4018/IJBDCN.2017010101

Rath, M., & Pattanayak, B. K. (2014). A methodical survey on real time applications in MANETS: Focussing On Key Issues. *International Conference on, High Performance Computing and Applications (IEEE ICHPCA),* 22-24. 10.1109/ICHPCA.2014.7045301

Rath, M., & Pattanayak, B. K. (2018). Monitoring of QoS in MANET Based Real Time Applications. In Information and Communication Technology for Intelligent Systems (ICTIS 2017): Vol. 2. ICTIS 2017. Smart Innovation, Systems and Technologies (vol. 84, pp. 579-586). Springer. doi:10.1007/978-3-319-63645-0_64

Rath, M., & Pattanayak, B. K. (2018). Monitoring of QoS in MANET Based Real Time Applications. In Information and Communication Technology for Intelligent Systems: Vol. 2. ICTIS. Smart Innovation, Systems and Technologies (vol. 84, pp. 579-586). Springer. doi:10.1007/978-3-319-63645-0_64

Rath, M., & Pattanayak, B. K. (2018). SCICS: A Soft Computing Based Intelligent Communication System in VANET. Smart Secure Systems – IoT and Analytics Perspective. *Communications in Computer and Information Science*, *808*, 255–261. doi:10.1007/978-981-10-7635-0_19

Rath, M., Pattanayak, B. K., & Pati, B. (2017). *Energetic Routing Protocol Design for Real-time Transmission in Mobile Ad hoc Network. In Computing and Network Sustainability, Lecture Notes in Networks and Systems* (Vol. 12). Singapore: Springer.

Rath, M., Rout, U. P., & Pujari, N. (2017). *Congestion Control Mechanism for Real Time Traffic in Mobile Adhoc Networks, Computer Communication, Networking and Internet Security. Lecture Notes in Networks and Systems* (Vol. 5). Singapore: Springer.

Rath, M., Swain, J., Pati, B., & Pattanayak, B. K. (2018). *Attacks and Control in MANET. In Handbook of Research on Network Forensics and Analysis Techniques* (pp. 19–37). IGI Global.

Rath, M. (2018c). Effective Routing in Mobile Ad-hoc Networks With Power and End-to-End Delay Optimization: Well Matched With Modern Digital IoT Technology Attacks and Control in MANET. In *Advances in Data Communications and Networking for Digital Business Transformation*. IGI Global. Doi:10.4018/978-1-5225-5323-6.ch007

Rath, M. (2018d). An Analytical Study of Security and Challenging Issues in Social Networking as an Emerging Connected Technology. In *Proceedings of 3rd International Conference on Internet of Things and Connected Technologies*. Malaviya National Institute of Technology. Retrieved from https://ssrn.com/abstract=3166509

Sahoo, J., & Rath, M. (2017). Study and Analysis of Smart Applications in Smart City Context. *2017 International Conference on Information Technology (ICIT)*, 225-228. 10.1109/ICIT.2017.38

Shah. (2016). Remote health care cyber-physical system: quality of service (QoS) challenges and opportunities. *IET Cyber-Physical Systems: Theory & Applications, 1*(1), 40-48. doi:10.1049/iet-cps.2016.0023

Sun, E., Zhang, X., & Li, Z. (2012). The Internet of Things (IOT) and cloud computing (CC) based tailings dam monitoring and pre-alarm system in mines. *Safety Science*, *50*(4), 811–815. doi:10.1016/j.ssci.2011.08.028

Sundaravadivel, Kougianos, Mohanty, & Ganapathiraju. (2018). Everything You Wanted to Know about Smart Health Care: Evaluating the Different Technologies and Components of the Internet of Things for Better Health. *IEEE Consumer Electronics Magazine, 7*(1), 18-28.

Vippalapalli, V., & Ananthula, S. (2016). Internet of things (IoT) based smart health care system. *International Conference on Signal Processing, Communication, Power and Embedded System (SCOPES)*, 1229-1233. 10.1109/SCOPES.2016.7955637

Zuhra, F. T., Abu Bakar, K., Ahmed, A., & Tunio, M. A. (2017). Routing protocols in wireless body sensor networks: A comprehensive survey. *Journal of Network and Computer Applications*, 73-97.

Chapter 12
Disaster Management Using Internet of Things

Meghna Sharma
The NorthCap University, India

Jagdeep Kaur
The NorthCap University, India

ABSTRACT

The problem of hazard detection and the robotic exploration of the hazardous environment is the need of the of the hour due to the continuous increase of the hazardous gases owing to the industry proliferation and modernization of the infrastructure. It includes radiological materials and toxic gases with long term harmful effects. The definition of a hazardous environment and extracting the parameters for the same is itself a complicated task. The chapter proposes the alarming solution to warn about the level of hazardous effects for a particular environment area. The need of the hour is to build complete systems that can autosense the hazardous environment even in low visibility environment and raise an alarm. The combination of IoT and machine learning can be best used for getting the real-time data and using the real-time data for analyzing the accurate current hazardous level as well as prediction of future hazards by reading the parameters for detection and also selecting the useful parameters from them.

INTRODUCTION

Internet of Things (IoT) can be explained as a network in which the connection of various types of devices which have electronics, sensors, and software, controllers embedded in them and connected for exchanging data. The connectivity in IoT is not limited to desktops, laptops, smart phones and tablets but covers any kind of daily usage objects like home appliances. The digital world can be directly converted to physical world for our convenience and controlling the world around us much more efficiently and effortlessly.

As studied by Gartner there is a tremendous increase of the use of IoT devices from 31% in one year, from approximately 8.4 billion in the year 2017 to the estimation of approximately 30 billion devices by 2020 (Gartner). Technically a fully fledged unit of IoT system consists of majorly four components consisting of sensors/devices with an interface for user and connection between the various devices and sensors for processing and transferring data. The technology roadmap for IoT is as shown below in Figure 1.

DOI: 10.4018/978-1-5225-7432-3.ch012

Figure 1. Technology roadmap of IoT

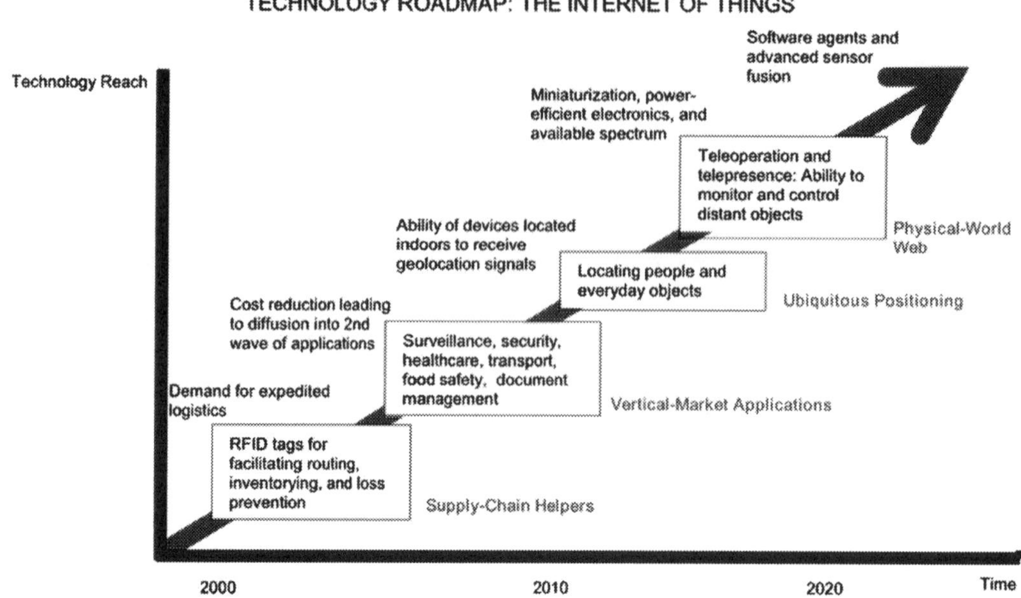

As the road map indicates IoT has come a long way. It started with demand for expatiating logistics with these of RFID tags for facilitating routing, inventory management, tracking of goods, monitoring of logistics and tasks which can be done automatically when data is read from RFID tag by the readers. After that came many applications like Surveillance, security, healthcare, food safety, document management and disaster management. Application areas for IoT started increasing though in the chapter major areas are covered. Use of IoT became prevalent after 2010 and further the future beyond this is ubiquitous computing where locating people and everyday objects is going to become easy. It can help in many aspects like tracking lost objects, stolen objects, tracking missing people but still intruding the privacy is a big issue which needs to be resolved. The future of IoT is physical web world connections with the ability to control and monitor distant objects. Use of software agents and advance sensor fusion is going to make humans rock with almost every work done remotely, ubiquitously and automatically with IoT. The sensors produce large amount of data which is collected through cloud platform and this data can be used in disaster management. Due to the high temporal frequency of the sensor data it is considered as the Big Data. There are many challenges associated with it like capturing and storing the sensor data and providing means for searching, utilizing and analyzing this data. So, in this cyber-physical era, the Big Data act as a bridge between the IoT and the internet. The different Big Data technologies like Hadoop, NoSql, and MapReduce etc can be used for IoT generated data. The Big Data generated provides an ample amount of opportunities for disaster Management. This Big Data consist of Geo-spatial sensor data, data generated by social networking sites etc. The main activities in Disaster Management are Preparedness, Response and Recovery and these phases are inter-related with each other as the success of response and recovery phases depends on the data collection during preparedness and prevention phases. For instance, the data generated is further processed and analyzed for various actions like raising an alarm or alerting the users or calibrating the system automatically without any manual intervention. This chapter proposes an IoT based system that can be used for disaster management in industries. The chapter is organized in the following sections:

- IoT and Big Data
- IoT in Disaster Management
- Big Data in Disaster Management
- Security of Big Data in Disaster Management
- Existing Scenarios
- Proposed Solution
- Conclusion

INTERNET OF THINGS (IoT) AND BIG DATA

The omnipresence of IoT and Big data gives opportunities to researchers to derive meaningful information form heterogeneous data collected from different sensors. The sensors generate large amount of data that can be analyzed and interpreted to help in decision making and control. The different sources of Big Data using IoT are:

- Sensors in smart phones
- Wearable devices
- Household gadgets
- Wi-Fi-enabled sensors

There are many challenges associated with IoT and Big Data. First is to process the big data &its acquisition, storage, analysis, updating, privacy and visualizations. Secondly, the temporal feature of the big data generated can be used for making real-time decisions. The descriptive and predictive analytics of the IoT generated data can really help in disaster management. The descriptive analytics describes the current situation and the predictive analytics helps in predicting future conditions.

INTERNET OF THINGS (IoT) IN DISASTER MANAGEMENT

A disaster can be defined as any physical event or human action which can lead to disruption in normal life damaging life and property to such an extent that it is difficult to cope up with it. The origin of any disaster can be man- made like environmental degradation and technological hazards or natural related to geological, hydro-meteorological and biological. Natural disasters include floods, cyclones, hailbursts, droughts, soil erosion, thunder etc. Geological disasters include landslides, earthquakes, large fire, dam failures, and mine fires etc. Biological disasters include epidemics. Now natural disasters are not much under our control though they can be detected various sensors depending on the application area. Man Made disasters are created by humans due to misuse of nature for their own benefit but it is proving to be hazardous to humans only. Chemical and Industrial disaster, nuclear disaster, fires, Oil spills, bomb blasts etc. are all man -made disasters. Disaster is disturbance in the balance of things that can be prevented or remedied with proactive approach. Any kind of disaster is it man-made or natural can be potentially management using the advanced technologies. Disaster Management is an attempt to inquire into the process of a potential damage (hazard) turning to disaster, to identify the causes and rectify the same.

The Internet of Things can also play a very important role in case of disaster with immense number of possibilities. IoT can be used for management of disasters like accidents in plants, mines and oil wells, detection of hazardous gases from mines and plants etc. Technology can't stop the occurrence of disasters especially man-made but use of IoT can be really helpful with data preparedness like prediction of any hazard or early warning for any disaster. In this way IoT can compensate for a poor infrastructure that puts developing and emerging countries in a particularly vulnerable position.

A very useful application of IoT in disaster management, can be the monitoring of fires caught in the forests. Sensors attached or embedded in the trees can help to check out the level of hazard after the fire is broke out affecting the level of pollution. Measurements of temperature level, moisture level and harmful gases like CO indicating carbon level can help in detecting the environment condition and effective measures to prevent it. Sensor data can help in checking the criticality based on the parameters studied on the data and thus can also alert the local population or any wild life for further action. Similar process can be used in factories or underground mines or manual scavenging where human life is working in unfavourable conditions risking their life. Measurement and analysis of critical parameters of hazard by sensing data can help to inform about the working conditions and level of hazard. IoT applications are not limited to these kind of applications but can also be used various other kinds of disasters also like measuring movements of earth which can help to some extent for calamities like earthquakes and tsunamis. Microwave sensors can be used for this application. There are other type of sensors like infrared sensors which can help in the detection and measurement of floods, continuous tracking people and things and so on.

Disaster management with wireless battery operated IoT devices can be done full preparedness to deal with it. Resiliency of the system is ensured in these systems so that in case any equipment failure due to any reasons should be able to recover and continues to operate without affecting the data. As robustness is much needed in IoT devices specially used for disaster management, preparedness for the case of any failure in conventional services for communication should be managed by limited communication services emergence micro message. So data resiliency and availability of effective alternate commination system must be taken into account when designing, creating and deploying the IoT systems for disaster managements. The level of hazards from the disasters decides the level of components of any IoT system.

Sensors attached to sense data for preparedness and resilience in disaster management is generally fixed at some points and has limited scope of measurement. The better option would some dynamic sensors with continuous streaming of data for further analysis. Autorobots with multiple sensors can prove to be an excellent solution to this. A simple arrangement of an auto-robot can be explained as shown in the Figure 2.

BIG DATA IN DISASTER MANAGEMENT

Disaster refers to man-made or natural accident. This chapter refers to man-made disasters only that may lead to loss of life and property. The three main phases (Rahman, 2017) of disaster management are:

Figure 2. Auto-robot with various sensors

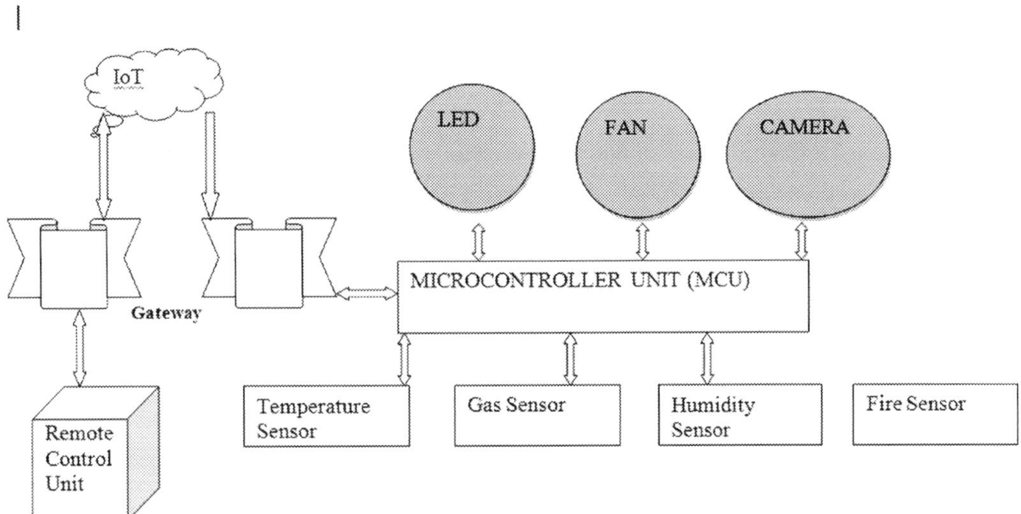

- Disaster Preparedness
- Disaster Response
- Disaster Recovery

These phases are explained as follows:

Disaster Preparedness

It denotes the methods used to prepare for and lessen the effects of disasters. It is a very difficult phase as it is very tough to model all effects of a disaster due to reliance on different variables. Big Data with high precision is required for such modeling. Big Data helps in early detection of floods, earthquake sensing, storms, hurricanes, Tsunami, hazardous gas leakage etc.

Disaster Response

There are three aspects where big data can help in disaster response as highlighted by Pu 2013; these are identifying the critical areas, real time situation analysis and identification of the most effective response based on historical data. The identification can be done with the help of advanced GPS system. The videos and images can be used for real time analysis. The crowd sourcing analysis can be used for identification of the affected areas.

Disaster Recovery

This phase mostly comes after the disaster has actually occurred. The frequent images taken by the satellites are an important source of big data and it must be processed at high speed for quick recovery process. As (Hayeshi, 2015) used spatiotemporal index to search the time series grid data for similar data. The post disaster data analysis can help in recovery in the future occurrence of such emergent situations.

SECURITY OF BIG DATA IN DISASTER MANAGEMENT

Seamless integration of different data sources and managing its security and privacy is still a daunting task. With each application varies the type of the data to be managed. As the data only is used for the analysis and strategy building, different preprocessing techniques must be enforced to ensure the consistency, accuracy and completeness for further decision making process. There are many challenges faced while doing data mining for the data generated in disaster management via IoT. Many data mining techniques like frequent pattern mining with association analysis, finding correlations among the various attributes as well as analyzing the trends in order to avoid or at least reduce the reoccurrences of disasters. The data which is transferred and stored in the network of the complete framework of disaster management must be taken care for its confidentiality, authenticity and privacy for realizing its security.

The Cloud Security Alliance (Group, 2013) has categorized security and privacy challenges into security related to infrastructure security, privacy of data, data management, integrity, and reactive security. Security of infrastructure can be implemented with secure programming in a distributed environment for unstructured as well as structured data generated as big data. Data needs to be encrypted for preserving its privacy. There has to be secure data storage with regular updation of transaction logs. Integrity and consistency of the data should be taken care. Proper validation, real time monitoring and filtering of the data should be done to handle reactive security. To a great extent regular monitoring of log data, network traffic, event management alerts, cyber attack patterns if any and any other information sources help in checking any anomaly or intrusion.

The security and privacy of the generated big data may include the following as discussed:

1. **Hadoop Security:** Hadoop is a distributed process framework and with its popularity as an environment for big data handling, security became a major concern and it was designed to operate in trusted environment only. The system is designed in such a way that can strongly prevent any hacker to get access to data in cloud. Authentication of the user is must to access the name node in the hadoop network infrastructure. Hashing techniques like SHA-256 are accepted to give good results for authentication. Random encryption techniques such as RSA, Rijndael, AES and RC6 have been also used on data in order that a hacker does not gain an access whole data. Use of encryption and decryption while transferring data in the network gives added security level.
2. **Cloud Security:** Data storage on clouds is one of the main problems nowadays. Service provider takes care of the security of the data. Again compression of the data, authentication of the user; encryption as well as decryption handle the secure access to big data on cloud platform. Authorized access with secure login credentials is must. Even during natural disaster cases automatic backup and recovery of data must be ensured with multiple backups and constant updations. Regular monitoring and auditing of network events is required to catch the intrusions. It is not easy to detect any intrusion and further applying prevention procedures on the traffic of data in the network. Analyzing Domain Name Server traffic, Internet Protocol flow records, Hypertext Transfer Protocol traffic and honey pot data (S. Marchal, 2014) help in managing the secure architecture regularly. Data correlation schemes are helpful in storage and processing of data in distributed environment. An

alert is generated in detection system if the metrics used for security score reaches beyond some threshold level of the security parameters and any malicious activity is there by monitoring traffic flow.

3. **Key Management:** Generation of keys for communicating between servers and using them for sharing information is again an issue for consideration. Keys for encryption and decryption should be encrypted too. Personal identifiable information is a big cause of concern as the data is generally shared frequently. Data is generally harvested for further analysis so strong security measures should be taken. As more than 80 percent of the big data is unstructured type, it's all the more difficult to ensure its safety.
4. **Anonymization:** Anonymization is one of the ways to ensure the privacy of the data by detaching the identification from the data and then transferring it in the network with secure channels. There are many traditional methods and hybrid techniques (Irudayasamy & Arockiam, 2015) to handle anonymity using various artificial techniques. Some technique is applied on the data for removal or hiding of any sensitive information and quite a tedious task for big data type of environments.

EXISTING SCENARIO

Many autonomous robots with different sensors are used for navigation and the main focus here is working of IoT for disaster management in low visibility environment specifically for measuring the environment conditions for harmful gases. In this particular set of conditions not much work is done as studied in the current scenario of research work but this area needs to be explored as it can be used for many applications like coal mining, manual scavenging, and night driving and so on. Presently most of the disaster management and monitoring is done through remotely operated robots except in military where autonomous robots also called as auto-robots are used for exploration of environment. Similarly autonomous robots can be used for detecting all the gas sources by proper planning of the navigation path of the mobile auto robot in reduced time and high accuracy without any manual intervention which can prove to very hazardous otherwise. No work is done in this area till date as studied in the literature.

Industrial disasters and its hazards on massive scale with its effect on the economic condition of workers, factories, and government are studied. The risk is very high and increases with gas, coal, electrical, and oil industries. Lot of research work is done in this domain with their own pros and cons. The research by L.Shu et al (L. Shu M. M., May 2017). Describes the use of Internet of Things for handling the industrial type of disasters. The major concern is the design for detection and monitoring of toxic gases (M. Mukherjee, Jan. 2017) (L. Shu M. M., Oct. 2016) in the gas generation facilities around the globe. One solution is given by Kim. Et al. with a simple client-server-based system model using Raspberry Pi to identify any hazardous gas in a gas factory (H. Kim, Sept. 2015). In another work AT Mega32 is used as sensor node for detecting hazardous gases (D. Spirjakin, Sept. 2015). Sensor node detects particles of dust in the gas leakage with the help of platinum micro This IoT-supported sensor node connects with the remote user or observer with ZigBee (https://en.wikipedia.org/wiki/Zigbee) for monitoring and analyzing the leakage of gases in its vicinity. Automation of gas leakage repairing work can be very well automated as explained by Guo. Et al. (X. Guo, May 2015). Generally in most of the papers use of ZigBee (https://en.wikipedia.org/wiki/Zigbee) is shown for remotely monitoring the leakage but one of the works also explained the usage of micro-drones for detecting gas leakage detection in an industrial area (V. Gallego, April 2015). This system uses micro drones to identify gases like Nitrogen Oxides (NOx) and Volatile Organic Compounds (VOCs) in gases. The complete network is connected with Global System for Mobile Communication (GSM) module. Disaster management is very crucial in the oil depots. The real time monitoring arrangement must be ensured for preventing any hazardous incident. RFID based system using RFID tags and readers have been designed in (Z. Du, Nov 2012) along with Virtual Private Networks (VPN), and the Internet. A fault diagnosis model which includes use of IoT in distributed environment is suggested by Chen. Et. al. (Chen, Sept. 2013). Smoke and LPG gas detection using Texas EZ430-RF2500 wireless module is also used (S. Nivedhitha, April 2013). Coal mine safety is also the kind of industry where safety monitoring and analysis is very much required. The main reasons for the disaster is power fluctuation, fire from organic gases, underground water intrusion etc. Chansala mining disaster is one of the worst incidents took place in recent times in India. More than 300 people including the miners died due to flooding in the mine. Many solutions are sought after specially considering IoT as most promising one. A cross platform based mobile information system for navigating the internal condition of coal mines (N. Yu, Dec. 2011). Investigation of reasoning based information sharing with automation of monitoring system is also (L. Jingxuan, Aug. 2011).A closed loop hypothetical system which monitors electro mechanical equipment along with integrated production control system is also used as a solution to disaster management (Dazhi, Aug. 2011). In one of the works (Abbas, Dec. 2014) Arduino is used as a key communicator between the sensors and users and senses the hazardous levels in industry.

Tactile sensors which are used to sense the obstacles used a mathematical model as proposed by Yuan et al. (Yuan Y., August,2015). It uses three dimensions force sensor but reliability is an issue with the proposed approach A fuzzy based mobile navigation robot is used for indoor environment (Dang, 2015) but the system can't work in harsh environment and when the obstacles are not static. Use of thermal cameras for night time navigation is proposed (Mouats, 2015) but they are static ones and give the information about the fixed angle and area of view. Smart mobile robot for security in low visible environment is proposed by Faisal et al. (Faisal, 2015) but can be further improved with the integration of neural network and fuzzy logic based system to construct smart security system. So in the overall research work either static sensor based systems are used or individually working for harsh environment or low visibility environment. The combination is not used where a system can do disaster management with accurate analysis in harsh as well as low visibility environment. Both hardware and software needs to be improved for the combination.

PROPOSED APPROACH

The problem of hazard detection and the robotic exploration of the hazardous environment is need the of the hour due to the continuous increase of the hazardous gases owing to the industry proliferation and modernization of the infrastructure . It includes radiological materials and toxic gases with long term harmful effects. The definition of a hazardous environment and extracting out the parameters for the same is itself a complicated task. The proposed approach aims to set up the alarming solution to warn about the level of hazardous effects for a particular environment area. The need of the hour is to build complete systems which can autosense the hazardous environment even in low visibility environment and raise an alarm. The combination of IoT and machine learning can be best used for getting the real time data and using the real time data for analyzing the accurate current hazardous level as well as prediction of future hazards by reading the parameters for detection and also selecting the useful parameters from them. The complete methodology can be explained in form of steps is as shown in Figure 3:

The key technologies consist of Global Positioning System, Cloud Server, Arduino, combination of MySQL and NoSQL databases. The big data management consists of following activities and tools that help in real time decision making:

- **Methods:** Spark and Storm tools, R Studio
- **Storage:** Hadoop, MongoDB
- **Processing:** Storm and Informatica
- **Representation:** Google Charts, Tableau

The following requirements must also be full filled for effective execution of the proposed system:

- **Connection:** The most important system requirement is the reliable connection between devices and the big data analytics.
- **QoS:** The effective management of sensors is required for providing Quality of Service.
- **Storage:** The facility to store large amount of heterogeneous data with a very latency for data analytics is also a prime system requirement.
- **Data Preprocessing:** For real time decision making data must be accurate and real time so suitable preprocessing is applied to remove any noise from the data

Figure 3. Complete cycle of disaster management with auto-robots

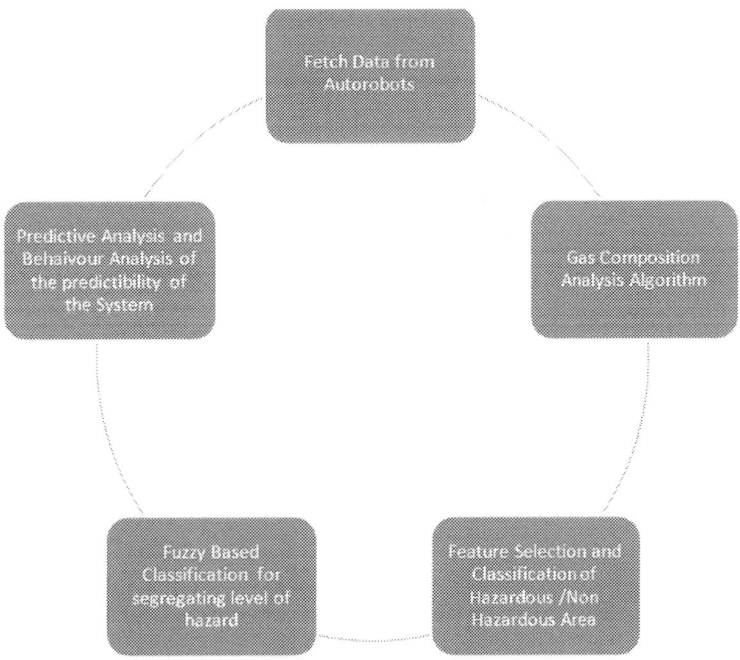

Innovation is combining the low visibility with hazardous environment detection. It can be very helpful in automation of manual scavenging, mining areas, under tunnel construction sites etc. It can be used to save many lives or at least give them the alarm to check the conditions they are working in and the effect on their health. However, many research challenges exist in the proposed integrated system that needs to be addressed for the success of the system:

CONCLUSION

This chapter starts with the overall idea of big data associated with IoT in disaster management. It covered the various domains of disaster management as well as security and privacy issues to be dealt with .Gradually the specific domain of use of auto robots in the low visibility areas and its usage in disaster management is discussed. The study of various approaches used to deal with disaster management using IoT is done for various types of industries. Further use of machine learning and data mining techniques to deal with disaster management in the domain is discussed .Many approaches are used but not for low visibility environment and using automatic robots. The approach which can be used in low visibility environment for detecting hazardous situation can help in many application areas and use of deep learning approaches can further enhance the process of classification of hazardous and non hazardous areas. Integration of autonomous robots with machine learning concepts can make full proof system for disaster management using Internet of things (IoT).

REFERENCES

Abbas, M. U. (2014). On the application of IoT) (Internet of Things) for securing industrial threats. In *Proc. IEEE 12th Int. Conf. on Frontiers of Information Technology* (pp. 37–40). IEEE.

Chen, J. L. (2013). Research on online fault diagnosis model based on IoT in process industry. *Advanced Information and Computer Technol. in Eng. and Manufacturing Environmental Eng.*, *765*, 2089–2092.

Dang, Z. Y. (2015). Fuzzy-based obstacle avoidance for a mobile robot navigation in indoor environment. In *Consumer Electronics-Taiwan (ICCE-TW), IEEE International Conference on* (pp. 55-56). IEEE.

Dazhi, D. (2011). Research on coal mine electromechanical equipment closedloopmanagement system based on IoTand information technology. In *Proc. IEEE 2nd Int. Conf. on Artificial Intelligence, Management Science and Electronic Commerce (AIMSEC)* (pp. 5101-5104). IEEE. 10.1109/AIMSEC.2011.6011237

Du, Z. Y. M. (2012). Design and implementation of safety management system for oil depot based on Internet of Things. In *Proc. IEEE Int. Conf. Green Comput. and Communication* (pp. 249–252). IEEE. 10.1109/GreenCom.2012.46

Faisal, M. M. (2015). Smart mobile robot for security of low visibility environment. In *Information Technology: Towards New Smart World (NSITNSW),5th National Symposium.* Chicago: IEEE.

Gallego, V. M. R. (2015). Unmanned aerial gas leakage localization and mapping using microdrones. In *Proc. IEEE Sensors Applications Symposium (SAS)* (pp. 1–6). IEEE. 10.1109/SAS.2015.7133629

GartnerE. (n.d.). Retrieved from https://www.gartner.com/newsroom/id/3598917

Group, C. S. (2013, April). *Expanded Top Ten Big Data Security and Privacy Challenges*. Academic Press.

Guo, X. Y. W. (2015). Design of WSN-based environment monitoring system on repair of gas leakage. In *Proc. IEEE 27th Chinese Control and Decision Conf. (CCDC)* (pp. 3340–3344). IEEE.

Irudayasamy, A., & Arockiam, L. (2015). Scalable multidimensional anonymization algorithm over big data using reduce on public cloud. *J. Theor. Appl. Inf. Technol.*, *74*, 221–231.

Jingxuan, L., S. J. (2011). The monitoring expert system of colliery safety production. In *Proc. IEEE Int. Conf. on Mechatronic Science, Electric Eng. and Computer (MEC)* (pp. 2592–2595). IEEE. 10.1109/MEC.2011.6026023

Kim, H. J. S. (2015). Design and implementation of gateways and sensor nodes for monitoring gas facilities. In *Proc. IEEE 4th Int. Conf. on Information Science and Industrial Applications (ISI)* (pp. 3–5). IEEE.

Marchal, S. J. X. (2014). A Big Data Architecture for Large Scale Security Monitoring. In Big Data (BigData Congress) (pp. 56-63). Anchorage, AK: Academic Press.

Mouats, T. A., Aouf, N., Chermak, L., & Richardson, M. A. (2015). Thermal stereo odometry for UAVs. *IEEE Sensors Journal*, *15*(11), 6335–6347. doi:10.1109/JSEN.2015.2456337

Mukherjee, M., Shu, L., Hu, L., Hancke, G. P., & Zhu, C. (2017). Sleep scheduling in industrial wireless sensor networks for toxic gas monitoring. *IEEE Wireless Communications*, *24*(9), 106–112. doi:10.1109/MWC.2017.1600072WC

Nivedhitha, S. A. P. (2013). Development of multipurpose gas leakage and fire detector with alarm system. In *Proc. IEEE/ACM Texas Instruments India Educators' Conf* (pp. 194–199). IEEE.

Özaslan, T. L., Loianno, G., Keller, J., Taylor, C. J., Kumar, V., Wozencraft, J. M., & Hood, T. (2017). Autonomous navigation and mapping for inspection of penstocks and tunnels with MAVs. *IEEE Robotics and Automation Letters*, *2*(3), 1740–1747. doi:10.1109/LRA.2017.2699790

Shu, M. M. (2017, May). Challenges and research issues of data management in IoT for large-scale petrochemical plants. *IEEE Systems Journal*, 1–15.

Shu, L., Mukherjee, M., & Wu, X. (2016). Toxic gas boundary area detection in large-scale petrochemical plants with industrial wireless sensor networks. *IEEE Communications Magazine*, *54*(10), 22–28. doi:10.1109/MCOM.2016.7588225

Spirjakin, D. A. M. (2015). Design of smart dust sensor node for combustible gas leakage monitoring. In *Proceedings of Federated Conf. on Computer Science and Information Systems(FedCSIS)* (pp. 1279–1283). Academic Press.

Yu, N. C. L. (2011). The development and application of crossplatformcoal mine mobile information system. *Proc. IEEE Int. Conf. on Computer Science and Netw. Technology, 3*, 1492–1496.

Yuan Y. G. J. (2015). Study of obstacle avoidance navigation robot control based on bland man tracing wall theory. In *Proceedings of IEEE international conference on Information and Automation* (pp. 398-403). IEEE.

Yuan, Y. G. (2015). *Study of obstacle avoidance navigation robot control based on bland man tracing wall theory*. IEEE.

Chapter 13
Tools and Platforms for Developing IoT Systems

Görkem Giray
Independent Researcher, Turkey

ABSTRACT

The internet of things (IoT) transforms the world in many ways. It combines many types of hardware and software with a variety of communication technologies to enable the development of innovative applications. A typical IoT system consists of IoT device, IoT gateway, IoT platform, and IoT application. Developing these elements and delivering an IoT system for fulfilling business requirements encompasses many activities to be executed and is not straightforward. To expedite these activities, some major vendors provide software development kits (SDK), integrated development environments (IDE), and utility tools for developing software to be executed on IoT devices/gateways. Moreover, these vendors utilize their cloud platforms to provide fundamental services, such as data storage, analytics, stream processing, for developing IoT systems. These vendors also developed IoT specific cloud-based services, such as connectivity and device management, to support IoT system development. This chapter presents an overview of tools and platforms provided by five major vendors.

INTRODUCTION

The Internet of Things (IoT) has attracted considerable interest in many various domains, including smart cities, retail, logistics, manufacturing, agriculture, and health. In line with this interest, designing and developing IoT systems have become mainstream. In theory, it is possible to develop an IoT system using many types of hardware, developing software with many tools and programming languages and even designing a special communication protocol for data exchange. On the other hand, using standard hardware and communication protocols, reusing software libraries and platforms have many advantages, including: (1) decrease in development time and hence time-to-market; (2) decrease in cost due to economies of scale; (3) interoperability with other systems via standards. This chapter attempts to provide an overview of some tools and platforms that can be used for developing software for the IoT. These tools encompass Software Development Kits (SDK), Integrated Development Environments (IDEs), utility tools for developers, and IoT platforms that provide some common basic functionalities for IoT systems.

DOI: 10.4018/978-1-5225-7432-3.ch013

Section 2 begins with an overview of the foundational concepts underlying the IoT and then presents the brief descriptions of the elements making up a typical IoT system. Section 3 summarizes the tools and platforms offered by major vendors (Amazon, Bosch, Google, IBM, and Microsoft) to develop IoT systems. Section 4 discusses the current state of software development for IoT devices, the fundamental services delivered by IoT platforms and capabilities offered by IoT platforms for handling IoT big data. Finally, Section 5 concludes the chapter.

BACKGROUND

The "IoT" concept and IoT systems make use of many concepts that are available in various disciplines, including software engineering, software architecture, and cloud computing. The following subsection titled "foundational concepts" summarizes these concepts and the relationships among them. The second subsection presents the main components of a typical IoT system.

Foundational Concepts

IoT systems are made up of many distributed components interacting via a network. To cope with the complexity of such a system, *abstraction* and *encapsulation* are key concepts. A group of functionality can be encapsulated and provided as services; which is the approach of *Service Oriented Architecture (SOA). Cloud computing* extends the scope of these services to infrastructures, platforms, even applications. The remainder of this section briefly describes these concepts and clarifies the relationships among these concepts.

Abstraction is one of the fundamental cognitive activity associated with problem-solving. Abstraction is a technique for coping with complexity. Abstraction means preserving essential and eliminating unessential information about an entity from a specific perspective for an objective. This helps to focus on the big picture and thus cope with the complexity. Encapsulation complements abstraction by hiding the internal functioning of an entity and providing an interface to exhibit the behavior of the entity. In short, an entity is known by its interface presenting its services to outside world and its internals is hidden from the outside world. The examples of such an entity vary in size and can be a procedure, a class, a layer, a library, even a platform. For instance, encapsulation in object-orientation is the packaging of attributes representing state and operations into a class and provide an interface to access the services provided by that class (Page-Jones, 1999). Figure 1 illustrates how an IoT device can be abstracted and represented as a class. Data and implementation details are encapsulated in the class; the operations of sending data and resetting are provided to the outside world.

Abstraction and encapsulation can be done at any level, at a micro level, such as a class, at a higher level, such as establishing layers while designing the architecture of a system. An architecture encompasses the major components and their interrelationships at a certain level of detail in line with the objective in drawing that architecture. Figure 2 illustrates how the components of an IoT system can be organized as layers to cope with complexity (Köksal & Tekinerdogan, 2017). Each layer has a group of cohesive responsibilities, such as security layer providing the security functionality for the system. Each layer encapsulates the implementation details necessary for fulfilling its responsibilities and communicates with the other layers through interfaces.

Figure 1. A sample abstraction of an IoT device

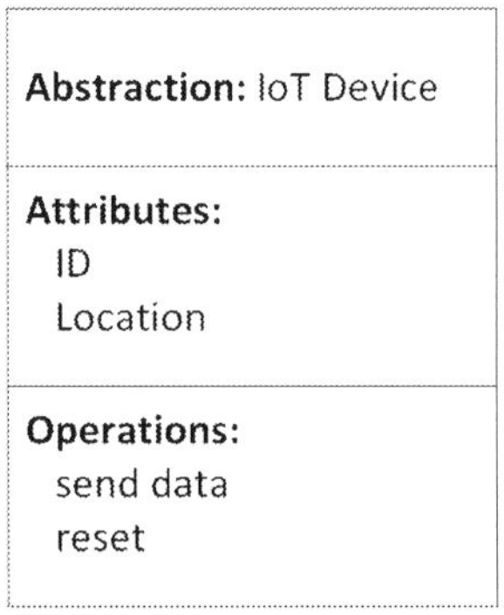

Abstraction: IoT Device
Attributes: ID Location
Operations: send data reset

Figure 2. A sample layered architecture for an IoT system
(adapted from (Köksal & Tekinerdogan, 2017))

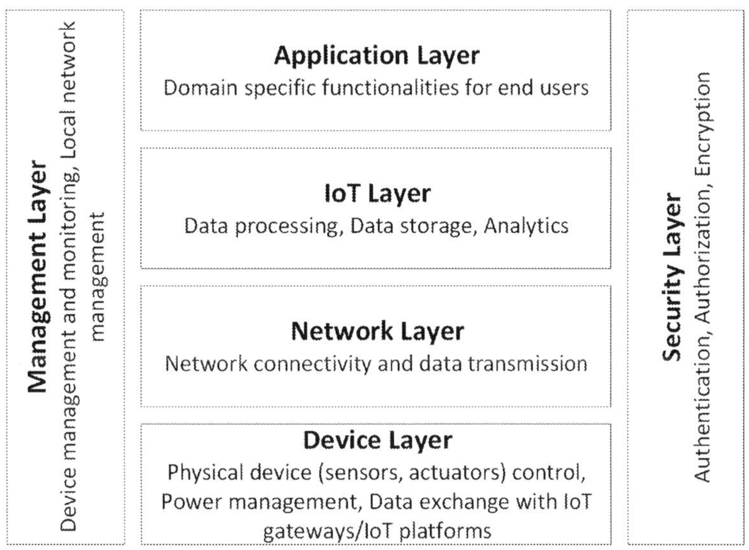

A *layered architecture* is a type of architectural style that partitions the concerns of a system into stacked layers (Meier, 2009). Architectural styles provide an abstract framework and a set of principles for a family of systems for shaping the architecture of a system (Meier, 2009). They promote design reuse and help architects in avoiding reinventing the wheel. SOA is another architectural style where complex and monolithic systems are decomposed into distributed components that provide and/or consume services (Bass et al., 2012). Service provider and consumer components can be developed using different programming languages and deployed on different platforms (Bass et al., 2012). These components can be deployed independently and can be part of different systems or even belong to different organizations (Bass et al., 2012). Their interfaces describe the services they provide (Bass et al., 2012). Two basic types of method to access web services are SOAP and REST. SOAP stands for "Simple Object Access Protocol" and specifies a communication protocol, which enables XML-based message exchange. REST (Representation State Transfer) is an architectural style rather than a protocol itself. It applies a few constraints to clarify communication and resource management.

With the advent of the Internet as a communication infrastructure and the design approach to provide functionality through services (SOA), many varieties of services have been made available to be used by both systems and end users worldwide. These services are designed to be consumed at different levels, as infrastructure, platform, and software. The umbrella term for this approach is *cloud computing*, which enables ubiquitous, convenient, on-demand access to a shared pool of configurable resources (e.g., servers, networking, databases, software, and more) (Mell & Grance, 2011). It provides five essential characteristics: namely on-demand self-service, broad network access, rapid flexibility on scalability, measured service, and resource pooling (Mell & Grance, 2011). Computing resources are pooled to serve multiple consumers using a multi-tenant model (Mell & Grance, 2011). Multi-tenancy is an approach to share a computing resource between multiple consumers by providing every consumer a dedicated share of the resource, which is isolated from other shares regarding performance and data privacy (Krebs et al., 2012).

Cloud computing services are mainly offered in three main types of models: *Infrastructure as a Service (IaaS)*, *Platform as a Service (PaaS)*, and *Software as a Service (SaaS)*. These service models determine the types of computing resources offered to consumers. A simplified view of three service models of cloud computing is displayed in Figure 3 and explained as follows.

- *IaaS* provides some fundamental computing resources, mostly computation, storage, and network. Consumers (generally engineers dealing with system and network) have significant control over operating systems, storage, and applications to be deployed; however, do not have control over the underlying hardware infrastructure (Mell & Grance, 2011). Some examples of IaaS include Amazon Web Services, Google Cloud Platform, and Microsoft Azure. IaaS provides an infrastructure to process (computing), store (storage), and exchange (network) a huge amount of data sensed by IoT devices, which is generally the case for IoT systems.
- *PaaS* provides some programming languages, libraries, services, and tools to develop and deploy applications on a cloud infrastructure for software developers (Mell & Grance, 2011). Developers have control over the applications to be developed and deployed as well as some configuration settings for the hosting environment; however, does not have any control over the infrastructure (Mell & Grance, 2011). Some examples of PaaS include Amazon Relational Database Service and Google App Engine. Generally, PaaS also provides some general purpose services, such as storage management, analytics, to be used by software developers. For instance, a storage management service (such as Amazon Relational Database Service) can use the storage services provided by an IaaS to physically store data and provide a number of services for developers to operate a database in the cloud. Briefly, common functionalities related to data storage are encapsulated as storage management services and provided to developers through APIs. Such common functionalities can be used by developers to store and analyze the huge amount of data produced and consumed by IoT systems. Moreover, some vendors (such as Amazon, Google, Microsoft) also provide some services at PaaS level specific to the IoT. Such services include device registry and device management.
- *SaaS* provides applications to be used through a web browser, mobile application, or a programming interface (Mell & Grance, 2011). Consumers (generally end users) do not have any control on the platform and infrastructure services; they can only control some application settings that can be changed through a user interface or programming interface. Some examples of SaaS include Gmail by Google and Office 365 by Microsoft.

Figure 3. Three service models of cloud computing

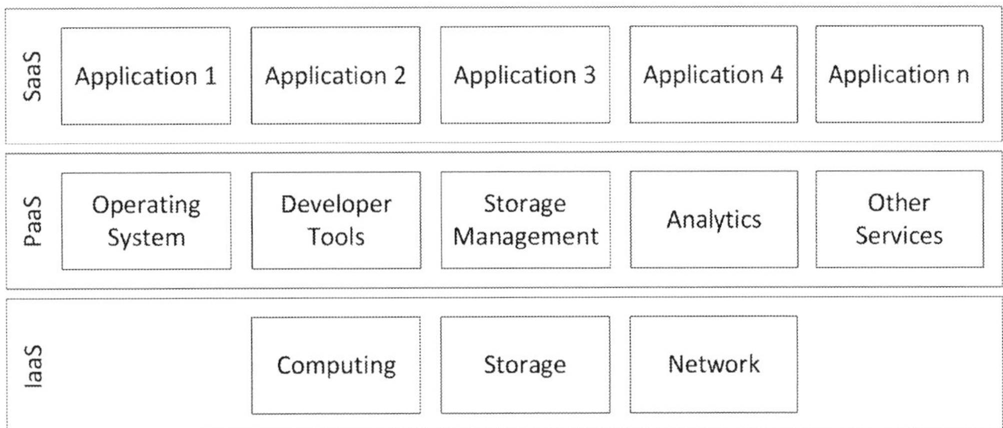

This chapter focuses on PaaS model of cloud computing since it can provide important benefits to software developers in developing IoT systems. Developers can abstract away the configuration details of the application server, operating system, storage, etc. and focus on the specific functionalities of the IoT system they work on. Moreover, reusing services brings time and cost savings.

An Overview of IoT Systems

IoT refers to the global network of IoT devices, which enables these devices to send and receive data. IoT utilizes the current Internet infrastructure, standards, and technologies to interconnect these IoT devices. Even though there are many ways of visualizing IoT systems, Figure 4 displays a simplified view of an IoT system.

IoT devices sense data from the real world, send them to an IoT platform directly or via an IoT gateway. Data may be processed, stored by an IoT platform and served to an IoT application for further processing to meet the specific needs of a domain.

The main elements of an IoT system, namely IoT device, IoT gateway, IoT platform, and IoT application are described briefly as below:

Figure 4. A simplified view of an IoT system

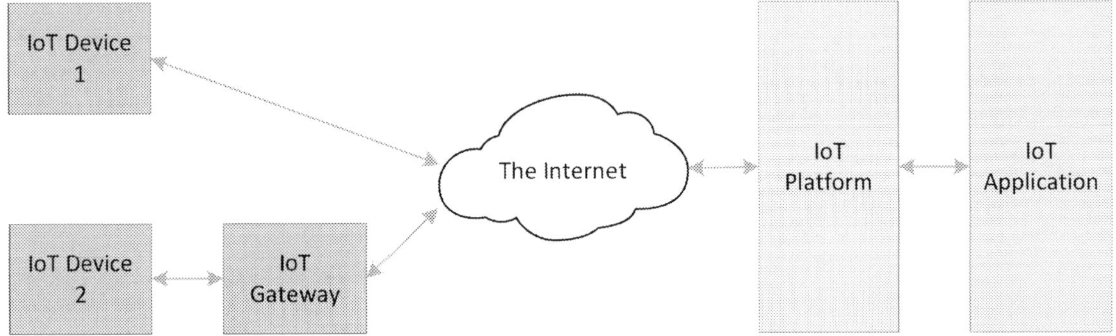

- **IoT device:** IoT devices (also called things, connected devices, smart devices, smart objects, etc.) are capable of sensing data from the real world and communicating these data electronically to an IoT gateway and/or to an IoT platform/application over a connection. Generally, IoT devices gather data through their sensors (e.g. temperature) and some of them take actions through their actuators (e.g. turn on air condition remotely). The capabilities of IoT devices differ, some of them can only sense some data whereas some others can process these data and send it through the Internet using a secure and Internet ready protocol.
- **IoT gateway:** IoT gateways play an intermediary role between IoT devices and IoT platforms. IoT gateways receive data from IoT devices, may translate, filter, aggregate, cleanse data and direct these data to IoT platforms. IoT gateways may translate data since IoT devices are not supporting an Internet ready protocol, such as AMQP, MQTT, and HTTPS. IoT gateways may filter, aggregate, and cleanse data to optimize bandwidth usage. The responsibilities of a gateway can be fulfilled using field and/or cloud gateways ("Microsoft Azure IoT Reference Architecture," 2018). As the name implies, field gateways are usually collocated with IoT devices and do some local processing before sending data to an IoT platform. Cloud gateways are software components managing communication with IoT devices/gateways and hosted in the cloud as a part of an IoT platform. The use of field and cloud gateways depends on the requirements and available resources in a specific project.
- **IoT platform:** IoT platform refers to a combination of some basic functionalities common to most IoT systems. These functionalities are generally delivered as PaaS and encompass computation, storage, analytics, device management, etc.
- **IoT application:** An IoT application is specific to a domain and implements the requirements of a specific business model. It utilizes IoT platform for common basic functionalities.
- **IoT system:** An IoT system (or IoT solution) is a composition of the elements explained above and fulfills some specific requirements. For instance, in an IoT system for waste management, sensors in containers (IoT devices) can sense data to detect rubbish levels in containers. These sensors can send these data to an IoT platform (possibly via IoT gateways) to have the trash collection routes optimized. An IoT application can visualize optimized routes for end users.

SOFTWARE DEVELOPMENT FOR THE IoT

As displayed in Figure 4, developing IoT systems involves the integration of various elements. Various IoT devices and IoT gateways have different computing, storage, and networking capabilities. These capabilities designate the limitations imposed on the software components that will run on these devices. Many cloud platforms (not IoT specific) provide various capabilities, which can be reused when developing software components for IoT systems. A particular array of competencies is required to develop each of these elements and bring these together to have a complete IoT system. Various vendors provide many types of tools and ready to use services in order to develop IoT systems much faster with a reasonable cost. It is reported that more than 450 vendors provide IoT platforms as well as some tools for developing software for IoT systems (Williams, 2017). This section provides the tools and capabilities offered by major vendors, namely Amazon, Bosch, Google, IBM, and Microsoft.

Amazon Web Services IoT Platform

Amazon Web Services (AWS) IoT platform enables IoT devices to connect to AWS platform services and IoT applications to interact with IoT devices. Figure 5 shows a simplified view of an IoT system using the tools/services provided by Amazon.

The *AWS IoT Device SDKs* ("AWS IoT Device SDK," n.d.) include some open-source libraries and a developer guide that enable IoT devices to connect, authenticate, and exchange data with AWS IoT platform using the MQTT, HTTP, or WebSockets protocols. The SDK supports Embedded C, JavaScript, Arduino Yun, Java, and Python. Developers can use one of these SDKs to develop software IoT device/gateway client software.

Message broker provides a secure mechanism for IoT devices, Amazon IoT platform, and IoT applications to exchange data. It supports MQTT and MQTT over WebSocket and provides an HTTP REST API for data exchange.

Rules engine processes (such as augment, filter) data and sends them to other services, such as to be stored by Amazon RDS, to be analyzed by Amazon QuickSight.

Device shadows service stores current and desired states of IoT devices in the AWS cloud. IoT devices can send their state data to device shadow service through the message broker to be used by other IoT devices, AWS services, and/or an IoT application. Similarly, AWS services and/or an IoT application can update the desired state of an IoT device using device shadow service. This desired state is sent to the corresponding IoT device immediately or when the device comes online if it is not connected to a network/the Internet at all time.

Device registry keeps track of the metadata of IoT devices. It establishes an identity for devices and manages devices' attributes and capabilities (such as a capability of reporting temperature and its unit of measure).

Security and identity service provides controlled access to services and resources. The message broker and rules engine use this service to exchange data securely with IoT devices and other services.

Figure 5. An IoT system architecture based on Amazon tools/services
(adapted from ("AWS IoT," 2018))

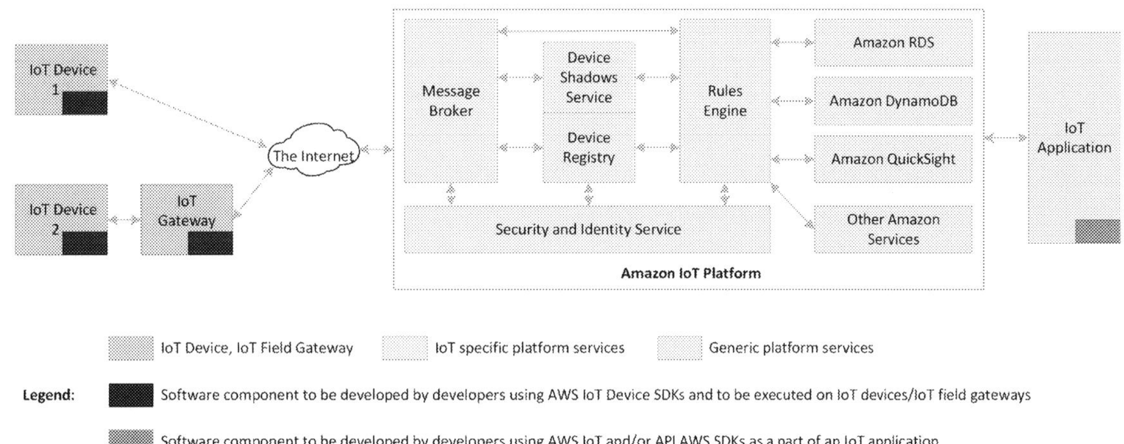

Message broker, rule engine, device shadows, device registry service, and security and identity service are platform services especially provided for IoT systems. These services can be combined with the rest of the AWS platform services, such as Amazon RDS and DynamoDB to store data, Amazon QuickSight to analyze data. Amazon provides AWS IoT API ("AWS Documentation," n.d.) and AWS SDKs ("Tools for Amazon Web Services," n.d.) to integrate IoT applications with AWS platform services. AWS IoT API enables developers to programmatically create and manage IoT devices, certificates, rules, and policies using HTTP or HTTPS requests. AWS SDKs include language-specific APIs and currently have support for programming languages such as Java, Node.js, Python, Ruby, Go, C++. A developer can use Eclipse IDE along with AWS SDK for Java ("AWS SDK for Java," n.d.) and AWS Toolkit for Eclipse ("AWS Toolkit for Eclipse," n.d.) to develop an IoT application interacting with AWS platform services. AWS Toolkit for Eclipse is an open source plug-in for the Eclipse Java IDE and aims to increase developer productivity by facilitating development, debugging, and deployment of Java applications.

Bosch IoT Suite

The Bosch IoT Suite ("Bosch IoT Suite," n.d.) is an IoT platform, which provides some basic capabilities needed to build IoT applications. These capabilities encompass management of IoT devices and gateways, secure access management, and data analysis. Bosch IoT Suite services provide its capabilities under six titles as displayed in Figure 6.

IoT Hub supports connectivity and messaging between IoT devices and platform.

IoT Things keeps track of the data on IoT devices. These data are able to manage life cycle of devices, to keep track of relationships among devices, and to make search on device data. The service provides a RESTful API and Java client for access and integration.

IoT Rollouts is a service for rolling out software updates to IoT devices and gateways. This service is compatible with Eclipse hawkBit's APIs ("Eclipse hawkBit," n.d.). hawkBit is a domain independent back-end framework for rolling out software updates to IoT devices and gateways. It aims to provide

Figure 6. An IoT system architecture based on Bosch tools/services

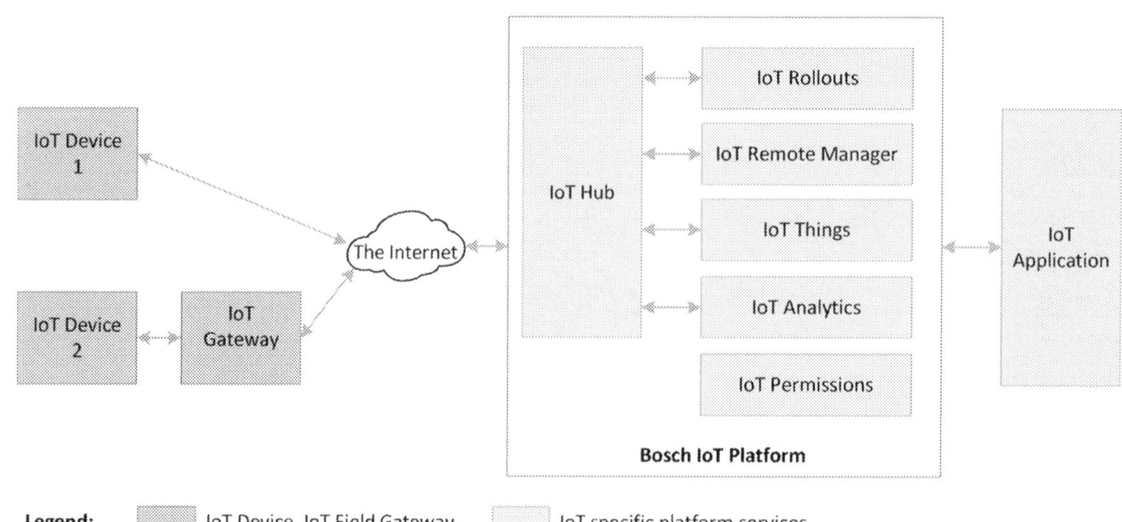

a base to develop services/applications for software updates independent from particular application domains and hence IoT applications.

IoT Remote Manager provides device management and monitoring capabilities for IoT gateways and IoT devices. It mainly offers remote management of applications (remote install, uninstall, update, configure), firmware and file update, remote configuration and provisioning, remote monitoring and diagnostics, and remote security administration.

IoT Analytics provides common analysis capabilities for processing device generated data to gain insights.

IoT Permissions enables the management of users, groups, roles, and applications including authorization and authentication. The service provides a RESTful HTTP API and Java client libraries to be used by IoT applications. An IoT application can register users, groups, roles, and applications at IoT Permissions along with the permissions granted. Afterwards, the IoT application can use this service to authenticate and authorize the incoming requests.

Google IoT Platform

Google utilizes its Cloud Platform to provide an IoT platform for IoT systems. Most of the components of this platform are independent of the IoT, such as storage and analytics; some of the components are offered for the IoT, such as Cloud IoT Core. Google Cloud Platform provides the following capabilities related to the IoT ("Overview of Internet of Things," 2018; "Cloud IoT Core," n.d.) (as displayed in Figure 7):

Cloud IoT Core provides services to manage IoT devices and process data being generated by those devices. Cloud IoT Core is composed of a device manager and a protocol bridge. The device manager is able to register IoT devices either manually through a console or programmatically. It establishes an identity for each device, provides a mechanism for authentication and maintains a configuration for each device. The protocol bridge enables the communication between IoT devices/gateways and Google Cloud Platform. It supports secure connection over MQTT. It passes telemetry to ingestion services for further processing.

Ingestion services classify and direct telemetry to other services. The other platform services and IoT applications can subscribe to specific streams of telemetry and ingestion services can direct correspond-

Figure 7. An IoT system architecture based on Google tools/services

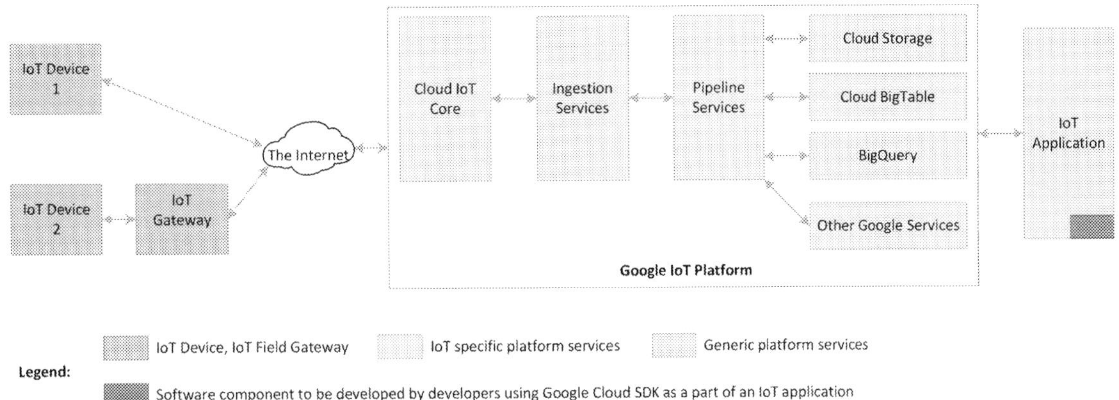

ing streams to these services/applications. Moreover, these services can buffer telemetry to handle data spikes. These services can be used through HTTPS REST APIs and gRPC ("GRPC," n.d.), an open source remote procedure call framework.

Pipeline services provide some capabilities to process data such as transformation, aggregation, and enrichment. For instance, captured data can be transformed to another unit of measure; can be aggregated with data received from other devices; can be enriched with other data about the device.

Storage services offer a variety of storage solutions ranging from storage for unstructured blobs of data (such as video or image) to key-value and relational databases.

Analytics services provide capabilities for analyzing accumulated data to look at trends and gain insight.

Google Cloud SDK ("Google Cloud SDK," n.d.) encompasses a set of tools, which enables management of services hosted on Google Cloud Platform.

Developers can use cloud platform services by making direct HTTP requests to Google Cloud APIs. These APIs expose a JSON REST interface. As an alternative, Google provides a client library ("API Client Libraries," n.d.) for all of its Cloud APIs that enables access for those using programming languages available. Currently, Java, .NET languages, Python, JavaScript, and Objective C are supported. More programming languages, including Go, Ruby, Node.js will be supported in the future.

IBM Watson IoT Platform

The IBM Watson IoT platform is a cloud-based service, which provides application access to IoT devices and data to create IoT systems. The platform can be used for managing devices, storing and accessing device data and connecting a variety of devices and gateways. MQTT and TLS protocols are used for secure communication with devices. Moreover, some services regarding analytics and data visualization are provided on this platform. The services provided by the platform can be classified under four areas as displayed in Figure 8 (Börnert et al., 2016):

Figure 8. An IoT System Architecture based on IBM tools/services

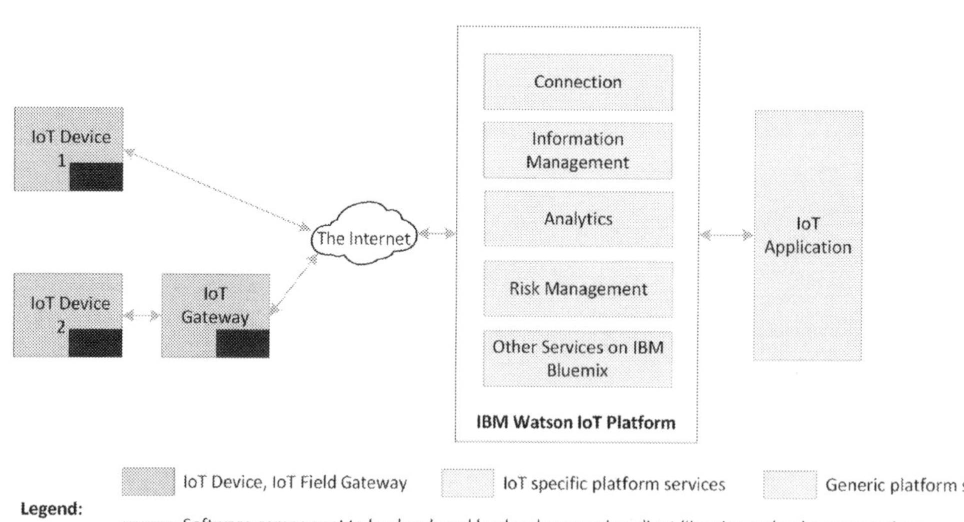

- *Connection* service is concerned with connecting and managing IoT devices. Device management capabilities include device reboot, firmware update, device diagnostics and metadata gathering, bulk device addition, and removal.
- *Information management* services are about data storage and transformation. These services provide access to real-time and historical data gathered from IoT devices.
- *Analytics* services provide some capabilities for processing and visualizing data.
- *Risk management* services are concerned with security, authentication, and prevention of fraud.

The Watson IoT Platform provides an HTTP REST API that provides access for IoT applications to: (1) manage (create, delete, update, list, view details) IoT devices; (2) diagnose IoT devices (retrieve and clear logs/device error codes); (3) determine connection problems (retrieve device connection logs); (4) view the last event for a specific device; (5) track usage by retrieving total amount of data used; (6) query service status.

Client libraries ("IBM Watson IoT – GitHub," n.d.) provide reusable code for developing software that runs on IoT devices and gateways to interact with Watson IoT Platform. The libraries are provided for different programming languages, namely C++, C#, embedded C, Java, mBed C++, Mode.js, Python. Although there are some differences among the features provided by the libraries for different programming languages, there are some main features provided, which can be summarized as follows:

- Connecting IoT devices/gateways with Watson IoT Platform
- Sending data using MQTT/HTTP
- Performing client side certificate based authentication
- Connecting IoT devices/gateways to Watson IoT Platform device management service
- Enabling devices/gateways to automatically reconnect to Watson IoT Platform while they are in a disconnected state

Microsoft Azure IoT Platform

Azure IoT device SDK is a set of libraries for developing software for IoT devices. The aim of the SDK is to facilitate sending messages to and receiving messages from the Azure IoT Hub service via a secure connection. The SDKs are open source and hosted on GitHub ("Microsoft Azure – GitHub," n.d.). The different variations of the SDK support different operating systems such as Windows, Linux, real-time operating systems (RTOS); a variety of programming languages, namely C, C#, Java, JavaScript, and Python; diverse data exchange protocols, such as AMQP, MQTT, HTTP/REST.

Azure IoT gateway SDK is a set of libraries, which enables the software development for IoT gateways. It is open source, based on standards, and runs on many types of hardware.

Azure IoT Gateway SDK creates a module pipeline for implementing the specific requirements of an IoT system. While existing modules decrease development and maintenance costs, customized modules also can be implemented. Figure 9 shows an example scenario. IoT device 1 and 2 can communicate via protocol 1 and 2 respectively. Both of these protocols are not Internet-ready and hence translated to an Internet ready protocol using a module (translate module). Afterwards, data are aggregated to optimize bandwidth usage (aggregate module) and sent to the Internet (send module) to an IoT platform.

Figure 9. An example scenario for IoT gateway implemented using modules

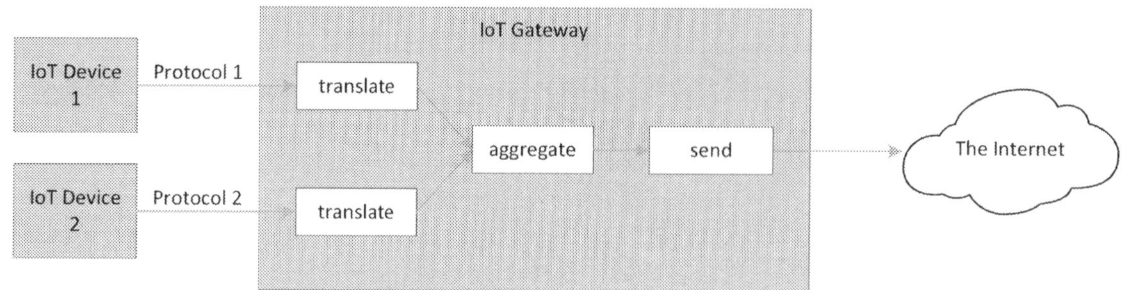

Azure IoT Services ("Microsoft Azure IoT Reference Architecture," 2018), displayed in Figure 10, refers to the IoT platform developed and maintained by Microsoft and offers some common services, such as storage, analytics, etc., for IoT applications.

Azure IoT Hub allows secure bidirectional communication between IoT devices and gateways. IoT Hub manages connections at transport protocol level, protects the communication path, authenticates and authorizes devices toward the system.

Provisioning API handles the device life cycle that enables to add and remove devices to an IoT system. This API implements the external interface to enable changes on device identity store and device registry.

Device identity, registry, and state store provide storage services for device data. Identity store provides security credentials for registered IoT devices. Registry stores descriptive information about devices along with some indexing capabilities for fast lookups. State store is for storing incoming data from devices to be used for the operations related to state data.

Stream processors facilitate data flow either by moving or routing data without any transformation or by performing complex event processing. For instance, a stream processor may listen only to special types of events; whereas another processor can perform complex event processing tasks such as data aggregation or analytics tasks such as detecting anomalies and generating alerts.

Analytics services offer processing capabilities for data streams. Moreover, machine learning algorithms are provided for predictive scenarios such as error detection.

Storage services encompass many types of databases, e.g., relational, big data, key-value, document, as well as blob storage for unstructured data for text or binary data at massive scale.

UX services provide some tools for visualizing data; for instance, Power BI to create dashboards and Bing Maps to display data on a map.

Business integration services are responsible for the integration of IoT platform with specific IoT applications.

DISCUSSION

While IoT system development may seem similar to web or mobile development, in practice it requires a broad spectrum of tools, technologies, and skills (Taivalsaari & Mikkonen, 2018). This broad spectrum should cover many aspects of embedded, web, and mobile software development. Moreover, the distributed nature of IoT devices might complicate software development, deployment, and maintenance.

Figure 10. An IoT System Architecture based on Microsoft tools/services

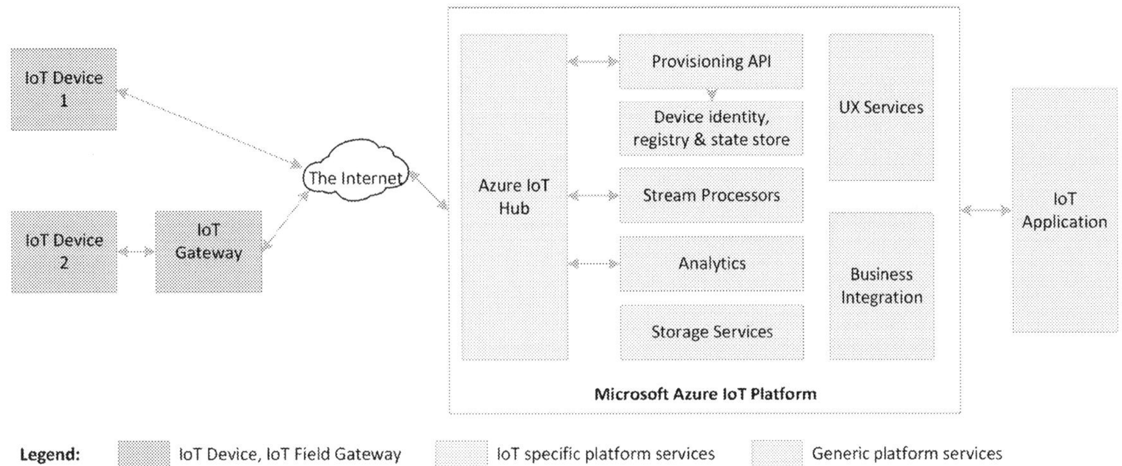

In some cases IoT devices may consist of various hardware platforms with different capabilities and development environments. Managing this heterogeneity through appropriate level of abstraction is another challenge. Huge volume of data collected via many IoT devices is another issue to be tackled. Cloud-based IoT platforms are important enablers of IoT system development. Such platforms provide many infrastructural services (Such as storing and processing big data) encapsulated in separate components with well-defined interfaces. Such components not only streamline IoT system development, but also reduce entry barriers by offering economic and scalable back-end services.

Software Development for IoT Devices

IoT devices are hardware platforms that provide limited programming and execution capabilities. Therefore, there are many challenges associated with programming, deploying, and maintaining software for IoT devices. Software development for IoT devices generally follows the approach of embedded programming in which the application developed is tightly coupled with the hardware platform. There are efforts to decouple applications from hardware platform by providing programming languages that enable higher levels of abstraction and virtual machines to isolate application from the underlying hardware platform (Ahmadighohandizi & Systä, 2016; Sivieri et al., 2016). Such efforts are also closely related to a recent trend called edge computing (Shi et al., 2016). Edge computing proposes to move the computing from IoT platforms to IoT devices and gateways whenever feasible. Such an approach requires the development of more complex software for IoT devices and gateways. To achieve this, developers need more capable tools and programming languages that provide higher level of abstraction. Kiuas is an effort towards providing a programming environment for IoT devices (Selonen & Taivalsaari, 2016). This cloud-based environment provides a visual and textual development environment in which developers develop code regarding IoT device management, sensor data collection and visualization, device actuation etc.

Deployment for IoT devices and gateways are another pain point which should be addressed. In-place deployment for a huge number of IoT devices with a big bang approach might be risky for many IoT systems. A possible problem with the production environment might cause serious damages. For IoT devices which can host and execute two separate versions of an application, old and new versions can co-exist for a period of time (blue-green deployment pattern (Fowler, 2010)). During this period, if a problem arises, the system can switch to the old version. The challenge of blue-green deployment pattern might be ensuring the synchronization of persistent data for old and new versions (Ahmadighohandizi & Systä, 2016).

Maintainability of software residing on IoT devices and gateways is another potential problem area. Various kinds of hardware platforms, protocols, architectures, programming languages make IoT systems complex and therefore difficult to understand, even for experienced developers (Corno et al., 2018). To address this challenge there are efforts to provide documentation techniques (such as code recipes in (Corno et al., 2018)) independent from programming languages and run-time environments. Enriching code with such documentation techniques can help developers to understand existing code and make software maintenance easier.

Building general purpose applications for IoT devices and making them available through an application store is another challenge for software development on IoT devices. Apart from specific applications running on IoT pre-defined devices, such applications should be much more flexible in handling heterogeneous hardware platforms and communication protocols. (Kubitza, 2016) proposes an IDE providing abstraction mechanisms for handling hardware heterogeneity to build general purpose applications for IoT devices.

IoT Platforms

IoT platforms are treated as important enablers and backbones for realizing IoT business cases and developing IoT systems ("IoT Analytics," 2015). Such IoT platforms offer some common fundamental services, which are abstracted as and encapsulated in components. Components provide access to their services by following the SOA approach and generally using REST architectural style. Such components in IoT domain provide services regarding connectivity, device management, security, and data storage.

A connectivity layer that is handling communication over different protocols is the gate of IoT platforms to IoT devices. Amazon's Message Broker, Bosch IoT Hub, Google Cloud IoT Core, IBM Connection service, and Azure IoT Hub provide secure mechanisms for data exchange between IoT devices/gateways and IoT platforms. Device management ensures IoT devices/gateways are running properly with up-to-date software installed on them ("IoT Analytics," 2015).

Device management capabilities encompass some common tasks such as device provisioning, remote configuration, management of software updates, and troubleshooting ("IoT Analytics," 2015). Such services are critical for the operation of an IoT system with thousands or even millions IoT devices/gateways. Amazon recently announced AWS Device Management component, which makes it easy to onboard, organize, monitor, and remotely manage IoT devices ("AWS IoT Device Management Overview," n.d.). Bosch IoT Rollouts service takes care of deploying software to IoT devices/gateways. IoT Remote Manager provides device management and monitoring capabilities for IoT devices/gateways. Google does not provide an explicit component dealing with device management. IBM Connection service and Microsoft Azure IoT Hub provide device management capabilities besides connectivity. Closely related with device management, IoT platforms involve some components for persisting IoT device/gateway metadata and state data. Amazon device registry keeps track of the metadata of IoT devices. Amazon device shadow service stores the current and desired states of IoT device and enables to update states of IoT devices through message broker. Bosch IoT platform keeps track of device metadata through IoT

Things component. Google IoT platform manages device metadata through device manager component present in Cloud IoT Core. Connection service in IBM Watson IoT platform includes some functionality regarding device metadata gathering. Microsoft Azure IoT platform handles device life cycle through Provisioning API and stores device metadata in device identity, registry, and state store.

Security, which is a cross-cutting concern for such platforms, is handled by various components. Amazon IoT platform has a separate security and identity service for controlling access to services and resources. Bosch IoT Permissions enables the management of users, groups, roles, and applications including authorization and authentication. Google Cloud IoT Core includes a mechanism for authentication. IBM Risk management services are concerned with security, authentication, and prevention of fraud. Microsoft Azure IoT Hub provides protection of communication path, device authentication and authorization.

Data storage is one of the pivotal requirements of an IoT platform. Generally, IoT platforms utilize existing storage solutions present on cloud platforms for storing IoT data. Bosch IoT platform is a platform specifically developed for IoT systems. This platform can run other general purpose cloud platforms, such as Amazon Web Services, and uses the storage services of these platforms, such as Amazon RDS and Amazon DynamoDB.

Many IoT systems have various analytics functionalities for processing IoT data and enabling informed actions. Such functionality is within the scope of big data analytics and discussed in the next subsection.

Handling IoT Big Data

As more and more data are digitized, the term "big data" is becoming more important for many domains as well as IoT. A growing number of IoT devices and related systems generate massive amounts of data. Relational databases do not meet all the requirements for the IoT, especially scalability requirements. Consequently there is a need for alternative approaches for processing and storing big data produced by IoT systems. As the IoT spreads over, distributed computing models and non-relational data storage approaches started to provide part of the solution. Having these on integrated cloud environments addresses the need for scalability required by IoT systems.

Amazon provides Amazon RDB for storing structured data and Amazon DynamoDB for unstructured data. Amazon QuickSight provide some functionalities for analyzing data. As mentioned earlier, Bosch IoT platform can be hosted on a general purpose cloud platform, such as Amazon Web Services, and use the storage and analytics capabilities of that platform. Moreover, Bosch IoT platform includes IoT Analytics component, which provides common analysis capabilities for processing device generated data to gain insights. Google, IBM, and Microsoft utilize general purpose storage and analytics components to store and analyze IoT big data. Some platforms also has some services to process streams of IoT data, such as stream processors of Microsoft Azure.

CONCLUSION

With more and more connected devices to be in use in forthcoming years, IoT is an active focus area for industry. In line with this trend, IoT systems meeting business requirements with reasonable cost have to be developed within an acceptable timeframe. The development of IoT systems is not straightforward and must be supported with a variety of tools and platforms. Cloud platform providers utilize their existing cloud services to form IoT specific platforms. Such platforms include IoT specific services, especially connectivity and device management. Big data storage and processing services are key for obtaining benefits from IoT data. As stated by (Wortmann, 2015), "the support of the latest and continuously evolving standards as well as the integration of adequate end-to-end tool chains even in the embedded software domain to enhance developer productivity represent further important challenges in the development of IoT platforms".

REFERENCES

Ahmadighohandizi, F., & Systä, K. (2016, September). Application development and deployment for IoT devices. In *European Conference on Service-Oriented and Cloud Computing* (pp. 74-85). Springer.

API Client Libraries | Google Developers. (n.d.). Retrieved from https://developers.google.com/api-client-library/

AWS Documentation - AWS IoT - API Reference. (n.d.). Retrieved from http://docs.aws.amazon.com/iot/latest/apireference/API_Operations.html

AWS IoT Developer Guide. (2018). Retrieved from https://docs.aws.amazon.com/iot/latest/developer-guide/iot-dg.pdf

AWS IoT Device Management Overview - Amazon Web Services. (n.d.). Retrieved from https://aws.amazon.com/tr/iot-device-management/

AWS IoT Device SDK. (n.d.). Retrieved from https://aws.amazon.com/iot-platform/sdk/

AWS SDK for Java. (n.d.). Retrieved from https://aws.amazon.com/sdk-for-java/

AWS Toolkit for Eclipse. (n.d.). Retrieved from https://aws.amazon.com/eclipse/

Bass, L., Clements, P., & Kazman, R. (2012). *Software Architecture in Practice* (3rd ed.). Addison-Wesley Professional.

Börnert, C., Clark, K., Daya, S., Debeaux, M., Diederichs, G., Gucer, V., ... Thole, J. (2016). *An Architectural and Practical Guide to IBM Hybrid Integration Platform*. IBM Redbooks.

Bosch IoT Suite. (n.d.). Retrieved from https://www.bosch-iot-suite.com/

Cloud IoT Core. (n.d.). Retrieved from https://cloud.google.com/iot-core/

Corno, F., De Russis, L., & Sáenz, J. P. (2018, May). Easing IoT development for novice programmers through code recipes. In *Proceedings of the 40th International Conference on Software Engineering: Software Engineering Education and Training* (pp. 13-16). ACM. 10.1145/3183377.3183385

Eclipse hawkBit. (n.d.). Retrieved from https://www.eclipse.org/hawkbit/

Fowler, M. (2010). *BlueGreenDeployment*. Retrieved from https://martinfowler.com/bliki/BlueGreenDeployment.html

Google CloudS. D. K. (n.d.). Retrieved from https://cloud.google.com/sdk/

GRPC. (n.d.). Retrieved from https://grpc.io/

IBM Watson IoT - GitHub. (n.d.). Retrieved from https://github.com/ibm-watson-iot/

IoT Analytics. (2015). *IoT Platforms - The central backbone for the Internet of Things*. Retrieved from https://iot-analytics.com/product/iot-platforms-white-paper/

Köksal, Ö., & Tekinerdogan, B. (2017). Feature-Driven Domain Analysis of Session Layer Protocols of Internet of Things. In *IEEE International Congress on Internet of Things (ICIOT)* (pp. 105-112). IEEE.

Krebs, R., Momm, C., & Kounev, S. (2012). Architectural Concerns in Multi-tenant SaaS Applications. *Closer*, *12*, 426–431.

Kubitza, T. (2016, November). Apps for Environments: Running Interoperable Apps in Smart Environments with the meSchup IoT Platform. In *International Workshop on Interoperability and Open-Source Solutions* (pp. 158-172). Springer.

Meier, J. D., Hill, D., Homer, A., Jason, T., Bansode, P., Wall, L., ... Bogawat, A. (2009). *Microsoft application architecture guide*. Microsoft Corporation.

Mell, P., & Grance, T. (2011). *The NIST definition of cloud computing*. NIST.

Microsoft Azure – GitHub. (n.d.). Retrieved from https://github.com/azure/

Microsoft Azure IoT Reference Architecture. Version 2.0. (2018). Retrieved from https://aka.ms/iotrefarchitecture

Overview of Internet of Things. (n.d.). Retrieved from https://cloud.google.com/solutions/iot-overview

Page-Jones, M. (1999). *Fundamentals of Object-Oriented Design in UML* (1st ed.). Addison-Wesley Professional.

Selonen, P., & Taivalsaari, A. (2016, August). Kiuas – IoT cloud environment for enabling the programmable world. In *Software Engineering and Advanced Applications (SEAA), 2016 42th Euromicro Conference on* (pp. 250-257). IEEE.

Shi, W., Cao, J., Zhang, Q., Li, Y., & Xu, L. (2016). Edge computing: Vision and challenges. *IEEE Internet of Things Journal*, *3*(5), 637–646. doi:10.1109/JIOT.2016.2579198

Sivieri, A., Mottola, L., & Cugola, G. (2016). Building internet of things software with eliot. *Computer Communications*, *89*, 141–153. doi:10.1016/j.comcom.2016.02.004

Taivalsaari, A., & Mikkonen, T. (2018, April). On the development of IoT systems. In *Fog and Mobile Edge Computing (FMEC), 2018 Third International Conference on* (pp. 13-19). IEEE. 10.1109/FMEC.2018.8364039

Tools for Amazon Web Services. (n.d.). Retrieved from https://aws.amazon.com/tools/?nc1=f_ls

Williams, Z. D. (2017). *IoT Platform Comparison: How the 450 providers stack up* [White paper]. Retrieved July 19, 2018, from https://iot-analytics.com/iot-platform-comparison-how-providers-stack-up/

Wortmann, F., & Flüchter, K. (2015). Internet of things. *Business & Information Systems Engineering*, *57*(3), 221–224. doi:10.100712599-015-0383-3

ADDITIONAL READING

Botta, A., De Donato, W., Persico, V., & Pescapé, A. (2016). Integration of cloud computing and internet of things: A survey. *Future Generation Computer Systems*, *56*, 684–700. doi:10.1016/j.future.2015.09.021

Giray, G., Tekinerdogan, B., & Tüzün, E. (2017). Adopting the Essence Framework to Derive a Practice Library for the Development of IoT Systems. In Z. Mahmood (Ed.), *Connected Environments for the Internet of Things* (pp. 151–168). Cham: Springer. doi:10.1007/978-3-319-70102-8_8

Giray, G., Tekinerdogan, B., & Tüzün, E. (2018). IoT System Development Methods. In Q. F. Hassan, A. R. Khan, & S. A. Madani (Eds.), *Internet of Things: Challenges, Advances and Applications* (pp. 141–159). Chapman & Hall/CRC Press.

Gorton, I., & Klein, J. (2015). Distribution, data, deployment: Software architecture convergence in big data systems. *IEEE Software*, *32*(3), 78–85. doi:10.1109/MS.2014.51

Grover, M., Malaska, T., Seidman, J., & Shapira, G. (2015). *Hadoop Application Architectures: Designing Real-World Big Data Applications*. O'Reilly Media, Inc.

Big data and cloud computing:Hashem, I. A. T., Yaqoob, I., Anuar, N. B., Mokhtar, S., Gani, A., & Khan, S. U. (2015). The rise of "big data" on cloud computing: Review and open research issues. *Information Systems*, *47*, 98–115. doi:10.1016/j.is.2014.07.006

Mistrík, I., Bahsoon, R., Ali, N., Heisel, M., & Maxim, B. (Eds.). (2017). *Software Architecture for Big Data and the Cloud*. Morgan Kaufmann.

Riggins, F. J., & Wamba, S. F. (2015, January). Research directions on the adoption, usage, and impact of the internet of things through the use of big data analytics. In *System Sciences (HICSS), 2015 48th Hawaii International Conference on* (pp. 1531-1540). IEEE. 10.1109/HICSS.2015.186

Software development for IoT:Taivalsaari, A., & Mikkonen, T. (2017). A roadmap to the programmable world: Software challenges in the IoT era. *IEEE Software*, *34*(1), 72–80. doi:10.1109/MS.2017.26

KEY TERMS AND DEFINITIONS

Communication Protocol: Communication protocols are formal descriptions of formats and rules for producing digital messages for electronic data exchange.

Device Management: Device management is the application of a set of methods, techniques, tools to manage IoT devices throughout their lifecycle. The fundamental activities of device management are provisioning and authentication, configuration and control, monitoring and diagnostics, and software updates and maintenance.

Integrated Development Environment (IDE): An IDE is an application, which provides some facilities (such as source editor, configuration management, builders, runtime, testing, debugger, etc.) to developers for software development.

IoT Application: An IoT application is specific to a domain and implements the requirements of a specific business model. It utilizes IoT platform for common basic functionalities.

IoT Device: IoT devices (also called as things, connected devices, smart devices, smart objects, etc.) are capable of sensing data from the real world and communicating these data electronically to an IoT gateway and/or to an IoT platform/application over a connection.

IoT Gateway: IoT gateways play an intermediary role between IoT devices and IoT platforms. IoT gateways receive data from IoT devices, may translate, filter, aggregate, cleanse data and direct these data to IoT platforms.

IoT Platform: IoT platform refers to a combination of some basic functionalities common to most IoT systems. These functionalities encompass computation, storage, analytics, device management, etc.

IoT System: An IoT system (or IoT solution) is a composition of the elements, namely IoT device, gateway, platform, application, and fulfill some specific requirements. For instance, an IoT system for waste management can detect rubbish levels in containers to optimize the trash collection routes.

Software Development Kit (SDK): An SDK supports developers for software development by providing some functionality in the form of a set of libraries and hence foster software reuse.

Chapter 14
An Internet of Things Ambient Light Monitoring System

Muhammad Hariz Abdul Manab
Universiti Teknologi PETRONAS, Malaysia

Micheal Drieberg
Universiti Teknologi PETRONAS, Malaysia

Azrina Abd Aziz
Universiti Teknologi PETRONAS, Malaysia

Patrick Sebastian
Universiti Teknologi PETRONAS, Malaysia

Hai Hiung Lo
Universiti Teknologi PETRONAS, Malaysia

ABSTRACT

Nowadays, the Internet of Things (IoT) technologies are ubiquitous and widely used to solve everyday challenges related to power usage consumption, environmental condition, automation, and many more. A scalable IoT-based ambient light monitoring system is designed to measure the ambient light intensity or illuminance of particular indoor areas, with an implementation in campus. This system is designed to measure the light measurement autonomously and continuously without human involvement. The end-users are able to access the real-time information of the collected data via internet through a cloud-based IoT platform with analytics capabilities. This system will provide significant benefits to the campus community in terms of creating a more conducive environment, increased productivity, and improved health condition. Furthermore, its implementation can be easily extended to other human spaces to create even greater benefits to society at large.

DOI: 10.4018/978-1-5225-7432-3.ch014

INTRODUCTION

The correct level of ambient light is crucial for various human activities to ensure comfort and good productivity. However, the ambient light illumination in a working or living space may not be at the optimal level due to the fact that there is normally little or no control provided to the users, resulting in either under or over illumination. Improper lighting control may result in energy wastage, loss of productivity or worse, adverse health and psychological effects.

Taking a university campus as a case study, it can be seen that the campus encompasses a large area and the lighting distributions are not exactly the same in all the campus' indoor areas. The unknown conditions of the indoor lighting levels may lead to energy wastage and unwanted health issues. Currently, the luminous data of the indoor ambient light is not easily attainable nor available. The application of light meter is not practical and can only provide limited readings due to its high cost and the need for manual operation, making any real-time monitoring of luminous data acquisition infeasible in the long term. Therefore, a real-time Internet of Things (IoT) based monitoring system is required and need to be developed in order to collect the data of the ambient light. Also, the data should be easily assessed anytime and anywhere through the Internet. With this system, the staffs and students are able to manage and control their lighting usage thus improving energy usage and ensuring a comfortable and good environment.

A scalable IoT system to remotely monitor the ambient light level in real-time inside the indoor areas of the campus that supports multiple sensors with low power consumption, is developed. The system is a remote system which uses the concept of IoT where the integration of everyday devices and the Internet takes place to provide big data for which analytics are applied to extract useful information. The end-users are able to access the real-time information of the collected data via internet through a cloud based IoT platform with analytics capabilities. The integrated system node consists of microcontroller board, second generation ambient light sensors, and communication device for wireless communication based on IEEE 802.11 (Wi-Fi). The measurement of the light intensity in SI unit of lux in certain indoor areas in campus will be taken and the data will then be collected and shared to the cloud based IoT platform via Wi-Fi. The data samples collected by the IoT system are evaluated and analyzed to determine the lighting conditions at the work and living areas.

This book chapter describes the design, development and implementation of a novel application of IoT, which is an ambient light monitoring system. Its outline includes the background, methodology, results and discussion, and conclusion. The objectives of this chapter is to enable readers to benefit from understanding the need for such an application, the current state-of-the-art development in the area of ambient light monitoring, the methodology used in the system design and component selections, and finally the data collection and analysis. They can then apply a similar design methodology to their own application domain. Readers will also be exposed to the system building blocks of an IoT application, including the actual hardware and software components.

BACKGROUND

This chapter covers the overview on smart environmental monitoring and the theory on ambient light. The related works on real-time environmental monitoring using IoT are also provided.

Introduction on Smart Environmental Monitoring Using IoT

The existence of IoT has revolutionized the way we do things in our daily life. Thanks to the rapid development of IoT technology, more and more smart systems are emerging around the world to provide solutions to domestic and industrial problems. Smart car, smart home and smart city are well-known applications of IoT. IoT is basically a technology that allows any devices to be connected to a network via the Internet and supports real-time data exchange among these devices. The abilities to connect many devices in various sizes and capabilities, share critical data ubiquitously and make an intelligent decision without or with minimal human intervention are the key features for smart systems. By using IoT technology, everyday devices in our homes are now able to monitor the environment continuously, inform on any peculiar event and react to the physical world as per instructed thus, providing more convenience and better security.

Smart environmental monitoring is one of the IoT applications that has garnered significant attention from the environmentalist and public. The idea of smart environmental monitoring is to collect physical data from the environment and perform analysis to prevent any potential risks. Natural disasters such as earthquakes, landslides and flood or environmental issues such as global warming, water pollution and air pollution can be mitigated if the environment is constantly and accurately monitored.

Generally, a smart environmental system is a system that has the capability to manage itself, and manipulate and analyze data. Smart environmental monitoring is also defined as an ecosystem of interacting devices integrated by embedded system, sensors, and internet network (Soliman et al, 2013). Sensors play an important role in smart environmental monitoring systems. The types of sensor to be used depend on the event to be monitored.

The environmental monitoring applications can be broadly divided into two types which are indoor and outdoor monitoring. Indoor monitoring systems are the systems deployed for building and workplace monitoring. Different types of sensors including temperature, light, humidity, and air quality sensors are used to gather environmental data. A popular example is the fire and smoke detection for indoor buildings. The outdoor monitoring systems on the other hand monitor the outdoor environments one application example is weather forecasting.

There are various benefits of smart ambient light monitoring systems. In indoor encapsulated areas, the lighting load contributes most to the total domestic load (Khera et al, 2015). Therefore, there is a rising need to provide an indoor ambient light monitoring in order to save electrical energy. On the other hand, ambient light monitoring system is also important for the study of light pollution, illumination engineering and agriculture (Sumriddetchkajorn, & Somboonkaew, 2010). The conventional work to collect or measure the light intensity is achieved using a lux meter. However, this manual approach can only provide limited readings and it's also expensive. The automated ambient light monitoring system is a preferable solution due to its reliability and accuracy.

Spaces which are under illuminated or over illuminated may also contribute to adverse health issues such as headaches, fatigue and stress (Lin, 2014). Over illumination is a term used when the lighting intensity is beyond the required level needed for a particular activity while under illumination is vice versa. An optimum lighting condition is crucial in order to have good work performance and to create a better work environment. Thus, a monitoring system for ambient light is required so that the occupants can be made aware and alerted to the environmental lighting changes, which enables them to undertake the appropriate decisions with regards to the optimum illumination level.

Background on Ambient Light

Ambient light can be classified into natural and artificial lights. The natural lights usually come from the sun while artificial lights include LED, fluorescent and incandescent lights. The illumination of particular areas no matter outdoor or indoor is contributed by the presence of ambient lights. Light intensity is an important parameter in many applications. For instance, office or living areas, quality photography pictures, solar charging or sunlight harvesting, and machine vision all require optimum lighting conditions.

The visible light spectrum perceived by the human eyes has wavelengths from 380 nm to 760 nm. Basically, light sources emit visible, infrared (IR) and ultraviolet (UV) radiation. So, the right choice of light sensor is important for the ambient light monitoring system design. The light sensor chosen must match the luminosity curve to match with the spectral sensitivity of human eyes.

The International Commission on Illumination luminosity function, also known as the V (λ), provides the visual sensitivity of the human eyes to lights at various wavelengths (Lee et al, 2015). Basically, there are two curves which are the photopic and scotopic curves. The photopic curve is a curve for the approximation of human eyes response under well-lighted conditions while the scotopic curve is for low-light conditions. Normally, the photopic curve will be used to match the response of the eye as the visual level is much better in well-lighted condition found in typical working environments (Lee et al, 2015). Therefore, the chosen sensor will need to match the photopic curve. The wavelength range for the photometric measurement will be taken from 380 nm – 710 nm. This range of photometric unit is the approximation of human eyes response under the photopic condition.

Each room's illumination should also be planned based on the correct illumination level. Table 1 provides the recommended illumination (Sinometer, 2012). Over or under illumination are both undesirable and should be avoided. Good lighting condition should be provided in order to enable people to accomplish the required tasks. The working environment can only be conducive with the correct level of lighting. The recommended illuminations are different even in the same area reflects the need of different amount of illumination for different tasks. Based on the table, it can be noted that detailed tasks such as electronic parts assembly line in the factory, forefront of show window in store and typing in the office require high illumination in the range of 1000 ~ 3000 lux. On the other hand, tasks that are more general like climbing the indoors stairs corridor in the store, packing work or walking the entrance passage in the factory and workout in the indoor gymnasium in the school only requires low illumination levels of below 300 lux. The correct level of ambient light is crucial for various human activities to ensure good productivity and comfortability. Its importance cannot be overstressed as improper lighting can result in energy wastage, loss of productivity and reduced comfortability.

Smart Environmental Monitoring Using IoT

In this section, the indoor and outdoor environmental monitoring applications using IoT are presented. Many researches have focused on the development of the smart environmental monitoring system using IoT. In (Qianqian et al, 2015), an indoor monitoring system using Arduino Yun was developed to monitor the air condition by measuring the humidity, temperature, volatile organic compounds (VOCs) concentration and dust particle density. The advantages of the project include its low cost, fairly accurate indoor air monitoring and easy data access from anywhere through Wi-Fi. However, the system is not scalable.

Another approach of smart monitoring system is in (Kelly et al, 2013). The system measures three parameters which are the attributes of hot water system, power consumption and the environmental

Table 1. The recommended illumination for different scenarios (Sinometer, 2012)

Scenarios	Tasks	Recommended Illumination (Lux)
Office	Conference and reception	200 to 750
	Clerical type work	700 to 1500
	Typing	1000 to 2000
Factory	Packing work and entrance	150 to 300
	Production line with visual work	300 to 750
	Inspection work	750 to 1500
	Small parts assembly line	1500 to 3000
Hotel	Public room	100 to 200
	Reception and cashier	220 to 1000
Store	Stairs corridor	150 to 200
	Show window	750 to 1500
	Forefront of show window	1500 to 3000
Hospital	Sickroom	100 to 200
	Medical examination room	300 to 750
	Operation theater	750 to 1500
School	Auditorium	100 to 300
	Class room	200 to 750
	Laboratory and library	500 to 1500

conditions in the house. The internetworking of ZigBee communication with IP network or Internet is truly the best method in order to make the system scalable, remotely accessible and reliable. All the data from the sensing units are able to be monitored from anywhere through the IoT website as long as the Internet connection is available. However, most of the hardware used in the system are customized thus limiting the choice in the hardware.

An environmental monitoring system capable of sensing environmental parameters including temperature, light level, humidity, concentrations of the harmful carbon monoxide and detecting earthquakes was developed in (Ibrahim et al, 2015). It uses the Raspberry-Pi with integration of various sensors. However, the system is not scalable as there is only one node and there was no discussion on how the system might be used with multiple nodes.

An IoT based farm environmental monitoring system for management and implementation of precision production was proposed in (Jiao et al, 2014). The system can continuously measure many agricultures related parameters including air temperature, humidity, light intensity and soil moisture. The node was custom build based around the Freescale microprocessor. The system was implemented in an orchard in Anhui Agricultural University and its operation was found to be stable and reliable. However, the complexity of both the hardware and software components of this system is very high.

In (Vijayakumar, & Ramya, 2015), an IoT real time monitoring of the water quality was developed. The system can measure temperature, PH, conductivity, turbidity and dissolved oxygen of the water. The node is based on the Raspberry-Pi, integrated with the corresponding sensors. However, the system is not scalable and it also has a high power consumption.

An environmental monitoring system for both water and air was developed in (Trancă et al, 2017). The measured parameters include air temperature, water depth and water temperature. It is based on the industrial NI wireless node integrating both analog and digital sensors. The advantages of this system include its low power, high architecture flexibility and also its ability to withstand the harsh industrial environments. However, the nodes have a high cost and there is also no internet connectivity.

An IoT environmental monitoring system consisting of the integration of water and soil quality monitoring was developed in (Ramesh et al, 2017). The system is aimed towards solving the serious issue of water contamination caused by waste in Thalassery, Kannur District, Kerala, India. It consists of the normal water quality sensors and also the soil quality sensors that can detect harmful heavy metals. The system also includes an alert feature and was implemented in Kerala, India. However, the cost of the sensors used and communication platform is high.

Table 2 summarizes the related works on smart environmental monitoring applications with their advantages and disadvantages.

METHODOLOGY

This section presents the methods and procedure that will be carried out throughout the developed system.

Table 2. Smart environmental monitoring systems description

Related Work	Description	Advantages	Disadvantages
Qianqian et al, 2015	Indoor air quality monitoring system using Arduino Yun	Low cost, accurate indoor air monitoring and easy data access	Not scalable
Kelly et al, 2013	Environmental condition monitoring in homes using custom ZigBee enabled nodes	Scalable, easy access and reliable	Custom nodes are difficult for others to replicate
Ibrahim et al, 2015	Environmental monitoring and earthquake detection system using Raspberry-Pi	Many sensing parameters such as temperature, humidity, light level and CO harmful air pollutant	Not scalable. The system has only one node
Jiao et al, 2014	An environmental monitoring system designed to measure soil temperature and moisture, air temperature, photosynthetic radiation and humidity	Many sensing parameters, has a stable and continuous sensing data and low-cost hardware	High hardware and software complexity
Vijayakumar, & Ramya, 2015	Monitoring of the water quality and user can access the data via Internet using Raspberry-Pi integrated with the sensors	User friendly, low cost, with processing and transmission capabilities using Wi-Fi	Not scalable and high power consumption
Trancă et al, 2017	An environmental monitoring system which include both air and water parameters using the industrial NI wireless node	Low power monitoring system with high architecture flexibility and can be used in industrial environments	High cost hardware used and no Internet accessibility
Ramesh et al, 2017	An IoT environmental monitoring system consisting of the integration of water and soil quality monitoring with alert system implemented in Kerala, India	The integration of several multi-sensor systems for one monitored parameter provides very detailed data	High cost hardware implementation in term of sensors used and communication platform

System Design and Development

There are two (2) main stages involved in the system design and development to build the ambient light monitoring system using IoT. The system focuses on monitoring light intensity at indoor areas. Figure 1 shows the block diagram of network structure of the system architecture. Stage one of the system is to transfer the data collected from sensor to the sensor node or sink node. The illumination intensity or lux reading is retrieved from multiple sensors connected to a sensor or sink node via a I2C communications protocol where these sensors are placed at different locations. Subsequently, the sensor node or sink node would then transfer the data collected to a platform for data analysis and monitoring. A comparison study was also done to determine the type of wireless sensor nodes (WSN) network architecture, embedded board for sink and sensor nodes, and the types of wireless communication. This is to ensure the best choice of devices to be used for developing the remote ambient light monitoring system.

In the developed system, the modules architectures of the main hardware components are illustrated in Figure 1. The Arduino Uno Board, Yun Shield and TSL2561 ambient light sensors would be combined to build the illumination monitoring system. The utilization of a Single Board Computer (SBC) of Arduino Boards which is based on an Atmel microcontroller with shields and sensor make the IoT application a reality (Matijevic, & Cvjetkovic, 2016).

Table 3 shows the features of the Arduino Uno board that is to be used. Based on the table, Arduino Uno has sufficient features to be utilized as a microcontroller for the system. The Digital inputs, serial communication functionality (SCL and SDA) and the clock speed is sufficient to design the monitoring system. Moreover, in order to enable the Arduino board or the system able to connect to the Internet, Yun Shield provides the functionalities extension and solves the problem of Internet connectivity like Wi-Fi, Ethernet and storage like use of SD card. In this instance, since all the data is stored in the Cloud, the storage extension provided by the Yun Shield would not to be used.

The Yun Shield module is a versatile module with Internet connectivity and can resolve the limited storage issue of the Arduino board. The core module of the Yun Shield is the Dragino HE. The HE module need only 200mA current when in full load, which makes it a low power consuming device. It

Figure 1. Block diagram of ambient light monitoring system

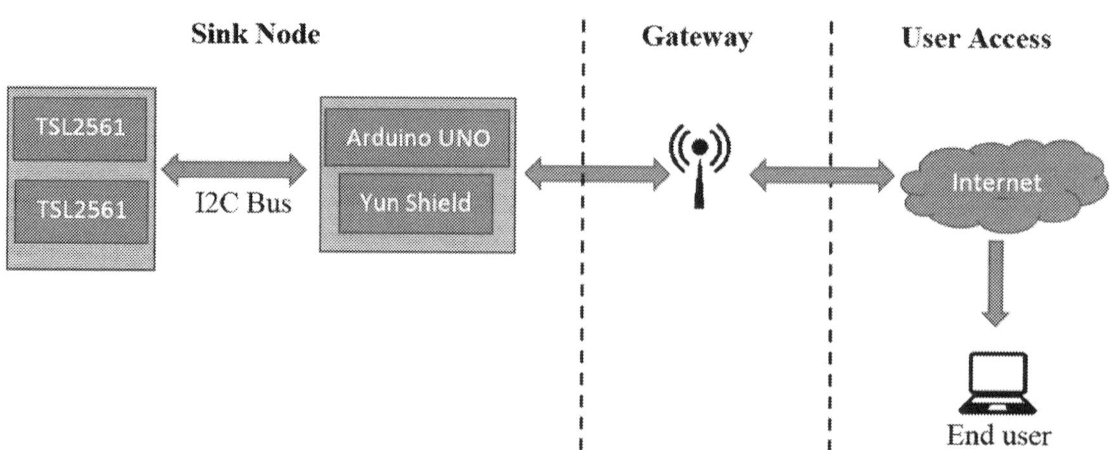

Table 3. Arduino Uno specifications (Matijevic, & Cvjetkovic, 2016)

Board/features	Uno details
AI	6 input,10 bits
DIO	14 I/O, 6 with PWM, 8 bits
Processor	AtMega 328
Clock	16Mhz
Flash	32 KB
SRAM	2 KB
EEPROM	1 KB

is powered by the Arduino Vin pins which means that the DC port (7V~15V) of Arduino board need to be used to power up the Yun Shield to prevent overheating of the hardware.

The Wi-fi and RJ-45 (used for Internet cable) interface are connected directly to the HE module for internetwork communication while SPI (Serial Peripheral Interface) and UART can also be used to communicate with the microcontroller. The sketches from the Arduino IDE can be uploaded using UART (universal asynchronous receiver/transmitter) interface, SPI or using Bridge class method by Wi-Fi interface. Table 4 shows the Yun Shield specifications and its ability to provide Internet connection for the system.

The TSL2561 light sensors will sense the light intensity and convert it to digital output before being sent to the sink node via I2C bus. The light sensors which read an analog input of light intensity measurement based on the empirical formula is converted to digital input before being sent to the microcontroller for data transmission. Each sensor has a different identifying address and unique ID in order to prevent address conflict during the data transmission via the I2C bus. For the TSL2561 light sensor, the maximum number of sensors that can be connected to one microcontroller is three sensors. In this developed system, only two sensors are used to collect the lux measurement which each sensor is designed to be in different position and distance in a fixed indoor location.

Light sensor TSL2561 is used by connecting it with the Arduino Uno to measure the intensity of the indoor light. The clock signal (SCL) pin and data signal (SDA) pin of the Uno Board is used for the data transmission between the TSL2561 and the Uno Board. In this context, the sensor works as a "slave" and communicates with the "master" chip which is the sensor node or sink node. The I2C communication protocol would allow multiple "slave" chips which are the sensors to communicate with the sink node respectively with the 3.3V power supply from the Uno Board.

Table 4. Yun Shield specifications (Geeetech, 2016)

Processor speed	400MHz, 24K MIPS
RAM	64 MB
Flash	16 MB
Network	150M Wifi 802.11 b/g/n
OS	Linux Open Source OpenWrt
Peripherals	1 x 10M/100M RJ45 Connector 1 x USB 2.0 host connector

The TSL2561 light sensor was chosen due to its accuracy in term of what exactly human eyes see or perceived and precise in measuring the lux thus allowing exact lux calculation. This choice is because of the different type of light energy spectrum that will be received by the sensor and the conventional light sensor cannot differentiate the different wavelengths of light such as sunlight and artificial light thus will capture the entire energy spectrum produced by different light sources and transform the input into a current (Pitigoi-Aron et al, 2005).

This sensor was selected because it matches the luminosity function, V (λ) curve (Lee et al, 2015). The spectral response comparison between the TSL2561 ambient light sensor and traditional light sensor for the photopic response measurement indicates that the relative spectral sensitivity between the human eye and ambient light sensor are approximately the same while it differs with the Si light sensor which indicates that the sensitivity of the Si sensor is not the same with human eye response. This is due to the characteristics of traditional light sensors which can only measure and respond strongly to infrared (IR) light, whereas the human eye is not capable of detecting light at that wavelength. When the intensity of the IR light is high, a significant error of measurement will occur due to the different response of the silicon light sensor and the human eye.

Table 5 provides the specifications of the TSL2561 ambient light sensor. However, it is only suitable to be used for indoor monitoring as the maximum light range detection is about 40k lux and for an indoor lighting environment, the maximum light range should not exceed 40k lux.

The significant characteristics of this sensor is its ability to mimic or approximates the human eye response towards light, commonly interpreted as illuminance measured in lux. It is a programmable light-to-digital converter that convert the light intensity to a digital signal output by using two integrating ADCs. It is manufactured by Texas Advanced Optoelectronic Solution (TAOS) company (Yong, 2011). This sensor can be used for various applications related with optical engineering. As the sensor consisted of two types of photodiodes, the currents produced by the photodiodes will be converted to a digital output (16-Bit Digital Output) that indicates the irradiance measured on each channel. The output from the sensor will be the input to the microprocessor, which will perform the derivation using specific calculation in order to get the illuminance or ambient light intensity in the lux SI unit.

The calculated lux will be approximately the same as seen by the human eye. This TSL2561 light sensor uses both of its diodes which are the full spectrum and IR. As the two of the photodiodes (Channel 0 and Channel 1) received input in a form of light, the current produced by the photodiodes will be converted into a digital signal by both of the ADCs simultaneously. After the conversion cycle is completed, the results are transferred to the data registers of both channels. The data transfer is double buffered to ensure no invalid data is registered or read. After the transfer is completed, a new conversion cycle will begin. The way the sensor approximates the human eye response towards light is by converting the outputs of the ADC from both channels to the lux unit. Channel 1's output is used to remove the effect of the IR component of light on Channel 0's output.

Table 5. TSL2561 features (Minghui et al, 2010)

Features	Details
Light range detection	0.1 - 40,000+ Lux
Diodes	Infrared and full spectrum
Voltage range	2.7 – 3.6V

Table 6 shows the formula used to obtain the value in lux unit. The formula is obtained through empirical testing using both fluorescent and incandescent light sources. The level of lux is directly proportional with the obtained voltage level. As the intensity is lowered, the obtained voltage will also be lower and vice versa (Sumriddetchkajorn, & Somboonkaew, 2010). The currents produced by the photodiodes of Channel 0 and Channel 1 are converted in form of illuminance measured in SI unit of lux. The value produced from Channel 0 and Channel 1 will be used in the empirical formula to obtain the value in lux. The responsivity of the photodiodes of Channel 0 and Channel 1 are different. For Channel 0, the photodiode captures both visible and infrared light (IR) while Channel 1 mainly captures only IR light.

Validation and Testing

Proceeding to next step of realizing the ambient light monitoring system using IoT, validation and testing is done for the system in order to make sure the data collected by the light sensors is accurate. The accuracy of the light sensors used in the system design is specified based on the datasheet values provided by the manufacturer, TAOS. A conventional digital lux meter is also used to compare the measurement results produced by the TSL2561 light sensors. Table 7 shows the electrical specification of the digital lux meter used in this project.

The TSL2561 light sensor is tested with different lighting intensity to measure its lux changes. The sensor is tested at high brightness when 4 tubes of fluorescent lamps are used as the sensor is fixed at 7ft or approximately 2.10m. During this test, there is no presence of natural light which is the sunlight. The reading with the use of two fluorescent lamps facing directly to the sensor from the upward position.

To enable I2C communication, the sensors need to be connected with the Uno Board using the SCL and SDA pins on the board. Figure 2 shows the connection of the sensors with the Uno Board. Basically, the sensors are only allocated with three addresses currently and each of the sensor will have a unique ID respectively. The address allocation is to prevent conflict during the data transmission between the sensors and sink node. The allocation of the address also need to be declared in the code in order to enable the sensors to work.

Table 6. Empirical formula of illuminance for TSL2561 light sensor (Yong, 2011)

$0 < c <= 0.52$	$E_v = 0.0315 \times c_0 - 0.0593 \times c_0 \times (c_1/c_0)^{1.4}$
$0.52 < c <= 0.65$	$E_v = 0.0229 \times c_0 - 0.0291 \times c_1$
$0.65 < c <= 0.80$	$E_v = 0.0157 \times c_0 - 0.0180 \times c_1$
$0.80 < c <= 1.30$	$E_v = 0.00338 \times c_0 - 0.00260 \times c_1$
$c > 1.30$	$E_v = 0$

Table 7. LX1010B conventional digital lux meter electrical specifications (Sinometer, 2012)

Range	Resolution	Accuracy (23 ± 5 °C)
0 – 2000 Lux	1 Lux	±(5%+2d)
2000 – 19990 Lux	10 Lux	±(5%+2d)
20000 – 50000 Lux	100 Lux	±(5%+2d)

Figure 2. Configuration setup of TSL2561 Sensors and Arduino Uno

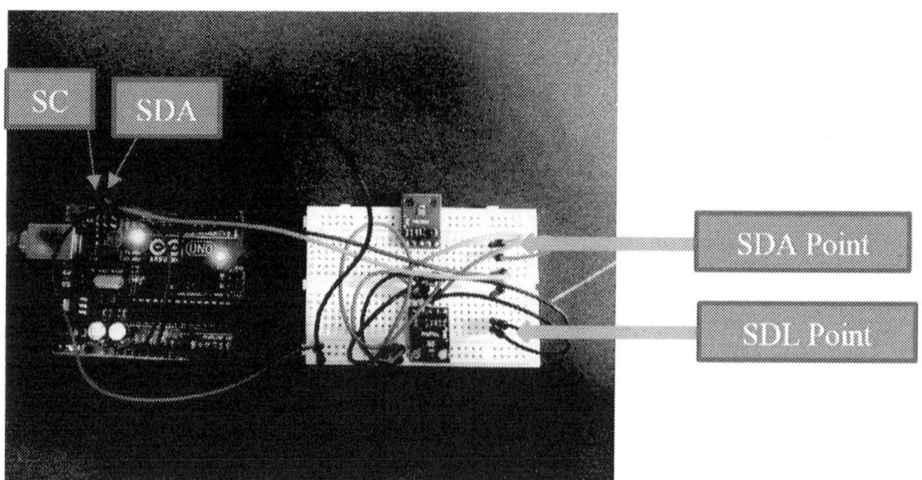

Data Collection and Analysis

Once the validation and testing of the sensors is done, the wireless connection mechanism is implemented to complete the overall IoT monitoring system. In this project work, a simple connectivity to the Internet is implemented by using the Wi-Fi interface of the Yun Shield to make the connection to the Internet. An Access Point (AP) is to be setup by the user in order for the Yun Shield to connect with it in order to be connected to the Internet. In this project, a software named Connectify is used for the computer to create the Wi-Fi hotspot to be the AP. After the Internet integration with the IoT ambient light monitoring system, the data collection can be performed. The light data is stored in the Cloud in order to enable the access of the data by the users anytime, anywhere using the Internet. Several data samples will be taken in order to evaluate the trends of the lighting condition in several indoor workspaces thus validating the reliability of the IoT monitoring system in terms of its data transmission and the accuracy. Figure 3 shows the wireless connection mechanism through the Internet.

Figure 3. Wireless connection mechanism

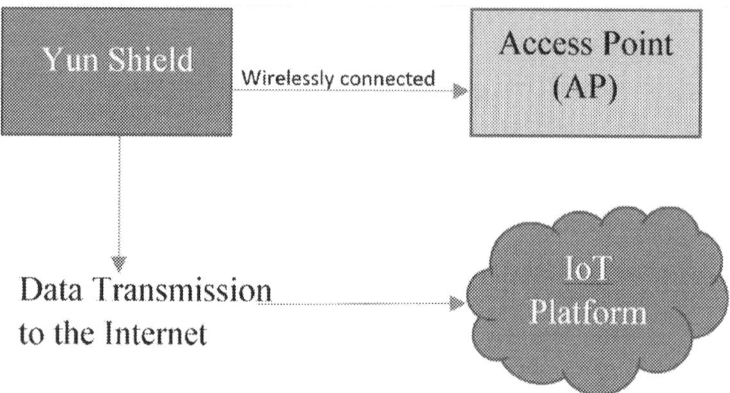

The data transmission from the monitoring system to the Cloud is performed by using an open IoT platform, which is ThingSpeak. In order to transfer the data collected by the light sensors to ThingSpeak, the Yun Shield is used as a Wi-Fi platform for the Uno Board to connect to the Internet wirelessly. Figure 4 shows the connection between the Yun Shield with Arduino Uno and the integration with the TSL2561 light sensors. The integrated system is powered up using the AC/DC adapter of 6V/300mA to ensure continuous operation as the monitoring activity runs continuously throughout a 24-hour time period.

After the hardware and software setup and configuration has been made, the data can be transferred to ThingSpeak. ThingSpeak platform is simple to be used and user friendly. In order to use ThingSpeak, a user account is created and a channel is also created to record the data sent. Figure 5 shows the channel

Figure 4. Yun shield with Arduino Uno board connection and integration with the TSL2561 light sensors

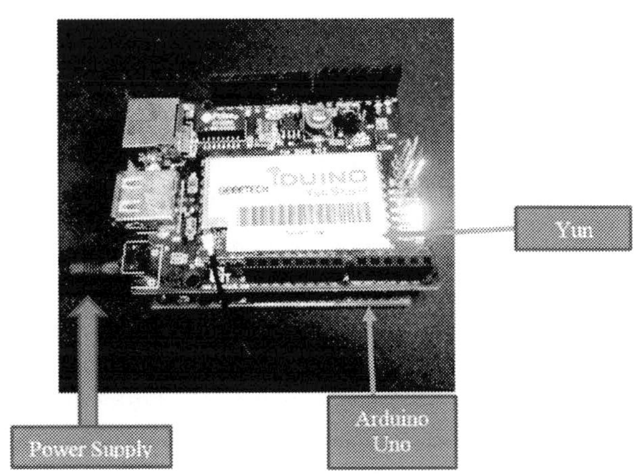

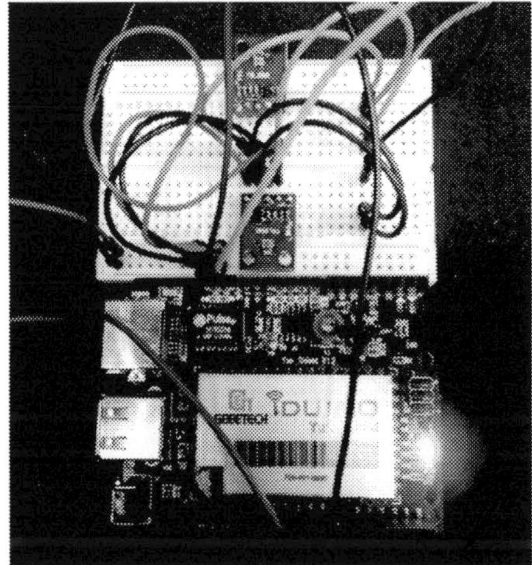

Figure 5. ThingSpeak channels, API keys, and data display

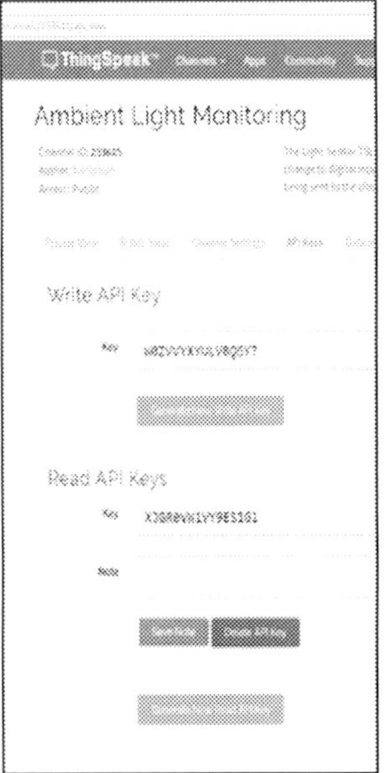

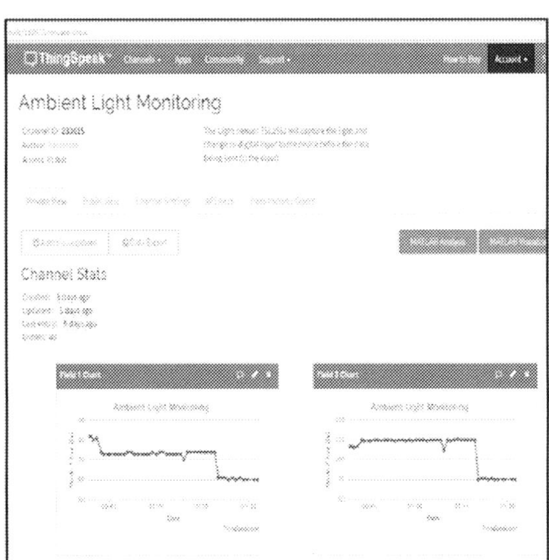

created by the user, API keys and data display in ThingSpeak. The data logging is running in the created channel during the monitoring activities. For this developmental work, the Ambient Light Monitoring Channel would be used for monitoring indoor ambient light. After a channel is created, the API key will be given as a verification key to access the channel. The API key is used in the coding for the transmission of data to the respective channel. The transmission time of the data collected by the system to the ThingSpeak channel would be at the precise 15s intervals and displayed accordingly.

RESULTS AND DISCUSSION

This section presents the results obtained and their discussion.

Validation and Testing

The results obtained from the developed ambient light monitoring system are presented in this section. The testing of the light sensor was performed to check whether it can accurately measure the illumination. Fluorescent light is used as an input to the light sensor. The sensor was configured to work in both bright lighting condition without causing sensor saturation and dim lighting condition without the need to increase sensor sensitivity manually.

For this project, the sensor is configured to automatically switch between low light and bright light condition. This is because the lighting condition is monitored over a 24-hour time period for different location of workplaces. With a 16 bit Analog-to-Digital converter, there are three resolution settings available for the sensor: 1) Highest resolution at a conversion time of 402 ms, 2) medium resolution with 101 ms conversion time, and 3) the lowest resolution but with the fastest 13 ms conversation time.

Validation of the light sensors and testing of the ambient light monitoring system using IoT with the indoor lighting condition in several working spaces is discussed here with the fastest 13ms conversion time.

Illuminance is the radiant flux density from visible radiation measured in lux. In this context, the wavelengths of visible radiation or visible light ranges from 390nm – 810nm. Basically, the illuminance from the light source will vary with the distance of the sensor. As the distance between the sensor and the light source increases, the illuminance will decrease. The accuracy and precision of the light sensor used is verified by comparing its illuminance value with the readings of a lux meter. From the datasheet of TSL2561, it was determined that the sensor was a suitable choice for our application of lighting measurement.

In order to have the accurate results using the ambient light monitoring system, the values measured by the TSL2561 light sensors are compared with the value measured by the LX1010B digital lux meter. This procedure is done to ensure that the IoT monitoring system gives accurate readings and the data collected are trustworthy during the monitoring activities or when the data logging is running. Table 8 shows the results of the of the TSL2561 light sensors sensitivity test.

From Table 8, the illuminance is produced directionally by two tubes of fluorescent lamps with length of 2ft. The results of the actual measurements are the average of three measurements taken by the LX1010B digital lux meter. Sensor1 (S1) and Sensor2 (S2) are the TSL2561 light sensors used to measure the illuminance produced by the luminaires (fluorescent lamps). The values measured by S1 and S2 are compared with the actual values measured by the digital lux meter to test its sensitivity towards the illuminance of the luminaires used in the indoor workplace. The illuminance is observed

Table 8. TSL2561 light sensor sensitivity test

Distance (ft.)	Actual (lx)	S1 (lx)	S2 (lx)	S1 Difference (lx)	S2 Difference (lx)	S1 Percentage error (%)	S2 Percentage error (%)
1	1238	1297	1276	59	38	4.77	3.07
2	577	590	605	13	28	2.25	4.85
3	253	264	266	11	13	4.35	5.14
4	179	188	185	9	6	5.03	3.35
5	138	143	145	5	7	3.62	5.07
6	119	125	122	6	3	5.04	2.52
7	94	95	99	1	3	1.06	5.32

to be decreasing as the distance of the measurement taken is increased thus it shows that illuminance is dependent on the distance. As the distance between the light source and the surface/object (the sensors and lux meter, respectively) increases, the illuminance produced by the light source will decrease. This relationship is stated as an Inverse square law in the study of illumination (Taylor, 2017)

$$E_v = I_v / d^2 \tag{1}$$

where E_v is the illuminance produced by the luminaire, I_v is the luminous intensity produced by the luminaire and d is the distance from the luminaire.

Figure 6 shows the light sensor sensitivity graph. From the figure, it can be seen that the deviation between the illuminance values produced by the light sensors and the actual readings of the digital lux

Figure 6. TSL2561 light sensor sensitivity graph

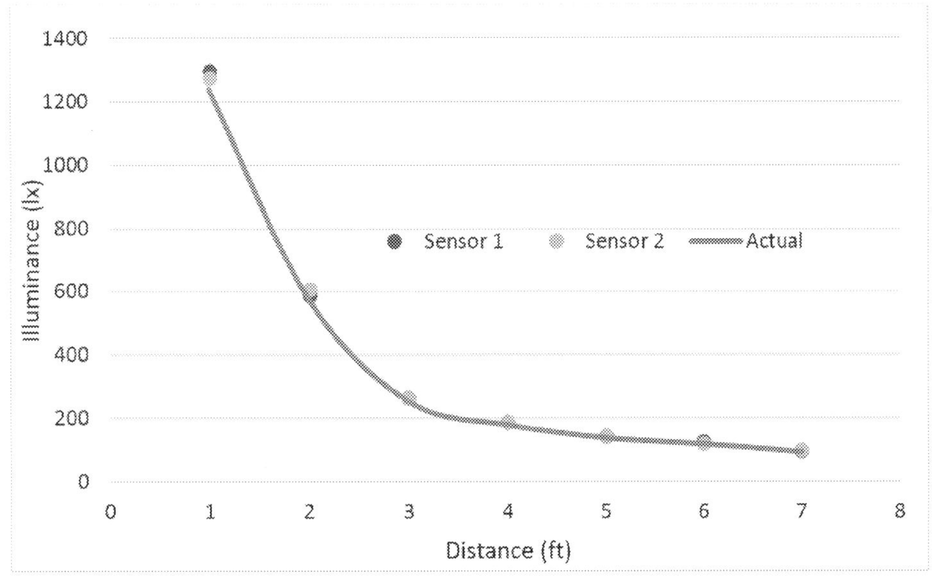

**For a more accurate representation see the electronic version.*

meter is small. Therefore, the readings from the light sensors is accurate and precise. The illuminance produced by the luminaires also decreases as the distance where the measurements taken increases. The tolerances of the light sensors are lower than 6% as shown in Table 8. The light sensitivity test has shown that the TSL2561 light sensor is suitable for the application of monitoring the lighting conditions in indoor workplaces on campus.

Although different quality and quantity of luminaires will give different readings of illuminance (Taylor, 2017), only the illuminance produced by the fluorescent lamp is studied in this project, as most of the luminaires found in the indoor workplaces on campus used are fluorescent lamps.

Ambient Light Monitoring System Testing

The ambient light monitoring system was tested at different indoor environment. In this project, two work areas with similar specifications at different indoor location is used to do the monitoring activity. The two work areas are denoted as Area 1 and Area 2, respectively. The collected data by the monitoring system is extracted from the ThingSpeak channel. The evaluation and analysis of the collected data samples is discussed in this section. Figure 7 shows the proposed prototype of the ambient light monitoring system.

To verify the accuracy and precision of the ambient light monitoring system, the system was tested. The monitoring system was fixed directionally at 7ft or 2.10m from the artificial light sources which illuminate the indoor working area. Figure 8 shows the TSL2561 light sensors positioning during the experiment. From the figure, it can be noted that the indoor work area is of 12ft by 6ft. The illumination or the light distribution of the work area is analysed here. Both Luminaire 1 and Luminaire 2 are composed of two tubes of fluorescent lamps with the same specifications. The positioning of the light sensors is based on the grid method (Hajibabaei, & Rasooli, 2014). S1 is represented by the green circle while S2

Figure 7. Prototype of ambient light monitoring system

Figure 8. TSL2561 light sensors positioning during experiment

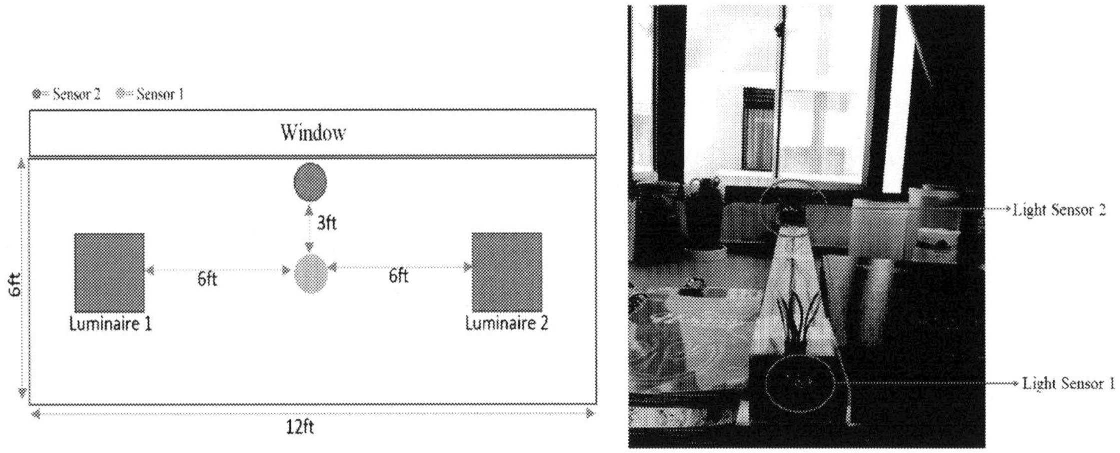

is represented by the blue circle. The distance between the sensors is fixed at 3ft with S2 positioned next to the window. S2 is located next to the window so as to differentiate it from the illuminance measured by S1 as the measurement taken by S1 is dominated by both Luminaire 1 and Luminaire 2 while the measurement taken by S2 is greatly affected by the natural light from the sun. S1 is positioned at the middle of the work area and is located about 6ft between Luminaire 1 and Luminaire 2. This setting is to ensure that the measurement taken by S1 is a true measurement value of the illuminance or lighting condition in the work area.

Table 9 shows the settings of the work areas. The monitoring activity at Area 1 and Area 2 were conducted on different days as the monitoring was done in 24-hour of time period and at different locations. The data collected by the monitoring system is taken every 60 seconds to ensure that sufficient data and measurements are collected for analysis. There were several data points missing from the data logged and it was suspected that the 15s transmission delay between the monitoring system and the ThingSpeak platform could be the cause.

Figure 9 shows the readings of the illumination recorded from S1 of Area 1, divided into two 12 hours monitoring graphs. From the first 12 hours' graph, the illuminance values recorded between 00:00 till 02:27 is in the range of 70 lx – 140 lx. This is the illuminance reading of the luminaires used to light the area. During this first 12 hours monitoring, the luminaires were switched on at 00:00 till 02:27. It can be seen at the time between 00:00 and 01:12, when the time where there was only one luminaire was used (either Luminaire 1 or Luminaire 2). Also, between 02:27 till 07:12, 0 lx was recorded as the luminaires

Table 9. Setting of the work areas

Work Area	Area (ft)	Luminaires	Location	Orientation	Monitoring date	Monitoring interval (s)	Transmission delay (s)
Area 1	12ft x 6ft	Two tubes of fluorescent lamp	Residential Village 5D-L1.1.4	250° from North	1.4.2017	60	15
Area 2	12ft x 6ft	Two tubes of fluorescent lamp	Residential Village 5D-L1.1.6	135° from North	2.4.2017	60	15

Figure 9. Area 1, Sensor 1: 1st and 2nd 12 hours monitoring graphs

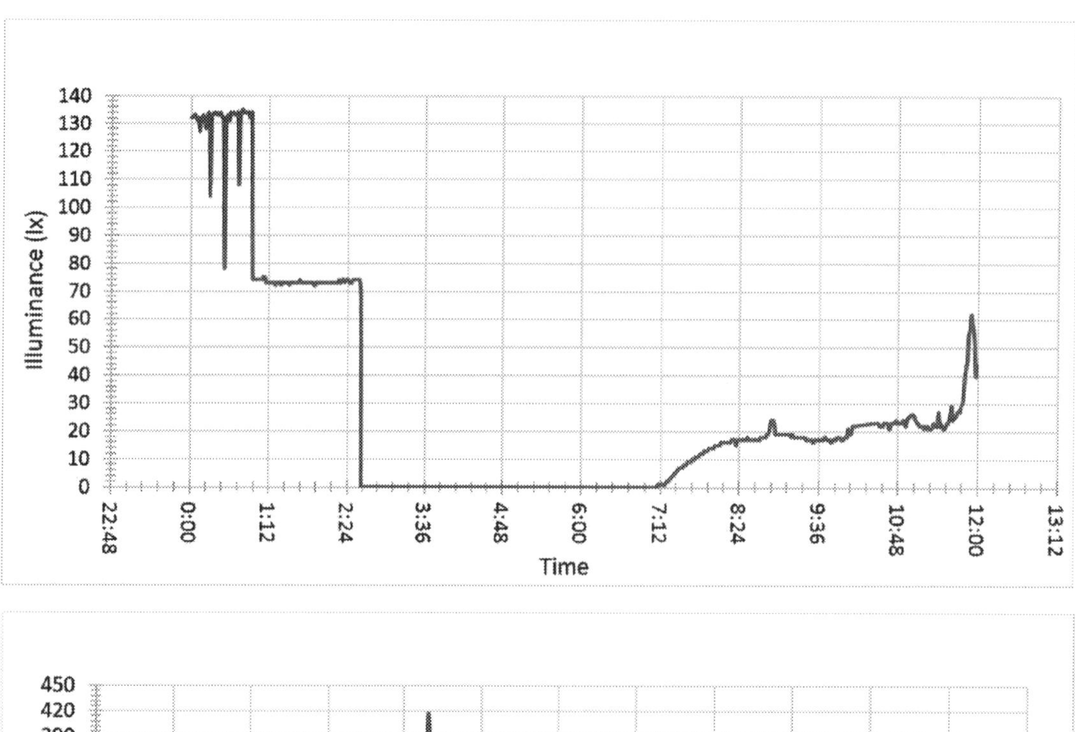

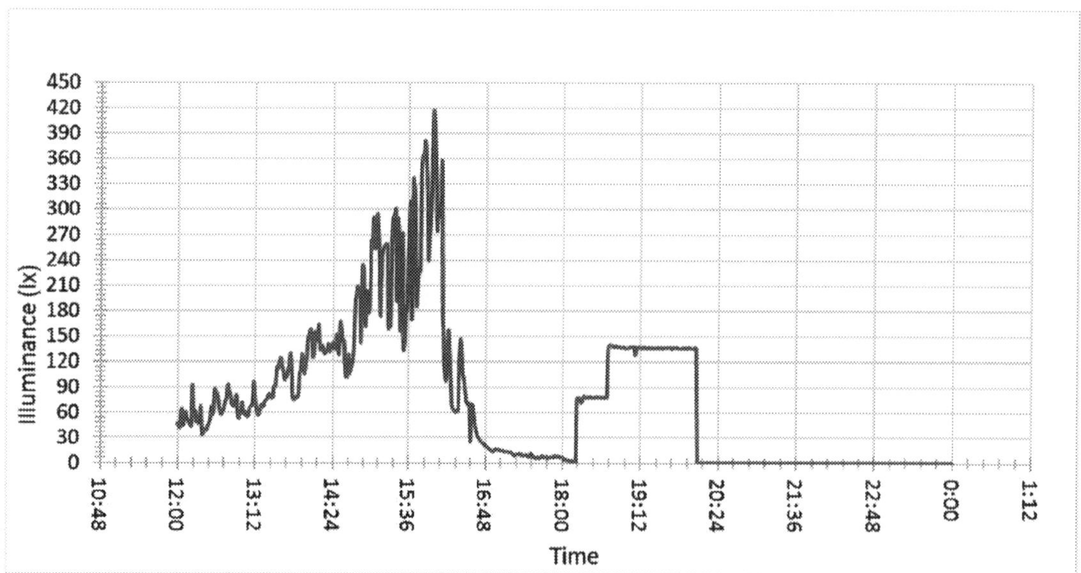

were switched off at 02:27. While between 07:12 till 12:00, the lux recorded is increasing from 1 lx to 70 lx, which are the readings of the ambient natural light as the sun rises.

Based on the second 12 hours' graph, from 12:00 till 18:14, the lux recorded by S1 is in the range of 1 lx – 420 lx. The trend is increasing until 15:58 (maximum of 416 lx was recorded) which indicated the sunlight illuminance is increasing over time. During this time period, neither Luminaire 1 nor Luminaire 2 is switched on. The illuminance measured comes only from the sun. From 18:14 till 18:43, either Luminaire 1 or Luminaire 2 is switched on as the lux recorded is between 70 lx – 80 lx while from 18:43 till 20:03, the lux recorded is between 130 lx – 140 lx, indicating that both Luminaire 1 and Luminaire 2 were on.

Figure 10 shows the readings of the illumination recorded from S2 of Area 1, divided into two 12 hours monitoring graphs. Referring to the figure, the illuminance values recorded between 00:00 till 02:27 is very similar to those obtained by S1. However, it is interesting to note that from 07:12 till 12:00, the illuminance values recorded are larger as S2 is placed next to the window. Between 15:07 and 16:04, as the sun shone brightly, there were points where the illuminance values recorded were 0 lx. This is where the light sensor was saturated. The maximum lux the sensor could measure was set at 20 klx, therefore when the illuminance exceeded 20 klx, the sensor was saturated and returned the 0 lx reading. The orientation of the room could greatly affect the illumination readings too. During the day, the lighting condition in Area 1 is dominated by the sun light and the usage of luminaires are only observed between 18:43 and 20:03. There are also readings of 0 lx recorded from both S1 and S2 indicating that the work area is in no light condition overnight after the lights were switched off.

Figure 10. Area 1, Sensor 2: 1st and 2nd 12 hours monitoring graphs

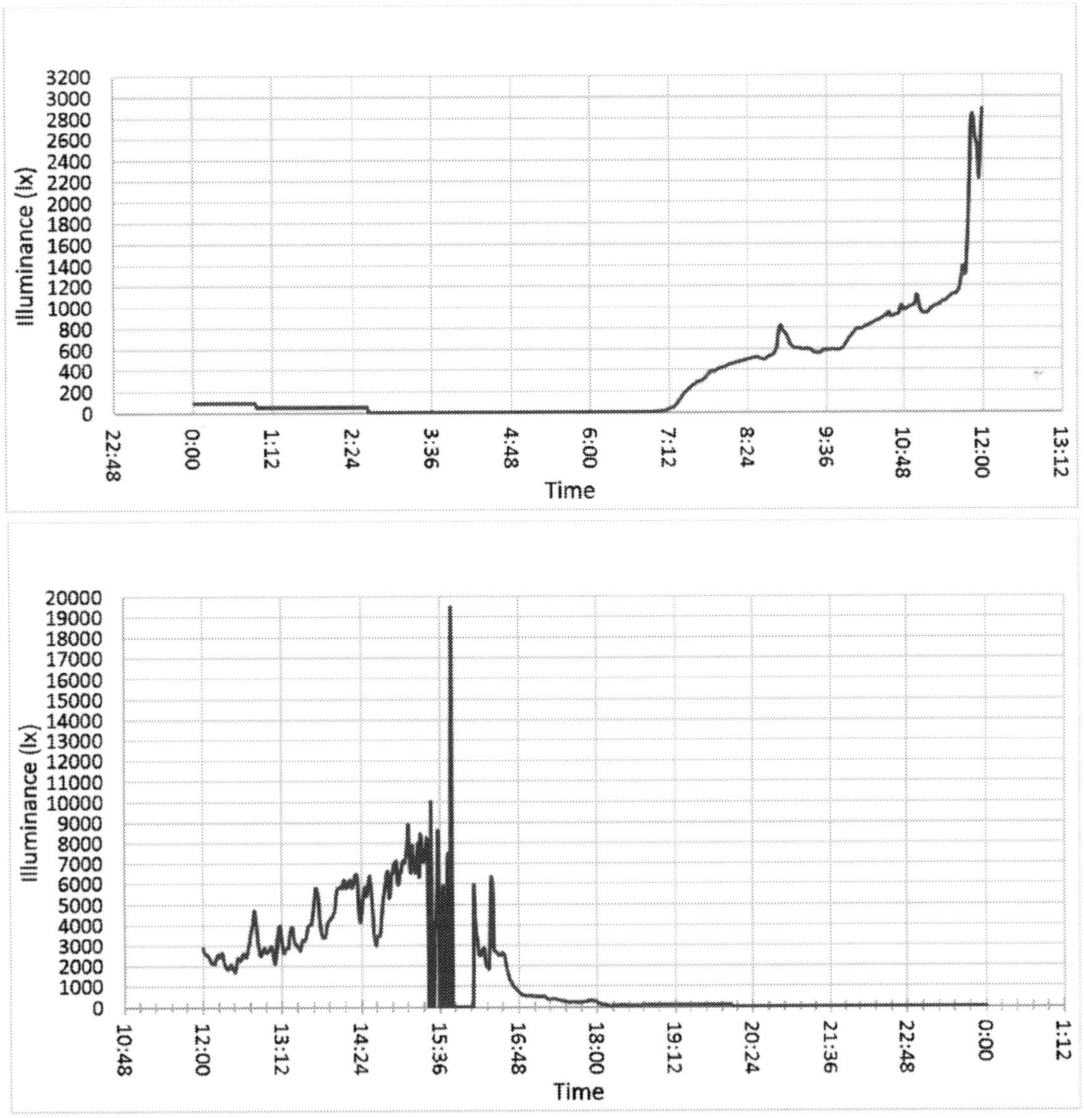

Figure 11 shows the readings of the illumination recorded from S1 and S2 of Area 2, 24 hours monitoring graphs. The time intervals where the usage of luminaires can be seen from time 00:00 till 03:20, 08:08 till 13:20 and 16:54 till 23:59. This is indicated by the relatively constant values recorded in the range of 140 lx – 170 lx. The luminaires were switched off from 13:30 till 16:45 and the values of 1 lx – 60 lx were recorded is due to the presence of sunlight. It is clear from the readings that, the values in

Figure 11. Area 2: S1 and S2 24 hours monitoring graphs

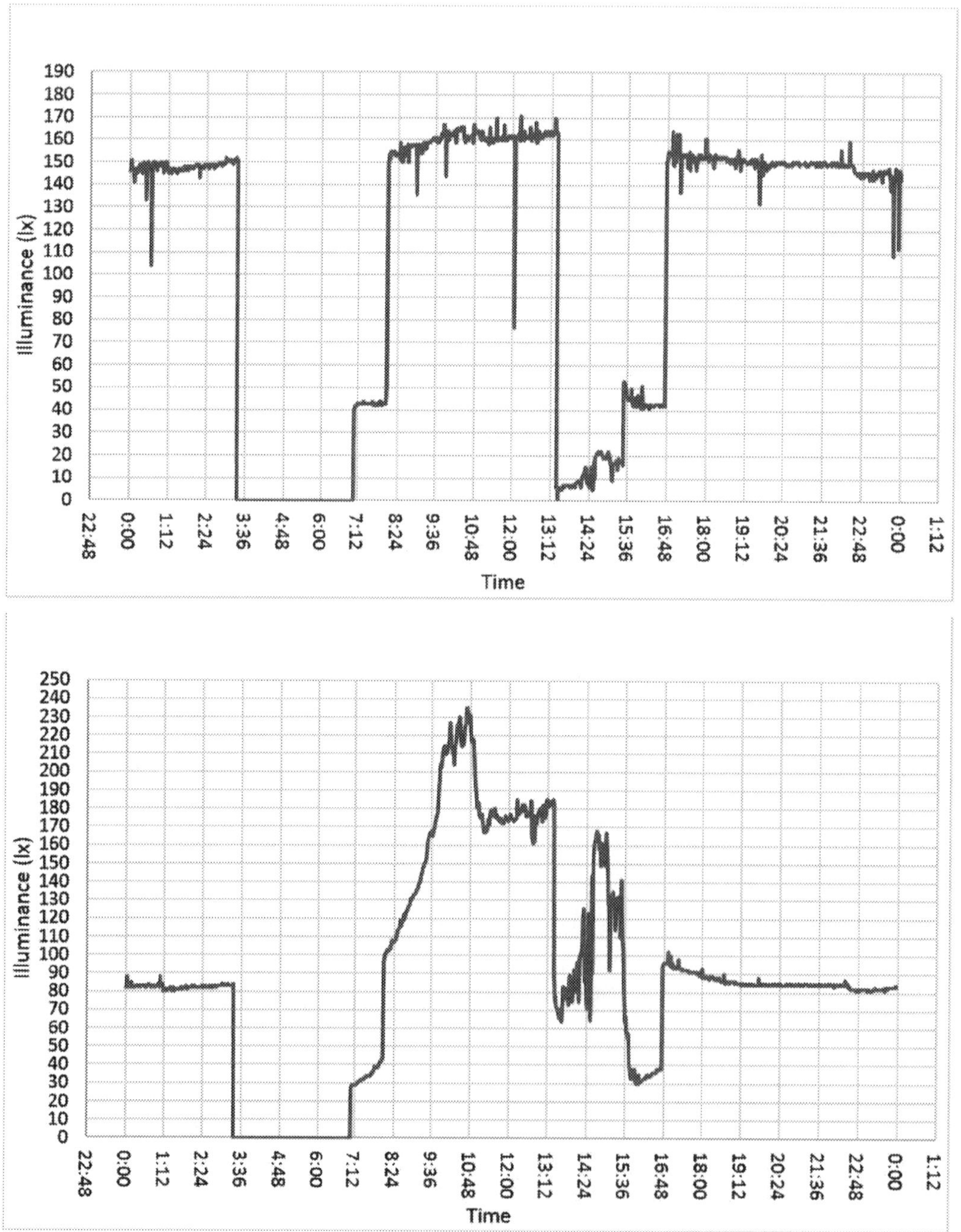

the range of 140 lx – 170 lx recorded are when both Luminaire 1 and Luminaire 2 were used. However, there were data points which shows discrete spikes due to the luminaire used, which is suspected to be caused by the fluorescent lamp having a low-level continuum of spectral power distribution (SPD) at specific wavelengths. As shown, the illumination recorded by S2 increases in the range of 27 lx – 231 lx at time 07:12 till 10:41 and in the range of 66 lx – 167 lx at time 13:34 till 15:00, due to the increasing of illuminance of the sunlight at the area.

Overall, the illumination of Area 1 is greatly dominated by the presence of sunlight as its illuminance frequently recorded readings that exceed 160 lx. The frequent readings of illuminance in the range of 130 lx to 160 lx in Area 2 shows that the lighting in the workspace there was mainly from the luminaires installed. These results have shown that the ambient lighting monitoring system can reliably provide accurate illumination measurements over an extended time period.

CONCLUSION

The design and development of the ambient light monitoring system using IoT discussed in this project is a simple but reliable and scalable monitoring system that can take measurement of the illuminance autonomously in a real-time without human involvement. It enables the long-term monitoring of the indoor ambient light remotely. The prototype which consist of several main components is a proof of concept of using IoT in environmental monitoring activity. Besides, the system can also provide access of the collected ambient light data anywhere to the users using through the Internet for any intervention work. The system that is implemented in the campus is able to promote a smart environment around the campus as well as giving the society an awareness in terms of the importance of the correct lighting levels that should be adopted for the various daily activities. The system is able to give a positive impact towards better productivity, comfortability and health. Other than that, the data samples taken automatically and continuously for several days at several indoor workplaces around campus can also provide a good insight into the different trends of lighting conditions and usage which are due to the artificial lights and natural light. The obtained data over a long period of time also prove the reliability of the ambient light monitoring system using IoT. Nevertheless, the lighting demands is subjective as it is changeable depending on the user's specific visual task. The TSL2561 light sensor, Arduino Uno, Yun Shield module and IoT platform are chosen based on their simplicity, robustness, reliability, scalability, and low power usage. The illumination data acquisition by ambient light monitoring system using IoT is extremely important for future intervention works such as to have an optimal lighting condition or even for energy harvesting purpose. Most importantly, such systems can help to create a better environment in terms of energy efficiency and conducive living and working spaces.

REFERENCES

Geeetech. (2016). *Yun Shield*. Retrieved from http://www.geeetech.com/wiki/index.php/Iduino_Yun_Shield

Hajibabaei, M., & Rasooli, E. (2014). Comparison of Different Methods of Measuring Illuminance in the Indoor of Office and Educational Buildings. *Jundishapur Journal of Health Sciences*, *6*(3), 1–5. doi:10.5812/jjhs.21720

Ibrahim, M., Elgamri, A., Babiker, S., & Mohamed, A. (2015). Internet of things based smart environmental monitoring using the raspberry-pi computer. In *Proceedings of Digital Information Processing and Communications (ICDIPC), 5th International Conference* (pp. 159-164). Academic Press. 10.1109/ICDIPC.2015.7323023

Jiao, J., Ma, H.-M., Qiao, Y., Du, Y.-L., Kong, W., & Wu, Z.-C. (2014). Design of farm environmental monitoring system based on the internet of things. *Advance Journal of Food Science and Technology*, *6*(3), 368–373. doi:10.19026/ajfst.6.38

Kelly, S. D. T., Suryadevara, N. K., & Mukhopadhyay, S. C. (2013). Towards the implementation of IoT for environmental condition monitoring in homes. *IEEE Sensors Journal*, *13*(10), 3846–3853. doi:10.1109/JSEN.2013.2263379

Khera, N., Gill, H., Dodwani, G., Celly, N., & Singh, S. (2015). Remote Condition Monitoring of Real-Time Light Intensity and Temperature Data. In *Proceedings of Advances in Computing and Communication Engineering (ICACCE), 2nd International Conference* (pp. 3-6). Academic Press. 10.1109/ICACCE.2015.111

Lee, W. J., Zhang, Z., Rau, S. H., Gammon, T., Johnson, B. C., & Beyreis, J. (2015). Arc Flash Light Intensity Measurement System Design. *IEEE Transactions on Industry Applications*, *51*(5), 4267–4274. doi:10.1109/TIA.2015.2431638

Lin, C.-C. (2014). Effect of noise intensity and illumination intensity on visual performance. *Perceptual and Motor Skills*, *19*(2), 441–454. doi:10.2466/26.24.PMS.119c20z1 PMID:25153619

Matijevic, M., & Cvjetkovic, V. (2016). Overview of architectures with Arduino boards as building blocks for data acquisition and control systems. In *Proceedings of Remote Engineering and Virtual Instrumentation (REV), 13th International Conference on* (pp. 56-63). Academic Press. 10.1109/REV.2016.7444440

Minghui, Y., Peng, Y., & Wangwang, S. (2010). Light Intensity Sensor Node Based on TSL2561. *Microcontrollers & Embedded Systems*, *10*(6), 38–40.

Pitigoi-Aron, R., Forke, U., & Viala, R. (2005). *U.S. Patent No. US6933486B2*. Santa Clara, CA: U.S. Patent and Trademark Office.

Qianqian, Y., Guangyao, Z., Wenhui, Q., Bin, Z., & Chiang, P. Y. (2015). Air-kare: A Wi-Fi based, multi-sensor, real-time indoor air quality monitor. In *Proceedings of Wireless Symposium (IWS), IEEE International* (pp. 1-4). IEEE. 10.1109/IEEE-IWS.2015.7164542

Ramesh, M. V., Nibi, K. V., Kurup, A., Mohan, R., Aiswarya, A., Arsha, A., & Sarang, P. R. (2017). Water quality monitoring and waste management using IoT. In *Proceedings of Global Humanitarian Technology Conference (GHTC), IEEE Conference* (pp. 1-7). IEEE. 10.1109/GHTC.2017.8239311

Sinometer. (2012). *LX1010B Mini Digital Lux Meter*. Retrieved from http://www.sinometer.com/?Environmental-Meters-category179.html

Soliman, M., Abiodun, T., Hamouda, T., Zhou, J., & Lung, C. H. (2013). Smart Home: Integrating Internet of Things with Web Services and Cloud Computing. In *Proceedings of Cloud Computing Technology and Science, IEEE 5th International Conference on* (pp. 317-320). IEEE.

Sumriddetchkajorn, S., & Somboonkaew, A. (2010). Low-cost cell-phone-based digital lux meter. *Proceedings of SPIE Advanced Sensor Systems and Applications*, *IV*, 1–6.

TaylorA. E. F. (2017). *Illumination Fundamentals*. Retrieved from https://optics.synopsys.com/lighttools/pdfs/illuminationfund.pdf

Trancă, D. C., Rosner, D., Curatu, R., Surpăteanu, A., Mocanu, M., Pardău, Ş., & Pălăcean, A. V. (2017). Industrial WSN node extension and measurement systems for air, water and environmental monitoring: IoT enabled environment monitoring using NI WSN nodes. In *Proceedings of Networking in Education and Research (RoEduNet), 16th RoEduNet Conference* (pp. 1-6). Academic Press.

Vijayakumar, N., & Ramya, R. (2015). The real time monitoring of water quality in IoT environment. In *Proceedings of Circuit, Power and Computing Technologies (ICCPCT), International Conference* (pp. 1-4). Academic Press.

Yong, H. (2011). Research of Real-Time Optical Intensity Sensing System with Wireless Sensor Network. In *Proceedings of Wireless Communications, Networking and Mobile Computing (WiCOM), 7th International Conference* (pp. 1-3). Academic Press. 10.1109/wicom.2011.6040362

Chapter 15
Challenges and Solutions of Big Data and IoT

Jayashree K.
Rajalaskshmi Engineering College, India

Abirami R.
Rajalaskshmi Engineering College, India

Rajeswari P.
Rajalaskshmi Engineering College, India

ABSTRACT

The successful development of big data and the internet of things (IoT) is increasing and influencing all areas of technologies and businesses. The rapid increase of more devices that are connected to IoT from which enormous amount of data are consumed indicates the way how big data is related with IoT. Since huge amount of data are obtained from different sources, analysis of these data involves much of processing at each and every level to extract knowledge for decision making process. To manage big data in a continuous network that keeps expanding leads to few issues related to data collection, data processing, analytics, and security. To address these issues, certain solution using bigdata approach in IoT are examined. Combining these two areas provides several opportunities developing new systems and identify advanced techniques to solve challenges on big data and IoT.

INTRODUCTION

Now a days Bigdata and Internet of Things (IoT) have emerge as the important areas in many developing countries with respect to various commercial, industry and also in other applications. The term IoT refers to connection of all physical devices in the world with the help of internet, by which most of the big data are gathered, aggregated and managed. Bigdata also helps in analyzing this data that is gathered and stored to obtain useful results. The driving force behind IoT and bigdata is analyzing and collecting the data based on consumer's actions, to predict what people would buy and why they buy that particular product. One of the example, is loyalty cards given in grocery shops and other commercial outlets. When

DOI: 10.4018/978-1-5225-7432-3.ch015

users use the card they would identify what and why people buy the product, this information can be helpful to improve the sales as well as profit (Gubbi et al., 2013).

Few commercial and government sectors work in the field of bigdata and IoT to identify the ways to improve the services in the field of agriculture, electricity, forestry, treatment of water and manufacturing sectors from where large amount of data is collected and also the ways to increase the profit rate. The major factors like low rejection rates, increased quality, low downtime, increased throughput, improved security and effective use of resources, labor remains the vital cause to implement IoT and Bigdata (Advantech).

Internet reconstructed the ways of business, global interactions and civilizing reformation. Presently, devices with the help of internet are used to control various automated gadgets paving a way to IoT. Thus even machines have become the users of internet, like the humans using web browsers. Researchers are attracted to IoT because of its increasing opportunities and challenges. It also has an vital impact on future technologies like network, communication and on infrastructure. Hence, the devices will be intelligently connected, controlled and managed. In-spite of few issues related to volume, velocity and variety, the concept of IoT became the most relevant topic because of the usage of mobile devices, various communication devices, embedded technologies, cloud computing concepts and data analytics are being widely used now a days. IoT provides services to any kind of application be it a simple or complex application. Even-though various definitions, contents and comparisons of concepts are given to IoT, it still remains to be a puzzling topic (Acharjya et al., 2016). Research work are being carried out in incorporating various technologies like computation intelligence and bigdata, so that management of data and knowledge discovery can be improved on huge applications like applications that deals with automation.(Mishra et al., 2015).

Knowledge discovery began by identifying how people process the information using frames, protocols, tags and networks. Based on processing of data, knowledge discovery is divided into four phases like a) knowledge acquisition, b)knowledge base, c) knowledge dissemination and d) knowledge application.

In the first stage which is knowledge acquisition, several standard and evaluation techniques are used to discover knowledge from the data. Then various experts systems and knowledge base are used to store the discovered knowledge of the data which is second phase (knowledge base). In knowledge dissemination phase, the data stored in knowledge base are analyzed so that useful information are obtained or extracted by searching documents, knowledge within documents and knowledge,this process is also called as knowledge extraction. Finally, the knowledge discovered has to be applied on several applications. All these phase are done repeatedly to extract he knowledge from the data. Knowledge exploration remains a research topic to deal with the issues related to it. (Kahani et al., 2015).

Thus, this chapter discusses the background of big data and IoT. It also discusses about various challenges of big data and IoT in detail with solution for issues. The various related work and application of big data and IoT would be addressed in this chapter.

BACKGROUND

IoT is a collection of networks which consists of various resources or devices like sensors, software, several electronic and communication devices which helps in collecting and transferring the data from one application to other in order to provide requested services to the users. It creates a better way to relate real world physical devices with software that is related to computers. The next big technology that influences the behavior of human beings in number of ways and factors is IoT. Since, tremendous amount of data is being obtained from IoT devices, various databases related to bigdata technology like SQL along with Hadoop, Column-oriented database, Hive, PIG, Wibidata, PLATFORA, SkyTree, Schema less databases otherwise called No-SQL databases, Streaming Big Data analytics, Big Data Lambda Architecture, Map-reduce concepts are used to store the data.(Kundhavai et al., 2016).

Few important factors of IoT which has impact on Bigdata are discussed below:

Big Data Storage

Basically, the reason behind using big data storage is that, it can manage, manipulate enormous amount of of data, and also expands its storage capacity whenever needed, also provides necessary operations to transfer the information or data to analytics tools. The format of the data varies, from structured data to unstructured data or even the combination of both, since the data are being collected from various sources, hence a proper data center is required to store and manipulate the different kinds of data. IoT has a absolute influence on the storage mechanism used by bigdata. Collecting IoT bigdata is the most difficult task because it is necessary to remove the duplicate data or redundant data before analyzing it. Once data is collected it is transferred through networks and maintained at data centers. To effectively handle the storage capacity, Bigdata several organizations make use of Platform as a Service (PaaS) which provides a platform to develop and run web based applications on cloud. But this IoT bigdata storage will be a issue as the rate the data grows is faster than it is expected.

Data Security Issues

The major concern in IoT is security where basic and standard methodologies cannot be used to overcome this issue. For example, imagine if the cameras installed in television and in security systems have some wi-fi access, how are we going to deal with the issues. Hence new techniques and methodologies have to be used. Challenges that are related to security are:

1. Secure processing of data in distributed environment.
2. Secure data centers.
3. Secure transactions.
4. Secure removing of redundant data.
5. Secure and scalable mining and analysis of data.
6. Access control.
7. Implementing real time security and so on.

An IoT application should follow a multilayered security and network methodology that will prevent the application from attacks and should not allows the attacks to scatter to other parts of network. To achieve it strict policies has to be maintained to access the network before connecting various IoT devices. Point to point and point to multi point encryption techniques like SDN that is Software defined networking technique can be used along with network access policies to avoid attacks.

Big Data Analytics

Analyzing the data and come to a conclusion about the information is called data analytics. Analytics on data plays a major role in many organizations in-terms of decision making process, and also in the field of science to experiment on models and theories. IoT Bigdata analytics helps to take decision in a better way during decision making process in many organizations. Big data analytics helps to get a clear view on business value and various ways the other organizations use the analytics process to achieve their business needs. According to Gartner, Big data is a collection of variety of data resource with enormous volume and velocity in which new techniques can be used to process the data that will be useful in decision making process. Volume is the size of the data. Data can be from various sources like social media, sensors, data generated from machines, structured or unstructured network data. Organizations using applications of IoT and bigdata will be loaded with terabytes of bigdata. Since the data are collected from various sources, different varieties of data be it structured, unstructured or semi-structured data like log files, dates, strings, audio, video 3D data are being stored. Velocity is the rate at which the data is being processed. For example, the rate in which data streams are obtained from different resources like mobiles, click streams are being processed. Mining and analyzing Bigdata provides a way to display patterns that are hidden, display correlations that are not identified and reveals other business data.

Impact on Day to Day Living

IoT bigdata gradually changes the lifestyle of the people. Few applications like i) Cameras installed in the cafeteria estimates the amount of time a person spends in that particular area, ii) Sensors in lecture rooms estimates the time staff takes the class and spends time on board which helps to measure the performance of the employee, iii) In home theater system can be set in such a way that whenever the person switch on the television their favorite movie can be played, iv) automatic switch off and on of electronic devices when there is nobody inside the home, v) A smart wrist band that is used by elder people which intimates them the nearby hospitals, in cases of emergency.

RELATED WORK

IoT and bigdata are two rapidly developing domains, which becomes a part of business and used in day to day applications. (Ejaz Ahmed et al., 2016)

An IoT based cyber systems was proposed by author C. Lee et al., which can increase the outcome of several industrial applications by using methodologies related to information analysis and knowledge collection. The system aims in analyzing the industrial data and combines several analytics components based on different modules in-order to achieve the requirements of business (Lee et al., 2015).

Berlian et al., has described a working model to monitor and analyze the huge amount of data, which are obtained from Internet of Underwater things (IoUT). MapReduce concept is utilized by the authors to manipulate the data, which proves to decreases the request execution time in comparison with SQL queries. In-spite of several advantages in the model, certain issues related to trust management protocol and in development of trust-based admission control for IoUT remains a major concern which has to be solved in near future.

Roman et al. has discussed on concepts like association of data, conclusions and knowledge acquisition process in the field of IoT big data management. They have also insisted about the future scope for IoT knowledge discovery. In another work they have discussed about a cognitive working model for IoT, that enhances the outcomes of symbolic derivations from the data that is collected, management of knowledge obtained while analyzing and simplifies the process of decision making.

Jorge came up with a architecture named distributed complex event processing system, for solving few issues like latency, updating remote policies, mobility and global system view. The architecture process data from various devices based on the type and location of device that is used for sending the data. Inorder to obtain solution for latency problems, processing has to be done either within the device or in nearby devices (Abbasil et al., 2017)

CHALLENGES

Issues Related to Big Data (Das et al., 2017)

One of the issue related to big data analytics is insufficient collaboration of databases, that organize the data as well as provides SQL queries in combination with packages related to analytics which provides facilities to process Non-SQL data such as data mining and statistical analyzes. Now a days data analysis are controlled as the data is been exported from the database, the exported data are allowed to perform non-SQL processing and the data are brought back finally. Issues like collection, processing in addition with reliability issues acts as a major concern in the field of IoT (Kaushik et al., 2012).

1. **Data Acquisition:** Data gathered from several resources like sensors, networks when analysed it is found to produce number of unwanted raw data. These unwanted data can be filtered out the amount of data can be reduced drastically. One major issue to be addressed is, when filtering the data useful information must not be filtered out or deleted.
2. The next issue is in terms of metadata, metadata has to be obtained automatically, in-order to identify what kind of data and how it is collected and measured. These data provides all minute information which helps to analyse the data in all the aspects where even minute information will be taken into account. Getting metadata requires multiple process like data acquisition, extraction of data or information and data cleaning, data integration, modelling and analysis of data, data interpretation and deployment, but only few process are given importance, whereas other process are left out (Che, 2013).
3. **Reliability Issues: When** the applications are deployed in the real time environment, IoT systems faces few challenges related to reliability. Issue raised while deploying the application are issues related to communication between devices due to signal, noise problem,fault tolerance in case if sensor or other devices fails, and in-terms of securing the network. In addition to it three major issues related to big data IoT systems are: i) authentication, ii) security, iii) uncertainty.
4. **Need of Data Management and Data Analytics:** Various software and hardware requirements are needed to manage and analyze the data. So there is a need to have better machines which will help in processing the data in parallel, so that analysis and management of data can be done simultaneously (Khushboo Wadhwani 2017).

5. **Need for Efficient Parallel Algorithms:** Advanced and efficient parallel algorithms need to be developed, so that time complexity while processing the data can be reduced from higher order complexity to lower order.
6. **Need for Better Adaptations to Classical Algorithms:** Inorder to handle major issues raised by big data, even simple or traditional algorithms can be used, which can reduce the effort put by the people to slove complex issues.
7. **Privacy and Security of the Data:** To strength the security and privacy policies, high level encryption techniques and algorithms has to be used.
8. **Need of Secure Cloud:** New techniques has to be used to safeguard and process the data that are stored in cloud.
9. **Increased Need to Store Data:** To overcome the issues related to storage cloud based solutions were used, but other issues like security, privacy, data integrity, data recovery or fault tolerance, control over data and vendor policies that arises needs to identify a technique to handle or solve the issues.
10. **Requires Massive Parallelism:** Data that are collected has to be stored and processing hence massive parallelism is required, which can be achieved by i) Processing the data over millions of servers, ii) Managing data over numerous devices, iii) Controlling and organizing new information model or infrastructure system like Map Reduce model which support distributed processing, yet new algorithms and methodologies are required to support parallelism.
11. **Needs Big Data Resource Management:** Traditionally used database like relational database are no longer and cannot be used to handle big data issues, due to scalability. To manage enormous amount of data non-relational data base like NO-SQL can be used to provide better storage, scalability and volume to maintain different formats of data.
12. **Need for using non-volatile memory:** Hard disk cannot be used to manage or handle huge data, in such cases advanced storage techniques for achieving high-performance in memory usage databases which uses key-value pair to access data has to be used.

IoT applications deals with connecting large number of devices, which will result in collection of enormous amount of which in turn has to be handled, managed and stored. Solution lies in using certain bigdata techniques hence, IoT and Bigdata are integrated together.

SOLUTIONS USING APPROACHES FOR BIG DATA CHALLENGES

1. **Heterogeneity:** Valuable information will not be obtained if the data collected are not in Heterogeneity format, because algorithms are capable of processing only homogeneous data or data in a specific format. Hence data has to be made into a single format to perform analytics in data. (Zicari et al., 2015). Map reduce techniques can be used to structure or format the data because it used key value pair to store the data in the memory (Lane et al., 2016).
2. **Inconsistency and Incompleteness of Data:** As data are collected form different sources and from different devices, there might be a chance to get incomplete and erroneous data. These issues has

to be handled and managed during analysis of data (Tole et al., 2013). Researches are still working on other challenges like effective representation of data, accessing it, and identify whether it is structured unstructured or semi structured data. Solution to remove inconsistency and noisy data is by applying certain Data pre-processing techniques like data cleaning, integration, transformation and data reduction (Keim et al., 2009).

3. **Scalability:** Scalability poses a major issue as the size of the data that is collected and stored increases day by day. Researchers are been done to identify the ways to handle scalability issue like handling the data by identifying the speed of the processor, but in some cases the volume of data expands rapidly than the processor speed (Ziczri et al.,2014). Basic traditional techniques and methodologies cannot be used to solve scalability problems especially in real time applications. Even hardware drives cannot be used as the amount of data collected will be very huge.To overcome this drives like Solid State Drives(SSD) and Pulse Code Modulation (PCM) can be used (Prakash et al., 2017). Grid computing can also be used to solve issues related to data and memory.
4. **Velocity of Data:** Data collected has to be processed very rapidly and the response has to be sent to the user quickly. Certain online learning approaches can be used to solve challenges in learning algorithms (Davidson et al.,2017).
5. **Timeliness:** It refers to the way the data collected from real time applications are filtered to manage the storage of the data (Monica et al., 2013).Using index structure techniques used in traffic management system can be utilized to handle the issue. If proper working model or methodologies are not used for analyzing the data, it will result in poor decision making process.
6. **Visualization:** Since huge amount of data are collected and stored, visualizing the data becomes a tedious task. Using existing methodologies leads to poor performance and response time. It is a must to adapt advanced techniques to over the issue (Guillermo et al., 2014). Communication between the data points should be managed so that the data can be aggregated and managed properly.
7. **Security:** Security platforms like Zscaler provides protection to IoT devices from security issues along with cloud based solutions. Zscaler allows to route through the traffic and prepare policy for the devices in such a way, it does not transfer the information to the unwanted or unnecessary servers. Data protection is a major issue related to security, if it is overcommed then organizations could analyze and monitor their own data (Prakash et al., 2017).

CONCLUSION

The idea of IoT allows even tiny devices like sensors to collect and transfer the information. This information will be helpful to the decision makers to take decisions in future by analyzing the huge amount of data that are gathered from various devices used in the application (Antonio et al., 2010). The heterogeneous data collected from various devices will lead to issues related to data management, like abstraction, classification, privacy and security (Martin et al., 2014). In addition to heterogeneous data, issues related to volume of data seems to be a challenge for IoT solution providers. Bigdata provides solutions for most of the challenges and provides an idea analyze data and discover related patterns and techniques to solve certain issues.(Abbasil et al., 2017) .

REFERENCES

Abbasi, M.A., Memon, Z.A., Syed, T.Q., Memon, J., & Alshbou, R. (2017). Addressing the Future Data Management Challenges in IoT: A Proposed Framework. *International Journal of Advanced Computer Science and Applications, 8*(5).

Acharjya, D.P., & Ahmed, K.P. (2016). A Survey on Big Data Analytics: Challenges, OpenResearch Issues and Tools. *International Journal of Advanced Computer Science and Applications, 7*(2).

Adrian. (2016). *Securing Hadoop: Technical Recommendations*. Academic Press.

Berlian, H. M., Sahputra, T. E. R., Ardi, B. J. W., Dzatmika, H. W., Besari, A. R. A., Sudibyo, A. W., & Sukaridhoto, S. (2016). Design and implementation of smart environment monitoring and analytics in real-time system framework based on internet of underwater things and big data. *International Electronics Symposium*, 403–408. 10.1109/ELECSYM.2016.7861040

Busold, C., Heuser, S., Sadeghi, A., & Asokan, N. (2015). Smart and Secure Cross-Device Apps for the Internet of Advanced Things. *International Conference on Financial Cryptography and Data Security*. 10.1007/978-3-662-47854-7_17

Che, D., Safran, M., & Peng, Z. (2013). From Big Data to Big Data Mining: Challenges, Issues, and Opportunities, Database Systems for Advanced Applications DASFAA Workshops. *Lecture Notes in Computer Science*, *7827*, 1–15. doi:10.1007/978-3-642-40270-8_1

Das, S. K., Mohanty, S., Barik, S., Nathrout, K., & Suman, H. (2017). Survey on Big Data and Its Challenges Related to IoT. *Proceedings of International Interdisciplinary Conference on Engineering Science & Management.*

Davidson & Plattner. (2017). *Ventures Big data Challenges and Opportunities*. Academic Press.

Gubbi, J., Buyya, R., Marusic, S., & Palaniswami, M. (2013). Internet of Things (IoT): A vision, architectural elements, and future directions. Future Generation Computer Systems, 29(7), 1645-1660.

Janakiraman. (2017). *Big Data Challenges*. Academic Press.

Kakhani, M.K., Kakhani, S., & Biradar, S.R. (2015). Research issues in bigdata analytics. *International Journal of Application or Innovation in Engineering & Management*, 228-232.

Kaushik, R. T., & Nahrsted, K. (2012). A data-centric cooling energy costs reduction approach for big data analytics cloud. *Proceedings of the International Conference on High Performance Computing, Networking, Storage and Analysis*. 10.1109/SC.2012.103

Keim, D. A., Mansmann, F., Schneidewind, J., & Ziegler, H. (2006). Challenges in visual data analysis. In *Tenth International Conference on Information Visualisation*. IEEE. 10.1109/IV.2006.31

Kundhavai, K. R., & Sridevi, S. (2016). IoT and Big Data - The Current and Future Technologies: A Review. *International Journal of Computer Science and Mobile Computing.*, *5*(1), 10–14.

Lafuente. (2014). *Big Data Security - Challenges & Solutions*. Academic Press.

Lee, C. K. M., Yeung, C. L., & Cheng, M. N. (2015). Research on IoT based Cyber Physical System for Industrial big data Analytics. *International Conference on Industrial Engineering and Engineering Management*, 1855–1859. 10.1109/IEEM.2015.7385969

Mantri, D. S., Prasad, N. R., & Prasad, R. (2016). Mobility and Heterogeneity Aware Cluster-Based Data Aggregation for Wireless Sensor Network. Wireless Personal Communications, 86(2), 975-993. doi:10.100711277-015-2965-2

Martin, H., Hermerschmidt, L., Kerpen, D., Häußling, H., Rumpe, B., & Wehrle, K. (2014). User-driven privacy enforcement for cloud-based services in the internet of things. *International Conference on Future Internet of Things and Cloud.*

Minch, R. P. (2015). Location privacy in the era of the internet of things and big data analytics. *48th Hawaii International Conference on System Sciences*, 1521–1530. 10.1109/HICSS.2015.185

Mishra, N., Lin, C., & Chang, H. (2015). A Cognitive Adopted Framework for IoT Big-Data Management and Knowledge Discovery Prospective. *International Journal of Distributed Sensor Networks, 2015*, 1–13. doi:10.1155/2015/718390

Monica, N., & Kumar, K.R. (n.d.). Survey on Big Data by Coordinating MapReduce to Integrate Variety of Data. *International Journal of Science and Research.*

Mukherjee, A., Paul, H. S., Dey, S., & Banerjee, A. (2014). Angels for distributed analytics in IoT. *IEEE World Forum on Internet of Things*, 565–570. 10.1109/WF-IoT.2014.6803230

Roman, R., Zhou, J., & Lopez, J. (2013). On the features and challenges of security and privacy in distributed internet of things. *Computer Networks*, *57*(10), 2266–2279. doi:10.1016/j.comnet.2012.12.018

Sicari, S., Rizzardi, A., Grieco, L. A., & Porisini, A. (2015). Security, privacy and trust in Internet of Things: The road ahead. *Computer Networks*, *76*, 146–164. doi:10.1016/j.comnet.2014.11.008

Tole, A. A. (2013). Big data challenges. *Database Syst.,* 31-40.

Valera, A. J., Zamora, A. M., & Skarmeta, A. F. G. (2010). An architecture based on internet of things to support mobility and security in medical environments. *7th IEEE Consumer Communications and Networking Conference*. 10.1109/CCNC.2010.5421661

Wadhwani. (2017). *Big Data Challenges and Solutions*. Technical Report.

Zicari, R.V. (2014). Big data: Challenges and opportunities. *Big Data Computing*, 104-128.

Chapter 16
Role of Big Data in Internet of Things Networks

Vijayalakshmi Saravanan
University of Waterloo, Canada

Fatima Hussain
Ryerson University, Canada

Naik Kshirasagar
University of Waterloo, Canada

ABSTRACT

With recent advancement in cyber-physical systems and technological revolutions, internet of things is the focus of research in industry as well as in academia. IoT is not only a research and technological revolution but in fact a revolution in our daily life. It is considered a new era of smart lifestyle and has a deep impact on everyday errands. Its applications include but are not limited to smart home, smart transportation, smart health, smart security, and smart surveillance. A large number of devices connected in all these application networks generates an enormous amount of data. This leads to problems in data storage, efficient data processing, and intelligent data analytics. In this chapter, the authors discuss the role of big data and related challenges in IoT networks and various data analytics platforms, used for the IoT domain. In addition to this, they present and discuss the architectural model of big data in IoT along with various future research challenges. Afterward, they discuss smart health and smart transportation as a case study to supplement the presented architectural model.

1. INTRODUCTION

The Internet-of-Things (IoT) concept traces its origins the back to late 90s and it referred to the interoperability of devices using RFID technology. With the explosion of cheap mobile devices with a wide array of sensors, IoT has transformed into a large-scale network of heterogeneous devices that are connected via wired or wireless internet. Today, a widely accepted definition of the modern IoT is "a network infrastructure comprised of interconnected "smart things" having self-healing and self-configuring

DOI: 10.4018/978-1-5225-7432-3.ch016

characteristics. These smart things refer to physical and virtual entities capable of sensing and gathering information, having smart interfaces with interoperability capability using standard communication technologies." (Xu, He and Li, 2014) & (van Kranenburg, 2007)).

This new revolution in terms of IoT has led to a generation of huge volumes of data contributed by billions of devices connected to the internet (Bloem et al., 2013; Tannahill & Jamshidi, 2014; Zikopoulos, Eaton, Deroos, Deutsch, & Lapis, 2012). Recent estimates suggest that several zettabytes (ZB) of data have been created and processed today, a quantity that vastly exceeds the data created and stored since the dawn of human civilization until 2003 (Chen, Mao and Liu, 2014). Naturally, such an explosion in generated data has mandated that Big Data storage, processing, and analytics technologies go hand-n-hand with the IoT, with Big Data tools today being an indispensable backbone for the operation of the IoT.

The creation of the new IoT has opened up new vistas in exploiting the power of information in ways never seen before. Efficient utilization of the massive volume of data generated by industrial sensors can help increase the efficiency of industrial manufacturing processes, while data from smart devices can enhance a wide variety of human experiences ranging from home environmental control to tailored social media content. Further, big data analytics can help governments and businesses make critical decisions and improve policy-making towards economic growth (Cebr, 2016).

The objective of this chapter is to present an overview of big data, its storage and processing which serve as key enablers for IoT applications. We discuss the concept of Big Data along with its importance in IoT, in section 2, followed by the architectural framework of the IoT in section 3. Section 4 covers state of the art techniques used in IoT applications. Afterward, we present two applications of IoT in intelligent transportation networks and healthcare services, as a case study in section 5. These case studies are used to illustrate the power of Big Data technologies coupled with the IoT framework. In section 6, we highlight challenges in the adaptation of Big Data in IoT, along with some future directions. We conclude the chapter in section 7.

2. IMPORTANCE OF BIG DATA INTERNET OF THINGS

This section provides a general overview of Big Data and its usability in the IoT domain. The notion of Big Data trails back to the realization of engines such as; Yahoo and Google and large-scale experiments performed by European Organization for Nuclear Research (CERN) supercollider (Arkady, Perera and Georgakopoulos, 2013). Today, with Cloud technologies, smartphones and massive social media networks, Big Data is a ubiquitous industry worth nearly 125 billion USD.

2.1. Big Data: The Definition

Big Data is usually characterized by five properties, referred to as the 5V's in Figure 1.

2.1.1 Volume

Typically, Big Data means massive volumes of data, usually in terabytes (TB), petabytes (PB), zettabytes (ZB) or more.

Figure 1. Characteristics of Big Data
(Dr. Asif Q. Gill 2012)

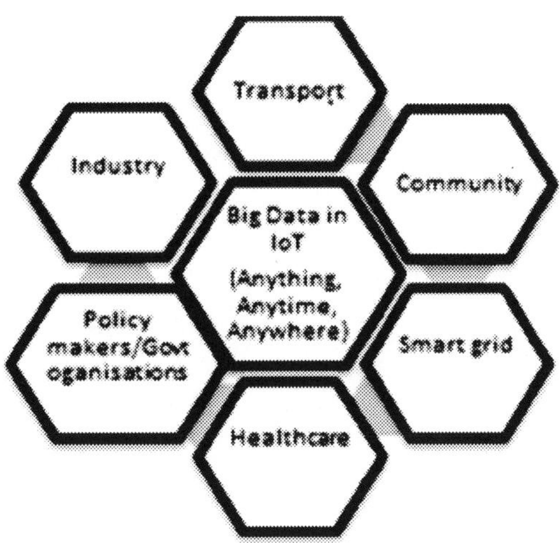

2.1.2. Variety

The data consists of a mixture of structured, unstructured and quasi-structured information, drawn from such vastly heterogeneous sources as RFID, web searches, social media, mobile sensors like GPS and accelerometers, high fidelity industrial sensors, video streaming etc.

2.1.3 Velocity

Big Data arrives at varying speeds ranging from milliseconds to days to years and has differing requirements on the speed with which it is to be processed.

2.1.5 Value

Some researchers consider value as a key characteristic of Big Data, with data being considered valuable if useful information (from a business or engineering perspective) can be extracted from large data sets where individual data points may not carry any value by themselves.

2.1.6 Veracity

It means accuracy and credibility of data. This becomes increasingly relevant when large numbers of users in the IoT may be reluctant to report truthful data due to privacy and security concerns.

2.2. IoT Landscape and Scope of Big Data

The explosive growth of the IoT landscape and the subsequent creation of large-scale cyber-physical-human networks has made Big Data tools critical to every IoT application. Data generated from devices were already big even before the arrival of IoT. Now, this data is projected to double every two years to reach an estimated 35 ZB (zettabytes) with more than 50 billion estimated devices by the year 2020. Figure 2 shows the exponential increase in the data generated from the IoT with the number of connected devices according to data from the McKinsey Global Institute. The factors driving more devices to join the IoT is clear: larger computing power (cloud computing) with lower cost, extensive wireless connectivity, and ease of low-power sensing.

Figure 3 shows the Gartner Hype Cycle for emerging technologies in 2014, revealing IoT to be among the most disruptive technologies in this decade and predicting the subsequent emergence of Big Data motivated by the extensive integration of IoT into everyday life. Today, big data is a disruptive technology and have the potential to create a potential for personal analytics and human-machine interaction that has never been encountered before. However, Big Data technologies must surmount several key barriers including standards, security and privacy, efficient storage and analysis and network infrastructure. In the following lines, we discuss the current state-of-the-art and associated challenges in processing, storage, and Big Data analytics, in the context of its role as a key enabler of IoT.

Big data architecture for IoT applications is important in the sense that it provides a reliable data-handling scheme, capable of being scaled and adapted by any type of infrastructure. Figure 4 depicts the three main high-level tasks that must be accomplished by the Big Data architecture.

- Data Collection

In the IoT paradigm, data is acquired from various resources such as the internet, social media, mobile sensors, RFID etc. as well as conventional database management systems like RDBMS. The volume of data acquired in this manner is in accordance with Moore's law (Forsth, 2012; Kurzweil & Grossman, 2005).

- Data Management

Several powerful Big Data technologies like MapReduce and NoSQL used to retrieve data effectively from heterogeneous sources and process it according to application needs

Figure 2. Availability of Data on Internet of Things
(Source: McKinsey Global Institute Analysis)

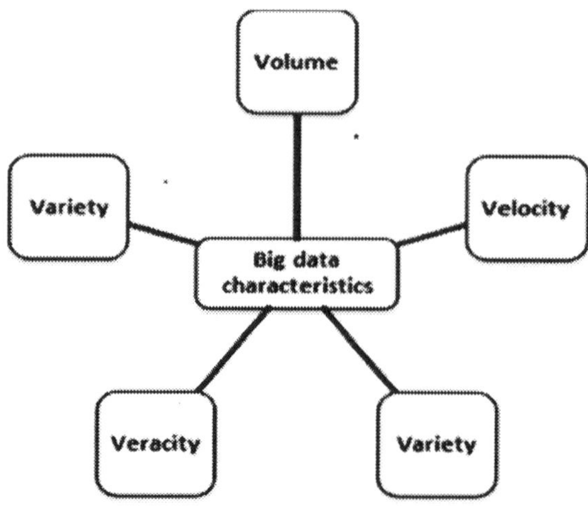

Figure 3.

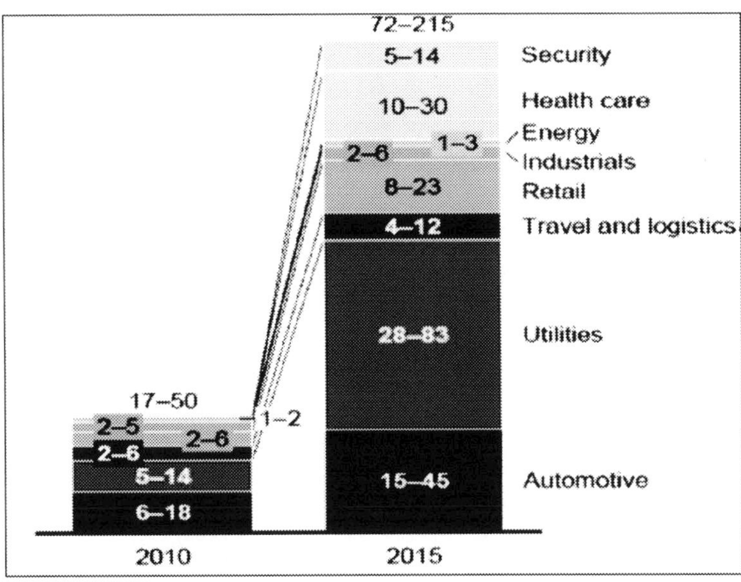

- Data Utilization

The processed data is mined using various learning techniques and is used to infer applicable information, which can be visualized and applied for prediction and analysis.

Figure 5 shows a sample of Big Data architecture for IoT (Figueiredo, 2015). In such typical architecture, data is collected from heterogeneous sources that may be unstructured is sent through streaming processed where it is processed, eventually becoming structured as it moves through the architecture. At this stage, the data is extracted for analytics, queries or visualization. Its complexity is characterized by various factors such as; available input and outputs and correlation among them, and the timescales involved (Suh, 2005; Xu, Wang, Bi, & Yu, 2014; Bi & Lang, 2007; Bi, Lang, Shen, & Wang, 2008; Bi & Zhang, 2011). Any Big Data architecture for IoT applications must possess the following characteristics (Figueiredo, 2015; Cecchinel et al., 2014).

3.1. Characteristics of Big Data in IoT Applications

3.1.1. Flexibility and Scalability

The architecture must be able to handle heterogeneous data from a variety of sources, as well as different data scales ranging from TB to ZB in terms of data volumes.

3.1.2. Reconfigurability

The architecture must, preferably, be remotely reconfigurable when deployed in on-site locations.

3.1.3. Interfacing

The architecture must support easy interfacing of devices both to retrieve data for analytics and visualization as well as for data collection. Heterogeneous devices such as smartphones, medical imagining devices, and implants, automotive sensors etc. must be an interface for IoT applications.

3.1.4. Storage

Efficient storage of data is critical for fast feature extraction and correlation studies to identify interrelated data. In the context of IoT, this is crucial to extract user preferences to provide value-added services such as product suggestions.

3.1.5. Batch Processing

This is essential to analyze large quantities of data quickly and efficiently.

3.1.6. Visualization

For some IoT applications, such as industrial process control, effective data visualization will provide operators with the ability to make better decisions in critical time-frames.

3.1.7. Reliability

A good architecture must be tolerant of human error, hardware failure, and data inaccuracies.

Figure 4. Big Data and IoT: High-Level Architecture
(Designed by the authors)

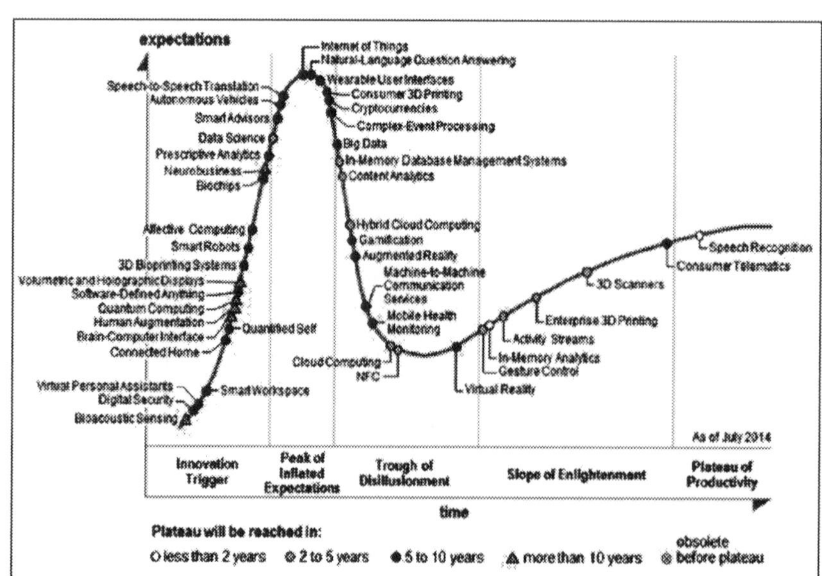

3.2. Task Models

The efficient implementation of Big Data architectures that can handle the rapidly growing volume of data also requires new task models that address the following challenges.

3.2.1. Task Parallelism

This refers to the breaking down of the non-sequential program segments into multiple tasks that are simultaneously executed on multiple cores. Due to the overheads associated with parallel programming languages, the complexity of parallel processing code increases. This calls for new architectural models and programming languages for task parallelism that reduce these overheads.

3.2.2. Data Parallelism

This refers to the simultaneous execution of a function on all elements of a dataset using multiple cores. With large and highly distributed datasets, the computational time for this operation increases due to the overhead associated with the need to distribute the code across many nodes for parallelized implementation. This calls for new ways to process data in parallel. The introduction of the Hadoop MapReduce programming model is one step in this direction.

To enable real-time IoT applications meeting the above architectural requirements, new big data techniques must be developed (Taylor, 2013). In the following sections, we will describe these techniques in more details

3.3. Architectural Challenges for Big Data in IoT

Though Big Data and associated tools/ technologies have been used for predictive analysis for many years (Earley, 2014), now it is facing many challenges because of new requirements of data storage and analytics of heterogeneous and massive volume of data generated from IoT devices. Advanced Big Data tools and techniques are being developed to sense and store data after being gathered from various IoT

Figure 5. Typical Big Data Architecture for IoT Applications
(Source: Figueiredo, 2015)

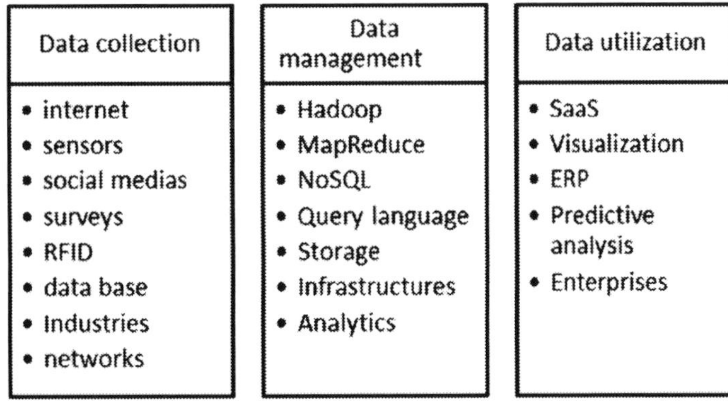

applications, adapting effectively to the dynamic nature of IoT enterprises. Many researchers have discussed the technical and architectural challenges associated with Big Data tools (Assuncao, Calheiros, Bianchi, Netto, and Buyya, 2014); most common challenges for various IoT applications are discussed in Hegeman et al. (2013). Bloem et al. (2013) discuss three main technical challenges - data scalability, data integration and ten core technologies to process data -. Besides the technical challenges presented by these authors, the integration of Big Data tools into IoT applications requires expertise in this domain. Currently, the lack of organization support is also a key challenge in this regard. In addition, lack of skill set and talent required for data analytics. (Forfas, 2014).

According to Moore's law, CPU performance gain doubles every 18 months. Nevertheless, the pace of growth of Big Data volumes has outpaced the processing speed, with the consequences that several architectures challenges lie ahead on the road to using Big Data effectively. The issue of systems being CPU intensive while being poor I/O intensive is a common challenge for both traditional and Big Data architectures. This motivates the need for massively and embarrassingly parallel paradigms. Due to the large volume of data, a variety of formats, representations, and models, I/O parallelism has become the key architecture challenge for Big Data. In recent years, distributed systems like the Hadoop and MapReduce have been widely adopted to address this challenge (Dean & Ghemawat, 2008). However, the use of Hadoop works with an assumption, that data does not share memory on a single machine. To overcome such challenges along with the rapidly growing volume of data, new task models that address both task and data parallelism must be developed.

4. TECHNIQUES AND TOOLS USED IN BIG DATA

A huge amount of data generated by IoT applications poses a critical challenge for high-performance computing industries to develop scalable and, parallelized solutions to process this data. The use of a wide array of techniques like machine learning, graph analysis, statistical analysis, and signal processing in conjunction with classical Big Data programming tools in present-day IoT applications has made it critical for programmers and software engineers to be well versed in a wide array of topics including domain-specific issues and scalable system programming. Scalable programming, distributed storage, parallelized programming, and multi-core execution have become especially relevant due to the need to analyze large volumes of heterogeneous data that go beyond available technologies.

4.1. Big Data Management Tools

In recent years, the following tools have been extensively used for big data processing, storage, and analytics.

4.1.1 MapReduce

Typical tools for MapReduce include Pig, Caffeine, Hadoop, Hive, S4, Kafka, MapR, Acunu, and Flume. Hadoop is the popular tool used nowadays. It supports Java and Python; the most widely used languages. PIG and PigLatin; being dataflow languages are specifically developed and used to simplify this MapReduce process.

4.1.2 Database Management

- **NoSQL:** MongoDB, CouchDB, Cassandra, Redis, BigTable, HBase, Hypertable, Voldemort, Riak, ZooKeeper
    - **HBase:** HBase is a column-oriented database built on HDFS and MapReduce jobs.
    - **BigTable:** It is a distributed, high performance, proprietary data storage system built on the Google file system (Chang et al., 2008).
- **Hive and HiveQL:** Is used to process ad-hoc queries for data in Hadoop. It supports HiveQL, which is like SQL but has comparatively less support than SQL.

4.1.3 Data Storage

HDFS (Hadoop distributed file system), S3 (Simple storage services)
Servers: EC2, Google App Engine, Elastic, Beanstalk, Heroku

4.1.4 Data Processing

R, Yahoo! Pipes, Mechanical Turk, Solr/Lucene, ElasticSearch, Datameer, BigSheets, Tinkerpop

We now examine two of the most popular Big Data processing frameworks, MapReduce and Hadoop, in detail.

4.2. MapReduce

It is a data processing computational framework applied to large datasets by employing distributed algorithms on clusters. This framework comprises user-defined Map and Reduce functions as well as a MapReduce library. Data is processed in parallel using map functions, whose output is sorted and processed by reducing functions. The MapReduce library parallelizes the data processing by breaking it down into smaller chunks that are processed using a master/slave implementation. Typically, the MapReduce framework is implemented in six steps as follows.

Step 1: Read data value from the Hadoop Distributed File Systems (HDFS).
Step 2: Split the task into small tasks.
Step 3: Input key/value pairs to Map function to generate intermediate key/value pairs.
Step 4: From the output of the Map function, identify and send all pairs with the same key to the Reduce function.
Step 5: Sort the input to the reduce function by key.
Step 6: Write the reduced output into the HDFS.

The slave tasks in this setup are processed parallel without communicating with one another. This framework, while allowing for efficient data parallelization, also handles load balancing, data distribution, and fault tolerance. Alternative MapReduce implementations have also been proposed by (Jiang et al. (2010); Chen et al. (2010); Mao et al. (2010b); Ranger et al. (2007b); Talbot et al. (2011) and Yoo et al. (2009)).

Several authors have explored optimization techniques for processing large numbers of datasets using multi-core processors. For example, two such optimization techniques on the Hadoop framework are proposed in Kumar et al. (2013). Several investigations regarding performance of multi-core processors has been done (Gough, Siddha, & Chen (2007); Saha et al. (2007); Boyd-Wickizer et.al. (2008); Zhu, Sreedhar, Hu, & Gao (2007)) and the performance bottlenecks that arise in systems using MapReduce libraries have also been explored (Mao, Morris, & Kaashoek, 2010a). A recent study showed that the Phoenix library results in a better performance than the PThreads used in multi-core processors (Ranger, Raghuraman, Penmetsa, Bradski, & Kozyrakis, 2007a). While some studies have pointed out the limitations of Hadoop implementations in dealing with data that has a high variety (J Dean et al. (2008) and D. Jiang (2014), hybrid architectures have been proposed (A. Abouzeid (2009); D. J. DeWitt (2013)) to overcome these drawbacks. The implementation of these architectures requires efficient processing techniques for structured and graph data.

4.3. Hadoop Model

The Hadoop model was developed to facilitate the parallel processing of large datasets on clusters. The Hadoop model can simultaneously run multiple tasks at a single node, allowing for an efficient multi-core implementation (Haggarty, Knottenbelt, & Bradley, 2009). Typically, a Hadoop model architecture comprises of a Hadoop Distributed File System (HDFS) for data storage coupled with a MapReduce framework for a large-scale data processing. Recently, a new Hadoop model as shown in Figure 6, known as the Hadoop NextGen-MapReduce model, comprising of the following components has been proposed.

4.3.1 Cluster

The cluster is the hardware component of this model, comprising of connected nodes (computers) that are partitioned into racks.

4.3.2 YARN

The YARN comprises three main components as shown in Figure 8, and provides the computational resources (such as processors and memory) that are required for the implementation of the Hadoop NextGen-MapReduce model.

- **Resource Manager:** Every cluster has one Resource Manager which allocates resources to all applications in the system. In other words, the Resource Manager acts as a Master node.
- **Node Manager:** Node Managers are slave nodes used as containers to run client application programs. There are several Node Managers in every cluster and can allocate various resources to the clusters. This allocation is performed on the available cores and the cluster's memory.
- **Client:** The client submits the application program to the Resource Manager to be processed.

4.3.3 HDFS

The HDFS is a distributed file storage system. The development of the HDFS was motivated by the issue of data locality. Locality refers to the scenario where the data to be processed is not located at the same node that processes it, leading to a decrease in parallel processing performance. The HDFS addressed this issue by allowing data to be processed at the same node in which it is stored, leading to increased processing speeds (White, 2009).

4.3.4 Storage

These are alternative storage options like the Simple Storage Service (S3) that may be used by certain applications.

4.3.5 MapReduce

The MapReduce implementation lies in this layer.

One drawback of the Hadoop model is that the Master Node may sometimes become unresponsive to file requests from the client nodes due to the increased number of Meta files in slave nodes, pertaining to additional tasks (Dong et al., 2012).

5. BIG DATA ANALYTICS: IoT APPLICATION CASE STUDIES

Due to advancements in the IoT and sensor technologies, Big Data analytics has become critical to process different data and make effective decisions based on the available information (Lee, Lapira, Bagheri, & Kao, 2013; King, Lyu, & Yang, 201; SAS, 2014). Big data analytics encompasses many analysis tools

Figure 6. Hadoop Architecture
(http://ercoppa.github.io/HadoopInternals/HadoopArchitectureOverview.html)

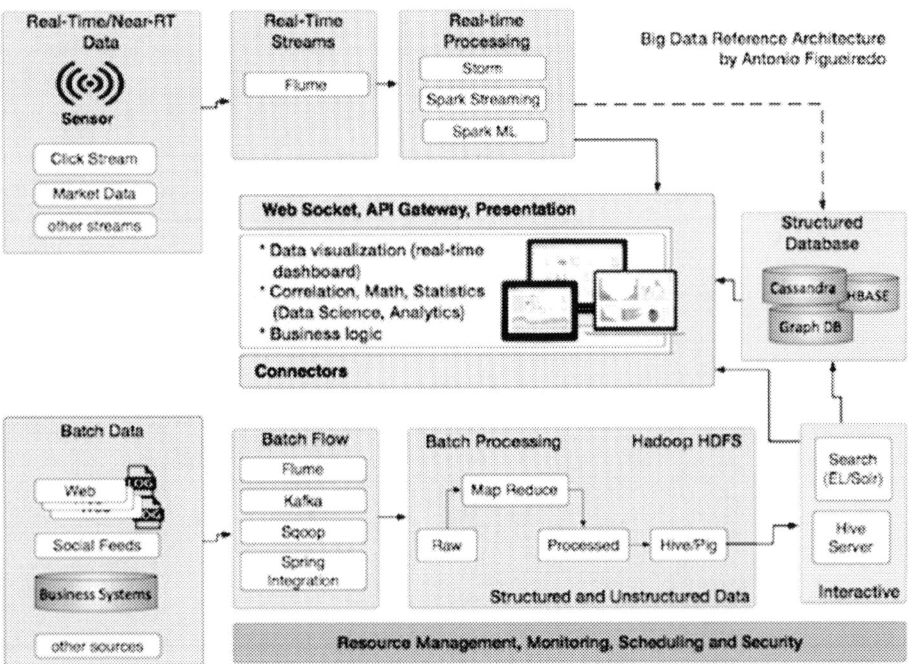

Figure 7. Hadoop NextGen-MapReduce Model (YARN)(http://ercoppa.github.io/HadoopInternals/HadoopArchitectureOverview.html)

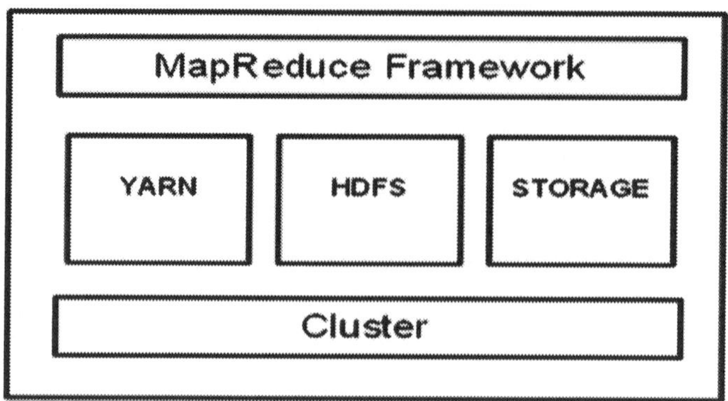

such as regression analysis, neural networks, cluster analysis and decision trees (Davis, 2014) and refers to analytical techniques and technologies that can handle extreme data models (Bloem et al., 2013). Typically, these techniques differ from classical data analytics techniques in that they combine tools like pattern recognition and machine learning with standard statistical tools. Rapid developments in big date analytics has made it currently possible to efficiently process large volumes of data (Barlow, 2013). This section discusses Big Data analytics in two IoT application domains - transportation networks and healthcare. Our aim is to illustrate how Big Data can help transform these specific domains. We also provide an overview of related problems and challenges. We do not attempt to compare different approaches. Rather, we seek to highlight the challenges of Big Data analytics in IoT using various sources from literature.

5.1. Smart Transportation System

Every year, traffic jams in the United States alone result in 7 billion wasted man hours and 3 billion gallons of wasted fuel, with an economic cost of over 160 billion USD (Lomax et al., 2015). Further, road crashes cause nearly 1.3 million fatalities and cost 518 billion USD annually (ASIRT, 2016). Increased information about road conditions like hazards and congestion provided to drivers real-time can lead to a more efficient use of the transportation network, minimizing traffic jams and crashes. Today, three main technological advances have contributed to the collection and dissemination of this information to drivers on the road. These technologies will form the cornerstone of future research in IoT-enabled Intelligent Transportation Systems (ITS).

5.1.1 Vehicles as Data Sources

Most vehicles are enabled with GPS systems and most drivers have smartphones, enabled with an array of sensors, connected to the internet. Therefore, drivers themselves have become sources of data that can be processed to extract useful information about road conditions. Several mobile applications like Waze have already successfully used this community-generated or crowdsourced data to provide vehicles with preferred routes and accurate estimates of travel time.

5.1.2 Vehicle-to-Vehicle Communication

The introduction of automated vehicles allows for direct Vehicle-to-Vehicle (V2V) communication of traffic conditions and vehicle data such as engine parameters over wireless networks. With this information, vehicles can jointly prevent or eliminate small-scale (microscopic) traffic jams and avoid collisions at a local level without need for external intervention from the traffic management centers. This frees up the resources of the traffic controllers to handle large-scale (macroscopic) problems like dynamically coordinating traffic lights, speed limits etc. to improve system efficiency at a large-scale level.

5.1.3 Vehicle-to-Infrastructure Communication

Traffic lights and other sensors on the road generate data regularly and communicate this data to traffic management centers. With Vehicle-to-Infrastructure (V2I) communication technology, this data can now be used to directly provide vehicles with useful information about their environment and provide early warning of accidents or other hazardous conditions. This information can then be exchanged among vehicles using V2V communication infrastructure to manage traffic at a microscopic level. Data communicated to a central traffic management center and combined with historical data and weather conditions to predict traffic jams and change traffic light sequences and road signs to reduce system-wide congestion.

The US Department of Transportation (Burt et al., 2014) predicts that volume of connected vehicle data in the United States will be of the order of 10 to 27 petabytes per second, if only Basic Safety Messages (BSM) are transmitted. This highlights the challenge for Big Data analytics in future transportation networks. The following are examples of the types of data will be collected and transmitted over IoT in future ITS.

- **Vehicle-Level:** GPS location, speed, acceleration, braking.
- **Infrastructure-Level:** Traffic light times, number of cars passing through in a time interval (traffic flow), dynamic speed limit settings, traffic density.
- **Ancillary Data:** Weather reports, road conditions, demographics, driver route choices, historical data.

Clearly, this data has high variety as well as volume. Therefore, efficient Big Data architectures must be developed to clean up bad data, eliminate redundant information and store the processed data efficiently for analytics. Several researchers have worked towards addressing this problem. For example, the TransDec (Transportation Decision-making) system was developed by the Integrated Media Systems Center (IMSC) at University of Southern California to efficiently store, analyze and visualize data from the Los Angeles Metropolitan Authority. Figure 8 shows the architecture of the TransDec system. In this architecture, data pertaining to road traffic (e.g., traffic density, traffic flow, road occupancy), public transportation (e.g., GPS locations, delay information), ramp meters and other events (e.g., collisions, casualties, ambulance arrival times) are acquired, aggregated and stored in the Microsoft Azure Cloud Platform (Jagadish et al., 2014). This data is then analyzed using several machine learning techniques to accurately predict traffic evolution patterns in various segments of the network.

5.2. Smart Transportation and Associated Challenges

With the introduction of new sources of data like automated vehicles and ancillary sensors, novel learning techniques that combine local vehicle-level data with system-level data like traffic density maps and road conditions to make accurate predictions about traffic patterns, travel times, likelihood of traffic jams etc. must be developed. The following are specific research directions for Big Data analytics in ITS.

5.2.1 Human-Level Applications and Tailored Services

With data like location and user behavioral patterns gathered from personal mobile devices, it is possible to match users with tailored services that foresee the user's needs at particular times of the day. New service providers can mine user data from social networks, smart home sensors and mobile devices to match users with carpooling or ride-sharing services. From the Big Data analytics perspective, this will require the development of learning algorithms that can derive useful information from multi-modal heterogeneous data that may not necessarily be linked to the user's transportation preferences, like weather data and home sensor data (Burt et al., 2014).

5.2.2 Network-Level Applications and Performance Optimization

While users will derive benefits like targeted transportation services from Big Data enabled ITS, traffic management centers can use this user generated data to improve network performance. In this domain, a key Big Data analytics challenge is in the development of accurate traffic prediction models from dynamic user data, road data and weather conditions. These models can then be used to design traffic light schedules, dynamic speed limits and other network-level controls to optimize network throughput. User route preference data also used to predict congested routes at a particular time and incentivize users to stay off the road at particular times or take routes other than their preferred one to minimize overall network travel time.

5.2.3 Security and Privacy

Some data like user GPS locations may be used by attackers to determine a user's identity (Jagadish et al., 2014). Therefore, data storage mechanisms that protect user privacy will be particularly relevant in ITS that are powered by crowdsourced data. The collection of large amounts of crowdsourced data also brings the challenge of identifying the veracity of this data, since users may report false data, especially on social networks, to protect their privacy. In this case, the large volume and redundancy of Big Data must be intelligently exploited to develop analytics algorithms that extract useful information by correcting for the errors associated with possibly inaccurate data.

The integration of Big Data analytics will transform ITS as it will contribute to billions of dollars being saved at the network-level and provide a more personalized and improved travel experience at the individual user-level.

5.3. Smart Health Care

In this section, we explore how Big Data and IoT-enabled technologies have drastically transformed healthcare applications to become more efficient. The availability of cheap and portable mobile sensors provides an opportunity for continuous monitoring of vital signs and other functions of the human body. With the next generation IoT technologies, information about a patient's health status will be available 24/7, opening up the potential for timely preventive as well as reactive care. Further, collection of patient data over longer periods of time can enhance diagnosis by providing the ability to study various trends that emerge in the data over time. In this section, we present an overview of IoT-enabled healthcare systems, personalized medicine and disease risk prediction.

Current health care systems use standalone desktops and laptops to capture, store and transfer patient data through an integrated healthcare infrastructure to primary care doctors, specialists and emergency responders. This data, usually referred to as an electronic health record, electronic medical record or personal health record/history (Häyrinen, K., et.al, 2008), usually comprises the medical history of the patient including test results, past ailments, medication provided etc. Today, with the ubiquity of smart-phones and other IoT devices combined with easy-to-use mobile applications, this data can further be expanded to reflect daily records of a patient's heart rate, stress levels, blood sugar, sleep activity, blood pressure and other vital signs. Further, a patient's dietary habits (intake of calories), exercise routine and other day-to-day activities can be incorporated to get a more complete picture of the patient's health (Swan, M., 2012).

In Feldman et al. (2012), it is predicted that data generated from healthcare applications will reach 25K petabytes in 2020. This large volume of data collected from various health care systems drives the big data challenges in this domain. Data generated from healthcare applications is typically very heterogeneous ranging from radiology records to daily heart rate trends and vastly differing arrival and processing time scales. While lab test result data is typically available every few months, data from personal patient monitors may arrive every hour or even every minute. Heterogeneity also arises in data storage, where data can be stored in spread sheet applications like Excel, databases and the Hadoop data storage system. Further, while traditional patient electronic health records are structure with tagged name, age and other fields, the vast majority of data available from personal monitoring devices is unstructured or semi-structured. Therefore, this data will first need to be converted to a structured form by a combination of machine learning and data mining techniques. The structured data can then be processed through healthcare software to analyze trends and allow doctors to take preventive action that reduce readmissions to hospitals (Figure 9).

In Islam et al. (2015), the analysis of this data is divided into single-condition and clustered condition analysis. In this framework, single-condition pertains to an individual disease or condition or parameter that is monitored. Examples of single-condition analysis include blood sugar or body temperature monitoring to ensure that these parameters are within desired limits. Clustered-condition deals with predicting trends across several diseases or conditions that are tied together. Preventive healthcare for conditions like heart attacks fall under this category. While single-condition analysis can be carried out locally, clustered-condition analysis requires the analysis of patterns in data collected over a considerable period. A variety of machine learning techniques need to be developed along with efficient parallelized implementations to accomplish this.

Figure 8. TransDec Architecture
Source: http://imsc.usc.edu/intelligent-transportation.html

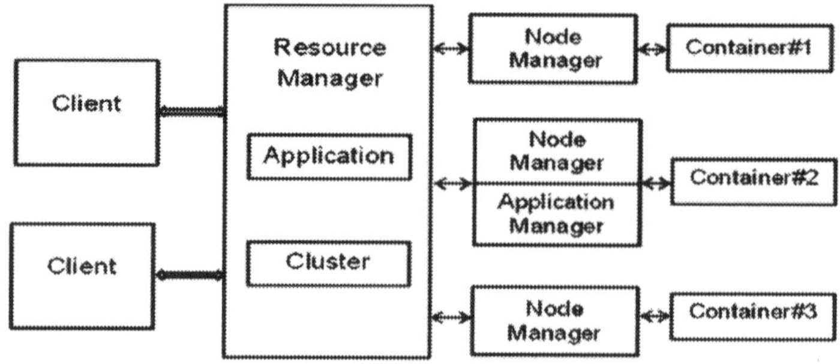

5.4 Smart Health and Associated Challenges

We posit that future research in IoT-enabled healthcare will involve the following key directions (Raghupathi et al., 2014).

5.4.1 Evidence-Based Patient-Oriented Personalized Medicine

Patient electronic health records, personal monitoring device data and clinical data will be used to provide personalized healthcare solutions, predict risk of certain health conditions and reduce readmission rates.

5.4.2 Large-Scale Analytics

Analysis of trends across data collected from many patients will be used to identify those at risk of particular conditions or in need of preventive care. These predictive analytics tools can be used for the prevention of chronic disease like diabetics.

5.4.3 Public Health

Rapid analysis of the spread of epidemics will enable faster response and prevent crises by driving accelerated drug discovery and vaccine development.

5.4.4 Genome Analysis

The advent of cost-effective genetic analysis tools will allow genetic data to augment patient profiles in making healthcare decisions.

5.4.5 Security and Privacy

While the benefits of Big Data in the healthcare domain are evident, attention must be paid to the information security and privacy issues that arise with storing and processing patient data. Further, regulatory issues like obtaining permission to use or share certain datasets require careful examination.

Figure 9. Big data & IoT in healthcare

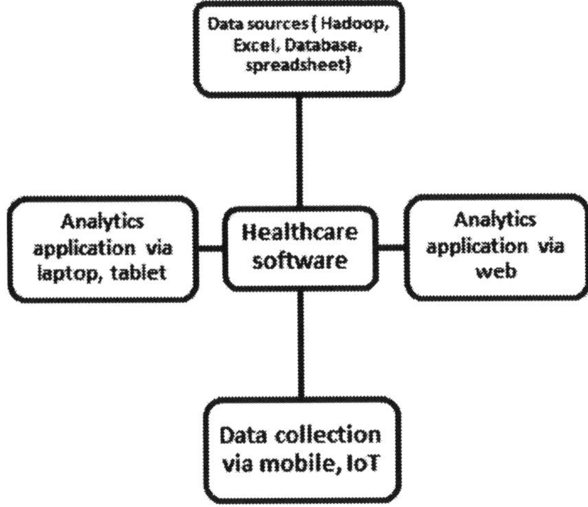

With the above-mentioned objectives, big data can revolutionize the healthcare system by supporting more genomics research, changing data into information, support healthcare providers and self-care, increasing general awareness of using integrated communication technologies and expanding the eco-system to provide efficient healthcare services.

6. CHALLENGES AND FUTURE DIRECTIONS

One area where further research is needed is analysis of a variety of social media platforms that could provide useful insight. Future research can also consider benchmarking social media data to other existing sources of information such as (server logs of web pages). Future researchers can also analyze how traffic statistics change on individual pages. This analysis can serve as a useful further measure of what the public is currently thinking. It can then be benchmarked against the results from social media data analysis.

7. CONCLUSION

IoT has revolutionized the future of infrastructure networks with the proliferation of many internet-enabled devices capable of being interconnected. However, the massive amount of heterogeneous data generated by the IoT has made the storage, processing and analysis of this data very challenging. Naturally, this calls for the inclusion of all those tools and techniques specific for Big Data analysis. This chapter presents a detailed overview of the architectural challenges for Big Data in IoT along with current tools for Big Data analytics, processing and storage. Big Data challenges in IoT are also illustrated via two emerging applications – smart transportation systems and smart healthcare. Although lots of research has been done in this domain but lots of more research and development is required in various categories such as; Big Data computer architecture, advanced storage techniques, I/O and data-driven techniques. Cloud computing, bio-inspired and quantum computing are few to mention.

ACKNOWLEDGMENT

First and foremost, the authors would like to thank "God Almighty". I, Vijayalakshmi Saravanan would like to express my special thanks to the "Schlumberger Foundation Faculty for the Future" (FFTF) who awarded me a Postdoctoral fellowship opportunity, which helped me in doing a lot of research, in the field of Computer Science and Engineering. During this chapter writing, I came to know many new things and innovative ideas in my research field. I am thankful to them. Last but not the least, my sincere thanks to my dear husband, Mohan Radhakrishnan and my beloved parents, G. Saravanan & S. Selvi who supported me a lot throughout the writing process that helped in the successful completion of this chapter. I also thank Sivaranjani S, University of Notre dame, US for the consistent support.

REFERENCES

Abouzeid, A., Bajda-Pawlikowski, K., Abadi, D., Silberschatz, A., & Rasin, A. (2009). HadoopDB: an architectural hybrid of MapReduce and DBMS technologies for analytical workloads. *Proceedings of the VLDB Endowment, 2*(1), 922-933. Retrieved on April 19, 2016 from http://www.vldb.org/pvldb/2/vldb09-861.pdf

Anuganti, V. (2012). Typical "big" data architecture. *Venu Anuganti Blog*. Retrieved on April 4, 2016 from http://venublog.com/2012/11/30/typical-big-data-architecture/

ASIRT. (n.d.). Retrieved from https://asirt.org/initiatives/informing-road-users/road-safety-facts/road-crash-statistics

Assuncao, M. D., Calheiros, R. N., Bianchi, S., Netto, M. A. S., & Buyya, R. (2014). Big Data and clouds: Trends and future directions. *Journal of Parallel and Distributed Computing*. doi:10.1016/j.jpdc.2014.08.003

Atzori, L., Iera, A., & Morabito, G. (2010). The internet of things: A survey. *Computer Networks, 54*(15), 2787–2805. doi:10.1016/j.comnet.2010.05.010

Barlow, M. (2013). *Real-time big data analytics: emerging architecture*. Sebastopol, CA: O'Reilly Media.

Bi, Z. M., & Lang, S. Y. T. (2007). A framework for CAD- and sensor-based robotic coating automation. *IEEE Transactions on Industrial Informatics, 3*(1), 84–91. doi:10.1109/TII.2007.891309

Bi, Z. M., Lang, S. Y. T., Shen, W. M., & Wang, L. (2008). Reconfigurable manufacturing systems: The state of the art. *International Journal of Production Research, 46*(4), 967–992. doi:10.1080/00207540600905646

Bi, Z. M., & Zhang, W. J. (2011). Modularity technology in manufacturing: Taxonomy and issues. *International Journal of Advanced Manufacturing Technology, 18*(5), 381–390. doi:10.1007001700170062

Bloem, J., van Doorn, M., Duivestein, S., van Manen, T., van Ommeren, E., & Sackdeva, S. (2013). *No more secrets with big data analytics*. Retrieved from http://vint.sogeti.com/wp-content/uploads/2013/11/Sogeti_NoMoreSecrets.pdf

Bloem, J., van Doorn, M., Duivestein, S., van Manen, T., van Ommeren, E., & Sackdeva, S. (2013). *No more secrets with big data analytics*. Retrieved from http://vint.sogeti.com/wp-content/uploads/ 2013/11/ Sogeti_NoMoreSecrets.pdf

Burt, M., Cuddy, M., & Razo, M. (2014). *Big Data's Implications for Transportation Operations: An Exploration.* US Department of Transportation White Paper. Retrieved from http://ntl.bts.gov/lib/55000/55000/55002/Big_Data_Implications_FHWA-JPO-14-157.pdf

Cebr. (2016). *The Value of Big Data and the Internet of Things to the UK Economy*. Cebr Report for SAS.

Cecchinel, C. (2014). An architecture to support the collection of big data in the internet of things. In *2014 IEEE World Congress on Services*. IEEE. 10.1109/SERVICES.2014.83

Chang, F., Dean, J., Ghemawat, S., Hsieh, W. C., Wallach, D. A., Burrows, M., & Gruber, R. E. (2008). BigTable: A distributed storage system for structured data. *ACM Trans. Comput. Syst., 26*(2), 4:1–4:26. Retrieved on April 4, 2016 from http://static.googleusercontent.com/media/research.google.com/en// archive/bigtable-osdi06.pdf

Chen, M., Mao, S., & Liu, Y. (2014). Big data: A survey. *Mobile Networks and Applications, 19*(2), 171–209. doi:10.100711036-013-0489-0

Chen, R., Chen, H., & Zang, B. (2010). Tiled-MapReduce: optimizing resource usages of data-parallel applications on multicore with tiling. In *Proceedings of the 19th International Conference on Parallel architectures and compilation techniques* (pp. 523-534). ACM. Retrieved on April 4, 2016 from http:// www.csee.ogi.edu/~zak/cs506-pslc/tiledmr.pdf

Da Xu, L., He, W., & Li, S. (2014). Internet of things in industries: A survey. *IEEE Transactions on Industrial Informatics, 10*(4), 2233–2243. doi:10.1109/TII.2014.2300753

Davenport, T. H., Barth, P., & Bean, R. (2012). How 'Big Data' is different. *MIT Sloan Management Review, 54*(1), 22–24. Retrieved from http://www.hbs.edu/faculty/Pages/item.aspx?num=43026

Davis, C. K. (2014). Beyond data and analytics. *Communications of the ACM, 57*(6), 39–41. doi:10.1145/2602326

Dean, J., & Ghemawat, S. (2008). MapReduce: simplified data processing on large clusters. *Communications of the ACM, 51*(1), 107-113. Retrieved on April 4, 2016 from http://static.googleusercontent.com/media/research.google.com/en//archive/mapreduce-osdi04.pdf

DeWitt, D. J., Halverson, A., Nehme, R., Shankar, S., Aguilar-Saborit, J., Avanes, A., & Gramling, J. (2013). Split query processing in polybase. In *Proceedings of the 2013 ACM SIGMOD International Conference on Management of Data* (pp. 1255-1266). ACM. Retrieved on April 4, 2016 from https:// pdfs.semanticscholar.org/3fd5/fdfd1a672a613de8a2b266676f577de9bcf1.pdf

Dong, B., Qiu, J., Zheng, Q., Zhong, X., Li, J., & Li, Y. (2010). A novel approach to improving the efficiency of storing and accessing small files on Hadoop: a case study by PowerPoint files. In *2010 IEEE International Conference on Services Computing* (pp. 65-72). IEEE. Retrieved on April 4, 2016 from http://ieeexplore.ieee.org/xpl/login.jsp?tp=&arnumber=5557216&url=http%3A%2F%2Fieeexpl ore.ieee.org%2Fxpls%2Fabs_all.jsp%3Farnumber%3D5557216

Dong, B., Zheng, Q., Tian, F., Chao, K.-M., Ma, R., & Anane, R. (2012). An optimized approach for storing and accessing small files on cloud storage. *Journal of Network and Computer Applications, 35*(6), 1847–1862. doi:10.1016/j.jnca.2012.07.009

Earley, S. (2014). *Big data and predictive analytics: What is new? IT Pro*. IEEE Computer Society.

Feldman, B., Martin, E. M., & Skotnes, T. (2012). Big Data in Healthcare Hype and Hope. *Dr. Bonnie, 360*.

Forfas. (2014). *Assessing the demand for big data and analytics skills 2013–2020*. Retrieved from http://www.forfas.ie/media/07052014- Assessing_the_Demand_for_Big_Data_and_Analytics_Skills- Publication.pdf

Figueiredo. (n.d.). *Keeping up with Big data*. Retrieved from https://www.linkedin.com/pulse/keeping-up-big-data-antonio-figueiredo

Forsyth Communications. (2012). *For big data analytics there's no such thing as too big the compelling economics and technology of big data computing*. Retrieved from http://www.cisco.com/c/dam/ en/us/solutions/data-center-virtualization/big_data_wp.pdf

Franks, B. (2012). *Taming the Big Data tidal wave: Finding opportunities in huge data streams with advanced analytics* (1st ed.). Wiley Publishing. doi:10.1002/9781119204275

Ghemawat, S., Gobioff, H., & Leung, S. T. (2003). The Google file system. *ACM SIGOPS Operating Systems Review, 37*(5), 29-43. Retrieved on April 4, 2016 from http://static.googleusercontent.com/media/research.google.com/en//archive/gfs-sosp2003.pdf

Gough, C., Siddha, S., & Chen, K. (2007). Kernel scalability—expanding the horizon beyond fine grain locks. *Proceedings of the Linux Symposium*, 153-165. Retrieved on April 4, 2016 from https://www.kernel.org/doc/ols/2007/ols2007v1-pages-153-166.pdf

Haggarty, O. J., Knottenbelt, W. J., & Bradley, J. T. (2009). Distributed response time analysis of GSPN models with MapReduce. *Simulation, 85*(8), 497–509. doi:10.1177/0037549709340785

Häyrinen, K., Saranto, K., & Nykänen, P. (2008). Definition, structure, content, use and impacts of electronic health records: A review of the research literature. *International Journal of Medical Informatics, 77*(5), 291–304. doi:10.1016/j.ijmedinf.2007.09.001 PMID:17951106

Hegeman, T., Ghit, B., Capota, M., HIdders, J., Epema, D., & Iosup, A. (2013). *The BTWorld use case for big data analytics: Description, MapReduce logical workflow, and empirical evaluation*. Retrieved from http://www.pds.ewi.tudelft.nl/~iosup/btworld-mapreduce-workflow13ieeebigdata.pdf

Islam, S. M. (2015). The internet of things for health care: A comprehensive survey. *IEEE Access: Practical Innovations, Open Solutions, 3*, 678–708. doi:10.1109/ACCESS.2015.2437951

Jagadish, H. V., Gehrke, J., Labrinidis, A., Papakonstantinou, Y., Patel, J. M., Ramakrishnan, R., & Shahabi, C. (2014). Big data and its technical challenges. *Communications of the ACM, 57*(7), 86–94. doi:10.1145/2611567

Jiang, D., Chen, G., Ooi, B. C., Tan, K. L., & Wu, S. (2014). epiC: an extensible and scalable system for processing big data. *Proceedings of the VLDB Endowment, 7*(7), 541-552. Retrieved on April 4, 2016 from http://www.nus.edu.sg/dpr/files/research_highlights/2015_01Jan_epiC.pdf

Jiang, W., Ravi, V. T., & Agrawal, G. (2010). A map-reduce system with an alternate API for multi-core environments. In *Proceedings of the 2010 10th IEEE/ACM International Conference on Cluster, Cloud and Grid Computing* (pp. 84-93). IEEE Computer Society. Retrieved on April 4, 2016 from http://web.cse.ohio-state.edu/~agrawal/allpapers/ccgrid10.pdf

King, I., Lyu, M. R., & Yang, H. (2013). *Online learning for big data analytics*. Retrieved from http://cci. drexel.edu/bigdata/bigdata2013/ieee.bigdata.tutorial.1.slides.pdf

Kumar, K. A., Gluck, J., Deshpande, A., & Lin, J. (2013). Hone: "scaling down" Hadoop on shared-memory systems. *Proc. VLDB Endow., 6*(12), 1354–1357. Retrieved on April 4, 2016 from http://www.vldb.org/pvldb/vol6/p1354-kumar.pdf

Kurzweil, R., & Grossman, T. (2005). *Fantastic voyage: Live long enough to live forever. Plume*. New York: Rodale Inc.

Lee, J., Lapira, E., Bagheri, B., & Kao, H. (2013). Recent advances and trends in predictive manufacturing systems in big data environment. *Manufacturing Letters, 1*(1), 38–41. doi:10.1016/j.mfglet.2013.09.005

Liu, X., Han, J., Zhong, Y., Han, C., & He, X. (2009). Implementing WebGIS on Hadoop: A case study of improving small file I/O performance on HDFS. In *IEEE International Conference on Cluster Computing and Workshops* (pp. 1-8). IEEE. Retrieved on April 4, 2016 from http://ieeexplore.ieee.org/stamp/stamp.jsp?tp=&arnumber=5289196

Lomax, T., Schrank, D., & Eisele, B. (2015). *Annual Urban Mobility Scorecard*. Retrieved from http://mobility.tamu.edu/ums/

Manyika, J., Chui, M., Brown, B., Bughin, J., Dobbs, R., Roxburgh, C., & Byers, A. H. (2011). *Big Data: The Next Frontier for Innovation, Competition and Productivity*. McKinsey Global Institute. Retrieved on April 4, 2016 from http://www.fujitsu.com/us/Images/03_Michael_Chui.pdf

Mao, Y., Morris, R., & Kaashoek, M. F. (2010). Optimizing MapReduce for multicore architectures. In *Computer Science and Artificial Intelligence Laboratory*. Massachusetts Institute of Technology, Tech. Rep. Retrieved on April 4, 2016 from http://citeseerx.ist.psu.edu/viewdoc/download;jsessionid=F539BF63A34B2D6D8F9B472F9A007144?doi=10.1.1.186.5309&rep=rep1&type=pdf

Raden, N. (2012). *Big data analytics architecture: Putting all your eggs in three baskets*. Hired Brains, Inc. Retrieved on April 4, 2016 from https://site.teradata.com/Microsite/raden-research-paper/landing/.ashx

Ranger, C., Raghuraman, R., Penmetsa, A., Bradski, G., & Kozyrakis, C. (2007). Evaluating MapReduce for multi-core and multiprocessor systems. In *IEEE 13th International Symposium on High Performance Computer Architecture HPCA 2007* (pp. 13-24). IEEE. Retrieved on April 4, 2016 from http://csl.stanford.edu/~christos/publications/2007.cmp_mapreduce.hpca.pdf

Saha, B., Adl-Tabatabai, A. R., Ghuloum, A., Rajagopalan, M., Hudson, R. L., Petersen, L., & Rohillah, A. (2007). Enabling scalability and performance in a large scale CMP environment. *ACM SIGOPS Operating Systems Review, 41*(3), 73-86. Retrieved on April 4, 2016 from http://leafpetersen.com/leaf/publications/eurosys2007/mcrt-eurosys.pdf

SAS. (2014). *Big data meets big data analytics: Three key technologies for extracting real-time business value from the big data that threatens to overwhelm traditional computing architectures*. Retrieved from http://www.sas.com/content/dam/SAS/en_us/doc/whitepaper1/big-data-meetsbig-data-analytics-105777.pdf

Schaller, R. R. (1997). Moore's law: Past, present, and future. *IEEE Spectrum, 34*(6), 52–59. doi:10.1109/6.591665

Schonlau, M. (2002). The clustergram: A graph for visualizing hierarchical and nonhierarchical cluster analyses. *Stata Journal, 2*(4), 391-402. Retrieved on April 4, 2016 from http://schonlau.net/publication/02stata_clustergram.pdf

Schultz, T. (2013). Turning healthcare challenges into big data opportunities: A use-case review across the pharmaceutical development lifecycle. *Bulletin of the American Society for Information Science and Technology*, *39*(5), 34–40. doi:10.1002/bult.2013.1720390508

Suh, N. P. (2005). *Complexity: theory and applications*. Oxford, UK: Oxford University Press.

Swan, M. (2012). Sensor mania! the internet of things, wearable computing, objective metrics, and the quantified self-2.0. *Journal of Sensor and Actuator Networks*, *1*(3), 217–253. doi:10.3390/jsan1030217

Talbot, J., Yoo, R. M., & Kozyrakis, C. (2011). Phoenix++: modular MapReduce for shared-memory systems. In *Proceedings of the Second International Workshop on MapReduce and its Applications* (pp. 9-16). ACM. Retrieved on April 4, 2016 from http://csl.stanford.edu/~christos/publications/2011.phoenixplus.mapreduce.pdf

Tannahill, B. K., & Jamshidi, M. (2014). Systems of systems and big data analytics – bridging the gap. *Computers & Electrical Engineering*, *40*(1), 2–15. doi:10.1016/j.compeleceng.2013.11.016

Taylor, J. (2013). *Delivering customer value faster with big data analytics*. Retrieved from http://www.fico.com/en/wp- content/secure_upload/DeliveringCustomerValueFasterWithBigDataAnalytics.pdf

Think Big Analytics. (2013). *Big data reference architecture*. Retrieved on April 4, 2016 from http://thinkbiganalytics.com/leading_big_data_technologies/big-data-reference-architecture/

van Kranenburg, R. (2007). *The Internet of Things: A Critique of Ambient Technology and the All-Seeing Network of RFID*. Amsterdam: Institute of Network Cultures.

Viégas, F. B., Wattenberg, M., & Dave, K. (2004). Studying cooperation and conflict between authors with history flow visualizations. In *Proceedings of the SIGCHI Conference on Human Factors in Computing Systems* (pp. 575-582). ACM. Retrieved on April 4, 2016 from http://alumni.media.mit.edu/~fviegas/papers/history_flow.pdf

Vijayalakshmi, S., Anpalagan, A., Kothari, D. P., Woungang, I., & Obaidat, M. S. (2014). An analytical study of resource division and its impact on power and performance of multi-core processors. *The Journal of Supercomputing*, *68*(3), 1265–1279. doi:10.100711227-014-1086-0

White, T. (2009). *Hadoop: The definitive guide* (1st ed.). O'Reilly Media, Inc. Retrieved on April 4, 2016 from http://ce.sysu.edu.cn/hope/UploadFiles/Education/2011/10/201110221516245419.pdf

Whitepaper. (2012). *Challenges and opportunities with BigData* (Tech. Rep.). Retrieved on April 4, 2016 from https://www.purdue.edu/discoverypark/cyber/assets/pdfs/BigDataWhitePaper.pdf

Xu, L. D., Wang, C., Bi, Z. M., & Yu, J. (2014). Object-oriented templates for automated assembly planning of complex products. *IEEE Transactions on Automation Science and Engineering*, *11*(2), 492–503. doi:10.1109/TASE.2012.2232652

Yoo, R. M., Romano, A., & Kozyrakis, C. (2009). Phoenix rebirth: Scalable MapReduce on a large-scale shared-memory system. In *Workload Characterization, 2009. IISWC 2009. IEEE International Symposium on* (pp. 198-207). IEEE. Retrieved on April 4, 2016 from http://csl.stanford.edu/~christos/publications/2009.scalable_phoenix.iiswc.pdf

Zaslavsky, A., Perera, C., & Georgakopoulos, D. (2013). *Sensing as a service and big data.* arXiv preprint arXiv:1301.0159

Zhu, W., Sreedhar, V. C., Hu, Z., & Gao, G. R. (2007). Synchronization state buffer: supporting efficient fine-grain synchronization on many-core architectures. *ACM SIGARCH Computer Architecture News*, *35*(2), 35-45. Retrieved on April 4, 2016 from http://www.capsl.udel.edu/pub/doc/papers/ISCA2007.pdf

Zikopoulos, P., Eaton, C., Deroos, D., Deutsch, T., & Lapis, G. (2012). *Understanding big data: Analytics for enterprise class Hadoop and streaming data*. New York: McGraw-Hill.

ADDITIONAL READING

Adamov, A. (2012). Distributed file system as a basis of data-intensive computing. *In Application of Information and Communication Technologies (AICT), 2012 6th International Conference on Application of Information and Communication Technologies (pp. 1-3).* IEEE. Retrieved on April 4, 2016 from http://ieeexplore.ieee.org/stamp/stamp.jsp?tp=&arnumber=6398484

Assuncao, M. D., Calheiros, R. N., Bianchi, S., Netto, M. A., & Buyya, R. (2013). Big Data computing and clouds: challenges, solutions, and future directions. *arXiv preprint arXiv:1312.4722*. Retrieved on April 4, 2016 from http://arxiv.org/pdf/1312.4722.pdf

Assunção, M. D., Calheiros, R. N., Bianchi, S., Netto, M. A., & Buyya, R. (2015). Big Data computing and clouds: Trends and future directions. *Journal of Parallel and Distributed Computing*, *79*, 3–15. doi:10.1016/j.jpdc.2014.08.003

Bahga, A., & Madisetti, V. K. (2012). Analyzing massive machine maintenance data in a computing cloud. *IEEE Transactions on Parallel and Distributed Systems*, *23*(10), 1831–1843. doi:10.1109/TPDS.2011.306

Bahga, A., & Madisetti, V. K. (2013). Performance evaluation approach for multi-tier cloud applications. *Journal of Software Engineering and Applications*, *6*(02), 74–83. doi:10.4236/jsea.2013.62012

Barbarossa, S., & Scutari, G. (2007). Bio-inspired sensor network design. *IEEE Signal Processing Magazine*, *24*(3), 26–35. doi:10.1109/MSP.2007.361599

Bekkerman, R., Bilenko, M., & Langford, J. (Eds.). (2011). *Scaling up machine learning: Parallel and distributed approaches.* Missing city, state: Cambridge University Press. Retrieved on April 4, 2016 from http://hunch.net/~large_scale_survey/SUML.pdf

Bertone, P., & Gerstein, M. (2001). Integrative data mining: the new direction in bioinformatics. *Engineering in Medicine and Biology Magazine, IEEE,20(4), 33-40.* Retrieved on April 4, 2016 from http://ieeexplore.ieee.org/stamp/stamp.jsp?arnumber=940042

Bryant, R. E. (2007). *Data-intensive supercomputing: The case for DISC.* Retrieved on April 4, 2016 from https://www.cs.cmu.edu/~bryant/pubdir/cmu-cs-07-128.pdf

Bryant, R. E. (2011). Data-intensive scalable computing for scientific applications. *Computing in Science & Engineering*, *13*(6), 25–33. doi:10.1109/MCSE.2011.73

Byungik Ahn, J. (2012). Neuron machine: Parallel and pipelined digital neurocomputing architecture. *In Computational Intelligence and Cybernetics (CyberneticsCom), 2012 IEEE International Conference on Computational Intelligence and Cybernetics (pp. 143-147).* IEEE. Retrieved on April 4, 2016 from http://ieeexplore.ieee.org/stamp/stamp.jsp?arnumber=6381635

Chang, F., Dean, J., Ghemawat, S., Hsieh, W. C., Wallach, D. A., Burrows, M., & Gruber, R. E. (2008). BigTable: A distributed storage system for structured data. *ACM Transactions on Computer Systems*, *26*(2), 4. doi:10.1145/1365815.1365816

Chen, C. P., & Zhang, C. Y. (2014). Data-intensive applications, challenges, techniques and technologies: A survey on Big Data. *Information Sciences*, *275*, 314–347. doi:10.1016/j.ins.2014.01.015

Chen, M., Mao, S., & Liu, Y. (2014). Big data: A survey. *Mobile Networks and Applications*, *19*(2), 171–209. doi:10.100711036-013-0489-0

Dean, J., & Ghemawat, S. (2008). MapReduce: Simplified data processing on large clusters. *Communications of the ACM*, *51*(1), 107–113. doi:10.1145/1327452.1327492

Del Río, S., López, V., Benítez, J. M., & Herrera, F. (2014). On the use of MapReduce for imbalanced big data using random forest. *Information Sciences*, *285*, 112–137. doi:10.1016/j.ins.2014.03.043

Di Ciaccio, A., Coli, M., & Ibanez, J. M. A. (Eds.). (2012). *Advanced statistical methods for the analysis of large data-sets.* Missing city, state: Springer Science & Business Media Retrieved on April 4, 2016 from http://www.springer.com/us/book/9783642210365

Forbes, N. (2000). Biologically inspired computing. *Computing in Science & Engineering*, *2*(6), 83–87. doi:10.1109/5992.881711

Fujimoto, Y., Fukuda, N., & Akabane, T. (1992). Massively parallel architectures for large scale neural network simulations. *IEEE Transactions on Neural Networks*, *3*(6), 876–888. doi:10.1109/72.165590 PMID:18276485

Garber, L. (2012). Using in-memory analytics to quickly crunch big data. *Computer*, *45*(10), 16–18. doi:10.1109/MC.2012.358

García, A. O., Bourov, S., Hammad, A., Hartmann, V., Jejkal, T., Otte, J. C., . . . Stotzka, R. (2011). Data-intensive analysis for scientific experiments at the large scale data facility. *In Large Data Analysis and Visualization (LDAV), 2011 IEEE Symposium on Large Data Analysis and Visualization (pp. 125-126).* IEEE. Retrieved on April 4, 2016 from http://ieeexplore.ieee.org/xpl/login.jsp?tp=&arnumber=6092331&url=http%3A%2F%2Fieeexplore.ieee.org%2Fxpls%2Fabs_all.jsp%3Farnumber%3D6092331

Ghemawat, S., Gobioff, H., & Leung, S. T. (2003). The Google file system. *In ACM SIGOPS operating systems review (Vol. 37, No. 5, pp. 29-43).* ACM. Retrieved on April 4, 2016 from http://static.googleusercontent.com/media/research.google.com/en//archive/gfs-sosp2003.pdf

Gillick, D., Faria, A., & DeNero, J. (2006). *MapReduce: Distributed computing for machine learning.* Berkley, Volume 18. Retrieved on April 4, 2016 from https://www.researchgate.net/profile/Dan_Gillick/publication/237563704_MapReduce_Distributed_Computing_for_Machine_Learning/links/551c00630cf20d5fbde24350.pdf

Gokhale, M., Cohen, J., Yoo, A., Miller, W. M., Jacob, A., Ulmer, C., & Pearce, R. (2008). Hardware technologies for high-performance data-intensive computing. *Computer*, *41*(4), 60–68. doi:10.1109/MC.2008.125

Gorton, I., Greenfield, P., Szalay, A., & Williams, R. (2008). Data-intensive computing in the 21st century. *Computer*, *41*(4), 30–32. doi:10.1109/MC.2008.122

Hashem, I. A. T., Yaqoob, I., Anuar, N. B., Mokhtar, S., Gani, A., & Khan, S. U. (2015). The rise of "big data" on cloud computing: Review and open research issues. *Information Systems, 47, 98-115.* Elsevier. Retrieved on April 4, 2016 from http://www.sciencedirect.com/science/article/pii/S0306437914001288

Jacobs, A. (2009). The pathologies of big data. *Communications of the ACM*, *52*(8), 36–44. doi:10.1145/1536616.1536632

Jagadish, H. V., Gehrke, J., Labrinidis, A., Papakonstantinou, Y., Patel, J. M., Ramakrishnan, R., & Shahabi, C. (2014). Big data and its technical challenges. *Communications of the ACM*, *57*(7), 86–94. doi:10.1145/2611567

Jagadish, H. V., Gehrke, J., Labrinidis, A., Papakonstantinou, Y., Patel, J. M., Ramakrishnan, R., & Shahabi, C. (2014). Big data and its technical challenges. *Communications of the ACM*, *57*(7), 86–94. doi:10.1145/2611567

Jiang, D., Ooi, B. C., Shi, L., & Wu, S. (2010). The performance of MapReduce: An in-depth study. *Proceedings of the VLDB Endowment, 3(1-2), 472-483.* VLDB Endowment. Retrieved on April 4, 2016 from http://www.vldb.org/pvldb/vldb2010/papers/E03.pdf

Jiang, D., Tung, A. K., & Chen, G. (2011). Map-join-reduce: Towards scalable and efficient data analysis on large clusters. *IEEE Transactions on Knowledge and Data Engineering*, *23*(9), 1299–1311. doi:10.1109/TKDE.2010.248

Jordan, J. M., & Lin, D. K. (2014). Statistics for big data: Are statisticians ready for big data? *Journal of the Chinese Statistical Association*, *52*(1), 133–149.

Kambatla, K., Kollias, G., Kumar, V., & Grama, A. (2014). Trends in big data analytics. *Journal of Parallel and Distributed Computing*, *74*(7), 2561–2573. doi:10.1016/j.jpdc.2014.01.003

Kasavajhala, V. (2011). Solid state drive vs. hard disk drive price and performance study. Proc. Dell Tech. White Paper, 8-9. Retrieved on April 4, 2016 from http://www.dell.com/downloads/global/products/pvaul/en/ssd_vs_hdd_price_and_performance_study.pdf

Kim, W. (2009). Parallel clustering algorithms: survey. CSC 8530 Parallel Algorithms, Spring 2009,Georgia State University, Atlanta, GA. Retrieved on April 4, 2016 from http://grid.cs.gsu.edu/~wkim/index_files/SurveyParallelClustering.html

Klemens, B. (Ed.). (2008). *Modeling with data: tools and techniques for scientific computing*. Missing city,state: Princeton University Press. Retrieved on April 4, 2016 from http://press.princeton.edu/titles/8706.html

Konwinski, A. (2009). Improving mapreduce performance in heterogeneous environments. Technical Report of EECS Department, University of California, Berkeley, no. UCB/EECS-2009-183. Retrieved on April 4, 2016 from http://digitalassets.lib.berkeley.edu/techreports/ucb/text/EECS-2009-183.pdf

Kouzes, R. T., Anderson, G. A., Elbert, S. T., Gorton, I., & Gracio, D. K. (2009). The changing paradigm of data-intensive computing. *Computer*, *42*(1), 26–34. doi:10.1109/MC.2009.26

Kraft, S., Casale, G., Jula, A., Kilpatrick, P., & Greer, D. (2012). Wiq: work-intensive query scheduling for in-memory database systems. *In 2012 IEEE 5th International Conference on Cloud Computing (CLOUD) (pp. 33-40). IEEE.* Retrieved on April 4, 2016 from http://ieeexplore.ieee.org/xpl/login.jsp?tp=&arnumber=6253486&url=http%3A%2F%2Fieeexplore.ieee.org%2Fxpls%2Fabs_all.jsp%3Farnumber%3D6253486

Landset, S., Khoshgoftaar, T. M., Richter, A. N., & Hasanin, T. (2015). A survey of open source tools for machine learning with big data in the Hadoop ecosystem. *Journal of Big Data*, *2*(1), 1–36. doi:10.118640537-015-0032-1

LaValle, S., Lesser, E., Shockley, R., Hopkins, M. S., & Kruschwitz, N. (2011). Big data, analytics and the path from insights to value. *MIT Sloan Management Review*, *52*(2), 21.

Liu, C., Yang, C., Zhang, X., & Chen, J. (2015). External integrity verification for outsourced big data in cloud and IoT: A big picture. *Future Generation Computer Systems*, *49*, 58–67. doi:10.1016/j.future.2014.08.007

Loughran, S., Calero, J. M. A., Farrell, A., Kirschnick, J., & Guijarro, J. (2012). Dynamic cloud deployment of a MapReduce architecture. *IEEE Internet Computing*, *16*(6), 40–50. doi:10.1109/MIC.2011.163

Lynch, C. (2008). Big data: How do your data grow? *Nature*, *455*(7209), 28–29. doi:10.1038/455028a PMID:18769419

Mackey, G., Sehrish, S., Bent, J., Lopez, J., Habib, S., & Wang, J. (2008). Introducing map-reduce to high end computing. *In Petascale Data Storage Workshop, 2008. PDSW'08. 3Rd (pp. 1-6).* IEEE. Retrieved on April 4, 2016 from http://ieeexplore.ieee.org/xpl/login.jsp?tp=&arnumber=4811889&url=http%3A%2F%2Fieeexplore.ieee.org%2Fxpls%2Fabs_all.jsp%3Farnumber%3D4811889

McAfee, A., Brynjolfsson, E., Davenport, T. H., Patil, D. J., & Barton, D. (2012). Big data. The management revolution. *Harvard Business Review*, *90*(10), 61–67. PMID:23074865

Nielsen, M. (2009). The Fourth Paradigm: Data-Intensive Scientific Discovery edited by Tony Hey, Stewart Tansley & Kristin Tolle. *Nature-London, 462(7274), 722-722.* Retrieved on April 4, 2016 from http://research.microsoft.com/en-us/collaboration/fourthparadigm/4th_paradigm_book_complete_lr.pdf

Pébay, P., Thompson, D., Bennett, J., & Mascarenhas, A. (2011). Design and performance of a scalable, parallel statistics toolkit. *In Parallel and Distributed Processing Workshops and Ph.D. Forum (IPDPSW), 2011 IEEE International Symposium on (pp. 1475-1484).* IEEE. Retrieved on April 4, 2016 from http://ieeexplore.ieee.org/xpl/login.jsp?tp=&arnumber=6009003&url=http%3A%2F%2Fieeexplore.ieee.org%2Fxpls%2Fabs_all.jsp%3Farnumber%3D6009003

Savitz, E. (2012). Gartner: 10 Critical Tech Trends for the Next Five Years. Retrieved on April 4, 2016 from http://www.forbes.com/sites/ericsavitz/2012/10/22/gartner-10-critical-tech-trends-for-the-next-five-years/#39e9ca1f4c6f

Shah, A. H. S., & Capellá, J. (2012). Good Data Won't Guarantee Good Decisions. *Harvard Business Review, The Magazine.* Retrieved on April 4, 2016 from http://hbr.org/2012/04/good-data-wont-guarantee-good-decisions/ar/1

Shvachko, K., Kuang, H., Radia, S., & Chansler, R. (2010). The Hadoop distributed file system. *In 2010 IEEE 26th Symposium on Mass Storage Systems and Technologies (MSST) (pp. 1-10)* Incline Village, NV. IEEE. Retrieved on April 4, 2016 from http://pages.cs.wisc.edu/~akella/CS838/F15/838-CloudPapers/hdfs.pdf

Szalay, A. (2011). Extreme data-intensive scientific computing. *Computing in Science & Engineering*, *13*(6), 34–41. doi:10.1109/MCSE.2011.74

Thusoo, A., Sarma, J. S., Jain, N., Shao, Z., Chakka, P., Anthony, S., & Murthy, R. (2009). Hive: A warehousing solution over a map-reduce framework. *Proceedings of the VLDB Endowment International Conference on Very Large Data Bases*, *2*(2), 1626–1629. doi:10.14778/1687553.1687609

Wu, X., Zhu, X., Wu, G. Q., & Ding, W. (2014). Data mining with big data. *IEEE Transactions on Knowledge and Data Engineering*, *26*(1), 97–107. doi:10.1109/TKDE.2013.109

Chapter 17
Role of Communication Technologies for Smart Applications in IoT

Garima Singh
Delhi Technological University, India

Gurjit Kaur
Delhi Technological University, India

ABSTRACT

New technologies like ICTs (information and communications technologies) are recognized as key players in building smart applications for IoT. The use of sensors and actuators can efficiently control the whole communication system and will provide application-based solutions for smart applications. ICT provides industry-leading cellular machine-to-machine (M2M) technologies including industrial-grade embedded modules with cloud platforms, long life spans, expert application development assistance, and more. ICT M2M connectivity helps utilities to lower down the operating costs by eliminating the need to deploy and maintain communications infrastructure separately.

INTERNET OF THINGS

Internet of Things (IoT) has emerged as the most promising technology of 5G communications. This 5G technology looks forward to interconnect trillions of devices around the sphere, IoT is going to play an important role in implementation of numerous applications like smart cities, intelligent transportation services, e-health, smart grids, and many others. All these applications of IoT provide improved quality of experience in everyday life activities. In IoT each and every device need to be connected to its utility gateway directly or indirectly to develop a successful IoT operation era. Consequently, this can be possible if devices have smart sensors equipped on them that will collect the real time data and will forward that to their network operation center for further processing.

DOI: 10.4018/978-1-5225-7432-3.ch017

Figure 1. Internet of Things

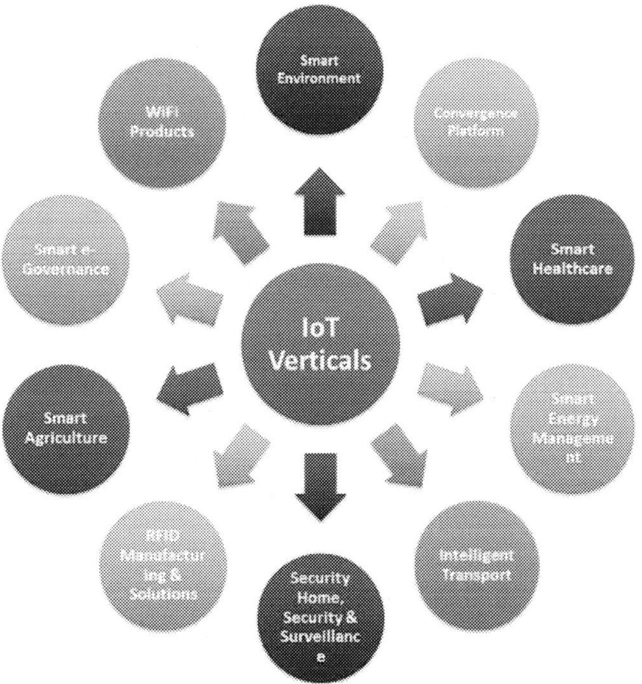

Requirement of IoT

IoT uses communication technologies to develop a flawless computing for everywhere. For this, we need to improve energy and communication technologies as they are the main requirements for IoT to work. To successfully operate communications in IoT network has to face many challenges for its successful operation. Many types of communication technologies are developed like cooperative communications, used for large network gains. However, this chapter focuses mainly on how each and every layer of IoT layered architecture will communicate.

Communication in IoT

Now, new smart antennas like adaptive antennas, receptive directional antennas, fractal antennas and plasma antennas are used for IoT communication. These antennas are made up of some new material and can be fixed in the objects. These new smart antennas support new advanced communications systems on chip. Transmission rates, Modulation schemes and transmission speed are main problems to be undertaken. To ensure the efficient mobility of billions of smart things new advanced communication paradigm need to be defined.

- **Application Layer:** This layer is first layer of architecture and includes the IoT applications. It is mainly responsible various applications delivery to different users in IoT.
- **Application Support and Management Layer:** Authorization is main function of this layer and also deals with the security, control and management of different IoT applications.

Figure 2. Major components of IoT

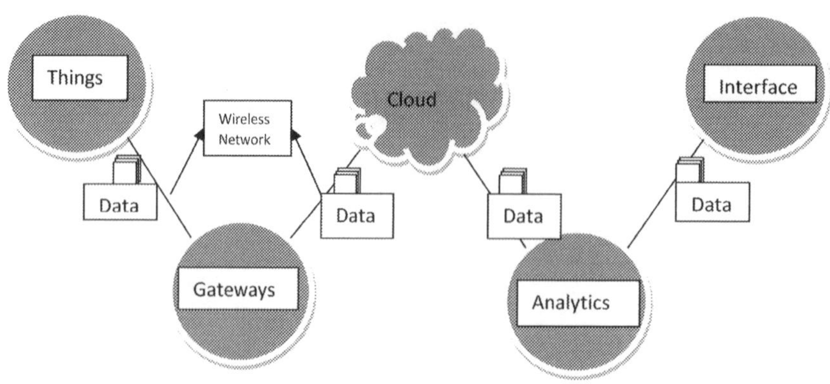

Figure 3. Cellular connectivity for the IoT

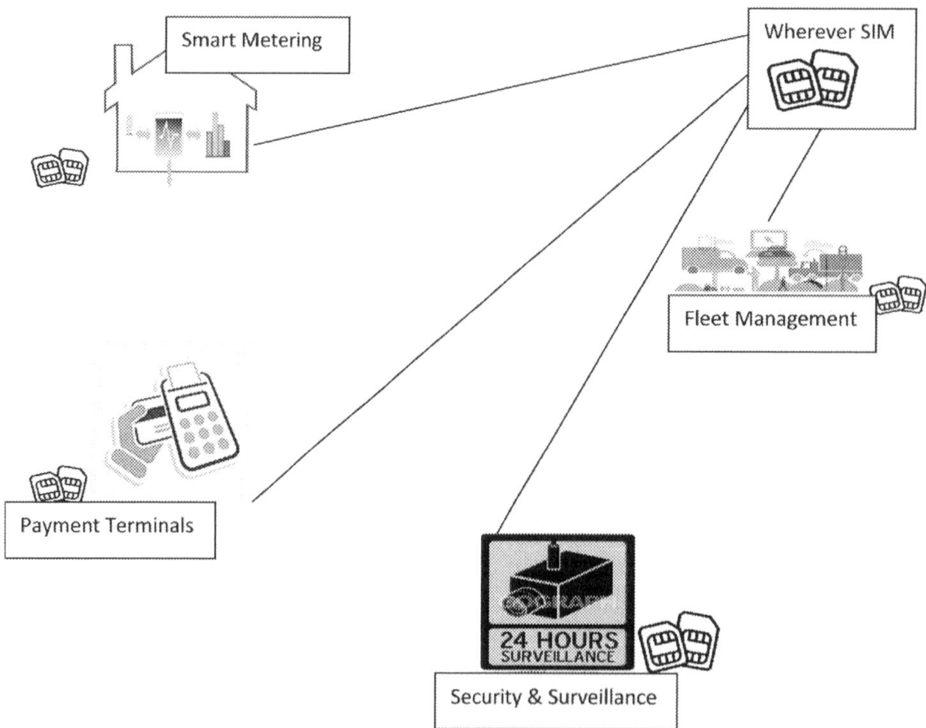

- **Services Layer:** This layer takes all the decisions related to the storage, monitoring, organization and visualization about the received information.
- **Communication Layer:** Communication between the different IoT devices and nodes is handled by this layer. Whenever required this layer also supports cross platform communication. Decisions regarding the quality of service and energy consumed in communication are made in this layer.
- **Network Layer:** This layer handles various networking protocols and access technologies to provide services to the wide range IoT applications. Networks on this layer can be private, public or

hybrid models which are built to support the communication requirements for latency, bandwidth or security.

- **Hardware Layer:** To gather the real time information in smart IoT applications sensors and other hardware like RFID tags and readers and embedded systems and others are required. Which is need to physically placed on the area from where information is required. This all is done on this layer. Many of these hardware elements provide identification, information collection (e.g. sensors), information storage (e.g. RFID tags), and information processing (e.g. embedded edge processors).
- **Environment Layer:** This layer includes places and objects needed to be detected and observed. These objects can be anything humans, cars, building and environmental factors also like humidity, temperature, etc.

Detailed seven layer communication scenario of layers of IoT is shown in Figure 1. The layer in single direction mainly but they can interact in both direction also in some cases. The layered communication process starts in manner that firstly application layer will ask for the identity of the authorized person to use IoT based smart application. If provide identity to the application layer is right and registered in the IoT database in the services layer, then only application will be open and one can get the required information. Next comes to the environment layer which is used to track the objects and can observe the places also which need to be observed. Environmental layer can track both static and movable objects like vehicles. The objects like buildings observed by environmental layer can have moving objects also like people walking inside the buildings. Hardware component like tracking devices, sensors, RFID readers and tags are placed in next hardware layer. These hardware components are used to transport live information about the places or object which is tracked. This tracked information is passed to the network layer. The network layer have multiple networks and these network has various technologies and access protocols like Zigbee, Wi-Fi, Z wave, Bluetooth and others.

Z Wave

Z-Wave protocol architecture is developed by ZenSys and promoted by the Z-Wave Alliance. Like Zigbee it is also low power consuming protocol. This is used mostly in light commercial environment and automation. Its communication protocol is open. The Z-wave is mainly used for reliable transfer of information from a control unit to one or more nodes in the IoT network. It has two types of devices, First is poll Controllers which send commands to the slaves, the second one is, which reply to the controller for the execution of the commands (Sarma and Girao, 2009) and ("Savings Trust", 2012).

Wi-Fi

Wi-Fi stands for wireless fidelity which belongs to the IEEE 802.11x standards. Nowadays it is the most popular communication mode used to connect devices to the Internet wirelessly. Devices like laptop, smart phone and all have Wi-Fi interfaces to connect with wireless router and get two way access of the Internet. The family of Wi-Fi standard allows establishing wireless network for small distances only. Wi-Fi has series types of networks like IEEE 802.11, IEEE 802.11a, IEEE 802.11b, IEEE 802.11g, IEEE 802.11n, IEEE 802.11e: QoS extension, IEEE 802.11f: extension for managing handover and

Figure 4. Layer IoT architecture

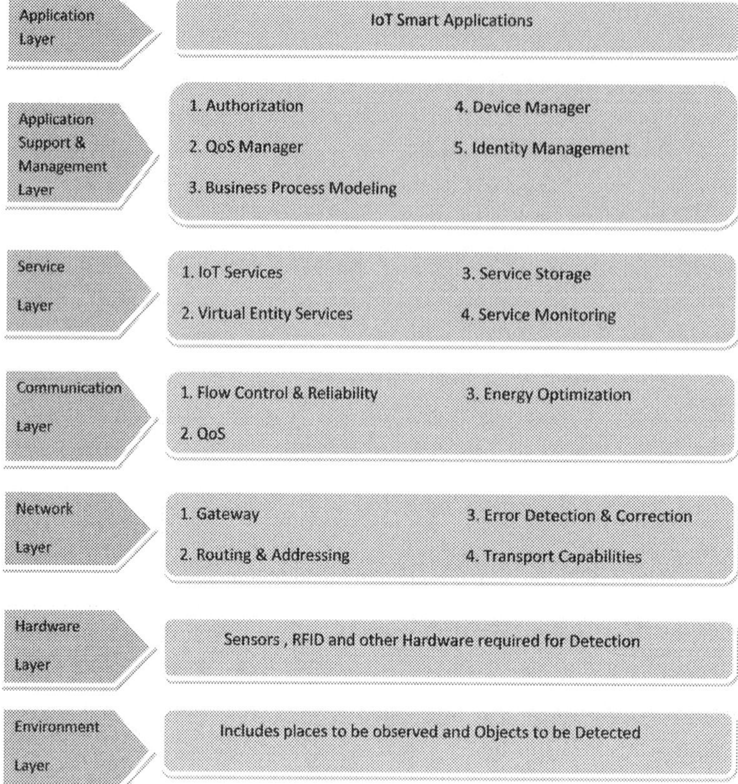

IEEE 802.11i security extension. The Wi-Fi group uses wan unlicensed spectrum of 2.4 GHz (ISM) band for its working.

Zigbee

The name of Zigbee comes out from bee's waggle dance as they make "zig" sound to communicate while flying to locate the pollen's location. Hence their communication network is formed in this way. It is a IoT data link protocol. Zigbee is a local area low power network protocol which operates at 2.4GHz frequency band. Zigbee works on IEEE802.15.4 standard. The main advantages of using Zigbee are (Lee, Su, and Shen, 2007):

- Zigbee works on low power standby mode and save large operational power in comparison of Bluetooth and WiFi. To make node work for 6 to 24 months two double A batteries are required.
- Along with low power Zigbee also operates at low data rate of 250kbps.
- It has a short data transmission range between 10 to 100 meters which can be further increased up to 1 to 3km by increasing the transmission power.
- It has very short delay profile as Zigbee takes only 15ms response time from sleep into working state and further a node takes 30ms to connect with the network.

- Zigbee has high capacity and can form large network of 65,000 nodes. These days, Zigbee is mainly used in wireless control networks and sensor in M2M and IoT because of its properties.

NFC

NFC is used as a wireless communication technology for short range i.e. for few inches only having technology principles similar to RFID. Through NFC data can be transmitted among devices only by bringing them together or touching them. However, NFC is used for more elaborative two-way communication using a tag to contain small amount of data. These tags can be read only or may be rewritable and also can be altered later if required like RFID tags. NFC operates mainly in three modes: card emulation mode (passive mode), reader/writer mode (active mode) and peer-topeer mode. NFC technology is vastly used in contactless payment systems, mobile phones and industrial applications. With the help of NFC it is easier to connect and control IoT devices in different environments like workplace and home. NFC supports Person-to-Person(P2P) network topology [(Porkodi and Bhuvaneswari, 2014) (Salman, 2015) (Affairs, 2015) (Azamuddin, 2015)].

Bluetooth

Bluetooth is a best model representing the upcoming technology and belongs to IEEE 802.15.1 standard. Bluetooth is mainly used for short range and it is a short and low-cost device of wireless radio technology. Bluetooth was first low power wireless communication protocol designed to replace short-range wired communications. It is used for sharing data for short distance also supports device's mobility which makes it enabler of the Internet of Things (IoT). Bluetooth has exceptional property of creating its very own personal area network while communicating. Bluetooth will discover and communicates to its neighbor devices without any need of line of sight that's why it is also acknowledged as WPAN (Wireless Personal Area Network). For this reason it is highly used in IoT because many IoT devices have limited power resources and would like to interconnect to the IoT (sensors, actuators, etc.) then Bluetooth will be best option for this. There is new version of Bluetooth mainly used in IoT i.e. Bluetooth 4.2, having few improvements (Decuir 2010). Bluetooth Classic took 10 years to connect with one billion devices, but Bluetooth Smart technology has been connected with billion of devices in a single year only and will grow even more in the coming years.

Bluetooth Smart technology can interact with Bluetooth enable devices like computers, tablets and smart phone's and gives industrial grade solutions. No extra dedicated expensive hubs are required to implement this as devices are already installed with this technology. This in turn reduces the complexity and cost of technology. These key features of smart Bluetooth are enabling IoT devices to give more affluent services to customers. Networking capabilities of Bluetooth Smart are making it as a stronger and most important factor in IoT world.

- To support flexible Internet connection options (IPv6/6LoWPAN or Bluetooth Smart Gateway) in IoT, this feature will help.
- This improved version has better Privacy Rights, high Energy Efficiency and improved Security Performance.
- Have high Throughput Speed and Packet Capacity which is highly required in IoT device communication.

Figure 5. Role of Bluetooth in IoT

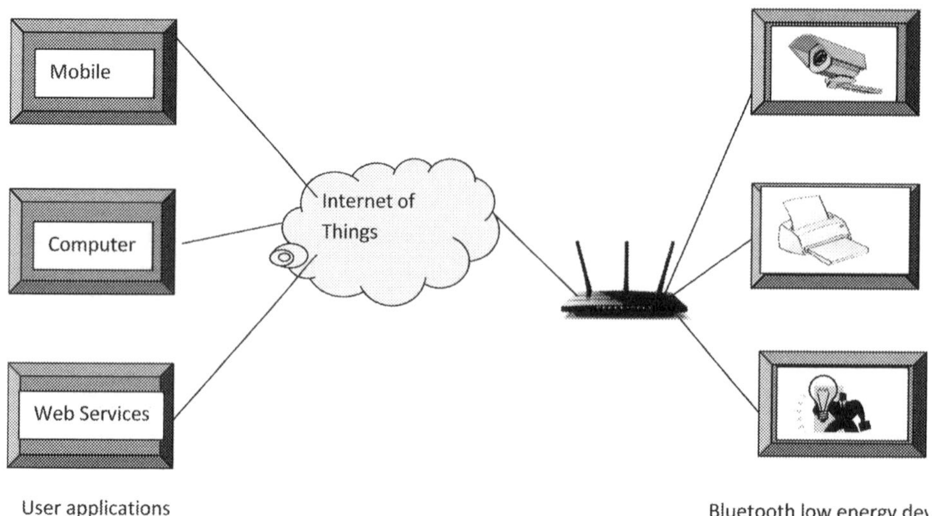

The real time information gathered by these access protocols is carried to the communication layer. The communication layer has IoT Web portal. Here, cross platform communication is done using different protocols like FTP, HTTP and others. All the real time information gathered at the communication layer is transmitted to the services layer. All the decisions related to the storage, monitoring and organization are made. The decisions about the visualization of the received information, resources allocation including creating virtual entities are also took place at service layer. After all this the received information is then transmitted f to the application support and management layer from service layer. Then finally this information is available to the authorized person sitting before the application user interface in the application layer. The authorized person can take the required decisions and also can request additional information from the application. It is most safe, most connected and lowest power specification yet. In addition to the above mentioned communication protocols there is one another communication technique used in IoT i.e. Cooperative Communication.

Figure 6. IoT technologies and protocol

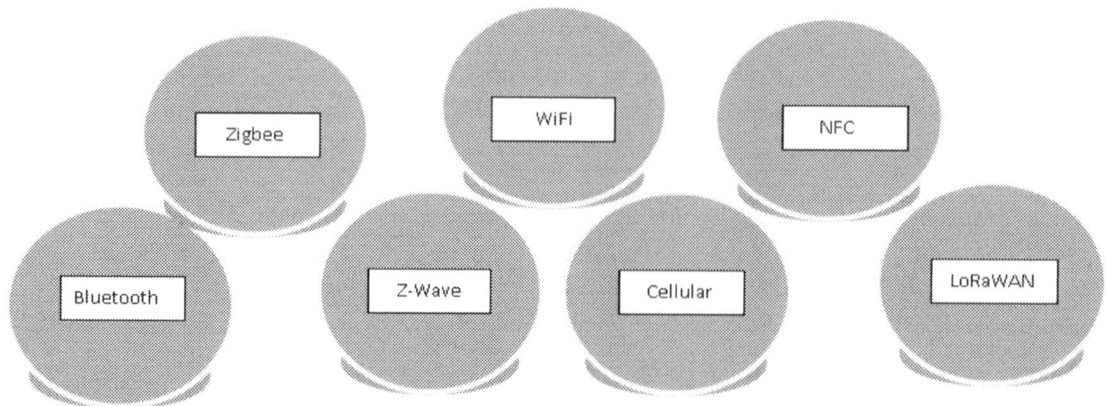

Cooperative Communication

Modern communication period has an important domain i.e. cooperative communications. Use of co-operative communication in IoT devices helps will help in sustaining the physical resources required for an IoT network. Cooperative mechanism is a relaying paradigm used for cooperative relaying of information. Using cooperative relaying for communication of IoT smart applications will increase the diversity in turn increasing reliability, data rates, signal-to-noise ratio (SNR) and in turn it will increase the successful hop count and the maximum distance travelled by the information symbols (Singh. Developing Inter-device transmission strategies are the main focus of researchers from the past few years. For successful transmission of data in a dense IoT networks having types of devices dispersed in an area will require a multi hop cooperative communications system. A symbol is needed to be transmitted in each slot of time in cooperative relaying methods. To achieve high information rate between source and destination nodes of IoT devices, have to go for multi relaying cooperative communication. Information transmitted from one hop to another assuming that at least one of the devices in each hop will be able to decode the information received from the IoT devices of the previous hop. The IoT devices which are receiving the information, at the same instant will act as the relay also. According to this scenario the data will reach to the destination in energy efficient manner (Jadaun and Singh, 2015). Cooperative relaying system can be further enhanced by incorporating the channel fading effects and broadcast nature of the wireless channels through diversity. Using cooperative communication we can narrow down the effects of multipath fading which is very common in wireless communication. Along with the existing diversity techniques such as frequency, temporal and spatial diversity, use of cooperative communication is also a novel technique used to achieve diversity by transmitting the information from IoT relaying devices. Through minimizing the effects of multipath fading one can improve the possibility of receiving the data correctly. There exists many types of relaying categorized based on the way they process the data like

- **Amplify-and-Forward (AF) Relay Scheme:** The information received at the intermediate node of IoT is decoded and then amplified also in AF relaying and then relayed to the next receiving node of IoT (Jadaun and Singh, 2015).

Figure 7. Cooperative communication

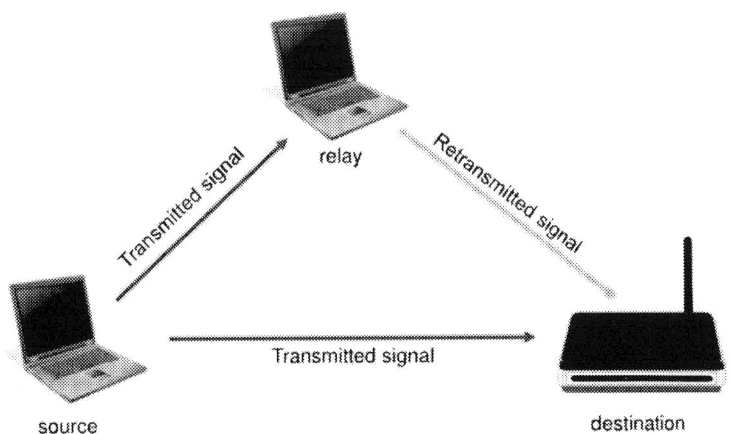

- **Decode-and-Forward (DF) Relay Scheme:** According to the DF relaying, the data received is successfully decoded first and the relayed to the next IoT node. If node is unable to decode the data successfully the it will not participate in cooperative relaying scheme (Singh and Jadaun, 2015).

Latest IoT Connectivity Solutions

There are many platforms which enable an end to end IoT connectivity to transmit and receive data between desired devices and clouds. This end to end IoT platform need to be scalable, secure, interoperable and also must be able of gathering the necessary data for companies which helps them in decision making and also supports remote monitoring, and tracking of their products.

To support this requirement, advancement of networking protocols is required like Gateway. Gateway is a network node that is used to connect two dissimilar networks with the help of different protocols. An IoT gateway is used to perform several crucial tasks like protocol translation, device connectivity, security, device management, filtering of data and processing, updating and more. The latest IoT gateway is working as a platform to run the application code for processing of the data making it as an intelligent element of IoT system.

Gateway is not limited to these functions only but they also carry an additional property of Web Bluetooth dashboard software which allows users to receive data on a browser and smart phones makes the IoT devices user friendly as shown in Figure 8.

The above given gateway have multiple configurations like Bluetooth, Wifi and Cellular, which helps the users to connect with local and remote devices and provides the required data and usability. This advanced gateway supports connectivity to USB, Ethernet and NFC. This type of advanced display gateway saves money and can perform different type functions with a single hardware inspite of multiple devices of hardware and software. The IoT device manufactures believe that information can be gathered quickly and processed easily with these of type of display gateway. So they find this a great solution of connectivity for IoT devices.

Figure 8. IoT gateways

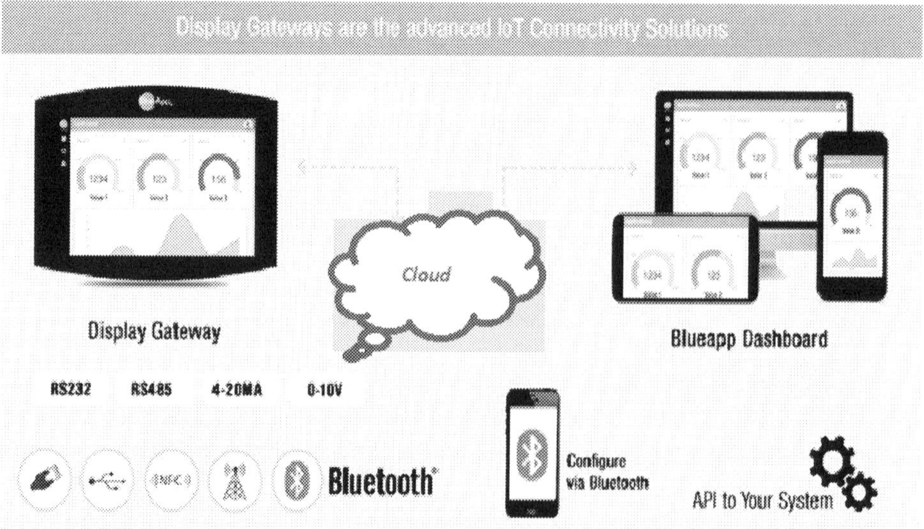

Smart Applications of IoT

Dairy Farming Industry

It's a big challenge for farming Industry to meet the needs of the ever-growing population worldwide. The current world's population is 7.5 billion but in the next 40 years it is expected to reach 9 billion. According to United Nation's Food and Agriculture Organization, to prevent massive famine in world the global food production will need to increase by 70%.

The major challenges faced by Farming Industry are:

- Limited availability of land, environmental issues, Lack and of resources and depletion of natural resources.
- Strong demand for more food as the world's population grows.
- Land management problems resulting from the preparation of the land to grow the crops to improper grazing practices.
- Government policies and intervention.

IoT Solutions are helping to resolve some of the challenges that farmers face for the growing population demand to be more productive in their farming process. This not only applies to crops but dairy farmers as well. Dairy farmers face the same demands as crop farmers to increase the productivity of dairy products like milk and yogurt and consumed meat products.

The farming industry has always adapted to new technology into their farming efforts to meet the heavy demands of population growth, but The Internet of Things is providing invaluable data that has not been available in recent years; this data can be analyzed to make better decisions in the farming industry and their farming strategies to improve productivity for higher yields.

Figure 9. Role of IoT in dairy farming industry

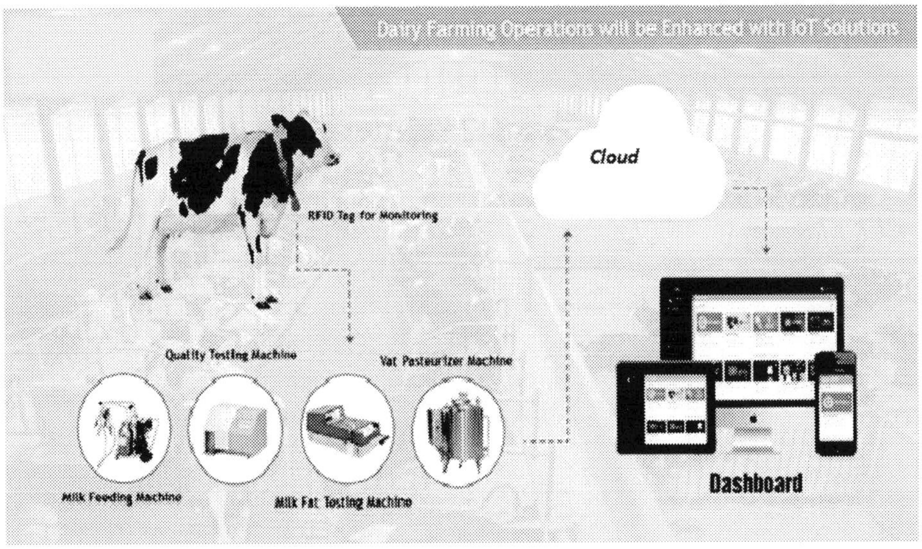

How the Farming industry is using technology to increase productivity:

- Tracking cattle movement and locations to prevent potential loss or theft.
- Measuring fertility of cows to make better decisions on breeding.
- Monitoring or Tracking of cows behavior, eating habits, health conditions etc
- Lactation and the use of robots to increase milk production.

The use of hardware and software can make the farming industry more productive to meet the challenges it faces by collecting different data points to improve the industry's production. This technology is also harmless to the environment and to the cattle so it appeals to many different people and groups, unlike the genetically modified hormones and other harmful and unnatural additives that are normally added to increase productivity.

Many hardware and software solutions are being used in many different industries to create innovative IoT solutions for collecting data, with our hardware solutions like BluTerm Adapters, Wifi, Bluetooth and Cellular Gateways and software solutions with mobile applications and a dashboard to analyze data. These IoT solutions for data collection are easy to integrate into any system and provide great reliability.

Supply Chain Management Process

Supply Chain Management consists of the identifying, tracking, acquiring and managing of products or resources required for any business and organization. The Internet of Things is taking the Supply Chain Management process to another level through improved and accurate tracking of the assets. The Tracking of goods in the supply chain management process is the most difficult and important task because we have to track large shipping containers or something so small that can fit in the palm of your hand. All the way through this process, things can be lost or stolen for which companies has to pay and will ultimately prevents them from being delivered to the consumer. This process affects a number of entities so exact location of goods is needed to be tracked which requires high speed connectivity system.

To make IoT effective in supply chain management services, we need a communication platform like gateways, hi-speed internet connectivity that can provide fast and real-time insights into the locations of goods and products like mobile apps which provide the most accurate visibility of goods with notifications from manufacturer to end consumer. This kind of platform is simple and easy to integrate into any supply chain system to get the exact data and display it on mobile application or web browser.

Smart Buildings Automate Operations

2017 turned to be a pivotal year for the Internet of Things as many industries have listened to themselves with this new technology that will streamline, enhance and have cost saving benefits to their business operations. Each and every business want to get registered with this new smart technology now like IoT to make themselves easily available for the customers. There are undoubtedly benefits of having smart capabilities in any industry ranging from Industrial and Device Manufacturing, Smart Homes, Smart Autos and Smart Buildings/Building Automation, and Retail. Building Automation is one industry that can use Connected Device and IoT Solutions that will save them money for years to come.

Figure 10. Role of IoT in supply chain management

A smart building is a structure that uses automated processes to control the building's operations including heating, ventilation, air conditioning, lighting, security and other systems. The goal of these smart capabilities is to save energy, report data, support energy grids, and mitigate environmental impacts.

Any building can be a smart building with the right technology, structures, and systems in place. Normally we think of a smart building as a medium to large buildings with the intended goal of saving energy through the different technologies and systems. Modest energy efficiency improvements to com-

Figure 11. Role of IoT in building automation

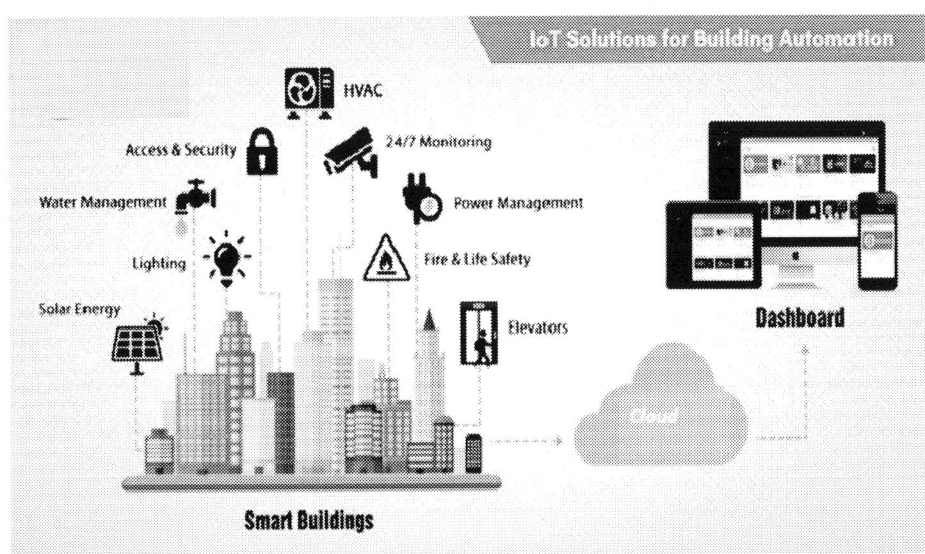

mercial buildings can save millions of dollars annually if owners implemented these smart solutions to their building plans. These saving would help in addressing any countries concern for the conservation of energy and help to cut down on the energy consumption of large buildings. A smart building can range from a smart home to a large commercial building, all playing a role to change the environment we live in to reduce unnecessary energy.

Buildings Automation Systems are needed to manage different functions that are crucial for the monitoring and maintenance of a building on a daily basis, when adding smart capabilities to the building, you're giving these buildings the ability to automatically make decisions to either turn on or off, adjust different systems to stay within set parameters or to alert building maintenance of systems that are not within the desired thresholds.

A smart building can also provide other functionality take for example a hospital, having smart capabilities adding to the building systems can be used to check in patients, guide the patient to the doctor's office or a medical area for testing and other medical needs, also tracking of patients. These are as small use cases, but these minor integrations into smart hospitals can improve the long waiting lines, and increase otherwise unhappy people whose experience at the medical facilities are not always timely. By having an increased streamlined hospital or medical physicality, doctors can spend more quality time with their patients. Tracking of patients can be an increased level of security especially for newborns or mentally ill patients. Technology like this sounds expensive, but it's not nearly expensive as it is to maintain a building without these capabilities. Smart building is cost effective because of their smart consumption of energy and accurate monitoring of energy flow and all this is practically possible with the help of IoT. The benefits of integrating an IoT solution into your existing building will have cost saving measures that will make up for the initial investment in the first year.

REFERENCES

Affairs, M. of E. n.d. (2015). Internet of Things in the Netherlands Applications trends and potential impact on radio spectrum.

Azamuddin Bin Ab Rahman, R. J. (2015). *Comparison of Internet of Things (IoT)*. Data Link Protocols.

Bandyopadhyay, D., & Sen, J. (2011). Internet of Things: Applications and Challenges in Technology and Standardization. *Wireless Personal Communications*, *58*(1), 49–69. doi:10.100711277-011-0288-5

Decuir, J. (2010). *Bluetooth 4.0: Low Energy, IEEE Annual Report*. Retrieved from http:// chapters. comsoc.org/vancouver/BTLER3.pdf

Jadaun, S. S., & Singh, G. (2015, May). Outage performance of cognitive multi relay networks with asymptotic analysis. In *Computing, Communication & Automation (ICCCA), 2015 International Conference on* (pp. 432-435). IEEE. 10.1109/CCAA.2015.7148415

Jadaun, S. S., & Singh, G. (2015, May). Outage Performance of Relay Assisted Cognitive Radio System With Asymptotic Analysis. *International Journal of Applied Engineering Research, 10*(3), 9757-9771.

Lee, J. S., Su, Y. W., & Shen, C. C. (2007). A comparative study of wireless protocols: Bluetooth, UWB, ZigBee, and Wi-Fi. *33rd Annual Conference of the IEEE Industrial Electronics Society (IECON 2007)*, 46–51.

Porkodi, R., & Bhuvaneswari, V. 2014. The Internet of Things (IoT) applications and communication enabling technology standards: An overview. *Intelligent Computing Applications (ICICA), 2014 International Conference on*, 324–329.

Salman, T. (2015). *Internet of Things Protocols and Standards*. Academic Press.

Sarma, A. C., & Girão, J. (2009). Identities in the future internet of things. *Wireless Personal Communications*, *49*(3), 353–363. doi:10.100711277-009-9697-0

Singh, G., & Jadaun, S. S. (2015, May). Cognitive relay network with asymptotic analysis. In *Computing, Communication & Automation (ICCCA), 2015 International Conference on* (pp. 1335-1338). IEEE. 10.1109/CCAA.2015.7148584

Singh, G., Kaur, G., Dwivedi, V. K., & Yadav, P. K. (n.d.). Development of coded-cooperation based multi-relay system for cognitive radio using mathematical modeling and its performance analysis. *Wireless Networks*, 1-7.

Chapter 18
Machine Learning, Data Mining for IoT-Based Systems

Ramgopal Kashyap
https://orcid.org/0000-0002-5352-1286
Amity University Chhattisgarh, India

ABSTRACT

This chapter will addresses challenges with the internet of things (IoT) and machine learning (ML), how a bit of the trouble of machine learning executions are recorded here and should be recalled while arranging the game plan, and the decision of right figuring. Existing examination in ML and IoT was centered around discovering how garbage in will convey garbage out, which is extraordinarily suitable for the extent of the enlightening list for machine learning. The quality, aggregate, availability, and decision of data are essential to the accomplishment of a machine learning game plan. Therefore, the point of this section is to give an outline of how the framework can utilize advancements alongside machine learning and difficulties get a kick out of the chance to understand the security challenges IoT can be bolstered. There are a few extensively unmistakable counts open for ML use. In spite of the way that counts can work in any nonexclusive conditions, there are specific standards available about which figuring would work best under which conditions.

INTRODUCTION

The Internet of Things (IoT) perspective is making through the general social event of perceiving and getting humbler scale and nano-contraptions dove in standard conditions and interconnected in low-control, lossy frameworks. The aggregate and consistency of certain contraptions construct all around requested and after that the rate of unforgiving data open for managing and examination exponentially grows-up. More than ever, conceivable strategies are required to treat data streams with the last goal to give a great illustration of recuperated information (Puthal, 2018). The significant information name was built up to mean the innovative work of data mining systems, what's more, affiliation structures to direct "volume, speed, grouping, and veracity" issues rising correctly when immense proportions of information make a joke of what's more, ought to control. Like this, Machine Learning (ML) is under-

DOI: 10.4018/978-1-5225-7432-3.ch018

stood to build unpalatable data and settle on needs to be arranged to decision help and computerization ("Special issue of Big Data Research Journal on "Giant Data and Neural Networks," 2018). Advance in ML estimations and change keeps running with advances of certain advances and Web-scale data affiliation structures, with the objective that specific focal spotlights have been passed on from the data examination reason behind the watching by some unimportant inadequacies are 'before clear concerning the creating multifaceted nature and heterogeneity of specific figuring difficulties. Mainly, the nonattendance of imperative, machine real depiction of yields from setting up ML structures is a perceptible cutoff for a possible abuse in entirely autonomic application conditions.

This fragment exhibits a general structure showing redesign standard ML examination on IoT data streams; relate semantic frameworks to information recuperated from the physical world, rather than inconsequential portrayal names. The key idea is to treat a typical ML plan issue like a levelheadedness drove resource introduction. Steps join producing a reason based depiction of quantifiable data dispersals and playing out fine-grained event attestation, misusing non-standard reasoning relationship for matchmaking (Rathore, Paul, Ahmad and Jeon, 2017). Each remark recommends a power giving the conceptualization and vocabulary to the particular taking in a territory, an influenced matchmaking on metadata set away in seeing and getting contraptions dove in an exceptional situation, lacking settled databases. Affirmation assignments float among devices which give unessential computational cutoff points. Stream thinking systems give the expecting to manage the flood of semantically remarked on invigorates gathered from low-level data, remembering the ultimate objective to interface with versatile setting attentive practices. Alongside this vision, creative examination frameworks related with data cleared by simple off-the-rack sensor contraptions can give solid results in event confirmation without requiring far-reaching computational resources. The methodology was tried and affirmed in a proper examination for road and headway opposing a certified educational gathering amassed for tests. Results were isolated from eminent ML figurings reviewing an authoritative objective to contemplate execution. The test campaign and early starter's groundwork assess both probability and plausibility of the differing strategies.

MOTIVATION

The standard motivation for this zone moves from the affirmation of honest to goodness cutoff focuses in the IoT, regardless of confirmation decreasing and accessibility interconnection invigorates physical structures, liberal data corpora show up without having amazingly the probability of destroying them from start to finish locally. Generally got data mining techniques to have two central detriments: i) they on a fundamental level do just about a social event errand and ii) their precision is widened whenever related on large data adds up to so making unfeasible an on-line examination (Yildirim, Birant and Alpyildiz, 2017). These sections foresee perceived the probability of seeing reasoning things: the IoT is deciphered likewise as recognized by the earth while is inconceivably secured the likelihood of settling on decisions and taking exercises locally after the perceiving forms. It should be seen as that in IoT conditions; information is collected through cut back scale contraptions identified with general things or sent in given situations and interconnected remotely. In a general sense, by the righteousness of their little measure, such demand has scarcest overseeing limits, a dash of securing and low-throughput correspondence restrict — they for the most part pass on repulsive data whose volume impacts fundamentally to be set to up by cutting-edge remote applications. A sharp comprehension of recuperated information diminishes estimations and possibly settles on decisions on what perceived, paying little identity to whether at a primitive stage. Standard machine learning frameworks have been, as it were, used for that; regardless, their huge deficiency is without a telling and first depiction of revealed events (Noel, 2016). IoT criticalness could update by explaining bona fide ask for, the data they gather and the conditions they make a plunge with brief, made what's more, semantically rich portrayals. The mix of the IoT and Semantic Web accomplishing the ensured Semantic Web of Things (SWoT). This perspective hopes to interface with novel classes of quick applications and affiliations grounded on Knowledge Representation (KR), misusing semantic-based revamp enlistments to interpret specific information starting from a specific event correspondingly, setting introduction. By right hand a shaped and machine-certifiable delineation in standard Semantic Web vernaculars, every social event yield could expect a non-obscure gigantic-ness (Jara et al., 2014). Also, clarification limits gave by the supporting semantic matchmaking grant to legitimize occurs, so expanding trust in structure response. If certain little scale devices are fit for capable onboard overseeing on the furtively recouped data, they can portray themselves and the setting where they are planned toward external contraptions what's more, applications. Would upgrade interoperability, flexibility, drawing in certain data based systems with high degrees of automaticity not yet allowed by ordinary IoT establishments and methodology. Machine learning, web on things and great information are reliant on one another while completing an exceptional development as found in figure 1.

Web of Things encourage joining between the physical world and computer correspondence systems, and applications, for example, foundation administration and ecological observing make protection and security procedures essential for future IoT frameworks. IoT frameworks need to ensure information protection and address security issues, for example, mocking assaults, interruptions, forswearing of administration assaults, circulated disavowal of administration assaults, sticking, listening in, and malware. For example, wearable gadgets that gather and send the client wellbeing information to the associated cell phone need to evade protection data spillage.

Figure 1. Machine learning interoperability

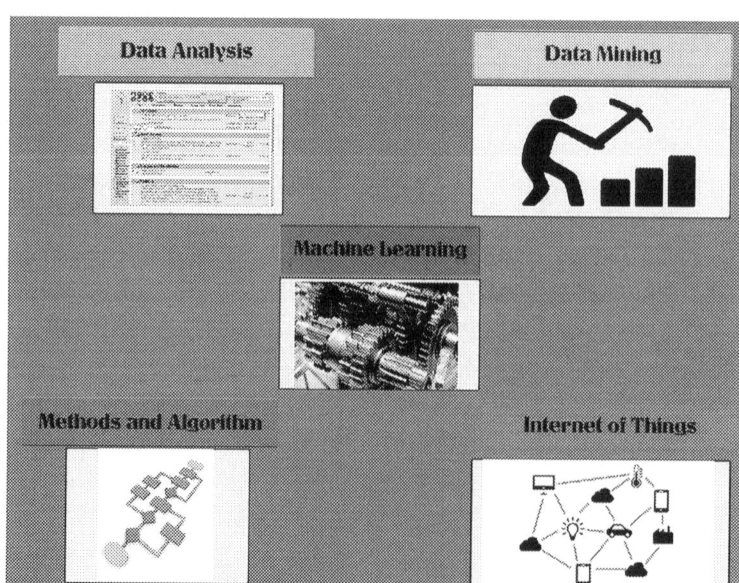

Machine Learning and IoT

It's for the most part restrictive for IoT gadgets with limited calculation, memory, radio transfer speed, and battery asset to execute computational-escalated and inactivity delicate security assignments, particularly under overwhelming information streams (Urquhart and Rodden, 2016). In any case, most existing security arrangements produce vast calculation and correspondence stack for IoT gadgets, for example, shoddy sensors with light-weight security insurances are usually more powerless against assaults than computer frameworks.

Forecast of Information Patterns

In this article, we explore the IoT confirmation, get to control, secure offloading, and malware identifications:

- Authentication enables IoT gadgets to recognize the source hubs and address the personality based assaults, for example, parodying and Sybil assaults.
- Access control counteracts unapproved clients to get to the IoT assets.
- Secure offloading methods empower IoT gadgets to utilize the calculation and capacity assets of the servers and edge gadgets for the computational-serious and inertness delicate errands.
- Malware recognition shields IoT gadgets from security spillage, control exhaustion, and system execution corruption against malware, for example, infections, worms, and Trojans with the improvement of ML and brilliant assaults, IoT gadgets need to pick the safeguard approach and decide the critical parameters in the security conventions for the tradeoff in the heterogeneous and dynamic systems. This undertaking is trying as an IoT gadget with confined assets more often than not experiences issues precisely assessing the current system and assault state in time.

Bunching of Information

The verification execution of the plan in is delicate to the test limit in the speculation test, which relies upon both the radio proliferation show and the mocking model. Such data is inaccessible for most open-air sensors, prompting a high false alert rate or miss location rate in the parodying identification. Machine learning systems (Kashyap and Piersson, 2018) including managed learning, unsupervised learning, and fortification learning have been generally connected to enhance security, for example, verification; get to control, against sticking offloading and malware location figure 2 shows how uncommon machine learning estimations give various results for that correct theory is required.

Supervised Learning System

Support vector machine (SVM), K-nearest neighbor (K-NN), neural network, deep neural network (DNN) can be utilized to mark the system activity, or application hints of IoT gadgets to construct the grouping or then again relapse demonstrate. For instance, IoT gadgets can utilize SVM to organize interruption and ridiculing assaults apply K-NN in the system interruption and malware recognitions, and use the neural system to recognize organize interruption and DoS assaults. IoT gadgets can connect devices in

Figure 2. Machine learning methods case astute result comparison

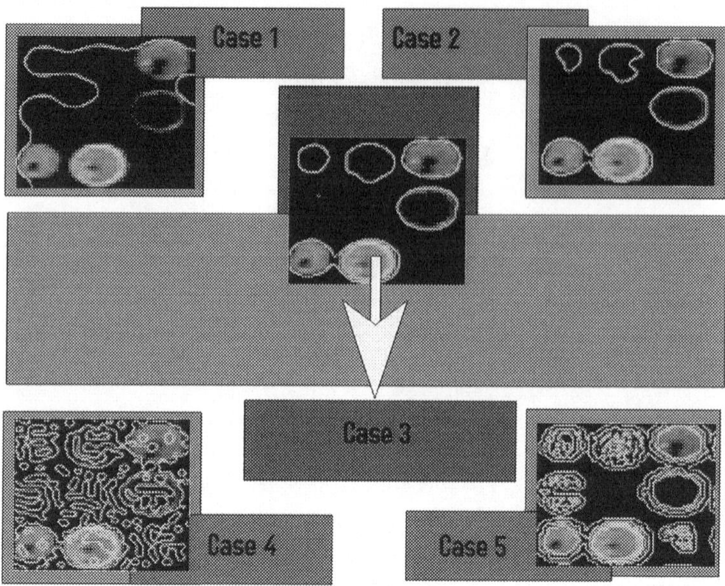

the interruption location, and irregular timberland classifier can be utilized to identify malware. IoT gadgets with adequate calculation and memory assets can use DNN to identify caricaturing assaults.

Unsupervised Learning System

Unsupervised learning does not require marked information in the supervised learning and explores the likeness between the unlabeled information to bunch them into various gatherings. For model, IoT gadgets can utilize multivariate connection investigation to recognize DoS assaults furthermore, apply IGMM in the PHY-layer validation with security assurance.

Reinforcement Learning System

Q-learning empowers an IoT gadget to pick the security conventions and additionally the key parameters against various assaults using experimentation. For instance, Q-learning as a model reinforcement learning method has been utilized to enhance the execution of the validation, hostile to sticking offloading, and malware identifications.

Learning-Based Access Control

It is trying to configuration get to control for IoT frameworks in heterogeneous systems with numerous sorts of hubs and multi-source information. ML strategies, for example, SVM, K-NN, and neural system have been utilized for interruption discovery. For example, the DoS assault identification as proposed in utilizes multivariate connection examination to extricate the geometrical relationships between system activity highlights. This plan builds the discovery exactness by 3.05% to 95.2% contrasted and the triangle region based closest neighbors approach with knowledge (Kashyap and Gautam, 2017). IoT gadgets, for example, sensors open air, as a rule, have a strict asset and calculation imperatives yielding difficulties for peculiarity interruption discovery strategies more often than not have corrupted identification execution in IoT framework. ML systems enable the form to lightweight get to control conventions to spare vitality and expand the lifetime of IoT frameworks. For instance, the anomaly recognition plot as created in applies K-NN to address the issue of unsupervised exception location in WSNs and offers adaptability to characterize anomalies with diminished vitality utilization. This plan can spare the most extreme vitality by 61.4% contrasted and the Centralized plan with comparable normal vitality utilization.

System Administration Advancements for IoT

It is extremely an expansive space, and there are many contending answers for the transference of information. Contrasts between arrangements originate from various guidelines and correspondence conventions connected in the segments which much of the time are not steady with each other. It can make troubles when choosing the parts for the IoT speculation's organizing because it is questionable which advancements will end up overwhelming renditions for the IoT segments. It would imply that picking the wrong innovation could turn out to be testing or exorbitant to supplant (Chen and Liu, 2016). Networking innovations, as a rule, can be partitioned into wired and remote advancements with regards to IoT, the remote advances are all the more fascinating because of the adaptability permitted by not associating things with wires into the web. Another grouping factor for the remote advancements is the inclusion region which can be separated into short range and long-extend advances. Short-run advances incorporate innovations with inclusion regions littler than an ordinary house whereas long-extend advances cover significantly more large regions. In some IoT cases, the short-extend advances can be more appropriate because of their better vitality productivity and lower costs (Wang, McMahan and Gallagher, 2015). This list contrast between short-extend advancements and long-ago innovations being the more drawn out inclusion region, generally bring down arrangement costs, an abnormal state of security and less demanding administration for long-ago advances. Short-go remote innovations incorporate both remote particular region organizing advancements and remote neighborhood advances. This innovation associate gadgets together inside little separations while WLAN advancements interface PCs together from a bigger territory, more often than not around the measure of a substantial building this require a switch to interface into the web. Short-extend remote advancements incorporate a wide range of innovations, for example, Bluetooth, ZigBee, Z-wave, Insteon, BACnet, Modbus, ANT, and Wi-Fi separate these advancements into four noteworthy application zones: client checking, home computerization, building mechanization and autos. Some short-run remote innovations can connect in different regions, for example, Wifi and Zigbee while different advances are more application territory particular, for example, BACnet and Modbus which utilized in building mechanization. Contrasts between advancements made from to the way that they work in various layers on the short-run remote innovation stack. Short-run remote innovation stack layer comprises from the physical layer, interface layer, arrange layer, transport layer and application layer. Specialized contrasts likewise originate from various working extents, frequencies and convention between operability (Hussain and Cambria, 2018). Long-extend remote correspondence in the IoT setting incorporates cell innovations and remote wide territory organizing advances. Cell innovation implies many interconnected transmitters each in charge of a specific zone or cell. Cell advancements are typically arranged in the ages beginning from the original of innovations (1G) to the present fourth era of advances (4G). The cutting-edge forward is the fifth era which is intended to sent from the year 2019 advances. The fifth era (5G) of cell innovations is extremely applicable to the IoT because it empowers significantly more effective correspondence. The 5G advancements give noteworthy upgrades in some gadgets associated, information rate, inclusion, and nature of administration estimates contrasted with the past fourth era innovations. The fifth era of cell advancements likewise give better security, portability, nature of administration bolster and worldwide reach than current innovations. Key wellspring of upgrades for 5G innovations is the utilization of higher frequencies called millimeter waves. Another factor for 5G enhancements is beamforming capacities and full duplex abilities, which mean centering transmission all the more insightfully and having the capacity to send two-way correspondences utilizing similar frequencies all the more effective (Tofan, 2014). Wide zone organizing innovations incorporate for instance Coronis, NWawe, and On-Ramp remote. Key highlights are wide inclusion region, proficient vitality utilization and utilization of low transmission capacity. Wide territory organize advances, and cell advances are good innovations where WAN advances are more suited for shorter range machine-to-machine, additionally called M2M correspondence, and current cell advances all the more longer-run correspondence with past referred to benefits contrasted with WAN advances.

Computing Paradigm for Machine Learning

The registering worldview for the IoT venture is an essential viewpoint in the IoT speculation, particularly when the extent of the created information approaches big data levels (Yao, 2014) contend that information administration is one of the greatest difficulties for IoT speculations because of the large measures of information that IoT venture can create. Distinctive processing ideal models incorporate for instance centralized server registering, pc figuring, distributed computing, and edge figuring, applications of machine learning shown in figure 3.

IoT speculations, the most intriguing figuring ideal models have distributed computing and edge processing. Distributed computing is a registering worldview where progressively versatile assets given over the web, and a significant part of the information handled elsewhere than where it made. Advantages of distributed computing incorporate versatility, valuing and high accessibility (Kashyap and Pierson,

Figure 3. Machine learning applications

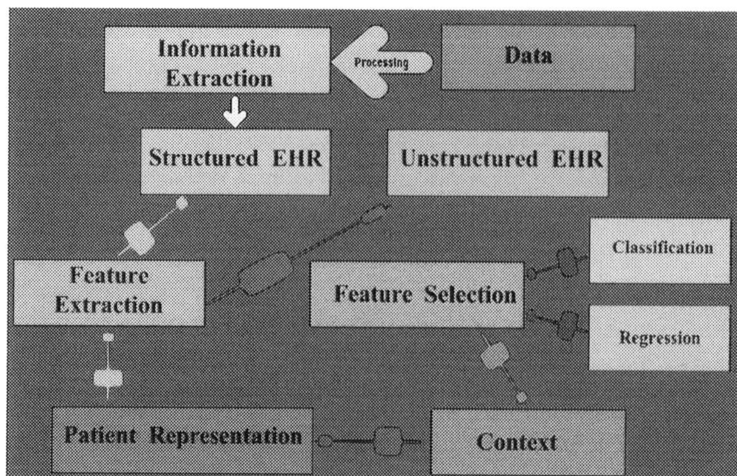

2018). Distributed computing enables clients to get too tall measures of assets, for example, preparing power, stockpiling, servers and applications on-request and pay by the utilized sum without the need to put resources into the IT foundation. Difficulties for distributed computing dependent on incorporate security, protection and a certain level of un-customizability of the cloud stages. One testing angle is further trouble in changing distributed computing suppliers due to the area of the information.

Cloud Figuring

It can order in three areas, private, open and a half and a half private distributed computing are given solely to one customer who permits more prominent control on security, information control, and more customization capacities. Outsider suppliers or clients themselves can give private mists. Open distributed computing is a processing administration given by an outsider where different customers, for the most part, share the equipment, which means servers, stockpiling frameworks and systems. Mixture registering is a blend of private cloud and open cloud. Principle contrast between these kinds of distributed computing is security. Private mists can open mists which as a rule can be in broad daylight utilize and can't be overseen just based by specific customer's needs (Kashyap and Tiwari, 2018). Cloud registering is partition in three administration levels: Software as a Service (SaaS), Platform as a Service (PaaS) and Infrastructure as a Service (IaaS). SaaS benefit demonstrates it gives clients access to applications without the need to work the IT foundation by any stretch of the imagination. It implies SaaS benefit show clients can buy an entrance to the application using a permit or a membership. SaaS benefit demonstrates clients the entire IT stack, which means application, middleware, database, working framework, virtualization, and IT framework foundation, as an administration. There are two classes of SaaS arrangements: level and vertical. Level SaaS arrangement gives application to particular capacity crosswise over various enterprises whereas vertical SaaS arrangement comprises from items customized to specific ventures. PaaS benefit show offers clients finish IT stack where they can run distinctive applications, yet the apps themselves excluded in the administration display. In this way, clients gain admittance to the middleware, database, working framework, virtualization and IT framework foundation which is required to have a domain where to run applications. IaaS benefit display gives clients the IT framework foundation and virtualization and the IaaS client set up the working frameworks and the critical applications themselves. (Dzbor, Stutt, Motta and Collins, 2007). Edge figuring, or mist registering as it can likewise b a figuring worldview where an enormous piece of information handling occurs close to the cause of the information at the edge of the system. Machine learning challenges like security, specific troubles, and interoperability shown in figure 4. For the event, for applications that don't give zone benefits the exchanging of zone information may have all the earmarks of being horrifying. In any case, an exchange may be tolerable tolerating uncovered in a confirmation approach.

Edge registering worldview comprises from putting a unit with preparing, putting away and dissecting abilities into the system. For instance, switches or switches with these capacities can be utilized as a haze hub. Haze hub, likewise called an IoT entryway gadget, imparts between different hubs in the system by utilizing some remote systems administration innovations introduced beforehand. The IoT door hub is likewise associated with the web so it can send and get information from the cloud stage. Edge figuring can be appropriate for instance in mechanical IoT situations where moving substantial measure of information into the cloud for preparing and over into the blue pencils and actuators probably won't be proficient due time or different requirements. Edge registering would then be able to be appropriate concerning constant investigation arrangements since it permits quicker response times. Activities

Figure 4. Challenges with machine learning

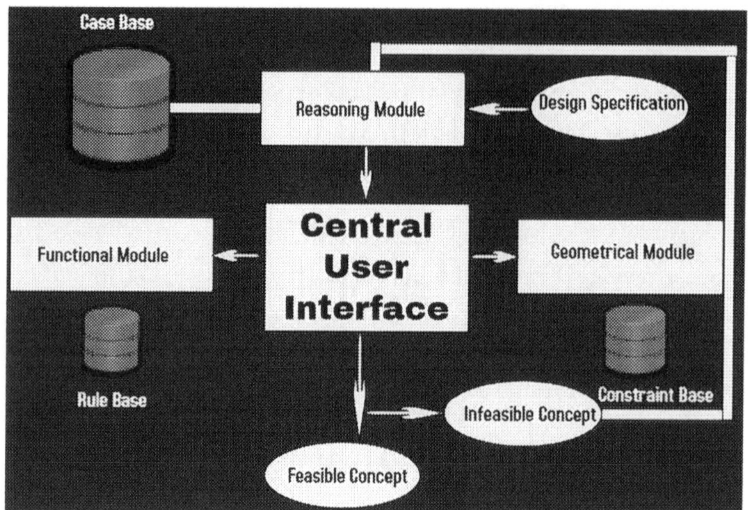

would be dependent on given standards in the system itself, and just certain information would be sent into the cloud stage for more profound examination. (Cisco, 2015) Benefits for edge figuring show up when the IoT setting requires quick reactions for information importance there is a low idleness prerequisite for correspondence. Edge registering is valuable in a circumstance where the system is expansive topographically, and there are a unique number of units associated with the system. Utilization of edge processing can likewise give some additional protection and security into the IoT venture since every one of the information doesn't need to be sent into the cloud stage and back. This likewise diminishes the required bandwidth and transmission costs if the information can be handled and acted inside the system. Edge figuring isn't selective of distributed computing, and there are fascinating conceivable outcomes in a mix of edge processing worldview into the as of now a mainstream pattern of grasping the distributed computing potential outcomes (Kim, 2018).

FOUNDATION

This domain quickly reviews contemplations on machine learning and description logics, recollecting a final goal to make the segment free and effortlessly sensible and it takes a gander at original related work.

Intelligence Layer in the IoT

Venture comprises from the information examination and central leadership after the information from the blue pencils in the detecting layer has been gathered and handled through the system layer. The normal popular expression Big Data is particularly connected to the IoT idea because of the large measures of information IoT blue pencils can create. An IoT venture can deliver large measures of information which can be considered as Big Data. One standard definition for Big Data is data with huge volume, assortment, and speed or essentially the three V's of information (Neath and Cavanaugh, 2011) as shown in figure 5.

Figure 5. Big data processing model

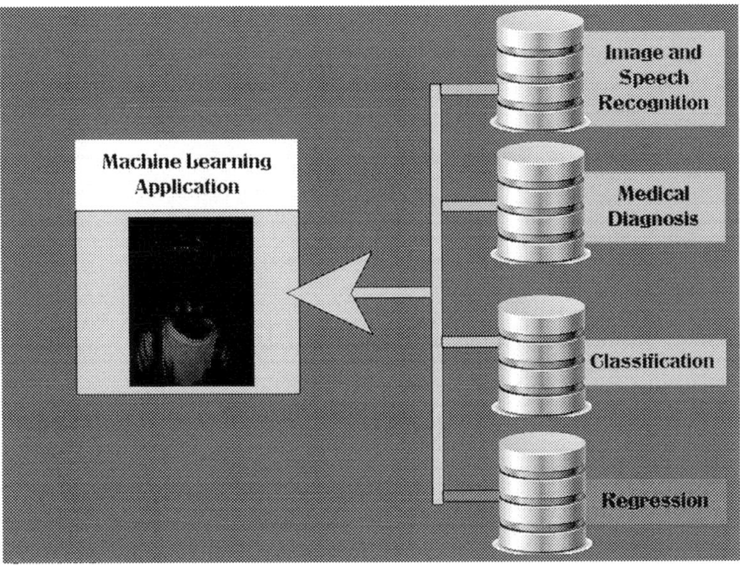

The Big Data component in numerous IoT venture implies that the insight layer is the most important perspective in the IoT speculation. Enter components in the insight layer are:

Analytic Solutions and Decision Support Systems

Artificial Intelligence Figure 5 portrays the insight layer of the IoT venture understanding what the gotten data means and capacity to settle on choices dependent on these discoveries are significant in the IoT setting without these capacities, the equipment and systems administration arrangements can't create noteworthy esteem. IoT speculation is an approach to gather a lot of information from different sources and to utilize expository answers to transform that information into experiences which at that point could be transformed into benefits (Kashyap, 2018). Refining the control level information is finished by utilizing examination arrangements which are usually called business knowledge or business investigation arrangements. Another important piece of the IoT venture is choosing how to deal with the information and how to settle on educated choices dependent on this information. Basic leadership in the IoT setting may require a type of choice emotionally supportive networks because of large measures of data created. On the off chance that the measure of data ascends over the human decision makers abilities even with applying choice emotionally supportive networks human-made reasoning arrangements may be required to remove all the possible incentive from the IoT speculation.

Decision Making

Examination implies breaking down information with the utilization of different strategies, systems, advancements, practices, and applications to have a clear comprehension of the circumstance. The objective of the expository arrangement is to transform data into bits of knowledge and permit activity dependent on those bits of knowledge. This is the motivation behind why logical arrangements are very basic viewpoint in the IoT speculation. Investigation consolidates perspectives from various fields, for example, data frameworks, software engineering, insights, and business. Regular terms utilized with regards to examination are business insight (BI) and business administration (BA). (Borisova, 2014) few perspectives to think about while breaking down investigation arrangements are information distribution center, information taking care of which are otherwise called extraction, change, stacking forms, database questioning, online expository handling and announcing and the distinctive instruments which to use in these procedures (Tiwari S., Gupta R.K., & Kashyap R., 2019).. The investigation can be partitioned into classes of clear examination, prescient investigation, and prescriptive investigation. Spellbinding investigation gives by and large lucidity to circumstances by giving general level answers from chronicled information. The graphics examination comprises from general rundowns of information properties and measurements, design disclosure, and division (Little, 2010).Prescient examination gives probabilistic responses to what may occur later on dependent on the chronicled information. These should be possible by some relapse examination or by characterization. The prescient examination is otherwise called determining or extrapolating from past information. Prescriptive examination incorporates both unmistakable and prescient investigation and produces distinctive choices to act dependent on the circumstance. Prescriptive examination computes various distinctive movements dependent on future activity by utilizing apparatuses from a few controls. Graphic examination answers what occurred previously though prescient investigation gives forecasts what may occur later on. The prescriptive examination takes both past kinds of an investigation into thought and gives significant responses to decision-making circumstances (Toivonen and Gross, 2015) the investigation arrangement in the IoT speculation is in charge of refining the vast crude information that originates from the blue pencils and different sources into significant data. (Zhang, Xiang, and Wang, 2010) notice multiprotocol capacities, de-centralization, enhanced security and data mining as a future element to be incorporated into the investigation arrangements. Multiprotocol capacities mean supporting diverse sorts of conventions and models both in accepting information and sending it. This element is exceptionally essential given the different principles and conventions in the IoT area. De-centralisation implies that sensors and information they created isn't attached to a single stage however that different kind of frameworks can collaborate and participate. Enhanced security is imperative for all levels in the IoT venture; however, investigation arrangements are likely the most basic part in the security for the entire IoT arrangement. Enhanced data mining capacities are required to examine past and current data all the more effectively with large measures of information produced by the IoT gadgets and from different sources (Punyavachira, 2013). The measure of information produced by the IoT arrangement may be big to the point that conventional investigation arrangements probably won't be satisfactory and particular big data arrangements must be incorporated into the knowledge layer of the IoT venture. Enormous data arrangements vary from common examination arrangements by their capacity to deal with bigger measures of more mind-boggling information by using for instance hugely parallel handling databases, information mining networks, disseminated databases, distributed computing, and versatile stockpiling frameworks. Difficulties with big data arrangements are security, integrational issues between customary social databases and NoSQL database frameworks, a prerequisite of more proficient answers for accelerate handling calculations and enhancement of information stockpiling.

Decision Support System (DSS)

It is an intelligent computer-based framework intended to enhance central leadership in complex circumstances where there is excessively information for people to process. A decision support system can likewise be connected to settle on the central leadership more goals and deliberate. The reason for diagnostic arrangements is to give better comprehension of the information which at that point makes the best open doors for central leadership. frameworks have been made which are usually eluded as choice emotionally supportive networks. Choice emotionally supportive networks can be utilized from various perspectives, for example, to settle on decisions between different alternatives, building distinctive choices for the procedure and even to recognize chances to make basic leadership circumstances (Huby, Cockram and Fleming, 2013). Decision models can be spoken to with three parts right off the bat, the inclination of goals besides the potential alternatives accessible. Thirdly, the measure of vulnerability in the model in regards to the impact of factors into the choice and the results. The general structure for a choice emotionally supportive network is three-separated application comprising from the database, backend-arrangement, and frontend-arrangement (Islam, 2018). The database stores all the required information, the backend essentially runs the required tasks, and the frontend composes the association between the client and the choice emotionally supportive network. DSS is a general term for any computer application intended to upgrade the client's capacity to decide. There are five general classes of DSS: interchanges driven DSS, information-driven DSS, report driven DSS, learning driven DSS, and model-driven DSS.

Artificial Intelligence (AI)

It is a subsection of software engineering which is centered on creating personal computers (PCs) capacities to coordinate people concerning knowledge. As of late, there has been a ton of enthusiasm for AI, and uniquely towards machine learning and all the conceivable application zones, AI could be utilized. Human-made intelligence connected in the IoT speculation is extremely intriguing because of the possibly large measures of information created by the IoT controls. This measure of enormous information can undoubtedly be excessively to include people in central leadership if the required activities must be made close continuously. The produced information can be so colossal and complex that people probably won't have the capacity to distinguish every single significant component in the information. In this manner, applying AI appears a legitimate component to consider in an IoT venture. IoT speculation can likewise be thought as a venture to embed blue pencils into a present framework to make changes to apply AI capacities. Human-made consciousness is where the point is to enhance PCs capacities in spaces where people have been altogether superior to machines, for example, learning, and imagination, arranging, thinking and central leadership (Sun and Betti, 2015). The point in human-made brainpower is to comprehend knowledge and after that make insightful PCs. Human-made intelligence comprises from a wide range of zones connected to human insight, for example, normal dialect handling, information portrayal, thinking, computer vision, mechanical technology, and machine learning. The field of AI joins a few trains, for example, software engineering, arithmetic, logic, brain science, etymology, financial matters, and science (Misra, Krishna, and Abraham, 2010). There are numerous subfields of AI, for example, apply autonomy, discourse preparing, arranging, master frameworks, which are firmly connected to choice emotionally supportive networks, artificial neural systems, transformative calculation, and machine learning. In the IoT setting the most interesting subfield of AI could be machine learning. Machine learning is a subset of AI which examines how to influence PCs to perform errands without expressly letting them know and making PCs make enhancements for their own by utilizing different calculations (Abdolkarimi, Abaei, and Mosavi, 2017) arranges machine learning calculations in five fundamental gatherings: imagery, connectionism, transformative, Bayesian and analogism. Every single one of these gatherings applies diverse sorts of calculations as their fundamental technique in machine learning. In imagery the calculation connected is different reasoning, in connectionism, it is back propagation, in developmental it is genetic programming, in Bayesian calculation Bayesian surmising is utilized as the fundamental strategy and in analogism, it bolsters vector machine. Different sorts of these calculations are utilized in zones, for example, administered learning, unsupervised learning, neural systems and strengthened learning. These calculations perform distinctively on various kinds of errands they are relegated (Hasan and Mishra, 2012). IoT venture where there are a huge number of blue pencils and actuators introduced into an organization's frameworks give a fascinating chance to apply human-made brainpower and particularly machine learning. Human-made brainpower could be utilized progressively central leadership in a circumstance where it would be inconceivable by human administrators to settle on choice as productively as machines (Coufal, 2016). Uncovering the IoT improved framework to machine learning gives chances to distinguish potential approaches to utilize the framework gainfully which probably won't be effectively found by people. Applying machine learning effectively into the IoT venture could therefore capable of finding fascinating discoveries which could conceivably then be connected either to expand deals or abatement operational expenses.

Information Mining

We abuse semantic web advancements for a few reasons right off the bat, semantics empowers an explicit depiction of the importance of sensor information in an organized way, with the goal that machines could comprehend it. Besides, it encourages interoperability for information joining since unrelated IoT information is changed over as indicated by a similar vocabulary (Hasan and Mishra, 2012). Thirdly, semantic thinking motors can be effectively utilized to find abnormal state deliberations from sensor information. Fourthly, setting mindfulness could be actualized utilizing semantic thinking. At long last, in principle, semantics facilitates the learning sharing and reuse of space learning skill which ought to evade the reexamination of the wheel. Each time a new area particular vocabulary is characterized.

Big Information Mine Information

The IoT information is a sort of informational collection, which incorporates that regular arrangement of preparing information, administration information, so this information is the principal focus of enormous information handling. Huge information starts with information securing at each step, which makes a first the web of things information interface, and guaranteeing the precision of the different circles. Huge information gets information on unit client hubs. However, the number of hubs develop exponentially, creating a lot of the web of things information, and requires more rational calculations for improvement (Kashyap, and Tiwari, 2017). The Internet of Things possesses information learning abilities that enable enormous information innovation to get the data from the immense Internet, and advance data limit, securing rate, and detecting strategies. The web of things learning strategies incorporate that situation learning, scale learning, informal learning and complex data adapting, so the web of things will take in the calculation stretched out to the setting, additionally progress information handling proficiency (Kashyap, R., 2019a). What's more, enormous information can play its claim focal points, which understand the synchronous improvement of informal learning and information investigation by dissecting techniques, for example, stream information, change point identification, and time arrangement forecast (Little, 2010). Customary information investigation has been not used to plan suitable learning capacities, while enormous information can be handled through a summed up model to the dispersed informational collection in the web of things, which can accomplish programmed information mining of complex systems, for example, picture order, dialect, right and content examination. Right now, the Lambda design empowers bunch information investigation of enormous information, which accomplishes the auspiciousness and assorted variety of the web of things information preparing, so the Lambda design is broadly utilized in Hadoop and Spark.

THE UTILIZATION OF ENORMOUS INFORMATION ON THE WEB OF THINGS

Enormous data delves profoundly into organized, semi-organized and unstructured data in an Internet of things information, and successfully organizes its inward information and recovers data significantly. The measure of information handled by huge information is billions, and the records framed by it achieve several billion (Schumaker, 2013). At present, enormous information is fundamentally connected to arrange deals, client visits, web-based life, portable information and such, which not just spare Internet of things information handling costs, yet also, enhance information gathering and advancement capacities.

Healthcare Industry

Enormous information predicts the patient's hospitalization; release what's more, treatment time by breaking down the therapeutic information and then the patient's connected records, to enhance the treatment impact. At that point, the healing center dependent on the mediation of huge information to diminish the patient's costly doctor's facility costs. A few doctor's facilities are growing new data items, fundamentally to gather quiet inpatient data and give alluring proposals and advantages to patients (Waoo, Kashyap & Jaiswal, 2010). As indicated by Internet insights, clinic treatment costs increment half every year, multiplying like clockwork, while the development of enormous information can decrease the aggregate expense of 60% predicts that as of the finish of 2020, individuals depend more on enormous information to keep clinic treatment costs down to 42% of the present circumstance. At present, Baidu has two noteworthy sorts of information accumulation frameworks, basically for client look portrayal of interest information, crawler information, and open web information (Ott and Houdek, 2014).What's more, enormous information employments an assortment of information preparing strategies to ace the healing facility's patient information and treatment information to frame an information investigation chain dependent on client connections to all the more likely anticipate the patient's treatment conduct, movement of the illness, furthermore, the future danger of sickness.

Financial Administrations Industry

Huge information enables budgetary administrations associations to mine information in profundity, and which make adjust money related information in general by tweaking client information. Among them, Apache arrange is the primary advancement of defense parcel exchanged system in the US Department, which is the start of the world wide web, and transmission control convention/web convention that is the most essential web convention, so the huge information Furthermore, a web of things additionally for the IP convention and TCP convention dependent on data correspondence. The use of enormous information in the money related field should start with the digitization of simple flags, and seal the information parcels of clients with the end goal to guarantee the security of money related information, with the goal that their business extension is more extensive, and the administration level is higher (Brookman, Rouge, Alva and Yeung, 2017).

Resource Investigation

Enormous information can improve the investigation of assets, which utilize constant creation information to enhance the operational proficiency of asset improvement undertakings, and make more great utilization of existing assets. Enormous information influences early recognizable proof of profitability advancements, which find different wellsprings of information that incorporate gas logging, quakes, tests, and gamma beams, and to set up a logical model of asset improvement (Tango, Minin, Tesauri and Montanari, 2010). At the equivalent time, enormous information breaks down the peculiarities in the penetrating procedure by the chronicled information of asset advancement with the end goal to enhance penetrating strategies, enhances resource usage and prescient support, and diminishes downtime. Moreover, enormous information takes into account a thorough building examination to better than anyone might have expected, which comprehend Earth's assets through successful information investigation. The effect of enormous information on the web of things is essentially reflected in the midstream also, downstream businesses of asset advancement, so as the examination and checking of continuous sensor information, the examination of unrefined petroleum lab parts results in the decrease of important time, which can diminish related expenses furthermore, the enhancement of forecast exactness (Zhang, 2016).

Retail and Coordination

Huge information utilizes radio frequency identification (RFID) innovation to track the pattern of coordination items conveniently, for example, labels, which can give retailers more exact and effective coordination data. In the meantime, huge information can enhance the exactness of stock administration data, and lessen the occurrence of robbery. Moreover, huge information can help coordination undertakings to acquire focused chances to streamline their coordination activities, which incorporate conveyance is estimating, course improvement and gauging of turnaround time. During the time spent coordination's administration, the organization can get more data, benefit level data, production network hazard data, sensor figure data, coordination and transmission data, and geographic data with enormous information innovation (Sądel and Śnieżyński, 2017). Enormous information can help the Internet of Things early distinguishing proof, physical measurements, faculty planning, active investigation, with the end goal to accomplish the extension of the Internet of things itself.

Profound Learning for the Web of Things

The multiplication of internetworked handy and implanted gadgets prompts dreams of the IoT, offering to ascend to a sensor-rich reality where physical things in our normal the condition is progressively enhanced with registering, detecting, and correspondence capacities. Such abilities guarantee to upset the collaborations between people and physical articles. Undoubtedly, critical research endeavors have been spent toward building more intelligent and more easy to use applications on portable and installed gadgets and sensors (Tango, Minin, Tesauri and Montanari, 2010). In the meantime, late advances in profound learning have enormously changed the manner, in which that is registering gadgets process human-driven substance, for example, pictures, video, and discourse, what's more, sound. Applying profound neural systems to IoT gadgets could in this manner realize an age of utilizations equipped for performing complex detecting and acknowledgment errands to help another domain of communications between people and their physical environment (Kashyap, R.,2019b). This article talks about four key examine inquiries toward the acknowledgment of such novel associations between people and (profound) learning-empowered physical things, specifically: What profound neural system structures can viably process and wire real info information for different IoT applications? How to lessen the asset utilization of profound learning models with the end goal that they can be proficiently conveyed on did asset oblige IoT gadgets? How to figure certainty estimations in the accuracy of profound learning forecasts for IoT applications? At long last, step by step instructions to limit the requirement for marked information in learning?

To expand on the above difficulties, first, see that IoT applications regularly rely upon joint effort among different sensors, which requires planning novel neural system structures for multisensory information combination. These structures ought to be ready to demonstrate complex connections among various tangible contributions over time and adequately encode highlights of real data sources that are appropriate to wanted acknowledgment and different errands. We survey a general profound learning structure, for this reason, called deep sense that gives a brought together yet the adjustable answer for the adapting needs of different IoT applications (Mawdsley, Tyson, Peressotti, Jong and Yaffe, 2009). It exhibits that specific mixes of profound neural system topologies are especially appropriate for gaining from sensor information. Second, IoT gadgets are typically low-end frameworks with restricted computational, vitality, and memory assets (Shukla R., Gupta R.K., & Kashyap R., 2019). One key obstacle in sending profound neural systems on IoT gadgets in this manner lies in the high asset request for prepared profound neural system models. While existing neural system pressure calculations can successfully decrease the number of model parameters, not these models prompt grid portrayals that can be productively executed on item IoT gadgets (Ghotekar, 2016). Ongoing work portrays an especially compelling profound learning pressure calculation, considered Deep IoT that can straightforwardly pack the structures of normally utilized profound neural systems. The compacted model can be conveyed on ware gadgets. An expansive extent of execution time, vitality and memory can be lessened with little impact on the last forecast precision. Third, unwavering quality affirmations are vital in digital physical and IoT applications. The requirement for advertising such confirmations call for all around aligned estimation of vulnerability related with learning results (Zhang, 2016). We present straightforward strategies for producing well-calibrated vulnerability gauges for the forecasts figured in profound neural systems, called RDeepSense. It accomplishes precisely and very much aligned estimations by changing the goal capacity to reflect expectation rightness steadfastly. At last, naming information for learning reasons for existing is tedious. One must show detecting gadgets to perceive articles and ideas without the advantage of (many) precedents, where ground truth esteems for such protests, what's more, ideas are given. Unsupervised what's more, semi-supervised arrangements are expected to fathom the test of learning with constrained marked and for the most part unlabeled examples while moving toward the execution of gaining from completely marked information (Chen, Liu, and Yang, 2016). We expand on these center issues, what's more, their rising answers for help establish a framework for building IoT frameworks advanced with successful, effective, what's more, solid profound realizing models.

Deep Learning Models for Sensor Data

A key research test toward the acknowledgment of learning-empowered IoT frameworks lies in the plan of profound neural system structures that can viably assess yields of intrigue from boisterous time-arrangement multisensory measurements. In spite of the expansive assortment of installed and portable registering assignments in IoT settings, one can, for the most part, arrange them into two regular sub-types: estimation undertakings and characterization assignments, contingent upon whether the expected results are persistent or straight out, individually. The inquiry thusly moves toward becoming regardless of whether general neural system engineering exists that can viably take in the structure of models required for estimation and grouping undertakings from sensor information. Such a general profound learning neural arrange engineering would, on a fundamental level, conquered disservices of the present approaches that depend on systematic model improvements or the utilization of hand-created built highlights (Houeland and Aamodt, 2017). Generally, for estimation-arranged issues, for example, following and confinement, sensor inputs are prepared based on the physical models of the marvels included. Sensors create estimations of physical amounts such as increasing speed and rakish speed. From these estimations, other physical amounts are inferred, (for example, dislodging through twofold coordination of increasing speed after some time). In any case, estimations of product sensors are loud. The commotion in estimations is nonlinear and may be associated after some time, which makes it hard to display. It is along these lines testing to separate flag from the clamor, prompting estimation mistakes and predisposition (Li, Jiang, Zhang, Pang and Huang, 2014). For characterization arranged issues, for example, action and setting acknowledgment, a common methodology is to figure proper highlights inferred from crude sensor information. These high-quality highlights are then nourished into a classifier for preparing. Structuring great hand-made highlights can be tedious; it requires broad investigations to sum up well to different settings, for example, unique sensor commotion designs and different client practices. A general profound learning system can successfully address both of the previously mentioned difficulties by consequently adjusting the scholarly a neural system to complex corresponded clamor designs while, in the meantime, uniting on the extraction of maximally hearty flag includes that are most suited for the job that needs to be done. An ongoing structure called deep sense shows a case for achievability of such a general arrangement. Deep sense incorporates convolution neural systems (CNN) and recurrent neural systems (RNNs). Tangible information sources are adjusted and isolated into time interims for handling time-arrangement information. For every interim, deep sense first applies an individual CNN to every sensor, encoding applicable nearby highlights inside the sensor's information stream. At that point, a (worldwide) CNN is connected on the separate yields to display collaborations among numerous sensors for successful sensor combination. Next, an RNN is connected to remove practical examples. Finally, either a relative change or a softmax yield is utilized, contingent upon regardless of whether we need to demonstrate an estimation or a characterization assignment (Schwab and Ray, 2017). This engineering takes care of the general issue of learning multisensory combination errands for reasons for estimation or then again grouping from time-arrangement information. For estimation-situated issues, deep sense takes in the solid framework what's more, clamor models to yield yields from boisterous sensor information straightforwardly. The neural system goes about as an inexact exchange work. For classification-oriented issues, the neural system goes about as a programmed highlight extractor encoding nearby, worldwide, and transient data. The focal thought of the model-based way to deal with oversee machine learning is to make a custom show uniquely fitted particularly to each new application. Once in a while, the model together with a detailed assembling calculation may stand out from a common machine learning system, while a huge piece of the time it won't. Normally, show based machine learning will be executed utilizing a model particular vernacular in which the model can be depicted utilizing decreased code, from which the thing finishing that model can be made hence (Dehestani et al., 2011) as showed up in figure 6 how exhibit base and case base model are expecting fundamental part in machine learning.

DISCUSSION

Basic learning is essential for overseeing unmistakably settled issues in computer vision and trademark vernacular managing, yet it normally does everything considered by using epic central processing unit and graphical processing unit resources. Standard vital learning methodologies aren't genuine to looking out for the challenges of the Internet of Things applications, regardless, since they can't have any effect a close level of computational resources. While using translated figuring and structure weight there will be a condition of reliable episodes. Push diminishing in structure or spotlight point size may pass on prohibited drops inexactness and accuracy. Immense learning is the best response for different examination and perceiving affirmation issues. Correctly when used with an eye to sparing system, memory, and power resources, important learning can pass on data to IoT contraptions. These structures join a critical number of passed on contraptions reliably making a high volume of data. Changing sorts of contraptions make particular sorts of data, prompting heterogeneous enlightening accumulations, yet the data typically joins timestamps and zone information. Finally, IoT applications must be proposed to drive forward hubbub in the data as a result of transmission and anchoring goofs. Fake care is expecting a

Figure 6. Model-based machine learning

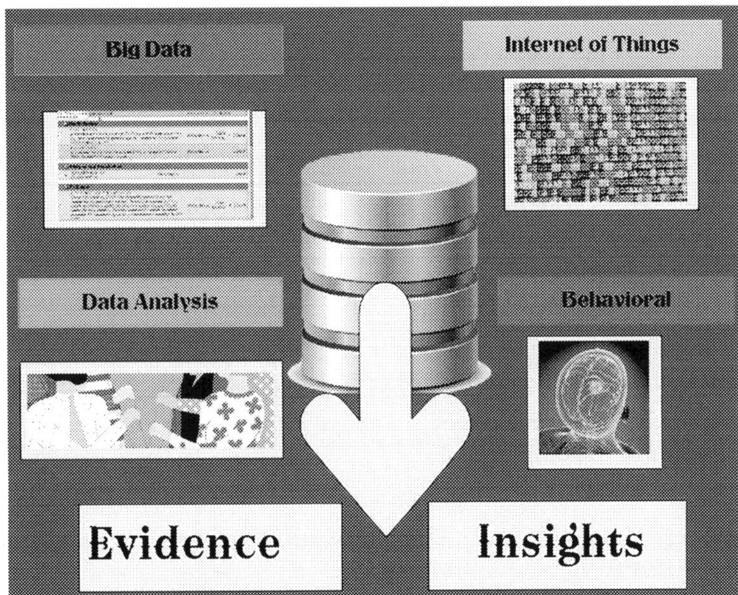

growing part in IoT applications and affiliations. Financing interests in IoT new affiliations that are using AI are up tenaciously. Affiliations have acquired different affiliations working at the relationship of AI and IoT over the latest two years. Additionally, crucial merchants of IoT deal with making PC programs are beginning at now offering cemented AI limits, for instance, machine learning-based examination. Artificial intelligence is expecting an including a part in IoT in light of its ability to quickly wring bits of picking up from data. Machine taking in, an AI movement, brings the ability to frequently see plans and perceive oddities in the data that shocking sensors and devices impact information, for instance, temperature, to weight, suppleness, air quality, vibration, and sound. The compelling blend of AI and IoT movement is helping affiliations avoid unconstrained downtime, increase working advantage, interface new things and affiliations, and enhance hazard affiliation. Big data sums and in this manner, people may require help from choice emotionally supportive networks and even computerized reasoning, so these perspectives are additionally important components to consider in the IoT speculation. The second research question was what the most important business measurements for the IoT venture are? Based on the writing three measurements were distinguished: IoT biological system, the plan of action decided for the venture and the application region of the speculation. IoT biological community is the network of the considerable number of organizations, authorities, and people collaborating in the IoT condition. Examination of the IoT biological community is essential for the IoT venture because the environment is a vital factor in the improvement of different innovations, models and conventions. Not understanding the IoT biological system can make difficulties if the picked IoT advancements, guidelines, and conventions. Plan of action is the applied model of the organization's business portraying how an organization makes, conveys and catches esteem. For the IoT venture, this is exceptionally essential since one noteworthy test in IoT speculations is the way to adapt the information got. The IoT innovations can anyway permit changes in the organization's plans of action which can be the best wellspring of the benefit of the IoT venture. Application territory of the venture is an important measurement of the IoT speculation because distinctive zones have enormously extraordinary necessities. Atzori et al. (2010) separate the application zones into four primary sections of transport and coordination, therapeutic services, brilliant condition, and individual and social area. Prerequisites for IoT interests in these application regions can vary for instance with venture needs, support costs, vitality utilization, information administration necessities and client association (Gubbi et al., 2013). The third research question was, does IoT speculation require further developed productivity investigation strategies because of the idea of these mechanical components and business measurements?

Conventional gainfulness investigation techniques, for example, clear, present esteem strategy, recompense strategy and inside rate of return strategy are usually connected strategies however probably won't be most appropriate for the IoT ventures because of the high vulnerability identified with the IoT speculations. Genuine choice valuation strategies anyway are more suited to incorporate the vulnerability of venture into the productivity examination. The examination of the gainfulness investigation techniques with a whole situation where add up to cost of proprietorship investigation was performed on two modern machines where one of the machines had IoT-capacities, and the other one didn't. In the light, the speculation case figured, and benefit investigation was performed utilizing the common gainfulness examination strategies and a genuine alternative valuation strategy for fluffy result technique. The aftereffects of the correlation of the benefit examination demonstrated that incorporating the vulnerability level in the gainfulness investigation is important for the IoT speculations. Counting the good choices found for the situation expanded the net present estimation of the speculation 5 percent, however, the accurate estimation of the true alternative valuation is showing the vulnerability related in the appraisals. This vulnerability can be utilized all the more effective in the venture procedure because of an incredible wellspring of the IoT speculations' qualities produced in the most dubious esteem sources which are difficult to gauge with conventional gainfulness investigation techniques. Consequences of the case show that accurate choice valuation is a conventional technique for breaking down IoT ventures since it can help recognize the most significant parts of various speculations which normally are the most unverifiable segments of the speculations. In this manner, including the good choice valuation in the benefits investigation of IoT speculations is a decent decision which can enable organizations to recognize the most potential esteem creating ventures which can here and there incorporate a lot of vulnerability. Consequences of the proposition show that organizations ought to think about IoT as a potential wellspring of an upper hand. IoT ventures can give organizations numerous choices either to robotize their present activity or even develop new items, administrations, and methods for working. Organizations ought to likewise incorporate good choice valuation strategies in their capital planning while breaking down IoT ventures.

CONCLUSION

The motivation behind the investigation was to break down the productivity examination of a general IoT speculation. Breaking down the productivity of an IoT speculation previously required investigating the components of the IoT venture. IoT speculation's investigation comprises for the most part from two sections: what data is basic from a business perspective and in what capacity should this data be given by the IoT innovation. Based on the past writing three mechanical layers and three business measurements were distinguished. In the wake of distinguishing the significant components of the IoT venture, various benefit techniques were broken down to think about how the IoT speculations productivity would be assessed ideally. Investigation of the unique gainfulness strategies finished with a genuine case with an IoT-competent mechanical machine. Principle look into the issue of the investigation was the assurance of profit for speculations for the IoT venture and based on that three research questions were framed. To start with, what are the principal mechanical components of an IoT speculation? Second, what are the most critical business measurements for the IoT venture? Third, does an IoT venture require further developed benefit examination strategies because of the idea of these innovative components and business measurements? The first and second research questions considered in the second section of the proposal, and the third research question examined in the third and fourth parts of the postulation. The first research question was what the fundamental innovative components of an IoT venture are? Based on the writing the three mechanical components of general IoT venture were recognized as detecting layer, organizing layer and insight layer. Detecting layer is where assembling all the data created by the information sources and following up on the information is finished. Detecting layer comprises from different edits and actuators. Key advances are radio recurrence recognizable proof innovation, close field correspondences innovation, and remote sensor systems. Systems administration layer is where the information is exchanged from the detecting layer into insight layer for investigation and central leadership with various systems administration advancements. There are many systems administration advances in the IoT worldview, for example, Wi-Fi, Bluetooth and the fifth era of cell advances. Another key part of the IoT speculation is the registering worldview. Distributed computing and edge registering offer intriguing conceivable outcomes for IoT interests in regions, for example, scaling capacities and speed while more conventional centralized computer processing gives more advantages in regions, for example, security. Knowledge layer comprises from the components identified with the investigation and central leadership, and it tends to be viewed as the most critical piece of the IoT venture. Enter advances in the insight layer incorporate examination answers for the IoT information, choice emotionally supportive networks for following up on that information and potentially some AI-answers for assuming control over a few sections of the basic leadership process when the measure of information achieves levels past human capacities. IoT ventures can be considered as a strategy to extricate information from different information sources, understanding the importance of that information and settling on choices and activities based on that information. The sum and speed of the potential IoT information can achieve effectively. Generally, organizations may underestimate the most intricate and potentially the most significant speculations because of the conventional productivity examination techniques' powerlessness to incorporate all the important parts of the IoT interests in the gainfulness investigation. Based from the aftereffects of the theory it very well may be presumed that in the IoT speculation's benefit investigation the good alternative valuation strategies ought to be connected because conventional gainfulness examination techniques are not ideally suited to break down all the important parts of IoT ventures without anyone else. From the aftereffects of the proposition it very well may be presumed that one angle which may diminish the market interest for IoT speculations may be the underestimating of the IoT ventures because of the failure to examine the benefit of IoT speculations accurately. This might be caused from to the high utilization of conventional productivity examination techniques which can exclude all the pertinent parts of the IoT interest in the benefits investigation. There are numerous confinements of the proposition. IoT is an exceptionally wide worldview so breaking down all the pertinent territories is very testing and was impractical in the extent of this proposition. Likewise, past writing of the IoT is intensely centered on building and software engineering spaces which cause difficulties in understanding the true capability of the IoT for the laymen of those fields. Another constraint of the proposition is the avoidance of security and protection parts of the IoT which are significant components of the IoT venture yet require further investigation than was conceivable in theory. There are many fascinating exploration territories in regards to productivity investigation of IoT speculations. Intriguing further research theme would be an examination of various genuine choice valuation strategies to one another in productivity investigation of IoT speculations. Another point would be administrative adaptability for instance in scaling the IoT speculations or the parts of reversibility in the IoT ventures. The likelihood to oversee IoT speculations and the chances to incorporate genuine alternatives in them would be a fascinating region of research, the adaptability of changing mechanical arrangements in the IoT speculation.

REFERENCES

Abdolkarimi, E., Abaei, G., & Mosavi, M. (2017). A wavelet-extreme learning machine for low-cost INS/GPS navigation system in high-speed applications. *GPS Solutions*, *22*(1), 15. doi:10.100710291-017-0682-x

Borisova, N. (2014). An Approach for Ontology-Based Information Extraction. *Information Technology and Control*, *12*(1). doi:10.1515/itc-2015-0007

Brookman, J., Rouge, P., Alva, A., & Yeung, C. (2017). Cross-Device Tracking: Measurement and Disclosures. *Proceedings On Privacy Enhancing Technologies*, *2017*(2). doi:10.1515/popets-2017-0020

Chen, W., Liu, T., & Yang, X. (2016). Reinforcement learning behaviors in sponsored search. *Applied Stochastic Models in Business and Industry*, *32*(3), 358–367. doi:10.1002/asmb.2157

Chen, Z., & Liu, B. (2016). Lifelong Machine Learning. *Synthesis Lectures On Artificial Intelligence And Machine Learning*, *10*(3), 1–145. doi:10.2200/S00737ED1V01Y201610AIM033

Coufal, D. (2016). On the convergence of kernel density estimates in particle filtering. *Kybernetika*, 735–756. doi:10.14736/kyb-2016-5-0735

Dehestani, D., Eftekhari, F., Guo, Y., Ling, S., Su, S., & Nguyen, H. (2011). Online Support Vector Machine Application for Model-Based Fault Detection and Isolation of HVAC System. *International Journal Of Machine Learning And Computing*, 66-72. doi:10.7763/ijmlc.2011.v1.10

Dzbor, M., Stutt, A., Motta, E., & Collins, T. (2007). Representations for semantic learning webs: Semantic Web technology in learning support. *Journal of Computer Assisted Learning*, *23*(1), 69–82. doi:10.1111/j.1365-2729.2007.00202.x

Ghotekar, N. (2016). Analysis and Data Mining of Call Detail Records using Big Data Technology. *IJARCCE*, *5*(12), 280–283. doi:10.17148/IJARCCE.2016.51264

Hasan, M., & Mishra, P. (2012). Robust Gesture Recognition Using Gaussian Distribution for Features Fitting. *International Journal Of Machine Learning And Computing*, 266-273. doi:10.7763/ijmlc.2012.v2.128

Houeland, T., & Aamodt, A. (2017). A learning system based on lazy metareasoning. *Progress In Artificial Intelligence*, *7*(2), 129–146. doi:10.100713748-017-0138-0

Huby, G., Cockram, J., & Fleming, M. (2013). Through-life Data Exploitation to Reduce Downtime and Costs. *Procedia CIRP*, *11*, 50–55. doi:10.1016/j.procir.2013.07.070

Hussain, A., & Cambria, E. (2018). Semi-supervised learning for big social data analysis. *Neurocomputing*, *275*, 1662–1673. doi:10.1016/j.neucom.2017.10.010

Internet of Things & Creation of the Fifth V of Big Data. (2017). *International Journal Of Science And Research*, *6*(1), 1363–1366. doi:10.21275/art20164394

Islam, N. (2018). *Business Intelligence and Analytics for Operational Efficiency*. SSRN Electronic Journal. doi:10.2139srn.3163429

Jara, A., Olivieri, A., Bocchi, Y., Jung, M., Kastner, W., & Skarmeta, A. (2014). Semantic Web of Things: An analysis of the application semantics for the IoT moving towards the IoT convergence. *International Journal of Web and Grid Services*, *10*(2/3), 244. doi:10.1504/IJWGS.2014.060260

Kashyap, R. (2018). Object boundary detection through robust active contour-based method with global information. *International Journal Of Image Mining*, *3*(1), 22. doi:10.1504/IJIM.2018.093008

Kashyap, R. (2019a). Security, Reliability, and Performance Assessment for Healthcare Biometrics. In D. Kisku, P. Gupta, & J. Sing (Eds.), Design and Implementation of Healthcare Biometric Systems (pp. 29-54). Hershey, PA: IGI Global. doi:10.4018/978-1-5225-7525-2.ch002

Kashyap, R. (2019b). Geospatial Big Data, Analytics and IoT: Challenges, Applications and Potential. In H. Das, R. Barik, H. Dubey & D. Sinha Roy (Eds.), Cloud Computing for Geospatial Big Data Analytics (pp. 191-213). Springer International Publishing.

Kashyap, R., & Gautam, P. (2017). 'Fast Medical Image Segmentation Using Energy-Based Method,' Biometrics. *Concepts, Methodologies, Tools, and Applications*, *3*(1), 1017–1042. doi:10.4018/978-1-5225-0983-7.ch040

Kashyap, R., & Piersson, A. D. (2018). Impact of Big Data on Security. In G. Shrivastava, P. Kumar, B. Gupta, S. Bala, & N. Dey (Eds.), *Handbook of Research on Network Forensics and Analysis Techniques* (pp. 283–299). Hershey, PA: IGI Global. doi:10.4018/978-1-5225-4100-4.ch015

Kashyap, R., & Piersson, A. D. (2018). Big Data Challenges and Solutions in the Medical Industries. In V. Tiwari, R. Thakur, B. Tiwari, & S. Gupta (Eds.), *Handbook of Research on Pattern Engineering System Development for Big Data Analytics* (pp. 1–24). Hershey, PA: IGI Global. doi:10.4018/978-1-5225-3870-7.ch001

Kashyap, R., & Tiwari, V. (2017). Energy-based active contour method for image segmentation. *International Journal of Electronic Healthcare*, *9*(2–3), 210–225. doi:10.1504/IJEH.2017.083165

Kashyap, R., & Tiwari, V. (2018). Active contours using global models for medical image segmentation. *International Journal of Computational Systems Engineering*, *4*(2/3), 195. doi:10.1504/IJCSYSE.2018.091404

Kim, L. (2018). DeepX: Deep Learning Accelerator for Restricted Boltzmann Machine Artificial Neural Networks. *IEEE Transactions on Neural Networks and Learning Systems*, *29*(5), 1441–1453. doi:10.1109/TNNLS.2017.2665555 PMID:28287986

Li, G., Jiang, S., Zhang, W., Pang, J., & Huang, Q. (2014). Online web video topic detection and tracking with semi-supervised learning. *Multimedia Systems*, *22*(1), 115–125. doi:10.100700530-014-0402-0

Little, B. (2010). Concerns with Learning-Management Systems and Virtual Learning Environments. *Elearn, 2010*(7), 2. doi:10.1145/1833513.1837142

Mawdsley, G., Tyson, A., Peressotti, C., Jong, R., & Yaffe, M. (2009). Accurate estimation of compressed breast thickness in mammography. *Medical Physics*, *36*(2), 577–586. doi:10.1118/1.3065068 PMID:19291997

Misra, S., Krishna, P., & Abraham, K. (2010). A stochastic learning automata-based solution for intrusion detection in vehicular ad hoc networks. *Security and Communication Networks*, *4*(6), 666–677. doi:10.1002ec.200

Neath, A., & Cavanaugh, J. (2011). The Bayesian information criterion: Background, derivation, and applications. *Wiley Interdisciplinary Reviews: Computational Statistics*, *4*(2), 199–203. doi:10.1002/wics.199

Noel, K. (2016). *Application of Machine Learning to Systematic Allocation Strategies*. SSRN Electronic Journal. doi:10.2139srn.2837664

Ott, D., & Houdek, F. (2014). Automatic Requirement Classification: Tackling Inconsistencies Between Requirements and Regulations. *International Journal of Semantic Computing*, *08*(01), 47–65. doi:10.1142/S1793351X14500020

Punyavachira, T. (2013). *Forecasting Stock Indices Movement Using Hybrid Model: A Comparison of Traditional and Machine Learning Approaches*. SSRN Electronic Journal. doi:10.2139srn.2416494

Puthal, D. (2018). Lattice-modeled Information Flow Control of Big Sensing Data Streams for Smart Health Application. *IEEE Internet of Things Journal*. doi:10.1109/jiot.2018.2805896

Rathore, M., Paul, A., Ahmad, A., & Jeon, G. (2017). IoT-Based Big Data. *International Journal on Semantic Web and Information Systems*, *13*(1), 28–47. doi:10.4018/IJSWIS.2017010103

Schumaker, R. (2013). Machine learning the harness track: Crowdsourcing and varying race history. *Decision Support Systems*, *54*(3), 1370–1379. doi:10.1016/j.dss.2012.12.013

Schwab, D., & Ray, S. (2017). Offline reinforcement learning with task hierarchies. *Machine Learning*, *106*(9-10), 1569–1598. doi:10.100710994-017-5650-8

Shukla, R., Gupta, R. K., & Kashyap, R. (2019). A multiphase pre-copy strategy for the virtual machine migration in cloud. In S. Satapathy, V. Bhateja, & S. Das (Eds.), *Smart Innovation, Systems and Technologies* (Vol. 104). Singapore: Springer. doi:10.1007/978-981-13-1921-1_43

Sun, H., & Betti, R. (2015). A Hybrid Optimization Algorithm with Bayesian Inference for Probabilistic Model Updating. *Computer-Aided Civil and Infrastructure Engineering*, *30*(8), 602–619. doi:10.1111/mice.12142

Tango, F., Minin, L., Tesauri, F., & Montanari, R. (2010). Field tests and machine learning approaches for refining algorithms and correlations of driver's model parameters. *Applied Ergonomics*, *41*(2), 211–224. doi:10.1016/j.apergo.2009.01.010 PMID:19286165

Tiwari, S., Gupta, R. K., & Kashyap, R. (2019). To enhance web response time using agglomerative clustering technique for web navigation recommendation. In H. Behera, J. Nayak, B. Naik, & A. Abraham (Eds.), *Computational Intelligence in Data Mining. Advances in Intelligent Systems and Computing* (Vol. 711). Singapore: Springer. doi:10.1007/978-981-10-8055-5_59

Tofan, C. (2014). Optimization Techniques of Decision Making - Decision Tree. *Advances In Social Sciences Research Journal*, *1*(5), 142–148. doi:10.14738/assrj.15.437

Toivonen, H., & Gross, O. (2015). Data mining and machine learning in computational creativity. *Wiley Interdisciplinary Reviews. Data Mining and Knowledge Discovery*, *5*(6), 265–275. doi:10.1002/widm.1170

Urquhart, L., & Rodden, T. (2016). *A Legal Turn in Human-Computer Interaction?* Towards Regulation by Design for the Internet of Things. SSRN Electronic Journal. doi:10.2139srn.2746467

Wang, D., McMahan, C., & Gallagher, C. (2015). A general regression framework for group testing data, which incorporates pool dilution effects. *Statistics in Medicine*, *34*(27), 3606–3621. doi:10.1002im.6578 PMID:26173957

Waoo, N., Kashyap, R., & Jaiswal, A. (2010). DNA nano array analysis using hierarchical quality threshold clustering. In *Proceedings of 2010 2nd IEEE International Conference on Information Management and Engineering* (pp. 81-85). IEEE. 10.1109/ICIME.2010.5477579

Waoo, N., Kashyap, R., & Jaiswal, A. (2010). DNA nanoarray analysis using hierarchical quality threshold clustering. In *2010 2nd IEEE International Conference on Information Management and Engineering*. IEEE.

Yao, M. (2014). Research on Learning Evidence Improvement for kNN Based Classification Algorithm. *International Journal Of Database Theory And Application*, *7*(1), 103–110. doi:10.14257/ijdta.2014.7.1.10

Yildirim, P., Birant, D., & Alpyildiz, T. (2017). Data mining and machine learning in the textile industry. *Wiley Interdisciplinary Reviews. Data Mining and Knowledge Discovery*, *8*(1), e1228. doi:10.1002/widm.1228

Zhang, B., Xiang, Y., & Wang, J. (2010). Information Filtering Algorithm Based on Semantic Understanding. *Dianzi Yu Xinxi Xuebao*, *32*(10), 2324–2330. doi:10.3724/SP.J.1146.2009.01393

Zhang, N. (2016). Semi-supervised extreme learning machine with wavelet kernel. *International Journal of Collaborative Intelligence*, *1*(4), 298. doi:10.1504/IJCI.2016.10004854

KEY TERMS AND DEFINITIONS

Artificial Intelligence: Computerized thinking is understanding appeared by machines, as opposed to the trademark learning appeared by individuals and changed animals. In programming designing, AI asks about is described as the examination of "sharp masters": any device that sees its condition and goes for broke exercises that intensify its danger of successfully achieving its objectives. Casually, the articulation "artificial intellectual competence" is associated when a machine mimics "emotional" limits that individuals interface with other human identities, for instance, "learning" and "basic reasoning."

Artificial Neural Network: An artificial neural network (ANN) is information taking care of perspective that is animated by the way tangible natural frameworks, for instance, the cerebrum, process information. The key segment of this perspective is the novel structure of the information taking care of the system. It is made out of a broad number of incredibly interconnected getting ready segments (neurons) filling in as one to deal with specific issues. ANNs, like people, learn by case. An ANN is intended for a specific application, for instance, plan affirmation or data gathering, through a learning strategy. Learning in regular structures incorporates changes as per the synaptic affiliations that exist between the neurons.

Chapter 19
Creating a Research Laboratory on Big Data and Internet of Things for the Study and Development of Digital Transformation

Vardan Mkrttchian
https://orcid.org/0000-0003-4871-5956
HHH University, Australia

Leyla Gamidullaeva
https://orcid.org/0000-0003-3042-7550
K.G. Razumovsky Moscow State University of Technologies and Management (FCU), Russia

Svetlana Panasenko
Plekhanov Russian University of Economics, Russia

Arman Sargsyan
National University of AC of Armenia, Armenia

ABSTRACT

This chapter discusses the problems associated with the design of the business model in the new context of big data and the internet of things to create a research laboratory for studying and improving digital transformations. The development of business prospects for IOT is due to two main trends: 1) the change of focus from IOT viewing primarily as a technology platform for viewing it as a business ecosystem and 2) the transition from focusing on the business model in general to the development of business models of ecosystems. In the chapter, the business model of the ecosystem is considered as a model consisting of signs fixed in ecosystems and focuses on creating the cost of the laboratory and fixing the value of the ecosystem in which the created laboratory operates.

DOI: 10.4018/978-1-5225-7432-3.ch019

INTRODUCTION

As shown by Wasser et al. (2014), the spectacular increase of the Web over the last twenty years should be overshadowed by the fact that the "things" that surround us are beginning to flow to us via the Internet. The Internet of Things (IoT) is a term that was invented 20 years ago by Kevin Ashton of Procter & Gamble. This term today are paradigms which examines the objects around us connected to the network, giving anyone access to information "at any time and in any place" (ITU, 2005, Gomez et al., 2013). IoT makes it possible to show the interrelation of objects ("things") for various purposes, including identification, communication, reading and data collection (Oriwoh et al., 2013). In this case objects ("things") can vary from mobile devices to common home objects embedded in systems for detection or communication using various technologies (Oriwoh et al., 2013; Gomez et al., 2013). IoT presents great opportunities for computations and communications. At the same time, the development of these opportunities is largely due to the development of dynamic technical innovations, sensory technologies, intellectual things, nanotechnology and miniaturization (ITU, 2005).

In the well-known strategic research program of the "Cluster of European Projects on the Internet of Things" (CERP-IoT, 2009), it is expected that IoT will change business, information and social processes and provide many unforeseen opportunities, in particular to create a research laboratory for studying and improving digital transformations. This will be facilitated by the observations of Kyriazis and Varvarigou (2013), that the dynamic, fast-changing and technology-rich digital environment of IoT allows the provision of value-added applications that use a variety of devices that facilitate services and information, which is very necessary to create a research laboratory for studying and improving digital transformations. Moreover, they add that, as technologies for IoT mature and become ubiquitous; the focus will be on approaches that make it possible to become smarter, more reliable and more autonomous, which coincides with the main goal of this chapter, creating a research laboratory for studying and improving digital transformations. However, there was practically no research on IoT and related business models from the ecosystem point of view, as limited research in IoT focused on the technological platform and business models of one firm (Uckelmann et al., 2011, Leminen et al., 2012). Therefore, in this chapter, we consider the design of a business model for creating a research laboratory for studying and improving digital transformations, as a technological and research process in the transition from business models of an individual company to networked and more complex ecosystem business models. In particular, the study focuses on problems that prevent the emergence of business models IoT.

Our conceptual study of creating a research laboratory for studying and improving digital transformations is organized as follows. First, after this brief introduction, we will consider the theoretical background of paradigm shifts in relation to ecosystems and business models related to IoT specifically for creating a research laboratory for studying and improving digital transformations. Secondly, we discuss the main problems of developing business models for IoT for a research laboratory for studying and improving digital transformations. Thirdly, we come to these tasks, offering the basis for creating a new tool for developing business models of ecosystems for the IoT by concluding a research laboratory for studying and improving digital transformations. Finally, in conclusion, we will consider our key implications. The IoT in the modern world are not simply connected with the opportunities of digital technologies but also largely based on them. This is exactly why the full-fledged successive industrial sector's digitization will become a platform for qualitative changes of the economy and long-term opportunities. Thus, the transition to digital technologies is inevitable, but from another perspective, this very transition cannot be the absolute goal. In this chapter, the authors aimed at providing a better understanding for IoT concept and its application benefits for former Soviet Union countries, for example – Russian Federation. The main problem is how the Russian Federation acts against the economically developed countries, which are the creators of IoT. This chapter mainly focuses on presenting the authors' views on how to sustain and increase competitive advantage of the Russian Federation by catching and implementing IoT. With IoT, Russian Federation gets a bigger share of the world manufacturing value chain. Recent trends of globalization are faced with the need to meet the constant global demand for new production technologies. To overcome this problem, the industry must ensure sustainable production. It is expected that, within the framework of the fourth stage of industrialization, a new approach in the IoT will ensure a greater integration of information and communication technologies (ICT) with industry. It leads to the intelligent and self-organized industry as well as, more flexible and efficient industrial goods.

During the first industrial revolution with the help of water and steam, the production was mechanized. The main driver of the second industrial revolution was electricity, which helped create mass production. At the center of the third revolution was electronics and information technologies that automated production. Due to the third industrial revolution there began a wide use of information technologies in the industry. The IoT is related with the development of Cyber Physical Systems. The fourth industrial revolution is the blending of technologies of the physical, digital and biological world, which creates new opportunities and affects political, social and economic systems. The fourth industrial revolution fundamentally transforms modern production, thanks to new technological achievements, including digitalization and robotization, artificial intelligence and the Internet of things (IoT), new materials and biotechnology. Due to these changes, production in developed countries again becomes the main source of prosperity and creation of new jobs.

Nowadays, development of intelligent instructional methods in connected settings, and guided appearance in experientially based learning have been investigated. Besides, due to the afforts of V. Mkrttchian, such courses were analyzed and additionally researched, and appeared in virtual classrooms within the framework of experiential learning.

BACKGROUND

Now in a networked environment, all organizations, including research laboratories, are becoming part of complex business ecosystems. All this becomes even more difficult when there is a transition from centralized to decentralized and distributed network structures (Barabasi, 2002; Möller et al., 2005). This is because each structure emphasizes its original activity in the ecosystem, and an ever-increasing level of complexity requires the emergence of systems of new types of values (Möller et al., 2005). In Muegge (2011) business ecosystems are considered as a form of participation "where organizations and individuals usually self-identify as ecosystems, both in their own internal discourse and in the identity of the brand that they convey to others." At the same time, the author points out that the business ecosystem belongs to the organizational structure of economic entities, for example, to our research laboratory for studying and improving digital transformations whose individual business activities are tied to a certain platform and that this platform is the organization of things.

This platform has a technological nature and is the basis of the created business ecosystem (Cusumano & Gawer, 2002). In Muegge (2011), this platform is shown as a set of technological blocks and additional assets that the organization as a whole and its individual members can use and consume to create additional products, technologies and services. In another work, Muegge (2013) presents the structure of a platform according to which the platform is already the organization of things (for example, technology and additional assets), the community is the organization of people, and the business ecosystem is the organization of economic entities. Thus, the core of the IOT ecosystem refers to the interconnection of the physical world of things with the virtual world of the Internet, software and hardware boards, and the standards commonly used to provide such interaction (Mazhelis et al. 2012).

Moore (1996) in his work defines the business ecosystem described above as "an economic community supported by the founding of interacting organizations and individuals". The business ecosystem includes customers, leading manufacturers, competitors and other interested parties. At the same time, it was revealed that leading and lucrative organizations exert a strong influence on evolutionary processes. Peltoniemi (2005), in his work on system theory, shows that "the system is more than the sum of its parts" and reminds us that the work of the system cannot be understood by studying its parts separated from the essence. In his work the author showed that the socio-economic system, such as the business ecosystem, but is a more complex adaptive system and that its participants-people develop through joint evolution with a greater environment, self-organization, the ability to create new relationships between themselves and of course to adaptation in the environment.

As noted above, this chapter addresses the problems associated with developing a business model in the new context of the Big Data and the Internet of things to create a research laboratory for studying and improving digital transformations. In this regard, to complete the background of the chapter, it is necessary to consider, how the transition from the business model of the organization to the business model of the ecosystem in which digital transformations occur.

A review of the literature has shown that since the early 2000s the new economic business model has gradually shifted to management concepts with general controlled management (Shafer et al., 2005). This new, very strong and broad concept immediately passed into the concept (Zott & Amit, 2008) and is becoming increasingly important (Demil & Lecocq, 2010). And the moment came when the academic re-search of business models began to be developed without the generally accepted idea of what modern business models should consist of el (Morris et al., 2005; Osterwalder et al., 2005; Schweizer, 2005). Right Zott, Amit and Massa (2011), arguing and proving that early researchers viewed the business model in a variety of ways, including a statement, description, presentation, architecture, conceptual tool or model, a structural template, a method, a template and a set of all these elements. In addition, they found that the business model is often studied without defining its concept.

The academic definition of business models has now changed markedly over the past decade. Achtenhagen, Melin and Naldi (2013) have shown that fundamental changes have taken place from "which business models" to the understanding of "for which business models." It is already generally known that a business model describes the way a particular organization is managed (Osterwalder et al. 2005; Rajala & Westerlund, 2008; Casadesus-Masanell & Ricart, 2010; Teece, 2010). It is noteworthy that Osterwalder, Pigneur and Tucci (2005) showed that "the business model is an indicator - an identifier of how the company conducts its business." At the same time, business models are understood as entities that break into components or different modules. Shafer, Smith, and Linder, (2005) found more than two dozen different components of the business model, divided into four main areas, and Osterwalder and Pigneur (2010) discuss different components in nine groups. Muegge (2012) uses a component view to provide a method for discovering business models for technology entrepreneurs.

Despite the fact that scientists are unified in their view of the business model as a design at the organization level, it is noted that it is part of the system (Rajala & Westerlund, 2008). In his work, Timmers (1998) describes the business model as product architecture, services and information flows", including a description of the various business participants and their role; Description of potential benefits for various business entities; and a description of the sources of income. The literature on business ecosystems points to the need for a deeper network review of business models (see Carbone, 2009, Muegge, 2013). Existing templates of business models and structures are adequate in addressing the problems faced by individual existing organizations, but less suitable for analyzing the interdependent nature of growth and the success of organizations that are developing in the same innovation ecosystem (Weiller & Neely, 2013). Given the development of the IoT area, it becomes clear that the interdependence associated with the fact that it is connected with other participants through technical and business ties is becoming increasingly significant and it is from these positions that the design of the business model is further made in the new context of Big Data and the Internet of Things to create a research laboratory for studying and improving digital transformations. By rapid implementation of information and communication technologies in manufacturing, the industrial process becomes smart and enables mass customization. Many researches today are devoted to the investigation of the technologies and processes concerned with IoT and its impact on economic development.

IoT supposes the use of network approach that is based on the ability of creating smart products and components. According to the same authors about IoT enables new implementation areas through the potential of IoT technologies such as powerful, flexible and affordable Cyber Physical Systems applications or extended applicability of Lean Production with various production types.

Bughin and Manyika (2015) assumed that the crucial impact factor in competition is related with the Internet of Things (IoT) which means that senior managers and company's members must act at the system level in order to be able to solve the challenges coming from the technological disruption.

IoT technologies' application has proved their effectiveness in terms of increasing European firm's competitive advantage not only in manufacturing sectors, but also in service fields such as retail, healthcare, travel and financial services (Piercy & Rich, 2009).

MAIN FOCUS OF THE CHAPTER

Issues, Controversies, Problems

Previous studies are almost silent about the problems associated with the monetization of IoT, that is, they do not talk about the traps of making money on the Internet of things. Moreover, there is no information about the problems associated with the design of the business model in the new context of Big Data and the Internet of things to create a research laboratory for studying and improving digital transformations. This is in the case; Wurster (2014) tried in his work to classify barriers that prevent organizations from moving forward in terms of making money with the help of IoT. It turns out that IoT has a significant technological impact, thus creating new problems for the organization. These problems are connected with the definition of horizontal needs and opportunities, it is necessary to solve the management task related to the internal alignment of the team of the organization to solve the problem of the conformity of technology and the goals of business developers and ways to overcome the market maturity problem for the new IoT technology. As will be shown later, we expanded this point of view and identified three new IOT tasks, including a variety of objects, immaturity of innovation and unstructured ecosystems. We identified these problems on the basis of a literature review and discussions with the IoT experts. Based on Muegge (2011), these problems are centered on the platform, the community of developers and business ecosystems associated with the formation of IoT ecosystem business models. This chapter focuses on solving these problems as a result of which the problems associated with the design of the business model in the new context of Big Data and the Internet of things to create a research laboratory for studying and improving digital transformations will be technically resolved (see below).

Next, we face the problem of the variety of objects associated with the difficulty of developing business models for IoT because of the many different types of connected objects and devices without generally accepted or emerging standards. As is known, the IoT is a network of interconnected objects (Evans, 2011), where everyone, from toothbrushes and sportswear to refrigerators and cars, will have an online presence. It is extremely difficult for them to standardize the interfaces with which they can connect to the Internet. In addition, there is another problem for management; there are almost endless ways to connect the object, thing, business and consumer (Leminen et al., 2012). Therefore, the number and structure of possible business models is growing. While recent estimates indicate that there are currently 20 billion connected devices, and by 2020 there will be 50 billion devices, more than 99 percent of physical objects that may one day join the network are still not connected (Evans, 2011). It turns out that the number of objects that will be part of the future of the Internet is just an unprecedented number of sites. But at the same time, Espada and colleagues (2011) note that more and more physical objects called "things" become available in digital format, thereby solving the above problem. Since these "virtual objects" are digital elements that have a specific purpose, they contain a series of data and can perform actions, integrate with other applications and physical "things," and they may require specific business logic (Espada et al., 2011).

The next problem is the inequality of innovations that relates to the current "mess" of emerging technologies and components created, but to this day unclaimed essential innovations of IoT, are still not ripe in products and services. Since they are not standardized or are modularly not ready for wider use. This often requires a lot of engineering work to combine them together in another application. Modularly not ready objects, including "components of plug and play" components, today are not in great demand, although they are prerequisites for the developing market. In addition, the design of the business model in the new context of Big Data and the Internet of things to create a research laboratory for studying and improving digital transformations will allow us to implement combined components, experiment and create products and services for the IoT ecosystem, and also learn the experience of the market in developing new demanded businesses -models. The popular model for today for the life cycle of the introduction of new technologies (Moore, 2006) recognizes five types of innovators, including innovators, early adopters, early majority, late majority and backward. In this chapter, the challenge is to move from early followers to the early majority, because the business model should allow "expanding" the business. Since early adopters are willing to tolerate the immaturity of innovation, but the early majority prefers to evaluate and buy whole products, including the product, ancillary products and any related services (Moore, 2006). This is in case when Downes and Nunes (2013) showed that the great opportunities provided by the new digital platforms based on IoT are the same. As new products are improved by several trial users and then quickly covered by the vast majority of the market. Again, the innovation must be mature enough that customers can quickly accept it.

The next problem that we solved in this chapter is unstructured ecosystems that do not have certain basic structures and management, do not have the role of stakeholders and do not have the logic of creating value. At the same time they will not be suitable or are not in demand by the participants of the new ecosystem. This is possible, for example, when there may be no IoT operators or potential customers. But in the future, the pursuit of new business opportunities requires opening up new relationships in new industries or expanding existing relationships takes time and is a problem for management. The complexity of the ecosystem is related to the number of participants (Möller et al., 2005), and the early ecosystem is an unstructured, chaotic and open area for participants. IoT is still in its infancy, just like on the Internet. The Internet has become the driving force behind the incredible wealth of competing and complementary business ecosystems that all use the Internet in different ways, such as an ecosystem tied to Amazon Web Services (AWS) or an ecosystem tied to Google's paid Google AdSense form, or an inhibitory ecosystem provided by open APIs and open data, or many business ecosystems tied to platforms developed at the community level. There is a need for business models that will shape IoT business ecosystems through the innovation of the business model itself (Carbone, 2009). However, it is still too early to talk about which of these will be important but evolving ecosystems in the IoT field, and which participants (participants) will become key players within them. Such interested parties can be, for example, a provider of objects / devices, a software infrastructure provider, a provider of hosted solutions or intelligent services, an IOT operator, a value-added service provider or a full service integrator, data collector / analyzer, or even an open source community (Carbone, 2009). Therefore, instead of focusing on key stakeholders, it may be better to focus on generating and fixing values in ecosystems. Unstructured IoT ecosystems necessitate IoT-based business models that help build and analyze the choice of ecosystems and business models and formulate this integrated value for stakeholders. So we approached Potential Solutions and Recommendations for the design of the business model in the new the context of the Big Data and the Internet of things to create a research laboratory for studying and improving digital transformations.

Solutions and Recommendations

Before developing recommendations and solutions, we assumed that modern managers could overcome the problems discussed above and be able to develop acceptable business models for IOT, but that provided that if they change their focus on the ecosystem approach of doing business and use the business design tools models that take into account the ecosystem nature of IoT, while temporarily forget the selfish goals of their organization. These possible efforts are analyzed below. A rapid development of virtual technologies in 2011-2018 has extended their applications, as well as their function essential for simulation (through the video games, especially). It is apparent that these technologies could be put at the service of education. The most obvious application is simulation, and we are indeed able to generate experiences of laboratories, repeatable and virtually infinitely variable. In addition, virtual practice and the development of computing technologies, both at the hardware level (more RAM (Random Access Memory) and HDD (Hard Disc Drive), new architecture of education), and the software level (new languages and paradigms) would permit the development of artificial intelligence. The research of virtual environment definitively dissolves any material thing in itself transforming it, and a developer/researcher has to use not material objects, but only their signs. A science studying signs and sign systems is semIoTics. This is a cognitive method, which structures the object, and promotes its understanding. SemIoTics is closely connected with other areas of expertise, concerning the study of systems. For example, it is in close touch with the theory of information science and technology, with the only difference that cybernetics studies dynamic and quantitative aspects of the relationships in the system, while semIoTics concerns steady-state and qualitative characteristics. The research of the semIoTic approach is useful for acquaintance with the theory of information, as these areas of expertise complement each other. Although being existed for many years, an IA is a new kind of technique able to compile data, and to reiterate the experiences taking into account the previous results (e.g., "a genetic algorithm", or "an algorithm of the neural network"). Thus, taking into account the evolution of these approaches, it is possible to design a system or a student able to conduct experiments with various parameters. This article is based on the educational principle that experimentation is the key to a good understanding, and that to be optimal an education must be adapted on a case-by-case basis. The aim of the paper consists in realization of a virtual environment, in which the students will be able to interact through avatars being their virtual alter-ego. This world will be "virtual", if there is a basis for the environment designed as follows:

- A classroom (allowing for working in a small group, with the avatar of a professor dedicated)
- A conference room (allowing for the relationship of a large number of individuals, multidisciplinary, and inter-university)
- A labor (allowing for the achievement of practical work)

The IA will be carried out by video capture, and modeling of the image of a student or a teacher, the aim being to make an anthropomorphic way. This will considerably improve the sensation of immersion, and in fact will facilitate learning. In addition, although there is the IA of "professor" type who can deliver lessons, there will be also IA, compiling data and, of course, it can be queried by the host to palliate a question blocking its immediate progress at the *t* moment.

Technical details will be provided later on in this paper, but the choices described here allow meeting the essential issues that are as follows:

- To be able to dispense the largest number of a particular teaching
- Make the teaching methods more flexible and scalable
- Facilitate the activity and the interdisciplinary learning

A term "a course of validation of knowledge acquired" would be possible to add to the system, based on the profiles of each avatar (experiments carried out, choice of courses or conferences, notes of professors, etc.), and a prioritization of avatars and their access to given functions of these validations (all under control of a teacher).

The design model is dividable into two essential modules:

- The system of video capture-
- The system of compiling data and creating the IA

The system of video capture will serve to the modeling of an image from 2D to 3D. It will include a hardware part, which is although still incomplete in its composition, it will require the employment of at least three cameras, and a monochrome part with a smooth edge for virtualization of the environment (place and component).

These few technical specificities arising from the choice of the implementation make use of the technique of triangulation in a mark prefix. This technology allows you to simulate the in-motion by extrapolation in the mark without having to perform a visual capture of the subject to be considered. Moreover, using this method, we could divest ourselves of hardware constraints (the level of definition of camera angles and specific).The software features, as well as the implementation, will be developed later in this article.

The IA will be focused on the assisted learning to interact with the students. At the same time, the students will pose questions to the SIA *(Student Interactive Assistant)*, which will be able to use the compilation of data available in the various databases of the system, as well as to find the answers through the course already "pre-designed" by a session of questions with the teachers' help. This last point deserves a clarification, namely, our RNS (*Regulatory News Service*) will be formed by the teachers who can ask questions of the IA, test its answers, change if necessary, or correct them.

This system of IA ensures a very high scalability, and an excellent level of customization. The aim of this approach is to find much more efficient teaching. The software features, as well as the implementation, will be developed in this chapter.

Figures 1 and 2 are dedicated to the hardware elements, and will show what part of the system will be supported by some physical element.

The user level will be implemented in two different versions: IA as a teacher, and IA as a student. The student version will include a menu displaying the SIA, and allowing to access a different space, classroom, conference rooms, work practice, etc., through a drop-down menu Then, the student will select/cancel the activation of the SIA, and for a better educational follow it will also be possible to consult a history of activity (courses or conferences followed, notes and laboratories), and a schedule of upcoming activities. The activities will be declined by name, topic, the responsible professor, and the level in the university curriculum (1st, 2nd years, etc.)

We hope that a term "a system of course suggestion" will be able to integrate to the SIA, as a function of the spread and the shortcomings of the student.

Figure 1. Illustration of Intelligent Agent (IA) server link to the image between the student servers (users), and the data file of the educational media library

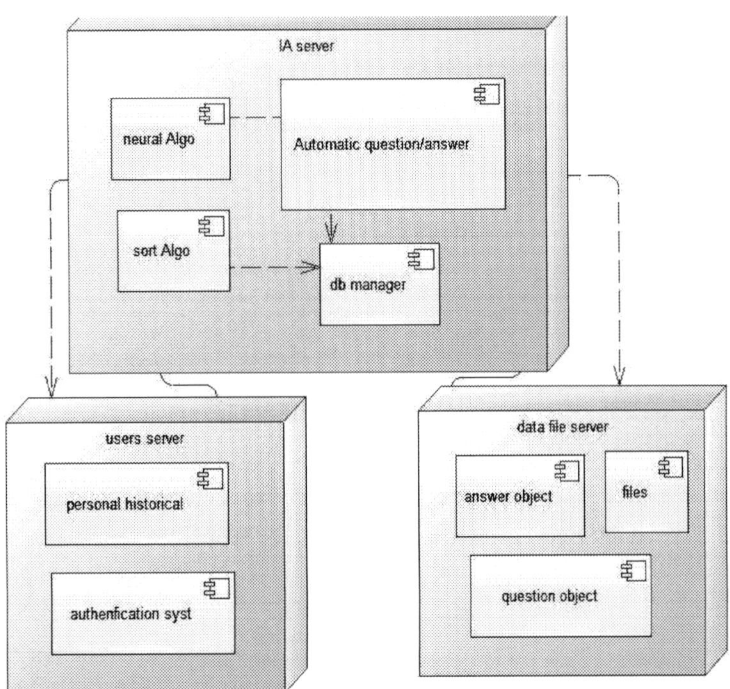

Figure 2. Illustration of Intelligent Agent (IA) server link to the virtual environment image of the 3D modeling server, and video capture hardware of the modification room

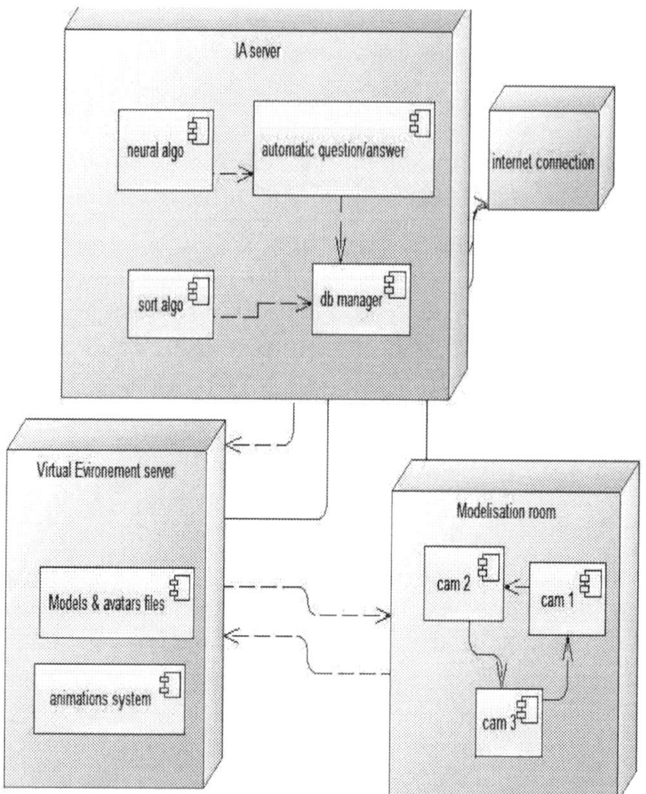

Assuming that managers could follow the path outlined above, and that they will need to shift their attention from the business model of their organization to the common ecosystem business models. Our research has shown that such a term has at least three interpretations:

- this term can refer to a business model with specific properties - in this case - a business embodied in ecosystem concepts (for example, the concept of a "green business model" that refers to environmentally-oriented parties and has specific "Green" qualities) (Westerlund, 2013);
- The ecosystem business model (or category of business models) can be shared by ecosystem participants (for example, the term "faceless semiconductor business model", which implies that all diskless semiconductor companies are more or less the same) (Low & Muegge, 2013);
- such a term may refer to a design at the level of analysis of a superior organization, which explains how the whole ecosystem works towards common goals, rather than as a business at the level of that organization (Battistella et al., 2013). However, the third interpretation usually refers to the structure and mechanisms of ecosystems, and not to the ecosystem as a business model (Ritala et al., 2013).

Our research has shown that such understandings of these different interpretations as different concepts these managers understand them as different views on the same phenomena. However, as our studies show, the business model of the ecosystem consists of a set of signs (Osterwalder and Pigneur, 2010) fixed in ecosystems that focus both on the method of creating and fixing the value of the organization, and on any part of the ecosystem method, creating and fixing the value of the ecosystem.

Attempts by our predecessors to define the IoT business ecosystem from a platform perspective (Mazhelis et al., 2012), but currently existing IoTs on individual solutions and applications reject the correctness of such solutions. Now, everyone approaches the understanding of IoT business models by considering the value for all participants of the IoT business ecosystem. This approach determines the value for all participants who use the IoT platform. Our research has shown that most vendors and telecom operators, as well as IOT platform vendors (for example, platform providers from machine to machine) are trying to formulate the value of IoT using this approach to develop their business models. However, the received business models are often biased towards the supplier and do not have drivers for the total value as one of the explicit components.

Our research has shown that we need built-in drivers, which determine the total cost of the entire ecosystem, in our case, the IoT research laboratory, and not for individual value drivers (that is, the value of a particular subject from specific applications or services). Therefore, our research is aimed at creating value and capturing values in business models from the level of organization to the level of ecosystems. The developed structure of the business model for IoT has a higher-level perspective to formulate the integrated value of IoT, rather than accessing the drivers of fragmented values. Our colleagues Weill and Vitale (2001) present a set of simple schemes designed to provide tools for developing e-business initiatives. Their "e-business electronic schemes" include three classes of components of the business model: participants (firm interests, customers, suppliers and allies), relationships and flows (money, information, product or service flows), we can confirm that the correctness of colleagues our research confirms.

Our research has shown as well Tapscott, Lowy and Ticoll (2000) offer a map of values for describing how the web is working. The value map displays all key classes of participants (partners, customers, suppliers) and price exchanges between them (tangible and intangible benefits and knowledge). Similarly, Gordin and Ackermans (2001) propose a conceptual approach to modeling, "the ontology of" e3-value "to determine how the economic value is created and exchanged in the network of participants. Their ontology raises a number of useful terms related to values, such as port values and port values. Muegge (2011) argues that the engine that drives innovation in the ecosystem is a cycle of resources from the platform to the business ecosystem, the developer community and back to the platform. He also argues that the development community is a value-creation (innovation) locus, and the business ecosystem is a value-capture locus (the commercialization of innovation).

The research has shown that the Allee (2000) network of values is creating economic value through dynamic and complex exchanges between organizations, suppliers, strategic partners, the community, customers and users. Our own studies have confirmed that such price exchanges can be displayed in block diagrams showing goods, services and revenue streams, as well as knowledge flows and value creation. Dynamics, which is visible from the point of view of network cost, is relevant even when describing business models at the level of an individual organization. For example, Casadesus-Masanell and Ricart (2010) argue that the business model consists of a set of management decisions and their consequences. Each choice can lead to different results; thus, they control dynamism. Moreover, they summarize three characteristics of a good business model: it is consistent with the organization's goals, it is self-excitation (that is, dynamic and cyclical), and it is reliable. These characteristics support the sustainability of business in ecosystems (Iansiti & Levien, 2002).

The analysis would be incomplete without mentioning the results of comparing the state of the digital economy in Australia and the Russian Federation, especially on digital transformation. As a result of the implementation of our project, it was established that Australia, developed by the level of the digital economy, can adopt the Russian experience of teaching the basics of digital transformation of participants in this process. We have established how the learning process takes place.

The two sides of digital transformation are centered on local hardware, software and infrastructure for a distributed virtual machine model, software as a service and cloud IT. This is the transition from the physically grounded world to the digital one. This is a digital transformation. This transformation consists of two parts: the technological side and the human side. Most business and IT leaders already have a technological side, but they do not pay attention to the human side: the understanding that effective digital transformation is related to how people adopt and use technology, at least as well as in technology itself. And this applies not only to people at the top of your organization, but to everyone who works for you, especially if they interact directly with customers.

According to research (Mkrttchian, et al, 2018) the achievement of a complete and successful digital transformation depends not only on the right technology, but also on:

- From the leaders. People at the top of your organization must lead the way through digital transformations, for example, using the same tools that they expect everyone else will use.
- From managing an employee's trip, exactly the way you manage your customer's trip. Each user expects that the online experience will be as smooth as that of the world's leading digital companies.

These are small tasks, but they are much easier to accomplish with an integrated, seamless and secure solution. Just like cloud IT solutions can help you improve the quality of customer service, it will also help you provide the best experience with employees. This can become a real impact on the business when first-line employees feel able to help their clients in new and exciting directions.

Two Critical Business Effects

Collaboration uses the collective mental capacity of your employees. Two main components are basic for collaborative technologies: the ability to work from virtually anywhere and the ability to work with simple intuitive solutions on almost any device. Premium solutions offer integrated tools that help everyone to contribute. They are easier to adapt to your specific needs and culture, they are easily scaled, they have more life cycles, and their creators usually offer better long-term support. And since they are more common, new employees may already know how to use them, which reduces the time and cost of training.

Creativity depends on the ability to find innovative solutions to existing problems. From there, it expands the possibilities of finding these solutions, finding and fixing problems and testing them again. Thus, the necessary tools for working together also help you stimulate creativity, simplifying the experiment and finding ideas that really work (Mkrttchian, et al, 2019).

Security and Management

Digital transformation has opened up new opportunities, but it has also raised increased security concerns. Triple H-Avatar helps protect data that has been trusted with intelligent, permanent protection that protects data on many devices and scenarios. A simplified IT environment also allows your IT team to create and manage employees' devices and services, which reduces the burden on members of your IT team.

Business creativity depends on the ability to find innovative solutions to existing problems. Fortunately, there is a simple answer: Triple H-Avatar meets the needs of the enterprise. It integrates all existing technologies and equipment to help employees be more creative and work together safely, namely:

- unlock creativity, helping its people to work with documents, voice and touch, all backed up by tools using AI and machine learning.
- provides the widest and deepest applications and services, as well as a universal tool for collaboration, giving its people the flexibility and choice in how they connect, exchange and communicate.
- simplifies IT by integrating management of users, devices, applications and services.
- helps protect customer data, company data and intellectual property with built-in intellectual protection.

Triple H-Avatar is designed for businesses with up to 50 users, but this is not limited, if necessary, the number of users can be increased to 3000. It combines all available resources with individual security and management functions. It also helps to expand the capabilities of employees, protect your business and simplify the management of IT, namely:

- helps your teams achieve more by better connecting employees, customers and suppliers.
- helps your employees work anywhere on any device.
- protects data on all devices with permanent protection.
- simplifies the configuration and management of employees' devices and services using a single IT console.

The concept of the Internet of things has recently gained incredible popularity. Unlike many other models that appeared in recent years, which were often too overpriced, the concept of the Internet of things already now has all the prerequisites for conquering the entire developed world. All sorts of sensors are everywhere: ubiquitous wireless access networks; effective data analysis tools; means of graphic visualization and much more. Even the very idea of how to realize all the advantages of the concept of the Internet of things can be staggering. For example, only one car with an automated control system receives from the sensors about 750 MB of information every second of the movement (Fig. 3.) Accordingly, the amount of data generated by the completely entangled communication networks of the city in one second will be measured in petabytes. Naturally, the city faces the question of where to store all these data.

FUTURE RESEARCH DIRECTIONS

Relevant literature shares the view on how business models in the new context of Big Data and the Internet of things to create a research laboratory for studying and improving digital transformations in the future will be about creating value and fixing value. The authors argue that managers can develop viable IoT business models, taking into account the different aspects associated with these two important tasks in the future, since in ecosystems, different value factors will always be. They include both individual and

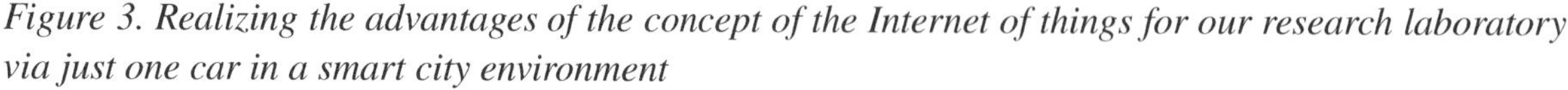

Figure 3. Realizing the advantages of the concept of the Internet of things for our research laboratory via just one car in a smart city environment

common motives of different participants, and also contribute to the birth of the ecosystem to meet the need for value creation, innovation and making money. In the future, it is expectable that the emphasis on shared value drivers is critical to creating an unbiased ecosystem. Without respect for the goals of other participants, long-term relationships cannot be built. However, each individual value driver will also serve as a motivational factor of individual significance. In the future, stability, cyber security and improved customer experience will be of great importance. In future studies, examples of cost drivers may be drivers that different participants can enter into the IoT ecosystem.

CONCLUSION

In this chapter, design-related business models in the new context of Big Data and the Internet of Things to create a research laboratory for studying and improving digital transformations, node values include various actors, actions or (automated) processes that are linked to other nodes to create value . In addition, these nodes can include autonomous subjects, such as intelligent sensors, pre-programmed machines and associated intellects (avatars).

Thus, the ecosystem is a connection with different node values; in addition to individual activities, automatic connections and processes, individuals or commercial and non-profit organizations, these valuable nodes can be groups of such organizations, networks of organizations or even groups of networks. In short, there is a significant heterogeneity of the nodes of value in the IoT ecosystems.

In this chapter, price exchanges relate to the exchange of meanings by different means, resources, knowledge and information. The exchange of values occurs between and within nodes with different values in the ecosystem, and exchanges can be described using different value streams. In fact, these streams show "how the engine works" by exchanging replay, knowledge, money and information in various ways, they describe the action that takes place in the business ecosystem to create and record the value. The exchange of value is crucial, because they also indicate how the revenues in the ecosystem are generated and distributed.

In this chapter, not all created values make sense from the point of view of commercialization. The extract of value refers to a part of the ecosystem that extracts value; in other words, it shows a meaningful value that can be monetized, and the corresponding nodes and exchanges that are necessary for creating and capturing value. Allocation of value is a useful concept, as it can help focus on the relevant part of the ecosystem. This part can be individual activities, automated processes, individuals or commercial and non-profit organizations or groups of such organizations, networks of organizations or even groups of networks and flows of values between these nodes. Value allocation is useful for determining the basic value and its main aspects in the ecosystem.

In this chapter, the concept of value creation illustrates how value is deliberately created and fixed in an ecosystem. That is, cost design is a general architecture that reflects the basic structure of the ecosystem business model. On the one hand, it provides the boundaries for the ecosystem and describes the entire object that creates and fixes the value. On the other hand, this is the sum of the four pillars of value and leads to a pattern of work. In this vein, cost design is a concept that is very similar to the concept of a business model. The difference is that although the "business model" is usually associated with the business model of the firm, the concept of value for use at the ecosystem level can be defined.

Thus, the authors argue that the "cost design" can better correspond to the context of ecosystems than the "business model". In addition, we believe that different value constructs can be classified, analyzed and compared similarly to different types of business model.

This analysis allowed building up a gateway for improvement the author's ideas about the design of intelligent agents as a model system for the development of a SocIoTechnology using a SemIoTics and Signs in virtual cloud-based lab.

ACKNOWLEDGMENT

The reported study was funded by RFBR according to the research project No. 18-010-00204.

REFERENCES

Achtenhagen, L., Melin, L., & Naldi, L. (2013). Dynamics of Business Models Strategizing, Critical Capability and Activities for Sustained Value Creation. *Long Range Planning*, *46*(6), 427–442. doi:10.1016/j.lrp.2013.04.002

Allee, V. (2000). Reconfiguring the Value Network. *The Journal of Business Strategy*, *21*(4), 36–39. doi:10.1108/eb040103

Barabasi, A.-L. (2002). *Linked: The New Science of Network*. Cambridge, UK: Perseus Publishing.

Battistella, C., Colucci, K., DeToni, A. F., & Nonino, F. (2013). Methodology of Business Ecosystems Network Analysis: A Case Study in Telecom Italia Future Centre. *Technological Forecasting and Social Change*, *80*(6), 1194–1210. doi:10.1016/j.techfore.2012.11.002

Carbone, P. (2009, February). The Emerging Promise of Business Ecosystems. *Open Source Business Resource,* 11-16. Retrieved from http://Timreview.CA/article/227

Casadesus Masanell, R., & Ricart, J. E. (2010). From Strategy to Business Models and onto Tactics. *Long Range Planning*, *43*(2), 195–215. doi:10.1016/j.lrp.2010.01.004

CERP-IoT. (2009). *Internet of Things Strategic Research Roadmap.* Cluster of European Projects. Retrieved from http://www.grifs-project.eu/data/File/CERP-IoT%20SRA_I-oT_v11.pdf

Cusumano, M. A., & Gawer, A. (2002). The Elements of Platform Leadership. *MIT Sloan Management Review*, *43*(3), 51–58.

Demil, B., & Lecoq, X. (2010). Business Model: Towarda Dynamic Consistency View of Strategy. *Long Range Planning*, *43*(2-3), 227–246. doi:10.1016/j.lrp.2010.02.004

Downes, L., & Nunes, P. F. (2013). Big-Bang Disruption. *Harvard Business Review*, *91*(3), 44–56.

Espada, J. P., Martínez, O. S., García-Bustelo, B. C. P., & Lovelle, J. M. C. (2011). Virtual Objects on the Internet of Things. *International Journal of Artificial Intelligence and Interactive Multimedia*, *1*(4), 24–30. doi:10.9781/ijimai.2011.144

Evans, D. (2011). *The Internet of Things-How the Next Evolution of the Internet Is Changing Everything*. Cisco Internet Business Solutions Group (IBSG) White Paper.

Gershenfeld, N., & Vasseur, J. P. (2014). As Objects Go Online: The Promise (And Pitfalls) of the Internet of Things. *Foreign Affairs*, *93*(2), 60–67.

Gomez, J., Huete, J. F., Hoyos, O., Perez, L., & Grigori, D. (2013). Interaction System Based on Internet of Things as Support for Education. *Procedia Computer Science*, *21*, 132–139. doi:10.1016/j.procs.2013.09.019

Gordijn, J., & Akkermans, H. (2001). Design and Evaluation of e-Business Models. *IEEE Intelligent Systems*, *16*(4), 11–17. doi:10.1109/5254.941353

Iansiti, M., & Levien, R. (2002). *Keynotes and Dominators:FramingOper-atingand Technology Strategy in a Business Ecosystem.* Harvard Business School Working Paper, No. 03-061. Cambridge, MA: Harvard Business School.

ITU. (2005). *The Internet of Things*. ITU Internet Reports. Retrieved from http://www.itu.int/osg/spu/publications/internetofthings/

Kyriazis, D., & Varvarigou, T. (2013). Smart, Autonomous and Reliable Internet of Things. *Procedia Computer Science*, *21*, 442–448. doi:10.1016/j.procs.2013.09.059

Leminen, S., Westerlund, M., Rajahonka, M., & Siuruainen, R. (2012). Towards IoT Ecosystems and Business Models. In S. Andreev, S. Balandin, & Y. Koucheryavy (Eds.), Internet of Things, Smart Spaces, and Next Generation Networking Lecture Notes in Computer Science (vol. 7469, pp. 15-26). Berlin: Springer. doi:10.1007/978-3-642-32686-8_2

Low, A., & Muegge, S. (2013). Keystone Business Models for Network Security Processors. *Technology Innovation Management Review, 3*(7), 25-33. Retrieved from http://timreview.ca/article/703

Mazhelis, O., Luoma, E., & Warma, H. (2012). Defining Internet of Things Ecosystem. In S. Andreev, S. Balandin, & Y. Koucheryavy (Eds.), Internet of Things, Smart Spaces, and Next Generation Networking–Lecture Notes in Computer Science (vol. 7469, pp. 1-14). Berlin: Springer. doi:10.1007/978-3-642-32686-8_1

Mkrttchian, V., Palatkin, I., Gamidullaeva, L., & Panasenko, S. (2018). About digital avatars for control systems using Big Data and Knowledge sharing in virtual industries. In A. Gyamfi & I. Williams (Eds.), *Big Data and Knowledge Sharing in Virtual Organizations* (pp. 46–59). Hershey, PA: IGI Global; doi:10.4018/978-1-5225-7519-1ch.04

Mkrttchian, V., Veretikhina, S., Gavrilova, O., Ioffe, A., Markosyan, S., & Chernyshenko, S. (2019). The comparison of Cross-cultural analysis of the green country - Australia and of the North Country – Russia: Cultures, small businesses, cross the barriers. In U. G. Benna (Ed.), *Industrial and Urban Growth Policies at the Sub-National, National, and Global Levels* (pp. 176–189). Hershey, PA: IGI Global. doi:10.4018/978-1-5225-7625-9

Möller, K., Rajala, A., & Svahn, S. (2005). Strategic Business Nets–Their Type and Management. *Journal of Business Research, 58*(9), 1274–1284. doi:10.1016/j.jbusres.2003.05.002

Moore, G. R. (2006). *Crossing the Chasm– Marketing and Selling Technology Products to Mainstream Customers (2nd ed.)*. Cornwall: Capstone Publishing Ltd.

Moore, J. F. (1996). *The Death of Competition: Leadership & Strategy in the Age of Business Ecosystems*. New York: Harper Business.

Morris, M., Schindehutte, M., & Allen, J. (2005). The Entrepreneur's Business Model: Towards Unified Perspective. *Journal of Business Research, 58*(6), 726–735. doi:10.1016/j.jbusres.2003.11.001

Muegge, S. (2011). Business Ecosystems as Institutions of Participation: A Systems Perspective on Community-Developed Platforms. *Technology Innovation Management Review, 1*(2), 4-13. Retrieved from http://timreview.ca/article/495

Muegge, S. (2012). Business Model Discovery by Technology Entrepreneurs. *Technology Innovation Management Review, 2*(4), 5-16. http://timreview.ca/article/545

Muegge, S. (2013). Platforms, Communities, and Business Ecosystems: Lessons Learned About Technology Entrepreneurship in an Interconnected World. *Technology Innovation Management Review, 3*(2), 5-15. Retrieved from http://timreview.ca/article/655

Oriwoh, E., Sant, P., & Epiphaniou, G. (2013). Guidelines for Internet of Things Deployment Approaches – The Thing Commandments. *Procedia Computer Science, 21*, 122-131. doi:10.1016/j.procs.2013.09.018

Osterwalder, A., & Pigneur, Y. (2010). *Business Model Generation: A Handbook for Visionaries, Game Changers, and Challengers*. Zurich, Switzerland: Business Model Foundry.

Osterwalder, A., Pigneur, Y., & Tucci, C. L. (2005). Clarifying Business Models: Origins, Present and Future of the Concept. *Communications of the Association for Information Science, 16*(1), 1-25. http://aisel.aisnet.org/cais/vol16/iss1/1

Peltoniemi, M. (2005). *Business Ecosystem: A Conceptual Model of an Organization Population from the Perspectives of Complexity and Evolution. Research Reports 18*. Tampere, Finland: E-Business Research Center.

Rajala, R., & Westerlund, M. (2008). Capability Perspective of Business Model Innovation: An Analysis in the Software Industry. *International Journal of Business Innovation and Research*, *2*(1), 71–89. doi:10.1504/IJBIR.2008.015936

Ritala, P., Agouridas, V., Assimakopoulos, D., & Gies, O. (2013). Value Creation and Capture Mechanisms in Innovation Ecosystems: A Comparative Case Study. *International Journal of Technology Management*, *63*(3), 244–267. doi:10.1504/IJTM.2013.056900

Schweizer, L. (2005). Concept and Evolution of Business Models. *Journal of General Management*, *31*(2), 37–56. doi:10.1177/030630700503100203

Shafer, S. M., Smith, H. J., & Linder, J. C. (2005). The Power of Business Models. *Business Horizons*, *48*(3), 199–207. doi:10.1016/j.bushor.2004.10.014

Tapscott, D., Lowy, A., & Ticoll, D. (2000). *Digital Capital: Harnessing the Power of Business Webs*. Cambridge, MA: Harvard Business School Press.

Teece, D. J. (2010). Business Models, Business Strategy and Innovation. *Long Range Planning*, *43*(2-3), 172–194. doi:10.1016/j.lrp.2009.07.003

Timmers, P. (1998). Business Models for Electronic Markets. *Electronic Markets*, *8*(2), 3–8. doi:10.1080/10196789800000016

Uckelmann, D., Harrison, M., & Michahelles, F. (2011). An Architectural Approach. Towards the Future Internet of Things. In D. Uckelmann, M. Harrison, & F. Michahelles (Eds.), *Architecting the Internet of Things* (pp. 1–24). Berlin: Springer. doi:10.1007/978-3-642-19157-2_1

Weill, P., & Vitale, M. R. (2001). *Placeto Space:Migrating to eBusiness Models*. Cambridge, MA: Harvard Business School Press.

Weiller, C., & Neely, A. (2013). *Business Model Design in an Ecosystem Context*. University of Cambridge Working Papers. Cambridge, UK: Cambridge Service Alliance.

Westerlund, M. (2013). TIM Lecture Series Green Business Models To Change The World: How Can Entrepreneurs Ride the Sustainability Wave? *Technology Innovation Management Review*, *3*(7), 53-57. Retrieved from http://timreview.ca/article/70

Wurster, L. F. (2014). *Emerging Technology Analysis: Software Licensing and Entitlement Management Is the Key to Monetizing the Internet of Things*. Gartner Research Report G00251790. Stamford, CT: Gartner, Inc.

Zott, C., & Amit, R. (2008). The Fit between Product Market Strategy and Business Model: Implications for Firm Performance. *Strategic Management Journal*, *29*(1), 1–26. doi:10.1002mj.642

Zott, C., Amit, R., & Massa, L. (2011). The Business Model: Recent Developments and Future Research. *Journal of Management*, *37*(4), 1019–1042. doi:10.1177/0149206311406265

ADDITIONAL READING

Mkrttchian, V. (2011). Use 'hhh" technology in transformative models of online education. In G. Kurubacak & T. Vokan Yuzer (Eds.), *Handbook of research on transformative online education and liberation: Models for social equality* (pp. 340–351). Hershey, PA: IGI Global. doi:10.4018/978-1-60960-046-4.ch018

Mkrttchian, V. (2012). Avatar manager and student reflective conversations as the base for describing meta-communication model. In U. Demiray, G. Kurubacak, & T. Vokan Yuzer (Eds.), *Meta-communication for reflective online conversations: Models for online education* (pp. 75–101). Hershey, PA: IGI Global. doi:10.4018/978-1-61350-071-2.ch005

Mkrttchian, V. (2013). Training of Avatar Moderator in Sliding Mode Control Environment for Virtual Project Management. In Enterprise Resource Planning: Concepts, Methodologies, Tools, and Applications (pp. 1376-1405). IRMA, IGI Global.

Mkrttchian, V. (2013). Cloud Platform for online Laboratory for Online Learning working in Sliding Mode. *Maldives Journal of Research, 1*, 12–19.

Mkrttchian, V. (2015). Modelling using of Triple H-Avatar Technology in online Multi-Cloud Platform Lab. In M. Khosrow-Pour (Ed.), *Encyclopedia of Information Science and Technology* (3rd ed., pp. 4162–4170). Hershey, PA: IGI Global. doi:10.4018/978-1-4666-5888-2.ch409

Mkrttchian, V., & Aleshina, E. (2017). *Sliding Mode in Intellectual Control and Communication: Emerging Research and Opportunities*. Hershey, PA, USA: IGI Global. doi:10.4018/978-1-5225-2292-8

Mkrttchian, V., Aysmontas, B., Uddin, M., Andreev, A., & Vorovchenko, N. (2015). The Academic views from Moscow Universities of the Cyber U-Learning on the Future of Online Education at Russia and Ukraine. In G. Eby & T. Vokan Yuzer (Eds.), *Identification, Evaluation, and Perceptions of Online Education Experts* (pp. 32–45). Hershey, PA: IGI Global. doi:10.4018/978-1-4666-8119-4.ch003

Mkrttchian, V., & Belyanina, L. (Eds.). (2018). *Handbook of Research on Students' Research Competence in Modern Educational Contexts*. Hershey, PA, USA: IGI Global. doi:10.4018/978-1-5225-3485-3

Mkrttchian, V., Bershadsky, A., Bozhday, A., & Fionova, L. (2015). Model in SM of DEE Based on Service Oriented Interactions at Dynamic Software Product Lines. In G. Eby & T. Vokan Yuzer (Eds.), *Identification, Evaluation, and Perceptions of Online Education Experts* (pp. 230–247). Hershey, PA: IGI Global. doi:10.4018/978-1-4666-8119-4.ch014

Mkrttchian, V., Bershadsky, A., Bozhday, A., Kataev, M., & Kataev, S. (Eds.). (2016). *Handbook of Research on Estimation and Control Techniques in E-Learning Systems*. Hershey, PA, USA: IGI Global. doi:10.4018/978-1-4666-9489-7

Mkrttchian, V., Kataev, M., Hwang, W., Bedi, S., & Fedotova, A. (2014). Using Plug-Avatars "hhh" Technology Education as Service-Oriented Virtual Learning Environment in Sliding Mode. In G. Eby & T. Vokan Yuzer (Eds.), *Emerging Priorities and Trends in Online Education: Communication, Pedagogy, and Technology*. Hershey, PA: IGI Global. doi:10.4018/978-1-4666-5162-3.ch004

Mkrttchian, V., Kataev, M., Shih, T., Kumar, M., & Fedotova, A. (2014, July-September). Avatars "HHH" Technology Education Cloud Platform on Sliding Mode Based Plug- Ontology as a Gateway to Improvement of Feedback Control Online Society. *International Journal of Information Communication Technologies and Human Development*, *6*(3), 13–31. doi:10.4018/ijicthd.2014070102

Mkrttchian, V., & Stephanova, G. (2013). Training of Avatar Moderator in Sliding Mode Control. In G. Eby & T. Vokan Yuzer (Eds.), *Project Management Approaches for Online Learning Design* (pp. 175–203). Hershey, PA: IGI Global. doi:10.4018/978-1-4666-2830-4.ch009

Mkrttchian, V., & Stephanova, G. (2013) Training of Avatar Moderator in Sliding Mode Control Environment for Virtual Project Management. In Romero, J.A. & other (Eds). Enterprise Resource Planning: Concepts, Methodologies, Tools, and Applications. (pp. 1376-1405) IRMA, IGI Global.

KEY TERMS AND DEFINITIONS

Business Model: Is a plan for the successful operation of a business, identifying sources of revenue, the intended customer base, products, and details of financing.

Design Tools: Are objects, media, or computer programs, which can be used to design. They may influence the process of production, expression and perception of design ideas and therefore need to be applied skillfully.

Digital Transformation: Is the profound transformation of business and organizational activities, processes, competencies and models to fully leverage the changes and opportunities of a mix of digital technologies and their accelerating impact across society in a strategic and prioritized way, with present and future.

Ecosystem: Is a complex network or interconnected system.

Internet of Things: Is the interconnection via the Internet of computing devices embedded in everyday objects, enabling them to send and receive data.

Online Multi-Cloud Platform Lab: A laboratory on the Internet, which is available on the multi-cloud platform and intended for research, training and development of forecasting.

Research Laboratory: Is for studying and improving digital transformations.

Triple H-AVATAR Technology: The technology of modeling and simulation based on known technology of Avatar used in the HHH University since 2010.

Chapter 20
Big Data Analytics and Internet of Things in Industrial Internet in Former Soviet Union Countries

Vardan Mkrttchian
https://orcid.org/0000-0003-4871-5956
HHH University, Australia

Leyla Gamidullaeva
https://orcid.org/0000-0003-3042-7550
Penza State University, Russia

Svetlana Panasenko
Plekhanov Russian University of Economics, Russia

Arman Sargsyan
National University of AC of Armenia, Armenia

ABSTRACT

The purpose of this chapter is to explore the integration of three new concepts—big data, internet of things, and internet signs—in the countries of the former Soviet Union. Further, the concept of big data is analyzed. The internet of things is analyzed. Information on semiotics is given, and it reduces to the notion of internet signs. Context concepts and the contribution of big data, internet of things, and internet of signs to contextual simplification are analyzed. The chapter briefly outlines some potential applications of the integration of these three concepts. The chapter briefly discusses the contribution of the study and gives some extensions. These applications included continuous monitoring of accounting data, continuous verification and validation, and use of big data, location information, and other data, for example, to control fraudsters in the countries of the former Soviet Union.

DOI: 10.4018/978-1-5225-7432-3.ch020

INTRODUCTION

The aim of this research is to show the possibilities of integrating three new concepts of the industrial Internet, namely the Big Data, the Internet of Things (IoT) and Internet Signs in the countries of the Former Soviet Union. The chapter shows that IoT, people and other participants generate "big data" and that "big data" and "Internet of things" can be used to create "Internet signs" in the former Soviet Union of the country. In addition, each of these three interrelated concepts is considered for their impact on the context and available context information. Cox and Ellsworth, (1997) first used the term "large data", referring to the use of large amounts of data to visualize the scientific data of their experiments. Diebold (2012)) used the term "Big Data in Statistics and Econometrics" back in 2000. Then the term "Big Data" showed a larger set of data, which was more than the norm. At present, this term has expanded, and includes a number of characteristics and the integration of different types of data and analyzes. According to this principle, a number of different sources have developed the term The aim of this research is to show the possibilities of integrating three new concepts of the industrial Internet, namely the Big Data, the Internet of Things (IoT) and Internet Signs in the countries of the Former Soviet Union. The chapter shows that IoT, people and other participants generate "big data" and that "big data" and "Internet of things" can be used to create "Internet signs" in the former Soviet Union of the country. In addition, each of these three interrelated concepts is considered for their impact on the context and available context information. Cox and Ellsworth, (1997) first used the term "large data", referring to the use of large amounts of data to visualize the scientific data of their experiments. Diebold (2012)) used the term "Big Data in Statistics and Econometrics" back in 2000. Then the term "Big Data" showed a larger set of data, which was more than the norm. At present, this term has expanded, and includes a number of characteristics and the integration of different types of data and analyzes. According to this principle, a number of different sources have developed the term "Big Data." Therefore, in our study, consider some of these definitions and summarize some of the similarities between them. Further, we will use these definitions to consider the contribution of some applications as "Big Data". Ashton (2009) showed that the term "Internet of Things" was introduced in 1999, and was originally intended to describe such a situation. Today computers - and, consequently, the Internet - are used by consumers - people for information.

"Big Data." Therefore, in our study, consider some of these definitions and summarize some of the similarities between them. Further, we will use these definitions to consider the contribution of some applications as "Big Data". Ashton (2009) showed that the term "Internet of Things" was introduced in 1999, and was originally intended to describe such a situation. Today computers - and, consequently, the Internet - are used by consumers - people for information.

The problem is that people have time, attention and accuracy very different and limited, which means that all their actions are ineffective in collecting data about things in the real world. Therefore, there was an idea to give computers their own means for gathering information so that they could see, hear and deceive the world for themselves. As a result, the "Internet of Things" provides an associated set of computer programs and sensors that, unlike people, work efficiently. Further, more "Internet Things" include data from people connected with the Internet, moving from "Internet of things" to "Internet of everything", SRA, (2009). Our study examines the expansion of the original concept, which made it possible to use it as a tool for reviewing the context.

The introduced concept of "Online Signs" O'Leary (2012a) is the subject of our study. The term and the concept of "Internet Signs" is due to the fact that in this case, that the data generated on the Internet from a very wide range of sources. These are devices in the "Internet of Things", it is information from social networks and other Internet sources that are associated with "big data", "signs" and "moods" on some O'Leary issues (2011). These "signs" generated by information related to the Internet provide "Internet signs". Introduction of the concept of "Internet Signs" allows you to expand and supplement the potential information about events and situations.

Currently, as our studies have shown, "Big Data" is a term that has emerged and is evolving to take into account the rapidly growing amounts of digital information generated by efforts to ensure that this analyzed information and its actual use of this data as a means increase productivity, create and promote innovation and improve the decision-making process. Our research has shown that "big data" as a collection of three words: volume, speed and diversity. Indicates an increase in the amount of data compared to traditional settings. Let's analyze each word - speed indicates that information is generated at a speed exceeding the speed of using traditional systems. Our research has revealed the presence of several new data forms that are of interest to organizations. In his work Zikopoulos et al. (2013) presented additional concepts of reliability and value in "Big Data". We have found that reliability refers to the accuracy, truthfulness and reliability of the data. "Value" means the potential for big data to provide an economically advantageous addition to the enterprise technology portfolio. We have found that "value" provides key cost-effective criteria in terms of determining whether "Big Data" should be used. We will further show that the development of "Big Data" also requires an infrastructure to support the collection, storage, processing and use of accumulated information.

In his work Teradata's Bawa (2011) suggested the idea that the number of applications that generate data that are avalanche-like increase and that the number of programs that write them for consumption has such a character. In his work, Bawa (2011) noted that the structure of these diverse data is very diverse and is a function of the program it creates. Our research has been proven. Given the growing volume of data, there is now a need for a massive analysis, and this analysis concerns accumulated data.

EMC has proposed in the future to introduce a service based on "Big Data" (BDaaS). But at the same time EMC revealed a variety of data, data complexity and less structured data. In addition, EMC (2012) emphasizes that data should be analyzed faster than in the past.

The introduction of this chapter showed that at the present time the data is becoming more diverse, more complex and less structured, it becomes necessary to process it quickly. Meeting such demanding requirements is a major challenge for traditional databases and the expansion of infrastructures. "Big Data" refers to new scalable architectures that meet these needs. "Big Data" mainly refers to massively distributed architectures and massively-parallel processing using blocks of creating products for managing and analyzing data.

The introduction of this chapter summarizes all the known definitions of "Big Data". These definitions are correlated and are consistent with the emphasis that the "Big Data", as currently conceived, is more than just "More" Data. "Big Data" also includes the increased speed with which data is generated, and with which enterprises must respond. "Big Data" also seems to consistently note the complexity, diversity and unstructured nature of the generated data. Accordingly, the analysis of such diverse and diverse data will also be diverse and diverse, since unevenness is required to eliminate ambiguity (Ashby, 1965). Finally, the EMC definition emphasizes the need for changes in information technology architectures, as a transition to more parallel processing takes place.

Nowadays, development of intelligent instructional methods in connected settings, and guided appearance in experientially based learning have been investigated. Besides, due to V. Mkrttchian, such courses were analyzed and additionally researched, and appeared in virtual classrooms within the framework of experiential learning. Previous research demonstrates that definition of experiential learning is broadly deciphered, investigated and bantered about, in any case, for this study purposes it is characterized as an organized learning exercises set through a planned mix of advancements and instructional strategies, for example, organized talks, coordinated composing assignments, and on location situations in nearby groups. Meta-communication is vital for distance learning. It helps to manage meta-level interactions in a virtual classroom, and to build a dynamic background of distance education. Collaborative learning impacts local and global communities. There are several types of meta-communication which provide different situations for reflection, so it's necessary to make an assessment of communication action concepts. This whole process needs a substantial commitment by educators, as well as a consistent level of engagement and motivation by both students and teachers. The reflection transform as cognitive and full of feeling improvement mean, especially as encouraged in electronic courses, was another idea for some students. The results of this study demonstrate that intelligent instructional methods can possibly encourage and broaden noteworthy realizing when executed in internet learning situations. In such classrooms, important learning comprises developing a limit for mindfulness through open doors for organized reflection, creating joint efforts to investigate individualized mindfulness, recognitions, understanding complex hypothetical ideas inside a cognitive transforming system, and applying intelligent material coming about, because of individual impressions and synergistic connections in both scholastic and "certifiable" connections.

BACKGROUND

Since the main theme of this chapter is devoted to 'Internet of Things' and the background is about them. In his work, Chui et al. (2010) that "sensors and drives built into physical objects - from tracks to pacemakers - are connected via wired and wireless networks using the same Internet Protocol (IP) that connects the Internet itself." This explains that the concept and term "Internet of things" generally refers to the notion that many different "things" are connected to the Internet and therefore can be connected with each other.

Our research has shown that "Things" can be sensors, databases, other devices or software. And the sensors may include pacemakers, location identifiers such as the Global Positioning System (GPS) and individual identification devices, such as RFID tags. In addition, sensors can provide various information characteristics, usually of interest to a particular setting. For example, RFID sensors can indicate the time and location, pacemakers' record information about the heart rate; other sensors can record the status of the element that tracks the sensor, the number of cars, the presence of an RFID tag and other information.

Experience shows that "Things" can be smart and be aware of other "Things". As a result, we see that in some cases, "Things" will want or need to communicate with other "things". One "Thing" can find the place of a related or interesting "Thing" and initiate a dialogue, collect information from each other and report the consequences of this information to any decision-maker. As an example, labeled vats of chemicals that can be spontaneously burned, if they are located side by side, could report this to a decision maker to facilitate the safe storage of these chemicals.

Also experience shows that "Things" can gather information and knowledge from their interaction with other "things". Things can either keep this information and knowledge at the local level, or transfer them to some place in the Cloud, where information will be widely available to others. For example, for hospital use of RIFD in patients, the tag usually only contains the patient number, and the patient information is stored on the secure server. Similarly, the use of RFID in cars often includes only the tag number (for example, paid devices). To this end, several information technology architectures are proposed for storing, analyzing and processing information about "things".

Experience also shows that "Things" are potentially autonomous, semi-autonomous or not autonomous. However, because "things" are connected on the web, they can become more autonomous, because they interact with other "things". In addition, the network composition and "things" can be more than individual "things", since "network effects" develop among "things", where the network information is ultimately greater than the information associated with any "thing". For example, O'Leary (2006, 2008) explored the concepts of the development of self-contained supply chains that unite many different sources of data and capabilities.

Our research has shown that "Internet of things" both stand-alone and network generate "big data". This is due to the fact that the data loss related to the "Internet of things" is very important for them. Because the sensors interact with the world, "Things", such as RFID tags, generate volumes and volumes of data. As a result, digital processing becomes a requirement for feasibility. The speed of data related to the "Internet of things", in comparison with the traditional processing of transactions, avalanche-like grows and can become uncontrollable, since sensors can continuously capture data.

It is clear that the variety of data related to the "Internet of things" is enormous, as the types of sensors expand and new, jittery data sources emerge. With such a variety, the reliability of data in the "Internet of things" will improve over time as the quality of the sensor improves and other data. For example, the use of RFID tags generates much more reliable information than before. Therefore, now such large amounts of data, combined with an increase in the data rate, along with an increase in the diversity of data, illustrate the push of the "Internet of things" to generate "Big Data ".

The foregoing introduction and the background suggest that it is more likely to unnecessarily restrict conversations about the "Internet of things", except for people, especially in a world where many "things" are the automation of people and most of the work of "things" for or about people. In addition, the "things" and the quality of the information they produce are affected by people. As a result, it is important to have a concept in the background that is more than just "things".

To summarize the foregoing, it is necessary to consider at the end of the background how the sensor data and people are integrated. For examples taken from the Western world, since such systems in the countries of the former Soviet Union are not yet effective and are not widespread. There are several systems available to inform drivers about traffic that have different manifestations on the Internet. For example, Sigalert.com provides a sensor analysis of traffic density on highways. In addition, there is quality information about traffic. For example, "Waze" is a social networking application that generates social traffic data. Users can provide information on hazards, traffic density, the location of the police and other data. Combining Waze with sensor media provides users with a unique understanding of traffic and context (danger, police, etc.). In addition, using data from both, the reliability of the data can be improved, which ultimately provides the user with increased value.

Internet as a development tools continues to be a benchmark in e-learning, taking advantage of constant technological developments. The "hhh" technology is an educational model placing a student at the center of learning activity, and establishing collaborative learning environments. Being a hybrid environment, the "hhh" model has integrated the best features of online and face to face learning environments by offering knowledge, experience, and different perspectives. The "hhh" model is a possible solution to bridge the gap between online and F2F learning environments encouraging transformative learning model. The "hhh" model increases and extends the connectivity, collaboration, and reflection. The "hhh" technology requires the appropriate pedagogy, information systems technology, collaboration zones, moderated chats, and flexible curriculum. The "hhh" technology redesigns and enhances the educational experience by better student engagement, and new avenues for student expression. The pattern of "hhh" technology makes students more assertive, directive, enthusiastic and motivated. This model is comprised of seven principles, which allow students to achieve meaningful learning in online learning environments. These principles are guidelines for developing the "hhh" technology learning model, connected with collaboration/interaction, curriculum, internet, synched learning opportunities, media curricular enhancements, and pedagogical implementation. This is the base of learning framework where it is necessary to focus on the learning goals, knowing that the experiences are first and foremost for educational purposes. In the "hhh" model, the collaboration zone or, in other words, the "hhh" technology learning content, includes students, experts and teachers in online classroom. The teachers have opportunity to augment their content knowledge by interacting with the subject matter experts. The "hhh" model allows greater engagement and enhanced opportunities for success by providing synched instructional learning opportunities and interacting live with explorers, educators, subject matter experts, and fellow users. Having a specific ultimate goal to tackle the above issues, and effectively create a contact with all trainees and their productive participation during the study, the educator system obliges data about the individual attributes of singular understudy (level of tension, respect toward oneself, character inspiration, etc.). With such data, the instructor will have the capacity to recognize the style of correspondence with each of the understudies, and to build up the most ideal methods for determining potential clashes, if any, in the learning methodology, strategies supporting and aiding learners in the event of trouble (Mkrttchian, et al, 2018) and (Mkrttchian, et al., 2019).The foregoing allowed us to expand the concept of the "Internet of things" to the unified notion of "Internet of people and things", to provide a wider base of connections and relationships, as a cyber-physical environment filled with things and people, as confirmed by the studies of the UK Future Internet Strategy Group, (2011) . Information based on people may include sensors that represent "people"; for example, capturing their location or other variables. In addition, information based on people can include social media, providing additional contextual information. In this notion "Internet of people and things" access and communication with other objects is provided in the appropriate context. This was confirmed by other researchers who introduced the concept of "the Internet of everything" (SRA, 2009), where virtually everyone is connected to the Internet and can communicate with everyone else.

MAIN FOCUS OF THE CHAPTER

Issues, Controversies, Problems, Solutions, and Recommendations

The term and concept of semiotic is the study of signs with a history that includes Greek philosophers, Ferdinand de Saussure, Charles Sanders Pierce, Joseph Schumpeter and others (Dorsey, 2003). But these concepts are associated with social and cultural problems. In his works, Chandler (2009) for the first time showed that semiotics is "a science that studies the role of signs as a part of social life". Before that, Culler (2005) in his work suggested that with semiotics, we think of "our social and cultural world as a series of iconic systems ..."

Our research has shown that different phenomena can cause signs. Eco (1978) in his "Theory of Semiotics" has developed a number of topics in semiotics, including formalized languages, written languages, the theory of texts, mass communication and other issues. Accordingly, signs penetrate into communication. In addition, semiotics is found in specific disciplines, including, for example, medical semiotics (Eco, 1978) and economics, such as an analysis of Schumpeter's business and business cycles, which seems to be parallel to Peirce's semiotic study (Swedberg, 2012). However, signs can also be obtained from non-linguistic information. For example, visual communication is also included in Eco (1978).

Semiotics was used to capture several types of symptoms (for example, "signs of symptoms"). For example, semiotics can be used to investigate the obvious "symptoms" of behavior and events. In his works Culler (1981) noted as part of semiotics, one can explore symptoms as signs of previous causes and seek to restore the history of some event. "Symptoms" provide "signs" of potential causes of behavior and events. In addition, changes in these symptoms can also be "signs." For example, symptoms may include blogs that suggest that something is wrong with some product. Accordingly, there is interest in determining how data can be used to obtain information about these symptoms and signs. For example, on the basis of available information, there may be "signs" of bankruptcy, fraud or reputation (Spangler et al., 2009).

Our research showed that interest in semiotics despite the manifestation of interest in the symptoms, Culler (2005) in his work noted "the attempts of semiotics to make explicit knowledge that allows signs to make sense ...". This explicit knowledge was created using several categories of information. For example, Eco (1978) proposed a number of categories of signs, including written language, natural language, cultural codes, aesthetic codes, taste codes and a number of others. To explicitly represent knowledge, several types of analysis may be required. To facilitate the use and integration with "big data" and "Internet of things", it usually requires the development of explicit knowledge. For example, explicit knowledge can be torn from blogs or other social networks (for example, O'Leary, 2011).

Our research has shown that information is generated by computer devices (for example, sensors) for people who control devices, often automating tasks previously performed by people. Accordingly, one of the prospects of our research is that these signs can be generated by these things. In particular, "Things" generate a wide range of measurements that can be used to provide insight into signs. For example, sensors that indicate the absence of available parking spaces indicate that the object is busy or that an event occurs.

As our studies in semiotics have shown, the analysis of "things" is limited, and was not connected with "things", but was associated with signs, symbols and concepts, it turned out that "things" are present and represent themselves. As Langer (1942) notes in his work - symbols are not proxy objects for their objects, but they are carriers of the concept of objects. Our research has shown that speaking of things, we have ideas about them, not about things themselves; and it is about the concept, and not what the symbols directly mean and show.

In our research, we interact with concepts and representations of "things". At the same time, "things" generate information about which signs about these "things" can be based. For example, in economics, semiotics used metrics based on issues such as price trends, sentiments and even slogans as a means of exploring phenomena such as behavior and events in the stock market (Dorsey, 2003). Ultimately, directly or indirectly, "things generate signs." A semiotics, in the analysis of Saussure, Chandler (2009) notes that "primacy is attached to relationships, not things - the meaning of signs is seen as lying in their systematic relationship to each other, and not derived from any inalienable reference to material things. " From the point of view of semiotics, "the relations between things generate signs." Similarly, in "Internet-things" the relations between "Things" play a key role in determining the signs. "Internet of things" will provide substantial data on these relationships. Thus, there is data on the "Thing" and data on the relationship between "Things" that generate "Big Data".

As a result, from the point of view of semiotics, and not for "Internet of things", there is interest in "Internet signs". Ultimately, the relationship between "things", the concepts of "things" and symptoms of behavior can serve as a basis for a better understanding of events, situations, behavior and other problems.

Our research showed that semiotics focused on human information. Signs based on this information generated by humans are built into the Internet, created from a wide range of other data, except sensors. For example, signs are in different Internet media, such as blogs, wikis, comments, messages, provides message analysis to find out which problems are most common, gives a summary of what is now a "trend." Such summaries of activities in social networks give signs of what is happening or is happening, including what events or situations are considered important or interesting.

In our studies, we found out that "signs" of information on the Internet act as symptoms or show problems. The researchers took the hidden information and knowledge available in blogs, and so on, and began to determine the nature of the "signs" in these media in order to make the signs and knowledge about them more explicit. Accordingly, these data sources record indicators and potential indicators of activity. This study can be interpreted as the result of the generation of signs from what is sometimes regarded as a data source in "Big Data".

As a result of the search, the context was defined (Dictionary.com) as a set of circumstances or facts that surround a particular event, situation, etc. First, consider the concepts of circumstances or facts. In the case of "big data" or "Internet of things" there would be significant data that could be used to describe circumstances or facts. Such data will precede, occur or occur with a specific event or situation. This would provide essential data as a basis for characterizing the context. Secondly, in the definition, the context is defined around an event or situation. As a result, one approach would be to define a model of the world surrounding specific events or situations that would help define the context. For example, Schilit and Theimer (1994) defined the context as consisting of a location, the identity of nearby objects and people, and changes in these objects. As another example, Schilit et al. (1994) show that an important part of the context / events includes the resources (resources) with whom you (the adjacent agents) and where you are (location). In his work, Day (2001) suggests that these definitions are too specific and that it is difficult to list the entire set of interesting variables a priori. Accordingly, he suggests such a definition "Context" is any information that can be used to describe a situation in essence. An entity is a person, place, or object that is considered relevant to the interaction between the user and the application, including the user and the application it. As a result, the definition of Day (2001) is that it is consistent with the use of the essential data available in the "Big Data" and "Internet of Things" to collect and analyze data about a particular event or situation.

Our research has shown that at one level the context is determined by a set of "preceding", "accompanying" and "subsequent" data. But as events occur, the data is generated from different sources. Capturing more different data leads to the fact that more "context" limits. If the context is captured using all available data, then "Big Data" should also be able to provide "Big Context". In this parameter, the "Big Context" will refer to access to significant amounts of data in different formats from different sources, situations or events, but integrated and available for use.

Accordingly, "Big Data" provides an opportunity to provide "more" context than traditional settings. As a result, the recent development in the "Big Data" was to try and integrate the data into context. As an example, as Earnandez notes (Eernandez, 2012), in the case of business transactions, a new perspective is to store "each transaction in the context of business activity, for example, pay, search or purchase, how well it was performed, who initiated it, where the user was, and much more. "

In the case of business settings, there may be theoretical structures or schemes that can facilitate the identification of the relevant variables and the expected relationships between them (for example, O'Leary, 1999). Thus, contextual identification variables are likely to require some consideration of events, situations or settings of interest. The user level will be implemented in two different versions: IA as a teacher, and IA as a student. The student version will include a menu displaying the SIA, and allowing to access a different space, classroom, conference rooms, work practice, etc., through a drop-down menu Then, the student will select/cancel the activation of the SIA, and for a better educational follow it will also be possible to consult a history of activity (courses or conferences followed, notes and laboratories), and a schedule of upcoming activities. The activities will be declined by name, topic, the responsible professor, and the level in the university curriculum (1st, 2nd years, etc.)

We hope that a term "a system of course suggestion" will be able to integrate to the SIA, as a function of the spread and the shortcomings of the student.

The instructor version will include, in addition to all the functions previously described, a space of creation of *"class room"* and *"conference room"*, for the professors may depend on their areas of expertise and re-index files, change the existing data bases, and record the students. Finally, the professors may cause the IA to choose a domain in a predefined list by the tab "lessons maker", the SIA will be asking questions, and they will get the answers, or more probably will choose the best one among a multiple choice, as well they will create new courses, and will advance the IA; and then by querying they can readjust the answers provided by the system (the same lesson can be redrafted without a limit).

In order to choose the most suitable language, we must define the most important points of the implementation:

- IA must be able to interact between themselves, and with the elements of their environment
- We must be able to virtualize elements in 3D in large quantities, and be able to easily change their properties
- We must ensure a stable interconnection and hose between our virtual environment, and the elements of the system (BDD (*Big Data Driver*), internet, and server student management).

Taking into account the first parameter, it is clear that we must opt for an object language as an element of the code for interaction between the objects, which can potentially be inherited from them, or from a common interface, and, thus, share the same properties. It is important to note, a data order of practice is quite significant, as all environments are immersive virtual (such as, our project), and are achieved with languages of the type object (most of these languages are derivatives of C++), which only certain properties are syntactic of different containers.

The aim being to achieve an academic order draft, non-referred to commercial, it appears simpler to stay on an object language easily reusable by the various actors of the project. We will also confine us to the three most commonly required ones (e.g., C++, JAVA, PYTHON) in our selection.

The second parameter, namely, the capacity to easily model an interactive environment in 3D, is excluded from the JAVA office, which only includes very little of bookstore planned for this effect. It is also to be noted, that a few existing ones are no longer maintained, and could involve some compatibility problems with the rest of the tools. Moreover, the JAVA has very little optimal memory, and the CPU (*Central Processing Unit*) eliminates this weakness by 3D language modeling.

Finally, the third point that we are interested in, is the interaction with the other elements of the system. We pushed to refuse the use of the PYTHON, which in fact is not the easiest of the elements to outsource, the fact that this is not a compiled language. And, therefore, adding another code to the elements would require rewriting the latter, and standardizing the development platforms which appear delicate for a project of referred interuniversity.

The discriminant analysis of each of the points previously quoted shows that only a language meets all our needs, the intellectual agent will thus be carried out in its major part in C++. That being fixed, we need to look to the libraries used. One of the first architectural points is the possibility to use 2D models, and then convert them to 3D, extrapolating their movement without having to achieve a new capture. In terms of CAD (*Computer-Aided Design*), and creation of 3D models, the C++ offers a large quantity of bookstore (SFML, OPENGL, SDK), but very little includes the concept of a "graph", which allows you to create a movie from a mark, a set of points, and physical characteristics of the object. Indeed, in most cases, animating an object needs to capture the image under several different angles, and with a high definition.

This function of a "graph" directs us toward the choice of the OGRE library in C++. Although it not only introduces this feature, it accounts with the QT library to make its obvious choice. QT is a library of interface creation which, by personal experience, is a tool extremely powerful, with many function annexes (such as device management, the management of network protocols), and extremely portable.

In summary, the language chosen will be the PPC, among which we will withhold the OGRE library for 3D modeling, and the QT library for the creation of the interface and the network map. At first, an object should be placed in a monochrome room, in order to guarantee the reliability of the measures. Our topic will be placed at the center of three cameras in rear view and the above. This shooting will help to define the sides of the object, and to define a notion of a footprint for our software. Once these first measures will be made, we can export our model, and then the time will come to define its place and properties in the virtual environment. The animation of the object will be through a selection of a point on the object itself, and their translation in the mark (our environment). A key concept to remember is that the pixel and the modification of the position of an element of the environment will change the value for each of the pixels; in this, the concept of congestion is unavoidable. It also tells us that the environment must be created first, piece by piece, and that its properties must be immutable. For example, if we want to recreate an experience, we must first recreate the part or all the avatars, starting with its proportions, and then add our object models. Once the models are added, we define their place and properties (size, weight, voltage, on/off). Finally, we will be able to allow avatars to take place in the room; they will be able to select their place according to their material needs and availability. The SIA will be 2D or 3D projection of an image of the subject taken with a simple camera; the rest of their properties and their animation arise from the same processes as for virtualization of objects. The PYHTON language is withheld in this part of the research, first of all because it is an object language, and therefore includable of C++, and especially because of its use in the CPU resource, its management of the registry, and its mathematical power of the fact of its non-variable font type (gained by personal experience) of the object language, the most appropriate for design and implementation of an artificial intelligence.

The bookshop restraint will be the LIBMATH, existing in all languages. As for the PYTHON, it includes a single function, especially for sorting, putting in a link with its non-aspect type. In addition, this language is not compiled to make it suitable to an adaptation time on actual parameters variable. Outside, this specific point is a major asset to the operation of the IA scalable, likely to be changed by the experience, and to use a new different area, namely, digital economy.

Our IA rests on two algorithms:

The first one is a sorting algorithm ("smooth sort"), which will classify the files in functions of their subject, their level of complexity, and their pedagogic relevance. It will be necessary, therefore, to upstream planned routines of classifications based on grids of evaluations (the criteria will be fixed by the pedagogical team). And then, once this first processing is performed, the sorting algorithm will take into account the number of consultation, possible comments on the document from students, and will establish a correlation between the activities carried out, and the contents of the documents.

The second algorithm will be an "algorithm of the neural network", which is pressed on the sorting performed; it is the choice of the student in terms of curriculum and activities, as well as of their questions, and their progress curve will be able to build a course (built on a model prefix by the pedagogical team). We opt in this case for the method of retro learning. Thus, the IA will possess models of databases built around a system of question/answer with a teacher (the IA asks a question, the teacher prepares a response, or chooses from a list of a multiple choice). These questions will be derived from the construction diagram of a course mentioned above; in a prime time this model will be as follows:

- Introduction, overview of the subject and its history
- Development, theorems, reference values, constant
- Document references
- Exercise and corrections

Figure 1. Example of a search engine implementing in the Certificate Practicing Planner (CPP)

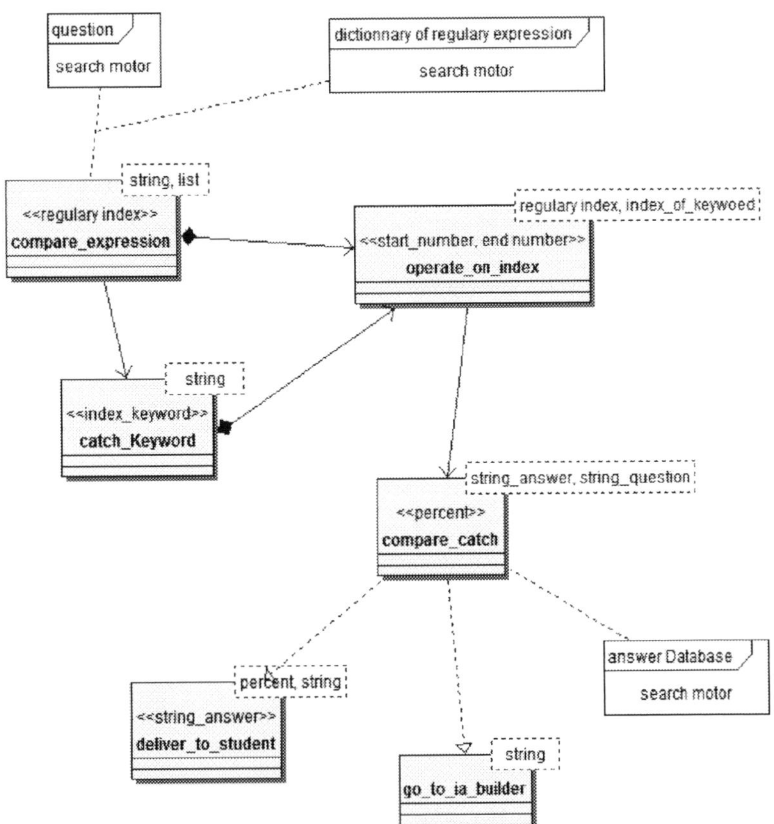

Figure 2. Illustration of the model operation for answering the system question to the Intelligent Agent (IA) on the basis of the disk, when the teacher has fully completed his question (created or regenerated files are treated as objects)

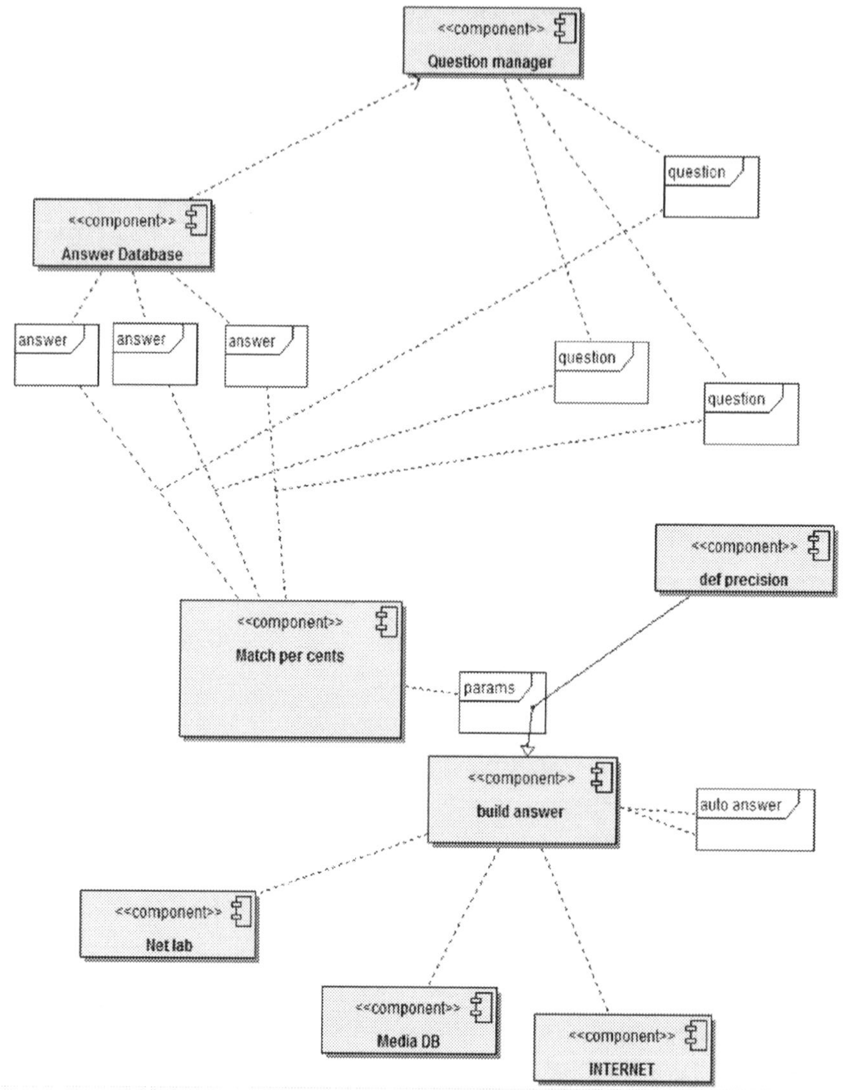

The teacher may amend, add, delete the data in the course prefabricated by the IA, and note the relevance of its response at any time, thus establishing a new scale of sorting in the document, and, therefore, inducing a new construction model. The IA will, thus, be able to renew itself in an autonomous way.

There will be, therefore, a multitude of IA versions based on the templates generated by its interaction with the students, in particular, and on the history and the curriculum of the students.

There are two essential functions of the IA: its learning ability (renewal), and its ability to return the knowledge on the way of structure and coherence. To fill these spots, it rests on two essential software elements:

Figure 3. Illustration of research of response of the IA to a question

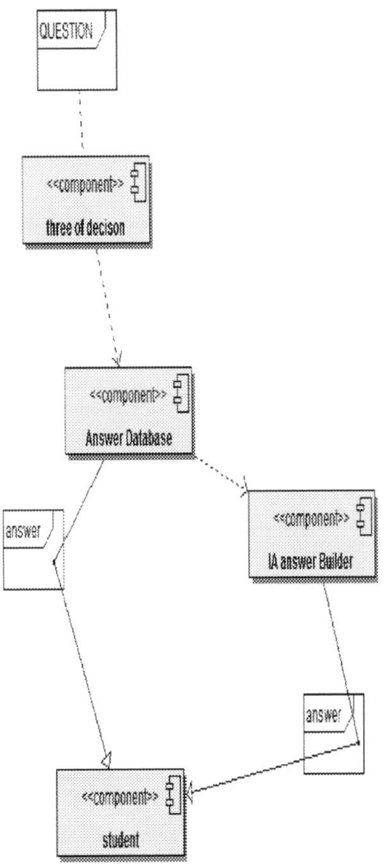

- The "search engine" using dictionaries, an evaluator of expression and combinations of decision tree will be able to assess the relevance of the proposed answers in the BDD of existing response, or to request the creation of a new answer.
- The "generator" response is the most essential element, which compiles the data, and uses the "algorithm of the neural network" based on the construction types already performed in this system, and a probabilistic shaft to provide a new answer.

Our research has shown that any discussion of the context in semiotics gives an idea of the context. Eco (1981) in his work emphasizes the importance of contexts, noting that the sign becomes only. Completely meaningful when it is inserted into a broader context " As another example, also noted by Eco (1981), ". I need to look for possible contexts that can make an expression ... understandable and reasonable. The very nature of signs postulates an active role on the part of their translator. «Our research has shown that semiotics offers terms that make information part of the context: meaningful, understandable and reasonable. "Value" implies that there is a model of how the functions of the world allow us to understand data in both the local and global contexts. "Intelligent" means that the relationship between data and the model can be understood. "Reasonable" indicates that the behavior of the data in the model corresponds to the required parameters. The new designs we have obtained, the Internet of Things and the Internet

Figure 4. Description of the databases' contents and links existing between them

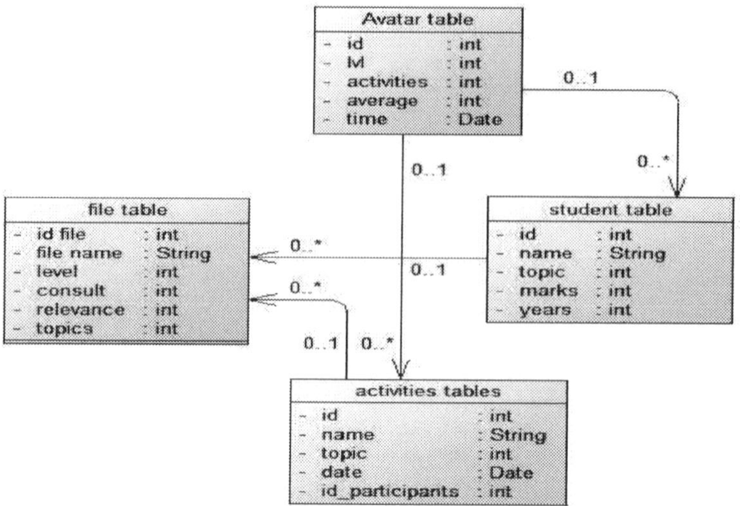

of Signs, can contribute to the definition of both local and larger contexts. For example, a context can be defined as a set of other "things" within some epsilon of a "thing" of concern. Since the Internet of Things forms a network, classical network approaches can be used to facilitate analysis. Alternatively, "things" can be grouped according to some model. Such models can have several relationships, such as a cascading grouping element. Such cascading groupings can be used to determine local and larger contexts. Industrial Internet in sharing use constructs such as the 'Internet of Things' and the 'Internet of Signs' can facilitate the definition of both local and larger contexts (figure 5).

FUTURE RESEARCH DIRECTIONS

This study can be expanded in the future in a number of ways. The chapter did not explore the role of business intelligence or the more classic data warehouse. This collection and analysis of data is usually more associated with traditional transaction data. however, data from the "internet of things" and "big data", which include social media and other forms of unstructured data, can be integrated into business intelligence and data warehouse, including internet signs.

CONCLUSION

The aim of this research was to show the possibilities of integrating three new concepts of the industrial Internet, namely the Big Data, the Internet of Things (IoT) and Internet Signs in the countries of the Former Soviet Union. The goal of the research is fulfilled; and ultimately, the authors affirms the following:

- "Internet of things" and people generate "big data". "Big data" and "Internet of things" can be used to create "Internet signs" in the countries of the former Soviet Union;

Figure 5. Industrial Internet in sharing use constructs such as the 'Internet of Things' and the 'Internet of Signs' can facilitate the definition of both local and larger contexts

Industrial Internet

WORLD MARKET	PILOT PROJECTS IN RUSSIA
IBM PTC GE Microsoft SAP Amazon Cisco	System integrators Foreign solution provider Software engineer
SCENARIOS OF USE	
User	**Goal**
Plants	Serviceability monitoring and optimization of equipment load
Logistic and transport companies	Transport optimization
Services and trade organizations	Analysis of clients' behavior, development of personal
Agricultural producers	Fields' monitoring, monitoring of cattle's health
Oil and gas companies	Percent increase in hydrocarbons' extraction

- Each of these three interrelated concepts is considered to influence the context and information available in the context of the countries of the former Soviet Union;
- A number of applications illustrating new concepts have been obtained, in particular, continuous monitoring of accounting data, continuous verification and validation and use of big data, location information and other data, for example for "scammers" in the countries of the former Soviet Union.
- It is established that sensors can capture information and store this information locally or place this information in some cloud system;
- There may be significant information about the sensor to be transmitted;
- Data are received in understanding and defining the context, it is shown that additional information based on the sign can be used as part of this context analysis;
- Additional models are proposed for understanding the context - from local to a broader context and cascading contexts;
- It is shown that, while the "Internet of Things" has received increasing attention, additional efforts should be directed to "Internet Signs" and "Internet of People and Things." Additional studies can focus on their use in matters such as context and better understanding of the relationship between different types of signs;
- New approaches to the use of "Big Data" are shown to facilitate audit or continuous financial provision as new and new data sources are received. In addition, as data volumes increase, new analytical approaches are likely to be required for auditing or continuous financial provision of "Big Data".

This analysis allowed building up a gateway for improvement the author's ideas about the design of intelligent agents as a model system for the development of a Sociotechnology using a Semiotics and Signs in virtual cloud-based lab;

- *Firstly, the database activity described all the activities proposed to the student (conferences, TP etc.), and the topic corresponds with the material relating to the activity, each activity having a unique ID. The field "ID of participants" identified the pupils, or the IA participated;*
- *Secondly, the table contains the name, ID (unique) of high years of university curriculum, the notes, and the field topic of the materials that the student has chosen to study;*
- *Thirdly, the table contains an index of all the files of educational order, with a unique ID, a classification by area and a level of complexity. This table also shows how many times a file has been consulted, and across the field "relevance" notes that the student has entered data to this document based on the answers given;*
- *Finally, the last table contains the data specific to each IA, its unique ID (generated from the ID of the student), the list of the activities in which it has participated, his "level" based on the notes, and the results obtained in various activities, the average the student's notes, and his time of presence during the conferences, and in the lab.*

ACKNOWLEDGMENT

The reported study was funded by RFBR according to the research project No. 18-010-00204.

REFERENCES

Ashby, R. (1965). *Introduction to Cybernetics*. John Wiley & Sons.

Ashton, K. (2009). *That Internet of Things' thing: in the real world, things matter more than ideas*. Retrieved from: http://www.rfid-journal.com/article/view/4986

Bawa, M. (2011). Multi-structured data: platform capabilities required for big data analytics. *Tetra data Aster – The Data Blog*. Retrieved from: http://www.asterdata.com/blog/2011/06/multi-structured-data-platform-capabilities-required-for-big-data-analytics/#Citation

Chandler, D. (2009). *Semiotics for beginners*. Retrieved from: http://www.aber.ac.uk/media/Documents/S4B/sem02.html

Chui, M., Loffler, M., & Roberts, R. (2010). The Internet of Things. *The McKinsey Quarterly*, *2*, 1–9.

Cox, M., Ellsworth, D. (1997). *Managing big data for scientific visualization*. ACM Sig graphs.

Culler, J. (1981). *The Pursuit of Signs*. Routledge.

Culler, J. (2005). *The Pursuit of Signs*. London: Routledge.

Dey, A. (2001). Understanding and using context. *Personal and Ubiquitous Computing*, *5*(1), 4–7. doi:10.1007007790170019

Diebold, F. X. (2012). *A personal perspective on the origin(s) and development of "Big Data": the phenomena, the term and the discipline*. Retrieved from: http://www.ssc.upenn.edu/~fdiebold/papers/paper112/Diebold_Big_Data.pdf

Dorsey, W. (2003). *Market semiotics: behavioral market diagnosis*. Retrieved from: http://www.marketsemiotics.com/docs/pdf/ MSBrochure.pdf

Eco, U. (1978). *A Theory of Semiotics*. Bloomington, IN: Indiana University Press.

Eco, U. (1981). The theory of signs and the role of the reader. *The Bulletin of the Midwest Modern Language Association*, *14*(1), 35–45. doi:10.2307/1314865

EMC. (2012). *Big data-as-a-service: a market and technology perspective*. Retrieved from: http://www.emc.com/collateral/software/wwhite-hite-ppapers/h10839-big-data-as-a-service-perspt.pdf,apers/h10839-big-data-as-a-service-perspt.pdf

Heil, A., Knoll, M., & Weis, T. (2007). The Internet of Things–context-based device federations. *Proceedings of the 40th Annual Hawaii International Conference on System Sciences (HICSS2007).*

Hernandez, P. (2012). App employs context for Big Data analytics efficiency. *Enterprise Apps Today*. Retrieved from: http://www.enterpriseappstoday.com/business-intelligence/app-employs-context-for-big-data-analytics-efficiency

Langer, S. (1942). *Philosophy in a NewKey: A Study in the Symbolism of Reason, Rite, and Art*. Cambridge, MA: Harvard University Press.

Mkrttchian, V., Palatkin, I., Gamidullaeva, L., & Panasenko, S. (2018). About digital avatars for control systems using Big Data and Knowledge sharing in virtual industries. In A. Gyamfi & I. Williams (Eds.), *Big Data and Knowledge Sharing in Virtual Organizations* (pp. 46–59). Hershey, PA: IGI Global; doi:10.4018/978-1-5225-7519-1ch.04

Mkrttchian, V., Veretikhina, S., Gavrilova, O., Ioffe, A., Markosyan, S., & Chernyshenko, S. (2019). The comparison of Cross-cultural analysis of the green country - Australia and of the North Country – Russia: Cultures, small businesses, cross the barriers. In U. G. Benna (Ed.), *Industrial and Urban Growth Policies at the Sub-National, National, and Global Levels* (pp. 176–189). Hershey, PA: IGI Global. doi:10.4018/978-1-5225-7625-9

Schilit, B., Adams, N., & Want, R. (1994).Context-aware computing applications. *First International Workshop on Mobil eComputing Systems and Applications*, 85–90.

Schilit, B., & Theime, M. (1994). Disseminate acting active *map in* formation to mobile hosts. *IEEE Network*, *8*(5), 22–32. doi:10.1109/65.313011

Spangler, S., Cheney, Proctor, L., Lelecu, A., Behal, A., He, B., & Davis, T. (2009). COBRA–mining web for corporate brand and deputation analysis. *Web Intelligence and Agent Systems*, *7*(3), 243–254.

SRA. (2009). *The Internet of Things Strategic Road Map*. Retrieved from: http://sintef.biz/upload/IKT/9022/CERP-IoT%20SRA_IoT_v11_pdf

Svedberg, R. (2012). Shum peter's theories of organizational entrepreneurship. In D. Hjorth (Ed.), *Handbook on Organizational Entrepreneurship* (pp. 31–48). Cheltenham, UK: Edward Elgar Publishing. doi:10.4337/9781781009055.00011

UK Future Internet Strategy Group. (2011). *Future Internet Report*. Retrieved from: https://connect.innovateuk.org/c/document_library/get_file?folderId=861750&name=DLFE–34705.pdf

Zikopoulos, P., DeRoos, D., Parasuraman, K., Deutsch, T., Corrigan, D., & Giles, J. (2013). *Harness the Power of Big Data*. McGraw-Hill.

Zikopoulos, P., Eaton, C., De Roos, D., Deutsch, T., & Lapis, G. (2012). *Understanding Big Data: Analytics for Enterprise Class Hadoopand Streaming Data*. McGraw-Hill.

ADDITIONAL READING

Mkrttchian, V. (2011). Use 'hhh" technology in transformative models of online education. In G. Kurubacak & T. Vokan Yuzer (Eds.), *Handbook of research on transformative online education and liberation: Models for social equality* (pp. 340–351). Hershey, PA: IGI Global. doi:10.4018/978-1-60960-046-4.ch018

Mkrttchian, V. (2012). Avatar manager and student reflective conversations as the base for describing meta-communication model. In U. Demiray, G. Kurubacak, & T. Vokan Yuzer (Eds.), *Meta-communication for reflective online conversations: Models for online education* (pp. 75–101). Hershey, PA: IGI Global. doi:10.4018/978-1-61350-071-2.ch005

Mkrttchian, V. (2013). Training of Avatar Moderator in Sliding Mode Control Environment for Virtual Project Management. In Enterprise Resource Planning: Concepts, Methodologies, Tools, and Applications (pp. 1376-1405). IRMA, IGI Global.

Mkrttchian, V. (2013). Cloud Platform for online Laboratory for Online Learning working in Sliding Mode. *Maldives Journal of Research*, *1*, 12–19.

Mkrttchian, V. (2015). Modelling using of Triple H-Avatar Technology in online Multi-Cloud Platform Lab. In M. Khosrow-Pour (Ed.), *Encyclopedia of Information Science and Technology* (3rd ed., pp. 4162–4170). Hershey, PA: IGI Global. doi:10.4018/978-1-4666-5888-2.ch409

Mkrttchian, V., & Aleshina, E. (2017). *Sliding Mode in Intellectual Control and Communication: Emerging Research and Opportunities*. Hershey, PA, USA: IGI Global. doi:10.4018/978-1-5225-2292-8

Mkrttchian, V., Aysmontas, B., Uddin, M., Andreev, A., & Vorovchenko, N. (2015). The Academic views from Moscow Universities of the Cyber U-Learning on the Future of Online Education at Russia and Ukraine. In G. Eby & T. Vokan Yuzer (Eds.), *Identification, Evaluation, and Perceptions of Online Education Experts* (pp. 32–45). Hershey, PA: IGI Global. doi:10.4018/978-1-4666-8119-4.ch003

Mkrttchian, V., & Belyanina, L. (Eds.). (2018). *Handbook of Research on Students' Research Competence in Modern Educational Contexts*. Hershey, PA, USA: IGI Global. doi:10.4018/978-1-5225-3485-3

Mkrttchian, V., Bershadsky, A., Bozhday, A., & Fionova, L. (2015). Model in SM of DEE Based on Service Oriented Interactions at Dynamic Software Product Lines. In G. Eby & T. Vokan Yuzer (Eds.), *Identification, Evaluation, and Perceptions of Online Education Experts* (pp. 230–247). Hershey, PA: IGI Global. doi:10.4018/978-1-4666-8119-4.ch014

Mkrttchian, V., Bershadsky, A., Bozhday, A., Kataev, M., & Kataev, S. (Eds.). (2016). *Handbook of Research on Estimation and Control Techniques in E-Learning Systems*. Hershey, PA, USA: IGI Global. doi:10.4018/978-1-4666-9489-7

Mkrttchian, V., Kataev, M., Hwang, W., Bedi, S., & Fedotova, A. (2014). Using Plug-Avatars "hhh" Technology Education as Service-Oriented Virtual Learning Environment in Sliding Mode. In G. Eby & T. Vokan Yuzer (Eds.), *Emerging Priorities and Trends in Online Education: Communication, Pedagogy, and Technology*. Hershey, PA: IGI Global. doi:10.4018/978-1-4666-5162-3.ch004

Mkrttchian, V., Kataev, M., Shih, T., Kumar, M., & Fedotova, A. (2014). Avatars "HHH" Technology Education Cloud Platform on Sliding Mode Based Plug- Ontology as a Gateway to Improvement of Feedback Control Online Society. *International Journal of Information Communication Technologies and Human Development*, *6*(3), 13–31. doi:10.4018/ijicthd.2014070102

Mkrttchian, V., & Stephanova, G. (2013). Training of Avatar Moderator in Sliding Mode Control. In G. Eby & T. Vokan Yuzer (Eds.), *Project Management Approaches for Online Learning Design* (pp. 175–203). Hershey, PA: IGI Global. doi:10.4018/978-1-4666-2830-4.ch009

Mkrttchian, V., & Stephanova, G. (2013) Training of Avatar Moderator in Sliding Mode Control Environment for Virtual Project Management. In Romero, J.A. & other (Eds). Enterprise Resource Planning: Concepts, Methodologies, Tools, and Applications. (pp. 1376-1405) IRMA, IGI Global.

KEY TERMS AND DEFINITIONS

Big Context: Is defined as a better understanding of how entities.

Big Data: Is extremely large data sets that may be analyzed computationally to reveal patterns, trends, and associations, especially relating to human behavior and interactions.

Context: Is the circumstances that form the setting for an event, statement, or idea, and in terms of which it can be fully understood.

Internet of Everything: Is a broad term that refers to devices and consumer products connected to the internet and outfitted with expanded digital features.

Internet of People and Things: Is a system of interrelated computing devices, mechanical and digital machines, objects, animals or people that are provided with unique identifiers (UIDs) and the ability to transfer data over a network without requiring human-to-human or human-to-computer interaction.

Internet of Signs: Is categories of signs, including written language, natural language, cultural codes, aesthetic codes, codes of tastes, and a number of others.

Internet of Things: Is the interconnection via the Internet of computing devices embedded in everyday objects, enabling them to send and receive data.

Semiotics: Is the study of signs and symbols and their use or interpretation.

Chapter 21
Green Internet of Things (G-IoT):
ICT Technologies, Principles, Applications, Projects, and Challenges

Arun Solanki
Gautam Buddha University, India

Anand Nayyar
Duy Tan University, Vietnam

ABSTRACT

Smart world is envisioned via the fusion of diverse technologies like sensor communications, cloud computing, internet of things, AI, machine and deep learning. No doubt, new technologies bring revolution and innovation in every aspect of human life, but they are accompanied by lots of limitations in terms of energy wastage, environmental hazards like carbon or other chemical emissions, extreme consumption of natural or renewable sources and greenhouse effects. In order to minimize the negative impact of these technologies on the environment, it is utmost important to move towards green technology. That is the reason researchers are working hard and moving towards green computing, ICT, and IoT. This chapter explores an in-depth analysis of principles of G-IoT, making significant progress towards improvising the quality of life and sustainable environment. In addition to this, the chapter outlines various Green ICT technologies explores potential towards diverse real-time areas and also highlights various challenges acting as a barrier towards G-IoT implementation in the real world.

INTRODUCTION AND EVOLUTION OF INTERNET OF THINGS

Information and Communication Technologies (ICT) have automated and simplified various routine tasks in the real world. Computers, these days, are playing a significant role in controlling and monitoring almost all aspects of the physical world. Information and Communication Technologies (ICT) have created a significant impact on all aspects of mankind right from basic living to transformation of an

DOI: 10.4018/978-1-5225-7432-3.ch021

"Industrial" to "Global Connected" society. Since the invention of the Internet almost 40 years ago by ARPANET (Kakabadse, Kouzmin, & Kakabads 2017), the word "Internet" is defined as network of networks, serving billions of users across the planet in 24x7 order. Indeed, an era has just started, where ubiquitous communications are becoming a reality. The internet has played a crucial role in enhancing and developing ICT sector. All the communications on the Internet take place in the manner of "Client-Server" architecture in which servers get the request from the users and process it and clients are a billion users getting the response from servers worldwide. Social Networks are regarded as the ultra-most modern trend to revolutionize the way information is generated and distributed across worldwide. In addition to this, Machine to Machine communication is also increasing in a consistent manner and now one machine utilizes the information generated from one machine like Sensors Communicating Online with the Server or Remote Monitoring Station. Everything around the world is getting connected. New ICT solutions are hitting on a routine basis, particularly, Internet of Things (IoT)., which is changing the way the people organize, interact and participate in various facets of society. Internet of Things is regarded as a flawless integration of users and devices to converge the physical realm with human-derived virtual environments. Internet of Things (IoT) is regarded as a worldwide network of physical objects intercommunication anywhere and everywhere cum anytime and every time.

IoT is mixture of two important components "Internet" and "Things". The simple explanation to this is, "Any device having the capability and is compatible to connect to the Internet will come under Things". Things can be called "Smart Devices", "Sensors", "Miscellaneous Objects" to communicate with one another and accessible anytime and from anywhere.

The term "Internet of Things" was coined by "Kevin Ashton" (Ashton, 2017) in 1999. IoT is rebranding the existing face of Machine to Machine (M2M) of today. According to Ashton "The IoT creates an intelligent environment using invisible network fabric that can be sensed, controlled and programmed. IoT-enabled products employ embedded technology that allows devices to communicate directly or indirectly with each other or the Internet" (Ashton, 2017).

Till date, 5 billion devices are connected to the Internet and are regarded as "Smart Connected" things. It is also predicted that by 2020, more than 50 billion devices will be connected and soon in next coming years, IoT will become almost 3 trillion-node networks worldwide (Santucci & Lange, 2008),(IERC,2018), (CASAGRAS, 2018).

Internet of Things: Definitions

IoT has become a "Global Concept" and various standard organizations have given definitions of IoT in a comprehensive manner. International Telecommunications Unit (ITU, 2018), (IETF, 2018), (NIST, 2018), defined the Internet of Things in their own words according to their application areas. Considering all the above-foresaid definitions defined by various standard organizations regarding IoT, one can find it really complex to understand the entire scenario and working of IoT and even with regard to basic methodologies and architecture of IoT. In a nutshell, IoT is a mix of two terms, "Internet and "Things/ Objects". Figure 1 shows the Ecosystem deriving Internet of Things.

Elements

Figure 2 represents all elements surrounding the IoT ecosystem (Lin, Yu, Zhang, Yang, Zhang & Zhao, 2017), (Atzori, Iera, & Morabito, 2010), (Suo, Wan, Zou, & Liu, 2012). IoT, primarily, comprise of six

Figure 1. Ecosystem deriving Internet of Things

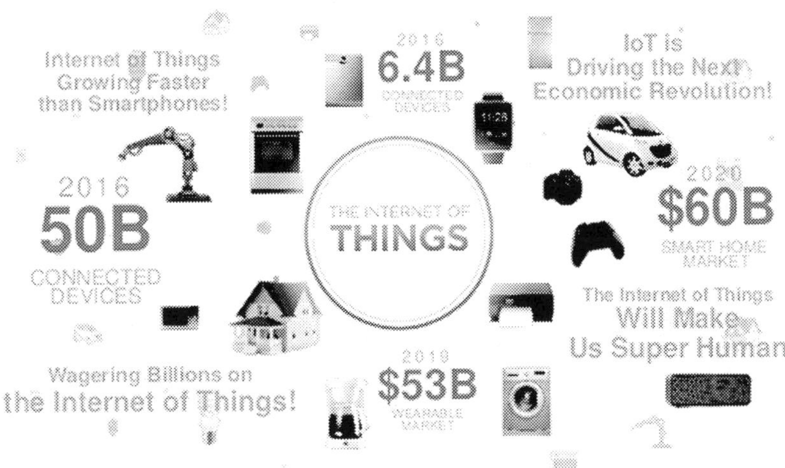

Figure 2. Elements of IoT

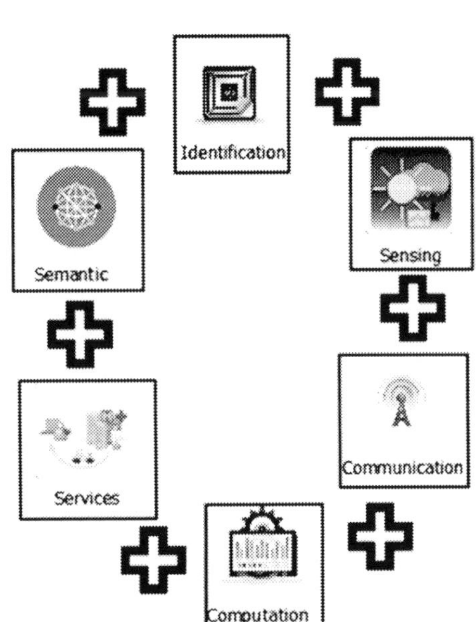

main elements: (1) Identification; (2) Sensing; (3) Communication Technologies; (4) Computation; (5) Services; (6) Semantic.

- **Identification:** The first and foremost element in IoT is identification. It performs the task of object naming and mapping services. In order to perform the identification process in IoT, various techniques are proposed like Ubiquitous Codes (uCode) and Electronic Product Codes (EPC). It is highly essential for IoT, to map a clear distinction between an address and object ID. Object ID can be marked as "OE1" for a sensor node and IP Address is the address of the object. Both identification and addressing are highly important in case of IoT for object identification when it comes to local network. Identification techniques play a crucial role to identify the IoT in a highly unique manner in the overall network.

- **Sensing:** In IoT, sensing is primarily concerned with collecting all varied information from specific sensor nodes operating within the network and sending it to the database, Cloud Server or Data centre. The captured data in the database is further utilized to perform analysis using various Data Analysis algorithms. Tons of sensors are available for IoT in terms of Healthcare, Environmental, Industrial, Wearable, Actuators etc.
- **Communication Technologies:** In order to connect all the sensor nodes to communicate with one another and transmit the data back, various communication technologies are linked up. Some of the typical communication protocols used by IoT devices are Wi-Fi, Bluetooth, ZigBee, Z-Wave etc. Traditionally RFID, RF technologies also used to perform Machine to Machine communication.
- **Computation:** IoT devices are equipped with intelligent hardware processing units to perform all tasks of processing, computation, and in-device hardware components communications. Hardware processing units like Microcontrollers, Microprocessors and even System on Chip (SoC), FPGA perform this task. In order to design and develop IoT, nowadays embedded chip companies have released lots of development boards in terms of Arduino (Puri, Nayyar, Le 2017) (Nayyar, & Puri, 2016), Freeduino, Raspberry Pi (Nayyar, & Puri, 2015), Intel Galileo (Nayyar &Puri, 2016), Beagle bone(Nayyar, 2016), (Nayyar, & Puri, 2016), (Nayyar, & Puri, 2015) CHIP, Orange Pi and many more. IoT devices are also making use of Real-Time Operating Systems (RTOS) like Contiki RTOS.

IoT devices are making strong utilization of diverse cloud platforms. Devices store and transmit the information of sensed data to cloud providers like Thingspeak.com to facilitate the users for real-time monitoring of devices.

- **Services:** IoT devices perform four different services like Identity-related services, Information Aggregation, Collaborative Aware and Ubiquitous Services. Identity-related services are related to the Identity detection of the object and map the real-world object to the virtual world. Information collected is in raw form, so it has to be summarized, processed and reported in proper form which is done by Information Aggregation services. The information gathered is to be further analyzed for all types of further decisions is done by Collaborative aware services. The only role of Ubiquitous services to make Collaborative services available anywhere and anytime as per the end user requirements.
- **Semantic:** In order to process all requested services by end users, it is highly important to capture all the data from various IoT devices in an intelligent manner and further analyzed to make efficient decisions. The semantic process is regarded as "Brain" of IoT and performs various tasks like Resource discovery, Resource Utilization, Information Modelling and Data Analysis. In order to perform semantic services, various techniques can be used like: Web Ontology Language (OWL), Resource Description Framework (RDF), Efficient XML Interchange (EXI) etc.

The Table 1 highlight various IoT Elements along with their respective support details.

Table 1. IoT elements

IoT Elements		Support
Identification	Addressing	IPV4, IPV6
	Naming	EPC, uCODE
Sensing		Wearable Sensor, RFID Tag, Acurator
Communication		WiFi, Bluetooth, IEEE 802.15.4,RFID, Thread,NFC, UWB,Neul
Computation	Software	OS(Tiny OS, Contiki)
	Hardware	Arduino, Raspbeery Pi Clouds(Hadoop etc)
Service		Energy Monitoring System, Smart Home, e-Health Care and Smart City etc.
Semantic		RDF,OWL,EXI

INTRODUCTION TO GREEN COMPUTING

The concept of Green Computing (Green IT or Green ICT as per IFG International Federation of Green ICT and IFG Standard) is defined as, "*study and practice of designing, manufacturing, utilizing and disposing of computers, laptops, servers and associated sub-units like keyboards, mouse, monitors, printers, hard disk and any other storage devices, communication systems, efficiently and highly effectively with either minimal or no impact on the natural environment*" (Kiruthika, & Parimala, 2017), (Murugesan, 2008), (Raza, Patle, & Arya,, 2012), (Ifgict, 2018). The primary objective of green computing is to eliminate the utilization of hazardous materials, enhance the energy efficiency of any sort of IT product in terms of durability and utilization, and above all promote recyclability and biodegradability of damaged products cum waste production of factories. Green computing lays a strong foundation for attaining economic feasibility and attaining better system performance by taking care of social and moral responsibilities.

The concept of "Green Computing" originated by US Environmental Protection Agency (EPA) in 1992 with the launch of voluntary labelling program, i.e. Energy Star, to promote energy efficiency in computer hardware. Till then to until now, many computers have an Energy Star Label, which is regarded as significant certification to promote green computing. On the same lines, green computing-based initiative was also taken by Swedish organization TCP Development via launch of TCO Certification program to promote the utilization of low emission components in terms of magnetism and electrical in

CRT based monitor, and on later stages, the program expanded and designed criteria for energy utilization, ergonomics, and utilization of hazardous material in construction.

(Murugesan, 2008), enlists the following points to be solved following Green Computing path:

- **Green Use:** Reduction in energy utilization of computers and misc. information systems along with their effective utilization in an environment-friendly manner.
- **Green Disposal:** Recycling and re-utilization of old computers along with refurbishing computer and other electronic equipment's.
- **Green Design:** Energy efficient and environmentally friendly design of computers, servers and other cooling equipment's.
- **Green Manufacturing:** Production and manufacturing of all sorts of computer and electronic equipment with less impact on the environment.

Green computing is highly beneficial in lots of parameters. Green computing is not only beneficial for businesses or end users but promotes positive effects on the environment, creating global impact over the country and in turn the whole world. Green computing promotes the tremendous reduction in energy wastage, low cost as well as waste reduction.

Green computing, is highly adapted by lots of IT organizations worldwide and the number is increasing two-fold every year because of the following trends:

- Explosive growth in Internet and ICT use.
- Increase in cooling requirements for equipment.
- Increase in cost of energy.
- Reduction in energy supply.
- Low server utilization rates.
- Increasing knowledge among people regarding the impact of ICT utilization on the environment.

The Concept of Green IoT (G-IoT)

Considering the adoption of Smart Technologies everywhere, IoT is now regarded as one of the top six "Innovative Civil Technologies" by National Intelligence Council (NIC) of U.S.A, foreseen by NIC, can impact U.S.A power grids. According to NIC, by the year 2025, almost all types of everything's used by everyone in terms of furniture, transportation, food items will have Internet nodes. But in order to promote sustainability in smart technologies to enable a sustainable smart world of the future, lots of attention has to be given with regard to energy efficiency in IoT based devices.

Green Internet of Things (G-IoT) is established on the same concept of IoT which contains smart and portable devices, communication protocols, architecture, but with the addition of energy efficient production paradigms in all products and services in order to reduce waste, efficient energy utilization, less toxic and carbon emission in the environment. As all devices operating in the smart world contain sensors of varied types to sense different sorts of information and communicate with each other, devices require lots of energy for smooth operations. Considering the adoption rate of IoT devices by organizations and end-users, the demand for energy is also increasing parallely. This makes, Green IoT, a significant area to focus as it is highly important to reduce energy consumption, to fulfil all the requirements of the smart world with regard to sustainability.

Considering the foremost requirement of energy efficiency, Green IoT is defined by (Shaikh, Zeadally &Exposito 2017) as the energy efficient actions which are used by IoT to reduce the greenhouse effect on IoT applications. The fig.3 gives an overview of technologies connected with Green IoT.

In order to satisfy the implementation of Green-IoT in the real world, Green IoT has to satisfy the environmentally friendly operational conditions. The following points highlight the principles of Green-IoT:

- **Switch Off Facilities Not Required**: In order to conserve energy, only those facilities which are required should operate and rest all other facilities should be turned off. Example: Implementation of Wake/Sleep algorithms should be implemented in sensor nodes, i.e. Sensor nodes wake up when data is required to be transmitted otherwise, sensor nodes go to sleep position to conserve energy utilization.
- **Utilization of Natural/Renewable Power Generation Sources**: Rather than to use limited sources of nature like coal, water; green power generation energy sources like Solar, Wind, Geothermal, biogas for generating power for using ICT equipment. In the near future, power generation is expected via wireless technology and biodegradable batteries.
- **Implementation of Advanced Communication Technologies**: In the recent years, advanced communication technologies are emerging like MIMO, 5G, CRAN (Cognitive Adhoc Radio Networks) which improvises frequency operation, modulation schemes, power utilization and overall spectral efficiency can be attained.
- **Energy Efficient Schemes and Minimize the Length for Data Path**: Deployment of energy-efficient routing protocols/techniques for enhancing the lifetime of IoT enabled devices to make the network run for a prolonged period of time. Information transmission should be performed, when

Figure 3. Green IoT

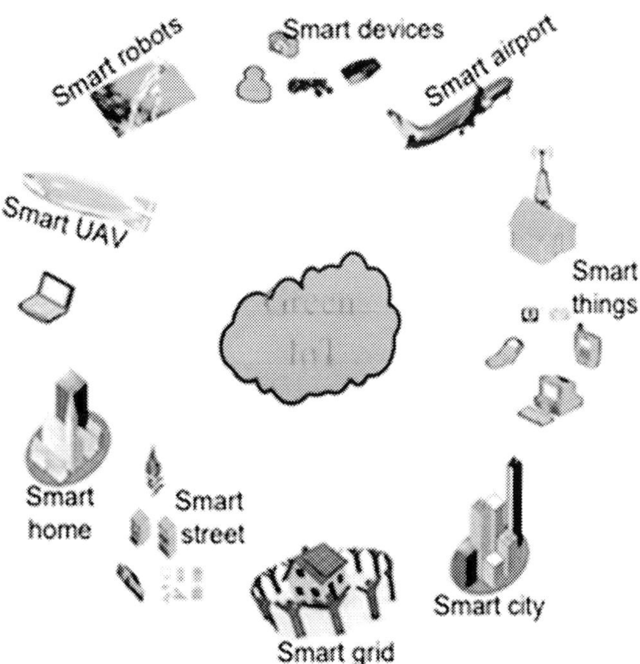

required. Implementation of cloud-based architecture reduces the data quantity to be transmitted by only transmitting sensitive/critical information.

- **Cloud-Based Implementations**: Migration of intelligent processing and storage devices to cloud, to generate G-IoT based data to overcome all challenges in terms of latency, bandwidth, security, and cost of operations.
- **Security Mechanisms**: Advanced security and privacy techniques implementation in G-IoT system for enhancing the reliability of overall G-IoT architecture.

ICT Enabling Green IoT

Green-IoT is supported by the strong backbone of ICT technologies. The ICT technologies enable Green IoT to perform all sorts of communication and transmission of information among all devices operating on the network. ICT technologies facilitate the end-users to store, transmit, access and update all sorts of information. Considering ICT, the following are the elements:

- **RFID (Radio Frequency Identification)**: RFID is regarded as a tiny electronic device, making use of electromagnetic fields to facilitate automatic identification and tags tracking attached to objects. RFID tags are classified into categories: Passive and Active. Passive tags gather energy from RFID readers within range via radio waves. Active tags, on the contrary, have inbuilt power source via battery and can fully operate at a distance of few hundred meters from the RFID reader. According to reports by world RFID market, RFID market is expected to touch the US $18.68 billion by end of the year 2026 with a significant CAGR rate of 12.3% (Ahson & Ilyas, 2017).
- **WSN (Wireless Sensor Network)**: Wireless sensor networks consist of spatially distributed devices, making use of smart sensors to sense information from physical or varied environments like Temperature, Humidity, Gases, Pressure, light intensity, etc. A sensor network comprises of few to tons of sensor nodes and every sensor node is equipped with a microprocessor, transducer, antenna and power source (Shah, Patel, Patel, Patel, & Jhaveri, 2018).
- **WPAN (Wireless Personal Area Network)**: Wireless Personal Area Network (WPAN) connects individual devices wirelessly in short range. WPAN facilitates interconnection of all different sorts of computing and communication devices that people can wear and carry around and WPAN measure's unique parameters of a person. In other words, WPAN technology is also entitled as "Plugging In" (Mor, Kumar & Sharma, 2018).
- **WBAN (Wireless Body Area Network)**: Wireless body area network facilitates interconnection of nodes, i.e. Sensors and Actuators attached to a person's body either via clothes or on the skin. All the nodes are connected via wireless medium and forms either star or multihop topology. WBAN is mostly used in medical technologies like Healthcare for measuring varied parameters of a patient like blood pressure, heartbeat, ECG etc. (Ramyaka, Durga, Sharma & Sharma, 2017).
- **HAN (Home Area Network)**: Home area network facilitates interconnection of all digital devices in user home like computers, telecommunication devices, TV's, handheld devices, gaming consoles, home video surveillance systems, kitchen equipment's to form an interconnected network to share information. HAN facilitates add-on advantages in terms of automation of repeated tasks, enhancement in personal productivity, personal security and above all interactive entertainment (Srinivas & Kale, 2017).

- **NAN (Neighborhood Area Network)**: Neighborhood area network (NAN) is regarded as a fusion of Wi-Fi hotspots and WLAN, which plays a strong role for all users to connect Internet instantly at a cheap price. It is generally designed and maintained by an individual to provide network services to specific people living at home. NANs cover only a small block close to 802.11 standard access points. NANs provide a strong way to extend neighbourhood Wi-Fi networks (Alohali, Kifayat, Shi, & Hurst, 2016).
- **M2M (Machine to Machine)**: Machine to Machine communication is emerging paradigm popularly termed as "Internet of Things (IoT)". M2M refers to a technology that lays a bridge of connectivity between wired and wireless devices and other devices of the same type. M2M facilitates end-users to capture data about varied events like temperature, inventory and other types of data. M2M can be applied in various scenarios like remote monitoring, control of assets and even Industry 4.0 gets facilitated via M2M (Holler, Tsiatsis, Mulligan, Karnouskos, & Boyle, 2014).
- **Cloud Computing**: Cloud computing is convenient, on-demand network which is available everywhere and it give access to different devices using a shared pool of different resources which include networks, servers, storage, application and services. Software as a Service (SaaS), Platform as a Service (PaaS) and Infrastructure as a service (IaaS) are the service models used by Cloud Computing. The cloud computing is deployed in Private, Public, Hybrid, and community models (Senyo, Addae & Boateng 2018).
- **Data Center**: A Data centre is termed as state-of-the-art facility that centralizes all IT organization's equipment's and act as information store to store, manage and backup all the data. Data centres are termed as critical network systems that are highly important for routine operations. The uptime of Data center demands range from 99.67% to 99.998%.The important components of data center are UPS (Uninterruptable Power Supply) - comprise of power sources to facilitate 24X7 round the clock power supply to keep data center's up and running; Environmental Control-Computer Room Air Conditioners (CRAC), Heating, Ventilation, and Air Conditioning systems (HVAC) and Air Exhaust Systems (AES); Security Hardware- biometrics and round the clock IP camera surveillance systems (Alaraifi, Molla & Deng 2012).

Green ICT Technologies

The Green ICT technologies outlined in this section are: Green RFID, Green WSN, Green Cloud Computing, Green Machine to Machine communication and Green Data Centres.

Green RFID

RFID technology lays a strong backbone as "Wireless System" for IoT. RFID technology comprises of several and tag readers (Pazowski, 2015), (Zhu, Leung, Shu, & Ngai, 2015), (Roselli, 2014), (Orecchini, Yang, Rida, Alimenti, Tentzeris, & Roselli, 2010) RFID tag consists of a small microchip attached to a radio used for sending and receiving signals with a Unique Identifier (UID) and wraps around with an adhesive sticker. RFID tags are used to store information with regard to the objects they are attached. The process of RFID works as the flow of information is initialized by an RFID tag reader via query signal transmission; it is followed by a response from RFID tags operating within the range. RFID tags have a very small transmission range, i.e. few meters and bands used by RFID technology for transmission are 124-135 kHz for low frequencies and 860-960 MHz for ultra-high frequencies. Considering

RFID technology, NFC (Near Field Communication) is regarded as the most promising technology and highly customer oriented as tag readers are integrated into mobile phones facilitating best interaction with the environment.

RFID technologies are utilized in the real world in terms of monitoring wildlife, forests, water resources monitoring, hotel rooms, waste disposal, etc. RFID technology faces some shortcomings in terms of recycling and sometimes security.

From the Green - IoT point of view, RFID tags (Lin, Yu, Zhang, Yang, Zhang & Zhao, 2017) should be reduced in size via utilization of biodegradable RFID (Duroc & Kaddour, 2012), (Thomas, 2008), (Al-Azzawi, Rigelsford, & Langley, 2018) printable RFID tags and even 3-D printed RFID tags. RFID technology, especially when designed for Green IoT should be integrated with energy efficient algorithms in order to optimize- tag detection, power consumption, collision avoidance and overhearing etc.

Green WSN

MEMS (Micro-Electromechanical Systems) and Wireless Communications fusion have laid strong evolution of Sensor Networks popularly termed as "Wireless Sensor Networks (WSNs). WSNs are playing a crucial role in recent times for advancement and strong adoption of Internet of Things (IoT) (Sahana, Singh, Kumar, & Das 2018), (Qian, & Wang, 2013).

WSNs are utilized in lots of real-time applications like Industrial monitoring, agriculture, environmental monitoring (Nayyar, Puri & Le, 2016) military, object detection, forestry and many others.

Wireless sensor networks comprise of few hundreds to tons of sensor nodes either static or mobile implemented in a geographical region to perform the task of sensing the data, processing, and computing and sending the data back to the base station for further analysis. The sensor nodes deployed forming WSN have the low processing power, limited memory, limited battery life and less communication range. Sensor nodes cooperate with each other in the self - organization manner and deliver the data to the base station in an ad hoc manner. Almost all the WSN commercial solutions are based on IEEE 802.15.4 standard covering physical and MAC layers for low-power and low-bit rate communications. The IEEE 802.15.4 specification doesn't include higher layers, which is significant for sensor nodes for accessing the Internet. In recent times, lots of energy efficient routing protocols based on clustering, multipath and hierarchical routing (Nayyar, & Gupta, 2014), (Nayyar, Puri & Le, 2016), (Kumar & Nayyar, 2014), (Sharma, Gupta, & Nayyar, 2014) are proposed for WSN based on Sleep-wake Strategy for improvising lifetime, but every protocol is having drawbacks in one way or another affecting the reliability and operational capacity of the entire sensor network.

Considering Green-IoT, WSN technology has to be given major attention, especially with regard to energy efficiency (Shaikh, Zeadally & Exposito 2017). Some of the following techniques need to be adopted to enhance the operational lifetime of the sensor nodes:

- Routing techniques, highly energy efficient for sensor communications (Nayyar, & Gupta, 2014), (Kumar & Nayyar, 2014).
- Utilization of natural energy sources like Solar, Wind or Wireless charging to power the sensor nodes deployed in real time.
- Adoption of optimization techniques like Swarm Intelligence based routing protocols (Nayyar, & Singh, 2017) for enhancing routing efficiency of sensor nodes and even minimizing delay and enhancing throughput of the sensor network.

- Data reduction mechanisms like (Aggregation, Adaptive Sampling, Compression and Network Coding)
- Efficiency in radio transmissions like modulation optimization, directional antennas, energy efficient cognitive radio and cooperative communication.

Green Cloud Computing

Internet of Things (IoT) is a special type of network comprising of physical objects or things, embedded with electronics, sensors, software and communications systems, enabling greater value and service via data exchange with manufacturers, operators and other connected devices (Stergiou, Psannis, Kim & Gupta, 2018). Data gathered by these devices requires mass storage, which is facilitated via utilization of "Cloud Computing". IoT, when combined with Cloud Computing, leads to new technology transformation, i.e. *Mobile Cloud Computing (MCC)*. Mobile Cloud Computing is getting improvised in terms of services, interface, ease of access and even security in the last few years with the increased usage of IoT.

Mobile Cloud Computing is elaborated in two aspects: (1) Infrastructure based; (2) Ad hoc Mobile Cloud. Infrastructure based cloud computing keeps the hardware static and provides all sorts of software, infrastructure, and platform-oriented services to users. Ad hoc Mobile cloud is emerging paradigm and overcomes all limitations of cloud computing in terms of delay and throughput. It is deployed over mobile ad hoc networks and facilitates execution of computation-intensive applications by utilizing resources of other mobile devices.

Considering Green-IoT, green cloud computing should include significant dimensions in terms of Environmental sustainability, energy efficiency and total cost of ownership (Shaikh, Zeadally & Exposito 2017), (Qiu, Shen & Chen, 2018), (Wibowo, & Wells,2018). The following factors to be considered for green cloud computing to make it highly functional for G-IoT implementation.

- Utilization and implementation of software and hardware consuming less energy while performing operations. Only those hardware devices and software solutions should be implemented consuming less energy with efficient resource utilization and providing efficient solutions in terms of efficiency to the end-users.
- Energy efficient algorithms to perform load balancing, fault tolerance, and resource allocation.
- Green Cloud Computing based approaches should be implemented using renewable energy sources on-site, dynamic provisioning, multi-tenancy and data center efficiency.

Green Machine to Machine Communications (M2M)

Advancements in IoT have led to innovations in diverse areas like wearable technologies, implantable sensors, embedded computing, intelligent systems, cloud computing that has enabled the design, implementation of advanced IoT systems like Cyber-Physical Systems (CPS). IoT has transformed the face of today's Cyber-Physical Systems and Machine to Machine communication. Machine to Machine (M2M) are technologies facilitating wired and wireless systems to communicate with other devices of the same standards. Machine to Machine systems focuses on Machine-type-communication (MTC) which means, no need for any sort of human intervention when devices are communicating with each other. With the fusion of WSN, RFID, M2M, network communications and advanced control theories, CPS systems are becoming advanced and broadening their roots in different areas.

Considering green-IoT, M2M communication is important, but the serious drawback is the consumption of energy in M2M is very high. In order to facilitate energy efficient M2M communications, which is the need of the hour for implementing Green IoT, the following parameters must be considered (Shaikh, Zeadally & Exposito 2017), (Wan, Chen, Xia & Zhou 2013), (Vo, Choi, Chang & Lee, 2010), (Alsamhi, Ma, Ansari, & Meng, 2018).

Adjustment of transmission power in highly intelligent manner.

- Design and development of energy efficient routing protocols via optimization techniques like Genetic Algorithms, Swarm Intelligence, and Fuzzy Logics etc.
- Deployment of energy saving mechanisms like protection from overloading and efficient resource allocation.
- Deployment of energy harvesting techniques like spectrum sensing, management and power optimization of Cognitive Radio.

Green Data Centers

The primary task performed by the data center is to manage, store, process and disseminates data and applications created by end users, IoT objects/things, systems, etc. Data center infrastructure is central to IT architecture, via which all content is shared, sourced as well as transmitted. Proper planning is required for implementing data center as its design is highly critical and other parameters like resilience, scalability, security and above all performance has to be carefully planned.

Data center operations are as follows:

- **Infrastructure Operations:** Deployment, maintaining, monitoring, updating and even patching of the server, storage systems and all types of network resources.
- **Security:** Procedures, tools, and technologies deployed to assure physical and data security from low to top level in the premises.
- **Power and Cooling:** Processes to ensure sufficient power is supplied and coolant systems are working for keeping data center operational 24x7 without any downtime.
- **Management:** Monitoring, implementing and enforcing policies regarding operations across all data center processes.

Considering Green-IoT, the following techniques are required to attain energy efficiency for environmental sustainability (Shaikh, Zeadally & Exposito 2017), (Zhang, & Ansari, 2012), (Wang & Khan, 2013), (Basmadjian, Bouvry, Costa, Gyarmati, Kliazovich, Lafond & Torres, 2015).

- Implementation of dynamic power management techniques like vSphere.
- Design and development of high energy efficient hardware.
- Implementation of modern energy efficient data center design architectures.
- Utilization of renewable energy sources like Wind, Solar, Water for powering and cooling data centres.
- Energy efficient communication techniques.

Green IoT: Current Initiatives

In the recent two decades, trends towards implementation of Green IoT technology is increasing. Lots of green projects are backed and funded by various organizations, agencies and even governments for deployment and testing of green technologies for IoT. In this section, we enlist some of the few Green IoT projects and standards laying a strong base for G-IoT advancements.

All over the world, lots of efforts are put by several organizations and governments to handle the situation of biohazards and implement techniques for minimizing carbon emissions using green technologies.

The following projects are started by respective organizations, governments as part of a Green IoT initiative to make the environment humanity friendly:

1. **Project EARTH**: Project EARTH (Energy Aware Radio and network technologies) was funded under FP7-ICT. The project was primarily proposed to handle all significant issues with regard to energy saving by enhancing the energy efficiency of mobile broadband systems by reducing CO2 emissions. Project EARTH has focused on mobile cellular systems, LTE, LTE-A as well as 3G (UMTS/HSPA) (Cordis, 2018), (Project earth, 2018). Results outlined from project EARTH were as follows:
   a. Deployment strategies& Network Architectures having high degree of energy efficiency.
   b. Novel network management schemes, highly adaptive to handle all sorts of load variations at regular intervals of time.
   c. Novel component designs with energy efficient adaptive operating points.
   d. Novel resource management protocols for multi-cell cooperative networking.
2. **Project TREND**: Project TREND (Towards Real Energy-efficient Network Design) is funded and supported by European Commission (EU). The objective behind TREND is to integrate all activities of all European organizations working in networking like R&D departments, manufacturers, and operational units to access the energy demand of telecom infrastructures and design and develop energy efficient and future-ready sustainable networks (Project TREND, 2018). Objectives:
   a. Develop a virtual center of excellence to work on issues with regard to energy-efficient networking and provide training, research and implement the new technologies and tools cum architectures.
   b. Strong collaboration between researchers and groups to design and propose novel things for energy efficient networking.
   c. Organize conferences and seminars for doing research in energy efficient networking outside Europe.
3. **TCGCC**: TCGCC (Technical Committee on Green Communications and Computing) was founded by the IEEE communication society to provide a strong base for research and to exchange ideas for proposing novel solutions for environmentally friendly green communications and computing. The main objective behind the development of this committee is to promote research and development to produce a green energy efficient environment. Design and development of novel hierarchical and distributed techniques with regard to energy distribution and management, energy harvesting, and novel architectures to optimize energy utilization in Adhoc and sensor networks, smart grids and green cloud computing and data centers, propose resource efficient cross-layer optimization methods and advanced signal processing techniques for energy-efficient transmission systems (TCGCC, 2018).

4. **GreenTouch**: GreenTouch consortium was developed by combining 30+ ICT companies, academic, and non-government research experts to design energy efficient techniques to enhance communications and data networks including the Internet and reduce carbon emission from ICT devices, platforms, and networks. The technical committee worked on three main technology areas: Mobile Networks; Services, Policies and Standards; Wired core and access networks (Green Touch, 2018).
5. **The Green Grid**: The Green Grid Association is non-profit, consortium of industry, end-users, policy makers, technology providers and utility companies, was formed with an objective to design and propose novel metrics, new build tools, and initiatives to enable ICT industries to improvise operations, reduce energy consumption and deliver enhanced sustainable products and services. The association is currently working on 15+ projects to improvise sustainability and promote green-IoT and computing in industries. The top projects underway by the Green Grid are Infrastructure Utility Effectiveness (IUE), Power Metrics for IT Equipment, Liquid Cooling, Open standard for Data center availability tool, Data center automation with a DCIM system and REDFISH API utilization(thegreengrid,2018).
6. **C2POWER**: C2POWER- Cognitive Radio and Cooperative Strategies for Power Saving in multi-standard wireless devices, the association include academic, research associations and telecom operators to improvise the energy efficiency of mobile handsets via two ways: (1) Cooperative technologies- allows nearby devices to work together in finding an efficient way to access Internet; (2) cognitive technologies to facilitate future terminals to become context-aware and smart(C2power,2018).
7. **Cool Silicon**: Cool Silicon was founded to enhance energy efficiency in ICT with the join collaboration of 60 companies cum research center's to increase energy efficiency for micro- and Nanotechnologies and communication systems to design and propose energy efficient sensors for IoT devices. Current projects involved in Cool Silicon are: Cool-RFID- Innovative RFID Sensor Tag; CoolCarbonConcentrate- Integration of carbon concentrate on electric and electronic systems; iCool: design and develop secure technology for energy efficient electronics (Cool Silicon,2018).
8. **GreenICN**: GreenICN- Architecture and Applications of Green Information Centric Networking were founded to propose a novel API for facilitating design and development of new applications and services to support European Union and Japanese for ICN adoption. GreenICN promotes the creation of the new, low-energy and information-centric Internet and even the test performance of real-world Green ICN applications (GreenICN,2018).

IoT: Standardization

In addition to this, to support Green IoT, various organizations are working on different projects to make it highly flexible, adaptable and dynamic for implementation. Example: Implementation of IPv6 on IoT devices like Sensors, RFID tags is currently undertaken by Internet Engineering Task Force (IETF) by proposing two standards: 6LoWPAN and Routing over Low power and Lossy Networks (ROLL). Other organizations like CEN, ISO, ETSI are also working consistently to improvise communication standards of IoT as well as to enhance privacy and facilitate next-generation M2M and energy efficient WSN networks.

Challenges Surrounding Green IoT

Fusion of ICT technologies and Green IoT will play a strong role in the environment to minimize the carbon emission and will, in turn, reduce pollution in large extent and ultimately the goal of cleaner world or green world will be achieved. Green IoT will play a crucial role in designing new business models and improvising existing methodologies and processes which will reduce the risks and will facilitate the mankind. But, G-IoT still has lots of challenges and shortcomings and requires significant improvements in diverse areas for strong real-time implementation.

The following are the challenges surrounding Green IoT, and acting as a barrier to growth in real-world implementations:

1. **Dedicated Green IoT Architectures**: Like any traditional networks like OSI, TCP/IP and even modern and advanced networks like 4G/5G/LTE, Green-IoT has no standardized architecture to facilitate communication across applications, networks, and different devices. It is also a real challenge to integrate the concept of "Energy Optimization or Efficiency or Enhancement" in architecture. In order to facilitate Green IoT, the ground rule is- both devices and protocols should be energy efficient and even the applications too so that impact over the environment can be highly low. As mentioned in the above section, collaborating all sorts of energy-optimized devices, applications and protocols in a single roof over novel architecture requires joint collaborative efforts and initiatives from academia, industry and specialized research institutions so that novel G-IoT architecture can be proposed and become operational in real-time.
2. **Green IoT Infrastructure**: Designing energy efficient infrastructure like Sensor Nodes requires strong planning, dedicated professional and novel re-design approach. Deploying a newly built infrastructure in real-time is also challenging as results are unknown. Currently, fewer initiatives and directions are done by researchers across the world in this area owing to the complexity and lack of support. Green IoT energy efficient infrastructure design and implementation are highly challenging both at the design level and implementation level.
3. **Green IoT Energy-Efficient Communication Protocols:** Another challenge surrounding Green-IoT is the facilitation of energy-efficient communication which is surrounded by lots of shortcomings like a consistent supply of energy and energy efficient routing protocols to enable end-to-end communication between devices. Lots of researchers are currently working to propose energy efficient techniques for IoT that can provide a strong outcome to Green IoT. Currently, energy sources like solar, wind, thermal seems to be highly promising for IoT.

In addition to the above, another issue concerning communication is scalability. In order to counterfeit this problem, two solutions are proposed: Tethering and Multihopping (Sharma, Navda, Ramjee, Padmanabhan, & Belding, 2009), (Han, & Ansari, 2014), (Hong., Xiao & Chong 2010). Via tethering, users can communicate with the host in an ad hoc manner, the host is connected directly to the Internet. Multihopping is regarded as an important technique to overcome the limitations of energy utilization and scalability. So, the novel solution is required to solve various challenges in Green IoT in terms of mobility, scalability, and energy efficient communications.

4. **Green IoT Security and Privacy Concerns**: The chief concern surrounding Internet of Things (IoT) in the last few years is security and privacy. To implement security techniques requires lots

of processing power and energy utilization. The design and development of techniques taking care of both energies as well as security are still under infant stage. As IoT utilizes devices like Sensors and RFID tags, both are resource constrained devices, it becomes really challenging to determine security mechanisms in Green IoT paradigm. In Green IoT, security should be given due preference and should be considered right from the design phase so that end to end communication between devices, i.e. M2M communication can be secure and no network threats of any sort like Man in the middle, spoofing, Denial of Service (DoS) should happen in Green IoT.

Considering the shortcomings, Green IoT is still in pre-development stages and lots of challenges are yet to be solved to make Green IoT highly sustainable and prevalent in the real world.

Green IoT Applications

With the help of technology, the dream of sustainability can be attained by taking right technological decisions with regard to innovations at the correct passage of time. So, technology can become an indispensable tool for sustainable development as it assures that people have access to clean water, energy efficient living without any toxic environment and natural resources are managed in the correct manner. In the recent times, people have started practicing "Go Green", "Live Green and Think Green" and then all has resulted in overall ICT based Green Computing. Green Computing, especially Green-IoT, extended the utilization of green products, green homes, recycling, use of renewable energy sources, etc. So, in a nutshell, G-IoT has a bright future in the near times and will influence the environment and energy utilization by (Shaikh, Zeadally & Exposito, 2017), (Zhu, Leung, Shu, & Ngai, 2015), (Prasad & Kumar, 2013). Considering the implementation of Green IoT in the real world, we classified applications of G-IoT in following six major areas: Healthcare, Industry, Smart cities, Transportation, and Energy. The figure 4 outlines various potential applications of Green IoT.

Figure 4. Applications: Green IoT

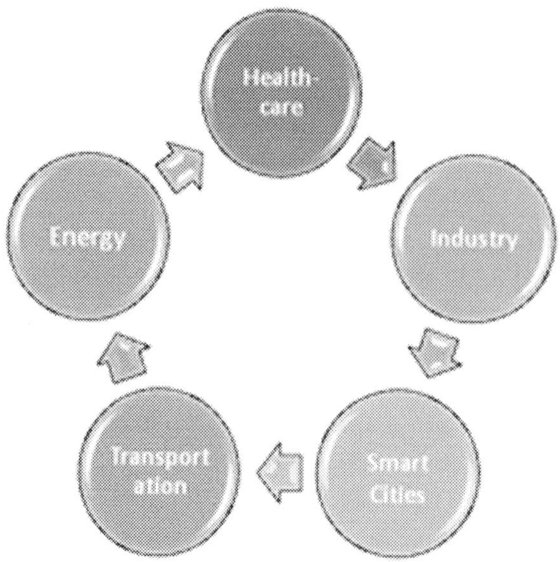

Healthcare

IoT technologies have changed the face of the healthcare sector in recent times with a substantial number of innovations and inventions. Lots of research is moving towards the direction to propose energy efficient IoT based healthcare solutions and making the dream of "Green Hospitals" come to reality.

The following are the G-IoT based approaches for healthcare sector (Mathew, Pillai, & Palade, 2018):

1. **Internet of m-Health Things (m-IoT)**: m-Health is a novel solution proposed for real-time monitoring of patient's health with the fusion of mobile computing, biosensors, communication technologies. M-IoT makes use of low power communication protocol, i.e. 6LoWPAN with 4G networks for Internet connectivity. the m-IoT based solution is highly successful for real-time tracking of the glucose level of patient and utilizes very low power for operation (Istepanian, Jovanov and Zhang, 2004)
2. **Smart WDA/WBAN Systems**: Sensors are the central point of healthcare IoT systems and perform all tasks of sensing of varied patient's health parameters for real-time monitoring and diagnosis. The sensors are integrated into wearable products and the heterogeneous nature of wearable products and medical sensors solves wide challenges for researchers and developers working in the area of Wireless Body Area Networks (WBAN). Smart WBAN systems make use of low power communication protocols like BLE (Bluetooth Low Energy) and keep systems up and running for a prolonged period of time (Chung, Lee & Jung, 2008).
3. **Remote Health Monitoring**: An IoT based approach can also be beneficial for remote health monitoring. The IoT based devices make use of RFID sensors to record the health status of the patient and this information is sent through sensor via the base station to the remote computer using the Internet. The person at the remote healthcare center can measure all parameters of a patient's body and the same can be communicated to the doctors via SMS alerts or online website. IoT based Remote Monitoring frameworks make use of low powered RFID, smart sensors and low power utilization communication protocols like RF or W-LAN make the system G-IoT compliant.

Industry

The next wave of Internet of Things is to interconnect smart machines, smart materials, products and make efficient utilization of sensed, processed and analyzed data, to enhance the potential of traditional factories to "*Industry 4.0"* by increasing overall production, quality output, flexibility via the reduction in energy consumption and resource utilization. The word "Industry 4.0" heralds the coming of a new industrial revolution via smart manufacturing and will be entitled as "Industrial Internet of Things (IIoT)" (Jeschke, Brecher, Meisen, Özdemir, & Eschert, 2017)

Industrial Internet of Things, makes sound commitments of operational efficiencies via automation, connectivity, and analytics.

Industrial Internet of Things (IIoT) has huge potential for early adoption by industry.

The following are G-IoT based approaches for Industry:

1. **Remote Monitoring of Assets**: Remote monitoring of assets is regarded as one of the most recommended Industry application. The stakeholders can monitor the presence, functioning, health, and output of their assets without any sort of location barriers. Remote monitoring based IoT solutions

can enable monitoring of tons of equipment like solar panels, energy meters, gas pipelines, production machines, factory outlets, etc. With IIoT and G-IoT, stakeholders can monitor the health of remote assets to make effective and quick decisions.

2. **Smart Robotics**: With Smart Robotics, factories can enable consistent production without any hiccup. The Smart Robotics is equipped with powerful and energy efficient sensors to enable them to keep the prototypes working with high precision. With smart robotics, companies can transform themselves into smart factories and all robots can be linked to private clouds.
3. **Industrial Smart Cities**: Industrial smart city deployment is multidimensional. The Industrial Smart city has the following benefits:
   a. Electronic traffic congestion management
   b. Public transit operations management.
   c. Improved operations management for water treatment plants for efficiencies.
   d. Infrastructure and operational monitoring of the electrical grid.
   e. Highly localized air quality monitoring and data collection, allowing correlation to traffic congestion and public health trends.

Smart Cities

The concept of the smart city is a fusion of Information and Communication Technology (ICT) along with connected objects to the Internet (Internet of Things) to optimize the city operations and services to provide smart connectivity to citizens. Smart cities enable city officials to have direct interaction with the community and the infrastructure of the city which facilitates monitoring what is happening around the city and how the city is progressing. Smart City applications also enable efficient management of urban flows and allow real-time responses from citizens. The global market for Smart Urban services will be around $400 billion by 2020. The following four factors contribute towards a precise definition of "Smart City":

1. Advanced digital technologies to communities and cities all around.
2. Utilization of ICT technologies for the transformation of life and working environments in the city.
3. Introduction and deployment of ICT techniques in every government department to facilitate automation in systems.
4. The territorialisation of practices that bridges ICT and people together for innovation enhancement.

The following are Green-IoT based approaches for Smart Cities (Zanella, Bui, Castellani, Vangelista, &Zorzi, 2014), (Shapiro, 2006), (Talari, Shafie-khah, Siano, Loia, Tommasetti, & Catalão, 2017), (Morello, Mukhopadhyay, Liu, Slomovitz, & Samantaray, (2017):

1. **Smart Buildings**: Smart Buildings are termed as "Digital Extensions" to all sorts of engineering and architectural activities. Smart Building is termed as structure facilitating automated processes to automatically control all sorts of building's operations like: Security, Lightning, Air conditioning, Heating, Ventilation, etc. A Smart building makes use of sensors, actuators, and microchips to manage everything. The utilization of sophisticated hardware facilities improvement in asset reliability, performance and in turn reduces energy utilization. The following points highlight the benefits of smart buildings:

a. **Predictive Maintenance:** Sensors can detect all sorts of technical performance of the building and can automatically activate the maintenance procedures in case of any sort of malfunction.
b. **Energy Saving:** Data sent by the sensors can be carefully analysed, doing prompt actions for temperature and lighting settings.
c. **Effective Monitoring:** With smart buildings, all the equipment's can be effectively monitored and can be replaced on time, making maintenance highly cheap and effective.
d. **Optimized Site Cleaning:** All sorts of presence sensors can optimize cleaning operations. The data sensed by sensors can alert facility manager to undertake all cleaning operations whenever or wherever required.
e. **Redesigned Space:** Sensors enable easy identification of the overused and underused area of the building and can recommend some adjustments by making use of modern techniques like Artificial Intelligence and Machine Learning.

2. **Smart Lightning**: Smart lightning is a new concept under IoT, whose primary objective is energy efficiency. Smart Lightning includes high-efficiency fixtures and automation controls to adjust in real time based on conditions when the area is empty or crowded. The advantages associated with smart lightning are: (1) Faster Deployment; (2) Reduction in all sorts of maintenance costs; (3) Public security; (4) Energy conservation; (5) highly customized.
3. **Smart Waste**: Considering the ill impact of demolition and construction, it is highly important to learn about the saving of time and cost in a project, by performance optimization and sustainability. Smart waste can be used across a supply chain, with organizations inputting site data relevant to them, for the stakeholders or contractor to report and analyse who can give the vital information to identify trends and areas of improvement.

Smart Waste Management helps the end users to measure, and report regarding construction site wastes, whether these waste materials can be retained, reused on site, or sent for recycling and processing.

Smart Waste Management has following advantages:

a. Compliance management with Duty of Care waste regulations.
b. Maximizes reuse and recycling of waste materials on site.
c. Smart Waste Management improves the recycling rate of an industry and the diversion of waste from landfill.

Energy

Internet of Things (IoT) is making a significant impact on the Energy sector. Technological advancements in the energy sector are moving at a strong pace to keep the pace with: cost for high-performance hardware is declining, while data transfer rates are improvising. IoT technology can leverage energy utility organizations to have better control over operations. As rebuilding of power grids is not possible, innovative technologies are coming up to enhance power quality and security. Considering buildings, implementation of sensors can reduce the cost to the significant level by monitoring temperature and lighting in case of non-usage of the specific area.

The following points highlight advantages with regard to the implementation of IoT in the energy sector (Shaikh, Zeadally & Exposito 2017), (Ajeeba, Thomas, & Rasheed, 2017):

1. **Energy Optimization:** With the combination of AI and Machine learning techniques, energy can be optimized and traded.
2. **Environmental Efficiency:** IoT in energy reduces costs and saves resources with smart energy management devices and environmental efficient technologies.
3. **Predictive Maintenance:** Prevent downtime, get proactive insights with customized alerts along with reports on energy status.

Considering Green IoT, the following approaches are highlighted for the energy sector:

1. **Zero-Net Buildings**: Zero-Net Buildings (ZNE), also known as zero-energy buildings. These buildings are highly energy efficient, and over a span of one year, generate on-site energy, by making use of renewable sources, in a quantity equal to or greater than amount of energy consumed.
2. **Smart Energy Grids**: IoT technology can improvise energy sector via the introduction of "Smart Energy Grids". These grids are highly beneficial for making energy utilization more efficient by providing the end-users with real-time bills. It's more efficient, greener, highly secure and reliable. The smart grid reduces the energy consumption with the monitoring, analysis, control, and communication capabilities which can maximize the throughput of the system. The electricity moves around the system in Smart Grid in an efficient and economical manner. It provides the economical electricity to the owners of home. Smart Grid optimizes the operation of the entire electrical grid. The new technologies like plug-in hybrid electric vehicles, various forms of distributed generation, solar energy, smart metering, lighting management systems, distribution automation are supported by Smart Grid.
3. **Smart Meters**: Smart Meter is regarded as "Intelligent IoT" enabled device to periodically record consumption of electric energy. These devices communicate the information to electricity service provider. This information is used for doing activities like monitoring and billing. There is a two-way communication between the Smart Meter and supplier. The customers are satisfied with the advantages like faster interaction, more control of their energy usage to save money and reduce carbon emissions. As everything is visible and transparent, utilities can optimize energy distribution and even act to shift demand loads. The Mobile communication infrastructure also provides a reliable connectivity option for smart metering infrastructure.

Transportation

The Internet of Things (IoT) is dramatically accelerating the pace of innovation in the transportation industry- especially the cars and trucks we drive every day. IoT is revolutionizing the modern world of travel via the use of sensors, applications for mobile devices and other technological advancements. From air travel to parking management systems, the IoT is helping to improve the efficiency and convenience of modern-day travel. Next generation intelligent transportation systems will optimize the movement of goods and people, improving economics, public safety, and the environment.

The Automation of roadways including railways, airways are creating substantial business opportunities to stakeholders. The passenger experience has been changed on these transportation mediums. The cargo and merchandise are tracked and delivered easily using IoT enabled transportation system.

The benefits in the area of Transportation via IoT include the following:

1. Improve the traveller experience, with more dependable transportation, enhanced customer services and better and more accurate communication and information.
2. Increase safety, by better understanding transit system operations through sensor data that tracks everything from anomalies in train speeds, roadway temperatures, aircraft part condition, to the number of cars waiting at an intersection.
3. Reduce congestion and energy use, through the use of real-time data to improve how officials scale resources to meet demand, with the agility to react quickly to fast-changing traffic patterns, or to address traffic impacts on fuel use, the environment, and regional economic competitiveness.
4. Improve operational performance, by proactively monitoring critical infrastructure and creating more efficient processes to reduce operating costs and improve system capacity.

Considering G-IoT, the following applications can be visualized with regard to Smart transportation (Shaikh, Zeadally & Exposito 2017):

1. **Smart Parking**: Smart Parking is used to utilize few resources as possible- like fuel, time and space. Smart Parking cum Intelligent Transportation systems is highly important for movement of people and goods. The Low-cost sensors use real time data to find the available slots in parking. These slots can be monitored from IoT enabled Smart Parking System. The usage of Smart Parking defiantly reduced the manual searching time, floor searching etc. The online payments and parking time notifications can be sent to the owner using Smart Parking System. A parking solution can greatly benefit both the user and the lot owner (Rao, 2017).
2. **Smart Transport Logistics**: The optimum traffic route is always available in a Smart Transport logistics. Smart Transport logistics always take care of intelligent infrastructures and results in faster movement of goods. Furthermore, smart technologies have enabled logistics and mobility companies to achieve greater efficiency through the use of better collaborative operation models. There are number of companies like Flipkart, Amazon and Alibaba is using the Smart Transport Logistics (Bektaş, Crainic, & Van Woensel, 2017). The following are the advantages of Smart Transport Logistics systems:
    a. Especially helpful for long-haul cargo operators and last-mile delivery providers
    b. Containers and packages can be tracked and environmental conditions monitored through onboard sensors
    c. Specialty shipping services to track cargo that is temperature-sensitive, hazardous or extremely valuable
    d. Prevention of theft and product damage
    e. Delivery, scheduling, and placement can be automated
    f. Using IoT for transport logistics ensures that products are delivered to the right place, at the time and in the right condition. It minimizes human intervention and reduces fuel costs.

CONCLUSION

Despite numerous advantages and societal advancements via utilization of ICT techniques, the 21st century technology solutions and their growth imply the access of the energy utilization and other resources, thereby, increasing the percentage of hazardous emission in the environment and waste. The ultimate goal of the modern society is to use the modern ICT technologies to save planet earth and to keep the planet sustainable living place for people. Implementing green technology will lead to less energy utilization and wastage which minimizes the negative impact on human health and the environment. Green technologies make use of fewer resources and energy and highly contribute towards sustainable development.

In this chapter, we reviewed the green perspective of the Internet of Things (IoT). G-IoT has tremendous potential to change and bring significant advantages to lots of areas and can make the world economy as Green Economy. The adoption of G-IoT promises useful results in areas like- Healthcare, Manufacturing Industry, Smart Cities, Energy, and Transportation. The chapter focusses on key ICT technologies like RFID, WSN, Machine to Machine (M2M), Cloud Computing, Data centre, which can contribute towards Green IoT and also highlight various current projects and standards contributing towards Green IoT.

To conclude, we believe that G-IoT can transform the planet earth and assist the people to live a better life. Many industries and research organizations are taking strong steps and investing heavily to undertake research on designing green hardware consuming less energy and propose standard G-IoT based architectures making the mankind's future brighter and sustainable.

REFERENCES

C2POWER. (n.d.). Retrieved from http://www.ict-c2power.eu/

Ahson, S. A., & Ilyas, M. (2017). *RFID Handbook: applications, technology, security, and privacy*. CRC Press.

Ajeeba, A. A., Thomas, A., & Rasheed, R. (2017). IoT Based Energy Meter Reading, Theft Detection and Disconnection. *International Research Journal of Engineering and Technology*.

Al-Azzawi, B. F., Rigelsford, J. M., & Langley, R. J. (2018). Investigations into improving the detectability of self-resonant RFID tags. *IET Microwaves, Antennas & Propagation*, *12*(9), 1519–1525. doi:10.1049/iet-map.2017.1205

Alaraifi, A., Molla, A., & Deng, H. (2012). An exploration of data center information systems. *Journal of Systems and Information Technology*, *14*(4), 353–370. doi:10.1108/13287261211279080

Alohali, B., Kifayat, K., Shi, Q., & Hurst, W. (2016). Group Authentication Scheme for Neighbourhood Area Networks (NANs) in Smart Grids. *Journal of Sensor and Actuator Networks*, *5*(2), 9. doi:10.3390/jsan5020009

Alsamhi, S. H., Ma, O., Ansari, M. S., & Meng, Q. (2018). *Greening Internet of Things for Smart Everythings with A Green-Environment Life: A Survey and Future Prospects*. arXiv preprint arXiv:1805.00844

Ashton, K. (2017). *That 'Internet of Things' Thing*. Retrieved June 14, 2018 from https://www.rfidjournal.com/articles/view?4986

Atzori, L., Iera, A., & Morabito, G. (2010). The internet of things: A survey. *Computer Networks*, *54*(15), 2787–2805. doi:10.1016/j.comnet.2010.05.010

Basmadjian, R., Bouvry, P., Costa, G., Gyarmati, L., Kliazovich, D., Lafond, S., ... Torres, J. (2015). Green data centers. In *Large-scale Distributed Systems and Energy Efficiency: A Holistic View*. John Wiley & Sons.

Bektaş, T., Crainic, T. G., & Van Woensel, T. (2017). From managing urban freight to smart city logistics networks. In Network Design and Optimization for Smart Cities (pp. 143-188). Academic Press. doi:10.1142/9789813200012_0007

CASAGRAS. (n.d.). Retrieved from http://www.i-o-t.org/post/CASAGRAS

Chung, W. Y., Lee, Y. D., & Jung, S. J. (2008). A wireless sensor network compatible wearable u-healthcare monitoring system using integrated ECG, accelerometer and SpO2. *Proc. 30th Annu. Int. Conf. IEEE Eng. Med. Biol. Soc. (EMBS)*, 1529–1532.

Cool Silicon. (n.d.). Retrieved from https://www.cool-silicon.de/start/

Duroc, Y., & Kaddour, D. (2012). RFID potential impacts and future evolution for green projects. *Energy Procedia*, *18*, 91–98. doi:10.1016/j.egypro.2012.05.021

GreenI. C. N. (n.d.). Retrieved from http://www.greenicn.org/

Green Touch. (n.d.). Retrieved from https://s3-us-west-2.amazonaws.com/belllabs-microsite-greentouch/index.html

Han, T., & Ansari, N. (2014). Powering mobile networks with green energy. *IEEE Wireless Communications*, *21*(1), 90–96. doi:10.1109/MWC.2014.6757901

Holler, J., Tsiatsis, V., Mulligan, C., Karnouskos, S., & Boyle, D. (2014). *From Machine-to-machine to the Internet of Things: Introduction to a New Age of Intelligence*. Academic Press.

Hong, L., Xiao, F. W., & Chong, P. H. (2010, September). Opportunistic relay selection in future green multihop cellular networks. In *Vehicular Technology Conference Fall (VTC 2010-Fall), 2010 IEEE 72nd* (pp. 1-5). IEEE. Retrieved from http://www.ifgict.org/

International Telecommunication Unit (ITU). (n.d.). Retrieved from https://www.itu.int/en/ITU-T/gsi/iot/Pages/default.aspx

Internet Engineering Task Force (IETF). (n.d.). Retrieved from https://www.ietf.org/topics/iot/

Istepanian, R. S. H., Jovanov, E., & Zhang, Y. T. (2004). Guest editorial introduction to the special section on m-health: Beyond seamless mobility and global wireless health-care connectivity. *IEEE Transactions on Information Technology in Biomedicine*, *8*(4), 405–414. doi:10.1109/TITB.2004.840019 PMID:15615031

Jeschke, S., Brecher, C., Meisen, T., Özdemir, D., & Eschert, T. (2017). Industrial internet of things and cyber manufacturing systems. In *Industrial Internet of Things* (pp. 3–19). Cham: Springer. doi:10.1007/978-3-319-42559-7_1

Jim Chase. (2013). *The Evolution of the Internet of Things*. Retrieved June 14, 2018 from http://www.ti.com/lit/ml/swrb028/swrb028.pdf

Kakabadse, A. K., Kouzmin, A., & Kakabadse, N. K. (2017). Current trends in internet use: e-communication, e-information, and e-commerce. In Creating Futures: Leading Change Through Information Systems (pp. 147-178). Routledge.

Kiruthika, K., & Parimala, R. (2017). Green Space & Computing Techniques: ECO-Friendly ICT Initiative. *International Journal of Engineering Science*.

Kumar, A., & Nayyar, A. (2014). Energy Efficient Routing Protocols for Wireless Sensor Networks (WSNs) based on Clustering. *International Journal of Scientific & Engineering Research*, *5*(6), 440–448.

Leung, V. (2015). Green internet of things for smart cities. *International workshop on smart cities and urban informatics*.

Lin, J., Yu, W., Zhang, N., Yang, X., Zhang, H., & Zhao, W. (2017). A survey on internet of things: Architecture, enabling technologies, security and privacy, and applications. *IEEE Internet of Things Journal*, *4*(5), 1125–1142. doi:10.1109/JIOT.2017.2683200

Mathew, P. S., Pillai, A. S., & Palade, V. (2018). Applications of IoT in Healthcare. In *Cognitive Computing for Big Data Systems Over IoT* (pp. 263–288). Cham: Springer. doi:10.1007/978-3-319-70688-7_11

Mor, K., Kumar, S., & Sharma, D. (2018). Ad-Hoc Wireless Sensor Network Based on IEEE 802.15. 4: Theoretical Review. *International Journal of Computer Sciences and Engineering, 6*(3), 219-224.

Morello, R., Mukhopadhyay, S. C., Liu, Z., Slomovitz, D., & Samantaray, S. R. (2017). Advances on Sensing Technologies for Smart Cities and Power Grids: A Review. *IEEE Sensors Journal*, *17*(23), 7596–7610. doi:10.1109/JSEN.2017.2735539

Murugesan, S. (2008). Harnessing Green IT: Principles and practices. *IT Professional*, *10*(1), 24–33. doi:10.1109/MITP.2008.10

National Institute of Standards and Technology (NIST). (n.d.). Retrieved from https://www.nist.gov/news-events/news/2016/07/nists-network-things-model-builds-foundation-help-define-internet-things

Nayyar, A. (2016). An Encyclopedia Coverage of Compiler's, Programmer's & Simulator's for 8051, PIC, AVR, ARM, Arduino Embedded Technologies. *International Journal of Reconfigurable and Embedded Systems*, *5*(1).

Nayyar, A., & Gupta, A. (2014). A comprehensive review of cluster-based energy efficient routing protocols in wireless sensor networks. *IJRCCT*, *3*(1), 104–110.

Nayyar, A., & Puri, E. V. (2016). A Review of Intel Galileo Development Board's Technology. *Int. Journal of Engineering Research and Applications*, *6*(3), 34–39.

Nayyar, A., & Puri, V. (2015). Raspberry Pi- A Small, Powerful, Cost Effective and Efficient Form Factor Computer: A Review. *International Journal of Advanced Research in Computer Science and Software Engineering*, *5*(12), 720–737.

Nayyar, A., & Puri, V. (2015, November). A review of Beaglebone Smart Board's-A Linux/Android powered low-cost development platform based on ARM technology. In *Future Generation Communication and Networking (FGCN), 2015 9th International Conference on* (pp. 55-63). IEEE.

Nayyar, A., & Puri, V. (2016). A Comprehensive Review of BeagleBone Technology: Smart Board Powered by ARM. *International Journal of Smart Home, 10*(4), 95–108. doi:10.14257/ijsh.2016.10.4.10

Nayyar, A., & Puri, V. (2016, March). A review of Arduino board's, Lilypad's & Arduino shields. In *Computing for Sustainable Global Development (INDIACom), 2016 3rd International Conference on* (pp. 1485-1492). IEEE.

Nayyar, A., Puri, V., & Le, D. N. (2016). A Comprehensive Review of Semiconductor-Type Gas Sensors for Environmental Monitoring. *Review of Computer Engineering Research, 3*(3), 55–64. doi:10.18488/journal.76/2016.3.3/76.3.55.64

Nayyar, A., & Singh, R. (2014). A comprehensive review of ant colony optimization (ACO) based energy-efficient routing protocols for wireless sensor networks. *International Journal of Wireless Networks and Broadband Technologies, 3*(3), 33–55. doi:10.4018/ijwnbt.2014070103

Nayyar, A., & Singh, R. (2017). Ant Colony Optimization (ACO) based Routing Protocols for Wireless Sensor Networks (WSN): A Survey. *Int. J. Adv. Comput. Sci. Appl, 8*, 148–155.

Nayyar, A., & Singh, R. (2017). Simulation and performance comparison of ant colony optimization (ACO) routing protocol with AODV, DSDV, DSR routing protocols of wireless sensor networks using NS-2 simulator. *American Journal of Intelligent Systems, 7*(1), 19–30.

Orecchini, G., Yang, L., Rida, A., Alimenti, F., Tentzeris, M. M., & Roselli, L. (2010). Green technologies and RFID: Present and future. *Applied Computational Electromagnetics Society Journal, 25*(3), 230–238.

Pazowski, P. (2015). Green computing: latest practices and technologies for ICT sustainability. In *Managing Intellectual Capital and Innovation for Sustainable and Inclusive Society, Joint International Conference* (pp. 1853-1860). Academic Press.

Prasad, S. S., & Kumar, C. (2013). A green and reliable internet of things. *Communications and Network, 5*(1), 44–48. doi:10.4236/cn.2013.51B011

ProjectTREND. (n.d.). Retrieved from http://www.fp7-trend.eu/

Project Earth. (n.d.). Retrieved from http://www.ict-earth.eu/

Puri, V., Nayyar, A., & Le, D. N. (2017). *Handbook of Ardunio: Technical and Practice*. Scholars Press.

Qian, Z. H., & Wang, Y. J. (2013). Internet of things-oriented wireless sensor networks review. *Dianzi Yu Xinxi Xuebao, 35*(1), 215–227. doi:10.3724/SP.J.1146.2012.00876

Qiu, C., Shen, H., & Chen, L. (2018). *Towards green cloud computing: Demand allocation and pricing policies for cloud service brokerage*. IEEE Transactions on Big Data. doi:10.1109/TBDATA.2018.2823330

Ramyaka, V. N., Durga, G. S., Sharma, D., & Sharma, P. K. (2017). Technologies and pplications of wireless body area network: a review. *Procedia Computer Science, 83*, 1274-1281.

Rao, Y. R. (2017). Automatic smart parking system using Internet of Things (IOT). *Int J EngTechnol Sci Res, 4*(5).

Raza, K., Patle, V. K., & Arya, S. (2012). A review on green computing for eco-friendly and sustainable it. *Journal of Computational Intelligence and Electronic Systems*, *1*(1), 3–16. doi:10.1166/jcies.2012.1023

Roselli, L. (Ed.). (2014). *Green RFID systems*. Cambridge University Press. doi:10.1017/CBO9781139343459

Sahana, S., Singh, K., Kumar, R., & Das, S. (2018). A Review of Underwater Wireless Sensor Network Routing Protocols and Challenges. In *Next-Generation Networks* (pp. 505–512). Singapore: Springer. doi:10.1007/978-981-10-6005-2_51

Santucci, G., & Lange, S. (2008). Internet of things in 2020: a roadmap for the future. *Information Society and Media Directorate-general of the European Commission (DG INFSO) & European Technology Platform on Smart Systems Integration (EPoSS) Report, 5*.

Senyo, P. K., Addae, E., & Boateng, R. (2018). Cloud computing research: A review of research themes, frameworks, methods and future research directions. *International Journal of Information Management*, *38*(1), 128–139. doi:10.1016/j.ijinfomgt.2017.07.007

Shah, P. S., Patel, N. N., Patel, D. M., Patel, D. P., & Jhaveri, R. H. (2018). Recent Research in Wireless Sensor Networks: A Trend Analysis. In *Information and Communication Technology for Sustainable Development* (pp. 87–95). Singapore: Springer. doi:10.1007/978-981-10-3932-4_10

Shaikh, F. K., Zeadally, S., & Exposito, E. (2017). Enabling technologies for green internet of things. *IEEE Systems Journal*, *11*(2), 983–994. doi:10.1109/JSYST.2015.2415194

Shapiro, J. M. (2006). Smart cities: Quality of life, productivity, and the growth effects of human capital. *The Review of Economics and Statistics*, *88*(2), 324–335. doi:10.1162/rest.88.2.324

Sharma, A., Navda, V., Ramjee, R., Padmanabhan, V. N., & Belding, E. M. (2009, December). Cool-tether: energy efficient on-the-fly Wi-Fi hot-spots using mobile phones. In *Proceedings of the 5th international conference on Emerging networking experiments and technologies* (pp. 109-120). ACM. 10.1145/1658939.1658952

Sharma, S., Gupta, M., & Nayyar, A. (2014). Review of Routing Techniques Driving Wireless Sensor Networks. *International Journal of Computer Science and Mobile Computing*, *3*(5), 112–122.

Sherly, J., & Somasundareswari, D. (2015). Internet of things based smart transportation systems. *International Research Journal of Engineering and Technology*, *2*(7), 1207–1210.

Srinivas, N., & Kale, V. S. (2017, July). Review of network technologies in intelligent power system. In *IEEE Region 10 Symposium (TENSYMP), 2017* (pp. 1-6). IEEE. 10.1109/TENCONSpring.2017.8069974

Stergiou, C., Psannis, K. E., Kim, B. G., & Gupta, B. (2018). Secure integration of IoT and cloud computing. *Future Generation Computer Systems*, *78*, 964–975. doi:10.1016/j.future.2016.11.031

Suo, H., Wan, J., Zou, C., & Liu, J. (2012, March). Security in the internet of things: a review. In Computer Science and Electronics Engineering (ICCSEE), 2012 international conference on (Vol. 3, pp. 648-651). IEEE. doi:10.1109/ICCSEE.2012.373

Talari, S., Shafie-khah, M., Siano, P., Loia, V., Tommasetti, A., & Catalão, J. P. (2017). A review of smart cities based on the internet of things concept. *Energies*, *10*(4), 421. doi:10.3390/en10040421

The Green Grid. (n.d.). Retrieved from https://www.thegreengrid.org

Thomas, V. M. (2008, May). Environmental implications of RFID. In *Electronics and the Environment, 2008. ISEE 2008. IEEE International Symposium on* (pp. 1-5). IEEE. 10.1109/ISEE.2008.4562916

TSCGCC. (n.d.). Retrieved from https://sites.google.com/site/gcccomsoc/

Vo, Q. D., Choi, J. P., Chang, H. M., & Lee, W. C. (2010, November). Green perspective cognitive radio-based M2M communications for smart meters. In *Information and Communication Technology Convergence (ICTC), 2010 International Conference on* (pp. 382-383). IEEE.

Wan, J., Chen, M., Xia, F., Di, L., & Zhou, K. (2013). From machine-to-machine communications towards cyber-physical systems. *Computer Science and Information Systems*, *10*(3), 1105–1128. doi:10.2298/CSIS120326018W

Wang, L., & Khan, S. U. (2013). Review of performance metrics for green data centers: A taxonomy study. *The Journal of Supercomputing*, *63*(3), 639–656. doi:10.100711227-011-0704-3

Wibowo, S., & Wells, M. (2018). Green Cloud Computing and Economics of the Cloud: Moving towards Sustainable Future. *GSTF Journal on Computing (JoC), 5*(1).

Zanella, A., Bui, N., Castellani, A., Vangelista, L., &Zorzi, M. (2014). Internet of things for smart cities. *IEEE Internet of Things Journal, 1*(1), 22-32.

Zhang, M., Yu, T., & Zhai, G. F. (2011). Smart transport system based on "The Internet of Things". *Applied Mechanics and Materials*, *48*, 1073–1076. doi:10.4028/www.scientific.net/AMM.48-49.1073

Zhang, Y., & Ansari, N. (2012). Green data centers. Handbook of Green Information and Communication Systems, 331.

Zhu, C., Leung, V. C., Shu, L., & Ngai, E. C. H. (2015). Green internet of things for smart world. *IEEE Access: Practical Innovations, Open Solutions*, *3*, 2151–2162. doi:10.1109/ACCESS.2015.2497312

Chapter 22
Artificial Neural Network Models for Large-Scale Data

Vo Ngoc Phu
Duy Tan University, Vietnam

Vo Thi Ngoc Tran
Ho Chi Minh City University of Technology, Vietnam

ABSTRACT

Artificial intelligence (ARTINT) and information have been famous fields for many years. A reason has been that many different areas have been promoted quickly based on the ARTINT and information, and they have created many significant values for many years. These crucial values have certainly been used more and more for many economies of the countries in the world, other sciences, companies, organizations, etc. Many massive corporations, big organizations, etc. have been established rapidly because these economies have been developed in the strongest way. Unsurprisingly, lots of information and large-scale data sets have been created clearly from these corporations, organizations, etc. This has been the major challenges for many commercial applications, studies, etc. to process and store them successfully. To handle this problem, many algorithms have been proposed for processing these big data sets.

INTRODUCTION

We have displayed the surveys of the massive data sets (MASSDSs) related to the Artificial Neural Network (ARTNEURNET) in this book chapter.

These above problems and challenges of the ARTNEURNET for the big data sets (BIGDSs) are very crucial as follows:

1. The large-scale data sets (LARSCDSs) have certainly been the massive advantages for the big corporations, the large-scale organizations, the economies of the countries in the world, etc.
2. There have been the massive positives of the MASSDSs for the different fields in the world.

DOI: 10.4018/978-1-5225-7432-3.ch022

3. People have spent too much time and cost of storing, handling the BIGDSs, and furthermore, of extracting the significant values from the LARSCDSs
4. People have considered how to reduce time and cost of (3) fully.
5. …etc.

We have also given an example of a novel model of the ARTNEURNET for the MASSDSs using the ARTNEURNET, and the multi-dimensional vectors (MULTDIMVECTs) of the opinion lexicons of the RUSSELL & RAO coefficient (RUSRAOC) through an international search engine – Google (GOOGSE) with the And and Or operator (ANDOROPs) in a sequential system (SEQSYS) and a parallel network system (PANETSYS).

We have implemented the problem so far by others as follows:

1. There have not been enough the algorithms, methods, models, and etc. of the ARTNEURNET for the MASSDSs yet to be applied to the different areas for the economies, countries, societies, corporations, organizations, and etc.
2. There have not been the algorithms, methods, models, and etc. of the ARTNEURNET for the LARSCDSs, which have been implemented in the SEQSYS and the PANETSYS.
3. The algorithms, methods, models, and etc. of the ARTNEURNET for the BIGDSs have already been developed with the small samples in the SEQSYS and the PANETSYS.
4. …etc.

We have given a novel model of an example of the ARTNEURNET of the semantic analysis (SEMANAL) for the MASSDSs in the SEQSYS and the PANETSYS.

We have been the main contributions of this book chapter to the problem from the surveys related to a lot of novel models of the ARTNEURNET for the MASSDSs as follows:

1. This book chapter has helped the readers have the information and knowledge about the ARTNEURNET for the BIGDSs certainly.
2. Most of the models of the LARSCDSs of the ARTNEURNET in the different areas have been displayed in both the SEQSYS and the PANETSYS on more details in the below sections.
3. According to the above information and knowledge, the readers (including scientists, researchers, CEO, managers, and etc.) can build, develop, and deploy the commercial applications, studies, and etc. so much.
4. The different techniques of the models have already been presented carefully.
5. We have also shown that a novel model of us for the MASSDS have been proposed successfully.
6. …etc.

We have already presented the contribution non-trivial as follows: A proposed model of the SEMANAL for the BIGDS has been developed in the SEQUENTS and the PANETSYS – the Cloudera environment with Hadoop Map (M) and Hadoop Reduce (R). This model has used the ARTNEURNET with the MULTDIMVECTs of the opinion lexicons (OPINLEXs) to classify the sentiments (positive, negative, or neutral) for the documents (1,000,000) of the testing data set (TESTDSET) based on the documents

(2,000,000) of the training data set (TRAINDSET) in English. We have calculated the semantic values of the terms (verbs, nouns, adjectives, adverbs, and etc.) in English by using the RUSSELL & RAO coefficient (RUSRAOC) through the GOOGSE with the ANDOROPs. In addition, we have already achieved 87.03% accuracy on the TESTDSET of this novel model.

We have already displayed the simple concepts in this book chapter:

1. Based on our opinion, Artificial Intelligence (people have called it as machine intelligence sometimes) has been machines, programs, and etc. which can perform many intelligent tasks such as learning from experience, adjusting to new inputs, implementing human-like tasks, etc.
2. According to our opinion, the ARTNEURNET has comprised a set of small units (or small nodes) which they have been called the artificial neurons (ARTNEURs) similar to the neurons in a biological brain of the Human. The ARTNEURs have been connected together, called the connections which have been like the synapses of the biological brain. They can transmit a signal from one ARTNEUR to another easily and quickly. Furthermore, one ARTNEUR can also receive a signal and it can also handle it fully, etc.
3. Based on our opinion, a big data set has been a set of records (or samples) which have been thousands of records and a large size. In addition, a massive data set has been a set of records (or samples) which have been millions of records, etc.
4. According to our opinion, a sequential environment has been an environment of the computer science which has only been a computer (or a node).
5. A parallel network environment has been an environment of the computer science which has been many computers (or a nodes) and at least a server (or many servers). Furthermore, they have been connected together. They have transmitted many signals to each other easily, quickly, fully, and etc. In addition, they can handle the signals in a parallel way at the same time.
6. …etc.

BACKGROUND

In this section, we have briefly shown the surveys related to our novel model, and in addition, we have also presented the TESTDSET and the TRAINDSET of this proposed model.

Based on the studies presented in this part, we have proved that calculating a valence and identifying a polarity of one word/phrase in English have also been used by the RRC.

We have been the studies related to the Point-wise Mutual Information measure (PMIMEA) in [(Aleksander Bai, & Hugo Hammer, 2014), (P.D.Turney, & M.L.Littman, 2002), (Robert Malouf, & Tony Mullen, 2017), (Christian Scheible, 2010), (Dame Jovanoski, & et al, 2015), (Amal Htait, & et al, 2016), (Xiaojun Wan, 2009), (Julian Brooke, & et al, 2009), (Tao Jiang, & et al, 2015), (Tan, S.; & Zhang, J.; 2007), (Weifu Du, & et al, 2010), (Ziqing Zhang, & et al, 2010), and (Guangwei Wang, & Kenji Araki, 2007)].

The authors have already presented the PMIMEA and the Jaccard coefficient (JACCCO) in the studies (Shi Feng, & et al, 2013) and (Nguyen Thi Thu An, & Masafumi Hagiwara, 2014).

The JACCCO was used in the surveys [(Nihalahmad R. Shikalgar, & Arati M. Dixit, 2014), (Xiang Ji, & et al, 2015), (Nazlia Omar, & et al, 2013), (Huina Mao, & et al, 2014), (Yong REN, & et al, 2014), (Oded Netzer, & et al, 2012), and (Yong Ren, & et al, 2011)].

The similarity measures have been presented to identify the opinion scores of the words in the works [(Vo Ngoc Phu, & et al, 2017a), (Vo Ngoc Phu, & et al, 2017b), (Vo Ngoc Phu, & et al, 2017c), (Vo Ngoc Phu, & et al, 2017d), and (Vo Ngoc Phu, & et al, 2017e)].

The surveys have presented the dictionaries in English in the studies [(English Dictionary of Lingoes, 2017), (Oxford English Dictionary, 2017), (Cambridge English Dictionary, 2017), (Longman English Dictionary, 2017), (Collins English Dictionary, 2017), and (MacMillan English Dictionary, 2017)]. In addition, they have been more than the 55,000 words (nouns, adjectives, verbs, and etc.) in English.

The RRC has been displayed in the surveys [(Seung-Seok Choi, & et al, 2010), (Donald A. Jackson, & et al, 1989), (Andréia da Silva Meyer, & et al, 2004), (S. M. Shafer, & D. F. Rogers, 2007), (S. C. Beer, & et al, 1992), (Daniel P. Faith, 1983), (Khan Md. Saiful Islam, & Bhaba R. Sarker, 2000), and (Eviatar Nevo, & et al, 2013)].

The authors have shown the vector space modeling (VSM) in the surveys [(Vaibhav Kant Singh, & Vinay Kumar Singh, 2015), (Víctor Carrera-Trejo, & et al, 2015), and (Pascal Soucy, & Guy W. Mineau, 2015)].

The works have presented the algorithms, applications, studies, and etc. to perform in a distributed way in a parallel network environment in [(Hadoop, 2017), (Apache, 2017), and (Cloudera, 2017)].

The ARTNEURNET has been displayed in the works [(R.J. Kuo, & et al, 2001), (K. P. Sudheer, & et al, 2002), (Carsten Peterson, & et al, 1994), (D.C. Park, & et al, 1991), (Kuo-lin Hsu, & et al, 1995), (Xin Yao, 1999), (B. Samanta, & K.R. Al-Balushi, 2003), (V Brusic, G Rudy, & et al, 1998), (Muriel Gevrey, & et al, 2003), (C. Charalambous, 1992), (K. P. Sudheer, & et al, 2002), (Zhi-Hua Zhou, & et al, 2002), (Laurent Magnier, & Fariborz Haghighat, 2010), (Sovan Lek, & J.F. Guégan, 1999), and (Kyoung-jae Kim, & Ingoo Han, 2000)].

There have been a lot of the surveys related to the SEMANAL for the MASSDSs in the SEQSYS and the PARNETSYS as follows: (Vo Ngoc Phu, & Phan Thi Tuoi, 2014), (Vo Ngoc Phu, & et al, 2017f), (Vo Ngoc Phu, & Vo Thi Ngoc Tran, 2017a), (Vo Ngoc Phu, & et al, 2017g), (Vo Ngoc Phu, & et al, 2017h), (Nguyen Duy Dat, & et al, 2017), (Vo Ngoc Phu, & et al, 2017i), (Vo Ngoc Phu, & Vo Thi Ngoc Tran, 2017b), (Vo Ngoc Phu, & Vo Thi Ngoc Tran, 2018a), (Vo Ngoc Phu, & Vo Thi Ngoc Tran, 2018b), (Vo Ngoc Phu, & Vo Thi Ngoc Tran, 2018c), (Vo Ngoc Phu, & et al, 2018), (Vo Ngoc Phu, & Vo Thi Ngoc Tran, 2018d), (Vo Ngoc Phu, & Vo Thi Ngoc Tran, 2018e), (Vo Ngoc Phu, & Vo Thi Ngoc Tran, 2018f), (Vo Ngoc Phu, & Vo Thi Ngoc Tran, 2018g), (Vo Ngoc Phu, & Vo Thi Ngoc Tran, 2018h), (Vo Ngoc Phu, & Vo Thi Ngoc Tran, 2018i), (Vo Ngoc Phu, & Vo Thi Ngoc Tran, 2018j)]

All the documents of the TESTDSET and the TRAINDSET have automatically been extracted from Facebook, websites, and social networks in English. Then, we have labeled positive and negative for them fully.

The TRAINDSET has been the 2,000,000 documents of the movie area including the 1,000,000 positive and the 1,000,000 negative in English.

The TESTDSET has been the 1,000,000 documents of the movie field comprising the 500,000 positive and the 500,000 negative.

MAIN FOCUS OF THE CHAPTER

Issues, Controversies, Problems

We have displayed all the possible novel approaches of the ARTNEURNET for the MASSDSs in the different fields.

We have considered that if a model successfully processes its data set over 500,000 samples - 1,000,000 records in a SEQSYS, this model can be used for the MASSDSs.

We have also considered that if a model is successfully implemented in a PARNETSYS, this model can be used for the LARSCDSs. The reason here has been that the PARNETSYSs have been used for the MASSDSs fully.

The novel models in this book chapter have been divided into the two environments: the SEQSYSs and the PARNETSYSs

There have not been a lot of the studies of the ARTNEURNET for the MASSDSs in the SEQSYS. We have displayed the ARTNEURNET surveys of the BIGDSs in the SEQSYS firstly as follows:

The authors used context-dependent pre-trained deep neural networks in the survey (George E. Dahl, & et al, 2012) for large-vocabulary speech recognition in using deep belief networks for phone recognition, etc.

A novel model was described how to train neural network for the LARSCDSs effectively in the study (Tomas Mikolov, & et al, 2011). The hash-based implementation of a maximum entropy model was introduced can be trained as a part of the neural network model, etc.

The authors displayed a proposed model related to deep neural networks to automate large-scale statistical analysis for the massive data applications in the work (Rongrong Zhang, & et al, 2017), etc.

The authors developed an application of pre-trained deep neural networks to large vocabulary speech recognition in the study (Navdeep Jaitly, & et al, 2012), etc.

The authors used SOM-based stratified sampling for data splitting for the artificial neural networks in the work (R.J.May, H.R.Maier, & G.C.Dandy, 2010), etc.

The authors presented a novel model of a pattern-recognition technique according to the ARTNEURNET for reduction of false positives in computerized detection of lung nodules in low-dose computed tomography in the survey (Kenji Suzuki, & et al, 2003), etc.

We have hoped that there are going to be many surveys of the ARTNEURNET for the MASSDSs in the SEQSYS more and more in the near future, etc.

Furthermore, we have presented the studies of the ARTNEURNET for the LARSCDSs in the PARNETSYS as follows:

The authors developed a neural network parallel algorithm in the work (N. Funabiki, & Y. Takefuji, 1992) for channel assignment problems in cellular radio networks, etc.

In the study (Leah L. Rogers, & Farid U. Dowla, 1994), the optimization of groundwater remediation was proposed by using the ARTNEURNET with parallel solute transport modeling, etc.

The authors used and designed massively distributed computers for the ARTNEURNET in the work (Tomas Nordstrom, & Bertil Svensson, 1992), etc.

The authors displayed distribution environment state estimation by using an ARTNEURNET approach for pseudo measurement modeling in the survey (Efthymios Manitsas, & et al, 2012), etc.

The survey developed a parallel neural network architecture for controlling hexapord robot locomotion in (Randall D. Beer, & et al, 2008), etc.

The authors proposed an application of the ARTNEURNET approach in the survey (Qi-quan Li, & et al, 2013). This survey developed a radial basis function neural networks model, combined with principal component analysis, to predict the spatial distribution of SOM content across China, etc.

The parallel environments were developed for implementing neural networks in the work (Manavendra Misra, 1997), etc.

The authors used MapReduce and Cascading Model for the parallelizing back-propagation Neural Network in the survey (Yang Liu, & et al, 2016), etc.

The work used the ARTNEURNET on massively distributed computer hardware in (Udo Seiffert, 2004), etc.

The multicore and GPU parallelization of neural networks were developed for face recognition in the work (Altaf Ahmad Huqqani, & et al, 2013), etc.

The authors designed and performed a distributed software for a hybrid neural network computation in the distributed virtual machine system in the study (Huiwei Guan, & et al, 2002), etc.

The authors used and designed massively distributed computers for the ARTNEURNET in the research (Tomas Nordström, & Bertil Svensson, 1992), etc.

In the "Solutions and Recommendations", we have shown a novel model for the BIGDSs of the ARTNEURNET of the SEMANAL in the SEQSYS and the PARNETSYS, etc.

SOLUTIONS AND RECOMMENDATIONS

We have proposed the significant basic principles as follows:

1. Each sentence has been m words/phrases in English.
2. The maximum number of one sentence in English has been m_max. It has meant that m has been less than m_max, or m has been as equal as m_max.
3. Each document has been n sentences in English.
4. The maximum number of one document in English has been n_max. It has meant that n has been less than n_max, or n has been as equal as n_max.
5. Each sentence has been transformed into one one-dimensional vector (ONEDIMVECT) in English. Therefore, the length of the vector has been m. When m has been less than m_max, each element of the vector from m to m_max-1 has been 0 (zero).
6. Each document in English has been transferred into one MULTDIMVECT. So, the MULTDIMVECT has been n rows and m columns. When n has been less than n_max, each element of the MULTDIMVECT from n to n_max-1 has been 0 (zero vector).

In this proposed survey, we have proposed a new model by using the ARTNEURNET with the MULTDIMVECTs of the sentiment lexicons (SENTLEXs) to classify the opinions (positive, negative, or neutral) of the documents in English in the SEQSYS and the PARNETSYS

We have been the most significant contributions of this novel model briefly as follows:

1. We have believed that the results of this novel approach can be used for many surveys, commercial applications, and etc.

2. The opinion scores of the words/phrases in English has been identified by using the RUSRAOC through the GOOGSE with the ANDOROPs on the Internet
3. We have developed the formulas for this proposed survey.
4. We have built the algorithms for this novel approach.
5. We have believed that we can certainly apply this study to other languages easily.
6. The ARTNEURNET has been applicable to the SEMANAL of the natural language processing, etc.
7. This proposed model has proved that the different areas of the scientific research can be related in many different ways.
8. This work has successfully handled millions of the documents in English for the SEMANAL.
9. The SEMANAL has been performed in the SEQSYS and the PARNETSYS
10. We have proposed the significant principles in this survey.
11. We have used the Cloudera distributed network environment (CLOUDISNETEN), the Hadoop Map-M and Hadoop Reduce-R for this novel work successfully.
12. We have believed that this proposed study can be applied to other parallel network systems successfully.
13. We have believed that we can apply this work to many different distributed network environment such as the CLOUDISNETEN, etc.
14. We have believed that we can apply this approach to many parallel functions such as the M and the R, etc.
15. We have developed the algorithms related to the ARTNEURNET in this novel approach.

a. Transferring the Documents Into the MULTDIMVECTs According to the SENTLEXs

We have been the 3 sections for this part as follows:

a.1. Calculating the Valence of the SENTLEXs

We have been at least the 55,000 terms comprising nouns, verbs, adjectives, and etc. in English.

We have identify the semantic score and the polarity of the words or the phrases in English for our basis English opinion dictionary (BEOD) by using the RUSRAOC.

We have been the PMIMEA of the two words wi and wj based on the survey [(Aleksander Bai, & Hugo Hammer, 2014), (P.D.Turney, & M.L.Littman, 2002), (Robert Malouf, & Tony Mullen, 2017), (Christian Scheible, 2010), (Dame Jovanoski, & et al, 2015), (Amal Htait, & et al, 2016), (Xiaojun Wan, 2009), (Julian Brooke, & et al, 2009), (Tao Jiang, & et al, 2015), (Tan, S.; & Zhang, J.; 2007), (Weifu Du, & et al, 2010), (Ziqing Zhang, & et al, 2010), (Guangwei Wang, & Kenji Araki, 2007), (Shi Feng, & et al, 2013), and (Nguyen Thi Thu An, & Masafumi Hagiwara, 2014)] as follows:

$$PMI\left(wi,wj\right)=\log_2\left(\frac{P\left(wi,wj\right)}{P\left(wi\right)\times P\left(wj\right)}\right) \quad (1)$$

and we have been the equation of the SO (sentiment orientation) of word wi

$$SO(wi) = PMI(wi, positive) - PMI(wi, negative) \tag{2}$$

We have been the positive and the negative of Eq. (2) in the works [(Aleksander Bai, & Hugo Hammer, 2014), (P.D.Turney, & M.L.Littman, 2002), (Robert Malouf, & Tony Mullen, 2017), (Christian Scheible, 2010), (Dame Jovanoski, & et al, 2015), (Amal Htait, & et al, 2016), (Xiaojun Wan, 2009), and (Julian Brooke, & et al, 2009)] as follows: negative = { nasty, negative, bad, unfortunate, poor, wrong, inferior}, and positive = {nice, good, excellent, positive, correct, fortunate, superior}.

The AltaVista search engine (ALTVISSE) was used in the PMIMEA in the studies [(P.D.Turney, & M.L.Littman, 2002), (Robert Malouf, & Tony Mullen, 2017), and (Dame Jovanoski, & et al, 2015)]. The authors were used the GOOGSE in the PMIMEA of the works [(Christian Scheible, 2010), (Amal Htait, & et al, 2016), and (Julian Brooke, & et al, 2009)]. The authors also used German in the study (Christian Scheible, 2010). Macedonian was also used in the survey (Dame Jovanoski, & et al, 2015). Arabic was used in the study (Amal Htait, & et al, 2016). Chinese was used in the work (Xiaojun Wan, 2009). Spanish was used in the survey (Julian Brooke, & et al, 2009).

The formula of the JACCCO of the two words wi and wj has been as follows:

$$Jaccard(wi, wj) = J(wi, wj) = \frac{|wi \cap wj|}{|wi \cup wj|} \tag{3}$$

and other type of the equation of the JACCCO of the two words wi and wj has been as follows:

$$Jaccard(wi, wj) = J(wi, wj) = sim(wi, wj) = \frac{F(wi, wj)}{F(wi) + F(wj) - F(wi, wj)} \tag{4}$$

and the SO of the word wi has been as follows:

$$SO(wi) = \sum Sim(wi, positive) - \sum Sim(wi, positive) \tag{5}$$

We have been the positive and the negative of Eq. (5) in English as follows: negative = {nasty, bad, poor, negative, wrong, unfortunate, inferior}, and positive = {good, nice, excellent, positive, fortunate, correct, superior}.

The authors used the JACCCO with the GOOGSE in English in the surveys [(Shi Feng, & et al, 2013), (Nguyen Thi Thu An, & Masafumi Hagiwara, 2014), and (Xiang Ji, & et al, 2015)]. The authors used the JACCCO in English in the studies (Nihalahmad R. Shikalgar, & Arati M. Dixit, 2014) and (Oded Netzer, & et al, 2012). The authors used the JACCCO in Chinese in the works (Yong REN, & et al, 2014) and (Yong Ren, & et al, 2011). The authors used the JACCCO in Arabic in the survey (Nazlia Omar, & et al, 2013). The authors used the JACCCO and the Chinese search engine in Chinese in the work (Huina Mao, & et al, 2014).

The authors used the Ochiai measure (OCHMEAS) through the GOOGSE with the ANDOROPs to identify the valences of the words in Vietnamese in the study (Vo Ngoc Phu, & et al, 2017a).

The opinion scores of the words in English were calculated by using the Cosine coefficient (COS-COE) through the GOOGSE with the ANDOROPs in the work (Vo Ngoc Phu, & et al, 2017b), etc. The semantic values of the words in English were identified by using the Sorensen coefficient (SORCOE) through the GOOGSE with the ANDOROPs in the research (Vo Ngoc Phu, & et al, 2017c), etc.

According to the above proofs, we have been the information as follows: The authors used the PMIMEA with the ALTVISSE in the languages such as English, Chinese and Japanese, and the authors used the PMIMEA with the GOOGSE in English. The authors used the JACCCO with the GOOGSE in English, Chinese, and Vietnamese. The authors used the OCHMEAS with the GOOGSE in Vietnamese. The authors used the COSCOE and SORCOE with the GOOGSE in English.

Based on the surveys [(Julia V. Ponomarenko, & et al, 2002), (Andréia da Silva Meyer, & et al, 2004), (Snežana Mladenović Drinić, & et al, 2008), (Tamás, Júlia; & et al, 2001), (Vo Ngoc Phu, & et al, 2017a), (Vo Ngoc Phu, & et al, 2017b), (Vo Ngoc Phu, & et al, 2017c), (Vo Ngoc Phu, & et al, 2017d), and (Vo Ngoc Phu, & et al, 2017e)], the PMIMEA, the JACCCO, the COSCOE, the OCHMEAS, the Tominato measure (TOMMEAS), and the RUSRAOC have been the similarity measures of the two words, and they can implement the same functions and the same characteristics. So, the RUSRAOC has been used in identifying the opinion scores of the words. Furthermore, we have proved that the RUSRAOC can be used in determining the semantic value of the word in English through the GOOGSE with the ANDOROPs.

We have been the equation of the RUSRAOC based on the surveys in [(Seung-Seok Choi, & et al, 2010), (Donald A. Jackson, & et al, 1989), (Andréia da Silva Meyer, & et al, 2004), (S. M. Shafer, & D. F. Rogers, 2007), (S. C. Beer, & et al, 1992), (Daniel P. Faith, 1983), (Khan Md. Saiful Islam, & Bhaba R. Sarker, 2000), and (Eviatar Nevo, & et al, 2013)] as follows:

$$RRC(a,b) = \frac{(a \cap b)}{(a \cap b) + (\neg a \cap b) + (a \cap \neg b) + (\neg a \cap \neg b)} \tag{6}$$

with a and b have been the vectors.

According Eq. (1), Eq. (2), Eq. (3), Eq. (4), Eq. (5), and Eq. (6), calculating the valence of the words/phrases in English and their polarity has been identified by using the novel formulas of the RUSRAOC through the GOOGSE.

In Eq. (6), when we have been one element of a only, a has been a word. When we have been one element of b only, b has been a word. In addition, in Eq. (6), we have replaced a by w1, and we have also replaced b by w2.

$$RRC(w1,w2) = \frac{P(w1,w2)}{P(w1,w2) + P(\neg w1,\neg w2) + P(\neg w1,w2) + P(w1,\neg w2)} \tag{7}$$

Eq. (1) has been similar to Eq. (7). Furthermore, in Eq. (2), we have replaced Eq. (1) by Eq. (7). We have been Eq. (8) as follows:

$$Valence\left(w\right) = SO\_RRC\left(w\right) = RRC\left(w, positive\_query\right) - RRC\left(w, negative\_query\right) \quad (8)$$

In Eq. (7), w1 has been replaced by w, and w2 has been replaced by position_query. We have been Eq. (9) as follows:

$$RRC\left(w, positive\_query\right) = \frac{P\left(w, positive\_query\right)}{A9} \quad (9)$$

with

$$A9 = P\left(w, positive\_query\right) + P(\neg w, \neg positive\_query) + P\left(\neg w, positive\_query\right) + P\left(w, \neg positive\_query\right)$$

In Eq. (7), w1 has been replaced by w, and w2 has been replaced by negative_query. We have been Eq. (10) as follows:

$$RRC\left(w, negative\_query\right) = \frac{P\left(w, negative\_query\right)}{A10} \quad (10)$$

with

$$A10 = P\left(w, negative\_query\right) + P(\neg w, \neg negative\_query) + P\left(\neg w, negative\_query\right) + P\left(w, \neg negative\_query\right)$$

We have been the information of w, w1, w2, P(w1, w2), and etc. as follows:

1. w, w1, and w2 have been the words/the phrases in English.
2. P(w1, w2) has been the number of the returned results in the GOOGSE by the keyword (w1 and w2). In addition, we have used the API of the GOOGSE to get the number of the returned results in the GOOGSE online by the keyword (w1 and w2).
3. P(w1) has been the number of the returned results in the GOOGSE by the keyword w1. Furthermore, we have used the API of the GOOGSE to get the number of the returned results in the GOOGSE online by the keyword w1.
4. P(w2) has been the number of the returned results in the GOOGSE by the keyword w2. Moreover, we have used the API of the GOOGSE to get the number of the returned results in the GOOGSE online by the keyword w2.
5. Valence(W) = SO_RRC(w) has been the opinion value of the word/the phrase w in English, and it has also been the SO of the word (or the phrase) by the RUSRAOC.

6. positive_query has been { active or good or positive or beautiful or strong or nice or excellent or fortunate or correct or superior } with the positive_query has been the group of the positive words in English.
7. negative_query has been { passive or bad or negative or ugly or week or nasty or poor or unfortunate or wrong or inferior } with the negative_query has been the group of the negative words in English.
8. P(w, positive_query) has been the number of the returned results in the GOOGSE by the keyword (positive_query and w). In addition, we have used the API of the GOOGSE to get the number of the returned results in the GOOGSE online by the keyword (positive_query and w)
9. P(w, negative_query) has been the number of the returned results in the GOOGSE by the keyword (negative _query and w). Furthermore, we have used the API of the GOOGSE to get the number of the returned results in the GOOGSE online by the keyword (negative_query and w)
10. P(w) has been the number of the returned results in the GOOGSE by the keyword w. Moreover, we have used the API of the GOOGSE to get the number of the returned results in the GOOGSE online by the keyword w.
11. P(¬w,positive_query) has been the number of the returned results in the GOOGSE by the keyword ((not w) and positive_query). In addition, we have used the API of the GOOGSE to get the number of the returned results in the GOOGSE online by the keyword ((not w) and positive_query).
12. P(w, ¬positive_query) has been the number of the returned results in the GOOGSE by the keyword: (w and (not (positive_query))). Moreover, we have used the API of the GOOGSE to receive the number of the returned results in the GOOGSE online using the keyword: (w and [not (positive_query)]).
13. P(¬w,¬positive_query) has been the returned results in the GOOGSE by the keyword: ([not w] and [not (positive_query)]). Furthermore, we have used the API of the GOOGSE to receive the returned results in the GOOGSE online using the keyword: ((not w) and (not (positive_query))).
14. P(¬w,negative_query) has been the returned results in the GOOGSE using the keyword: ((not w) and negative_query). Moreover, we have used the API of the GOOGSE to receive the returned results in the GOOGSE online using the keyword: ((not w) and negative_query).
15. P(w,¬negative_query) has been the returned results in the GOOGSE using the keyword: (w and (not (negative_query))). In addition, we have used the API of the GOOGSE to receive the returned results in the GOOGSE online using the keyword: (w and (not (negative_query))).
16. P(¬w,¬negative_query) has been the returned results in the GOOGSE using the keyword: ((not w) and (not (negative_query))). Furthermore, we have used the API of the GOOGSE to receive the returned results in the GOOGSE online using the keyword: ((not w) and (not (negative_query))).

We have identified the semantic score of the word w in English according to the proximity of positive_query with w, the remote of positive_query with w, the proximity of negative_query with w, and the remote of negative_query with w.

When the value RRC(w, positive_query) has been as equal as 1, the word w in English has been the nearest of positive_query.

When the value RRC (w, positive_query) has been as equal as 0, the word w in English has been the farthest of positive_query.

When the value RRC (w, positive_query) has been greater than 0, and the value RRC (w, positive_query) has been less than 1 or as equal as 1, the word w in English has belonged to positive_query being the positive group of the words in English.

When the value RRC (w, negative_query) has been as equal as 1, the word w in English has been the nearest of negative_query.

When the value RRC (w, negative_query) has been as equal as 0, the word w in English has been the farthest of negative_query.

When the value RRC (w, negative_query) has been greater 0, and the value RRC (w, negative_query) has been less than 1 or as equal as 1, the word w in English has belonged to negative_query being the negative group of the words in English.

Therefore, the semantic value of the word w in English has been the value (RRC (w, positive_query)-RRC (w, negative_query)), and in addition, the Eq. (8) has been the equation for identifying the sentiment score of the word w in English

The information of the value RRC has been as follows:

1. RRC (w, positive_query) has been greater than 0 or as equal as 0, and RRC (w, positive_query) has been less than 1 or as equal as 1.
2. RRC (w, negative_query) has been greater than 0 or as equal as 0, and RRC (w, negative_query) has been less than 1 or as equal as 1.
3. When the value RRC (w, positive_query) has been as equal as 0, and the value RRC(w, negative_query) has been as equal as 0, the value SO_RRC(w) has been as equal as 0.
4. When the value RRC (w, positive_query) has been as equal as 1, and the value RRC (w, negative_query) has been as equal as 0, the value SO_RRC(w) has been as equal as 0.
5. When the value RRC (w, positive_query) has been as equal as 0, and the value RRC (w, negative_query) has been as equal as 1, the value SO_RRC(w) has been as equal as -1.
6. When the value RRC (w, positive_query) has been as equal as 1, and the value RRC (w, negative_query) has been as equal as 1, the value SO_RRC(w) has been as equal as 0

Thus, the value SO_ RRC (w) $\geq$ -1 and SO_ RRC (w) $\leq$ 1.

When the value SO_RRC (w) has been greater than 0, the word w in English has been the positive polarity.

When the value SO_RRC (w) has been less than 0, the word w in English has been the negative polarity.

When the value SO_RRC (w) has been as equal as 0, the word w in English has been the neutral polarity.

Furthermore, the opinion score of the word w in English has been SO_ RRC (w).

We have identified the valence and the polarity of the word/the phrase w in English by using a training corpus of approximately one hundred billion words of the web sites, social networks, and etc. in English that have been indexed by the GOOGSE on the internet. The ALTVISSE has been chosen because it has been a NEAR operator. However, the ALTVISSE has been no longer.

In this survey, we have used the GOOGSE which has not been a NEAR operator. The GOOGSE has used the ANDOROPs. The results of identifying the semantic value of the word w in English by using the GOOGSE have been similar to the results of the opinion score of the word w in English by using the ALTVISSE

The BEOD has been more the 55,000 words/phrases in English, and the BEOD has been stored in Microsoft SQL Server 2008 R2.

a.2. Transferring the Documents Into the MULTDIMVECTs in the SEQSYS

In this section, we have transformed the documents of the TESTDSET and the TRAINDSET into the MULTDIMVECTs in the SEQSYS.

We have presented how to transfer one document in English into one MULTDIMVECT according to the SENTLEXs in the SEQSYS firstly. Then, we have applied this to transfer all the documents of the TESTDSET and the TRAINDSET into MULTDIMVECTs in the SEQSYS.

We have proposed the algorithm 1 to transfer one document in English into MULTDIMVECT based on the SENTLEXs in the SEQSYS

Input: one English document

Output one MULTDIMVECT based on the SENTLEXs

1. This document has been separated into the n sentences
2. We have repeated each sentence in the sentences as follows:
3. This sentence has been separated into the n_n meaningful words (or meaningful phrases);
4. We have repeated each term in the n_n terms as follows:
5. We have gotten the semantic value of this term according to the BEOD;
6. Add this term (term, valence) into the one one-dimensional vector;
7. End Repeat- End (4);
8. Add one one-dimensional vector (corresponding to this sentence) into the MULTDIMVECT;
9. End Repeat – End (2);
10. Return the MULTDIMVECT;

a.3. Transferring the Documents Into the MULTDIMVECTs in the PARNETSYS

We have transformed the documents of the TESTDSET and the TRAINDSET into the MULTDIMVECTs in the PARNETSYS

We have displayed how to transfer one document in English into one MULTDIMVECT according to the SENTLEXs in the CLOUDISNETEN. The input of the M in the CLOUDISNETEN has been one document, the SENTLEXs of the BEOD. The output of the M has been one ONEDIMVECT (corresponding to one sentence of this document). The input of the R has been the output of the M. So, the output of the R has been one MULTDIMVECT (corresponding to this document). Then, we have applied this part to transform all the documents of the TESTDSET and the TRAINDSET into the MULTDIMVECTs in the CLOUDISNETEN.

In the M phase:

Input: One document in English ; The SENTLEXs of the BEOD.

Output: one ONEDIMVECT;

1. Input One English document; and the SENTLEXs of the BEOD into the M in the CLOUDISNETEN.
2. This document has been separated into the sentences;
3. We have repeated each sentence in the sentences as follows:
4. This sentence has been separated into the n_n meaningful words (or meaningful phrases)
5. Each term in the n_n terms, do repeat:
6. Get valence of this term based on the BEOD;

7. Add this term into the ONEDIMVECT;
8. End Repeat – End (5);
9. Return this ONEDIMVECT;
10. The output of the M has been this ONEDIMVECT;

In the R phase:
Input: one ONEDIMVECT of the M (the input of the R has been the output of the M)
Output: one MULTDIMVECT (corresponding to one English document)

1. Receive one ONEDIMVECT of the M
2. Add this ONEDIMVECT into the MULTDIMVECT;
3. Return the MULTDIMVECT;

b. Implementing the ARTNEURNET in the SEQSYS and the PARNETSYS

We have been the two parts of this section as follows: The SEMANAL for the documents of the SEQSYS has been displayed in the first part. The SEMANAL for the documents of the SEQSYS has been presented in the second part.

There have been the two groups of the TRAINDSET as follows: The first group has included the positive documents, and the second group has been the negative documents. The first group has been called the positive cluster, and the second group has been called the negative cluster.

All the documents in both the first group and the second group have gone through the segmentation of words and stop-words removal. Then, they have been transferred into the MULTDIMVECTs (vector representation).

The positive documents of the positive cluster have been transformed into the positive MULTDIMVECTs which have been called the positive multi-dimensional vector group (POSMULTDIMVECTGR).

The negative documents of the negative cluster have been transformed into the negative MULTDIMVECTs which have been called the negative multi-dimensional vector group (NEGMULTDIMVECTGR).

Therefore, the TRAINDSET has been the POSMULTDIMVECTGR and the NEGMULTDIMVECTGR.

We have transformed all documents in English into the MULTDIMVECTs in the SEQSYS similar to (a.2), and we have also transferred all the documents in English into the MULTDIMVECTs in the PARNETSYS similar to (a.3).

b.1. The ARTNEURNET in the SEQSYS

The documents of the TESTDSET have been transformed into the MULTDIMVECTs: Each document of the TESTDSET has been transferred into each MULTDIMVECT (each sentence of one document of the TESTDSET has been transformed into the ONEDIMVECT in the SEQSYS similar to (a.2)).

The positive documents of the TRAINDSET have been transferred into the positive MULTDIMVECTs in the SEQSYS, called POSMULTDIMVECTGR: Each document of the positive documents of the TRAINDSET has been transformed into the ONEDIMVECT in the SEQSYS similar to (a.2)).

The negative documents of the TRAINDSET have been transferred into the negative MULTDIMVECTs in the SEQSYS, called NEGMULTDIMVECTGR: Each document of the negative documents of the TRAINDSET has been transformed into the ONEDIMVECT in the SEQSYS similar to (a.2)).

We have performed this part as follows: The ARTNEURNET has been implemented to classify one MULTDIMVECT (called A) of the TESTDSET into either the NEGMULTDIMVECTGR or the POSMULTDIMVECTGR. When A has been classified into the POSMULTDIMVECTGR, this document (corresponding to A) has been the positive polarity. When A has been classified into the NEGMULTDIMVECTGR, this document (corresponding to A) has been the negative polarity. When A has been classified into neither the NEGMULTDIMVECTGR nor the POSMULTDIMVECTGR, this document (corresponding to A) has been the neutral polarity.

We have developed the algorithms to perform the ARTNEURNET in the SEQSYS.

We have proposed the algorithm 2 to transfer one document in English into one MULTDIMVECT in the SEQSYS: Each document has been separated into the sentences. Each sentence of one document has been transformed into one ONEDIMVECT in the SEQSYS based on (a.2). We have inserted all the ONEDIMVECTs of the sentences into one MULTDIMVECT.

Input: one English document

Output: one MULTDIMVECT

1. Split the English document into many separate sentences based on "." Or "!" or "?";
2. Each sentence in the n sentences of this document, do repeat:
3. Transfer this sentence into one ONEDIMVECT based on (a.2);
4. Add the transferred vector into one MULTDIMVECT
5. End Repeat – End (2)
6. Return one MULTDIMVECT;

We have built the algorithm 3 to create the POSMULTDIMVECTGR in the SEQSYS: Each document of the positive documents of the TRAINDSET has been separated into the sentences. Each sentence of the document has been transferred into one ONEDIMVECT in the SEQSYS according to (a.2). We have inserted all the ONEDIMVECTs of the sentences of the document into one ONEDIMVECT of the document. Then, the positive documents of the TRAINDSET have been transferred into the positive MULTDIMVECTs.

Input: the positive English documents of the TRAINDSET.

Output: the positive vector group POSMULTDIMVECTGR

1. Each document of the positive document of the TRAINDSET, do repeat:
2. OneMultiDimensionalVector:= Call Algorithm 1 with the positive English document of the TRAINDSET;
3. Add OneMultiDimensionalVector into POSMULTDIMVECTGR;
4. End Repeat – End (1)
5. Return POSMULTDIMVECTGR;

We have proposed the algorithm 4 to create the NEGMULTDIMVECTGR in the SEQSYS: Each documents of the negative documents of the TRAINDSET has been separated into the sentences. Each sentence of the document has been transferred into one ONEDIMVECT in the SEQSYS according to (a.2). We have inserted all the ONEDIMVECTs of the sentences of the document into one ONEDIMVECT of the document. Then, the negative documents of the TRAINDSET have been transformed into the negative MULTDIMVECTs.

Input: the negative English documents of the TRAINDSET.
Output: the negative vector group NEGMULTDIMVECTGR

1. Each document in the negative documents of the TRAINDSET, do repeat:
2. OneMultiDimensionalVector:= Call Algorithm 1 with the negative English document of the TRAINDSET;
3. Add OneMultiDimensionalVector into NEGMULTDIMVECTGR ;
4. End Repeat – End (1);
5. Return NEGMULTDIMVECTGR;

We have developed the algorithm 5 to classify one MULTDIMVECT (corresponding to one document of the TESTDSET) into either the NEGMULTDIMVECTGR or the POSMULTDIMVECTGR in the SEQSYS

Input: one MULTDIMVECT A (corresponding to one English document of the TESTDSET), the POSMULTDIMVECTGR and the NEGMULTDIMVECTGR;

Output: positive, negative, neutral;

1. Implement the ARTNEURNET based on the ARTNEURNET of the surveys [53-67] with the input has been one MULTDIMVECT (corresponding to one English document of the TESTDSET), the POSMULTDIMVECTGR, and the NEGMULTDIMVECTGR;
2. With the results of (1), If the vector is clustered into the positive vector group Then Return positive;
3. Else If the vector is clustered into the negative vector group Then Return negative; End If – End (2)
4. Return neutral;

The ARTNEURNET has used the Euclidean distance to calculate the distance between two vectors

b.2. The ARTNEURNET in the PARNETSYS

All the documents of the TESTDSET and the TRAINDSET have been transformed into all the MULTDIMVECTs in the CLOUDISNETEN.

We have transformed the documents of the TESTDSET into all the MULTDIMVECTs by using the M and the R in the CLOUDISNETEN for the purpose of shortening the execution time of this task.

We have transferred the documents of the TRAINDSET into all the MULTDIMVECTs by using the M and the R in the CLOUDISNETEN for the purpose of shortening the execution time of this task.

The positive documents of the TRAINDSET have been transformed into the positive MULTDIMVECTs in the CLOUDISNETEN, called POSMULTDIMVECTGR

The negative documents of the TRAINDSET have been transformed into the negative MULTDIMVECTs in the CLOUDISNETEN, called NEGMULTDIMVECTGR

We have done this part in Figure 1 as follows: One MULTDIMVECT (called A) of the document of the TESTDSET has been classified into either the NEGMULTDIMVECTGR or the POSMULTDIMVECTGR using the ARTNEURNET in the CLOUDISNETEN. When A has been classified into the POSMULTDIMVECTGR, the document (corresponding to A) has been the positive polarity. When A has been classified into the NEGMULTDIMVECTGR, the document (corresponding to A) has been the negative polarity. When A has been classified into neither the NEGMULTDIMVECTGR nor the POSMULTDIMVECTGR, the document (corresponding to A) has been the neutral polarity.

Transferring each document in English into one MULTDIMVECT in the CLOUDISNETEN has been presented in Figure 2. This has been the two phases: the M, and the R. Moreover, the input of the M has been on document, and the output of the M has been many components of a MULTDIMVECT corresponding to the document. This document, the input of the M, has been separated into the sentences. Each sentence in the document has been transformed into one ONEDIMVECT based on (a.3). This has been repeated for all the sentences of the document until all the sentences have been transformed into all the ONEDIMVECTs of the document. Then, the M of the CLOUDISNETEN has automatically transferred the ONEDIMVECT into the R. The input of the R has been the output of the M, and this input has comprised the components (corresponding the ONEDIMVECTs) of the MULTDIMVECT. The output of the R has been a MULTDIMVECT corresponding to the document. In the R of the CLOUDISNETEN, these ONEDIMVECTs have been added into one MULTDIMVECT.

The documents of the TESTDSET have been transferred into the MULTDIMVECTs based on Figure 2.

The ARTNEURNET in the CLOUDISNETEN has been the two main phases: the first main phase has been the M phase in the CLOUDISNETEN, and the second main phase has been the R phase in the CLOUDISNETEN.

In the M of the CLOUDISNETEN, the input of this phase has been the MULTDIMVECT of one English document (which has been classified), the POSMULTDIMVECTGR and the NEGMULTDIMVECTGR. The output of the phase has been the classifying results of the MULTDIMVECT of the document into either the NEGMULTDIMVECTGR or the POSMULTDIMVECTGR.

In the R of the CLOUDISNETEN, the input of the phase has been the output of the M of the CLOUDISNETEN, and this input has been the classifying results of the MULTDIMVECT of the document into either the NEGMULTDIMVECTGR or the POSMULTDIMVECTGR. The output of the phase has been the result of the SEMANAL of the document into either the positive polarity, the negative polarity, or the neutral polarity.

In the R phase, when the MULTDIMVECT has been classified into the POSMULTDIMVECTGR, this document has been classified as the positive semantic. When the MULTDIMVECT has been classified into the NEGMULTDIMVECTGR, this document has been classified as the negative opinion. When the MULTDIMVECT has been classified into neither the NEGMULTDIMVECTGR nor the POSMULTDIMVECTGR, this document has been classified as the neutral sentiment.

In the M phase: We have implemented this phase in Figure 3. The ARTNEURNET in the CLOUDISNETEN has been based on the ARTNEURNET of the surveys [(R.J. Kuo, & et al, 2001), (K. P. Sudheer, & et al, 2002), (Carsten Peterson, & et al, 1994), (D.C. Park, & et al, 1991), (Kuo-lin Hsu, & et al, 1995), (Xin Yao, 1999), (B. Samanta, & K.R. Al-Balushi, 2003), (V Brusic, G Rudy, & et al, 1998), (Muriel Gevrey, & et al, 2003), (C. Charalambous, 1992), (K. P. Sudheer, & et al, 2002), (Zhi-Hua Zhou, & et al, 2002), (Laurent Magnier, & Fariborz Haghighat, 2010), (Sovan Lek, & J.F. Guégan, 1999), and (Kyoung-jae Kim, & Ingoo Han, 2000)]. This input has been one MULTDIMVECT of the TESTDSET, the NEGMULTDIMVECTGR and the POSMULTDIMVECTGR of the TRAINDSET. The output of the ARTNEURNET has been the classifying result of the MULTDIMVECT into either the NEGMULTDIMVECTGR or the POSMULTDIMVECTGR.

The main ideas of the ARTNEURNET have been presented one more details.

The ARTNEURNET in our model has included the learning stage and the testing stage. An overview of our ARTNEURNET has been in Figure 4.

In Figure 4, the input of neural network has been a multi-dimensional vector X and the output of network has been +1 or -1. When the output has been +1, this vector of the input has been classified into the POSMULTDIMVECTGR. When the output has been -1, this vector of the input has been classified into the NEGMULTDIMVECTGR

Our learning stage: in this stage, we have used the positive vectors of the POSMULTDIMVECTGR and the negative vectors of the NEGMULTDIMVECTGR to identify the parameters of our neural network, such as weights, outputs, etc.

Our testing stage: with the parameters of our neural network, each vector of the TESTDSET has been the input of our neural network. The following Algorithm 6 is the basic algorithm of the supervised learning of our neural network.

Supervised learning can be considered as mapping approximately: X → Y, where X is the set of problems and Y is the corresponding set of solutions to that problem. The samples (x, y) with x = (x1, x2,..., Xn) ∈ X, y = (yl, y2,..., Ym) ∈ Y be given.

Input: x = (x1, x2,..., Xn) ∈ X,
Output: y = (yl, y2,..., Ym) ∈ Y

begin

1. Build the appropriate structure for neural network, for example with (n+1) neurons input (n neurons for input variables and 1 neuron for threshold x0), m output neurons, and initialize the weights of the network links.
2. Input one vector x in the X training data set input into network
3. Calculate the output vector o of network.
4. Compare the expected output vector y (is the given result of training data set) with the output vector o which network generated; if can be then identify error
5. Adjust the weights in some way so that in the next time, when inputs vector x to the network, the output vector o will resemble y more.
6. Can repeat step 2 to step 5 if want, until converging. The evaluation of error can perform in many different ways, using the most used instant error: Err = (o - y), or Err = | o - y |; mean squared error (MSE: mean-square error): Err = (o- y) 2/2;

end;

There have been two types of errors in the evaluation of a neural network. Firstly, called as clear error, assess approximately the training samples of a network have been trained. Second, called as test error, assess the ability of a total process of a network has been trained, the ability to react with the new input vector.

In this study, we have used back-propagation algorithm of neural network for our new model.

The main ideal of the back-propagation algorithm: we have wanted to train a multi-layer feed-forward network by gradient descent to approximate an unknown function, based on some training data consisting of pairs (x,t). The vector x has represented a pattern of input to the network, and the vector t the corresponding target (desired output). As we have seen before, the overall gradient with respect to the entire training set has been just the sum of the gradients for each pattern; in what follows we would therefore describe how to compute the gradient for just a single training pattern. As before, we would number the units, and denote the weight from unit j to unit i by wij.

Definitions

The error signal for unit j: $\delta_j = -\partial E / \partial net_j$

The (negative) gradient for weight wij: $\nabla \mathcal{M}^{s3} = -9E / 9\mathcal{M}^{s3}$

The set of nodes anterior to unit i: $A_i = \left\{ j : \exists w_{ij} \right\}$

The set of nodes posterior to unit j: $P_j = \left\{ i : \exists w_{ij} \right\}$

The Gradient

As we did for linear networks before, we expand the gradient into two factors by use of the chain rule:

$$\Delta w_{ij} = -\frac{\partial E}{\partial net_i} \frac{\partial net_i}{\partial w_{ij}}$$

The first factor is the error of unit i. The second is

$$\frac{\partial net_i}{\partial w_{ij}} = \frac{\partial}{\partial w_{ij}} \sum_{k \in A_i} w_{ik} y_k = y_j$$

Putting the two together, we get

$$\Delta w_{ij} = \delta_i y_j$$

To compute this gradient, we thus need to know the activity and the error for all relevant nodes in the network.

Forward Activation

The activity of the input units is determined by the network's external input x. For all other units, the activity is propagated forward:

$$y_i = f_i \left(\sum_{j \in A_i} w_{ij} y_j \right)$$

Before the activity of unit i can be calculated, the activity of all its anterior nodes (forming the set Ai) must be known. Since feedforward networks do not contain cycles, there is an ordering of nodes from input to output that respects this condition.

Calculating Output Error

Assuming that we are using the sum-squared loss

$$E = \frac{1}{2}\sum_{o}\left(t_o - y_o\right)^2$$

the error for output unit o is simply

$$\delta_o = t_o - y_o$$

Error Backpropagation

For hidden units, we must propagate the error back from the output nodes (hence the name of the algorithm). Again using the chain rule, we can expand the error of a hidden unit in terms of its posterior nodes:

$$\delta_j = -\sum_{i \in P_j} \frac{\partial E}{\partial net_i} \frac{\partial net_i}{\partial y_j} \frac{\partial y_j}{\partial net_j}$$

Of the three factors inside the sum, the first is just the error of node i. The second is

$$\frac{\partial net_i}{\partial y_j} = \frac{\partial}{\partial y_j} \sum_{k \in A_i} w_{ik} y_k = w_{ij}$$

while the third is the derivative of node j's activation function:

$$\frac{\partial y_j}{\partial net_j} = \frac{\partial f_j(net_j)}{\partial net_j} = f_j'(net_j)$$

For hidden units h that use the tanh activation function, we can make use of the special identity

$$f_h'(net_h) = 1 - y_h^2$$

Putting all the pieces together we get

$$\delta_j = f_j'(net_j) \sum_{i \in P_j} \delta_i w_{ij}$$

In order to calculate the error for unit j, we must first know the error of all its posterior nodes (forming the set Pj). Again, as long as there are no cycles in the network, there is an ordering of nodes from the output back to the input that respects this condition. For example, we can simply use the reverse of the order in which activity was propagated forward.

After finishing to cluster the multi-dimensional vector into either the POSMULTDIMVECTGR or the NEGMULTDIMVECTGR, the M has transferred this results into the R in the Cloudera system.

In the R phase:

This phase has been performed in Figure 5: After receiving the classifying result of the M, the R has labeled the opinion polarity for the MULTDIMVECT which has been classified. Then, the output of the R has returned the semantic polarity of one document (corresponding to the MULTDIMVECT) of the TESTDSET. When the MULTDIMVECT has been classified into the POSMULTDIMVECTGR, the document has been the positive polarity. When the MULTDIMVECT has been classified into the NEGMULTDIMVECTGR, the document has been the negative polarity. When the MULTDIMVECT has not been classified into the NEGMULTDIMVECTGR and the POSMULTDIMVECTGR, the document has been the neutral polarity.

We have used an Accuracy (A) measure to identify the accuracy of the results of the SEMANAL of this model.

The Java programming language (JAVAPRL) has been used to program for saving the TESTDSET and the TRAINDSET, and for performing our proposed model to classify the documents of the TESTDSET into either the positive, the negative, or the neutral.

The configuration of each server (each node) has been: Intel® Server Board S1200V3RPS, Intel® Pentium® Processor G3220 (3M Cache, 3.00 GHz), 2GB PC3-10600 ECC 1333 MHz LP Unbuffered DIMMs.

The operating system of each node (each server) has been the Cloudera.

The SEQSYS in this novel survey has been 1 node (1 server). The JAVAPRL has been used in programming the ARTNEURNET.

We have implemented the ARTNEURNET in the CLOUDISNETEN: This CLOUDISNETEN has included the 9 nodes (9 servers). The JAVAPRL has been used in programming the application of the ARTNEURNET in the CLOUDISNETEN. All the 9 nodes have been the same configuration information.

The results of the documents of the TESTDSET have been displayed in Table 1.

The accuracy of the SEMANAL of the documents of the TESTDSET has been presented in Table 2.

Table 1. The results of the documents of the TESTDSET

	Testing Dataset	Correct Classification	Incorrect Classification
Negative	500,000	434,759	65,241
Positive	500,000	435,541	64,459
Summary	1,000,000	870,300	129,700

Table 2. The accuracy of the SEMANAL of the documents of the TESTDSET

Proposed Model	Class	Accuracy
Our new model	Negative	87.03%
	Positive	

The average execution times of the SEMANAL of our novel model for the documents of the TESTDSET have been shown in Table 3.

Although our new model has been tested on our English data set, it can be applied to other languages certainly.

In this book chapter, our novel model has been tested on the 1,000,000 documents in English of the TESTDSET which has been very small. However, this novel approach can be applied to many large-scale data sets with millions of the documents in English in the shortest time.

In this work, we have developed a novel model to classify the opinions (positive, negative, or neutral) of the documents using the ARTNEURNET in the SEQSYS and the CLOUDISNETEN with the M and the R.

In Table 2, we have already achieved 87.03% accuracy of the TESTDSET of the novel model.

In Table 3, we have been the information of the average execution times of the SEMANAL of our proposed model as follows:

1. The average execution time of the SEMANAL of the ARTNEURNET in the SEQSYS has been 5,261,792 seconds /1,000,000 English documents, and it has been greater than the average execution time of the SEMANAL of the ARTNEURNET in the CLOUDISNETEN – 3 nodes which has been 1,538,736 seconds /1,000,000 documents in English.
2. The time of the SEMANAL of the ARTNEURNET in the CLOUDISNETEN – 9 nodes which has been 611,784 seconds /1,000,000 documents in English has been the shortest time.
3. The average execution time of the SEMANAL of the ARTNEURNET in the CLOUDISNETEN – 6 nodes has been 854,373 seconds /1,000,000 documents in English.

The time of the ARTNEURNET in the CLOUDISNETEN has been dependent on the performance of the CLOUDISNETEN, and it has also been dependent on the performance of each server of the CLOUDISNETEN. It has also been dependent on the number of the nodes (servers) of the CLOUDISNETEN.

FUTURE RESEARCH DIRECTIONS

From those results of this novel model and according to the above proofs, we are going to study this model for applying to billions of English documents in both the SE and the PNE. In addition, we are

Table 3. The average execution times of the SEMANAL of our novel model for the documents of the TESTDSET

	The Average Times of the Classification /1,000,000 English Documents
The ARTNEURNET in the sequential environment	5,261,792 seconds
The ARTNEURNET in the CLOUDISNETEN – 3 nodes	1,538,736 seconds
The ARTNEURNET in the CLOUDISNETEN – 6 nodes	854,373 seconds
The ARTNEURNET in the CLOUDISNETEN – 9 nodes	611,784 seconds

also going to research this approach for being performed in the PNE with over 50 nodes. Furthermore, the accuracy of this new computational model can be studied to improve certainly.

From the results of this chapter, many algorithms, methods, models, and etc. are going to be developed more and more for handling the massive data sets fully in the near future.

CONCLUSION

In this book chapter, we have already presented the simple concepts of the ARTNEURNET, the BIGDSs, and etc. We have also shown the importance of the ARTNEURNET, the MASSDSs, and etc. in the world. The problems and challenges of the ARTNEURNET, the MASSDSs, and etc. have also displayed on more details, etc.

We have already given an example of the ARTNEURNET of the SEMANAL for the LARSCDSs in this book chapter using the ARTNEURNET, and the MULTDIMVECTs of the SENTLEXs of the RUSRAOC through the GOOGSE with the ANDOROPs in the SEQSYS and the PANETSYS.

From the results of the proposed model, based on our opinion, the ARTNEURNET, the artificial intelligence, the machine learning, and etc. are very crucial for the MASSDS certainly. We believe that there are going to have many important contributions of the ARTNEURNET, the artificial intelligence, the machine learning, and etc. for the BIGDSs fully and successfully.

In addition, this novel model can process billions of the documents in English of the SEMANAL for a MASSDS.

Many algorithms, methods, models, and etc. are going to be developed for the BIGDSs to be applied to the different fields from the results of the proposed approach. This is very significant for many organizations, economies, governments, countries, commercial applications, researches, and etc. in the world.

ACKNOWLEDGMENT

This book chapter has been funded by Institute of Research and Development of Duy Tan University-DTU in Da Nang city in Vietnam

REFERENCES

Andréia da Silva, M., Antonio, A. F. G., Pereira de Souza, A., & Lopes de Souza, C. Jr. (2004). Comparison of similarity coefficients used for cluster analysis with dominant markers in maize (Zea maysL). *Genetics and Molecular Biology*, *27*(1), 83–91. doi:10.1590/S1415-47572004000100014

Andréia da Silva, M., Antonio, A. F. G., Pereira de Souza, A., & Lopes de Souza, C. Jr. (2004). Comparison of similarity coefficients used for cluster analysis with dominant markers in maize (Zea mays L). *Genetics and Molecular Biology*, *27*(1). doi:10.1590/S1415-47572004000100014

Apache. (2017). Retrieved from http://apache.org

Bai, A., & Hammer, H. (2014). Constructing sentiment lexicons in Norwegian from a large text corpus. *2014 IEEE 17th International Conference on Computational Science and Engineering*. DOI: 10.1109/CSE.2014.73

Beer, R. D., Chiel, H. J., Quinn, R. D., Espenschied, K. S., & Larsson, P. (2008). A Distributed Neural Network Architecture for Hexapod Robot Locomotion. *Neural Computation*, *4*(3), 356–365. doi:10.1162/neco.1992.4.3.356

Beer, S. C., Goffreda, J., Phillips, T. D., Murphy, J. P., & Sorrells, M. E. (1992). Assessment of Genetic Variation in Avena sterilis using Morphologicall Traits, Isozymes, and RFLPs. *Crop Science*, *33*(6), 1386–1393. doi:10.2135/cropsci1993.0011183X003300060051x

Brooke, J., Tofiloski, M., & Taboada, M. (2009). Cross-Linguistic Sentiment Analysis: From English to Spanish. *International Conference RANLP 2009*, 50–54.

Brusic, V., Rudy, G., Honeyman, G., Hammer, J., & Harrison, L. (1998). Prediction of MHC class II-binding peptides using an evolutionary algorithm and artificial neural network. *Bioinformatics (Oxford, England)*, *14*(2), 121–130. doi:10.1093/bioinformatics/14.2.121 PMID:9545443

Carrera-Trejo, V., Sidorov, G., Miranda-Jiménez, S., Ibarra, M. M., & Martínez, R. C. (2015). Latent Dirichlet Allocation complement in the vector space model for Multi-Label Text Classification. *International Journal of Combinatorial Optimization Problems and Informatics*, *6*(1), 7–19.

Charalambous, C. (1992). Conjugate gradient algorithm for efficient training of artificial neural networks. *IEE Proceedings. Part G. Circuits, Devices and Systems*, *139*(3), 301–310. doi:10.1049/ip-g-2.1992.0050

Choi, S.-S., Cha, S.-H., & Tappert, C. C. (2010). A Survey of Binary Similarity and Distance Measures. *Systemics, Cybernetics and Informatics*, *8*(1).

Cloudera. (2017). Retrieved from http://www.cloudera.com

Dahl, G. E., Yu, D., Deng, L., & Acero, A. (2012). Context-Dependent Pre-Trained Deep Neural Networks for Large-Vocabulary Speech Recognition. *IEEE Transactions on Audio, Speech, and Language Processing*, *20*(1), 30–42. doi:10.1109/TASL.2011.2134090

Dat, Phu, & Chau, Tran, & Nguyen. (2017). STING Algorithm used English Sentiment Classification in A Parallel Environment. *International Journal of Pattern Recognition and Artificial Intelligence*, *31*(7). doi:10.11420218001417500215

DictionaryC. E. (2017). Retrieved from http://dictionary.cambridge.org/

DictionaryC. E. (2017). Retrieved from http://www.collinsdictionary.com/dictionary/english

DictionaryL. E. (2017). Retrieved from http://www.ldoceonline.com/

DictionaryO. E. (2017). Retrieved from http://www.oxforddictionaries.com/

Drinić, S. M., Nikolić, A., & Perić, V. (2008). Cluster Analysis of Soybean Genotypes Based on RAPD Markers. *Proceedings. 43rd Croatian and 3rd International Symposium on Agriculture*, 367-370.

Du, W., Tan, S., Cheng, X., & Yun, X. (2010). Adapting Information Bottleneck Method for Automatic Construction of Domain-oriented Sentiment Lexicon. WSDM'10, New York, NY. doi:10.1145/1718487.1718502

English Dictionary of Lingoes. (2017). Retrieved from http://www.lingoes.net/

Faith, D. P. (1983). Asymmetric binary similarity measures. *Oecologia, 57*(3), 287–290. doi:10.1007/BF00377169 PMID:28309352

Feng, S., Le Zhang, B. L. D. W., Yu, G., & Wong, K.-F. (2013). Is Twitter A Better Corpus for Measuring Sentiment Similarity? *Proceedings of the 2013 Conference on Empirical Methods in Natural Language Processing*, 897–902.

Funabiki & Takefuji. (1992). A neural network parallel algorithm for channel assignment problems in cellular radio networks. *IEEE Transactions on Vehicular Technology, 41*(4), 430-437. Doi:10.1109/25.182594

Gevrey, M., Dimopoulos, I., & Lek, S. (2003). Review and comparison of methods to study the contribution of variables in artificial neural network models. *Ecological Modelling, 160*(3), 249–264. doi:10.1016/S0304-3800(02)00257-0

Guan, H., Li, C.-K., Cheung, T.-Y., Yu, S., & Tong, W. (2002). Design and implementation of a parallel software for hybrid neural network computation in PVM environment. *Proceedings of Third International Conference on Signal Processing (ICSP'96)*. DOI: 10.1109/ICSIGP.1996.566591

Hadoop. (2017). Retrieved from http://hadoop.apache.org

Hernández-Ugalde, J. A., Mora-Urpí, J., & Rocha, O. J. (2011). Genetic relationships among wild and cultivated populations of peach palm (Bactris gasipaes Kunth, Palmae): Evidence for multiple independent domestication events. *Genetic Resources and Crop Evolution, 58*(4), 571–583. doi:10.100710722-010-9600-6

Hsu, K., Gupta, H. V., & Sorooshian, S. (1995). Artificial Neural Network Modeling of the Rainfall-Runoff Process. *Water Resources Research, 31*(10), 2517–2530. doi:10.1029/95WR01955

Htait, A., Fournier, S., & Bellot, P. (2016). LSIS at SemEval-2016 Task 7: Using Web Search Engines for English and Arabic Unsupervised Sentiment Intensity Prediction. *Proceedings of SemEval-2016*, 481–485. 10.18653/v1/S16-1076

Huqqani, A. A., Schikuta, E., Ye, S., & Chen, P. (2013). Multicore and GPU Parallelization of Neural Networks for Face Recognition. *Procedia Computer Science, 18*, 349–358. doi:10.1016/j.procs.2013.05.198

Islam & Sarker. (2000). A similarity coefficient Measure And Machine-Parts Grouping In Cellular Manufacturing Systems. *International Journal Of Production Research*. Http://Dx.Doi.Org/10.1080/002075400189374

Jackson, Somers, & Harvey. (1989). Similarity Coefficients: Measures of Co-Occurrence and Association or Simply Measures of Occurrence? *American Naturalist, 133*(3).

Jaitly, N., Nguyen, P., Senior, A., & Vanhoucke, V. (2012). Application of Pretrained Deep Neural Networks to Large Vocabulary Speech Recognition. *13th Annual Conference of the International Speech Communication Association*, 2578-2581.

Ji, X., Chun, S. A., Wei, Z., & Geller, J. (2015). Twitter sentiment classification for measuring public health concerns. *Social Network Analysis and Mining*, *5*(1), 13. doi:10.100713278-015-0253-5

Jiang, T., Jiang, J., Dai, Y., & Li, A. (2015). Micro–blog Emotion Orientation Analysis Algorithm Based on Tibetan and Chinese Mixed Text. *International Symposium on Social Science (ISSS 2015)*. 10.2991/isss-15.2015.39

Jovanoski, D., Pachovski, V., & Nakov, P. (2015). Sentiment Analysis in Twitter for Macedonian. Proceedings of Recent Advances in Natural Language Processing, 249–257.

Kuo, R. J., Chen, C. H., & Hwang, Y. C. (2001). An intelligent stock trading decision support system through integration of genetic algorithm based fuzzy neural network and artificial neural network. *Fuzzy Sets and Systems*, *118*(1), 21–45. doi:10.1016/S0165-0114(98)00399-6

Kyoung-jae, K., & Han, I. (2000). Genetic algorithms approach to feature discretization in artificial neural networks for the prediction of stock price index. *Expert Systems with Applications*, *19*(2), 125–132. doi:10.1016/S0957-4174(00)00027-0

Lek, S., & Guégan, J. F. (1999). Artificial neural networks as a tool in ecological modelling, an introduction. *Ecological Modelling*, *120*(2–3), 65–73. doi:10.1016/S0304-3800(99)00092-7

Li, Q., Yue, T., Wang, C., Zhang, W., Yu, Y., Li, B., ... Bai, G. (2013). Spatially distributed modeling of soil organic matter across China: An application of artificial neural network approach. *Catena*, *104*, 210–218. doi:10.1016/j.catena.2012.11.012

Liu, Y., Jing, W., & Xu, L. (2016). Parallelizing Backpropagation Neural Network Using MapReduce and Cascading Model. *Computational Intelligence and Neuroscience*, *2016*, 1–11. doi:10.1155/2016/2842780 PMID:27217823

MacMillanE. D. (2017). Retrieved from http://www.macmillandictionary.com/

Magnier, L., & Haghighat, F. (2010). Multiobjective optimization of building design using TRNSYS simulations, genetic algorithm, and Artificial Neural Network. *Building and Environment*, *45*(3), 739–746. doi:10.1016/j.buildenv.2009.08.016

Malouf, R., & Mullen, T. (2017). Graph-based user classification for informal online political discourse. *Proceedings of the 1st Workshop on Information Credibility on the Web*, 1-8.

Manitsas, Singh, Pal, & Strbac. (2012). Distribution System State Estimation Using an Artificial Neural Network Approach for Pseudo Measurement Modeling. *IEEE Transactions on Power Systems, 27*(4), 1888-1896. Doi:10.1109/TPWRS.2012.2187804

Mao, G. Wang, & Bollen. (2014). Automatic Construction of Financial Semantic Orientation Lexicon from Large-Scale Chinese News Corpus. In *7th Financial Risks International Forum*. Institut Louis Bachelier.

May, R. J., Maier, H. R., & Dandy, G. C. (2010). Data splitting for artificial neural networks using SOM-based stratified sampling. *Neural Networks*, *23*(2), 283–294. doi:10.1016/j.neunet.2009.11.009 PMID:19959327

Mikolov, T., Deoras, A., Povey, D., Burget, L., & Cernocky, J. (2011). Strategies for Training Large Scale Neural Network Language Models. *2011 IEEE Workshop on Automatic Speech Recognition and Understanding (ASRU)*, 196-201. 10.1109/ASRU.2011.6163930

Misra, M. (1997). Parallel Environments for Implementing Neural Networks. *Neural Computing Surveys*, *1*, 48–60.

Netzer, O., Feldman, R., Goldenberg, J., & Fresko, M. (2012). Mine Your Own Business: Market-Structure Surveillance Through Text Mining. *Marketing Science*, *31*(3), 521–543. doi:10.1287/mksc.1120.0713

Nevo, E., Fragman, O., Dafni, A., & Beiles, A. (2013). Biodiversity And Interslope Divergence Of Vascular Plants Caused By Microclimatic Differences At "Evolution Canyon", Lower Nahal Oren, Mount Carmel, Israel. *Israel Journal of Plant Sciences*, *47*(1), 49–59. doi:10.1080/07929978.1999.10676751

Nguyen, T. T. A., & Hagiwara, M. (2014). Adjective-Based Estimation of Short Sentence's Impression. *Proceedings of the 5th Kanesi Engineering and Emotion Research; International Conference*.

Nordström, T., & Svensson, B. (1992). Using and Designing Massively Parallel Computers for Artificial Neural Networks. *Journal of Parallel and Distributed Computing*, *14*(3), 260–285. doi:10.1016/0743-7315(92)90068-X

Nordström, T., & Svensson, B. (1992). Using and designing massively parallel computers for artificial neural networks. *Journal of Parallel and Distributed Computing*, *14*(3), 260–285. doi:10.1016/0743-7315(92)90068-X

Omar, N., Albared, M., Al-Shabi, A. Q., & Al-Moslmi, T. (2013). Ensemble of Classification algorithms for Subjectivity and Sentiment Analysis of Arabic Customers' Reviews. *International Journal of Advancements in Computing Technology*, 5.

Park, D. C., El-Sharkawi, M. A., Marks, R. J., Atlas, L. E., & Damborg, M. J. (1991). Electric load forecasting using an artificial neural network. *IEEE Transactions on Power Systems*, *6*(2). doi:10.1109/59.76685

Peterson, C., Rögnvaldsson, T., & Lönnblad, L. (1994). JETNET 3.0—A versatile artificial neural network package. *Computer Physics Communications*, *81*(1–2), 185–220. doi:10.1016/0010-4655(94)90120-1

Phu, Chau, Ngoc, & Duy. (2017g). A C4.5 algorithm for english emotional classification. *Evolving Systems*. doi:10.100712530-017-9180-1

Phu, V. N., Dat, N. D., Vo, T. N. T., Vo, T. N. C., & Nguyen, T. A. (2017f). Fuzzy C-means for english sentiment classification in a distributed system. *International Journal of Applied Intelligence*, *46*(3), 717–738. doi:10.100710489-016-0858-z

Phu, V. N., & Tuoi, P. T. (2014). Sentiment classification using Enhanced Contextual Valence Shifters. *International Conference on Asian Language Processing (IALP)*, 224-229. 10.1109/IALP.2014.6973485

Phu, V. N., Vo, T. N. C., Dat, N. D., Vo, T. N. T., & Nguyen, T. A. (2017b). *A Valences-Totaling Model for English Sentiment Classification. International Journal of Knowledge and Information Systems.* doi:10.100710115-017-1054-0

Phu, V. N., Vo, T. N. C., & Vo, T. N. T. (2017c). *Shifting Semantic Values of English Phrases for Classification. International Journal of Speech Technology.* doi:10.100710772-017-9420-6

Phu, V. N., Vo, T. N. C., & Vo, T. N. T. (2017i). *SVM for English Semantic Classification in Parallel Environment. International Journal of Speech Technology.* doi:10.100710772-017-9421-5

Phu, V. N., Vo, T. N. C., Vo, T. N. T., & Dat, N. D. (2017a). *A Vietnamese adjective emotion dictionary based on exploitation of Vietnamese language characteristics. International Journal of Artificial Intelligence Review.* doi:10.100710462-017-9538-6

Phu, V. N., Vo, T. N. C., Vo, T. N. T., Dat, N. D., & Khanh, L. D. D. (2017d). *A Valence-Totaling Model for Vietnamese Sentiment Classification. International Journal of Evolving Systems.* doi:10.100712530-017-9187-7

Phu, V. N., Vo, T. N. C., Vo, T. N. T., Dat, N. D., & Khanh, L. D. D. (2017e). *Semantic Lexicons of English Nouns for Classification. International Journal of Evolving Systems.* doi:10.100712530-017-9188-6

Phu, V. N., & Vo, T. N. T. (2017a). *English Sentiment Classification using Only the Sentiment Lexicons with a JOHNSON Coefficient in a Parallel Network Environment.* American Journal of Engineering and Applied Sciences. doi:10.3844/ajeassp.2017

Phu, V. N., & Vo, T. N. T. (2017b). *A STING Algorithm and Multi-dimensional Vectors Used for English Sentiment Classification in a Distributed System. American Journal of Engineering and Applied Sciences.* doi:10.3844/ajeassp.2017

Phu, V. N., & Vo, T. N. T. (2018a). English Sentiment Classification using A Gower-2 Coefficient and A Genetic Algorithm with A Fitness-proportionate Selection in a Parallel Network Environment. *Journal of Theoretical and Applied Information Technology, 96*(4), 1-50.

Phu, V. N., & Vo, T. N. T. (2018b). English sentiment classification using a Fager & MacGowan coefficient and a genetic algorithm with a rank selection in a parallel network environment. *International Journal of Computer Modelling and New Technologies, 22*(1), 57-112.

Phu, V. N., & Vo, T. N. T. (2018c). Latent Semantic Analysis using A Dennis Coefficient for English Sentiment Classification in A Parallel System. *International Journal of Computers, Communications and Control, 13*(3), 390-410.

Phu, V. N., & Vo, T. N. T. (2018d). English Sentiment Classification using A BIRCH Algorithm and The Sentiment Lexicons-Based One-dimentional Vectors in a Parallel Network Environment. *International Journal of Computer Modelling and New Technologies, 22*(1).

Phu, V. N., & Vo, T. N. T. (2018e). A Fuzzy C-Means Algorithm and Sentiment-Lexicons-based Multi-dimensional Vectors Of A SOKAL & SNEATH-IV Coefficient Used For English Sentiment Classification. *International Journal of Theoretical and Applied Information Technology, 96*(10).

Phu, V. N., & Vo, T. N. T. (2018f). A Self-Training - Based Model using A K-NN Algorithm and The Sentiment Lexicons - Based Multi-dimensional Vectors of A S6 coefficient for Sentiment Classification. *International Journal of Theoretical and Applied Information Technology, 96*(10).

Phu, V. N., & Vo, T. N. T. (2018g). The Multi-dimensional Vectors and An Yule-II Measure Used for A Self-Organizing Map Algorithm of English Sentiment Classification in A Distributed Environment. *Journal of Theoretical and Applied Information Technology, 96*(10).

Phu, V. N., & Vo, T. N. T. (2018h). Sentiment Classification using The Sentiment Scores Of Lexicons Based on A Kuhns-II Coefficient in English. International Journal of Tomography & Simulation, 31(3).

Phu, V. N., & Vo, T. N. T. (2018i). K-Medoids algorithm used for english sentiment classification in a distributed system. *Computer Modelling and New Technologies, 22*(1), 20-39.

Phu, V. N., & Vo, T. N. T. (2018j). A Reformed K-Nearest Neighbors Algorithm for Big Data Sets. *Journal of Computer Science*. Retrieved from http://thescipub.com/abstract/10.3844/ofsp.11819

Phu, V. N., Vo, T. N. T., & Max, J. (2018). A CURE Algorithm for Vietnamese Sentiment Classification in a Parallel Environment. *International Journal of Computer Science*. Retrieved from http://thescipub.com/abstract/10.3844/ofsp.11906

Phu, V. N., Vo, T. N. T., Vo, T. N. C., Dat, N. D., & Khanh, L. D. D. (2017h). A Decision Tree using ID3 Algorithm for English Semantic Analysis. *International Journal of Speech Technology*. doi:10.100710772-017-9429-x

Ponomarenko, J. V., Bourne, P. E., & Shindyalov, I. N. (2002). Building an automated classification of DNA-binding protein domains. *Bioinformatics (Oxford, England), 18*(Suppl 2), S192–S201. doi:10.1093/bioinformatics/18.suppl_2.S192 PMID:12386003

Ren, Y., Kaji, N., Yoshinaga, N., Toyoda, M., & Kitsuregawa, M. (2011). Sentiment Classification in Resource-Scarce Languages by using Label Propagation. In *Proceedings of the 25th Pacific Asia Conference on Language, Information and Computation*. Institute of Digital Enhancement of Cognitive Processing, Waseda University.

Rogers, L. L., & Dowla, F. U. (1994). Optimization of groundwater remediation using artificial neural networks with parallel solute transport modeling. *Water Resources Research, 30*(2), 457–481. doi:10.1029/93WR01494

Samanta, B., & Al-Balushi, K. R. (2003). Artificial Neural Network Based Fault Diagnostics Of Rolling Element Bearings Using Time-Domain Features. *Mechanical Systems and Signal Processing, 17*(2), 317–328. doi:10.1006/mssp.2001.1462

Scheible, C. (2010). Sentiment Translation through Lexicon Induction. *Proceedings of the ACL 2010 Student Research Workshop*, 25–30.

Seiffert, U. (2004). Artificial Neural Networks on Massively Parallel Computer Hardware. *Neurocomputing, 57*, 135–150. doi:10.1016/j.neucom.2004.01.011

S. M. Shafer, & D. F. Rogers. (2007). Similarity and distance measures for cellular manufacturing. Part II. An extension and comparison. *International Journal of Production Research, 31*(6). doi:10.1080/00207549308956793

Shikalgar & Dixit. (2014). JIBCA: Jaccard Index based Clustering Algorithm for Mining Online Review. *International Journal of Computer Applications, 105*(15).

Singh & Singh. (2015). Vector Space Model: An Information Retrieval System. *Int. J. Adv. Engg. Res. Studies, 4*(2), 141-143.

Soucy, P., & Mineau, G. W. (2015). Beyond TFIDF Weighting for Text Categorization in the Vector Space Model. *Proceedings of the 19th International Joint Conference on Artificial Intelligence*, 1130-1135.

Sudheer, K. P., Gosain, A. K., Mohana Rangan, D., & Saheb, S. M. (2002). Modelling evaporation using an artificial neural network algorithm. *Hydrological Processes, 16*(16), 3189–3202. doi:10.1002/hyp.1096

Sudheer, K. P., Gosain, A. K., & Ramasastri, K. S. (2002). A data-driven algorithm for constructing artificial neural network rainfall-runoff models. *Hydrological Processes*. doi:10.1002/hyp.554

Suzuki, Armato III, Li, Sone, & Doi. (2003). Massive training artificial neural network (MTANN) for reduction of false positives in computerized detection of lung nodules in low-dose computed tomography. *The International Journal of Medical Physics Research and Practice, 30*(7), 1602-1617.

Tamás, J., Podani, J., & Csontos, P. (2001). An extension of presence/absence coefficients to abundance data:a new look at absence. *Journal of Vegetation Science, 12*(3), 401–410. doi:10.2307/3236854

Tan, S., & Zhang, J. (2007). An empirical study of sentiment analysis for Chinese documents. *Expert Systems with Applications*. doi:10.1016/j.eswa.2007.05.028

Turney, P. D., & Littman, M. L. (2002). *Unsupervised Learning of Semantic Orientation from a Hundred-Billion-Word Corpus*. arXiv:cs/0212012

Wan, X. (2009). Co-Training for Cross-Lingual Sentiment Classification. *Proceedings of the 47th Annual Meeting of the ACL and the 4th IJCNLP of the AFNLP*, 235–243.

Wang, G., & Araki, K. (2007). Modifying SO-PMI for Japanese Weblog Opinion Mining by Using a Balancing Factor and Detecting Neutral Expressions. *Proceedings of NAACL HLT 2007*, 189–192. 10.3115/1614108.1614156

Yao, X. (1999). Evolving artificial neural networks. *Proceedings of the IEEE, 87*(9). doi:10.1109/5.784219

Yong, R., Nobuhiro, K., Naoki, Y., & Masaru, K. (2014). Sentiment Classification in Under-Resourced Languages Using Graph-based Semi-supervised Learning Methods. *IEICE Transactions on Information and Systems, E97–D*(4). doi:10.1587/transinf.E97.D.1

Zhang, R., Deng, W., & Zhu, M. Y. (2017). Using Deep Neural Networks to Automate Large Scale Statistical Analysis for Big Data Applications. *Proceedings of Machine Learning Research, 77*, 311–326.

Zhang, Z., Ye, Q., Zheng, W., & Li, Y. (2010). Sentiment Classification for Consumer Word-of-Mouth in Chinese: Comparison between Supervised and Unsupervised Approaches. *The 2010 International Conference on E-Business Intelligence*.

Zhou, Z.-H., Wu, J., & Tang, W. (2002). Ensembling neural networks: Many could be better than all. *Artificial Intelligence*, *137*(1–2), 239–263. doi:10.1016/S0004-3702(02)00190-X

APPENDIX 1: ABBREVIATIONS

Artificial Intelligence: ARTINT
large-scale data sets: LARSCDSs
big data sets: BIGDSs
massive data sets: MASSDSs
sequential system: SEQSYS
parallel network system: PARNETSYS
multi-dimensional vectors: MULTDIMVECTs
RUSSELL & RAO coefficient: RUSRAOC
international search engine – Google: GOOGSE
And and Or operator: ANDOROPs
semantic analysis: SEMANAL
testing data set: TESTDSET
training data set: TRAINDSET
Artificial Neural Network: ARTNEURNET
artificial neurons: ARTNEURs
Point-wise Mutual Information measure: PMIMEA
unsupervised learning: UNSUPLERN
sentiment orientation: SO
Jaccard coefficient: JACCCO
one-dimensional vector: ONEDIMVECT
sentiment lexicons: SENTLEXs
positive multi-dimensional vector group: POSMULTDIMVECTGR
negative multi-dimensional vector group: NEGMULTDIMVECTGR
Cosine coefficient: COSCOE
Ochiai measure: OCHMEAS
Sorensen coefficient: SORCOE
Tominato measure: TOMMEAS
Cloudera distributed network environment: CLOUDISNETEN
Hadoop Map: M
Hadoop Reduce: R
basis English opinion dictionary: BEOD
Sentiment orientation: SO
AltaVista search engine: ALTVISSE
Bing search engine: BINGSE
Java programming language: JAVAPRL

APPENDIX 2: FIGURES

Figure 1. The ARTNEURNET in the Parallel Network Environment.

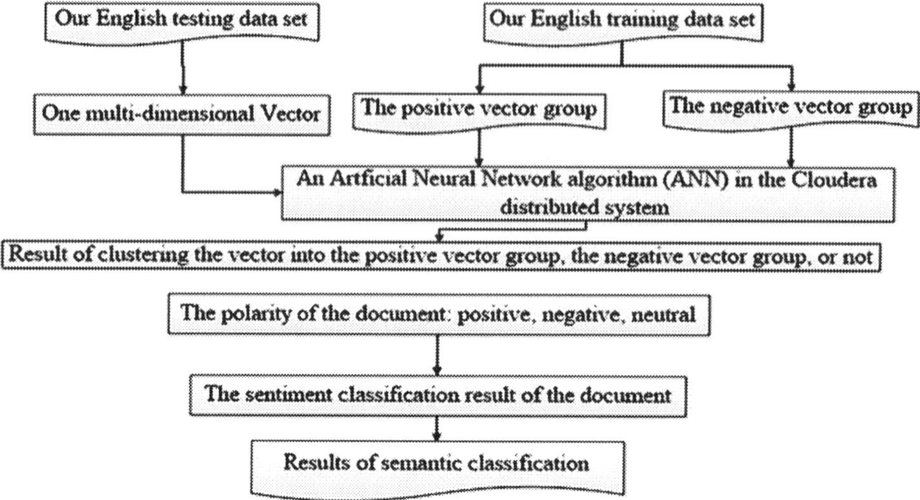

Figure 2. Transforming each English document into one MULTDIMVECT in the CLOUDISNETEN

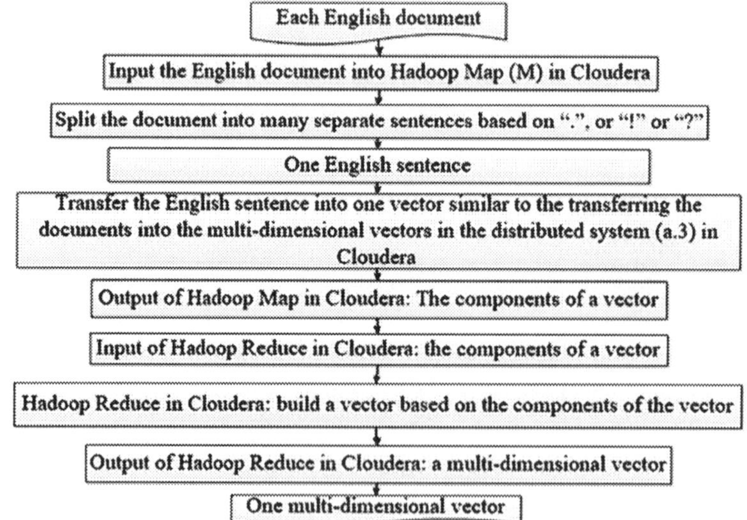

Figure 3. The ARTNEURNET in the M of the CLOUDISNETEN

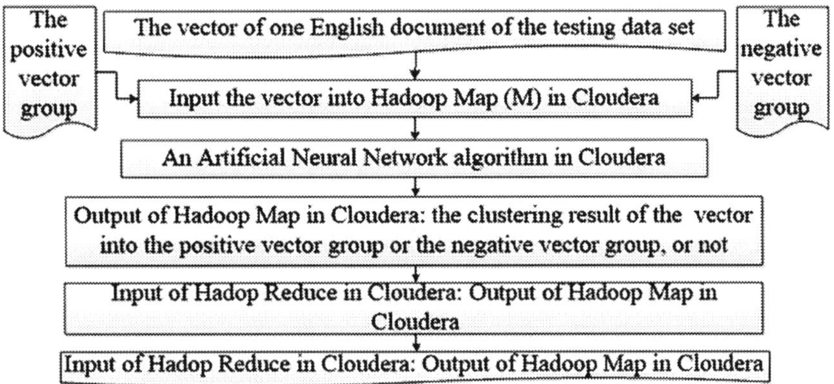

Figure 4. Overview of neural network

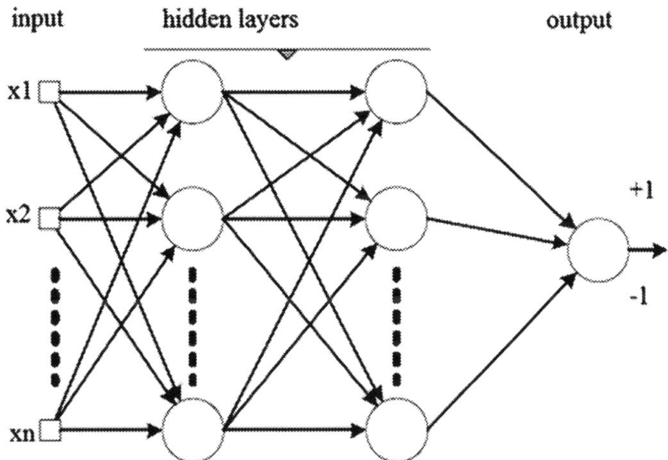

Figure 5. The ARTNEURNET in the R of the CLOUDISNETEN

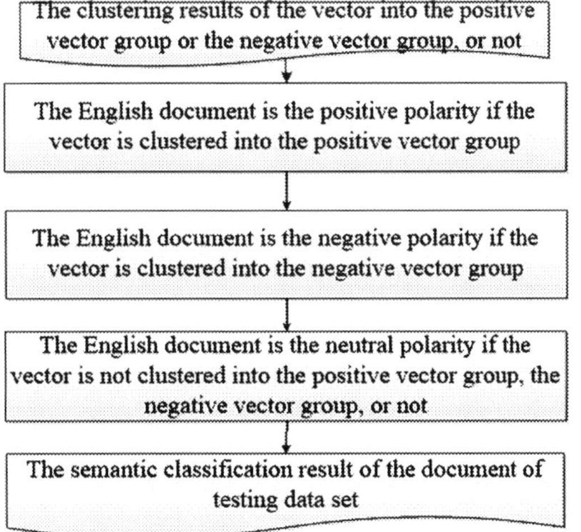

Chapter 23
Personal Data Privacy and Protection in the Meeting, Incentive, Convention, and Exhibition (MICE) Industry

M. Fevzi Esen
Istanbul Medeniyet University, Turkey

Eda Kocabas
Istanbul Medeniyet University, Turkey

ABSTRACT

With the new developments in information technologies, personal and business data have become easily accessible through different channels. The huge amounts of personal data across global networks and databases have provided crucial benefits in a scientific manner and many business opportunities, also in the meeting, incentive, convention, and exhibition (MICE) industry. In this chapter, the authors focus on the analysis of MICE industry with regards to the new regulation (GDPR) of personal data protection of all EU citizens and how the industry professionals can adapt their way of business in light of this new regulation. The authors conducted an online interview with five different meetings industry professionals to have more insight about the data produced with its content and new regulations applied to the industry. The importance of personal data privacy and protection is discussed, and the most suitable anonymization techniques for personal data privacy are proposed.

INTRODUCTION

New technologies changed open or private data in personal or business environments. The big amounts of gigabytes and terabytes of disseminated personal or business data across global networks and databases have brought significant advantages for scientific understanding and business opportunities. Since the individuals are more involved in information and communication practices, they produce various forms of distributed and persistent data in different dimensions and structures. Moreover, data about the objects

DOI: 10.4018/978-1-5225-7432-3.ch023

of physical life is also migrated to virtual environments and this data is combined and aggregated with online data (Brown & Marsden, 2013). This reality creates the phases of data lifecycle including the processes of collecting, saving, storing, reporting, sharing, analyzing and interpreting data.

Digitalization has allowed all individuals to contribute to worldwide big data mass. An estimated of 1.8 ZB data is produced in 2011 and this number is expected to reach approximately 90 ZB by 2020 (Jeon, 2012). It is expected that personal data can generate an economic benefit of $387 billion annually by 2020 (Liem & Petropoulos, 2016). Consumers create enormous data stream during their communication, searches, transactions and travels through connected devices. They leave a digital footprint behind that contains their personal information. Seventy five percent of digitally created data is composed of personal data and almost seventy percent of consumers take action to protect their privacies across all industries (Cooper et al., 2016). This reality generates personal data privacy concerns and the need of safeguarding data. Only in the U.S. A., more than $2 billion is spent to assure personal data privacy and protection (Khatibloo et. al., 2016). Despite of increasing volume of data creation every second, traditional systems have failed to resolve issues related to privacy while enabling data to be used effectively (Izu et al., 2014).

The increase in the amount of electronic data makes information systems necessary to evaluate various data types that are not held in relational databases but which contain hierarchical and semantic labels. While structured data following a data model and organized as relational tables are stored in analytically configured databases, unstructured data have a complexity in a dynamic range of its sources that may come from social media shares, mobile data, e-mails and text messages, sensor data and semantic web which are kept in specialized database systems. In order to discover knowledge from structured and unstructured data, the technologies have been developed that can systematically transform data and manage it in appropriate databases and integrate it with other data sources.

Data sharing among individuals, institutions and countries arises the problem of conflict of interest between data owners and holders against data owners. The issue of personal data privacy protection has been addressed in various national and international regulations within this context.

Personal data, as an asset, with its growing financial value has a crucial role in modern economies. Companies invest in data technologies to transform their business processes through digital intelligence for gaining a competitive advantage. According to International Association of Privacy Professionals and EY (IAPP-EY) Report on data privacy governance of 2017, companies spend a mean of $5 million in adaptation of their products and services for personal data privacy protection. Estimated data privacy spent per employee rose from $124 to $147 in 2017 (IAPP-EY, 2017). Moreover, more than three quarters of consumers believe that most companies are not able to handle personal data privacy protection and its related issues (PwC, 2017).

In tourism industries, a huge amount of data is derived from sales-booking processes and traditional distribution channels such as web sites, call centers, press releases, and customer relationship. Approximately 20% of structured data come from hotel management, customer relationships and blog content management systems (Xiang & Fesenmaier, 2016:18). In addition, search records, location data, social media messages, photographs and videos, GPS signals and the data which many tourists share during their travels with their technological devices are created every day. From the surveys applied to inbound or outbound visitors to the private records of the guests in hotels that relate to various tourism activities fall within the definition of data privacy protection.

Many tourists share their virtual and physical activities voluntarily or without giving their consents. Most of online and offline applications collect and analyze the records of their personal data with the awareness of its owners. As of 2017, the cost of intentional or unintentional disclosure of private information as a breach reaches to $124 per record in hospitality industry (IBM, 2017). Furthermore, there is a 33.1% maturity level and awareness of organizations, a score below an average percentage of 34.4%, to meet global data privacy and protection standards in hospitality and leisure industry (DLA, 2018). These facts increased the value of personal data management and created an expertise field on life cycle of personal data sharing and disclosure processes.

Data owners put responsibility to service providers and governments regarding the management of personal information in a digital data environment. A wide range of definitions and regulations are set concerning personal data privacy and its protection. The General Data Protection Regulation (GDPR) sets obligations for companies that enable to understand data privacy risks of consumers' private information. GDPR adopts strict regulations on collecting, accessing, transferring, sharing and free movement of personal data. In addition, organizations take complete responsibility for compliance with data privacy and in case of disobedience to regulations, an organization may face administrative penalties of up to 4% of company's annual total revenues under the regulation.

International meeting, incentive, conference and exhibitions (MICE) is an industry that generates huge revenues for cities and benefits from tourism and hospitality industries. It consists of a variety of related sectors such as accommodation, food and beverage, transport and activity providers, public relations, trade and distribution. This indicates that data generating mechanisms which have an integrated use of various data sources including users, devices and operations, exist in MICE industry. For this reason, like in any other sector, there is an increase in reliance on technology and personal data sharing based on trust and collaboration. Privacy concerns are shown as a serious issue that prevents to share personal data for tourism research in all of the sectors related to tourism (Li et al., 2018).

The chapter is organized as follows: Section 1 gives the definition and general highlights of MICE industry. Section 2 provides how much and what kind of data are produced within MICE industry and section 3 explains general data protection regulation on data privacy and protection and its implications on MICE industry. Section 4 defines potential solutions for personal data privacy protection within data processing phase. Finally, Section 5 concludes the chapter and give some ideas for further research.

BACKGROUND

Although the meeting industry can be seen as a new emerging and fast-growing industry, it can be seen the first examples of conventional activities and events even from the Ancient Greek and Roman Period. The Meeting, Incentive, Convention And Exhibition (MICE) industry goes back to the time that the Romans had the Forum in which the meetings took place and the Coliseum where the events took place. During that time, there was neither professional meeting organizers nor educational background of the people organizing events. However, in today's world, there is an increasing need among clients, employers, and governments to have a set of competency standards to which professionals must follow.

The term MICE or MI (Meeting Industry) was introduced in 2006 in collaboration with the key industry players including International Congress & Convention Association (ICCA), the Meetings Professional International (MPI), Reeds Travel Exhibitions and the World Tourism Organization (UNWTO) for creating a strong industrial image (Smagina, 2017).

MICE is also an industry which combines many different sectors' activities under one umbrella. The acronym "MICE" is referred to describe the particular type of tourism group travelling for a particular purpose (Gurkina, 2013). In other words, it is related to classical tourism movements, and also includes business-related movements to a different destination for specific reason such as scientific meetings, huge conventions, exhibitions and company incentives. MICE Industry is also known as shortly meeting or event industry. They all refer to the similar type of activities. Krugman and Wright (2007) state that a global meeting, convention or exhibition forms temporary global communities in the host destination generally in a foreign land.

MICE is a multifaceted industry that has an effect to and is affected by many different sectors like health, medicine, law, agriculture, science and many more. According to International Congress and Convention Association (ICCA), MICE has enormously become one of the top industries in terms of growth rate, economic benefit to the nations as well as creating a positive image of a destination.

The main aims of the industry are all about bringing people together face-to-face, exchanging ideas and information, discussing and in some cases negotiating, and building friendships and closer business relationships, encouraging better performance by individuals and organizations (Rogers, 2008). Briefly, MICE industry is a multifaceted, fast growing industry with variety of layers (Davidson & Turner, 2017). Besides, with various regulations and the increase in governmental and corporate bodies' engagement into the meetings, the structure of the meeting industry has become much more diverse and hard to manage. Fenich (2015) uses MEEC (Meetings, Expositions, Events and Conventions) instead of MICE which is an ever evolving industry globally. Rogers (2008) described the MICE industry as quite diverse and multifaceted, as well. The following list provides some insight into MICE divisions or segments:

- Conventions and Meetings
- Expositions
- Corporate Events
- Festivals & Social Events
- Religious Events & Special Events
- Mega-Events & Retail Events
- Sporting Events (occurring relatively infrequently)

With an initial starting point of the regional meeting industry in North America and Europe, it is now undoubtedly an international industry which captivates really huge investments across all over the world (Rogers, 2008). The fast growth in industry and commerce boosts the requirement of meetings among business people and professionals, focused to share and discuss new ideas or knowledge (Spiller, 2002).

MICE industry stakeholders are formed as two groups; suppliers and buyers. The supplier side includes venues, destinations, agencies, intermediaries and many others. The buyer side can be a corporate, association, public sector and entrepreneurs. We can classify the meetings market according to many different segments such as; by the size of the meetings, kind of attendees and the aim of the meetings. However, meeting suppliers prefer to segment the clients or meeting planners into two different groups; corporate and non-corporate market (ICCA, 2013). Corporate market represents for "for profit" organizations who have events during the year and non-corporate market refers to for non-profit establishments like institutions, professional societies or associations and a lot more. They have different destination selection processes and criteria. However, in common, they firstly look for the destinations providing higher quality of meeting and accommodation facilities with easy access from all over the world. As shown in Figure 1, meetings are classified into two different dimensions and they include corporate and association meetings.

Figure 1. International meeting types
(ICCA, 2017)

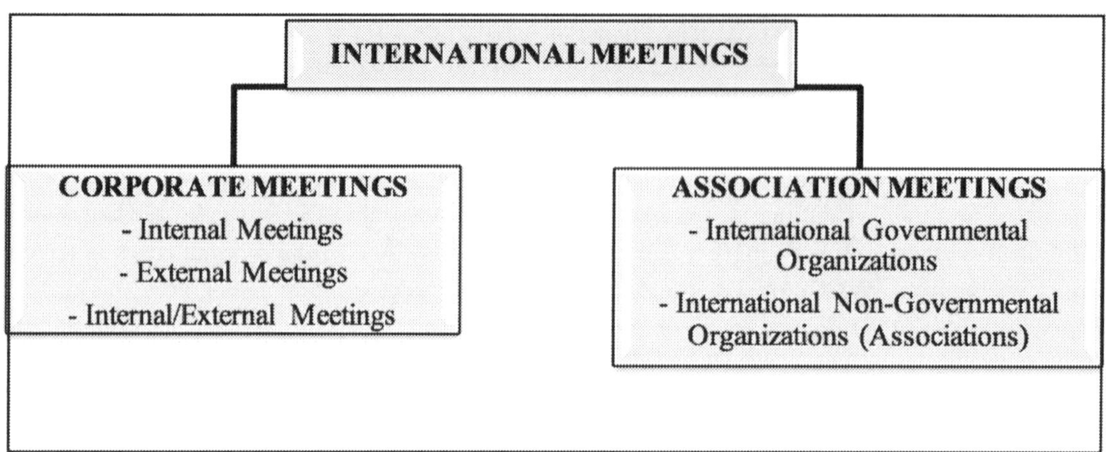

There has been organized 115.000 meetings for the last ten years in MICE (Davidson & Turner, 2017). The ICCA report of 2017 shows that the world meeting destinations captured totally 12,558 rotating international association meetings. The ICCA database consists of almost 21,000 regular meeting series with 220,000 meeting editions by 11,500 international associations. Therefore, it can be easily said that this is the industry in a rapid and huge growth (Davidson & Turner, 2017). Top 10 countries who hosted most of the association meetings in their homeland are presented in Table 1.

Technological development is a great opportunity for the MICE industry to be more innovative, inspirational and time-efficient in organizing meetings, events or exhibitions. On the other hand, it is a challenge because of the fact that the industry generates a huge amount of data and it has to protect it to avoid misusing of personal information. Sometimes, it is very difficult to achieve it during the age of technology and Internet of Things (IOT).

Table 1. 2017 ICCA statistics report/ Top 10 countries

ICCA Ranking 2017	Country/Territory	Number of Meetings
1	U.S.A.	941
2	Germany	682
3	U.K	592
4	Spain	564
5	Italy	515
6	France	506
7	Japan	414
8	China-P.R.	376
9	Canada	360
10	Netherlands	307

(ICCA, 2017)

The existing researches on MICE industry generally touch on five basic areas which are economic impact of meetings, site-selection process, destination marketing through national offices such as Convention and Visitors Bureaus (CVBs), new enhancements and innovation in meeting technologies (Sikosek, 2012). This situation generates a big amount of data to the industry representatives. The type of information created through these ways could be national member organizations' details, phone numbers, personal e-mails, ID, credit card, address details and a lot more. Therefore, it feeds the sector in creating online & face to face new networking opportunities through the personal information shared by different bodies such as meeting organizers, ICCA staff and other sources.

HOW BIG IS THE DATA PRODUCED WITHIN MICE INDUSTRY?

MICE industry is one of the most important industries with massive data which can be highly utilizable for various purposes (Kim et al., 2016). In the past, the MICE industry representatives have tried to implement smart technologies like RFID and NFC; however, it was unsuccessful because of the fact that internet world and technological developments were very slow. Despite being produced vast data sourced from the events or meetings' participants like tradeshow visitors, supplying companies, no systematical tool for gathering, storing or improving those data was applied in MICE industry.

Variety of establishments from different MICE sub-industries shape their business activities with various technologies which can gather, process, group and analyze tremendous amount of data sets so as to gain value from them. General data collection in MICE industry includes the tracking of clients, such as targeted promotional activities, predictive and user attitude analysis converting personal data into a useful resource (Voigt & Von dem Bussche, 2017).

MICE, as a multifaceted and fast-growing industry, produces a huge amount of data. The data is produced by leading meeting industry organizations like ICCA and MPI, tradeshow organizers, MICE agencies and destination marketing organizations.

In order to define data in MICE industry, it is a common tool in following and tracking some useful information in regards to reaching the targeted meetings' location history, subject details, national representatives, local ambassadors, hosting organizations and contact details of sponsors that supported those meetings, events or exhibitions in previous years. ICCA has an enormous database consisting of thousands of international associations information. ICCA has also established big data platform which is also synchronized with Google Scholar and Microsoft Academic Search so that the industry professionals who are active members of ICCA can easily benefit from this source to gain potential meeting clients to their home destinations.

ICCA has also been collecting and researching wide-ranging data of the world association and society conferences, meetings or congresses since over fifty years. ICCA database includes detailed association and meeting profiles with the knowledge of the previous meetings location as all of the meetings must have rotation pattern, meeting or association requirements and other important aspects of almost 20.000 worldwide conventions, meetings or conferences. Harris (2018) states that only in IMEX fair – Frankfurt, it is engaged with more than 200k events, 180m marketing e-mails, 20m registrations, more than 2500 customers with 40k regular users.

As stated in the previous section, the meetings industry has more than 20.000 meetings' full profile data. All of these numbers state that MICE industry produces a very large, complex and accessible data for all the professionals. As a result, controlling personal data privacy is a very complex and hard issue, if any data management systems are not applied by the data controllers.

Instead of using traditional survey results to predict the future movements of target groups, personal data provides a variety of information about the clients and suppliers in most of the leading industries as it is in the MICE industry. This creates more synchronized, correct and homogenous data for the benefit of the meeting destinations. Meeting industry professionals who are actively following and applying big data privacy and protection strategies gain a higher position as today's improvement requires to handle the personal data privacy (Song & Liu, 2017).

We conducted an online interview with five different meetings industry professionals to have some insights about the data produced with its content and the new regulations applied to the industry. The respondents include a senior manager from ICCA, the head of Vienna Convention Bureau, the managing partner at one of the international MICE agencies which also has a branch in Turkey, high-level manager at one of the Convention & Visitors Bureau (CVB) in Turkey and lastly high-level manager from one of the convention centers in Turkey. The following questions were asked during the interview:

Question 1: How does MICE Industry achieve to manage data privacy and protection issues and what are the most frequently encountered cases in regards to data privacy and protection management in the industry?

Question 2: What kind of data does the industry produce? (please describe attributes such as personal data, corporate data, meeting data and etc...)

Question 3: Do you have any suggestion of tools used for protecting data in MICE industry?

Question 4: What is your comment on GDPR-General Data Protection Regulation which will be applied by 25th of May, 2018? Will it really affect the way of business that the industry follows?

The responses to the Question 2 overall tell that the personal data such as identity card details, the clients' country of origin, telephone, e-mail address, office contact details, and apart from these data, the general data such as potential meeting organizers, name of the event, venue, name of the associations, responsible high-level people such as the positions of the participants (CEO, senior manager, staff etc.) are generated. The data collected during the event, meeting or exhibition registrations includes some kind of special information such as physical state, food preferences and allergic sensitization and etc.

Apart from the data that industry specifically produce, there is also a common personal data which almost all of the industries store with the assistance of ongoing client interactions or activities (Salvarci et al., 2015). Identity and credit card details, address information, telephones, e-mails, websites, and such information can be grouped as the personal information.

Recently, many corporations have become experts in the area of storing and analyzing the broader extent of data on tourists' accommodation activities, buying actions and the client information so as to deliver more efficient and higher quality of services (Song & Liu, 2017). They can easily deduce their clients' personal tendency from the posts, photos and videos shared via social channels.

The personal information unstructuredly collected through social media posts, downloaded mobile applications, internet statistics, blogs, web server logs and location-based records provides an opportunity to the industry suppliers like hotels, venues or airline companies in their strategic decision-making processes (Esen & Turkay, 2017). Besides, most of the travelers carry technological devices and share some videos, photos, current locations and social media posts while they are travelling. The data produced during their trips equals to %80 of the total data used in effective tourism planning in the world.

The other traditional distribution channels to collect personal information may be sales and reservation transactions, websites, call centers, press releases and guest relations (Esen & Turkay, 2017). Collecting the correct information about the clients leads the marketing team of a specific company to the direct business goals and this can also minimize the inefficiency resulted from missing information (Salvarci et al., 2015).

Apart from personal data generation, the meeting industry also has different types of sensitive data such as presentations done during the meetings, keynote speakers data, meeting reports confidential to outsiders who did not attend the meeting.

Use of big data has increased among corporate and non-corporate establishments and it has become a common source for their strategic decisions. In parallel with this increase, there is also a bad rise in personal data privacy concerns and misusing of these information. According to Song and Liu (2017), the extensive usage of big data by transportation, travel, accommodation and other tourism related bodies provides them with having knowledge on clients' preferences on a broader perspective and assists investing in different businesses within the next years.

The global dimension of big data and the transnational nature of companies or networks holding the data call for a discussion in an international context, even though legal and ethical issues often have a strongly local component (Eurostat, 2017). Therefore, big data can provide to connect missing links in the traditional data sets, and this can assist data owners to make use of the data more efficiently and systematically. However, having or providing data brings some responsibilities to them. Businesses need to protect the personal information in their database from the other parties. They need to be loyal to the confidentiality agreement with the clients. However, nowadays, with the huge amount of data and transactions between the clients and suppliers, it becomes difficult to manage and protect the clients' personal information. It creates a major critical risk with a likely dramatic impact on the trust users put into them (Eurostat, 2017).

HOW TO AND WHY WE SHOULD PROTECT THE PRIVACY OF PERSONAL DATA IN MICE?

Personal data is an economic property and the new currency of the digitalized world (Moerel, 2014). In MICE industry, the scope of personal data varies when compared the industry with other data producing industries such the retailing industry or tourism industry. Despite of the fact that MICE is closely interrelated with tourism industry, the data produced within these industries quite differs.

As described in the previous section, personal data in MICE industry include the personal information such as identity card details, the clients' country of origin, telephone, e-mail address, office contact details as well as the general data such as potential meeting organizers, name of the event, venue, name of the associations and tenures. Meeting reports, presentations of key note speakers, attendance details of meetings are the data specifically generated from the MICE industry.

Smart phones and other mobile devices have transformed the society greatly in the past decade. In the upcoming periods, IOT (Internet of Things) will take the role to completely change the way people live and also the industries directly related with human activities such as the MICE industry. Meeting venues, accommodation sites, special events and tradeshows are the areas affected by this change.

The customers of the meeting industry consist of organizations, associations, agencies, and conference entrepreneurs and their personal information is more valuable than the suppliers side (Meeting Venues, CVBs, PCOs and etc.) as the buyers decide or lead where it will be the next meeting destination of their companies, association or governmental organizations. It is really crucial to reach their contact information to make them convince that their destination perfectly matches the buyers' meeting requirements and expectations.

It is obvious that the new information technologies create many opportunities. Nevertheless, that is also a reason that these technologies can cause new risks or responsibilities (Moerel, 2014). On one hand, the technological development in the industry has powerful and positive effect on outputs of all designed activities, meetings, shows and many more. However, on the other hand, access to any type of information including personal one has become easier because of the improvements on technology. It is stated that technology destroys trust and people can easily get access to the information they need through GPS directions, online transactions and conference registrations (Terry, 2015). These concerns stem from reselling clients' information to the alternate market for Big Data (Martin, 2015).

General Data Protection Regulation (GDPR) limits the illegal information transactions to 3rd parties. Since being exposed to mass-mailing is not preferable by most of the delegates or participants, there is an increase in reliance on technology and personal data sharing based on trust and collaboration between industry professionals in MICE industry. As of the 25th of May 2018, The EU General Data Protection Regulation (GDPR) has been adapted in all the industries especially in meetings & events industry that produces a huge amount of personal data from two sides; both the buyers and suppliers. The primary purpose of GDPR is to ensure the privacy of all European Citizens' personal information and activities in an enormously digital data-driven world leading to different scales of security threats felt by the meeting professionals. The new data protection law will change the way of business, from storing e-mail addresses to promoting the next meeting or product as well as from the largest conferences and trade shows to the smallest meetings, every sized-meeting involving EU citizens.

GDPR process is managed by data controller officer who would be a responsible person from data flow within or outside of the organization (ICCA Congress, 2017). However, according to the interviews with five key industry professionals, there is a common argument from their responses to question 4 that GDPR will not really affect the industry businesses and like the other laws requirements, industry professionals will be following the same way of to do their businesses.

Violation of confidentiality agreement in personal data privacy frequently occurs in the meeting industry especially within the private entities whose main aim is to make profit. Potential misuse of personal data in the meeting industry can be listed as following:

- Destination mass-marketing and for promotional purposes,
- Industry research and surveys,
- Event or meeting invitation,
- Hiring decisions,
- Social marketing,
- TPS and telephone marketing,
- B2B Marketing,
- Research and Development,
- Advertising and promotion campaigns,
- Sales management,

With the new EU GDPR, the industry professionals need to get consent from the data owners to save and use their personal data. The leading organizations in the industry like ICCA, UIA or MPI, which would potentially control clients-engaged companies, website operators and application providers. By using technological ways of control such as sensors, they can follow how the produced data was firstly gathered as well as in which way the data is distributed to the third parties.

The responses to question 3, "Do you have any suggestion of tools used for protecting data in MICE industry?" mainly tell that a reliable data privacy protection method is a must for MICE industry and it is stated that personal data must be anonymized for business and organizational purposes. The data stores should also be kept with separate online sections that only provide access to authorized person in the company. Besides, the company staff should be aware of the fact that these data must not be shared with the third parties. The data used during the specific project should be removed from all of the system or anonymized to decrease privacy risks.

For interview question 1, "How does MICE Industry achieve to manage data privacy and protection issues and what are the most frequently encountered cases in regards to data privacy and protection management in the industry?", industry representatives responded that the data protection is totally related to the company in subject. The adaptation to the EU law is the first step that the organizations need to take. Systematically, the data should be in review and necessary changes need to be completed by the responsible team. Another response from the agency tells that the agency makes a confidentiality agreement with the clients, and there is a serious results if one of the bodies do not abide the agreement. The agency removes data in one month after the business is done so that no data waste occurs.

GDPR makes necessary for the industry companies and organizations to do ongoing investments in technologies and data management practices to protect their data properly. In the following section, detailed techniques for personal data privacy and protection are discussed.

TECHNIQUES FOR PERSONAL DATA PRIVACY PROTECTION

European Data Protection Supervisor (EDPS) defines data privacy protection as information and communication technologies that are developed in consideration of technology, privacy and confidentiality in order to protect the data at every step of the design from the very beginning (EDPS, 2010). This ensures all necessary controls implemented and maintained within the data lifecycle by taking the impact of a system or process on the privacy of individuals into account. The definition of privacy pertains to the data that cannot be traced to an individual and does not constitute an intrusion (Vaidya et al., 2006).

Economic and social costs of lack of personal data privacy protection are increasing. Despite a variation among the countries, the average cost of personal data breaches reached $158 in 2016 (IBM, 2017). Companies may also suffer from misuse or lose of consumers' personal data and may face loss of current and potential customers, profit decrease, penalties or other sanctions. Technological advancements provide an opportunity for companies and individuals to balance their benefits in compliance with the guidelines and regulations (Romanosky & Acquisti, 2009).

Sustainable mechanisms that enable appropriate use and management of personal information depend on the availability of information technologies, business models and logical – physical architecture of databases. Data life cycle that consists of data generation & collection, data storage and data processing stages, plays an important role to classify aforementioned mechanisms (Mehmood et al., 2016) (Figure 2). At this point, data privacy protection begins with a detailed examination of existing data types and structures, and the identification of the perceptions, expectations and sensitivity levels of the parties.

Figure 2. Data life cycle
(Mehmood, et al., 2016)

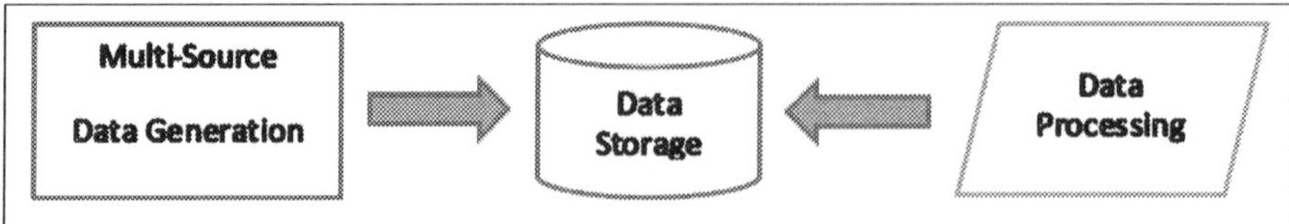

Data life cycle stages differentiate the mechanisms of data privacy protection. The main purpose of data privacy and protection can be either preventing unauthorized access or minimizing data transfer and storage, or anonymizing the data or providing data security (Gurses and Danezis, 2012).

For data generation phase, gathering data from reliable and reputable sources is the essential element of data privacy. In this phase, data owner aims to minimize the risks of third-party access to his personal data as much as possible. Some security measures like trusted source of information or other digital certificates, limited access control, encryption of data fields (personal information identifier) can be implemented to keep personal data from being released (Alshboul et al., 2015). Data storage phase includes storing and managing data. Secure communications between services and customers, the storage designs with hardware security chips that have been adapted for both servers and peripherals, cryptographic signatures over BIOS, firewalls, networking equipments and non-computing resources constitute hardware structure that affect data privacy and security. The security of other IT structures such as satellites, secured building space, internet service providers (ISPs) also enhances personal data privacy and protection. Dividing datasets vertically or horizontally, performing hardware and software encryption, developing physical security measures and adopting security protocols regarding access control are the ways of protecting personal data privacy on data storages (Aldossary & Allen, 2016).

Data processing phase refers to systematic collection, transmission and extraction of data. Once the raw data are collected, they need to be processed and transformed into information. The collected data are first passed through a pre-processing (filtering, normalization, etc.) stage and then converted into information by various algorithms depending on the nature of the data. The disclosure of personal data in a secure manner and extracting information from personal data without violating personal data privacy rules represent important stages of data processing (Mehmood et al., 2016).

In order to produce valuable information and insights for businesses, the first step is managing and organizing data processes effectively. These processes may vary according to the sector or industry. For example, while a hotel processes personal data regarding payment for hotel services for a visitor who travels for MICE purposes, a company may engage in processing the records of entries of a visitor into exhibition or conference rooms during an exhibition or fair which is organized for military defense and aerospace technologies.

During the data processing stage, transmission and disclosure of the data must be handled privately due to the security vulnerabilities and threats related to data. At this point, some balance techniques are designed to protect the security and confidentiality of individuals while benefiting from the contributions of personal data. Data anonymization is one of the solutions produced to ensure the balance of benefits and the security of personal data (Kaaniche & Laurent, 2017). By anonymization, personal identifiable information including descriptive and subjective properties is either removed or encrypted. Thus, accessing to identifiers and data subject regarding personal data cannot be possible. This ensures to produce valuable outputs for companies as well as simultaneously protecting personal data privacy.

Data Privacy

Privacy refers to an entitlement of an individual to determine the information shared with others regarding his or her condition (Torra, 2017). Privacy is a measure of control for individuals about their personal information. Race and ethnic origin, religion, sexual life, personal believes and interests, membership to community, convictions and the other data relating to idiosyncratic behaviors or opinions of individuals and their family members are under the principles of data privacy. According to European Community Privacy Guideline of 1995, privacy only applies to "individually identifiable data" and it is a human right for individuals. The risk of the identification of individuals in any data disclosed is also under the scope of data privacy.

Privacy must ensure that any data that gives knowledge about a specific person and cannot be traced to an individual. Privacy reflects various types of information relating to an identifiable person like social security and passport numbers, demographic and financial records, personal preferences, browsing history, biometrics, passwords, contact information, memberships, views etc.; but herein there is a difference between privacy and sensitivity of data in terms of the definition of personal data. According to EU Directive on data protection, privacy is a subset of personal data which refers to the data that is avoided from being disclosed without one's permission whereas sensitivity is defined by legislative processes (EC, 1995).

Personal data privacy may be breached by following (Katal et al., 2013):

- Combining personal data with external datasets may reveal new information regarding individuals. Disclosure of this information may not be preferred due to the personal privacy reasons.
- Companies almost always collect personal data to enhance customers' experiences and turn data into a business value. Such concerns can lead to misuse of personal data.
- Personal data are not stored in a physical or virtual location properly and data leakage or data loss occurred during data transferring, storage or processing.

The main concepts of data privacy are anonymity, unlinkability and disclosure. Anonymity enables unidentifiably of subjects by replacing the subjects which consist same attributes. This assures that personal data can be generated, stored and processed without disclosing his or her identity and the relationships. Unlinkability is a sufficient condition of anonymity that refers whether identifiers and attributes of personal data are related or not. Pfitzman and Hansen (2007) define unlinkability as not being able to establish relationship between the owner and the data in their proposed terminology. For example, as shown in Figure 3, thermal SPA or a wellness center specialized in treating elderly people aged between 65 and 80 years old with musculoskeletal system disorders, makes three day hotel reservations to increase loyalty of its customers for incentive tourism purposes on a regular basis. The hotel requests personal ID and passport number, age, gender and special needs of customers to complete registration process. In case of lack of privacy concerns, one may can link data attributes and find a priori-knowledge about sending company and its customer group. This may also allow one to develop customer win strategies. Disclosing personal data which are identifiable and linkable is the other concept of data privacy. Lambert (1993) discusses identity, attribute and membership disclosure which facilitate various inferences about individuals' characteristics before the data disclosure.

Figure 3. Concepts of data privacy
(Figure is formed by authors)

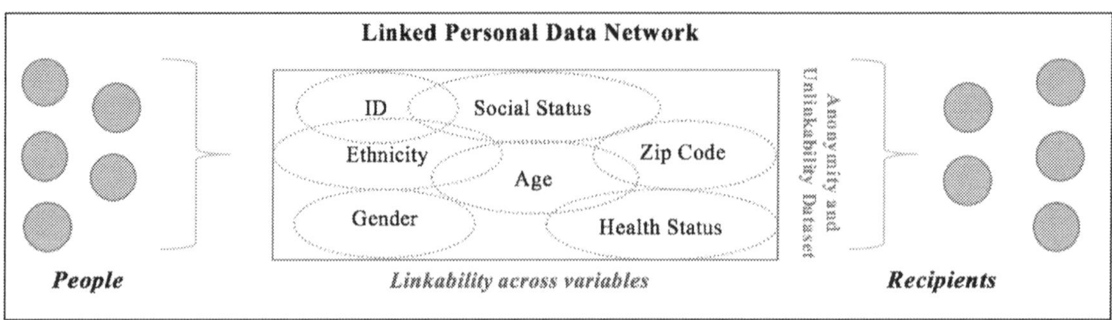

In order to ensure which data must be anonymized and which data can be disclosed, identification of personal data is a necessity. Ciriani et al. (2007) identify four groups of data attributes:

- **Explicit Identifiers (EI):** These data attributes which can pinpoint an individual directly. ID, passport and social security number, name – surname are the examples of explicit identifiers.
- **Quasi-Identifiers (QI):** Data attributes that can identify an individual are defined as quasi – identifiers. Phone numbers, demographic information, zip code, birth date are generally publicly available for various purposes such as research, marketing, public relations, planning etc. According to researches almost 90% of U.S. population can be identified by looking only at quasi – identifiers, e.g., birth date, zip code and gender (Ras and Tsay, 2009).
- **Sensitive Data:** GDPR (2018) defines the personal data with specific conditions as sensitive data. Religious beliefs, physical or mental health condition, ethnic origin, financial status, genetic or biometric data contain confidential information about data owner.
- **Non-Sensitive Data:** The personal data that are not related to the given sensitive data categories is treated as non-sensitive data.

Logical representation of the attributes of tourist data is given in Table 2. Most hotels keep huge amounts of customer data with various attributes. This data need to be separated from sensitive data and thus nobody can link an individual and his/her specific data. Data anonymization aims to break the connection between the attributes and the combinations of the attributes (Koot, 2012). EI and QI identify a unique individual. Samarati et al. (1998) state that if QI is known by recipients, dropping EI is not enough for anonymization.

Table 2. Tourist data list

Explicit Identifiers		Quasi-Identifiers		Sensitive Data		
ID	**Name**	**Gender**	**Zip Code**	**Race/Ethnic Origin**	**Credit Card Information**	**Religion**
1	Dany	Male	48917	Hispanic	4803230012678109	Jewish
2	Amy	Female	69002	White American	1290326790809578	Christian

Data Protection

European Union (2012) mandated that appropriate technologies which are accessible by its owners, must be implemented to protect personal data privacy even after the collection and storage of data by providers and every individual must have the right to delete or access his/her data. Data protection identifies the management of personal data and relies on privacy related regulations for specific sectors (Kaaniche & Laurent, 2017). For example, while the Health Insurance Portability and Accountability Act of 1996 (HIPAA) identifies data protection as "the standards to protect health information of individuals", Information and Communication Technology (ICT) standards (ISO/IEC) refers to all administrative and technical measures that are to be taken to guard against unintentional or unauthorized disclosure, destruction or modification of personal data. Freedom of Information and Protection of Privacy Act (FIPPA) in Canada also defines protection of personal data privacy within the concept of how, when and which personal data are collected and what obligations do the parties have for disclosure of personal information (FIPPA, 1996).

Data protection is a task of protecting personal or sensitive data which are complex and widely distributed. It is a legal concept in law for controlling individuals' data to ensure privacy. The aim is to regulate data flows cross-border and balance freedom of information and data consumers (EDP, 2016). Protection of personal data is a necessity for social order, consumer confidence, fundamental rights and freedom. Data anonymization is one of the technical solutions produced to maintain privacy balance (EU, 2016).

GDPR (2018) separates personal data protection into general protection and special protection of personal data. General protection refers to the protection of personal data with the norms aimed at protection of personality rights and privacy. Special protection is the provision of a number of national and international legal norms that regulate the protection of personal data.

Protection of personal data in legal practice is assumed to be the processing of personal data. In most practices, data processing is defined as the operations upon personal data such as collecting, storing, transforming, disclosing, sharing and transferring through automatic or non-automatic systems. GDPR (2018) gives a direct reference to the use of anonymization mechanisms for protecting personal data privacy and it puts emphasis on anonymization as protection measures for protection of identity.

While determining the way of protection, the following questions can provide information functionality and balance value of information to community and personal privacy (Blyth and Kovacich, 2006):

- What types of personal data are being processed?
- What is the purpose of collecting data?
- What is the location of data processing?
- What are the security levels or level of impact of personal data?
- What are the data subjects (customers, respondents, clients etc.) and data attributes (fields or characteristics?
- What are the phases of personal data processing?
- Who are the recipients of data?
- What is the cost of processing data?
- What happens if the personal information is no longer available?
- What is the cost of data loss?

- What happens if the third parties get the information?
- Is privacy protection required by law and if so, what happens if we disobey the laws?
- What do we need to meet legislative requirements (technical, ethical or organizational)?

Ensuring Personal Data Privacy: Data Anonymization

It is possible to prevent the intrusion of the confidential data by making various changes on the data or by providing access to the data in a restricted manner (Verykios et al., 2004). Data anonymization is a process which generates solutions for threats and privacy problems that are related to personal data. The purpose is to provide solutions for sharing and disclosing data safely and securely towards business goals and objectives. Personal data can only be available to everyone to access by disclosure. Opening data without any constraints for public or private use, provides opportunities to develop new products and services and create new policies as much as obtaining data flow between businesses, government bodies and other parties.

Considering the benefits of use of personal data and its basic role in international economic order with its privacy and confidentiality issues, data anonymization emerges as one of the technical solutions to protect the balance of utility and privacy. Spiekerman and Cranor (2009) state that data anonymization provides the highest degree of privacy for the data provider. Sweeney (2002); Lin and Cheng (2009) propose data anonymization as one of the best techniques to provide personal data privacy when compared to the other methods. Esayas (2015) states that data anonymization is a necessity for information security and it can serve as a safe harbour to fulfill data privacy obligations.

As shown in Figure 4, tourists generate various types of personal data regarding their business travels, exhibitions, conferences or other meetings. Raw data can also be standardized consistent with regulatory policies and company's ethical code. For example, when attendants register for a conference abroad, they also book accommodation online and they are asked to share their personal information such as passport number, contact and payment information, flight number, meal requests etc. as well as submission of personal information to conference chair. During the conference, RFID or NFC badges or wearable cards are given to participants to track their registrations, their accesses to events and meeting rooms,

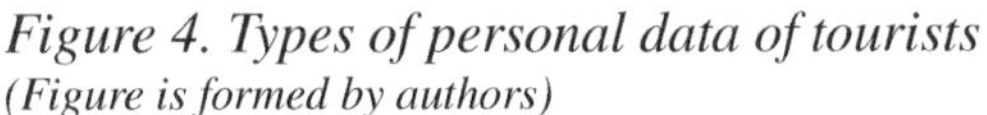

Figure 4. Types of personal data of tourists
(Figure is formed by authors)

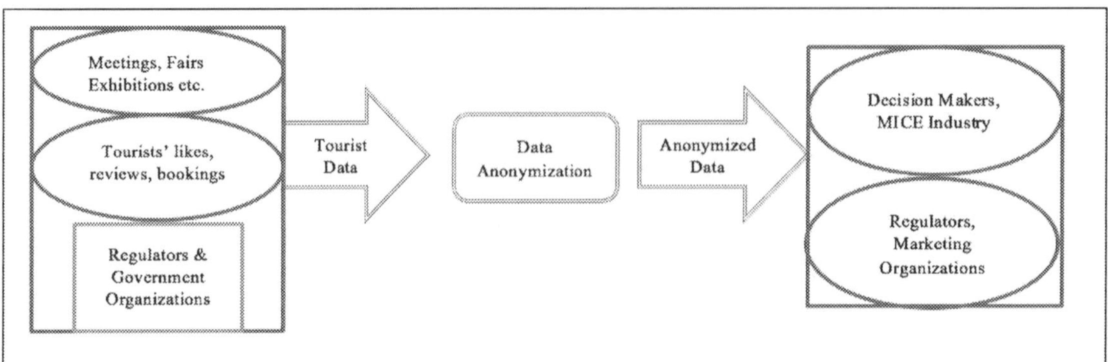

cashless payment, their interactive networks, marketing content and so on. All of this mentioned data are personal and subject to data privacy. In order to protect data privacy, the identities of participants and any other sensitive data are removed from the datasets by applying data anonymization. This also helps decision makers and MICE industry to make descriptive and inferential statistics without revealing any sensitive or private information.

It is important to note that anonymous data and anonymized data have different meanings. While anonymous data refers to data that cannot be associated with a particular person, anonymized data is associated with a person in the preceding, but no longer associated with the person. The recipient of the information cannot identify an individual by using anonymized data.

The main disadvantage of data anonymization is the emergence of unique identifiers by combining several variables. For example, a dataset containing tourist records with three different variables such as customers' residence, age group and special needs. Since the identity of the person cannot be identified by looking at just one of the variables, combinations of descriptive variables (namely, EI and QI in this example) can help to pinpoint a specific individual. Just looking the identifiers as given, it is likely to easily identify the customer without giving further details. In order to prevent this situation, either generalizing one or more identifiers (instead of naming customers' residence, county or state may be given) or anonymizing would be possible.

The first step in data anonymization is to get rid of identifiers. Afterwards, anonymization is performed to minimize the risk of information disclosure by considering the data combinations. At this point, we can divide data anonymization techniques into four parts. These techniques can be combined with one another to create different anonymization techniques (Venkataramanan and Shriram, 2017):

1. Attribute and Record Suppression,
2. Top - Bottom Coding and Global Recoding,
3. Micro-Aggregation,
4. Adding Noise,
5. Data Swapping,

When determining appropriate techniques, the purpose of anonymization, the clarity of data and the type of data (nominal, ordinal or interval-ratio) that are to be anonymized, must be considered. In this chapter, we only focus on popular anonymization techniques which are considered important for MICE industries, without addressing pertubative - nonpertubative techniques and their differences.

Attribute and Record Suppression

Suppression techniques refer to removing, withholding or deleting one or more variables / records (the entire column or row) completely from the dataset. In attribute suppression, sensitive attributes are removed as a single cell, tuple or entire column from the dataset. For example, in Table 3, the table is anonymized by removing the sensitive data "booking number" from the dataset. Since it is not possible to recover any information regarding the attribute, attribute suppression is considered as one of the strongest anonymization technique (Alfaro et al., 2011).

Unlike the other methods, instead of the entire column (variable), only specific records are removed from the dataset in record suppression. This technique is applicable when a record (row) is unique and it

Table 3. Suppressing "booking number" attribute

Residence Zip Code	Gender	Age	Booking Number
48102	Female	45	4903EF
33569	Female	39	560M60
67120	Male	53	62JB89

contains singular attributes. Outlier records which are unique may lead identification of individuals. For example, as shown in Table 4, a dataset that contains registration information of participants from many countries to a special conference may have only one single participant from a single country. In this case, it is suitable to remove the single record rather than removing "participant's country" from the dataset.

These techniques can be used, if:

- The data set includes high-level descriptors (explicit identifiers or sensitive data),
- The data are too sensitive and shall not be disclosed,
- The data are not relevant for analytic use (not interpretable),
- No other protection methods are available.

Top-Bottom Coding and Global Recoding

Top–bottom coding and global recoding techniques are the main concepts of data generalization. In data generalization, data privacy protection is provided by combining the attributes into a more general category. These methods can be reviewed as a non-perturbative data anonymization method (Torra, 2017).

Top and bottom coding technique aggregates the values of attributes into predefined categories (Torra, 2017). For example, in Table 5, we classified "age" attribute into ten year groups and we coded participants' countries as low-income, middle-income and high-income etc.). The technique is suitable for numerical or ordinal variables. When top coding is applied, the highest values are put together, and in the same way, the lowest values are put together to create new categories. Then, the dataset is rearranged according to the new categories created (Hundepool et al., 2008).

In global recording, discrete or continuous numerical variables can be aggregated into a predefined class. Here, the various categories can be changed to form just one category. For example, customers with disabilities or illnesses personally complete their registration forms and must declare their conditions in accordance with the rules. As shown in Table 6, these two adjacent categories can be combined

Table 4. Suppressing the record

Country	Gender	Special Needs	Check-in Date
USA	Male	No	03/11/2018
USA	Female	No	03/11/2018
HR	Female	No	02/11/2018
USA	Male	No	03/11/2018
USA	Female	No	02/11/2018

Table 5. An example of top and bottom coding technique

Tourist	Country	New Coded -Country	Age	New Coded-Age	Hotel Reservation
1	Germany	High-Income	35	30 – 40	Yes
2	Norway	High-Income	43	40 – 50	No
3	Croatia	Middle-Income	37	30 – 40	Yes
4	Serbia	Middle-Income	48	40 – 50	No
5	Somalia	Low-Income	50	40 – 50	Yes
6	USA	High-Income	33	30 – 40	Yes
7	Canada	High-Income	45	40 – 50	Yes

Table 6. Illness and disability anonymized dataset

Participant	Illness	Disability	Coded- Special Conditions	Marital Status	Coded – Marital Status
1	None	Vision Loss	Visual Impairment	Separated	Separated or Divorced
2	Asthma	None	Chronic Illness	Divorced	Separated or Divorced
3	Epilepsy	None	Chronic Illness	Divorced	Separated or Divorced
4	Chronic Fatigue	None	Chronic Illness	Single	Single
5	None	MS	Physical Impairment	Separated	Separated or Divorced

Note: The categories should be designed in pursuant to statistical classification for analysis purposes.

into a single category named as "special conditions". The same conditions also apply to "marital status". It should be noted that global recoding is applied not only to the attribute that has an identifying effect but also to the entire data set.

Micro-Aggregation

Micro-aggregation is a perturbative technique which reduces the utility of data by creating new singular combinations in the dataset. The statistical values of the created dataset should be the same as the calculated values of the original set (Oommen & Fayyoumi, 2008). The technique aims to sort the records into a meaningful order (ascending or descending) and then to allocate the whole dataset to a certain number of subclasses. The choice of sorting method depends on how the data is dispersed (heterogeneously or homogeneously). The technique is suitable for numerical, ordinal or nominal variables. The values for each record in the subclasses are obtained by averaging the values of the records in the same subclass. The records belonging to the same subclass have the same values. Thus, all attribute values are replaced by the calculated average values. The subclasses contain at least number k of records where k denotes a threshold value. The minimum value of k should be 3 and the subclasses are constructed to provide maximum similarity between the records (ICO, 2008).

In order to perform micro-aggregation, dataset must be split into k subclasses containing at least n records. For each subclass, the average value of each subclass is calculated by averaging all n . Afterwards, the values of each record are replaced by the average of the group that the record belongs. In

Table 7. Micro-aggregated variables

Participant	Payment for Hotel Services ($)	Micro-Aggregated Payment	Average Duration of Call Service (Seconds)	Micro-Aggregated Average Duration	Number of Room Service Usage (Numbers)	Micro-Aggregated Number of Room Service
1	3000	2686.66	68	98	12	8.33
2	2260	2686.66	124	98	1	2.33
3	1820	1523.33	56	40.33	4	2.33
4	4200	3958.33	102	98	8	8.33
5	3750	3958.33	330	300	22	25
6	1500	1523.33	428	300	37	25
7	1250	1523.33	38	40.33	5	8.33
8	2800	2686.66	27	40.33	2	2.33
9	3925	3958.33	142	300	16	25

Table 7, the data of the participants accommodated in hotel for an exhibition are given. To prevent identity disclosure of the participants, micro-aggregation anonymization technique is applied to dataset. For "payment for hotel services", the participants are sorted in ascending order and then, the participants are arranged in groups (subclasses) with at least three participants as following: {3,6,7}, {1,2,8}, {4,5,9}. The average values of each class are calculated and the mean values of the groups are appointed to each record as shown in Table 7. Disadvantage of replacing observed values with micro-aggregated ones is to omit statistical inferences and the general structure of original data (Defays and Anwar, 1998).

Adding Noise

Adding noise is applied to numerical values and the original values are changed by positive or negative deterioration with adding or multiplying a random value at certain ratios to quantitative attributes that are required to be protected. Typically, the random value ε follows normal distribution with zero mean and positive variance ∂^2 (Kadampur and Somayajulu, 2010). In Table 8, random variable is generated with $\pm 5\%$ deviation for tourists' hotel payments data to ensure privacy.

Adding noise does not change the mean of attribute, but may increase the variance in the dataset. However, this method does not work in which the dataset has highly scattered data or outliers. Statistical characteristics of dataset may be lost if the procedure is applied.

Data Swapping

Data swapping refers to permutation or shuffling that rearranges data by exchanging the values. The swapped new data do not correspond to original values. This technique can be a feasible solution for masking data while obtaining personal information. It is also mainly designed for variables that can be categorized and the main idea is to transform the values of private records by swapping between the records. Prior to the execution of the procedure, eligibility of the attributes, swap ratio of the records and which pairs are the most appropriate for data swapping should be determined.

Table 8. Adding noise to hotel payment data

Tourist	Hotel Payment (X)	Random Variable (ε)	New Value With Noise $(Z = X + \varepsilon)$
1	1200	50	1250
2	2000	2	2002
3	3050	-147	2903
4	1248	55	1303
5	500	-6	494
6	1315	-15	1300
7	1770	-39	1731
8	980	49	1029
9	330	-7	323

The advantages and disadvantages of this technique can be listed as follows (Moore, 1996):

1. It masks the accurate information about the individuals and removes the relationship between the record and individual,
2. It is very easy to program and perform,
3. It can be applied on one or more variables,
4. It is appropriate for both categorical and continuous variables,
5. Arbitrary swaps can create unusual combinations of the records.
6. The statistical comparison of the two datasets (original and swapped) may require additional tests. The storage and computation stages may take extra time and effort.
7. The technique may weaken the statistical relationship between the variables. It also may distort the regression and correlation test results of the variables.

The dataset of tourists which are registered in hotel facilities is presented in Table 9. To construct a data swap structure, first, we swap ethnic origins within occupation. The ethnic origins of the customers 1 and 4; 2 and 5; 3 and 7 are swapped. Second, we swap the occupations within each ethnic origin. Similarly, customer 1's and customer 3's occupation are swapped; as well as customer 2's and customer 7's. The same number of records should be swapped within each class (Dalenius and Reiss, 1982).

In order to swap continuous variables, the other variants of data swapping such as rank based proximity and enhanced swap procedures have been suggested (Moore, 1996).

CONCLUSION

Various data structures such as longitudinal data, transactional data, multidimensional or relational data, streaming or dynamic data have been produced from tourist activities, especially from MICE industry. While protecting personal data privacy, the most appropriate data anonymization techniques which deal with data structures, semantics and utility of data, regulations, business environment, privacy require-

Table 9. Tourists' ethnic origin and occupation attributes swap

Customer	Ethnic Origin	After Swap (Ethnic Origin)	Occupation	After Swap (Occupation)	Number of Services Registered
1	W	A	Art Photographer	Geologist	2
2	A	W	Architect	Geologist	4
3	W	A	Geologist	Art Photographer	4
4	A	W	Art Photographer	Art Photographer	3
5	W	A	Architect	Architect	5
6	A	A	Architect	Architect	7
7	A	W	Geologist	Architect	6

ments and knowledge discovery should be preferred. By data anonymization, it must be ensured that the confidentiality of the data is preserved, data transparency requirements and legal obligations are met throughout the data lifecycle processes.

As stressed by Cavoukian (2011), data privacy must be the default mode of operations. In this way, personal data privacy protection mechanisms need to be developed from the very beginning of the operations of an organization. While executing this task, two dimensions of personal data privacy (user and holder privacy) must be considered together and most relevant approach (data-driven or computation-driven) should be adopted by designing software systems and engineering strategies on personal data privacy.

Personal data privacy protection can be assumed as optimization under various constraints. In order to achieve optimal privacy of personal data, the tradeoff between utility and privacy is a challenging issue. Moreover, in big data scenarios, "how data anonymization techniques could be applied to streaming personal data or big-data related sources such as check-ins, rate and reviews, travel flows, tourists' spatial behaviors within or without the conference, event, exhibition etc., and other digital footprints in MICE industry" is a cumbersome process. Powerful data privacy tools that detect personal privacy breaches and combine diverse sources of tourism activities are most important aspects of personal data privacy protection. These tools should preserve the statistical inferences of original dataset.

The subject of anonymization processes and the protection of personal data requires multidisciplinary approaches. Developing only technical methods or taking only legal measures can lead to an overprotective, obstructive, or negligent situation. Therefore, the scope and limits of personal data privacy protection should be considered as a specific solution and the nature of the data (whether it consists of sensitive data or not), data classifications by data subjects and privacy levels, the variety and size of the data should be known.

With the new data protection framework of EPDS (2018), "data protection by design" and "privacy enhanced technologies" become mandatory tools for a better protection. While all data protection requirements must be considered in the design process, also the design decisions must take account of the data protection features of the chosen technological approaches. Modules and functions for re-use should be chosen so that they do not perform processing operations, including the collection of data which are not necessary for the purpose of the system. Adequate measures should be designed into IT systems that allow adequate management of retention time and perform necessary subsequent actions such as e.g. anonymization or deletion. Furthermore, additional safeguards should be used such as encryption and multi-level access controls to mitigate high risk processing if a dataset especially consists of tourists' sensitive data e.g. physical/mental health data, financial data, racial/ethnic origin, political opinion or other sensitive data. Besides that, the information channels must be open between the parties (data owner and holder) and IT systems can be directly accessible to the individuals while data is processed. The system should be able to provide the information about data processing via its interface.

The organizations also have some obligations to provide following elements of the processing operations to its users. The identity of personal data holders (the organization or authorized legal representatives or any other organizations which have controllership responsibility) and the type of personal data which are being processed, the purposes of collecting and processing personal data and the definition of recipients of the personal data are the key questions to be asked. The responsibility of meeting and event organisers must continue in regards to the data they have previously, especially combining both their own data and those gathered from the third parties. The GDPR is broad yet it gives duty to the meeting organizers to get permission for benefiting from the data, having a responsible manner before and after an event.

EU GDPR is a crucial regulation to protect the tourists' personal data. The intense tourist or delegate flow in MICE industry also leads to an immense sharing of sensitive data. To control or manage the data privacy, ethical mechanisms also needs to be developed and the meeting industry should comply the data to GDPR.

REFERENCES

Aldossary, S., & Allen, W. (2016). Data security, privacy, availability and integrity in cloud computing: Issues and current solutions. *International Journal of Advanced Computer Science and Applications*, *7*(4), 485–498. doi:10.14569/IJACSA.2016.070464

Alshboul, Y., Wang, Y., & Nepali, R. K. (2015, August). *Big data life cycle: threats and security model.* Paper presented at the 21st Americas Conference on Information Systems, Fajardo, Puerto Rico.

Blyth, A., & Kovacich, G. L. (2006). *Information Assurance*. Springer.

Brown, I., & Marsden, C. T. (2013). *Regulating Code: Good Governance and Better Regulation in the Information Age*. The MIT Press.

Cavoukian, A. (2011). *Privacy by design. The 7 foundational principles in Privacy by Design. Strong privacy protection now, and well into the future*. Retrieved from https://www.ipc.on.ca/wp-content/uploads/Resources/7foundationalprinciples.pdf

Cooper, T., Maitland, A., Siu, J., & Wei, K. (2016). *Guarding and growing personal data value: Accenture Report on Personal Data*. Retrieved from https://www.accenture.com/

Davidson, R., & Turner, A. (2017). *IBTM World Trends Watch Report*. Reed Exhibitions.

Defays, D., & Anwar, M. N. (1998). Masking microdata using micro-aggregation. *Journal of Official Statistics*, *14*(4), 449–461.

Directive 95/46/EC of the European Parliament, and the Council of 24 October 1995 on the protection of individuals with regard to the processing of personal data and on the free movement of such data. *Official Journal of the European Communities*, No I. (281):31-50, Oct. 24 1995.

DLA-PIPPER. (2018). *Piperglobal Data Privacy Snapshot 2018: How does your organisation compare?* Retrieved from https://www.dlapiper.com/

EDPS. (2010). *Opinion on privacy in the digital age: "Privacy by Design" as a key tool to ensure citizens' trust in ICTs*. Retrieved from https://secure.edps.europa.eu/EDPSWEB/webdav/site/mySite/shared/Documents/EDPS/PressNews/Press/2010/EDPS-2010-06_Privacy%20in%20digital%20age_EN.pdf

EDPS. (2018). *Guidelines on the protection of personal data in IT governance and IT management of EU institutions*. Retrieved from https://edps.europa.eu/sites/edp/files/publication/it_governance_management_en.pdf

Esayas, S. Y. (2015). The role of anonymisation and pseudonymisation under the EU data privacy rules: Beyond the 'all or nothing' approach. *European Journal of Law And Technology*, *6*(2). Retrieved from http://ejlt.org/article/view/378/569

Esen, M. F., & Turkay, B. (2017). Big data applications in tourism industries. *Journal of Tourism and Gastronomy Studies*, *5*(4), 92–115. doi:10.21325/jotags.2017.140

European Union. (2012). *The Reform of Data Protection of 2012*. Retrieved from https://edps.europa.eu/

European Union. (2016). *European Union agency for network and information security, guidelines for smes on the security of personal data processing*. Retrieved from https://www.enisa.europa.eu/publications/guidelines-for-smes-on-the-security-of-personal-data-processing

Eurostat. (2017). *Early adopters of big data*. European Union Statistical Working Paper. doi:10.2785/762729

Fenich, G. G. (2015). *Planning and Management of Meetings, Expositions, Events, and Conventions*. London, UK: Pearson Education Limited.

FIPPA. c. F.31, R.S.O. (1990). *The freedom of information and protection of privacy act*. Retrieved from http://www.bclaws.ca/

Garcia Alfaro, J., Navarro Arribas, G., Cavalli, A., & Leneutre, J. (2011). Data privacy management and autonomous spontaneous security. In *Proceedings of 5th International Workshop, Dpm 2010 and 3rd International Workshop, SETOP* (vol. 5). Athens, Greece: Springer Science & Business Media. 10.1007/978-3-642-19348-4

Gurkina, A. (2013). *Travel experience in hotels for MICE industry* (Bachelor's thesis). Haaga-Helia University of Applied Sciences, Finland.

Gurses, S., & Danezis, G. (2012). *A critical review of ten years of privacy technology*. Retrieved from https://homes.esat.kuleuven.be

Harris, P. (2018, May). *GDPR: The steps event planners need to follow*. Paper presented at The Trade Show of Imex Frankfurt, Frankfurt, Germany.

Hundepool, A., Van de Wetering, A., Ramaswamy, R., Franconi, L., Polettini, S., Capobianchi, A., . . . Giessing, S. (2008). *μ- ARGUS version 4.2 User's Manuel*. Retrieved from https://ec.europa.eu/eurostat/cros/page/essnet_en

IMEX Group. (2018). *IMEX Frankfurt trade show 2018 show statistics.* Retrieved from https://www.imex-frankfurt.com/show-stats

Information Commissioner's Office (ICO). (2008). *Privacy by Design.* Retrieved from http://ico.org.uk/for_organisations/data_protection/topic_guides/~/media/documents/pdb_report_html/

International Congress and Convention Association. (2013). *A Modern History of International Association Meetings.* Retrieved from https://www.iccaworld.org

Jeon, Y. H. (2012). Impact of big data: Networking considerations and case study. *International Journal of Computer Science and Network Security*, *12*(12), 30–34.

Kaaniche, N., & Laurent, M. (2017). Data security and privacy preservation in cloud storage environments based on cryptographic mechanisms. *Computer Communications*, *111*(10), 120–141. doi:10.1016/j.comcom.2017.07.006

Kadampur, M. A., & Somayajulu, D. V. L. N. (2010). A noise addition scheme in decision tree for, privacy preserving data mining. *Journal of Computers*, *2*(1), 137–144.

Katal, M. W., & Goudar, R. H. (2013). Big data: issues, challenges, tools and good practices. In *Proceedings of IEEE International Conference Contemporary Computing* (*vol. 6*, pp. 404–409). Uttar Pradesh, India: Jaypee Institute of Information Technology & University of Florida. 10.1109/IC3.2013.6612229

Khatibloo, F., Sridharan, S., Stanhope, J., Joyce, R., Liu, S., & Turley, C. (2016). *Consumer Data: beyond first and third party decoding the value of four consumer data types.* Retrieved form https://www.forrester.com/

Kim, S., Park, S., Sun, M. R., & Lee, J. H. (2016). A study of smart beacon-based Meeting, Incentive trip, Convention, Exhibition and Event (MICE) services using big data. In *Proceedings of Information Technology and Quantitative Management (ITQM 2016)* (Vol. 91, pp. 761–768). Seoul, South Korea: National Information Society Agency. doi:10.1016/j.procs.2016.07.072

Koot, M. R. (2012). *Measuring and Predicting Anonymity.* University of Amsterdam. Retrieved from https://pure.uva.nl/

Krugman, C., & Wright, R. R. (2007). *Global meetings and exhibitions.* Hoboken, NJ: John Wiley & Sons, Inc.

Lambert, D. (1993). Measures of disclosure risk and harm. *Journal of Official Statistics*, *9*(2), 313–331.

Liem, C., & Petropoulos, P. (2016). The economic value of personal data for online platforms, firms and consumers. *The London School of Economics Business Review.* Retrieved from http://blogs.lse.ac.uk/businessreview/2016/01/19/

Lin, J. L., & Cheng, Y. W. (2009). Privacy preserving item set mining through noisy items. *Elsevier Expert Systems with Applications*, *36*(3), 5711–5717. doi:10.1016/j.eswa.2008.06.052

Martin, K. E. (2015). Ethical issues in the big data industry. *MIS Quarterly Executive*, *14*(2), 67–85.

Mehmood, A., Natgunanathan, I., Xiang, Y., Hua, G., & Guo, S. (2016). Protection of big data privacy. *IEEE Access: Practical Innovations, Open Solutions*, *4*, 1821–1834. doi:10.1109/ACCESS.2016.2558446

Moerel, L. (2014, February). *Big data protection how to make the draft eu regulation on data protection future proof.* Lecture delivered during the public acceptance of the appointment of professor of Global ICT Law at Tilburg University, Tillburg, The Netherlands.

O'Hara, K. (2016). The seven veils of privacy. *IEEE Internet Computing, 20*(2), 86–91. doi:10.1109/MIC.2016.34

Oommen, B. J., & Fayyoumi, E. (2008). Enhancing Micro-Aggregation Technique by Utilizing Dependence-Based Information in Secure Statistical Databases. In Y. Mu, W. Susilo, & J. Seberry (Eds.), *Information Security and Privacy* (pp. 404–418). Berlin: Springer. doi:10.1007/978-3-540-70500-0_30

Pfitzmann, A., & Hansen, M. (2007). *Anonymity, unlinkability, unobservability, pseudonymity, and identity management – a consolidated proposal for terminology.* Retrieved from http://citeseerx.ist.psu.edu/

Ponemon Institute and IBM. (2017). *Cost of Data Breach Study: Global Overview, Benchmark Research.* Retrieved from http://www.ibm.com

PwC. (2017). *Consumer Intelligence Series: Protect.me.* Retrieved from https://www.pwc.com

Rogers, T. (2008). *Conferences and Conventions: A global industry* (2nd ed.). Oxford, UK: Elsevier. doi:10.1016/B978-0-7506-8544-3.50009-4

Romanosky, S., & Acquisti, A. (2009). Privacy costs and personal data protection: Economic and legal perspectives, *24. Berkeley Technology Law Journal, 24*(3), 1061–1102.

Salvarci, T., Manap, N. S., Davras, G., & Dolmaci, N. (2015). Privacy of personal information in tourism sector. *International Journal of Human Sciences, 12*(1), 236–254. doi:10.14687/ijhs.v12i1.2988

Samarati, P., & Sweeney, L. (1998). Generalizing data to provide anonymity when disclosing information. In *Proceedings of the 17th ACM SIGACT –SIGMOD-SIGARD Symposium on Principles of Database Systems.* New York: Association of Computing Machinery. 10.1145/275487.275508

Sanders, E., Mackenzie, C., Sirk, M., & Pittet, A. (2017, November). *Is your business ready for GDPR and e-privacy regulatory changes?* Paper presented at the 56th annual congress of International Congress and Convention Association (ICCA), Prague, Czech Republic.

Sikošek, M. (2012). A Review of Research in Meetings Management: Some Issues and Challenges. *Academica Turistica, 5*(2), 61–76.

Smagina, N. (2017). The internationalization of the Meetings, Incentives, Conventions and Exhibitions (MICE) industry: Its influences on the actors in the tourism business activity. *Journal of Economics and Management, 27*(1), 95–113.

Song, H., & Liu, H. (2017). Predicting tourist demand using big data. In Z. Xiang & D. R. Fesenmaier (Eds.), *Analytics in Smart Tourism Design, Tourism on the Verge* (pp. 13–29). Springer International Publishing.

Spiekerman, S., & Cranor, L. F. (2009). Engineering privacy. *IEEE Transactions on Software Engineering, 35*(1), 67–82. doi:10.1109/TSE.2008.88

Sweeney, L. (2002). K-anonymity: A model for protecting privacy. *International Journal of Uncertainty, Fuzziness and Knowledge-based Systems*, *10*(5), 557–570. doi:10.1142/S0218488502001648

The International Association of Privacy Professionals. (2017). *IAPP-EY annual privacy governance report.* Retrieved from https://iapp.org/

Top Banana and the Institute of Internal Communication. (2015). *Technology destroying trust in business- but events can fix it.* Retrieved from http://www.meetpie.com/Modules/NewsModule/newsdetails.aspx?t=Technology-destroying-trust-in-business-but-events-can-fix-it&newsid=20501

Torra, V. (2017). *Data privacy: foundations, new developments and the big data challenge*. New York: Springer. doi:10.1007/978-3-319-57358-8

Vaidya, J., Clifton, C., & Zhu, M. (2006). *Privacy preserving data mining*. Springer.

Venkataramanan, N., & Shriram, A. (2017). Data privacy: principles and practice. Boca Raton, FL: CRC Press: Taylor and Francis Group.

Voigt, P., & Von dem Bussche, A. (2017). *The EU general data protection regulation (GDPR): A practical guide*. Berlin, Germany: Springer International Publishing. doi:10.1007/978-3-319-57959-7

Z. W., &, L. S. (2009). *Advances in intelligent information systems: Studies in computational intelligence*. Berlin, Germany: Springer International Publishing.

KEY TERMS AND DEFINITIONS

Attribute and Record Suppression: In attribute suppression, sensitive attributes are removed as a single cell, tuple or entire column from the dataset. Instead of the entire column (variable), only specific records are removed from the dataset in record suppression.

Big Data: In MICE industry, it is a common tool in following and tracking some useful information in regards to reaching the targeted meetings' location history, subject details, national representatives, local ambassadors, hosting organizations and contact details of sponsors that supported those meetings, events or exhibitions.

Data Privacy: The term refers to the confidentiality of information that one has and other parties are not allowed to share it without a consent of the data owner. Privacy is a measure of control for individuals about their personal information.

Data Protection and Anonymization: Data protection is a task of safeguarding personal or sensitive data which are complex and widely distributed. Data anonymization is a process which generates solutions for threats and privacy problems that are related to personal data.

Data Swapping and Micro-Aggregation: Data swapping refers to permutation or shuffling that rearranges data by exchanging the values. Micro-aggregation is a perturbative technique which reduces the utility of data by creating new singular combinations in the dataset.

Global Recoding: In global recording, discrete or continuous numerical variables can be aggregated into a predefined class.

MICE Industry: MICE is an industry that refers to meetings, incentives, conventions, and exhibitions.

Noise Adding: This is applied to numerical values and the original values are changed by positive or negative deterioration with adding or multiplying a random value at certain ratios to quantitative attributes that are required to be protected.

Personal Data: It is the data that needs to be protected if the subject person does not prefer to share it with other parties.

Chapter 24
Public Administration Curriculum-Based Big Data Policy-Analytic Epistemology:
Symbolic IoT Action-Learning Solution Model

Emmanuel N. A. Tetteh
Norwich University, USA & Action Learning, Action Research Association, USA

ABSTRACT

The equilibration that underscores the internet of things (IoT) and big data analytics (BDA) cannot be underestimated at the behest of real-life social challenges and significant policy data generated to redress the concerns of epistemic communities, such as political policy actors, stakeholders, and the citizenry. The cognitive balancing of new information gathered by BDA and assimilated across the IoT is at the crossroads of ascertaining how the growing increases of such BDA can be better managed to transition from the big data state of disequilibration to reach a more stable equilibrium of policy data usefulness. In the quest for explicating the equilibration of policy data usefulness, an account of the curriculum-based MPA policy analysis and analytics concentration program at Norwich University is described as a case example of big data policy-analytic epistemology. The case study offers a symbolic ideology of an IoT action-learning solution model as a recommendation for fostering the stable equilibration of policy data usefulness.

ORGANIZATION BACKGROUND

This section provides an introductory viewpoint of the background on the case history of the organization underscoring the experiential learning context of the curriculum-based Master of Public Administration (MPA) Policy Analysis and Analytics (PAA) concentration program at Norwich University (NU). Since its inception in 1819, NU, founded by Captain Alden Partridge, a former United States Military Academy Superintendent, has remained well-committed to the philosophy of experiential learning for preparation

DOI: 10.4018/978-1-5225-7432-3.ch024

of traditional-age and nontraditional-age students in a Corps of Cadets and as civilians to advance future societal leadership, service professionalism, and business industries (Norwich University, 2014a). Building upon the works of Dewey, Lewin, and Piaget, Kolb (1984) made a significant contribution to the experiential learning theorization model. According to Kolb, experiential learning fosters the creation of knowledge through critical thinking and persistent adaptation to community engagement, as can be attested to or derived by the process of concrete experience, and also modified by reflective learning, conceptual evaluation, and active investigation (Bergsteiner, Avery, & Neumann, 2010; Kolb, 1984).

By simplifying Kolb's theorization, the experiential learning model has been conceptualized as "an experience or problem situation; a reflective phase in which the learner examines the experience and creates learning from his/her reflection; and an application phase in which the new knowledge or skills are applied to a new problem or situation" (National Institute of Food and Agriculture, 2017, p. 1). As a coeducational institution of experiential learning pedagogy and andragogy in Northfield, Vermont, as well as one of America's six senior military institutions of higher learning and the initiation of the Reserve Officers' Training Corps (ROTC), NU offers various traditional learning and distance-learning baccalaureate and graduate degree programs to approximately 3,500 students (Norwich University, 2015).

Recognizing its enormous contribution to the ROTC, along with its training of military officers and non-military learners for various careers in the business enterprise, government agencies, and military service, as well as for the pursuit of academic degrees, NU has evolved in many significant ways over its almost 200 years. In 2014, it began the *Forging the Future* initiative in preparation for its bicentennial celebration in 2019 (Norwich University, 2010, 2014a). This five-year campaign for the bicentennial celebration is geared toward fostering an increased level of innovative learning atmosphere through high-tech pedagogical and restructuring of top-notch facilities to contribute to the university's vitality of service innovation to the nation (Norwich University, 2014a).

In keeping with the *Forging the Future* campaign initiatives and in alignment with its mission mandate, NU's College of Graduate and Continuing Studies (CGCS) has resoundingly remained more committed to providing lifelong learners with dynamic experiential learning model. This dynamic experiential learning paradigm is structured on the balance between learners' real-life challenges and the application of:

- A collaborative action-learning model;
- Action research modalities;
- Knowledge and process management protocols;
- Public service leadership via the traditional face-to-face teaching/learning model and the open and distance learning (ODL) framework of fostering pragmatic learning (Norwich University, 2014b).

Accredited by the New England Association of Schools and Colleges, the University's Board of Trustees adopted its mission mandate as:

To give our youth an education that shall be American in its character–to enable them to act as well as to think–to execute as well as to conceive–'to tolerate all opinions when reason is left free to combat them' – to make moral, patriotic, efficient, and useful citizens, and to qualify them for all those high responsibilities resting upon a citizen in this free republic. (Norwich University, 2010, p. 22)

By way of operationalizing this mission mandate, the essential linkages between the NU mission mandate and its organizational governance structure are to stimulate core objectives, as well as to facilitate effective decision making, policy-making process, career capacity building, functioning systems development, public service values' enhancement, and translation of these initiatives into the most effective and efficient delivery of services. It thus goes to show that the management of organizational core objectives and relationships within levels of management, task performances, and adaptation to the organization's changing environment could coordinate the dynamic dimensional structures of the organizational functioning systems to shape its governance structure. An organization's functioning systems reflect the dynamic dimension of its symbolic governance structure involving the hierarchical or democratic pattern of activities and behaviors, the relationships among the levels of people in authority, the reporting system that shapes task performances, and adaptation to its changing environment (Fuller, 2008).

As opposed to a hierarchical government structure, NU organizational culture is characterized by shared governance (Norwich University, 2014b) as epitomized by a democratic governance structure model in keeping with its strategic mission mandate. A hierarchical government structure model entails a president-to-management decision-making process, whereas the context of accountability, authority, and information-sharing model is mainly a one-way flow from the top that works downward. The democratic governance structure model, however, fosters a participatory form of the information-sharing model and promotes a circular-structure accountability model of disseminating the decision-making process (Tetteh, 2004). Thus, there is a higher level of equilibration in the decision-making process within the democratic governance structure model.

As the CGCS embarks upon disseminating NU mission mandate, one of the seven MPA program concentrations, the PAA concentration, has been developed in recognition of the need to equip graduate-level students with the knowledge base and technical know-how regarding the methods of policy analysis for handling Big Data policy-analytic epistemology via the Internet of Things (IoT) ecosystem platform of the ODL framework. Epistemology generally deals with the questions concerning the nature, scope, and sources of the systems of adequate and inadequate knowledge that shape the reality of human worldviews. The Big Data policy-analytic epistemology is, therefore, an intended inquiry into ways that the large ever-increasing Big Data across the epistemic communities can be better explored using data analysis software tools via the IoT ecosystem framework to shape a public policy decision-making process. Unlike the other six MPA program concentrations (i.e., Criminal Justice, Public Works, Municipal Governance, International Development and Influence, Nonprofit Management, Fiscal Management), the PAA concentration is unique in that it has an accompanying web-based data analytic lab for the facilitation of Big Data analytics (BDA).

SETTING THE STAGE

This section provides an overview of the case vignette into the data epistemology that shapes the MPA curriculum-based BDA of the IoT ecosystem framework. With the appointment of Dr. Rosemarie Pelletier, MPA and Information Security and Assurance Program Director, and under the collaborative support of Dr. William Clements, Vice President and Dean of College of Graduate and Continuing Studies (CGCS), the PAA concentration were developed with unique curriculum-based BDA methods of policy analysis. The MPA curriculum-based BDA methods of policy analysis involve a wide range of data analysis software tools and data analysis methodologies (Pelletier & Tetteh, 2015) employed in the analysis of public policy data epistemology.

Public Policy Data Epistemology

The public policy data epistemology recognizes the power of the IoT ecosystem framework for which the equilibration of the BDA is facilitated. This allows for the continuum of evolving Big Data of the multifaceted public, organizational, and humankind problems or situational needs that permeate and transcend all fabric of the human society to be tackled for problem resolution. By way of tackling such an array of complex issues, the MPA curriculum-based BDA focuses on extensive methods of policy analysis at the systems level of the epistemic communities and the interactions of system-level decisions on public policy and its effects. The policy-related research is thus intended to explore BDA epistemology of policy structure, analytic process, and policy outcomes related to organizational service delivery systems as funded by public and nonprofit sources.

Equilibration of BDA Epistemology of the Epistemic Communities

The BDA epistemology entails fostering the equilibration of coherent and consistent policy data analysis that structure the analysis of Big Data shaping the uncultivated data and the cultivated data via the use of data analytics software tools across the IoT ecosystem framework to aid in the symbolic ideology of IoT action-learning solution. The equilibration of coherent and consistent policy data analysis focuses on the accessibility of policy decision making, the acceptability of policy decision, the availability of policy, and the usability of policy initiatives. It also includes distributive policy channels, cost-benefit analysis of policy initiatives, efficiency, and effectiveness of policy initiatives. It cites the use of quantitative and qualitative approaches as suitable methods of inquiry to redress policy dilemmas and urban planning problems of the epistemic communities. It thus indicates that the identification and analysis of policy problems involve a comprehensive understanding of the complex policy issues of the epistemic communities and the applicable policy analysis methods for handling multidimensional policy data cases. Therefore, the would-be public administrators and/or policy analysts are expected to possess a working knowledge of the various software tools for the facilitation of BDA epistemology toward problem resolution and policy decision making in the public sector and nonprofit arena of the epistemic communities (Tetteh, Core Faculty Lead, Policy Analysis and Analytics concentration, 2015c).

CASE DESCRIPTION

Device Entities to Support the IoT Ecosystem Framework of the Epistemic Communities

In this case study chapter, the importance of emerging data analytic relevance of ranking job functions and data analysis software tools structured as device entities to support the IoT ecosystem framework of the epistemic communities are explored. The means by which such data analysis software tools are used via the IoT ecosystem framework of the epistemic communities in policy data analysis within the age of BDA to account for an innovative curriculum-based PAA program model in public administration are also explored. The IoT ecosystem framework encompasses cross-domain of all components of data analytics software tools, tech-enabled systems or systemic technologies, and techno-politics data of the epistemic communities. The IoT ecosystem framework enables governments, businesses, and consumers to create BDA values by connecting to their IoT devices using the systemic technologies, including cloud computing, application layers, remotes, dashboards, data storage, networks, gateways, analytics, and security infrastructures (Farooq & Kunz, 2017; Zdravković et al., 2018).

Epistemic Communities

The seminary work of Adler and Haas (1992) and Haas (1992) underscored the definitional orientation of the epistemic communities as a network of political policy actors, stakeholders, citizenry, and service professionals with inherent capabilities whose ethos of shared knowledge are shaped by policy-relevant knowledge, policy coordination, policy analytic data, policy innovation, a shared set of principled belief systems, mutual expectations, social action, and shared interpretations. For Haas (1992), the epistemic communities play an essential role in explaining the network of policy-relevant cause-and-effect relationships, elucidate the intricate connection between policy issues, delineate policy self-interest, and aid in the policy-relevant formation. In recent years, the legal profession and related sectors for career advancement (e.g., legal occupations, tech businesses, public service careers, government, state and city jobs) have all called for the emerging workforce of the epistemic communities to be prepared for data analytic relevance of ranking job functions in the age of BDA (EY Building a Better Working World, 2014; Frey & Osborne, 2017).

Data Analytic Relevance of Ranking Job Functions in the Epistemic Communities

Data analytic relevance of ranking job functions in the epistemic communities include analytic data networking for legal coding, the hermeneutics of data analysis, the depiction of data visualization, data process management, and automated concept or subject indexing text and classification for retrieval (Francesconi & Peruginelli, 2007; Koniaris, Anagnostopoulos, & Vassiliou, 2017; Zhang & Koppaka, 2007). An *analytic data network for legal coding* engages in strategic data coding of litigation analytics to unlock data-driven perceptions into case litigation and associated case laws, historical insights, and trends toward strengthening case strategy and managing client expectations for case outcomes (Koniaris et al., 2017). The *hermeneutics of data analysis* focuses on the utilization of various data analysis methods and interpretations to shape public policy decision making and stakeholder insight of data findings' usefulness.

The *depiction of data visualization* involves the efforts of policy data analysts and decision makers to help stakeholders to understand the significance of data findings using data visualization software to create mind maps, concept mappings, graphical mappings, pie charts, data tables, and infographics to understand policy data to aid in streamlining a policy decision-making process. *Data process management* entails the management of procuring, authenticating, loading, guarding, and processing required policy data to ensure user-friendliness, dependability, and data usefulness for stakeholder administrative process. *Automated concept or subject indexing text and classification for retrieval* is conceptualized as:

Denotes non-intellectual, machine-based processes of subject indexing as defined by the library science community: derived and assigned indexing using both alphabetical and classification indexing systems, for the purposes of improved information retrieval. The rationale for combining them into one entry is the fact that the underlying machine-based principles are rather similar, especially when it comes to application to textual documents. (Golub, 2017, para. 12)

Other functional areas include symbolism of data simulations, semantics-based legal citation network viewers, legislation network construction, a network of instrument data analytic citation, and policy codification of network data analysis of legal basis (Francesconi & Peruginelli, 2007; Koniaris et al., 2017; Zhang & Koppaka, 2007). The *symbolism of data simulations* involves data modeling, mapping, and simplifying, using the executions of a system of symbolism, depictions, and those of metaphorical constructs to convey data findings' reports. The *semantics-based legal citation network viewer* involves the use of legal research tools to generate citation relevance between policy cases and issues within the legal and judicial field of practice to enable the legal professionals identify broad-range of case citations more efficiently and streamlined legal case research for attorneys, legal scholars, and judges (Zhang & Koppaka, 2007). *Legislation network construction* is comprised of the legal collection, classification, and analysis of a several normative-focused policies, issues-based information gathering, and legal case documents derived from legal document databases that are cross-referred to one another to aid in the promulgation of laws by legislators and policymakers (Francesconi & Peruginelli, 2007; Koniaris et al., 2017).

The *network of instrument data analytic citation* focuses on deploying the predictive data analytics of a broad range methods to identify patterns and distinctive trends in data to attain increased valuation concerning ways to operationalize BDA to drive strategic organizational analysis of value propositions and forecast trends for embedded data analytics across organizational culture, technical dimensions, and data analytics infrastructure (Chen, 2013; Halper, 2014). Thus, predictive data analytics for a network of instrument data analytics citation is instrumental in predicting functional data, operational strategies, cultural dynamics, and forecasting future trends for organizational vitality. The *policy codification of network data analysis of legal basis* provides policy analytic data procedure of application framework guidelines for the adoption of network security, reliability rules, interoperability, operational procedures, suspected control system vulnerabilities, and network codes that are embedded into regulatory data structures.

Additional areas of data analytic relevance for career functions in the epistemic communities include concept-based searching, ranking, and analytic indexing techniques; equilibration of knowledge-based data epistemology and analytic management systems; network of regulations analyst and data pragmatism; representation model for legal case data analysis; and comprehensive legal ontology of authority data codification (Ashley, 2009; Karmakar & Swarnakar, 2017; Koniaris et al., 2017; Mazzega, Bourcier, & Boulet, 2009). *Concept-based searching, ranking, and analytic indexing techniques* entail data search engine indexing of the accurate information retrieval storage system, along with document clustering to optimize speed and performance during search queries for relevant documents (Karmakar & Swarnakar, 2017). The *equilibration of knowledge-based data epistemology and analytic management system* focuses on the strategic inquiry of the leveraging of cloud-based BDA and the balancing of premeditated exploration to successfully gather and handle BDA and information management that can be readily made accessible for enhanced decision making in organizations (Shorfuzzaman, 2017).

The *network of regulations analyst and data pragmatism* involves data information asset management; regulations concerning the construction, design, and production of work equipment; and compliance framework. The *representation model for legal case data analysis* focuses on the quality of representation and legal services provided to clientele shaped by information-rich data analysis of case law model and application. The *comprehensive legal ontology of authority data codification* involves the process of arranging laws or rules according to established precedence, critical functional systems of judicial rulings, cross-case analogies, case-based legal reasoning, and representative decision justifications' application (Ashley, 2009; Bagby & Mullen, 2007).

Daunting Challenges of the Equilibration of Data Deontological and Teleological Hermeneutics

The importance of data analytics that considers the IoT ecosystem in the period of Big Data can be, in part, reminiscent to the growing concern that public policy problems and associated data analytic software devices are becoming increasingly enormous, but the policy decision makers' quest for data management solutions is also becoming somewhat more elusive. The linkages between IoT data analytic demand and policy data supply are thus faced with daunting challenges for policy decision makers who want to gain some degree of hermeneutical insight into the data analytical viewpoints and vice versa. The public policy analysis that implicates the policy decision-making framework, however, might require the equilibration of data deontological and teleological hermeneutics being shaped by the epistemological inquisition into the BDA (Ashley, 2009). The equilibration of data deontological hermeneutics tends to focus on the balance between the ontology of analogical BDA and the means by which the rightness or wrongness of data analytics might be conceived to implicate the sense-making process of the BDA to aid a formidable data interpretation.

The equilibration of data teleological hermeneutics focuses on the alignment between the fitness or suitability of challenging policy data interest interpretation and the ontological interpretation of analogical BDA epistemology. It thus follows that one way to make a better sense of the BDA is to know the best ways to handle the immense knowledge intended to be made from the data analytic stimulations (Kettl, 2018). The ontological interpretation of analogical BDA is therefore structured on the premise that no one has a monopoly on the epistemology of knowledge inquisition, and that "the *gap* between what we [*may*] *know*—and what we can agree that we [*might*] *know*—and what we [*might*] *need* to *know* is [becoming increasily] enormous" (emphasis added, Kettl, 2018, p. 2). Thus, due to its unique, cutting-edge program innovation, the PAA concentration offered through the ODL dashboard in the MPA degree program at NU is discussed to account for the importance of BDA as a framework for the symbolic ideology of IoT policy action-learning solutions' mechanism of the epistemic communities.

PUBLIC ADMINISTRATION BIG DATA EPISTEMIC COMMUNITY POLICYMAKING

Gaps in Data-Driven Policies of the Epistemic Community in Public Administration Field

More than two decades ago, Thomas (1997) argued that the epistemic community idea had not made inroads into the field of public administration. There appears, however, to be an emerging paradigm shift in the domain of public service management for which Big Data are being generated to tackle public policy issues of the epistemic communities (Cinquegrani, 2002; Dunlop, 2017; Wu & He, 2009). The enterprise of the prefix "public" in public administration (PA) is highly diverse, multitask-oriented, and shaped by variation of sectors whose spheres of operation encompass agencies, public policy creativities, and service policy delivery systems publicly funded with the transactional resources of the city, state, government, and citizenry of the epistemic communities (Basu, 2016; Fard, 2012; Van Der Waldt, 2014).

The service policy delivery systems are characterized by data-driven policies and service-linkages rooted in the public values and stakeholder interests, as well as the balance between the political ideology and technical dimensions of system changes geared toward providing policy-based services and programs to the epistemic communities (Melaville, Blank, & Asayesh, 1993). It thus follows that the domain of the "public" in PA is not only at the *heart* of PA, but it is also shaped by the data epistemology and ideology of politics and social values of service functionality, policymaking, and budgetary resources to serve the public good. This data epistemology that structures the public good is operationalized in stakeholder ideals to which societal civility, democratic governance systems, interest groups, public service, values of the citizenry, situational needs of society, and functional systems of a democratic society can be said to shape the public policy decision-making processes.

Dynamic Challenges in the Data-Driven Policymaking Process

The functional systems of a democratic society tend to reflect the operationalization of dynamic policy-making process that shapes democratic governance systems, organizational governance structure, and the socio-economic sectors, including education, nonprofit, for-profit or the proprietary sectors. The dynamics of a policymaking process involve deeply held values, different perceptions regarding the causes of social problems, and appropriate service policy impact that is responsive to those problems within the domain of the political propositions or the ideological policy needs of the epistemic communities. Deficiencies in the data-driven policies as shaped by the imposition of public service values, for which the service policy delivery systems are operationalized to meet the needs satisfaction of the epistemic communities, can thus create problems for the public policy decision-making processes. In other words, the dynamics of data-driven policies generated to shape important policy development and implementation processes can be productive while some aspects might be ineffective in addressing the desirable goals of the epistemic communities' policy interests.

Contextual Equilibration Challenges Structuring Data-Driven Policymaking Functionality Process

The political proposition of a data-driven policy dynamic might introspect sound as atypical concerning the equilibration challenges that structure the ideological values, perceptions, and beliefs of the epistemic communities. The policymaking processes, however, might occasionally seem to be self-centered toward gaining egocentric policy agendas of the epistemic communities. It may be argued otherwise, but the explicit representation of the data-driven policy interests inherent within the epistemic communities might show adversary policy interests that often undermine the potential strength of the citizenry's various needs. The context of this adversarial relationship, while posing a threat to the data-driven policy interests of the epistemic communities, may also revolutionize the service policy delivery systems toward meeting the citizenry's satisfaction. Therefore, the crucial goal is to bridge the growing gap between the productive elements of the data-driven policies and the climate of service operation toward forecasting collaborative service policies and decisions to satisfy the needs of the society at large. Figure 1 illustrates the dynamics of equilibration that structure the PA domain of the Big Data-driven policy perception that impacts social action of public policy decision-making processes within the epistemic communities.

The contextual working capabilities of the "public" in PA are administered or executed by the "administration" component of the Big Data-driven policies in the PA, so it can also be said that it is this "administration" aspect of the PA that gives the soul of PA its systemic administration functionality. However, the systemic "administration" functionality of PA often gets caught up in the multiplicity of data-driven epistemic community policies due to the competing needs of the public and interfaces with budgetary resource limitations. This tends to raise questions regarding the ways to ensure that the budgetary resource limitations are adequately and equitably used to meet the variations of stakeholders' policy interests or to satisfy the public needs of the epistemic communities. Response to such needs-based questions calls for the equilibration of BDA epistemology as a symbolic ideology of the IoT action-learning solution model that structures the connections between the "public" and "administration" components in the PA of the epistemic communities. The equilibration of BDA epistemology as the symbolic ideology of the IoT action-learning solution model is thus characterized by the contextual and topological data analytic paradigms that shape the instrumentality framework of data management.

Contextual Instrumentalities of Topological Data Analytic Paradigms of the Internet of Things

In the policymaking, analysis, and implementation processes depicted in Figure 1, both qualitative textual data analysis and quantitative statistical data analysis rely upon contextual and topological data analytic paradigms of political ideology and policy action-learning data management instrumentality framework. The topological data analytic paradigms are intended to transport data understanding beyond the "plain meaning" of words to diagnose that words or the worldviews of the epistemic communities can mean

Figure 1. Domain of data-driven policy perception impacting social action of public policy decision-making processes in the epistemic communities

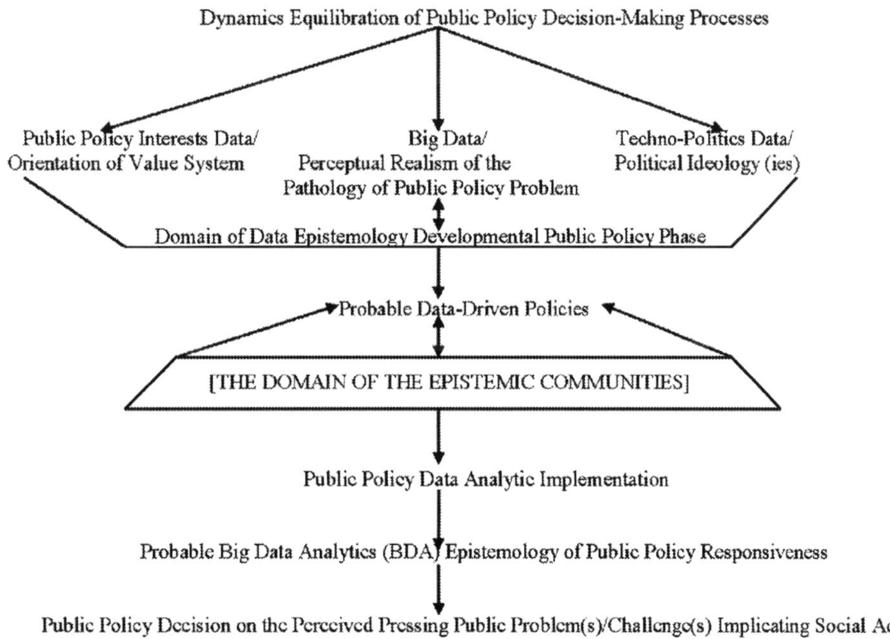

many things. Those meanings surrounding the words or worldviews, however, must be consistent and coherent to shape policy data such that the meaning of a specific word or worldview might need to be shaped by the other words around it (Fard, 2012; Krim, Gentimis, & Chintakunta, 2016). Probably the best known standard topological data analytic paradigm is the use of symbolic data isomorphic interactions of metaphorical computation or metaphorical concept mapping, which is an implied comparison that uses a word or phrase figuratively applied to one object to convey something different (Bench-Capon & Gordon, 2009; Tetteh, 2010, 2015a). Metaphors are used in the qualitative data analysis as symbolic data isomorphic interactions to serve as: (i) data-condensing or data-reducing devices, (b) pattern-making or data-building devices, (c) decentering or symbolic kaleidoscopic devices, and (d) the means or vehicles for connecting data to theory (Miles, Huberman, & Saldaña, 2014).

As a core, lead faculty, and senior lecturer since the inception of the development of the data analytics courses in the PAA concentration at NU, Tetteh (2015b) has always held the notion that the décor of the symbolic ideology of IoT instrumentalities that may structure analytic data paradigms can be conceived by methods of action-learning solutions and policy data statistics to help mitigate the pressing social issues facing policy stakeholders. Moreover, the plethora of policy data generated through the policy-making process can make better sense to stakeholders if it is translated into policy statistics and descriptive policies to inform further action-learning solutions of policy implementation. Policymaking and planning can therefore be viewed as structured by complex bureaucratic contexts and cross-sector collaborations. To comprehend such policy complexity, the policy-student administrator must develop a policy capacity of bureaucratic expertise for data-based policy analysis in keeping with the values of public service governance. Pertinent to the capacity building of bureaucratic expertise, the would-be policy analyst is thus expected to gain practical knowledge and insight into the multifaceted issues and political ideologies that shape policy action learning, planning, formation, and dissemination processes.

CURRENT FOCUSED CHALLENGES

Curriculum-Based Big Data Policy-Analytic Epistemology Model in Norwich University MPA Policy Analysis and Analytics Concentration

Heuristic Epistemology of Big Data Analytics Framework

The Norwich MPA PAA concentration recognizes the role of Big Data analytics (BDA) epistemology as a framework for heuristic epistemology, wherein industry-based and community-based Big Data are made useful based on hands-on data analysis findings and reports to policy decision makers. For Armstrong (2009), the heuristic epistemology "comprises of three symbiotic and heuristic modalities, namely, the Triad of *Apperception, Appraisal*, and *Appropriation*, undergirded by the understanding that the notion of truth is a type of virtue" (emphasis added, p. 1). These "virtuous truth" data-driven policies can thus be conceived of as the equilibration of coherent and consistent data-generated knowledge of the contextual data triangulation structuring apperception, appraisal, and appropriation techniques that underscores the worldviews of the epistemic communities.

Therefore, through the facilitation of apperception, appraisal, and appropriation processes, such data triangulation techniques are intended to ensure that the equilibration of coherent validation and consistent cross-verification of the "virtuous truth" data-driven policies is generated from the epistemic communities' worldviews via the IoT ecosystem framework. Given the complexity of BDA epistemology for which such contextual data triangulation techniques are thus warranted, Armstrong (2009) asserted that the heuristic epistemology "seeks to bring to light the contributing causes of divergence and divisiveness over opposing truth claims, which, in turn, hinder the knowing process of moving from error or ignorance to truth appropriated" (p. 2). However, when valid "virtuous truth" is gathered from the epistemic communities' worldviews, it can offer credence to the equilibration of the data-driven policies.

Discrepant Policy Case Challenges of the Epistemic Communities

The challenge is that the discrepant policy cases inherent in the epistemic communities' data worldviews can offer information-rich viewpoints and thus should not be ignored if the "virtuous truth" data-driven policies are intended to meet the threshold of the coherent validation and consistent cross-verification processes. Consequently, the means by which the "divergence and divisiveness over opposing truth claims" can be handled to shape the public policy data are imperative for ensuring that all of the voices that shape the varied, competing, and complex self-interests of the epistemic communities are given careful consideration in the facilitation of the BDA epistemology as symbolic ideology of IoT action-learning solution model.

Equilibration of Apperception, Appraisal, and Appropriation Techniques

The *apperception technique* serves as a fulcrum for redirecting the discrepant policy cases that shape the divergence and divisiveness data in a manner that can complement the enrichment of the epistemic communities' data worldviews. For Armstrong (2009), the *appraisal technique* "diverts the object of enquiry to the subject [by] assessing one's level of apperception and appropriation in order to ensure that the other two modalities do not become static" (p. 3), but is instead useful in enhancing the policy data worldviews of the epistemic communities. The *appropriation technique* fosters data authentication process of the transfer of data-driven policies to the policy data know-how of shaping a policy decision-making process to implicate social action for the epistemic communities'shared interests.

In the quest of facilitating the equilibration of apperception, appraisal, and appropriation techniques, the emerging powerful computer-assisted software applications and the importance of IoT data mining, data matrix, data reconstruction, data filtering, data recording, data reduction, and data visualization techniques, to name just a few, can be resourcefully useful. With the increasing availability of substantial analytic databases, data analytics software and the computer-assisted software program applications are intended to create a framework for the Norwich MPA PAA concentration by providing a hands-on, cutting-edge innovation of online learning coupled with a data analytic tech-enabled lab known as the *virtual action learning big analytic data* (VAL-BAD) lab.

Virtual Action Learning Big Analytic Data and Computer-Assisted Software Application

Data mining entails "digging" around in large analytic databases to discover relationships among variables of interests, or sometimes until the researcher finds a statistical association that "demonstrates" something of value to demonstrate. *Data matrix* allows the use of computer-assisted software for storing information-rich Big Data to facilitate the coordination in locating of data, data filtering, data coding, data reduction, data reconstruction, data recording, and data visualization. The *data reconstruction* identifies, organizes, and manages the disconnect of intricate and integral data from the compressed sensed data using a network-coding-based file system to regenerate code as its distributed storage coding scheme and creates categorization that fits the coding boundary values and multi-layers of neural network to provide a streamline data summary report for policy decision makers (Chen, 2013; Li & Deng, 2014).

Data filtering involves the process of delineating, identifying, and rectifying outlier values and errors in the analytic data from big raw data to make the analytic data clean for further processing. The *data reduction* has been conceived as "an umbrella term for a suite of technologies—including compression, deduplication, and thin provisioning—that serve to reduce the storage capacity required to handle a given data set" (Pure Storage, 2018, para. 1). *Data visualization* represents the depiction of the data report using graphical models, mind-maps, concept mapping, and other visual portraits to aid data policy formulation and understanding for decision makers.

In the VAL-BAD lab, students begin to use data analysis tools such as Excel, SPSS, and R Statistical Analysis, and then move to explore the online-based Dedoose software application by utilizing relevant policy research methods for statistical analysis, policy planning, and policy problem resolution. The *SPSS* is a statistical data analysis software application for analyzing quantitative data and reporting systems. The *R statistical analysis* is free data analytic software that offers a wide range of statistical applications. The *Dedoose software* is a cloud-based data analytic computing application for collaborative data analysis of qualitative and mixed methods research. Data innovation, however, requires hands-on knowledge based on readily available state-of-the-art industry data analytic software, so students must also be exposed to emerging computer-assisted data analysis software such as NVivo, CAT (Coding Analysis Toolkit), NUDIST, HyperResearch, and Atlas-ti.

The *NVivo software* is an advanced data analytic application for analyzing qualitative and mixed methods research. *CAT* is a free web-based statistical data analytic tool. *NUDIST* and *HyperResearch* are powerful data analysis software used to analyze qualitative data. *Atlas-ti* is a cloud-based data analytic application for analyzing qualitative and mixed methods research. Throughout the PAA concentration, students are expected to work concurrently via the VAL-BAD lab, which is intended to expose them to the data analysis tools, as well as to policy research methods and data analysis techniques. The problems researched and analyzed in the VAL-BAD lab come from "real-world" work with community-based industries, corporations, various government agencies, and entities. Students, faculty, and representatives from "partner" organizations are expected to work together in the VAL-BAD lab to research and analyze data, write reflective reports and publish when required or become necessary to support stakeholders or policy decision makers.

Throughout the courses taken in the PAA concentration, students develop and keep an *Action-Learning Policy Data Analysis Casebook* (RALPDAC) of their hands-on action learning experiences of the VAL-BAD lab. Thus, the drafted RALPDAC is intended to showcase the interplay between course-based learning and work-based learning evident in students' functional resume and consolidation into a potential White Paper publication for career advancement. Students often pursue an education that does not translate into readily gained work industry experience concerning innovative ways of handling vast information. A function resume exposes students to the critical knowledge base on emerging theoretical propositions, as well as to the practical methods of handling trends in industry-led knowledge and data analysis experience. Table 1 provides synopses of the courses offered in the Norwich MPA PAA concentration.

Table 1. Summary of MPA 36-credit degree policy analysis and analytics curriculum-based Big Data policy analytic program model

AD 511: Foundations of Public Administration and Policy--(6 Credits) Among others, this course is intended to introduce students to the theories of public administration, administrative ethics, service accountability, leadership roles, democratic governance systems, organizational governance structure, strategic planning, policy research, critical analysis, and political ideology as implicated by data-driven policies.
AD 545: Politics, Policy, and Planning--(6 Credits) Among others, this course is designed to introduce students to the methods of policy-data analysis software applications such as Excel and SPSS to facilitate the analysis of policy statistics, policy planning, policy resolution, utilization of real-time policy data sets, and implications of politics and action learning in the policy-making process. *This course has an accompanying VAL-BAD lab.*
AD 555: Methods of Policy Analysis--(6 Credits) Among others, this course provides students the opportunity to explore in greater depths the methods of projection analysis, chi-square test, hypothesis testing, and policy analysis techniques using crosscutting research strategies, identifying and gathering data, data analysis, establishing evaluation criteria, and identifying alternatives. *This course has an accompanying VAL-BAD lab.*
AD 565: Policy and Policy Implementation--(6 Credits) Among others, this course is intended to examine data-driven policy complexities and functions at the organizational governance structure level, planning, formulation, iterative process, forecasting activities and effects, evaluation, and implementation, that implicate the behavior of policy actions and adoption. *This course has an accompanying VAL-BAD lab.*
AD 575: Tools for Policy Analysis--(6 Credits) Among others, this course is intended to utilize BDA software tools such as Excel, Dedoose, SPSS, and R applications in examining and analyzing policy cases of the nonprofit sector, sociopolitical environments, and at the federal, state, regional, and urban government levels to aid policy recommendations and implementations to support public policy decision-makers. *This course has an accompanying VAL-BAD lab.*
AD: 585 Economics and Decision Making--(6 Credits) Among others, this course is intended to introduce students to the data-driven policies that implicate a broader scope of administrative leadership, decision-making principles and strategies, financial management, and economic policies as might be utilized by public sector leaders and service industries to shape the state of the economy at both the domestic and global sectors of advancing service innovation. *This course has an accompanying VAL-BAD lab.*

Norwich University (2018). *Online Master of Public Administration Curriculum: Policy Analysis and Analytics Concentration.* Northfield, VT: Author. Retrieved from https://online.norwich.edu/academic-programs/masters/public-administration/overview.

SOLUTIONS AND RECOMMENDATIONS

Equilibration of Big Data Analytics Epistemology of Symbolic Ideology of the Internet of Things Action-Learning Solutions

Since the development of the policy analytics data courses of NU's PAA concentration, it can be conceived that the IoT ecosystem framework has become somewhat confronted with gigantic mountains of BDA epistemology for public administration. This is not, however, due to the discipline of public administration having a monopoly on knowledge (Van Der Waldt, 2014) regarding everything that must be done or whether this is the only field of inquiry that has the know-how (Kettl, 2018). Instead, common ground must be found concerning ways to engage in meaningful BDA epistemology of action-learning solutions. Policy makers are inundated with increasing heaps of Big Data (Kettl, 2018), but some known epistemology data, although not intended, might not only consist of data outliers, inaccurate observations, or perhaps illogical reasoning.

Equilibration of Idiographic and Nomothetic Explanations

It is necessary to make data analytic evidence and accuracy convey the equilibration of idiographic and nomothetic explanations. The idiographic explanation provides insight into the unique, peculiar, and distinctive causes of specific events, actions, or particular conditions of an individual or a single aspect of a situation within the epistemic community. The nomothetic explanation offers an overall or generalized insight into the causal factors among variables or the relationship between elements of conditions or events across the epistemic communities. Consistent with Armstrong's (2009) idea regarding "divergence and divisiveness over opposing truth claims" (p. 2), the data outliers, inaccurate observations, and illogical reasoning can thus be addressed using the equilibria triangulation of apperception, appraisal, and appropriation techniques.

Action Learning Solution

There is an oversupply of vast piles of Big Data across the IoT ecosystem framework (Kettl, 2018; Mohammadi, Al-Fuqaha, Sorour, & Guizani, 2018). It is perhaps for this that the equilibration of BDA epistemology must be shaped by the symbolic ideology of action-learning solutions of insightful precision for the restructuring of the right kind of questions to enable policy decision makers to reach reasonable policy problem resolutions. An action learning solution fosters collaborative methods of reflective practice inquiry, structured in policy data analysis of reflective thought processes and guided by the equilibration of data epistemology directed at tackling context-specific policy issues, capacity building, and coaching mechanism tailored to BDA epistemology of the epistemic communities.

Equilibration, Disequilibration, and Stable Equilibrium of Big Data Analytics Epistemology

Piaget conceived the three models of equilibration (i.e., state of equilibrium, state of disequilibration, more stable equilibrium or re-equilibration) (Boom, 2009; Piaget, 1985) for tackling all questions regarding human cognitive development. Such models can also be adapted to serve as alignment mechanisms for the symbolic ideology of IoT action-learning solution of BDA epistemology. Serving as alignment mechanisms implies that there must be a symbiotic relationship between the three models of equilibration, the triangulation of apperception, appraisal, and appropriation techniques, and the symbolic ideology of IoT action-learning solution of the BDA epistemology. The symbolic ideology of an IoT action-learning solution has become a framework for Big Data gathering, stimulation of techno-politics data, data learning device, and containment of data epistemology ideologies (Gutiérrez-Rubí & Sarsanedas, 2016; Kurban, Peña-López, & Haberer, 2017; Mohammadi et al., 2018).

Techno-politics data can be viewed as policy-based ideological data shaped and garnered by critical informants, political policy actors, citizenry, stakeholders, people, individuals, and/or functional intellectuals whose worldviews are aligned to the context of renewed self-interests, public spheres of politics, management of political action, and understanding of political communication dynamics (Dunlop, 2017; Gutiérrez-Rubí & Sarsanedas, 2016; Kellner, 1998). At the *equilibrium state level*, the modes of thought across the IoT that structure the epistemic communities' worldviews tend to shape techno-politics data.

The *disequilibration state level* tends to foster the identification of shortcomings inherent in the data outliers, inaccurate observation, or illogical reasoning that surfaced during the equilibrium state level to make data analytics evidence and accuracy convey the equilibration of idiographic and nomothetic explanations. This can then lead the epistemic communities to the more *stable equilibrium* or *re-equilibration levels*, at which point the elimination of shortcomings inherent in the data outliers, inaccurate observation, or illogical reasoning that surfaced during the equilibrium levels can bring about the symbolic ideology of IoT action-learning solution. The BDA epistemology ideologies can be conceived as being embedded into the conceptual scheme of political ideology orientation (Gutiérrez-Rubí& Sarsanedas, 2016; Kurban et al., 2017), so it is imperative that the models of equilibration should be aligned with the idealism of political ideology to better facilitate policy data coordination via the symbolic IoT action-learning solution of the BDA epistemology processes.

Conceptual Action-Learning Epistemologies of Political Ideology Scheme

In his 2000 work on *American Government,* Wilson provided a conceptual scheme of political ideology by operationally defining it as "A coherent and consistent set of beliefs about who ought to rule, what principles rulers ought to obey, and what policies rulers ought to pursue" (p. 73). From the standpoint of the Wilsonian operational definition, it can be deciphered that three action-learning epistemologies of conceptual scheme structure the idealism of political ideology: *who ought to rule*[1], *what principles rulers ought to obey*[2], and *what policies rulers ought to pursue*[3]. Consistent with the Wilsonian operational definition, Ball and Dagger (2014) conceptualized political ideology as:

A fairly coherent and comprehensive set of ideas that explains and evaluates social conditions, helps people understand their place in society, and provides a program for social and political action. An ideology, more precisely, performs four functions for people who hold it: the (1) explanatory, (2) evaluative, (3) orientative, and (4) programmatic functions. (p.5)

Thus, the policy data coordination requires the interplay of a coherent and consistent set of beliefs structuring the systemic "administration" functionality of executing and disseminating explanation, evaluation, policy orientation, and policy program initiation to satisfy the needs of the epistemic communities.

Five Action-Learning "P" Epistemology Orientations of the IoT Symbolic Ideology Framework

As depicted in Figure 2, the interplay of policy data coordination is also structured by the three political ideology schemes and triangulation techniques, as well as in responsive alignment with the equilibration, disequilibration, and stable equilibration levels, to aid the facilitation of the symbolic ideology of IoT action-learning solution of the BDA epistemology processes. The symbolic ideology of an IoT action-learning solution is also shaped by the transactional resources of symbolic capital power, which are characterized as a type of policy action, and the source, channel, substance, and directionality of policy initiatives (Fuller, 2008; Nataliia & Elena, 2015). By expanding upon the work of Kettl (2018), it is therefore essential to offer that the action-learning solutions should be reflective of the following five action-learning “P” orientations of the symbolic ideology of IoT ontology to facilitate the equilibration of BDA epistemology processes better:

1. **Policy-Focused Inquisition (PFI):** To what extent can the IoT action-learning solutions of techno-politics data and historical data shaping BDA teach about one’s future policy actions?
2. **Prediction-Based Collaborative Inquisition (PBCI):** In what ways can the collaborative efforts of stakeholders make better policy decisions from the IoT action-learning solutions structuring the predictive BDA of techno-politics to shape knowledge production that implicates positive or constructive results?
3. **Production of Knowledge-Oriented Inquisition (PKOI):** To what extent has the positive implication of knowledge production been accomplished, and how can improvements be made with the IoT action-learning solutions that structure the productive techno-politics data in shaping policy actions?
4. **Potential Risk Management-Based Inquisition (PRMBI):** What, if any, are the potential symbolic ideologies of IoT action-learning solutions that structure techno-politic data challenges and undermine stakeholders’ original intentions? Can these ideologies impede the action-learning solutions that shape policy data actions?

Figure 2. Equilibration schemes of political ideology facilitation of symbolic IoT action-learning solution of the big data analytics (BDA) epistemology of the epistemic communities

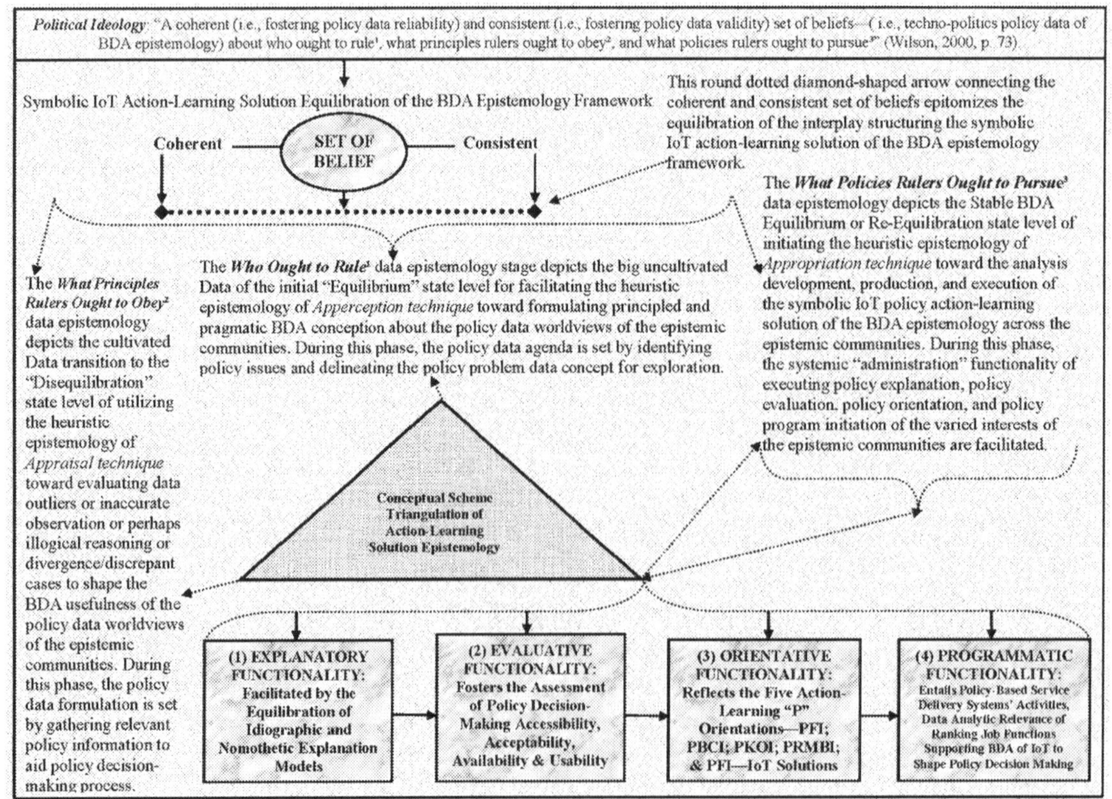

5. **Pliability-Focused Inquisition (PFI):** In what ways can the collaborative efforts of stakeholders' symbolic ideology of IoT action-learning solutions of data capacity building be improved? How can stakeholders recover when bad things unexpectedly happen to impede the action-learning solutions shaping policy data actions?

CONCLUSION

The dynamic power of the IoT ecosystem framework has become the most effective and efficient way for facilitating BDA as a channel by which people interact, learn, work, communicate, and do business with one another. Emerging data analytic software is becoming increasingly productive for policy analysts, researchers, students, and knowledge workers who design productive services and generate knowledge for organizations, governments, business enterprises, and industrial services for the benefit of epistemic communities. Epistemic communities have become knowledge-based technology service economies, with a growing number of companies and institutions attracting customers through the power of the IoT ecosystem framework.

The IoT ecosystem has created a framework of easy access to information-rich Big Data that are shaping the systemic way of analyzing data. The impact of the IoT ecosystem framework of delivery of teaching/learning across the institutions of higher education has offered knowledge acquisition that will better serve the career needs of the epistemic communities. In response to the Obama Administration's policy initiatives, institutions of higher education have been pursuing combinations of underlying assumptions regarding which educational options they should offer; how, where, and when they should offer them; and for whom they should be offered so they can prepare students for gainful employment. The PAA concentration is essential to core policy action-learning models across the epistemic communities of planning, analyzing, administering, managing policies, and preparing students for policy analytic jobs to redress pressing social issues inherent within the epistemic communities.

Of the related persistent public policy issue—whether one should consider the ramifications of political policy ideologies disseminated through television programs—such as news reports on Sony hacking, the White House hacking, the power going down around the DC area, or perhaps the 2016 Democratic National Committee email hacking, it is quite apparent that Big Data management, policy data creation, and data-driven cybersecurity threats are all interconnected. Governmental entities, corporations, nonprofits all collect Big Data, but it has only recently come to light that these BDA have the potential to be used for something other than their primary purposes. Local governments continuously collect information, and social media gather information. What happens to the information gathered and how can such Big Data shape public policy decisions? Can public administrators use the information first to craft policy and then evaluate that policy in an iterative process? (Pelletier & Tetteh, 2015). These lead to the necessity and emergence of the PAA concentration regarding the use of data-driven policies to facilitate epistemological inquisitions into BDA to determine:

- Are the BDA epistemology securely held?
- Can the BDA epistemology be manipulated in such a way as to create new false records and cause harm?
- Can the public infrastructure be at risk due to the collection of BDA epistemology that is partially analyzed but not securely held?

Courses in the PAA concentration are thus designed to ensure that before moving onto the next seminar, all students understand and use the various quantitative statistical analysis software and qualitative computer-assisted software applications when exploring and examining the impact of politics on policy learning and action planning. Therefore, by using the symbolic ideology of IoT action-learning solution to facilitate the BDA epistemology processes, one can gather the policy data necessary to determine the outcome of public policy decision making for the benefit of epistemic communities.

REFERENCES

Adler, E., & Haas, P. M. (1992). Conclusion: Epistemic communities, world order, and the creation of a reflective research program. *International Organization*, *46*(1), 367–390. doi:10.1017/S0020818300001533

Armstrong, M. C. C. (2009). Heuristic epistemology to limit divisiveness. *Journal of Dharma*, *34*(2), 207–220. Retrieved from http://www.dharmaramjournals.in/ArticleDetails.aspx?AID=690

Ashley, K. D. (2009). Ontological requirements for analogical, teleological, and hypothetical legal reasoning. *Proceedings of the 12th International Conference on Artificial Intelligence and Law–ICAIL '09,* 1–10. 10.1145/1568234.1568236

Bagby, J. W., & Mullen, T. (2007). Legal ontology of sales law application to ecommerce. *Artificial Intelligence and Law*, *15*(2), 155–170. doi:10.100710506-007-9027-3

Ball, T., & Dagger, R. (2014). Political ideologies and the democratic ideal (9th ed.). New York, NY: Pearson.

Basu, R. (2016). The discipline of public administration today: New perspectives. *The Indian Journal of Public Administration*, *62*(1), 1–8. doi:10.1177/0019556120160101

Bench-Capon, T., & Gordon, T. F. (2009). Isomorphism and argumentation. *Proceedings of the 12th International Conference on Artificial Intelligence and Law–ICAIL '09,* 11–20. doi: 10.1145/1568234.1568237

Bergsteiner, H., Avery, G. C., & Neumann, R. (2010). Kolb's experiential learning model: Critique from a modelling perspective. *Studies in Continuing Education*, *32*(1), 29–46. doi:10.1080/01580370903534355

Boom, J. (2009). Piaget on equilibration. In U. Müller, J. I. M. Carpendale, & L. Smith (Eds.), The Cambridge companion to Piaget (pp. 132–149). New York: Cambridge University Press. doi:10.1017/CCOL9780521898584.006

Chen, L. (2013). *Digital functions and data reconstruction: Digital–discrete methods*. New York: Springer. doi:10.1007/978-1-4614-5638-4

Cinquegrani, R. (2002). Futurist networks: Cases of epistemic community? *Futures, 34*, 779–783. doi:10.1016/S0016–3287(02)00020–4

Dunlop, C. A. (2017). The irony of epistemic learning: Epistemic communities, policy learning and the case of Europe's hormones saga. *Policy & Society, 36*(2), 215–232. doi:.2017.1322260 doi:10.1080/14494035

EY Building a Better Working World. (2014, April). *Big Data: Changing the way businesses compete and operate* (Insights on Governance, Risk and Compliance Report). Ernst & Young Global Limited. Retrieved from http://www.ey.com/us/en/home/library

Fard, H. D. (2012). Research paradigms in public administration. *International Journal of the Humanities, 19*(4), 55–108. Retrieved from http://eijh-old.modares.ac.ir/article_10524.html

Farooq, M. O., & Kunz, T. (2017). *IoT-RF: A routing framework for the Internet of Things*. Paper presented at the IEEE 28th Annual International Symposium on Personal, Indoor, and Mobile Radio Communications (PIMRC), Montreal, QC, Canada. Retrieved from https://ieeexplore.ieee.org/document/8292730/

Francesconi, E., & Peruginelli, G. (2007). Searching and retrieving legal literature through automated semantic indexing. *Proceedings of the 11th International Conference on Artificial intelligence and Law–ICAIL '07,* 131–139. 10.1145/1276318.1276343

Frey, C. B., & Osborne, M. A. (2017). The future of employment: How susceptible are jobs to computerisation? *Technological Forecasting and Social Change, 114*(1), 254–280. doi:10.1016/j.techfore.2016.08.019

Fuller, S. R. (2008). Organizational symbolism: A multidimensional conceptualization. *The Journal of Global Business and Management, 4*(2), 168–174. Retrieved from http://www.jgbm.org/page/ previous_V4-2.htm

Golub, K. (2017, October 16). *Encyclopedia of knowledge organization: Automatic subject indexing of text* [ISKO Version 1.0]. Retrieved from http://www.isko.org/cyclo/automatic

Gutiérrez-Rubí, A., & Sarsanedas, O. (2016, June 20). *Technopolitics and the new territories for political action* [Interview]. London, UK: Democracia Abierta/OpenDemocracy. Retrieved from https://www.opendemocracy.net/democraciaabierta/antoni-guti-rrez-rub-oleguer-sarsanedas/tecnopolitics-and-new-territories-for-poli

Haas, P. M. (1992). Introduction: Epistemic communities and international policy coordination. *International Organization, 46*(1), 1–35. doi:10.1017/S0020818300001442

Halper, F. (2014). Predictive analytics for business advantage [TDWI Best Practices Report]. *The Data Warehousing Institute (TDWI) Research*. Retrieved from https://tdwi.org/research/list/research-and-resources.aspx

Karmakar, S., & Swarnakar, S. (2017). New concept-based indexing technique for search engine. *Indian Journal of Science and Technology, 10*(18), 1–10. doi:10.17485/ijst/2017/v10i18/114018

Kellner, D. (1998). Intellectuals, the new public spheres, and techno-politics. In C. Toulouse & T. W. Luke (Eds.), *The politics of cyberspace* (pp. 167–186). New York, NY: Routledge.

Kettl, D. (2018). *Little bites of Big Data for public policy*. Thousand Oaks, CA: Sage.

Kolb, D. A. (1984). *Experiential learning: Experience as the source of learning and development*. Prentice–Hall.

Koniaris, M., Anagnostopoulos, I., & Vassiliou, Y. (2017). Network analysis in the legal domain: A complex model for European Union legal sources. *Journal of Complex Networks, 32*(1), 1–17. doi:10.1093/comnet/cnx029

Krim, H., Gentimis, T., & Chintakunta, H. (2016). Discovering the whole by the coarse: A topological paradigm for data analysis. *IEEE Signal Processing Magazine, 33*(2), 95–104. doi:.2015.2510703 doi:10.1109/MSP

Kurban, C., Peña–López, I., & Haberer, M. (2017, February). What is technopolitics? A conceptual scheme for understanding politics in the digital age. *IDP. Revista de Internet, Derecho y Ciencia Política, 24*, 3–20. Retrieved from http://edcp.blogs.uoc.edu/20170524-article-what-is-technopolitics-a-conceptual-scheme-for-understanding-politics-in-the-digital-age/

Li, K., & Deng, Y. (2014). Accelerating the reconstruction process in network coding storage system by leveraging data temperature. In C. H.Hsu, X. Shi & V. Salapura (Eds.), *Lecture Notes in Computer Science: Vol. 8707. Network and Parallel Computing* (pp. 510–521). Berlin: Springer.

Mazzega, P., Bourcier, D., & Boulet, R. (2009). The network of French legal codes. *Proceedings of the 12th International Conference on Artificial Intelligence and Law—ICAIL '09,* 236–237. doi:10.1145/1568234.1568271

Melaville, A., Blank, M. J., & Asayesh, G. (1993). *Together we can: A guide for crafting a profamily system of education and human services*. Washington, DC: Center for the Study of Social Policy and the Institute for Educational Leadership.

Miles, M. B., Huberman, A. M., & Saldaña, J. (2014). *Qualitative data analysis: A methods sourcebook* (3rd ed.). Thousand Oaks, CA: Sage.

Mohammadi, M., Al-Fuqaha, A. I., Sorour, S., & Guizani, M. (2018, June 06). Deep learning for IoT Big Data and streaming analytics: A survey. In *IEEE Communications Surveys and Tutorials* (Early Access). Retrieved from https://ieeexplore.ieee.org/ document/8373692/

Nataliia, L., & Elena, F. (2015). Internet of things as a symbolic resource of power. *Procedia: Social and Behavioral Sciences*, *166*, 521–525. doi:10.1016/j.sbspro.2014.12.565

National Institute of Food and Agriculture—United States Department of Agriculture. (2017, July 6). *Experiential learning model.* Washington, DC: Author. Retrieved from https://nifa.usda. gov/resources

Norwich University. (2010, July 31). *Norwich University 2010 NEASC self–study*. Northfield, VT: Author.

Norwich University (2014a, July). *NU2019 strategic plan update: Building on the past...strengthening our future*. Northfield, VT: Author.

Norwich University. (2014b). *College of Graduate and Continuing Studies (CGCS): Faculty Manual 2014–2015*. Northfield, VT: Author.

Norwich University (2015, August 15). *Interim/fifth year report*. Northfield, VT: Author.

Norwich University. (2018). *Online Master of Public Administration curriculum: Policy analysis and analytics concentration*. Northfield, VT: Author. Retrieved from https://online.norwich.edu/ academic-programs/masters/public-administration/overview

Pelletier, R. A., & Tetteh, E. N. A. (2015). *Policy Analysis and Analytics Concentration, Master of Public Administration Program, College of Graduate and Continuing Studies, Norwich University*. Northfield, VT: Norwich University.

Piaget, J. (1985). *The equilibration of cognitive structures: The central problem of intellectual development*. Chicago: University of Chicago Press. (Original work published 1975)

Pure Storage. (2018). *What is data reduction?* Retrieved from https://www.purestorage.com/fr/resources/glossary/data–reduction.html

Shorfuzzaman, M. (2017). Leveraging cloud-based Big Data analytics in knowledge management for enhanced decision making in organizations. *International Journal of Distributed and Parallel Systems*, *8*(1), 1–13. doi:10.5121/ijdps.2017.8101

Tetteh, E. N. A. (2004). *Theories of democratic governance in the institutions of higher education*. New York: iUniverse.

Tetteh, E. N. A. (2010). *Communal photosynthesis: Metaphor-based heuristic study of service-learners' symbolic interactionism in security management*. Ann Arbor, MI: ProQuest LLC/UMI Dissertation.

Tetteh, E. N. A. (2015a). Communal–photosynthesis metaphor: Autobiographical action–research journeys and heuristic–action–learning frameworks of living educational theories. *ALARj*, *21*(1), 148–176.

Tetteh, E. N. A. (2015b). *Overview of AD 545 course: Politics, policy, and planning (Policy Analysis and Analytics Concentration, Master of Public Administration Program, College of Graduate and Continuing Studies, Norwich University)*. Northfield, VT: Norwich University.

Tetteh, E. N. A. (2015c). *Overview of AD 555 course: Methods of policy analysis (Policy Analysis and Analytics Concentration, Master of Public Administration Program, College of Graduate and Continuing Studies, Norwich University)*. Northfield, VT: Norwich University.

Thomas, C. W. (1997, April 1). Public management as interagency cooperation: Testing epistemic community theory at the domestic level. *Journal of Public Administration: Research and Theory*, *7*(2), 221–246. doi:10.1093/oxfordjournals.jpart.a024347

Van der Waldt, G. (2014). Public administration teaching and interdisciplinarity: Considering the consequences. *Teaching Public Administration, 32*(2), 169–193. doi: 14523285 doi:10.1177/01447394

Wilson, J. Q. (2000). *American government: A brief version* (5th ed.). Boston, MA: Houghton Mifflin.

Wu, X., & He, J. (2009). Paradigm shift in public administration: Implications for teaching professional training programs. *Public Administration Review*, *69*(s1), S21–S28. doi:10.1111/j.1540-6210.2009.02085.x

Zdravković, M., Zdravković, J., Aubry, A., Moalla, N., Guedria, W., & Sarraipa, J. (2018). Domain framework for implementation of open IoT ecosystems. *International Journal of Production Research*, *56*(7), 2552–2569. doi:10.1080/00207543.2017.1385870

Zhang, P., & Koppaka, L. (2007). Semantics–based legal citation network. *Proceedings of the 11th International Conference on Artificial intelligence and Law–ICAIL '07*, 123–130. doi: 10.1145/1276318.1276342

KEY TERMS AND DEFINITIONS

Data Deontological Hermeneutics: The interpretation of data regarding the means by which the rightness or wrongness of data analytics might be conceived to implicate the sense-making process of big data analytics.

Data Teleological Hermeneutics: The alignment, fitness, or suitability of challenging the interpretation of data structuring big data analytics.

Disequilibration: The unbalancing of big data analytics across the IoT created by the shortcomings inherent in the divergence or discrepant cases of data, data outliers, or inaccurate observation or illogical reasoning.

Equilibration: The balancing of big data analytics created by the initial stage of policy data analysis across the IoT.

Epistemic Communities: A network of the ethos of political policy actors, stakeholders, the citizenry, and professionals with the data capacity of shared knowledge, policy-relevant knowledge, policy analytic data, policy coordination, policy innovation, principled belief systems, mutual expectations, collective action, and shared interpretations.

Heuristic Epistemology: The equilibration of coherent and consistent data-generated knowledge of the data triangulation structuring apperception, appraisal, and appropriation techniques that underscores the worldviews of the epistemic communities.

Political Ideology: The balancing of a coherent and consistent set of policy beliefs and techno-politic data interest that implicates public policy data epistemology.

Public Policy Data Epistemology: The problem resolution continuum of evolving big data analytics of complex situational needs and public policy issues of organization and citizenry across the power of the IoT ecosystem framework of the epistemic communities.

Stable Equilibration/Re-Equilibration: The rebalancing of big data analytics created by the elimination of shortcomings inherent in the divergence or discrepant cases of data, data outliers, or inaccurate observations or illogical reasoning to contribute to the IoT action-learning solution.

Compilation of References

Aazam, M., & Huh, E. N. (2014). Fog computing and smart gateway based communication for cloud of things. *Proceedings - 2014 International Conference on Future Internet of Things and Cloud,* 464–470.

Aazam, M., Khan, I., Alsaffar, A. A., & Huh, E. (2014). *Cloud of Things : Integrating Internet of Things and cloud computing and the issues involved*. Academic Press.

Abbas, M. U. (2014). On the application of IoT) (Internet of Things) for securing industrial threats. In *Proc. IEEE 12th Int. Conf. on Frontiers of Information Technology* (pp. 37–40). IEEE.

Abbasi, M.A., Memon, Z.A., Syed, T.Q., Memon, J., & Alshbou, R. (2017). Addressing the Future Data Management Challenges in IoT: A Proposed Framework. *International Journal of Advanced Computer Science and Applications, 8*(5).

Abdolkarimi, E., Abaei, G., & Mosavi, M. (2017). A wavelet-extreme learning machine for low-cost INS/GPS navigation system in high-speed applications. *GPS Solutions*, *22*(1), 15. doi:10.100710291-017-0682-x

Abouzeid, A., Bajda-Pawlikowski, K., Abadi, D., Silberschatz, A., & Rasin, A. (2009). HadoopDB: an architectural hybrid of MapReduce and DBMS technologies for analytical workloads. *Proceedings of the VLDB Endowment, 2*(1), 922-933. Retrieved on April 19, 2016 from http://www.vldb.org/pvldb/2/vldb09-861.pdf

Acetech. (2013). Internet Privacy. Options for adequate realization. In J. Buchmann (Ed.), *Interdisciplinary perspectives on internet applications and privacy options*. Heidelberg: Springer Verlag.

Acharjya, D.P., & Ahmed, K.P. (2016). A Survey on Big Data Analytics: Challenges, OpenResearch Issues and Tools. *International Journal of Advanced Computer Science and Applications, 7*(2).

Achtenhagen, L., Melin, L., & Naldi, L. (2013). Dynamics of Business Models Strategizing, Critical Capability and Activities for Sustained Value Creation. *Long Range Planning*, *46*(6), 427–442. doi:10.1016/j.lrp.2013.04.002

Acquisti, A., Brandimarte, L., & Loewenstein, G. (2015). Privacy and human behavior in the age of information. *Science*, *347*(6221), 509–514. doi:10.1126cience.aaa1465 PMID:25635091

Adame, T., Bel, A., Carreras, A., Melià-Seguí, J., Oliver, M., & Pous, R. (2018). CUIDATS: An RFID–WSN hybrid monitoring system for smart health care environments. *Future Generation Computer Systems*, *78*(2), 602–615. doi:10.1016/j.future.2016.12.023

Adibi, Mobasher, & Tofigh. (2016). LTE networking: Extending the reach for sensors in mHealth applications. *Transactions on Emerging Telecommunications Technologies*.

Adler, E., & Haas, P. M. (1992). Conclusion: Epistemic communities, world order, and the creation of a reflective research program. *International Organization*, *46*(1), 367–390. doi:10.1017/S0020818300001533

Adrian. (2016). *Securing Hadoop: Technical Recommendations*. Academic Press.

Affairs, M. of E. n.d. (2015). Internet of Things in the Netherlands Applications trends and potential impact on radio spectrum.

Agnellutti, C. (2014). *Big Data: An Exploration of Opportunities, Values, and Privacy Issues*. New York: Nova Science Publishers, Inc.

Aguaded-Ramírez, E. (2017). Smart city and Intercultural Education. *Procedia: Social and Behavioral Sciences*, *237*, 326–333. doi:10.1016/j.sbspro.2017.02.010

Ahamed, J., & Rajan, A. V. (2016). Internet of Things (IoT): Application systems and security vulnerabilities. *2016 5th International Conference on Electronic Devices, Systems and Applications (ICEDSA)*, 1-5. 10.1109/ICEDSA.2016.7818534

Ahmadighohandizi, F., & Systä, K. (2016, September). Application development and deployment for IoT devices. In *European Conference on Service-Oriented and Cloud Computing* (pp. 74-85). Springer.

Ahmed, E., Yaqoob, I., Hashem, I. A. T., Khan, I., Ahmed, A. I. A., Imran, M., & Vasilakos, A. V. (2017). The role of big data analytics in Internet of Things. *Computer Networks*, *129*, 459–471. doi:10.1016/j.comnet.2017.06.013

Ahson, S. A., & Ilyas, M. (2017). *RFID Handbook: applications, technology, security, and privacy*. CRC Press.

Ahvenniemi, H., Huovila, A., Pinto-Seppä, I., & Airaksinen, M. (2017). What are the differences between sustainable and smart cities? *Cities (London, England)*, *60*, 234–245. doi:10.1016/j.cities.2016.09.009

Ajeeba, A. A., Thomas, A., & Rasheed, R. (2017). IoT Based Energy Meter Reading, Theft Detection and Disconnection. *International Research Journal of Engineering and Technology*.

Akoka, J., Comyn-Wattiau, I., & Laoufi, N. (2017). Research on Big Data–A systematic mapping study. *Computer Standards & Interfaces*, *54*, 105–115. doi:10.1016/j.csi.2017.01.004

Al Nuaimi, E., Al Neyadi, H., Mohamed, N., & Al-Jaroodi, J. (2015). Applications of big data to smart cities. *Journal of Internet Services and Applications*, *6*(1), 25. doi:10.118613174-015-0041-5

Alaba, F. A., Othman, M., Hashem, I. A. T., & Alotaibi, F. (2017). Internet of Things security: A survey. *Journal of Network and Computer Applications*, *88*, 10–28. doi:10.1016/j.jnca.2017.04.002

Alaraifi, A., Molla, A., & Deng, H. (2012). An exploration of data center information systems. *Journal of Systems and Information Technology*, *14*(4), 353–370. doi:10.1108/13287261211279080

Al-Azzawi, B. F., Rigelsford, J. M., & Langley, R. J. (2018). Investigations into improving the detectability of self-resonant RFID tags. *IET Microwaves, Antennas & Propagation*, *12*(9), 1519–1525. doi:10.1049/iet-map.2017.1205

Albreem, M. A., El-Saleh, A. A., Isa, M., Salah, W., Jusoh, M., Azizan, M. M., & Ali, A. (2017). Green internet of things (IoT): An overview. In: Smart Instrumentation, Measurement and Application (ICSIMA), 2017 IEEE 4th International Conference on. IEEE, 2017. p. 1-6.

Aldossary, S., & Allen, W. (2016). Data security, privacy, availability and integrity in cloud computing: Issues and current solutions. *International Journal of Advanced Computer Science and Applications*, *7*(4), 485–498. doi:10.14569/IJACSA.2016.070464

Alelaiwi, A., Alghamdi, A. Shorfuzzaman, M., Rawashdeh, M., Hossain, M.S. & Muhammad, G. (2015). Enhanced engineering education using smart class environment. *Computers in Human Behavior, 51(Part B)*, 852-856.

Alharthi, A., Krotov, V., & Bowman, M. (2017). Addressing barriers to big data. *Business Horizons*, *60*(3), 285–292. doi:10.1016/j.bushor.2017.01.002

Alkhamisi, A., Nazmudeen, M. S. H., & Buhari, S. M. (2016). A cross-layer framework for sensor data aggregation for IoT applications in smart cities. *2016 IEEE International Smart Cities Conference (ISC2)*, 1-6. 10.1109/ISC2.2016.7580853

Allee, V. (2000). Reconfiguring the Value Network. *The Journal of Business Strategy*, *21*(4), 36–39. doi:10.1108/eb040103

Allseen Alliance. (2017). *AllJoyn Framework*. Retrieved May 1, 2017, from https://allseenalliance.org/framework

Alohali, B., Kifayat, K., Shi, Q., & Hurst, W. (2016). Group Authentication Scheme for Neighbourhood Area Networks (NANs) in Smart Grids. *Journal of Sensor and Actuator Networks*, *5*(2), 9. doi:10.3390/jsan5020009

Alohali, B., Merabti, M., & Kifayat, K. (2014). A Cloud of Things (CoT) Based Security for Home Area Network (HAN) in the Smart Grid. *2014 Eighth International Conference on Next Generation Mobile Apps, Services and Technologies*, 326-330. 10.1109/NGMAST.2014.50

Aloi, G., Caliciuri, G., Fortino, G., Gravina, R., Pace, P., Russo, W., & Savaglio, C. (2017). Enabling IoT interoperability through opportunistic smartphone-based mobile gateways. *Journal of Network and Computer Applications, 81*, 74–84. doi:10.1016/j.jnca.2016.10.013

Alsabti, K., Ranka, S., & Singh, V. (1997). An efficient k-means clustering algorithm. *Electrical Engineering and Computer Science*, *43*. Retrieved from http://surface.syr.edu/eecs/43

Alsamhi, S. H., Ma, O., Ansari, M. S., & Meng, Q. (2018). *Greening Internet of Things for Smart Everythings with A Green-Environment Life: A Survey and Future Prospects.* arXiv preprint arXiv:1805.00844

Alshawish, R. A., Alfagih, S. A., & Musbah, M. S. (2016, September). Big data applications in smart cities. In International Conference on Engineering & MIS (ICEMIS) (pp. 1-7). IEEE.

Alshboul, Y., Wang, Y., & Nepali, R. K. (2015, August). *Big data life cycle: threats and security model.* Paper presented at the 21st Americas Conference on Information Systems, Fajardo, Puerto Rico.

Amazon. (2018). *AWS IoT Services Overview - Amazon Web Services*. Retrieved May 15, 2018, from https://aws.amazon.com/iot/?nc1=h_ls

Andréia da Silva, M., Antonio, A. F. G., Pereira de Souza, A., & Lopes de Souza, C. Jr. (2004). Comparison of similarity coefficients used for cluster analysis with dominant markers in maize (Zea maysL). *Genetics and Molecular Biology*, *27*(1), 83–91. doi:10.1590/S1415-47572004000100014

Angelidou, M. (2015). Smart cities: A conjuncture of four forces. *Cities (London, England)*, *47*, 95–106. doi:10.1016/j.cities.2015.05.004

Anshari, M., & Alas, Y. (2015). Smartphones habits, necessities, and big data challenges. *The Journal of High Technology Management Research*, *26*(2), 177–185. doi:10.1016/j.hitech.2015.09.005

Anuganti, V. (2012). Typical "big" data architecture. *Venu Anuganti Blog*. Retrieved on April 4, 2016 from http://venublog.com/2012/11/30/typical-big-data-architecture/

Apache. (2017). Retrieved from http://apache.org

API Client Libraries | Google Developers. (n.d.). Retrieved from https://developers.google.com/api-client-library/

Archenaa, J., & Mary Anita, E. A. (2015). A Survey of Big Data Analytics in Healthcare and Government. *Procedia Computer Science, 50*, 408-413. doi:10.1016/j.procs.2015.04.021

Aribas, E., & Daglarli, E. (2017). Realtime object detection in IoT (Internet of Things) devices. *25th Signal Processing and Communications Applications Conference (SIU)*, 1-6. 10.1109/SIU.2017.7960690

Armstrong, M. C. C. (2009). Heuristic epistemology to limit divisiveness. *Journal of Dharma*, *34*(2), 207–220. Retrieved from http://www.dharmaramjournals.in/ArticleDetails.aspx?AID=690

Arora, B., & Rahman, Z. (2016). Using Big Data Analytics for Competitive Advantage. *International Journal of Innovative Research and Development*, *5*(2).

Ashby, R. (1965). *Introduction to Cybernetics*. John Wiley & Sons.

Ashley, K. D. (2009). Ontological requirements for analogical, teleological, and hypothetical legal reasoning. *Proceedings of the 12th International Conference on Artificial Intelligence and Law–ICAIL '09*, 1–10. 10.1145/1568234.1568236

Ashton, K. (2009). *That Internet of Things' thing: in the real world, things matter more than ideas*. Retrieved from: http://www.rfid-journal.com/article/view/4986

Ashton, K. (2017). *That 'Internet of Things' Thing*. Retrieved June 14, 2018 from https://www.rfidjournal.com/articles/view?4986

ASIRT. (n.d.). Retrieved from https://asirt.org/initiatives/informing-road-users/road-safety-facts/road-crash-statistics

Assuncao, M. D., Calheiros, R. N., Bianchi, S., Netto, M. A. S., & Buyya, R. (2014). Big Data and clouds: Trends and future directions. *Journal of Parallel and Distributed Computing*. doi:10.1016/j.jpdc.2014.08.003

Atzori, L., Iera, A., & Morabito, G. (2010). The Internet of Things: A survey. *Computer Networks*, *54*(15), 2787–2805. doi:10.1016/j.comnet.2010.05.010

Avijit, K., & Chinnaiyan, R. (2018). IOT for Smart Cities. International Journal of Scientific Research in Computer Science. *Engineering and Information Technology*, *3*(4), 1126–1139.

AWS Documentation - AWS IoT - API Reference. (n.d.). Retrieved from http://docs.aws.amazon.com/iot/latest/apireference/API_Operations.html

AWS IoT Developer Guide. (2018). Retrieved from https://docs.aws.amazon.com/iot/latest/developerguide/iot-dg.pdf

AWS IoT Device Management Overview - Amazon Web Services. (n.d.). Retrieved from https://aws.amazon.com/tr/iot-device-management/

AWS IoT Device SDK. (n.d.). Retrieved from https://aws.amazon.com/iot-platform/sdk/

AWS SDK for Java. (n.d.). Retrieved from https://aws.amazon.com/sdk-for-java/

AWS Toolkit for Eclipse. (n.d.). Retrieved from https://aws.amazon.com/eclipse/

Aydin, G., Hallac, I. R., & Karakus, B. (2015). Architecture and Implementation of a Scalable Sensor Data Storage and Analysis System Using Cloud Computing and Big Data Technologies. *Journal of Sensors*, *2015*, 1–11. doi:10.1155/2015/834217

Azamuddin Bin Ab Rahman, R. J. (2015). *Comparison of Internet of Things (IoT)*. Data Link Protocols.

Bagby, J. W., & Mullen, T. (2007). Legal ontology of sales law application to ecommerce. *Artificial Intelligence and Law*, *15*(2), 155–170. doi:10.100710506-007-9027-3

Bagnoli, V. (2015). Competition for the Effectiveness of Big Data Benefits. *IIC-International Review of Intellectual Property and Competition Law*, *46*(6), 629–631. doi:10.100740319-015-0382-4

Bai, A., & Hammer, H. (2014). Constructing sentiment lexicons in Norwegian from a large text corpus. *2014 IEEE 17th International Conference on Computational Science and Engineering*. DOI: 10.1109/CSE.2014.73

Ball, T., & Dagger, R. (2014). Political ideologies and the democratic ideal (9th ed.). New York, NY: Pearson.

Bandyopadhyay, D., & Sen, J. (2011). Internet of things: Applications and challenges in technology and standardization. *Wireless Personal Communications*, *58*(1), 49–69. doi:10.100711277-011-0288-5

Bandyopadhyay, S., & Maulik, U. (2002). An evolutionary technique based on K-Means algorithm for optimal clustering in RN. *Information Sciences*, *146*(1–4), 221–237. doi:10.1016/S0020-0255(02)00208-6

Barabasi, A.-L. (2002). *Linked: The New Science of Network*. Cambridge, UK: Perseus Publishing.

Barcena, M. B., Wueest, C., & Lau, H. (2014). *How safe is your quantified self*. Mountain View, CA: Symantech.

Barkham, R., Bokhari, S., & Saiz, A. (2018). *Urban Big Data: City Management and Real Estate Markets*. New York, NY: GovLab Digest.

Barlow, M. (2013). *Real-time big data analytics: emerging architecture*. Sebastopol, CA: O'Reilly Media.

Bartsch, M., & Dienlin, T. (2016). Control your Facebook: An analysis of online privacy literacy. *Computers in Human Behavior*, *56*, 147–154. doi:10.1016/j.chb.2015.11.022

Basmadjian, R., Bouvry, P., Costa, G., Gyarmati, L., Kliazovich, D., Lafond, S., ... Torres, J. (2015). Green data centers. In *Large-scale Distributed Systems and Energy Efficiency: A Holistic View*. John Wiley & Sons.

Bass, L., Clements, P., & Kazman, R. (2012). *Software Architecture in Practice* (3rd ed.). Addison-Wesley Professional.

Basu, R. (2016). The discipline of public administration today: New perspectives. *The Indian Journal of Public Administration*, *62*(1), 1–8. doi:10.1177/0019556120160101

Battistella, C., Colucci, K., DeToni, A. F., & Nonino, F. (2013). Methodology of Business Ecosystems Network Analysis: A Case Study in Telecom Italia Future Centre. *Technological Forecasting and Social Change*, *80*(6), 1194–1210. doi:10.1016/j.techfore.2012.11.002

Batty, M. (2013). Big data, smart cities and city planning. *Dialogues in Human Geography*, *3*(3), 274–279. doi:10.1177/2043820613513390 PMID:29472982

Batty, M., Axhausen, K. W., Giannotti, F., Pozdnoukhov, A., Bazzani, A., Wachowicz, M., ... Portugali, Y. (2012). Smart cities of the future. *The European Physical Journal. Special Topics*, *214*(1), 481–518. doi:10.1140/epjst/e2012-01703-3

Bawa, M. (2011). Multi-structured data: platform capabilities required for big data analytics. *Tetra data Aster – The Data Blog*. Retrieved from: http://www.asterdata.com/blog/2011/06/multi-structured-data-platform-capabilities-required-for-big-data-analytics/#Citation

Beer, R. D., Chiel, H. J., Quinn, R. D., Espenschied, K. S., & Larsson, P. (2008). A Distributed Neural Network Architecture for Hexapod Robot Locomotion. *Neural Computation*, *4*(3), 356–365. doi:10.1162/neco.1992.4.3.356

Beer, S. C., Goffreda, J., Phillips, T. D., Murphy, J. P., & Sorrells, M. E. (1992). Assessment of Genetic Variation in Avena sterilis using Morphologicall Traits, Isozymes, and RFLPs. *Crop Science*, *33*(6), 1386–1393. doi:10.2135/cropsci1993.0011183X003300060051x

Bektaş, T., Crainic, T. G., & Van Woensel, T. (2017). From managing urban freight to smart city logistics networks. In Network Design and Optimization for Smart Cities (pp. 143-188). Academic Press. doi:10.1142/9789813200012_0007

Beligianni, F., Alamaniotis, M., Fevgas, A., Tsompanopoulou, P., Bozanis, P., & Tsoukalas, L. H. (2016). An internet of things architecture for preserving privacy of energy consumption. *Mediterranean Conference on Power Generation, Transmission, Distribution and Energy Conversion (MedPower 2016)*, 1-7. 10.1049/cp.2016.1096

Bello-Orgaz, G., Jung, J. J., & Camacho, D. (2016). Social big data: Recent achievements and new challenges. *Information Fusion*, *28*, 45–59. doi:10.1016/j.inffus.2015.08.005

Ben Alaya, M., Banouar, Y., Monteil, T., Chassot, C., & Drira, K. (2014). OM2M: Extensible ETSI-compliant M2M service platform with self-configuration capability. *Procedia Computer Science*, *32*, 1079–1086. doi:10.1016/j.procs.2014.05.536

Bench-Capon, T., & Gordon, T. F. (2009). Isomorphism and argumentation. *Proceedings of the 12th International Conference on Artificial Intelligence and Law–ICAIL '09,* 11–20. doi: 10.1145/1568234.1568237

Bergamaschi, S., Carlini, E., Ceci, M., Furletti, B., Giannotti, F., Malerba, D., ... Perego, R. (2016). Big Data Research in Italy: A Perspective. *Engineering*, *2*(2), 163–170. doi:10.1016/J.ENG.2016.02.011

Bergsteiner, H., Avery, G. C., & Neumann, R. (2010). Kolb's experiential learning model: Critique from a modelling perspective. *Studies in Continuing Education*, *32*(1), 29–46. doi:10.1080/01580370903534355

Berlian, H. M., Sahputra, T. E. R., Ardi, B. J. W., Dzatmika, H. W., Besari, A. R. A., Sudibyo, A. W., & Sukaridhoto, S. (2016). Design and implementation of smart environment monitoring and analytics in real-time system framework based on internet of underwater things and big data. *International Electronics Symposium*, 403–408. 10.1109/ELECSYM.2016.7861040

Bettencourt, L. M. (2014). The uses of big data in cities. *Big Data*, *2*(1), 12–22. doi:10.1089/big.2013.0042 PMID:27447307

Beyer, M. (2011). *Gartner Says Solving 'Big Data' Challenge Involves More Than Just Managing Volumes of Data.* Gartner.

Beyer, M. A., & Laney, D. (2012). *The importance of 'big data': a definition.* Gartner.

Bhargava, D., & Sinha, M. (2012). Design and implementation of agent based inter process synchronization manager. *International Journal of Computers and Applications*, *46*(21), 17–22.

Bibri, S. E. (2018). The IoT for Smart Sustainable Cities of the Future: An Analytical Framework for Sensor-Based Big Data Applications for Environmental Sustainability. *Sustainable Cities and Society*, *38*, 230–253. doi:10.1016/j.scs.2017.12.034

Bi, Z. M., & Lang, S. Y. T. (2007). A framework for CAD- and sensor-based robotic coating automation. *IEEE Transactions on Industrial Informatics*, *3*(1), 84–91. doi:10.1109/TII.2007.891309

Bi, Z. M., Lang, S. Y. T., Shen, W. M., & Wang, L. (2008). Reconfigurable manufacturing systems: The state of the art. *International Journal of Production Research*, *46*(4), 967–992. doi:10.1080/00207540600905646

Bi, Z. M., & Zhang, W. J. (2011). Modularity technology in manufacturing: Taxonomy and issues. *International Journal of Advanced Manufacturing Technology*, *18*(5), 381–390. doi:10.1007001700170062

Bi, Z., & Cochran, D. (2014). Big data analytics with applications. *Journal of Management Analytics*, *1*(4), 249–265. doi:10.1080/23270012.2014.992985

Bloem, J., van Doorn, M., Duivestein, S., van Manen, T., van Ommeren, E., & Sackdeva, S. (2013). *No more secrets with big data analytics.* Retrieved from http://vint.sogeti.com/wp-content/uploads/ 2013/11/Sogeti_NoMoreSecrets.pdf

Blyth, A., & Kovacich, G. L. (2006). *Information Assurance.* Springer.

Bonomi, F., Milito, R., Natarajan, P., & Zhu, J. (2014). Big Data and Internet of Things: A Roadmap for Smart Environments. In Studies in Computational Intelligence (Vol. 546). Cham: Springer International Publishing.

Bonomi, F., Milito, R., Zhu, J., & Addepalli, S. (2012). Fog Computing and Its Role in the Internet of Things. In *Proceedings of the First Edition of the MCC Workshop on Mobile Cloud Computing* (pp. 13–16). New York: ACM. 10.1145/2342509.2342513

Boom, J. (2009). Piaget on equilibration. In U. Müller, J. I. M. Carpendale, & L. Smith (Eds.), The Cambridge companion to Piaget (pp. 132–149). New York: Cambridge University Press. doi:10.1017/CCOL9780521898584.006

Borisova, N. (2014). An Approach for Ontology-Based Information Extraction. *Information Technology and Control, 12*(1). doi:10.1515/itc-2015-0007

Bormann, C. M. E. A. K. (2014). *Terminology for Constrained-Node Networks RFC 7228*. Retrieved August 12, 2016, from https://tools.ietf.org/html/rfc7228#section-2.3.2

Börnert, C., Clark, K., Daya, S., Debeaux, M., Diederichs, G., Gucer, V., ... Thole, J. (2016). *An Architectural and Practical Guide to IBM Hybrid Integration Platform*. IBM Redbooks.

Bosch IoT Suite. (n.d.). Retrieved from https://www.bosch-iot-suite.com/

Botta, A., de Donato, W., Persico, V., & Pescape, A. (2014). On the Integration of Cloud Computing and Internet of Things. In *2014 International Conference on Future Internet of Things and Cloud* (Vol. 56, pp. 23–30). IEEE. 10.1109/FiCloud.2014.14

Bousquet, J., Kuh, D., Bewick, M., Standberg, T., & Farrell, J. (2015). Operational definition of Active and Healthy Ageing (AHA): A conceptual framework. *The Journal of Nutrition, Health & Aging, 19*(9), 955–960. doi:10.100712603-015-0589-6

boyd, D., & Hargittai, E. (2010). Facebook privacy settings: Who cares. *First Monday, 15*(8), 1-23.

Boyd, D. (2010). Austin, Texas: Making Sense of Privacy and Publicity. In SXSW; Retrieved from http://www.danah.org/papers/talks/2010/SXSW2010.html

Briedis, M., Webb, J., & Fraser, M. (2016). *Improving the Communication of Privacy Information for Consumers*. Retrieved from Sydney https://goo.gl/zWZS3T

Brooke, J., Tofiloski, M., & Taboada, M. (2009). Cross-Linguistic Sentiment Analysis: From English to Spanish. *International Conference RANLP 2009*, 50–54.

Brookman, J., Rouge, P., Alva, A., & Yeung, C. (2017). Cross-Device Tracking: Measurement and Disclosures. *Proceedings On Privacy Enhancing Technologies, 2017*(2). doi:10.1515/popets-2017-0020

Brown, & Marsden, C. T. (2013). *Regulating code: Good governance and better regulation in the information age*. Cambridge: MIT Press.

Brown, E. (2016). *Who Needs the Internet of Things*. Retrieved May 2018, from https://www.linux.com/news/who-needs-internet-things

Brown, I., & Marsden, C. T. (2013). *Regulating Code: Good Governance and Better Regulation in the Information Age*. The MIT Press.

Brusic, V., Rudy, G., Honeyman, G., Hammer, J., & Harrison, L. (1998). Prediction of MHC class II-binding peptides using an evolutionary algorithm and artificial neural network. *Bioinformatics (Oxford, England), 14*(2), 121–130. doi:10.1093/bioinformatics/14.2.121 PMID:9545443

Buntz, B. (2016). *Why Chicago is a Smart City King*. Retrieved 08 January, 2018 from http://www.ioti.com/smart-cities/why-chicago-smart-city-king

Burt, M., Cuddy, M., & Razo, M. (2014). *Big Data's Implications for Transportation Operations: An Exploration.* US Department of Transportation White Paper. Retrieved from http://ntl.bts.gov/lib/55000/55000/55002/Big_Data_Implications_FHWA-JPO-14-157.pdf

Busold, C., Heuser, S., Sadeghi, A., & Asokan, N. (2015). Smart and Secure Cross-Device Apps for the Internet of Advanced Things. *International Conference on Financial Cryptography and Data Security.* 10.1007/978-3-662-47854-7_17

C2POWER. (n.d.). Retrieved from http://www.ict-c2power.eu/

Calvillo, C. F., Sánchez-Miralles, A., & Villar, J. (2016). Energy management and planning in smart cities. *Renewable & Sustainable Energy Reviews, 55*, 273–287. doi:10.1016/j.rser.2015.10.133

Cao, Y., Chen, S., Hou, P., & Brown, D. (2015). FAST: A fog computing assisted distributed analytics system to monitor fall for stroke mitigation. In *2015 IEEE International Conference on Networking, Architecture and Storage (NAS)* (pp. 2–11). IEEE. 10.1109/NAS.2015.7255196

Capgemini. (2012). Measuring Organizational Maturity in Predictive Analytics: the First Step to Enabling the Vision. *Resource.*

Capozzoli, A., Piscitelli, M. S., & Brandi, S. (2017). Mining typical load profiles in buildings to support energy management in the smart city context. *Energy Procedia, 134*, 865–874. doi:10.1016/j.egypro.2017.09.545

Carbone, P. (2009, February). The Emerging Promise of Business Ecosystems. *Open Source Business Resource,* 11-16. Retrieved from http://Timreview.CA/article/227

Cardellini, V., Grassi, V., Lo Presti, F., & Nardelli, M. (2017). Optimal Operator Replication and Placement for Distributed Stream Processing Systems. *Performance Evaluation Review, 44*(4), 11–22. doi:10.1145/3092819.3092823

Caron, X., Bosua, R., Maynard, S. B., & Ahmad, A. (2016). The Internet of Things (IoT) and its impact on individual privacy: An Australian perspective. *Computer Law & Security Review, 32*(1), 4–15. doi:10.1016/j.clsr.2015.12.001

Carrera-Trejo, V., Sidorov, G., Miranda-Jiménez, S., Ibarra, M. M., & Martínez, R. C. (2015). Latent Dirichlet Allocation complement in the vector space model for Multi-Label Text Classification. *International Journal of Combinatorial Optimization Problems and Informatics, 6*(1), 7–19.

Casadesus Masanell, R., & Ricart, J. E. (2010). From Strategy to Business Models and onto Tactics. *Long Range Planning, 43*(2), 195–215. doi:10.1016/j.lrp.2010.01.004

CASAGRAS. (n.d.). Retrieved from http://www.i-o-t.org/post/CASAGRAS

Casanovas, P., De Koker, L., Mendelson, D., & Watts, D. (2017). Regulation of Big Data: Perspectives on strategy, policy, law and privacy. *Health and Technology,* 1–15. doi:10.100712553-017-0190-6

CAVIAR Test Case Scenarios. (2003). Retrieved, May 2018 from http://homepages.inf.ed.ac.uk/rbf/CAVIARDATA1/

Cavoukian, A. (2011). *Privacy by design. The 7 foundational principles in Privacy by Design. Strong privacy protection now, and well into the future.* Retrieved from https://www.ipc.on.ca/wp-content/uploads/Resources/7foundational principles.pdf

Cavoukian, A. (2009). *Privacy by design: The 7 foundational principles. implementation and mapping of fair information practices.* Canada: Information and Privacy Commissioner of Ontario.

Cavoukian, A., & Jonas, J. (2012). *Privacy by Design in the Age of Big Data.* Ontario, Canada: Information & Privacy Commissioner.

Cebr. (2016). *The Value of Big Data and the Internet of Things to the UK Economy*. Cebr Report for SAS.

Cecchinel, C. (2014). An architecture to support the collection of big data in the internet of things. In *2014 IEEE World Congress on Services*. IEEE. 10.1109/SERVICES.2014.83

Cenedese, A., Zanella, A., Vangelista, L., & Zorzi, M. (2014). Padova smart City: An urban Internet of Things experimentation. *Proceeding of IEEE International Symposium on a World of Wireless, Mobile and Multimedia Networks 2014, WoWMoM 2014*. 10.1109/WoWMoM.2014.6918931

CERP-IoT. (2009). *Internet of Things Strategic Research Roadmap*. Cluster of European Projects. Retrieved from http://www.grifs-project.eu/data/File/CERP-IoT%20SRA_I-oT_v11.pdf

Chandler, D. (2009). *Semiotics for beginners*. Retrieved from: http://www.aber.ac.uk/media/Documents/S4B/sem02.html

Chang, F., Dean, J., Ghemawat, S., Hsieh, W. C., Wallach, D. A., Burrows, M., & Gruber, R. E. (2008). BigTable: A distributed storage system for structured data. *ACM Trans. Comput. Syst., 26*(2), 4:1–4:26. Retrieved on April 4, 2016 from http://static.googleusercontent.com/media/research.google.com/en//archive/bigtable-osdi06.pdf

Change Detection Dataset. (2015). Retrieved, March 2018, from http://changedetection.net/

Charalambous, C. (1992). Conjugate gradient algorithm for efficient training of artificial neural networks. *IEE Proceedings. Part G. Circuits, Devices and Systems, 139*(3), 301–310. doi:10.1049/ip-g-2.1992.0050

Chaudhry, A., Crowcroft, J., Howard, H., Madhavapeddy, A., Mortier, R., Haddadi, H., & McAuley, D. (2015, August). Personal data: thinking inside the box. In *Proceedings of the fifth decennial Aarhus conference on critical alternatives* (pp. 29-32). Aarhus University Press.

Che, D., Safran, M., & Peng, Z. (2013). From Big Data to Big Data Mining: Challenges, Issues, and Opportunities, Database Systems for Advanced Applications DASFAA Workshops. *Lecture Notes in Computer Science, 7827*, 1–15. doi:10.1007/978-3-642-40270-8_1

Chen, R., Chen, H., & Zang, B. (2010). Tiled-MapReduce: optimizing resource usages of data-parallel applications on multicore with tiling. In *Proceedings of the 19th International Conference on Parallel architectures and compilation techniques* (pp. 523-534). ACM. Retrieved on April 4, 2016 from http://www.csee.ogi.edu/~zak/cs506-pslc/tiledmr.pdf

Chen, H., Chiang, R. H. L., & Storey, V. C. (2012). Business intelligence and analytics: From big data to big impact. *Management Information Systems Quarterly, 36*(4), 1165–1188. doi:10.2307/41703503

Chen, J. L. (2013). Research on online fault diagnosis model based on IoT in process industry. *Advanced Information and Computer Technol. in Eng. and Manufacturing Environmental Eng., 765*, 2089–2092.

Chen, L. (2013). *Digital functions and data reconstruction: Digital–discrete methods*. New York: Springer. doi:10.1007/978-1-4614-5638-4

Chen, M., Mao, S., & Liu, Y. (2014). Big data: A survey. *Mobile Networks and Applications, 19*(2), 171–209. doi:10.100711036-013-0489-0

Chen, M., Mao, S., Zhang, Y., & Leung, V. C. M. (2014). *Big Data*. Cham, Germany: Springer International Publishing. doi:10.1007/978-3-319-06245-7

Chen, S., Xu, H., Liu, D., Hu, B., & Wang, H. (2014). A Vision of IoT: Applications, Challenges, and Opportunities With China Perspective. *IEEE Internet of Things Journal, 1*(4), 349–359. doi:10.1109/JIOT.2014.2337336

Chen, W., Liu, T., & Yang, X. (2016). Reinforcement learning behaviors in sponsored search. *Applied Stochastic Models in Business and Industry, 32*(3), 358–367. doi:10.1002/asmb.2157

Chen, Y., Ardila-Gomez, A., & Frame, G. (2017). Achieving energy savings by intelligent transportation systems investments in the context of smart cities. *Transportation Research Part D, Transport and Environment*, *54*, 381–396. doi:10.1016/j.trd.2017.06.008

Chen, Z., & Liu, B. (2016). Lifelong Machine Learning. *Synthesis Lectures On Artificial Intelligence And Machine Learning*, *10*(3), 1–145. doi:10.2200/S00737ED1V01Y201610AIM033

Choi, S.-S., Cha, S.-H., & Tappert, C. C. (2010). A Survey of Binary Similarity and Distance Measures. *Systemics, Cybernetics and Informatics, 8*(1).

Chourabi, H., Nam, T., Walker, S., Gil-Garcia, J. R., Mellouli, S., Nahon, K., . . . Scholl, H. J. (2012, January). Understanding smart cities: An integrative framework. In 2012 45th Hawaii International Conference on System Science (HICSS) (pp. 2289-2297). IEEE.

Christiansen, L. (2011). Personal privacy and Internet marketing: An impossible conflict or a marriage made in heaven? *Business Horizons*, *54*(6), 509–514. doi:10.1016/j.bushor.2011.06.002

Christl, W., Kopp, K., & Riechert, P. U. (2017). How companies use personal information against people: Automated Disadvantage, Personalized Persuasion, and the Societal Ramifications of the Commercial Use of Personal Information. *Cracked Labs*. Retrieved from https://crackedlabs.org/en/data-against-people

Christl, W., & Spiekerman, S. (2016). *Networks of control: A report on corporate surveillance, digital tracking, big data & privacy*. Vienna, Austria: Facultas.

Christovich, M. M. (2016). Why should we care what Fitbit shares-a proposed statutory solution to protect sensitive personal fitness information. *Hastings Communication & Entertainment Law Journal*, *38*, 91–116.

Chudik, A., Kapetanios, G., & Pesaran, M. H. (2016). *Big Data Analytics: A New Perspective*. Federal Reserve Bank of Dallas Globalization and Monetary Policy Institute.

Chui, M., Loffler, M., & Roberts, R. (2010). The Internet of Things. *The McKinsey Quarterly*, *2*, 1–9.

Chung, W. Y., Lee, Y. D., & Jung, S. J. (2008). A wireless sensor network compatible wearable u-healthcare monitoring system using integrated ECG, accelerometer and SpO2. *Proc. 30th Annu. Int. Conf. IEEE Eng. Med. Biol. Soc. (EMBS)*, 1529–1532.

Chunli, L. (2012). *Intelligent transportation based on the Internet of Things*. Paper presented at the 2012 2nd International Conference on Consumer Electronics, Communications and Networks (CECNet).

Cinquegrani, R. (2002). Futurist networks: Cases of epistemic community? *Futures, 34*, 779–783. doi:10.1016/S0016–3287(02)00020–4

Cisco. (2018). *Cisco Global Cloud Index: Forecast and Methodology, 2016–2021*. White Paper.

Cities Digest. (2017). *Smart City Moscow*. CitiesDigest. Retrieved from https://www.citiesdigest.com/2017/07/03/smart-city-moscow

Clarke, R. (1999). Introduction to dataveillance and information privacy, and definitions of terms. Retrieved from http://www.rogerclarke.com/DV/CACM88.html

Clarke, R. (1988). Information technology and dataveillance. *Communications of the ACM*, *31*(5), 498–512. doi:10.1145/42411.42413

Clarke, R. (2014b). The Prospects for Consumer-Oriented Social Media. *Organizacija*, *47*(4), 219–230. doi:10.2478/orga-2014-0024

Clausing, D., & Holmes, M. (2010). Technology readiness. *Research Technology Management*, *53*(4), 52–59. doi:10.1080/08956308.2010.11657640

Cloud IoT Core. (n.d.). Retrieved from https://cloud.google.com/iot-core/

Cloudera. (2017). Retrieved from http://www.cloudera.com

CMD. (2014). *Digital Canberra: Action Plan 2014-2018*. Retrieved from http://www.cmd.act.gov.au/__data/assets/pdf_file/0006/565566/digcbractionplan_print.pdf

Coleman, S. Y. (2016). Data-Mining Opportunities for Small and Medium Enterprises with Official Statistics in the UK. *Journal of Official Statistics*, *32*(4), 849–865. doi:10.1515/jos-2016-0044

Coleman, S., Göb, R., Manco, G., Pievatolo, A., Tort-Martorell, X., & Reis, M. S. (2016). How Can SMEs Benefit from Big Data? Challenges and a Path Forward. *Quality and Reliability Engineering International*, *32*(6), 2151–2164. doi:10.1002/qre.2008

Colombo, A. W., Bangemann, T., Karnouskos, S., Delsing, J., Stluka, P., Harrison, R., & Lastra, J. L. (2014). *Industrial cloud-based cyber-physical systems*. The IMC-AESOP Approach. doi:10.1007/978-3-319-05624-1

Commission, E. (2017). *Annual Report on European SMEs 2015/2016 – SME recovery continues*. Academic Press.

Commission, E. (2013). Business Opportunities. *Big Data*.

Consoli, S., Presutti, V., Recupero, D. R., Nuzzolese, A. G., Peroni, S., & Gangemi, A. (2017). Producing linked data for smart cities: The case of Catania. *Big Data Research*, *7*, 1–15. doi:10.1016/j.bdr.2016.10.001

Conti, M., Dehghantanha, A., Franke, K., & Watson, S. (2018). Internet of Things security and forensics: Challenges and opportunities. *Future Generation Computer Systems*, *78*, 544–546. doi:10.1016/j.future.2017.07.060

Cool Silicon. (n.d.). Retrieved from https://www.cool-silicon.de/start/

Cooper, T., Maitland, A., Siu, J., & Wei, K. (2016). *Guarding and growing personal data value: Accenture Report on Personal Data*. Retrieved from https://www.accenture.com/

Corno, F., De Russis, L., & Sáenz, J. P. (2018, May). Easing IoT development for novice programmers through code recipes. In *Proceedings of the 40th International Conference on Software Engineering: Software Engineering Education and Training* (pp. 13-16). ACM. 10.1145/3183377.3183385

Correia, J., & Compeau, D. (2017). Information Privacy Awareness (IPA): A Review of the Use, Definition and Measurement of IPA. *Paper presented at the Proceedings of the 50th Hawaii International Conference on System Sciences*, Hawaii. Retrieved from http://hdl.handle.net/10125/41646

Coufal, D. (2016). On the convergence of kernel density estimates in particle filtering. *Kybernetika*, 735–756. doi:10.14736/kyb-2016-5-0735

Cox, M., Ellsworth, D. (1997). *Managing big data for scientific visualization*. ACM Sig graphs.

Crawford, K., & Schultz, J. (2014). Big data and due process: Toward a framework to redress predictive privacy harms. *Boston College Law Review. Boston College. Law School*, *55*(1), 39–92.

Crow, G., Wiles, R., Heath, S., & Charles, V. (2006). Research ethics and data quality: The implications of informed consent. *International Journal of Social Research Methodology*, *9*(2), 83–95. doi:10.1080/13645570600595231

Cui, L., Yu, F. R., & Yan, Q. (2016). When big data meets software-defined networking: SDN for big data and big data for SDN. IEEE Netw., 30, 58–65.

Cui, L., Xie, G., Qu, Y., Gao, L., & Yang, Y. (2018). Security and Privacy in Smart Cities: Challenges and Opportunities. *IEEE Access: Practical Innovations, Open Solutions*, *6*, 46134–46145. doi:10.1109/ACCESS.2018.2853985

Culkin, N., & Smith, D. (2000). An emotional business: A guide to understanding the motivations of small business decision takers. *Qualitative Market Research*, *3*(3), 145–157. doi:10.1108/13522750010333898

Culler, J. (1981). *The Pursuit of Signs*. Routledge.

Culler, J. (2005). *The Pursuit of Signs*. London: Routledge.

Culver, S. H., & Grizzle, A. (2017). *Survey on privacy in media and information literacy with youth perspectives*. Paris: UNESCO.

Cumgeek. (2017). *Hong Kong becomes a Smart City*. (in Russian) Retrieved from https://cumgeek.com/articles/gonkong-skoro-stanet-umnym-gorodom

Custers, B. (2016). Click here to consent forever: Expiry dates for informed consent. *Big Data & Society, 3*(1).

Cusumano, M. A., & Gawer, A. (2002). The Elements of Platform Leadership. *MIT Sloan Management Review*, *43*(3), 51–58.

Da Xu, L., He, W., & Li, S. (2014). Internet of things in industries: A survey. *IEEE Transactions on Industrial Informatics, 10*(4), 2233–2243. doi:10.1109/TII.2014.2300753

Dahl, G. E., Yu, D., Deng, L., & Acero, A. (2012). Context-Dependent Pre-Trained Deep Neural Networks for Large-Vocabulary Speech Recognition. *IEEE Transactions on Audio, Speech, and Language Processing*, *20*(1), 30–42. doi:10.1109/TASL.2011.2134090

Dang, Z. Y. (2015). Fuzzy-based obstacle avoidance for a mobile robot navigation in indoor environment. In *Consumer Electronics-Taiwan (ICCE-TW), IEEE International Conference on* (pp. 55-56). IEEE.

Das, S. (2013). Technology for Smart Home. In *Proceedings of International Conference on VLSI, Communication, Advanced Devices, Signals & Systems and Networking (VCASAN-2013)* (pp. 7-12). Springer, India. Retrieved from http://www.springer.com/978-81-322-1523-3

Das, S. K., Mohanty, S., Barik, S., Nathrout, K., & Suman, H. (2017). Survey on Big Data and Its Challenges Related to IoT. *Proceedings of International Interdisciplinary Conference on Engineering Science & Management.*

Dat, N. D., Phu, V. N., Vo, T. N. C., Vo, T. N. T., & Nguyen, T. A. (2017). STING Algorithm used English Sentiment Classification in A Parallel Environment. International Journal of Pattern Recognition and Artificial Intelligence, 31(7). doi:10.1142/S0218001417500215

Data privacy Lab, IQSS, Harvard University. (n.d.). White Paper. Retrieved 21 December 2018 from https://dataprivacylab.org/projects/pgp/1021-1.pdf

Dat, Phu, & Chau, Tran, & Nguyen. (2017). STING Algorithm used English Sentiment Classification in A Parallel Environment. *International Journal of Pattern Recognition and Artificial Intelligence*, *31*(7). doi:10.114202180014175002l5

Davenport, T. H., Barth, P., & Bean, R. (2012). How 'Big Data' is different. *MIT Sloan Management Review*, *54*(1), 22–24. Retrieved from http://www.hbs.edu/faculty/Pages/item.aspx?num=43026

Davidson & Plattner. (2017). *Ventures Big data Challenges and Opportunities*. Academic Press.

Davidson, R., & Turner, A. (2017). *IBTM World Trends Watch Report*. Reed Exhibitions.

Davis, C. K. (2014). Beyond data and analytics. *Communications of the ACM*, *57*(6), 39–41. doi:10.1145/2602326

Dazhi, D. (2011). Research on coal mine electromechanical equipment closedloopmanagement system based on IoTand information technology. In *Proc. IEEE 2nd Int. Conf. on Artificial Intelligence, Management Science and Electronic Commerce (AIMSEC)* (pp. 5101-5104). IEEE. 10.1109/AIMSEC.2011.6011237

De Santo, A., & Gaspoz, C. (2015). *Influence of risks and privacy literacy on coping responses to privacy threats.* Paper presented at the In Proceedings of the 20th Association Information Management Conference. Retrieved from http://bit.ly/2dGrUfk

Dean, J., & Ghemawat, S. (2008). MapReduce: simplified data processing on large clusters. *Communications of the ACM, 51*(1), 107-113. Retrieved on April 4, 2016 from http://static.googleusercontent.com/media/research.google.com/en//archive/mapreduce-osdi04.pdf

Debatin, B. (2011). Ethics, privacy, and self-restraint in social networking. In R. L. Trepte (Ed.), Privacy online (pp. 47-60). Berlin: Springer. doi:10.1007/978-3-642-21521-6_5

Decuir, J. (2010). *Bluetooth 4.0: Low Energy, IEEE Annual Report.* Retrieved from http:// chapters.comsoc.org/vancouver/BTLER3.pdf

Defays, D., & Anwar, M. N. (1998). Masking microdata using micro-aggregation. *Journal of Official Statistics, 14*(4), 449–461.

Dehestani, D., Eftekhari, F., Guo, Y., Ling, S., Su, S., & Nguyen, H. (2011). Online Support Vector Machine Application for Model-Based Fault Detection and Isolation of HVAC System. *International Journal Of Machine Learning And Computing*, 66-72. doi:10.7763/ijmlc.2011.v1.10

Del Chiappa, G., & Baggio, R. (2015). Knowledge transfer in smart tourism destinations: Analyzing the effects of a network structure. *Journal of Destination Marketing & Management, 4*(3), 145–150. doi:10.1016/j.jdmm.2015.02.001

Delft, The Netherlands. (2015). *Delft Smart City.* Retrieved from https://www.delft.nl/Bedrijven/Stad_van_innovatie/Delft_Smart_City

Demil, B., & Lecoq, X. (2010). Business Model: Towarda Dynamic Consistency View of Strategy. *Long Range Planning, 43*(2-3), 227–246. doi:10.1016/j.lrp.2010.02.004

Detection and Ranging for the Internet of Things. (2018). Retrieved April 2018, from http://www.kritikalsolutions.com/internet-of-things

DeWitt, D. J., Halverson, A., Nehme, R., Shankar, S., Aguilar-Saborit, J., Avanes, A., & Gramling, J. (2013). Split query processing in polybase. In *Proceedings of the 2013 ACM SIGMOD International Conference on Management of Data* (pp. 1255-1266). ACM. Retrieved on April 4, 2016 from https://pdfs.semanticscholar.org/3fd5/fdfd1a672a613de8a2b266676f577de9bcf1.pdf

Dey, A. (2001). Understanding and using context. *Personal and Ubiquitous Computing, 5*(1), 4–7. doi:10.1007007790170019

Dhaka, V. S., & Vyas, S. (2014). Analysis of Server Performance with Different Techniques of Virtual Databases. *Journal of Emerging Trends in Computing and Information Sciences, 5*(10).

Dhungana, D., Engelbrecht, G., Parreira, J. X., Schuster, A., & Valerio, D. (2015). Aspern smart ICT: Data analytics and privacy challenges in a smart city. *2015 IEEE 2nd World Forum on Internet of Things (WF-IoT),* 447-452. 10.1109/WF-IoT.2015.7389096

Diallo, S. Y., Herencia-zapana, H., Padilla, J. J., & Tolk, A. (2011). *Understanding Interoperability.* Academic Press.

DictionaryC. E. (2017). Retrieved from http://dictionary.cambridge.org/

DictionaryC. E. (2017). Retrieved from http://www.collinsdictionary.com/dictionary/english

DictionaryL. E. (2017). Retrieved from http://www.ldoceonline.com/

DictionaryO. E. (2017). Retrieved from http://www.oxforddictionaries.com/

Diebold, F. X. (2012). *A personal perspective on the origin(s) and development of "Big Data": the phenomena, the term and the discipline*. Retrieved from: http://www.ssc.upenn.edu/~fdiebold/papers/paper112/Diebold_Big_Data.pdf

Ding, D., Conti, M., & Solanas, A. (2016). A smart health application and its related privacy issues. *2016 Smart City Security and Privacy Workshop (SCSP-W)*, 1-5. 10.1109/SCSPW.2016.7509558

Directive 95/46/EC of the European Parliament, and the Council of 24 October 1995 on the protection of individuals with regard to the processing of personal data and on the free movement of such data. *Official Journal of the European Communities*, No I. (281):31-50, Oct. 24 1995.

DLA-PIPPER. (2018). *Piperglobal Data Privacy Snapshot 2018: How does your organisation compare?* Retrieved from https://www.dlapiper.com/

Dlodlo, N. (2015). The internet of things in transportation in south Africa. In *2015 International Conference on Emerging Trends in Networks and Computer Communications*. IEEE.

Donato, C. (2016). Buenos Aires Preserves Old Charm by Becoming a Smart City. *SAP News Center*. Retrieved from http://news.sap.com/buenos-aires-preserves-old-charm-by-becoming-a-smart-city/

Dong, B., Qiu, J., Zheng, Q., Zhong, X., Li, J., & Li, Y. (2010). A novel approach to improving the efficiency of storing and accessing small files on Hadoop: a case study by PowerPoint files. In *2010 IEEE International Conference on Services Computing* (pp. 65-72). IEEE. Retrieved on April 4, 2016 from http://ieeexplore.ieee.org/xpl/login.jsp?tp=&arnumber=5557216&url=http%3A%2F%2Fieeexplore.ieee.org%2Fxpls%2Fabs_all.jsp%3Farnumber%3D5557216

Dong, B., Zheng, Q., Tian, F., Chao, K.-M., Ma, R., & Anane, R. (2012). An optimized approach for storing and accessing small files on cloud storage. *Journal of Network and Computer Applications*, *35*(6), 1847–1862. doi:10.1016/j.jnca.2012.07.009

Doran, D., Gokhale, S., & Dagnino, A. (2013). Human sensing for smart cities. In *Proceedings of the 2013 IEEE/ACM International Conference on Advances in Social Networks Analysis and Mining* (pp. 1323-1330). ACM.

Dorsey, W. (2003). *Market semiotics: behavioral market diagnosis*. Retrieved from: http://www.marketsemiotics.com/docs/pdf/ MSBrochure.pdf

Downes, L., & Nunes, P. F. (2013). Big-Bang Disruption. *Harvard Business Review*, *91*(3), 44–56.

Drinić, S. M., Nikolić, A., & Perić, V. (2008). Cluster Analysis of Soybean Genotypes Based on RAPD Markers. *Proceedings. 43rd Croatian and 3rd International Symposium on Agriculture*, 367-370.

Du, W., Tan, S., Cheng, X., & Yun, X. (2010). Adapting Information Bottleneck Method for Automatic Construction of Domain-oriented Sentiment Lexicon. WSDM'10, New York, NY. doi:10.1145/1718487.1718502

Du, Z. Y. M. (2012). Design and implementation of safety management system for oil depot based on Internet of Things. In *Proc. IEEE Int. Conf. Green Comput. and Communication* (pp. 249–252). IEEE. 10.1109/GreenCom.2012.46

Dunlop, C. A. (2017). The irony of epistemic learning: Epistemic communities, policy learning and the case of Europe's hormones saga. *Policy & Society, 36*(2), 215–232. doi:.2017.1322260 doi:10.1080/14494035

Duroc, Y., & Kaddour, D. (2012). RFID potential impacts and future evolution for green projects. *Energy Procedia, 18*, 91–98. doi:10.1016/j.egypro.2012.05.021

Dutcher, J. (2014). What is Big data? Retrieved from https://datascience.berkeley.edu/what-is-big-data/

Dutton, W. H. (2013). The Internet of things. doi:https://ssrn.com/abstract=2324902 or doi:10.2139srn.2324902

Dzbor, M., Stutt, A., Motta, E., & Collins, T. (2007). Representations for semantic learning webs: Semantic Web technology in learning support. *Journal of Computer Assisted Learning, 23*(1), 69–82. doi:10.1111/j.1365-2729.2007.00202.x

Earley, S. (2014). *Big data and predictive analytics: What is new? IT Pro*. IEEE Computer Society.

Eclipse hawkBit. (n.d.). Retrieved from https://www.eclipse.org/hawkbit/

Economist. (2016). *The world`s most livable cities*. Retrieved from https://www.economist.com/blogs/graphicdetail/2016/08/daily-chart-14

Eco, U. (1978). *A Theory of Semiotics*. Bloomington, IN: Indiana University Press.

Eco, U. (1981). The theory of signs and the role of the reader. *The Bulletin of the Midwest Modern Language Association, 14*(1), 35–45. doi:10.2307/1314865

Edosio, U. Z. (2014). Big data Analytics and its Application in E-commerce. *E-Commerce Technologies, 1*. Retrieved from https://www.researchgate.net/publication/264129339_Big_Data_Analytics_and_its_Application_in_E-Commerce

EDPS. (2010). *Opinion on privacy in the digital age: "Privacy by Design" as a key tool to ensure citizens' trust in ICTs*. Retrieved from https://secure.edps.europa.eu/EDPSWEB/webdav/site/mySite/shared/Documents/EDPS/PressNews/Press/2010/EDPS-2010-06_Privacy%20in%20digital%20age_EN.pdf

EDPS. (2018). *Guidelines on the protection of personal data in IT governance and IT management of EU institutions*. Retrieved from https://edps.europa.eu/sites/edp/files/publication/it_governance_management_en.pdf

Ekanayake, B. N. B., Halgamuge, M. N., & Syed, A. (January 2018). Review: Security and Privacy Issues of Fog Computing for the Internet of Things (IoT). In *Lecture Notes on Data Engineering and Communications Technologies Cognitive Computing for Big Data Systems Over IoT, Frameworks, Tools and Applications* (Vol. 14). Springer. doi:10.1007/978-3-319-70688-7_7

Elgendy, N., & Elragal, A. (2014, July). Big data analytics: a literature review paper. In *Industrial Conference on Data Mining* (pp. 214-227). Springer, Cham.

Elhoseny, H., Elhoseny, M., Riad, A. M., & Hassanien, A. E. (2018, February). A framework for big data analysis in smart cities. In *International Conference on Advanced Machine Learning Technologies and Applications* (pp. 405-414). Springer, Cham. 10.1007/978-3-319-74690-6_40

EMC. (2012). *Big data-as-a-service: a market and technology perspective*. Retrieved from: http://www.emc.com/collateral/software/wwhite-hite-ppapers/h10839-big-data-as-a-service-perspt.pdf,apers/h10839-big-data-as-a-service-perspt.pdf

Enabling Detection and Ranging for the Internet of Things and Beyond. (2018). Retrieved May 2018, from https://leddartech.com/enabling-detection-and-ranging-for-the-internet-of-things-and-beyond/

Endsley, M. R. (1988). Situation awareness global assessment technique (SAGAT). *Paper presented at the IEEE Aerospace and Electronics Conference, 1988. NAECON 1988.*

Endsley, M. R. (1995a). Measurement of Situation Awareness in Dynamic Systems. *Human Factors, 37*(1), 65–84. doi:10.1518/001872095779049499

Endsley, M. R. (1995b). Toward a Theory of Situation Awareness in Dynamic Systems. *Human Factors, 37*(1), 32–64. doi:10.1518/001872095779049543

English Dictionary of Lingoes. (2017). Retrieved from http://www.lingoes.net/

Esayas, S. Y. (2015). The role of anonymisation and pseudonymisation under the EU data privacy rules: Beyond the 'all or nothing' approach. *European Journal of Law And Technology, 6*(2). Retrieved from http://ejlt.org/article/view/378/569

Esen, M. F., & Turkay, B. (2017). Big data applications in tourism industries. *Journal of Tourism and Gastronomy Studies, 5*(4), 92–115. doi:10.21325/jotags.2017.140

Espada, J. P., Martínez, O. S., García-Bustelo, B. C. P., & Lovelle, J. M. C. (2011). Virtual Objects on the Internet of Things. *International Journal of Artificial Intelligence and Interactive Multimedia, 1*(4), 24–30. doi:10.9781/ijimai.2011.144

ETSI. (2013). *Interoperability Best Practices*. Retrieved from https://portal.etsi.org/CTI/Downloads/ETSIApproach/IOT_Best_Practices.pdf

Etzioni, A. (2010). Is Transparency the Best Disinfectant? *Journal of Political Philosophy, 18*(4), 389–404. doi:10.1111/j.1467-9760.2010.00366.x

Etzioni, A. (2015). *A Cyber Age Privacy Doctrine: policy and practice*. New York: Palgrave Macmillan. doi:10.1057/9781137513960

EU Smartcities. (2017). *The Hague- Smart communities market place*. Retrieved from https://eu-smartcities.eu/place/hague

European Commission. (2016). *General Data Protection Regulation*. Retrieved from https://goo.gl/JxYRUK

European Commission. (2017). *The Internet of Things | Digital Single Market*. Retrieved May 12, 2018, from https://ec.europa.eu/digital-single-market/en/research-innovation-iot

European Commission. (n.d.). Strategic Energy Technology Plan. Retrieved from https://ec.europa.eu/energy/en/topics/technology-and-innovation/strategic-energy-technology-plan

European Union. (2012). *The Reform of Data Protection of 2012*. Retrieved from https://edps.europa.eu/

European Union. (2016). *European Union agency for network and information security, guidelines for smes on the security of personal data processing*. Retrieved from https://www.enisa.europa.eu/publications/guidelines-for-smes-on-the-security-of-personal-data-processing

Eurostat. (2017). *Early adopters of big data*. European Union Statistical Working Paper. doi:10.2785/762729

Evans, D. (2011). *The Internet of Things-How the Next Evolution of the Internet Is Changing Everything*. Cisco Internet Business Solutions Group (IBSG) White Paper.

EY Building a Better Working World. (2014, April). *Big Data: Changing the way businesses compete and operate* (Insights on Governance, Risk and Compliance Report). Ernst & Young Global Limited. Retrieved from http://www.ey.com/us/en/home/library

Faber. (1994). Clustering and the Continuous k-Means Algorithm. *Los Alamos Science, 22*.

Faisal, M. M. (2015). Smart mobile robot for security of low visibility environment. In *Information Technology: Towards New Smart World (NSITNSW),5th National Symposium*. Chicago: IEEE.

Faith, D. P. (1983). Asymmetric binary similarity measures. *Oecologia, 57*(3), 287–290. doi:10.1007/BF00377169 PMID:28309352

Fan, W., & Bifet, A. (2013). Mining big data: current status, and forecast to the future. ACM *sIGKDD Explorations Newsletter*, *14*(2), 1-5.

Farahani, B., Firouzi, F., Chang, V., Badaroglu, M., Constant, N., & Mankodiya, K. (2018). Towards fog-driven IoT eHealth: Promises and challenges of IoT in medicine and healthcare. *Future Generation Computer Systems, 78*(2), 659-676.

Farahani, B., Firouzi, F., Chang, V., Badaroglu, M., Constant, N., & Mankodiya, K. (2017). Towards fog-driven IoT eHealth: Promises and challenges of IoT in medicine and healthcare. *Future Generation Computer Systems*. doi:10.1016/j.future.2017.04.036

Fard, H. D. (2012). Research paradigms in public administration. *International Journal of the Humanities*, *19*(4), 55–108. Retrieved from http://eijh-old.modares.ac.ir/article_10524.html

Farooq, M. O., & Kunz, T. (2017). *IoT-RF: A routing framework for the Internet of Things*. Paper presented at the IEEE 28th Annual International Symposium on Personal, Indoor, and Mobile Radio Communications (PIMRC), Montreal, QC, Canada. Retrieved from https://ieeexplore.ieee.org/document/8292730/

Federal Trade Commission. (2015). *Internet of things: privacy and security in a connected world*. Retrieved from https://goo.gl/qAhiAH

Feldman, B., Martin, E. M., & Skotnes, T. (2012). Big Data in Healthcare Hype and Hope. *Dr. Bonnie, 360*.

Felzenszwalb, F., Girshick, R. B., McAllester, D., & Ramanan, D. (2010). Object detection with discriminatively trained part based models. *IEEE Transactions on Pattern Analysis and Machine Intelligence*, *32*(9), 1627–1645. doi:10.1109/TPAMI.2009.167 PMID:20634557

Feng, S., Le Zhang, B. L. D. W., Yu, G., & Wong, K.-F. (2013). Is Twitter A Better Corpus for Measuring Sentiment Similarity? *Proceedings of the 2013 Conference on Empirical Methods in Natural Language Processing*, 897–902.

Fenich, G. G. (2015). *Planning and Management of Meetings, Expositions, Events, and Conventions*. London, UK: Pearson Education Limited.

Fereidooni, H., Frassetto, T., Miettinen, M., Sadeghi, A.-R., & Conti, M. (2017). Fitness Trackers: Fit for Health but Unfit for Security and Privacy. *Paper presented at the Connected Health Applications, Systems and Engineering Technologies (CHASE) Conference*. IEEE.

Fernández-Ares, A., Mora, A. M., Arenas, M. G., García-Sanchez, P., Romero, G., Rivas, V., ... Merelo, J. J. (2017). Studying real traffic and mobility scenarios for a Smart City using a new monitoring and tracking system. *Future Generation Computer Systems*, *76*, 163–179. doi:10.1016/j.future.2016.11.021

Fertik, M. (Feb.1 2013). The Rich See a Different Internet Than the Poor. *Scientific American*. Retrieved from https://goo.gl/gVLnxK

Figueiredo. (n.d.). *Keeping up with Big data*. Retrieved from https://www.linkedin.com/pulse/keeping-up-big-data-antonio-figueiredo

Finlay, D. (2016). Article Seven - Connected Health Approaches to Wound Monitoring. In J. Davis, A. McLister, J. Cundell, & D. Finlay (Eds.), *Smart Bandage Technologies* (pp. 229–244). Academic Press. doi:10.1016/B978-0-12-803762-1.00007-2

FIPPA. c. F.31, R.S.O. (1990). *The freedom of information and protection of privacy act*. Retrieved from http://www.bclaws.ca/

FI-WARE Consortium. (2012). *FI-WARE Architecture*, *2004*. doi:10.1002/ejoc.201200111

Fiware. (2017). Retrieved May 1, 2017, from https://www.fiware.org/tag/iot/

Flohr, F., & Gavrila, M. (2016). *Daimler Pedestrian Segmentation Benchmark Dataset*. Retrieved, May 2018 from, http://www.gavrila.net/Datasets/Daimler_Pedestrian_Benchmark_D/daimler_pedestrian_benchmark_d.html

Forfas. (2014). *Assessing the demand for big data and analytics skills 2013–2020*. Retrieved from http://www.forfas.ie/media/07052014- Assessing_the_Demand_for_Big_Data_and_Analytics_Skills- Publication.pdf

Forkan, A. R. M., Khalil, I., Ibaida, A., & Member, Z. T. (2015). BDCaM: Big Data for Context-Aware monitoring-a personalized knowledge discovery framework for assisted healthcare. *IEEE Transactions on Cloud Computing*.

Forkan, A., Khalil, I., & Tari, Z. (2014). CoCaMAAL: A cloud-oriented context-aware middleware in ambient assisted living. *Future Generation Computer Systems*, *35*, 114–127. doi:10.1016/j.future.2013.07.009

Fornaciari, F. (2014). Pricey privacy: Framing the economy of information in the digital age. *First Monday*, *19*(12). doi:10.5210/fm.v19i12.5008

Forsyth Communications. (2012). *For big data analytics there's no such thing as too big the compelling economics and technology of big data computing*. Retrieved from http://www.cisco.com/c/dam/ en/us/solutions/data-center-virtualization/big_data_wp.pdf

FowlerM. (2010). *BlueGreenDeployment*. Retrieved from https://martinfowler.com/bliki/BlueGreenDeployment.html

Francesconi, E., & Peruginelli, G. (2007). Searching and retrieving legal literature through automated semantic indexing. *Proceedings of the 11th International Conference on Artificial intelligence and Law–ICAIL '07,* 131–139. 10.1145/1276318.1276343

Frank, P. (2014). The Dark Market for Personal Data. *The New York Times*. Retrieved from https://goo.gl/v5k5Kf

Franks, B. (2012). *Taming the Big Data tidal wave: Finding opportunities in huge data streams with advanced analytics* (1st ed.). Wiley Publishing. doi:10.1002/9781119204275

Frey, C. B., & Osborne, M. A. (2017). The future of employment: How susceptible are jobs to computerisation? *Technological Forecasting and Social Change*, *114*(1), 254–280. doi:10.1016/j.techfore.2016.08.019

Fuller, S. R. (2008). Organizational symbolism: A multidimensional conceptualization. *The Journal of Global Business and Management*, *4*(2), 168–174. Retrieved from http://www.jgbm.org/page/ previous_V4-2.htm

Funabiki & Takefuji. (1992). A neural network parallel algorithm for channel assignment problems in cellular radio networks. *IEEE Transactions on Vehicular Technology, 41*(4), 430-437. Doi:10.1109/25.182594

Furht, B., & Villanustre, F. (2016). Introduction to big data. In B. Furht & F. Villanustre (Eds.), *Big Data Technology and Application* (pp. 3–11). Cham: Springer International Publishing. doi:10.1007/978-3-319-44550-2_1

Gallego, V. M. R. (2015). Unmanned aerial gas leakage localization and mapping using microdrones. In *Proc. IEEE Sensors Applications Symposium (SAS)* (pp. 1–6). IEEE. 10.1109/SAS.2015.7133629

Ganti, R. K., Ye, F., & Lei, H. (2011). Mobile crowdsensing: Current state and future challenges. *IEEE Communications Magazine*, *49*(11), 32–39. doi:10.1109/MCOM.2011.6069707

Gantz, J. & Reinsel, D. (2011). Extracting value from chaos. *IDC iView Report*.

Ganzha, M., Paprzycki, M., Pawlowski, W., Szmeja, P., & Wasielewska, K. (2016). Semantic Technologies for the IoT-An Inter-IoT Perspective. In *Internet-of-Things Design and Implementation (IoTDI), 2016 IEEE First International Conference on* (pp. 271–276). Academic Press. 10.1109/IoTDI.2015.22

Ganzha, M., Paprzycki, M., Pawłowski, W., Szmeja, P., & Wasielewska, K. (2017). Semantic interoperability in the Internet of Things: An overview from the INTER-IoT perspective. *Journal of Network and Computer Applications*, *81*, 111–124. doi:10.1016/j.jnca.2016.08.007

Ganzha, M., Paprzycki, M., Pawłowski, W., Szmeja, P., & Wasielewska, K. (2018). Towards Semantic Interoperability Between Internet of Things Platforms BT - Integration, Interconnection, and Interoperability of IoT Systems. In R. Gravina, C. E. Palau, M. Manso, A. Liotta, & G. Fortino (Eds.), (pp. 103–127). Cham: Springer International Publishing; doi:10.1007/978-3-319-61300-0_6

Garcia Alfaro, J., Navarro Arribas, G., Cavalli, A., & Leneutre, J. (2011). Data privacy management and autonomous spontaneous security. In *Proceedings of 5th International Workshop, Dpm 2010 and 3rd International Workshop, SETOP* (vol. 5). Athens, Greece: Springer Science & Business Media. 10.1007/978-3-642-19348-4

Gartner. (2013). IT Glossary. Retrieved from https://www.gartner.com/it-glossary/big-data/

Gartner. (2015). Gartner says 6.4 billion connected things will be in use in 2016, up 30 percent from. Retrieved from https://www.gartner.com/newsroom/id/3165317

Gartner. (2017). Gartner Says 8.4 Billion Connected "Things" Will Be in Use in 2017, Up 31 Percent From 2016. Retrieved from https://www.gartner.com/newsroom/id/3598917

GartnerE. (n.d.). Retrieved from https://www.gartner.com/newsroom/id/3598917

Gasser, U., & Schultz, J. (2015). Governance of online intermediaries: Observation from series of national case studies. *The Berkman Centre for Internet & Society Research publication series No. 2015-5.* doi:10.2139srn.2566364

Geeetech. (2016). *Yun Shield.* Retrieved from http://www.geeetech.com/wiki/index.php/Iduino_Yun_Shield

Geneiatakis, D., Kounelis, I., Neisse, R., Nai-Fovino, I., Steri, G., & Baldini, G. (2017). Security and privacy issues for an IoT based smart home. *2017 40th International Convention on Information and Communication Technology, Electronics and Microelectronics (MIPRO)*, 1292-1297. 10.23919/MIPRO.2017.7973622

Gershenfeld, N., & Vasseur, J. P. (2014). As Objects Go Online: The Promise (And Pitfalls) of the Internet of Things. *Foreign Affairs*, *93*(2), 60–67.

Gevrey, M., Dimopoulos, I., & Lek, S. (2003). Review and comparison of methods to study the contribution of variables in artificial neural network models. *Ecological Modelling*, *160*(3), 249–264. doi:10.1016/S0304-3800(02)00257-0

Gharavi, H., & Ghafurian, R. (2011). Smart grid: The electric energy system of the future. *Proceedings of the IEEE*, *99*(6), 917–921. doi:10.1109/JPROC.2011.2124210

Ghemawat, S., Gobioff, H., & Leung, S. T. (2003). The Google file system. *ACM SIGOPS Operating Systems Review*, *37*(5), 29-43. Retrieved on April 4, 2016 from http://static.googleusercontent.com/media/research.google.com/en//archive/gfs-sosp2003.pdf

Ghosh, R., Komma, S. P. R., & Simmhan, Y. (2018). *Adaptive Energy-aware Scheduling of Dynamic Event Analytics across Edge and Cloud Resources*. Academic Press.

Ghotekar, N. (2016). Analysis and Data Mining of Call Detail Records using Big Data Technology. *IJARCCE*, *5*(12), 280–283. doi:10.17148/IJARCCE.2016.51264

Giaretta, A., Balasubramaniam, S., & Conti, M. (2016). Security vulnerabilities and countermeasures for target localization in bio-nanothings communication networks. *IEEE Transactions on Information Forensics and Security*, *11*(4), 665–676. doi:10.1109/TIFS.2015.2505632

Giuliano, Mazzenga, Neri, & Vegni. (2017). Security Access Protocols in IoT Capillary Networks. *IEEE Internet of Things Journal, 4*(3), 645-657.

Glasser, M., Bailey, N., McMillan, A., Goff, E., Morrell, M. J., Nam, Y., ... Da Xu, L. (2014). Multimodal Low-Invasive System for Sleep Quality Monitoring and Improvement BT - Beyond the Internet of Things: Everything Interconnected. *Sleep*, *49*(6), 261–274. doi:10.1164/rccm.169.1160

Godoe, P., & Johansen, T. (2012). Understanding adoption of new technologies: Technology readiness and technology acceptance as an integrated concept. *Journal of European Psychology Students*, *3*(1).

Goebel, R., Norman, A., & Karanasios, S. (2015). *Exploring the Value of Business Analytics Solutions for SMEs*. Association for Information Systems AIS Electronic Library (AISeL).

Golub, K. (2017, October 16). *Encyclopedia of knowledge organization: Automatic subject indexing of text* [ISKO Version 1.0]. Retrieved from http://www.isko.org/cyclo/automatic

Gomez, J., Huete, J. F., Hoyos, O., Perez, L., & Grigori, D. (2013). Interaction System Based on Internet of Things as Support for Education. *Procedia Computer Science*, *21*, 132–139. doi:10.1016/j.procs.2013.09.019

Google CloudS. D. K. (n.d.). Retrieved from https://cloud.google.com/sdk/

Google. (2017). *Google Cloud IoT*. Retrieved May 15, 2018, from https://cloud.google.com/iot-core/

Gordijn, J., & Akkermans, H. (2001). Design and Evaluation of e-Business Models. *IEEE Intelligent Systems*, *16*(4), 11–17. doi:10.1109/5254.941353

Gough, C., Siddha, S., & Chen, K. (2007). Kernel scalability—expanding the horizon beyond fine grain locks. *Proceedings of the Linux Symposium,* 153-165. Retrieved on April 4, 2016 from https://www.kernel.org/doc/ols/2007/ols2007v1-pages-153-166.pdf

Graham, T. (2016). Smart city Malmo. *EIB*. Retrieved from http://www.eib.org/attachments/documents/smart_city_initiatives_and_projects_in_malmo_sweden_en.pdf

Gravina, R., Manso, M., & Liotta, A. (2018). *Integration, Interconnection, and Interoperability of IoT Systems* (R. Gravina, C. E. Palau, M. Manso, A. Liotta, & G. Fortino, Eds.). Cham: Springer International Publishing. doi:10.1007/978-3-319-61300-0

Green Touch. (n.d.). Retrieved from https://s3-us-west-2.amazonaws.com/belllabs-microsite-greentouch/index.html

GreenI. C. N. (n.d.). Retrieved from http://www.greenicn.org/

Group, C. S. (2013, April). *Expanded Top Ten Big Data Security and Privacy Challenges*. Academic Press.

Groves, P., Kayyali, B., Knott, D., & Van Kuiken, S. (2013). The 'big data' revolution in healthcare. *The McKinsey Quarterly*, *2*(3).

GRPC. (n.d.). Retrieved from https://grpc.io/

Guan, H., Li, C.-K., Cheung, T.-Y., Yu, S., & Tong, W. (2002). Design and implementation of a parallel software for hybrid neural network computation in PVM environment. *Proceedings of Third International Conference on Signal Processing (ICSP'96)*. DOI: 10.1109/ICSIGP.1996.566591

Gubbi, J., Buyya, R., Marusic, S., & Palaniswami, M. (2013). Internet of Things (IoT): A vision, architectural elements, and future directions. Future Generation Computer Systems, 29(7), 1645-1660.

Gubbi, J., Buyya, R., Marusic, S., & Palaniswami, M. (2013). Internet of Things (IoT): A vision architectural elements and future directions. *Future Generation Computer Systems*, *29*(7), 1645–1660. doi:10.1016/j.future.2013.01.010

Guo, X. Y. W. (2015). Design of WSN-based environment monitoring system on repair of gas leakage. In *Proc. IEEE 27th Chinese Control and Decision Conf. (CCDC)* (pp. 3340–3344). IEEE.

Guo, Z., Karimian, N., Tehranipoor, M. M., & Forte, D. (2016). Hardware security meets biometrics for the age of IoT. *2016 IEEE International Symposium on Circuits and Systems (ISCAS)*, 1318-1321. 10.1109/ISCAS.2016.7527491

Gupta, A., Mohammad, A., Syed, A., & Halgamuge, M. N. (2016). A Comparative Study of Classification Algorithms using Data Mining: Crime and Accidents in Denver City the USA. *International Journal of Advanced Computer Science and Applications*, *7*(7), 374–381. doi:10.14569/IJACSA.2016.070753

Gurkina, A. (2013). *Travel experience in hotels for MICE industry* (Bachelor's thesis). Haaga-Helia University of Applied Sciences, Finland.

Gurses, S., & Danezis, G. (2012). *A critical review of ten years of privacy technology*. Retrieved from https://homes.esat.kuleuven.be

Gutiérrez-Rubí, A., & Sarsanedas, O. (2016, June 20). *Technopolitics and the new territories for political action* [Interview]. London, UK: Democracia Abierta/OpenDemocracy. Retrieved from https://www.opendemocracy.net/democraciaabierta/antoni-guti-rrez-rub-oleguer-sarsanedas/tecnopolitics-and-new-territories-for-poli

Haas, P. M. (1992). Introduction: Epistemic communities and international policy coordination. *International Organization*, *46*(1), 1–35. doi:10.1017/S0020818300001442

Hadoop. (2017). Retrieved from http://hadoop.apache.org

Haggarty, O. J., Knottenbelt, W. J., & Bradley, J. T. (2009). Distributed response time analysis of GSPN models with MapReduce. *Simulation*, *85*(8), 497–509. doi:10.1177/0037549709340785

Hajibabaei, M., & Rasooli, E. (2014). Comparison of Different Methods of Measuring Illuminance in the Indoor of Office and Educational Buildings. *Jundishapur Journal of Health Sciences*, *6*(3), 1–5. doi:10.5812/jjhs.21720

Halper, F. (2014). Predictive analytics for business advantage [TDWI Best Practices Report]. *The Data Warehousing Institute (TDWI) Research*. Retrieved from https://tdwi.org/research/list/research-and-resources.aspx

Hamerly, G., & Elkan, C. (2002). Alternatives to the k-means algorithm that find better clusterings. *CIKM '02 Proceedings of the eleventh international conference on Information and knowledge management*, 600-607.

Handte, M., Foell, S., Wagner, S., Kortuem, G., & Marrón, P. (2016). An Internet-of-Things enabled connected navigation system for urban bus rider. *IEEE Internet Things Journal*, *3*(5), 735–744. doi:10.1109/JIOT.2016.2554146

Hanke, S., Mayer, C., Hoeftberger, O., Boos, H., Wichert, R., & Tazari, M.-R. … Furfari, F. (2011). universAAL -- An Open and Consolidated AAL Platform. In R. Wichert & B. Eberhardt (Eds.), Ambient Assisted Living: 4. AAL-Kongress 2011 (pp. 127–140). Berlin: Springer Berlin Heidelberg. doi:10.1007/978-3-642-18167-2_10

Hans van der Veer, A. W. (2008). *Achieving Technical Interoperability - the ETSI Approach*. Academic Press.

Hans, G. (2012). Privacy Policies, Terms of Service, and FTC Enforcement: Broadening Unfairness Regulation for a New Era. *Michigan Telecommunications and Technology Law Review*, *19*, 163.

Han, T., & Ansari, N. (2014). Powering mobile networks with green energy. *IEEE Wireless Communications*, *21*(1), 90–96. doi:10.1109/MWC.2014.6757901

Haque, M., Murshed, M., & Paul, M. (2008). On stable dynamic background generation technique using gaussian mixture models for robust object detection. *5th International Conference on Advanced Video and Signal Based Surveillance*, 41–48. 10.1109/AVSS.2008.12

Harris, P. (2018, May). *GDPR: The steps event planners need to follow.* Paper presented at The Trade Show of Imex Frankfurt, Frankfurt, Germany.

Hasan, M., & Mishra, P. (2012). Robust Gesture Recognition Using Gaussian Distribution for Features Fitting. *International Journal Of Machine Learning And Computing*, 266-273. doi:10.7763/ijmlc.2012.v2.128

Hashem, I. A. T., Chang, V., Anuar, N. B., Adewole, K., Yaqoob, I., Gani, A., ... Chiroma, H. (2016). The role of big data in smart city. *International Journal of Information Management*, *36*(5), 748–758. doi:10.1016/j.ijinfomgt.2016.05.002

Hashem, I. A. T., Yaqoob, I., Anuar, N. B., Mokhtar, S., Gani, A., & Ullah Khan, S. (2015). The rise of "big data" on cloud computing: Review and open research issues. *Information Systems*, *47*, 98–115. doi:10.1016/j.is.2014.07.006

Haynes, D. (2015). *Risk and regulation of access to personal data on online social networking services in the UK.* Unpublished doctoral dissertation, City University London, London. Retrieved from http://openaccess.city.ac.uk/11972/

Haynes, D., & Robinson, L. (2015). Defining user risk in social networking services. *Aslib Journal of Information Management*, *67*(1), 94–115. doi:10.1108/AJIM-07-2014-0087

Häyrinen, K., Saranto, K., & Nykänen, P. (2008). Definition, structure, content, use and impacts of electronic health records: A review of the research literature. *International Journal of Medical Informatics*, *77*(5), 291–304. doi:10.1016/j.ijmedinf.2007.09.001 PMID:17951106

Hegeman, T., Ghit, B., Capota, M., HIdders, J., Epema, D., & Iosup, A. (2013). *The BTWorld use case for big data analytics: Description, MapReduce logical workflow, and empirical evaluation.* Retrieved from http://www.pds.ewi.tudelft.nl/~iosup/btworld-mapreduce-workflow13ieeebigdata.pdf

Heil, A., Knoll, M., & Weis, T. (2007). The Internet of Things–context-based device federations. *Proceedings of the 40th Annual Hawaii International Conference on System Sciences (HICSS2007).*

Helberger, N. (2016). Profiling and Targeting Consumers in the Internet of Things – A New Challenge for Consumer Law. *SSRN Electronic Journal*. doi:10.2139srn.2728717

Helsinki Smart Region. (2016). Retrieved from https://www.helsinkismart.fi

Hernandez, P. (2012). App employs context for Big Data analytics efficiency. *Enterprise Apps Today.* Retrieved from: http://www.enterpriseappstoday.com/business-intelligence/app-employs-context-for-big-data-analytics-efficiency

Hernández-Ugalde, J. A., Mora-Urpí, J., & Rocha, O. J. (2011). Genetic relationships among wild and cultivated populations of peach palm (Bactris gasipaes Kunth, Palmae): Evidence for multiple independent domestication events. *Genetic Resources and Crop Evolution*, *58*(4), 571–583. doi:10.100710722-010-9600-6

Hirawat, A., & Bhargava, D. (2015). Enhanced accident detection system using safety application for emergency in mobile environment: Safeme. In *Proceedings of Fourth International Conference on Soft Computing for Problem Solving* (pp. 177-183). Springer New Delhi. 10.1007/978-81-322-2220-0_14

Hodo, E. (2016). Threat analysis of IoT networks using artificial neural network intrusion detection system. *2016 International Symposium on Networks, Computers and Communications (ISNCC)*, 1-6. 10.1109/ISNCC.2016.7746067

Holler, J., Tsiatsis, V., Mulligan, C., Avesand, S., Karnouskos, S., & Boyle, D. (2014). *From Machine-to-machine to the Internet of Things: Introduction to a New Age of Intelligence.* Cambridge: Academic Press.

Hong, L., Xiao, F. W., & Chong, P. H. (2010, September). Opportunistic relay selection in future green multihop cellular networks. In *Vehicular Technology Conference Fall (VTC 2010-Fall), 2010 IEEE 72nd* (pp. 1-5). IEEE. Retrieved from http://www.ifgict.org/

Hong, S., Kim, D., Park, S., Jung, W., & Kim, E. (2010). SNAIL: An IP-based wireless sensor network approach to the internet of things. *IEEE Wireless Communications*, *17*(6), 34–42. doi:10.1109/MWC.2010.5675776

Hossain, Islam, Ali, Kwak, & Hasan. (2017). An Internet of Things-based health prescription assistant and its security system design. *Future Generation Computer Systems.*

Houeland, T., & Aamodt, A. (2017). A learning system based on lazy metareasoning. *Progress In Artificial Intelligence*, 7(2), 129–146. doi:10.100713748-017-0138-0

Hsu, K., Gupta, H. V., & Sorooshian, S. (1995). Artificial Neural Network Modeling of the Rainfall-Runoff Process. *Water Resources Research*, *31*(10), 2517–2530. doi:10.1029/95WR01955

Htait, A., Fournier, S., & Bellot, P. (2016). LSIS at SemEval-2016 Task 7: Using Web Search Engines for English and Arabic Unsupervised Sentiment Intensity Prediction. *Proceedings of SemEval-2016*, 481–485. 10.18653/v1/S16-1076

Huang, Ng, Rong, & Li. (2005). Automated variable weighting in k-means type clustering. *IEEE Transactions on Pattern Analysis and Machine Intelligence, 27*(5). Doi:10.1109/TPAMI.2005.95

Huang, C., Lu, R., & Choo, K. K. R. (2017). Vehicular Fog Computing: Architecture, Use Case, and Security and Forensic Challenges. *IEEE Communications Magazine*, *55*(11), 105–111. doi:10.1109/MCOM.2017.1700322

Huang, Z. (1998). Extensions to the k-Means Algorithm for Clustering Large Data Sets with Categorical Values. *Data Mining and Knowledge Discovery*, *2*(3), 283–304. doi:10.1023/A:1009769707641

Huby, G., Cockram, J., & Fleming, M. (2013). Through-life Data Exploitation to Reduce Downtime and Costs. *Procedia CIRP*, *11*, 50–55. doi:10.1016/j.procir.2013.07.070

Hui, T. K., Sherratt, R. S., & Sánchez, D. D. (2017). Major requirements for building Smart Homes in Smart Cities based on Internet of Things technologies. *Future Generation Computer Systems*, *76*, 358–369. doi:10.1016/j.future.2016.10.026

Hu, L., & Giang, N. (2017). IoT-Driven Automated Object Detection Algorithm for Urban Surveillance Systems in Smart Cities. *IEEE Internet of Things Journal*, *5*(2), 747–754. doi:10.1109/JIOT.2017.2705560

Hundepool, A., Van de Wetering, A., Ramaswamy, R., Franconi, L., Polettini, S., Capobianchi, A., . . . Giessing, S. (2008). *μ- ARGUS version 4.2 User's Manuel.* Retrieved from https://ec.europa.eu/eurostat/cros/page/essnet_en

Hu, P., Member, S., Ning, H., Member, S., Qiu, T., & Member, S. (2017). Security and Privacy Preservation Scheme of Face Identification and Resolution Framework Using Fog Computing in .... *Security and Privacy Preservation Scheme of Face Identification and Resolution Framework Using Fog Computing in Internet of Things*, *4*, 1143–1155.

Huqqani, A. A., Schikuta, E., Ye, S., & Chen, P. (2013). Multicore and GPU Parallelization of Neural Networks for Face Recognition. *Procedia Computer Science*, *18*, 349–358. doi:10.1016/j.procs.2013.05.198

Hussain, A., & Rao, W. (2015). Health and emergency-care platform for the elderly and disabled people in the Smart City. *Journal of Systems and Software, 110*, 253-263.

Hussain, A., & Cambria, E. (2018). Semi-supervised learning for big social data analysis. *Neurocomputing*, *275*, 1662–1673. doi:10.1016/j.neucom.2017.10.010

Iansiti, M., & Levien, R. (2002). *Keynotes and Dominators:FramingOper-atingand Technology Strategy in a Business Ecosystem.* Harvard Business School Working Paper, No. 03-061. Cambridge, MA: Harvard Business School.

IBM Watson IoT - GitHub. (n.d.). Retrieved from https://github.com/ibm-watson-iot/

Ibrahim, M., Elgamri, A., Babiker, S., & Mohamed, A. (2015). Internet of things based smart environmental monitoring using the raspberry-pi computer. In *Proceedings of Digital Information Processing and Communications (ICDIPC), 5th International Conference* (pp. 159-164). Academic Press. 10.1109/ICDIPC.2015.7323023

IMEX Group. (2018). *IMEX Frankfurt trade show 2018 show statistics.* Retrieved from https://www.imex-frankfurt.com/show-stats

Information Commissioner's Office (ICO). (2008). *Privacy by Design.* Retrieved from http://ico.org.uk/for_organisations/data_protection/topic_guides/~/media/documents/pdb_report_html/

Initialization, S. B. (SBI) dataset. (2015). Retrieved, April 2018, from, http://sbmi2015.na.icar.cnr.it/

InterIoT. (2016). Retrieved June 1, 2017, from http://www.inter-iot-project.eu/

International Congress and Convention Association. (2013). *A Modern History of International Association Meetings.* Retrieved from https://www.iccaworld.org

International Telecommunication Unit (ITU). (n.d.). Retrieved from https://www.itu.int/en/ITU-T/gsi/iot/Pages/default.aspx

Internet Engineering Task Force (IETF). (n.d.). Retrieved from https://www.ietf.org/topics/iot/

Internet of Things & Creation of the Fifth V of Big Data. (2017). *International Journal Of Science And Research, 6*(1), 1363–1366. doi:10.21275/art20164394

Internet of Things. (2017). Retrieved, May 2018 from, https://arxiv.org/ftp/arxiv/papers/1708/1708.04560.pdf

IoT Analytics. (2015). *IoT Platforms - The central backbone for the Internet of Things.* Retrieved from https://iot-analytics.com/product/iot-platforms-white-paper/

Irudayasamy, A., & Arockiam, L. (2015). Scalable multidimensional anonymization algorithm over big data using reduce on public cloud. *J. Theor. Appl. Inf. Technol., 74*, 221–231.

Işık, Ö., Jones, M. C., & Sidorova, A. (2013). Business intelligence success: The roles of BI capabilities and decision. *Information & Management, 50*(1), 13–23. doi:10.1016/j.im.2012.12.001

Islam & Sarker. (2000). A similarity coefficient Measure And Machine-Parts Grouping In Cellular Manufacturing Systems. *International Journal Of Production Research.* Http://Dx.Doi.Org/10.1080/002075400189374

Islam, N. (2018). *Business Intelligence and Analytics for Operational Efficiency*. SSRN Electronic Journal. doi:10.2139srn.3163429

Islam, S. M. (2015). The internet of things for health care: A comprehensive survey. *IEEE Access: Practical Innovations, Open Solutions, 3*, 678–708. doi:10.1109/ACCESS.2015.2437951

Istepanian, R. S. H., Jovanov, E., & Zhang, Y. T. (2004). Guest editorial introduction to the special section on m-health: Beyond seamless mobility and global wireless health-care connectivity. *IEEE Transactions on Information Technology in Biomedicine, 8*(4), 405–414. doi:10.1109/TITB.2004.840019 PMID:15615031

ITU. (2005). *The Internet of Things.* ITU Internet Reports. Retrieved from http://www.itu.int/osg/spu/publications/internetofthings/

Jackson, Somers, & Harvey. (1989). Similarity Coefficients: Measures of Co-Occurrence and Association or Simply Measures of Occurrence? *American Naturalist, 133*(3).

Jacoby, M., Antonić, A., Kreiner, K., Łapacz, R., & Pielorz, J. (2016). Semantic Interoperability as Key to IoT Platform Federation. In *International Workshop on Interoperability and Open-Source Solutions* (pp. 3–19). Academic Press.

Jadaun, S. S., & Singh, G. (2015, May). Outage performance of cognitive multi relay networks with asymptotic analysis. In *Computing, Communication & Automation (ICCCA), 2015 International Conference on* (pp. 432-435). IEEE. 10.1109/CCAA.2015.7148415

Jadaun, S. S., & Singh, G. (2015, May). Outage Performance of Relay Assisted Cognitive Radio System With Asymptotic Analysis. *International Journal of Applied Engineering Research, 10*(3), 9757-9771.

Jagadish, H. V., Gehrke, J., Labrinidis, A., Papakonstantinou, Y., Patel, J. M., Ramakrishnan, R., & Shahabi, C. (2014). Big data and its technical challenges. *Communications of the ACM, 57*(7), 86–94. doi:10.1145/2611567

Jain, A. K. (2010). Data clustering: 50 years beyond K-means. *Pattern Recognition Letters, 31*(8), 651–666. doi:10.1016/j.patrec.2009.09.011

Jain, H., & Jain, R. (2017, March). Big data in weather forecasting: Applications and challenges. In *2017 International Conference on Big Data Analytics and Computational Intelligence (ICBDAC)* (pp. 138-142). IEEE.

Jaitly, N., Nguyen, P., Senior, A., & Vanhoucke, V. (2012). Application of Pretrained Deep Neural Networks to Large Vocabulary Speech Recognition. *13th Annual Conference of the International Speech Communication Association*, 2578-2581.

Janakiraman. (2017). *Big Data Challenges*. Academic Press.

Janssen, M., Estevez, E., & Janowski, T. (2014). Interoperability in big, open, and linked data-organizational maturity, capabilities, and data portfolios. *Computer, 47*(10), 44–49. doi:10.1109/MC.2014.290

Janssen, M., van der Voort, H., & Wahyudi, A. (2017). Factors influencing big data decision-making quality. *Journal of Business Research, 70*, 338–345. doi:10.1016/j.jbusres.2016.08.007

Jara, A. J., Genoud, D., & Bocchi, Y. (2014). Big data in smart cities: From poisson to human dynamics. *Proceedings - 2014 IEEE 28th International Conference on Advanced Information Networking and Applications Workshops*, 785–790.

Jara, A., Olivieri, A., Bocchi, Y., Jung, M., Kastner, W., & Skarmeta, A. (2014). Semantic Web of Things: An analysis of the application semantics for the IoT moving towards the IoT convergence. *International Journal of Web and Grid Services, 10*(2/3), 244. doi:10.1504/IJWGS.2014.060260

Jaradat, M., Jarrah, M., Bousselham, A., Jararweh, Y., & Al-Ayyoub, M. (2015). The internet of energy: Smart sensor networks and big data management for smart grid. *Procedia Computer Science, 56*(6), 592–597. doi:10.1016/j.procs.2015.07.250

Jeon, Y. H. (2012). Impact of big data: Networking considerations and case study. *International Journal of Computer Science and Network Security, 12*(12), 30–34.

Jeschke, S., Brecher, C., Meisen, T., Özdemir, D., & Eschert, T. (2017). Industrial internet of things and cyber manufacturing systems. In *Industrial Internet of Things* (pp. 3–19). Cham: Springer. doi:10.1007/978-3-319-42559-7_1

Jeste, Blazer, Buckwalter, Cassidy, Fishman, Gwyther, … Feather. (2016). Age-Friendly Communities Initiative: Public Health Approach to Promoting Successful Aging. *The American Journal of Geriatric Psychiatry, 24*(12), 1158-1170.

Jia, L., Hall, D., & Song, J. (2015). The conceptualization of data-driven decision making capability. In *Proceedings of the Twenty-First Americas Conference on Information Systems*, Puerto Rico, August 13–15.

Jiang, D., Chen, G., Ooi, B. C., Tan, K. L., & Wu, S. (2014). epiC: an extensible and scalable system for processing big data. *Proceedings of the VLDB Endowment, 7*(7), 541-552. Retrieved on April 4, 2016 from http://www.nus.edu.sg/dpr/files/research_highlights/2015_01Jan_epiC.pdf

Jiang, W., Ravi, V. T., & Agrawal, G. (2010). A map-reduce system with an alternate API for multi-core environments. In *Proceedings of the 2010 10th IEEE/ACM International Conference on Cluster, Cloud and Grid Computing* (pp. 84-93). IEEE Computer Society. Retrieved on April 4, 2016 from http://web.cse.ohio-state.edu/~agrawal/allpapers/ccgrid10.pdf

Jiang, J., & Gallupe, R. B. (2015). Environmental scanning and business insight capability: the role of business analytics and knowledge integration. In *Proceedings of the Twenty-First Americas Conference on Information Systems*, Puerto Rico, August 13–15.

Jiang, L., Da Xu, L., Cai, H., Jiang, Z., Bu, F., & Xu, B. (2014). An IoT-Oriented Data Storage Framework in Cloud Computing Platform. *Industrial Informatics. IEEE Transactions On, 10*(2), 1443–1451.

Jiang, T., Jiang, J., Dai, Y., & Li, A. (2015). Micro–blog Emotion Orientation Analysis Algorithm Based on Tibetan and Chinese Mixed Text. *International Symposium on Social Science (ISSS 2015).* 10.2991/isss-15.2015.39

Jiao, J., Ma, H.-M., Qiao, Y., Du, Y.-L., Kong, W., & Wu, Z.-C. (2014). Design of farm environmental monitoring system based on the internet of things. *Advance Journal of Food Science and Technology, 6*(3), 368–373. doi:10.19026/ajfst.6.38

Jim Chase. (2013). *The Evolution of the Internet of Things.* Retrieved June 14, 2018 from http://www.ti.com/lit/ml/swrb028/swrb028.pdf

Jin, D., Hannon, C., Li, Z., Cortes, P., Ramaraju, S., Burgess, P., ... Shahidehpour, M. (2016). Smart street lighting system: A platform for innovative smart city applications and a new frontier for cyber-security. *The Electricity Journal, 29*(10), 28–35. doi:10.1016/j.tej.2016.11.011

Jing, Ng, & Huang. (2007). An Entropy Weighting k-Means Algorithm for Subspace Clustering of High-Dimensional Sparse Data. *IEEE Transactions on Knowledge and Data Engineering, 19*(8). Doi:10.1109/TKDE.2007.1048

Jingxuan, L., S. J. (2011). The monitoring expert system of colliery safety production. In *Proc. IEEE Int. Conf. on Mechatronic Science, Electric Eng. and Computer (MEC)* (pp. 2592–2595). IEEE. 10.1109/MEC.2011.6026023

Ji, X., Chun, S. A., Wei, Z., & Geller, J. (2015). Twitter sentiment classification for measuring public health concerns. *Social Network Analysis and Mining, 5*(1), 13. doi:10.100713278-015-0253-5

Joshi, S., Saxena, S., Godbole, T., & Shreya. (2015). Developing Smart Cities: An Integrated Framework. *Procedia Computer Science, 93*, 902–909. doi:10.1016/j.procs.2016.07.258

Jovanoski, D., Pachovski, V., & Nakov, P. (2015). Sentiment Analysis in Twitter for Macedonian. Proceedings of Recent Advances in Natural Language Processing, 249–257.

Joy, J., & Gerla, M. (2017). Internet of Vehicles and Autonomous Connected Car - Privacy and Security Issues. *2017 26th International Conference on Computer Communication and Networks (ICCCN),* 1-9. 10.1109/ICCCN.2017.8038391

Juang & Rabiner. (1990). The segmental K-means algorithm for estimating parameters of hidden Markov models. *IEEE Transactions on Acoustics, Speech, and Signal Processing, 38*(9). Doi:10.1109/29.60082

Jung, C. R. (2009). Efficient background subtraction and shadow removal for monochromatic video sequences. *IEEE Transactions on Multimedia, 11*(3), 571–577. doi:10.1109/TMM.2009.2012924

KAA. (2018). *Kaa IoT Development Platform overview.* Retrieved May 18, 2018, from https://www.kaaproject.org/

Kaaniche, N., & Laurent, M. (2017). Data security and privacy preservation in cloud storage environments based on cryptographic mechanisms. *Computer Communications*, *111*(10), 120–141. doi:10.1016/j.comcom.2017.07.006

Kadampur, M. A., & Somayajulu, D. V. L. N. (2010). A noise addition scheme in decision tree for, privacy preserving data mining. *Journal of Computers*, *2*(1), 137–144.

Kakabadse, A. K., Kouzmin, A., & Kakabadse, N. K. (2017). Current trends in internet use: e-communication, e-information, and e-commerce. In Creating Futures: Leading Change Through Information Systems (pp. 147-178). Routledge.

Kakhani, M.K., Kakhani, S., & Biradar, S.R. (2015). Research issues in bigdata analytics. *International Journal of Application or Innovation in Engineering & Management*, 228-232.

Kaklauskas & Gudauskas. (1991). *Intelligent decision-support systems and the Internet of Things for the smart built environment*. Elsevier BV.

Kalid, S., Syed, A., Mohammad, A., & Halgamuge, M. N. (2017). Big-Data NoSQL Databases: Comparison and Analysis of "Big-Table", "DynamoDB", and "Cassandra". *IEEE 2nd International Conference on Big Data Analysis (ICBDA'17)*, 89-93.

Kang, Y., Park, I., Rhee, J., & Lee, Y. (2016). MongoDB-based Repository Design for IoT- generated RFID / Sensor Big Data. *IEEE Sensors Journal*, *16*(2), 485–497. doi:10.1109/JSEN.2015.2483499

Kanungo, Mount, Netanyahu, Piatko, Silverman, & Wu. (2002). An efficient k-means clustering algorithm: analysis and implementation. *IEEE Transactions on Pattern Analysis and Machine Intelligence*, *24*(7). Doi:10.1109/TPAMI.2002.1017616

Karine, K. (2017). How industry can help us fight against botnets: Notes on regulating private-sector intervention. *International Review of Law Computers & Technology*, *31*(1), 105–130. doi:10.1080/13600869.2017.1275274

Karmakar, S., & Swarnakar, S. (2017). New concept-based indexing technique for search engine. *Indian Journal of Science and Technology*, *10*(18), 1–10. doi:10.17485/ijst/2017/v10i18/114018

Kashyap, R. (2019a). Security, Reliability, and Performance Assessment for Healthcare Biometrics. In D. Kisku, P. Gupta, & J. Sing (Eds.), Design and Implementation of Healthcare Biometric Systems (pp. 29-54). Hershey, PA: IGI Global. doi:10.4018/978-1-5225-7525-2.ch002

Kashyap, R. (2019b). Geospatial Big Data, Analytics and IoT: Challenges, Applications and Potential. In H. Das, R. Barik, H. Dubey & D. Sinha Roy (Eds.), Cloud Computing for Geospatial Big Data Analytics (pp. 191-213). Springer International Publishing.

Kashyap, R. (2018). Object boundary detection through robust active contour-based method with global information. *International Journal Of Image Mining*, *3*(1), 22. doi:10.1504/IJIM.2018.093008

Kashyap, R., & Gautam, P. (2017). 'Fast Medical Image Segmentation Using Energy-Based Method,' Biometrics. *Concepts, Methodologies, Tools, and Applications*, *3*(1), 1017–1042. doi:10.4018/978-1-5225-0983-7.ch040

Kashyap, R., & Piersson, A. D. (2018). Big Data Challenges and Solutions in the Medical Industries. In V. Tiwari, R. Thakur, B. Tiwari, & S. Gupta (Eds.), *Handbook of Research on Pattern Engineering System Development for Big Data Analytics* (pp. 1–24). Hershey, PA: IGI Global. doi:10.4018/978-1-5225-3870-7.ch001

Kashyap, R., & Piersson, A. D. (2018). Impact of Big Data on Security. In G. Shrivastava, P. Kumar, B. Gupta, S. Bala, & N. Dey (Eds.), *Handbook of Research on Network Forensics and Analysis Techniques* (pp. 283–299). Hershey, PA: IGI Global. doi:10.4018/978-1-5225-4100-4.ch015

Kashyap, R., & Tiwari, V. (2017). Energy-based active contour method for image segmentation. *International Journal of Electronic Healthcare, 9*(2–3), 210–225. doi:10.1504/IJEH.2017.083165

Kashyap, R., & Tiwari, V. (2018). Active contours using global models for medical image segmentation. *International Journal of Computational Systems Engineering, 4*(2/3), 195. doi:10.1504/IJCSYSE.2018.091404

Katal, M. W., & Goudar, R. H. (2013). Big data: issues, challenges, tools and good practices. In *Proceedings of IEEE International Conference Contemporary Computing* (*vol. 6*, pp. 404–409). Uttar Pradesh, India: Jaypee Institute of Information Technology & University of Florida. 10.1109/IC3.2013.6612229

Kaur, M. J., & Maheshwari, P. (2016, March). Building smart cities applications using IoT and cloud-based architectures. In *2016 International Conference on Industrial Informatics and Computer Systems (CIICS)* (pp. 1-5). IEEE. 10.1109/ICCSII.2016.7462433

Kaushik, R. T., & Nahrsted, K. (2012). A data-centric cooling energy costs reduction approach for big data analytics cloud. *Proceedings of the International Conference on High Performance Computing, Networking, Storage and Analysis*. 10.1109/SC.2012.103

Keim, D. A., Mansmann, F., Schneidewind, J., & Ziegler, H. (2006). Challenges in visual data analysis. In *Tenth International Conference on Information Visualisation*. IEEE. 10.1109/IV.2006.31

Kellner, D. (1998). Intellectuals, the new public spheres, and techno-politics. In C. Toulouse & T. W. Luke (Eds.), *The politics of cyberspace* (pp. 167–186). New York, NY: Routledge.

Kelly, S. D. T., Suryadevara, N. K., & Mukhopadhyay, S. C. (2013). Towards the implementation of IoT for environmental condition monitoring in homes. *IEEE Sensors Journal, 13*(10), 3846–3853. doi:10.1109/JSEN.2013.2263379

Kettl, D. (2018). *Little bites of Big Data for public policy*. Thousand Oaks, CA: Sage.

Khan, Z., Anjum, A., & Kiani, S. L. (2013, December). Cloud based big data analytics for smart future cities. In *Proceedings of the 2013 IEEE/ACM 6th international conference on utility and cloud computing* (pp. 381-386). IEEE Computer Society. 10.1109/UCC.2013.77

Khatibloo, F., Sridharan, S., Stanhope, J., Joyce, R., Liu, S., & Turley, C. (2016). *Consumer Data: beyond first and third party decoding the value of four consumer data types*. Retrieved form https://www.forrester.com/

Khatoun, R., & Zeadally, S. (2017). Cybersecurity and Privacy Solutions in Smart Cities. *IEEE Communications Magazine, 55*(3), 51–59. doi:10.1109/MCOM.2017.1600297CM

Khera, N., Gill, H., Dodwani, G., Celly, N., & Singh, S. (2015). Remote Condition Monitoring of Real-Time Light Intensity and Temperature Data. In *Proceedings of Advances in Computing and Communication Engineering (ICACCE), 2nd International Conference* (pp. 3-6). Academic Press. 10.1109/ICACCE.2015.111

Kim, H. J. S. (2015). Design and implementation of gateways and sensor nodes for monitoring gas facilities. In *Proc. IEEE 4th Int. Conf. on Information Science and Industrial Applications (ISI)* (pp. 3–5). IEEE.

Kim, T. H., Ramos, C., & Mohammed, S. (2017). Smart city and IoT.

Kim, J. T. (2017). Analyses of secure authentication scheme for the smart home system based on the internet on things. *2017 International Conference on Applied System Innovation (ICASI)*, 335-336. 10.1109/ICASI.2017.7988420

Kim, L. (2018). DeepX: Deep Learning Accelerator for Restricted Boltzmann Machine Artificial Neural Networks. *IEEE Transactions on Neural Networks and Learning Systems, 29*(5), 1441–1453. doi:10.1109/TNNLS.2017.2665555 PMID:28287986

Kim, S., Park, S., Sun, M. R., & Lee, J. H. (2016). A study of smart beacon-based Meeting, Incentive trip, Convention, Exhibition and Event (MICE) services using big data. In *Proceedings of Information Technology and Quantitative Management (ITQM 2016)* (Vol. 91, pp. 761–768). Seoul, South Korea: National Information Society Agency. doi:10.1016/j.procs.2016.07.072

King, I., Lyu, M. R., & Yang, H. (2013). *Online learning for big data analytics*. Retrieved from http://cci. drexel.edu/bigdata/bigdata2013/ieee.bigdata.tutorial.1.slides.pdf

King, N. J., & Forder, J. (2016). Data analytics and consumer profiling: Finding appropriate privacy principles for discovered data. *Computer Law & Security Review*, *32*(5), 696–714. doi:10.1016/j.clsr.2016.05.002

Kiruthika, K., & Parimala, R. (2017). Green Space & Computing Techniques: ECO-Friendly ICT Initiative. *International Journal of Engineering Science*.

Kitchin, R. (2014). *The data revolution: Big data, open data, data infrastructures and their consequences*. Los Angeles: Sage.

Kitchin, R. (2014). The real-time city? Big data and smart urbanism. *GeoJournal*, *79*(1), 1–14. doi:10.100710708-013-9516-8

Köksal, Ö., & Tekinerdogan, B. (2017). Feature-Driven Domain Analysis of Session Layer Protocols of Internet of Things. In *IEEE International Congress on Internet of Things (ICIOT)* (pp. 105-112). IEEE.

Kolb, D. A. (1984). *Experiential learning: Experience as the source of learning and development*. Prentice–Hall.

Koniaris, M., Anagnostopoulos, I., & Vassiliou, Y. (2017). Network analysis in the legal domain: A complex model for European Union legal sources. *Journal of Complex Networks, 32*(1), 1–17. doi:10.1093/comnet/cnx029

Koot, M. R. (2012). *Measuring and Predicting Anonymity*. University of Amsterdam. Retrieved from https://pure.uva.nl/

Kovacs, E., Bauer, M., Kim, J., Yun, J., Le Gall, F., & Zhao, M. (2016). Standards-Based Worldwide Semantic Interoperability for IoT. *IEEE Communications Magazine*, *54*(12), 40–46. doi:10.1109/MCOM.2016.1600460CM

Krco, S., Pokric, B., & Carrez, F. (2014). Designing IoT architecture (s): A European perspective. In *Internet of Things (WF-IoT), 2014 IEEE World Forum on* (pp. 79–84). IEEE.

Krebs, R., Momm, C., & Kounev, S. (2012). Architectural Concerns in Multi-tenant SaaS Applications. *Closer*, *12*, 426–431.

Kreps, J. (2014). *Questioning the Lambda Architecture - O'Reilly Media*. Retrieved May 8, 2018, from https://www.oreilly.com/ideas/questioning-the-lambda-architecture

Kreutz, D., Ramos, F. M. V., Verissimo, P. E., Rothenberg, C. E., Azodolmolky, S., & Uhlig, S. (2015). Software-defined networking: A comprehensive survey. *Proceedings of the IEEE, 103*(1), 14–76. doi:10.1109/JPROC.2014.2371999

Krim, H., Gentimis, T., & Chintakunta, H. (2016). Discovering the whole by the coarse: A topological paradigm for data analysis. *IEEE Signal Processing Magazine, 33*(2), 95–104. doi:.2015.2510703 doi:10.1109/MSP

Krishna, & Narasimha Murty. (1999). Genetic K-means algorithm. *IEEE Transactions on Systems, Man, and Cybernetics, Part B (Cybernetics)*, *29*(3). Doi:10.1109/3477.764879

Krugman, C., & Wright, R. R. (2007). *Global meetings and exhibitions.* Hoboken, NJ: John Wiley & Sons, Inc.

Kubitza, T. (2016, November). Apps for Environments: Running Interoperable Apps in Smart Environments with the meSchup IoT Platform. In *International Workshop on Interoperability and Open-Source Solutions* (pp. 158-172). Springer.

Kumar, K. A., Gluck, J., Deshpande, A., & Lin, J. (2013). Hone: "scaling down" Hadoop on shared-memory systems. *Proc. VLDB Endow., 6*(12), 1354–1357. Retrieved on April 4, 2016 from http://www.vldb.org/pvldb/vol6/p1354-kumar.pdf

Kumar, A., & Nayyar, A. (2014). Energy Efficient Routing Protocols for Wireless Sensor Networks (WSNs) based on Clustering. *International Journal of Scientific & Engineering Research, 5*(6), 440–448.

Kumar, R., & Prabu, S. (2016). Smart healthcare monitoring system for rural area using IoT. *International Journal of Pharmacy & Technology, 8*(4), 21821–21826.

Kundhavai, K. R., & Sridevi, S. (2016). IoT and Big Data - The Current and Future Technologies: A Review. *International Journal of Computer Science and Mobile Computing., 5*(1), 10–14.

Kung, L., Kung, H., Jones-Framer, A., & Wang, Y. (2015). Managing big data for firm performance: a configurational approach. In *Proceedings of the Twenty-First Americas Conference on Information Systems*, Puerto Rico, August 13–15.

Kuo, R. J., Chen, C. H., & Hwang, Y. C. (2001). An intelligent stock trading decision support system through integration of genetic algorithm based fuzzy neural network and artificial neural network. *Fuzzy Sets and Systems, 118*(1), 21–45. doi:10.1016/S0165-0114(98)00399-6

Kurban, C., Peña–López, I., & Haberer, M. (2017, February). What is technopolitics? A conceptual scheme for understanding politics in the digital age. *IDP. Revista de Internet, Derecho y Ciencia Política, 24*, 3–20. Retrieved from http://edcp.blogs.uoc.edu/20170524-article-what-is-technopolitics-a-conceptual-scheme-for-understanding-politics-in-the-digital-age/

Kurzweil, R., & Grossman, T. (2005). *Fantastic voyage: Live long enough to live forever. Plume*. New York: Rodale Inc.

Kwon, O., Lee, N., & Shin, B. (2014). Data quality management, data usage experience and acquisition intention of big data analytics. *International Journal of Information Management, 34*(3), 387–394.

Kwon, O., Lee, N., & Shin, B. (2014). Data quality management, data usage experience, and acquisition intention of big data analytics. *International Journal of Information Management, 34*(3), 387–394. doi:10.1016/j.ijinfomgt.2014.02.002

Kyoung-jae, K., & Han, I. (2000). Genetic algorithms approach to feature discretization in artificial neural networks for the prediction of stock price index. *Expert Systems with Applications, 19*(2), 125–132. doi:10.1016/S0957-4174(00)00027-0

Kyriazis, D., & Varvarigou, T. (2013). Smart, Autonomous and Reliable Internet of Things. *Procedia Computer Science, 21*, 442–448. doi:10.1016/j.procs.2013.09.059

Lacey, D., & James, B. E. (2010). Review of availability of advice on security for small/medium sized organisations. *Retrieved, 2*(28), 2013.

Lafuente. (2014). *Big Data Security - Challenges & Solutions*. Academic Press.

Lambert, D. (1993). Measures of disclosure risk and harm. *Journal of Official Statistics, 9*(2), 313–331.

Lambiotte, R., & Kosinski, M. (2014). Tracking the digital footprints of personality. *Proceedings of the IEEE, 102*(12), 1934–1939. doi:10.1109/JPROC.2014.2359054

Laney, D. (2001). 3D data management: Controlling data volume, velocity, and variety. *Gartner*. Retrieved from http://blogs.gartner.com/doug-laney/files/2012/01/ad949-3D-Data-Management-Controlling-Data-Volume-Velocity-and-Variety.pdf

Langer, S. (1942). *Philosophy in a NewKey: A Study in the Symbolism of Reason, Rite, and Art*. Cambridge, MA: Harvard University Press.

Langheinrich, M. (2002). A privacy awareness system for ubiquitous computing environments. In H. L. E. G. Borriello (Ed.), *International conference on Ubiquitous Computing*. Springer. 10.1007/3-540-45809-3_19

Lee, J. S., Su, Y. W., & Shen, C. C. (2007). A comparative study of wireless protocols: Bluetooth, UWB, ZigBee, and Wi-Fi. *33rd Annual Conference of the IEEE Industrial Electronics Society (IECON 2007)*, 46–51.

Lee, C. K. M., Yeung, C. L., & Cheng, M. N. (2015). Research on IoT based Cyber Physical System for Industrial big data Analytics. *International Conference on Industrial Engineering and Engineering Management*, 1855–1859. 10.1109/IEEM.2015.7385969

Lee, C., & Zappaterra, L. (2014). Kwanghee Choi and Hyeong-Ah Choi, "Securing smart home: Technologies, security challenges, and security requirements. *2014 IEEE Conference on Communications and Network Security*, 67-72.

Lee, I. (2017). Big data: Dimensions, evolution, impacts, and challenges. *Business Horizons*, *60*(3), 293–303. doi:10.1016/j.bushor.2017.01.004

Lee, I., & Lee, K. (2015). The Internet of Things (IoT): Applications, investments, and challenges for enterprises. *Business Horizons*, *58*(4), 431–440. doi:10.1016/j.bushor.2015.03.008

Lee, J., Lapira, E., Bagheri, B., & Kao, H. (2013). Recent advances and trends in predictive manufacturing systems in big data environment. *Manufacturing Letters*, *1*(1), 38–41. doi:10.1016/j.mfglet.2013.09.005

Lee, W. J., Zhang, Z., Rau, S. H., Gammon, T., Johnson, B. C., & Beyreis, J. (2015). Arc Flash Light Intensity Measurement System Design. *IEEE Transactions on Industry Applications*, *51*(5), 4267–4274. doi:10.1109/TIA.2015.2431638

Lehikoinen, J. T. (2008). Theory and Application of the Privacy Regulation Model. In J. Lumsden (Ed.), *Handbook of Research on User Interface Design and Evaluation for Mobile Technology* (pp. 863–876). Hershey, PA: IGI Global; doi:10.4018/978-1-59904-871-0.ch051

Lek, S., & Guégan, J. F. (1999). Artificial neural networks as a tool in ecological modelling, an introduction. *Ecological Modelling*, *120*(2–3), 65–73. doi:10.1016/S0304-3800(99)00092-7

Lella, J., Mandla, V. R., & Zhu, X. (2017). Solid waste collection/transport optimization and vegetation land cover estimation using Geographic Information System (GIS): A case study of a proposed smart-city. *Sustainable Cities and Society*, *35*, 336–349. doi:10.1016/j.scs.2017.08.023

Leminen, S., Westerlund, M., Rajahonka, M., & Siuruainen, R. (2012). Towards IoT Ecosystems and Business Models. In S. Andreev, S. Balandin, & Y. Koucheryavy (Eds.), Internet of Things, Smart Spaces, and Next Generation Networking Lecture Notes in Computer Science (vol. 7469, pp. 15-26). Berlin: Springer. doi:10.1007/978-3-642-32686-8_2

Lemov, R. (2016). Big data is people: why big data is actually small personal and very human. *Aeon*. Retrieved from https://goo.gl/gRsu8L

Leung, V. (2015). Green internet of things for smart cities. *International workshop on smart cities and urban informatics*.

Li, K., & Deng, Y. (2014). Accelerating the reconstruction process in network coding storage system by leveraging data temperature. In C. H.Hsu, X. Shi & V. Salapura (Eds.), *Lecture Notes in Computer Science: Vol. 8707. Network and Parallel Computing* (pp. 510–521). Berlin: Springer.

Li, Song, & Zeng. (n.d.). Policy-based Secure and Trustworthy Sensing for an Internet of Things in Smart Cities. *IEEE Internet of Things Journal*.

Li, B., Tian, B., Yao, Q., & Wang, K. (2012). A vehicle license plate recognition system based on analysis of maximally stable extremal regions. In *Proceedings of 9th IEEE Int. Conference Network Sensors Control (pp.* 399-404). 10.1109/ICNSC.2012.6204952

Liem, C., & Petropoulos, P. (2016). The economic value of personal data for online platforms, firms and consumers. *The London School of Economics Business Review.* Retrieved from http://blogs.lse.ac.uk/businessreview/2016/01/19/

Li, G., Jiang, S., Zhang, W., Pang, J., & Huang, Q. (2014). Online web video topic detection and tracking with semi-supervised learning. *Multimedia Systems*, *22*(1), 115–125. doi:10.100700530-014-0402-0

Likas, A., Vlassis, N., & Verbeek, J. J. (2003). The global k-means clustering algorithm. *Pattern Recognition*, *36*(2), 451–461. doi:10.1016/S0031-3203(02)00060-2

Lin, Yu, Zhang, Yang, Zhang, & Zhao. (n.d.). A Survey on Internet of Things: Architecture, Enabling Technologies, Security and Privacy, and Applications. *IEEE Internet of Things Journal.*

Lin, C.-C. (2014). Effect of noise intensity and illumination intensity on visual performance. *Perceptual and Motor Skills*, *19*(2), 441–454. doi:10.2466/26.24.PMS.119c20z1 PMID:25153619

Lin, J. L., & Cheng, Y. W. (2009). Privacy preserving item set mining through noisy items. *Elsevier Expert Systems with Applications*, *36*(3), 5711–5717. doi:10.1016/j.eswa.2008.06.052

Lin, J., Yu, W., Zhang, N., Yang, X., Zhang, H., & Zhao, W. (2017). A survey on internet of things: Architecture, enabling technologies, security and privacy, and applications. *IEEE Internet of Things Journal*, *4*(5), 1125–1142. doi:10.1109/JIOT.2017.2683200

Linux Foundation. (2017). *IoTivity*. Retrieved May 1, 2017, from https://www.iotivity.org/

Lippell, H. (2016). Big Data in the Media and Entertainment Sectors. In *New Horizons for a Data-Driven Economy* (pp. 245–259). Cham: Springer.

Li, Q., Yue, T., Wang, C., Zhang, W., Yu, Y., Li, B., ... Bai, G. (2013). Spatially distributed modeling of soil organic matter across China: An application of artificial neural network approach. *Catena*, *104*, 210–218. doi:10.1016/j.catena.2012.11.012

Little, B. (2010). Concerns with Learning-Management Systems and Virtual Learning Environments. *Elearn, 2010*(7), 2. doi:10.1145/1833513.1837142

Liu, X., Han, J., Zhong, Y., Han, C., & He, X. (2009). Implementing WebGIS on Hadoop: A case study of improving small file I/O performance on HDFS. In *IEEE International Conference on Cluster Computing and Workshops* (pp. 1-8). IEEE. Retrieved on April 4, 2016 from http://ieeexplore.ieee.org/stamp/stamp.jsp?tp=&arnumber=5289196

Liu, C., Marchewka, J. T., Lu, J., & Yu, C. S. (2005). Beyond concern—A privacy-trust-behavioral intention model of electronic commerce. *Information & Management*, *42*(2), 289–304. doi:10.1016/j.im.2004.01.003

Liu, Y., Jing, W., & Xu, L. (2016). Parallelizing Backpropagation Neural Network Using MapReduce and Cascading Model. *Computational Intelligence and Neuroscience*, *2016*, 1–11. doi:10.1155/2016/2842780 PMID:27217823

Lo, B. P., Ip, H., & Yang, G.-Z. (2016). Transforming health care: Body sensor networks, wearables, and the Internet of Things. *IEEE Pulse*, *7*(1), 4–8. doi:10.1109/MPUL.2015.2498474 PMID:26799719

Lomax, T., Schrank, D., & Eisele, B. (2015). *Annual Urban Mobility Scorecard.* Retrieved from http://mobility.tamu.edu/ums/

Lomotey, Pry, & Sriramoju. (2017). Wearable IoT data stream traceability in a distributed health information system. *Pervasive and Mobile Computing, 40*, 692-707.

Low, A., & Muegge, S. (2013). Keystone Business Models for Network Security Processors. *Technology Innovation Management Review, 3*(7), 25-33. Retrieved from http://timreview.ca/article/703

Lugmayr, A., Stockleben, B., Scheib, C., Mailaparampil, M., Mesia, N., & Ranta, H. (2016). *A Comprehensive Survey on Big-Data Research and its Implications-What is Really'New'in Big Data?-IT's Cognitive Big Data!* Paper presented at the PACIS.

Lupton, D. (2014). You are your data: Self-tracking practices and concepts of data. In S. Selke (Ed.) Lifelogging (pp. 61-79). doi:10.1007/978-3-658-13137-1_4

Lupton, D. (2015). *Digital sociology*. London: Routledge.

Lupton, D. (2016). *The quantified self*. Malden, MA: Polity Press.

Lupton, D., & Williamson, B. (2017). The datafied child: The dataveillance of children and implications for their rights. *New Media & Society, 19*(5), 780–794. doi:10.1177/1461444816686328

Mach, P., & Becvar, Z. (2017). Mobile Edge Computing: A Survey on Architecture and Computation Offloading. *IEEE Communications Surveys and Tutorials, 19*(3), 1628–1656. doi:10.1109/COMST.2017.2682318

MacMillanE. D. (2017). Retrieved from http://www.macmillandictionary.com/

Magnier, L., & Haghighat, F. (2010). Multiobjective optimization of building design using TRNSYS simulations, genetic algorithm, and Artificial Neural Network. *Building and Environment, 45*(3), 739–746. doi:10.1016/j.buildenv.2009.08.016

Mahmood, T., & Afzal, U. (2013, December). Security analytics: Big data analytics for cybersecurity: A review of trends, techniques and tools. In *2013 2nd national conference on Information assurance (NCIA)* (pp. 129-134). IEEE.

Mai, V., & Khalil, I. (2017). Design and implementation of a secure cloud-based billing model for smart meters as an Internet of Things using homomorphic cryptography. *Future Generation Computer Systems, 72*, 327–338. doi:10.1016/j.future.2016.06.003

Majeed, A., Haq, A. U., Jamal, A., Bhana, R., Banigo, F., & Baadel, S. (2016). Internet of everything (IoE) exploiting organisational inside threats: Global network of smart devices (GNSD). *IEEE International Symposium on Systems Engineering (ISSE)*, 1-7. 10.1109/SysEng.2016.7753152

Maki, H., Ogawa, H., Matsuoka, S., Yonezawa, Y., & Caldwell, W. M. (2011). A daily living activity remote monitoring system for solitary elderly people. In *Proceedings of 2011 annual international conference of the IEEE engineering in medicine and biology society* (pp. 5608–5611). 10.1109/IEMBS.2011.6091357

Malouf, R., & Mullen, T. (2017). Graph-based user classification for informal online political discourse. *Proceedings of the 1st Workshop on Information Credibility on the Web*, 1-8.

Mamata, R. B. P. (2018). Communication Improvement and Traffic Control Based on V2I in Smart City Framework. *International Journal of Vehicular Telematics and Infotainment Systems, 2*(1).

Manitsas, Singh, Pal, & Strbac. (2012). Distribution System State Estimation Using an Artificial Neural Network Approach for Pseudo Measurement Modeling. *IEEE Transactions on Power Systems, 27*(4), 1888-1896. Doi:10.1109/TPWRS.2012.2187804

Mantelero, A. (2014). The future of consumer data protection in the EU Re-thinking the "notice and consent" paradigm in the new era of predictive analytics. *Computer Law & Security Review, 30*(6), 643–660. doi:10.1016/j.clsr.2014.09.004

Mantri, D. S., Prasad, N. R., & Prasad, R. (2016). Mobility and Heterogeneity Aware Cluster-Based Data Aggregation for Wireless Sensor Network. Wireless Personal Communications, 86(2), 975-993. doi:10.100711277-015-2965-2

Manyika, J., Chui, M., Brown, B., Bughin, J., Dobbs, R., Roxburgh, C., & Byers, A. H. (2011). *Big Data: The Next Frontier for Innovation, Competition and Productivity.* McKinsey Global Institute. Retrieved on April 4, 2016 from http://www.fujitsu.com/us/Images/03_Michael_Chui.pdf

Mao, G. Wang, & Bollen. (2014). Automatic Construction of Financial Semantic Orientation Lexicon from Large-Scale Chinese News Corpus. In *7th Financial Risks International Forum.* Institut Louis Bachelier.

Mao, Y., Morris, R., & Kaashoek, M. F. (2010). Optimizing MapReduce for multicore architectures. In *Computer Science and Artificial Intelligence Laboratory.* Massachusetts Institute of Technology, Tech. Rep. Retrieved on April 4, 2016 from http://citeseerx.ist.psu.edu/viewdoc/download;jsessionid=F539BF63A34B2D6D8F9B472F9A007144?doi=10.1.1.186.5309&rep=rep1&type=pdf

Marchal, S. J. X. (2014). A Big Data Architecture for Large Scale Security Monitoring. In Big Data (BigData Congress) (pp. 56-63). Anchorage, AK: Academic Press.

Marjani, M., Nasaruddin, F., Gani, A., Karim, A., Hashem, I. A. T., Siddiqa, A., & Yaqoob, I. (2017). Big IoT data analytics: Architecture, opportunities, and open research challenges. *IEEE Access: Practical Innovations, Open Solutions*, *5*, 5247–5261.

Marshalls, A. (2016). How Toronto is becoming a smarter city. *Torontoist.* Retrieved from http://torontoist.com/2016/06/how-toronto-is-becoming-a-smarter-city

Martin, H., Hermerschmidt, L., Kerpen, D., Häußling, H., Rumpe, B., & Wehrle, K. (2014). User-driven privacy enforcement for cloud-based services in the internet of things. *International Conference on Future Internet of Things and Cloud.*

Martin, K. E. (2015). Ethical issues in the big data industry. *MIS Quarterly Executive*, *14*(2), 67–85.

Marz, N., & Warren, J. (2015). *Big data: principles and best practices of scalable realtime data systems.* Shelter Island, NY: Manning, cop. Retrieved from http://nathanmarz.com/about/

Mathew, P. S., Pillai, A. S., & Palade, V. (2018). Applications of IoT in Healthcare. In *Cognitive Computing for Big Data Systems Over IoT* (pp. 263–288). Cham: Springer. doi:10.1007/978-3-319-70688-7_11

Matijevic, M., & Cvjetkovic, V. (2016). Overview of architectures with Arduino boards as building blocks for data acquisition and control systems. In *Proceedings of Remote Engineering and Virtual Instrumentation (REV), 13th International Conference on* (pp. 56-63). Academic Press. 10.1109/REV.2016.7444440

Mawdsley, G., Tyson, A., Peressotti, C., Jong, R., & Yaffe, M. (2009). Accurate estimation of compressed breast thickness in mammography. *Medical Physics*, *36*(2), 577–586. doi:10.1118/1.3065068 PMID:19291997

May, R. J., Maier, H. R., & Dandy, G. C. (2010). Data splitting for artificial neural networks using SOM-based stratified sampling. *Neural Networks*, *23*(2), 283–294. doi:10.1016/j.neunet.2009.11.009 PMID:19959327

Mazhelis, O., Luoma, E., & Warma, H. (2012). Defining Internet of Things Ecosystem. In S. Andreev, S. Balandin, & Y. Koucheryavy (Eds.), Internet of Things, Smart Spaces, and Next Generation Networking–Lecture Notes in Computer Science (vol. 7469, pp. 1-14). Berlin: Springer. doi:10.1007/978-3-642-32686-8_1

Mazzega, P., Bourcier, D., & Boulet, R. (2009). The network of French legal codes. *Proceedings of the 12th International Conference on Artificial Intelligence and Law—ICAIL '09*, 236–237. doi: 10.1145/1568234.1568271

McDonald, A. M., & Cranor, L. F. (2009). The cost of reading privacy policies. *A Journal of Law and Policy for the Information Society*, *4*(3), 543-568.

McKeown, N., Anderson, T., Balakrishnan, H., Parulkar, G., Peterson, L., Rexford, J., ... Turner, J. (2008). OpenFlow: Enabling innovation in campus networks. *Computer Communication Review*, *38*(2), 69–74. doi:10.1145/1355734.1355746

McKinsey Global Institute. (2015). *The Internet of Things : Mapping the Value Beyond the Hype*. Author.

Meena, N. K., Parashar, S., Swarnkar, A., Gupta, N., Niazi, K. R., & Bansal, R. C. (2017). Mobile Power Infrastructure Planning and Operational Management for Smart City Applications. *Energy Procedia*, *142*, 2202–2207. doi:10.1016/j.egypro.2017.12.589

Mehmood, A., Natgunanathan, I., Xiang, Y., Hua, G., & Guo, S. (2016). Protection of big data privacy. *IEEE Access: Practical Innovations, Open Solutions*, *4*, 1821–1834. doi:10.1109/ACCESS.2016.2558446

Meier, J. D., Hill, D., Homer, A., Jason, T., Bansode, P., Wall, L., ... Bogawat, A. (2009). *Microsoft application architecture guide*. Microsoft Corporation.

Melaville, A., Blank, M. J., & Asayesh, G. (1993). *Together we can: A guide for crafting a profamily system of education and human services*. Washington, DC: Center for the Study of Social Policy and the Institute for Educational Leadership.

Mell, P., & Grance, T. (2011). *The NIST definition of cloud computing*. NIST.

Melo, S., Macedo, J., & Baptista, P. (2017). Guiding cities to pursue a smart mobility paradigm: An example from vehicle routing guidance and its traffic and operational effects. *Research in Transportation Economics*, *65*, 24–33. doi:10.1016/j.retrec.2017.09.007

Meyer, R. (2015, September 25). Could a Bank Deny Your Loan Based on Your Facebook Friends? *The Atlantic*. Retrieved from https://goo.gl/HauP6P

Miah, S. J., Vu, H. Q., Gammack, J., & McGrath, M. (2017). A big data analytics method for tourist behaviour analysis. *Information & Management*, *54*(6), 771–785. doi:10.1016/j.im.2016.11.011

Michael, M. G., & Michael, K. A. (2007). A Note on Uberveillance, From Dataveillance to Überveillance and the Realpolitik of the Transparent Society. In *The Second Workshop on Social Implications of National Security*, Wollongong, Australia, October 29. Retrieved from https://ro.uow.edu.au/infopapers/560/

Michael, K. (2015). Wearables and Lifelogging: The socioethical implications. *IEEE Consumer Electronics Magazine*, *4*(2), 79–81. doi:10.1109/MCE.2015.2392998

Michael, K. (2017). Implantable Medical Device Tells All: Uberveillance Gets to the Heart of the Matter. *IEEE Consumer Electronics Magazine*, *6*(4), 107–115. doi:10.1109/MCE.2017.2714279

Michael, K., & Miller, K. W. (2013). Big data: New opportunities and new challenges. *Computer*, *46*(6), 22–24. doi:10.1109/MC.2013.196

Michalik, P., Stofa, J., & Zolotova, I. (2014, January). Concept definition for Big Data architecture in the education system. In *2014 IEEE 12th International Symposium on Applied Machine Intelligence and Informatics (SAMI)* (pp. 331-334). IEEE. 10.1109/SAMI.2014.6822433

Microsoft Azure – GitHub. (n.d.). Retrieved from https://github.com/azure/

Microsoft Azure IoT Reference Architecture. Version 2.0. (2018). Retrieved from https://aka.ms/iotrefarchitecture

Microsoft. (2016). *Azure IoT Hub | Microsoft Azure*. Retrieved May 15, 2018, from https://azure.microsoft.com/en-us/services/iot-hub/

Mikolov, T., Deoras, A., Povey, D., Burget, L., & Cernocky, J. (2011). Strategies for Training Large Scale Neural Network Language Models. *2011 IEEE Workshop on Automatic Speech Recognition and Understanding (ASRU)*, 196-201. 10.1109/ASRU.2011.6163930

Miles, M. B., Huberman, A. M., & Saldaña, J. (2014). *Qualitative data analysis: A methods sourcebook* (3rd ed.). Thousand Oaks, CA: Sage.

Minbo, L., Zhu, Z., & Guangyu, C. (2013). Information Service System Of Agriculture IoT. *Automatika (Zagreb)*, *54*(4), 415–426. doi:10.7305/automatika.54-4.413

Minch, R. P. (2015). Location privacy in the era of the internet of things and big data analytics. *48th Hawaii International Conference on System Sciences*, 1521–1530. 10.1109/HICSS.2015.185

Mineraud, J., Mazhelis, O., Su, X., & Tarkoma, S. (2016). A gap analysis of Internet-of-Things platforms. *Computer Communications*, *89*, 5–16. doi:10.1016/j.comcom.2016.03.015

Minghui, Y., Peng, Y., & Wangwang, S. (2010). Light Intensity Sensor Node Based on TSL2561. *Microcontrollers & Embedded Systems*, *10*(6), 38–40.

Mishra, D., Gunasekaran, A., Childe, S. J., Papadopoulos, T., Dubey, R., & Wamba, S. (2016). Vision, applications and future challenges of Internet of Things: A bibliometric study of the recent literature. *Industrial Management & Data Systems*, *116*(7), 1331–1355. doi:10.1108/IMDS-11-2015-0478

Mishra, N., Lin, C., & Chang, H. (2015). A Cognitive Adopted Framework for IoT Big-Data Management and Knowledge Discovery Prospective. *International Journal of Distributed Sensor Networks*, *2015*, 1–13. doi:10.1155/2015/718390

Misra, M. (1997). Parallel Environments for Implementing Neural Networks. *Neural Computing Surveys*, *1*, 48–60.

Misra, S., Krishna, P., & Abraham, K. (2010). A stochastic learning automata-based solution for intrusion detection in vehicular ad hoc networks. *Security and Communication Networks*, *4*(6), 666–677. doi:10.1002ec.200

Mkrttchian, V., Palatkin, I., Gamidullaeva, L., & Panasenko, S. (2018). About digital avatars for control systems using Big Data and Knowledge sharing in virtual industries. In A. Gyamfi & I. Williams (Eds.), *Big Data and Knowledge Sharing in Virtual Organizations* (pp. 46–59). Hershey, PA: IGI Global; doi:10.4018/978-1-5225-7519-1ch.04

Mkrttchian, V., Veretikhina, S., Gavrilova, O., Ioffe, A., Markosyan, S., & Chernyshenko, S. (2019). The comparison of Cross-cultural analysis of the green country - Australia and of the North Country – Russia: Cultures, small businesses, cross the barriers. In U. G. Benna (Ed.), *Industrial and Urban Growth Policies at the Sub-National, National, and Global Levels* (pp. 176–189). Hershey, PA: IGI Global. doi:10.4018/978-1-5225-7625-9

Moerel, L. (2014, February). *Big data protection how to make the draft eu regulation on data protection future proof*. Lecture delivered during the public acceptance of the appointment of professor of Global ICT Law at Tilburg University, Tillburg, The Netherlands.

Mohamed, N., & Al-Jaroodi, J. (2014, July). Real-time big data analytics: Applications and challenges. In *2014 International Conference on High Performance Computing & Simulation (HPCS)* (pp. 305-310). IEEE.

Mohammadi, M., Al-Fuqaha, A. I., Sorour, S., & Guizani, M. (2018, June 06). Deep learning for IoT Big Data and streaming analytics: A survey. In *IEEE Communications Surveys and Tutorials* (Early Access). Retrieved from https://ieeexplore.ieee.org/ document/8373692/

Mohd Selamat, S. A., Prakoonwit, S., Sahandi, R., Khan, W., & Ramachandran, M. (2018). Big data analytics—A review of data-mining models for small and medium enterprises in the transportation sector. *Wiley Interdisciplinary Reviews. Data Mining and Knowledge Discovery*, *8*(3), e1238. doi:10.1002/widm.1238

Mohsen Nia & Jha. (n.d.). A Comprehensive Study of Security of Internet-of-Things. *IEEE Transactions on Emerging Topics in Computing*.

Molina, B. (2014). Empowering smart cities through interoperable Sensor Network Enablers. Academic Press. doi:10.1109/SMC.2014.6973876

Möller, K., Rajala, A., & Svahn, S. (2005). Strategic Business Nets–Their Type and Management. *Journal of Business Research*, *58*(9), 1274–1284. doi:10.1016/j.jbusres.2003.05.002

Moncrief, M. (2015, August 15). Your Facebook friends could make or break that loan application. *The Sydney Morning Herald*. Retrieved from https://goo.gl/szE4Aj

Monica, N., & Kumar, K.R. (n.d.). Survey on Big Data by Coordinating MapReduce to Integrate Variety of Data. *International Journal of Science and Research*.

Monzon, A. (2015, May). Smart cities concept and challenges: Bases for the assessment of smart city projects. In *2015 International Conference on Smart Cities and Green ICT Systems (SMARTGREENS)* (pp. 1-11). IEEE.

Moore, G. R. (2006). *Crossing the Chasm– Marketing and Selling Technology Products to Mainstream Customers (2nd ed.)*. Cornwall: Capstone Publishing Ltd.

Moore, J. F. (1996). *The Death of Competition: Leadership & Strategy in the Age of Business Ecosystems*. New York: Harper Business.

Mor, K., Kumar, S., & Sharma, D. (2018). Ad-Hoc Wireless Sensor Network Based on IEEE 802.15. 4: Theoretical Review. *International Journal of Computer Sciences and Engineering, 6*(3), 219-224.

Morabito, R., Petrolo, R., Loscrì, V., & Mitton, N. (2018). LEGIoT: A Lightweight Edge Gateway for the Internet of Things. *Future Generation Computer Systems*, *81*, 1–15. doi:10.1016/j.future.2017.10.011

Morello, R., Mukhopadhyay, S. C., Liu, Z., Slomovitz, D., & Samantaray, S. R. (2017). Advances on Sensing Technologies for Smart Cities and Power Grids: A Review. *IEEE Sensors Journal*, *17*(23), 7596–7610. doi:10.1109/JSEN.2017.2735539

Moreno, M. V., Terroso-Sáenz, F., González-Vidal, A., Valdés-Vela, M., Skarmeta, A. F., Zamora, M. A., & Chang, V. (2017). Applicability of big data techniques to smart cities deployments. *IEEE Transactions on Industrial Informatics*, *13*(2), 800–809. doi:10.1109/TII.2016.2605581

Morgan, B., & Yeung, K. (2007). *An introduction to Law and Regulation*. Cambridge: Cambridge University Press. doi:10.1017/CBO9780511801112

Morris, M., Schindehutte, M., & Allen, J. (2005). The Entrepreneur's Business Model: Towards Unified Perspective. *Journal of Business Research*, *58*(6), 726–735. doi:10.1016/j.jbusres.2003.11.001

Mouats, T. A., Aouf, N., Chermak, L., & Richardson, M. A. (2015). Thermal stereo odometry for UAVs. *IEEE Sensors Journal*, *15*(11), 6335–6347. doi:10.1109/JSEN.2015.2456337

Moumena, A., Mohamed, C., & Mohamed, N. (2012). Challenges in Middleware Solutions for the Internet of Things. *Proc. of The 2012 International Conference on Collaboration Technologies and Systems (CTS 2012)*.

Muegge, S. (2011). Business Ecosystems as Institutions of Participation: A Systems Perspective on Community-Developed Platforms. *Technology Innovation Management Review, 1*(2), 4-13. Retrieved from http://timreview.ca/article/495

Muegge, S. (2012). Business Model Discovery by Technology Entrepreneurs. *Technology Innovation Management Review, 2*(4), 5-16. http://timreview.ca/article/545

Muegge, S. (2013). Platforms, Communities, and Business Ecosystems: Lessons Learned About Technology Entrepreneurship in an Interconnected World. *Technology Innovation Management Review, 3*(2), 5-15. Retrieved from http://timreview.ca/article/655

Mukherjee, A., Paul, H. S., Dey, S., & Banerjee, A. (2014). Angels for distributed analytics in IoT. *IEEE World Forum on Internet of Things*, 565–570. 10.1109/WF-IoT.2014.6803230

Mukherjee, M., Shu, L., Hu, L., Hancke, G. P., & Zhu, C. (2017). Sleep scheduling in industrial wireless sensor networks for toxic gas monitoring. *IEEE Wireless Communications*, *24*(9), 106–112. doi:10.1109/MWC.2017.1600072WC

Mulgan, R. (2000). Comparing accountability in the public and private sectors. *Australian Journal of Public Administration*, *59*(1), 87–97. doi:10.1111/1467-8500.00142

Munugala, Brar, Syed, Mohammad, & Halgamuge. (2017). The Much Needed Security and Data Reforms of Cloud Computing in Medical Data Storage. In *Applying Big Data Analytics in Bioinformatics and Medicine*. IGI Global.

Murugesan, S. (2008). Harnessing Green IT: Principles and practices. *IT Professional*, *10*(1), 24–33. doi:10.1109/MITP.2008.10

Nambiar, R., Bhardwaj, R., Sethi, A., & Vargheese, R. (2013). A look at challenges and opportunities of Big Data analytics in healthcare. In *IEEE International Conference on Big Data*, Santa Clara, October 6-9. 10.1109/BigData.2013.6691753

Nataliia, L., & Elena, F. (2015). Internet of things as a symbolic resource of power. *Procedia: Social and Behavioral Sciences*, *166*, 521–525. doi:10.1016/j.sbspro.2014.12.565

National Institute of Food and Agriculture—United States Department of Agriculture. (2017, July 6). *Experiential learning model.* Washington, DC: Author. Retrieved from https://nifa.usda. gov/resources

National Institute of Standards and Technology (NIST). (n.d.). Retrieved from https://www.nist.gov/news-events/news/2016/07/nists-network-things-model-builds-foundation-help-define-internet-things

Navetta, D. (2013). Legal Implications of Big Data, a Primer. *Computer & Internet Lawyer*, *11*(3), 14–19.

Nayyar, A., & Puri, V. (2015, November). A review of Beaglebone Smart Board's-A Linux/Android powered low-cost development platform based on ARM technology. In *Future Generation Communication and Networking (FGCN), 2015 9th International Conference on* (pp. 55-63). IEEE.

Nayyar, A., & Puri, V. (2016, March). A review of Arduino board's, Lilypad's & Arduino shields. In *Computing for Sustainable Global Development (INDIACom), 2016 3rd International Conference on* (pp. 1485-1492). IEEE.

Nayyar, A. (2016). An Encyclopedia Coverage of Compiler's, Programmer's & Simulator's for 8051, PIC, AVR, ARM, Arduino Embedded Technologies. *International Journal of Reconfigurable and Embedded Systems*, *5*(1).

Nayyar, A., & Gupta, A. (2014). A comprehensive review of cluster-based energy efficient routing protocols in wireless sensor networks. *IJRCCT*, *3*(1), 104–110.

Nayyar, A., & Puri, E. V. (2016). A Review of Intel Galileo Development Board's Technology. *Int. Journal of Engineering Research and Applications*, *6*(3), 34–39.

Nayyar, A., & Puri, V. (2015). Raspberry Pi- A Small, Powerful, Cost Effective and Efficient Form Factor Computer: A Review. *International Journal of Advanced Research in Computer Science and Software Engineering*, *5*(12), 720–737.

Nayyar, A., & Puri, V. (2016). A Comprehensive Review of BeagleBone Technology: Smart Board Powered by ARM. *International Journal of Smart Home*, *10*(4), 95–108. doi:10.14257/ijsh.2016.10.4.10

Nayyar, A., Puri, V., & Le, D. N. (2016). A Comprehensive Review of Semiconductor-Type Gas Sensors for Environmental Monitoring. *Review of Computer Engineering Research*, *3*(3), 55–64. doi:10.18488/journal.76/2016.3.3/76.3.55.64

Nayyar, A., & Singh, R. (2014). A comprehensive review of ant colony optimization (ACO) based energy-efficient routing protocols for wireless sensor networks. *International Journal of Wireless Networks and Broadband Technologies*, *3*(3), 33–55. doi:10.4018/ijwnbt.2014070103

Nayyar, A., & Singh, R. (2017). Ant Colony Optimization (ACO) based Routing Protocols for Wireless Sensor Networks (WSN): A Survey. *Int. J. Adv. Comput. Sci. Appl*, *8*, 148–155.

Nayyar, A., & Singh, R. (2017). Simulation and performance comparison of ant colony optimization (ACO) routing protocol with AODV, DSDV, DSR routing protocols of wireless sensor networks using NS-2 simulator. *American Journal of Intelligent Systems*, *7*(1), 19–30.

Neath, A., & Cavanaugh, J. (2011). The Bayesian information criterion: Background, derivation, and applications. *Wiley Interdisciplinary Reviews: Computational Statistics*, *4*(2), 199–203. doi:10.1002/wics.199

Neff, G., & Nafus, D. (2016). *The Self-Tracking*. Cambridge, MA: MIT Press. doi:10.7551/mitpress/10421.001.0001

Neirotti, P., De Marco, A., Cagliano, A. C., Mangano, G., & Scorrano, F. (2014). Current trends in Smart City initiatives: Some stylised facts. *Cities (London, England)*, *38*, 25–36. doi:10.1016/j.cities.2013.12.010

Netzer, O., Feldman, R., Goldenberg, J., & Fresko, M. (2012). Mine Your Own Business: Market-Structure Surveillance Through Text Mining. *Marketing Science*, *31*(3), 521–543. doi:10.1287/mksc.1120.0713

Nevo, E., Fragman, O., Dafni, A., & Beiles, A. (2013). Biodiversity And Interslope Divergence Of Vascular Plants Caused By Microclimatic Differences At "Evolution Canyon", Lower Nahal Oren, Mount Carmel, Israel. *Israel Journal of Plant Sciences*, *47*(1), 49–59. doi:10.1080/07929978.1999.10676751

Newell, P. B. (1995). Perspectives on privacy. *Journal of Environmental Psychology*, *15*(2), 87–104. doi:10.1016/0272-4944(95)90018-7

Nguyen, T. T. A., & Hagiwara, M. (2014). Adjective-Based Estimation of Short Sentence's Impression. *Proceedings of the 5th Kanesi Engineering and Emotion Research; International Conference*.

Nissenbaum, H. (2004). Privacy as contextual integrity. *Washington Law Review (Seattle, Wash.)*, *79*, 119.

Nivedhitha, S. A. P. (2013). Development of multipurpose gas leakage and fire detector with alarm system. In *Proc. IEEE/ACM Texas Instruments India Educators' Conf* (pp. 194–199). IEEE.

Noel, K. (2016). *Application of Machine Learning to Systematic Allocation Strategies*. SSRN Electronic Journal. doi:10.2139srn.2837664

Nordström, T., & Svensson, B. (1992). Using and Designing Massively Parallel Computers for Artificial Neural Networks. *Journal of Parallel and Distributed Computing*, *14*(3), 260–285. doi:10.1016/0743-7315(92)90068-X

Norwich University (2014a, July). *NU2019 strategic plan update: Building on the past...strengthening our future*. Northfield, VT: Author.

Norwich University (2015, August 15). *Interim/fifth year report*. Northfield, VT: Author.

Norwich University. (2010, July 31). *Norwich University 2010 NEASC self-study*. Northfield, VT: Author.

Norwich University. (2014b). *College of Graduate and Continuing Studies (CGCS): Faculty Manual 2014–2015*. Northfield, VT: Author.

Norwich University. (2018). *Online Master of Public Administration curriculum: Policy analysis and analytics concentration*. Northfield, VT: Author. Retrieved from https://online.norwich.edu/ academic-programs/masters/public-administration/overview

O'Hara, K. (2016). The seven veils of privacy. *IEEE Internet Computing*, *20*(2), 86–91. doi:10.1109/MIC.2016.34

OECD. (1980). *OECD Guidelines on the Protection of Privacy and Transborder Flows of Personal Data*. Retrieved 21 December 2018 from http://www.oecd.org/internet/ieconomy/oecdguidelinesontheprotectionofprivacyandtransborderflowsofpersonaldata.htm

Office of the Australian Information Commissioner. (2014). *Privacy fact sheet 17: Australia Privacy Principles* Retrieved from https://goo.gl/ZSswXH

Office of the Australian Information Commissioner. (2017). *Australian Community Attitudes to Privacy Survey 2017*. Retrieved from https://goo.gl/7zembF

Office of the Privacy Commissioner. (2015, December 21). *Report of the privacy commissioner under section 61B of the privacy and personal information protection act 1988*.

OGC Senor. (2016). *OGC Sensor Things API standard specification*. Retrieved April 2018, from http://www.opengeospatial.org/standards/sensorthings

Oh, S. R., & Kim, Y. G. (2017). Security Requirements Analysis for the IoT. *2017 International Conference on Platform Technology and Service (PlatCon)*, 1-6.

Ojha, M., & Mathur, K. (2016, March). Proposed application of big data analytics in healthcare at Maharaja Yeshwantrao Hospital. In *2016 3rd MEC International Conference on Big Data and Smart City (ICBDSC)* (pp. 1-7). IEEE.

Oko, Y. (2016). Bangkok strives to be 'smart city' to ease traffic. *Asian Review*. Retrieved from http://asia.nikkei.com/Business/Trends/Bangkok-strives-to-be-smart-city-to-ease-traffic

Omar, N., Albared, M., Al-Shabi, A. Q., & Al-Moslmi, T. (2013). Ensemble of Classification algorithms for Subjectivity and Sentiment Analysis of Arabic Customers' Reviews. *International Journal of Advancements in Computing Technology*, 5.

Omnes, N., Bouillon, M., Fromentoux, G., & Le Grand, O. (2015). A programmable and virtualized network & IT infrastructure for the internet of things: How can NFV & SDN help for facing the upcoming challenges. In *Intelligence in Next Generation Networks (ICIN), 2015 18th International Conference on* (pp. 64–69). Academic Press.

Omoronyia, I. (2016). The case for privacy awareness requirements. *International Journal of Secure Software Engineering*, *7*(2), 19–36. doi:10.4018/IJSSE.2016040102

Oommen, B. J., & Fayyoumi, E. (2008). Enhancing Micro-Aggregation Technique by Utilizing Dependence-Based Information in Secure Statistical Databases. In Y. Mu, W. Susilo, & J. Seberry (Eds.), *Information Security and Privacy* (pp. 404–418). Berlin: Springer. doi:10.1007/978-3-540-70500-0_30

OpenFog Consortium Architecture Working Group. (2017, February). OpenFog Reference Architecture for Fog Computing. *OpenFogConsortium*, 1–162.

Orecchini, G., Yang, L., Rida, A., Alimenti, F., Tentzeris, M. M., & Roselli, L. (2010). Green technologies and RFID: Present and future. *Applied Computational Electromagnetics Society Journal*, *25*(3), 230–238.

Oriwoh, E., Sant, P., & Epiphaniou, G. (2013). Guidelines for Internet of Things Deployment Approaches – The Thing Commandments. *Procedia Computer Science, 21*, 122-131. doi:10.1016/j.procs.2013.09.018

Osterwalder, A., Pigneur, Y., & Tucci, C. L. (2005). Clarifying Business Models: Origins, Present and Future of the Concept. *Communications of the Association for Information Science, 16*(1), 1-25. http://aisel.aisnet.org/cais/vol16/iss1/1

Osterwalder, A., & Pigneur, Y. (2010). *Business Model Generation: A Handbook for Visionaries, Game Changers, and Challengers*. Zurich, Switzerland: Business Model Foundry.

Ott, D., & Houdek, F. (2014). Automatic Requirement Classification: Tackling Inconsistencies Between Requirements and Regulations. *International Journal of Semantic Computing, 08*(01), 47–65. doi:10.1142/S1793351X14500020

Oussous, A., Benjelloun, F.Z., Lahcen, A.A. & Belfkih, S. (in press). Big Data technologies: A survey. *Journal of King Saud University – Computer and Information Sciences*.

Overview of Internet of Things. (2018). Retrieved, June 2018 from https://cloud.google.com/solutions/iot-overview

Overview of Internet of Things. (n.d.). Retrieved from https://cloud.google.com/solutions/iot-overview

Özaslan, T. L., Loianno, G., Keller, J., Taylor, C. J., Kumar, V., Wozencraft, J. M., & Hood, T. (2017). Autonomous navigation and mapping for inspection of penstocks and tunnels with MAVs. *IEEE Robotics and Automation Letters, 2*(3), 1740–1747. doi:10.1109/LRA.2017.2699790

Pacheco, J., Satam, S., Hariri, S., Grijalva, C., & Berkenbrock, H. (2016). IoT Security Development Framework for building trustworthy Smart car services. *2016 IEEE Conference on Intelligence and Security Informatics (ISI)*, 237-242. 10.1109/ISI.2016.7745481

Page-Jones, M. (1999). *Fundamentals of Object-Oriented Design in UML* (1st ed.). Addison-Wesley Professional.

Pantelis, K., & Aija, L. (2013, October). Understanding the value of (big) data. In *2013 IEEE International Conference on Big Data* (pp. 38-42). IEEE.

Pan, Y., Tian, Y., Liu, X., Gu, D., & Hua, G. (2016). Urban big data and the development of city intelligence. *Engineering, 2*(2), 171–178. doi:10.1016/J.ENG.2016.02.003

Parasuraman, A., & Colby, C. L. (2015). An updated and streamlined technology readiness index: TRI 2.0. *Journal of Service Research, 18*(1), 59–74. doi:10.1177/1094670514539730

Parasuraman, A., & Grewal, D. (2000). The impact of technology on the quality-value-loyalty chain: A research agenda. *Journal of the Academy of Marketing Science, 28*(1), 168–174. doi:10.1177/0092070300281015

Park, D. C., El-Sharkawi, M. A., Marks, R. J., Atlas, L. E., & Damborg, M. J. (1991). Electric load forecasting using an artificial neural network. *IEEE Transactions on Power Systems, 6*(2). doi:10.1109/59.76685

Park, Y. J. (2013). Digital literacy and privacy behavior online. *Communication Research, 40*(2), 215–236. doi:10.1177/0093650211418338

Patel, P., Intizar Ali, M., & Sheth, A. (2017). On Using the Intelligent Edge for IoT Analytics. *IEEE Intelligent Systems, 32*(5), 64–69. doi:10.1109/MIS.2017.3711653

Pattanayak, B., & Rath, M. (2014). A Mobile Agent Based Intrusion Detection System Architecture For Mobile Ad Hoc Networks. *Journal of Computational Science, 10*(6), 970–975. doi:10.3844/jcssp.2014.970.975

Pazowski, P. (2015). Green computing: latest practices and technologies for ICT sustainability. In *Managing Intellectual Capital and Innovation for Sustainable and Inclusive Society, Joint International Conference* (pp. 1853-1860). Academic Press.

Pelletier, R. A., & Tetteh, E. N. A. (2015). *Policy Analysis and Analytics Concentration, Master of Public Administration Program, College of Graduate and Continuing Studies, Norwich University*. Northfield, VT: Norwich University.

Peltoniemi, M. (2005). *Business Ecosystem: A Conceptual Model of an Organization Population from the Perspectives of Complexity and Evolution. Research Reports 18*. Tampere, Finland: E-Business Research Center.

Peña, J. M., Lozano, J. A., & Larrañaga, P. (1999). An empirical comparison of four initialization methods for the K-Means algorithm. *Pattern Recognition Letters*, *20*(10), 1027–1040. doi:10.1016/S0167-8655(99)00069-0

Perera, C., Liu, C. H., Jayawardena, S., & Chen, M. (2014). A survey on internet of things from industrial market perspective. *IEEE Access : Practical Innovations, Open Solutions*, *2*, 1660–1679. doi:10.1109/ACCESS.2015.2389854

Perera, C., Talagala, D., Liu, C. H., & Estrella, J. C. (2016). *Energy Efficient Location and Activity-aware On-Demand Mobile Distributed Sensing Platform for Sensing as a Service in IoT Clouds*. Academic Press.

Perera, C., Zaslavsky, A., Christen, P., & Georgakopoulos, D. (2014). Context aware computing for the internet of things: A survey. *IEEE Communications Surveys and Tutorials*, *16*(1), 414–454. doi:10.1109/SURV.2013.042313.00197

Peter, S., & Gopal, R. K. (2016). Multi-level authentication system for smart home-security analysis and implementation. *2016 International Conference on Inventive Computation Technologies (ICICT)*, 1-7. 10.1109/INVENTIVE.2016.7824790

Peterson, C., Rögnvaldsson, T., & Lönnblad, L. (1994). JETNET 3.0—A versatile artificial neural network package. *Computer Physics Communications*, *81*(1–2), 185–220. doi:10.1016/0010-4655(94)90120-1

Petronio, S. (2002). *Boundaries of privacy: Dialectic of disclosure*. Albany, NY: State University of New York Press.

Pfitzmann, A., & Hansen, M. (2007). *Anonymity, unlinkability, unobservability, pseudonymity, and identity management – a consolidated proposal for terminology*. Retrieved from http://citeseerx.ist.psu.edu/

Phu, Chau, Ngoc, & Duy. (2017g). A C4.5 algorithm for english emotional classification. *Evolving Systems*. doi:10.100712530-017-9180-1

Phu, V. N., & Vo, T. N. T. (2017a). English Sentiment Classification using Only the Sentiment Lexicons with a JOHNSON Coefficient in a Parallel Network Environment. American Journal of Engineering and Applied Sciences. doi:10.3844/ajeassp.2017

Phu, V. N., & Vo, T. N. T. (2018a). English Sentiment Classification using A Gower-2 Coefficient and A Genetic Algorithm with A Fitness-proportionate Selection in a Parallel Network Environment. *Journal of Theoretical and Applied Information Technology*, *96*(4), 1-50.

Phu, V. N., & Vo, T. N. T. (2018a). Sentiment Classification using The Sentiment Scores Of Lexicons Based on A Kuhns-II Coefficient in English. International Journal of Tomography & Simulation, 31(3).

Phu, V. N., & Vo, T. N. T. (2018b). English sentiment classification using a Fager & MacGowan coefficient and a genetic algorithm with a rank selection in a parallel network environment. *International Journal of Computer Modelling and New Technologies*, *22*(1), 57-112.

Phu, V. N., & Vo, T. N. T. (2018b). The Multi-dimensional Vectors and An Yule-II Measure Used for A Self-Organizing Map Algorithm of English Sentiment Classification in A Distributed Environment. *Journal of Theoretical and Applied Information Technology*, *96*(10).

Phu, V. N., & Vo, T. N. T. (2018c). English Sentiment Classification using A Gower-2 Coefficient and A Genetic Algorithm with A Fitness-proportionate Selection in a Parallel Network Environment. *Journal of Theoretical and Applied Information Technology*, *96*(4), 1-50.

Phu, V. N., & Vo, T. N. T. (2018c). Latent Semantic Analysis using A Dennis Coefficient for English Sentiment Classification in A Parallel System. *International Journal of Computers, Communications and Control, 13*(3), 390-410.

Phu, V. N., & Vo, T. N. T. (2018d). English Sentiment Classification using A BIRCH Algorithm and The Sentiment Lexicons-Based One-dimentional Vectors in a Parallel Network Environment. *International Journal of Computer Modelling and New Technologies, 22*(1).

Phu, V. N., & Vo, T. N. T. (2018d). Latent Semantic Analysis using A Dennis Coefficient for English Sentiment Classification in A Parallel System. *International Journal of Computers, Communications and Control, 13*(3), 390-410.

Phu, V. N., & Vo, T. N. T. (2018e). A Fuzzy C-Means Algorithm and Sentiment-Lexicons-based Multi-dimensional Vectors Of A SOKAL & SNEATH-IV Coefficient Used For English Sentiment Classification. *International Journal of Theoretical and Applied Information Technology, 96*(10).

Phu, V. N., & Vo, T. N. T. (2018e). English sentiment classification using a Fager & MacGowan coefficient and a genetic algorithm with a rank selection in a parallel network environment. *International Journal of Computer Modelling and New Technologies*, *22*(1), 57-112.

Phu, V. N., & Vo, T. N. T. (2018f). A Self-Training - Based Model using A K-NN Algorithm and The Sentiment Lexicons - Based Multi-dimensional Vectors of A S6 coefficient for Sentiment Classification. *International Journal of Theoretical and Applied Information Technology, 96*(10).

Phu, V. N., & Vo, T. N. T. (2018f). English Sentiment Classification using A BIRCH Algorithm and The Sentiment Lexicons-Based One-dimentional Vectors in a Parallel Network Environment. *International Journal of Computer Modelling and New Technologies*, *22*(1).

Phu, V. N., & Vo, T. N. T. (2018g). A Fuzzy C-Means Algorithm and Sentiment-Lexicons-based Multi-dimensional Vectors Of A SOKAL & SNEATH-IV Coefficient Used For English Sentiment Classification. *International Journal of Theoretical and Applied Information Technology*, *96*(10).

Phu, V. N., & Vo, T. N. T. (2018g). The Multi-dimensional Vectors and An Yule-II Measure Used for A Self-Organizing Map Algorithm of English Sentiment Classification in A Distributed Environment. *Journal of Theoretical and Applied Information Technology, 96*(10).

Phu, V. N., & Vo, T. N. T. (2018h). Sentiment Classification using The Sentiment Scores Of Lexicons Based on A Kuhns-II Coefficient in English. International Journal of Tomography & Simulation, 31(3).

Phu, V. N., & Vo, T. N. T. (2018h). The Bag-Of-Words Vectors And A Sokal & Sneath-Iv Coefficient Used For A K-Means Algorithm Of English Sentiment Classification In A Parallel System. *Journal of Theoretical and Applied Information Technology*, *96*(15), 1-30.

Phu, V. N., & Vo, T. N. T. (2018i). A Co-Training Model Using A Fuzzy C-Means Algorithm, A K-Means Algorithm And The Sentiment Lexicons - Based Multi-Dimensional Vectors Of An Otsuka Coefficient For English Sentiment Classification. *Journal of Theoretical and Applied Information Technology*, *96*(15), 1-29.

Phu, V. N., & Vo, T. N. T. (2018i). K-Medoids algorithm used for english sentiment classification in a distributed system. *Computer Modelling and New Technologies, 22*(1), 20-39.

Phu, V. N., & Vo, T. N. T. (2018j). A Reformed K-Nearest Neighbors Algorithm for Big Data Sets. *Journal of Computer Science*. Retrieved from http://thescipub.com/abstract/10.3844/ofsp.11819

Phu, V. N., & Vo, T. N. T. (2018j). A Self-Training - Based Model using A K-NN Algorithm and The Sentiment Lexicons - Based Multi-dimensional Vectors of A S6 coefficient for Sentiment Classification. *International Journal of Theoretical and Applied Information Technology*, *96*(10).

Phu, V. N., & Vo, T. N. T. (2018k). English Sentiment Classification using An Ochiai similarity measure and The One-dimensional Vectors in a Parallel Network Environment. International Journal of Tomography & Simulation, 31(3).

Phu, V. N., & Vo, T. N. T. (2018l). English Sentiment Classification using An YULEQ similarity measure and The One-dimensional Vectors in a Parallel Network Environment. *Journal of Theoretical and Applied Information Technology*, *6*(11).

Phu, V. N., & Vo, T. N. T. (2018m). The Binary Bits And The Sentiment Lexicons Based On An Yules Sigma Coefficient Used For Sentiment Classification In English. *Journal of Theoretical and Applied Information Technology*, 96(15), 1-36.

Phu, V. N., Vo, T. N. C., & Vo, T. N. T. (2017c). Shifting Semantic Values of English Phrases for Classification. International Journal of Speech Technology. doi:10.1007/S13772-017-9420-6

Phu, V. N., Vo, T. N. C., Dat, N. D., Vo, T. N. T., & Nguyen, T. A. (2017b). A Valences-Totaling Model for English Sentiment Classification. International Journal of Knowledge and Information Systems. doi:10.100710115-017-1054-0

Phu, V. N., Vo, T. N. C., Vo, T. N. T., & Dat, N. D. (2017a). A Vietnamese adjective emotion dictionary based on exploitation of Vietnamese language characteristics. International Journal of Artificial Intelligence Review. doi:10.1007/S13462-017-9538-6

Phu, V. N., Vo, T. N. C., Vo, T. N. T., Dat, N. D., & Khanh, L. D. D. (2017d). A Valence-Totaling Model for Vietnamese Sentiment Classification. International Journal of Evolving Systems. doi:10.100712530-017-9187-7

Phu, V. N., Vo, T. N. C., Vo, T. N. T., Dat, N. D., & Khanh, L. D. D. (2017e). Semantic Lexicons of English Nouns for Classification. International Journal of Evolving Systems. doi:10.100712530-017-9188-6

Phu, V. N., Vo, T. N. T., & Max, J. (2018). A CURE Algorithm for Vietnamese Sentiment Classification in a Parallel Environment. *International Journal of Computer Science*. Retrieved from http://thescipub.com/abstract/10.3844/ofsp.11906

Phu, V. N., Dat, N. D., Vo, T. N. T., Vo, T. N. C., & Nguyen, T. A. (2017f). Fuzzy C-means for english sentiment classification in a distributed system. *International Journal of Applied Intelligence*, *46*(3), 717–738. doi:10.100710489-016-0858-z

Phu, V. N., & Tuoi, P. T. (2014). Sentiment classification using Enhanced Contextual Valence Shifters. *International Conference on Asian Language Processing (IALP)*, 224-229. 10.1109/IALP.2014.6973485

Phu, V. N., Vo, T. N. C., & Vo, T. N. T. (2017c). *Shifting Semantic Values of English Phrases for Classification. International Journal of Speech Technology*. doi:10.100710772-017-9420-6

Phu, V. N., Vo, T. N. C., & Vo, T. N. T. (2017g). *SVM for English Semantic Classification in Parallel Environment. International Journal of Speech Technology*. doi:10.100710772-017-9421-5

Phu, V. N., Vo, T. N. C., Vo, T. N. T., & Dat, N. D. (2017a). *A Vietnamese adjective emotion dictionary based on exploitation of Vietnamese language characteristics. International Journal of Artificial Intelligence Review*. doi:10.100710462-017-9538-6

Phu, V. N., Vo, T. N. T., Vo, T. N. C., Dat, N. D., & Khanh, L. D. D. (2017h). A Decision Tree using ID3 Algorithm for English Semantic Analysis. *International Journal of Speech Technology*. doi:10.100710772-017-9429-x

Piaget, J. (1985). *The equilibration of cognitive structures: The central problem of intellectual development*. Chicago: University of Chicago Press. (Original work published 1975)

Pierson, J. (2012). Online privacy in social media: A conceptual exploration of empowerment and vulnerability. *Communications & Stratégies*, *88*(4), 99–120.

Pingo, Z., & Narayan, B. (2016). When Personal Data Becomes Open Data: An Exploration of Lifelogging, User Privacy, and Implications for Privacy Literacy. In R. A. Morishima & C. Liew (Ed.), Digital Libraries: Knowledge, Information, and Data in an Open Access Society (pp. 3-9). Cham: Springer.

Pishva, D. (2017). Internet of Things: Security and privacy issues and possible solution. *2017 19th International Conference on Advanced Communication Technology (ICACT)*, 797-808. 10.23919/ICACT.2017.7890229

Pitigoi-Aron, R., Forke, U., & Viala, R. (2005). *U.S. Patent No. US6933486B2*. Santa Clara, CA: U.S. Patent and Trademark Office.

Poggio, A., & Tomaso, D. (2016). *The Center for Biological & Computational Learning (CBCL)*. Retrieved, May 2018, from http://cbcl.mit.edu/software-datasets/CarData.html

Ponemon Institute and IBM. (2017). *Cost of Data Breach Study: Global Overview, Benchmark Research*. Retrieved from http://www.ibm.com

Ponomarenko, J. V., Bourne, P. E., & Shindyalov, I. N. (2002). Building an automated classification of DNA-binding protein domains. *Bioinformatics (Oxford, England)*, *18*(Suppl 2), S192–S201. doi:10.1093/bioinformatics/18.suppl_2.S192 PMID:12386003

Poppe, K., Wolfert, S., & Verdouw, C. N. (2015). A European Perspective on the Economics of Big Data. *OECD*. Retrieved from https://www.oecd.org/tad/events/Autumn15_Journal_Poppe.et.al.pdf

Porkodi, R., & Bhuvaneswari, V. 2014. The Internet of Things (IoT) applications and communication enabling technology standards: An overview. *Intelligent Computing Applications (ICICA), 2014 International Conference on*, 324–329.

Porter, M. E., & Heppelmann, J. E. (2014). How smart, connected products are transforming competition. *Harvard Business Review*, *92*(11), 64–88.

Pramanik, M. I., Lau, R. Y., Demirkan, H., & Azad, M. A. K. (2017). Smart health: Big data enabled health paradigm within smart cities. *Expert Systems with Applications*, *87*, 370–383. doi:10.1016/j.eswa.2017.06.027

Prasad, S. S., & Kumar, C. (2013). A green and reliable internet of things. *Communications and Network*, *5*(1), 44–48. doi:10.4236/cn.2013.51B011

Probst, L., Frideres, L., Demetri, D., Vomhof, B., Lonkeu, O.-K., & Luxembourg, P. (2014). Business Innovation Observatory - Customer Experience. *European Union.*

Project Earth. (n.d.). Retrieved from http://www.ict-earth.eu/

ProjectTREND. (n.d.). Retrieved from http://www.fp7-trend.eu/

Punyavachira, T. (2013). *Forecasting Stock Indices Movement Using Hybrid Model: A Comparison of Traditional and Machine Learning Approaches*. SSRN Electronic Journal. doi:10.2139srn.2416494

Pure Storage. (2018). *What is data reduction?* Retrieved from https://www.purestorage.com/fr/resources/ glossary/data–reduction.html

Puri, V., Nayyar, A., & Le, D. N. (2017). *Handbook of Ardunio: Technical and Practice*. Scholars Press.

Pusala, M. K., Salehi, M. A., Katukuri, J. R., Xie, Y., & Raghavan, V. (2016). *Massive Data Analysis: Tasks, Tools, Applications, and Challenges, Big Data Analytics*. Springer.

Puthal, D. (2018). Lattice-modeled Information Flow Control of Big Sensing Data Streams for Smart Health Application. *IEEE Internet of Things Journal*. doi:10.1109/jiot.2018.2805896

PwC. (2017). *Consumer Intelligence Series: Protect.me*. Retrieved from https://www.pwc.com

Qianqian, Y., Guangyao, Z., Wenhui, Q., Bin, Z., & Chiang, P. Y. (2015). Air-kare: A Wi-Fi based, multi-sensor, real-time indoor air quality monitor. In *Proceedings of Wireless Symposium (IWS), IEEE International* (pp. 1-4). IEEE. 10.1109/IEEE-IWS.2015.7164542

Qian, Z. H., & Wang, Y. J. (2013). Internet of things-oriented wireless sensor networks review. *Dianzi Yu Xinxi Xuebao, 35*(1), 215–227. doi:10.3724/SP.J.1146.2012.00876

Qiu, C., Shen, H., & Chen, L. (2018). *Towards green cloud computing: Demand allocation and pricing policies for cloud service brokerage*. IEEE Transactions on Big Data. doi:10.1109/TBDATA.2018.2823330

Qiu, H. J. F., Ho, I. W. H., Tse, C. K., & Xie, Y. (2015). A Methodology for Studying 802.11p VANET Broadcasting Performance With Practical Vehicle Distribution. *IEEE Transactions on Vehicular Technology*, *64*(10), 4756–4769. doi:10.1109/TVT.2014.2367037

Quack, T., & Gool, L. (2008). Object Recognition for the Internet of Things. *Lecture Notes in Computer Science, 4952*, 230–246.

Raden, N. (2012). *Big data analytics architecture: Putting all your eggs in three baskets*. Hired Brains, Inc. Retrieved on April 4, 2016 from https://site.teradata.com/Microsite/raden-research-paper/landing/.ashx

Rahim, A., Forkan, M., Khalil, I., & Atiquzzaman, M. (2017). ViSiBiD: A learning model for early discovery and real-time prediction of severe clinical events using vital signs as big data. *Computer Networks*, *113*, 244–257. doi:10.1016/j.comnet.2016.12.019

Rahmat, A., Syadiah, N., & Subur, B. (2016). Smart Coastal City: Sea Pollution Awareness for People in Surabaya Waterfront City. *Procedia: Social and Behavioral Sciences*, *227*, 770–777. doi:10.1016/j.sbspro.2016.06.144

Raja, L., & Vyas, S. (2018). The Study of Technological Development in the Field of Smart Farming. *Smart Farming Technologies for Sustainable Agricultural Development, 1*.

Rajala, R., & Westerlund, M. (2008). Capability Perspective of Business Model Innovation: An Analysis in the Software Industry. *International Journal of Business Innovation and Research*, *2*(1), 71–89. doi:10.1504/IJBIR.2008.015936

Rajaraman, V. (2016). Big Data Analytics. *Resonance*, *21*(8), 695–716. doi:10.100712045-016-0376-7

Ramesh, M. V., Nibi, K. V., Kurup, A., Mohan, R., Aiswarya, A., Arsha, A., & Sarang, P. R. (2017). Water quality monitoring and waste management using IoT. In *Proceedings of Global Humanitarian Technology Conference (GHTC), IEEE Conference* (pp. 1-7). IEEE. 10.1109/GHTC.2017.8239311

Ramyaka, V. N., Durga, G. S., Sharma, D., & Sharma, P. K. (2017). Technologies and pplications of wireless body area network: a review. *Procedia Computer Science, 83*, 1274-1281.

Ranger, C., Raghuraman, R., Penmetsa, A., Bradski, G., & Kozyrakis, C. (2007). Evaluating MapReduce for multi-core and multiprocessor systems. In *IEEE 13th International Symposium on High Performance Computer Architecture HPCA 2007* (pp. 13-24). IEEE. Retrieved on April 4, 2016 from http://csl.stanford.edu/~christos/publications/2007.cmp_mapreduce.hpca.pdf

Rao, Y. R. (2017). Automatic smart parking system using Internet of Things (IOT). *Int J EngTechnol Sci Res, 4*(5).

Rappa, M. (2003). Business models on the web. In *Managing the Digital Enterprise*. Retrieved from http://digitalenterprise.org/privacy/privacy.html

Rath, M. (2018a). An Exhaustive Study and Analysis of Assorted Application and Challenges in Fog Computing and Emerging Ubiquitous Computing Technology. *International Journal of Applied Evolutionary Computation, 9*(2), 17-32. Retrieved from www.igi-global.com/ijaec

Rath, M. (2018b). A Methodical Analysis of Application of Emerging Ubiquitous Computing Technology With Fog Computing and IoT in Diversified Fields and Challenges of Cloud Computing. *International Journal of Information Communication Technologies and Human Development, 10*(2). Doi:10.4018/978-1-5225-4100-4.ch002

Rath, M. (2018c). Effective Routing in Mobile Ad-hoc Networks With Power and End-to-End Delay Optimization: Well Matched With Modern Digital IoT Technology Attacks and Control in MANET. In *Advances in Data Communications and Networking for Digital Business Transformation*. IGI Global. Doi:10.4018/978-1-5225-5323-6.ch007

Rath, M. (2018d). An Analytical Study of Security and Challenging Issues in Social Networking as an Emerging Connected Technology. In *Proceedings of 3rd International Conference on Internet of Things and Connected Technologies*. Malaviya National Institute of Technology. Retrieved from https://ssrn.com/abstract=3166509

Rath, M. (2018e). Smart Traffic Management System for Traffic Control using Automated Mechanical and Electronic Devices. *I Mater. Sci. Eng., 377*. /10.1088/1757-899X/377/1/012201

Rath, M., & Oreku, G. S. (2018). Security Issues in Mobile Devices and Mobile Adhoc Networks. In Mobile Technologies and Socio-Economic Development in Emerging Nations. IGI Global. doi:10.4018/978-1-5225-4029-8.ch009

Rath, M., & Panda, M. R. (2017). MAQ system development in mobile ad-hoc networks using mobile agents. *IEEE 2nd International Conference on Contemporary Computing and Informatics (IC3I)*, 794-798.

Rath, M., & Panigrahi, C. (2016). Prioritization of Security Measures at the Junction of MANET and IoT. In *Second International Conference on Information and Communication Technology for Competitive Strategies*. ACM Publication. 10.1145/2905055.2905187

Rath, M., & Pattanayak, B. K. (2014). A methodical survey on real time applications in MANETS: Focussing On Key Issues. *International Conference on, High Performance Computing and Applications (IEEE ICHPCA)*, 22-24. 10.1109/ICHPCA.2014.7045301

Rath, M., & Pattanayak, B. K. (2018). Monitoring of QoS in MANET Based Real Time Applications. In Information and Communication Technology for Intelligent Systems (ICTIS 2017): Vol. 2. ICTIS 2017. Smart Innovation, Systems and Technologies (vol. 84, pp. 579-586). Springer. doi:10.1007/978-3-319-63645-0_64

Rath, M., Pati, B., & Pattanayak, B. (2015). Delay and power based network assessment of network layer protocols in MANET. *2015 Intern-ational Conference on Control, Instrumentation, Communication and Computational Technologies (IEEE ICCICCT)*, 682-686. 10.1109/ICCICCT.2015.7475365

Rath, M., Pati, B., & Pattanayak, B. (2016). Comparative analysis of AODV routing protocols based on network performance parameters in Mobile Adhoc Networks. In Foundations and Frontiers in Computer, Communication and Electrical Engineering (pp. 461-466). CRC Press, Taylor & Francis.

Rath, M., Pati, B., & Pattanayak, B. (2016). QoS Satisfaction in MANET Based Real Time Applications. *International Journal of Control Theory and Applications, 9*(7), 3069-3083.

Rath, M., Pati, B., & Pattanayak, B. K. (2016). Inter-Layer Communication Based QoS Platform for Real Time Multimedia Applications in MANET. Wireless Communications, Signal Processing and Networking (IEEE WiSPNET), 613-617. doi:10.1109/WiSPNET.2016.7566203

Rath, M., Pati, B., & Pattanayak, B. K. (2018). Relevance of Soft Computing Techniques in the Significant Management of Wireless Sensor Networks. In Soft Computing in Wireless Sensor Networks (pp. 86-106). Chapman and Hall/CRC, Taylor & Francis Group. doi:10.1201/9780429438639-4

Rath, M. (2017). Resource provision and QoS support with added security for client side applications in cloud computing. *International Journal of Information Technology*, *9*(3), 1–8.

Rath, M., & Pati, B. (2017). *Load balanced routing scheme for MANETs with power and delay optimization. International Journal of Communication Network and Distributed Systems*, 19.

Rath, M., Pati, B., & Pattanayak, B. (2015). Energy Competent Routing Protocol Design in MANET with Real time Application Provision. *International Journal of Business Data Communications and Networking, IGI Global*, *11*(1), 50–60. doi:10.4018/IJBDCN.2015010105

Rath, M., Pati, B., & Pattanayak, B. (2016). Energy Efficient MANET Protocol Using Cross Layer Design for Military Applications. *Defence Science Journal*, *66*(2), 146. doi:10.14429/dsj.66.9705

Rath, M., Pati, B., & Pattanayak, B. (2016). Resource Reservation and Improved QoS for Real Time Applications in MANET. *Indian Journal of Science and Technology*, *9*(36). doi:10.17485/ijst/2016/v9i36/100910

Rath, M., Pati, B., & Pattanayak, B. K. (2017). Cross layer based QoS platform for multimedia transmission in MANET. *11th International Conference on Intelligent Systems and Control (ISCO)*, 402-407. 10.1109/ISCO.2017.7856026

Rath, M., Pati, B., & Pattanayak, B. K. (2019). Mobile Agent-Based Improved Traffic Control System in VANET. In A. Krishna, K. Srikantaiah, & C. Naveena (Eds.), *Integrated Intelligent Computing, Communication and Security. Studies in Computational Intelligence* (Vol. 771). Singapore: Springer. doi:10.1007/978-981-10-8797-4_28

Rath, M., & Pattanayak, B. (2016). A Contemporary Survey and Analysis of Delay and Power Based Routing Protocols in MANET. *Journal of Engineering and Applied Sciences (Asian Research Publishing Network)*, *11*(1), 536–540.

Rath, M., & Pattanayak, B. (2017). MAQ:A Mobile Agent Based QoS Platform for MANETs. *International Journal of Business Data Communications and Networking, IGI Global*, *13*(1), 1–8. doi:10.4018/IJBDCN.2017010101

Rath, M., & Pattanayak, B. K. (2018). SCICS: A Soft Computing Based Intelligent Communication System in VANET. Smart Secure Systems – IoT and Analytics Perspective. *Communications in Computer and Information Science*, *808*, 255–261. doi:10.1007/978-981-10-7635-0_19

Rath, M., Pattanayak, B. K., & Pati, B. (2017). *Energetic Routing Protocol Design for Real-time Transmission in Mobile Ad hoc Network. In Computing and Network Sustainability, Lecture Notes in Networks and Systems* (Vol. 12). Singapore: Springer.

Rath, M., Rout, U. P., & Pujari, N. (2017). *Congestion Control Mechanism for Real Time Traffic in Mobile Adhoc Networks, Computer Communication, Networking and Internet Security. Lecture Notes in Networks and Systems* (Vol. 5). Singapore: Springer.

Rath, M., Swain, J., Pati, B., & Pattanayak, B. K. (2018). *Attacks and Control in MANET. In Handbook of Research on Network Forensics and Analysis Techniques* (pp. 19–37). IGI Global.

Rathore, M. M., Ahmad, A., Paul, A., & Rho, S. (2016). Urban planning and building smart cities based on the Internet of Things using Big Data analytics. *Computer Networks*, *101*(3), 63–80. doi:10.1016/j.comnet.2015.12.023

Rathore, M., Paul, A., Ahmad, A., & Jeon, G. (2017). IoT-Based Big Data. *International Journal on Semantic Web and Information Systems*, *13*(1), 28–47. doi:10.4018/IJSWIS.2017010103

Ratnikova, L. (2015). 11 Ecological initiatives in megapolicies. *Recyclemag*. Retrieved from http://recyclemag.ru/article/11-ekologicheskih-initsiativ-mirovyh-megapolisov

Raza, K., Patle, V. K., & Arya, S. (2012). A review on green computing for eco-friendly and sustainable it. *Journal of Computational Intelligence and Electronic Systems*, *1*(1), 3–16. doi:10.1166/jcies.2012.1023

Razzaque, M. A., Milojevic-Jevric, M., Palade, A., & Clarke, S. (2016). Middleware for Internet of Things: A Survey. *IEEE Internet of Things Journal*, *3*(1), 70–95. doi:10.1109/JIOT.2015.2498900

Ren, J., Guo, Y., Liu, Q., & Zhang, Y. (2018). Distributed and Efficient Object Detection in Edge Computing: Challenges and Solutions. *IEEE Network*, *1*, 1–7.

Ren, Y., Kaji, N., Yoshinaga, N., Toyoda, M., & Kitsuregawa, M. (2011). Sentiment Classification in Resource-Scarce Languages by using Label Propagation. In *Proceedings of the 25th Pacific Asia Conference on Language, Information and Computation*. Institute of Digital Enhancement of Cognitive Processing, Waseda University.

Richardson, M., Bosua, R., Clark, K., Webb, J., Ahmad, A., & Maynard, S. (2017a). Towards responsive regulation of the Internet of Things: Australian perspectives. *Internet Policy Review, 6*(1).

Riggins, F. J., & Wamba, S. F. (2015). *Research directions on the adoption, usage, and impact of the internet of things through the use of big data analytics.* Paper presented at the System Sciences (HICSS), 2015 48th Hawaii International Conference on. 10.1109/HICSS.2015.186

Right Sensors for Object Tracking. (2016). Retrieved April 2018, from https://www.hcltech.com/blogs/right-sensors-object-tracking-iot-part-1

Rights, E. U. A. F. (2016). *Handbook on European data protection law*. Retrieved from http://fra.europa.eu/en/publication/2014/handbook-european-data-protection-law

Ritala, P., Agouridas, V., Assimakopoulos, D., & Gies, O. (2013). Value Creation and Capture Mechanisms in Innovation Ecosystems: A Comparative Case Study. *International Journal of Technology Management*, *63*(3), 244–267. doi:10.1504/IJTM.2013.056900

Rizwan, P., Suresh, K., & Babu, M. R. (2016). Real-time smart traffic management system for smart cities by using Internet of Things and big data. In *2016 International Conference on Emerging Technological Trends (ICETT)* (pp. 1–7). Academic Press. doi:10.1109/ICETT.2016.7873660

Robles, R. J., & Kim, T. H. (2010). Applications, systems and methods in smart home technology. *Int. Journal of Advanced Science And Technology, 15.*

Rogers, L. L., & Dowla, F. U. (1994). Optimization of groundwater remediation using artificial neural networks with parallel solute transport modeling. *Water Resources Research*, *30*(2), 457–481. doi:10.1029/93WR01494

Rogers, T. (2008). *Conferences and Conventions: A global industry* (2nd ed.). Oxford, UK: Elsevier. doi:10.1016/B978-0-7506-8544-3.50009-4

Romanosky, S., & Acquisti, A. (2009). Privacy costs and personal data protection: Economic and legal perspectives, *24. Berkeley Technology Law Journal*, *24*(3), 1061–1102.

Roman, R., Zhou, J., & Lopez, J. (2013). On the features and challenges of security and privacy in distributed internet of things. *Computer Networks*, *57*(10), 2266–2279. doi:10.1016/j.comnet.2012.12.018

Ronen, E., Shamir, A., Weingarten, A. O., & O'Flynn, C. (2017). IoT Goes Nuclear: Creating a ZigBee Chain Reaction. *2017 IEEE Symposium on Security and Privacy (SP)*, 195-212. 10.1109/SP.2017.14

Rosati, U., & Conti, S. (2016). What is a smart city project? An urban model or a corporate business plan? *Procedia: Social and Behavioral Sciences*, *223*, 968–973. doi:10.1016/j.sbspro.2016.05.332

Rose, B. (2014). The Best Fitness Tracker for Every Need. *Gizmodo*. Retrieved 21 December 2018 from https://www.gizmodo.com.au/2014/12/the-best-fitness-tracker-for-every-exercise/

Roselli, L. (Ed.). (2014). *Green RFID systems*. Cambridge University Press. doi:10.1017/CBO9781139343459

Rosenblat, A., Kneese, T., & boyd, d. (2014). *Networked Employment Discrimination*. Data & Society Research Institute. Retrieved 21 December 2018 from doi:10.2139srn.2543507

Rotman, D. (2009). *Are You Looking At Me? Social Media and Privacy Literacy*. Paper presented at the 4th iSchool Conference 2009, Chapel Hill, NC. Retrieved 21 December 2018 from http://hdl.handle.net/2142/15339

S. M. Shafer, & D. F. Rogers. (2007). Similarity and distance measures for cellular manufacturing. Part II. An extension and comparison. *International Journal of Production Research, 31*(6). doi:10.1080/00207549308956793

Sacco, D., Motta, G., You, L., Bertolazzo, N., Chen, C., Pavia, U., & Pv, P. (2013). *Smart cities, urban sensing and big data: mining geo-location in social networks*. Salerno, Italy: AICA.

Saha, B., Adl-Tabatabai, A. R., Ghuloum, A., Rajagopalan, M., Hudson, R. L., Petersen, L., & Rohillah, A. (2007). Enabling scalability and performance in a large scale CMP environment. *ACM SIGOPS Operating Systems Review, 41*(3), 73-86. Retrieved on April 4, 2016 from http://leafpetersen.com/leaf/publications/eurosys2007/mcrt-eurosys.pdf

Sahana, S., Singh, K., Kumar, R., & Das, S. (2018). A Review of Underwater Wireless Sensor Network Routing Protocols and Challenges. In *Next-Generation Networks* (pp. 505–512). Singapore: Springer. doi:10.1007/978-981-10-6005-2_51

Sahoo, J., & Rath, M. (2017). Study and Analysis of Smart Applications in Smart City Context. *2017 International Conference on Information Technology (ICIT)*, 225-228. 10.1109/ICIT.2017.38

Salman, T. (2015). *Internet of Things Protocols and Standards*. Academic Press.

Salvarci, T., Manap, N. S., Davras, G., & Dolmaci, N. (2015). Privacy of personal information in tourism sector. *International Journal of Human Sciences*, *12*(1), 236–254. doi:10.14687/ijhs.v12i1.2988

Samanta, B., & Al-Balushi, K. R. (2003). Artificial Neural Network Based Fault Diagnostics Of Rolling Element Bearings Using Time-Domain Features. *Mechanical Systems and Signal Processing*, *17*(2), 317–328. doi:10.1006/mssp.2001.1462

Samarati, P., & Sweeney, L. (1998). Generalizing data to provide anonymity when disclosing information. In *Proceedings of the 17th ACM SIGACT –SIGMOD-SIGARD Symposium on Principles of Database Systems*. New York: Association of Computing Machinery. 10.1145/275487.275508

Sanaz, R., Moosavi, R., Mohammad, R., & Yang, P. Tenhunen, h. (2014). Pervasive Health Monitoring Based on Internet of Things: Two Case Studies. *Wireless Mobile Communication and Healthcare (Mobihealth) 2014 EAI 4th International Conference*, 275-278.

Sanders, E., Mackenzie, C., Sirk, M., & Pittet, A. (2017, November). *Is your business ready for GDPR and e-privacy regulatory changes?* Paper presented at the 56th annual congress of International Congress and Convention Association (ICCA), Prague, Czech Republic.

Santana-Mancilla, P. C., Echeverría, M. A. M., Santos, J. C. R., Castellanos, J. A. N. C., & Díaz, A. P. S. (2013). Towards Smart Education: Ambient Intelligence in the Mexican Classrooms. *Procedia: Social and Behavioral Sciences*, *106*, 3141–3148. doi:10.1016/j.sbspro.2013.12.363

Santucci, G., & Lange, S. (2008). Internet of things in 2020: a roadmap for the future. *Information Society and Media Directorate-general of the European Commission (DG INFSO) & European Technology Platform on Smart Systems Integration (EPoSS) Report, 5.*

Sarabia-Jacome, D., Belsa, A., Palau, C. E., & Esteve, M. (2018). Exploiting IoT Data and Smart City Services for Chronic Obstructive Pulmonary Diseases Risk Factors Monitoring. In *2018 IEEE International Conference on Cloud Engineering (IC2E)* (pp. 351–356). IEEE. doi:10.1109/IC2E.2018.00060

Sarma, A. C., & Girão, J. (2009). Identities in the future internet of things. *Wireless Personal Communications*, *49*(3), 353–363. doi:10.100711277-009-9697-0

SAS. (2014). *Big data meets big data analytics: Three key technologies for extracting real-time business value from the big data that threatens to overwhelm traditional computing architectures.* Retrieved from http://www.sas.com/content/dam/SAS/en_us/doc/whitepaper1/big-data-meetsbig-data-analytics-105777.pdf

Scarpato, N., Pieroni, A., Di Nunzio, L., & Fallucchi, F. (2017). E-health-IoT universe: A review. *Management*, *21*(44), 46.

Schaller, R. R. (1997). Moore's law: Past, present, and future. *IEEE Spectrum*, *34*(6), 52–59. doi:10.1109/6.591665

Scheible, C. (2010). Sentiment Translation through Lexicon Induction. *Proceedings of the ACL 2010 Student Research Workshop*, 25–30.

Schilit, B., Adams, N., & Want, R. (1994).Context-aware computing applications. *First International Workshop on Mobil eComputing Systems and Applications*, 85–90.

Schilit, B., & Theime, M. (1994). Disseminate acting active *map in* formation to mobile hosts. *IEEE Network*, *8*(5), 22–32. doi:10.1109/65.313011

Schneier, B. (2010). A taxonomy of social networking data. *Security & Privacy, IEEE*, *8*(4), 88–88. doi:10.1109/MSP.2010.118

Schneier, B. (2015). *Data and Goliath: The hidden battles to collect your data and control your world.* New York: WW Norton & Company.

Schönfeld, M., Heil, R., & Bittner, L. (2017). Big Data in a Farm- Smart Farming. In *Big Data in Context* (pp. 109–120). Springer.

Schonlau, M. (2002). The clustergram: A graph for visualizing hierarchical and nonhierarchical cluster analyses. *Stata Journal, 2*(4), 391-402. Retrieved on April 4, 2016 from http://schonlau.net/publication/02stata_clustergram.pdf

Schultz, T. (2013). Turning healthcare challenges into big data opportunities: A use-case review across the pharmaceutical development lifecycle. *Bulletin of the American Society for Information Science and Technology*, *39*(5), 34–40. doi:10.1002/bult.2013.1720390508

Schumaker, R. (2013). Machine learning the harness track: Crowdsourcing and varying race history. *Decision Support Systems*, *54*(3), 1370–1379. doi:10.1016/j.dss.2012.12.013

Schwab, D., & Ray, S. (2017). Offline reinforcement learning with task hierarchies. *Machine Learning*, *106*(9-10), 1569–1598. doi:10.100710994-017-5650-8

Schwartz, P. M., & Solove, D. J. (2011). PII problem: Privacy and a new concept of personally identifiable information, the. *New York University Law Review*, *86*, 1814.

Schweizer, L. (2005). Concept and Evolution of Business Models. *Journal of General Management*, *31*(2), 37–56. doi:10.1177/030630700503100203

Seiffert, U. (2004). Artificial Neural Networks on Massively Parallel Computer Hardware. *Neurocomputing*, *57*, 135–150. doi:10.1016/j.neucom.2004.01.011

Selonen, P., & Taivalsaari, A. (2016, August). Kiuas – IoT cloud environment for enabling the programmable world. In *Software Engineering and Advanced Applications (SEAA), 2016 42th Euromicro Conference on* (pp. 250-257). IEEE.

Senyo, P. K., Addae, E., & Boateng, R. (2018). Cloud computing research: A review of research themes, frameworks, methods and future research directions. *International Journal of Information Management*, *38*(1), 128–139. doi:10.1016/j.ijinfomgt.2017.07.007

Shafer, S. M., Smith, H. J., & Linder, J. C. (2005). The Power of Business Models. *Business Horizons*, *48*(3), 199–207. doi:10.1016/j.bushor.2004.10.014

Shah. (2016). Remote health care cyber-physical system: quality of service (QoS) challenges and opportunities. *IET Cyber-Physical Systems: Theory & Applications, 1*(1), 40-48. doi:10.1049/iet-cps.2016.0023

Shah, P. S., Patel, N. N., Patel, D. M., Patel, D. P., & Jhaveri, R. H. (2018). Recent Research in Wireless Sensor Networks: A Trend Analysis. In *Information and Communication Technology for Sustainable Development* (pp. 87–95). Singapore: Springer. doi:10.1007/978-981-10-3932-4_10

Shahzadi, R., Ferzund, J., Tausif, M., & Suryani, M. A. (2016). Internet of Things based Expert System for Smart Agriculture. *International Journal of Advanced Computer Science and Applications*, *7*(9), 341–350.

Shaikh, F. K., Zeadally, S., & Exposito, E. (2017). Enabling technologies for green internet of things. *IEEE Systems Journal*, *11*(2), 983–994. doi:10.1109/JSYST.2015.2415194

Shanthamallu, U. S., Spanias, A., Tepedelenlioglu, C., & Stanley, M. (2017). *A brief survey of machine learning methods and their sensor and IoT applications.* Paper presented at the Information, Intelligence, Systems & Applications (IISA), 2017 8th International Conference on. 10.1109/IISA.2017.8316459

Shapiro, J. M. (2006). Smart cities: Quality of life, productivity, and the growth effects of human capital. *The Review of Economics and Statistics*, *88*(2), 324–335. doi:10.1162/rest.88.2.324

Sharma, L., & Lohan, N. (2017) Performance enhancement through Handling of false classification in video surveillance. *Journal of Pure and applied Science & Technology, 7*(2), 9-17.

Sharma, L., & Yadav, D. (2016). Fisher's Linear Discriminant Ratio based Threshold for Moving Human Detection in Thermal Video. *Infrared Physics and Technology, 78*, 118-128.

Sharma, A., Navda, V., Ramjee, R., Padmanabhan, V. N., & Belding, E. M. (2009, December). Cool-tether: energy efficient on-the-fly Wi-Fi hot-spots using mobile phones. In *Proceedings of the 5th international conference on Emerging networking experiments and technologies* (pp. 109-120). ACM. 10.1145/1658939.1658952

Sharma, L. (2018). *Object Detection with Background Subtraction. LAP LAMBERT Academic Publishing.*

Sharma, L., Yadav, D., & Bharti, S. (2015). An improved method for visual surveillance using background subtraction technique. *2nd Int. Conf. on Signal Processing and Integrated Networks (SPIN)*, 421-426. 10.1109/SPIN.2015.7095253

Sharma, S., Gupta, M., & Nayyar, A. (2014). Review of Routing Techniques Driving Wireless Sensor Networks. *International Journal of Computer Science and Mobile Computing*, *3*(5), 112–122.

Shelby, Z., & Hartke, K. C. B. (2014). *The Constrained Application Protocol (CoAP) - RFC 7252*. Retrieved July 15, 2016, from http://coap.technology/

Sherly, J., & Somasundareswari, D. (2015). Internet of things based smart transportation systems. *International Research Journal of Engineering and Technology*, *2*(7), 1207–1210.

Shikalgar & Dixit. (2014). JIBCA: Jaccard Index based Clustering Algorithm for Mining Online Review. *International Journal of Computer Applications, 105*(15).

Shi, W., Cao, J., Zhang, Q., Li, Y., & Xu, L. (2016). Edge computing: Vision and challenges. *IEEE Internet of Things Journal*, *3*(5), 637–646. doi:10.1109/JIOT.2016.2579198

Shorfuzzaman, M. (2017). Leveraging cloud-based Big Data analytics in knowledge management for enhanced decision making in organizations. *International Journal of Distributed and Parallel Systems*, *8*(1), 1–13. doi:10.5121/ijdps.2017.8101

Shu, M. M. (2017, May). Challenges and research issues of data management in IoT for large-scale petrochemical plants. *IEEE Systems Journal*, 1–15.

Shukla, R., Gupta, R. K., & Kashyap, R. (2019). A multiphase pre-copy strategy for the virtual machine migration in cloud. In S. Satapathy, V. Bhateja, & S. Das (Eds.), *Smart Innovation, Systems and Technologies* (Vol. 104). Singapore: Springer. doi:10.1007/978-981-13-1921-1_43

Shu, L., Mukherjee, M., & Wu, X. (2016). Toxic gas boundary area detection in large-scale petrochemical plants with industrial wireless sensor networks. *IEEE Communications Magazine*, *54*(10), 22–28. doi:10.1109/MCOM.2016.7588225

Sicari, S., Rizzardi, A., Grieco, L. A., & Porisini, A. (2015). Security, privacy and trust in Internet of Things: The road ahead. *Computer Networks*, *76*, 146–164. doi:10.1016/j.comnet.2014.11.008

Sikošek, M. (2012). A Review of Research in Meetings Management: Some Issues and Challenges. *Academica Turistica*, *5*(2), 61–76.

Sim, I., Liginlal, D., & Khansa, L. (2012). Information Privacy Situation Awareness: Construct and Validation. *Journal of Computer Information Systems*, *53*(1), 57–64. doi:10.1080/08874417.2012.11645597

Singh & Singh. (2015). Vector Space Model: An Information Retrieval System. *Int. J. Adv. Engg. Res. Studies, 4*(2), 141-143.

Singh, G., & Jadaun, S. S. (2015, May). Cognitive relay network with asymptotic analysis. In *Computing, Communication & Automation (ICCCA), 2015 International Conference on* (pp. 1335-1338). IEEE. 10.1109/CCAA.2015.7148584

Singh, G., Kaur, G., Dwivedi, V. K., & Yadav, P. K. (n.d.). Development of coded-cooperation based multi-relay system for cognitive radio using mathematical modeling and its performance analysis. *Wireless Networks*, 1-7.

Singh, M., Halgamuge, M. N., Ekici, G., & Jayasekara, C. S. (January 2018). A Review on Security and Privacy Challenges of Big Data. In *Lecture Notes on Data Engineering and Communications Technologies Cognitive Computing for Big Data Systems Over IoT, Frameworks, Tools and Applications* (Vol. 14). Springer. doi:10.1007/978-3-319-70688-7_8

Sinometer. (2012). *LX1010B Mini Digital Lux Meter*. Retrieved from http://www.sinometer.com/?Environmental-Meters-category179.html

Sivieri, A., Mottola, L., & Cugola, G. (2016). Building internet of things software with eliot. *Computer Communications*, *89*, 141–153. doi:10.1016/j.comcom.2016.02.004

Skarlat, O., Nardelli, M., Schulte, S., Borkowski, M., & Leitner, P. (2017). Optimized IoT service placement in the fog. *Service Oriented Computing and Applications, 11*(4), 427–443. doi:10.100711761-017-0219-8

Skublics, S., & White, P. (2013). *Teaching Smalltalk as a first programming language.* ACM SIGCSE Bulletin.

Smagina, N. (2017). The internationalization of the Meetings, Incentives, Conventions and Exhibitions (MICE) industry: Its influences on the actors in the tourism business activity. *Journal of Economics and Management, 27*(1), 95–113.

Smart Cities Council. (n.d.). Pike research. Retrieved from http://smartcitiescouncil.com/tags/pike-research

Smart Dubai. (2016). *Smart Dubai.* Retrieved from http://www.smartdubai.ae

Sofia2. (2017). Retrieved June 1, 2017, from http://sofia2.com/

Solanas, A., Patsakis, C., Conti, M., Vlachos, I. S., Ramos, V., Falcone, F., ... Martinez-Balleste, A. (2014). Smart health: A context-aware health paradigm within smart cities. *IEEE Communications Magazine, 52*(8), 74–81. doi:10.1109/MCOM.2014.6871673

Soliman, M., Abiodun, T., Hamouda, T., Zhou, J., & Lung, C. H. (2013). Smart Home: Integrating Internet of Things with Web Services and Cloud Computing. In *Proceedings of Cloud Computing Technology and Science, IEEE 5th International Conference on* (pp. 317-320). IEEE.

Solove, D. J. (2006). A taxonomy of privacy. *University of Pennsylvania Law Review, 154*(3), 477–564. doi:10.2307/40041279

Solove, D. J. (2012b). Privacy self-management and the consent dilemma. *Harvard Law Review, 126*, 1880–1903.

Solove, D. J., & Schwartz, P. M. (2014). *Consumer Privacy and Data Protection* (5th ed.). New York: Wolters Kluwer.

Song, H., & Liu, H. (2017). Predicting tourist demand using big data. In Z. Xiang & D. R. Fesenmaier (Eds.), *Analytics in Smart Tourism Design, Tourism on the Verge* (pp. 13–29). Springer International Publishing.

Soucy, P., & Mineau, G. W. (2015). Beyond TFIDF Weighting for Text Categorization in the Vector Space Model. *Proceedings of the 19th International Joint Conference on Artificial Intelligence*, 1130-1135.

Soursos, S., Zarko, I. P., Zwickl, P., Gojmerac, I., Bianchi, G., & Carrozzo, G. (2016). Towards the cross-domain interoperability of IoT platforms. In *2016 European Conference on Networks and Communications (EuCNC)* (pp. 398–402). Academic Press. 10.1109/EuCNC.2016.7561070

Souza, A., Figueredo, M., Cacho, N., Araújo, D., & Prolo, C. A. (2016). Using Big Data and Real-Time Analytics to Support Smart City Initiatives. *IFAC-PapersOnLine, 49*(30), 257–262. doi:10.1016/j.ifacol.2016.11.121

Spangler, S., Cheney, Proctor, L., Lelecu, A., Behal, A., He, B., & Davis, T. (2009). COBRA–mining web for corporate brand and deputation analysis. *Web Intelligence and Agent Systems, 7*(3), 243–254.

Sphinx. (2018). *ParaDrop - Enabling Edge Computing at the Extreme Edge — paradrop 0.11.2 documentation.* Retrieved May 23, 2018, from http://paradrop.readthedocs.io/en/latest/index.html

Spiekerman, S., & Cranor, L. F. (2009). Engineering privacy. *IEEE Transactions on Software Engineering, 35*(1), 67–82. doi:10.1109/TSE.2008.88

Spirjakin, D. A. M. (2015). Design of smart dust sensor node for combustible gas leakage monitoring. In *Proceedings of Federated Conf. on Computer Science and Information Systems(FedCSIS)* (pp. 1279–1283). Academic Press.

SRA. (2009). *The Internet of Things Strategic Road Map.* Retrieved from: http://sintef.biz/upload/IKT/9022/CERP-IoT%20SRA_IoT_v11_pdf

Sravanthi, K., & Reddy, T. S. (2015). Applications of Big data in Various Fields. *International Journal of Computer Science and Information Technologies*, *6*(5), 4629–4632.

Srinivas, N., & Kale, V. S. (2017, July). Review of network technologies in intelligent power system. In *IEEE Region 10 Symposium (TENSYMP), 2017* (pp. 1-6). IEEE. 10.1109/TENCONSpring.2017.8069974

Srinivasan, R., Mohan, A., & Srinivasan, P. (2016). Privacy conscious architecture for improving emergency response in smart cities. *2016 Smart City Security and Privacy Workshop (SCSP-W)*, 1-5. 10.1109/SCSPW.2016.7509559

Srivastava, S., Bisht, A., & Narayan, N. (2017). Safety and security in smart cities using artificial intelligence — A review. *2017 7th International Conference on Cloud Computing, Data Science & Engineering - Confluence*, 130-133. 10.1109/CONFLUENCE.2017.7943136

Stadtentwicklung. (2015). *Smart City Strategy Berlin. State Department for Urban Development and the Environment*. Retrieved from http://www.stadtentwicklung.berlin.de/planen/foren_initiativen/smart-city/download/Strategie_Smart_City_Berlin_en.pdf

Sta, H. B. (2016). Quality and the efficiency of data in "Smart-Cities". *Future Generation Computer Systems*, *74*, 409–416. doi:10.1016/j.future.2016.12.021

Stauffer, C., & Grimson, W. E. L. (1999). Adaptive background mixture models for real-time tracking. *IEEE Computer Society Conference on Computer Vision and Pattern Recognition*, 2, 246–252 10.1109/CVPR.1999.784637

Steenbruggen, J., Tranos, E., & Nijkamp, P. (2015). Data from mobile phone operators: A tool for smarter cities? *Telecommunications Policy*, *39*(3), 335–346. doi:10.1016/j.telpol.2014.04.001

Stergiou, C., Psannis, K. E., Kim, B. G., & Gupta, B. (2018). Secure integration of IoT and cloud computing. *Future Generation Computer Systems*, *78*, 964–975. doi:10.1016/j.future.2016.11.031

Stimmel, C. L. (2014). *Big Data Analytics Strategies for the Smart Grid*. CRC Press. doi:10.1201/b17228

Strohbach, M., Ziekow, H., Gazis, V., & Akiva, N. (2015). *Towards a big data analytics framework for IoT and smart city applications. In Modeling and processing for next-generation big-data technologies* (pp. 257–282). Springer.

Su & Chou. (2001). A modified version of the K-means algorithm with a distance based on cluster symmetry. *IEEE Transactions on Pattern Analysis and Machine Intelligence*, *23*(6). Doi:10.1109/34.927466

Su, F., & Peng, Y. (2016). The research of big data architecture on telecom industry. In *2016 16th International Symposium on Communications and Information Technologies (ISCIT)*. IEEE. doi:10.1109/ISCIT.2016.7751636

Su, K., Li, J., & Fu, H. (2011, September). Smart city and the applications. In *2011 International Conference on Electronics, Communications and Control (ICECC)* (pp. 1028-1031). IEEE. 10.1109/ICECC.2011.6066743

Sudheer, K. P., Gosain, A. K., Mohana Rangan, D., & Saheb, S. M. (2002). Modelling evaporation using an artificial neural network algorithm. *Hydrological Processes*, *16*(16), 3189–3202. doi:10.1002/hyp.1096

Sudheer, K. P., Gosain, A. K., & Ramasastri, K. S. (2002). A data-driven algorithm for constructing artificial neural network rainfall-runoff models. *Hydrological Processes*. doi:10.1002/hyp.554

Suh, N. P. (2005). *Complexity: theory and applications*. Oxford, UK: Oxford University Press.

Sumriddetchkajorn, S., & Somboonkaew, A. (2010). Low-cost cell-phone-based digital lux meter. *Proceedings of SPIE Advanced Sensor Systems and Applications*, *IV*, 1–6.

Sun, C. (2012). Application of RFID technology for logistics on internet of things. *AASRI Procedia*, *1*, 106–111. doi:10.1016/j.aasri.2012.06.019

Sundaravadivel, Kougianos, Mohanty, & Ganapathiraju. (2018). Everything You Wanted to Know about Smart Health Care: Evaluating the Different Technologies and Components of the Internet of Things for Better Health. *IEEE Consumer Electronics Magazine, 7*(1), 18-28.

Sun, E., Zhang, X., & Li, Z. (2012). The Internet of Things (IOT) and cloud computing (CC) based tailings dam monitoring and pre-alarm system in mines. *Safety Science*, *50*(4), 811–815. doi:10.1016/j.ssci.2011.08.028

Sun, H., & Betti, R. (2015). A Hybrid Optimization Algorithm with Bayesian Inference for Probabilistic Model Updating. *Computer-Aided Civil and Infrastructure Engineering*, *30*(8), 602–619. doi:10.1111/mice.12142

Sun, Y., Song, H., Jara, A. J., & Bie, R. (2016). Internet of things and big data analytics for smart and connected communities. *IEEE Access : Practical Innovations, Open Solutions*, *4*, 766–773. doi:10.1109/ACCESS.2016.2529723

Sun, Y., Wu, L., Wu, S., Li, S., Zhang, T., Zhang, L., ... Xiong, Y. (2015). Security and Privacy in the Internet of Vehicles. *2015 International Conference on Identification, Information, and Knowledge in the Internet of Things (IIKI)*, 116-121. 10.1109/IIKI.2015.33

Suo, H., Wan, J., Zou, C., & Liu, J. (2012, March). Security in the internet of things: a review. In Computer Science and Electronics Engineering (ICCSEE), 2012 international conference on (Vol. 3, pp. 648-651). IEEE. doi:10.1109/ICCSEE.2012.373

Supriya, M., & Deepa, A. J. (2017). A Survey on Prediction Using Big Data Analytics. *International Journal of Big Data and Analytics in Healthcare*, *2*(1), 1–15. doi:10.4018/IJBDAH.2017010101

Susanti, R., Soetomo, S., Buchori, I., & Brotosunaryo, P. M. (2016). Smart Growth, Smart City and Density: In Search of The Appropriate Indicator for Residential Density in Indonesia. *Procedia: Social and Behavioral Sciences*, *227*, 194–201. doi:10.1016/j.sbspro.2016.06.062

Suzuki, Armato III, Li, Sone, & Doi. (2003). Massive training artificial neural network (MTANN) for reduction of false positives in computerized detection of lung nodules in low-dose computed tomography. *The International Journal of Medical Physics Research and Practice, 30*(7), 1602-1617.

Svantesson, D., & Clarke, R. (2010). A best practice model for e-consumer protection. *Computer Law & Security Review*, *26*(1), 31–37. doi:10.1016/j.clsr.2009.11.006

Svedberg, R. (2012). Shum peter's theories of organizational entrepreneurship. In D. Hjorth (Ed.), *Handbook on Organizational Entrepreneurship* (pp. 31–48). Cheltenham, UK: Edward Elgar Publishing. doi:10.4337/9781781009055.00011

Swan, M. (2012). Sensor mania! the internet of things, wearable computing, objective metrics, and the quantified self-2.0. *Journal of Sensor and Actuator Networks*, *1*(3), 217–253. doi:10.3390/jsan1030217

Sweeney, L., Abu, A., & Winn, J. (2013). *Identifying participants in the personal genome project by name*. Academic Press.

Sweeney, L. (2002). K-anonymity: A model for protecting privacy. *International Journal of Uncertainty, Fuzziness and Knowledge-based Systems*, *10*(5), 557–570. doi:10.1142/S0218488502001648

Taivalsaari, A., & Mikkonen, T. (2018, April). On the development of IoT systems. In *Fog and Mobile Edge Computing (FMEC), 2018 Third International Conference on* (pp. 13-19). IEEE. 10.1109/FMEC.2018.8364039

Talari, S., Shafie-khah, M., Siano, P., Loia, V., Tommasetti, A., & Catalão, J. P. (2017). A review of smart cities based on the internet of things concept. *Energies*, *10*(4), 421. doi:10.3390/en10040421

Talbot, J., Yoo, R. M., & Kozyrakis, C. (2011). Phoenix++: modular MapReduce for shared-memory systems. In *Proceedings of the Second International Workshop on MapReduce and its Applications* (pp. 9-16). ACM. Retrieved on April 4, 2016 from http://csl.stanford.edu/~christos/publications/2011.phoenixplus.mapreduce.pdf

Tamás, J., Podani, J., & Csontos, P. (2001). An extension of presence/absence coefficients to abundance data:a new look at absence. *Journal of Vegetation Science*, *12*(3), 401–410. doi:10.2307/3236854

Tan, L., & Wang, N. (2010). Future Internet: The Internet of Things. In *Advanced Computer Theory and Engineering (ICACTE), 3rd International Conference* (pp. 376–380). Academic Press.

Tango, F., Minin, L., Tesauri, F., & Montanari, R. (2010). Field tests and machine learning approaches for refining algorithms and correlations of driver's model parameters. *Applied Ergonomics*, *41*(2), 211–224. doi:10.1016/j.apergo.2009.01.010 PMID:19286165

Tannahill, B. K., & Jamshidi, M. (2014). Systems of systems and big data analytics – bridging the gap. *Computers & Electrical Engineering*, *40*(1), 2–15. doi:10.1016/j.compeleceng.2013.11.016

Tanque, M., & Foxwell, H. J. (2014). *Big Data and Cloud Computing: A Review of Supply Chain Capabilities and Challenges*. Retrieved from http://linkinghub.elsevier.com/retrieve/pii/B9780124071926000091

Tan, S., & Zhang, J. (2007). An empirical study of sentiment analysis for Chinese documents. *Expert Systems with Applications*. doi:10.1016/j.eswa.2007.05.028

Tao, F., Cheng, Y., Da Xu, L., Zhang, L., & Li, B. H. (2014). CCIoT-CMfg: Cloud computing and internet of things-based cloud manufacturing service system. *IEEE Transactions on Industrial Informatics*, *10*(2), 1435–1442. doi:10.1109/TII.2014.2306383

Tapscott, D., Lowy, A., & Ticoll, D. (2000). *Digital Capital: Harnessing the Power of Business Webs*. Cambridge, MA: Harvard Business School Press.

Taylor, J. (2013). *Delivering customer value faster with big data analytics*. Retrieved from http://www.fico.com/en/wp- content/secure_upload/DeliveringCustomerValueFasterWithBigDataAnalytics.pdf

TaylorA. E. F. (2017). *Illumination Fundamentals*. Retrieved from https://optics.synopsys.com/lighttools/pdfs/illuminationfund.pdf

Tayyaba, S. K., Shah, M. A., Khan, O. A., & Ahmed, A. W. (2017). Software Defined Network (SDN) Based Internet of Things (IoT): A Road Ahead. In *Proceedings of the International Conference on Future Networks and Distributed Systems* (p. 10). ACM. 10.1145/3102304.3102319

Teece, D. J. (2010). Business Models, Business Strategy and Innovation. *Long Range Planning*, *43*(2-3), 172–194. doi:10.1016/j.lrp.2009.07.003

Telecommunication Standarization Sector of ITU. (2014). *Common requirements and capabilities of a gateway for Internet of things applications*. Retrieved from https://www.itu.int/rec/T-REC-Y.2067/en

Terms of Service Didn't Read. (2017). *I have read and agree to the Terms is the biggest lie on the web. We aim to fix that.* Retrieved 21 December 2018 from https://tosdr.org/index.html

Tetteh, E. N. A. (2004). *Theories of democratic governance in the institutions of higher education*. New York: iUniverse.

Tetteh, E. N. A. (2010). *Communal photosynthesis: Metaphor-based heuristic study of service-learners' symbolic interactionism in security management*. Ann Arbor, MI: ProQuest LLC/UMI Dissertation.

Tetteh, E. N. A. (2015a). Communal–photosynthesis metaphor: Autobiographical action–research journeys and heuristic–action–learning frameworks of living educational theories. *ALARj*, *21*(1), 148–176.

Tetteh, E. N. A. (2015b). *Overview of AD 545 course: Politics, policy, and planning (Policy Analysis and Analytics Concentration, Master of Public Administration Program, College of Graduate and Continuing Studies, Norwich University).* Northfield, VT: Norwich University.

Tetteh, E. N. A. (2015c). *Overview of AD 555 course: Methods of policy analysis (Policy Analysis and Analytics Concentration, Master of Public Administration Program, College of Graduate and Continuing Studies, Norwich University).* Northfield, VT: Norwich University.

The Green Grid. (n.d.). Retrieved from https://www.thegreengrid.org

The International Association of Privacy Professionals. (2017). *IAPP-EY annual privacy governance report.* Retrieved from https://iapp.org/

The Open Innotation Tool Dataset. (2016). *Dataset from MIT lab.* Retrieved, March 2018, from http://labelme.csail.mit.edu/Release3.0/browserTools/php/dataset.php

Think Big Analytics. (2013). *Big data reference architecture.* Retrieved on April 4, 2016 from http://thinkbiganalytics.com/leading_big_data_technologies/big-data-reference-architecture/

Thomas, V. M. (2008, May). Environmental implications of RFID. In *Electronics and the Environment, 2008. ISEE 2008. IEEE International Symposium on* (pp. 1-5). IEEE. 10.1109/ISEE.2008.4562916

Thomas, C. W. (1997, April 1). Public management as interagency cooperation: Testing epistemic community theory at the domestic level. *Journal of Public Administration: Research and Theory*, *7*(2), 221–246. doi:10.1093/oxfordjournals.jpart.a024347

Timmers, P. (1998). Business Models for Electronic Markets. *Electronic Markets*, *8*(2), 3–8. doi:10.1080/10196789800000016

Tiwari, S., Gupta, R. K., & Kashyap, R. (2019). To enhance web response time using agglomerative clustering technique for web navigation recommendation. In H. Behera, J. Nayak, B. Naik, & A. Abraham (Eds.), *Computational Intelligence in Data Mining. Advances in Intelligent Systems and Computing* (Vol. 711). Singapore: Springer. doi:10.1007/978-981-10-8055-5_59

Tofan, C. (2014). Optimization Techniques of Decision Making - Decision Tree. *Advances In Social Sciences Research Journal*, *1*(5), 142–148. doi:10.14738/assrj.15.437

Toivonen, H., & Gross, O. (2015). Data mining and machine learning in computational creativity. *Wiley Interdisciplinary Reviews. Data Mining and Knowledge Discovery*, *5*(6), 265–275. doi:10.1002/widm.1170

Tole, A. A. (2013). Big data challenges. *Database Syst.*, 31-40.

Tools for Amazon Web Services. (n.d.). Retrieved from https://aws.amazon.com/tools/?nc1=f_ls

Top Banana and the Institute of Internal Communication. (2015). *Technology destroying trust in business- but events can fix it.* Retrieved from http://www.meetpie.com/Modules/NewsModule/newsdetails.aspx?t=Technology-destroying-trust-in-business-but-events-can-fix-it&newsid=20501

Torra, V. (2017). *Data privacy: foundations, new developments and the big data challenge.* New York: Springer. doi:10.1007/978-3-319-57358-8

Torre, I., Sanchez, O. R., Koceva, F., & Adorni, G. (2017). Supporting users to take informed decisions on privacy settings of personal devices. *Personal and Ubiquitous Computing*, 1–20.

Townsend, A. M. (2013). *Smart cities: Big data, civic hackers, and the quest for a new utopia*. New York: WW Norton & Company.

Toyama, K., Krumm, J., Brumitt, B., & Meyers, B. (1999). Wallflower: principles and practice of background maintenance. *7th International Conference on Computer Vision,* 255–261. 10.1109/ICCV.1999.791228

Tragos, E. Z. (2014). Enabling reliable and secure IoT-based smart city applications. *2014 IEEE International Conference on Pervasive Computing and Communication Workshops (PERCOM WORKSHOPS),* 111-116. 10.1109/PerComW.2014.6815175

Trancă, D. C., Rosner, D., Curatu, R., Surpăteanu, A., Mocanu, M., Pardău, Ş., & Pălăcean, A. V. (2017). Industrial WSN node extension and measurement systems for air, water and environmental monitoring: IoT enabled environment monitoring using NI WSN nodes. In *Proceedings of Networking in Education and Research (RoEduNet), 16th RoEduNet Conference* (pp. 1-6). Academic Press.

Travis, A., & Arthur, C. (2014, May 13). EU court backs 'right to be forgotten': Google must amend results on request. *The Guardian.* Retrieved from https://www.theguardian.com/technology/2014/may/13/right-to-be-forgotten-eu-court-google-search-results

TSCGCC. (n.d.). Retrieved from https://sites.google.com/site/gcccomsoc/

Tschofenig, H., Arkko, J., & Thaler, D. D. M. (2015). *Architectural Considerations in Smart Object Networking - RFC 7452.* Retrieved from https://tools.ietf.org/pdf/rfc7452.pdf

Tuan, N., Mohammad, G., Rahmani, T., & Westerlund, L. (2015). Fault Tolerant and Scalable IoT-based Architecture for Health Monitoring. *Sensors Applications Symposium (SAS)*, 1-6.

Tuninetti Ferrari, A. (2017). *Big Data: balancing the web user's and the service provider's rights in the Big Data era* (Unpublished doctoral thesis). Università degli Studi di Parma. Dipartimento di Giurisprudenza. Retrieved 21 December 2018 from http://dspace-unipr.cineca.it/handle/1889/3333

Turban, E., King, D., Sharda, R., & Delen, D. (2013). *Business intelligence: a managerial perspective on analytics.* Prentice Hall.

Turney, P. D., & Littman, M. L. (2002). *Unsupervised Learning of Semantic Orientation from a Hundred-Billion-Word Corpus.* arXiv:cs/0212012

Uckelmann, D., Harrison, M., & Michahelles, F. (2011). An Architectural Approach. Towards the Future Internet of Things. In D. Uckelmann, M. Harrison, & F. Michahelles (Eds.), *Architecting the Internet of Things* (pp. 1–24). Berlin: Springer. doi:10.1007/978-3-642-19157-2_1

Uesugi, Sh. (2014). *Kappa Architecture - Where Every Thing Is A Stream.* Retrieved May 4, 2018, from http://milinda.pathirage.org/kappa-architecture.com/

UK Future Internet Strategy Group. (2011). *Future Internet Report.* Retrieved from: https://connect.innovateuk.org/c/document_library/get_file?folderId=861750&name=DLFE–34705.pdf

Ullah, F., Habib, M. A., Farhan, M., Khalid, S., Durrani, M. Y., & Jabbar, S. (2017). Semantic interoperability for big-data in heterogeneous IoT infrastructure for healthcare. *Sustainable Cities and Society, 34*, 90–96. doi:10.1016/j.scs.2017.06.010

United Nations. (2012). *World urbanization prospects; the 2011 revision.* New York: Department of Economic and Social Affairs.

Urquhart, L., & Rodden, T. (2016). *A Legal Turn in Human-Computer Interaction?* Towards Regulation by Design for the Internet of Things. SSRN Electronic Journal. doi:10.2139srn.2746467

Vaidya, J., Clifton, C., & Zhu, M. (2006). *Privacy preserving data mining*. Springer.

Valera, A. J., Zamora, A. M., & Skarmeta, A. F. G. (2010). An architecture based on internet of things to support mobility and security in medical environments. *7th IEEE Consumer Communications and Networking Conference*. 10.1109/CCNC.2010.5421661

van de Pas, J., van Bussel, G. J., Veenstra, M., & Jorna, F. (2015). Digital data and the city: An exploration of the building blocks of a smart city architecture. In D. Baker & W. Evans (Eds.), *Digital Information Strategies: From Applications and Content to Libraries* (pp. 185–198). Chandos Publishing.

Van der Waldt, G. (2014). Public administration teaching and interdisciplinarity: Considering the consequences. *Teaching Public Administration, 32*(2), 169–193. doi: 14523285 doi:10.1177/01447394

van Kranenburg, R. (2007). *The Internet of Things: A Critique of Ambient Technology and the All-Seeing Network of RFID*. Amsterdam: Institute of Network Cultures.

Van Kranenburg, R., & Bassi, A. (2012). IoT challenges. *Communications in Mobile Computing*, *1*(1), 9. doi:10.1186/2192-1121-1-9

van Zoonen, L. (2016). Privacy concerns in smart cities. *Government Information Quarterly*, *33*(3), 471–480. doi:10.1016/j.giq.2016.06.004

Vargas, V., Syed, A., Mohammad, A., & Halgamuge, M. N. (2016). Pentaho and Jaspersoft: A Comparative Study of Business Intelligence Open Source Tools Processing Big Data to Evaluate Performances. *International Journal of Advanced Computer Science and Applications*, *7*(10), 20–29.

Vattapparamban, E., Güvenç, İ., Yurekli, A. İ., Akkaya, K., & Uluağaç, S. (2016). Drones for smart cities: Issues in cybersecurity, privacy, and public safety. *2016 International Wireless Communications and Mobile Computing Conference (IWCMC)*, 216-221. 10.1109/IWCMC.2016.7577060

Vegvesen. (2015). *Smart Bodo*. Retrieved from https://www.vegvesen.no/_attachment/1103917/binary/1076326?fast_title=Visjonen+om+verdens+smarteste+by+%E2%80%93+SMART +Bod%C3%B8+-+Asgeir+Jordbru.pdf

Venkataramanan, N., & Shriram, A. (2017). Data privacy: principles and practice. Boca Raton, FL: CRC Press: Taylor and Francis Group.

Vidiasova, L., Kachurina, P., & Cronemberger, P. (2017). Smart Cities Prospects from the Results of the World Practice Expert Benchmarking. *Procedia Computer Science, 119*, 269–277. doi:10.1016/j.procs.2017.11.185

Viégas, F. B., Wattenberg, M., & Dave, K. (2004). Studying cooperation and conflict between authors with history flow visualizations. In *Proceedings of the SIGCHI Conference on Human Factors in Computing Systems* (pp. 575-582). ACM. Retrieved on April 4, 2016 from http://alumni.media.mit.edu/~fviegas/papers/history_flow.pdf

Vijayakumar, N., & Ramya, R. (2015). The real time monitoring of water quality in IoT environment. In *Proceedings of Circuit, Power and Computing Technologies (ICCPCT), International Conference* (pp. 1-4). Academic Press.

Vijayalakshmi, S., Anpalagan, A., Kothari, D. P., Woungang, I., & Obaidat, M. S. (2014). An analytical study of resource division and its impact on power and performance of multi-core processors. *The Journal of Supercomputing*, *68*(3), 1265–1279. doi:10.100711227-014-1086-0

Vippalapalli, V., & Ananthula, S. (2016). Internet of things (IoT) based smart health care system. *International Conference on Signal Processing, Communication, Power and Embedded System (SCOPES)*, 1229-1233. 10.1109/SCOPES.2016.7955637

Vo, Q. D., Choi, J. P., Chang, H. M., & Lee, W. C. (2010, November). Green perspective cognitive radio-based M2M communications for smart meters. In *Information and Communication Technology Convergence (ICTC), 2010 International Conference on* (pp. 382-383). IEEE.

Voigt, P., & Von dem Bussche, A. (2017). *The EU general data protection regulation (GDPR): A practical guide*. Berlin, Germany: Springer International Publishing. doi:10.1007/978-3-319-57959-7

Vyas, V., Saxena, S., & Bhargava, D. (2015). Mind Reading by Face Recognition Using Security Enhancement Model. In *Proceedings of Fourth International Conference on Soft Computing for Problem Solving* (pp. 173-180). Springer New Delhi. 10.1007/978-81-322-2217-0_15

Wadhwani. (2017). *Big Data Challenges and Solutions*. Technical Report.

Wagstaff, K., Cardie, C., Rogers, S., & Schroedl, S. (2001). Constrained K-means Clustering with Background Knowledge. *Proceedings of the Eighteenth International Conference on Machine Learning*, 577-584.

Wallhoff, F., & München, T. (2000). *FGNet Facial Emotions and Expressions Database*. Retrieved, May 2018, from http://www-prima.inrialpes.fr/FGnet/html/benchmarks.html

Wang, X., Wang, J. T., Zhang, X., & Song, J. (2013). *A multiple communication standards compatible IoT system for medical usage*. Paper presented at the 2013 IEEE Faible Tension Faible Consommation. 10.1109/FTFC.2013.6577775

Wang, D., McMahan, C., & Gallagher, C. (2015). A general regression framework for group testing data, which incorporates pool dilution effects. *Statistics in Medicine*, *34*(27), 3606–3621. doi:10.1002im.6578 PMID:26173957

Wang, F. (2014). Scanning the Issue and Beyond; Parallel driving with software vehicular robots for safety and smartness. *IEEE Transactions on Intelligent Transportation Systems*, *15*(4), 1381–1387. doi:10.1109/TITS.2014.2342451

Wang, G., & Araki, K. (2007). Modifying SO-PMI for Japanese Weblog Opinion Mining by Using a Balancing Factor and Detecting Neutral Expressions. *Proceedings of NAACL HLT 2007*, 189–192. 10.3115/1614108.1614156

Wang, L., & Khan, S. U. (2013). Review of performance metrics for green data centers: A taxonomy study. *The Journal of Supercomputing*, *63*(3), 639–656. doi:10.100711227-011-0704-3

Wanichayapong, N., Pruthipunyaskul, W., Pattara-Atikom, W., & Chaovalit, P. (2011, August). Social-based traffic information extraction and classification. In *2011 11th International Conference on ITS Telecommunications (ITST)* (pp. 107-112). IEEE.

Wanigasooriya, Halgamuge, & Mohamad. (2017). The Analyzes of Anticancer Drug Sensitivity of Lung Cancer Cell Lines by Using Machine Learning Clustering Techniques. *International Journal of Advanced Computer Science and Applications, 8*(9).

Wan, J., Chen, M., Xia, F., Di, L., & Zhou, K. (2013). From machine-to-machine communications towards cyber-physical systems. *Computer Science and Information Systems*, *10*(3), 1105–1128. doi:10.2298/CSIS120326018W

Wan, X. (2009). Co-Training for Cross-Lingual Sentiment Classification. *Proceedings of the 47th Annual Meeting of the ACL and the 4th IJCNLP of the AFNLP*, 235–243.

Waoo, N., Kashyap, R., & Jaiswal, A. (2010). DNA nanoarray analysis using hierarchical quality threshold clustering. In *2010 2nd IEEE International Conference on Information Management and Engineering*. IEEE.

Waoo, N., Kashyap, R., & Jaiswal, A. (2010). DNA nano array analysis using hierarchical quality threshold clustering. In *Proceedings of 2010 2nd IEEE International Conference on Information Management and Engineering* (pp. 81-85). IEEE. 10.1109/ICIME.2010.5477579

Warren, S., & Brandeis, L. (1890). The right to privacy. *Harvard Law Review, 4*(5), 193-220. Retrieved 21 December 2018 from https://www.cs.cornell.edu/~shmat/courses/cs5436/warren-brandeis.pdf

Washburn, D., Sindhu, U., Balaouras, S., Dines, R. A., Hayes, N., & Nelson, L. E. (2009). *Helping CIOs understand "smart city" initiatives*. Cambridge: Forrester.

Weber, R. (2010). Internet of Things – New security and privacy challenges. *Computer Law & Security Review*, *26*(1), 23–30. doi:10.1016/j.clsr.2009.11.008

Weber, R. (2015). Internet of things: Privacy issues revisited. *Computer Law & Security Review*, *31*(5), 618–627. doi:10.1016/j.clsr.2015.07.002

Weiller, C., & Neely, A. (2013). *Business Model Design in an Ecosystem Context*. University of Cambridge Working Papers. Cambridge, UK: Cambridge Service Alliance.

Weill, P., & Vitale, M. R. (2001). *Placeto Space:Migrating to eBusiness Models*. Cambridge, MA: Harvard Business School Press.

Westerlund, M. (2013). TIM Lecture Series Green Business Models To Change The World: How Can Entrepreneurs Ride the Sustainability Wave? *Technology Innovation Management Review, 3*(7), 53-57. Retrieved from http://timreview.ca/article/70

Westin, A. F. (1967). *Privacy and freedom*. New York: Athenaeum.

White, T. (2009). *Hadoop: The definitive guide* (1st ed.). O'Reilly Media, Inc. Retrieved on April 4, 2016 from http://ce.sysu.edu.cn/hope/UploadFiles/Education/2011/10/201110221516245419.pdf

Whitepaper. (2012). *Challenges and opportunities with BigData* (Tech. Rep.). Retrieved on April 4, 2016 from https://www.purdue.edu/discoverypark/cyber/assets/pdfs/BigDataWhitePaper.pdf

Whitmore, A., Agarwal, A., & Da Xu, L. (2015). The Internet of Things—A survey of topics and trends. *Information Systems Frontiers*, *17*(2), 261–274. doi:10.100710796-014-9489-2

Wibowo, S., & Wells, M. (2018). Green Cloud Computing and Economics of the Cloud: Moving towards Sustainable Future. *GSTF Journal on Computing (JoC), 5*(1).

Williams, Z. D. (2017). *IoT Platform Comparison: How the 450 providers stack up* [White paper]. Retrieved July 19, 2018, from https://iot-analytics.com/iot-platform-comparison-how-providers-stack-up/

Wilson, J. Q. (2000). *American government: A brief version* (5th ed.). Boston, MA: Houghton Mifflin.

Wolfert, S., Ge, L., Verdouw, C., & Bogaardt, M. J. (2017). Big data in smart farming–a review. *Agricultural Systems, 153*, 69-80. Retrieved from https://www.sciencedirect.com/science/article/pii/S0308521X16303754

Woodward, W. A., Gray, H. L., & Elliott, A. C. (2017). *Applied Time Series Analysis with R*. CRC press.

World Bank. (n.d.). Retrieved from data.worldbank.org/indicator/SP.URB.TOTL.IN.ZS?end=2015&start=1960&view=chart

World Economic Forum. (2015). *Industrial Internet of Things: Unleashing the Potential of Connected Products and Services*. Retrieved from http://www3.weforum.org/docs/WEFUSA_IndustrialInternet_Report2015.pdf

Wortmann, F., & Flüchter, K. (2015). Internet of things. *Business & Information Systems Engineering*, *57*(3), 221–224. doi:10.100712599-015-0383-3

Wurster, L. F. (2014). *Emerging Technology Analysis: Software Licensing and Entitlement Management Is the Key to Monetizing the Internet of Things*. Gartner Research Report G00251790. Stamford, CT: Gartner, Inc.

Wu, X., & He, J. (2009). Paradigm shift in public administration: Implications for teaching professional training programs. *Public Administration Review*, *69*(s1), S21–S28. doi:10.1111/j.1540-6210.2009.02085.x

Wu, Y., Zhang, W., Shen, J., Mo, Z., & Peng, Y. (2018). Smart City with Chinese Characteristics against the Background of Big Data: Idea, Action and Risk. *Journal of Cleaner Production*, *173*, 60–66. doi:10.1016/j.jclepro.2017.01.047

Xia, H., Wang, Y., Huang, Y., & Shah, A. (2017). "Our Privacy Needs to be Protected at All Costs": Crowd Workers' Privacy Experiences on Amazon Mechanical Turk. *ACM Human Computer Interaction*, *1*(2), 22. doi:10.1145/3134748

Xu, H., Dinev, T., Smith, J., & Hart, P. (2011). Information privacy concerns: Linking individual perceptions with institutional privacy assurances. *Journal of the Association for Information Systems*, *12*(12), 798–824. doi:10.17705/1jais.00281

Xu, L. D., Wang, C., Bi, Z. M., & Yu, J. (2014). Object-oriented templates for automated assembly planning of complex products. *IEEE Transactions on Automation Science and Engineering*, *11*(2), 492–503. doi:10.1109/TASE.2012.2232652

Yacchirema, D., Palau, C., & Esteve, M. (2016). Smart IoT Gateway For Heterogeneous Devices Interoperability. *IEEE Latin America Transactions*, *14*(8), 3900–3906. doi:10.1109/TLA.2016.7786378

Yacchirema, D., Sarabia-Jácome, D., Palau, C. E., & Esteve, M. (2018). A Smart System for sleep monitoring by integrating IoT with big data analytics. *IEEE Access: Practical Innovations, Open Solutions*, *1*. doi:10.1109/ACCESS.2018.2849822

Yadav, D., Sharma, L., & Bharti, S. (2014). *Moving Object Detection in Real-Time Visual Surveillance using Background Subtraction Technique. In 14th International conference on Hybrid Intelligent Systems (HIS2014)* (pp. 79–84). IEEE.

Yadav, D., & Singh, K. (2015). A Combined Approach of Kullback-Leibler Divergence Method and Background Subtraction for Moving Object Detection in Thermal Video. *Infrared Physics and Technology, Elsevier*, *76*, 21–31. doi:10.1016/j.infrared.2015.12.027

Yadav, D., & Singh, K. (2015). Moving Object Detection for Visual Surveillance Using Quasi-Euclidian Distance, IC3T-2015. *LNCS, Advances in Intelligent Systems and Computing Series, Springer*, *381*, 225–233. doi:10.1007/978-81-322-2526-3_25

Yadav, S. A., Kumar, S. R., Sharma, S., & Singh, A. (2016). A review of possibilities and solutions of cyber attacks in smart grids. *2016 International Conference on Innovation and Challenges in Cyber Security (ICICCS-INBUSH)*, 60-63. 10.1109/ICICCS.2016.7542359

Yang, Zhao, Zhang, Lin, & Yu. (2017). Toward a Gaussian-Mixture Model-Based Detection Scheme Against Data Integrity Attacks in the Smart Grid. *IEEE Internet of Things Journal, 4*(1), 147-161.

Yang, J., Han, Y., Wang, Y., Jiang, B., Lv, Z., & Song, H. (in press). Optimization of real-time traffic network assignment based on IoT data using DBN and clustering model in smart city. *Future Generation Computer Systems*.

Yao, M. Z. (2011). Self-protection of online privacy: A behavioral approach. In R. L. Trepte S. (Ed.), Privacy Online (pp. 111-125). Berlin: Springer. doi:10.1007/978-3-642-21521-6_9

Yao, M. (2014). Research on Learning Evidence Improvement for kNN Based Classification Algorithm. *International Journal Of Database Theory And Application*, *7*(1), 103–110. doi:10.14257/ijdta.2014.7.1.10

Yao, X. (1999). Evolving artificial neural networks. *Proceedings of the IEEE*, *87*(9). doi:10.1109/5.784219

Yaqoob, I., Hashem, I. A. T., Gani, A., Mokhtar, S., Ahmed, E., Anuar, N. B., & Vasilakos, A. V. (2016). Big data: From beginning to future. *International Journal of Information Management*, *36*(6), 1231–1247. doi:10.1016/j.ijinfomgt.2016.07.009

Yildirim, P., Birant, D., & Alpyildiz, T. (2017). Data mining and machine learning in the textile industry. *Wiley Interdisciplinary Reviews. Data Mining and Knowledge Discovery*, *8*(1), e1228. doi:10.1002/widm.1228

Yin, D., & Kosar, T. (2011). A data-aware workflow scheduling algorithm for heterogeneous distributed systems. *International Conference on High Performance Computing & Simulation*, 114–120. 10.1109/HPCSim.2011.5999814

Yin, J., Sharma, P., Gorton, I., & Akyoli, B. (2013, March). Large-scale data challenges in future power grids. In *2013 IEEE Seventh International Symposium on Service-Oriented System Engineering* (pp. 324-328). IEEE.

Yong, H. (2011). Research of Real-Time Optical Intensity Sensing System with Wireless Sensor Network. In *Proceedings of Wireless Communications, Networking and Mobile Computing (WiCOM), 7th International Conference* (pp. 1-3). Academic Press. 10.1109/wicom.2011.6040362

Yong, R., Nobuhiro, K., Naoki, Y., & Masaru, K. (2014). Sentiment Classification in Under-Resourced Languages Using Graph-based Semi-supervised Learning Methods. *IEICE Transactions on Information and Systems*, *E97–D*(4). doi:10.1587/transinf.E97.D.1

Yoo, R. M., Romano, A., & Kozyrakis, C. (2009). Phoenix rebirth: Scalable MapReduce on a large-scale shared-memory system. In *Workload Characterization, 2009. IISWC 2009. IEEE International Symposium on* (pp. 198-207). IEEE. Retrieved on April 4, 2016 from http://csl.stanford.edu/~christos/publications/2009.scalable_phoenix.iiswc.pdf

Yuan Y. G. J. (2015). Study of obstacle avoidance navigation robot control based on bland man tracing wall theory. In *Proceedings of IEEE international conference on Information and Automation* (pp. 398-403). IEEE.

Yuan, Y. G. (2015). *Study of obstacle avoidance navigation robot control based on bland man tracing wall theory*. IEEE.

Yu, N. C. L. (2011). The development and application of crossplatformcoal mine mobile information system. *Proc. IEEE Int. Conf. on Computer Science and Netw. Technology, 3*, 1492–1496.

Z. W., &, L. S. (2009). *Advances in intelligent information systems: Studies in computational intelligence*. Berlin, Germany: Springer International Publishing.

Zanella, A., Bui, N., Castellani, A., Vangelista, L., &Zorzi, M. (2014). Internet of things for smart cities. *IEEE Internet of Things Journal, 1*(1), 22-32.

Zanella, A., Bui, N., Castellani, A., Vangelista, L., & Zorzi, M. (2014). Internet of things for smart cities. *IEEE Internet of Things Journal*, *1*(1), 22–32. doi:10.1109/JIOT.2014.2306328

Zarpelão, B. B., Miani, R. S., Kawakani, C. T., & de Alvarenga, S. C. (2017). A survey of intrusion detection in Internet of Things. *Journal of Network and Computer Applications*, *84*, 25–37. doi:10.1016/j.jnca.2017.02.009

Zaslavsky, A., Perera, C., & Georgakopoulos, D. (2013). *Sensing as a service and big data*. arXiv preprint arXiv:1301.0159

Zaslavsky, A., Perera, C., & Georgakopoulos, D. (2012). Sensing as a Service and Big Data. *Proceedings of the International Conference on Advances in Cloud Computing (ACC-2012)*, 21–29.

Zdravković, M., Zdravković, J., Aubry, A., Moalla, N., Guedria, W., & Sarraipa, J. (2018). Domain framework for implementation of open IoT ecosystems. *International Journal of Production Research*, *56*(7), 2552–2569. doi:10.1080/00207543.2017.1385870

Zhang, Y., & Ansari, N. (2012). Green data centers. Handbook of Green Information and Communication Systems, 331.

Zhang, Z., Ye, Q., Zheng, W., & Li, Y. (2010). Sentiment Classification for Consumer Word-of-Mouth in Chinese: Comparison between Supervised and Unsupervised Approaches. *The 2010 International Conference on E-Business Intelligence*.

Zhang, B., Xiang, Y., & Wang, J. (2010). Information Filtering Algorithm Based on Semantic Understanding. *Dianzi Yu Xinxi Xuebao*, *32*(10), 2324–2330. doi:10.3724/SP.J.1146.2009.01393

Zhang, K., Ni, J., Yang, K., Liang, X., Ren, J., & Shen, X. S. (2017). Security and Privacy in Smart City Applications: Challenges and Solutions. *IEEE Communications Magazine*, *55*(1), 122–129. doi:10.1109/MCOM.2017.1600267CM

Zhang, M., Yu, T., & Zhai, G. F. (2011). Smart transport system based on "The Internet of Things". *Applied Mechanics and Materials*, *48*, 1073–1076. doi:10.4028/www.scientific.net/AMM.48-49.1073

Zhang, N. (2016). Semi-supervised extreme learning machine with wavelet kernel. *International Journal of Collaborative Intelligence*, *1*(4), 298. doi:10.1504/IJCI.2016.10004854

Zhang, P., & Koppaka, L. (2007). Semantics–based legal citation network. *Proceedings of the 11th International Conference on Artificial intelligence and Law–ICAIL '07,* 123–130. doi: 10.1145/1276318.1276342

Zhang, R., Deng, W., & Zhu, M. Y. (2017). Using Deep Neural Networks to Automate Large Scale Statistical Analysis for Big Data Applications. *Proceedings of Machine Learning Research*, *77*, 311–326.

Zheng, X., Chen, W., Wang, P., Shen, D., Chen, S., Wang, X., ... Yang, L. (2016). Big data for social transportation. *IEEE Transactions on Intelligent Transportation Systems*, *17*(3), 620–630.

Zhou, W., & Piramuthu, S. (2014). *Security/privacy of wearable fitness tracking IoT devices*. Paper presented at the 9th Iberian Conference on Information Systems and Technologies (CISTI), Barcelona, Spain. 10.1109/CISTI.2014.6877073

Zhou, J., Cao, Z., Dong, X., & Vasilakos, A. V. (2017). Security and privacy for cloud-based IoT: Challenges. *IEEE Communications Magazine*, *55*(1), 26–33. doi:10.1109/MCOM.2017.1600363CM

Zhou, K., Fu, C., & Yang, S. (2016). Big data driven smart energy management: From big data to big insights. *Renewable & Sustainable Energy Reviews*, *56*, 215–225. doi:10.1016/j.rser.2015.11.050

Zhou, Z.-H., Wu, J., & Tang, W. (2002). Ensembling neural networks: Many could be better than all. *Artificial Intelligence*, *137*(1–2), 239–263. doi:10.1016/S0004-3702(02)00190-X

Zhu, W., Sreedhar, V. C., Hu, Z., & Gao, G. R. (2007). Synchronization state buffer: supporting efficient fine-grain synchronization on many-core architectures. *ACM SIGARCH Computer Architecture News, 35*(2), 35-45. Retrieved on April 4, 2016 from http://www.capsl.udel.edu/pub/doc/papers/ISCA2007.pdf

Zhu, C., Leung, V. C., Shu, L., & Ngai, E. C. H. (2015). Green internet of things for smart world. *IEEE Access: Practical Innovations, Open Solutions*, *3*, 2151–2162. doi:10.1109/ACCESS.2015.2497312

Zicari, R.V. (2014). Big data: Challenges and opportunities. *Big Data Computing*, 104-128.

Ziegeldorf, J. H., Morchon, O. G., & Wehrle, K. (2014). Privacy in the Internet of Things: Threats and challenges. *Security and Communication Networks*, *7*(12), 2728–2742. doi:10.1002ec.795

Zikopoulos, P., DeRoos, D., Parasuraman, K., Deutsch, T., Corrigan, D., & Giles, J. (2013). *Harness the Power of Big Data*. McGraw-Hill.

Zikopoulos, P., Eaton, C., De Roos, D., Deutsch, T., & Lapis, G. (2012). *Understanding Big Data: Analytics for Enterprise Class Hadoopand Streaming Data*. McGraw-Hill.

Zikopoulos, P., Eaton, C., Deroos, D., Deutsch, T., & Lapis, G. (2012). *Understanding big data: Analytics for enterprise class Hadoop and streaming data*. New York: McGraw-Hill.

Zohora, F. T., Khan, M. R. R., Bhuiyan, M. F. R., & Das, A. K. (2017). Enhancing the capabilities of IoT based fog and cloud infrastructures for time sensitive events. *ICECOS 2017 - Proceeding of 2017 International Conference on Electrical Engineering and Computer Science: Sustaining the Cultural Heritage Toward the Smart Environment for Better Future*, 224–230.

Zott, C., & Amit, R. (2008). The Fit between Product Market Strategy and Business Model: Implications for Firm Performance. *Strategic Management Journal*, *29*(1), 1–26. doi:10.1002mj.642

Zott, C., Amit, R., & Massa, L. (2011). The Business Model: Recent Developments and Future Research. *Journal of Management*, *37*(4), 1019–1042. doi:10.1177/0149206311406265

Zuhra, F. T., Abu Bakar, K., Ahmed, A., & Tunio, M. A. (2017). Routing protocols in wireless body sensor networks: A comprehensive survey. *Journal of Network and Computer Applications*, 73-97.

About the Contributors

Gurjit Kaur, a bright scholar, gold medalist throughout including B.Tech and M.Tech and president awardee has spent over 15 years of her academic career towards research and teaching in the field of Electronics and Communication. She is having distinction of receiving a Gold medal by former President of India A P J Abdul Kalam for being overall topper of the Punjab Technical University, Jalandhar by securing 82% marks. She has been a topper throughout her academic career. She earned her Ph.D. degree from Panjab University, Chandigarh in 2010 and her M. Tech from PEC University of Technology, Chandigarh in 2003 with distinction. Presently Dr Kaur is working as an Associate Professor at Delhi Technological University, Delhi, India. Prior to that she was working as an Assistant Professor in the School of Information and Communication Technology, Gautam Buddha University, Greater Noida, India. Her research interests include Optical CDMA, Wireless Communication system, high-speed interconnect and IOT. Her name has been listed in Marquis Who's Who in Science and Technology, USA. She has published more than 70 papers in journals and conferences, authored one book on Optical Communication, and one book chapter on WiMax of Florida Atlantic University, published by CRC Press. Besides this, she has presented her research work as short courses/tutorials in many national and international conferences. She served as a reviewer of various journals like IEEE transactions on communication etc. Dr Kaur is recipient of Prof. Indira Parikh 50 Women in Education Leader Award in world Education Congress, Mumbai, India in 2017. She also received Bharat Vikas Award by Institute of Self Reliance in National Seminar on Diversity of Cultural and Social Environment at Bhubneswar, Odisha, in 2017. She worked as a convener for two international conferences i.e. International ICIAICT 2012 which was organized by CSI, Noida Chapter and International conference EPPICTM 2012 which was organized in collaboration with MTMI, USA, University of Maryland Eastern Shore, USA and Frostburg State University, USA at School of Information and Communication Technology, Gautam Buddha University, Greater Noida, India.

Pradeep Tomar is working as Assistant Professor in the School of Information and Communication Technology, Gautam Buddha University, Greater Noida, U.P., India since 2009. Dr. Tomar earned his Ph.D. from MDU, Rohtak, Haryana, India. Before joining Gautam Buddha University, he worked as a Software Engineer in a multi-national company, Noida and lecturer in M. D. University, Rohtak, Haryana and Kurukshetra University, Kurukshetra, Haryana. Dr. Tomar has good teaching, research and software development experience as well as vast administrative experience at university level on various posts like research coordinator, examination coordinator, admission coordinator, programme coordinator, time table coordinators, proctor and hostel warden. Dr. Tomar is also a member of Computer Society of India (CSI), Indian Society for Technical Education (ISTE), Indian Science Congress Association

(ISCA), International Association of Computer Science and Information Technology (IACSIT) and International Association of Engineers (IAENG). Dr. Tomar has qualified the National Eligibility Test (NET) for Lecturership in Computer Applications in 2003, Microsoft Certified Professional (MCP) in 2008, SUN Certified JAVA Programmer (SCJP) for the JAVA platform, standard edition 5.0 in 2008 and qualified the IBM Certified Database Associate - DB2 9 Fundamentals in 2010. Dr. Tomar has been awarded with Bharat Jyoti Award by India International Friendship Society in the field of Technology in 2012 and Bharat Vikas Award by Institute of Self Reliance in National Seminar on Diversity of Cultural and Social Environment at Bhubneswar, Odisha, in 2017. He has been awarded for the Best Computer Faculty award by Govt. of Pondicherry and ASDF society. His biography is published in Who's Who Reference Asia, Volume II. Dr. Tomar has been awarded distinguished Research Award from Institute for Global Business Research for his work in "A Web Based Stock Selection Decision Support System for Investment Portfolio Management in 2018. Several technical sessions in national and international conferences had been chaired by Dr. Tomar and he delivered expert talks at FDP, workshops, national and international conferences. Three conferences have been organized by Dr. Tomar: one national conference with COMMUNE group and two international conferences, in which one international ICIAICT 2012 was organized by CSI, Noida Chapter and second international conference 2012 EPPICTM was organized in collaboration with MTMI, USA, University of Maryland Eastern Shore, USA and Frostburg State University, USA at School of Information and Communication Technology, Gautam Buddha University, Greater Noida, India. Apart from teaching, he is running a programming club for ICT students and he is guiding various research scholars in the areas of Software Engineering, reusability of code, soft computing technique, big Data and IoT. His major current research interest is in Component-Based Software Engineering. He is working as Co investigator in sponsored research project in High throughput design, synthesis and validation of TALENs for targeted Genome Engineering, funded by Department of Biotechnology, Ministry of Science and Technology Government of India New. Two books "Teaching of Mathematics" and "Communication and Information Technology" at national levels and Examining Cloud Computing Technologies through the Internet of Things (IoT) at international level have been authored by Dr. Tomar. He has also contributed more than 100 papers/articles in national/international journals and conferences. He served as a member of the editorial board and reviewer for various Journals and national/international conferences.

* * *

Azrina Abd Aziz received her Bachelor Degree in Electrical and Electronic Engineering (Hons) from University of Queensland, Australia in 1997 and her MSc. in System Level Integration from the Institute for System Level Integration (ISLI), Scotland in 2003. She then completed her Ph.D. in Electrical and Computer Systems Engineering at Monash University, Melbourne, Australia in 2014. Her recent research interests focus on energy-efficient techniques for topology control in wireless sensor networks (WSNs), wireless body area networks (WBANs) for biomedical applications and biometrics for identity authentication and recognition.

Muhammad Hariz Abdul Manab received the B.Eng degree from Universiti Teknologi Petronas, Perak in 2017 in Electrical and Electronic Engineering. Currently, he is working as a product engineer at Intel Penang Malaysia.

Deepshikha Bhargava has rich experience of 18+ years as an academician. At present working as Professor, University of Petroleum & Energy Studies (UPES), Dehradun. Earlier she was Director & Head, Amity Institute of Information Technology, Amity University Rajasthan, Jaipur. Published 15 books and 50+ research papers in Journals and Conference Proceedings of International & National repute. Professional Member ACM-USA, IACSIT, Singapore; CSTA, ACM-USA; CSI; ISLE; and Project Management Institute (PMI). Also member of Reviewer & Editorial Board of 10+ SCI indexed International Journals. She has supervised two PhD (awarded). Her area of research includes Nature Inspired computation, Software agents, Soft Computing and Knowledge Management. She has been Visiting Professor at Université des Mascareignes (UDM), Ministry of Education and Human Resources, Tertiary Education and Scientific Research, Mauritius. At present she is Chairman- CSI Jaipur Chapter. She has received the award "Distinguished Professor" by CSI Mumbai, "Nobel Contribution in Education" in Jaipur & "Late Smt. Nani Devi-Narayan Swaroop Bhargava Puraskar" for Outstanding contribution in Research, in year 2013. Also Best paper award in session at IEEE International Conference at Bangkok, Thailand in 2012. She has also awarded by Ministry of Human Resources & Development (Dept. of Education), Govt. of India in year 1992. Recently awarded "Outstanding Woman Educator & Scholar Award" at Women's Day Awards & Celebration 2015 organized by National Foundation for Entrepreneurship Development (NFED), Coimbatore, Tamil Nadu.

Anjali Chaudhary is working as Assistant professor in Department of Computer Science & Engineering, School of Engineering and Technology, Noida International University, Greater Noida, Uttar Pradesh, India since September 2014. She has earned her masters degree, M.Tech. (Specialization in Software Engineering) from School of Information and Communication Technology, Gautam Buddha University, Greater Noida, UP. Ms. Anjali has also worked as a guest faculty in school of Information and Communication technology, Gautam Buddha University, Greater Noida, India. Apart from teaching experience Ms. Anjali has attended and co-ordinated many workshops, seminars & quiz competitions at university level. She has been member of organizing committee of national/international conference at university level. Ms. Anjali has presented 02 papers in international conference. She has 1 paper published in international conference and 1 paper published in international journal. She has been served as reviewer member for Research & Reviews: Discrete Mathematical Structures Vol 3, No 1 (2016). She is also nominee member of CSI (Computer Society of India).

Shravani Devarakonda received her Diploma degree followed by bachelor's degree in Electronics and Communication Engineering at Jawaharlal Nehru University, India in 2013, after she worked as a Graduate Engineer Apprentice (GEA) at Electronics Corporation of India Limited from 2014 to 2015 and Master of Information Technology degree from Charles Sturt University, Melbourne, in 2018. Her main research incorporates with Internet of Things (IoT), Network Security, and Forensics.

Onur Dogan graduated from the Sakarya University with a Bachelor's Degree in Industrial Engineering in 2010 and received a Master's Degree in Management Engineering from the Istanbul Technical University in 2013. He is a Ph.D. candidate in the same university. He studied on intelligent decision support system, lean manufacturing and quality approaches such as QFD, FMEA or DOE during the master thesis. His PhD research interests include process mining, data mining and fuzzy sets. He studied at Universitat Politecnica de Valencia as a visitor researcher for a 12-month research project.

Micheal Drieberg received the B.Eng. degree from Universiti Sains Malaysia, Penang, Malaysia, in 2001, the M.Sc. degree from Universiti Teknologi PETRONAS, Seri Iskandar, Malaysia, in 2005, and the Ph.D. degree from Victoria University, Melbourne, Australia, in 2011, all in electrical and electronics engineering. He is currently a Senior Lecturer with the Department of Electrical and Electronics Engineering, Universiti Teknologi PETRONAS. His research interests include radio resource management, medium access control protocols, energy harvesting communications, and performance analysis for wireless and sensor networks. Dr. Drieberg has published and served as a reviewer for several high impact journals and flagship conferences. He has also made several contributions to the wireless broadband standards group.

Fevzi Esen has received his M.A. and Ph.D. in quantitative sciences from Istanbul University. He now works at Istanbul Medeniyet University, Faculty of Tourism, as assistant professor. His main interest fields are: data mining, statistics and big data applications in tourism industries.

Leyla Gamidullaeva holds a PhD in Economics. She is Doctoral Candidate and Associate Professor at the Department of Management and Economic Security of Penza State University, Russia. L. Gamidullaeva is currently a head of the department of Applied and Business Informatics at K.G. Razumovsky Moscow State University of technologies and management (Penza branch). She has authored over 200 refereed publications and over ten books. She writes and presents widely on issues of innovation management, regional economic growth, institutional theory, knowledge management, networking and collaboration.

Görkem Giray is a software engineer and an independent researcher. Dr. Giray obtained his BSc degree (1999) and PhD degree (2011) in Computer Engineering from Ege University, İzmir, Turkey. He obtained his MBA degree from Koç University, Istanbul, in 2001. He has been working in various software engineering positions since 2000. He has also been delivering courses in software engineering since 2013.

Regel Gonzalez-Usach received her M.Sc. in Telecommunication at the Universitat Politècnica de Valencia, focused on networking, electronics and systems. She pursued her thesis at the University of Stuttgart under the topic of Multipath TCP and Future Internet. She is currently performing a Ph.D on Networking and Internet of Things at the Universitat Politècnica de Valencia in Spain. Her research activities and interests cover Future Internet, Internet of Things, Big Data, Fog Computing, Multipath TCP, AAL and software applications.

Omer Faruk Gurcan graduated with a BS from Selçuk University in 2006, a MS from the İstanbul Technical University and now continues PhD in Industrial Engineering Program in İstanbul Technical University. His research interests are focused on knowledge management, statistical analysis, data mining and machine learning.

Malka Halgamuge is a Researcher in the Department of Electrical and Electronic Engineering of the University of Melbourne. She has also obtained her Ph.D. from the same department in 2007. She also a Senior Lecturer (casual) at the Charles Sturt University, Melbourne. She is passionate about research and teaching university students (Lifesciences, Big Data/Data Science, Natural Disaster, Wireless

Communication). She has published more than 80 peer-reviewed technical articles attracting over 818 Google Scholar Citations with h-index = 14 and her Research Gate RG Score is 32.32. She is currently supervising 2 PhD students at the University of Melbourne and 3 PhD students completed their theses in 2013 and 2015 with her as the main supervisor. She successfully sought 7 short-term research fellowships at premier Universities in the World.

Matilde Julian received her M.Sc. in Telecommunication and Biomedical Engineering and her Ph.D at the Universitat Politècnica de Valencia. Her research activities and interests cover a wide range of subjects related to biomedical signal processing, clinical applications, Future Internet, Internet of Things and AAL.

Jayashree K. is an Engineer by qualification, having done her Doctorate in the area of Web services Fault Management from Anna University, Chennai and Masters in Embedded System Technologies from Anna University and Bachelors in Computer Science and Engineering from Madras University. She is presently Associate Professor in the Department of Computer Science and Engineering at Rajalakshmi Engineering College, affiliated to Anna University Chennai. Her areas of interest include Web services, Cloud Computing, Data Mining and distributed computing. She is a member of ACM, CSI.

Ramgopal Kashyap has areas of interest in image processing, pattern recognition, and machine learning. He has published many research papers, and book chapters in international journals and conferences like Springer, Inderscience, Elsevier, ACM, and IGI-Global indexed by Science Citation Index (SCI) and Scopus (Elsevier). He has Reviewed Research Papers in the Science Citation Index Expanded, Springer Journals and Editorial Board Member and conferences programme committee member of the IEEE, Springer international conferences and journals held in countries: Czech Republic, Switzerland, UAE, Australia, Hungary, Poland, Taiwan, Denmark, India, USA, UK, Austria, and Turkey. He has written many book chapters published by IGI Global, USA.

Eda Kocabas is currently working at Istanbul Medeniyet University as a Research assistant in Istanbul, Turkey. She has received her B.A. in Tourism Administration at Boğaziçi University in 2014. She has worked at the official destination marketing bureau of Istanbul. She now holds Master of Arts in social sciences from Istanbul University. Her research interest areas include Destination Marketing and Branding, Sustainable Conventions & Meeting, and Alternative Tourism Studies.

Hai Hiung Lo received the B.Eng. degree in Electrical and Electronics Engineering from the University of Leicester, Leicester City, UK in 1996, then worked as an engineer for 2 years before proceeding to further his study and obtained the M.Sc. degree in Computer Engineering from the University of Minnesota – Twin Cities, Minneapolis, USA in 2005. He is currently a Lecturer with the Department of Electrical and Electronics Engineering, Universiti Teknologi PETRONAS. His research interests include VLSI Design, Computer System Architecture, and Embedded Systems Design. Mr. Hai Hiung, Lo has published and served as a reviewer for several flagship conferences.

Nirvikar Lohan has done his Ph.D in Computer Science Engineering and presently working as Associate Professor in College of Engineering Roorkee, Uttarakhand, India. He is having more than 17 years of experience in research and academics and also conducted several conferences, workshops and FDP programs. He is presently guiding 5 Ph.D students and guided more than 10 M.Tech Students. His primary research interests are image processing and computer vision, wireless networks, Internet of Things, Big data.

Vardan Mkrttchian received his Doctorate of Sciences (Engineering) in Control Systems from Lomonosov Moscow State University (former USSR). Dr. Vardan Mkrttchian taught for undergraduate and graduate student's courses of control system, information sciences and technology, at the Astrakhan State University (Russian Federation), where he was is the Professor of the Information Systems (www.aspu.ru) six years. Now he is full professor in CAD department of Penza State University (www.pnzgu.ru). He is currently chief executive of HHH University, Australia and team leader of the international academics (www.hhhuniversity.com). He also serves as executive director of the HHH Technology Incorporation. Professor Vardan Mkrttchian has authored over 400 refereed publications. He is the author of over twenty books published of IGI Global, included ten books indexed of SCOPUS in IT, Control System, Digital Economy, and Education Technology. He is also has authored more than 200 articles published in various conference proceedings and journals.

Azeem Mohammad is a Director of Charles Sturt University Study Centre at Melbourne. Azeem has over 20 years' experience in higher education sector which includes teaching, management and research. He has number of publications in knowledge management, Data sciences. His experience including variety of skill set ranging from researcher, lecturer to senior level manager. His research interests include data sciences, AI, decision making and education management.

Siti Aishah Mohd Selamat is a Ph.D. candidate with particular interests in data science, strategic studies, and business management. Prior to enrolling at Bournemouth University, she has had 10 years of working experience in both general and IT project management in Singapore, Indonesia, and Malaysia. She holds an M.B.A in IT Management and B.A. in Business Management from the University of Bedfordshire and also, an Advanced Diploma and Diploma in IT from Informatics Institute Singapore. Her Ph.D. delves in developing an automatised analytic solution for Small-Medium Enterprises (SMEs) in the context of the transportation sector.

Kshirasagar Naik is an Associate Professor in the Department of Electrical and Computer Engineering at the University of Waterloo. He has also been a member of IEEE since 1994. His research interests include computer network protocols, wireless and mobile communication systems, sensor networks, peer-to-peer networks, cognitive radio systems and energy saving in hand-held devices and data centers. Delay tolerant networks, body-area networks, mHealth (mobile health) and eHealth applications, vehicular networks, and intelligent transportation systems are also areas of research that interest Professor Naik.

Bhuva Narayan is a Senior Lecturer and Course Coordinator in the Information and Knowledge Management Program at the University of Technology Sydney (UTS), Sydney, Australia. She has an MLIS from the iSchool at the University of Pittsburgh and a PhD from the Queensland University of Technology, Australia. Her research interests are in information behaviour, human learning, design thinking, digital social media, privacy literacy, and in social justice issues.

Anand Nayyar (Academician, Researcher, Author, Writer, Inventor, Innovator, Scientist, Consultant, and Orator) received MCA from Punjabi University, Patiala in 2008 with Gold Medal and Distinction. He has done his Ph.D. in Computer Science from Desh Bhagat University, Mandi Gobindgarh in 2017 in Wireless Sensor Networks, Swarm Intelligence, and Network Simulation. He has published more than 300 Research Papers and 25 Books of Computer Science. He is working in the area of WSN, Swarm Intelligence, IoT, and Machine Learning.

Carlos Palau received his M.Sc. and Ph.D (Dr.Ing.) degrees, both in telecommunication engineering, from the Universitat Politécnica de Valencia in 1993 and 1997, respectively. He is Full Professor in the Escuela Técnica Superior de Ingenieros de Telecomunicación at the Universitat Politecnica de Valencia. He has more than 18 years of experience in the ICT research area in the area of Networking. He has collaborated extensively in the R&D of multimedia streaming, security, networking and wireless communications for government agencies, defence and European Commission. Currently he is leading the ITC-30 project Inter-IoT, focused in the achievement of global interoperability in IoT. He is author and co-author of more than 120 research papers and member of the TPC of several IEEE, ACM and IFIP conferences. He is Senior Member of IEEE.

Svetlana Panasenko received higher economic education in 1992 at the Stavropol Polytechnic Institute with a degree in Economics and management, from 1992 to 1996 she worked as a chief economist in business organizations, in 2007 she received a degree of doctor of economic Sciences at the North Caucasus state technical University, where from 2007 to 2010 she worked as a Professor at the faculty of Economics and Finance. In 2015, she received a master's degree in practical psychology from Moscow state University of psychology and education. Since 2010 she has been accepted to the position of Professor at the Plekhanov Russian state University in Moscow and currently holds the position of head of the Department of trade policy at this University. She writes and widely represents the issues of e-Commerce, Neurotechnology, marketing and management in the digital economy. She is the author of works on the analysis of export-import relations between Russia and other countries, innovative approaches to the development of various sectors of the economy (Espacios, 2018).

Zablon Pingo holds Bachelors degree and Masters in Information science. He is currently a PhD candidate at the University of Technology Sydney. His research interests are in privacy issues surrounding information technologies including, social media, Big data and Internet of Things. He is also a sessional lecturer at University of Technology Insearch teaching digital literacies.

Simant Prakoonwit received his MSc and PhD from Imperial College London. Currently he is an Associate Professor in the Department of Creative Technology, Faculty of Science and Technology, Bournemouth University, UK. He works on several research projects related to artificial intelligence, big data, assitive technologies and biomedical engineering. Dr Prakoonwit has won several awards, e.g. the IEEE Innovation and Creativity Prize Award, Brunel Research Initiative Enterprise Fund Award, Bedfordshire's Rising Star/Research Investment Programme Award, best papers at conferences and invitations to submit to journal's special issues.

Abirami R. is currently working as Assistant Professor in Department of Computer Science and Engineering at Rajalakshmi Engineering College, Chennai. She pursued her Master degree in Computer Science and Engineering in Rajalakshmi Engineering College and completed the course in 2016. She received a gold medal for her outstanding performance in academics. She has a keen interest in Computer Science and passion for research in the field of Bigdata.

Mamata Rath, M.Tech, Ph.D (Comp.Sc), has twelve years of experience in teaching as well as in research and her research interests include Mobile Adhoc Networks, Internet of Things, Ubiquitous Computing, VANET and Computer Security. She has authored a number of research articles, both in Journals and International Conferences as well as book chapters. She has been working as Organiser for International Conferences such as ICACIE-2016,ICACIE-2017 and IEEE ANTS-2017.She has also reviewed some important research article for reputed publishers.

David Sarabia received his M.Sc. degree in Communications Technologies, Systems and Networks from the Universitat Politécnica de Valencia in 2016. He is currently performing a Ph.D in the Escuela Técnica Superior de Ingenieros de Telecomunicación at the Universitat Politècnica de València, Spain. His research activities and interests cover Internet of Things, Big Data, Cloud Computing, Fog Computing, and Machine Learning.

Vijayalakshmi Saravanan received her Ph.D. in Computer Science and Engineering from VIT University, India under Erasmus Mundus Fellowship (EURECA) as research exchange student at Mälardalen University, Sweden and visiting researcher at Ryerson University, Canada. She was working as an Assistant Professor in Practice at the University of Texas, San Antonio (UTSA) in the Department of Computer Science. Prior to this, she was a Postdoctoral Associate at UB (University at Buffalo), The State University of New York, USA and University of Waterloo, Canada under the prestigious "Schlumberger Faculty for the Future" Fellowship award (2015-2017). She is having 10 years of teaching experience in two premier Universities VIT and Amrita Vishwa Vidyapeetham, India. Dr. Saravanan has published many technical articles in scholarly international journal and conferences. She is serving as the technical reviewer and program committee member for reputed conference & journals such as GHC, SIGCSE, and Springer. Her research interests include Power-Aware Processor Design, Big Data, IoT and Computer Architecture. She is a Senior Member of IEEE & ACM, CSI, Ex-Chair for IEEE-WIE VIT affinity group, India (2009-2015), NPA (National Postdoctoral Association) Annual Meetings committee, Workshop/ IIA Co-Chair (2017-2018) and a Board member of N2WOMEN (Networking Networking Women).

Patrick Sebastian is currently a Senior Lecturer in the Electrical and Electronic Engineering Department at Universiti Teknologi PETRONAS (UTP). He received his PhD in Parameteric Tracking with Spatial Extraction Across An Array of Cameras from Middlesex University, London. He has interests in the areas of Computer Architectures, Embedded systems, Image Processing and Video Surveillance. Prior to his current appointment, Patrick was a Senior Engineer at Penang Seagate Industries Malaysia.

Lavanya Sharma has done Ph.D from Uttarakhand Technical University, India in 2018 and M.Tech (Computer Science & Engineering) in 2013 from Maharashi Dayanand University, Haryana, India. She is a recipient of several prestigious awards during her academic career. She also received TEQIP scholarship during her Ph.D. She has contributed in academic research and published several papers in

International conferences & International journals including IEEE, Inderscience, Elsevier, Springer and many more. She has authored a text book on Object Detection with Background Subtraction and also contributed as Technical Committee member and organized Springer's ICACDS conferences 2016 & 2018 held in India. Her primary research interests are image processing and computer vision, vehicular Adhoc network, mobile Adhoc networks, Internet of Things. Her vision is to promote teaching & research, providing a highly competitive and productive environment in academic and research areas with tremendous growing opportunities for the society and her country.

Meghna Sharma is pursuing her Ph.D. from YMCA University, Faridabad, India. She received her M.Tech. degree from Guru Jambheshwar University, Hissar and B.E. from Chhotu Ram State College, Murthal. She has a total of 15 years of experience in Teaching and Research. She is working as Assistant Professor (Selection Grade) in The NorthCap University(NCU), Gurugram. Before she came on board at NCU, Ms Meghna worked as a scientist in ISRO. She is a recipient of the Science Award conferred by the Government of Haryana in 2007. Her interest is in Data Mining, Machine Learning, Big Data Analytics, DBMS.

Garima Singh is working as Research scholar in Delhi Technical University, Delhi. She passed her BE degree by First class with Honors in Electronics and Communication Engineering at Sharda University in 2013 and received her ME (Electronics and Communication) from Jaypee Institute of Information and Technology in 2015. She has been the topper throughout her academic carrier and has the distinction of receiving an A+ for her ME thesis. Her professional experience and research are in the area of Cognitive Radio, Cooperative Communication, Optical and Wireless Communication System. She has several publications in International SCI indexed Journals and conferences and book chapters with IGI and CRC press.

Arun Solanki is working in the School of Information and Communication Technology at Gautam Buddha University, Greater Noida. He completed his Ph.D. in 2014 from Gautam Buddha University, Greater Noida in Expert Systems. He has completed his M.Tech. from YMCA Engg. College Faridabad in 2008. He has published more than 30 research papers in reputed international Journal and international conferences. He has delivered more than ten expert lectures in reputed organization institutions. More than 50 M.Tech. dissertations have been submitted in his guidance. His main research areas include the expert system, web development, and Image processing. He has organized international conferences in Gautam Buddha University. Many other programs like the workshop, FDP, etc. are also organized under his guidance.

Emmanuel Tetteh is a Core, Lead Faculty, and Senior Lecturer of the MPA Policy Analysis and Analytics concentration program in the College of Graduate and Continuing Studies at Norwich University. He is recently hired as a faculty member in the College of Humanities and Social Sciences at Grand Canyon University. Also, he is an Adjunct Professor at the Metropolitan College of New York (MCNY) and The College of New Rochelle. Dr. Tetteh also served as a faculty member in the School of Public Service Leadership at Capella University where he taught and mentored doctoral candidates. Dr. Tetteh holds a Bachelor of Professional Studies' degree in Human Services and a Master of Science's degree in Administration from MCNY, as well as a Ph.D. degree in Public Policy and Administration from Walden University. Through action learning/action research (AL/AR), and program evaluation projects, Dr. Tetteh developed and coined the metaphor of "Communal Photosynthesis (CP)" phenomenon in 2001. Dr. Tetteh has recently also developed an intriguing action research model grounded in the systemic thinking of his CP metaphor. Dr. Tetteh offered a personal reflection on the meaning of AL/AR and introduced the "creative-reflective methodology" unraveling the Identify, Act, Reflect, Evaluate, and Produce (IAREP) model for participatory action research. As of 2013, Dr. Tetteh has maintained a unanimous election as the International Vice President of Action Learning, Action Research Association (ALARA), Ltd.

Sonali Vyas is serving as academician for around a decade. Currently, she is working as Assistant Professor (AP-II) at Amity Institute of Information Technology, Amity University Rajasthan. Her research interests include Database Virtualization, Data Mining, and Big Data Analytics. She is a professional member of IEEE, ACM-India, IFERP, IAENG, SCRS, and IJERT. She is a guest editor in a special issue of "Elsevier International Journal of Computer and Electrical Engineering (CAEE)". She is also a member of Editorial board of International Journal of Engineering Research in Computer Science and Engineering (IJERCSE) and Member of National Advisory Board at ICASETM-17 and reviewer of many referred national and international journals. She has authored an ample number of research papers in refereed journals/conference proceedings. At present, she is supervising four Ph.D. research scholars in the field of Bio-Inspired Computation, Data Mining, Big Data Analytics and IoT. She also supervised M.Tech. Dissertations in Computer Science. She also served as project supervisor of many Postgraduate and undergraduate students.

Diana Yacchirema received the M.Sc. (Hons.) degree in Management of Communications and Information Technology from the Escuela Politécnica Nacional (EPN), Quito, Ecuador, in 2009 and the M.Sc. degree in Communications Technologies, Systems and Networks from the Universitat Politècnica de Valéncia (UPV), Valencia, Spain, in 2011. She is currently working toward the Ph.D degree in telecommunications engineering with the Distributed Real Time Systems and Applications Research Group, UPV. Her research activities and interests include a wide range of subjects related to Internet of Things, sensor networks, big data, cloud computing, edge computing and network security. She was the recipient of the Best Academic Record Award from the EPN, in 2009.

Index

N

O

P

R

S

T

U

V

W

Z

IGI Global books are available in three unique pricing formats:
Print Only, E-Book Only, or Print + E-Book. Shipping fees apply.

www.igi-global.com

Recommended Reference Books

ISBN: 978-1-6831-8016-6
© 2017; 197 pp.
List Price: $180

ISBN: 978-1-5225-1034-5
© 2017; 350 pp.
List Price: $200

ISBN: 978-1-5225-2973-6
© 2018 ; 286 pp.
List Price: $205

ISBN: 978-1-5225-2589-9
© 2017; 602 pp.
List Price: $345

ISBN: 978-1-5225-2229-4
© 2016; 1,093 pp.
List Price: $465

ISBN: 978-1-5225-2857-9
© 2018; 538 pp.
List Price: $265

Do you want to stay current on the latest research trends, product announcements, news and special offers?
Join IGI Global's mailing list today and start enjoying exclusive perks sent only to IGI Global members.
Add your name to the list at **www.igi-global.com/newsletters.**

Publisher of Peer-Reviewed, Timely, and Innovative Academic Research

www.igi-global.com Sign up at www.igi-global.com/newsletters facebook.com/igiglobal twitter.com/igiglobal  linkedin.com/igiglobal